White & Summers U.C.C. HB—a

*American Casebook Series*

*Hornbook Series and Basic Legal Texts*

*Nutshell Series*

*of*

# WEST PUBLISHING COMPANY

## St. Paul, Minnesota 55102

---

## ACCOUNTING

Fiflis and Kripke's Cases on Accounting for Business Lawyers, 687 pages, 1971.

## ADMINISTRATIVE LAW

Davis' Basic Text on Administrative Law 3rd Ed., 617 pages, 1972.

Davis' Cases, Text and Problems on Administrative Law, 5th Ed., about 625 pages, 1973.

Gellhorn's Administrative Law in a Nutshell, 336 pages, 1972.

## ADMIRALTY

Healy and Currie's Cases on Admiralty, 872 pages, 1965.

## AGENCY

Seavey and Hall's Cases on Agency, 431 pages, 1956.

Seavey's Text on Agency, 329 pages, 1964.

See Agency-Partnership.

## AGENCY PARTNERSHIP

Henn's Cases on Agency, Partnership and Other Unincorporated Business Enterprises, 396 pages, 1972.

Seavey, Reuschlein & Hall's Cases on Agency and Partnership, 599 pages, 1962.

Steffen's Cases on Agency and Partnership, 3rd Ed., 733 pages, 1969.

## ANTITRUST LAW

Oppenheim's Cases on Robinson-Patman Act, Pamphlet, 295 pages, 1967.

Oppenheim and Weston's Cases on Antitrust, 3rd Ed., 952 pages, 1968.

Oppenheim and Weston's Supplement, 1972.

## BANKRUPTCY

MacLachlan's Text on Bankruptcy, 500 pages, 1956.

See Creditors' Rights.

Selected Commercial Statutes, about 1000 pages, 1973.

## BILLS AND NOTES

Aigler and Steinheimer's Cases on Bills and Notes, 670 pages, 1962.

Britton's Text on Bills and Notes, 2nd Ed., 794 pages, 1961.

See Commercial Transactions.

See Negotiable Instruments.

## BUSINESS ORGANIZATIONS

See Agency-Partnership.

See Corporations.

## CIVIL PROCEDURE

See Pleading and Procedure.

## CLINICAL TEACHING

Freeman and Weihofen's Cases on Clinical Law Training—Interviewing and Counseling, 506 pages, 1972.

## COMMERCIAL PAPER

See Bills and Notes.

See Commercial Transactions.

See Negotiable Instruments.

## COMMERCIAL TRANSACTIONS

Speidel, Summers and White's Teaching Materials on Commercial Transactions, 1144 pages, 1969.

Murray and White's Problem Teaching Materials on Commercial Transactions, about 300 pages, 1973.

White and Summers Text on the Uniform Commercial Code, 1054 pages, 1972.

Selected Commercial Statutes, about 1000 pages, 1973.

See Negotiable Instruments.

See Sales.

I

## COMMON LAW PLEADING

Koffler and Reppy's Text on Common Law Pleading, 663 pages, 1969.

McBaine's Cases, Introduction to Civil Procedure, 399 pages, 1950.

Shipman's Text on Common Law Pleading, 3rd Ed., 644 pages, 1923.

## COMMUNITY PROPERTY

Burby's Cases on Community Property, 4th Ed., 342 pages, 1955.

Huie's Texas Cases on Marital Property Rights, 681 pages, 1966.

Verrall and Sammis' Cases on California Community Property, 2nd Ed., 398 pages, 1971.

## CONFLICT OF LAWS

Cramton and Currie's Cases—Comments—Questions on Conflicts, 915 pages, 1968.

Ehrenzweig's Text on Conflicts, 824 pages, 1962.

Ehrenzweig's Conflicts in a Nutshell, 2nd Ed., 392 pages, 1970.

Ehrenzweig and Louisell's Jurisdiction in a Nutshell, 3rd Ed., about 255 pages, 1973.

Goodrich's Text on Conflict of Laws, 4th Ed., 483 pages, 1964.

Scoles and Weintraub's Cases on Conflict of Laws, 2nd Ed., 966 pages 1972.

## CONSTITUTIONAL LAW

Lockhart, Kamisar and Choper's Cases — Comments — Questions on Constitutional Law, 3rd Ed., 1,487 pages, 1970.

Lockhart, Kamisar and Choper's Cases on The American Constitution, 3rd Ed., 1970.

Lockhart, Kamisar and Choper's Annual Supplement.

See Constitutional Rights and Liberties.

## CONSTITUTIONAL RIGHTS & LIBERTIES

Lockhart, Kamisar and Choper's Cases on Constitutional Rights and Liberties, 3rd Ed., 1970.

Lockhart, Kamisar and Choper's Annual Supplement.

## CONSUMER CREDIT

Kripke's Cases on Consumer Credit, 454 pages, 1970.

Schrag's Cases on Consumer Credit, 2nd Ed., Pamphlet reprint from Cooper, et al. Law and Poverty, 2nd Ed., about 175 pages, 1973.

## CONTRACTS

Calamari & Perillo's Text on Contracts, 621 pages, 1970.

Corbin's Cases on Contracts, 3rd Ed., 1381 pages, 1947. 1953 Supplement, 36 pages.

Corbin's Text on Contracts, Student Edition, 1224 pages, 1952.

Freedman's Cases on Contracts, 658 pages, 1973.

Fuller and Eisenberg's Cases on Contracts, 1043 pages, 1972.

Jackson's Cases on Contract Law in a Modern Society, about 1400 pages, 1973.

Simpson's Cases on Contracts, 592 pages, 1956.

Simpson's Text on Contracts, 2nd Ed., 510 pages, 1965.

White and Summer's Text on the Uniform Commercial Code, 1054 pages, 1972.

## COPYRIGHT

Nimmer's Cases on Copyright and Other Aspects of Law Pertaining to Literary, Musical and Artistic Works, 828 pages, 1971.

Nimmer's 1972 Supplement.

## CORPORATIONS

Henn's Text on Corporations, 2nd Ed., 956 pages, 1970.

Stevens and Henn's Statutes, Cases on Corporations and Other Business Enterprises, 1448 pages, 1965.

Stevens and Henn's Practice Projects Supplement, 81 pages, 1965.

## CORRECTIONS

Krantz' Cases on the Law of Corrections and Prisoners' Rights, about 1085 pages, 1973.

## CREDIT TRANSACTIONS

Maxwell & Riesenfeld's California Cases on Security Transactions, 371 pages, 1957.

Maxwell & Riesenfeld's Supplement, 68 pages, 1963.

## CREDITORS' RIGHTS

Epstein's Teaching Materials on Debtor-Creditor Relations, 525 pages, 1973.

Epstein's Debtor-Creditor Relations in a Nutshell, 309 pages, 1973.

Riesenfeld's Cases on Creditors' Remedies and Debtors' Protection, 669 pages, 1967.

Riesenfeld's Case and Statutory Supplement, 1972.

## CRIMINAL LAW

Dix and Sharlot's Cases on Criminal Law, about 1350 pages, 1973.

LaFave and Scott's Text on Criminal Law, 763 pages, 1972.

Miller's Text on Criminal Law, 649 pages, 1934.

Stumberg's Texas Cases on Criminal Law, 505 pages, 1954.

Stumberg and Maloney's Texas Cases Supplement, 117 pages, 1965.

## CRIMINAL PROCEDURE

Hall, Kamisar, LaFave and Israel's Cases on Modern Criminal Procedure, 3rd Ed., 1456 pages, 1969.

Hall, Kamisar, LaFave and Israel's Cases on Basic Criminal Procedure, 3rd Ed., 617 pages, 1969.

Hall, Kamisar, LaFave, and Israel's Annual Criminal Procedure Supplement.

Israels and LaFave's Constitutional Criminal Procedure in a Nutshell, 423 pages, 1971.

Federal Rules of Civil-Appellate-Criminal Procedure, Law School Edition, 296 pages, 1973.

## DAMAGES

Crane's Cases on Damages, 3rd Ed., 337 pages, 1955.

McCormick's Text on Damages, 811 pages, 1935.

See Remedies.

## DECEDENTS ESTATES

See Wills, Intestate Succession, Trusts, Gifts and Future Interests.

## DICTIONARIES

Black's, one volume.

Bouvier's, two volumes.

## DOMESTIC RELATIONS

Clark's Cases on Domestic Relations, 870 pages, 1965.

Clark's Text on Domestic Relations, 754 pages, 1968.

Paulsen's Cases on Family Law and Poverty, 2nd Ed., Pamphlet reprint from Cooper, et al. Law and Poverty, 2nd Ed., about 266 pages, 1973.

See Juvenile Courts.

## EQUITY

Cook's Cases on Equity, 4th Ed., 1192 pp., 1948.

McClintock's Text on Equity, 2nd Ed., 643 pages, 1948.

Van Hecke, Leavell and Nelson's Cases on Equitable Remedies and Restitution, 2nd Ed., 717 pages, 1973.

See Remedies.

## EVIDENCE

Broun and Meisenholder's Problems in Evidence, about 155 pages, 1973.

Cleary and Strong's Cases on Evidence, 967 pages, 1969.

McCormick, Elliott & Sutton's Cases on Evidence, 4th Ed., 1088 pages, 1971.

McCormick, Cleary, et al., Text on Evidence, 2nd Ed., 938 pages, 1972.

Rothstein's Evidence in a Nutshell, 406 pages, 1970.

## FEDERAL ESTATE AND GIFT TAXATION

See Taxation.

## FEDERAL INCOME TAXATION

See Taxation.

## FEDERAL JURISDICTION AND PROCEDURE

Currie's Cases on Federal Courts, 823 pages, 1968.

Currie's Supplement, 1973.

Ehrenzweig and Louisell's Jurisdiction in a Nutshell, 3rd Ed., about 255 pages, 1973.

Forrester, Currier and Moye's Cases on Federal Jurisdiction and Procedure, 2nd Ed., 933 pages, 1970.

Forrester, Currier and Moye's Supplement, 1973.

Wright's Text on Federal Courts, 2nd Ed., 745 pages, 1970.

Wright's Supplement, 1972.

## FUTURE INTERESTS

Gulliver's Cases on Future Interests, 624 pages, 1959.

Powell's Cases on Future Interests, 3rd Ed., 1961.

Simes Text on Future Interests, 2nd Ed., 355 pages, 1966.

See Wills, Intestate Succession, Trusts, Gifts and Future Interests.

## GRATUITOUS TRANSFERS

See Wills, Intestate Succession, Trusts, Gifts and Future Interests.

## HOUSING AND URBAN DEVELOPMENT

Berger's Cases on Housing, 2nd Ed., Pamphlet reprint from Cooper, et al. Law and Poverty, 2nd Ed., about 210 pages, 1973.

Krasnowiecki's Cases on Housing and Urban Development, 697 pages, 1969.

Krasnowiecki's Statutory Supplement 1969.

See Land Use.

## INSURANCE

Keeton's Cases on Basic Insurance Law, 655 pages, 1960.

Keeton's Basic Text on Insurance Law, 712 pages, 1971.

Keeton's Case Supplement to Keeton's Basic Text, 398 pages, 1971.

Keeton's Programmed Problems in Insurance Law, 243 pages, 1972.

Keeton & Keeton's Compensation Systems, Pamphlet Reprint from Keeton & Keeton's Cases on Torts, 85 pages, 1971.

Vance's Text on Insurance, 3rd Ed., 1290 pages, 1951.

## INTERNATIONAL LAW

Friedmann, Lissitzyn and Pugh's Cases on International Law, 1,205 pages, 1969.

Friedmann, Lissitzyn and Pugh's Supplement, 1972.

## INTRODUCTION TO LAW

Fryer and Orentlicher's Cases on Legal Method and Legal System, 1,043 pages, 1967.

Kempin's Historical Introduction to Anglo-American Law in a Nutshell, 2nd Ed., 280 pages, 1973.

Kimball's Historical Introduction to Legal System, 610 pages, 1966.

Kinyon's Introduction to Law Study and Law Examinations in a Nutshell, 389 pages, 1971.

Smith's Cases on Development of Legal Institutions, 757 pages, 1965.

See Legal Method.

## JURISPRUDENCE

Christie's Text and Readings on Jurisprudence—The Philosophy of Law, about 1050 pages, 1973.

Wu's Cases on Jurisprudence, 719 pages, 1958.

## JUVENILE JUSTICE

Fox's Cases on Modern Juvenile Justice, 1012 pages, 1972.

Fox's The Law of Juvenile Courts in a Nutshell, 286 pages, 1971.

## LABOR LAW

Oberer and Hanslowe's Cases on Labor Law, 1091 pages, 1972.

Oberer and Hanslowe's Statutory Supplement, 1972.

Sovern's Cases on Racial Discrimination in Employment, 2nd Ed., Pamphlet reprint from Cooper et al. Law and Poverty, 2nd Ed., about 160 pages, 1973.

## LAND USE

Beuscher and Wright's Cases on Land Use, 788 pages, 1969.

Hagman's Cases on Public Planning and Control of Urban and Land Development, about 1025 pages, 1973.

Hagman's Text on Urban Planning and Land Development Control Law, 559 pages, 1971.

## LEGAL BIBLIOGRAPHY

Cohen's Legal Research in a Nutshell, 2nd Ed., 259 pages, 1971.

How To Find The Law, with Special Chapters on Legal Writing, 6th Ed., 313 pages, 1965.

How To Find The Law Student Problem Book.

Rombauer's Legal Problem Solving, 2nd Ed., 212 pages, 1973.

Rombauer's Problem Supplement.

## LEGAL ETHICS

Mellinkoff's Text on The Conscience of a Lawyer, 304 pages, 1973.

Pirsig's Cases on Professional Responsibility, 2nd Ed., 447 pages, 1970.

## LEGAL HISTORY

Kempin's Historical Introduction to Anglo-American Law in a Nutshell, 2nd Ed., 280 pages, 1973.

Kimball's Historical Introduction to Legal System, 610 pages, 1966.

Radin's Text on Anglo-American Legal History, 612 pages, 1936.

Smith's Cases on Development of Legal Institutions, 757 pages, 1965.

## LEGAL INTERVIEWING AND COUNSELING

See Clinical Teaching.

## LEGAL METHOD—LEGAL SYSTEM

Fryer and Orentlicher's Cases on Legal Method and Legal System, 1043 pages, 1966.

See Introduction to Law.

## LEGAL PROCESS

See Legal Method.

## LEGAL PROFESSION

See Legal Ethics.

## LEGAL WRITING STYLE

Weihofen's Text on Legal Writing Style, 323 pages, 1961.
See Legal Bibliography.

## LEGISLATION

Nutting, Elliott and Dickerson's Cases on Legislation, 4th Ed., 631 pages, 1969.

## LOCAL GOVERNMENT LAW

Michelman and Sandalow's Cases on Government in Urban Areas, 1216 pages, 1970.
Michelman and Sandalow's 1972 Supplement.
Stason and Kauper's Cases on Municipal Corporations, 3rd Ed., 692 pages, 1959.
See Land Use.

## MASS COMMUNICATION LAW

Gillmor and Barron's Cases on Mass Communication Law, 853 pages, 1969.
Gillmor and Barron's 1971 Supplement.

## MORTGAGES

Osborne's Cases on Secured Transactions, 559 pages, 1967.
Osborne's Text on Mortgages, 2nd Ed., 805 pages, 1970.
See Sales.
See Secured Transactions.

## MUNICIPAL CORPORATIONS

See Local Government Law.

## NATURAL RESOURCES

Trelease, Bloomenthal and Geraud's Cases on Natural Resources, 1131 pages, 1965.

## NEGOTIABLE INSTRUMENTS

Nordstrom and Clovis' Problems on Commercial Paper, 458 pages, 1972.
See Commercial Transactions.

## OFFICE PRACTICE

A.B.A. Lawyer's Handbook, 557 pages, 1962.
See Clinical Teaching.

## OIL AND GAS

Hemingway's Text on Oil and Gas, 486 pages, 1971.
Huie, Woodward and Smith's Cases on Oil and Gas, 2nd Ed., 955 pages, 1972.
See Natural Resources.

## PARTNERSHIP

Crane and Bromberg's Text on Partnership, 695 pages, 1968.
See Agency-Partnership.

## PATENTS

Choate's Cases on Patents, 1060 pages, 1973.

## PERSONAL PROPERTY

Aigler, Smith and Tefft's Cases on Property, 2 Vols., 1339 pages, 1960.
Bigelow's Cases on Personal Property, 3rd Ed., 507 pages, 1942.
Fryer's Readings on Personal Property, 3rd Ed., 1184 pages, 1938.

## PLEADING AND PROCEDURE

Brown, Karlen, Meisenholder, Stevens, and Vestal's Cases on Procedure Before Trial, 784 pages, 1968.
Cleary's Cases on Pleading, 2d Ed., 434 pages, 1958.
Cound, Friedenthal and Miller's Cases on Civil Procedure, 1075 pages, 1968.
Cound, Friedenthal and Miller's Cases on Pleading, Discovery and Joinder, 643 pages, 1968.
Cound, Friedenthal and Miller's Civil Procedure Supplement, 1972.
Ehrenzweig and Louisell's Jurisdiction in a Nutshell, 3rd Ed., about 255 pages, 1973.
Elliott & Karlen's Cases on Pleading, 441 pages, 1961.
Hodges, Jones and Elliott's Cases on Texas Trial and Appellate Procedure, 623 pages, 1965.
Hodges, Jones, Elliott and Thode's Cases on Texas Judicial Process Prior to Trial, 935 pages, 1966.
Karlen and Joiner's Cases on Trials and Appeals, 536 pages, 1971.
Karlen's Procedure Before Trial in a Nutshell, 258 pages, 1972.
McBaine's Cases on Introduction to Civil Procedure, 399 pages, 1950.
Federal Rules of Civil-Appellate-Criminal Procedure, Law School Edition, 296 pages, 1973.

## POVERTY LAW

Cooper, Dodyk, Berger, Paulsen, Schrag and Sovern's Cases on Law and Poverty, 2nd Ed., about 1165 pages, 1973.

Cooper and Dodyk's Cases on Income Maintenance, 2nd Ed., Pamphlet reprint from Cooper, et al. Law and Poverty, 2nd Ed., about 400 pages, 1973.

LaFrance, Schroeder, Bennett and Boyd's Text on Law and the Poor, about 520 pages, 1973.

## REAL PROPERTY

Aigler, Smith & Tefft's Cases on Property, 2 Vols., 1339 pages, 1960.

Berger's Cases on Housing, Pamphlet reprint from Dodyk, et al. Law and Poverty, 277 pages, 1969.

Browder, Cunningham & Julin's Cases on Basic Property Law, 2d Ed., 1397 pages, 1973.

Burby's Text on Real Property, 3rd Ed., 490 pages, 1965.

Jacobs' Cases on Landlord and Tenant, 2nd Ed., 815 pages, 1941.

Moynihan's Introduction to Real Property, 254 pages, 1962.

Phipps' Titles in a Nutshell—The Calculus of Interests, 277 pages, 1968.

Smith and Boyer's Survey of the Law of Property, 2nd Ed., 510 pages, 1971.

See Housing and Urban Development.

## REMEDIES

Cribbet's Cases on Judicial Remedies, 762 pages, 1954.

Dobb's Text, on Remedies, 1067 pages, 1973.

Van Hecke, Leavell and Nelson's Cases on Equitable Remedies and Restitution, 2nd Ed., 717 pages, 1973.

Wright's Cases on Remedies, 498 pages, 1955.

York and Bauman's Cases on Remedies, 2nd Ed., about 1500 pages, 1973.

See Equity.

## RESTITUTION

See Equity.
See Remedies.

## REVIEW MATERIALS

Ballantine's Problems.
Burby's Law Refreshers.
Smith Reviews.

## SALES

Nordstrom's Text on Sales, 600 pages, 1970.

Nordstrom and Lattin's Problems on Sales and Secured Transactions, 809 pages, 1968.

See Commercial Transactions.

## SECURED TRANSACTIONS

Henson's Text on Secured Transactions, about 350 pages, 1973.

See Commercial Transactions.
See Sales.

## SURETYSHIP AND GUARANTY

Osborne's Cases on Suretyship, 221 pages, 1966.

Simpson's Cases on Suretyship, 538 pages, 1942.

## TAXATION

Chommie's Text on Federal Income Taxation, 2nd Ed., about 1000 pages, 1973.

Hellerstein's Cases on State and Local Taxation, 3rd Ed., 741 pages, 1969.

Kragen & McNulty's Cases on Federal Income Taxation, 1,182 pages, 1970.

Lowndes & Kramer's Text on Federal Estate and Gift Taxes, 2nd Ed., 951 pages, 1962.

McNulty's Federal Income Taxation in a Nutshell, 322 pages, 1972.

Rice's Problems in Federal Estate & Gift Taxation, 2nd Ed., 496 pages, 1972.

Rice's Problems in Federal Income Taxation, 2nd Ed., 589 pages, 1971.

## TORTS

Green, Pedrick, Rahl, Thode, Hawkins and Smith's Cases on Torts, 1311 pages, 1968.

Green, Pedrick, Rahl, Thode, Hawkins and Smith's Cases on Injuries to Relations, 466 pages, 1968.

Keeton and Keeton's Cases on Torts, 1193 pages, 1971.

Prosser's Text on Torts, 4th Ed., 1208 pages, 1971.

## TRADE REGULATION

See Anti-Trust Law.
See Unfair Trade Practices.

## TRIAL AND APPELLATE PRACTICE

See Pleading and Procedure.

## TRUSTS

Bogert's Text on Trusts, 5th Ed., about 535 pages, 1973.

Powell's Cases on Trusts and Wills, 639 pages, 1960.

See Wills, Intestate Succession, Trusts, Gifts and Future Interests.

## UNFAIR TRADE PRACTICES

Oppenheim's Cases on Unfair Trade Practices, 783 pages, 1965.

Oppenheim and Weston's Supplement.

Oppenheim's Robinson-Patman Act Pamphlet, 295 pages, 1967.

## WATER LAW

Trelease's Cases on Water Law, 364 pages, 1967.

## WILLS

Atkinson's Text on Wills, 2nd Ed., 975 pages, 1953.

Mennell's Cases on California Decedents' Estates, 566 pages, 1973.

Turrentine's Cases on Wills, 2nd Ed., 483 pages, 1962.

See Wills, Intestate Succession, Trusts, Gifts and Future Interests.

## WILLS, INTESTATE SUCCESSION, TRUSTS, GIFTS AND FUTURE INTERESTS

Gulliver, Clark, Lusky and Murphy's Cases on Gratuitous Transfers: Wills, Intestate Succession, Trusts, Gifts and Future Interests, 1017 pages, 1967.

## WORKMEN'S COMPENSATION

Malone and Plant's Cases on Workmen's Compensation, 622 pages, 1963.

# HANDBOOK

## OF THE LAW UNDER THE

# UNIFORM COMMERCIAL CODE

By

**JAMES J. WHITE**

Professor of Law, University of Michigan

and

**ROBERT S. SUMMERS**

Professor of Law, Cornell University

**HORNBOOK SERIES**

ST. PAUL, MINN.

WEST PUBLISHING CO.

1972

White & Summers U.C.C. HB
1st Reprint—1973

WE HEREBY AFFECTIONATELY DEDICATE
THIS WORK TO OUR PARENTS

| | |
|---|---|
| Leland C. White | Orson W. Summers |
| and | and |
| Vernie B. White | Estella R. Summers |
| of | of |
| Harlan, Iowa | Halfway, Oregon |

WHO MUST ULTIMATELY
SHARE SOME OF THE BLAME

\*

# PREFACE

The libraries include many one-volume treatises that answer all the questions no one ever asks and answer none of the questions that everyone asks. And some pages of treatises in statutory fields offer little beyond statutory paraphrase. Further, while in our system statutory law tends to be transformed into case law, the treatises often relegate cases to footnote status. At least we have done our work on this book mindful of these flaws; only the readers can say whether we have avoided them ourselves. Of course, a treatise on the Uniform Commercial Code must lay out basic content and collect and analyze the rapidly growing case law. We have, as well, sought to identify and treat real questions, and have forced ourselves to take positions on some important issues as yet unresolved in the cases.

This book is designed for two audiences, law students and practitioners. To a certain extent those audiences have different needs. For example, we include footnotes plump with citations for the practitioner; and for student and practitioner alike we offer our best effort at exposition of the law. Doubtless the experienced practitioner and the advanced student will find some of our exposition too elemental, and the beginning student will surely find some of it too complex. We console ourselves that treatise writers who try to do only a thousand pages on a body of law as large as the Uniform Commercial Code must and should make compromises. Certainly it would have been unwise to treat only the exciting frontier questions. And it would have been similarly unwise to dwell only on what is basic.

As the table of contents will disclose, the book is organized in the same fashion as the Code and proceeds through the Articles from first to last. We have omitted consideration of one Article (Article 8); we have made relatively short work of others (Articles 4, 5, and 6), and have dealt in a comparatively generous way with several (Articles 2, 3 and 9). We have strayed, too, into adjoining law as relevant (mainly the Bankruptcy Act and the Federal Bills of Lading Act). We believe we have concentrated our efforts in ways that reflect not only the student's but also the lawyer's needs. For example, most lawyers can practice in relative ignorance of Article 8 without fear of a malpractice suit, but the same is not at all true with respect to Article 9. To the extent our guesses are incorrect we hope to hear from our readers.

A final word about our collaboration. One of us was in a position to do more on the book than the other. That other felt the order of the authors' names should reflect this fact, and was insistent. But,

# PREFACE

(a few differences over policy aside) the authors are jointly and severally liable for any and all blunders, mistakes, or other deficiencies. Each went over the work of the other, and there were numerous discussions and meetings (not wholly without refreshment). So here it is. We hope it helps.

J. J. W.
R. S. S.

October, 1972

P. S.  We do not treat pre-Code case law to any significant extent, a decision forced on us by limitations of space and time. Certainly it is not our view that the Code displaces all pre-Code cases.

# ACKNOWLEDGMENTS

Professor White gratefully acknowledges the dedication, skill and effort of the following students at the University of Michigan Law School, each of whom contributed significantly to the preparation of this book: Ron Brot, '71, Bruce Chadwick, '72, Mike Huotari, '72, Gail Miller, '71, Dick McCarthy, '71, George McKeegan, '72, Gary McRay, '72, Susan Wright, '71, Gretchen Steadry '73 and Robert A. Rowan '73.

Professor White also gratefully acknowledges the super-human effort of First-Sergeant Kathie Cohn.

Professor Summers gratefully acknowledges the dedication, skill and effort of the following students of the Cornell University School of Law, each of whom contributed significantly to the preparation of this book: James A. DeMent, Jr., '72, Robert A. Hillman, '72, Derek W. Hunt, '72, Charles M. Adelman, '73, and Kelly T. Hynes, '73. Professor Summers also wishes to record his indebtedness and gratitude to Mrs. Ann B. Pendleton, head of the Cornell Law School Secretarial Staff and to Mrs. Jylanda Diles, Mrs. Barbara A. Haueisen, and Miss Susan Capogrossi of the Cornell Law School Secretarial Staff. In addition, Professor Summers wishes to express his sincere thanks to Professor Harry Bitner, Cornell Law Librarian, and to librarians Alan Diefenbach and Robert Oakley. Finally, an expression of profound gratitude is due W. Ray Forrester, Dean of the Cornell Law School, for his encouragement and support throughout this three year project. It has indeed been a privilege and a pleasure to work on books in the atmosphere prevailing during his deanship.

Both Professor White and Professor Summers wish to express special gratitude to Mr. James A. DeMent, Jr., Cornell Law School, Class of 1972. Mr. DeMent performed yeoman service throughout, and took on a great many of the technical chores involved in preparing the final manuscript for the printer.

\*

# SUMMARY OF CONTENTS

## THE UNIFORM COMMERCIAL CODE— AN INTRODUCTION

### ARTICLE TWO

| Chapter | Page |
|---|---|
| 1. Offer, Acceptance, and Consideration | 21 |
| 2. Statute of Frauds and Parol Evidence Rule | 43 |
| 3. Terms of the Contract | 82 |
| 4. Unconscionability | 112 |
| 5. Risk of Loss | 134 |
| 6. Buyer's Remedies for Repudiation, for Nondelivery and for Failure to Deliver Conforming Goods (Which the Buyer Refused to Keep) | 167 |
| 7. Seller's Remedies | 207 |
| 8. Rejection, Revocation of Acceptance, Cure and Acceptance | 246 |
| 9. Warranty | 271 |
| 10. Damages for Breach of Warranty | 306 |
| 11. Defenses to Warranty Actions | 326 |
| 12. Disclaimers of Warranty Liability and Modification of Buyer's Remedies | 349 |

### ARTICLES THREE and FOUR

| Chapter | Page |
|---|---|
| 13. The Negotiable Instrument: Party's Contract Liability; Discharge; and the Underlying Obligation | 397 |
| 14. The Holder in Due Course | 456 |
| 15. Liabilities Associated With Stolen (and Lost) Instruments; Forged Signatures | 492 |
| 16. NSF, Forged Drawer's Signature, and Negligence | 519 |
| 17. The Payor Bank and Its Customer | 551 |

### ARTICLES FIVE and SIX

| Chapter | Page |
|---|---|
| 18. Letters of Credit | 601 |
| 19. Bulk Transfers | 640 |

### ARTICLE SEVEN

| Chapter | Page |
|---|---|
| 20. Storage of Goods Covered by Warehouse Receipts—Rights and Liabilities of Parties, Including Purchasers and Lenders | 667 |
| 21. Carriage of Goods Covered by Bills of Lading—Rights and Liabilities of Parties, Including Purchasers and Lenders | 710 |

# SUMMARY OF CONTENTS

# ARTICLE NINE

| Chapter | | Page |
|---|---|---|
| 22. | Scope of Article Nine | 754 |
| 23. | Creation and Perfection of Enforceable Article Nine Interests | 785 |
| 24. | The Bankruptcy Trustee vs. The Article Nine Claimant | 864 |
| 25. | Priority Conflicts: Mainty 9–307—9–313 | 899 |
| 26. | Default and Its Consequences | 954 |
| **Table of Cases** | | 1009 |
| **Table of Statutes** | | 1031 |
| **Index** | | 1063 |

# TABLE OF CONTENTS

## THE UNIFORM COMMERCIAL CODE—
## AN INTRODUCTION

| Sec. | | Page |
|---|---|---|
| 1. | Nature and Origins | 1 |
| 2. | Commercial Law Not Covered; Freedom of Contract | 5 |
| 3. | Variations in Enactment and in Interpretation; Conflict of Laws Rules | 7 |
| 4. | Aids to Interpretation and Construction | 8 |
| 5. | Aids in Drafting Documents Under the Code | 19 |
| 6. | A Note on Article One | 19 |

## ARTICLE TWO

### CHAPTER 1. OFFER, ACCEPTANCE, AND CONSIDERATION

| 1–1. | Introduction | 21 |
|---|---|---|
| 1–2. | Battle of the Forms Under Section 2–207 | 23 |
| 1–3. | Firm Offers | 33 |
| 1–4. | Methods of Acceptance | 34 |
| 1–5. | Contract Modification, Waiver, and Estoppel | 36 |

### CHAPTER 2. STATUTE OF FRAUDS AND PAROL
### EVIDENCE RULE

| 2–1. | Introduction | 43 |
|---|---|---|
| 2–2. | Transactions to Which Statute Applies; Other UCC Statutes of Frauds | 44 |
| 2–3. | General Structure of Statute; Consequences of Compliance and Noncompliance | 46 |
| 2–4. | Satisfying the Statute with a Writing | 51 |
| 2–5. | Satisfying Statutory Exceptions to the Writing Requirement | 54 |
| 2–6. | Satisfying Nonstatutory Exceptions to the Writing Requirement | 59 |
| 2–7. | Procedural and Remedial Matters | 60 |
| 2–8. | Statutes of Frauds—An Evaluation | 63 |
| 2–9. | The Parol Evidence Rule—Does It Give Preference to Written Evidence of Contract Terms? | 65 |
| 2–10. | Substantive Aspects of the Parol Evidence Rule—Problems of Interpretation | 68 |
| 2–11. | Judge-Made Exceptions to the Parol Evidence Rule | 75 |
| 2–12. | "Merger" Clauses and the Parol Evidence Rule | 76 |

# TABLE OF CONTENTS

## CHAPTER 3. TERMS OF THE CONTRACT

| Sec. | | Page |
|------|---|------|
| 3–1. | Introduction | 82 |
| 3–2. | Terms Supplied by Express Agreement of the Parties | 82 |
| 3–3. | Terms Supplied by Course of Dealing, Usage of Trade, and Course of Performance | 84 |
| 3–4. | Terms Supplied by Gap Filler Provisions of Article Two and General Law—Introduction | 88 |
| 3–5. | Article Two Gap Fillers on Delivery Terms (Herein, too, of Seller's Proper Tender of Delivery) | 88 |
| 3–6. | Article Two Gap Fillers on Payment Terms (Herein, too, of Buyer's Tender of Payment) | 95 |
| 3–7. | Article Two Gap Fillers on Price | 98 |
| 3–8. | Article Two Gap Fillers on Quantity (Especially in Requirements Contracts) | 103 |
| 3–9. | Mandatory Terms Under Article Two—Limits on Freedom of Contract | 109 |

## CHAPTER 4. UNCONSCIONABILITY

| | | |
|------|---|------|
| 4–1. | Introduction | 112 |
| 4–2. | Unconscionability in General | 113 |
| 4–3. | Procedural Unconscionability | 118 |
| 4–4. | Substantive Unconscionability | 119 |
| 4–5. | —— Excessive Price | 120 |
| 4–6. | —— Remedy Meddling | 125 |
| 4–7. | Relation of Procedural to Substantive Unconscionability | 128 |
| 4–8. | Form of Relief | 130 |

## CHAPTER 5. RISK OF LOSS

| | | |
|------|---|------|
| 5–1. | Introduction | 134 |
| 5–2. | 2–509(1), Contracts Contemplating Transportation by Carrier | 140 |
| 5–3. | 2–509(2), Goods Held by a Bailee | 144 |
| 5–4. | 2–509(3), The Residue | 145 |
| 5–5. | 2–510, Effect of Breach on Risk of Loss | 146 |
| 5–6. | Subrogation | 150 |
| 5–7. | Restrictions and Limitations Upon the Doctrine of Subrogation | 158 |
| 5–8. | Contribution—Introduction | 161 |
| 5–9. | —— Other Insurance Clauses | 163 |
| 5–10. | —— Conflicts Between Other Insurance Clauses | 164 |

# TABLE OF CONTENTS

## CHAPTER 6. BUYER'S REMEDIES FOR REPUDIATION, FOR NONDELIVERY AND FOR FAILURE TO DELIVER CONFORMING GOODS (WHICH THE BUYER REFUSED TO KEEP)

| Sec. | | Page |
|---|---|---|
| 6–1. | Introduction | 167 |
| 6–2. | Repudiation, Nondelivery, and Other Occasions for Resort to a Remedy | 168 |
| 6–3. | Cover, 2–712 | 175 |
| 6–4. | Contract-Market Damages, 2–713 | 180 |
| 6–5. | Buyer's Incidental and Consequential Damages | 192 |
| 6–6. | Specific Performance | 192 |
| 6–7. | The Buyer's Possible Responses to Repudiation | 196 |

## CHAPTER 7. SELLER'S REMEDIES

| 7–1. | Introduction, 2–703 | 207 |
|---|---|---|
| 7–2. | Action for the Price, 2–709 | 208 |
| 7–3. | —— Goods Accepted | 210 |
| 7–4. | —— Lost or Damaged Goods | 213 |
| 7–5. | —— Goods Not Reasonably Resalable | 213 |
| 7–6. | Seller's Resale, 2–706 | 216 |
| 7–7. | Damages for Nondelivery or Repudiation, 2–708(1) | 220 |
| 7–8. | Lost Profits, 2–708(2) | 225 |
| 7–9. | —— The Lost Volume Seller | 226 |
| 7–10. | —— Components and Jobber Sellers | 227 |
| 7–11. | —— Other Cases | 229 |
| 7–12. | —— Is 2–708(1) Ever Too Generous? | 232 |
| 7–13. | —— The Formula | 234 |
| 7–14. | Seller's Rights and Obligations With Respect to Unidentified and Incomplete Goods, 2–704 | 238 |
| 7–15. | Unpaid Seller's Goods-Oriented Remedies on Buyer's Insolvency | 241 |

## CHAPTER 8. REJECTION, REVOCATION OF ACCEPTANCE, CURE AND ACCEPTANCE

| 8–1. | Introduction | 246 |
|---|---|---|
| 8–2. | Acceptance, 2–606 | 249 |
| 8–3. | Rejection and Revocation of Acceptance, 2–601, 2–608, 2–612 | 253 |
| 8–4. | Cure, 2–508 | 266 |

## CHAPTER 9. WARRANTY

| 9–1. | Introduction | 271 |
|---|---|---|
| 9–2. | Express Warranties, 2–313 | 273 |
| 9–3. | —— What Words or Symbols? | 274 |

# TABLE OF CONTENTS

Sec.                                                                                        Page

9–4.   —— When and Where? Basis of the Bargain ............ 277

9–5.   —— Samples and Models ............ 282

9–6.   The Implied Warranty of Merchantability, 2–314—Introduction ............ 286

9–7.   —— Merchantability Defined ............ 289

9–8.   —— Causation ............ 295

9–9.   Fitness for Particular Purpose, 2–315 ............ 296

9–10.   The Warranties of Title and Against Infringement, 2–312  299

9–11.   —— Cause of Action ............ 299

9–12.   —— Disclaimer ............ 303

## CHAPTER 10. DAMAGES FOR BREACH OF WARRANTY

10–1.   Introduction ............ 306

10–2.   Damages for Breach of Warranty—The Basic Formula, 2–714(1) and (2) ............ 307

10–3.   —— Incidental Damages, 2–715(1) ............ 312

10–4.   —— Consequential Damages ............ 314

## CHAPTER 11. DEFENSES TO WARRANTY ACTIONS

11–1.   Introduction ............ 326

11–2.   Lack of Privity as a Defense to a Warranty Cause of Action ............ 327

11–3.   Privity—Personal Injury ............ 329

11–4.   —— Property Damage ............ 332

11–5.   —— Economic Loss—Loss of the Bargain and Profits .. 333

11–6.   —— Express Warranty ............ 335

11–7.   Defenses Based Upon Plaintiff's Contributory Behavior  335

11–8.   Statute of Limitations ............ 339

11–9.   Buyer's Failure to Give Notice as a Defense to Actions for Breach of Warranty ............ 343

## CHAPTER 12. DISCLAIMERS OF WARRANTY LIABILITY AND MODIFICATION OF BUYER'S REMEDIES

12–1.   Introduction ............ 349

12–2.   Disclaimers of Express Warranties, 2–316(1) ............ 351

12–3.   —— Conflict Within Written Agreement ............ 352

12–4.   —— Oral Warranties Made Prior to the Written Agreement ............ 354

12–5.   Disclaimers of Implied Warranties—Explicit Disclaimers of Implied Warranties, 2–316(2) ............ 356

12–6.   —— Other Methods ............ 364

12–7.   Cumulation and Conflict of Warranties, 2–317 ............ 372

12–8.   Modification or Limitation of Remedies, 2–719 ............ 375

12–9.   —— How to Limit the Buyer's Remedies, 2–719(1) .... 376

12–10. —— Failure of Stipulated Remedy to Achieve Its Essential Purpose, 2–719(2) _____ 379

12–11. —— Unconscionable Limitation of Remedy, 2–719(3) and 2–302 _____ 383

12–12. —— Use of 2–719(3) to Invalidate an Otherwise Valid Disclaimer _____ 392

# ARTICLES THREE and FOUR

## CHAPTER 13. THE NEGOTIABLE INSTRUMENT: PARTY'S CONTRACT LIABILITY; DISCHARGE; AND THE UNDERLYING OBLIGATION

13–1. Introduction _____ 397

13–2. Signature: Requirement and Form _____ 399

13–3. Some Agency Questions—Principal's Liability for Signature by Agent, 3–403(1), 3–404 _____ 400

13–4. —— Personal Liability of the Agent on Instruments Allegedly Signed in a "Representative Capacity" 403

13–5. —— Parol Evidence to Show Representative Capacity, 3–403(2)(b) _____ 406

13–6. Contractual Liability—Parties to an Instrument _____ 408

13–7. —— Liability of the Maker, 3–413(1) _____ 408

13–8. —— Liability of the Acceptor, 3–413, 3–412, 3–411, 3–410, 3–409 _____ 410

13–9. —— Liability of the Drawer, 3–413(2) _____ 411

13–10. —— Liability of the Indorser, 3–414 _____ 413

13–11. Warranty Liabilities _____ 425

13–12. Accommodation Parties, 3–415, 3–416, 3–606, General Liability of Article Three Surety _____ 425

13–13. —— Establishing Suretyship Status—Form of Signature and Parol Evidence, 3–415(3), 3–415(4), 3–416 _____ 429

13–14. —— Suretyship Defenses, 3–606 and Beyond _____ 432

13–15. —— Effect of Surety's Consent or Creditor's Reservation of Rights, 3–606(1), 3–606(2) _____ 436

13–16. —— Relationship Between Surety and Principal, Subrogation, Reimbursement and 3–415(5) _____ 438

13–17. —— Right of Surety to Assert Principal's Defenses _____ 440

13–18. Discharge, 3–601, 3–603, 3–605 _____ 443

13–19. —— Cancellation and Renunciation, 3–605 _____ 446

13–20. —— The Underlying Obligation, Suspension, and Discharge, 3–802 _____ 448

13–21. —— Discharge of a Disputed Obligation by Tender of a Check in "Full Satisfaction", 1–207 _____ 452

13–22. Lost or Stolen Instruments, 3–804 _____ 454

# TABLE OF CONTENTS

## CHAPTER 14.  THE HOLDER IN DUE COURSE

Sec.    Page

14–1.     Introduction .................................................... 456
14–2.     Holder in Due Course Defined ............................ 458
14–3.     ——— Holder ................................................ 458
14–4.     ——— Instrument ............................................ 459
14–5.     ——— Value .................................................. 465
14–6.     ——— Good Faith and Without Notice .................... 471
14–7.     The Payee as a Holder in Due Course .................. 478
14–8.     Judge-Made Limitations on the Holder in Due Course Doctrine—Close Connectedness .............................. 479
14–9.     Legislative Limitations on the Holder in Due Course Doctrine .................................................... 484
14–10.    Rights of the Holder in Due Course .................... 486
14–11.    Rights of a Holder Who is Not a Holder in Due Course .. 490

## CHAPTER 15.  LIABILITIES ASSOCIATED WITH STOLEN (AND LOST) INSTRUMENTS;  FORGED SIGNATURES

15–1.     Introduction .................................................... 492
15–2.     Drawer's Liability on Stolen (and Lost) Instruments, 3–804 ........................................................ 496
15–3.     Drawee's Liability to Drawer for Paying Over a Forged Indorsement, 4–401 ...................................... 498
15–4.     Conversion: Liability of Drawee and Other Banks to the "Owner" of a Stolen Instrument for Cashing or Otherwise Dealing With the Instrument, 3–419 ............. 499
15–5.     Stolen Checks and Notes—Warranty Liability, 4–207, 3–417 ........................................................ 509
15–6.     Conclusion .................................................... 517

## CHAPTER 16.  NSF, FORGED DRAWER'S SIGNATURE, AND NEGLIGENCE

16–1.     Introduction .................................................... 519
16–2.     Checks Bearing Forged Drawer's Signature ............ 519
16–3.     NSF Checks .................................................. 529
16–4.     Final Payment ................................................ 530
16–5.     Negligence .................................................... 537
16–6.     Negligence, 3–406 ............................................ 537
16–7.     Negligence, 4–406 ............................................ 539
16–8.     Impostors and Fictitious Payees .......................... 541
16–9.     Conclusion .................................................... 550

## CHAPTER 17.  THE PAYOR BANK AND ITS CUSTOMER

17–1.     Introduction .................................................... 551
17–2.     The Deposit Contract and Permissible Variation of Code Provisions, 4–103 ...................................... 552

# TABLE OF CONTENTS

17–3. When Bank May Charge Customer's Account, 4–401, 4–404, 4–405 _____ 558

17–4. The Bank's Liability to Its Customer for Wrongful Dishonor, 4–402 _____ 566

17–5. The Customer's Right to Stop Payment, 4–403 _____ 574

17–6. Payor Bank's Liability for Its Failure to Follow a Legitimate Stop Order, 4–403(3); Its Right to Subrogation on Improper Payment, 4–407 _____ 580

17–7. Priorities in the Customer's Bank Account, 4–303 _____ 588

## ARTICLES FIVE and SIX

### CHAPTER 18.   LETTERS OF CREDIT

18–1. Introduction _____ 601

18–2. Legal Nature of the Letter of Credit _____ 607

18–3. Relevant Sources of Law and Freedom of Contract _____ 608

18–4. Setting up a Valid Irrevocable Letter of Credit Arrangement Pursuant to Article Five; Valid and Invalid Terms; Variation by Agreement; Time the Credit Becomes "Established" _____ 615

18–5. An Inventory of Ways that a Valid, Irrevocable, and Established Letter of Credit Arrangement May Breakdown or Otherwise Go Astray _____ 618

18–6. Actual or Prospective Breakdowns Adversely Affecting the Beneficiary in the First Instance (Herein mainly of issuer's wrongful dishonor) _____ 619

18–7. Actual or Prospective Breakdowns Adversely Affecting the Customer in the First Instance (Herein mainly of issuer's wrongful honor, and of beneficiary nonperformance of the underlying contract) _____ 628

18–8. Actual or Prospective Breakdowns Adversely Affecting the Issuer (Herein mainly of wrongful honor) _____ 632

18–9. Transfer and Assignment of Letters of Credit and Rights Thereunder; Back to Back Credits (Letters of credit as financing devices) _____ 633

### CHAPTER 19.   BULK TRANSFERS

19–1. Introduction _____ 640

19–2. Bulk Transfers to Which Article Six of the Code Applies 644

19–3. Requirements of Article Six—Ways the Parties to a Bulk Transfer May Fail to Comply _____ 649

19–4. "Individual" Remedies of Transferor's Creditors in Event of Noncompliance _____ 653

19–5. "Individual" Remedies of Transferor's Creditors in Event of Compliance _____ 657

# TABLE OF CONTENTS

Sec.                                                               Page

19–6.   Conflicts Between Transferor's Creditors and Third Parties—Some Problems of Priority .......... 661

19–7.   Individual Creditor's Recovery v. Collective Remedies—An Addendum .......... 662

# ARTICLE SEVEN

## CHAPTER 20. STORAGE OF GOODS COVERED BY WAREHOUSE RECEIPTS—RIGHTS AND LIABILITIES OF PARTIES, INCLUDING PURCHASERS AND LENDERS

20–1.   Introduction .......... 667

20–2.   Scope and Structure of Article Seven .......... 668

20–3.   Rights of Storer Against Warehouseman .......... 671

20–4.   Rights of Purchaser of Warehouse Receipts .......... 682

20–5.   Rights of Pledgee of Warehouse Receipts .......... 697

## CHAPTER 21. CARRIAGE OF GOODS COVERED BY BILLS OF LADING—RIGHTS AND LIABILITIES OF PARTIES, INCLUDING PURCHASERS AND LENDERS

21–1.   Introduction .......... 710

21–2.   Law Applicable to Carriage of Goods and to Bills of Lading .......... 711

21–3.   Rights of Shipper Against Carrier .......... 713

21–4.   Rights of Purchasers of Bills of Lading .......... 741

21–5.   Rights of Pledgees of Bills of Lading .......... 750

# ARTICLE NINE

## CHAPTER 22. SCOPE OF ARTICLE NINE

22–1.   Introduction .......... 754

22–2.   The Basic Article Nine Scope Provision, 9–102(1) .......... 757

22–3.   —— Security Interest or Lease? .......... 759

22–4.   —— Consignments as Security Interests (Herein, too, of 2–326) .......... 765

22–5.   Surety's Subrogation Rights Not a Security Interest .......... 769

22–6.   Extent Article Nine Applies to Realty Interests .......... 771

22–7.   A Note on the 9–104 Exclusions .......... 773

22–8.   Applicability of Article Nine to Sales of Accounts, Contract Rights and Chattel Paper .......... 775

22–9.   Conflict of Laws Problems .......... 778

22–10.   Applicability of Article Nine to "Security Interests" that Arise Under Article Two on Sales .......... 780

22–11.   State and Federal Law that Over-Rides Article Nine .......... 782

# TABLE OF CONTENTS

## CHAPTER 23. CREATION AND PERFECTION OF ENFORCEABLE ARTICLE NINE INTERESTS

Sec. | | Page
23–1. | Introduction | 785
23–2. | Creation of Valid and Enforceable Article Nine Security Interests—General | 786
23–3. | The Agreement and Signed Writing Requirements, 9–203, 9–204 | 786
23–4. | Value and Debtor Rights | 791
23–5. | Perfection in General | 796
23–6. | Automatic Perfection | 797
23–7. | —— Purchase Money Interests in Farm Equipment and Consumer Goods, 9–302(1) (c) and (d) | 798
23–8. | —— Certain Accounts and Contract Rights, 9–302(1) (e) | 805
23–9. | —— Miscellaneous Automatic Perfection Provisions, 9–304(4) and (5), 9–306 | 809
23–10. | Perfection by Possession, 9–305 | 814
23–11. | Perfection by Filing—Places to File | 818
23–12. | —— Where to File? | 820
23–13. | —— Classifying the Collateral | 823
23–14. | —— Place of Business | 825
23–15. | —— Effect of Filings Made in the Wrong Place, 9–401 (2) | 829
23–16. | —— What to File? The Financing Statement, 9–402 | 833
23–17. | Perfection in Multiple State Transactions, 9–103 | 846
23–18. | —— Nonmobile, Tangible Goods | 847
23–19. | —— Mobile Goods, 9–103(2) | 852
23–20. | —— Intangibles, 9–103(1) and (2) | 854
23–21. | —— Automobiles and Other Vehicles Covered by Certificates of Title, 9–103(4) | 855
23–22. | Conclusion | 862

## CHAPTER 24. THE BANKRUPTCY TRUSTEE VS. THE ARTICLE NINE CLAIMANT

24–1. | Introduction | 864
24–2. | Failure to Create Security Valid and Enforceable Against the Debtor—Trustee's Rights Under Section 70(a) and 70(c) | 866
24–3. | Lack of Perfection as of Date of Bankruptcy—Trustee's Rights Under 70(c) | 867
24–4. | Delayed Perfection—Trustee's Possible Right to Avoid as Preferential Under Section 60 | 871
24–5. | "Floating Liens"—Trustee's Possible Right to Avoid as Preferential Under Section 60 | 876

# TABLE OF CONTENTS

Sec. Page

24-6. Security Interests in "Proceeds"—Trustee's Possible Right to Avoid as Preferential or as Otherwise Invalid 883

24-7. Debtor's Payments to Secured Creditor—Trustee's Possible Right to Avoid as Preferential Under Section 60 888

24-8. Some Extraordinary and Bizarre Avoidances Under Sections 67(a) and 70(e) 889

24-9. The Article Nine Security Transfer as a "Fraudulent Conveyance" Under Sections 70(e) or 67(d) 892

24-10. Attacks by the Trustee on the Underlying Debt Itself 897

## CHAPTER 25. PRIORITY CONFLICTS: MAINLY 9-307—9-313

25-1. Introduction 899

25-2. Rights of the Secured Creditor vis-a-vis Unsecured Creditors With and Without Judicial Liens, 9-201, 9-301 901

25-3. Basic Priorities—Among Secured Creditors, 9-312 903

25-4. —— First in Time, First in Right, 9-312(5) 905

25-5. —— Second in Time, First in Right, Purchase Money Security Interests, 9-312(3) and (4) 913

25-6. —— Security Interests in Crops, 9-312(2) 922

25-7. Priorities in Fixtures Between Real Estate Claimants and Secured Creditors, 9-313 924

25-8. Fixtures—What is a Fixture? 924

25-9. —— The Routine 9-313 Cases 927

25-10. —— Some Interpretative Snarls in 9-313 931

25-11. —— Proposed Changes in 9-313 935

25-12. Priority of Purchasers of Goods, 9-307 938

25-13. —— 9-307(1) and Buyers in the Ordinary Course of Business 940

25-14. —— Consumer Purchasers of Consumer Goods, 9-307 (2) 943

25-15. —— Relationship Between 2-403 and 9-307 944

25-16. —— Special Problems Involving Vehicles, Aircraft and Non-Code Recording Acts 946

25-17. Purchasers of Chattel Paper and Non-negotiable Instruments, 9-308 949

25-18. Purchasers of Instruments and Documents, 9-309 952

## CHAPTER 26. DEFAULT AND ITS CONSEQUENCES

26-1. Introduction 954

26-2. Defining "Default" 956

26-3. —— Acceleration Clauses 958

26-4. Creditor's Alternatives Upon Default 961

26-5. Repossession 966

26-6. —— Self-Help 966

26-7. —— Judicial Action 975

26-8. Strict Foreclosure 977

# TABLE OF CONTENTS

| Sec. | | Page |
|---|---|---|
| 26–9. | Resale of Repossessed Collateral | 981 |
| 26–10. | —— The Notice Requirement | 983 |
| 26–11. | —— Commercially Reasonable | 987 |
| 26–12. | Consequences of Creditor Misbehavior | 995 |
| 26–13. | Creditor Misbehavior—Criminal or Tort Liability | 995 |
| 26–14. | —— Liability Under the UCC, § 9–507(1) | 997 |
| 26–15. | —— Denial of a Deficiency | 1000 |

**Table of Cases** _____ 1009

**Table of Statutes** _____ 1031

**Index** _____ 1063

†

# HANDBOOK

## ON THE

# UNIFORM COMMERCIAL CODE

---

## THE UNIFORM COMMERCIAL CODE—
## AN INTRODUCTION

*Analysis*

Sec.
1. Nature and Origins.
2. Commercial Law Not Covered; Freedom of Contract.
3. Variations in Enactment and in Interpretation; Conflict of Laws Rules.
4. Aids to Interpretation and Construction.
5. Aids in Drafting Documents Under the Code.
6. A Note on Article One.

## § 1. Nature and Origins

Today the Uniform Commercial Code, 1962 Official Text with variations, is law in all states but Louisiana and is also law in the District of Columbia and the Virgin Islands.[1] The Code is law in these jurisdictions by virtue of "local," jurisdiction by jurisdiction, enactment. The United States Congress has not enacted the Code as general federal statutory law,[2] although it did enact the Code for the District of Columbia.[3] The Code is divided into ten articles as follows:

Article 1. General Provisions
Article 2. Sales
Article 3. Commercial Paper
Article 4. Bank Deposits and Collections

---

1. The jurisdictions enacting the Uniform Commercial Code and the date of such enactment are listed in 1 U.L.A. XXXVII (Master ed. 1968) (Table 1). Unless otherwise indicated, all references to the Uniform Commercial Code hereafter in this book are to the 1962 Official Text. Variations between this Text and the enacted law are traceable to two factors. First, nearly all states made some amendments to the Code upon enactment. Second, a number of states enacted earlier versions of the Code, versions which vary only slightly from the 1962 Official Text. For those states, see Permanent Editorial Board for the Uniform Commercial Code, Report No. 1 (1962); id., Report No. 2 (1965).

2. From the beginning, there has been some agitation for federal enactment. See, e. g., Braucher, Federal Enactment of the Uniform Commercial Code, 16 Law & Contemp.Prob. 100 (1951); Schnader, The Uniform Commercial Code—Today and Tomorrow, 22 Bus. Law. 229, 232 (1966).

3. D.C.Code Ann. §§ 28:1–101 to 28:10–104 (1967).

**1**

Article 5.    Letters of Credit

Article 6.    Bulk Transfers

Article 7.    Warehouse Receipts, Bills of Lading and Other Documents of Title

Article 8.    Investment Securities

Article 9.    Secured Transactions; Sales of Accounts, Contract Rights and Chattel Paper

Article 10.   Effective Date and Repealer

In all but Article Ten, the Articles are subdivided into "Parts." Thus, in Article One there are two "Parts," while in Article Two there are seven. Each Part is in turn subdivided into "sections." Sections are numbered in the 1962 Official Text in a manner that indicates both Article and Part. Thus, section 2–206 on "Offer and Acceptance in Formation of Contract" is in Article Two, Part Two. The first number of a section always indicates the Article and the second number the Part within that Article in which the section appears. The Official Text of the Code includes "Official Comments" on each section. The enacting jurisdictions did not enact these comments, although they did enact the section headings and the sections (except insofar as they amended the Official Text, a topic which will be considered below). The various jurisdictions, on enacting the Code, followed the arrangement and sequence of the Official Text. In almost all instances, they also preserved the Code's numbering system. For example, in the great State of Oregon, a seven appears before the first digit in the Code's numbering system and a zero after the last digit. Otherwise the Code's numbering system is left intact. Thus, in Oregon, 1–101 is 71.1010.[4]

The National Conference of Commissioners on Uniform State Laws [5] was the originating sponsor of the Code.[6] The Code was not the first venture of the Conference into the field of commercial law reform. The Conference had earlier sponsored a number of "uniform acts" in this field. Such of these acts as were adopted in one or more jurisdictions are listed below, with dates of promulgation:

| | |
|---|---|
| Uniform Negotiable Instruments Law | 1896 |
| Uniform Warehouse Receipts Act | 1906 |
| Uniform Sales Act | 1906 |
| Uniform Bills of Lading Act | 1909 |
| Uniform Stock Transfer Act | 1909 |
| Uniform Conditional Sales Act | 1918 |
| Uniform Trust Receipts Act | 1933 |

All states adopted the Uniform Negotiable Instruments Law and the Uniform Warehouse Receipts Act. Roughly two-thirds of the

4.  Ore.Rev.Stat. § 71.1010 (1972).

5.  Dunham, A History of the National Conference of Commissioners on Uniform State Laws, 30 Law & Contemp. Prob. 233 (1965).

6.  Schnader, A Short History of the Preparation and Enactment of the Uniform Commercial Code, 22 U.Miami L.Rev. 1 (1967).

states adopted the Uniform Sales Act and the Uniform Trust Receipts Act. The other acts were less well received.[7]

By the late 1930's, the foregoing uniform acts had become outdated. Changes had occurred in the patterns of commercial activity prevalent when the acts were promulgated. Also, wholly new patterns had emerged which gave rise to new kinds of legal needs.[8] Moreover, a major objective of the "uniform acts" had been to promote uniformity. But not all states enacted the acts, and the courts of the states rendered countless nonuniform "judicial amendments." By 1940, there was growing interest in commercial law reform. The Conference was already at work revising the old Uniform Sales Act and was giving consideration to a revision of the Uniform Negotiable Instruments Law.[9]

In 1940, Mr. William A. Schnader conceived the idea of a comprehensive commercial code that would modernize and displace the old uniform acts. That same year, with the support and advice of Professor Karl N. Llewellyn, Mr. Schnader, as President of the National Conference of Commissioners on Uniform State Laws, persuaded the Conference to adopt a proposal to prepare a comprehensive code.[10] Shortly thereafter, Schnader and others sought the co-sponsorship of the American Law Institute. Initially, the Institute agreed only to co-sponsor a revision of the old Uniform Sales Act, but on December 1, 1944 the two organizations formally agreed to co-sponsor a Uniform Commercial Code project, with Professor Karl N. Llewellyn of the Columbia Law School as its "Chief Reporter" and Soia Mentschikoff as Associate Chief Reporter. The co-sponsors also set up a supervisory Editorial Board of five members which was later enlarged. Professor Llewellyn then chose various individuals to serve as principal draftsmen of the main Code Articles:[11]

| | |
|---|---|
| Article 1. | Karl N. Llewellyn |
| Article 2. | Karl N. Llewellyn |
| Article 3. | William L. Prosser |
| Article 4. | Fairfax Leary, Jr. |
| Article 5. | Fredrich Kessler |
| Article 6. | Charles Bunn |
| Article 7. | Louis B. Schwartz |
| Article 8. | Soia Mentschikoff |
| Article 9. | Allison Dunham and Grant Gilmore |

7. See R. Braucher & A. Sutherland, Commercial Transactions, Selected Statutes x-xi (1964 ed.) (Table of Statutes Adopted).

8. Llewellyn, Why We Need the Uniform Commercial Code, 10 U.Fla.L.Rev. 367 (1957).

9. Malcolm, The Uniform Commercial Code in the United States, 12 Int'l & Comp.L.Q. 226, 229 (1963).

10. Schnader, A Short History of the Preparation and Enactment of the Uniform Commercial Code, 22 U.Miami L. Rev. 1 (1967).

11. Interesting reflections of Llewellyn on some of these selections appear in W. Twining, The Karl Llewellyn Papers 97–102 (1968).

Between 1944 and 1950, the foregoing team formulated (not without extensive consultation) the first complete draft of the Code. The co-sponsors then circulated this draft widely for comment. After revision, the co-sponsors promulgated the first Official Text of the Code in September of 1951 and published it as the "1952 Official Text." [12] In 1953, Pennsylvania became the first state to enact the Code, effective July 1, 1954. In February of 1953, the New York State Legislature and Governor Thomas Dewey referred the Code to the New York State Law Revision Commission (located at the Cornell Law School) for study and recommendations. Between 1953 and 1955, the Commission dropped all other work and spent several hundred thousand dollars studying the Code. In the end, the Commission concluded that the Code idea was a good one but that New York should not enact it without extensive revision.[13] Meanwhile, the Code's Editorial Board had been studying the Commission's work (as well as proposals for revision from other sources) and in 1956 the Board recommended numerous changes in the 1952 Official Text.[14] In 1957, the co-sponsors promulgated a 1957 Official Text that embodied numerous changes, many of which were based on the Commission's study. Another Official Text was promulgated in 1958, and still another one in 1962. The latter two made relatively minor changes in the 1957 Official Text.

Meanwhile, Massachusetts became the second state to enact the Code in September 1957. By 1960, Kentucky, Connecticut, New Hampshire, and Rhode Island had followed suit. In 1961, eight more states joined the fold. In 1962, there were four more, including New York. In 1963, there were eleven more enacting states, in 1964 one, in 1965 thirteen, and in 1966 five more. By 1968, the Code was effective in forty-nine states, the District of Columbia, and the Virgin Islands.[15] Louisiana remains the only state not to have adopted the Code.

In 1961 the Code sponsors set up a Permanent Editorial Board for the Code which continues in operation to this day.[16] Since its first written report in October 31, 1962, the Board has made two further reports.[17] The Board has been concerned mainly with two tasks:

12. Schnader, A Short History of the Uniform Commercial Code, 22 U.Miami L.Rev. 1 (1967); Mentschikoff, The Uniform Commercial Code: An Experiment in Democracy in Drafting, 36 A.B.A.J. 419 (1950).

13. N.Y.State Law Revision Comm'n, 1956 Report 68 (1956); Symposium, Panel Discussion on the Uniform Commercial Code Report of the New York Law Revision Commission, 12 Bus.Law. 49 (1956).

14. ALI & National Conference of Commissioners on Uniform State Laws, 1956 Recommendations of the Editorial Board for the Uniform Commercial Code (1957).

15. 1 U.L.A. XXXVII (Master ed. 1968) (Table 1).

16. Schnader, The Permanent Editorial Board for the Uniform Commercial Code: Can It Accomplish Its Object?, 3 Am.Bus.L.J. 137 (1965).

17. Permanent Editorial Board for the Uniform Commercial Code, Report No. 2 (1965); Permanent Editorial Board for the Uniform Commercial Code, Report No. 3 (1966).

(*1*) promoting uniformity in state by state enactment and interpretation of the Code and (*2*) evaluating and preparing proposals for revision of the 1962 Official Text. During the late 1960's and early 1970's, the Board devoted great energy to revision of Article Nine on personal property security.[18] Eventually, the American Law Institute and the National Conference of Commissioners on Uniform State Laws approved a revised Article Nine which West Publishing Co. published in 1972 as part of a new 1972 Official Text of the entire Code (incorporating all officially approved amendments thereto).

No one has published an authentic "inside" story on the evolution of the Code. Judged by its reception in the enacting jurisdictions, the Code is the most spectacular success story in the history of American law. We do know that the design and text of the Code bears the inimitable imprint of its chief draftsman, Karl N. Llewellyn,[19] and that his wife, Soia Mentschikoff, had a major hand in the entire project. We know, too, that many individuals whose names have not appeared so prominently as draftsmen or as reporters had great influence on aspects of the final product. One example is Professor Rudolf B. Schlesinger of the Cornell Law School who was not only responsible for the idea of a Permanent Editorial Board,[20] but also provided most of the ideas for the radical revision of Article Five on letters of credit that appeared in the 1957 Official Text.[21] A less obvious example is the extensive work of Professor Robert Braucher of the Harvard Law School (now Mr. Justice Braucher). His work began in the 1940's and continues to this date. We know, too, that politically and in other ways, William A. Schnader of the Philadelphia Bar was the Code's prime mover. It seems safe to say that without his efforts, the Code would not have come into being. Llewellyn and Schnader are now dead (deceased 1962 and 1969, respectively), a fact that imposes a real handicap on anyone who seeks to prepare an authentic history of the Code project. We note that a British scholar, Professor William Twining, has catalogued Llewellyn's papers at the University of Chicago Law School and that he has also developed an interest in writing a history of the Code project.[22]

## § 2. Commercial Law Not Covered; Freedom of Contract

The Uniform Commercial Code does not apply to the sale of realty nor to security interests in realty (except fixtures), yet these are undeniably commercial matters. The Code does not apply to the formation, performance, and enforcement of insurance contracts. It does

18. Permanent Editorial Board for the Uniform Commercial Code, Review Committee for Article 9 of the Uniform Commercial Code, Final Report (1971).

19. Gilmore, In Memoriam: Karl Llewellyn, 71 Yale L.J. 813 (1962).

20. Schlesinger, Problems of Codification of Commercial Law, 1 N.Y.State Law Revision Comm'n, 1955 Report 31–104 (1955).

21. Schlesinger, Study of Uniform Commercial Code Article 5—Documentary Letters of Credit, 3 N.Y.State Law Revision Comm'n, 1955 Report 1569–1719 (1955).

22. W. Twining, The Karl Llewellyn Papers (1968).

not apply to suretyship transactions (except where the surety is a party to a negotiable instrument). It does not govern bankruptcy. It does not define legal tender. It is not a comprehensive codification of commercial law. The Code does not even cover all aspects of transactions to which its provisions do apply. For example, it includes several innovative provisions on the formation of sales contracts,[23] but it still leaves most issues of contract formation to general contract law. To cite one more example, the Code includes provisions on a purchaser's title to goods, but one of these provisions turns on the distinction between void and voidable title,[24] a distinction that requires courts to invoke non-Code law. Section 1–103 is probably the most important single provision in the Code. It reads:

> Unless displaced by the particular provisions of this Act, the principles of law and equity, including the law merchant and the law relative to capacity to contract, principal and agent, estoppel, fraud, misrepresentation, duress, coercion, mistake, bankruptcy, or other validating or invalidating cause shall supplement its provisions.

As Professor Grant Gilmore once put it, the Code "derives from the common law" and "assumes the continuing existence of a large body of pre-Code and non-Code law on which it rests for support," without which the Code "could not survive." [25] Much of the pre-Code and non-Code law to which Professor Gilmore refers is case law from such fields as contracts, agency, and property.

Of course, federal commercial law overrides the Code. The Federal Bills of Lading Act is illustrative.[26] So, too, is the Carmack Amendment [27] to the Interstate Commerce Act. Federal *regulatory* law overrides the Code, too. Today there are federal regulatory statutes such as the National Consumer Credit Protection Act,[28] and federal statutes are even being proposed to regulate automobile manufacturer's warranties. Similarly, there is a growing body of *state* regulatory law that also overrides the Code. Thus, there are state retail instalment sales acts, state usury laws, state laws on consumer credit, and so on. The Code itself includes a few regulatory provisions.[29]

Finally, most of the Code's provisions are not mandatory. That is, the parties may vary their effect or displace them altogether, for freedom of contract is the rule rather than the exception.[30] Most

**23.** Uniform Commercial Code §§ 2–201 to 2–210 [hereinafter cited by section number only].

**24.** § 2–403.

**25.** Gilmore, Article 9: What It Does for the Past, 26 La.L.Rev. 285, 285–286 (1966).

**26.** Act of Aug. 29, 1916, ch. 415, §§ 1 et seq., 39 Stat. 538, as amended, 49 U.S.C.A. §§ 81 et seq. (1970).

**27.** Act of Feb. 4, 1887, ch. 104, Pt. 1, § 20, par. (11), 24 Stat. 386, as amended, 49 U.S.C.A. § 20, par. (11) (1970).

**28.** Act of May 29, 1968, Pub.L. No. 90–321, §§ 101 et seq., 82 Stat. 146, 15 U.S.C.A. §§ 1601 et seq., (1970), 18 U.S. C.A. §§ 891 et seq. (1970).

**29.** E. g., §§ 2–302; 9–501(3).

**30.** Bunn, Freedom of Contract Under the Uniform Commercial Code, 2 B.C. Ind. & Com.L.Rev. 59 (1960).

commercial law is therefore not in the Code at all but in private agreements, including course of dealing, usage of trade, and course of performance.

## § 3.　Variations in Enactment and in Interpretation;　Conflict of Laws Rules

The Uniform Commercial Code is not uniform.　By 1967, the various jurisdictions enacting the Code had made approximately 775 separate amendments to it.[31]　Article Nine on security interests in personal property was the chief victim of nonuniform amendments.　As of December 15, 1966, 47 of the 54 sections in the Article had been amended;[32] California, especially, liberally rewrote or deleted segments of it.　Article Six on bulk transfers was also the subject of many nonuniform amendments.　New York amended Article Five in a way that renders it inapplicable to many letter of credit transactions, and yet New York does more letter of credit business than any other state.

Another source of nonuniformity lies in the various "optional" provisions in the Official Texts of the Code.　Thus, for example, section 9–401 offers enacting states three alternatives with respect to the place for filing of financing statements.　Section 7–403(1)(b) offers two versions as to who has the burden of proving the bailee's negligence.　Section 6–106 imposes a duty on the bulk transferee to see that the transferor's creditors are paid off, but it is wholly optional.　Section 2–318 includes three optional versions on third party beneficiaries of warranties.　And the Code includes still other optional provisions.　In every instance, some states have adopted one version while other states have adopted another.[33]

So-called "open-ended" drafting is another source of nonuniformity.　In Articles Two and Nine, the draftsman used such phrases as "commercial reasonableness" and "good faith."　That different courts will give such phrases different meanings should surprise no one.　And, after any uniform law has been on the books for very long, disparate judicial interpretation and construction of even quite detailed provisions becomes another major source of nonuniformity.[34]　Up until now, relatively few Code sections have been the subject of judicial interpretation and construction in more than one jurisdiction, but even the small returns so far reveal some conflicts,[35] several of which we discuss later in this book.

31.　Schnader, A Short History of the Preparation and Enactment of the Uniform Commercial Code, 22 U.Miami L. Rev. 1, 10 (1967).

32.　Permanent Editorial Board for the Uniform Commercial Code, Report No. 3 at x (1966).

33.　Enactments of optional provisions are set forth generally in 1–3 U.L.A.

(Master ed. 1968) (Uniform Commercial Code).

34.　Note, Disparate Judicial Construction of the Uniform Commercial Code —The Need for Federal Legislation, 1969 Utah L.Rev. 722.

35.　Id. at 726–36.

The foregoing sources of nonuniformity signify that the Code's conflict of laws rules may become important. Section 1–105 sets forth the basic Code provisions:

(1) Except as provided hereafter in this section, when a transaction bears a reasonable relation to this state, and also to another state or nation the parties may agree that the law either of this state or of such other state or nation shall govern their rights and duties. Failing such agreement this Act applies to transactions bearing an appropriate relation to this state.

(2) Where one of the following provisions of this Act specifies the applicable law, that provision governs and a contrary agreement is effective only to the extent permitted by the law (including the conflict of laws rules) so specified:

Rights of creditors against sold goods. Section 2–402.
Applicability of the Article on Bank Deposits and Collections. Section 4–102.
Bulk transfers subject to the Article on Bulk Transfers. Section 6–102.
Applicability of the Article on Investment Securities. Section 8–106.
Policy and scope of the Article on Secured Transactions. Sections 9–102 and 9–103.

Various scholars of the conflict of laws have offered their thoughts on 1–105, and we have collected some of their writings in the footnote.[36] Later in this book we also address ourselves to specific conflicts problems in the contexts in which they arise.

## § 4.  Aids to Interpretation and Construction

The principal aids to interpretation and construction of the Code are these:

Case law
Prior drafts and prior official texts
Other legislative history
    —New York Law Revision Commission Reports
    —State legislative hearings and committee reports
Official Comments to each section
Periodic Reports of the Permanent Editorial Board
Rules of interpretation and construction
Treatises and other secondary sources

36. Nordstrom & Ramerman, The Uniform Commercial Code and the Choice of Law, 1969 Duke L.J. 623; Tuchler, Boundaries to Party Autonomy in the Uniform Commercial Code: A Radical View, 11 St. Louis L.J. 180 (1967); Weintraub, Choice of Law in Secured Personal Property Transactions: The Impact of Article 9 of the Uniform Commercial Code, 68 Mich.L.Rev. 683 (1970); Weintraub, Choice of Law for Products Liability: The Impact of the Uniform Commercial Code and Recent Developments in Conflicts Analysis, 44 Texas L.Rev. 1429 (1966).

We will now discuss each of the foregoing types of aids and will emphasize pitfalls in the use of each.[37]

## CASE LAW

There is now a substantial body of case law interpreting and construing the Code, but on many sections there is either no case at all or only one or two cases. Courts in the same state will likely follow the footsteps of their predecessors, even where those footsteps have gone astray. Some theorists believe the Code is a "true Code" and therefore would hold that every case must be resolved in light of the text itself, prior interpretations to the contrary notwithstanding.[38] We find no evidence that courts are departing from *stare decisis* notions in this way.

Is a Code case in another jurisdiction entitled to special weight because of the policy of uniformity in commercial law? From time to time a court bows to this policy,[39] but in most cases the court seems more concerned that its decision be right than that it be parallel with another state's. Certainly there are Code decisions that other courts should not follow.[40]

## PRIOR DRAFTS AND PRIOR OFFICIAL TEXTS
## WITH COMMENTS

Prior drafts and prior official texts of the Code with comments sometimes cast light on the enacted text. The main prior drafts and official texts with comments are:

1949 Proposed Draft with Comments
1950 Proposed Draft with Comments
1951 Final Text with Comments, Amendments in May, 1951, Amendments in September, 1951
1952 Official Text with Comments
1953 Changes Recommended by a Meeting of the Enlarged Editorial Board (Part A, Part B)
1956 Recommendations of the Enlarged Editorial Board
1957 Official Text with Comments; Supplement to the 1957 Official Edition of the Code
1958 Official Text with Comments
1962 Amendments to the Uniform Commercial Code in Report No. 2 of the Permanent Editorial Board for the Uniform Commercial Code
1962 Official Text with Comments

The foregoing materials are available in many law school libraries, in some county bar association libraries, and in the libraries

---

37. See generally Braucher, Legislative History of the Uniform Commercial Code, 58 Colum.L.Rev. 798 (1958).

38. Hawkland, Uniform Commercial "Code" Methodology, 1962 U.Ill.L.F. 291.

39. E. g., Evans v. Everett, 10 N.C.App. 435, 179 S.E.2d 120, 8 UCC Rep.Serv. 1361 (1971).

40. E. g., Roto-Lith, Ltd. v. F. P. Bartlett & Co., 297 F.2d 497, 1 UCC Rep. Serv. 73 (1st Cir. 1962).

of some lawyers. Today, lawyers make relatively little use of prior drafts and prior official texts in applying enacted Code language. At least two factors explain this. These materials are not as accessible to lawyers as are the usual aids to interpretation and construction. Further, lawyers cannot base reliable inferences as to the intended meaning of enacted text on changes made from prior versions of that text. Any inference may be unreliable because "frequently matters . . . [were] omitted as being implicit without statement and language . . . changed or added solely for clarity." This quote comes from a section in the 1952 Official Text: "Prior drafts of text and comments may not be used to ascertain legislative intent." [41] Subsequently the co-sponsors deleted this language from the Official Text. In our opinion, they should have left it in.

## NEW YORK LAW REVISION COMMISSION HEARINGS, STUDIES, AND REPORTS

The New York Law Revision Commission's study and report on the Code had a major impact on the final Official Texts. The Commission held public hearings, published specific studies on each Article, and made a final report with recommendations. All this material is conveniently bound in six volumes of the Commission's work for the years 1954 to 1956.[42] To see the very great impact that the Commission's work had, it is only necessary to compare the 1952 Official Text and 1953 Recommended Changes of the Enlarged Editorial Board with the 1956 Recommendations of the Enlarged Editorial Board and the 1957 Official Text. Usually, the explanation for a change in a section during this period can be traced in part to a criticism or suggestion appearing in the New York Law Revision Commission Reports.[43]

Today, courts frequently cite the Commission's work in interpreting and construing the Code. We think this source is generally of greater value to the lawyer than prior drafts and prior official texts with comments. The hearings and studies that the Commission published cast light on what the Code draftsmen were trying to do in the first place. And, as we have noted, the criticisms and suggestions that the Commission published often explain subsequent changes in the Official Text. The lawyer who regularly works with the Code should have access to the Commission's volumes and be aware that he can readily run down all Commission comments on a particular section by checking the relevant indices.[44]

41. ALI & National Conference of Commissioners on Uniform State Laws, Uniform Commercial Code Official Draft § 1–102(3) (g) (Text and Comments ed. 1952).

42. 1–2 N.Y.State Law Revision Comm'n, 1954 Report (1954); 1–3 N.Y.State Law Revision Comm'n, 1955 Report (1955); N.Y.State Law Revision Comm'n, 1956 Report (1956).

43. Symposium, Panel Discussion on the Uniform Commercial Code Report of the New York Law Revision Commission, 12 Bus.Law. 49 (1956).

44. 2 N.Y.State Law Revision Comm'n, 1954 Report 1503 (1954) (Table of References to Sections of the Uniform Commercial Code); N.Y.State Law Revision Comm'n, 1956 Report 259 (1956) (Table of Uniform Commercial Code References).

## STATE LEGISLATIVE HEARINGS, STUDIES, AND REPORTS

The most immediate legislative history behind particular state enactments lies in any local hearings, studies, or reports that preceded these enactments. Many states did not hold any such hearings or publish any such reports. But in at least twenty-two states, materials of this nature are available, and the lawyer can sometimes consult them with profit.[45] They are specially valuable in explaining any nonuniform amendments these states have made.[46] California, for example, was the principal offendor against the Code's goal of uniformity, and the origin of many of its amendments can be traced to a bound volume entitled "Sixth Progress Report to the Legislature by the Senate Fact Finding Committee on the Judiciary—Part I, The Uniform Commercial Code (1959–61)."

## OFFICIAL COMMENTS TO CODE SECTIONS

The Official Comments appended to each section of the 1962 Official Text of the Code are by far the most useful aids to interpretation and construction.[47] The courts take to the comments like ducks take to water even though the legislatures did not enact the Code comments. The lawyer must have a separate set of Code comments at hand. Karl N. Llewellyn explained the purposes of the comments in these terms:

> Every provision should show its reason on its face. Every body of provisions should display on their face their organizing principle. The rationale of this is that construction and application are intellectually impossible except with reference to *some* reason and theory of purpose and organization. Borderline, doubtful, or uncontemplated cases are inevitable. Reasonably uniform interpretation by judges of different schooling, learning and skill is tremendously furthered if the reason which guides application of the same language is the *same* reason in all cases. A patent reason, moreover, tremendously decreases the leeway open to the skilful advocate for persuasive distortion or misapplication of the language; it requires that any contention, to be successfully persuasive, must make some kind of sense *in terms of the reason;* it provides a real stimulus toward,

**45.** M. Ezer, Uniform Commercial Code Bibliography—1966 at 70–74 (1966).

**46.** Sometimes the lawyer can find a law review article that explains nonuniform amendments enacted in his state. See, e. g., Penney, New York Revisits the Code: Some Variations in the New York Enactment of the Uniform Commercial Code, 62 Colum.L. Rev. 992 (1962); Ruud, The Texas Legislative History of the Uniform Commercial Code, 44 Texas L.Rev. 597 (1966).

**47.** Skilton, Some Comments on the Comments to the Uniform Commercial Code, 1966 Wis.L.Rev. 597.

though not an assurance of, corrective growth rather than straitjacketing of the Code by way of case-law.[48]

We will offer caveats on the use of Code comments and then review several court decisions that refused to follow applicable comments. First, in each comment, there are cross-references to relevant definitions and to cognate Code sections. Sometimes these references are not exhaustive. For example, the cross-references in the comments to 2–316 fail to mention that a crucial term in 2–316 ("conspicuous") is defined in 1–201(10). Second, some comments deal with the meaning of sections different from, or in addition to, the ones to which they are appended. For example, Comment 2 to 2–312 deals with 2–607, and Comment 2 to 9–303(2) also deals with 9–304 (5). Third and most important, the comments depart from the text in two different ways. They sometimes expand on, and therefore go beyond, the text, and they sometimes restrict or narrow the meaning of the text.[49] The explanation for this is partly political. When opponents of a draft section prevailed against the draftsman, the draftsman would sometimes revise the draft accordingly, but seek to preserve the old draft in the comments.[50] In some instances, the comments are sounder than the text, and in others, they are not. But disparity or no, most courts follow the comments.

We have found a handful of exceptional cases in which courts refused to follow a comment at variance with the text. In one, the court refused to use a comment to expand the fictitious payee doctrine[51] and stated that "the plain language of the statute cannot be varied by reference to the comments."[52] In another case, the court applied the bulk transfer provisions of Article Six to the sale of a restaurant, cocktail lounge, and bar although the relevant comments are to the contrary.[53] The court simply remarked that the comment "is not controlling."[54] Still another court refused to extend 2–318 despite the comment's[55] generous invitation to do so. The court said, "The comment to the Code . . . which is the basis for the argument that the language of 2–318 is precatory only was never enacted

48. Personal Papers of Karl Llewellyn, Item J. VI 1. e. 5 (1944) (unpublished manuscript on file at the University of Chicago Law School). See also 1 N.Y.State Law Revision Comm'n, 1955 Report 158–59 (1955).

49. On the use of the comments in making "negative inference" arguments, see Skilton, Some Comments on the Comments to the Uniform Commercial Code, 1966 Wis.L.Rev. 597, 621–27.

50. Llewellyn, Why a Commercial Code?, 22 Tenn.L.Rev. 779, 782 (1953).

51. § 3–405, Comment 4.

52. Wright v. Bank of California, N.A., 276 Cal.App.2d 485, 490, 81 Cal.Rptr. 11, 14, 6 UCC Rep.Serv. 1165, 1170 (1st Dist. 1969).

53. § 6–102, Comment 2.

54. Zinni v. One Township Line Corp., 36 Pa.D. & C.2d 297, 299, 3 UCC Rep. Serv. 305, 307 (C.P.1965).

55. § 2–318, Comment 3.

by the Pennsylvania legislature." [56] In a few other cases, the courts failed to follow the comments.[57]

Certainly the comments are not entitled to as much weight as ordinary legislative history.[58] In some states the comments were not placed before the enacting body prior to adoption of the Code. Indeed, some of the present comments were not even in existence at the time the section to which they are now appended was adopted.[59] Furthermore, much of the Code is highly technical "lawyer's" law. If the average legislator did not understand the intricacies of Article Four or Article Nine at the time of enactment, it is likely that he did not grasp the relevant comments either.

### PERIODIC REPORTS OF THE PERMANENT EDITORIAL BOARD

The first Report of the Permanent Editorial Board appeared on October 31, 1962.[60] Since that time, two further reports have been published.[61] These reports can aid the lawyer in several ways. They include proposed amendments to Code sections that the Board itself recommends. They include the text of nonuniform amendments that the Board rejects and the Board's reasons for rejection. Also, Report No. 3 (1966) further includes actual "amendments to the Official Comments which are deemed desirable in light of experience under the Code." [62] The Board has power to amend the comments without referring them for review to the various jurisdictions in which the Code is in force. But we think the authoritative force of *ex post facto* comments must be less than that of the comments actually appended to sections of the Official Text at the time of enactment. Of course, these *ex post facto* comments will doubtless influence some courts, and properly so. Even though they cannot constitute legislative history, they may still have value for their intrinsic sense.

One other task of the Permanent Editorial Board is worthy of note. The Board prepares and files *amicus curiae* briefs in important cases.[63] Obviously, a lawyer's chances are better when the Board supports his side of an important case. To the Board, though,

---

56. Miller v. Preitz, 422 Pa. 383, 393, 221 A.2d 320, 325, 3 UCC Rep.Serv. 557, 562 (1966).

57. See, e. g., Phoenix Die Casting Co. v. Manufacturers & Traders Trust Co., 50 Misc.2d 152, 269 N.Y.S.2d 890, 3 UCC Rep.Serv. 519 (Sup.Ct.1966); UHR v. 3361, Inc., 21 Pa.D. & C.2d 348, 1 UCC Rep.Serv. 314 (C.P.1960).

58. See generally Skilton, Some Comments on the Comments to the Uniform Commercial Code, 1966 Wis.L. Rev. 597.

59. Permanent Editorial Board for the Uniform Commercial Code, Report No. 3 at 1–28 (1966).

60. Permanent Editorial Board for the Uniform Commercial Code, Report No. 1 (1962).

61. Permanent Editorial Board for the Uniform Commercial Code, Report No. 2 (1965); Permanent Editorial Board for the Uniform Commercial Code, Report No. 3 (1966).

62. Permanent Editorial Board for the Uniform Commercial Code, Report No. 3 at 21 (1966).

63. Dezendorf, How the Code's Permanent Editorial Board is Functioning, 22 Bus.Law. 227, 228 (1966).

*amicus* briefs are one means of helping to assure consistency and uniformity in Code law.

## RULES OF INTERPRETATION AND CONSTRUCTION

When all else fails the lawyer may turn to rules of interpretation and construction. The Code's Chief Reporter, Karl N. Llewellyn, once sought to demonstrate that for every rule of construction some court had invoked, another court had invoked a different rule with opposite effect.[64] There are treatises on these rules, and section 1–102 of the Code itself sets forth a general rule:

(1) This Act shall be liberally construed and applied to promote its underlying purposes and policies.

(2) Underlying purposes and policies of this Act are

(a) to simplify, clarify and modernize the law governing commercial transactions;

(b) to permit the continued expansion of commercial practices through custom, usage and agreement of the parties;

(c) to make uniform the law among the various jurisdictions.

(3) The effect of provisions of this Act may be varied by agreement, except as otherwise provided in this Act and except that the obligations of good faith, diligence, reasonableness and care prescribed by this Act may not be disclaimed by agreement but the parties may by agreement determine the standards by which the performance of such obligations is to be measured if such standards are not manifestly unreasonable.

(4) The presence in certain provisions of this Act of the words "unless otherwise agreed" or words of similar import does not imply that the effect of other provisions may not be varied by agreement under subsection (3).

(5) In this Act unless the context otherwise requires

(a) words in the singular number include the plural, and in the plural include the singular;

(b) words of the masculine gender include the feminine and the neuter, and when the sense so indicates words of the neuter gender may refer to any gender.

Section 1–102(2) does not exhaustively specify all the Code's underlying purposes. A further one is simply that the law of commercial transactions be, so far as reasonable, liberal and nontechnical. A great many Code sections evidence this underlying purpose. For in-

---

64. Llewellyn, Remarks on the Theory of Appellate Decision and the Rules or Canons About How Statutes are to be Construed, 3 Vand.L.Rev. 395 (1950).

stance, the Code "de-formalizes" the requirements for the formation of contracts in Article Two,[65] for the creation of letters of credit in Article Five,[66] and for the creation and perfection of security interests in Article Nine.[67] The Code is not merely nontechnical, but it is anti-technical in its pervasive de-emphasis of the title concept in Article Two.[68] The Code also rejects the perfect tender rule in sales law, once an open refuge for the technically minded.[69] The general obligation of good faith that 1–203 imposes and the numerous provisions which turn on commercial reasonableness additionally bespeak the liberalizing spirit of the Code. So, too, does 1–106 which provides that the "remedies provided by this Act shall be liberally administered."

Thus, the Code is to be liberally construed to further its underlying purposes, one of which is to liberalize ("de-technicalize") important branches of commercial law. Many courts seem to have understood this, either from reading 1–102 or from reading specific Code sections liberal in spirit, or both. Courts have already cited 1–102 in many cases. But, in these same cases, they have usually also cited a more specific section of liberalizing ilk such as 9–110 which validates a description in financing statements when it "reasonably identifies" the collateral,[70] 9–402(5) which validates financing statements that contain only minor errors,[71] 2–204(1) which provides that a contract for sale may be made in any manner sufficient to show agreement,[72] 2–401 which states that Article Two applies irrespective of title to the goods,[73] and so on.

Because courts so commonly cite not only 1–102, but also some more specific liberalizing section, it is difficult to know whether 1–102 is having any independent influence as a rule of liberal interpretation and construction. But at least two cases so far do indicate that it does have a life of its own. In Minsel v. El Rancho Mobile Home Center, Inc.,[74] the Michigan Court of Appeals was invited to construe 2–602 narrowly and technically to deny purchasers of a mobile home the right to throw the goods back at the seller. Specifically, the sellers argued that because the buyers continued to live in the mobile home for a period after they gave notice of rejection, this constituted "an

65. E. g., §§ 2–201; 2–204; 2–206 to 2–209.

66. §§ 5–104; 5–105.

67. §§ 9–110; 9–203; 9–204; 9–402.

68. §§ 2–401; 2–401, Comment 1.

69. §§ 2–504; 2–508; 2–601; 2–608; 2–612.

70. In re Bloomingdale Milling Co., 4 UCC Rep.Serv. 256 (Ref.Dec.W.D.Mich. 1966).

71. E. g., In re Uptown Variety, 6 UCC Rep.Serv. 221 (Ref.Dec.D.Ore.1969). For

a case that goes quite far without even citing section 1–102, see Rooney v. Mason, 394 F.2d 250, 5 UCC Rep.Serv. 308 (10th Cir. 1968).

72. Graulich Caterer, Inc. v. Hans Holterbosch, Inc., 101 N.J.Super. 61, 71, 243 A.2d 253, 259, 5 UCC Rep.Serv. 440, 448 (App.Div.1968).

73. Chrysler Credit Corp. v. Sharp, 56 Misc.2d 261, 288 N.Y.S.2d 525, 5 UCC Rep.Serv. 226 (Sup.Ct.1968).

74. Minsel v. El Rancho Mobile Home Center, Inc., 32 Mich.App. 10, 188 N.W. 2d 9, 9 UCC Rep.Serv. 448 (1971).

exercise of ownership by the buyer" under 2–602(2) (a) and was therefore "wrongful as against the seller." Technically, this continued used of the mobile home did seem to be an "exercise of ownership" under the statutory language, and no other specific section liberalizes this language. Yet under all the circumstances, the buyers' course of action was entirely reasonable. Accordingly, the court held for the buyers and cited 1–102 in support of its decision. Indeed, the court even spoke of a "rule of reasonableness evident throughout the UCC." [75]

In a second case, Baillie Lumber Co., Inc. v. Kincaid Carolina Corp.,[76] the North Carolina Court of Appeals refused to allow a buyer to spring an accord and satisfaction defense on the seller. The buyer claimed this defense because he had mailed checks to the seller marked "First instalment of agreed settlement," and the seller had cashed them. The court refused to find an accord and satisfaction and, in so holding, did not rely solely on the fact that the seller wrote "with reservation of all our rights" on the checks before cashing them, an inscription that specifically saves the seller's rights under 1–207. The court instead emphasized that "we are required to liberally construe" the Code.[77] Indeed, the last paragraph of the opinion suggests that even if the seller had not inscribed the checks before cashing them, the result would have been the same.[78] Certainly there are few pre-Code doctrines any more technical than the doctrine that cashing a check on which the drawer has written "payment in full" constitutes an accord and satisfaction.

Besides 1–102, we have already alluded to the existence of 1–106 which provides that Code remedies are to be liberally administered:

> (1) The remedies provided by this Act shall be liberally administered to the end that the aggrieved party may be put in as good a position as if the other party had fully performed but neither consequential or special nor penal damages may be had except as specifically provided in this Act or by other rule of law.

> (2) Any right or obligation declared by this Act is enforceable by action unless the provision declaring it specifies a different and limited effect.

Certainly 1–106 is in the same spirit as 1–102. The case law under 1–106 to date affords little basis for useful comment. Section 1–106 has only been cited in approximately two dozen cases, and in none did it figure prominently.

The comment to 1–102 also includes a further rule of construction, namely that Code provisions be extended by analogy when their

**75.** Id. at 14, 188 N.W.2d at 11, 9 UCC Rep.Serv. at 451.

**76.** Baillie Lumber Co. v. Kincaid Carolina Corp. 4 N.C. App. 342, 167 S.E.2d 85, 6 UCC Rep.Serv. 480 (1969).

**77.** Id. at 353, 167 S.E.2d at 92–93, 6 UCC Rep.Serv. at 484.

**78.** Id. at 353, 167 S.E.2d at 93, 6 UCC Rep.Serv. at 484.

rationale justifies this.[79] In several cases to date, the courts have extended Code sections by analogy,[80] but it is too early to tell whether courts are in fact abandoning their revered doctrine that statutes are to be narrowly construed.

## TREATISES AND OTHER SECONDARY LITERATURE

Today there is a large volume of Code literature. Here we will be highly selective and will, with few exceptions, list only books.[81] We recommend, in particular, the following generalized treatments on specific Articles:

### Article Two

R. Duesenberg & L. King, Sales and Bulk Transfers Under the Uniform Commercial Code (1966)

W. Hawkland, A Transactional Guide to the Uniform Commercial Code (1964)

R. Nordstrom, Handbook of the Law of Sales (1970)

State Bar of California, Sales and Bulk Transfers (1965)

Peters, Remedies for Breach of Contracts Relating to the Sale of Goods Under the Uniform Commercial Code: A Roadmap for Article Two, 73 Yale L.J. 199 (1963)

### Article Three

F. Beutel, Beutel's Brannan Negotiable Instruments Law (7th ed. 1948)

W. Britton, Handbook of the Law of Bills and Notes (2d ed. 1961)

C. Bunn, H. Snead, R. Speidel, An Introduction to the Uniform Commercial Code, ch. 11 to 13 (1964)

W. Hawkland, Commercial Paper (1959)

T. Paton, Paton's Digest (4th ed. 1940)

E. Peters, Commercial Transactions, ch. 8 (1971)

L. Simpson, Handbook on the Law of Suretyship (1950)

R. Speidel, R. Summers, J. White, Teaching Materials on Commercial Transactions, ch. 39 to 43 (1969)

---

79. See generally Traynor, Statutes Revolving in Common-Law Orbits, 17 Catholic U.L.Rev. 401 (1968); Note, The Uniform Commercial Code as a Premise for Judicial Reasoning, 65 Colum.L.Rev. 880 (1965).

80. E. g., Transatlantic Financing Corp. v. United States, 363 F.2d 312, 3 UCC Rep.Serv. 401 (D.C.Cir. 1966) (sections 2–614(1) and 2–615(a) applied to charter party contract); Vitromar Piece Dye Works v. Lawrence of London, Ltd., 119 Ill.App. 2d 301, 256 N.E.2d 135, 7 UCC Rep.Serv. 487 (1970) (section 2–607 applied to service contract);

Hunt Foods & Indus., Inc. v. Doliner, 26 App.Div.2d 41, 270 N.Y.S.2d 937, 3 UCC Rep.Serv. 597 (1st Dep't 1966) (section 2–202 applied to sale of securities); A. Alport & Sons, Inc. v. Hotel Evans, Inc., 65 Misc.2d 374, 317 N.Y. S.2d 937, 8 UCC Rep.Serv. 1040 (Sup. Ct.1970) (sections 3–414, 3–415 and 3–511(b) applied to determine liability on nonnegotiable instrument).

81. All the articles through 1966 are conveniently collected in M. Ezer, Uniform Commercial Code Bibliography— 1966 (1966).

R. Steinheimer, Michigan Negotiable Instruments Law and the Uniform Commercial Code (1960)

Barak, The Uniform Commercial Code—Commercial Paper: An Outsider's View, 3 Israel L.Rev. 7 (1968)

Bunn, Bank Collections Under the Uniform Commercial Code, 1964 Wis.L.Rev. 278

Felsenfeld, Some Ruminations About Remedies In Consumer-Credit Transactions, 8 B.C.Ind. & Com.L.Rev. 535 (1967)

Hawkland, The Effect of UCC § 1–207 on the Doctrine of Accord and Satisfaction by Conditional Check, 74 Com.L.J. 329 (1969)

Penney, A Summary of Articles 3 and 4 and Their Impact in New York, 48 Cornell L.Q. 47 (1962)

Peters, Suretyship Under Article 3 of the Uniform Commercial Code, 77 Yale L.J. 833 (1968)

White, Some Petty Complaints About Article Three, 65 Mich.L.Rev. 1315 (1967)

Comment, Allocation of Losses From Check Forgeries Under the Law of Negotiable Instruments and the Uniform Commercial Code, 62 Yale L.J. 417 (1953)

The Law of Indorsement and Transfer of Checks, 78 Banking L.J. 185 (1961)

## Article Four

J. Clarke, H. Bailey, R. Young, Bank Deposits and Collection (3d ed. 1963)

A. H. Michie, Banks and Banking (1950)

Leary, Check Handling Under Article Four of the UCC, 49 Marq.L. Rev. 331 (1965)

Malcolm, Article 4—A Battle with Complexity, 1952 Wis.L.Rev. 265

Malcolm, Reflections on West Side Bank: A Draftsman's View, 18 Catholic U.L.Rev. 23 (1968)

Penney, Bank Statements, Cancelled Checks, and Article Four in the Electronics Age, 65 Mich.L.Rev. 1341 (1967)

Comment, Uniform Commercial Code—Article Four—Process of Posting Not Complete Until Midnight Deadline, 20 S.C.L.Rev. 118 (1968)

Note, Final Payment and the Process of Posting Under the Uniform Commercial Code, 68 Colum.L.Rev. 349 (1968)

## Article Five

G. Gilmore & C. Black, The Law of Admiralty, ch. III (1957)

B. Kozolchyk, Commercial Letters of Credit in the Americas (1966)

W. Ward & H. Harfield, Bank Credits and Acceptances (4th ed. 1958)

Harfield, Code Treatment of Letters of Credit, 48 Cornell L.Q. 92 (1962)

Harfield, Practice Commentary, N.Y. U.C.C. §§ 5–101 to 5–117 (McKinney 1964) (passim)

Schlesinger, Study of Uniform Commercial Code Article Five—Documentary Letters of Credit, 3 N.Y.State Law Revision Comm'n, 1955 Report 1571–1719 (1955)

### Article Six

R. Duesenberg & L. King, Sales and Bulk Transfers Under the Uniform Commercial Code (1966)

State Bar of California, Sales and Bulk Transfers (1965)

### Article Seven

R. Braucher, Documents of Title Under the Uniform Commercial Code (1958)

Boshkoff, Documents of Title: A Comparison of the Uniform Commercial Code and other Uniform Acts with Emphasis on Michigan Law, 59 Mich.L.Rev. 711 (1961)

Ruud, Warehouse Receipts, Bills of Lading and Other Documents of Title, 16 Ark.L.Rev. 81 (1961)

### Article Nine

P. Coogan, W. Hogan, D. Vagts, Secured Transactions Under the Uniform Commercial Code (1963)

G. Gilmore, Security Interests in Personal Property (1965)

### § 5. Aids in Drafting Documents Under the Code

Lawyers who work in the field of commercial law must draft many different kinds of documents. Fortunately, there are now several useful form books on the Code:

Anderson's Uniform Commercial Code Legal Forms (1961)

D. Carroll & F. Whiteside, Forms for Commercial Transactions under the Uniform Commercial Code (1964)

F. Hart, Drafting Techniques Under the Uniform Commercial Code (1962)

F. Hart & W. Willier, Forms and Procedures Under the Uniform Commercial Code (1963)

R. Henson & W. Davenport, Uniform Laws Annotated, Uniform Commercial Code Forms and Materials, vols. 4–5 (1968)

### § 6. A Note on Article One

The Code is divided into ten Articles. Article One consists of two Parts and a total of eighteen sections. Some of these sections deal with rather basic matters, specifically, rules of construction,[82]

---

82.  §§ 1–102(1); 1–106.

freedom of contract,[83] conflict of laws,[84] the obligation of good faith,[85] a general statute of frauds for personalty,[86] definitions of terms that recur throughout the Code,[87] and supplemental general principles.[88] In addition, the Article includes a miscellany of other provisions.[89] Except insofar as we have already discussed these sections in this general introduction, we take them up at appropriate points in ensuing chapters.

83. §§ 1–102(3), (4).

84. § 1–105.

85. § 1–203.

86. § 1–206.

87. §§ 1–201; 1–205.

88. § 1–103.

89. §§ 1–101 (short title); 1–104 (construction against implicit repeal); 1–107 (waiver or renunciation of claim or right after breach); 1–108 (severability); 1–109 (section captions); 1–202 (prima facie evidence by third party documents); 1–204 (time; reasonable time; "seasonably"); 1–207 (performance or acceptance under reservation of rights); 1–208 (option to accelerate at will); 1–209 (subordinated obligations).

# CHAPTER 1

# OFFER, ACCEPTANCE, AND CONSIDERATION
## (And Scope of Article Two)

*Analysis*

Sec.
1–1. Introduction.
1–2. Battle of the Forms Under Section 2–207.
1–3. Firm Offers.
1–4. Methods of Acceptance.
1–5. Contract Modification, Waiver, and Estoppel.

## § 1–1  Introduction

Before turning to the provisions of Article Two on offer, acceptance, and consideration, we first outline its scope and structure. Section 2–102 provides:

> Unless the context otherwise requires, this Article applies to transactions in goods; it does not apply to any transaction which although in the form of an unconditional contract to sell or present sale is intended to operate only as a security transaction nor does this Article impair or repeal any statute regulating sales to consumers, farmers or other specified classes of buyers.

Various provisions of Article Two, including several that deal with offer, acceptance, and consideration (for instance, sections 2–204, 2–205, and 2–206) apply only to the "sale of goods," rather than to "transactions in goods." This inconsistency does not seem to have caused the courts any trouble. It should be added that 2–105, 2–106, and 2–107 define "goods," "sale," "contract for sale," and other key terms relevant to the scope of the Article. In a vast miscellany of cases, the courts have construed and interpreted these key terms. We do not propose to canvass those cases.[1]

Article Two includes 104 provisions subsumed under the following seven "Part" headings:

Part 1.  Short Title, General Construction and Subject Matter

Part 2.  Form, Formation and Readjustment of Contract

Part 3.  General Obligation and Construction of the Contract

Part 4.  Title, Creditors and Good Faith Purchasers

Part 5.  Performance

Part 6.  Breach, Repudiation and Excuse

Part 7.  Remedies

---

1.  A comprehensive index to these cases appears in Uniform Commercial Code Reporting Service "Finding Aid" ¶¶ 2102–2107 (Callaghan & Co. 1972).

It should be apparent that the draftsmen of Article Two patterned the sequence of sections in the Article after the sequence of events in sales.

Some of the Article Two provisions on the formation of contracts [2] for the sale of goods have not only radically altered sales law but have influenced the new Restatement, Second, Contracts as well.[3] In most fundamental terms Article Two expands our conception of contract. It makes contracts easier to form, and it imposes a wider range of obligations than before. Contract formation is easier in several ways. Parties may form a contract through conduct rather than merely through the exchange of communications constituting "offer and acceptance." Section 2–204 says, "A contract may be made in any manner sufficient to show agreement, including conduct by the parties which recognizes the existence of such a contract." Sections 2–206(1), 2–207(1), and 2–207(3) expressly allow for the formation of contracts partly or wholly on the basis of such conduct. Further, Article Two reduces the formalities required for contract formation. The statute of frauds (section 2–201) requires only a writing that "indicates" a contract was made, and 1–107, 2–205, and 2–209(1) abandon the requirement that an acceptance must coincide precisely with all terms of the offer. Section 2–204 states that "even though one or more terms are left open, a contract for sale does not fail for indefiniteness if the parties have intended to make a contract and there is a reasonably certain basis for giving an appropriate remedy." As we will see, Article Two itself helps provide this "reasonably certain basis" through numerous provisions which fill gaps in an agreement that might otherwise fail for indefiniteness.

Article Two contracts are also more expansive in content than before. Thus 1–201(11) defines "contract" as the "total legal obligation which results from the parties' agreement," and 1–201(3) defines "agreement" to mean "the bargain of the parties in fact as found in their language or by implication from other circumstances, including course of dealing, or usage of trade or course of performance as provided in this Act." Sections 1–205 and 2–208 define course of dealing, usage of trade, and course of performance. The Code therefore feeds into sales agreements much that is not made express by the parties. Section 1–103 on supplemental general principles also feeds general contract law on "implied conditions" into Article Two sales contracts. Further the Code imposes obligations of good faith which

---

2.  See Part Two of Article Two of the Code. See also Hawkland, Major Changes Under the Uniform Commercial Code in the Formation and Terms of Sales Contracts, 10 Prac.Law 73 (May, 1964); Murray, Contracts: A New Design for the Agreement Process, 53 Cornell L.Rev. 785 (1968); Project, Uniform Commercial Code and Contract Law: Some Selected Problems, 105 U.Pa.L.Rev. 836 (1957); Note, Creation of Contracts Under the Uniform Commercial Code, 13 U.Pitt.L.Rev. 750 (1952).

3.  See Braucher, Freedom of Contract and the Second Restatement, 78 Yale L.J. 598 (1969); Murray, Contracts: A New Design for the Agreement Process, 53 Cornell L.Rev. 785 (1968).

may be thought of as part of any Article Two contract.[4]  And Article Two broadens the notion of contract insofar as section 2–202 on parol evidence permits parties to prove "extrinsic" terms not provable under various pre-Code versions of the parol evidence rule.

We will consider the most important aspects of Article Two's broadened concept of contract in the remainder of this chapter.

### § 1–2   Battle of the Forms Under Section 2–207

It is a sad fact that many sales contracts are not fully bargained, not carefully drafted, and not understandingly signed or otherwise acknowledged by both parties.  Often here is what happens:  underlings of seller and buyer each sit in their respective offices with a telephone and a stack of form contracts.  Seller's lawyer has drafted seller's forms to give him advantage.  Buyer's lawyer has drafted buyer's forms to give him advantage.  The two sets of forms naturally diverge.  They may diverge not only in substantive terms but also in permissible methods of contract formation.

The process of "contracting" begins with underling telephoning underling or with the dispatch of a form.  When the process ends, there will usually be two forms involved, seller's and buyer's, and each form may even be signed by both underlings.  The deal will coincide with respect to the few bargained terms such as price, quality and quantity terms, and delivery terms.  But on other terms, the respective forms will diverge in important respects.  Frequently this will pose no problem, for the deal will go forward without breakdown.  But sometimes the parties will fall into dispute even before the occasion for performance.  More often, one or both will perform or start to perform and a dispute will break out.  In all such cases the parties will then haul out their forms and read them—perhaps for the first time and they will find that their forms diverge.  Is there a contract?  If so, what are its terms?

Section 2–207 is the Code draftsmen's solution to the battle of the forms.[5]  The section reads in full:

> (1) A definite and seasonable expression of acceptance or a written confirmation which is sent within a reasonable time operates as an acceptance even though it states terms

---

4.  Summers, "Good Faith" in General Contract Law and the Sales Provisions of the Uniform Commercial Code, 54 Va.L.Rev. 195 (1968).  See Restatement, Second, Contracts § 231 (Tent. Draft No. 5, 1970).

5.  On section 2–207 generally, see Apsey, The Battle of the Forms, 34 Notre Dame Law. 556 (1959); Davenport, How to Handle Sales of Goods: The Problem of Conflicting Purchase Orders and Acceptances and New Concepts in Contract Law, 19 Bus.Law. 75 (1963); Lipman, On Winning the Battle of the Forms: An Analysis of Section 2–207 of the Uniform Commercial Code, 24 Bus.Law. 789 (1969); Murray, Intention Over Terms: An Exploration of UCC 2–207 and New Section 60, Restatement of Contracts, 37 Fordham L.Rev. 317 (1969); Comment, Non-Conforming Acceptances Under Section 2–207 of the Uniform Commercial Code: An End to the Battle of the Forms, 30 U.Chi.L.Rev. 540 (1963).  Cf. 1 N.Y.State Law Revision Comm'n, 1954 Report 119 et seq. (1954).

additional to or different from those offered or agreed upon, unless acceptance is expressly made conditional on assent to the additional or different terms.

(2) The additional terms are to be construed as proposals for addition to the contract. Between merchants such terms become part of the contract unless:

> (a) the offer expressly limits acceptance to the terms of the offer;
>
> (b) they materially alter it; or
>
> (c) notification of objection to them has already been given or is given within a reasonable time after notice of them is received.

(3) Conduct by both parties which recognizes the existence of a contract is sufficient to establish a contract for sale although the writings of the parties do not otherwise establish a contract. In such case the terms of the particular contract consist of those terms on which the writings of the parties agree, together with any supplementary terms incorporated under any other provisions of this Act.

Unfortunately the foregoing section is in one respect like the amphibious tank that was originally designed to fight in the swamps, but was ultimately sent to fight in the desert. The original draftsman of 2–207 designed it to keep the welsher in the contract. He had cases like Poel v. Brunswick Balke-Collender Co.[6] in mind. There the seller's underling sent the buyer's underling an offer. The buyer's underling sent back its own order form which happened to coincide with the seller's terms except in one minor respect. It added: "The acceptance of this order you must in any event promptly acknowledge." Thereafter, the seller failed to acknowledge, and the buyer for other reasons backed out. When the seller sued the buyer, the court held that the buyer's order form did not constitute an acceptance. At common law an acceptance had to be a mirror image of the offer. The buyer's form therefore could not be an acceptance; it was a counter-offer. Section 2–207 was initially designed primarily to change the result in such cases. It rejects the common law mirror image rule and converts the common law counteroffer into an acceptance under 2–207(1).

But unfortunately the courts have had to press 2–207 into service not just to hold the welsher in. Parties to sales deals much more often call on courts to use 2–207 to decide the terms of their contract after they exchange documents, perform, or start to perform and then fall into dispute. This is not only a different but also a more difficult problem for the law than that of keeping the welsher in.

**6.** 216 N.Y. 310, 110 N.E. 619 (1915). See also In re Marcalus Mfg. Co., 120 F.Supp. 784 (D.N.J.1954) (request for acknowledgment in acceptance renders it a counter-offer); Watts v. Carter & Sons, Inc., 207 App.Div. 656, 202 N.Y.S. 852 (2d Dep't 1924) (seller's forms used in purported acceptance added terms which seemingly would be implied anyhow).

The law as to terms must be sophisticated enough to nullify the efforts of fine-print lawyers, it must be sufficiently reliance-oriented to protect the legitimate expectations of the parties, and it must be fair and even handed.  It must not give one side the whole loaf, especially on nonnegotiated matters.

Not only does 2–207 suffer from being designed for the swamps yet called on to fight in the desert, it also suffers because the desert terrain has proved to be so varied.  We discuss seven significantly different types of cases with which 2–207 must deal.  We believe each type arises often in real life; section 2–207 deals with several well, with others not so well.  (We number these cases with some fear, for we realize that those who can analyze do, and that those who cannot, number.)  The seven are:

(*1*)  Cases in which the parties send printed forms to one another, and a crucial term is covered one way in one form and the other way in the other form.  (Assume, for example, that buyer's form states that seller warrants the goods to be of a certain kind and seller's form disclaims all warranties.)

(*2*)  Cases in which a crucial term is found in the first form sent (the offer), but no term on that question appears in the second.

(*3*)  Cases in which a crucial term is found in the second form (the acceptance), but there is no consistent or conflicting term in the first.

(*4*)  Cases in which at least one form contains a term that provides that no contract will be formed unless the other party accedes to all of the terms on that form and offers no others.

(*5*)  Cases in which there is a prior oral agreement.  (In cases (*1*) through (*4*) we have assumed that there may be prior oral negotiations but that no oral agreement was reached before parties sent their forms.)

(*6*)  Cases in which the parties do not use forms but send a variety of messages and letters and conduct intermittent oral negotiations that ultimately produce an agreement.

(*7*)  Cases in which the second form differs so radically from the first that it does not constitute an "acceptance."

In our discussion on the foregoing types of cases, a pervasive problem will be this:  how may 2–207 be interpreted so as not to give an unearned and unfair advantage to the contracting party who by pure happenstance sends the first or in other cases the second form?  When the parties to the contract send their forms blindly and after a cursory examination of the bargained terms file the forms they receive, it makes no sense to give one an advantage over the other simply because he mailed the first form.  Yet avoiding apparent favoritism under 2–207 is a difficult task.

### 1.   *Conflicting Terms Found in First and Second Forms*

Assume that buyer sends a purchase order which provides that any dispute will be governed by arbitration.  Seller responds with an acknowledgment which provides that any disputes will not be resolved by arbitration.  If the bargained terms on the purchase order and acknowledgment agree, we would find that the seller's document is a definite and seasonable expression of acceptance under 2–207 and that a contract has been formed by the exchange of the documents.  We would thus bind the welsher who seeks to get out of the contract before either performs.

Assume however that the seller ships the goods, buyer receives and pays for them, and the parties fall into dispute about their quality.  Does the contract call for arbitration or does it not?  Buyer will argue that his document was the offer (and it would appear to us that his document was in fact the offer since it was sent first) and that seller's document operated as an acceptance of all of the terms on buyer's form.  Furthermore buyer will correctly point out that seller's term (no arbitration) was not an additional term which could come into their contract under 2–207(2) but was a "different" term and therefore could not become part of the contract.[7]

First, the seller might respond that his document differed from the buyer's so substantially that it did not constitute an "acceptance" under 2–207(1).  In our view, it is clear that a document may be an acceptance under 2–207(1) and yet differ substantially from the offer.  But how much?  Certainly there is some limit.  We think that in the usual "purchase order-acknowledgment" context the forms do not approach this limit at least if the forms do not diverge as to price, quality, quantity, or delivery terms, but only as to unbargained terms on the reverse side concerning remedies, arbitration, and the like.  Thus here we would reject seller's argument.

Second, the seller can argue that his acceptance was "expressly made conditional on assent to the additional or different terms."  This argument finds some support in the infamous case, Roto-Lith, Ltd v. F. P. Bartlett & Co.,[8] where the Court of Appeals for the First Circuit held that a responding document "which states a condition

---

7.   For cases involving arbitration clauses, see Southeastern Enameling Corp. v. General Bronze Corp., 434 F.2d 330, 8 UCC Rep.Serv. 469 (5th Cir. 1970) (clause became part of the contract; not merely an exchange of forms); Universal Oil Products Co. v. S. C. M. Corp., 313 F.Supp. 905, 7 UCC Rep. Serv. 813 (D.Conn.1970) (clause became part of contract; not merely an exchange of forms); Campanelli v. Conservas Altamira, S.A., 86 Nev. 838, 477 P.2d 870, 8 UCC Rep.Serv. 693 (1970) (clause became part of the con-

tract); In re Barclay Knitwear Co., 8 UCC Rep.Serv. 44 (N.Y.Sup.Ct.1970) (clause did not become part of the contract; not merely an exchange of forms); Trafalgar Square, Ltd. v. Reeves Bros., Inc., 35 App.Div.2d 194, 315 N.Y.S.2d 239, 8 UCC Rep.Serv. 343 (1st Dep't 1970) (clause became a part of the contract).

8.   Roto-Lith, Ltd. v. F. P. Bartlett & Co., 297 F.2d 497, 1 UCC Rep.Serv. 73 (1st Cir. 1962).

materially altering the obligation solely to the disadvantage of the offeror" was expressly conditional. We would reject that argument also, for it is inconsistent with our interpretation of the word "acceptance" in 2–207(1) and contrary to the draftsman's policy stated above to whittle down the counter-offer rule and form contracts more readily than under the common law.

Third, seller can argue that his acceptance is only an acceptance of the terms on which the two documents agree. This argument finds no explicit support in 2–207, but it finds some support in Comment 6:

> If no answer is received within a reasonable time after additional terms are proposed, it is both fair and commercially sound to assume that their inclusion has been assented to. Where clauses on confirming forms sent by both parties conflict each party must be assumed to object to a clause of the other conflicting with one on the confirmation sent by himself. As a result the requirement that there be notice of objection which is found in subsection (2) is satisfied and the conflicting terms do not become a part of the contract. The contract then consists of the terms originally expressly agreed to, terms on which the confirmations agree, and terms supplied by this Act, including subsection (2). The written confirmation is also subject to Section 2–201. Under that section a failure to respond permits enforcement of a prior oral agreement; under this section a failure to respond permits additional terms to become part of the agreement.

The buyer will be quick to point out that the language from the comment appears to deal principally with 2–207(2). That section is addressed only to the question whether additional terms in the acceptance are to become part of the contract. He will argue that the comment does not apply to conflicting terms insofar as those terms appear in the offer and not in the acceptance.

We would resolve this case by reference to the comment, and would find that the two terms cancel one another. On our view the seller's form was an acceptance only of terms in the offer which did not conflict with any terms in the acceptance. Thus the ultimate deal would not include an arbitration clause unless the usage of trade, course of performance, or course of dealing supplies one. The Code does not expressly authorize this result, but it does not bar it either.

This outcome favors neither party. But if the buyer-offeror's argument be accepted, the offeror will almost always get his own terms. If, on the other hand, the *Roto Lith* decision be followed, and the second document is not an acceptance or is expressly conditional and therefore cannot "operate" as an acceptance, the second party will almost always get his own terms because the second document will constitute a counter-offer accepted by performance. We believe that neither of these results is sound, and we would not give either party a term when their documents conflict as to that term. We recognize that the Code may then provide a term substantially identical to one of those rejected. So be it. At least a term so supplied has the merit of being a term that the draftsmen considered fair.

### 2. *Term Found in the First but Not the Second Form*

Assume that buyer sends a document to seller and that the document provides for arbitration. Seller sends back an acknowledgment that is silent on the question of arbitration. Buyer's argument in this case will be the same as in Case 1: "seller's document was an acceptance of the terms on my document including the one dealing with arbitration." Moreover buyer will point out that Comment 6 which caused him trouble in Case 1 does not operate in this circumstance since there are no terms on the forms that "conflict."

Despite the fact that this outcome gives the buyer-offeror an unearned advantage, we think that he is correct and that terms contained in his document which are not contradicted by the acceptance become part of the contract. If we were more bold, we would find that seller's document is only an "acceptance" of those terms on which both documents agree. However, there is no basis in the Code, in the comments, or in the statutory history for such a conclusion, and accordingly we reject it even though we would write the law differently if we could do so.

### 3. *Term Found in Second (Acceptance) but Not in First Form*

This is the problem of the *Roto Lith* case.[9] In that case the buyer sent a purchase order to seller. Subsequently seller returned an acknowledgment that contained a disclaimer. The court ultimately found that the seller's document was "expressly conditional" and therefore not an acceptance but a counter-offer, accepted by the buyer's performance in receiving and using the goods. Under that case the seller got all of his terms, disclaimer included.

We too would find the second document to be an acceptance and would reject the *Roto Lith* assumption that it was expressly conditional and therefore a counter-offer. Rather we would find that a contract was formed upon the exchange of documents without reference to the subsequent performance. This case differs from Case 2 in that the acceptor (offeree) does not get all of his terms in the contract under subsection (1). Rather any terms in his acceptance that did not appear in the offer must pass through subsection (2) of 2–207 to become part of the contract. That subsection reads in full as follows:

The additional terms are to be construed as proposals for addition to the contract. Between merchants such terms become part of the contract unless:

(a) the offer expressly limits acceptance to the terms of the offer;

9. Id. at 500, 1 UCC Rep.Serv. at 76.

    (b)  they materially alter it; or

    (c)  notification of objection to them has already been given or is given within a reasonable time after notice of them is received.

Doubtless the parties in our case are merchants, but a disclaimer "materially alters" the contract, and the disclaimer would not become part of the contract.

    4.  *At Least One Form Insists on All Its Terms and Prohibits a Contract on Any Other Terms*

Assume that seller sends a document to buyer which states that any contract formed as a result of an exchange of documents must consist of all the terms in seller's form and no others. In any case in which such language appears in either the offering document or the accepting one, we would find that no contract was formed merely by the exchange of documents. But let us assume the parties go on and perform.

A court can proceed to contract formation in one of two ways. First, a court can take the common law, *Roto Lith*, approach, that is, find that the second document is a counter-offer and hold that subsequent performance by the party who sent the first document constitutes acceptance. This approach gives one party (who fortuitously sent the second document) all of his terms. The Code draftsmen have chosen not to take this approach. They proceed on to contract formation via section 2-207(3) which reads in full as follows:

> Conduct by both parties which recognizes the existence of a contract is sufficient to establish a contract for sale although the writings of the parties do not otherwise establish a contract. In such case the terms of the particular contract consist of those terms on which the writings of the parties agree, together with any supplementary terms incorporated under any other provisions of this Act.

Note that contract formation under subsection (3) gives neither party the relevant terms in his document, but fills out the contract with the standardized provisions of Article Two. As a practical matter this solution may put a seller at a disadvantage, for he will often wish to undertake less responsibility for the quality of his goods than the Code imposes or else wish to limit his damages liability more narrowly than would the Code.

After *Roto Lith* revealed this problem fully, the Code's Permanent Editorial Board offered a new Comment 7 to 2-207 which reads in full as follows:

> In many cases, as where goods are shipped, accepted and paid for before any dispute arises, there is no question whether a contract has been made. In such cases, where the writings of the parties do not establish a contract, it is not necessary to determine which act or document constituted

the offer and which the acceptance.  See 2–204.  The only
question is what terms are included in the contract and subsection (3) furnishes the governing rule.

One might argue with some justification that the comment is an *ex
post facto* attempt to alter and shore up what has proved in *Roto Lith*
to be an unsatisfactory statutory scheme.  Be that as it may, the comment offers a certain and sensible rule that should alleviate the pains
most courts would feel with 2–207 in cases of the type under consideration.  Allegedly the comment was written by Professor Braucher
who has since been endowed with the right to make law in Massachusetts as a member of the Supreme Judicial Court.  Presumably
he was as wise then as he is now.

### 5.  *Prior Oral Agreement*

In these cases the parties first reach an oral agreement covering
the essence of the deal.  Thereafter, one or both sends a "confirmation" form that includes terms different from or additional to those
that the parties previously agreed on orally.  If the parties file the
forms as usual without reading them and go ahead and perform, and
if a dispute then arises, is there a contract?  If so, on what terms?

Here it is tempting to say that 2–207(1) does not apply at all because the section contemplates contract formation by offer and acceptance, and the offer and acceptance already occurred orally prior
to the exchange of forms.  By the same token, 2–207(3) would not
apply, for it contemplates contract formation through performance,
and here the contract was already formed orally prior to performance.  Thus, it would seem that a court should not resort to 2–207
either to form the contract or to determine terms in any case in which
the parties actually entered an oral agreement prior to their form-
shuffling exercises.

Yet Comment 1 to 2–207 indicates the drafters did intend at least
that sections 2–207(1) and (2) apply "where an agreement has been
reached orally  .  .  .  and is followed by one or both of the parties sending formal memoranda embodying the terms so far agreed
and adding terms not discussed."  Section 2–207(1) uses the word
"confirmation":

> A definite and reasonable expression of acceptance or a writ-
> ten confirmation which is sent within a reasonable time op-
> erates as an acceptance even though it states terms addition-
> al to or different from those offered or agreed upon, unless
> acceptance is expressly made conditional on assent to the ad-
> ditional or different terms.

Moreover, 2–207(1) speaks of a confirmation that operates as an acceptance despite the fact that it states terms additional to or different from those agreed upon.  Thus, prior oral agreement cases in
which one or both of the parties follow up with a confirmation form
are to be run through 2–207(1) and (2) with whatever results those

subsections dictate.  A recent Michigan court of appeals case is in accord.  In American Parts Co. v. American Arbitration Association,[10] the parties had initially reached an oral understanding.  The seller had thereafter sent a confirmation form which purportedly recited the contract terms (including quantity), added an arbitration clause, and provided that the entire form would become controlling if the "buyer accepts all or any part of the goods herein described."  The buyer allegedly refused to accept the entire contract quantity of goods, and the seller then sought arbitration.  The buyer sought a stay of arbitration, and the seller moved for summary judgment.  In denying summary judgment the court recognized that under 2–207 (1) a confirmation form can constitute an "acceptance" even where there has already been an oral offer and acceptance.  As a corollary, certain additional terms in the confirmation may become (retroactively, as it were) a part of the original contract by virtue of the operation of 2–207(2).[11]  But the Michigan court also noted differences between those forms falling in 2–207(1) that are confirmations and those that are not.[12]

### 6.  *Non-Form Agreements*

In this type of case there is no pattern, or at least no continuous pattern of exchange of printed forms.  One party may send a typewritten one.  The parties may initially exchange printed forms that differ so substantially that the second cannot be an acceptance; then one party responds further with a letter or a typed form or some such, yet the parties never write down their agreement in one document.  If one of the parties walks away, or worse yet, if both perform and then something goes wrong, is there a contract?  If so, what are its terms?  We believe that all such cases will continue to be resolved under general contract law via section 1–103 and that only that part of 2–207(1) after the comma is relevant.  The case of Construction Aggregates Corp. v. Hewitt Robins, Inc. is illustrative.[13]  The case is not a typical battle of the form situation; the parties appeared to have negotiated most (if not all) of the terms of the contract, to have consulted their lawyers about the terms, and to have corresponded with one another orally and in writing about various terms.  Thus it is not a case in which only the parties' documents pass in the mail like ships in the night and then are placed in files until a difficulty arises under the contract; here there was real bargaining.  The court found that one of the seller's latter transmissions constituted a counter-offer which the buyer had accepted by seeking to make only one change in it and by failing to raise any other objections to it.  The court found that the seller's "acceptance" was expressly conditional under the last clause of 2–207(1) and that the buyer assented to those conditions.  Thus we do not have the case in which the parties went on with

10.  8 Mich.App. 156, 154 N.W.2d 5, 6 UCC Rep.Serv. 119 (1967).

11.  Id. at 172, 154 N.W.2d at 14, 6 UCC Rep.Serv. at 129.

12.  Id. at 174, 154 N.W.2d at 15, 6 UCC Rep.Serv. at 131.

13.  404 F.2d 505, 6 UCC Rep.Serv. 112 (7th Cir. 1969).

performance in the face of two conflicting documents. Rather we have a case in which (or so the court found) the parties reached a bargained agreement on all the terms.

We well understand that a clever lawyer can make a colorable claim that every case falls within our sixth classification, is therefore beyond the reach of 2–207, and adrift on the murky sea of common law. We hope that courts will reject such arguments and will only rarely permit buyers and sellers who communicate principally through printed purchase order-acknowledgment forms to escape the grip of 2–207. Absent further legislative action, we believe that judicial use of 2–207 in such cases is still the best avenue for the development of a certain and consistent body of law.

But what are those "rare" cases in which the courts may properly permit the parties to escape the grip of 2–207 altogether? We follow the example of legislatures, and leave this hard question entirely to the courts.

### 7. *Second Form Not an Acceptance*

Not all return documents are 2–207(1) "acceptances." If the return document diverges significantly as to a dickered term, it cannot be a 2–207(1) acceptance. For example, if the purchase order calls for the sale of 200,000 pounds of lard at ten cents a pound and the acknowledgment responds with 200,000 pounds at fifteen cents a pound, the second document is not an acceptance under 2–207(1), and no contract is formed via the exchange of forms. If the parties thereafter fall into dispute before either performs, no one has liability for not performing. If, on the other hand, the parties perform and the question arises as to what the contract is, we would follow Comment 7 (1966 version) and proceed directly to subsection (3). There, as we have seen, the parties will get the terms on which their documents agree plus those that the Code offers.

### CONCLUSION

It is unfortunate that the draftsmen did not originally design 2–207 for the terrain upon which it was ultimately to do battle. We hope that the foregoing analysis will help the lawyer and the courts apply 2–207 as intelligently as possible. We see no way to apply 2–207 that does not in some cases give an unearned and unfair advantage to the person who happens to send the first, or in some cases the second, document. We hope that the Code's Permanent Editorial Board will have a go at redrafting 2–207 sometime in the next decade and that they will devise a section that will more often take parties into subsection (3).

Under the present state of the law we believe that there is no language that a lawyer can put on a form that will always assure his client of forming a contract on his client's own terms. For example, such efforts will always be frustrated if the responsive document is expressly conditional on assent to that document's terms, for the parties will then be thrown into subsection (3) and there the client will not get his own term unless some other section of the Code gives it to him. In our judgment that is the right outcome. If the client must have a term, he should bargain with the other party for it, and if he cannot strike a bargain with the other party for that term, he should not get it by his lawyer's sleight of hand. If he must have the term but cannot strike a bargain for it, his only answer may be to raise his price, buy insurance, or as a last resort, have a couple of extra martinis every evening and capitalize his corporation more thinly than he otherwise would.

## § 1–3   Firm Offers

In the long history of contract law, courts have allowed many an offeror to withdraw his offer in bad faith with impunity. Under the common law of contracts, courts said "an offeror can always withdraw his offer if he received no consideration for it." But under the Code, 2–205 limits the offeror's privilege to withdraw:

> An offer by a merchant to buy or sell goods in a signed writing which by its terms gives assurance that it will be held open is not revocable, for lack of consideration, during the time stated or if no time is stated for a reasonable time, but in no event may such period of irrevocability exceed three months; but any such term of assurance on a form supplied by the offeree must be separately signed by the offeror.

This section only applies if (1) there has actually been an offer (2) by a merchant (3) in a signed writing (4) which gives assurance that it will be held open. After three months any such firm offer lapses, but the Code does not say how this time period is to be computed. Section 2–205 closes with the proviso that any firm offer on a form supplied by the offeree must be separately signed by the offeror. The purpose of this proviso is to protect "against entrapment of an offeror by a printed clause on the offeree's form, such as 'All offers are to be irrevocable for 30 days.'" [14]

Thus 2–205 enables the offeror to make a "gift" of a firm offer. That is, the offeree need not give any consideration. He need not buy an option if the offer satisfies 2–205.

Section 2–205 is intended mainly to limit the power of an offeror to withdraw his firm offer in circumstances in which the offeree reasonably relies on the offer's firmness. A famous pre-Code controversy is this: [15] a prospective prime contractor secures what he takes to be a firm offer from a sub, and he uses it in computing his overall prime contract bid. The prospective prime contractor wins the prime contract and then seeks to accept the sub's bid whereupon the sub withdraws. Some pre-Code courts held that the sub can withdraw

14. 1 N.Y.State Law Revision Comm'n, 1955 Report 615 (1955).

15. See Schultz, The Firm Offer Puzzle: A Study of Business Practice in the Construction Industry, 19 U.Chi.L.Rev. 237 (1952).

because an offeror can always withdraw an offer for which he received no consideration.[16]   And some courts also held that the doctrine of promissory estoppel is of no avail to the prime, for this doctrine does not apply to the "formation" of contracts.[17]   Section 2–205 will change the result in such cases.   When 2–205's terms are not met, the offeree is still entitled to fall back on governing decisions of courts which have held that promissory estoppel is applicable.[18]   Or the offeree may be able to invoke the new Restatement, Second, Contracts. It provides that "an offer which the offeror should reasonably expect to induce action or forbearance of a substantial character by the offeree before acceptance and which does so induce is binding as an option contract to the extent necessary to avoid injustice." [19]   Certainly 2–205 should not be interpreted to prevent offerees from invoking promissory estoppel or Restatement doctrine.   The section is not addressed to cases where there is a substitute for consideration.

Section 2–205 presupposes that the offeror has made an offer. The Code does not define "offer," and courts must resort to extra-Code contract law via 1–103 to determine whether a party has made an offer.   Section 2–205 merely converts a common law offer into a firm offer.   To be a firm offer under 2–205, the offer must, among other things, "give assurance that it will be held open."   Only one Code case under the section is worth noting.   In Coronis Associates v. Gordon Construction Co.,[20] the appellate division of the New Jersey Supreme Court held that the following language did not give the assurance required for an offer to be firm under 2–205: "We are pleased to offer   .   .   .   (goods at quoted prices)   .   .   .   .   Thank you   .   .   .   for this opportunity to quote." [21]   In our view it is easy enough to imagine offers that do satisfy the 2–205 "assurance" requirement: "This offer is firm and will remain open for three months."

## § 1–4   Methods of Acceptance

The Code continues the offeror's common law right to specify that his offer may be accepted only in a given manner.   But if the offeror does not so specify, section 2–206(1) (a) provides that offers generally invite acceptance "in any manner and by any medium reasonable in the circumstances."   Thus the means of communicating an acceptance need not be identical with that of the offer.[22]   Telegraph-

---

16.   1 A. Corbin, Corbin on Contracts §§ 38, 51 (1963).

17.   E. g., James Baird Co. v. Gimbel Bros., 64 F.2d 344 (2d Cir. 1933).

18.   E. g., Hoffman v. Red Owl Stores, Inc., 26 Wis.2d 683, 133 N.W.2d 267 (1965) (negotiating party who has not yet made an offer still cannot break off with impunity if he has induced other party reasonably to rely).

19.   Restatement, Second, Contracts § 90 (Tent.Draft No. 2, 1965).

20.   90 N.J.Super. 69, 216 A.2d 246, 3 UCC Rep.Serv. 42 (App.Div.1966).

21.   Id. at 72, 216 A.2d at 248, 3 UCC Rep.Serv. at 43.

22.   See Murray, Contracts: A New Design for the Agreement Process, 53 Cornell L.Rev. 785, 793 (1968).

ed offers do not require telegraphed acceptances, unless reason so demands.

An offer may clearly call for acceptance by return promise or clearly call for acceptance by a specified act. When so, then the acceptance must take the specified form. But an offer may also be ambiguous as to whether it calls for one or the other.[23] Some courts have given effect to a "presumption" that such an offer calls for acceptance by return promise. Section 2–206(1) (a) appears to eliminate this presumption and to permit acceptance either by return promise or by performance, whichever is reasonable. Thus, a seller who merely ships ordered goods and so accepts, cuts off the buyer's power to revoke his offer, whereas absent 2–206(1) (a) a court might hold that the buyer has power to revoke unless and until the seller makes a return promissory acceptance.

To form a contract it is not even necessary under 2–206(1) (a) that the seller's shipment constituting the acceptance be conforming goods. Of course, the seller also breaches if he ships nonconforming goods.[24] One authority has it that this novelty is to provide a weapon against the so-called "unilateral contract trick." [25] Under prior law a seller could play this trick by shipping nonconforming goods and, when he was sued by the buyer, assert "no contract" since the shipment of nonconforming goods was not the act called for by the offer. Under 2–206(1) (b) the seller's defense will fail and the buyer will have a good claim for breach of contract.

Section 2–206(2) provides that "where the beginning of a requested performance is a reasonable mode of acceptance an offeror who is not notified of acceptance within a reasonable time may treat the offer as having lapsed before acceptance." Presumably this provision suspends the power of the offeror to revoke his offer for a period of time, a power that revives if the performing offeree does not notify the offeror within a reasonable time after the offeree commences performance. Comment 3 to 2–206 suggests that under this section a bilateral contract is formed when the offeree begins performance, but that the offeror's liability thereunder is subject to the condition that the offeree duly notify the offeror of his acceptance. However, the text of the section is not confined to bilateral contract possibilities, and it may also apply to explicit offers for acts—"unilateral offers"—and so protect a performing unilateral offeree against arbitrary revocation prior to completion of performance.[26]

One federal district court case poses an interesting question concerning the overlap between sections 2–206 and 2–207 on additional terms in the acceptance. In Universal Oil Products Co. v. S.C.M.

23.  See, e. g., Davis v. Jacoby, 1 Cal.2d 370, 34 P.2d 1026 (1934).

24.  See 1 N.Y.State Law Revision Comm'n, 1955 Report 623 (1955).

25.  W. Hawkland, Sales & Bulk Sales 6–7 (2d ed. 1958).

26.  See Restatement of Contracts § 45 (1932).

Corp.,[27] the seller sent a written offer to the buyer that did not contain a provision for arbitration of any disputes. The buyer responded with a written purchase order that did contain a provision for arbitration. The court treated the buyer's order as a counter-offer, rather than as an acceptance with a proposal for additional terms under 2–207(1) and (2). Since the seller shipped the goods pursuant to the buyer's order, the court found that the seller thereby accepted the counter-offer and became bound to arbitrate. The court purported to rely on that part of 2–206(1) (b) which provides that a seller may accept an order from a buyer for prompt shipment either by prompt shipment or by a prompt promise to ship. Although 2–206(1) (b) is broad enough to cover this case, the court's reliance on it is misplaced. The case involves a "battle of the forms" problem, and the Code draftsmen formulated 2–207 to deal with that problem.[28] If the case involves an exchange of forms, section 2–207 generally governs. The court should have decided the instant case under 2–207.[29]

### § 1–5  Contract Modification, Waiver, and Estoppel

Contracts for sale do not thereafter always remain fixed and unchanged. The parties may subsequently modify their contract by agreement or by conduct amounting to waiver or estoppel. Section 2–209 of Article Two and supplemental general law via 1–103 together define the requirements for modification, waiver, and estoppel. A court may also use section 2–302 on unconscionability and 1–203 on good faith to police modifying agreements for overreaching, as we will see.

The five subsections of 2–209 provide:

(1) An agreement modifying a contract within this Article needs no consideration to be binding.

(2) A signed agreement which excludes modification or rescission except by a signed writing cannot be otherwise modified or rescinded, but except as between merchants such a requirement on a form supplied by the merchant must be separately signed by the other party.

(3) The requirements of the statute of frauds section of this Article (Section 2–201) must be satisfied if the contract as modified is within its provisions.

(4) Although an attempt at modification or rescission does not satisfy the requirements of subsection (2) or (3) it can operate as a waiver.

(5) A party who has made a waiver affecting an executory portion of the contract may retract the waiver by reasonable notification received by the other party that strict

---

**27.**  313 F.Supp. 905, 7 UCC Rep.Serv. 813 (D.Conn.1970).

**28.**  See § 2–207, Comment 1; but see prior drafts of § 2–207, especially the

1952 Official Draft and December 1954 Recommendations of the Editorial Board.

**29.**  See Section 1–2 supra.

performance will be required of any term waived, unless the retraction would be unjust in view of a material change of position in reliance on the waiver.

The foregoing subsections of 2–209 and the problems with which they deal are of immense practical significance. This is partly because the occasions and pressures for contract changes are numerous and diverse. A contract modifier may be motivated by changed circumstances, unforeseen circumstances, or mere change of mind. And not all contract modifiers are honest. Some are extortionists, some are profiteers, and some are chiselers.[30] As we will see, 2–209 has rather less to say about the problem of overreaching than about formal requirements for the validity of modifications.

## FORMAL REQUIREMENTS

Here we consider the applicable law of consideration and any relevant writing requirements, contractual or statutory. The different ways in which a contract may be changed should be distinguished. In 2–209 an agreement that changes a prior contract is called a modification and is distinguished from waivers of both the "election" and the "estoppel" variety. There are at least three main types of modifying agreements: (*1*) explicit ones, (*2*) conduct in which the other party acquiesces constituting a course of performance at variance with the terms of the contract, and (*3*) conduct by both parties not constituting a course of performance but which may be fairly construed as a modifying agreement under either the Code's expansive definition of agreement or under 2–204(1). In the second and third types of cases parties may inadvertently modify, and it behooves contracting parties to read their mail. In Gateway Co. v. Charlotte Theatres [31] the parties reduced their agreement to writing. The buyer then sent the contract back to the seller with a cover letter directing attention to a modifying proposal that the seller install the air conditioners by a given date. The seller did not respond but went ahead and performed, though not by the specified date. The court held that the parties had modified their original contract to require earlier performance, and it warned that contracting parties cannot safely follow William Randolph Hearst's maxim: "Throw it in the wastebasket—every letter answers itself in a couple of weeks."

Of course, a modifying agreement is one thing, an enforceable modifying agreement is quite another. The Code reduces the formalities for a valid modification: under 2–209(1) consideration is unnecessary. Thus, the parties may modify free of any inflexibilities of the so-called preexisting duty rule. According to this rule, the prospective beneficiary of a modification must give or promise to give something to the other party beyond what he was under a duty to give under the original contract. Otherwise he could not enforce

---

**30.** See generally, Levie, The Interpretation of Contracts in New York Under the Uniform Commercial Code, 10 N.Y. L.F. 350, 355–61 (1964).

**31.** 297 F.2d 483 (1st Cir. 1961).

the prospective benefit. Reason and justice do not require an inflexible rule here. Occasions commonly arise in which it is neither unreasonable nor unjust to allow a party to benefit from a modification without in effect paying something further. For example, the parties may modify and set a date for contract performance earlier than that set in the prior agreement, and this may benefit the one party without imposing any burden whatsoever on the other. When so, there is no reason why the beneficiary should have to pay for the change. The same is true with respect to some extensions of time for performance, some changes in place of performance, and many other possible types of modifications. Section 2–209(1) repeals the preexisting duty rule, and in effect permits the consideration given to support the original contract to serve also to support the modified contract.

Assuming that a party can establish a modifying agreement, must he show that it was reduced to writing? Section 2–209(3) states that "[t]he requirements of the statute of frauds section of this Article (2–201) must be satisfied if the contract as modified is within its provisions." The impact of this provision is not clear. We see at least the following possible interpretations: (*1*) that if the original contract was within 2–201, any modification thereof must also be in writing; (*2*) that a modification must be in writing if the term it adds brings the entire deal within 2–201 for the first time, as where the price is modified from $400 to $500; (*3*) that a modification must be in writing if it falls in 2–201 on its own; (*4*) that the modification must be in writing if it changes the quantity term of an original agreement that fell within 2–201; and (*5*) some combination of the foregoing. Given the purposes of the basic statute of frauds section 2–201, we believe interpretations (*2*), (*3*), and (*4*) are each justified, subject, of course, to the exceptions in 2–201 itself and to any general supplemental principles of estoppel. One court appears to have adopted interpretation (*1*) above. In Asco Mining Co. v. Gross Mining Co.,[32] allegedly the seller orally extended the time for the buyer to pay, and the court flatly stated that this violated 2–209(3). One of us does not concur. The original deal was in writing, which alone was enough to "afford a basis for believing that the offered oral evidence rests on a real transaction." [33] Moreover, the oral change did not relate to the quantity term, the only one required to be in writing under 2–201 itself. Rather, it related to time for payment, which could have been shown through oral proof, if omitted from the original contract. The *Asco* court did recognize that the buyer might still prevail on retrial despite noncompliance with the statute of frauds, provided the buyer could prove an estoppel waiver under 2–209(4) and (5).

The parties can provide in their original agreement that its terms may be modified only in writing. Section 2–209(2) specifically validates such a clause. Observe that such a clause goes far beyond 2–209(3) and 2–201, for these sections only require a writing in certain

32.  3 UCC Rep.Serv. 293 (Pa.C.P.1965).    33.  § 2–201, Comment 1.

cases in which the sale involves a price of $500 or more. Already there are several Code cases on the effect of contract clauses requiring that modifications be in writing. In one the court ignored a stipulation that any modification not only be in writing but also signed by both parties.[34] In a second the court indicated that the party benefiting from the clause could (if he acted specifically with reference to it) waive it.[35] In a third the court suggested that a party could be estopped to set up such a clause, even if he did not specifically waive it. In this third case, Knutson Shipbuilding Corp. v. Rogers Construction Corp.,[36] the buyer gave an oral order for "extras" in the face of a clause seemingly requiring such orders to be in writing. The seller provided the extras and was awarded compensation therefor. The result is consistent with 2-209(4), (5), and 1-103.

Section 2-209(4) states that "[a]lthough an attempt at modification or rescission does not satisfy the requirements of subsection (2) or (3), it can operate as a waiver." Moreover, 2-209(5) provides that the waiving party may not retract his waiver "as to an executory portion of the contract" if this would be "unjust in view of a material change of position in reliance on the waiver." What "consideration" and "writing" requirements are there with respect to waivers, if any? In our opinion if the elements of an estoppel waiver are present, the relying party should not be prejudiced by failure to give consideration or by the oral nature of the waiver, and we believe sections 2-209(5) and 1-103 accord with our view. But what if the elements of an estoppel are not present? As for "consideration," there is pre- and post-Code authority that a party must give something in return for the waiver of a substantial right.[37] Section 2-209(1) does not in so many words change this doctrine, for 2-209 dispenses with consideration only in regard to modification agreements, not in regard to waivers. Any possible further requirement that the waiver be in writing could only derive from a contract clause, for 2-209(3) and 2-201 on the Code's statute of frauds do not apply to waivers. However, the parties may, as in the *Asco* case, provide that "no waiver . . . shall bind . . . unless in writing." But this clause itself may be waived.

## POLICING PROBLEMS

Contract modifications and waivers are notorious for the policing problems they generate. While most modifications are legitimate, some are not. A party who asserts a modification may simply be a liar. And if in fact no modification or waiver ever occurred, then we may hope that the judge or jury will discover as much. The actuality

---

34. In re Estate of Upchurch, —— Tenn. App. ——, 466 S.W.2d 886, 9 UCC Rep. Serv. 580 (1970).

35. C.I.T. Corp. v. Jonnet, 3 UCC Rep. Serv. 321 (Pa.C.P.1965), aff'd, 419 Pa. 435, 214 A.2d 620, 3 UCC Rep.Serv. 968 (1965).

36. 6 UCC Rep.Serv. 323 (N.Y.Sup.Ct. 1969).

37. See, e. g., Rennie & Laughlin, Inc. v. Chrysler Corp., 242 F.2d 208 (9th Cir. 1957).

of a modification or waiver may be conceded, but the aggrieved party may claim nonetheless that he was the victim of bad faith, open extortion, profiteering, chiseling, or the like, and that this conduct renders the modification or waiver invalid and of no legal force or effect. Section 2–209 is itself silent on policing problems, but the comments acknowledge them. And judges can use Code sections 1–203 and 2–302 on bad faith and unconscionability to police against the extortionist, the profiteer, the chiseler, the dishonest "compromiser," and others who unjustly demand modifications or waivers.

The extortionist is perhaps most familiar: "Pay me more or I won't finish making the goods and you won't be able to open up your new business on the scheduled date." The seller may thus get the buyer over a barrel and extort a higher price or some other concession. The wrong is aggravated if the extortionist insists on concessions that he sought but did not get in the negotiations leading up to the contract in the first place. Aggravated or not, extorted modifications or waivers are not enforceable under the Code. Courts can hold that they are in bad faith under 1–203 or unconscionable under 2–302, or both. Of course, in pre-Code days, courts could use the consideration doctrine to police against extortion: [38] "You gave no new consideration for the concession and you had a preexisting duty to do everything you are to do under the modified arrangement, hence the concession is unenforceable." While 2–209(1) withdraws this weapon, sections 1–203 and 2–302 should be adequate policing weapons. Moreover, the extortionist can no longer hope to sustain a modification or waiver by giving a new consideration merely technical in character (a "horse, hawk, or robe" [39]).

The profiteer is one who takes unfair advantage of market shift to exact a price adjustment that will enhance his profit on the contract (as opposed merely to enabling him to maintain his original profit). Thus when the market price falls significantly below the original contract price, the buyer may say to the seller: "Reduce the price or I will buy elsewhere and you will have to sue me if you want to recoup." Of course, profiteering is seldom so blatant as this. But blatant or not, courts should not uphold modifications that are nothing but sheer profiteering, unless there is some recognized commercial practice that sanctions them in the particular trade. Here, too, courts may resort to 1–203 and 2–302.

One kind of chiseler may be characterized as a chap who "takes a contract, usually by the low bid, at an unrealistic low price in the hope of making up the difference by overcharging on extras or forcing a modification." [40] Anytime the aggrieved party can actually prove

---

38. See generally, Patterson, An Apology for Consideration, 58 Colum.L.Rev. 929, 936–39 (1958).

39. Pinnel's Case, 5 Coke's Reps. 117a (C.P.1602).

40. Levie, The Interpretation of Contracts in New York Under the Uniform Commercial Code, 10 N.Y.L.F. 350, 357 (1964).

that the other party is in fact such a chiseler, the court should invoke 1–203 or 2–302 and not enforce the modification.

The "dishonest compromiser" is one who conjures up a dispute over the meaning of the original contract, not really believing in his position, but hoping to secure a favorable "compromise settlement." This wrong can take a variety of aggravated forms. For example, the dishonest compromiser may also seek to take advantage of the notorious "conditional check cashing rule" according to which the cashing of a check offered in settlement constitutes acceptance of the proposed settlement. (The check itself may include an inscription on it to that effect.) Courts have sought to police dishonest compromises by insisting that the dispute be "in good faith" and "honest" in origin.[41] Under the Code courts may similarly invoke 1–203. And, it is to be hoped that courts will utilize 1–203 and 2–302 to mitigate the rigors of the conditional check cashing rule.

How may a contracting party rebut a charge of extortion, profiteering, chiseling, or the like? Comment 2 to 2–209 suggests one approach:

> Subsection (1) provides that an agreement modifying a sales contract needs no consideration to be binding.
>
> However, modifications made thereunder must meet the test of good faith imposed by this Act. The effective use of bad faith to escape performance on the original contract terms is barred, and the extortion of a "modification" without legitimate commercial reason is ineffective as a violation of the duty of good faith. Nor can a mere technical consideration support a modification made in bad faith.
>
> The test of "good faith" between merchants or as against merchants includes "observance of reasonable commercial standards of fair dealing in the trade" (Section 2–103), and may in some situations require an objectively demonstrable reason for seeking a modification. But such matters as a market shift which makes performance come to involve a loss may provide such a reason even though there is no such unforeseen difficulty as would make out a legal excuse from performance under Sections 2–615 and 2–616.

The facts of Skinner v. Tober Foreign Motors Inc.,[42] illustrate one kind of modification or waiver that will stand up under the Code. The buyer of an airplane expected to pay for it out of earnings from its use, a fact known to the seller. The engine developed difficulties not covered by the seller's warranty. The buyer told the seller he could not afford both to keep up on his monthly payments to the seller and make the repairs. The buyer even offered to return the plane

---

41. See, e. g., Berger v. Lane, 190 Cal. 443, 450–51, 213 P. 45, 49 (1923); DeMars v. Musser-Sauntry Land, Logging & Mfg. Co., 37 Minn. 418, 419, 35 N.W. 1, 2 (1887).

42. 345 Mass. 429, 187 N.E.2d 669, 1 UCC Rep.Serv. 1 (1963).

in exchange for a release from any further obligations.  Instead, the seller proposed a reduction in payments with an extension of the payment period, and the buyer agreed.  Later the court refused to let the seller disaffirm this modification.  Although the buyer gave no new consideration for the modification, he plainly did not overreach the seller in any way.  The buyer also had a good business reason for seeking the modification, and both sides benefited.

The *Skinner* opinion, as well as others like it should help courts sort out modifications that are honest and just from those that involve extortion, profiteering, chiseling, or the like.

# CHAPTER 2

# STATUTE OF FRAUDS AND PAROL EVIDENCE RULE

*Analysis*

**Sec.**

2–1. Introduction.

2–2. Transactions to Which Statute Applies; Other UCC Statutes of Frauds.

2–3. General Structure of Statute; Consequences of Compliance and Noncompliance.

2–4. Satisfying the Statute with a Writing.

2–5. Satisfying Statutory Exceptions to the Writing Requirement.

2–6. Satisfying Nonstatutory Exceptions to the Writing Requirement.

2–7. Procedural and Remedial Matters.

2–8. Statutes of Frauds—An Evaluation.

2–9. The Parol Evidence Rule—Does It Give Preference to Written Evidence of Contract Terms?

2–10. Substantive Aspects of the Parol Evidence Rule—Problems of Interpretation.

2–11. Judge-Made Exceptions to the Parol Evidence Rule.

2–12. "Merger" Clauses and the Parol Evidence Rule.

## § 2–1 Introduction

The year: 1676. The place: Old Marston, Oxfordshire, England. Egbert, a Marstonian, owned a fighting cock named Fiste. John sued Egbert, alleging that Egbert had orally promised to sell Fiste to him in exchange for a hundred shillings, a "deal" which John's friend, Harold, claimed he overheard. Egbert denied all this. At the end of the lawsuit John prevailed, though in truth the deal between John and Egbert never took place. But the court did not permit Egbert to testify, even to rebut the testimony of Harold, John's friend. In 1676 courts did not permit parties to a lawsuit to testify. Moreover, courts in that day had no power to throw out jury verdicts manifestly contrary to the evidence.[1] Egbert's case and others (real and imagined) offended the Goddess of Justice. What to do? The next year (1677), Parliament passed a famous "statute of frauds" which required that certain contracts for the sale of goods be in writing to be enforceable. All this to combat "fraude and perjurie."[2]

In Colonial America and after, state legislatures and courts followed suit. In the Twentieth Century, section four of the Uniform

---

1. Willis, The Statute of Frauds—A Legal Anachronism, 3 Ind.L.J. 427, 429–32 (1928).

2. Costigan, The Date and Authorship of the Statute of Frauds, 26 Harv.L. Rev. 329 (1913); Hening, The Original Drafts of the Statute of Frauds and Their Authors, 61 U.Pa.L.Rev. 283 (1913); Stephen & Pollock, Section Seventeen of the Statute of Frauds, 1 L.Q.Rev. 1 (1885).

43

Sales Act became law in most states.[3] Yet the law also eventually permitted parties to lawsuits to testify on their own behalf, both in England and in America. Further, both in England and America the law eventually gave courts certain powers to deal with unreasonable jury verdicts. And in 1954 the British Parliament repealed its 1677 statute of frauds for the sale of goods.[4] However, those state-side law professors who, in the 1940's and 1950's, evolved the Uniform Commercial Code did not follow suit. They kept the spirit of '77 alive in section 2–201 of the Code. Section 2–201(1) provides that "a contract for the sale of goods for the price of $500 or more is not enforceable by way of action or defense unless there is some writing sufficient to indicate that a contract for sale has been made." The Code draftsmen kept this writing requirement because they saw it as a means to the end of combatting perjured testimony in contract cases.

The soundness of this basic means-end hypothesis was questioned in England early on.[5] And when English law abandoned the rules of evidence precluding "party" testimony and developed rules for judicial control of unreasonable jury verdicts, part of the original rationale for the statute of frauds for goods faded. Yet the statute remained until 1954 in England, and it is still much alive in the United States today. Tons of pre-Code and post-Code case law testify to the significance of this whole topic for lawyers.

## § 2–2 Transactions to Which Statute Applies; Other UCC Statutes of Frauds

Section 2–201 does not apply to the sale of realty as such.[6] It does not apply to the rendering of services for a price.[7] It does not apply

---

3. Uniform Sales Act § 4. Statute of Frauds:

(1) A contract to sell or a sale of any goods or choses in action of the value of five hundred dollars or upwards shall not be enforceable by action unless the buyer shall accept part of the goods or choses in action so contracted to be sold or sold, and actually receive the same, or give something in earnest to bind the contract, or in part payment, or unless some note or memorandum in writing of the contract or sale be signed by the party to be charged or his agent in that behalf.

(2) The provisions of this section apply to every such contract or sale, notwithstanding that the goods may be intended to be delivered at some future time or may not at the time of such contract or sale be actually made, procured, or provided, or fit or ready for delivery, or some act may be requisite for the making or completing thereof, or rendering the same fit for delivery; but if the goods are to be manufactured by the seller especially for the buyer and are not suitable for sale to others in the ordinary course of the seller's business, the provisions of this section shall not apply.

(3) There is an acceptance of goods within the meaning of this section when the buyer, either before or after delivery of the goods, expresses by words or conduct his assent to becoming the owner of those specific goods.

4. Grunfield, Law Reform (Enforcement of Contracts) Act, 1954, 17 Mod.L.Rev. 451 (1954).

5. Child v. Godalphin, 1 Dick. 39 (1723).

6. For pre-Code cases on the borderline between realty and personalty, see, e. g., L. Vold, The Law of Sales 96–99 (2d ed. 1959) and the cases cited therein.

7. National Historic Shrines Foundation, Inc. v. Dali, 4 UCC Rep.Serv. 71 (N.Y.Sup.Ct.1967).

to the sale of corporate stocks and bonds or to choses in action generally.[8] It does not apply to contracts of employment or brokerage even when these look to the sale of goods.[9] Rather, the section applies to a "contract for the sale of goods for the price of $500 or more." Section 2–106(1) defines a "sale" as "the passing of title from the seller to the buyer for a price," and 2–105(1) defines "goods" generally to mean "all things (including specially manufactured goods) movable at the time of identification to the contract for sale." It is easy to imagine clear cases to which the foregoing language applies. But as with any legal language, borderline cases can arise. When does property cease to be realty and become goods for purposes of 2–201? Consider a contract for the sale of standing timber, for the sale of a building to be removed from the land, or for the sale of minerals to be extracted. Sections 2–105(1) and 2–107(1) make it clear that these are all "contracts for the sale of goods" at least "if they are to be severed by the seller." Section 2–107(2) also explicitly treats contracts for the sale of growing crops as contracts for the sale of goods.

But experience affords many examples of borderline cases for which the Code's scope provisions do not explicitly cater. Doubtless some courts will rely on pre-Code case law to resolve these cases. For example, when two parties bargain for several items each at a price lower than $500, but when taken together exceed $500, is there one sale to which the statute applies or several sales to which the statute does not apply?[10] When one party orally agrees to sell his business to another, including an inventory of goods as well as a franchise, goodwill and the like, does the statute apply?[11] When a party transfers both goods and services in the same transaction, does the statute apply?[12] Many courts have tended to narrow the scope of pre-Code versions of the statute by refusing to apply it in borderline cases.[13] This practice is certainly understandable if the special needs for a statute of frauds back in 1677 no longer apply today, if the very idea of such a statute rests on a faulty means-end hypothesis, and if there are still other objections to the statute.[14] Also, if all these things are true, perhaps it follows *a fortiori* that courts should not extend 2–201 by analogy.[15] Rational extension by analogy re-

8.   But see § 8–319.

9.   Stone v. Krylon, Inc., 141 F.Supp. 785 (E.D.Pa.1956); Brown v. Lee, 242 Ark. 122, 412 S.W.2d 273 (1967).

10.   2 A. Corbin, Corbin on Contracts § 475 (1950) [hereinafter cited as Corbin on Contracts] and cases cited therein.

11.   Cf. Foster v. Colorado Radio Corp., 381 F.2d 222, 4 UCC Rep.Serv. 446 (10th Cir. 1967).

12.   2 Corbin on Contracts § 476.

13.   See Corbin, The Uniform Commercial Code—Sales; Should It Be Enacted?, 59 Yale L.J. 821, 832–33 (1950).

14.   For further discussion of these "ifs," see Sections 2–7 and 2–8 infra.

15.   § 1–102, Comment 1:

Courts . . . have recognized the policies embodied in an act as applicable in reason to subject-matter which was not expressly included in the language of the act . . . they have done the same where reason and policy so required, even where the subject-matter had been intentionally excluded from the act in general. . . .

quires not merely that the reason behind a rule "extend" to a new situation but also that the quality of that reason be sound.[16] Where a rule rests on a reason that is itself questionable, the case for extension is weaker. This is all the more true of a statute long under fire.

A party who escapes 2–201 may still be confronted with 1–206 which imposes a writing requirement for the enforceability of certain contracts for the "sale of personal property" other than goods.[17] The Code also includes a specific writing requirement for sales of securities [18] and for security agreements.[19] And 5–104(1) and (2) incorporate a kind of statute of frauds requirement for certain credits or letters of credit.

Finally, 2–201(1) applies not only to oral agreements that fall within its provisions in the first instance. It applies as well to future oral modifications of such contracts. Section 2–209(3) states explicitly that "the requirements of the statute of frauds . . . must be satisfied if the contract as modified is within its provisions." Section 2–209(4) takes some of the bite out of 2–209(3), for it permits a noncomplying oral modification to "operate as a waiver." [20]

## § 2–3   General Structure of Statute;  Consequences of Compliance and Noncompliance

The entire text of 2–201 is set forth below: [21]

(1) Except as otherwise provided in this section a contract for the sale of goods for the price of $500 or more is not enforceable by way of action or defense unless there is some writing sufficient to indicate that a contract for sale has been made between the parties and signed by the party against whom enforcement is sought or by his authorized agent or broker. A writing is not insufficient because it omits or incorrectly states a term agreed upon but the contract is not enforceable under this paragraph beyond the quantity of goods shown in such writing.

16. Traynor, Statutes Revolving in Common-law Orbits, 17 Catholic U.L. Rev. 401 (1968); Note, The Uniform Commercial Code as a Premise for Judicial Reasoning, 65 Colum.L.Rev. 880 (1965).

17. § 1–206:

(1) Except in the cases described in subsection (2) of this section a contract for the sale of personal property is not enforceable by way of action or defense beyond five thousand dollars in amount or value of remedy unless there is some writing which indicates that a contract for sale has been made between the parties at a defined or stated price, reasonably identifies the subject matter, and is signed by the party against whom enforcement is sought or by his authorized agent.

(2) Subsection (1) of this section does not apply to contracts for the sale of goods (Section 2–201) nor of securities (Section 8–319) nor to security agreements (Section 9–203).

See also Note, The Uniform Commercial Code, Section 1–206—A New Departure in the Statute of Frauds?, 70 Yale L.J. 603 (1961).

18. § 8–319.

19. § 9–203.

20. Cf. C.I.T. Corp. v. Jonnet, 419 Pa. 435, 214 A.2d 620, 3 UCC Rep.Serv. 968 (1965).

21. § 2–201.

(2) Between merchants if within a reasonable time a writing in confirmation of the contract and sufficient against the sender is received and the party receiving it has reason to know its contents, it satisfies the requirements of subsection (1) against such party unless written notice of objection to its contents is given within 10 days after it is received.

(3) A contract which does not satisfy the requirements of subsection (1) but which is valid in other respects is enforceable

    (a) if the goods are to be specially manufactured for the buyer and are not suitable for sale to others in the ordinary course of the seller's business and the seller, before notice of repudiation is received and under circumstances which reasonably indicate that the goods are for the buyer, has made either a substantial beginning of their manufacture or commitments for their procurement; or

    (b) if the party against whom enforcement is sought admits in his pleading, testimony or otherwise in court that a contract for sale was made, but the contract is not enforceable under this provision beyond the quantity of goods admitted; or

    (c) with respect to goods for which payment has been made and accepted or which have been received and accepted (Sec. 2–606).

The general rule is set forth in subsection 1 and requires that there be "some writing sufficient to indicate that a contract for sale has been made between the parties and signed by the party against whom enforcement is sought." There are both statutory and non-statutory exceptions to the foregoing general rule. The first statutory exception is not a full-fledged one, for it merely ameliorates the writing requirement. A writing is still required, but it need not be signed by the party to be charged. The character of this exception is best understood in light of the form of fraud it was designed to combat. Assume that Orval Orfed and Len Lemhi orally agree over the telephone that Orfed will sell Lemhi 1000 bushels of wheat at $40 a bushel. Orfed, the seller, thereafter sends a signed confirmatory memorandum to Lemhi reciting the terms of the deal, a common practice in such transactions. Such a memo would be good against Orfed under 2–201 should Orfed back out and Lemhi sue him for damages. But absent 2–201(2) the confirmatory memo would not be good against Lemhi, for it is not signed by him as required by 2–201(1). Thus Lemhi would be free to sit back and "play the market." If at delivery date the cost of wheat had fallen to some level below $40 a bushel, and he wanted to buy elsewhere, he could back out, whereas Orfed could not back out, at least so far as the statute of frauds goes, should the market rise. Section 2–201(2) is designed to prevent the Lemhis of the world from taking advantage of the Orfeds. It says that a memo good against Orfed will also be good against Lemhi provided that (1) both are merchants,[22] (2) the memo is sent by Orfed to Lemhi within a reasonable time (after the phone call?), (3) the memo by its terms "confirms" the oral contract, (4) the memo is good against Orfed under 2–201(1), (5) Lemhi receives it, (6) Lemhi has "reason to know its contents," and (7) Lemhi does not object to its contents within ten days of receipt. This carefully circumscribed section thus seeks to combat one form of fraud which pre-Code versions of the statute of frauds actually facilitate. At the same time 2–201(2) itself encourages the common and wise business practice of sending memoranda confirming oral deals, for the section obviates a disadvantage to which the sender would otherwise be subject.[23]

The second statutory exception to the writing requirement of 2–201(1) is more full-fledged. Section 2–201(3)(a) dispenses with a writing in certain cases where the seller significantly relies on an oral contract to specially manufacture goods for the buyer. The third exception is embodied in 2–201(3)(b) and provides that an oral contract falling in 2–201(1) becomes enforceable against a party if he "admits in his pleading, testimony or otherwise in court that a contract for sale was made." The fourth statutory exception appears in 2–201(3)(c) and provides for enforceability "with respect to goods for which payment has been made and accepted or which have been received and accepted." To say that an oral contract is "enforceable" because it falls into one of the foregoing four statutory exceptions is not the same as to say that it is enforceable to the full extent of the entire terms of the actual oral contract.

If past case law is any indicator, the foregoing four statutory exceptions are not the whole story. At the time of the Code's general reception, courts had carved out other exceptions to the writing requirements of pre-Code statutes of frauds.[24] According to some courts, a party cannot invoke the statute actually to perpetrate a fraud,[25] nor can a party invoke the statute if the elements of an equitable estoppel could be shown against him.[26] These exceptions survive enactment of the Code. Section 1–103 explicitly incorporates "supplemental general principles" on fraud and estoppel, and 1–203 states that "every contract or duty within this act imposes an obliga-

---

**22.** § 2–104. See Cook Grains, Inc. v. Fallis, 239 Ark. 962, 395 S.W.2d 555, 2 UCC Rep.Serv. 1141 (1965).

**23.** For a general discussion, see Llewellyn, Memorandum Replying to the Report and Memorandum of Task Group 1 of the Special Committee of the Commerce and Industry Association of New York, Inc., on the Uniform Commercial Code, 1 N.Y. State Law Revision Comm'n, 1954 Report 106, 109–11 (1954).

**24.** See, e. g., L. Vold, Law of Sales 90–93 (2d ed. 1959) and cases cited therein.

**25.** See, e. g., Piper v. Fosher, 121 Ind. 407, 23 N.E. 269 (1889).

**26.** See Section 2–6 infra.

tion of good faith in its performance or enforcement." [27]    Even so, lawyers accustomed to relying on pre-Code statutes of frauds case law should be wary, for 2–201 makes many changes in the pre-Code statutory law.[28]    Cases good under pre-Code statutes of frauds do not automatically remain good law under the Code version.

So much for the general rule of 2–201 and its various exceptions, statutory and nonstatutory.    In Sections 2–4, 2–5, and 2–6 of this Chapter, we will explore the rule and its exceptions more fully.

### General Consequences of Compliance and Noncompliance

A plaintiff who wants to enforce an alleged oral contract and who can hold up a memo satisfying 2–201(1) does not necessarily have much to write home about.    A complying memo is not boon in the way a noncomplying memo is bane.    Absent applicable exceptions, the plaintiff simply loses if he fails to produce a complying memo. But a complying memo is not equivalent to victory.    Of course, a complying memo might be a complete embodiment of the deal, be duly signed by both parties, and be attested by forty Bishops.    If the memo is of this variety, then it is indeed boon, for a fact-finder will decide upon the existence and the terms of the alleged oral agreement merely by looking to the complying memo itself.    But most statute of frauds cases are not of this kind; in most, the memo is either nonexistent or sketchy.    And whether sketchy or not, the theory is that a complying memo itself is not conclusive proof of the existence of the oral contract, let alone of its terms.    Beyond producing a memo "sufficient to indicate that a contract for sale has been made between the parties," the plaintiff must still persuade the trier of fact that the parties did make an oral contract and that its terms were thus and so.[29]    By parity of analysis, a defendant who unsuccessfully pleads the defense of the Statute of Frauds may still "defend on the facts" and prevail, that is, he may still persuade the trier of fact that no contract was ever made.

What else follows from noncompliance?    The theory is that noncompliance merely renders the oral contract unenforceable, not void.[30] This distinction can be significant in various ways.    A valid (not void) oral contract that is currently or was once unenforceable under the statute by one or the other parties may still have value.    A pro-

---

27.  Summers, "Good Faith" in General Contract Law and the Sales Provision of the Uniform Commercial Code, 54 Va.L.Rev. 195 (1968).

28.  But see Oswald v. Allen, 285 F. Supp. 488, 492–93, 5 UCC Rep.Serv. 712, 716 (S.D.N.Y.1968):

Section 85, subd. 1(a) of the New York Personal Property Law . . . was replaced by § 2–201 of the Uniform Commercial Code which amended, but did not change the substance of the law.

29.  For a dubious case on this point, see Harry Winston, Inc. v. Robert Simon, Inc., 4 UCC Rep.Serv. 482 (N. Y.Sup.Ct.1967).

30.  1 S. Williston, Sales §§ 71A, 72A (Rev. ed. 1948).    See UCC § 2–201, Comment 4:

Failure to satisfy the requirements of this section does not render the contract void for all purposes, but merely prevents it from being judicially enforced in favor of a party to the contract.

spective defendant might for instance send a prospective plaintiff a letter in which he acknowledges the oral contract and signs his name! The oral contract would then become not merely "not void," but enforceable too. Moreover, from the fact an oral contract is not enforceable by one party for lack of a required memo, it does not follow that the other party cannot enforce it, for he may have a complying memo. Yet prospective enforceability of an initially unenforceable oral contract does not turn solely on the production of complying memos. As we have seen,[31] an initially unenforceable oral contract may later become enforceable to some extent if one party prepares to perform,[32] admits the contract in litigation,[33] or partly performs.[34] All this would be legally impossible if oral contracts, initially unenforceable under the statute of frauds, were void. Professor Corbin has discussed a number of other ways in which an oral contract, unenforceable under the statute of frauds but not void, may be legally significant.[35] For example, this "contract" may prevent a buyer who takes control of the goods from being a trespasser. It may enable a party to the oral contract to show in a quasi-contractual action that he conferred a benefit on the defendant pursuant to an agreement, so that he was not an officious volunteer and therefore is truly entitled to quasi-contractual relief.[36]

It is sometimes said that the statute of frauds is a rule of substantive law and not a rule of evidence. It is not clear what this means. The temptation to call the statute a rule of evidence derives from the possibility that it can operate to preclude testimony in a court case. A party may be able to convince a court that the plaintiff's memo does not satisfy the statute and that he cannot satisfy it in any other way, so that the plaintiff is thereby precluded from offering any further oral evidence as to the existence and terms of the oral contract. But not just any rule which operates to affect the materiality and therefore the admissibility of evidence should for this reason be called a rule of evidence. For every rule of law can affect the materiality and therefore the admissibility of evidence. A true rule of evidence operates to exclude a given type of evidence, for example hearsay, but permits the relevant legal rights to be established by still other kinds of evidence. When a statute of frauds applies to render an oral contract unenforceable, however, the theory is that no other evidence can make the contract enforceable. Consequently, some courts have remarked that "the statute is not a mere rule of evidence, but a limitation of judicial authority to afford a remedy." [37]

---

31. See text accompanying note 21 supra.

32. § 2–201(3) (a).

33. § 2–201(3) (b).

34. § 2–201(3) (c).

35. 2 Corbin on Contracts § 279 et seq.

36. Id. § 288.

37. Id. § 279 n. 34: "The statute is not a mere rule of evidence, but a limitation of judicial authority to afford a remedy." See Safe Deposit & Trust Co. v. Diamond Coal & Coke Co., 234 Pa. 100, 83 A. 54 (1912).

## § 2–4   Satisfying the Statute with a Writing

To satisfy the statute with a writing a party need only (*1*) produce a writing, (*2*) signed by the party to be charged, which (*3*) recites a quantity term.

According to one pre-Code judicial doctrine, a party need not produce a complying memo if he can prove that the writing once existed but was somehow lost, misplaced, or destroyed.[38]  Section 2–201 does not expressly sanction this doctrine, but pre-Code statutes did not either.  Doubtless it remains good law even under 2–201 in some states.  To satisfy 2–201(1), must the writing consist of one piece of paper?  Presumably several writings can be pieced together to satisfy the requirement, writings which taken alone would not be sufficient.[39]  Moreover, it appears that the writing or writings need not be sent with intent to acknowledge a contract.  Indeed, one of the writings taken together to satisfy the statute may even be disputatious.[40]  Further, a writing or writings sufficient to satisfy the statute with respect to a principal oral contract may also be sufficient with respect to a separate but ancillary oral contract.[41]

The writing must be "signed by the party against whom enforcement is sought or by his authorized agent or broker." [42]  What counts as a signature has generated a good deal of litigation.  The Code expressly "deformalizes" the signature requirement.[43]  Even a letterhead will do, provided it "authenticates" the writing.

It is not necessary that the writing state all the terms of the contract, or even that it state any of them accurately.  It must state a quantity term, and if that quantity term proves lower than the quantity actually agreed upon as shown in oral proof, the contract will be enforceable only to the extent of the quantity specified in the writing.[44]  Thus, under 2–201 the general theory is that the success-

---

**38.**  See 2 Corbin on Contracts § 529.

**39.**  Cf. Reich v. Helen Harper, Inc., 3 UCC Rep.Serv. 1048 (N.Y.Civ.Ct.1966).

**40.**  Id.

**41.**  Conner v. May, 444 S.W.2d 948, 7 UCC Rep.Serv. 185 (Tex.Civ.App. 1969).

**42.**  § 2–201(1).

**43.**  Section 2–201, Comment 1, defines "signed" as including "any authentication which identifies the party to be charged."  Section 1—201(39) states: " 'Signed' includes any symbol executed or adopted by a party with present intention to authenticate a writing," and section 1–201, Comment 39, further explains:

Authentication may be printed, stamped or written; it may be by initials or by thumbprint.  It may be on any part of the document and in appropriate cases may be found in a billhead or letterhead.  No catalog of possible authentications can be complete and the court must use common sense and commercial experience in passing upon these matters.  The question always is whether the symbol was executed by the party with present intention to authenticate the writing.

See Romani v. Harris, 255 Md. 389, 258 A.2d 187, 7 UCC Rep.Serv. 194 (Ct. App.1969).  See also Reich v. Helen Harper, Inc., 3 UCC Rep.Serv. 1048 (N.Y.Civ.Ct.1966).

**44.**  All the commentators say the memo must state a quantitative term.  However, a close reading of section 2–201 indicates that all the commentators may be wrong.  An alternative interpretation of the language is that only if the writing states a quantitative term is that term determinative.

ful plaintiff recovers on an oral contract, not on a written one. It is not unnatural, however, for the inexperienced to inquire why, if there is to be a statute of frauds at all, it should not require all terms of a deal to be in writing. The explanations are several. First, such a requirement would be unrealistic. Businessmen do not and will not act by legal ritual. For convenience they often send sketchy memos and notes to one another. They may even choose to leave price and quality out of a writing. Indeed, the Code itself includes "suppletive" terms on price and quality which apply in the absence of contrary agreement of the parties.[45] Second, a requirement that all or most of the terms be in writing can itself be easily turned into an instrument of fraud. As Karl N. Llewellyn said before the New York Law Revision Commission:

> It was pointed out that the statute of frauds provision, the number of which is 2–201, made a tremendous innovation in the law. It does, and thank God it does. It was pointed out that the statute of frauds provision—at least I presume it was; it is in Mr. Fifield's memorandum—changes the necessary memo of the transaction, where a memo is required—that is, in cases under $500. It frees the memo from the necessity of laying down every term of the agreement and indeed requires the memo only to state specifically the single term of quantity.

> Now, just take a look for a moment at what the statute of frauds has raised in the way of trouble and see whether this isn't a wise and at the same time a very safe provision. What you have got as a requirement under the Code is that there shall be no doubt that there was a contract for sale. That is No. 1. Secondly, that you can't enforce it beyond the quantity stated. You can be inaccurate about other things or leave them out, mostly—price, for example, you can leave out. You refer to the market—you have to keep the jury from going crazy. You can't swear too much of a price onto a guy when there is a market around to test whether or not it is likely that that was the term agreed upon.

> But here is the kind of thing you get under the present law, and I submit that it is something to raise any commercial man's hair. Talk about uncertainty—no matter how perfect a memorandum is, though signed by both sides, the law is clear, and it is clear, I think, in every state that has a statute of frauds, that the fellow who doesn't want the contract enforced can say, "Sure, we made a contract. Sure, that is the memorandum I signed. But there was a term we agreed upon which is not in that memorandum." And he can give all evidence as to that term and nobody can keep

---

**45.** Llewellyn, Memorandum Replying to the Report and Memorandum of Task Group 1 of the Special Committee of the Commerce and Industry Association of New York, Inc., on the Uniform Commercial Code, 1 N.Y.State Law Revision Comm'n, 1954 Report 106, 117–18 (1954).

it from being given.  He goes to the jury on whether it was agreed, and if it was agreed, the contract is unenforceable.

Why, nothing is safe—nothing is safe!  There can always be evidence that there was not included in the memorandum an extra term, and the parol evidence rule is no protection against it.

We regard this as commercial outrage.  We think that if there was ever an instrument of fraud, that strange interpretation of the old statute which has become universal is an instrument of fraud.  We turn to the exact opposite and say, as long as you are sure you have got a deal, go to the jury as you would in any other case, and we say the risk is very small, and here is why the risk is very small.  You can't be sued under the memo for more than the quantity stated, which puts a top limit on what you could possibly be stuck with, and the whole practice of all intelligent business is to confirm in detail or make careful written contracts so that the number of cases in which defective memos will actually come into operation not only is already almost nugatory, but is decreasing by the minute.[46]

The primary job of the writing required by 2–201(1), then, is "[t]o indicate that a contract for sale has been made."  Perhaps the clearest case of a writing that so "indicates" is one which appears on its face to incorporate any and all conceivable terms a contract of that kind might include and which is signed by both parties and dated contemporaneously with the alleged real transaction which the writing is supposed to "indicate."  Very few litigated cases will be so clear.  Such cases will be settled.  And contrary to what is sometimes assumed, even if the plaintiff produces a writing so overwhelmingly "indicative" of a contract, the defendant may still deny and prove there was no contract.  For the theory of the writing sufficient under 2–201(1) is not that it conclusively proves the existence of the contract but that it affords the trier of fact something reliable to go on in addition to the mere oral testimony of the plaintiff.

Does "sufficient to indicate" imply a standard of proof stronger than, equivalent to, or weaker than "by the balance of probabilities?"  The comments to 2–201 offer two separate elaborations which are not identical:

All that is required is that the writing afford a basis for believing that the offered oral evidence rests on a real transaction.[47]

[I]t must evidence a contract for the sale of goods.[48]

---

46.  Id. at 163–64.

47.  § 1–201, Comment 1.

48.  Id.

Also Professor Karl Llewellyn, draftsman of 2–201, offered these translations at different times before the New York Law Revision Commission:

> [Plaintiff may proceed] once there is given enough of a memorandum to document the presence of a deal.[49]

> What the section does . . . is to require some objective guaranty, other than word, of mouth that there really has been some deal.[50]

There shall be no doubt that a contract was made.[51]

Plainly, this last of Llewellyn's formulations must be considered a slip of the tongue (or pen). The spirit of his other formulations and of the comments seems to be that "sufficient to indicate" is roughly equivalent to "more probably than not," rather than "no doubt."

To date the case law on the "sufficient to indicate" rubric is not plentiful. The cases can arise from two sources: (1) direct interpretations of 2–201(1) and (2) interpretations of 2–201(2) which inevitably address themselves to 2–201(1). The latter interpretations are necessarily a source of relevant case law because the confirmatory memo under 2–201(2) must satisfy 2–201(1). So far, two cases have held memos insufficient to indicate that a contract had been made. Both failed because of essentially "futuristic" language in the memo. In the first, the memo included the language: "It is our intention to award you a contract." [52] In the second, the writing recited: ". . . tentative deposit on tentative purchase." [53]

Even when the writing satisfies 2–201(1) or (2), the plaintiff cannot enforce any oral contract he is able to prove beyond the quantity term shown in the writing. This can itself arm the defendant with a sword of fraud, for he can, of course, dishonorably choose to insist on the written quantity limitation when the oral evidence plainly shows a contract for much more.

## § 2–5　Satisfying Statutory Exceptions to the Writing Requirement

Section 2–201(2) states:

> Between merchants if within a reasonable time a writing in confirmation of the contract and sufficient against the sender is received and the party receiving it has reason to know its contents, it satisfies the requirements of subsection

---

**49.** Llewellyn, Memorandum Replying to the Report and Memorandum of Task Group 1 of the Special Committee of the Commerce and Industry Association of New York, Inc., on the Uniform Commercial Code, 1 N.Y. State Law Revision Comm'n, 1954 Report 106, 111 (1954).

**50.** Id. at 119.

**51.** Id. at 163. See generally Note, Sufficiency of the Writing and Neces-

sity for a Signature in the Statute of Frauds of the Uniform Commercial Code, 4 U.San Fran.L.Rev. 177 (1969).

**52.** John H. Wickersham Eng'r & Constr., Inc. v. Arbutus Steel Co., 1 UCC Rep.Serv. 49, 50 (Pa.C.P.1962).

**53.** Arcuri v. Weiss, 198 Pa.Super. 506, 507, 184 A.2d 24, 25, 1 UCC Rep.Serv. 45, 46 (1962).

> (1) against such party unless written notice of objection to its contents is given within 10 days after it is received.

Section 2–201(2) [54] may be viewed as a kind of exception to the writing requirement of 2–201(1), [55] for while 2–201(2) requires a written confirmation, it need not be signed by the party to be charged. Note first that the writing must be "sufficient against the sender," that is, it must be signed by him and state a quantity. [56]

When is a memorandum sent "in confirmation of the contract?" As we have seen, 2–201(1) has comparable language which requires that the writing be "sufficient to indicate" a contract. Admittedly this latter language is not identical with the former, but it is submitted that our earlier analysis of the meaning of the "sufficient to indicate" language [57] applies to the "in confirmation" language of 2–201 (2). An early case under 2–201(2) sets a rational standard. In Harry Rubin & Sons v. Consolidated Pipe Co., [58] the buyer sent a letter to the seller that referred to the buyer's earlier oral "order" as a closed deal rather than merely as a pending offer. The court rejected seller's argument that because the buyer used the word "order" in his letter rather than "agreement" or "contract," the letter was not a writing "in confirmation of a contract sufficient to satisfy 2–201(2)." [59] The court perceived that the true test was whether "the writing offered a basis for believing that the offered oral evidence rested on a real transaction" and observed that the buyer "must still sustain the burden of persuading the trier of fact that the contracts were in fact made prior to the written confirmation." [60]

Section 2–201(3) provides:

> A contract which does not satisfy the requirements of subsection (1) but which is valid in other respects is enforceable
>
> (a) if the goods are to be specially manufactured for the buyer and are not suitable for sale to others in the ordinary course of the seller's business and the seller, before notice of repudiation is received and under circumstances which reasonably indicate that the goods are for the buyer, has made either a substantial beginning of their manufacture or commitments for their procurement; or

54. § 2–201(2):

Between merchants if within a reasonable time a writing in confirmation of the contract and sufficient against the sender is received and the party receiving it has reason to know its contents, it satisfies the requirements of subsection (1) against such party unless written notice of objection to its contents is given within 10 days after it is received.

55. See text accompanying note 22 supra.

56. See text accompanying note 22 supra.

57. See text accompanying notes 47–51 supra.

58. 396 Pa. 506, 153 A.2d 472, 1 UCC Rep.Serv. 40 (1959).

59. Id. at 511, 153 A.2d at 475, 1 UCC Rep.Serv. at 43.

60. Id. at 512, 153 A.2d at 476, 1 UCC Rep.Serv. at 44.

  (b) if the party against whom enforcement is sought admits in his pleading, testimony or otherwise in court that a contract for sale was made, but the contract is not enforceable under this provision beyond the quantity of goods admitted; or

  (c) with respect to goods for which payment has been made and accepted or which have been received and accepted (Sec. 2–606).

Subsections 2–201(3) (a), (b), and (c) all contemplate enforcement of certain oral contracts absent a writing. But in each of these exceptions, a valid oral contract must be proved, plus something more. This "something more" varies in each of the exceptions, but each has this in common: it is a kind of special indicator that a contract, albeit oral, was in fact made. Sellers do not produce custom-made goods just to pass the time of day. Parties do not admit contracts lightly in open court, nor do they ordinarily confer gratuitous benefits on others, except perhaps at Christmas.

The 2–201(3) (a) exception to the writing requirement applies only if the plaintiff-seller can prove the valid oral contract and prove that (*1*) the goods are to be specially manufactured for the buyer, (*2*) they are not suitable for sale to others in the ordinary course of seller's business, (*3*) seller made either a substantial beginning of their manufacture or commitments for their procurement, (*4*) seller's beginnings or commitments occurred under circumstances which reasonably indicate the goods are for buyer, and (*5*) these beginnings or commitments occurred before seller received a notice of repudiation from the buyer. Some commentators have suggested that where the oral contract calls for delivery of divisible or only apportionable units, the seller can enforce it only as to that unit (or units) with respect to which seller has made either a substantial beginning of manufacture or commitments for their procurement.[61] This view is contrary to interpretations of comparable pre-Code statutes of frauds, and judicial adherence to it would be a step backward.[62] If the seller must still prove his oral contract, and if the fact-finder is to be trusted to find or not to find the contract itself, why should the fact-finder not also be trusted to determine the quantity too, once the plaintiff has satisfied the fact-finder that a real transaction exists? True, 2–201(1) does provide that the oral contract is not enforceable beyond the quantity shown in the writing. But the theory of a statute of frauds is that a writing is somehow sacrosanct; small wonder, therefore, that a quantity term appearing in a writing is accorded some special effect. Section 2–201(3) (a) dispenses with a writing, and it does not expressly limit recovery to units on which work was begun or for which commitments were made. True, a specific quantity limitation appears in 2–201(3) (b) involving admissions in pleading or in open court. One way to reconcile the presence of a quantity limit in that

61. R. Nordstrom, Handbook of the Law of Sales § 27 (1970).

62. 2 Corbin on Contracts § 477.

subsection with the absence of such a limit in 2–201(3) (a) is to say that the kind of reliance contemplated by 2–201(3) (a) is a better indicator of the existence of a real transaction than is a flustered oral admission in court that a real contract exists and that there is therefore less justification for a quantity limit in 2–201(3) (a) than in 2–201(3) (b).

We turn now to the exception in 2–201(1) (3) (b).  This subsection, like 2–201(1) and 2–201(2) reflects the desire of Code draftsmen to have their cake and eat it too, that is, to have both a statute of frauds requirement and a requirement that cannot, in particular cases, be turned into an instrument of fraud.  Comments 7 to 2–201 explains that under this subsection it is "no longer possible to admit the contract in court and still treat the statute as a defense." Certainly it makes an open mockery of the statute to permit the defendant to use the statute effectively as a defense, yet in pleadings or in open court admit a contract!  This subsection tells him that, whatever be the facts, he must keep his mouth shut if he wants to rely on the statute.  And, of course, many a silent man has been a defrauder.  A more sensible version of 2–201(3) (b) would have required that a party setting up the defense must also, via admissible evidence, at least make out a *prima facie* case that a contract did not exist.[63]

In In re Particle Reduction Board Corp.,[64] a bankruptcy court applied 2–201(3) (b) against a party who sold goods to the bankrupt and admitted in open court that he "guessed" the transaction was a sale and not a lease, but that he still wanted "his" goods back because the bankrupt buyer had not paid for them.[65]  Bankruptcy courts may require less by way of an admission than other courts in non-bankruptcy cases, for third party interests are at stake.

As already indicated, 2–201(3) (b) makes it possible for a defendant also to lose his defense of the statute of frauds via an admission at the pleading stage.  Can he, similarly, win his case at the pleading stage by, for instance, demurring to a complaint that alleges an oral contract within 2–201(1) and by appending a sworn affidavit denying that an oral contract was never made?  We believe defendants can no longer prevail in this fashion.  Certainly the language of 2–201(3) (b) is broad enough to require that all cases go to trial so far as a statute of frauds defense is concerned, for 2–201(3) (b) contemplates the possibility that an oral contract within the statute may become enforceable by virtue of an admission in "open court" on cross-examination.  One recent New York lower court case and a

---

**63.** Admittedly, this would involve proving a negative, but not all negatives are difficult to prove, and plaintiff would not be permitted recovery without sufficient affirmative proof of an oral contract.

**64.** 5 UCC Rep.Serv. 242 (Ref.Dec.E.D. Pa.1968).

**65.** It should be noted that one court has said, correctly, that an admission in a demurrer is not the type of admission contemplated by section 2–201(3) (b).  See Beter v. Helman, 41 Westmoreland Co.L.J. 7 (Pa.C.P.1958).

Georgia case support this interpretation.[66]  A realist might argue that this cuts the heart right out of the writing requirement of 2–201(1). If the plaintiff makes enough hay on cross-examination to get past defendant's motion for a directed verdict, then the case will go to the jury.  The jury will be most unlikely to divide the issues into: (1) a statute of frauds issue and (2) an issue of whether the oral contract was ever made.  Instead, the jury will decide the entire case on the basis of whether it thinks the parties really made a deal, and the defendant's statute of frauds defense will lose any and all independent significance it supposedly had.

The exception to the writing requirement in 2–201(3)(c) provides that "a contract which does not satisfy the requirement of subsection (1) but which is valid in other respects is enforceable with respect to goods for which payment has been made and accepted or which have been received and accepted (Sec. 2–206)."[67]  This subsection expressly limits enforceability only to the apportionable part of goods that the buyer has received and accepted, and so changes prior law.[68]  In Haken v. Scheffler,[69] the buyer had not actually accepted all brick, stone, and mill irons that the seller had delivered, yet the buyer's acceptance and use of part of them plainly indicated the existence of a real transaction between the parties.  Accordingly, the Court held that 2–201(3)(c) was satisfied.

Some courts have had to consider whether a down payment on a single nondivisible unit transaction indicates a contract and permits the party making the payment to prove and recover in full on his oral contract.  A court might say that 2–201(3)(c) is not satisfied, because payment must be made in full with respect to the single unit. Williamson v. Martz,[70] a Pennsylvania lower court case, so held.  Other courts (correctly, in our opinion) have gone the other way.[71]  Lockwood v. Smigel[72] is illustrative.  There the court held that a $100 down payment on an $11,000 Rolls Royce brought 2–201(3)(c) into play and permitted the seller to try to prove his oral contract for the whole.

In several Code cases the defendant's lawyer appears to have urged a statute of frauds defense even though the case quite obviously fell within the 2–201(3)(c) exception.[73]  What constitutes an "ac-

**66.** Garrison v. Piatt, 113 Ga.App. 94, 147 S.E.2d 374, 3 UCC Rep.Serv. 296 (1966); Weiss v. Wolin, 303 N.Y.S.2d 940, 6 UCC Rep.Serv. 1097 (Sup.Ct. 1969).

**67.** See generally, Note, The Doctrine of Part Performance Under UCC Sections 2–201 and 8–319, 9 B.C.Ind. & Com.L.Rev. 355 (1968).

**68.** 2 Corbin on Contracts § 482.

**69.** Haken v. Scheffler, 24 Mich.App. 196, 180 N.W.2d 206, 8 UCC Rep.Serv. 349 (1970).

**70.** 11 Pa.D. & C.2d 33 (C.P.1956).

**71.** Starr v. Freeport Dodge, Inc., 54 Misc.2d 271, 282 N.Y.S.2d 58, 4 UCC Rep.Serv. 644 (Sup.Ct.1967).

**72.** 18 Cal.App.3d 800, 96 Cal.Rptr. 289, 9 UCC Rep.Serv. 452 (2d Dist.1971).

**73.** Associated Hardware Supply Co. v. Big Wheel Distrib. Co., 355 F.2d 114, 3 UCC Rep.Serv. 1 (3d Cir. 1965); Blowers v. First Nat'l Bank, 45 Ala. App. 485, 232 So.2d 666, 7 UCC Rep. Serv. 668 (1970); Motors Ins. Corp. v. Safeco Ins. Co., 412 S.W.2d 584, 4

ceptance" generated disputes in at least two other cases.[74]  Some courts appear to have approached this question through the acceptance sections of Part Six of Article Two, and this is exactly what they are invited to do by virtue of the reference to 2–206 in 2–201(3) (c). We hope that courts will be sympathetic to plaintiffs' arguments that acceptance has occurred and, at least in this context, err on the side of finding acceptance readily.

### § 2–6  Satisfying Nonstatutory Exceptions to the Writing Requirement

In pre-Code days there were judge-made exceptions to the writing requirement.  There is every reason to believe these remain good law, post-Code.[75]  It is not difficult to imagine oral contracts which do not satisfy the writing requirement and do not fall into any of the explicit statutory exceptions, but which nonetheless cry out for enforcement.  It is well to put one such case, based as it is on the facts of an actual case.[76]

Assume that Grower raises fruit and orally contracts to sell his fruit to Canner who agrees to pick the fruit.  The day for Canner to come and pick arrives, but he does not show up.  Grower frantically seeks to induce Canner to pick, yet Canner refuses.  Within two or three days Grower stops trying to procure another buyer and has a local jobber pick the fruit.  Assume that Grower has acted reasonably and that while he was seeking another buyer, a good part of the fruit became overripe and had to be disposed of as hog-feed.  In the foregoing case there was no writing, and the oral deal would not have fallen into any of the exceptions to 2–201(3).  Yet there is authority that in such cases a statute of frauds will not operate as a bar, provided the plaintiff establishes the elements of an estoppel.[77]  According to one view, the plaintiff establishes an estoppel when he shows that: (1) the defendant promised to perform, (2) the plaintiff reasonably relied on this promise, and (3) the plaintiff would suffer either an "unconscionable injury or unjust enrichment" from refusal

UCC Rep.Serv. 192 (Ky.Ct.App.1967); Roe v. Flamegas Indus. Corp., 16 Mich. App. 210, 167 N.W.2d 835, 6 UCC Rep. Serv. 502 (1969); Clark Grave Vault Co. v. Mealtime Foods, Inc., 5 UCC Rep.Serv. 597 (Pa.C.P.1967).

74.  Harry Winston Inc. v. Waldfogel, 292 F.Supp. 473, 5 UCC Rep. 1241 (S. D.N.Y.1968); Julian C. Cohen Salvage Corp. v. Eastern Elec. Sales Co., 205 Pa.Super. 26, 206 A.2d 331, 2 UCC Rep. Serv. 432 (1965).  Note also that acceptance is to be defined within the context of the sale of goods.  Lease transactions must be distinguished. On this point, see Blowers v. First Nat'l Bank, 45 Ala.App. 485, 232 So. 2d 666, 7 UCC Rep.Serv. 668 (1970).

The use of goods on trial may also pose a special problem.  See Harry Winston, Inc. v. Waldfogel, 292 F. Supp. 473, 5 UCC Rep.Serv. 1241 (S. D.N.Y.1968).

75.  See also L. Vold, The Law of Sales, 94 (2d ed. 1959) and cases cited therein.

76.  Mosekian v. Davis Canning Co., 229 Cal.App.2d 118, 40 Cal.Rptr. 157 (5th Dist.1964).  See Annot., 48 A.L.R.2d 1069 (1956).

77.  Note, The Doctrine of Equitable Estoppel and the Statute of Frauds, 66 Mich.L.Rev. 170 (1967).

to enforce the contract.[78]  Some courts require that the unconscionable injury or unjust enrichment be especially serious.[79]  And some courts require that the defendant deceitfully promise to perform.[80]  Indeed, some states do not even recognize an estoppel exception to the statutes of frauds requirement.[81]

The estoppel exception enters the Code via section 1–103:

> Unless displaced by the particular provisions of this Act, the principles of law and equity, including the law merchant and the law relative to capacity to contract, principal and agent, estoppel, fraud, misrepresentation, duress, coercion, mistake, bankruptcy, or other validating or invalidating cause shall supplement its provisions.

Furthermore, 1–203 provides: "Every contract or duty within this Act imposes an obligation of good faith in its performance or enforcement."  The foregoing provisions authorize the use of estoppel concepts against a party who unjustifiably misleads another party, however innocently.  These provisions may also be used to combat the defendant who otherwise acts in bad faith or fraudulently in setting up the statute as a defense.[82]  Of course, careful judges will not permit these nonstatutory exceptions to 2–201 to unduly narrow the scope for continued operation of 2–201 itself.

## § 2–7  Procedural and Remedial Matters

If a defendant chooses to invoke the defense of the statute of frauds, how is he to raise it procedurally?  On this the Code is silent.  The "modern trend" is said to be that the defendant must affirmatively plead the statute.[83]  It is important to consider how a disputed statute of frauds defense might be tried, for in a particular case this can make all the difference.  Assume that as a matter of procedure the statute of frauds defense has been properly raised.  The plaintiff will then have the burden at trial of introducing evidence of a legally sufficient writing or evidence establishing that the case falls into an exception to 2–201.  Absent one or both of these, the theory is that the defendant will prevail on a motion to dismiss (or other appropriate procedural moves).

As we suggested earlier,[84] this theory will often not prove out.  As a part of his effort to introduce a legally sufficient writing (or

78.  Mosekian v. Davis Canning Co., 229 Cal.App.2d 118, 40 Cal.Rptr. 157 (5th Dist.1964).

79.  E. g., Irving Tier Co. v. Griffin, 244 Cal.App.2d 852, 53 Cal.Rptr. 469 (1st Dist. 1965).

80.  E. g., Ozier v. Haines, 411 Ill. 160, 103 N.E.2d 485 (1952).

81.  E. g., Polka v. May, 383 Pa. 80, 84, 118 A.2d 154, 156 (1955) ("principle of estoppel may not be invoked against the operation of the statute of frauds.")

82.  See Summers, "Good Faith" in General Contract Law and the Sales Provisions of the Uniform Commercial Code, 54 Va.L.Rev. 195, 259 (1968).

83.  F. James, Civil Procedure § 4.8 (1965).

84.  See text following note 66 supra.

evidence of an exception), plaintiff may be able to introduce convincing evidence that an oral contract was in fact made between the parties.[85]   Certainly those many judges already skeptical of statutes of frauds will then be very much disposed to find a way to let the entire case go to the jury, especially since under the Code, the theory is that the successful plaintiff recovers on an oral contract (when enforceable) even when he produces a complying writing.[86]

But would not the defendant always be able to keep the plaintiff's evidence of the oral contract out on the ground that it is technically irrelevant on the question whether the statute of frauds is met? First, the plaintiff's order of proof in presenting his "case in chief" is *discretionary* with the judge.[87]   Moreover, many plaintiffs will argue that proof of the oral contract is itself relevant to the statute of frauds issue.   To be sufficient under 2–201, a signed writing must be sufficient to "indicate" that a contract between the parties was made. Many a signed writing will or will not be "sufficient to indicate that a contract was made" depending on whether the alleged oral contract was simple or complex.   Whether the alleged oral contract was simple or complex cannot be ascertained without hearing some of the plaintiff's evidence.

Furthermore, the plaintiff may convince the court that his oral evidence of the contract is properly admitted and heard even when he is not seeking to show a sufficient writing.   He may urge that he is entitled to put his entire case into evidence, all preliminary to calling the defendant and seeking to force his admission that a contract pursuant to 2–201(3)(b) exists.[88]   Suppose the defendant still denies the contract.   Can plaintiff get to the jury on the theory that defendant's denial is not credible in the face of plaintiff's overriding evidence?   Subsection 2–201(3)(b) requires the defendant to admit the contract, and we believe incredible denial may constitute an admission.[89]

The topic of remedies is more fully explored elsewhere in this book.[90]   Here we consider only remedial problems specially related to the statute of frauds.   Section 2–201 is silent on remedial matters. Assume a court decides that the plaintiff's oral contract is unenforce-

---

85.   There are many pre-Code cases where the trial court had all the evidence before it when it ruled on a statute of frauds issue.   See e. g., General Overseas Corp. v. Republic Pictures Int'l Corp., 74 F.Supp. 698 (S.D.N.Y.1947).   For examples of Code cases where this is so, see Oswald v. Allen, 285 F.Supp. 488, 5 UCC Rep. Serv. 712 (S.D.N.Y.1968); Arcuri v. Weiss, 198 Pa.Super. 506, 184 A.2d 24, 1 UCC Rep.Serv. 45 (1962).

86.   It is difficult to find recent cases in which the courts have upheld a statute of frauds defense in the face

of convincing oral evidence of the contract itself.

87.   C. McCormick, Law of Evidence § 58 (1954).

88.   Cf. Garrison v. Piatt, 113 Ga.App. 94, 147 S.E.2d 374, 3 UCC Rep.Serv. 296 (1966).

89.   See Spiering v. Fairmont Foods Co., 424 F.2d 337, 7 UCC Rep.Serv. 450 (7th Cir. 1970).   Cf. Garrison v. Piatt, 113 Ga.App. 94, 147 S.E.2d 374, 3 UCC Rep. Serv. 296 (1966).

90.   See Chs. 6 and 7 infra.

able in part or in full under 2–201, yet the plaintiff shows that he conferred a benefit on the repudiating defendant. Prior law permits the plaintiff to recover the reasonable value in money of any benefit he has conferred.[91] Does the plaintiff have a right to specific restitution of the very thing conferred upon the defendant? Some pre-Code case law suggests as much.[92]

Courts may read 2–201 in ways that generate serious "apportionment" problems. Suppose a buyer agrees to an oral contract for the purchase of a used truck which seller agrees to equip with a rack and trailer, all for a total price of $5,000, with buyer to pay $2500 on delivery of the truck and $2500 on delivery of the rack and trailer. Assume also that the truck is worth significantly more than the rack and trailer. Buyer repudiates after paying the $2500 and receiving the truck. If the seller is willing to let the buyer keep the truck, but wants fair value therefor, how might he get his fair value? If the oral agreement had apportioned the price among the three items, the just thing would be for the court to use the price tag the parties had placed on the truck. Purists might object that this would involve enforcing the oral contract contrary to the statute of frauds, but if the buyer wants to keep the truck and the seller is willing, then neither party can sensibly object to this use of the price term of the unenforceable oral contract. Since the parties did not apportion the total price, the parties will be forced to use some other method for determining the amount seller receives. Market value, as determined by comparable sales of comparable vehicles, is the most likely alternative.

Suppose the buyer can show that if the seller had fully performed, it would have cost the seller a total of $6000 (valuing the truck at $4000 and assigning a cost of $2000 to the construction of the rack and trailer). Here the seller might seek $4000 for the truck (less the $2500 down payment), but the buyer might urge that the seller's recovery should not exceed the "contract rate," that is, the seller should recover no more than ⅘ of $5,000 or $3,333. This is the more defensible of the two alternatives, unless the defendant is to be punished for repudiating and setting up the statute of frauds. Under 2–201(3)(c) the oral agreement is enforceable at least to the extent of goods received and accepted, and here the defendant received and accepted the truck. If the contract is to be enforced against him to that extent, he should be allowed to show the oral contract price in his favor to reduce plaintiff's recovery to an amount consistent with the contract rate, pre-Code case law to the contrary notwithstanding.[93]

Occasionally, a buyer makes a down payment on an oral contract within the statute, but repudiates and sues to get his down payment back. Assume the seller does not want to invoke 2–201(3)(c), but does want to keep the down payment. Can he? A few courts, in pre-

---

91. 2 Corbin on Contracts §§ 326–27. See Annot., 21 A.L.R.3d 9 (1968).

92. 2 Corbin on Contracts § 330.

93. Id. § 327 and cases cited therein.

Code cases, seem to have said yes,[94] but these results are inconsistent not only with the letter of contract theory, but also with the spirit of restitutionary theory.  The seller has been enriched.  The seller should not be allowed to retain this benefit, for he has no enforceable contract claim to it.  Moreover, the buyer is not a volunteer conferring a benefit gratuitously, rather the down payment was paid in contemplation of the performance of a contract unenforceable under the statute of frauds.

### § 2–8    Statutes of Frauds—An Evaluation

There are at least four relevant forms of courtroom fraud:  (*1*) a plaintiff might convince a fact-finder that he and the defendant made an oral contract when in fact they did not;  (*2*) a plaintiff might convince a fact-finder that the terms of an admitted contract were actually more favorable to the plaintiff than those in fact agreed on;  (*3*) a defendant might convince a fact-finder that the parties did not enter an oral contract when in fact they did;  or (*4*) the defendant might convince a fact-finder that the actual terms of an admitted contract were more favorable to him than those in fact agreed on.  The motive for any such fraud is usually economic; a plaintiff wants something for less (or nothing), or defendant wants out of a deal because of a break in the market or because of some change in his own plans.  Occasionally the motive is not economic.  One party might simply become "fed up" with the other, or come to dislike him, or to like some other supplier better, and so on.  When a fraudulent party succeeds, reactions of outrage are likely.  Just such reactions led to the enactment of the first statute of frauds given that (*1*) a party was not then allowed to testify even to rebut perjured oral testimony of a third party ("friend" of the other party, no doubt) and (*2*) judges had little or no effective control over unreasonable jury findings.[95]

Thus the theory of statutes of frauds, past and present, is that they are means to the end of preventing successful courtroom perjury.  The means to this end is simply the requirement of a writing signed by the party to be charged.  Doubtless this requirement operates in some cases to block what would otherwise be successful perjury.  But, the fact that "A" may in *some* cases serve as the means to "B" is hardly sufficient to justify calling A a means to B.  Of course, a legal requirement cannot be devised which would be an absolute guarantee against all perjury, but the statute of frauds writing requirement is, at least in the opinion of one of your authors, so far from any kind of guarantee against successful perjury that it is inappropriate even to call it a means to fraud prevention at all.

A "writing signed by the party against whom enforcement is sought" is hardly self-authenticating.  Forgery is always a possibility, especially in a continuing relationship.  While forgery may be more difficult to achieve than perjury, the difference is hardly monu-

---

**94.**  Id. § 332.                    **95.**  See Section 2–1 supra.

mental. More fundamental, an admittedly authentic signed writing "sufficient to indicate that a contract for sale has been made" is commonly still far from conclusive evidence that a contract for sale was made. Such a writing can easily exist despite the fact no oral contract was ever made. For example, the party who signed the writing might have done so for convenience during preliminary negotiations in advance of the time when the parties actually contemplated an agreement. Even if the signed writing is authentic, and even if it does, in fact, "indicate" a real deal, fraud may still occur. The defendant may still persuasively lie to the jury either as to the existence of the contract or as to its terms. Further, if neither party can produce a signed writing, it does not even tend to follow that the parties did not make an oral contract. Indeed, if they did actually make an oral contract, it seems more probable than not that in the inception of the contract no signed writing would exist! Moreover, in many real deals, oral though they be, the parties might thereafter refrain from reducing terms to writing because of a belief that a man's word is as good as his bond.

A true "means to an end" surely should not serve commonly as a means to disserve that end [96] either. Yet, centuries of experience and tons of case law testify that a statute of frauds can be an instrument of perjury and fraud. The possibility that plaintiffs must conjure up forged writings and perjured oral contracts out of whole cloth is unreal. These plaintiffs would be most unlikely to survive cross-examination, motions for directed verdict, and a jury's own scrutiny. But the possibility that defendants might get out of actual contracts simply for lack of a signed writing is not unreal at all. In sum, the "abuse potential" of a statute of frauds is great. This fact, more than any other, probably accounts for the disfavor in which many judges have held statutes of frauds. Yet some theorists have defended statutes of frauds on the basis that it is harder for a party to succeed at forgery than at perjury and that writing requirements imposed by law have the salutary effect of encouraging parties to put at least the terms of important deals into writing. One of your authors (White) wants to take this line. He says he sees a lot of fraud in court and thinks something should be done about it. (As a matter of fact White disagrees with almost all of the argument in the four foregoing paragraphs. He believes that faulty memories combine with greed and dishonesty to render much testimony by interested parties inaccurate. He believes forgery is a much less frequent occurrence and favors any rule that stimulates parties to write down their deals. Moreover he believes that the statute of frauds is consistent with laymen's ideas about serious contract, that is, no writing, no enforcement.)

Of the total number of oral contracts in any given year, in the overwhelming percentage the parties either perform for business reasons or permit cancellation for business reasons.[97] Of the remainder,

---

96. Burdick, A Statute for Promoting Fraud, 16 Colum.L.Rev. 273 (1916).

97. On the practice of permitting cancellation, see Macaulay, Non-Contrac-

some fall into either statutory or nonstatutory exceptions to the statute and thus remain or become enforceable. What of those that do not? Does the statute make a real difference as to disposition of very many of them? It seems unlikely that it does. Few will get to court, and of those that do, usually the judge or jury will have all the evidence as to the existence or nonexistence of the oral contract out in the open for all to see and evaluate, and it seems highly likely that in most cases it is this evidence that will make the difference, one way or the other, especially since 2–201(3) (b) allows the fruits of courtroom cross-examination to stand in the place of a writing.

### § 2–9   The Parol Evidence Rule—Does It Give Preference to Written Evidence of Contract Terms?

The law should give effect to the contract. In an important kind of trouble case, the parties dispute over contract terms. The contract might be entirely oral, or it might be partly oral and partly in writing. If the contract is not unenforceable under the statute of frauds,[98] a court will have to ascertain its terms. Partly to guard against the uncertainties of litigation over oral contract terms, parties frequently undertake to put their contracts in writing. But there can be no magic in this. One party may later contend that the writing does not embody the terms agreed on; a writing cannot prevent disputes over terms. Moreover, a writing cannot by itself tell us what any of the terms really were. A writing is only potential evidence to be introduced in court, should the parties go to court to resolve a dispute over terms.

Courts are frequently called on to resolve disputes over terms. The novice might expect that the process of adjudication here would be the same as in any other type of case in which facts are disputed: the parties would introduce all relevant evidence as to terms, including any writing, and the trier of fact would then determine what terms the parties actually contracted for. Also there would be the usual division of labor between judge and jury. Judges would, for example, rule on relevancy and admissibility, and they would be empowered to grant a motion for a non-suit, for a directed verdict, or for a judgment *n. o. v.* Thus, the usual protections against unreasonable jury determinations would be available to help assure that in

tual Relations in Business: A Preliminary Study, 28 Am.Soc.Rev. 55 (1963). And, on the general effects of a statute of frauds, see Note, The Statute of Frauds and the Business Community: A Re-appraisal in Light of Prevailing Practices, 66 Yale L.J. 1038 (1957).

98. Some of the basic differences between a statute of frauds requirement and a parol evidence rule should be noted. The former requires a certain kind of agreement to be partly in writing to be legally enforceable, but the latter imposes no such requirement. The latter, in effect, gives special preference to a writing in determining the terms of the agreement where both written and oral evidence are proffered, but the former does not have this effect except in regard to any quantity term in the writing. Finally, the parties may satisfy the former requirement without ever having made a contract, but the latter presupposes a contract and is concerned only with what its terms are.

the end, the court gives effect to the contract of the parties as actually agreed.

But Anglo-American law does not handle all disputes over contract terms in this way. Our courts apply a so-called "parol evidence rule" [99] when some of the evidence of terms is embodied in a writing. The usual effect of this is to give preference to the written version of terms. Writings are more reliable than memories to show contract terms, and forgery is supposedly easier to detect than is lying on the witness stand. These are the principal premises of a parol evidence rule. Early critics of the rule challenged these premises and emphasized that the rule is inconsistent with our usual processes of proof. If juries are to be "trusted" in disputes over contract terms not involving writings, then why should they not hear all the evidence, even where writings are involved, and decide accordingly? The debate still rages. [100]

Many versions of a parol evidence are possible; here, we focus solely on that version adopted in Article Two of the Code.

Section 2–202 provides:

> Terms with respect to which the confirmatory memoranda of the parties agree or which are otherwise set forth in a writing intended by the parties as a final expression of their agreement with respect to such terms as are included therein may not be contradicted by evidence of any prior agreement or of a contemporaneous oral agreement but may be explained or supplemented
>
> (a) by course of dealing or usage of trade (Section 1–205) or by course of performance (Section 2–208) ; and
>
> (b) by evidence of consistent additional terms unless the court finds the writing to have been intended also as a complete and exclusive statement of the terms of the agreement.

As we earlier indicated,[101] a rule of this nature is supposed to provide added assurance that the court will arrive at the truth as to disputed terms.[102] In substance the "rule" says, that if the court finds the writing to have been intended as a complete and exclusive statement of the terms of the agreement, then the writing alone constitutes the contract. This is to say no more than if X is the contract,

**99.** See 3 Corbin on Contracts §§ 573–96.

**100.** For example, compare Comment, The Parol Evidence Rule: A Conservative View, 19 U.Chi.L.Rev. 348 (1952) with Note, The Parol Evidence Rule: Is It Necessary?, 44 N.Y.U.L.Rev. 972 (1969). See generally Sweet, Contract Making and Parol Evidence: Diagnosis and Treatment of a Sick Rule, 53 Cornell L.Rev. 1036 (1968).

**101.** See text accompanying note 99 supra.

**102.** Of course, the rule may have bearing in such nonlitigation contexts as counselling and negotiation, too. See Sweet, Contract Making and Parol Evidence: Diagnosis and Treatment of a Sick Rule, 53 Cornell L.Rev. 1036, 1044–47 (1968).

then X is the contract. As a corollary, the rule also says that to the extent the writing incorporates terms the parties agreed on, then the writing controls as to those terms and anything contradictory or inconsistent is of no force or effect. This is to say no more than to the extent X is the contract, X is the contract to that extent. Thus it is not appropriate to say that the *substantive* aspects of the parol evidence rule give preference to written evidence of terms. As between the writing and other evidence as to terms, the substantive aspects of the rule are neutral. The theory is that either the writing or the other evidence may control terms, depending on which represents the agreement of the parties.

As the late Professor McCormick taught, the division of functions between judge and jury in administering the rule can "give preference" to written evidence over oral evidence of contract terms.[103] So, too, can allocations of burden of proof. Section 2–202 does not state very clearly what the division of functions is supposed to be. But the way the rule is worded, the trial is certainly not to be a free-wheeling affair in which the parties may introduce before the jury all evidence of terms, including the writing, with the jury then to decide on terms. Rather, it is plain from the rule and from prior history of similar rules that some of the evidence is to be heard initially only by the judge and that he may invoke the rule to keep this evidence from the jury. The evidence that is in this way subject to exclusion will usually be oral evidence. Indeed, before a judge can invoke a parol evidence rule at all, he must first admit a writing into evidence before the jury. If he thereafter excludes oral evidence of terms on the basis of the parol evidence rule, he gives preference to the writing already in evidence, for he does not permit the jury to consider the oral evidence in deciding on terms.

But when can the judge invoke 2–202 to exclude oral evidence of terms extrinsic to those in the writing? First, he may exclude the evidence if he finds that the parties intended the writing to be a *complete and exclusive* statement of the terms of the agreement (unless it be evidence of course of dealing, usage of trade, or course of performance introduced only to explain or supplement the writing). Code and comments both state that the question of completeness and exclusivity is for the judge.[104] Second, the judge may exclude evidence of terms extrinsic to those set forth in the writing if he decides that the writing is a final written expression as to these terms and that the other evidence contradicts these terms. The Code does not say that this question is for the judge, but if "completeness and exclusivity" is for the judge, then whether a writing is a final written expression as to the terms it does include would be for the judge, for

103. McCormick, The Parol Evidence Rule as a Procedural Device for Control of the Jury, 41 Yale L.J. 365 (1932).

104. §§ 2–202(b); 2–202, Comment 3. See Whirlpool Corp. v. Regis Leasing Corp., 29 App.Div.2d 395, 288 N.Y.S. 2d 337, 5 UCC Rep.Serv. 94 (1st Dep't 1968); Conner v. May, 444 S.W.2d 948, 7 UCC Rep.Serv. 185 (Tex.Civ.App. 1969).

the greater ordinarily includes the lesser. The issue of contradictoriness is also for the judge since it is hardly factual in nature. Third, in passing on any parol evidence rule objection, the judge may decide that the proffered evidence of terms extrinsic to the writing is simply not credible, and he may exclude it on that ground alone. Section 2–202 is silent on this, but Professor McCormick thought that the "real service" of the parol evidence rule was here.[105]

The foregoing division of functions between judge and jury in the administration of 2–202 inevitably operates to favor written evidence of terms. Yet there is no necessary identity between a writing and the actual deal. A writing can be inaccurate. Worse yet, it can be forged. Because no writing can necessarily embody the true terms of an agreement, because juries are already subject to substantial judicial controls,[106] because individual jurors are today better educated,[107] and because the foregoing division of functions between judge and jury perhaps unduly favors the party standing on the writing,[108] it may be that courts should devise rules on burden of proof that operate to counterbalance the special preference that the foregoing division of functions gives to written evidence of terms. Thus a party who stands on the writing as a complete and exclusive embodiment of the contract might be required to shoulder the burden of proving completeness and exclusivity to the judge's satisfaction. With the burden thus allocated, any time the evidence on these issues was in equipoise, the party opposed to admissibility would lose, thereby paving the way for the jury to hear and consider the extrinsic evidence in relation to the writing. Some commentators [109] and at least two courts [110] agree that 2–202 abolishes any presumption that a writing apparently complete on its face is complete and exclusive. This should make it easier for a court to impose the burden of proving completeness and exclusively on the party who stands on the writing. We would also impose the burden of proving that confirmatory memoranda agree as to a term, or that a writing is a final written expression as to a term, on the party opposing the admission of allegedly contradictory extrinsic evidence.

## § 2–10    Substantive Aspects of the Parol Evidence Rule—Problems of Interpretation

There is already a significant body of case law interpreting the language of 2–202 in its "substantive" aspects. First of all, to constitute a "writing" for parol evidence rule purposes, it is not neces-

---

105. C. McCormick, Handbook of the Law of Evidence 440 (1954). See also Annot., 10 A.L.R.2d 720 (1950).

106. F. James, Civil Procedure §§ 7.12–7.22 (1965).

107. Just meet one on the street!

108. See text accompanying note 103 supra.

109. 1 N.Y. State Law Revision Comm'n, 1955 Report 598 (1955).

110. Michael Schiavone & Sons, Inc. v. Securalloy Co., 312 F.Supp. 801, 7 UCC Rep.Serv. 674 (D.Conn.1970); Symonds v. Adler Restaurant Equip. Co., 6 UCC Rep.Serv. 808 (Okla.1969).

sary that it be the one and only writing in the case. Parties may express their agreement in several writings.[111] Under 2–202, if two contradictory but contemporaneous writings are involved, the judge may admit both with the jury to decide which embodies the actual agreement.[112] Where one writing is prior it may not be admitted if it contradicts a subsequent writing that is either a complete and exclusive statement of all terms or a final expression of some terms.

If the judge finds that the writing is a "complete and exclusive" statement of the contract terms, then he may not admit evidence even of terms that do not contradict terms in the writing. The language of 2–202 does not expressly set forth "tests" by which the judge is to determine whether the writing is a complete and exclusive statement of the terms of the contract. Over the years, various courts have devised different tests. One of these is the so-called "four corners" test by which the trial judge simply looks at what is within the four corners of the writing and decides if the writing looks complete.[113] The structure of section 2–202 seems less congenial to this test than earlier versions of the parol evidence rule. As we have noted, the section does not appear to adopt any presumption that the entire agreement is embodied in the writing. Rather, the presumption seems to be that unless proven otherwise, the writing does not include all the terms. A four corners test thrives more readily under a rule that presumes full embodiment in the writing unless only partial embodiment is proved.[114] Further, Comment 3 to 2–202 may reject a four corners test.[115] Such a test is not only somewhat ostrich-like, but is basically question-begging in character. It elevates what is at best only a general inferential maxim into a rule of law, yet the very question is whether, in the particular circumstances, the parties actually intended a complete and exclusive written statement of their agreement. A judge alone should be willing to go beyond the four corners and hear other evidence on the issue of completeness and exclusivity. The comments to 2–202 recognize this. Comment 3 says, "If the additional terms are such that, if agreed upon, they would certainly have been included in the document in the view of

---

111. Cf. Stern & Co. v. State Loan & Finance Corp., 238 F.Supp. 901, 2 UCC Rep.Serv. 721 (D.Dela.1965).

112. General Equip. Mfrs. v. Bible Press, Inc., 10 Mich.App. 676, 160 N.W. 2d 370, 5 UCC Rep.Serv. 822 (1968).

113. E. g., Anchor Cas. Co. v. Bird Island Produce, Inc., 249 Minn. 137, 82 N.W.2d 48 (1957). Of course, a four corners test is double-edged. In some cases it will be quite obvious from the writing alone that the writing is not a complete and exclusive statement of the contract terms. See, e. g., Hull-Dobbs, Inc. v. Mallicoat, 57 Tenn.App. 100, 415 S.W.2d 344, 3 UCC Rep.Serv. 1032 (1966).

114. See note 109 supra.

115. § 2–202, Comment 3:

Under paragraph (b) consistent additional terms, not reduced to writing, may be proved unless the court finds that the writing was intended by both parties as a complete and exclusive statement of all the terms. If the additional terms are such that, if agreed upon, they would certainly have been included in the document in the view of the court, then evidence of their alleged making must be kept from the trier of fact.

the court, then evidence of their alleged making must be kept from the trier of fact." Before a judge can decide any such question, arguably he must go beyond the four corners of the writing and actually hear the proffered evidence as to "additional terms." We believe a judge should take a similar approach to the question of whether a writing constitutes a "final written expression" as to some part of a total agreement. He should not simply look at the writing alone but should consider all proferred evidence on the issue of finality as to the terms involved.

Section 2–202 provides that certain agreed upon terms may not be *contradicted* by evidence of any prior agreement or of a contemporaneous oral agreement. What are "terms"? Section 1–201(42) defines "terms" to mean "that portion of an agreement which relates to a particular matter." The Code in 1–201(3) defines "agreement" to mean "the bargain of the parties in fact as found in their language or by implication from other circumstances. . . ." If a writing is silent as to a particular matter, then one can argue that it includes no "term" thereon and that extrinsic evidence of an alleged term covering the matter is not "contradictory" of anything in the writing and is admissible. In Hunt Foods & Industries, Inc. v. Doliner,[116] the writing appeared to be an unconditional option to purchase defendant's stock that the plaintiff might exercise at any time prior to its expiry. The writing said nothing at all about any condition. Defendant claimed the parties had orally agreed that the option was conditional, specifically, that it could only be exercised if the defendant used a prior offer of the plaintiff to solicit higher offers, and defendant sought to introduce extrinsic evidence to this effect. The court upheld the defendant, and proclaimed that (*1*) the evidence of the alleged extrinsic term (the condition) did not contradict a term of the writing, and (*2*) as evidence of a *consistent* additional term, the evidence was admissible inasmuch as it was not evidence of a term that would "certainly" have been included in the writing if actually agreed upon.[117] We do not agree that the oral condition did not contradict a specific term of the writing. The written option was unconditional, and the oral evidence rendered it conditional. We believe a better way to deal with the facts of *Hunt Foods* would be to say that 2–202 simply does not apply at all unless the parties intend their writing to be a "final expression of their agreement with respect to such terms as are included therein." Another approach would be to say that the parol evidence rule simply does not bar evidence that the legal effectiveness of a writing was conditioned on the occurrence of an external event that did not occur. Some courts have sanctioned

116.   26 App.Div.2d 41, 270 N.Y.S.2d 937, 3 UCC Rep.Serv. 597 (1st Dep't 1966), noted in 66 Colum.L.Rev. 1370 (1966). For extended discussion of this case, see Broude, The Consumer and the Parol Evidence Rule: Section 2–202 of the Uniform Commercial Code, 1970 Duke L.J. 881, 890–99.

117.   But see text accompanying note 133 infra.

the introduction of parol evidence on this approach even where the writing includes a merger clause.[118]

Suppose a writing says nothing of express warranties in regard to a given matter and includes no disclaimers. The plaintiff then seeks to introduce extrinsic evidence to prove an express oral warranty. May the defendant keep this evidence from the trier of fact on the ground that it contradicts a term *in the writing*? Presumably not, if the *Hunt Foods* theory of contradictoriness be followed. This would not necessarily mean that the plaintiff would be home free, for the judge might still keep the evidence out on the ground that if such an additional term had been agreed upon, it would most certainly have been embodied in the writing. On the other hand, if the writing includes an express warranty on a given matter and a party seeks to introduce evidence of a different extrinsic warranty on that matter, or if the writing includes a disclaimer and a party seeks to introduce evidence of an extrinsic express warranty, a court following *Hunt Foods* might well bar the evidence as "contradictory." Of course, if the disclaimer is legally ineffective under 2–316, then it cannot be contradictory, for it does not "exist." [119] At least one court has said that a disclaimer does not exist if the parties did not specifically bargain for it.[120] Section 2–316 does not expressly require as much for the existence of a disclaimer. Sometimes courts will indulge themselves in a distinction between an agreement and an inducement to enter the agreement, all in order to rationalize the admission of extrinsic evidence that contradicts the writing. This has already been done under 2–202. Thus in Hull Dobbs, Inc. v. Mallicoat,[121] the parties signed a writing covering the sale of a car that said "warranties, representations and promises" were not legally effective. Yet the court justified its admission of parol testimony as to representations concerning the condition of the car:

> The Security Agreement states that it constitutes the entire "agreement" between the parties but as to "warranties, representations and promises" the language is that they are not "to be binding on any *assignee*" of the seller. Since the "agreement" and "representations, warranties and promises" are treated as being separate and distinct and representations as to the condition of property sold are not generally considered a part of the agreement but an inducement to the execution of the sale agreement, we can not say the parties intended the Security Agreement to be a final statement of the terms of the sale. Representations as to the con-

---

118.  Luther Williams, Jr., Inc. v. Johnson, 229 A.2d 163 (D.C.Ct.App.1967). See also 1 N.Y. State Law Revision Comm'n, 1955 Report 683 (1955); 3 Corbin on Contracts § 590.

119.  Hertz Commercial Leasing Corp. v. Transportation Credit Clearing House, 59 Misc.2d 226, 298 N.Y.S.2d 392, 6 UCC Rep.Serv. 132 (Co.Ct.1969), rev'd on other grounds, 64 Misc.2d 910, 316 N.Y.S.2d 585 (App.Term.1970).

120.  Id.

121.  57 Tenn.App. 100, 415 S.W.2d 344, 3 UCC Rep.Serv. 1032 (1966).

dition of the car are not inconsistent with any provision of the contract even if it should be held that the Security Agreement was intended as a final statement of the terms of the sale.[122]

Since the agreement was labeled a security agreement, it seems defensible for the court to say that the parties did not intend it as a final written expression with respect to the sales aspects of the deal. Or, the court might have rested its decision on a misrepresentation theory.[123]

Suppose a writing includes an express warranty, or disclaims express warranties. May the plaintiff introduce evidence to prove an implied warranty? Some cases indicate that the answer is yes, even where the writing is not silent on the general subject of warranties. A distinction is drawn between express and implied warranties, and it is said that an implied warranty is not a *term* of the *agreement* at all but arises by operation of law, and that the parol evidence rule excludes only evidence of extrinsic *terms*.[124]

Courts besides the *Hunt Foods* court have also had to consider what "contradicts" means in 2–202. The usual terms of a written bill of sale are not contradicted by evidence of an oral term providing for security.[125] A writing providing for the sale of cattle is not contradicted by evidence of an oral term providing that the seller would feed the cattle in a certain manner prior to delivery.[126] Terms in the writing ("Discount and payment periods will start from verbal modification hereof shall be effective") were contradicted by the proffered evidence of the alleged extrinsic term (the seller would "supervise installation, fully check out all equipment, provide operational training . . . and notify . . . that the plant was fully equipped, installed and operational" before the buyer would be obligated to pay the plaintiff).[127] This decision is difficult to reconcile with the *Hunt Foods* theory of contradictoriness and with those cases which permit a party to show that the legal effect of a writing was dependent upon the occurrence of a "condition precedent to the entire contract" which did occur.

Under 2–202 whenever the judge finds that evidence of the alleged extrinsic term is not evidence of a term that contradicts a term in the writing, this evidence may, if of a "consistent additional term," be used to supplement the writing, provided the judge does not find that the term, if agreed upon, would certainly have been includ-

122. Id. at 104, 415 S.W.2d at 346, 3 UCC Rep.Serv. at 1033–34.

123. See Section 2–11 infra.

124. 1 N.Y. State Law Revision Comm'n, 1955 Report 415 (1955). Cf. Nettles v. Imperial Distribs., Inc., 152 W.Va. 9, 159 S.E.2d 206 (1968).

125. McDown v. Wilson, 426 S.W.2d 112, 6 UCC Rep.Serv. 317 (Mo.App. 1968).

126. Conner v. May, 444 S.W.2d 948, 7 UCC Rep.Serv. 185 (Tex.Civ.App. 1969).

127. Whirlpool Corp. v. Regis Leasing Corp., 29 App.Div.2d 395, 288 N.Y.S. 2d 337, 5 UCC Rep.Serv. 94 (1st Dep't 1968).

ed in the writing.[128]   One court has stressed that the more complete a writing appears to be on its face, the less likely it is that any extrinsic term was agreed upon, even if consistent with the writing.[129]

Even if the writing is a "complete and exclusive" statement of the terms of the agreement, parties may still introduce course of dealing, usage of trade, or course of performance to explain or supplement the agreement.[130]  This is so even where the language of the agreement is unambiguous on its face.   As Comment 2 to section 2–202 puts it:

> Paragraph (a) [of section 2–202] makes admissible evidence of course of dealing, usage of trade and course of performance to explain or supplement the terms of any writing stating the agreement of the parties in order that the true understanding of the parties as to the agreement may be reached.  Such writings are to be read on the assumption that the course of prior dealings between the parties and the usages of trade were taken for granted when the document was phrased.  Unless carefully negated they have become an element of the meaning of the words used.  Similarly, the course of actual performance by the parties is considered the best indication of what they intended the writing to mean.

There are two aptly illustrative court decisions so far.   In one, the court held that the words "delivery June–August" could be shown to have acquired a special meaning in the retail clothing trade that ruled out delivery of the entire lot in August.[131]  In the other case, the court held that the words "thirty-six inch steel" could be shown to have acquired by trade usage a special meaning such that delivery of thirty-seven inch steel constituted performance.[132]

In Division of Triple T Service, Inc. v. Mobil Oil Corp.,[133] the parties expressly agreed that a franchising arrangement would "terminate at the end of any current period (original or renewal) by notice from either party to the other, given not less than 90 days prior to such termination. . . ."  The franchisee claimed that trade usage showed that franchisors could only terminate "for cause."  The court said that such a condition would be "inconsistent" with the express terms of the contract and that evidence of the inconsistent

---

128.  See, e. g., § 2–202, Comment 3.

129.  Whirlpool Corp. v. Regis Leasing Corp., 29 App.Div.2d 395, 288 N.Y.S.2d 337, 5 UCC Rep.Serv. 94 (1st Dep't 1968).

130.  See generally Levie, Trade Usage and Custom Under the Common Law on the Uniform Commercial Code, 40 N.Y.U.L.Rev. 1101 (1965).

131.  Warren's Kiddie Shoppe, Inc. v. Casual Slacks, Inc., 120 Ga.App. 578,

171 S.E.2d 643, 7 UCC Rep.Serv. 166 (1969).

132.  Decker Steel Co. v. Exchange Nat'l Bank, 330 F.2d 82 (7th Cir. 1964).  The interesting trial record of this case is partially reprinted in R. Speidel, R. Summers & J. White, Commercial Transactions 490–97 (1969).

133.  60 Misc.2d 720, 304 N.Y.S.2d 191, 6 UCC Rep.Serv. 1011 (Sup.Ct.1969).

trade usage therefore could not be admitted. Can this case be reconciled with *Hunt Foods*?[134] In *Triple T*, the court emphasized that the express agreement treated "the entire area of termination," but in *Hunt Foods* the agreement said nothing about any condition on the right to exercise the option. Also, oral testimony may be more "admissibility-worthy" than mere evidence of general trade usage. Certainly, oral testimony is less remote from the specific transaction.

Can evidence of trade usage be introduced to *add* an additional term to the writing? Section 2–202(b) is drafted broadly enough to permit this. Furthermore, in Provident Tradesmen's Bank & Trust Co. v. Pemberton,[135] the court utilized evidence of trade usage to add an additional term to the writing, namely, that the plaintiff-lender owed a duty to notify the defendant-dealer if the dealer's customer let the insurance lapse on the car sold him. There was also evidence of a prior course of dealing between the parties sanctioning this duty to give notice. Yet the written agreement between the lender and the dealer was entirely silent on the matter. If the plaintiff had wanted to negate or exclude such a term, it could easily have drafted a contract clause to that effect. In the absence of a contract clause, courts will likely permit parties to use course of dealing, usage of trade, and course of performance to establish *additional* terms.[136]

So-called "course of performance" evidence may explain or supplement language in a writing, for it shows how the parties themselves interpreted their own deal. In one important case, Associated Hardware Supply Co. v. Big Wheel Distributing Co.,[137] the court relied on "course of performance" evidence in concluding that a buyer bought at a price of "dealer catalogue less 11%." The buyer claimed that the agreed price was really "cost plus 10% on warehouse shipments and cost plus 5% on factory shipments." The buyer was billed on the basis of "dealer catalogue less 11%" and made payments at that rate. The court thought this was a course of performance which showed that the buyer acquiesced in the seller's pricing term. It is not clear from the opinion, however, whether the buyer argued that its course of performance merely constituted acquiescence in a mode of payment rather than assent to the seller's pricing term. The buyer probably should have prevailed on this argument, especially given his allegation that the seller had assured him during relevant times that "dealer catalogue less 11%" would reduce to a price equivalent to "cost plus 10%." The court did send the buyer's counterclaim back for trial on whether the seller had thus defrauded the buyer, even though the court concluded that a contract had in fact been formed between the parties on the basis of the seller's price.

134. 26 App.Div.2d 41, 270 N.Y.S.2d 937, 3 UCC Rep.Serv. 597 (1st Dep't 1966).

135. 196 Pa.Super. 180, 173 A.2d 780, 1 UCC Rep.Serv. 57 (1961).

136. Levie, The Interpretation of Contracts in New York under the Uniform Commercial Code, 10 N.Y.L.F. 350, 368–72 (1964).

137. 355 F.2d 114, 3 UCC Rep.Serv. 1 (3d Cir. 1966).

Of course, parties may attach special meanings to the words they use without resort to usage of trade or course of dealing. One court allowed extrinsic evidence to show that "500 tons" really meant "up to 500 tons," [138] and properly so. In another case, the court interpreted a covenant not to sue a defendant in the business of giving hair treatments to apply only to injuries to the plaintiff's hair and scalp but not to the plaintiff's ear, even though the covenant was broad enough to cover ear injuries.[139]

### § 2–11  Judge-Made Exceptions to the Parol Evidence Rule

Over many decades, courts have fashioned numerous exceptions to the parol evidence rule. Each exception is canvassed in Professor Corbin's treatise,[140] and except insofar as the wording of 2–202 renders any exception redundant, each remains good law under the Code via 1–103. The fraud exception is the most important. It is often said that a party may not invoke the parol evidence rule in order to shield his own fraud.[141] Fraud may also serve as a basis for rescission or for affirmative relief. It will be recalled that in Associated Hardware Supply Co. v. Big Wheel Distributing Co.,[142] the court sent buyer's counterclaim back for retrial on the issue of whether the seller fraudulently told the buyer that "dealer catalogue less 11%" was equivalent to "cost plus 10%" and thereby induced the buyer to enter into or go forward with the deal.[143] Insofar as any such representations were oral, they were *dehors* the writing which the court said constituted the contract. Of course, the buyer might try to introduce them not to show fraud, but to show the meaning of the words in the contract, and this is permissible under 2–202. Yet, the buyer might go beyond this and show fraud, too.

Courts should be wary of turning the fraud exception into an exception that swallows up the entire parol evidence rule. A party should not be allowed to introduce his evidence of an alleged extrinsic term merely by alleging fraud. The judge should hold a preliminary hearing away from the jury to determine whether the party offering the evidence really is seeking to show fraudulent misrepresentation or fraudulent nondisclosure. If the judge concludes that any misrepresentation or nondisclosure is wholly innocent, then he should not admit the evidence under the fraud exception to the parol evidence rule. This is not to say, however, that the judge should not admit the evidence on any ground. It may still be admissible to show that the parties attached a special meaning to contract words.

---

138. Michael Schiavone & Sons, Inc. v. Securalloy Co., 312 F.Supp. 801, 7 UCC Rep.Serv. 674 (D.Conn.1970).

139. Ciunci v. Wella Corp., 26 App.Div. 2d 109, 271 N.Y.S.2d 317, 3 UCC Rep. Serv. 811 (1st Dep't 1966).

140. See 3 Corbin on Contracts §§ 573–621 (rev. ed. 1960).

141. See generally Sweet, Promissory Fraud and the Parol Evidence Rule, 49 Calif.L.Rev. 877 (1961).

142. 355 F.2d 114, 3 UCC Rep.Serv. 1 (3d Cir. 1966).

143. See text accompanying note 137 supra.

Mistake is a second judge-made exception to the parol evidence rule, and courts are continuing to apply it post-Code.[144] Indeed, it has already been held that the exception applies not only to mutual mistake but to unilateral mistake as well.[145]

### § 2–12 "Merger" Clauses and the Parol Evidence Rule

The language of section 2–202 should be quoted again in full:

> Terms with respect to which the confirmatory memoranda of the parties agree or which are otherwise set forth in a writing intended by the parties as a final expression of their agreement with respect to such terms as are included therein may not be contradicted by evidence of any prior agreement or of a contemporaneous oral agreement but may be explained or supplemented
>
> > (a) by course of dealing or usage of trade (Section 1–205) or by course of performance (Section 2–208); and
> >
> > (b) by evidence of consistent additional terms unless the court finds the writing to have been intended also as a complete and exclusive statement of the terms of the agreement.

This statutory language does not bar all evidence extrinsic to a writing already in evidence. A court may decide that the writing is not a "final written expression" as to any terms and admit the evidence. A court may decide that the writing is a final written expression of some terms, but not a "complete and exclusive" statement of all terms, and admit evidence of "consistent additional terms." A court may decide that the writing is a final written expression as to terms and also that the writing is a "complete and exclusive statement," yet admit evidence of course of dealing, usage of trade, or course of performance to "explain" the meaning of terms in the writing. Under judge-made exceptions to 2–202 a court may also admit evidence extrinsic to the writing. But can the parties, by contract, preclude the introduction of evidence at trial to show terms outside the writing? So-called "merger" clauses are generally valid. We offer the following illustrative clause which we believe would be valid and effective (so far as it goes): "THIS AGREEMENT SIGNED BY BOTH PARTIES AND SO INITIALED BY BOTH PARTIES IN THE MARGIN OPPOSITE THIS PARAGRAPH CONSTITUTES A FINAL WRITTEN EXRESSION OF ALL THE TERMS OF THIS AGREEMENT AND IS A COMPLETE AND EXCLUSIVE STATEMENT OF THOSE TERMS."

This language should be effective to preclude a judge from admitting extrinsic evidence on a theory that the writing is not a final written expression. It should also preclude a judge from admitting

---

144. Braund, Inc. v. White, 486 P.2d 50, 9 UCC Rep.Serv. 183 (Alas.1971).

145. General Equip. Mfgs. v. Bible Press, Inc., 10 Mich.App. 676, 160 N. W.2d 370, 5 UCC Rep.Serv. 822 (1968).

evidence on a theory that the writing is not a complete and exclusive statement of the contract terms. The foregoing clause would not, however, keep out *all* extrinsic evidence out. It would not keep out evidence of course of dealing, usage of trade, or course of performance introduced to explain the meaning of contract terms. Perhaps a more specific clause would do this job. Moreover, it would not keep out evidence introduced to impose rights and duties that arise by operation of law. Implied warranties are the prime example. If the parties want to disclaim or exclude these, they must take further steps. In addition, the foregoing contract language would not bar evidence introduced to fit the case in such judge-made exceptions to the parol evidence rule as mistake or fraud.[146]

Merger clauses are widely used and have special value in two classic situations aptly illustrated by recent cases. In the first situation, the parties negotiate over a period of time, making and withdrawing numerous proposals. They finally reach an agreement and reduce it to writing. Here there is special need for a merger clause to protect against the risk that one party will, honestly or dishonestly, seek to resurrect some proposal that did not show up in the final writing. In the recent Oklahoma Court of Appeals case of Holton v. Bivens,[147] the parties had negotiated extensively over the purchase and sale of a used bulldozer. They finally entered into a written agreement that included this language: "No oral agreement, guaranty, promise, representation or warranty shall be binding."

Thereafter a dispute arose, and the trial court allowed the buyer to introduce evidence of an express oral warranty.[148] The appellate court reversed.[149] It cited the foregoing merger clause and emphasized that "[e]very person should have the right to rely upon written contracts. Allowing testimony of oral agreements in contradiction thereof can only result in confusion concerning the reliability of the writing." [150]

In the second classic situation, the seller's over-enthusiastic salesman makes unauthorized oral representations to the buyer who thereafter signs a written agreement that does not include these representations. Here the seller needs protection against the risks that later a dispute will arise and that the buyer will seek to introduce evidence of the unauthorized oral representations to enhance his legal rights against the seller. Sellers can insert merger clauses to protect against this risk. In addition to the usual merger language, sellers are well advised to include some such wording as this: "AND ANY AND ALL REPRESENTATIONS, PROMISES, WARRANTIES OR STATEMENTS BY SELLER'S AGENT THAT DIFFER IN ANY WAY FROM THE TERMS OF THIS WRITTEN AGREEMENT SHALL BE GIVEN NO FORCE OR EFFECT." The clause in Santos v. Mid-

---

146. See Section 2–11 supra.

147. 9 UCC Rep.Serv. 836 (Okla.Ct.App. 1971). This case was not reported officially by express order of the court.

148. Id. at 837.

149. Id. at 838.

150. Id.

Continent Refrigerator Co.[151] did not include this further language, but it proved effective nonetheless.  Lessee leased a freezing unit to hold frozen foods for sale in his store.  The written contract provided that the lease would terminate on certain conditions that did not include an option by the lessee to terminate at any time he determined that frozen foods would not sell at his store.  Yet the lessee sought to terminate for lack of sales.  On motion for summary judgment, the lessee admitted the foregoing contract but presented an affidavit in which he claimed that lessor's salesman had orally assured the lessee that he would have such an option.  The trial court entered judgment for the lessor, and the Texas Court of Civil Appeals affirmed,[152] citing the following contract language: "It is expressly understood and agreed that there are no conditions of the terms of this contract other than those herein expressly carried out." [153]  There was also an express disclaimer of warranties of fitness for any particular purposes.

But parties cannot always rely on merger clauses, even well drawn ones; we now consider several ways around them.  First, it is often said that a merger clause will not keep out evidence of true fraud.  In neither of the two cases just discussed did the party seeking to introduce the extrinsic evidence actually claim fraud.  The case law as a whole is in conflict on whether merger clauses preclude extrinsic evidence of fraud.  Some courts have readily admitted the evidence on the theory that "fraud vitiates all." [154]  Other courts have refused to admit the evidence and have stressed that a party simply should not sign an agreement with a merger clause in it where that agreement also includes terms inconsistent with what the extrinsic evidence would allegedly show.[155]  This is in the nature of a "contributory negligence" justification for upholding the merger clause against charges of fraud.  There is a further possible justification, too.  Parties sometimes try to get out of what they later come to see as bad bargains.  Doubtless in some cases these justifications should carry the day.  But we think some courts have gone too far in permitting parties to use merger clauses as shields against alleged fraud.  Where the alleged victim is a consumer and not a businessman, and where there is little chance of profiteering or weasling, we think it overly harsh to deny the alleged victim of fraud a chance to prove his case.  In our view the recent decision in Holland Furnace Co. v. Williams [156] is questionable.

151.  469 S.W.2d 24, 9 UCC Rep.Serv. 587 (Tex.Civ.App.1971).

152.  Id.

153.  Id. at 26, 9 UCC Rep.Serv. at 589. Cf. Thorman v. Polytemp, Inc., 2 UCC Rep.Serv. 772 (N.Y.Co.Ct.1965).

154.  E. g., Coson v. Roehl, 63 Wash.2d 384, 387 P.2d 541 (1963); Angerosa v. White Co., 248 App.Div. 425, 290 N.Y. S. 204 (4th Dep't 1936); Super-Cold Southwest Co. v. Willis, 219 S.W.2d 144 (Tex.Civ.App.1949).

The seller, of course, may even quite explicitly seek to disclaim liability for fraud.  Generally, courts refuse to uphold such disclaimers.  See, e. g., President and Directors of Manhattan Co. v. Monogram Associates, Inc., 276 App.Div. 766, 92 N.Y.S.2d 579 (2d Dep't 1949).  But, for an aberrational episode, see Case Note, 25 Brooklyn L.Rev. 126 (1959).

155.  E. g., 80th Division Veterans' Ass'n v. Johnson, 100 Pa.Super. 447, 159 A. 467 (1931).

156.  179 Kan. 321, 295 P.2d 672 (1956).

There, the seller was allowed to recover the price of a gas burner. The court held that it would be no defense that seller's own agent, to induce the defendant to buy a new furnace, had fraudulently represented to the defendant that the furnace he had been using would emit carbon monoxide into his house. The court reasoned that the merger clause left the defendant "bound to know" that the agent did not have authority to make any representations about the defendant's own furnace.[157] In our view, the seller should not be empowered in this way to take the benefit of a contract with a third party and at the same time throw the risks of his own agent's fraud off on that very same third party. Even if this is to be generally possible, it should not be possible where, as in the *Holland Furnace* case, the agent's fraud did not even concern qualities of the product to be sold but rather the buyer's own alleged needs. Some cases arise the other way around with the buyer suing the seller for fraud and seeking damages measured by loss of bargain. One commentator has offered the meritorious proposal that courts should protect the seller relying on conspicuous merger clauses from all damage liability, but leave him "vulnerable to restitutionary actions, and also subject to defenses," should the seller sue for the price.[158]

Second, Code rules on bad faith might be used to attack a merger clause, although bad faith is not necessarily the same as fraud. Consider the following partly hypothetical case.[159] Buyer butchers and sells poultry for Kosher poultry markets in the area. Buyer's competitors can produce larger volumes and therefore sell at lower prices. To meet this competition, buyer enters negotiations with seller for processing equipment which will enable buyer to produce larger volumes. Seller visits buyer's plant and learns that the equipment is to be for "Kosher operation." Yet the contract later signed says nothing of "Kosher operation" and includes the following conspicuous merger clause which buyer specifically signs: "I understand that the contract between the parties consists solely of this written agreement and that there are no implied warranties whatsoever." The equipment is delivered and it turns out not to be for a Kosher operation. If buyer refuses to pay the price or seeks damages, he will want to prove an express oral warranty of fitness for a particular purpose. And a court might permit him to do this, for seller inserted the merger clause, so far as the Kosher operation warranty was concerned, in bad faith (at least if the seller and not just the seller's salesman knew of "Kosher operation"). In other words, he was fully aware of the buyers' needs and knowingly tried to spring a legalism on him as an excuse for not meeting these needs. This violates the general and non-

---

157. Id. at 324, 295 P.2d at 674.

158. Comment, Special Provisions in Contracts to Exclude Contentions Based upon Parol Evidence, 32 Ill.L. Rev. 938, 948 (1938). This theory (also appearing in Restatement, Second, Agency § 260 (1958)) has been applied in some cases. See, e. g., Super-Cold Southwest Co. v. Willis, 219 S.W.2d 144 (Tex.Civ.App.1949).

159. Cf. Berk v. Gordon Johnson Co., 232 F.Supp. 682, 2 UCC Rep.Serv. 240 (E.D.Mich.1964).

variable obligation of good faith performance imposed by section 1–203 of the Code.[160]   If the buyer fails in this attack on the merger clause, he might also consider a further possibility.   That is, he might try to introduce evidence that "Kosher operation" was a fundamental assumption on which the agreement was based.   According to Professor Corbin, a respectable tradition permits proof of such assumptions, at least in the absence of a merger clause.[161]   If, given the nature of the deal, it would be natural for the parties to leave the assumption unstated, then perhaps a merger clause should make no difference.

Third, section 2–302 on unconscionability might be invoked to invalidate a merger clause in a proper case.   For example, cases such as Champlin v. Transport Motor Co.[162] would be good law under the Code.   In that case, the writing, a conditional sales contract between a dealer and one of its salesmen, provided for the sale of a car to the salesman, who was to pay certain monthly instalments.   The writing also provided that "[n]o warranties, representations or agreements have been made by the seller unless specifically set forth herein."   Yet, the parties admitted that the sale was a device whereby the dealer would be able to procure chattel paper that he could transfer to a finance company in return for a much needed advance "owing to the almost total collapse of business generally in the automobile business in and around Spokane in 1932." [163]   It was also undisputed that the dealer orally agreed to "hold his salesman harmless" in the transaction so that he would not ultimately be liable for the payments.[164]   The evidence also showed that the dealer had forced his salesmen to choose either to give up their jobs or to go along with the deal outlined.   Plaintiff salesman went along, but when he failed to make the payments, the finance company repossessed the car he had been forced to buy ("trading in" his own therefor), thereby leaving him carless in the end.   All in all he judged he lost $500, and, despite vigorous efforts by the dealer to invoke the parol evidence rule, the court allowed the salesman to recover this amount from the dealer under the oral extrinsic hold-harmless clause.   The court stressed that "there was here undoubted business compulsion exerted upon respondent." [165]   Presumably section 2–302 contemplates duress as one form of procedural unconscionability.[166]   Certainly 1–103 can be invoked against duress.

A fourth way around a merger clause is to allege and prove that, because of mistake, the writing does not reflect the actual agreement

---

160.   Farnsworth, Good Faith Performance and Commercial Reasonableness under the Uniform Commercial Code, 30 U.Chi.L.Rev. 666 (1963).

161.   3 Corbin on Contracts § 590.

162.   177 Wash. 659, 33 P.2d 82 (1934).

163.   Id. at 660, 33 P.2d at 82.

164.   Id. at 661, 33 P.2d at 83.

165.   Id. at 663, 33 P.2d at 84.

166.   On the concept of procedural unconscionability, see Leff, Unconscionability and the Code—The Emperor's New Clause, 115 U.Pa.L.Rev. 485 (1967).

of the parties. In such cases, courts may actually reform the writing to make it conform to the agreement.[167]

Finally, it may be possible for a court to interpret or construe a merger clause so that it does not apply to the alleged extrinsic understanding. A court may torture the language of the clause.[168] Or, it may simply hold that the clause is of limited scope and silent on the matter at hand. Or, the court may conclude that the parties made two separate contracts, with the merger clause applicable only to the one at hand but not to the other. Thus, in an illustrative case,[169] the court, in referring to a merger clause, remarked:

> This paragraph is intended to buttress rights accruing under the royalty contract—to cut off defenses otherwise open. But no defense to claims under this contract is now made; it is admitted that plaintiff is entitled to recover every dollar it claims. The issue here is solely as to defendant's right to counterclaim for damages suffered under another contract. The fact that this other contract relates to what is, in important aspects, the same transaction, does not extend this fifteenth paragraph to the destruction of that other contract. Its effect is limited to the contract sued upon.[170]

Merger clauses do not apply to subsequent modifications. The parties are always free to modify their prior agreements, though they may specify that this can be done only by taking specific steps.[171] And they may even waive these steps.[172]

---

**167.** See Stephenson v. Ketchikan Spruce Mills, Inc., 412 P.2d 496 (Alas. 1966).

**168.** See Hartsfield, The "Merger Clause" and the Parol Evidence Rule, 27 Texas L.Rev. 361 (1949); Comment, Special Provisions in Contracts to Exclude Contentions Based upon Parol Evidence, 32 Ill.L.Rev. 938 (1938).

**169.** Champlin Refining Co. v. Gasoline Products Co., 29 F.2d 331 (1st Cir. 1928).

**170.** Id. at 337.

**171.** In re Estate of Upchurch, —— Tenn.App. ——, 466 S.W.2d 886, 9 UCC Rep.Serv. 580 (1971).

**172.** See Section 1–5 supra.

# CHAPTER 3

# TERMS OF THE CONTRACT
## (Including the Law of Tender)

*Analysis*

Sec.

3–1.  Introduction.

3–2.  Terms Supplied by Express Agreement of the Parties.

3–3.  Terms Supplied by Course of Dealing, Usage of Trade, and Course of Performance.

3–4.  Terms Supplied by Gap Filler Provisions of Article Two and General Law—Introduction.

3–5.  Article Two Gap Fillers on Delivery Terms (Herein, too, of Seller's Proper Tender of Delivery).

3–6.  Article Two Gap Fillers on Payment Terms (Herein, too, of Buyer's Tender of Payment).

3–7.  Article Two Gap Fillers on Price.

3–8.  Article Two Gap Fillers on Quantity (Especially in Requirements Contracts).

3–9.  Mandatory Terms Under Article Two—Limits on Freedom of Contract.

## § 3–1  Introduction

In this chapter we use "terms" to include express and implied promises, conditions, provisos, and presuppositions that bind the parties. We will survey the nature and sources of contract terms (each section will treat a different basic source), identify the outer boundaries of freedom of contract under Article Two, and state the Code law applicable when parties do not expressly agree on delivery and payment terms, or price, or on quantity (requirements and output contracts). We will also consider the Code provisions on seller's tender of delivery and buyer's tender of payment (concurrent conditions).[1]

## § 3–2  Terms Supplied by Express Agreement of the Parties

The general rule is that parties are free to make their own contracts for the sale and purchase of goods. Section 1–102(3) provides:

> The effect of provisions of this Act may be varied by agreement, except as otherwise provided in this Act and except that the obligations of good faith, diligence, reasonableness and care prescribed by this Act may not be disclaimed by agreement but the parties may by agreement determine the standards by which the performance of such obligations is to be measured if such standards are not manifestly unreasonable.

---

1. Related chapters on terms are Chapter 9 on Warranties, Chapter 5 on Risk of Loss, and Chapter 4 on Un- conscionability, as well as Section 1–2 of Chapter 1 on the Battle of the Forms.

82

The gist of the foregoing language is, of course, that freedom of contract is the rule rather than the exception.[2]   This reading is further reinforced by 1–102(4) which states:

> The presence in certain provisions of this Act of the words "unless otherwise agreed" or words of similar import does not imply that the effect of other provisions may not be varied by agreement under subsection (3).

The Code defines the word "agreement." Thus, when 1–102(3) states that provisions of this Act may be varied by "agreement," this means by "the bargain of the parties in fact as found in their language or by implication from other circumstances, including course of dealing or usage of trade or course of performance." The parties can generally vary or supersede Code provisions without doing so explicitly. The express agreement may be silent on a matter, yet usage of trade, course of dealing, or course of performance may fill the gap. Indeed, under 1–102(3), "circumstances," may fill gaps too, even when they fall short of what constitutes usage of trade, course of dealing, or course of performance. Consider this example: section 2–308 states in part that "unless otherwise agreed the place for delivery of goods is the seller's place of business." But what if the seller contracts to sell goods to a distant buyer and nothing is expressly said about delivery terms? May the seller insist that under 2–308 the buyer must pick the goods up at the seller's place of business? Or is the buyer entitled to have the seller ship them? The "circumstance" that the buyer is in a far off city, even without other factors, may induce a court to say that the seller has contracted (*1*) to deliver the goods to a carrier and (*2*) to comply with 2–504 in so doing.

The parties will often contract expressly as to quality, quantity, price, and some aspects of delivery and payment. In general, their agreement without more will be sufficient to displace any otherwise applicable Code provisions. But to displace some Code provisions, the parties must follow specified procedures. For example, the Code implies a warranty of merchantability in 2–314. To vary this provision by contrary agreement, the parties must jump through the hoops specified in 2–316(2) and (3).

However, freedom of contract under Article Two is not unlimited. There are several substantive provisions in the Article the effect of which parties may not vary by agreement, no matter how explicit.[3] We will review these in Section 3–9 on terms mandatorily supplied by Article Two.

---

2. See generally Bunn, Freedom of Contract Under the Uniform Commercial Code, 2 B.C.Ind. & Com.L.Rev. 59 (1960).

3. See § 1–205, Comment 4.

### § 3–3  Terms Supplied by Course of Dealing, Usage of Trade, and Course of Performance

The agreement of the parties includes that part of their bargain found in course of dealing, usage of trade, or course of performance.[4] These sources are relevant not only to the interpretation of express contract terms, but may themselves constitute contract terms. And these sources may not only supplement or qualify express terms, but in appropriate circumstances may even override express terms.

The Code defines course of dealing in 1–205(1):

> A course of dealing is a sequence of previous conduct between the parties to a particular transaction which is fairly to be regarded as establishing a common basis of understanding for interpreting their expressions and other conduct.

The Code defines usage of trade in 1–205(2):

> A usage of trade is any practice or method of dealing having such regularity of observance in a place, vocation or trade as to justify an expectation that it will be observed with respect to the transaction in question.

Note particularly that it is not necessary for both parties to be consciously aware of the trade usage. It is enough if the trade usage is such as to "justify an expectation" of its observance.

Course of performance is defined in 2–208(1):

> Where the contract for sale involves repeated occasions for performance by either party with knowledge of the nature of the performance and opportunity for objection to it by the other, any course of performance accepted or acquiesced in without objection shall be relevant to determine the meaning of the agreement.

It would appear that course of performance refers either to conduct alone or conduct plus communications, but not to communications alone. It is clear from the language of 2–208(1) and Comment 4 that a single occasion of conduct cannot constitute a *course* of performance. Also, for a party to be charged with the legal effect of a course of performance, he must at least know of that performance. It is not enough for him to fail to object to or to acquiesce in that of which he ought to have knowledge. In this basic respect course of performance differs from usage of trade.

What is the legal effect of course of dealing and its cohorts, once proved? First, they may add to the express terms of the agreement.[5]

---

**4.** See Carroll, New Perspectives on Usage of Trade, 12 B.C.Ind. & Com.L. Rev. 139, 154–78 (1970); Levie, Trade Usage and Custom Under the Common Law and the Uniform Commercial Code, 40 N.Y.U.L.Rev. 1101 (1965); Levie, The Interpretation of Contracts in New York Under the Uniform Commercial Code, 10 N.Y.L.F. 350 (1964). See generally Note, Custom and Trade Usage: Its Application to Commercial Dealings and the Common Law, 55 Colum.L.Rev. 1192 (1955).

**5.** §§ 1–205(3); 2–208(1), (3).

For example, they may import an additional term imposing a duty on one party to give a notice to the other in a given situation, even though the express agreement is silent on the matter.[6] Or they may impose a duty on one party to seek a given remedy within a given time period, even though the express agreement is silent on remedies.[7] They may even add a warranty, as under 2–314(3).

Second, course of dealing, usage of trade, or course of performance may give particular meaning to the language of the agreement.[8] Thus each may contradict or supersede the ordinary lay meaning of words used in an agreement. If the parties contract with reference to a trade usage that imports a meaning different from the ordinary lay meaning of words used, so much the worse for the lay meaning. The trade usage will control. For example, a deal for a "thousand rabbits" may actually call for delivery of twelve hundred rabbits.[9]

Third, course of dealing and its cohorts may cut down or even subtract whole terms from the express agreement of the parties. Section 1–105 says that course of dealing and usage of trade may "qualify" the express terms of the agreement. Thus, "delivery June–August" may be qualified by trade usage to require deliveries spread through these two months rather than all at once.[10] And 2–208(1) on course of performance is drafted broadly enough to allow for the same kind of effect. A major function of course of performance, together with the law of modification and waiver, is to help cut down or subtract express terms altogether.[11] Section 2–208(3) says that a course of performance inconsistent with any term of the agreement "shall be relevant to show a waiver or modification" of that term.[12] A modification is an agreement. But since 2–204 permits agreements to be formed by conduct alone, a modifying agreement can be formed by course of performance.[13] Of course, it would have to comply with 2–209 to be effective, for 2–208(3) provides as much.

Fourth, when course of dealing and its cohorts in some way become part of the agreement, they, like express terms, supersede or vary the effect of *Code* provisions that would otherwise govern. For example, an express contract disclaimer may not be required to dis-

6. See Provident Tradesmens Bank & Trust Co. v. Pemberton, 196 Pa.Super. 180, 173 A.2d 780, 1 UCC Rep.Serv. 57 (1961).

7. See Valley Nat'l Bank v. Babylon Chrysler-Plymouth, Inc., 53 Misc.2d 1029, 280 N.Y.S.2d 786, 4 UCC Rep. Serv. 385 (Sup.Ct.1967), aff'd 28 App. Div.2d 1092, 284 N.Y.S.2d 849, 4 UCC Rep.Serv. 732 (2d Dep't 1967).

8. §§ 1–205(3); 2–202; 2–208(1). See also §§ 1–205, Comment 4; 2–202, Comment 2.

9. Smith v. Wilson, 3 B. & Ad. 728, 110 Eng.Rep. 266 (K.B.1832).

10. Warren's Kiddie Shoppe, Inc. v. Casual Slacks, Inc., 120 Ga.App. 578, 171 S.E.2d 643, 7 UCC Rep.Serv. 166 (1969). Cf. Michael Schiavone & Sons, Inc. v. Securalloy Co., 312 F.Supp. 801, 7 UCC Rep.Serv. 674 (D.Conn.1970).

11. Indeed, course of performance may even help form a contract. See §§ 2–204; 2–206; 2–207(3).

12. To be effective, some waivers must be in writing. See § 1–107.

13. Accord Levie, The Interpretation of Controls in New York Under the Uniform Commercial Code, 10 N.Y.L.F. 350, 355–56 (1964).

claim the warranty of merchantability that section 2–314 "implies" in contracts for sale of goods.  Section 2–316(3) (c) makes it plain that a course of dealing or usage of trade or performance can operate to disclaim, too.[14]

What legal impact do course of dealing, usage of trade, and course of performance have on each other in event of conflict?  Section 1–205 (4) states:

> The express terms of an agreement and an applicable course of dealing or usage of trade shall be construed wherever reasonable as consistent with each other; but when such construction is unreasonable express terms control both course of dealing and usage of trade and course of dealing controls usage of trade.

Section 2–208(2) states:

> The express terms of the agreement and any such course of performance, as well as any course of dealing and usage of trade, shall be construed whenever reasonable as consistent with each other; but when such construction is unreasonable, express terms shall control course of performance and course of performance shall control both course of dealing and usage of trade (Section 1–205).

As we have already seen, the provision that express terms control inconsistent course of dealing and its cohorts really cannot be taken at face value.  But course of dealing does override usage of trade, and course of performance overrides both course of dealing and usage of trade.  Course of dealing between the parties is, in a sense, "closer" to their expectations than general trade usage and should prevail over it.  And course of performance should prevail over both, for it is later in time and, in the words of Comment 1 to 2–208, "parties themselves know best what they have meant by their words of agreement and their action under that agreement is the best indication of what that meaning was."

A further basic question concerns matters of proof.  As we have already seen,[15] the parol evidence rule may be a hurdle.  What are the tests for admissibility of evidence of course of dealing, usage of trade, and course of performance?  It is possible to glean these tests from a close review of the relevant definitional subsections.[16]  Problems may arise with respect to the tests for admissibility of trade usage in particular, for it is likely to be confused with "custom," and the law has long encumbered proof of custom with stringent requirements.[17]  The courts at common law said that a custom must be lawful,

---

14.  Section 2–316(3) (c) provides "[A]n implied warranty can also be excluded or modified by course of dealing or course of performance or usage of trade."

15.  See Ch. 2, text accompanying notes 130–139 supra.

16.  §§ 1–205(1), (2); 2–208(1).

17.  See generally Levie, Trade Usage and Custom Under the Common Law and the Uniform Commercial Code, 40 N.Y.U.L.Rev. 1101 (1965).

reasonable, well known, certain, precise, universal, ancient, and continuous,[18] though courts did not always apply these tests consistently. Code requirements for proof of trade usage are far less stringent. Of course, the usage must be lawful. It need not be reasonable, yet it cannot be unconscionable under 2-302. A trade usage that second hand automobile dealers always set odometers back could not survive 2-302 on unconscionability.[19] A usage of trade need not be well known, let alone "universal." It is enough if it has "such regularity of observance in a place, vocation or trade as to justify an expectation that it will be observed with respect to the transaction in question."[20] Comments 5 and 7 to 1-205 add these two glosses: the usage must be observed by "the great majority of decent dealers, even though dissidents ready to cut corners do not agree" and "usages may be either general to the trade or particular to a special branch of trade." The language of 1-205(2) does not require that the usage be certain and precise; it merely requires that the usage be "any practice or method of dealing." Comment 9 is more expansive:

> In cases of a well-established line of usage varying from the general rules of this Act where the precise amount of the variation has not been worked out into a single standard, the party relying on the usage is entitled, in any event, to the minimum variation demonstrated. The whole is not to be disregarded because no particular line of detail has been established. In case a dominant pattern has been fairly evidenced, the party relying on the usage is entitled under this section to go to the trier of fact on the question of whether such dominant pattern has been incorporated into the agreement.

Proof of course of dealing or course of performance seldom requires resort to expert witnesses and poses no special problem under the hearsay rule in the law of evidence. This is not so of usage of trade. To prove it, a party must usually call on an expert; and when a party seeks to prove a trade code,[21] hearsay problems may arise. However, exceptions to the hearsay rule permit introduction of trade codes upon proper proof.[22]

---

18. Id. at 1103.

19. See, e. g., Boise Dodge, Inc. v. Clark, 92 Idaho 902, 453 P.2d 551 (1969).

20. § 1-205(2).

21. A published trade code does not necessarily constitute a usage of trade within section 1-205. It must meet the tests of that section. Cf. Emco Mills v. Isbrandtsen Co., 210 F.2d 319 (8th Cir. 1954) (evidence contradictory on whether grain dealer association rules actually reflected a trade custom). Even though the evidence establishes a trade code that is also a trade usage within section 1-205, it still may not be a trade code binding on both parties. Compare the pre-Code case of Midland Lumber & Coal Co. v. Bean, 180 Minn. 531, 231 N.W. 206 (1930) (a party not familiar with a lumber association's rules not bound by them) with the later case of Tomlinson Lumber Sales, Inc. v. J. D. Harrold Co., 263 Minn. 470, 117 N.W. 2d 203 (1962) (a party familiar with such rules was bound).

22. For consideration of the hearsay problems involved in proving that a trade code constitutes a trade usage, see Decker Steel Co. v. The Exchange

Who has the burden of proof? The Code does not say. Yet courts are likely to impose the burden of proof on the party who seeks to benefit from evidence of course of dealing, trade usage, or course of performance.[23]   It does not follow, however, that the party who has this burden of proof should also have the burden of proof on parol evidence rule issues under 2–202.   Thus if the opposing party seeks to bar admission of evidence under 2–202, he should shoulder the burden of proof on this issue.[24]

### § 3–4   Terms Supplied by Gap Filler Provisions of Article Two and General Law—Introduction

Contracts often have gaps in them intentional or inadvertent. Some gaps are more or less complete, others only partial.   Article Two of the Code includes numerous gap filler provisions which taken together constitute a kind of standardized statutory contract. Of course, the parties can vary the effect of these provisions by agreement.[25] These provisions only come into play when the agreement of the parties (including course of dealing and its cohorts) is silent.   We will consider the most important gap filler provisions of Article Two in the next four sections of this chapter.

### § 3–5   Article Two Gap Fillers on Delivery Terms (Herein, too, of Seller's Proper Tender of Delivery)

In commercial deals, a seller and buyer who reside in the same general area usually agree explicitly on the time and place of delivery. The same is true when the parties reside at a distance, except that they often use shorthand symbols such as F.O.B. and C.I.F. to indicate some of the delivery terms.   The Code includes elaborate definitions for these shorthand symbols.[26]   But what if the parties do not agree, expressly or impliedly, on delivery terms, and there is no applicable usage of trade, course of dealing, or course of performance?   In this set of circumstances, the Code's gap filler provisions on delivery will

Nat'l Bank, 330 F.2d 82 (7th Cir. 1964). For a graphic presentation of the process, see the trial transcript of Decker Steel Co. v. Exchange Nat'l Bank, 330 F.2d 82 (7th Cir. 1964), reprinted in R. Speidel, R. Summers & J. White, Commercial Transactions 489–97 (1969).

23.   Generally the party who asserts the existence of a trade usage or the like and benefits from its proof has the burden of proving it.   See Restatement of Contracts § 247 (1932) and annotations contained therein.   See also UCC § 1–205(6); Bigham, Presumptions, Burden of Proof and the Uniform Commercial Code, 21 Vand.L.Rev. 177 (1968); Note, The Law of Evidence in the Uniform Commercial Code, 1 Ga. L.Rev. 44 (1966).

24.   See Section 2–9 supra.

25.   E. g., §§ 2–204 (quantity); 2–305 (price); 2–306 (quantity); 2–308 (place of delivery); 2–309 (time of delivery); 2–310 (time and place for payment); 2–503 (tender by seller); 2–509 (risk of loss); 2–511 (tender by buyer); 2–513 (buyer's inspection).   See generally Farnsworth, Disputes over Omissions in Contracts, 68 Colum.L.Rev. 860 (1968); Lenhoff, Optional Terms and Required Terms in the Law of Contracts, 45 Mich.L.Rev. 39 (1946).

26.   See, e. g., §§ 2–319; 2–320; 2–321– 322.   See generally Farnsworth, Documentary Drafts Under the Uniform Commercial Code, 22 Bus.Law. 479 (1967).

control.  These provisions also control where the parties initially agree on delivery terms but thereafter waive them.

Section 2–309(1) provides that unless otherwise agreed, the time for delivery shall be a "reasonable time."  What is reasonable will vary with the case depending on such factors as the nature of goods to be delivered,[27] the purpose for which they are to be used,[28] the extent of seller's knowledge of buyer's intentions,[29] transportation conditions,[30] the nature of the market,[31] and so on.  The timing of seller's tender of delivery must be reasonable not only as to date but as to hour.  Section 2–503(1) states that "tender must be at a reasonable hour, and if it is of goods they must be kept available for the period necessary to enable the buyer to take possession."  The parties may expressly agree that one or the other has the option to specify the time for delivery.  If they do not so agree, the Code makes clear that "specifications or arrangements relating to shipment are at the seller's option." [32]  This does not permit seller to ship at any time he chooses; his choice must be in good faith and commercially reasonable.[33]

Unless he has a lawful excuse,[34] a seller breaches if he fails to make timely delivery or tender thereof.[35]  On the other hand, the buyer breaches if he refuses to receive a timely tender, provided the tender is proper in other respects.[36]  However, Code comments indicate that where the time for delivery is a reasonable time, the seller must usually take steps to nail down a specific delivery date before he can put the buyer in breach for refusal to receive the goods.[37]  Two kinds of cases can arise: ones in which the deal is wholly silent as to time and ones in which the parties originally agreed on a time (or a method for determining it) but thereafter waived it.  In both types of cases, Comment 5 to 2–309 seems to require that the seller propose to the buyer a date after which the seller's duty to tender will expire and the buyer will be in breach for refusal to accept tender theretofore made or proposed.  Comment 6 indicates that if the buyer does not respond to the seller's time proposal, this constitutes acquiescence in it and buyer defaults if he refuses to accept tender on or before then.  If the buyer responds but rejects the seller's reasonable proposal and

**27.**  E. g., Kutner-Goldstein Co. v. Workman, 112 Cal.App. 132, 296 P. 313 (4th Dist. 1931).

**28.**  See, e. g., Kutner-Goldstein v. Workman, 112 Cal.App. 132, 296 P. 313 (4th Dist. 1931).

**29.**  Id.

**30.**  See, e. g., Mendelson-Zeller Co., Inc. v. Joseph Wedner & Son Co., 29 Agri.Dec. 470, 7 UCC Rep.Serv. 1045 (1970).

**31.**  § 1–204(2).

**32.**  § 2–311(2).

**33.**  § 2–311(1).

**34.**  As where the buyer repudiates.  See e. g., § 2–610, Southern Pac. Milling Co. v. Billiwhack Stock Farm, Ltd., 50 Cal.App.2d 79, 122 P.2d 650 (2d Dist. 1942).

**35.**  § 2–301.  The breach may or may not be a total breach.  See § 2–612(3).

**36.**  §§ 2–301; 2–602, Comment 3.  The breach may or may not be a total breach.  See § 2–612(3).

**37.**  § 2–309, Comments 5, 6.

insists on undue delay, "a question of flat breach" arises. Both Comments 5 and 6 to 2–309(1) are somewhat obscure, and both go beyond the actual text of the section, yet we believe they are sound. Where time for delivery is no more specific than a "reasonable time," it is generally only just to require that the seller nail this time down and give the buyer an opportunity to go along before the seller charges the buyer with breach.

The contract of the parties may be wholly silent on the place for delivery. Section 2–308 generally fills this gap with the seller's place of business as the place for delivery.[38] Often, however, the gap will only be partial. In an important class of cases, the contract will either require or authorize the seller to ship the goods, but will not require the seller to deliver them at a particular destination. The most common of these contracts are those which include the symbols "F.O.B. seller's plant" or "F.O.B. seller's city." The place of delivery in such contracts (and those that include equivalent language) is the place where the facilities of seller's carrier are located, for the seller must "put the goods into the possession of the carrier." [39] In the jargon of commercial lawyers, a contract that requires or authorizes the seller to send the goods to the buyer but does not require that he deliver them at any particular destination is called a "shipment contract." Generally, in shipment contracts, risk of loss passes to the buyer at the point of shipment, which is also the point of "delivery," [40] while in "destination contracts" (seller must deliver at a particular destination) risk passes upon seller's tender at destination.[41] From the agreement of the parties and surrounding circumstances it will usually be possible to tell (1) whether the seller is authorized to send the goods (the fact the parties are at a distance will usually be enough) and (2) whether the contract is of the shipment or the destination variety. Where the contract is silent, Code comments state a presumption that the parties intended a shipment contract. The Code case law is not enlightening on what it takes to overcome this presumption.[42] The place of delivery in a contract that includes destination symbols such

---

38. But section 2–308, quoted in full, reads as follows:

    Unless otherwise agreed

    (a) the place for delivery of goods is the seller's place of business or if he has none his residence; but

    (b) in a contract for sale of identified goods which to the knowledge of the parties at the time of contracting are in some other place, that place is the place for their delivery; and

    (c) documents of title may be delivered through customary banking channels.

    A code case applying section 2–308(b) is Haken v. Scheffler, 24 Mich.App. 196, 180 N.W.2d 206, 8 UCC Rep.Serv. 349 (1970).

39. § 2–504(a).

40. § 2–509(1) (a).

41. § 2–509(1) (b). Of course the parties may vary these risk allocations by agreement. See § 2–509(4); Consolidated Bottling Co. v. Jaco Equip. Corp., 442 F.2d 660, 8 UCC Rep.Serv. 966 (2d Cir. 1971).

42. See, e. g., Electric Regulator Corp. v. Sterling Extruder Corp., 280 F. Supp. 550, 4 UCC Rep.Serv. 1025 (D. Conn.1968) ("ship to" with address does not overcome presumption). See also Ninth St. E., Ltd. v. Harrison, 5 Conn. Cir. 597, 259 A.2d 772, 7 UCC Rep.Serv. 171 (1968). Cf. § 2–503, Comment 5.

as "F.O.B. buyer's plant" or equivalent language is, of course, the named destination point.

In the absence of a lawful excuse the seller's failure to tender delivery at the proper place constitutes breach on his part.[43] On the other hand the buyer's refusal to take delivery at the proper place generally constitutes breach on his part, provided seller's tender is proper in other respects.[44] The seller may tender delivery both at the proper time and at the proper place, but still fail to make a proper tender under 2–503. And if the seller fails to make a proper tender, generally he not only incurs liability for breach but also deprives himself of any power to put the buyer in breach for failure to take delivery. Beyond offering to deliver at the proper time and place, what else must a seller do to make a proper tender? The parties are free to agree on what else the seller must do. In the absence of such agreement, the Code fills this gap with several requirements. Section 2–503(1) states that the seller must "put and hold conforming goods at the buyer's disposition and give the buyer notification reasonably necessary to enable him to take delivery." Normally the seller's invoice will satisfy the notice requirements.

In addition, where the seller is required to send the goods to the buyer under a shipment contract in which risk of loss passes to the buyer on seller's due delivery to the carrier,[45] unless otherwise agreed the seller must, under 2–504:

(a) put the goods in the possession of such a carrier and make such a contract for their transportation as may be reasonable having regard to the nature of the goods and other circumstances of the case; and

(b) obtain and promptly deliver or tender in due form any document necessary to enable the buyer to obtain possession of the goods or otherwise required by the agreement or by usage of trade; and

(c) promptly notify the buyer of the shipment.

Failure to notify the buyer under paragraph (c) or to make a proper contract under paragraph (a) is a ground for rejection only if material delay or loss ensues.[46]

The first of the foregoing requirements is that the seller make a proper contract of carriage, a requirement designed to help assure that the goods will arrive not only in timely fashion, but in good condition as well. The buyer needs this protection, for in a shipment contract he has the risk of loss in transit and becomes liable for the price to the extent the goods are lost or damaged.[47] Thus if the seller does

---

**43.** § 2–301. The breach may or may not be total. See § 2–612(3).

**44.** §§ 2–301; 2–507(1); 2–602, Comment 3. Again, it need not be a total breach. See § 2–612(3).

**45.** § 2–509(1) (a).

**46.** § 2–504.

**47.** § 2–509(1) (a); Ninth St. E., Ltd. v. Harrison, 5 Conn.Cir. 597, 259 A.2d 772, 7 UCC Rep.Serv. 171 (1968) (seller entitled to price where goods lost or damaged in transit under term providing F.O.B. seller's place of business).

not make a proper contract of carriage, risk of loss remains on him, and properly so. Furthermore, if the seller does not make a proper contract of carriage, he thereby fails to make a proper tender, too. Section 2–503(2), on what constitutes proper tender, requires the seller in a shipment contract to comply with 2–504.[48] A seller can fail to comply with 2–504 in many ways. Thus he might fail to select a direct route,[49] to arrange for suitable vehicles,[50] to arrange for proper loading,[51] to declare the proper valuation for insurance purposes,[52] and more.[53]

In a shipment contract the seller must comply with section 2–504 as part of his tender responsibilities. Where the seller does comply, his compliance should reduce the chances that anything untoward will happen to the goods in transit and will thus protect the buyer, for the buyer has the risk of loss in transit in a shipment contract. But the Code does not provide comparable protection for the buyer in a destination contract. And he does not, under the law, need it. If nonconforming goods arrive in a destination contract, the buyer may simply reject them.[54] He is not liable for the price since he does not have the risk of loss in transit.[55] The seller retains this risk and has full responsibility for delivering conforming goods to the buyer at destination (unless otherwise agreed).

Even if the seller in a shipment contract delivers conforming goods to the carrier at the proper time and place and even if the seller makes a proper contract for their transportation, he must, unless otherwise agreed, do still more to complete his proper tender. He must see that at destination the goods are made available for inspection, for unless the buyer contracts it away he is entitled to inspect before either payment or acceptance.[56] While this conclusion may appear contrary to the language of section 2–507, it is firmly grounded in the wording of sections 2–310 and 2–513. But if the buyer on inspection finds that the goods do not conform, it does not follow that the seller is in breach and that the buyer is entitled to reject. The seller would not be in breach and the buyer would not be entitled to reject if the nonconformity on arrival is traceable to something that occurred during transit for which the seller is not responsible. If the

48. § 2–503(2) says: "Where the case is within the next section respecting shipment tender requires that the seller comply with its provisions."

49. See, e. g., Rosenberg Bros. & Co. v. F. S. Buffum Co., 234 N.Y. 338, 137 N.E. 609 (1922).

50. See, e. g., Best Foods, Inc. v. Mitsubishi Shoji Kaisha, Ltd., 224 App.Div. 24, 229 N.Y.S. 364 (1st Dep't 1928).

51. Cf. Madeirense Do Brasil, S.A. v. Stulman-Emrick Lumber Co., 147 F.2d 399 (2d Cir. 1945).

52. See, e. g., Lopez v. Henry Isaacs, Inc., 210 App.Div. 601, 206 N.Y.S. 405 (1st Dep't 1924).

53. See § 2–505(2). On whether there must be a causal relation between any loss in transit and the seller's default under section 2–504, see 1 N.Y. State Law Revision Comm'n, 1955 Report 472 (1955).

54. § 2–601. For exceptions to this principle, see §§ 2–612; 2–508; 2–504.

55. § 2–509(1) (b).

56. §§ 2–310(b); 2–513(1).

seller delivered conforming goods to the carrier, he would not be in breach and the buyer would not be entitled to reject for nonconformity on arrival.   Any nonconformity would be traceable to something that occurred during transit for which seller was not responsible.   In a shipment contract the buyer has the risk of loss in transit.

In a shipment contract seller's delivery and buyer's payment are not concurrent conditions.   For events to be such it must be possible for them to occur at the same time.   But in a shipment contract, delivery technically occurs at the point of shipment,[57] yet payment is not due until after the goods become available for inspection at destination.[58]   Delivery and payment therefore cannot be concurrent conditions.

Even though the goods have become available for inspection the buyer is still not obligated to pay in a shipment contract unless and until he has a reasonable opportunity to inspect, and the seller tenders any documents "necessary to enable buyer to obtain possession of the goods." [59]   Commonly, no such documents will be involved, for the seller will ship pursuant to a nonnegotiable bill of lading naming buyer as consignee or the like.   Under such a bill the carrier may deliver to the buyer without demanding the bill.   But under 2–505 the seller can have the carrier issue a negotiable bill of lading to seller's order or a nonnegotiable bill of lading naming the seller as consignee.   By the terms of such a bill in either form (or in comparable form), the seller retains power over the goods, for the carrier is thereby bound to follow the seller's instructions.[60]   Through this control a seller can reduce the risk that buyer will get the goods without paying or at least without making satisfactory arrangements to pay.   Of course if the deal is on credit, there is no occasion for the seller to retain control.   It should be added that the seller can retain control through the form of the bill of lading and yet arrange for the buyer to inspect.   The seller may authorize the buyer to inspect while the goods are still in the hands of the carrier and therefore under seller's control.[61]

So far we have only considered what the Code requires for the seller to make a proper tender of delivery when the contract calls for him to tender delivery of *goods* but is otherwise silent on one or more aspects of this tender.   But sometimes the seller will contract to tender delivery through tender of *documents* covering the goods.   Comment 5 to 2–503(5) states that tender of documents as the mode of delivery is "never required except where there is an express contract term or it is plainly implicit in the peculiar circumstances of the case or in a usage of trade."   Domestic contracts calling for delivery through tender of documents are infrequent.   Such contracts usually involve so-called "documentary sales" in which the buyer agrees to pay cash when seller's agent presents a sight draft and bill of lading

57.   §§ 2–319(1) (a); 2–503; 2–504.

58.   §§ 2–310(b); 2–513.

59.   § 2–504(b).

60.   §§ 2–505; 7–303(1); 7–403(1).

61.   See § 2–310, Comment 2.

covering the goods.[62]   To make a proper tender of delivery through tender of documents (absent contrary agreement), the seller must deliver the documents at the buyer's city.[63]   The time for delivery is a "reasonable time." [64]   The seller may send the documents through customary banking channels,[65] and he must tender "all documents" in "correct form." [66]   Once the seller does all these things under a contract calling for the buyer to pay when the seller's agent presents a sight draft and documents, he has discharged his delivery obligations and become entitled to payment "at the time and place at which the buyer is to receive the documents regardless of where the goods are to be received." [67]   The buyer has no right to inspect the goods prior to accepting and paying for the documents, unless he has expressly reserved this right in the contract.[68]

It must not be thought that documents of title can figure in what constitutes a proper tender only where the contract calls for tender of delivery by tendering *documents*.   Earlier we explained that in the so-called "shipment contract," [69] in which the seller is required to tender *goods* to the buyer, the seller must, unless otherwise agreed, "obtain and promptly deliver or tender in due form any document necessary to enable the buyer to obtain possession of the goods." [70]   If documents are necessary, and seller fails to tender them, his tender will not be proper under sections 2–503(1) and (2) and 2–504, even though he has already made delivery at the point of shipment.   Similarly in a destination contract the seller may, as part of his overall duty to make a proper tender of goods, also be required to tender documents covering them.[71]   Even after the goods are transported under either a shipment or a destination contract calling for delivery of goods, the seller remains responsible for two things:  (*1*) he must offer the buyer a reasonable opportunity to inspect, and (*2*) he must offer to relinquish any control he has retained over the goods through documents of title. Not until these things are done can the seller put the buyer in breach for failure to accept and pay.[72]

---

62.  On the nature of documentary sales, see further Ch. 18 infra.

63.  §§ 2–310(a) ;  2–310, Comment 3. See also §§ 2–308(c) ; 2–308, Comment 3.

64.  § 2–309(1).

65.  § 2–503(5) (b).

66.  § 2–503(5) (a).  There is a tradition of strictness in regard to documentary tenders.  See, e. g., Mitsubishi Goshi Kaisha v. J. Aron & Co., 16 F.2d 185 (2d Cir. 1926).  But compare Section 18–5 infra.

67.  § 2–310(c).

68.  §§ 2–310(c) ; 2–513(3) (b).

69.  See text accompanying notes 46–53 supra.

70.  § 2–504(b).

71.  § 2–503(3).

72.  The language of section 2–511(1) is not well chosen.  It reads: "Unless otherwise agreed tender of payment is a condition to the seller's duty to tender and complete any delivery."  The word delivery is inapt for shipment contracts, for in them the seller has technically already delivered at point of shipment.  Thus he no longer has any delivery obligation, though he must arrange for relinquishing any control retained.  See § 2–504(b).

Nearly all the Code law on seller's delivery and tender of delivery is gap filling law.  The parties are free to agree as they wish and the Code applies only to fill gaps.  The Code's gap fillers may seem somewhat strict.  But the Code itself also includes three distinct types of sections that modify and thus ameliorate the strictness of its gap fillers on tender.  First, in some circumstances the seller's duty to tender delivery may be excused altogether.  This will be so, for example, when "presupposed conditions" of the contract fail.[73]  Second, in some circumstances the seller is allowed to tender through a substitute carrier or in a substitute manner.  When he does so, the substitute tender is considered the real thing.[74]  Third, even though the seller's noncomplying tender is not excused and is not a permissible substitute, the tender may in some circumstances still be sufficient at least to preclude rejection.[75]

## § 3–6   Article Two Gap Fillers on Payment Terms (Herein, too, of Buyer's Tender of Payment)

Section 2–507(1) provides that seller's proper tender of delivery entitles him to "payment according to the contract."  But as we shall see, payment has numerous aspects, and the contract of the parties may be silent on one or all of them.  The Code includes numerous gap filler sections on payment.  If the agreement is silent, must the buyer pay cash or is he entitled to an extension of credit?  The Code fills this gap by requiring that the buyer pay cash on the barrelhead.[76]  The buyer must bargain for credit.  This may seem surprising, for in most commercial sales in which the parties do address this question, the seller extends credit.

When and where must the buyer pay cash?  If the deal is silent, 2–310(a) states that "payment is due at the time and place at which the buyer is to receive the goods even though the place of shipment is the place of delivery."[77]  Section 2–503(1) (a) suggests that the place of receipt is where the buyer is to take physical possession of the goods.  Frequently the time and place for payment will be the time and place where the seller is to make delivery, for this will be the "time and place at which the buyer is to receive the goods."  But frequently this will not be true.  That is, frequently the time and place where the buyer is to receive the goods will not be the same as the time and place for seller's "delivery."  In an important class of

73.  § 2–615.

74.  § 2–614.

75.  "Failure to notify the buyer  .  .  . or to make a proper contract  .  .  . is a ground for rejection only if material delay or loss ensues."  § 2–504. This is further discussed in Ch. 18 infra.

76.  §§ 2–310(a);  2–507(1);  2–507, Comment 2.

77.  Southwest Engineering Co. v. Martin Tractor Co., 205 Kan. 684, 473 P.2d 18, 7 UCC Rep.Serv. 1288 (1970) (court invoked section 2–310 to fill gap with payment on delivery term).  In an installment deal where the parties leave duration unspecified, there is authority that the court should look to the nature of the contract and to whatever the parties agreed to, orally or not.  See J. W. Knapp v. Sinas, 19 Mich.App. 427, 172 N.W.2d 867, 7 UCC Rep.Serv. 176 (1969).

cases the seller will not by contract be required to deliver them at any particular destination. In 2–504 "shipment contracts," the time and place of delivery is at seller's city or place of business, and this is obviously not where the buyer is actually to receive and take possession of the goods. The comments to 2–310(a) indicate that the section was drafted in light of the possibility that time and place of delivery might differ from time and place of receipt.[78] In the absence of contrary agreement, 2–513 provides that the buyer is entitled to inspect prior to payment, a right that he should not have to exercise by traveling to the seller's city to inspect at the time and place the seller delivers to the carrier. The Code draftsmen therefore deferred the buyer's duty to pay until the time and place of his receipt, a point at which he may conveniently exercise his customary right of inspection prior to payment.

But it must not be assumed that the buyer is entitled to withhold his payment not only until after he has had occasion to inspect at his place of receipt but also until after he has taken full possession and control of the goods. Absent contrary agreement, the Code theory is that the buyer is entitled to full possession and control over the goods only where he concurrently tenders payment. Put differently, while the seller must make the goods available for inspection, "he is not required to give up possession of the goods until he has received payment," [79] assuming, of course, that he has not agreed to extend credit.

What if buyer discovers what he thinks to be a breach of warranty? Can the buyer withhold part of his payment and still insist that the seller relinquish possession of the goods? Of course, if the seller admits the breach of warranty, he may readily agree to buyer's proposal to withhold part of the payment and no problem will arise. But assuming that the seller denies the breach of warranty, nothing in the Code on tender requires that he give up the goods in return for the reduced payment. Accordingly, if the buyer should refuse acceptance, except on his reduced terms, the seller would not be in breach for refusing to relinquish possession of the goods.[80] The seller should not be forced to give up the goods in return for the lower payment since more often than not the goods will prove to be conforming (most sellers perform most of the time), and if the buyer pays in full, both parties will then more often than not be in the position they expected to be in after performance.

Thus buyer's payment and seller's relinquishment of full possession and control are "concurrent conditions," absent contrary agreement. Even though the time and place where the buyer is to receive the goods is in a city far away from the seller's place of business, the seller can still retain full possession and control over the goods by procuring a document of title from the carrier in appropriate form, for example, a negotiable bill of lading to his own order or a nonne-

---

78.  See, e. g., § 2–310, Comment 1.

79.  § 2–310, Comment 2.

80.  If buyer has received the goods, 2–717 lets him tender a reduced price.

gotiable bill of lading naming himself as consignee.[81]   Documents in such form require the carrier to obey instructions from the seller as to disposition of the goods.[82]   The seller must be careful to assure that the carrier allows the buyer a reasonable opportunity to inspect. The buyer is entitled to inspect unless he explicitly gives up the right or agrees to a C. O. D. payment term or a term which, in the language of section 2–513(3), calls for "payment against documents of title, except where such payment is due only after the goods are to become available for inspection."   It must be admitted that there is a conflict between this language and section 2–310(c) which reads:

> [I]f delivery is authorized and made by way of documents of title otherwise than by subsection (b) then payment is due at the time and place at which the buyer is to receive the documents regardless of where the goods are to be received.

According to 2–513(3) the buyer does not give up his right to inspect before payment even when he agrees to pay against documents if "such payment is due only after the goods are to become available for inspection."   The parties may agree that the documents shall be held in the buyer's city until after the goods also arrive there.   When they do so agree, Code comments [83] as well as the text of 2–513(3) indicate that the buyer may inspect before payment, 2–310(c) to the contrary notwithstanding.

In the absence of contrary agreement, then, the buyer must tender payment at the time and place where he is to receive the goods and must also furnish facilities reasonably suited to delivery of the goods.[84]   Unless performance of these duties is excused, the buyer's failure in these respects will put him in breach.[85]   On the other hand if he does perform these duties, but the seller fails in his own corresponding duties, the seller will be in breach.[86]   What exactly must the buyer tender when he tenders payment?   Sections 2–511(2) and (3) fill any such gap in the contract:

> (2) Tender of payment is sufficient when made by any means or in any manner current in the ordinary course of business unless the seller demands payment in legal tender and gives any extension of time reasonably necessary to procure it.

> (3) Subject to the provisions of this Act on the effect of an instrument on an obligation (Section 3–802), payment by check is conditional and is defeated as between the parties by dishonor of the check on due presentment.

---

81.  §§ 2–310(b); 2–505.

82.  §§ 2–505(1); 7–303(1) (a), (b); 7–403 (1).

83.  §§ 2–310(a), Comment 4; 2–513, Comment 5.

84.  § 2–503(1) (b).

85.  §§ 2–301; 2–507; 2–511.   The breach may or may not be a total breach.   See e. g., § 2–612(3).

86.  §§ 2–301; 2–507.   The breach may or may not be a total breach.   See, e. g., § 2–612(3).

Tender of payment in the form of a check is only a conditionally valid tender. As between seller and buyer, the seller is entitled to reassert dominion over the goods if the buyer has acquired them by giving a check which is later dishonored.[87] There is some case authority that the seller must reassert dominion within ten days after the check is dishonored.[88] But, except where the buyer is insolvent, the Code does not expressly impose this ten-day limit.[89]

## § 3–7  Article Two Gap Fillers on Price

In most contracts for the sale of goods the parties expressly agree on a price. In this way they shift the risks of a fluctuating market. As Professor Prosser once put it (before torts became his *idée maîtresse*):

A prospective seller, who owns a thousand bushels of wheat, is necessarily subject to the risk that, before he sells, the market value of the wheat will decline, and he will receive less for it than it is now worth. A prospective buyer, who requires a thousand bushels of wheat, is correspondingly subject to the risk that before he buys the market will go up, and the wheat will cost him more than he would now have to pay. When the two agree upon a contract for the sale of the wheat at a price of one dollar per bushel, these risks are exchanged. It is now the seller who assumes the risk that the market will rise, and that he will have lost a profit; the buyer who assumes the risk that the market will go down, and the bargain prove to be a bad one. If the contract is for future delivery, the situation is the same, except that the seller doubtless feels more acutely the hardship of delivering wheat at one dollar, when its value has risen to one dollar and fifty cents, or the buyer regrets more poignantly his bad judgment if the market has fallen to fifty cents.[90]

Yet in a particular case businessmen may choose not to exchange the risks. Instead, they may choose to leave the price term entirely open or leave it to be determined in the future by some specified procedure. Parties do this for a variety of reasons, but one of the most common is simply that the seller thinks the market may rise and wants therefore to be able to sell at that higher price, while the buyer thinks the market may fall and therefore wants to be able to buy at that

---

**87.** §§ 2–507(2); 2–511(2), (3); In re Mort Co., 208 F.Supp. 309, 1 UCC Rep. Serv. 166 (E.D.Pa.1962).

**88.** In re Helms Veneer Corp., 287 F. Supp. 840, 5 UCC Rep.Serv. 977 (W.D. Va.1968); see also § 2–507, Comment 3.

**89.** Compare § 2–702 with § 2–507(2). For further discussion of the unpaid seller's goods-oriented remedies when

the buyer fails to pay, see Section 7–15 infra.

**90.** Prosser, Open Price in Contracts for Sale of Goods, 16 Minn.L.Rev. 733, 733 (1932). See also Note, UCC Section 2–305(1) (c): Open Price Terms and the Intention of the Parties in Sales Contracts, 1 Valpariso U.L.Rev. 381 (1967). Cf. 1 N.Y. State Law Revision Comm'n, 1955 Report 662–67 (1955).

lower price.   Obviously, to buyers who buy for purposes of manufacture or resale, a fixed price term can prove disastrous over any lengthy period, for if the market significantly falls during that period, his competitors will buy at the lower market price, undersell him, and possibly drive him out of business.

Section 2–305 of the Code recognizes these economic facts of life. It reads:

(1)   The parties if they so intend can conclude a contract for sale even though the price is not settled.   In such a case the price is a reasonable price at the time for delivery if

(a)   nothing is said as to price; or

(b)   the price is left to be agreed by the parties and they fail to agree; or

(c)   the price is to be fixed in terms of some agreed market or other standard as set or recorded by a third person or agency and it is not so set or recorded.

(2)   A price to be fixed by the seller or by the buyer means a price for him to fix in good faith.

(3)   When a price left to be fixed otherwise than by agreement of the parties fails to be fixed through fault of one party the other may at his option treat the contract as cancelled or himself fix a reasonable price.

(4)   Where, however, the parties intend not to be bound unless the price be fixed or agreed and it is not fixed or agreed there is no contract.   In such a case the buyer must return any goods already received or if unable so to do must pay their reasonable value at the time of delivery and the seller must return any portion of the price paid on account.

Section 2–305 has a contract formation aspect and a gap filling aspect.   Our focus will be on the latter, although their relationship dictates discussion of both.   The question whether a court is to fill a gap in light of 2–305 cannot even arise unless the court decides that the parties "intended" a contract under the first sentence of that section.   Yet a court's willingness to say as much may turn partly on the nature of any gap to be filled.   Indeed, a court cannot hold that the parties made a contract unless there is a "reasonably certain basis for granting an appropriate remedy for breach." [91]   If no price can be set, there will be no way to compute damages based either on contract-market differentials, on the difference between the contract price and the cost of cover (in the case of an aggrieved buyer), or

91.   § 2–204(3).   Royal Store Fixture Co. v. Bucci, 48 Pa.D. & C.2d 696, 7 UCC Rep.Serv. 1193 (Co.Ct.1969) (nature of store fixtures and refrigeration equipment to be sold left unspecified and only price stated was "at prices competitive with other manufacturer's equipment of equality and specifications"; held, too indefinite to constitute a contract).

on the difference between the contract price and a resale price (in the case of an aggrieved seller).

Price gaps may be complete or partial. Here, a "partial" gap is one in which the parties have specified how the price is ultimately to be determined but the method has failed. Section 2–305(1) (a) governs complete gaps. Sections 2–305(1) (b) and (c) and 2–305(2) and (3) govern partial gaps. Whether or not a gap exists may itself be the subject of dispute. The case of Associated Hardware Supply Co. v. Big Wheel Distributing Co.[92] involved such a dispute. There the buyer proposed a price of cost plus ten percent. The seller billed the buyer for goods delivered at "dealer catalogue prices less 11%," which the seller allegedly told the buyer was equivalent to cost plus ten percent. In fact the two were not equivalent. The seller's representation was either fraudulent or mistaken. If fraudulent, the buyer would be entitled to retain the goods and pay only their reasonable value, as the court recognized.[93] But if a mistake, then although the parties failed to agree on a price, the court thought the buyer's acceptance of the goods constituted acquiesence in the seller's price proposal. Here the court seems to have erred, for on the facts alleged the buyer only acquiesed in a method of billing, not a price, and the court should have turned to 2–305.[94]

When there is a gap as to price, 2–305 directs the court to determine "a reasonable price," provided the parties intended a contract. Note that the section says "a reasonable price" and not "fair market value of the goods." In many instances these two would not be identical. For example, evidence of a prior course of dealing between the parties might show a price below or above market. Without more, a court could justifiably hold in these circumstances that the course of dealing price is the "reasonable price." [95] In the "complete" gap cases, the courts utilize various forms of evidence. If there is sufficient evidence of price based on course of dealing, course of performance, or usage of trade, this will determine "reasonable price" whether or not that price is equivalent to market price. Indeed, with such evidence it may even be said that there is no "gap" at all in the agreement of the parties. Absent evidence of this nature, the court will ordinarily have to determine fair market price at the time and place of delivery.[96]

---

92. 355 F.2d 114, 3 UCC Rep.Serv. 1 (3d Cir. 1966).

93. Id. at 120, 3 UCC Rep.Serv. at 8–9.

94. Compare Hollywood Wholesale Elec. Co. v. Jack Baskin, Inc., 146 Cal.App.2d 399, 303 P.2d 1049 (2d Dist.1956) (buyer's acceptance of goods at invoiced price without objection held to bind buyer to that price), with Lamberta v. Smiling Jim Potato Co., 25 Agri.Dec. 1181, 3 UCC Rep.Serv. 981 (1966) (use of reasonable price did not bind buyer to invoice price).

95. Cf. Columbus Milk Producers' Co-op. v. Department of Agriculture, 48 Wis. 2d 451, 180 N.W.2d 617, 8 UCC Rep. Serv. 481 (1970) (course of dealing held basis for price at the general going rate).

96. Section 2–305 says "at the time for delivery." Presumably this also means at the place for delivery.

The "partial gap" cases are those in which the parties have specified a method for determining the price but that method has failed. It is important to distinguish complete gap from partial gap cases, for what would constitute a reasonable price in the two types of cases is not necessarily the same. In complete gap cases a court is more on its own, and properly so. But in at least some partial gap cases, what the court considers a reasonable price should be influenced to some extent by the price it thinks would have been set had the parties been successful with the method they agreed to.

The kinds of methods which parties may agree to for setting the price are highly varied. First, they may simply agree to agree between themselves on a price at a later date. Some courts invalidated such agreements as too indefinite.[97] But the Code validates such agreements, provided the parties intend to contract and there is a reasonably certain basis for granting an appropriate remedy.[98] In such cases courts are to fill the gap with a reasonable price. Sometimes the parties will agree that one of them is to fix the price. Here the agreed method may fail for either of two quite different reasons. The appointed party may fail to set any price, or he may set a price in bad faith. If his failure was owing to his own fault, 2–305 provides that the other party may "himself fix a reasonable price." But if the failure to fix a price was not the fault of either party, then the Code empowers the court to fix a reasonable price. If the party who is to fix the price fixes it in bad faith, the court will substitute a reasonable price; 2–305(2) provides that a "price to be fixed by the seller or by the buyer means a price for him to fix in good faith." [99]

The parties may also agree to set a price by reference to costs of one of parties. For example, a seller may be empowered to charge the buyer "cost plus ten percent." When this method of pricing fails, a court under 2–305(1) may supply a reasonable price.

The parties may agree to set the price by methods that do not require either party to act further. Thus they may agree that the price will be the prevailing market price at a given time and place, or that the price will be equivalent to prices charged by a competitor or group of competitors. In Columbus Milk Producers' Co-op v. Department of Agriculture,[100] the Wisconsin Supreme Court had before it a case in which the parties had not expressly agreed that farmers would be paid the "going rate" for milk, yet their course of dealing, course of performance, and usage of trade did show such an agreement. Thus all the court had to do was grant damages accordingly, for the buyer had not paid the going rate.

**97.** See, e. g., Sun Printing & Publishing Ass'n v. Remington Paper & Power Co., 235 N.Y. 338, 139 N.E. 470 (1923).

**98.** §§ 2–204(3); 2–305.

**99.** See Columbus Milk Producers' Co-op. v. Department of Agriculture, 48 Wis.2d 451, 180 N.W.2d 617, 8 UCC Rep.Serv. 481 (1970) (court set price where buyer originally had set it in bad faith).

**100.** 48 Wis.2d 451, 180 N.W.2d 617, 8 UCC Rep.Serv. 481 (1970).

Sometimes the parties agree that the contract price will be based on quotations in a trade journal or similar index. Then, the journal ceases publication or ceases publishing the needed quotations.[101] Here, too, 2–305 empowers the court to ascertain a reasonable price and fill the gap accordingly. Contracts may also provide for arbitration of the price.[102] Whenever the arbitration process fails to get underway or breaks down, the court may or may not be faced with a 2–305 issue. It may be asked only to direct that arbitration proceed.

If the court is to fill a price gap with a reasonable price consisting of a market price, when and where is this price to be ascertained? Under 2–305, this price is to be determined "at the time for delivery." The defendant will want to make sure that he does not end up having to overcompensate the plaintiff. For example, if the contract calls for a plaintiff buyer to pay freight costs, he should not be permitted to show a 2–305 price equivalent to market price at his home city, for that price would reflect the cost of transporting goods to his city.[103]

The foregoing discussion presupposes that the parties intended to contract and that the facts afford a reasonably certain basis for granting an appropriate remedy.[104] But what is a "reasonably certain basis"? Comment 4 to section 2–305 states:

> The section recognizes that there may be cases in which a particular person's judgment is not chosen merely as a barometer or index of a fair price but is an essential condition to the parties' intent to make any contract at all. For example, the case where a known and trusted expert is to "value" a particular painting for which there is no market standard differs sharply from the situation where a named expert is to determine the grade of cotton, and the difference would support a finding that in the one the parties did not intend to make a binding agreement if that expert were unavailable whereas in the other they did so intend. Other circumstances would of course affect the validity of such a finding.

Consider the recent case of Interstate Plywood Sales Co. v. Interstate Container Corp.[105] in light of the above comment. The defendant agreed to sell plywood to the plaintiff over a period of time at a contract price equivalent to market price based on prices published by five other plywood mills. Thereafter some of the mills went out of business or failed to publish any relevant prices. The court defined the issue in these terms: "Whether the five-mill pricing formula was designed to be the only binding means of setting price, or whether the

---

101. See, e. g., American Car & Foundry Co. v. East Jordan Furnace Co., 275 F. 786 (7th Cir. 1921).

102. Compare Ch. 1, note 7 and accompanying text supra.

103. See Section 6–4 infra.

104. See generally Note, UCC Section 2–305(1) (c): Open Price Terms and the Intention of the Parties in Sales Contracts, 1 Valparaiso U.L.Rev. 381 (1967).

105. 331 F.2d 449 (9th Cir. 1964).

contract called for sales of plywood at the general market price, with the five-mill formula being merely a guide thereto?" [106]   In other words, was the case more like the sale of a painting with the price to be set by an expert appraiser, than like a sale of cotton priced according to grade but with an expert to determine grade?   The plywood case arose prior to the effective date of the Code in California, and the court decided that the parties' intent to be bound was conditioned on the availability of a price based on the five-mill formula; since this price could not be determined, the deal could not be enforced.   Consequently the seller was free to sell his plywood elsewhere.   In our view, the parties chose a specific means of determining price merely as a "barometer or index of a fair price" rather than as "an essential condition to the parties intent to make any contract at all." [107]   There were numerous other comparable mill prices that could have been used as an index of a fair price.   We believe that under 2–305, the court should not have let the seller out.   Virtually all relevant factors indicated that the parties intended an ongoing contractual relationship.   Moreover, there was a reasonably certain basis for granting an appropriate remedy.

## § 3–8   Article Two Gap Fillers on Quantity (Especially in Requirements Contracts)

At one end of the spectrum it is possible for an open or indefinite quantity term to be completely indefinite.   Thus, two parties unknown to each other may each enter a wholly new business in a wholly new trade.   Thereafter they may enter an agreement by the terms of which one is to sell to the other all of his "requirements." [108]   Here no one may be able to forecast the extent of such requirements.   At the other end of the spectrum, the parties may own established businesses and state maxima and minima in their agreement on the basis of past experience.   Most requirements contracts (quantity measured by buyer's needs) fall somewhere between these extremes.   In one type, the seller at a specified price, agrees to supply all of the buyer's "needs" for sand and gravel, or for potatoes, or for eggs, and so on, over a given period.   If the buyer's business is an established one, if the needs of that business fluctuate little, and if the seller has been dealing with the buyer over time, a court can judge after breach or repudiation what the buyer might have ordered during the remaining life of the contract, multiply this quantity by the contract price, and arrive at a total contract price to be used for computing damages.   But some cases fall at that end of the spectrum where there is little basis on which to compute quantity.   Indeed the price term may be left open as well, and the parties may thereby compound the difficulty.   Yet

106.   Id. at 452.

107.   § 2–305, Comment 4.

108.   For earlier discussions, see Havighurst & Berman, Requirement and Output Contracts, 27 Ill.L.Rev. 1 (1932); Note, Requirements Contracts: Problems of Drafting and Construction, 78 Harv.L.Rev. 1212 (1965); Note, Requirements Contracts under the Uniform Commercial Code, 102 U.Pa.L. Rev. 654 (1954); Annot., 26 A.L.R.2d 1099 (1952).

even quite indefinite requirements contracts may be attractive to a buyer insofar as they assure him of a source of supply, allow him to meet the fluctuating needs of his business, and offer the economies and conveniences of dealing with only one supplier. To the seller, the contract may offer assurance of a market outlet, facilitate efficient scheduling of business activity, and save storage and marketing costs. It is only when a dispute arises that the intrinsic indefiniteness of the agreement causes trouble.

The law on requirements contracts is almost entirely judge-made and will remain so post-Code. A requirements contract may under all the circumstances simply be too indefinite to afford a basis for any remedy. But some courts have invalidated agreements that were in fact definite enough to afford a basis for computing damages.[109] In some of these cases one party had taken unfair advantage of the other, for instance by ordering a vastly increased amount during a sharp price rise. But invalidation is a clumsy tool for policing purposes.[110] And despite the inherent indefiniteness of requirements contracts, most courts have validated them. By the late 1950's, when the Code was widely proposed for adoption, some courts had also devised policing doctrines that enabled them to curb abuses under requirements contracts without resorting to the blunderbuss of invalidation.[111] The Code leaves this case law on policing intact.

While the Code does not validate requirements contracts in so many words, section 2–204(3) provides that "even though one or more terms are left open a contract for sale does not fail for indefiniteness if the parties have intended to make a contract and there is a reasonably certain basis for giving an appropriate remedy." These statutory conditions are satisfied in all but the most unusual requirements contract. In addition, 2–306(1), which is essentially a policing provision, presupposes the validity of requirements contracts.[112] Thus the Code generally validates requirements contracts. A party who seeks to invalidate a particular requirements contract therefore bears a heavy burden. And the mere existence of an open quantity term does not support invalidation, since indefiniteness is inherent in requirements contracts.

Validity aside, courts must still police against abuses. Abuses commonly take one of three forms: (1) unjustified increases in requirements, (2) unjustified decreases, and (3) unjustified withdrawal of either the buyer or the seller. In policing against abuses, a court will set quantities and thus fill "gaps" in the contract. In addition to

109. E. g., Interstate Plywood Sales Co. v. Interstate Container Corp., 331 F.2d 449 (9th Cir. 1964).

110. Compare text accompanying notes 112–140 infra.

111. E. g., Sylvan Crest Sand & Gravel Co. v. United States, 150 F.2d 642 (2d Cir. 1945). Cf. Simons v. American

Dry Ginger Ale Co., 335 Mass. 521, 140 N.E.2d 649 (1957).

112. Moreover, section 2–306, Comment 1, implies that contracts to supply the requirements of "dealers or distributers" are generally valid although many such buyers are just entering business or are ones whose business needs fluctuate markedly.

the policing tools available in the case law (which we shall return to), courts may invoke 2–306(1):

> A term which measures the quantity by the output of the seller or the requirements of the buyer means such actual output or requirements as may occur in good faith, except that no quantity unreasonably disproportionate to any stated estimate or in the absence of a stated estimate to any normal or otherwise comparable prior output or requirements may be tendered or demanded.

Under this section, claimed requirements may constitute an abuse if they (*1*) are not actual, (*2*) are not in good faith, or (*3*) are unreasonably disproportionate to any stated estimate or to any normal or otherwise comparable prior requirements. So far only one court has construed 2–306(1).[113] In one case, the court applied it even though it was plainly inapplicable. Gruschus v. C. R. Davis Contracting Co.[114] did not involve a requirements contract. Rather, the seller agreed to supply a definite but indeterminate amount of sand and aggregate—namely, all that the buyer needed to do a highway paving job. The seller supplied 10,875 tons in excess of the quantity needed and apparently demanded payment for most of this excess. The New Mexico courts disallowed this claim on the ground that the excess was not delivered in good faith and was "unreasonably disproportionate" to the requirements for which it was delivered. Actually the court could have cut the seller's claim down simply by invoking contract language that called only for whatever amount (indeterminate at time of contracting) the buyer needed in order to do the paving.

In a batch of pre- and post-Code cases, the buyer substantially increased his "requirements" over a relatively short period of time.[115] Such action may or may not constitute an abuse. And if an abuse, a court may or may not invalidate the contract altogether. As already indicated, the Code expressly affords means of policing that do not require invalidation. In nearly all of the cases the seller contended that he was not obligated to supply the increase. In resolving these cases, courts usually take a variety of factors into account, but in some cases one factor will be more or less decisive. For example, to avoid liability for an increase it is usually enough for a seller to show that the buyer was not buying solely for his current actual needs but was, for in-

113.  Romine v. Savannah Steel Co., 117 Ga.App. 353, 160 S.E.2d 659, 5 UCC Rep.Serv. 103 (1968).

114.  75 N.M. 649, 409 P.2d 500, 2 UCC Rep.Serv. 1080 (1965), aff'd on second appeal, 77 N.M. 614, 426 P.2d 589 (1967). Cf. Romine, Inc. v. Savannah Steel Co., 117 Ga.App. 353, 160 S.E.2d 659, 5 UCC Rep.Serv. 103 (1968).

115.  Examples of pre-Code cases include Johnston Pie Co. v. Acme Egg & Poultry Co., 74 Cal.App.2d 376, 168 P.2d 762 (2d Dist.1946); W. M. McElwain Co. v. Fisher, 260 S.W. 544 (Mo.Ct.App. 1924). For an example of a post-Code case, see Massachusetts Gas & Electric Light Supply Corp. v. V–M Corp., 387 F.2d 605, 4 UCC Rep.Serv. 897 (1st Cir. 1967).

stance, stockpiling or speculating.[116]   Even where the buyer's increased requirements truly reflect the current needs of his business, the case law indicates that the seller may still avoid liability for the increase by showing some combination of the following: (*1*) that he had no reasonable basis on which to forecast the requested increase; [117] (*2*) that the increase itself was quite substantial; [118]   (*3*) that the market price of the goods rose considerably above the price at which the seller had been selling to the buyer; [119]  (*4*) that this striking market shift was itself fortuitous; [120]   (*5*) that the contract as a whole favored the buyer; [121]  and (*6*) that the buyer increased his "requirements" solely to take advantage of his favorable price term, rather than because of a mistaken estimate,[122] a technological breakthrough, or the like.   Of course, a seller need not show *all* the foregoing factors to avoid liability for the increase, but the more the better.

The seller's own reason for refusing to supply the increase can help his case as well.   For example, if he can show that he refused to supply the increase not only because of the unprofitability of doing so, but also because of unforeseen factors that impaired his own capacity to produce, he will strengthen his position in the eyes of a court.[123] He may even be able to invoke 2–615 to excuse his nondelivery.   Any time he can do this, he will not need the special protections afforded sellers under requirements contracts.

Are all the foregoing factors relevant under the Code?   It would appear so.   Certainly 2–306(1) is drafted very broadly.   An increase must be in good faith.   Among other things, this rules out increases that do not represent *genuine* increases in the buyer's requirements. It also rules out increases that the buyer knows to be beyond the spirit of the deal.   Further, 2–306 requires that increases not be "unreasonably disproportionate" to any stated estimate or to any normal or otherwise comparable prior requirements.   The word "unreasonably" allows for the interplay of almost any factor a court properly considers relevant.   An increase might be in good faith, yet

116. See, e. g., Massachusetts Gas & Elec. Light Supply Corp. v. V–M Corp., 387 F.2d 605, 4 UCC Rep.Serv. 897 (1st Cir. 1967).

117. Compare American Trading Co. v. National Fibre & Installation Co., 31 Del. 258, 114 A. 67 (1921), with Marx v. American Malting Co., 169 F. 582 (6th Cir. 1909), and New York Cent. Iron Works Co. v. United States Radiator Co., 174 N.Y. 331, 66 N.E. 967 (1903).

118. See, e. g., Asahel Wheeler Co. v. Mendleson, 180 App.Div. 9, 167 N.Y.S. 435 (3d Dep't 1917); Moore v. American Molasses Co., 106 Misc. 263, 174 N.Y.S. 440 (Sup.Ct.1919).

119. See, e. g., Asahel Wheeler Co. v. Mendleson, 180 App.Div. 9, 167 N.Y.S.

435 (3d Dep't 1917); Moore v. American Molasses Co., 106 Misc. 263, 174 N.Y.S. 440 (Sup.Ct.1919).

120. See, e. g., Anaheim Sugar Co. v. T. W. Jenkins & Co., 274 F. 504 (9th Cir. 1921); Smith v. Donk Bros. Coal & Coke Co., 260 S.W. 545 (Mo.Ct.App. 1924).

121. Under the Code, even greater significance can be attached to this factor than before.   See § 2–302.

122. See Sherman Mach. & Iron Works v. Carey, Lombard & Co., 100 Okla. 29, 227 P. 110 (1924).

123. See, e. g., Sheesley v. Bisbee Linseed Co., 337 Pa. 197, 10 A.2d 401 (1940).

unreasonably disproportionate to prior requirements. This presumably changes the pre-Code law of some states in which courts sanctioned unforeseeable and very large increases within a rather short time.[124] Yet it codifies the law of certain other states.[125]

Sellers are not, however, automatically entitled to resist demands of buyers for any and all large increases. Sellers sometimes have reason to anticipate large increases. In agreeing to a fixed price, sellers also take the risk of a market rise, and the rise itself may not be substantial. Further, buyers sometimes have reasons for increased requirements in addition to or other than the desire to take advantage of the market. Finally, the very *raison d'être* of a requirements contract is to allow a buyer some flexibility in the size of his orders. In a proper case a court may sanction a sizeable increase. Indeed, where the increase is gradual and the buyer is not acting in bad faith, a court may permit an increase that is extremely large. In one pre-Code case,[126] the court enforced a contract under which the buyer's orders for bread gradually increased from fifty or sixty loaves to three or four thousand loaves per week.[127] Presumably the case would be decided in the same way under the Code.

A policing problem can also arise where a requirements buyer *decreases* his orders significantly over a relatively short period. Of course, if it transpires that the buyer is actually procuring his requirements more cheaply elsewhere, this is bad faith, and the courts will find that it constitutes breach. Where the market price of the required goods falls below that which the buyer contracted to pay the seller, the buyer may be tempted to try to get out. Some buyers may pretend for a time not to have any requirements at all. Doubtless courts will impose liability when they discover as much.[128] Some buyers have simply sought cheaper *substitute* products. Here the cases point in different directions, some for the buyer[129] and some against him,[130] depending on whether the court finds the buyer to have purchased the substitute in good faith. Presumably if a buyer drastically reduces his requirements solely to cut losses on the very requirements contract in question, a court will hold him in breach.

124. See, e. g., New York Cent. Iron Works Co. v. United States Radiator Co., 174 N.Y. 331, 66 N.E. 967 (1903) (court upheld buyer when his needs more than doubled in a short time and prices rose dramatically).

125. See, e. g., Andrews Coal Co. v. Board of Directors, 151 La. 695, 92 So. 303 (1922).

126. Ehrenworth v. George F. Stuhmer & Co., 229 N.Y. 210, 128 N.E. 108 (1920).

127. See also Anaheim Sugar Co. v. T. W. Jenkins, 274 F. 504 (9th Cir. 1921); Johnston Pie Co. v. Acme Egg & Poultry Co., 74 Cal.App.2d 376, 168 P.2d 762 (2d Dist.1946).

128. See, e. g., Fort Wayne Corrugated Paper Co. v. Anchor Hocking Glass Corp., 130 F.2d 471 (3d Cir. 1942) (dictum).

129. Cf. Southwest Natural Gas Co. v. Oklahoma Portland Cement Co., 102 F.2d 630 (10th Cir. 1939); Helena Light & R. Co. v. Northern Pac. R. Co., 57 Mont. 93, 186 P. 702 (1920).

130. Compare Loudenback Fertilizer Co. v. Tennessee Phosphate Co., 121 F. 298 (6th Cir. 1903), with Southwest Natural Gas Co. v. Oklahoma Portland Cement Co., 102 F.2d 630 (10th Cir. 1939).

Certainly there is dictum to this effect.[131]   Unless the seller has agreed (expressly or impliedly) to bear the risk of market breaks, then a requirements contract should at least protect him against this risk. Code comments are in accord; a reduction "merely to curtail losses" is not in good faith.[132]

A buyer may go out of business altogether and hope to escape a burdensome requirements contract in this way.   But if he only re-organizes the form of his business, a court will surely see through this and hold him liable on the contract.   A court might also hold him liable if he seeks to sell his entire business in a falling market without requiring his purchaser to assume any obligations under the require-ments contract.[133]   There is even authority that a buyer may not de-liberately evade his obligation by simply abandoning his business.[134] Of course, if the buyer is insolvent, his legal liability is unlikely to be worth much.

The seller's case against a buyer who decreases or ceases his re-quirements is all the more appealing when the seller shows he was not able to anticipate the buyer's action and had even expended sig-nificant sums or otherwise relied on promises of the buyer in pre-paring to meet the buyer's needs.   It will also help the seller if he shows that the buyer knew of this reliance.[135]

Yet it is not true that buyers may never decrease or cease their requirements.   Both pre-Code cases and 2–306(1) allow "good faith" reductions and even abandonment.   Thus, it is not bad faith for a buyer to reduce his orders where his own business needs have ac-tually fallen off.[136]   Similarly it is not bad faith to reduce orders be-cause of a decision to take advantage of a technological advance.[137] Nor is it bad faith to cut orders because of new government regula-tions or a strike, or some other event beyond the buyer's control, provided that the buyer did not assume the risk of its occurrence.[138] Doubtless there are other ways to negate bad faith as well.   Who has the burden of proof on the issue of bad faith?   One view is that the party who is to benefit from a showing of bad faith must prove it.[139] Thus a seller claiming breach would have to show that the buyer de-creased his orders in bad faith.

131.  HML Corp. v. General Foods Corp., 365 F.2d 77 (3d Cir. 1966); M. W. Kellogg Co. v. Standard Steel Fabricating Co., 189 F.2d 629 (10th Cir. 1951).

132.  § 2–306, Comment 2.

133.  See, e. g., Texas Indus. v. Brown, 218 F.2d 510 (5th Cir. 1955).

134.  See, e. g., Wells v. Alexandre, 130 N.Y. 642, 29 N.E. 142 (1891).

135.  See, e. g., Diamond Alkali Co. v. P. C. Tomson & Co., 35 F.2d 117 (3d Cir. 1929).

136.  See § 2–306, Comment 2.   Royal Paper Box Co. v. E. R. Apt Shoe Co., 290 Mass. 207, 195 N.E. 96 (1935); Helena Light & R. v. Northern Pac. R., 57 Mont. 93, 186 P. 702 (1920).

137.  See, e. g., Southwest Natural Gas Co. v. Oklahoma Portland Cement Co., 102 F.2d 630 (10th Cir. 1939).

138.  See, e. g., Cragin Prods. Co. v. Fitch, 6 F.2d 557 (8th Cir. 1925).

139.  See HML Corp. v. General Foods Corp., 365 F.2d 77 (3d Cir. 1966).

Section 2–306(1) limits a buyer to reductions that are not "unreasonably disproportionate to any normal or otherwise comparable prior requirements." Does this language preclude good faith reductions that are highly disproportionate to normal prior requirements? Presumably not. Even drastic good faith reductions are not unreasonably disproportionate.[140]

### § 3–9   Mandatory Terms Under Article Two—Limits on Freedom of Contract

The parties can, by agreement, displace most provisions of Article Two. This is certainly so of all gap filler provisions.[141] But certain other provisions are exceptions to the general principle of freedom of contract prevailing in Article Two. Section 1–102(3) provides that the parties may not "disclaim" their Code obligations of "good faith, diligence, reasonableness and care." Some provisions explicitly state that they cannot be varied by contrary agreement.[142] A number of others explicitly state they are variable.[143] These types pose no problem. But what of the sections that are not specifically flagged as variable or nonvariable?

It is clear that some of these provisions cannot be varied by agreement, despite the general green light in section 1–102(3) and the statement in the comments that the "residual rule is that the effect of all provisions of the act may be varied by agreement." [144] An obvious example is section 2–201 on the Statute of Frauds; the comments state that this section is not variable even though the text is silent.[145] An equally obvious example of a nonvariable provision not so flagged is 2–302 on unconscionability. Section 2–719(3) on unconscionable remedy limitations is also unflagged. Not all unflagged provisions are obviously nonvariable. On the contrary, most are obviously variable. Yet if the unflagged provisions include some that are variable and some that are not, and if the unflagged provisions are not all obviously one or the other, then it becomes necessary to articulate criteria for deciding the less obvious cases. For example, can the parties dispense with the notice of breach required by 2–607 (3)(a)? May they vary the burden of proof imposed by 2–607(4)? To date there is very little case law on this general problem, and we can only offer a general approach. Article Two embodies a general presumption that, absent a strong countervailing policy, the contract language of the parties should prevail.[146] But what should count as a

---

140. As yet there are no cases directly in point. Cf. Romine, Inc. v. Savannah Steel Co., 117 Ga.App. 353, 160 S.E.2d 659, 5 UCC Rep.Serv. 103 (1968); Note, Requirements Contracts Under the Uniform Commercial Code, 102 U.Pa.L.Rev. 654, 664–66 (1954).

141. See Sections 3–5 to 3–8 supra.

142. See, e. g., §§ 1–102(3); 1–105(2); 1–204(1); 2–210(1); 2–318; 2–718(1); 2–719(3).

143. See, e. g., §§ 2–206; 2–305; 2–306 (2); 2–307; 2–308; 2–309; 2–310; 2–311; 2–503; 2–504; 2–507; 2–509; 2–511.

144. § 1–102, Comment 3.

145. § 1–102, Comment 2.

146. § 1–102.

strong countervailing policy? One clue would be to consider whether the explicitly nonvariable provisions of Article Two reflect any general policies which the draftsmen considered strong enough to override any provisions of the parties to the contrary. Several general policies are immediately apparent. For example, several of the nonvariable provisions of Article Two are intended to prevent one party from taking undue advantage of the other, as by striking an unconscionable bargain,[147] unfairly upsetting justifiable reliance,[148] or acting in bad faith.[149] Judged by this criterion, an unflagged provision requiring notice of breach, such as 2–607(3)(a), ought not to be considered variable. Without the notice afforded by section 2–607(3), a seller might find himself relatively defenseless against a claim for consequential damages. Absent notice, he might not have any opportunity to inspect the consequences of the alleged breach, and evidence thereof might thus be left entirely in the province of the alleged aggrieved party. But with such notice, the seller might have been able to take steps to minimize his damages.[150] Thus, to allow a buyer to impose a "no notice" clause on the seller in the teeth of section 2–607 might be to permit the buyer to take undue advantage of the seller in the event of breach, a result in conflict with a general policy underlying a number of the explicitly nonvariable provisions of Article Two.

But the category of strong overriding policies includes more than just those policies that groups of explicitly nonvariable provisions have in common. Some unflagged provisions are doubtless nonvariable quite without regard to whether they manifest a policy reflected in a group of explicitly nonvariable provisions. For example, several Code sections purportedly protect the interests of third parties.[151] In earlier drafts of 1–102, a subsection provided that "[e]xcept as otherwise provided by this Act the rights and duties of a third party may not be adversely varied by an agreement to which he is not a party or by which he is not otherwise bound."[152] This subsection was eventually deleted only because it was thought unnecessary. Thus, while most of Article Two's specific third party protection provisions are unflagged, they should plainly be considered nonvariable. Consider a further type: those sections designed to serve some basic economic policy of similarly broad social significance but which do not directly concern third parties. For example, it can be argued that the parties ought not to be permitted to vary 2–709 by agreement to allow the seller to recover the price in just any case he wishes

---

**147.** § 2–302.

**148.** See, e. g., § 2–609(1).

**149.** § 1–203.

**150.** See, e. g., Texas Motor Coaches v. A. C. F. Motors Co., 154 F.2d 91 (3d Cir. 1946).

**151.** E. g., §§ 2–210(1); 2–403; 2–502; 2–702.

**152.** A case decided under this section is Girard Trust Corn Exch. Bank v. Warren Lepley Ford, Inc., 12 Pa.D. & C.2d 351, 1 UCC Rep.Serv. 495 (C.P. 1957).

so to stipulate.   Section 2–709 restricts the action for the price in the interest of preventing economic waste.   As Llewellyn put it: [153]

> .   .   .   But then decently admeasured damages are all a seller needs, and are just what a seller needs, when the mercantile buyer repudiates.   It is, indeed, social wisdom .   .   .   [to require the seller] in most cases which have not involved shipment to a distant point, to dispose of whatever goods may have come into existence or into his warehouse; that is its business, and the buyer's prospective inability has already been evidenced.   To force such goods on the buyer, where they are reasonably marketable by the seller, is social waste.   .   .   .

Despite the generality of 2–718 and 2–719, a court could justifiably refuse to enforce a contract clause giving the seller the price against a distant buyer where the goods never left the seller's warehouse and the seller could have readily resold them for a reasonable sum.[154]

The foregoing, then, represents a suggested approach that courts might take in deciding whether a policy behind a provision is of the kind that renders it nonvariable.   It should be added that 1–102(3) states that the "obligations of good faith, diligence, reasonableness and care prescribed by this Act may not be disclaimed by agreement." Thus the Code imposes these obligations in every contract for the sale of goods.   But section 1–102(3) goes on to say that "the parties may by agreement determine the standards by which the performance of such obligations is to be measured if such standards are not manifestly unreasonable."

153.   Llewellyn, Through Title to Contract and a Bit Beyond, 15 N.Y.U.L.Q. 159, 176–77 (1938).

154.   Cf. Frank Le Roux, Inc. v. Burns, 4 Wash.App. 165, 8 UCC Rep.Serv. 818 (1971).

# CHAPTER 4

# UNCONSCIONABILITY

*Analysis*

Sec.
4–1. Introduction.
4–2. Unconscionability in General.
4–3. Procedural Unconscionability.
4–4. Substantive Unconscionability.
4–5. —— Excessive Price.
4–6. —— Remedy Meddling.
4–7. Relation of Procedural to Substantive Unconscionability.
4–8. Form of Relief.

## § 4–1  Introduction

In an early draft of this chapter we attempted to discuss all of the legal doctrines courts use in policing sales. By "policing" we meant a court's refusal to enforce all the terms of a contract, or its award of damages against the naughty party to the contract either because that party engaged in fraud or kindred conduct in procuring the other party's agreement or because the terms as agreed upon were oppressive, contrary to public policy, or illegal. We soon discovered that a radically diverse array of legal doctrine fits under the "policing" umbrella. Not only do fraud and unconscionability fit there but so do the tort of misrepresentation, some warranty liability, illegality, and various statutory duties that the federal Consumer Credit Protection Act,[1] the Retail Installment Sales Acts, and the Uniform Consumer Credit Code impose. Despite our best efforts, we were unable to tame all of this doctrine—certainly not for purposes of a single chapter in this book. The task demands a book of its own. Here we can only catalogue most of the policing doctrines as a prelude to digging into the U.C.C. unconscionability section at length. These opening paragraphs on cognate policing doctrines will remind the reader that unconscionability is only one member of a large family of doctrines that restrict unbridled freedom of contract and protect against numerous forms of advantage taking.

Fraud is a most ancient and well-recognized doctrine [2]—one that is at least a first cousin to the doctrine of unconscionability—but today law schools, treatise writers, lawyers, and courts are in their own ways neglectful of fraud theory. Indeed it is now common place for lawyers to sue for breach of warranty and negligence, and entirely omit a count in fraud even when that theory might be the most plausible avenue of relief. Unlike unconscionability, the gist of which is often said to be *defensive*, fraud is often a plaintiff's weapon as well as a defendant's. Presumably most fraud is more

---

1. 15 U.S.C.A. §§ 1601–1681 (1970).

2. See W. Prosser, Law of Torts § 105 (4th ed. 1971).

heinous than unconscionable conduct and would also constitute unconscionable behavior that could be attacked under 2–302, but the reverse is not necessarily true. To prove fraud, one typically must show that the misstatement or other behavior of the defendant (*1*) related to a material matter of fact, (*2*) was made deceitfully with intent to induce reliance, (*3*) induced justifiable reliance (*4*) as a result of which the other party suffered damage.[3] Fraud is a case law doctrine and our four part list of elements will not hold true in all states or in all circumstances.

Closely allied to fraud are liability for misrepresentation and for breach of an express warranty. Depending upon local law, the plaintiff's case in fraud or misrepresentation may be identical but this is not necessarily so. The plaintiff may find that he can prove misrepresentation without proof of some of the factors that he must prove in order to sustain a case of fraud.[4] Likewise, express warranty liability flows much more readily from a merely inaccurate statement than does fraud liability.[5]

The Code also offers 1–203, which imposes a general obligation of good faith, as a weapon against various forms of advantage taking.[6] One of us has sought elsewhere to corral that complex obligation.[7] It goes without saying that a lawyer may also invoke various notions long recognized in general contract law, such as undue influence, duress, and mistake to combat contractual over-reaching. Finally, a contract term may be illegal because it violates the usury statutes or the provisions in the Uniform Consumer Credit Code or other statutes which explicitly outlaw certain terms.

No lawyer who seeks to undo a contract or to recover damages on the basis of unconscionability should rely exclusively on that doctrine until he has considered and rejected each of the foregoing possibilities. A careful lawyer who seeks to assert that a contract or term is unconscionable will also test his facts against the various cognate doctrines we have just catalogued. One of your authors believes that the lawyer should also consider the possibility that we are today witnessing the emergence of a new tort that might be called "wrongfully inducing another to contract." The contours of this tort must await more cases; perhaps in the second edition of this book we will devote an entire chapter to it.

## § 4–2    Unconscionability in General

For at least two hundred years equity courts have refused to grant specific enforcement of contracts so unconscionable "as no man

---

3. Id. at 685–86.

4. Id. at 683–85.

5. Id. at 686–87.

6. Section 1–201(19) supplies a general definition of good faith, and section 2–103 imposes an additional standard for merchants in Article Two transactions.

7. Summers, "Good Faith" in General Contract Law and the Sales Provisions of the Uniform Commercial Code, 54 Va.L.Rev. 195 (1968).

in his senses and not under delusion would make on the one hand, and as no honest and fair man would accept on the other." [8]   Section 2–302 of the Uniform Commercial Code has enshrined the doctrine of unconscionability in the statutory law of all but three of our states.[9]   The section reads in full as follows:

(1) If the court as a matter of law finds the contract or any clause of the contract to have been unconscionable at the time it was made the court may refuse to enforce the contract, or it may enforce the remainder of the contract without the unconscionable clause, or it may so limit the application of any unconscionable clause as to avoid any unconscionable result.

(2) When it is claimed or appears to the court that the contract or any clause thereof may be unconscionable the parties shall be afforded a reasonable opportunity to present evidence as to its commercial setting, purpose and effect to aid the court in making the determination.

By way of preamble let us lay out the battlefield upon which the 2–302 battles are being fought.   Most parties who assert 2–302 and virtually all who have used it successfully in reported cases have been consumers.   Most of these successful consumer litigants have been poor or otherwise disadvantaged.   Since much current literature suggests that the low-income consumer is often the victim of sharp practices,[10] it is not surprising that the targets of the unconscionability doctrine are usually plaintiff-creditors and credit sellers.   The courts have not been receptive to pleas of unconscionability by one merchant against another.[11]   Presumably, few busi-

---

8. Earl of Chesterfield v. Janssen, 28 Eng.Rep. 82, 100 (Ch.1750).

9. California and North Carolina omit section 2–302.  Louisiana has not enacted the Code.

10. See, e. g., H. Black, Buy Now Pay Later (1967); D. Caplovitz, The Poor Pay More (1969); W. Magnuson & J. Carper, The Dark Side of the Marketplace (1968).

11. See, e. g., Asco Mining Co. v. Gross Contracting Co., 3 UCC Rep.Serv. 293 (Pa.C.P.1965) (trial court erroneously submitted question to jury);  Sinkoff Beverage Co. v. Jos. Schlitz Brewing Co., 51 Misc.2d 446, 273 N.Y.S.2d 364, 3 UCC Rep.Serv. 733 (Sup.Ct.1966) (unilateral termination clause not unconscionable when utilized against attorney);  Rossotti Lithograph Corp. v. Townsend, 50 Pa.D. & C.2d 451, 8 UCC Rep.Serv. 1217 (C.P.1970) (motion for new trial dismissed because unconscionability not raised as affirmative

defense);  Division of the Triple T Serv., Inc. v. Mobile Oil Corp., 60 Misc.2d 720, 304 N.Y.S.2d 191, 6 UCC Rep.Serv. 1011 (Sup.Ct.1969) (termination clause calling for 90-day notice not unconscionable), aff'd mem., 34 App.Div.2d 618, 311 N.Y.S.2d 961 (2d Dept.1970).  But see Fairfield Lease Corp. v. Umberto, 7 UCC Rep.Serv. 1181 (N.Y.Civ.Ct.1970) (lease agreement containing harsh clauses is unconscionable and unenforceable);  cf. Fairfield Lease Corp. v. George Umbrella Co., 8 UCC Rep.Serv. 184 (N.Y.Civ.Ct.1970) (defendant's motion for summary judgment denied).  See also In re Elkins-Dell Mfg. Co., 253 F.Supp. 864, 3 UCC Rep.Serv. 386 (E.D.Pa.1966) (referee improperly invalidated security agreements solely on basis of terms of contract without considering circumstances);  Fairfield Lease Corp. v. Marsi Dress Corp., 60 Misc.2d 363, 303 N.Y.S.2d 179 (Civ.Ct.1969).  Businessmen receive a more sympathetic reception for claims that damage provisions or warranty disclaimers are

nessmen and middle-class cash purchasers are victims of the kinds of gross advantage-taking that usually calls forth 2–302.

This sketch of the battlefield is only a tentative one based upon appellate reports to date. But one thing is certain—unconscionability is a legal doctrine undergoing rapid evolution. Whatever its meaning (a matter of some difficulty to which we will turn next), and whatever the drafters' intent, section 2–302 embodies an idea whose time has arrived.

Today upwards of a hundred published opinions rely on 2–302 either wholly or in part. Although courts of only six jurisdictions (New York, New Jersey, New Hampshire, District of Columbia, Illinois, and Wisconsin) have actually refused to enforce a contract or term because it violated 2–302, the extensive litigation in New York, the incorporation of the doctrine into the Uniform Consumer Credit Code (sections 5.108 and 6.111), and the new-found judicial and legislative compassion for the consumer all foretell that 2–302 will lead a lively life in the courts in the next few decades.[12]

Before exploring the substance of the unconscionability doctrine, we will consider some of its procedural facets. Subsection (1) assigns the issue of unconscionability exclusively to the judge.[13] At least one court has said that the defendant must plead the issue as an affirmative defense, that is, the court cannot find unconscionability *sua sponte*.[14] Furthermore, the defendant must show that the

unconscionable. See, e. g., Granite Worsted Mills, Inc. v. Aaronson Cowen, Ltd., 29 App.Div.2d 303, 287 N.Y.S.2d 765, 5 UCC Rep.Serv. 98 (1968) (affirming arbitrator's refusal to enforce unconscionable consequential damage clause), rev'd on other grounds, 25 N.Y.2d 451, 255 N.E.2d 168 (1969); Electronics Corp. of America v. Lear Jet Corp., 55 Misc.2d 1066, 286 N.Y.S.2d 711, 4 UCC Rep.Serv. 647 (Sup.Ct.1967) (defendant's motion for summary judgment denied in face of plaintiff's claim of unconscionable warranty limitations); Denkin v. Sterner, 10 Pa.D. & C.2d 203, 1 UCC Rep.Serv. 173 (C.P.1956) (petition to open judgment granted on claim that damage provisions were unconscionable); United States Leasing Corp. v. Franklin Plaza Apartments Inc., 65 Misc.2d 1082, 319 N.Y.S.2d 531, 8 UCC Rep.Serv. 1026 (Civ.Ct.1971) (motion for summary judgment denied on basis of defendant's claim of unconscionable warranty disclaimers). For a discussion of unconscionability in the context of warranty disclaimers and remedy limitations, see Ch. 12 infra.

12. For a sample of the voluminous literature on section 2–302, see Braucher, The Unconscionable Contract or Term, 31 U.Pitt.L.Rev. 337 (1970); Davenport, Unconscionability and the Uniform Commercial Code, 22 U.Miami L.Rev. 121 (1967); Ellinghaus, In Defense of Unconscionability, 78 Yale L.J. 757 (1969); Leff, Unconscionability and the Code—The Emperor's New Clause, 115 U.Pa.L.Rev. 485 (1967); Leff, Unconscionability and the Crowd—Consumers and The Common Law Tradition, 31 U.Pitt.L.Rev. 349 (1970); Murray, Unconscionability: Unconscionability, 31 U.Pitt.L.Rev. 1 (1969); Shulkin, Unconscionability—The Code, The Court and the Consumer, 9 B.C.Ind. & Com.L.Rev. 367 (1968); Spanogle, Analyzing Unconscionability Problems, 117 U.Pa.L.Rev. 931 (1969); Speidel, Unconscionability, Assent and Consumer Protection, 31 U.Pitt.L.Rev. 359 (1970).

13. UCCC § 5.108 similarly reserves these issues for the court, but the Consumer Credit Protection Act, 15 U.S.C.A. §§ 1601–81, 1640 (1970), leaves questions concerning nondisclosure of credit terms to the jury.

14. Asco Mining Co. v. Gross Contracting Co., 3 UCC Rep.Serv. 293 (Pa.C.P. 1965).

contract or clause was unconscionable at the time the contract was made, not just that it was unconscionable by hindsight.[15] The section specifically authorizes three forms of relief: (*1*) the court may refuse to enforce the entire contract, (*2*) or a part of it, or (*3*) the court may limit the application of a particular clause to prevent an unconscionable result. Thus it appears that the doctrine is in the nature of an affirmative defense and is not usually intended as a basis for damage recovery. (There are other and as yet undeveloped possibilities for other remedies such as injunction and punitive damages.) [16]

Subsection (2) permits the alleged oppressor to show that the contract or clause was reasonable in light of the commercial setting. On at least two occasions appellate courts have reversed findings of unconscionability because the trial court failed to offer such an opportunity to the alleged oppressor.[17]

Neither the Code nor the comments define the word *unconscionable*. Comment 1 to 2–302 suggests a litmus test for unconscionability which seems reasonably workable at first glance:

> [W]hether, in the light of the general commercial background and the commercial needs of the particular trade or case, the clauses involved are so one-sided as to be unconscionable under the circumstances existing at the time of the making of the contract.

The comment continues:

> The principle is one of the prevention of oppression and unfair surprise . . . and not of disturbance of allocation of risks because of superior bargaining power.

Experimentation with even a single case shows this litmus to be useless; in no sense is the comment an objective definition of the word. It is simply a string of hopelessly subjective synonyms laden with a heavy "value" burden: "oppression," "unfair," or "one-sided." To the extent that the comment gives a message, it is an ambiguous one, for it acknowledges that the court in some circumstances has the power to overturn various clauses in a contract, but it assures us that the purpose is not to disturb the allocation of risks. How a court can refuse to enforce certain contracts which were formerly enforceable and not at the same time disturb the allocation of the risk because of superior bargaining power, is difficult to see.

The sad fact for lawyers is that neither the Code, the cases, nor the pages of this treatise offer a useful, operational definition

---

15. Sinkoff Beverage Co. v. Jos. Schlitz Brewing Co., 51 Misc.2d 446, 273 N.Y. S.2d 364, 3 UCC Rep.Serv. 733 (Sup. Ct.1966).

16. See notes 90–91, 99–109 and accompanying text infra.

17. In re Elkins-Dell Mfg. Co., 253 F. Supp. 864, 3 UCC Rep.Serv. 386 (E.D. Pa.1966) (remanded to referee in bankruptcy); E. F. Lynch, Inc. v. Piccirilli, 28 Mass.App.Dec. 49, 5 UCC Rep.Serv. 830 (1964).

of unconscionability.   However, the writings of Professor Leff [18] and others suggest a framework for the analysis of unconscionability problems, and the case law which is growing like Topsy is beginning to give meaning to the concept in certain circumstances and to suggest those general areas in which the courts will be moved to find unconscionability.   Professor Leff has distinguished between "bargaining naughtiness" (procedural unconscionability) and overly harsh terms (substantive unconscionability).[19]   Substantive unconscionability involves those one-sided terms of a contract from which a party seeks relief (for instance, "I have the right to cut off one of your child's fingers for each day you are in default"), while procedural unconscionability deals with the process of making a contract— "bargaining naughtiness" (for instance, "Just sign here; the small print on the back is only our standard form").   Each of these branches of unconscionability has common-law cousins; procedural unconscionability looks much like fraud or duress during contract formation, and substantive unconscionability reminds us of contracts or clauses contrary to public policy or illegal.   The two branches of unconscionability can perhaps best be seen in Williams v. Walker-Thomas Furniture Co.,[20] an early, and still the preeminent, case concerning section 2–302.

Although *Walker-Thomas* arose in the District of Columbia before the UCC had become effective in that jurisdiction, Judge Skelly Wright noted that Congress had enacted 2–302, and he relied upon it in his decision.   The appellant Mrs. Williams was a welfare mother with seven children and a monthly income of $218; she had purchased $1800 of merchandise from Walker-Thomas over a period of several years.   For each purchase Mrs. Williams signed an installment contract which included a highly complex cross-collateral agreement.   This device provided that each payment would be credited pro rata to all purchases which Mrs. Williams had ever made from the store and which she had not paid for in full.[21]   In other words, until the customer reduced her balance to zero, the store retained a security interest in every item it had sold her.   Mrs. Williams' last purchase was a stereo set which cost $514.95.   After she had paid the store more than $1400, Mrs. Williams defaulted, and the store filed an action to replevy all the items it had sold her.   The trial court granted the judgment, and the Municipal Court of Appeals affirmed.

18.  Leff, Unconscionability and The Code—The Emperor's New Clause, 115 U.Pa.L.Rev. 485 (1967).

19.  Id. at 487.

20.  350 F.2d 445, 2 UCC Rep.Serv. 955 (D.C.Cir. 1965).

21.  The cross-collateral clause reads as follows:

The amount of each periodical installment payment to be made by [purchaser] to the Company under this present lease shall be inclusive of and not in addition to the amount of each installment payment to be made by [purchaser] under such prior leases, bills or accounts; *and all payments now and hereafter made by [purchaser] shall be credited pro rata on all outstanding leases, bills and accounts* due the Company by [purchaser] at the time each such payment is made.

Id. at 447, 2 UCC Rep.Serv. at 956 (emphasis added by the court).

The Circuit Court of Appeals reversed the lower courts' holdings and remanded for findings on the issue of unconscionability.[22]

In discussing the standards courts must apply to determine whether a contract is unconscionable, Judge Wright touched upon both aspects of unconscionability:

> Unconscionability has generally been recognized to include an absence of meaningful choice on the part of one of the parties together with contract terms which are unreasonably favorable to the other party.[23]

A "meaningful choice" or its absence presumably bears upon procedural unconscionability; to characterize a clause as "unreasonably favorable" to one party is probably to say that it is substantively unconscionable to the other party.

## § 4–3  Procedural Unconscionability

A judicial finding of lack of "meaningful choice," that is, of procedural unconscionability, is usually founded upon a recipe consisting of one or more parts of assumed consumer ignorance and several parts of seller's guile.  In *Walker-Thomas*, Judge Wright emphasized the defendant's lack of education and the use of fine print by the seller in his contract form.[24]  The cross-collateral clause the seller used in that case is so hard to understand that it regularly baffles first year law students who have occasion to read it in their contracts course.  In Jefferson Credit Corp. v. Marcano,[25] a buyer who had "at best a sketchy knowledge of the English language"[26] signed an automobile installment sales contract which waived the implied warranties of merchantability and fitness for a particular purpose.  The court found "it can be stated with a fair degree of certainty"[27] that the buyer neither knew nor understood that he had made such waivers, even though they were printed in large black type.[28]

Thus, the assumption of consumer ignorance may, among other things, be based upon his proven inability to read the language in which the contract was printed, his proven lack of education or upon his status as a poor person.  One can question whether such middle-

22. Id. at 450, 2 UCC Rep.Serv. at 960.

23. Id. at 449, 2 UCC Rep.Serv. at 958.

24. Id.

25. 60 Misc.2d 138, 302 N.Y.S.2d 390, 6 UCC Rep.Serv. 602 (Civ.Ct.1969).

26. Id. at 141, 302 N.Y.S.2d at 393, 6 UCC Rep.Serv. at 605.

27. Id. at 141, 302 N.Y.S.2d at 393–94, 6 UCC Rep.Serv. at 605.

28. Other cases involving non-English speaking consumers include: Kabro Constr. Corp. v. Carire, 2 CCH Poverty L.Rep. ¶10,808 (N.Y.Civ.Ct. Jan. 7, 1970); Central Budget Corp. v. Sanchez, 53 Misc.2d 620, 279 N.Y.S.2d 391, 4 UCC Rep.Serv. 69 (Sup.Ct.1967); Frostifresh Corp. v. Reynoso, 52 Misc. 2d 26, 274 N.Y.S.2d 757, 3 UCC Rep. Serv. 1058 (Dist.Ct.1966), rev'd per curiam, 54 Misc.2d 119, 281 N.Y.S.2d 964, 4 UCC Rep.Serv. 300 (App.Term. 1967) (to allow reasonable profit, service and finance charges in addition to cost).  See notes 34–43 and accompanying text infra.

class assumptions of the ignorance of ADC mothers are warranted, but courts willingly seem to indulge such assumptions. Seller's guile often takes the form of a clause difficult to understand and placed in fine print on the rear of the contract. But it may also take the form of fraud, sharp practice, high pressure salesmanship, and so on.

Explicit in this recipe of procedural unconscionability, of course, is the proposition that a clause procedurally unconscionable with respect to one person may not be unconscionable with respect to another who is better endowed with intelligence and education, or the monetary trappings from which courts will infer such intelligence and education. Several troublesome points lay just beneath the surface in those opinions which discuss procedural unconscionability. The opinions often emphasize the lack of bargaining power on the part of the consumer-debtor. Although these statements have usually been made in opinions dealing with consumers who are ignorant, poor, or both, the courts have not limited their discussion of bargaining power to such circumstances, and of course, even an intelligent middle-class consumer has little bargaining power in a one-on-one situation against a sizeable organization.[29] The middle-class consumer's bargaining power presumably derives from his ability to shop and, if necessary, to whipsaw his sellers by using the offer of one as a bargaining lever against another. One can hope that courts will not be carried away by the "bargaining power" and "fine print" language of some of the opinions and so strike down the terms of garden variety contracts signed by middle-class consumers. Certainly, the draftsmen did not intend 2–302 to invalidate such contracts wholesale. Although there may be good reason for departure from our fictional assumptions that a consumer who signs a long contract knows its terms, in general such a departure should be made by the legislatures after due consideration of the consequences and not by judicial stretching of the unconscionability doctrine.

## § 4–4   Substantive Unconscionability

Passing to the question of substantive unconscionability, what do the cases disclose? Most of the cases in which the courts have found clauses to be substantively unconscionable can be lumped under one of two headings: excessive-price cases and cases in which the creditor unduly restricted the debtor's remedies or unduly expanded his own remedial rights. Here we will consider only the cases falling under these headings. Doubtless other similarly significant categories of cases are just around the corner.

---

**29.** Cf. Henningsen v. Bloomfield Motors, Inc., 32 N.J. 358, 161 A.2d 69 (1960), in which the New Jersey Supreme Court held that a middle-class automobile purchaser had no real bargaining power when all auto manufacturers disclaim warranties on form contracts. This was not a section 2–302 case.

## § 4–5   Substantive Unconscionability—Excessive Price

The preeminent case holding that excessive price can render a contract unconscionable is American Home Improvement, Inc. v. MacIver.[30]   MacIver, who may well have been a skin-flinted New England Scotchman, signed an installment contract for the installation of windows and home siding.   When the seller sued for payment, the court held that the contract was unenforceable because the seller had failed to comply with a state disclosure statute [31] and, alternatively, because the excessive price rendered the contract unconscionable. The court accepted the defendant's allegation that the goods sold and services rendered were worth $959 and concluded that the additional $800 of commission and $809 of finance charge resulted in an excessive price.[32]   The court also noted that the buyers "received little or nothing of value" since the plaintiffs did not perform the contract.[33]

In the second price case, Frostifresh Corp. v. Reynoso,[34] a Spanish-speaking consumer purchased a freezer for a total time price of $1,145.88.   The defendants signed an installment contract written in English, but the salesman neither translated nor explained the contract to them.   The cash sales price for the freezer was $900 and its wholesale cost to the plaintiff had been $348.   Without citing either *Walker-Thomas* or *MacIver*, the court found under 2–302 "that the sale of the appliance at the price and terms indicated in this contract is shocking to the conscience." [35]   The court was also influenced by the fact that the salesman had advised the buyers that the appliance would cost them nothing because they would be paid bonuses or commissions of $25 on each of the sales which were made to their friends.

Three other New York cases have reaffirmed the *Frostifresh* decision, and a New Jersey case has followed it.   In State ex rel. Lefkowitz v. ITM, Inc.[36] the court enjoined a comprehensive referral sales scheme which included price-value disparities comparable to that in the *MacIver* case.   The prices charged in the retail installment contracts varied from two to six times the seller's unit costs, and the purchase price-market value ratio ranged to $2\frac{1}{2}$.[37]   Jones v. Star Credit Corp.[38] held that:

> under the circumstances of this case, the sale of a freezer unit having a retail value of $300 for $900 ($1,439.69 includ-

**30.**   105 N.H. 435, 201 A.2d 886, 2 UCC Rep.Serv. 235 (1964).

**31.**   Id. at 438–39, 201 A.2d at 888, 2 UCC Rep.Serv. at 237.

**32.**   Id. at 439, 201 A.2d at 888, 2 UCC Rep.Serv. at 237.

**33.**   Id. at 439, 201 A.2d at 889, 2 UCC Rep.Serv. at 238.

**34.**   52 Misc.2d 26, 274 N.Y.S.2d 757, 3 UCC Rep.Serv. 1058 (Dist.Ct.1966), rev'd on issue of relief, 54 Misc.2d 119,

281 N.Y.S.2d 964, 4 UCC Rep.Serv. 300 (App.Term 1967).

**35.**   52 Misc.2d at 27, 274 N.Y.S.2d at 759, 3 UCC Rep.Serv. at 1059.

**36.**   52 Misc.2d at 39, 275 N.Y.S.2d 303, 3 UCC Rep.Serv. 775 (Sup.Ct.1966).

**37.**   Id. at 53, 275 N.Y.S.2d at 320, 3 UCC Rep.Serv. at 792.

**38.**   59 Misc.2d 189, 298 N.Y.S.2d 264, 6 UCC Rep.Serv. 76 (Sup.Ct.1969).

ing credit charges and $18 sales tax) is unconscionable as a matter of law.[39]

The purchaser had very limited financial resources and that fact was known to the door-to-door salesman. According to the court this difference in financial status of seller and buyer caused a "gross inequality of bargaining power."[40] In a third case, Central Budget Corp. v. Sanchez,[41] because "[e]xcessively high prices may constitute unconscionable contractual provisions within the meaning of Sec. 2–302,"[42] the plaintiff-assignee was denied summary judgment on his automobile sales contract action so that the defendant might present evidence showing unconscionability of price.[43]

Toker v. Westerman [44] follows the familiar pattern of a defendant who purchased an appliance from a door-to-door salesman at a very high price. In that case the defendant had purchased a refrigerator-freezer for a cash price of $899.98. The total price including interest, insurance, *etc.* was $1,229.76. At trial an appliance dealer had testified that the freezer in question was known in the trade as a "stripped unit" and that a reasonable retail price at the time of the sale would have been between $350.00 and $400.00. The holding of the court rests exclusively on excessiveness of the price, and it reads as follows:

> Suffice it to say that in the instant case the court finds as shocking and therefore unconscionable, the sale of goods for approximately two and one-half times their reasonable retail value. This is particularly so where, as here, the sale was made by a door-to-door salesman for a dealer who therefore would have less overhead expense than a dealer maintaining a store or showroom.[45]

The foregoing cases clearly do not mark the end of the development of the idea that excessive price can render a contract un-

---

39. Id. at 191–92, 298 N.Y.S.2d at 266, 6 UCC Rep.Serv. at 78–79.

40. Id. at 192, 298 N.Y.S.2d at 267, 6 UCC Rep.Serv. at 79.

41. 53 Misc.2d 620, 279 N.Y.S.2d 391, 4 UCC Rep.Serv. 69 (Civ.Ct.1967).

42. Id. at 621, 279 N.Y.S.2d at 392, 4 UCC Rep.Serv. at 70.

43. Id. at 622, 279 N.Y.S.2d at 393, 4 UCC Rep.Serv. at 71.
    A trial court in New Jersey found an excessive price to be unconscionable in a case in which the price charged for a freezer was more than 2½ times its fair market value. Toker v. Perl, 103 N.J.Super. 500, 247 A.2d 701, 5 UCC Rep.Serv. 1170 (Law Div.

1968). However, this was an alternative holding since the court also found that the contract was unenforceable because it had been procured by fraud —the buyers believed that they were contracting only for food, but in fact the salesman procured their signatures on a contract for a freezer also. On appeal, the Superior Court, Appellate Division, affirmed solely on the ground of fraud and refused to express an opinion on the unconscionability question. 108 N.J.Super. 129, 260 A.2d 244, 7 UCC Rep.Serv. 194 (App.Div.1970).

44. 113 N.J.Super. 452, 274 A.2d 78, 8 UCC Rep.Serv. 798 (Dist.Ct.1970).

45. Id. at 454, 274 A.2d at 80, 8 UCC Rep.Serv. at 799–800.

conscionable. This idea is also embodied in the UCCC,[46] and one suspects that it may be the unarticulated premise that explains cases such as *Walker-Thomas*. Certainly excessiveness of price will continue to be an important battle ground in the unconscionability war.

Determining which prices are "excessive" and which are not is an uncertain task since a court may use any one of several possible standards to measure price. The price might be said to be excessive because it returns too great a profit to the seller, or because it yields too great a return on the seller's invested capital, or because it is a substantially higher price than other merchants similarly or unsimilarly situated charge for like items. The courts in *MacIver* and *Frostifresh* used the crudest of all suggested tests: a price may be excessive merely because the mark-up is very large.[47] In *MacIver* the court determined that the price was excessive simply because the defendants were obligated to pay $2,568.60 for goods and services whose wholesale value was $959.00.[48] The New Hampshire court apparently did not consider whether the seller made any profit or what other merchants charged for comparable siding.

In three other cases, State ex rel. Lefkowitz v. ITM, Inc.,[49] Jones v. Star Credit Corp.,[50] and Toker v. Westerman,[51] courts found prices to be excessive because they were higher than those charged by other merchants for the same or similar goods.[52] In *Westerman* the buyer proved that prices of competitors were lower. In *Jones* the court noted that the consumers were obligated to pay $1,439.69 ($539.60 of which was finance charges) for a refrigerator which

---

46. UCCC § 6.111(3) (c).

47. In *Frostifresh* the court stated that "[t]he service charge, which almost equals the price of the appliance is in and of itself indicative of the oppression which was practiced on these defendants." 52 Misc.2d at 27, 274 N.Y.S.2d at 759, 3 UCC Rep.Serv. at 1059.

In General Motors Acceptance Corp. v. Thomas, 2 CCH Poverty L. Rep. ¶ 11,306, No. 68–MI–166065 (Cook City Cir.Ct. Mar. 19, 1970), an Illinois trial court appears to have taken the vaguest approach of all. In that case plaintiff finance company, upon defendant's default, repossessed and sold a car purchased under a retail installment contract. The court held that the plaintiff could not recover the deficiency balance on the ground that the contract was unconscionable and unenforceable under section 2–302 because the car was not in good working order.

48. 105 N.H. at 439, 201 A.2d at 888, 2 UCC Rep.Serv. at 238. The court's method of determining the value of the goods and services was at best questionable. The sloppiness of the decision can perhaps be explained partially by the failure of plaintiff's attorney to file a brief.

49. 52 Misc.2d 39, 275 N.Y.S.2d 303, 3 UCC Rep.Serv. 775 (Sup.Ct.1966).

50. 59 Misc.2d 189, 298 N.Y.S.2d 264, 6 UCC Rep.Serv. 76 (Sup.Ct.1969).

51. 113 N.J.Super. 452, 274 A.2d 78, 8 UCC Rep.Serv. 798 (Dist.Ct.1970).

52. A lower court in a third case, Toker v. Perl, 103 N.J.Super. 500, 247 A.2d 701, 5 UCC Rep.Serv. 1171 (Law Div. 1968), aff'd on other grounds, 108 N.J. Super. 129, 260 A.2d 244, 7 UCC Rep. Serv. 194 (App.Div.1970), also found a price to be excessive by comparing it to prices charged by other stores. See notes 42–43 and accompanying text supra.

was sold for $300 by W. T. Grant stores.[53]  Similarly, in *ITM* it was shown that appliances were being sold by the door-to-door salesmen at two to three times the prices charged at stores in the same shopping center in which defendant's offices were located.[54]

If section 2–302 is not to run merchants out of low income locations, it is unfair to compare the ghetto seller's prices to those of the suburban seller without some adjustment for the substantially different costs, terms and conditions.[55]  Any standard which is adopted must give the ghetto merchant due consideration for his added credit risks and for other legitimate expenses which are greater than those experienced by the suburban merchant.  Thus, some have suggested that a court should only compare the prices of similar goods sold by similar sellers under similar circumstances.[56]  Indeed, section 6.111(3) (c) of the UCCC has set up the following test:

> gross disparity between the price of the property or services sold or leased and the value of the property or services measured by the price at which similar property or services are readily obtainable in credit transactions by like buyers or lessees  .   .   .

The difficulty with this test is that both the defendant seller and the one whose prices set the standard may be making monopoly profits.  By establishing some permissible net return on invested capital or net profit on each sale after taxes as the standard, the courts could enable ghetto merchants to charge prices high enough to make a living without exploiting unsophisticated shoppers.  Of course, such a standard would not be without its drawbacks.  In the first place the ghetto merchant might make his net profit appear to be less than it really is by paying excessive salaries to himself and his relative-employees or by otherwise distorting his expenses.  Second the party asserting the unconscionability defense would be required to bear a nearly impossible factual burden if he had to prove that the opposing party made an excessive profit on the sale in order to win.

The case of Patterson v. Walker-Thomas Furniture Co.[57] well illustrates the difficulties facing a defendant-buyer who attempts to sustain a claim of excessive price.  In that case, the court affirmed the trial court's denial of defendant's request for interrogatories, for a subpoena *duces tecum*, and for the appointment of a special master or expert witness to establish the value of the goods.  The appellate court found that excessive price would be an element of un-

---

53.  59 Misc.2d at 190, 298 N.Y.S.2d at 265, 6 UCC Rep.Serv. at 77 ; interview with George Nager, attorney for plaintiffs, March, 1970.  This was a suit for declaratory relief by the buyers.

54.  Interview with Mark Walsh, Office of the Attorney General, New York State, March, 1970.

55.  It should be noted that only two of the excessive price cases, *Jones* and *Frostifresh*, involved ghetto neighborhoods.

56.  It appears that in *Jones*, *ITM*, and *Toker* the courts employed this narrower comparison.

57.  277 A.2d 111, 9 UCC Rep.Serv. 27 (D.C.Ct.App.1971).

conscionability and that certain aspects about the price were discoverable, but it held:

> An unsupported conclusory allegation in the answer that a contract is unenforceable as unconscionable is not enough. Sufficient facts surrounding the "commercial setting, purpose and effect" of a contract at the time it was made should be alleged so that the court may form a judgment as to the existence of a valid claim of unconscionability and the extent to which discovery of evidence to support that claim should be allowed.[58]

The court goes on to discuss "fraud, duress or coercion" at the time of making the contract and states that such facts must be alleged to permit discovery of matters having to do with excessive price. If those are not the necessary allegations, it is unclear from the opinion what the defendant must allege in his answer in order to entitle him to discovery on the question of excessive price.

A reasonable alternative to placing the entire burden of establishing excessive price on the party asserting unconscionability would be for the court to allow that party to make out a *prima facie* case either by showing a markup of two or three times, or by showing that the price at which the product was sold was two or three times greater than at least one other available price—in the ghetto or elsewhere. Indeed, in the four cases in which courts have found prices to be unconscionably excessive under section 2–302, the contract price to "market value" ratio has varied from 2:1 to 3:1.[59] After the buyer makes out his *prima facie* case, then the plaintiff-merchant would be permitted under 2–302(2) to rebut the buyer's case by showing that his net return or net profit was not excessive.

Judicial thinking on excessive price is still in the embryonic stage; it is certain that the issue of price will loom large in the unconscionability recipe, but the standard by which "excessiveness" is to be measured is far from settled.

---

58. Id. at 114, 9 UCC Rep.Serv. at 31.

59. The *Frostifresh* case did not discuss market value but did show that there was a $552 mark-up from the seller's cost of $348. 52 Misc.2d at 27, 274 N.Y.S.2d at 759, 3 UCC Rep.Serv. at 1059. It is reasonable to assume that the market value of the refrigerator was no more than $450, half the $900 purchase price. In Toker v. Perl, 103 N.J.Super. 500, 247 A.2d 701, 5 UCC Rep.Serv. 1171 (Law Div.1968), where the purchase price was $900 for a refrigerator, and in Jones v. Star Credit Corp., 59 Misc.2d 189, 298 N.Y.S.2d 264, 6 UCC Rep.Serv. 76 (Sup.Ct. 1969), where the purchase price was $900, the market value was found to be only $300 each.

Students of comparative law may be struck by the similarity of this 2:1 ratio to the Roman civil law doctrine of *laesio enormis*. This Christian moralistic doctrine, which goes back to the days of Diocletian (Corpus Juris Civilis, C. 4.44.2) allowed rescission of a contract whenever the value of an item equalled less than half the price. See Dawson, Economic Duress and the Fair Exchange in French and German Law, 11 Tul.L.Rev. 345, 364–66 (1937).

### § 4–6  Substantive Unconscionability—Remedy Meddling

Allegedly unconscionable remedy meddling is the other big battleground in the case law to date.  A creditor-seller's contractual meddling with his own and his buyer's rights and remedies upon default can take a variety of forms.  Typically, a credit seller will attempt to set liquidated damages for nonacceptance,[60] limit his liability for consequential damages,[61] and disclaim some or all of his warranty liability.[62]  He also may include a waiver of defense clause,[63] and if the sale is on secured credit, he may include a clause which gives him a right to repossess if he "deems himself insecure." [64] In addition there are a variety of other more egregious examples such as consent to jurisdiction of a court far distant from the buyer's home.

The Code invites judicial scrutiny of liquidated damages clauses. Section 2–718(1) provides, in part, "A term fixing unreasonably large liquidated damages is void as a penalty."  In an early Code case, the trial court struck down a liquidated damage clause on the ground that it was unconscionable.[65]  More recently, a Wisconsin trial court dismissed a car dealer's action to recover liquidated damages for nonacceptance, amounting to twenty percent of the contract price.[66]  Among other things, the court found that the liquidated damages clause was unconscionable under section 2–302 because the parties had unequal bargaining power arising from the fact that most car dealers impose similar clauses and thus eliminate the buyer's freedom of choice.

The Code also explicitly incorporates the unconscionability concept into 2–719(3) as follows:

> Consequential damages may be limited or excluded unless the limitation or exclusion is unconscionable.  Limitation of consequential damages for injury to the person in the case of consumer goods is prima facie unconscionable but limitation of damages where the loss is commercial is not.

There are also cases holding that warranty disclaimers are to be tested against 2–302.[67]  Judicial hostility to disclaimers is, of course, understandable.  What is somewhat surprising is that the

---

60.  See § 2–718.

61.  See § 2–719(3) discussed in Sections 12–8 through 12–12 infra.

62.  See § 2–316 discussed in Sections 12–2 through 12–6 infra.

63.  See § 9–206(1).

64.  See § 1–208 discussed in Ch. 26 infra.

65.  Denkin v. Sterner, 10 Pa.D. & C.2d 203, 1 UCC Rep.Serv. 173 (C.P.1956). While the court applied the Code and

used the word "unconscionable," it did not refer to section 2–302.

66.  Hult Chevrolet, Inc. v. Meier, 2 CCH Poverty L.Rep. ¶ 10,283, No. 124–489 (Wis.Cir.Ct.1969).  The court also found that the contract violated a Wisconsin truth-in-selling statute and a statute setting five percent as a liquidated damages ceiling for nonacceptance.

67.  For a discussion of warranty disclaimers and 2–302, see Section 12–11 infra.

courts feel free to analyze these cases under 2–302 and without any reference whatsoever to section 2–316. Section 2–316 could easily be construed as an explicit and statutory definition of unconscionability in the disclaimer area which the draftsmen carved out and set down in some detail because they well realized that this would be an area of dispute between buyers and sellers, and they did not wish to leave courts free to make inconsistent and nonuniform judgments on their own under 2–302.[68]

It is not clear from the cases whether counsel for sellers have argued that 2–316 applies to the exclusion of 2–302, but it is clear from the cases cited in the comments to 2–302 that the draftsmen envisioned the possibility that 2–302 would apply. Moreover the courts have so far applied 2–302 here. Indeed, the court in Electronics Corporation of America v. Lear Jet Corp.[69] held that even business buyers must be given the right to present proof that a complete disclaimer was unconscionable. In Jefferson Credit Corp. v. Marcano[70] the court said that a disclaimer that arguably complied with 2–316 was ineffective because of 2–302:

> It is my opinion that the lack of equality between the bargaining parties, the contract clauses under which the defendants unwittingly and unknowingly waived both the warranty of merchantability and the warranty of fitness for the purpose for which the motor vehicle was purchased and the defective condition of the motor vehicle, are sufficient to render the contract unenforceable under the provisions of the Uniform Commercial Code, Sec. 2–302 as between Francisco and Maria Marcano and the Fiesta Motors Corp.[71]

In that case the defendants, who could read only Spanish, had signed a printed form of a retail installment contract which limited all warranties to a thirty-day guarantee. The car was defective but the dealer managed to persuade the buyers to keep the car for thirty days. After that time he denied any further responsibility.[72] Of course the court could have reached the same result on the basis of

---

68. See Section 12–11 infra.

69. 55 Misc.2d 1066, 286 N.Y.S.2d 711, 4 UCC Rep.Serv. 647 (Sup.Ct.1967). The New York court was applying Massachusetts law in this case, but the Code was in effect in both states.

70. 60 Misc.2d 138, 302 N.Y.S.2d 390, 6 UCC Rep.Serv. 602 (Sup.Ct.1969).

71. Id. at 142, 302 N.Y.S.2d at 394–95, 6 UCC Rep.Serv. at 606.

72. When the buyers defaulted on the payments, the car was repossessed by the plaintiff, the dealer's assignee. The assignee sold the car to the dealer at a private sale six months after the purchase for one-fourth its original cost. While these facts were sufficient to prevent the dealer from enforcing the contract, the plaintiff in the case was the assignee. Thus the court had to go on to hold under section 9–504(5) that the "sale" by the assignee to the assignor (dealer) was a transfer, not a sale, of the collateral from a secured party to the guarantor. Id. at 148, 302 N.Y.S.2d at 345–46, 6 UCC Rep.Serv. at 608. Therefore, the assignee gave up its rights with the transfer and could not enforce the obligation.

2–316 by simply holding that the disclaimer of implied warranty of merchantability was not sufficiently "conspicuous" to a non-English reading party and was therefore ineffective under 2–316.

In Unico v. Owen [73] the New Jersey Supreme Court used 2–302 to strike down a waiver of defense clause in a retail installment sale contract which had been assigned to a finance company. Defendants had signed a contract to purchase 140 stereo albums and a stereo set from the Universal Stereo Corporation for a total price of $849.72. The seller immediately assigned the contract and note to Unico, but delivered only twelve albums and the stereo before it became insolvent. When the buyers refused to make any additional payments, the assignee, Unico, sued them on the note and on the contract. The court construed the language of 9–206(1)—"subject to any statute or decision which establishes a different rule for buyers or lessees of consumer goods"—to authorize its determination that waiver-of-defense clauses are unconscionable.[74]

A series of New York cases have refused to enforce clauses in consumer sales contracts which grant exclusive jurisdiction to a court distant from the consumer's home.[75] Another New York case, Robinson v. Jefferson Credit Corp.,[76] found unconscionable conduct on the part of the seller which took place after contract formation. Because it deemed itself insecure, the assignee of a retail installment contract refused to return a repossessed car after collecting past due payments, late charges, and repossession fees from the buyer. The court held that this refusal was unconscionable because it did not meet the standard of commercially reasonable conduct.[77]

It is hardly surprising that the Code provisions on remedies and limitations of remedies have caused so much conflict. It is here that the smiling salesman most easily puts one over on the consumer at a time when neither the salesman nor the consumer contemplates default. Surely this kind of litigation will increase in volume and intensity as consumers become better represented and more aggressive.[78] Doubtless other patterns of substantive unconscionability will

---

73.  50 N.J. 101, 232 A.2d 405, 4 UCC Rep.Serv. 542 (1967).

74.  Id. at 125, 232 A.2d at 418, 4 UCC Rep.Serv. at 560.

75.  Paragon Homes, Inc. v. Carter, 56 Misc.2d 463, 288 N.Y.S.2d 817, 4 UCC Rep.Serv. 1144 (Sup.Ct.1968), aff'd per curiam, 30 App.Div.2d 1052, 295 N.Y. S.2d 606, 5 UCC Rep.Serv. 991 (2d Dep't 1968), relied solely on section 2–302. Paragon Homes of New England, Inc. v. Langlois, 4 UCC Rep. Serv. 16 (N.Y.Sup.Ct.1967), and Paragon Homes of Midwest, Inc. v. Crace, 4 UCC Rep.Serv. 19 (N.Y.Sup.Ct.1967), reached the same conclusion through the doctrine of *forum non conveniens* and in dicta.

76.  4 UCC Rep.Serv. 15 (N.Y.Sup.Ct. 1967).

77.  Id. at 16.

78.  Recently the New York City Civil Court upheld an installment contract in which the obligee reserved the right to enter a judgment without notice in event of nonpayment. Gimbel Bros., Inc. v. Swift, 62 Misc.2d 156, 307 N. Y.S.2d 952, 7 UCC Rep.Serv. 300 (Civ. Ct.1970). In the course of the opinion, the court laid out an interesting test for section 2–302:

The doctrine of unconscionability is not a charter of economic anarchy . . . . A promisor can be relieved of his obligation . . . only when the transaction affronts the sense of

also develop; we do not suggest that price and remedies are the end of the story.

## § 4–7  Relation of Procedural to Substantive Unconscionability

Almost all of the foregoing cases exhibit creditor behavior that may be regarded as both procedurally and substantially unconscionable. At the very least the clause upon which the seller or creditor relies is printed on his own form, often on the back in small print, and the seller rarely calls it to the buyer's attention. Frequently, as in Jefferson Credit Corp. v. Marcano,[79] the consumer is poorly educated, and sometimes the contract is not even in his own language.

Two problems not yet resolved by existing case law are these: First, it is not clear whether some form of procedural unconscionability must be present for a court to find a clause or contract unconscionable at all within the meaning of 2–302. Second, and on the other hand, it is not clear whether "superconscionable" procedural conduct (that is, big print or different colored print for tough clauses) will take the curse off what would otherwise be a substantively unconscionable contract term under 2–302.

It is at least arguable that the courts in American Home Improvement v. MacIver[80] and Toker v. Westerman[81] found contracts unconscionable without any evidence of procedural unconscionability. In MacIver the buyers were apparently middle-class homeowners living in New Hampshire. Although an alternative holding relies on the fact that there were blanks in the contract at the time the party signed, there is no suggestion that the buyer was misled by these blanks or that the blanks were improperly filled in at a later time. In Toker v. Westerman there is no suggestion of procedural unconscionability whatever.[82]

Most courts take a "balancing approach" to the unconscionability question, and to tip the scales in favor of unconscionability, most courts seem to require a certain quantum of procedural plus a certain quantum of substantive unconscionability. At least one case, Patterson v. Walker-Thomas Furniture Co., Inc.,[83] may hold that ex-

---

decency without which business is mere predation and the administration of justice an exercise in bookkeeping.

62 Misc.2d at 158, 307 N.Y.S.2d at 954, 7 UCC Rep.Serv. at 301.

79.  60 Misc.2d 138, 302 N.Y.S.2d 390, 6 UCC Rep.Serv. 602 (Civ.Ct.1969). See notes 25–29 and accompanying text supra.

80.  105 N.H. 435, 201 A.2d 886, 2 UCC Rep.Serv. 235 (1964). See notes 30–33 and accompanying text supra.

81.  113 N.J.Super. 452, 274 A.2d 78, 8 UCC Rep.Serv. 798 (Dist.Ct.1970).

82.  See also Milford Finance Corp. v. Lucas, 45 Mass.App.Dec. 53, 8 UCC Rep.Serv. 801 (Mass.App.1970) (case remanded; court found it unnecessary to decide whether excessive price alone is sufficient for a finding of unconscionability).

83.  277 A.2d 111, 9 UCC Rep.Serv. 27 (D.C.Ct.App.1971).

cessive price alone is insufficient. After denying defendant's appeal in that case, the court concluded as follows:

> It cannot be said that the goods were grossly overpriced merely from an examination of the prices which appear on the face of the contracts. No other term of the contract is alleged to be unconscionable, nor is an absence of a meaningful choice claimed. *We hold that the two elements of which unconscionability is comprised; namely, an absence of meaningful choice and contract terms unreasonably favorable to the other party, must be particularized in some detail before a merchant is required to divulge his pricing policies* through interrogatories or through the production of records in court. An answer, such as the one here, asserting the affirmative defense of unconscionability only on the basis of the stated conclusion that the price is excessive is insufficient.[84]

It is not clear from the quoted holding whether excessive price alone is never enough. The court might only be saying that the allegations and the proof were insufficient. In our view the court holds that one must show some procedural unconscionability and that a high price, no matter how excessive, is not sufficient in and of itself. Finally it appears that a contract that is one hundred pounds substantively unconscionable may require only two pounds of procedural unconscionability to render it unenforceable and vice versa. If our interpretation of Patterson v. Walker-Thomas, on the one hand, and *MacIver* and *Westerman,* on the other, is accurate, the cases are in conflict. We favor the latter interpretation, namely, that excessiveness of the price is alone a sufficient basis for finding a contract unconscionable.

The courts have not yet given a clear answer to the question whether a creditor can make a substantively harsh clause enforceable by prominently placing it in the contract or by having the purchaser separately initial it. Certainly there is support in the Code (for instance, sections 2–316 and 2–209) for validating a clause that would be unenforceable if buried in fine print by making it conspicuous or by specifically focusing the consumer's attention on it. But it is unlikely that any device, short of a jack-in-the-box, can really capture the consumer's undivided attention. Given his notorious unwillingness to read his contracts and given that the consumer-buyer will usually see the contract for the first time after he has decided to buy the product, it seems most unlikely that big print and contrasting colors will do much to change the consumer's behavior. If our only goal is to reveal the sad state of his rights to him at the outset, but not actually to afford him relief from that status, then separate initialling should be sufficient to remove the curse from an

---

84.  Id. at 114, 9 UCC Rep.Serv. at 32
(emphasis added).

otherwise unconscionable contract. However, courts doubtless delude themselves when they assume that the prominence of a printed clause brings it to the buyer's attention and thus gives him a more "meaningful choice."

## § 4–8    Form of Relief

When the equity courts found contracts to be unconscionable, they refused specific enforcement.[85] The remedial tools available to a modern court under section 2–302 are of a similar equitable nature: the court may refuse to enforce the entire contract, it may refuse to enforce an unconscionable term, or it may limit the application of the terms so as to avoid an unconscionable result. Since the cases which have held contracts to be unconscionable have so far involved buyers for the most part, the most common obligation the courts have refused to enforce has been the payment of the contract price.

Courts occasionally have refused in terms to enforce contracts *in toto*. However in one of these cases, Jefferson Credit Corp. v. Marcano,[86] the defendants had already partially performed by making payments. Two other cases involved anticipatory repudiation. In Kabro Construction Corp. v. Carire [87] and Hult Chevrolet, Inc. v. Meier,[88] the sellers sought to enforce liquidated damage clauses against consumers who breached retail-installment contracts before any goods or services had been provided. Thus, while some courts have refused to require obligees of unconscionable contracts to pay the full contract price, these obligees have not received the benefit of the contracts without expense.[89]

In State ex rel. Lefkowitz v. ITM, Inc.,[90] a whole series of retail installment contracts which were part of a comprehensive scheme were declared unenforceable under 2–302 through an action brought by the Attorney General pursuant to a New York statute.[91] This type

---

85.   See Earl of Chesterfield v. Janssen, 28 Eng.Rep. 82 (Ch. 1750).

86.   60 Misc.2d 138, 302 N.Y.S.2d 390, 6 UCC Rep.Serv. 602 (1969). See notes 25–29 and accompanying text supra. The defendants had paid over $600 toward the total contract price of $4100 plus $300 finance charges. The court refused to enforce the contract in Toker v. Perl, 103 N.J.Super. 500, 247 A.2d 701, 5 UCC Rep.Serv. 1171 (Law Div.1968). However, on appeal the unconscionability issue was held to be unnecessary to the final determination. 108 N.J.Super. 129, 260 A. 2d 244, 7 UCC Rep.Serv. 194 (App.Div. 1970). See note 43 supra.

87.   2 CCH Poverty Law Rep. ¶ 10,808 (N.Y.Civ.Ct. Jan. 7, 1970). This case also involved a construction of 2–718.

88.   2 CCH Poverty Law Rep. ¶ 10,283, No. 124–489 (Wis.Cir.Ct. 1969). This case also involved state statutes regarding "truth-in-selling" and limitations on automobile sales penalty clauses. See note 66 and accompanying text supra.

89.   While the seller did not perform at all in American Home Improvement Co. v. MacIver, 105 N.H. 435, 201 A.2d 886, 2 UCC Rep.Serv. 235 (1964), it is not clear whether the buyers had made any payments.

90.   52 Misc.2d 39, 275 N.Y.S.2d 303, 3 UCC Rep.Serv. 775 (Sup.Ct.1966). See notes 36–37 and accompanying text supra.

91.   Id. at 41, 275 N.Y.S.2d at 309, 3 UCC Rep.Serv. at 776.

of injunctive decree, in which a seller is enjoined from enforcing unconscionable contracts, can be useful to buyers since they need only plead as a defense facts showing that the particular transaction conforms to the circumstances involved in the injunctive proceeding. In many instances, of course, the buyers will have already made a significant number of payments under the contract.

In a few cases, courts have limited their relief to nullifying only a single term of a contract. Thus in Unico v. Owen,[92] a waiver of defense clause was not enforced, and in Paragon Homes, Inc. v. Carter[93] a clause subjecting the parties to a foreign jurisdiction was nullified. The result in each case, however, was that the court refused to enforce any part of the contract. In *Unico*, without the waiver of defense clause the assignee was left subject to a valid defense to the entire obligation. Finding itself without jurisdiction in *Paragon Homes*, the New York court dismissed the entire action. Thus, relief from a single term can be a totally effective remedy for the defendant.

In 1663 an English court had before it a party who had been tricked into agreeing to pay one hundred pounds for a horse worth only eight. The court required him only to pay the reasonable value.[94] Under 2–302 modern courts have likewise reformed contracts in order to avoid unconscionable results. For example, the trial court in Frostifresh Corp. v. Reynoso[95] ruled that because the total price of $1,145.88 for a refrigerator-freezer was unconscionable, the buyer would only be obligated to pay $348, the seller's cost. However the appellate court ruled that the seller was entitled to the net cost plus a reasonable profit, necessary expenses, and reasonable finance charges.[96] Jones v. Star Credit Corp.[97] took a slightly different approach. Finding that the buyers had already paid over $600 towards a freezer with a retail value of $300, the court "reformed and amended" the contract "by changing the payments called for therein to equal the amount of payment actually so paid."[98] The result is thus similar to that achieved in cases where courts have refused to enforce contracts on which payments have already been made.

---

92. 50 N.J. 101, 232 A.2d 405, 4 UCC Rep.Serv. 542 (1967). See notes 73–74 and accompanying text supra.

93. 56 Misc.2d 463, 288 N.Y.S.2d 817, 4 UCC Rep.Serv. 1144 (Sup.Ct.1968). See note 75 and accompanying text supra.

94. James v. Morgan, 83 Eng.Rep. 323 (K.B. 1663). The defendant had agreed to pay a barley corn for each nail in the horse's shoe, doubling the number of grains with each nail. The 32 nails resulted in an obligation for four thousand bushels, equal to one hundred pounds sterling.

95. 52 Misc.2d 26, 274 N.Y.S.2d 757, 3 UCC Rep.Serv. 1058 (Dist.Ct.1966), rev'd on issue of relief, 54 Misc.2d 119, 281 N.Y.S.2d 964, 4 UCC Rep. Serv. 300 (App.Term 1967). See notes 34–35 and accompanying text supra.

96. 54 Misc.2d 119, 281 N.Y.S.2d 964, 4 UCC Rep.Serv. 300 (App.Term 1967).

97. 59 Misc.2d 189, 298 N.Y.S.2d 264, 6 UCC Rep.Serv. 300 (App.Term 1967). notes 38–40 and accompanying text supra.

98. 59 Misc.2d at 193, 298 N.Y.S.2d at 268, 6 UCC Rep.Serv. at 80.

An occasional reformation or denial of the price is not an effective method of deterring a seller bent on a pattern of unconscionable behavior. As the New York Court of Appeals stated in relation to sales practices involving actual fraud:

> In the calculation of his expected profits, the wrongdoer is likely to allow for a certain amount of money which will have to be returned to those victims who object too vigorously, and he will be perfectly content to bear the additional cost of litigation as the price for continuing his illicit business.[99]

That court's solution was to allow punitive damages.[100] For the same reasons, it would be desirable to impose punitive damages in certain unconscionability cases.

There are two main barriers to the implementation of such a policy. First, punitive damages are generally not available in an action for breach of contract.[101] This rule, however, relates only to actions seeking compensation for breach. Unconscionability is not a breach, but rather conduct analogous to fraud that renders the agreement void and unenforceable. The rule is well established that punitive damages are appropriate in cases involving malicious, wanton, or reckless fraud.[102] For example, punitive damages were awarded in District Motor Co. v. Rodill [103] when a salesman set back the odometer on a used car and sold it as new. It would be a natural extension of these principles to grant punitive damages in situations where one party engages in behavior that is a first cousin to fraud and knowingly enters into a contract which unconscionably benefits him (as when a refrigerator dealer leads an unsophisticated buyer to believe that the price for the item is a "good deal" when in reality it is two or three times the going market price).[104] Arguably, therefore, the doctrine which bars punitive damage recoveries to contract litigants ought not bar a counterclaim for such a recovery even though defendant asserts unconscionability as a defense to a contract claim.

99. Walker v. Sheldon, 10 N.Y.2d 401, 406, 179 N.E.2d 497, 499 (1961).

100. Id. at 406, 179 N.E.2d at 500.

101. C. McCormick, Law of Damages § 137 (1935); 5 A. Corbin, Corbin on Contracts § 1077 (1964).

102. See Walker v. Sheldon, 10 N.Y.2d 401, 179 N.E.2d 497 (1961); C. McCormick, Law of Damages § 81 (1935); Rice, Exemplary Damages in Private Consumer Actions, 55 Iowa L.Rev. 307 (1969). The Rice article provides a fine background to the use of punitive damages in sales cases. It should be noted that a few states allow punitive damages in cases involving simple fraud. See, e. g., Monroe v. Bankers Life & Cas. Co., 232 S.C. 363, 102 S.E. 2d 207 (1958); Annot., 165 A.L.R. 614 (1946).

103. 88 A.2d 489 (D.C.Ct.App.1952).

104. For arguments opposing the use of exemplary damages in consumer protection cases, see Rice, Exemplary Damages in Private Consumer Actions, 55 Iowa L.Rev. 307, 340 (1969).

Section 1–106(1) of the Code presents a second obstacle:

[N]either consequential or special nor penal damages may be had except as specifically provided in this Act or by other rule of law.

As the New York Appellate Division, First Department has pointed out, section 2–302 does not explicitly provide any damage remedy for victims of unconscionable contracts. For that reason the court denied punitive damage recoveries under 2–302.[105] Thus, any court wishing to award punitive damages for unconscionable conduct will have to rely on section 1–103 [106] and the last phrase in section 1–106 allowing punitive damages when they are authorized by "other rule of law." [107] The court will have to find or make up the "other rule of law," by extrapolation from the fraud cases. Indeed, the New Jersey Supreme Court in Unico v. Owen [108] used similar language in 9–206(1) [109] to provide consumer protection in addition to that specifically delineated by the Code.

**105.** Pearson v. National Budgeting Sys., Inc., 31 App.Div.2d 792, 297 N.Y. S.2d 59, 6 UCC Rep.Serv. 81 (1st Dep't 1969).

**106.** § 1–103 reads as follows:

Unless displaced by the particular provisions of this Act, the principles of law and equity, including the law merchant and the law relative to capacity to contract, principal and agent, estoppel, fraud, misrepresentation, duress, coercion, mistake, bankruptcy, or other validating or invalidating cause shall supplement its provisions.

**107.** The pertinent part of section 1–106 (1) reads as follows: "neither consequential or special nor penal damages may be had except as specifically provided in this Act or by other rule of law."

**108.** 50 N.J. 101, 232 A.2d 405, 4 UCC Rep.Serv. 542 (1967). See notes 73–74 and accompanying text supra.

**109.** § 9–206(1) reads as follows:

Subject to any statute or decision which establishes a different rule for buyers or lessees of consumer goods, an agreement by a buyer or lessee that he will not assert against an assignee any claim or defense which he may have against the seller or lessor is enforceable . . . .

# CHAPTER 5

# RISK OF LOSS

*Analysis*

Sec.
5–1. Introduction.
5–2. 2–509(1), Contracts Contemplating Transportation by Carrier.
5–3. 2–509(2), Goods Held by a Bailee.
5–4. 2–509(3), The Residue.
5–5. 2–510, Effect of Breach on Risk of Loss.
5–6. Subrogation.
5–7. Restrictions and Limitations Upon the Doctrine of Subrogation.
5–8. Contribution—Introduction.
5–9. —— Other Insurance Clauses.
5–10. —— Conflicts Between Other Insurance Clauses.

## § 5–1  Introduction

It is not news that the travel of goods from seller to buyer is today a perilous one in the United States and even more perilous when the goods must travel overseas. The carrier may lose the goods; his employees may injure or destroy them; thieves may steal them and, of course, fire, storm, shipwreck, or other acts of God may take toll. When goods are lost or damaged without the fault of the buyer or seller, the law might allocate the loss between them in a variety of ways. First the law might simply put the loss on the one who suffered it and foreclose him from suing the other party. Such a rule would be rather crude, for it would mean seller would bear the loss in one case and the buyer in another although the circumstances of both were identical, except, for example, that buyer's check had arrived a little sooner in one case than in the other. A second possibility would be to prorate the loss between the parties and ask each to bear part of it. The final possibility, and the one the Code has adopted, is to allocate the entire loss to one party depending upon: (*1*) the parties' agreement, (*2*) whether one party or the other is in breach, and (*3*) the moment in the transaction when the loss occurred.

At the outset one should understand the legal consequences of casting risk of loss on one party or the other. To say that buyer had the risk of loss at the time the goods were destroyed is to say that he is liable under 2–709 for the price. To say that seller had the risk of loss at the time the goods were destroyed is to say that he is liable in damages to the buyer for nondelivery unless he tenders a performance in replacement for the destroyed goods.[1]

---

1. Section 2–613 states an exception for the limited use of goods damaged without fault of either party before risk of loss passes to the buyer and when "the contract requires for its performance goods identified when the contract is made . . . ." In that narrow circumstance section 2–613 frees the seller from his obligation "if the loss is total," and if the loss is

Sections 2–509 and 2–510 are the basic risk of loss provisions in Article Two of the Uniform Commercial Code. The wise lawyer will enter those sections first through 2–509(4) which states in part:

The provisions of this section are subject to contrary agreement of the parties. . . .

The Code invites any lawyer who drafts a contract for the sale of goods to include a clause that specifically allocates the risk of loss between the buyer and the seller. There is no magic in 2–509 and 2–510, and there is no reason why the parties cannot agree to some other allocation. As we will see, the parties may specifically allocate risk by a clause which specifies the allocation in so many words or they may do so by the selection of symbols such as "C.I.F." and "F.O.B.," which under the Code have special risk of loss meaning.

In some ways the basic provisions of 2–509 and 2–510 are the most radical departure from prior law in Article Two. The prior law, section 22 of the Uniform Sales Act, provided in general that the party who had title or property in the goods also had the risk of loss.[2] The usual job of the court in a risk of loss case under the

partial, it gives the buyer the option to treat the contract as voided or to accept the goods with due allowance for the deterioration. That limited exception to the risk of loss rule applies only in the case of "goods whose continuing existence is presupposed by the agreement." § 2–613, Comment 1. It has no application to the typical case in which the seller is selling garden variety goods to a buyer under a usual sale of goods contract.

2. One who would retrace the risk of loss through the Uniform Sales Act had to go first to section 22, then to section 18, and finally to section 19. Section 22 provided that unless the parties otherwise agreed, the goods remained at the seller's risk until "the property therein transferred to the buyer" but that once the property had transferred to the buyer the goods were at the buyer's risk whether "delivery" had been made or not. Section 18 defined the terms used in section 22 by providing that the "property" in "specific or ascertained goods" passed when the contracting parties intended it to pass. Section 19 in turn stated a series of presumptions about the parties' intention with respect to title when that intention was not otherwise made clear. Thus section 22 stated that risk follows "property" (or title), that the property passes normally when the parties intend it to pass, and that the parties' presumed intention is to be found in section 19. The four most important

presumptions or rules contained in section 19 read as follows:

Rule 1. Where there is an unconditional contract to sell specific goods, in a deliverable state, the property in the goods passes to the buyer when the contract is made and it is immaterial whether the time of payment, or the time of delivery, or both, be postponed.

Rule 2. Where there is a contract to sell specific goods and the seller is bound to do something to the goods, for the purpose of putting them into a deliverable state, the property does not pass until such thing be done.

\* \* \*

Rule 4. (1) Where there is a contract to sell unascertained or future goods by description, and goods of that description and in a deliverable state are unconditionally appropriated to the contract, . . . the property in the goods thereupon passes to the buyer . . . . (2) Where, in pursuance of a contract to sell, the seller delivers the goods to . . . a carrier . . . for the purpose of transmission to . . . the buyer, he is presumed to have unconditionally appropriated the goods to the contract, except in the cases provided for in the next rule. . . .

Rule 5. If the contract to sell requires the seller to deliver the goods to the buyer, or at a particular place, or to pay the freight or cost of transportation to the buyer, or to a particular place, the property does not pass until the goods have been deliv-

Uniform Sales Act was therefore to determine whether buyer or seller had title to the goods at the time they were lost, stolen, or destroyed.  If the seller still had title, in general he had to bear the loss and could not recover the price from the buyer; if title had passed, the buyer usually was liable for the price and thus bore the risk.  Who had title and what caused title to pass from the seller to the buyer were often mysteries to both the lawyers and the courts.  These questions were bountiful sources of litigation and controversy.[3]  Speaking before the New York Law Revision Commission, Professor Llewellyn summarized the status of the law under the Uniform Sales Act and set forth his hopes for Article Two:

> May I say one other thing in that connection, and say it without any hesitancy at all for the record?  The number of lawyers who have an accurate knowledge of sales law is extremely small in these United States.  My brother Bacon has taught sales law for 28 years.  When he says it isn't too difficult to determine where the court will decide the title is or isn't or is going to be or should be, he is speaking a truth within limits for people who have taught sales law for 28 years.  I submit to you, sir, that there are not many of them.

> The ordinary lawyer, except for odds and ends of people who have specialized in this field, finds sales law as uncertain and as confused as you yourselves found it, if you are lawyers, when you finished the course in sales and wondered what the deuce you were going to do about an examination in confusion, dealing apparently with confused material and perhaps a confused professor.

> It is a body of law in which we just do not know our way around, and the thing that has been criticized, the elimination of the passing of title or the place where it is to pass, as the vital, focal factor for the courts to think about, is one of the great clarifications that has been offered to the law of these United States over many years.

> The way in which one comes to see that is not by praising the Code.  The way in which one comes to see that is to turn to the only body of truly commercial sales law which operates almost entirely without use of the concept of title.  There you have a body of sales law which is clean, clear, guidesome, which it is almost impossible to misconstrue, and which practically pays no attention to title at all.  That is the law of the C.I.F. contract, and the inspira-

---

ered to the buyer or reached the place agreed upon.

3.  A cursory search for cases turned up fifty-nine pre-Code reported appellate opinions in which a main issue of controversy was the risk of loss question. See, e. g., Midway Motors v. Pernworth, 141 Cal.App.2d Supp. 929, 296 P.2d 130 (1956); Lott v. Delmar, 2 N.J. 229, 66 A.2d 25 (1949); Groves v. Warren, 226 N.Y. 459, 123 N.E. 659 (1919); Parish & Parish Mining Co. v. Serodino, Inc., 52 Tenn.App. 196, 372 S.W.2d 433 (1963); Gillingham v. Phelps, 5 Wash.2d 410, 105 P.2d 825 (1940).

tion of the law of the C.I.F. contract is the inspiration at least to try to bring it home to ordinary sales law, that just doesn't happen to be overseas and confined to a few people; that is what has led to the plan of the Code, working in terms of the facts, what the parties really thought about, and what the issues really are.

So that, far from giving any excuse on behalf of the drafting staff or the supporting organizations for the elimination of the title concept as the center of the sales chapter, we bring it before you as what we conceive to be a true contribution and a true opportunity to bring a difficult, useful troubled body of law within the compass of anybody any time, anyhow.

Speaking to you, sir, as one law teacher to another, I suggest that this is going to be a great contribution to the law students of the United States. I think they can really learn their sales, and learn it fast, if you will give them Article 2.[4]

In Llewellyn's eyes the draftsmen's chief policy was to make the law certain. Above all, 2–509 and 2–510 were to be certain and clear to lawyers and to courts. We believe the draftsmen succeeded admirably. Sections 2–509 and 2–510 have so far produced only a small fraction of the litigation produced under the Uniform Sales Act during a comparable period, and the decisions under 2–509 and 2–510 are generally sound and accurate interpretations of the draftsmen's intent.[5]

---

4. 1 N.Y. State Law Revision Comm'n 1954 Report 160–61 (1954).

5. Section 2–509 has produced only a trickle of cases. See Ellis v. Bell Aerospace Corp., 315 F.Supp. 221, 7 UCC Rep.Serv. 918 (D.Ore.1970) (buyer had not yet received possession of helicopter at time of crash; risk on seller); Electric Regulator Corp. v. Sterling Extruder Corp., 280 F.Supp. 550, 4 UCC Rep.Serv. 1025 (D.Conn.1968) ("F.O.B., Norwalk, Connecticut" rendered contract a "shipment" contract and caused risk to pass at Norwalk notwithstanding instruction for seller to "ship to" addresses supplied by buyer); Ninth St. E., Ltd. v. Harrison, 5 Conn.Cir. 597, 259 A.2d 772, 7 UCC Rep.Serv. 171 (1968) ("F.O.B., shipment" contract passed risk of loss to buyer when seller duly placed the goods in possession of a carrier and made a reasonable contract for their transportation); Whately v. Tetrault, 29 Mass.App.Dec. 112, 5 UCC Rep. Serv. 838 (1964) (arrangement by buy-er's agent with bailee to pick up goods on the following day amounted to an acknowledgment by bailee of buyer's right to possession and cast risk of loss upon buyer while goods were in the possession of bailee); Conte v. Styli, 26 Mass.App.Dec. 73, 4 UCC Rep. Serv. 737 (1963) (since possession had passed to buyer at the time of destruction, buyer liable for the price; court applied the Code but did not cite section 2–509(3)); Deitch v. Shamash, 56 Misc.2d 875, 290 N.Y.S.2d 137, 5 UCC Rep.Serv. 109 (Civ.Ct.1968) (goods which disappeared before completion of tender were at seller's risk; passage of title not relevant); cf. Sandlin v. First Nat'l Bank, 20 Ohio App. 2d 200, 253 N.E.2d 313, 7 UCC Rep. Serv. 31 (1969) (seller who shipped coins to defendant bank at buyer's request had interest in the coins by reason of the sale and dishonor of buyer's check and was entitled to determination of whether defendant had exercised degree of care required of a gratuitous bailee).

Subsidiary policies in 2–509 and 2–510 place the loss upon the one most likely to have insured against it and most likely to take precautions to protect against loss.[6] Usually this will be the party who controls possession of the goods. Under the Uniform Sales Act, however, title—and therefore risk—would often jump to the buyer after the goods had become identified to the contract even though they were still in the seller's possession.[7] Thus, despite the fact that the goods might still be in the seller's warehouse, guarded by the seller's watchman, and covered by the seller's insurance, the risk would often be on the buyer under the Uniform Sales Act. The Code draftsmen altered this rule; in Comment 3 to 2–509 they explained: "[Our] underlying theory . . . is that a merchant who is to make physical delivery at his own place continues meanwhile to control the goods and can be expected to insure his interest in them. The buyer, on the other hand, has no control of the goods and it is extremely unlikely that he will carry insurance on goods not yet in his possession." The draftsman's intent to place the loss on the insurance company itself is further evidenced by the anti-subrogation provisions in 2–510 to be discussed in Section 5–7 below.

Section 2–509 divides sales contracts into three basic categories and provides rules for the allocation of risk of loss in each case.[8]

---

6. § 2–509, Comment 3 reads, in part:

The underlying theory of this rule is that a merchant who is to make physical delivery at his own place continues meanwhile to control the goods and can be expected to insure his interest in them. The buyer, on the other hand, has no control of the goods and it is extremely unlikely that he will carry insurance on goods not yet in his possession.

For an argument that this policy is based on assumptions that are not always valid, see 1 N.Y. State Law Revision Comm'n, 1954 Report 102 (1954). (In some trades merchants customarily do not insure goods which are awaiting delivery.)

7. Under the rules specified in section 19 of the Uniform Sales Act (note 2 supra), the "property" and thus the risk of loss would often pass to the buyer when the goods were put in a "deliverable state" or were "unconditionally appropriated" to the contract by the seller. Goods might reach such a state long before they passed into the buyer's possession. See, e. g., Lott v. Delmar, 142 N.J.Eq. 298, 59 A.2d 832 (1948), aff'd, 2 N.J. 229, 66 A.2d 25 (1949); Groves v. Warren, 226 N.Y. 459, 123 N.E. 659 (1919).

8. Section 2–509 went through only modest change from its appearance in the early drafts to its present form.

In the 1949 draft it read as follows:

Risk of Loss in the Absence of Breach.
(1) Where the contract requires or authorizes the seller to ship the goods
(a) if it does not require him to deliver at destination, the risk of loss passes to the buyer when the goods are duly delivered to the carrier even though the shipment is under reservation; but
(b) if it does require him to deliver at destination the risk of loss passes to the buyer when the goods are there duly tendered. In neither case does risk of loss turn on the time of delivery of documents of title.

(2) Where the case is not within subsection (1) and the goods are not held by a bailee to be delivered without being moved (subsection (4) of Section 2–503), the risk of loss passes to the buyer on his receipt of the goods if the seller is a merchant; otherwise the risk passes to the buyer on tender of delivery.

(3) The provisions of this section are subject to contrary agreement of the parties and to the provisions of this Article on sale on approval (Section 2–327).

Subsection (1) covers those cases in which the "contract requires or authorizes the seller to ship the goods by carrier." Most business contracts for the sale of goods fall within subsection (1). Subsection (2) covers the less frequent cases in which "goods are held by a bailee to be delivered without being moved. . . ." Subsection (3) is the residuary clause which covers all other cases. Important among the cases covered by subsection (3) are those in which the buyer is, by the contract, to pick up the purchased goods at the seller's place of business. Below we will consider each of these categories separately and will dwell on some of the interpretative difficulties that may arise under them. Some of the points we raise below are law school questions only; some are real practical

In 1956 the New York Law Revision Commission criticized the section as follows:

1. It was suggested that it is not clear whether subsection (1) applies where the contract requires seller to deliver the goods by his own truck.

2. The opinion was stated that

(a) In a case where the contract calls for shipment and requires buyer to deliver at destination, risk of loss should not pass to buyer until buyer's receipt of the goods except that if buyer had accepted a document of title covering the goods, risk of loss should pass to the buyer on arrival of the goods at destination.

(b) In a case where the goods are held by a bailee to be delivered without being moved, risk of loss should pass to a buyer only (i) on receipt by the buyer (not tender by seller) of a negotiable document of title or (ii) where seller tenders and buyer receives a nonnegotiable document of title or a direction to the bailee to deliver, at the time (after receipt by buyer of the nonnegotiable document or the direction to the bailee) when buyer notifies the bailee, except that the risk will not pass if the bailee refuses to obey the direction; an express provision to this effect should be incorporated in Section 2–509, and the cross-reference to Section 2–503 deleted;

(c) In a case where the contract does not authorize seller to ship by carrier, and the case is not one where the goods are held by a bailee to be delivered without being moved, the risk of loss should not pass to buyer upon tender, and the time of its passing should not depend on whether seller is a merchant; however, some limitation of a rule holding risk of loss of conforming goods on seller until buyer receives them is desirable;

(d) The clause at the end of subsection (1), "In neither case does risk of loss turn on the time of delivery of documents of title" is confusing, since receipt of the goods may be effected by receipt of documents of title; the clause should be deleted;

(e) In paragraph (a) of subsection (1), a cross-reference to Section 2–505 would be helpful;

(f) In cases where conforming goods are duly rendered and rejected, the risk of loss and the burden of disposing of the goods (or of suffering loss by reason of deterioration or obsolescence) should be located together; the burden of disposition is placed on seller to the extent that his remedy for the price (Section 2–709) is limited, and the rules of Sections 2–509, 2–510 and 2–709 should be harmonized.

(g) The seller should not be permitted to hold indefinitely at buyer's risk conforming goods that were wrongfully rejected. (See Section 2–709(1) (a)).

N.Y.State Law Revision Comm'n, 1956 Report 386 (1956).

Subsection (1) was revised to make clear that it does not apply to "shipment" in the seller's own trucks and to eliminate the confusing postamble. Subsection (2) was inserted to spell out the rules governing risk of loss when the goods were in the hands of a bailee. Subsections (2) and (3) were renumbered (3) and (4) respectively, and a cross reference to section 2–510 was inserted in (4).

In the 1956 draft, section 2–509 appeared in substantially its present form.

difficulties. An analysis of appellate opinions indicates that 2–509 and 2–510 are fulfilling the fondest hopes of the draftsmen.

### § 5–2 2–509(1), Contracts Contemplating Transportation by Carrier

Section 2–509(1) reads in full as follows:

Where the contract requires or authorizes the seller to ship the goods by carrier

> (a) if it does not require him to deliver them at a particular destination, the risk of loss passes to the buyer when the goods are duly delivered to the carrier even though the shipment is under reservation (Section 2–505); but

> (b) if it does require him to deliver them at a particular destination and the goods are there duly tendered while in the possession of the carrier, the risk of loss passes to the buyer when the goods are there duly so tendered as to enable the buyer to take delivery.

One should read 2–509(1) in conjunction with 2–319 on F.O.B. and F.A.S. terms and 2–320 on C.I.F. and C. & F. terms.[9] Some of the provisions of 2–319 and 2–320 are more explicit statements of the generalized terms of 2–509(1).

The usual purchase order and confirmation will contain a statement that the shipment is to be made "F.O.B. seller's place of business," a shipment contract, or "F.O.B. the buyer's place of business," a destination contract. By incorporating trade terms as code symbols in 2–319 and stating their risk of loss consequences in 2–319 and 2–509, the draftsmen have given us a simple solution to the bulk of risk of loss problems. If the contract reads "F.O.B. seller's place of business," 2–319(1) (a) indicates that the seller must there "ship the goods in the manner provided in this Article (Section 2–504) and bear the expense and risk of putting them into the possession of the carrier." Section 2–319(1) (b) tells us that under an "F.O.B. the place of destination" contract, the seller must "at his own expense and risk transport the goods to that place and there tender delivery of them. . . ." The negative implication of the quoted provi-

---

**9.** § 2–319(1) reads as follows:

Unless otherwise agreed the term F.O.B. (which means "free on board") at a named place, even though used only in connection with the stated price, is a delivery term under which

(a) when the term is F.O.B. the place of shipment, the seller must at that place ship the goods in the manner provided in this Article (Section 2–504) and bear the expense and risk of putting them into the possession of the carrier; or

(b) when the term is F.O.B. the place of destination, the seller must at his own expense and risk transport the goods to that place and there tender delivery of them in the manner provided in this Article (Section 2–503);

(c) when under either (a) or (b) the term is also F.O.B. vessel, car or other vehicle, the seller must in addition at his own expense and risk load the goods on board. If the term is F.O.B. vessel the buyer must name the vessel and in an appropriate case the seller must comply with the provisions of this Article on the form of bill of lading (Section 2–323).

sion from 2–319(1) (a), Comment 1 [10] to 2–504, and the decided cases [11] make it clear that the F.O.B. seller's place of business contract is one in which the seller is *not* obliged to deliver at a "particular destination" but rather that such a contract is a "shipment" contract in which the seller's only obligations are to make an appropriate contract for shipment and to get conforming goods into the possession of the carrier. Thus under the provisions of 2–509(1) (a) the risk in such a case passes to the buyer when the goods are "duly delivered to the carrier." Conversely, when the contract reads "F. O.B. *buyer's* place of business," both 2–509(1) (b) and 2–319(1) (b) make it clear that the risk does not pass to the buyer until the goods are tendered to the buyer at the place of destination.

Since the Code has adopted trade symbols already in use by businessmen, one will find only infrequent cases in which businessmen who contemplate transportation have not used those words and have left their lawyers and the courts without a clear legal principle under 2–509 and 2–319 or 2–320. Note that 2–509(1) (a) requires that the seller "duly" deliver the goods to the carrier. If, for example, the seller loads them improperly or if he makes a contract which is not proper under 2–504(a), he does not duly deliver and risk will not pass.[12]

The F.O.B. term in a sales contract controls risk of loss even where another term in the contract instructs the seller to "ship to Omaha." Assume for example a contract between a North Dakota

---

**10.** § 2–504, Comment 1 reads:

The section [2–504] is limited to "shipment" contracts as contrasted with "destination" contracts or contracts for delivery at the place where the goods are located. The general principles embodied in this section [2–504] cover the special cases of F.O.B. point of shipment contracts and C.I.F. and C. & F. contracts. Under the preceding section [2–503] on manner of tender of delivery, due tender by the seller requires that he comply with the requirements of this section [2–504] in appropriate cases.

**11.** See, e. g., Electric Regulator Corp. v. Sterling Extruder Corp., 280 F.Supp. 550, 4 UCC Rep.Serv. 1025 (D.Conn. 1968); Ninth St. E., Ltd. v. Harrison, 5 Conn.Cir. 597, 259 A.2d 772, 7 UCC Rep.Serv. 171 (1968).

**12.** If the seller loads the goods properly and makes a proper contract for their shipment with the carrier but fails to comply with either (b) or (c) of 2–504 (tender of necessary documents and notification of the buyer of shipment) the effect upon the risk of loss is unclear. Certainly one could read the due delivery requirement of 2–509 and the "ship the goods in the manner provided in this Article (Section 2–504)" in 2–319(1) (a) to mean that the seller must comply with all parts of 2–504 before the risk jumps: but that is not a necessary reading of those terms. It is equally plausible to find that risk passes as soon as the goods are delivered even though the seller fails in his duty to notify the buyer. Of course the seller should bear any loss which results from his failure to notify.

Suppose that in contravention of normal trade practices seller ships goods "F.O.B., place of shipment" and fails to "promptly notify" the buyer of the shipment. If the goods are subsequently destroyed under circumstances bearing no causal relationship to the shipper's failure to notify, does the shipper bear the risk? We think not.

Section 2–504 grants the buyer a right of rejection if material loss or delay ensues from the failure to notify, but the Code treats our situation ambiguously. If the buyer had had notice of the shipment, he would have been powerless to prevent the loss, yet he would have borne the risk. We believe the buyer should have the risk in our hypothetical also.

seller and a New York buyer which provides: "F.O.B., N.D. . . . ship to 145 Bank Ave., New York, N. Y. 00001." In such cases buyers have occasionally argued that the "ship to N. Y." term made the contract into a destination contract or, at minimum rendered it ambiguous. The courts have properly rejected these arguments;[13] all shipment contracts must contain a term that tells the seller where he is to ship the goods. He cannot make an appropriate contract for a shipment if the buyer has not told him the place to which to ship them. Thus virtually all contracts properly regarded as shipment contracts because they provide for a term "F.O.B. place of shipment" will also include the name of the destination to which seller is to make a contract for shipment; they remain "shipment" contracts.

A more serious problem under 2–509 is presented by the unusual case in which the sales contract does not contain an F.O.B. term, but contains language that arguably substitutes for that term. Consider, for example, the case in which there is no F.O.B. term but the contract states "seller shall pay freight". The buyer can argue that such a payment term is consistent with an F.O.B. destination contract and that the court should therefore find the contract to be an F.O.B. destination contract. Although the buyer's argument might have prevailed under the Uniform Sales Act,[14] there is ample evidence that the draftsmen of the Code intended a different result. Comment 5 to 2–503 states that the contract in question would normally be regarded as a shipment, not a destination contract, and goes on as follows:

> For the purposes of subsections (2) and (3) there is omitted from this Article the rule under prior uniform legislation that a term requiring the seller to pay the freight or cost of transportation to the buyer is equivalent to an agreement by the seller to deliver to the buyer or at an agreed destination. This omission is with the specific intention of negating the rule, for under this Article the "shipment" contract is regarded as the normal one and the "destination" contract as the variant type. The seller is not obligated to deliver at a named destination and bear the concurrent risk of loss until arrival, unless he has specifically agreed so to deliver or the commercial understanding of the terms used by the parties contemplates such delivery.

13. See, e. g., Electric Regulator Corp. v. Sterling Extruder Corp., 280 F.Supp. 550, 4 UCC Rep.Serv. 1025 (D.Conn. 1968).

14. Under the Uniform Sales Act § 19, Rule 5, the seller was presumed to have retained title and thus the risk if he was obliged to pay the freight. See, e. g., Pulkrabek v. Banker's Mortg. Corp., 115 Ore. 379, 238 P. 347 (1925) (where seller is required to prepay freight, title does not pass until arrival at destination). See also Madeirense Do Brasil S/A v. Stulman-Emrick Lumber Co., 147 F.2d 399 (2d Cir. 1945), cert. denied 325 U.S. 861 (1945) (C. & F. contract an exception to ordinary rule that payment of freight by seller implies that parties intend no passage of title until goods reach destination to which freight is paid).

Thus a contract which contains neither an F.O.B. term nor any other term explicitly allocating loss is a "shipment" contract. This is so although the seller has agreed to pay the shipment cost. Of course there will still be cases in which it will be unclear whether the parties have used terms tantamount to "F.O.B. place of destination" or which otherwise constitute an agreement with respect to risk of loss. In such cases the buyer must show that the included language deviates from the presumed shipment contract. The location of risk in contracts which use language equivalent to "F.O.B. destination" but which fail to employ those precise words is difficult to predict.

The New York Law Revision Commission considered the case in which the seller agrees to absorb only part of the transportation expense. When a seller seeks to meet the competition of another seller nearer to the buyer, this problem may arise as follows: a Gary, Indiana seller competes with a Pittsburgh seller for the east coast market. The Gary seller may quote a price plus freight from Pittsburgh. The commissioners concluded that although the seller's price absorbs part of the transportation expense, he has not agreed to deliver at a particular destination and consequently, under subsection (1) (a) risk passes to the buyer when the goods are "duly delivered to the carrier." [15]

In sum, the parties, in a contract contemplating carriage, must *explicitly* agree to a destination contract by using "F.O.B. buyer's place of business" or equivalent language. Otherwise, the contract will be a "shipment" contract.

A remaining problem of minimal significance in 2–509(1) is that of defining the word "carrier." Section 2–509(1) covers only those cases in which the contract "requires or authorizes the seller to ship the goods by *carrier*." If the contract obliges the seller to ship the goods in his own truck, the risk of loss would be governed by subsection (3) not by subsection (1), for there would be no shipment by carrier. We can conceive highly ambiguous contracts which would lie on the border line between subsection (1) and subsection (3). Consider for example a contract which provides "F.O.B. place of shipment" but also states that the seller would ship in his own truck. If one interprets such a contract to mean that the seller has an option to ship in his own truck, or by carrier, then the contract is under subsection 1 since it is one which at least "authorizes" shipment by carrier. If one decides that the contract obliges the seller to carry the goods himself and prohibits shipment by carrier, the seller might still argue that the "F.O.B. shipping point" term is an agreement by the parties (authorized by 2–509(4)) that risk shifts to buyer when the goods are loaded on seller's truck. If we are to follow the policy of 2–509(3) discussed below we should reject seller's argument.

Since the Code does not define "carrier" it is unclear how far the term reaches.[16] Surely it covers railroads, commercial air car-

15.  1 N.Y. State Law Revision Comm'n, 1955 Report 488 (1955).

16.  Other definitions to which one might turn, such as those in the Interstate

riers, and truckers. Does it also cover the United States mail? Although the United States mail does not normally come to mind when one speaks of a "carrier," we can see no reason why it should not be regarded as a carrier for this purpose. One mailing a package has given up possession and control as fully as one who has shipped by rail; his insurance coverage is not likely to differ greatly in the two cases, and we see no other reason to distinguish them.

## § 5–3  2–509(2), Goods Held by a Bailee

Section 2–509(2) reads in full as follows:

Where the goods are held by a bailee to be delivered without being moved, the risk of loss passes to the buyer

> (a) on his receipt of a negotiable document of title covering the goods; or

> (b) on acknowledgment by the bailee of the buyer's right to possession of the goods; or

> (c) after his receipt of a nonnegotiable document of title or other written direction to deliver, as provided in subsection (4) (b) of Section 2–503.

Although problems do not arise as frequently under subsection (2) as under subsection (1), the courts which have dealt with 2–509(2) have experienced relatively little difficulty.[17]

The only important interpretive difficulties concern the word "bailee" and the interpretation of (2) (c). If one limits his consideration to (2) (c), it will appear that risk of loss passes to a buyer upon his "receipt" (the acquisition of physical possession) of a nonnegotiable document. However, one who takes care to follow out the cross-reference to (4) (b) of section 2–503 finds that "risk of loss of the goods and of any failure by the bailee to honor the nonnegotiable document of title or to obey the direction remains on the seller until the buyer has had reasonable time to present the document or direction . . . ."

The most common circumstance under which subsection (2) will be applied is that in which the goods are in the hands of a professional bailee (for instance, a warehouseman) and the seller passes a negotiable or a non-negotiable document of title covering the goods to the buyer. That case is simple enough. One question remains, however. Can the seller ever be a "bailee" as the word is used in subsection (2)?[18] The facts in a pre-Code case, Courtin v. Sharp,[19] well

Commerce Act, 49 U.S.C.A. § 1(3) (1970), seem aimed at the particular subjects of those acts and offer no reliable basis for analogy.

17. See, e. g., Whately v. Tetrault, 29 Mass.App.Dec. 112, 5 UCC Rep.Serv. 838 (1964).

18. Consider this definition in section 7–102(1) (a): "'Bailee' means the person who by a warehouse receipt, bill of lading or other document of title acknowledges possession of goods and contracts to deliver them."

The choice of the word "bailee" in a section full of references to buyers and sellers and the presence of subsection 2–509(3) to deal with the case in which seller possesses goods already bought by buyer both suggest that the word "bailee" does not include sellers in possession.

19. 280 F.2d 345 (5th Cir. 1960).

illustrate the problem. There seller had reached an agreement with buyer for the sale of a colt. The parties had agreed that the seller would hold the colt for the buyer and, depending upon the terms of the payment of the price, would or would not charge him a fee for stabling the colt. The colt was killed without any fault on the part of the seller, and the seller sued the buyer for the purchase price. In such a case the seller could certainly argue that he was a bailee and that risk had passed since he had acknowledged the buyer's "right" to possession of goods under (2) (b). The case would be a particularly appealing one for that argument if the seller were receiving payment from the buyer for the boarding of the horse.

We believe that such an interpretation of the word bailee should be rejected by the courts, and except in circumstances which we cannot now conceive, a seller should not ever be regarded as a bailee. To allow sellers in possession of goods already sold to argue that they are bailees and that the risk of loss in such cases is governed by subsection (2) would undermine one of the basic policies of the Code's risk of loss scheme. As we have pointed out, the draftsmen intended to leave the risk on the seller in many circumstances in which the risk would have jumped to the buyer under prior law. The theory was that a seller with possession should have the burden of taking care of the goods and is more likely to insure them against loss.

If we accept such sellers' arguments, that is, that they are bailees under subsection (2) because of their possession of the goods sold or because of a clause in the sale's agreement, we will be back where we started from, for in bailee cases the risk jumps under (2) (b) on his "acknowledgment" of the buyer's right to possession. By hypothesis our seller has acknowledged the buyer's right and is simply holding the goods at buyer's disposal. Thus, to accomplish the draftsmen's purpose and leave risk on the seller in possession, we believe that one should find only non-sellers to be "bailees" as that term is used in 2–509(2). Notwithstanding the fact that a seller retains possession of goods already sold and that he has a term in his sale's contract which characterizes him as a "bailee," we would argue that he is not a bailee for the purposes of subsection (2) of 2–509 and would analyze his situation under subsection (1) or subsection (3) of 2–509.

## § 5–4   2–509(3), The Residue

Section 2–509(3) reads in full as follows:

> In any case not within subsection (1) or (2), the risk of loss passes to the buyer on his receipt of the goods if the seller is a merchant; otherwise the risk passes to the buyer on tender of delivery.

The subsection sets out two rules: one for merchant sellers and another for nonmerchant sellers.[20] In the former case, the risk re-

---

**20.** Section 2–104 defines merchant as follows:

(1) "Merchant" means a person who deals in goods of the kind or otherwise by his occupation holds himself out as having knowledge or skill peculiar to the practices or goods involved in the transaction or to whom

mains on the seller until the buyer "receives" the goods.[21]  Receipt in this case means taking physical possession of the goods (2–103(1) (c) ), and thus a merchant seller who retains physical possession may bear the risk of loss long after title has passed and long after he has received his money.  Note that this would also cover the case in which the seller ships in his own truck and does not use a carrier.  Although 2–103(1) (c) defines receipt as "taking physical possession," one may still find interpretative difficulties if he digs deeply enough into that language.  For example, could one argue in Courtin v. Sharp [22] that when the seller agreed to board the horse for a fee, he had commenced to act as the buyer's agent and had so "received" the goods?  Clearly a buyer could receive goods through an agent; presumably all corporate buyers can only receive through the acts of their human agents.  Courtin v. Sharp presents such an appealing case for that argument that we are afraid to predict how it might come out.  Courts considering such questions should keep in mind the policy of the Code to retain the risk on the insured seller, and except in extraordinary cases, as for example those when the buyer and seller formally change their relationship and buyer pays the seller to keep an item, they should not find receipt on behalf of the buyer in the acts of the seller.

Finally, we reiterate that 2–509 is subject "to contrary agreement of the parties" and to the provisions "on sale or approval." [23] The parties will often wish to spell out their rights with respect to loss in their sales contracts.  These attempts at private legislation should be recognized and carried out by the courts.[24]

## § 5–5   2–510, Effect of Breach on Risk of Loss

The draftsmen never clearly articulated why the party in breach should bear the risk of loss in certain circumstances when he would not bear that risk were he not in breach.[25]  Apart from the curb-

---

such knowledge or skill may be attributed by his employment of an agent or broker or other intermediary who by his occupation holds himself out as having such knowledge or skill.

**21.**  See Ellis v. Bell Aerospace Corp., 315 F.Supp. 221, 7 UCC Rep.Serv. 918 (D.Ore.1970) (buyer had not received possession of goods at time of destruction ; risk on seller).

**22.**  280 F.2d 345 (5th Cir. 1960).

**23.**  § 2–509(4) reads as follows:

The provisions of this section are subject to contrary agreement of the parties and to the provisions of this Article on sale on approval (Section 2–327) and on effect of breach on risk of loss (Section 2–510).

**24.**  In unusual circumstances, a contract term in fine print which casts

an unexpected burden on an ignorant party might be held unconscionable. Between businessmen who are able to insure against nearly all risks, the court should be most hesitant to find a risk allocating clause to be unconscionable.

**25.**  § 2–510 reads as follows:

(1) Where a tender or delivery of goods so fails to conform to the contract as to give a right of rejection the risk of their loss remains on the seller until cure or acceptance.

(2) Where the buyer rightfully revokes acceptance he may to the extent of any deficiency in his effective insurance coverage treat the risk of loss as having rested on the seller from the beginning.

(3) Where the buyer as to conforming goods already identified to the

stone equity of the provision and the statutory and case law tradition of placing the loss on one who was in breach,[26] it is not clear why breach by one party dictates a deviation from the rules of 2–509. Note that 2–510 is considerably out of phase with the policies of 2–509. First, it places the risk of loss on the one who does not have possession, who does not have control, and who, in the circumstances there covered, would be least likely to insure.   To some extent this result under 2–510 is mitigated by the fact that it will not operate in certain circumstances when the party seeking to invoke it has insurance to cover the loss.[27]   Second, because 2–510's application turns on such difficult legal judgments as whether the goods conform, and whether there has been a repudiation, it conflicts with the basic policy of 2–509, to set down clear and certain rules.

Whatever the policy that supports 2–510, it has produced little appellate litigation.[28]   Under subsection (1) risk of loss will remain

contract for sale repudiates or is otherwise in breach before risk of their loss has passed to him, the seller may to the extent of any deficiency in his effective insurance coverage treat the risk of loss as resting on the buyer for a commercially reasonable time.

**26.**  The Uniform Sales Act made breach specifically relevant only when delivery was delayed by the fault of a party.  Section 22(b) of the Sales Act reads:

Where delivery has been delayed through the fault of either the buyer or the seller the goods are at the risk of the party in fault as regards any loss which might not have occurred but for such fault.

See, e. g., Shilling v. Campbell, 38 Ill.App. 2d 180, 186 N.E.2d 782 (1962) (buyer's failure to pick up soybeans placed them at his risk); Baltimore & O. R. R. Co. v. Carter, 133 Md. 551, 105 A. 760 (1919) (seller may recover for goods lost while awaiting inspection by buyer where it appears the loss would not have occurred but for buyer's failure of duty); Schenning v. Devere & Schloegel Lumber Co., 173 Wis. 20, 180 N.W. 136 (1920) (buyer is responsible for loss caused by his failure to give timely shipping instructions).

**27.**  See Section 5–7 infra.

Professor John Honnold discussed the matter before the New York Law Revision Commission:

Subsection (3) of Section 2–510 is much more revolutionary.  It reads as follows:

(3) Where the buyer as to conforming goods already identified to

the contract for sale repudiates or is otherwise in breach before risk of their loss has passed to him, the seller may to the extent of any deficiency in his effective insurance coverage treat the risk of loss as resting on the buyer.

This provision would drastically change present law and to a substantial extent would undercut other provisions of the Code which were designed to place the risk of loss on the person who is in possession of the goods.  Its scope is enhanced by the ease with which the Code permits goods to be "identified" to a contract prior to delivery or shipment.  Unlike present law, under Section 2–501 of the Code identification can be performed by seller alone and without assent by buyer.  Under the Code, seller's setting goods aside for buyer prior to shipment or delivery and without notification to or other contact with buyer would constitute "identification".

Section 2–510(3), it will be noted, contains the crucial provision that after such identification, if buyer "repudiates or is otherwise in breach," buyer will bear the risk of loss to the extent that seller is uninsured.  The impact of this provision can best be seen with the aid of concrete examples.

1 N.Y. State Law Revision Comm'n, 1955 Report 496 (1955).

**28.**  The only reported cases which we have found are McKnight v. Bellamy, 248 Ark. 27, 449 S.W.2d 706, 7 UCC Rep.Serv. 287 (1970) (buyer entitled to return of purchase price of goods lost while they were in seller's possession after seller had breached); William F. Wilke, Inc. v. Cummins Diesel En-

(until there has been cure or acceptance) on the seller who makes a tender or delivery so defective as to give "a right of rejection." The operation of this subsection is well illustrated by William F. Wilke, Inc. v. Cummins Diesel Engines, Inc.[29]

Only one quirk of significance remains in 2–510(1). The subsection causes risk to remain on seller only when seller's nonconformity is serious enough to give the buyer a right of rejection. Nonconformities which do not substantially impair installment contracts and defects in tender which result from the seller's having made an improper shipment contract but which do not cause substantial delay (2–504) do not give a right of rejection and are therefore not sufficient to cause the risk of loss to remain on the seller.[30] That is simple enough until one compares the language of 2–510 with that in 2–709 on the action for the price. Above we have suggested that 2–709 must be read together with the risk of loss provisions since if the risk has passed to the buyer and the goods are destroyed, he is then liable for the price under 2–709(1) (a). To pose our problem, assume a case in which the seller ships goods that are part of an installment contract and contain an insubstantial defect under an F.O.B. shipment contract. Since the buyer has no right to reject (2–612), the risk passes to him under 2–509, and 2–510(1) does not interfere with that passage. The seller would have a cause of action for the price against the buyer if the goods were destroyed *en route*. Unfortunately, however, 2–709(1) (a) gives a cause of action only in the case in which "conforming goods" are lost or damaged. By hypothesis the goods in question were not conforming, and there's the rub. Sections 2–509 and 2–510 say that the risk is on the buyer, but 2–709 deprives seller of the usual mode of recovery.[31]

The proper result is for a court to bend 2–709(1) (a) to conform to the apparent intention of the draftsmen and allow the seller to recover the price in cases in which defective goods are destroyed,

gines, Inc., 252 Md. 611, 250 A.2d 886, 6 UCC Rep.Serv. 45 (1969) (seller who had delivered nonconforming goods bore risk of loss in absence of proof that damage was owing to any negligence on part of buyer); Portal Galleries, Inc. v. Tomar Products, Inc., 60 Misc.2d 523, 302 N.Y.S.2d 871, 6 UCC Rep.Serv. 1047 (Sup.Ct.1969) (seller who had manifested intention to abandon the contract and had rendered it unenforceable could not hold buyer liable in damages for difference between value of paintings covered by contract and destroyed in fire and an alleged deficiency in effective insurance coverage).

29. 252 Md. 611, 250 A.2d 886, 6 UCC Rep.Serv. 45 (1969).

30. Note that section 2–510(1) comes into action only upon a breach such as "to give a right of rejection."

31. This ellipsis apparently resulted when section 2–510 was modified in response to New York Law Revision Commission criticism; thus the risk remained on seller only when the nonconformity was serious enough to give a right to reject. See 1 N.Y. State Law Revision Comm'n, 1955 Report 494 (1955). Section 2–709 should have been modified to accommodate this change. The seller should have been authorized to recover the price of goods destroyed unless they were so defective as to entitle buyer to reject.

provided the defect is not one which would give rise to a right to a reject.

Section 2–510(2) throws the risk back upon the seller's shoulders when the buyer "rightfully revokes acceptance." [32] The section seems simple enough, but one should note that it will not help the buyer where he accepts defective goods and attempts to revoke acceptance only after they have been lost or stolen or otherwise injured. Transfer of the risk back to the seller occurs only when there is rightful revocation of acceptance. Section 2–608(2) requires that a buyer revoke acceptance "before any substantial change in condition of the goods which is not caused by their own defects." Thus if the goods are destroyed after acceptance but before revocation, the buyer's power to revoke and so use 2–510(2) is foreclosed.

Section 2–510(3) will cause the risk to jump to a buyer who repudiates or "is otherwise in breach." The risk jumps, however, only if the following four additional conditions are met: (1) goods are conforming, (2) they are "already" identified to the contract, (3) to the extent that the loss is not covered by seller's insurance, and (4) loss occurs within a commercially reasonable time (presumably from the repudiation or other breach). The application of this subsection may be somewhat more troublesome because the lawyer must determine whether a "commercially reasonable time has passed" and he will have to determine not only that the goods are conforming, but also that the buyer has breached. Still, subsection (3) seems a rather unremarkable provision.

A question of at least passing interest presented by both subsection (2) and subsection (3) of 2–510 is the effect of the language in those sections "to the extent of any deficiency in his effective insurance coverage." These are essentially antisubrogation clauses which place the loss on any insurance company. For a discussion of those clauses see Section 5–7 below. At the beginning of the discussion of 2–510, we raised the question whether buyer or seller's fault (that is his breach of the contract) ought to be relevant in determining who bears the risk loss. Note that other kinds of fault, namely those causally connected with the destruction of the goods, will sometimes determine who bears the loss and may take the transaction entirely out of the 2–509, 2–510 scheme. If, for example, risk has passed from seller to buyer under 2–509(3) because the seller had tendered delivery to the buyer, and the goods are then destroyed because of the negligence of the seller, at minimum buyer should be freed from his obligation to pay the price, and it would be appropriate to give him a cause of action for damages as well. Note also that seller's misbehavior can affect the risk in other ways. If, for example, he loads conforming goods on a railway car but loads them in a negligent fashion so that they will inevitably be destroyed, the risk does not pass to the buyer under 2–509(1) because he fails to "duly" deliver. Cases

---

32. For a discussion of rejection and revocation, see Ch. 8 infra.

governed by 2–509 and 2–510 are rarely those in which there is a causal connection between the buyer's or seller's act and the destruction of the goods. For the most part we are concerned in this chapter with cases in which neither party is at fault except to the extent that he may be in breach of contract.

## § 5–6  Subrogation

Insurers often attempt to subrogate themselves to the claims which their insureds have against third parties. Although the Code deals only incidentally with insurance, subrogation is a topic of great concern for merchants who store or ship goods. Our focus in this section will be on subrogation in the sales context, on cases in which the insurer of buyer or of seller is pursuing the other party to the sales transaction.

For our purposes subrogation is the insurer's assertion of his insured's right against a third party (the carrier, the other party to the sales transaction, or some third party) for the loss for which he has reimbursed his insured. At the outset one should understand certain conditions which must be met before the insurer will have any right of subrogation. He must have reimbursed the insured for the loss. The insured must in fact have a cause of action somehow related to the insured loss against a third party. The subrogation right is an equitable one, and it normally need not be stated in the agreement between the insured and the insurer.[33] However, as we will see, a clause that details the right will often be helpful and occasionally necessary if the insurer is to have a right to be subrogated to all of the rights of his insured.[34]

---

33. See Liverpool Steam Co. v. Phoenix Ins. Co., 129 U.S. 397 (1889) (insurer of goods, upon paying to insured total or partial amount of loss, becomes subrogated in a corresponding amount to insured's right of action against carrier even without formal assignment to express stipulation); Trinity Universal Ins. Co. v. Moore, 134 A.2d 333 (D.C.Ct.App.1957) (insurer's right of subrogation does not depend upon actual, formal assignment since equity instantly confers upon insurer who has paid the same rights which belonged to policyholder); Employer's Mut. Liab. Ins. Co. v. Griffin Constr. Co., 280 S.W.2d 179, (Ky.Ct.App.1955) (upon payment of loss equitable right of subrogation operates regardless of formal assignment or express stipulation thereof in policy); Knight v. Calvert Fire Ins. Co., 268 S.W.2d 53 (Mo. Ct.App.1954) (since subrogation arises by operation of law, it is immaterial whether insurance policy expressly provides for subrogation). See generally 16 G. Couch, Cyclopedia of Insurance Law §§ 61:19—:20 (2d ed. 1966).

34. The insurance clause set out below is illustrative of a specific provision binding the insured to cooperate in the company's assertion of a right to subrogation:

Company's Right of Recovery: In the event of any payment under this policy, the Insured shall execute and deliver instruments and papers and do whatever else is necessary to secure the subrogation rights of the Company. The Insured shall do nothing after loss to prejudice such rights. However, the Company specifically waives its rights of subrogation against all the subsidiary and affiliated companies of the Insured. Any release from liability, other than as provided in Section 19, entered into prior to loss hereunder by the Insured shall not affect this policy or the right of the Insured to recover hereunder. At the option of the Company, the Insured will execute a loan agreement, to the extent of any loss collectible under this policy. Said loan will bear no interest and will be repayable only

The law of subrogation has enjoyed an irregular and episodic growth in sales law and in analogous areas. The unsatisfactory state of the law is well illustrated by the English and American cases discussing subrogation of an insurer to the rights of a seller of real property on the one hand and a mortgagee on the other against buyer and mortgagor respectively. Assume that the mortgagee or the seller has insurance on the land and buildings, that the policy protects only his own interest, the property is destroyed while part of the mortgage debt or purchase price remains unpaid, and the insured mortgagee or seller collects his insurance. If there were no insurance, destruction of the property would not discharge the mortgagor from the mortgage debt, nor, in the land contract case, would it discharge the buyer's obligation to pay the price.[35] When there is insurance the large majority of the American courts treat the two cases differently. They find that the buyer of real property is entitled "to the benefit" of the seller's insurance and therefore that the insurer is not entitled to be subrogated to the seller's suit against the buyer for the price of the real estate which has been destroyed.[36] On the other hand the American courts find that a mortgagor is not entitled to "the benefit" of the mortgagee's insurance and that the mortgagee's insurer is subrogated to the mortgagee's rights against the mortgagor on the debt.[37] The financing seller on the one hand and the financing mort-

in the event and to the extent of the net recovery affected from any party believed to be liable for said loss, the Insured will at the Company's request and expense make claim upon and institute legal proceedings against any party which the Company believes to be liable for such loss, and will use all proper and reasonable means to recover the same, under the exclusive direction and control of the Company.

35. At least five different theories allocating the burden of fortuitous losses between seller and buyer have been advanced in real property law. The view most widely accepted was first enunciated in Paine v. Meller, 6 Ver. 349 (Ch. 1801), that from the time the seller-buyer relation arises the burden of loss is on the buyer even though the seller may be in possession. 3 American Law of Property § 11:30 (A. Casner ed. 1952).

36. See, e. g., Alabama Farm Bureau Mut. Ins. Serv., Inc. v. Nixon, 268 Ala. 271, 105 So.2d 643 (1958) (if property was insured by seller, generally he holds insurance money as trustee for purchaser); Williams v. Lilley, 67 Conn. 50, 34 A. 765 (1895) (lessee, on subsequently exercising option of purchase, entitled to have balance of insurance money in lessor's hands credited as payment on price); cf. Brown-

ell v. Board of Educ., 239 N.Y. 369, 146 N.E. 630 (1925) (denying claim of buyer to benefits of seller's insurance where risk of loss was not in buyer since contract of sale permitted him to withdraw from contract in event of destruction of property). See generally King, Subrogation Under Contracts Insuring Property, 30 Texas L.Rev. 62, 77 (1951); Case Note, 25 Colum. L.Rev. 477 (1925); Case Note, 34 Yale L.J. 87 (1924); Annot., 37 A.L.R. 1324 (1925).

37. See, e. g., Carpenter v. Providence Washington Ins. Co., 41 U.S. (16 Pet.) 495 (1842) (payment of insurance does not discharge debt and insurer is entitled to be subrogated to rights of mortgagee under the mortgage); Hackett v. Cash, 196 Ala. 403, 72 So. 52 (1916) (under policy covering only mortgagee's interest, insurer paying loss or damage suffered in respect to mortgaged property is subrogated to mortgagee's right against mortgagor); Fields v. Western Millers Mut. Fire Ins. Co., 265 App.Div. 891, 37 N.Y.S.2d 757 (3d Dep't 1942), aff'd 290 N.Y. 209, 48 N.E.2d 489 (1943) (insurer is entitled to be subrogated to rights of mortgagee upon payment of loss to him, where policy is issued to him, procured by him, and so written as to cover his interest only). See generally W. Vance, Insurance § 130

gagee on the other are often in identical economic positions; the risk of the insurer may be identical in both cases. Why the courts distinguish the two cases is a mystery. With that kind of confusion as to real property where the law is "mature and well developed," one can hardly rejoice at the prospect of a swim in the turbulent waters of sales law. We will do our best to keep the reader afloat.

The general classes of rights to which the insurer may wish to be subrogated in a sales contract can be divided into two groups. The first are the rights of the insured to recover from the carrier or some other party for his negligent or other destruction of the goods in question. Second are rights, commonly called collateral rights, against third parties who did not necessarily have anything to do with the destruction of the goods. An illustration of the second class is the seller's cause of action against the buyer for the price of goods destroyed at a time when the risk of loss was on the buyer's shoulders.[38]

A court faced with a subrogation situation in the sales transaction has three alternate ways of dividing the loss. Consider for example a case in which the insurance company has paid a seller-insured for conforming goods destroyed after risk had passed to buyer. If the insurer seeks to be subrogated to the seller's rights to the price against the buyer, what outcome? The Court could: (*1*) permit the insurance company to recover from the buyer and so place the loss on the buyer; (*2*) deny the insurance company the right to recover from the buyer, but permit the seller (who had already received the insurance proceeds) to recover from him and so be doubly compensated; or (*3*) bar both the insurance company and the seller from recovery and so place the loss on the insurance company. Although outcome two is one apparently reached in a number of automobile accident cases,[39] it has nothing to commend it, and it has been regularly rejected by the courts in sales and analogous cases.[40] The choice be-

---

(3d ed. 1951); 16 G. Couch, Cyclopedia of Insurance Law § 61:355 (2d ed. 1966).

**38.** In view of the fact that most courts allow subrogation to collateral as well as rights for the direct recovery for the injury caused, one normally need not worry about distinguishing the two classifications. However there is a third class of cases which may cause lawyers trouble. These are causes of action so far removed from the insured injury that they are not even "collaterally" attached to it. For example, is an insurer subrogated to a buyer's cause of action under section 2–714 for breach of contract as to goods which were destroyed after buyer incurred some expenses in attempted repair?

**39.** See Conard, Insurance Rates and Regulations in 15 L.Quad.Notes 14 (Fall 1970) (statement to N.Y. Joint Legis.Comm. on Ins. Rates & Regulations).

**40.** See, e. g., In re Future Mfg. Cooperative, Inc., 165 F.Supp. 111 (N.D. Cal.1958) (rejecting the second alternative because it contravenes public policy against double recovery and against placing insured in position where he might be tempted to cause loss or act carelessly); Standard Accident Ins. Co. v. Pellecchia, 15 N.J. 162, 104 A. 2d 288 (1954) (situation deemed contrary to public policy not only by reason of unfairness but because of inducement to fraud); Kernochan v. New York Bowery Fire Ins. Co., 17 N.Y. 428, 442 (1858) ("no man should

comes one between outcomes one and three: to put the loss on the buyer or on the insurance company? The argument in favor of denying subrogation and so leaving the loss on the insurance company, runs as follows: the insurance company has calculated its risk and has received its premium for taking that risk. Now that the feared event has come to pass, the insurer should not be permitted to cast its loss on another's shoulders when it has already received payment for bearing that loss. An answer to that argument is that the contract between the insured and the insurer is a "personal" one and that the court should not interfere with their agreement. If the insurer agreed to pay the insured but only on the understanding that the insurer would have the right to assert the insured's claims against third persons, then the courts should not interfere. A less doctrinal but possibly persuasive answer to the argument is that the insurer is not receiving a windfall but that its rates will be affected and ultimately set by reference not just to its losses, but to its net losses after subrogation recoveries—but for the subrogation right its premium would have been higher. Whether there is empirical support for this argument that the premium will vary in relation to the subrogation right, we cannot say.[41] Except for the modest inroads made by the 2–510

be allowed to bargain for an advantage to arise from the destruction of life or property"). But see Alexandra Restaurant, Inc. v. New Hampshire Ins. Co., 272 App.Div. 346, 71 N.Y.S.2d 515 (1st Dep't 1947), aff'd, 297 N.Y. 858, 79 N.E.2d 268 (1948) (court permitted insured lessee whose landlord repaired fire damage under obligation in lease to recover also from insurer). See generally King, Subrogation Under Contracts Insuring Property, 30 Texas L.Rev. 62, 71 (1951); Note, Subrogation of the Insurer to Collateral Rights of the Insured, 28 Colum.L.Rev. 202 (1928).

**41.** A great deal of relevant data are unavailable and no uniformity exists among the subrogation practices of insurers. Mr. Horn reports:

The various rating bureaus are not required to provide subrogation recovery data for the insurance departments in support of rate filings, nor is the information required of insurers under individual deviating filings. In either case the loss experience must to some extent be justified, but the loss experience used is net of all salvage and other recoveries. Insurance department actuaries are aware that subrogation recoveries are relatively large for certain classes of insurance but they know that the loss experience used in the various rating for-

mulas has already taken the collections into account.

R. Horn, Subrogation in Insurance Theory and Practice 149 (1964). Nevertheless Horn believes:

It is sometimes argued that subrogation is a 'windfall' to the insured, since it plays no (or only a minor) role in rate construction. The term 'windfall gain' is virtually always used to refer to some sort of unearned or unexpected gain and presumably this is what supporters of the proposition have in mind. It is submitted that such an argument overlooks two salient points: (1) subrogation does enter rate structures by serving to reduce losses upon which they are predicated; and (2) the insurer does indeed *earn* any gain which might result from loss recovery efficiency over and above that implicitly assumed in such rate structures.

\* \* \*

On the basis of the empirical data presented in this study, it seems true that aggregated subrogation collections for the responding companies are *relatively* unimportant for some broad classes of insurance. It may be, therefore, that subrogation need not enter the rate structures directly for these classes, especially if several years are used for a rate base thereby minimizing the relative effect of lag pursuant to the calendar-year reporting of recoveries.

antisubrogation clause and by cases like In re Future Manufacturing Cooperative, Inc.,[42] discussed below, the insurer in sales transactions usually is successfully subrogated to his insured's rights. When the insurer is seeking to be subrogated to so-called *noncollateral* rights, that is, to be subrogated to the cause of action in negligence or otherwise against the one who in fact caused the injury, the courts unanimously allow subrogation.[43] Why the courts have found these cases so easy is not clear. Perhaps we are seeing only the desire to punish the wrongdoer; perhaps the courts' actions arise from the hope that the wrongdoer can be made to act with greater care if he knows he will have to bear the loss. In any event the cases agree; the insurer is subrogated to the insured's rights to recover for the injury caused.

Although the courts are not unanimous in permitting an insurer to be subrogated to the so-called *collateral* rights of the insured (for instance, price of goods destroyed, indebtedness secured by goods de-

Id. at 190–91. See Case Note, 72 Harv. L.Rev. 1380, 1382 (1959) where the commentator suggests:

However, if the insurance company was in fact paid to assume the risk of loss to the extent of the unpaid balance without allowing for the possibility of subrogation, it seems it should be considered the primary obligor. The insurance company's business is bearing such risks, compensated by premiums which, by taking such losses into account, efficiently spread the loss among those who benefit from the activity out of which the loss arose. Although in any given case the vendee not only may be an efficient risk-spreader itself but may in fact already have spread the risk, the usual conditional-sales contract involves a vendee with slight economic resources.

The coverage of the policy in the absence of a specific clause can be best discerned by examination of the premiums that have been charged. It might seem that since the prior commitment of the vendee to bear the loss is definite, the insurance company was paid only to cover the risk of the coincidence of a fire and the vendee's inability to pay. However, in the infrequent case in which the vendor desires a "single-interest" policy, the practice of insurers is to charge the same premium per 1,000 dollars of coverage as for the standard fire-insurance policy under which there is no subrogation to collateral rights. Only when the vendor assures the company that he will proceed against the vendee prior to making a claim on the policy are the premiums reduced. Furthermore, since the information as to the premiums charged and as to

whether the premiums are determined with reference to any collateral rights of the insured is peculiarly within the knowledge of the insurance company, it seems reasonable in the present case to assume, unless proved otherwise, that the insurance company has charged for assumption of the broader risk. On the other hand, it is clear that an insurance company should have the right to select the particular risk it desires to bear. Thus, if the policy either specifically provides for the right of subrogation to collateral rights, or if the rate of premiums is in fact commensurate with such a right, the insurance company should prevail over the vendee.

**42.** 165 F.Supp. 111 (N.D.Cal.1958).

**43.** See, e. g., D. M. Picton & Co. v. United States, 96 F.Supp. 1010 (E.D. Tex.1950) (insurers subrogated by operation of law to all causes of action of tugboat owners against United States); Miller v. Newark Fire Ins. Co., 12 La.App. 315, 125 So. 150 (1929) (insurer subrogated to insured's rights against garage owners for stolen auto); Home Ins. Co. v. Bishop, 140 Me. 72, 34 A.2d 22 (1943) (insurer who paid loss is subrogated to any claim insured had against person whose tortious act caused injury or who, for any other reason, is liable to owner therefor); Lucas v. Garrett, 209 S.C. 521, 41 S.E.2d 212 (1947) (insurer issuing fire insurance policy to owner of goods, upon payment of loss occurring while goods were being transported by common carrier, is subrogated to all rights of owner against carrier) (dictum).

stroyed), the large majority of the cases permit subrogation to such rights.[44] These cases are well illustrated by Home Insurance Co. v. Bishop,[45] a case in which the court concluded that the insurance company was "substituted for the mortgagee and in legal effect has purchased its rights." After the debtor destroyed the insured automobile, the court authorized the insurance company of the creditor to be subrogated to the creditor-insured's rights on the buyer's note. The minority position, denying subrogation to collateral rights, is best articulated by Judge Goodman in In re Future Manufacturing Co-

44. See, e. g., Atlantic Mut. Ins. Co. v. Cooney, 303 F.2d 253 (9th Cir. 1962) (insurer subrogated to insured's rights against carrier or bailee on bailee's express agreement to be responsible for loss); United States Fidelity & Guar. Co. v. Slifkin, 200 F.Supp. 563 (N.D. Ala.1961) (consignor's insurers subrogated to rights of consignors against consignee); Chicago, St. L. & N. O. R. R. Co. v. Pullman So. Car. Co., 139 U.S. 79 (1891) (lessor-lessee); Meyer Koulish Co. v. Cannon, 213 Cal.App.2d 419, 28 Cal.Rptr. 757 (2d Dist. 1963) (insurer subrogated to insured's contract claim); Hartford Fire Ins. Co. v. Payne, 199 Iowa 1008, 203 N.W. 4 (1925) (shipper-carrier); Twin City Fire Ins. Co. v. Walter B. Hannah, Inc., 444 S.W.2d 131 (Ky.Ct.App.1969) (seller-buyer); Nobbe v. Equity Fire Ins. Co., 210 Minn. 93, 297 N.W. 349 (1941) (lien); Home Ins. Co. v. Bishop, 140 Me. 72, 34 A.2d 22 (1943) (insurer of seller's assignee held subrogated to latter's right to recover from endorser of note given by buyer whose interest under policy had been forfeited); American Equitable Assurance Co. v. Newman, 132 Mont. 63, 313 P.2d 1023 (1957) (buyer-seller); Interstate Ice & Power Corp. v. United States Fire Ins. Co., 243 N.Y. 95, 152 N.E. 476 (1926) (seller's insurer subrogated to claim against conditional buyer to whom insurer had denied liability on the policy) (dictum); Commercial Union Fire Ins. Co. v. Kelly, 389 P.2d 641 (Okla.1964) (lessor-lessee); National Fire Ins. Co. v. Mogan, 186 Ore. 285, 206 P.2d 963 (1949) (bailor-bailee); F. H. Vahlsing, Inc. v. Hartford Fire Ins. Co., 108 S.W.2d 947 (Tex.Civ.App.1937) (lessor-lessee).

The following cases allow the third party the benefit of the insured's insurance: In re Future Mfg. Co-op., Inc., 165 F.Supp. 111 (N.D.Cal.1958) (conditional sale); Gard v. Razanskas, 248 Iowa 1333, 85 N.W.2d 612 (1957) (option to purchase); Brady v. Welsh, 200 Iowa 44, 204 N.W. 235 (1925) (buyer-seller); Automatic Sprinkler Corp. of America v. Robinson-Slagle Lumber Co., 147 So. 542 (La.App.1933) (conditional sale); Eastern Restaurant Equip. Co. v. Tecci, 347 Mass. 148, 196 N.E.2d 869 (1964) (conditional sale). See generally King, Subrogation Under Contracts Insuring Property, 30 Texas L.Rev. 62, 81 (1951); Note, Subrogation of the Insurer to Collateral Rights of the Insured, 28 Colum.L.Rev. 202 (1928); Case Note, 72 Harv.L.Rev. 1380 (1959); Case Note, 20 Md.L.Rev. 161 (1960).

In Royal Zenith Corp. v. Citizens Publications, Inc., 179 N.W.2d 340 (Iowa 1970) (pre-Code). Justice Uhlenhopp of the Supreme Court of Iowa comments on the problem in dictum as follows:

> In a particular case the task is to divine, from what the parties said and did and the nature of the transaction, which one of them they intended should be the ultimate risk taker—who should be primarily and who secondarily responsible if loss occurred. A salient fact may demonstrate what that intention was. In the seller-buyer situation, if the buyer is to obtain insurance at his own expense for the seller's protection, and does so, plainly that insurer is intended to bear the loss as among the three parties. In the consignment situation, if the consignment contract recites as to the consignee, "Risks of loss or damage from all hazards of any kind, with or without negligence on your part is yours," manifestly the consignee has the burden of loss as opposed to the consignor and his insurer. In the bailment situation, if the storage contract provides the storage company guarantees against loss by fire to the extent it receives payment from its insurer, clearly that insurer bears the ultimate loss to the extent of its limits, though the depositor also maintains insurance.

179 N.W.2d at 346 (citations omitted).

45. 140 Me. 72, 77, 34 A.2d 22, 24 (1943).

operative, Inc.[46]   In that case the insurance company paid the unpaid portion of the purchase price to the seller and then sought to enforce the seller's right to the price against the estate of the bankrupt buyer.   The sales contract provided that the bankrupt buyer would insure the equipment in favor of the seller against fire.   After a thorough discussion of the policy and a careful consideration of the real property precedents described above, the court concluded, "While a rule giving the vendee the benefit of the vendor's insurance may run counter to the normal concept of an insurance policy as a personal contract between the insurer and the assured, this theoretical objection does not weigh as heavily as the equitable considerations in favoring the vendee." [47]   The court denied the subrogation claim.

But for the large body of real property case law which prohibits subrogation and gives one party the "benefit" of the other's insurance and but for the praise such cases have received from the commentators,[48] one could dismiss *Future Manufacturing* and the few other cases like it as aberrations.[49]   The care and persuasiveness with which Judge Goodman writes adds substantially to the weight of his decision.   Nevertheless, we regard the *Future Manufacturing* outcome as undesirable.   We believe that the court's premise, namely that the insurance company would get a windfall if, having received

---

**46.**   165 F.Supp. 111 (N.D.Cal.1958).

**47.**   Id. at 116.

**48.**   Several commentators have criticized the doctrine of subrogation. Professors Harper and James conclude as follows:

Subrogation tends to be wasteful in a society whose judicial machinery is already overtaxed.   It is often allowed in situations where it simply takes money from one of a man's pockets and puts it in one of his others, or where cross claims for subrogation will occur frequently and cancel out. It sometimes takes a loss out of machinery for distributing it and throws it back on an individual who cannot distribute losses at all.   It probably accomplishes little of the admonitory function.   It is an inappropriate weapon for punishment.   Altogether it is a far, far thing from the fair-haired boy it is so often assumed to be.

2 F. Harper & F. James, The Law of Torts § 25.23 at 1360 (1956).

Professor Gilmore observes:

The argument for insurer's subrogation seems, when first put forward, extremely plausible.   Only on reflection does the argument become suspect.   That seems to be, in a nutshell, the common law history.   When the subrogation argument was first put forward, in the early days of insurance law, it was accepted almost without question.   The nineteenth century cases, English and American, consistently accepted the subrogation rule with respect not only to tort claims but also to various types of contract claims.   The twentieth century story has been quite different.   The rule of subrogation to tort claims has maintained itself in the case law, but has been subjected to increasingly hostile and effective criticism.   The recent cases which have considered insurer's claims to be subrogated to contract rights have, on the whole, been unsympathetic to the claims.   Although there has been some diversity of result, it seems fair to say that the case law trend has been to give the uninsured contract obligor the benefit of the other party's insurance.   In sum, the history which the proponent of the subrogation rule could point to is mostly ancient history; current history lets him down.

2 G. Gilmore, Security Interests in Personal Property § 42.7.2 at 1149–50 (1965).

See generally Case Note, 72 Harv.L. Rev. 1380 (1959); Case Note, 20 Md.L. Rev. 161 (1960).

**49.**   See note 43 supra.

its premium, it also had a right to subrogation may be inaccurate. We find little authority to support Professor Gilmore's assertion that the current "case law trend has been to give the uninsured contract obligor the benefit of the other party's insurance." [50]

Moreover, Harper and James' assumptions about "overtaxing" [51] the courts with subrogation cases are not supported by any data known to us and seem naive in a day and age when the bulk of all cases and the large bulk of all sales cases are settled, not tried. We think that the rights of insured and insurer to transfer assets (such as claims against third parties) between them should not be disturbed except in cases such as 2–510(2) and (3) where the legislature has made the judgment that there should be no subrogation.

There are at least two important situations in which even Judge Goodman might permit subrogation. First the court states that the insurer could save his right to subrogation "by including a clause in the policy specifically subrogating it to the vendor's right to recover the purchase price from the vendee." [52] Until one examines the policy at issue in *Future Manufacturing*, that seems a safe and certain out for the insurer. The policy in that case contained a clause which provided that upon "payment under this policy, the Company shall be subrogated to all the Assured's rights of recovery therefor against any person or organization. . . ." [53] It appears to us that the insurer in *Future Manufacturing* had already done exactly what Judge Goodman states that an insurer must do in order to preserve his rights of subrogation. One familiar with that line of 20th Century pre-Code cases [54] in which courts repeatedly stated that parties could disclaim their warranty liability but found they had simply "not chosen the right language" in the case before the court might accuse Judge Goodman of speaking with forked tongue. A wise insurance counsel will now include a careful and detailed subrogation clause in the policy, but a cautious counsel will read Judge Goodman's statement as the gratuitous dictum it is and will not warrant to his client that the clause will preserve the insurer's right to be subrogated to collateral rights of the insured.

Secondly, Judge Goodman states that the insurer did not seek to be subrogated to seller's cause of action for buyer's breach of his promise to insure. He does not indicate what the outcome would have been had the insurer sought to be subrogated to that claim, but it is conceivable that he would have classified that right as a "non-collateral" right to which the insurer could have been subrogated.

**50.** 2 G. Gilmore, Security Interests in Personal Property § 42.7.2 at 1150 (1965).

**51.** 2 F. Harper & F. James, The Law of Torts § 25.23 at 1360 (1957).

**52.** In re Future Mfg. Cooperative, Inc., 165 F.Supp. 111, 116 (C.D.Cal. 1958).

**53.** Id. at 112.

**54.** See, e. g., Wade v. Chariot Trailer Co., 331 Mich. 576, 50 N.W.2d 162 (1951); Bekkevold v. Potts, 173 Minn. 87, 216 N.W. 790 (1927).

In summary, the insurer's right of subrogation to a cause of action against one who wrongfully destroyed goods is universally recognized. *Future Manufacturing* to the contrary notwithstanding, the majority of cases dealing with personal property finds that insurers are subrogated to the collateral rights of the insured as well. However, there are a variety of limits and restrictions upon the doctrine with which the lawyer should be familiar.

## § 5–7 Restrictions and Limitations Upon the Doctrine of Subrogation

An important restriction upon the application of the subrogation doctrine, and one easily overlooked, is the case in which the third party against whom the insured would have a cause of action is also a beneficiary of the insurance policy. Consider, for example, United States Fidelity & Guaranty Co. v. Slifkin.[55] Slifkin was a diamond merchant who held goods of others on consignment for resale. His insurance policy covered not only his own interest in the goods, but also those "in trust or on commission," and those "held by him in any capacity whether or not the insured is liable for the loss thereof." [56] The court found that the consignors of the stolen diamonds were third-party beneficiaries of Slifkin's policy. In such circumstances Slifkin's insurer had no cause of action against the consignors because those persons in effect were insured under the same policy.

Subsections 2–510(2) and (3) throw the risk of loss back upon the breaching seller and forward on to the repudiating buyer in certain circumstances. However, they transfer that risk only "to the extent of any deficiency in [the aggrieved party's] effective insurance coverage." The effect of the language is to deprive the insurance company of certain of the subrogation rights which the insured buyer or seller would have had but for the language in subsections (2) and (3) of 2–510.[57] Since 2–510(2) and (3) give the aggrieved *but fully insured* party no claim, the aggrieved party's in-

---

55. 200 F.Supp. 563 (N.D.Ala.1961).

56. Id. at 574.

57. See generally Professor Honnold writing for the New York Law Revision Commission:

Subsections (2) and (3) of Section 2–510 in the Code have a common provision which is unique in the treatment of risk of loss. The essence of the provision is that if one of the parties is in breach of the contract, the aggrieved party 'may, to the extent of any deficiency in his effective insurance coverage, treat the risk of loss as resting on' the defaulting party. It will be noted that this section has no impact on the rules of Section 2–509 which control risk in the absence of breach. Only if risk would be thrown on the party in breach by Section 2–510 does this provision operate to hold

risk on the innocent party to the extent of his insurance.

The result has some resemblance to decisions giving to one party with risk of loss the benefit of insurance taken by the other party. The theory is, however, quite different. Instead of transferring the proceeds of the policy to the party who has risk of loss, the Code transfers risk to the party with insurance. This difference in approach avoids any possibility that the insurer, after paying on the insurance, will seek subrogation to the insured's rights on the sales contract against the party in breach. Since, under the Code the insured party has the risk of loss, he has no contract rights against the other party to which the insurer can be subrogated.
1 N.Y. State Law Revision Comm'n, 1955 Report 499 (1955).

surer who only steps into the insured's shoes finds that he too has no cause of action. In short the proper analysis is to say that there is no cause of action to which the insurer can be subrogated.

Assume, for example, that seller has a contract to sell $10,000 of goods to buyer. The goods are identified under the contract, but they are in the possession of seller and are covered by seller's insurance. Buyer repudiates the contract and shortly thereafter the goods are destroyed. Under the terms of 2–510(3), the seller could treat the buyer as having the risk of loss if the seller were uninsured. Since he is fully insured, there is no "deficiency in his effective insurance coverage," and subsection (3) does not operate at all. Thus, seller's insurance company pays the entire loss to seller and has no cause of action against buyer.

But what of the insurer whose policy is specifically designed to counteract 2–510(2) and (3) or of the party who is only partially insured? In the former case, the insurance contract might provide that the insurance coverage is "ineffective as long as the buyer or the seller, as the case may be, has a cause of action for the price or for contract damages against the other party." The policy might also provide that the insurer would lend the insured the amount of his loss pending the outcome of the litigation. Under such circumstances, is there a "deficiency" in the "effective insurance coverage"? Professor Gilmore has argued, we think persuasively, that 2–510(2) and (3) set down rules of public policy which cannot be varied by the agreement of the parties.[58] That we believe to be the most probable meaning of the last sentence of Comment 3 to 2–510: "This section merely distributes the risk of loss as stated and is not intended to be disturbed by any subrogation of an insurer."

Thus we believe that attempts to deprive one party to the sales transaction of the benefits of the other's insurance in the circumstances covered by 2–510(2) and (3) should be rejected by the courts whether those attempts take the form of fancy footwork in the policy or of fictional loans.[59]

Consider the second case, one in which the seller has an insurance contract with policy limits of $10,000 and a contract for the sale of $20,000 worth of goods. The goods are destroyed in seller's hands shortly after the buyer repudiates the contract. Clearly there is a deficiency in the effective insurance coverage to the extent of $10,000 and to that extent seller should recover from buyer. May the insurer not step forward and claim that $10,000 under his subrogation rights? If he does so, seller has a "deficiency in his effective insurance" of yet another $10,000. But to allow him to take a second $10,000 out of the buyer's skin would violate the purpose of

**58.** 2 G. Gilmore, Security Interests in Personal Property § 42.7.2 at 1150–51 (1965).

**59.** Insurers sometimes advance the insured the amount of loss to the extent of the insurer's liability. The loan is repayable only in the event and to the extent of any net recovery by the insured. See generally 16 G. Couch, Cyclopedia of Insurance Law § 61:72 (2d ed. 1966).

2–510 (to give one party the "benefit" of the other's insurance). If on the other hand we allow the insurer to have the $10,000 but do not allow seller to sue buyer for a second $10,000, the seller will be in a worse position for having insured than he would have been in had he had no insurance but had contracted with a solvent-buyer defendant; in the latter case he would collect $20,000 from buyer and keep it all.

The correct outcome in such circumstances is to find that the buyer has a cause of action against the seller for the difference between the price and his insurance coverage and to deny the insurer's plea for subrogation to that claim. Quite logically the insurer can claim subrogation to the claim for the first $10,000, the amount paid to the insured, but there is no cause of action against the buyer on that part since it is fully insured. To put it another way, we think the transaction should be regarded as two separate claims. Part one is a loss of $10,000 as to which the seller carries full insurance, has no deficiency, and therefore has no claim under 2–510(3) against the buyer. Part two is a loss of $10,000 as to which there is no insurance. Since this claim is uninsured, the insurer has no more right to be subrogated to it than he has to an infinite variety of other claims unrelated to losses he has insured. Any other outcome produces inconsistencies with the outcomes in analogous cases under 2–510 and conflicts with the policy of 2–510(2) and (3).

One finds an analogous limitation on subrogation in 9–207(2)(b) which reads in part as follows:

> [T]he risk of accidental loss or damage is on the debtor to the extent of any deficiency in any effective insurance coverage.  .  .  .

The negative implication of the quoted language is that when goods which have been pledged to a creditor are destroyed, the loss is on his insurance company. If there is no insurance, then the loss is on the debtor. As in 2–510, absent an agreement to the contrary, the insurance company has no right of subrogation because there is no cause of action on the part of the debtor to which the insurance company can be subrogated. Whether the parties can change this outcome by contract is even more clouded under 9–207 than it is under 2–510. Under 2–510 one at least gets the help of the last sentence in Comment 3 which, with a little stretching, seems to be a statement of public policy against subrogation in that circumstance.[60] In 9–207 one gets no such help, and indeed 9–207(2) is prefaced by the clause

---

**60.** § 2–510, Comment 3 reads as follows:

> In cases where there has been a breach of the contract, if the one in control of the goods is the aggrieved party, whatever loss or damage may prove to be uncovered by his insurance falls upon the contract breaker under subsections (2) and (3) rather than upon him. The word "effective" as applied to insurance coverage in those subsections is used to meet the case of supervening insolvency of the insurer. The "deficiency" referred to in the text means such deficiency in the insurance coverage as exists without subrogation. This section merely distributes the risk of loss as stated and is not intended to be disturbed by any subrogation of an insurer.

"unless otherwise agreed." We find Professor Gilmore's argument that the "unless otherwise agreed" language refers to other parts of subsection (2) to be plausible but not persuasive.[61] If the draftsmen had intended to state a rule of public policy which the parties could not alter, they chose a most unusual way to state it in 9–207(2). We conclude that the insured and the insurer should not be permitted to alter the antisubrogation outcome in 9–207, but we are not confident of the intention of the draftsmen here.

A final and thoroughly intriguing limitation upon the subrogation right is found in bills of lading commonly used by railroads and other common carriers. When one reads the insurance policy provisions that the insurer "shall have all causes of action under the sun which belong to the insured and shall not be obliged to 'benefit' any third party" and compares that language with the bill of lading which states that the carrier shall "under all circumstances without fail, until hell freezes over, have the benefit of all insurance purchased by anyone with whom he deals," he is put in mind of two young boys trying to determine who gets first at bat by going up the bat hand-over-hand until finally one of them cannot get all four fingers on the top of the bat and so loses. The question becomes whose medicine is more powerful, the railroad's which says it benefits from shipper's insurance or the insurer's which says it may recover from the railroad. In general the shipper's insurer seems to have prevailed.[62]

## § 5–8   Contribution—Introduction

Contribution among insurers is an obscure topic little touched on in law school but of considerable importance to many lawyers. In modern consumer and commercial transactions there are a variety of circumstances in which one insurer will seek contribution against another. Assume, for example, that the driver of an automobile runs into a telephone pole and breaks his arm. He incurs $500 of hospital and medical bills. Through his employer he has Blue Cross and Blue Shield which are liable for the $500 bill, and in his automobile policy there is a medical payments clause which obligates his automobile insurer to pay the same $500. If Blue Cross and Blue Shield pay, may they seek contribution from the automobile insurer? A similar case may arise when the consignor of goods placed in the hands of the consignee carries insurance on those goods, and the consignee also covers the consignor's losses. In effect, the consignor's interest is twice insured, once by his own policy and once by the policy of his consignee.

---

**61.** 2 G. Gilmore, Security Interests in Personal Property § 42.7.2 at 1152 (1965).

**62.** See, e. g., Hartford Fire Ins. Co. v. Payne, 199 Iowa 1008, 203 N.W. 4 (1925) (absent contrary stipulation, shipper's insurer is subrogated to shipper's claim against carrier). See also

Luckenbach v. W. J. McCahan Sugar Co., 248 U.S. 139 (1918) (upholding validity of loan receipt device by which insurer made advance to insured as a loan, taking in return loan receipt providing that loan is repayable only to extent of recovery from carrier).

Three conditions must exist for a right to contribution: two or more insurers must insure the *same loss* by the *same insured*.[63] To sharpen your appreciation of the limitations on the right of contribution, consider a typical sales transaction. Seller has agreed to sell fifteen lathes to buyer. Seller has a manufacturer's output policy which covers his interest in goods (on his premises during manufacture) and in transit to buyer. Buyer also has a policy which covers goods on his premises and goods in transit to him. If the goods are destroyed in transit, and buyer's insurer pays buyer, does buyer's insurer have a cause of action against seller's insurer for contribution? Usually the answer will be no. Because the buyer's policy insured only buyer's loss and the seller's policy insured only seller's loss, the two do not cover the same loss and there is no right of contribution. Of course, if we change the facts slightly so that seller's policy covered not only "seller" but also "seller's customers" then the conditions for contribution would exist. Note that in the case in which there are two insurers but they do not cover the same loss to the same insured, there is still a possibility that the *entire loss* will be transferred from one insurer to another through a subrogation cause of action which we have discussed above.

Even if two insurers have insured the same person and their policies cover the same goods, there will be no right of contribution if the policies cover different risks. If, for example, one insurer protects against robbery at gunpoint and another protects only against loss resulting from locusts or the plague, there will be no contribution between them. Do not, then, confuse contribution with subrogation; the latter may exist anytime an insurer pays a party who himself has a claim against the other party in that transaction. The former occurs only when two or more insurers cover the same loss to one insured.

A second problem which one should distinguish from contribution arises when there are several claimants whose losses exceed the available insurance. Assume, for example, that one or more insurance policies cover the goods belonging to three sellers and that the combined policy limits of the policies are $150,000 but the combined loss is $200,000. In that case there is no problem of contribution among the insurers; each of the insurers will be required to pay an amount equal to his own policy limits into the pot.[64] The legal question is how to divide this pot among the insureds who have suffered an aggregate loss of $200,000.

Before one undertakes an examination of the real world of insurance contribution, a world horribly complicated by the clever

63. See, e. g., Southern Sur. Co. v. Commercial Cas. Ins. Co., 31 F.2d 817 (3d Cir. 1929), cert. denied 280 U.S. 577 (1929); Dietzel v. Patron's Mut. Fire Ins. Co., 232 Mich. 415, 205 N.W. 149 (1925); Lucas v. Garrett, 209 S.C. 521, 41 S.E.2d 212 (1947).

64. See, e. g., Hinson v. British Am. Assurance Co., 43 F.Supp. 951 (W.D. La.1942); Niagra Fire Ins. Co. v. D. Heenan & Co., 181 Ill. 575, 54 N.E. 1052 (1899); Ogden v. East River Ins. Co., 50 N.Y. 388 (1872).

work of insurance lawyers, he should understand how contribution might work if the lawyer's hand was stayed. Assume, for example, that goods are shipped from seller to buyer under circumstances in which buyer has the risk of loss. Buyer has an insurance policy with limits of $50,000 which covers his loss, and seller has a policy which covers not only his own losses but also the losses of his buyers. The seller's policy has limits of $100,000. Assume that goods worth $10,000 are stolen in transit. How is the loss divided between the two insurers? Absent clauses in the policies which produce a different result, the losses are prorated according to the policy limits. Thus the seller's insurer would pay two thirds of the loss ($6,666), and the buyer's insurer would pay one third ($3,333). This division of responsibility is founded upon the assumption that the insurer with the high liability limits received a correspondingly higher premium.

## § 5-9 Contribution—Other Insurance Clauses

Of course, life is not as simple as we have described it, and insurers and their lawyers early realized the possibility of reducing their own liability in contribution situations by putting clauses in their insurance policies. These clauses, known as "other" insurance clauses, attempt by various means to require that the insured claim last and least from the company whose policy contains the clause. The various forms which "other insurance clauses" take are as follows:

(1) "Escape" clauses provide that the insurance obligation is null and void if other valid and collectible insurance exists:

The insurance contained in this policy is not applicable to any person with respect to any loss against which he has other valid and collectible insurance.

In the more ancient cases, if all conflicting insurance policies contained escape clauses, all escaped; no insurer paid anything even though the insured had paid the premiums.[65] This result was hardly what the insured had bargained for, and modern cases reject that result.[66] Because newer policy forms do not use "escape" clauses, the problem is now rarely presented.

(2) "Pro rata" clauses obligate the insurer to pay ratably with the other insurer in the same proportion as the face value of its policy bears to the total available coverage of all other valid and collectible insurance:

If the insured or any other interested party carries other insurance covering such loss as is cov-

65. See, e. g., Phoenix Ins. Co. v. Copeland, 90 Ala. 386, 8 So. 48 (1890); Sugg v. Hartford Fire Ins. Co., 98 N.C. 143, 3 S.E. 732 (1887) (insured entitled to no protection though he paid both premiums).

66. See, e. g., Waddell v. Road Transp. & Gen. Ins. Co., [1932] 2 K.B. 563 (1931); see generally Note, Automobile Liability Insurance—Effect of Double Coverage and "Other Insurance" Clauses, 38 Minn.L.Rev. 838, 850–51 (1954).

ered by this policy, the company shall not be liable for a greater proportion of any such loss than the amount applicable thereto as hereby insured, bears to the total amount of all valid and collectible insurance covering such loss.[67]

(3) "Excess" clauses provide essentially that other insurers pay first. In theory a policy with an excess clause pays only when all other insurance has paid to its policy limits:

If there is other insurance against a loss covered under this policy the insurance provided under this policy shall be excess insurance over any other valid and collectible insurance.[68]

## § 5–10   Contribution—Conflicts Between Other Insurance Clauses

Insofar as we are able to tell from the cases, it is an unusual case today in which only one out of two competing insurance policies will have an other insurance clause and an even rarer case in which neither policy will have an other insurance clause. Thus, the courts are now often called upon to decide whose lawyer witchcraft will govern when the other insurance clauses in the two competing policies conflict. The problem is easy enough if both policies contain a pro rata clause; parties simply prorate the loss according to the policy limits. There is also little difficulty if both policies contain an excess clause or if both policies contain an escape clause. In those two instances neither clause is effective and the insurers prorate.[69]

What of the case in which one policy provides that the losses shall be prorated, and the other policy provides that it pays only after all other insurance has been exhausted (excess)? For reasons which are not clear to us, the courts have generally upheld the excess clause in competition with pro rata clauses.[70] The courts often fail

---

67. For a case dealing with the quoted clause, see United States Fidelity & Guar. Co. v. Slifkin, 200 F.Supp. 563, 576 (N.D.Ala.1961).

68. For a case dealing with excess clauses, see Citizens Mut. Auto. Ins. Co. v. Liberty Mut. Ins. Co., 273 F.2d 189 (6th Cir. 1959).

69. See, e. g., Insurance Co. of Texas v. Employers Liab. Assurance Co., 163 F.Supp. 143 (S.D.Cal.1958); Oil Base, Inc. v. Transport Indem. Co., 143 Cal. App.2d 453, 299 P.2d 952 (2d Dist. 1956); Consolidated Shippers, Inc. v. Pacific Employers Ins. Co., 45 Cal.App. 2d 288, 114 P.2d 34 (2d Dist. 1941). But see Hartford Steam Boiler Insp. & Ins. Co. v. Cochran Oil Mill & Ginnery Co., 26 Ga.App. 288, 105 S.E. 856 (1921).

70. See, e. g., Citizens Mut. Auto. Ins. Co. v. Liberty Mut. Ins. Co., 273 F.2d 189 (6th Cir. 1959); Employer's Liab. Assurance Corp. v. Fireman's Fund Ins. Group, 262 F.2d 239 (D.C.Cir. 1958); McFarland v. Chicago Express, Inc., 200 F.2d 5 (7th Cir. 1952); American Auto. Ins. Co. v. Republic Indem. Co. of America, 52 Cal.2d 507, 341 P. 2d 675 (1959). Contra, Lamb-Weston, Inc. v. Oregon Auto Ins. Co., 219 Ore. 110, 129, 341 P.2d 110, 119 (1959), modified on issue of proration of damages, 219 Ore. 129, 346 P.2d 643 (1959) (pro rata v. excess) where the court said, "In our opinion, whether one policy uses one clause or another, when any come in conflict with the 'other insurance' clause of another insurer, regardless of the nature of the clause, they are in fact repugnant and each should be rejected in toto." Cf.

to realize it, but such holdings in effect find the pro rata clause of the competing policy invalid.[71] Why one policy's terms should be favored over its competitor is unclear. If the court is faced with the need to invalidate one clause or the other, it would seem that the most equitable result should prevail, and that result in our opinion would usually be a proration. Indeed the best solution would be to disregard both clauses since they conflict and to resolve the dispute by proration.

No majority rule has emerged in the conflict between pro rata and escape clauses. However several courts have held that a pro rata clause governed when it conflicted with an escape clause on the theory that the escape clause would deny the insured the amount of insurance for which he had bargained and paid.[72] The courts will generally prorate in a conflict between an excess clause and an escape clause.[73]

The foregoing discussion and the cases cited in the footnotes will be only a starter for students and for lawyers with contribution problems. We omit discussion of some of the doctrine which we believe to be less important,[74] and we treat the rest with a com-

Oregon Auto Ins. Co. v. United States Fidelity & Guar. Co., 195 F.2d 958 (9th Cir. 1952) (proration ordered between excess clause and escape clause). See also Continental Cas. Co. v. Weekes, 74 So.2d 367 (Fla.1954); New Amsterdam Cas. Co. v. Certain Underwriters at Lloyds', 56 Ill.App.2d 224, 205 N.E.2d 735, rev'd 34 Ill.2d 424, 216 N.E.2d 665 (1965); Beattie v. American Auto Ins. Co., 338 Mass. 526, 156 N.E.2d 49 (1959); Woodrich Constr. Co. v. Indemnity Ins. Co. of North America, 252 Minn. 86, 89 N.W. 2d 412 (1959); Arditi v. Massachusetts Bonding & Ins. Co., 315 S.W.2d 736 (Mo.1958); Cosmopoliton Mut. Ins. Co. v. Continental Cas. Co., 28 N.J. 554, 147 A.2d 529 (1959).

The critics have given mixed reviews to the minority "Oregon theory": Watson, The "Other Insurance" Dilemma, 54 Ill.B.J. 486 (1966) (unfavorable); Note, Current Coverage in Automobile Liability Insurance, 65 Colum. L.Rev. 319 (1965) (favorable); Note, Automobile Liability Insurance—Effect of Double Coverage and "Other Insurance" Clauses, 38 Minn.L.Rev. 838 (1954) (favorable).

71. See, e. g., United Serv. Auto Ass'n v. Russom, 241 F.2d 296 (5th Cir. 1957); General Ins. Co. of America v. Western Fire & Cas. Co., 241 F.2d 289 (5th Cir.), cert. denied 354 U.S. 909 (1957); Mountain States Mut. Cas. Co. v. American Cas. Co., 135 Mont. 475, 342 P.2d 748 (1959).

72. For cases favoring pro rata provisions, see Peerless Cas. Co. v. Continental Cas. Co., 144 Cal.App.2d 617, 301 P.2d 602 (1st Dist.1956); Air Transport Mfg. Co. v. Employers' Liab. Assurance Corp., 91 Cal.App.2d 129, 204 P.2d 647 (2d Dist.1949).

73. See Zurich Gen. Accident & Liab. Ins. Co. v. Clamor, 124 F.2d 717 (7th Cir. 1941); Continental Cas. Co. v. Curtis Publishing Co., 94 F.2d 710 (3d Cir. 1938).

74. The difference between blanket and specific insurance has been a continuing source of trouble in the contribution field. Frequently insurers argue that their policies are "blanket," that their competitors are "specific," and therefore that the specific policy should pay first. Courts have had great difficulty in distinguishing specific policies from blanket policies and when they have been able to distinguish them, they have not agreed upon methods of proration. For a sample of cases wrestling with these problems, see Page v. Sun Ins. Office, 74 F. 203 (8th Cir. 1896); Pearl Assur. Co. v. Hartford Fire Ins. Co., 239 Ala. 515, 195 So. 747 (1940); Schmaelzle v. London & L. Fire Ins. Co., 75 Conn. 397, 53 A. 863 (1903); Haley v. Dorchester Mut. Ins. Co., 83 Mass. (1 Allen) 536 (1861); Ogden v. East River Ins. Co., 50 N.Y. 388 (1872). See generally Note, Contribution Between Insurers on Partially Concurrent Obligations, 40 Harv.L.Rev. 878 (1927).

paratively broad brush. We are satisfied if the student or the lawyer beginning his research understands the various clauses which may be relevant to a contribution conflict and perceives the differences between contribution and subrogation.[75] To reiterate, contribution exists only when two or more insurers insure the same insured for the same loss.

---

75. For an excellent discussion of subrogation and contribution, see United States Fidelity & Guar. Co. v. Slifkin, 200 F.Supp. 563 (N.D.Ala.1961).

# CHAPTER 6

# BUYER'S REMEDIES FOR REPUDIATION, FOR NONDELIVERY AND FOR FAILURE TO DELIVER CONFORMING GOODS (WHICH THE BUYER REFUSED TO KEEP)

*Analysis*

Sec.
6–1. Introduction.
6–2. Repudiation, Nondelivery, and Other Occasions for Resort to a Remedy.
6–3. Cover, 2–712.
6–4. Contract-Market Damages, 2–713.
6–5. Buyer's Incidental and Consequential Damages.
6–6. Specific Performance.
6–7. The Buyer's Possible Responses to Repudiation.

## § 6–1  Introduction

Buyer's remedies for breach of contract have been a topic for study from time immemorial. Generations of students have wrestled with the problems of the proper time and place for measuring the market and with the baffling opinion in Hadley v. Baxendale.[1] The Uniform Commercial Code combines ancient learning with some ideas of Professor Llewellyn to produce an impressive collage of buyer's remedies. The types of cases to which this chapter is addressed are those in which the seller has repudiated, or has otherwise wrongfully failed to deliver, or has delivered nonconforming goods which the buyer has properly refused to keep. Section 2–711,[2] an index of the buyer's alternative remedies, tells us that the buyer may cover (2–712), recover damages for nondelivery (2–713), or, in a proper case, secure

---

1. 9 Exch. 341 (1845).

2. § 2–711 provides (emphasis added):

(1) Where the seller fails to make delivery or repudiates or the buyer rightfully rejects or justifiably revokes acceptance then with respect to any goods involved, and with respect to the whole if the breach goes to the whole contract (Section 2–612), the buyer may cancel and whether or not he has done so may in addition to recovering so much of the price as has been paid

   (a) "cover" and have damages under the next section as to all the goods affected whether or not they have been identified to the contract; or

   (b) recover damages for non-delivery as provided in this Article (Section 2–713).

(2) Where the seller fails to deliver or repudiates the buyer may also

   (a) if the goods have been identified recover them as provided in this Article (Section 2–502); or

   (b) in a proper case obtain specific performance or replevy the goods as provided in this Article (Section 2–716).

(3) On rightful rejection or justifiable revocation of acceptance a buyer has a *security interest* in goods in his possession or control for any payments made on their inspection, receipt, transportation, care and custody and may hold such goods and resell them in like manner as an aggrieved seller (Section 2–706).

specific performance or replevin (2–716).[3] Two important buyer's remedies that we have treated in Chapter 8 rather than here are rejection (2–601) and revocation of acceptance (2–608). Also, we will not treat damages for breach in regard to accepted goods (2–714) here; we have covered that important remedy in Chapter 10 on warranty damages.

## § 6–2    Repudiation, Nondelivery, and Other Occasions for Resort to a Remedy

Although a variety of factors may explain nondelivery, its occurrence is simple enough. The seller simply fails to deliver, and absent a lawful excuse an occasion thus arises for the buyer to seek a remedy. Also, delivery of nonconforming goods is, in the usual case, readily determined. (We will consider what constitutes a breach of warranty in Chapter 9.) Some breaches are easy to prove; if without excuse the seller fails to deliver at all or fails to deliver on time, his breach is clear. On the other hand, if he delivers arguably nonconforming goods or if he makes pre-delivery rumblings which might be interpreted as a repudiation of the contract, the task of the buyer's lawyer will be harder. In this section we will consider what constitutes an anticipatory repudiation. Although our principal concern in this chapter will be with buyer's remedies, in this section we will treat not only buyer's repudiation but also seller's repudiation. The Code provisions on anticipatory repudiation and on the damages to which a repudiatee is entitled are pure joy to teachers intent upon persecuting their students; and are doubtless pure hell to many students. The complexity of these provisions intimidates judges too, many of whom tend to ignore the difficult problems.

The threshold issue in many anticipatory repudiation cases is whether the words or acts of the prospective defendant constitute an anticipatory repudiation at all. If the lawyer incorrectly advises his client that the other party has repudiated and instructs the client that he may turn elsewhere for cover or that he may cease his own performance, his client may himself be liable for anticipatory repudiation or for breach of the contract at the time performance becomes due. A clever and well advised prospective defendant who does not wish to forfeit the contract but is currently unable to perform, is likely to transmit thoroughly ambiguous signals to the other party. He may, for example, be a seller begging for but not demanding some form of increased payment for his performance,[4] or he may be a

3. Another alternative that might be considered a buyer's remedy is found in section 2–502, "Buyer's Right to Goods on Seller's Insolvency." This section indicates that if the seller becomes insolvent within ten days after receiving the first installment on their price, the buyer may recover those goods identified to the contract (under § 2–501) if he tenders the unpaid

balance of the price. Subsection (2), however, restricts the application of 2–502 in the situation where the buyer himself identifies the goods to the contract. Section 2–502 is discussed more fully in conjunction with specific performance (2–716) in Section 6–6 supra.

4. See, e. g., Reliance Cooperage Corp. v. Treat, 195 F.2d 977 (8th Cir. 1952).

buyer suffering a severely restricted cash flow who wants the seller to continue performance and who fully hopes to be able to pay after performance despite clouds of bankruptcy ominously gathering over his head. The lawyer must decide whether the seller's chiseling for a higher price or the buyer's equivocal expression of inability to perform constitute anticipatory repudiation.

Before we seek to define what is and what is not an anticipatory repudiation, we will consider an important Code innovation designed to relieve the lawyer of anxiety in these circumstances. Section 2–609 [5] authorizes one party upon "reasonable grounds for insecurity" to "demand adequate assurance of due performance and until he receives such assurance . . . if commercially reasonable suspend any performance for which he has not received the agreed return." [6] Subsection (4) provides that a prospective repudiator's "failure to provide within a reasonable time not exceeding thirty days an assurance of due performance" constitutes a "repudiation of the contract." All this makes the job of the lawyer easier. He need no longer trust the courts to grapple with the fictions of implied promises [7] or to slosh around in mushy notions of insolvency.[8] If his client is in a position to wait a month after receipt of an ambiguous statement that might constitute a repudiation, he need only demand adequate assurance of performance and wait out the month. Of course 2–609 itself poses problems: What are reasonable grounds for insecurity? When has a party given an adequate assurance of due performance? When is it commercially reasonable to suspend performance while awaiting assurance?

Not surprisingly, subsection (2) tells us to define both "reasonableness" and "adequacy" by "commercial standards," and Comment 3 reminds us of the pervasive obligation of good faith.[9] The Code cases

---

5.  § 2–609:

(1) A contract for sale imposes an obligation on each party that the other's expectation of receiving due performance will not be impaired. When reasonable grounds for insecurity arise with respect to the performance of either party the other may in writing demand adequate assurance of due performance and until he receives such assurance may if commercially reasonable suspend any performance for which he has not already received the agreed return.

(2) Between merchants the reasonableness of grounds for insecurity and the adequacy of any assurance offered shall be determined according to commercial standards.

(3) Acceptance of any improper delivery or payment does not prejudice the aggrieved party's right to demand adequate assurance of future performance.

(4) After receipt of a justified demand failure to provide within a reasonable time not exceeding thirty days such assurance of due performance as is adequate under the circumstances of the particular case is a repudiation of the contract.

6.  § 2–609(1).

7.  Hochster v. De la Tour; 2 El. & Bl. 678 (1853). Cf. Frost v. Knight, L.R. 7 Ex. 111 (1792); Restatement of Contracts § 318, comment a (1932).

8.  Rock-Ola Mfg. Corp. v. Leopold, 98 F.2d 196 (5th Cir. 1938).

9.  Professor Honnold comments that 2–609 gives the court broad discretion to determine what are reasonable grounds and that the comments provide guidelines for a properly conservative application of the section to balance two conflicting interests: (1) pro-

give a clue to the meaning of "commercial standards" here. In Lock-wood-Conditionaire Corp. v. Education Audio Visual, Inc.,[10] plaintiff seller of air conditioners sued the buyer for damages for withholding the price. After installation, the equipment failed to function properly and buyer demanded written assurance of due performance. Since plaintiff did not respond with adequate assurance, the court denied its claim for relief (although granting leave to reapply after a fair test of the equipment in the next summer). Unless the courts unduly restrict 2–609 by limiting the grounds for "insecurity," 2–609 will largely solve the lawyer's pre-Code dilemma about what to advise his client upon an apparent repudiation.[11]

In some cases clients will not wait for 2–609 to run its course, and the lawyer will be called upon to decide whether the other party has "repudiated." Section 2–610 [12] does not introduce any new tests,

---

viding certainty that the promisor will not breach, and (2) flagrant use of 2–609 as a weapon to avoid unpleasant contracts. 1 N.Y. State Law Revision Comm'n, 1955 Report 537 (1955).

To illustrate "reasonable grounds" and "adequate assurance" Comment 4 cites two pre-Code cases which together illustrate the intended commercial standards. According to Comment 4, reasonable grounds for insecurity would exist in a case like Corn Products Refining Co. v. Fasola, 94 N.J. 181, 109 A. 505 (1920) where a buyer who customarily took advantage of a ten-day payment discount failed to make his usual ten-day payment. As to the adequacy of assurance, the comment states that sending a good credit report from a banker and expressing an ability and willingness to pay within thirty days should be satisfactory. Comment 4 also expressly requires that the satisfaction of a party requesting "assurance" must be based on reason and not caprice. James B. Berry's Sons Co. v. Monark Gasoline & Oil Co., 32 F.2d 74 (8th Cir. 1929).

10. 3 UCC Rep.Serv. 354 (N.Y.Sup.Ct. 1966). See also Appeal of Productions Unlimited, Inc., 3 UCC Rep.Serv. 620 (VACAB 1966) (government can insist upon film owner's certificate that films were not available for use in public television concurrent with hospital use).

11. One court, in what seems a flight of fancy unauthorized by anything in the Code, has made the use of 2–609 obligatory in one case. In Wrightstone, Inc. v. Motter, 1 UCC Rep.Serv. 170 (Pa.C.P.1961), plaintiff-seller exercised his rights on an acceleration

clause in an installment sales contract and note. The clause was one which gave seller the right to declare a default if he felt himself "insecure." After repossession and resale, seller sued purchaser for a deficiency. The court apparently believed that 2–609 governed the case and decided that plaintiff himself had repudiated the contract by terminating the contract and repossessing without demanding adequate assurance. Thus the court concluded:

Defendants have a legal defense in that they were not permitted to give assurances of their performance of the contract before action to terminate the contract was taken by the plaintiff. They should have an opportunity to show, if they can, that they were injured by being deprived of that opportunity. In other words the rights and remedies of the aggrieved party to an anticipatory breach becomes applicable to this situation.

1 UCC Rep.Serv. at 172.

12. § 2–610:

When either party repudiates the contract with respect to a performance not yet due the loss of which will substantially impair the value of the contract to the other, the aggrieved party may

    (a) for a commercially reasonable time await performance by the repudiating party; or

    (b) resort to any remedy for breach (Section 2–703 or 2–711), even though he has notified the repudiating party that he would await the latter's performance and has urged retraction; and

but Comment 1 to 2–610 summarizes the general common law definition:

> .  .  .  anticipatory repudiation centers upon an overt communication of intention or an action which renders performance impossible or demonstrates a clear determination not to continue with performance.[13]

Like the common law, the Code allows for nonverbal repudiation by "action which reasonably indicates a rejection of the continuing obligation," and is consistent with section 318 of the Restatement of Contracts.[14]

What kind of statement or conduct is a repudiation? The easiest case is where a party makes his own performance impossible, as where a seller resells unique goods to another before time for performance.[15] However, Comment 2 to 2–610 indicates that repudiation may occur short of actual impossibility. Where on the spectrum between impossibility and inconvenience is the line which divides "repudiation" from "non-repudiation"? Comment 2 to 2–610 does little more than paraphrase the issue; it states that a demand for greater performance than agreed upon constitutes a repudiation "when under a fair reading it amounts to a statement of intention not to perform except on conditions which go beyond the contract." [16] Suppose, for example, that a seller contracts to sell 10,000 bushels of soybeans at $2.00/bushel and then phones to tell the buyer that he is not sure he can perform unless the buyer can meet the then current price of

(c) in either case suspend his own performance or proceed in accordance with the provisions of this Article on the seller's right to identify goods to the contract notwithstanding breach or to salvage unfinished goods (Section 2–704).

13. See also 4 A. Corbin, Corbin on Contracts, § 973 (1951); 11 S. Williston, Williston on Contracts, §§ 1322–23 (3d ed. 1968).

14. Restatement of Contracts § 318 (1932):

Except in the cases of a contract originally unilateral and not conditional on some future performance by the promisee, and of a contract originally bilateral that has become unilateral and similarly unconditional by full performance by one party, any of the following acts, done without justification by a promisor in a contract before he [has breached by failure to render performance or by hindering performance by the other party] constitutes an anticipatory repudiation which is a total breach of contract:

(a) a positive statement to the promisee or other person having a right under the contract, indicating that the promisor will not or cannot substantially perform his contractual duties;

(b) transferring or contracting to transfer to a third person an interest in specific land, goods, or in any other thing essential for the substantial performance of his contractual duties;

(c) any voluntary affirmative act which renders substantial performance of his contractual duties impossible, or apparently impossible.

15. Allen v. Wolf River Lumber Co., 169 Wis. 253, 172 N.W. 158 (1919) (defendant sold a limited amount of peeled bark which plaintiff had previously arranged to purchase).

16. Professor Patterson comments in 1 N.Y. State Law Revision Comm'n, 1955 Report 669, 672 (1955) that the Code continues prior law as to extra-contract demands, citing Estes v. Curtiss Aeroplane & Motor Corp., 191 App.Div. 719, 182 N.Y.S. 25 (4th Dep't 1920) aff'd. without opinion, 232 N.Y. 572, 134 N.E. 576 (1922); Wester v. Casein Co., 206 N.Y. 506, 100 N.E. 488 (1912).

$2.15/bushel. There are hundreds, perhaps a thousand, ways in which a clever chiseler might communicate his proposition. If he is foolish enough to say, "I won't ship unless you pay me $2.15," he has repudiated. If, on the other hand, all he does is to carry on at great length about how others are now getting $2.15 and about the financial difficulties that he will suffer if he is forced to deliver at $2.00, he probably has not repudiated. In these cases we have no litmus test to tell when the seller's demands for additional pay or other performance or his refusal to perform become sufficiently unequivocal to amount to repudiation.

A second kind of repudiation occurs when one of the parties simply announces an intention not to perform. Comment 1 to 2–610 appears to retain the common law requirement that a statement of intention not to perform must be positive and unequivocal. An indefinite statement as to future contingencies will not constitute a repudiation. An old case, but still probably the leading one on the requisite certainty of a repudiation, is Dingley v. Oler,[17] where a defendant-seller declined to deliver ice to the plaintiff-buyer because of an increase in the market price but instead suggested two alternative courses of action.[18] Declining to find a repudiation, the court explained:

> [a]lthough . . . they decline to ship the ice that season, it is accompanied with the expression of alternative intention, and that is, to ship it, as must be understood, during that season, if and when the market price should reach the point which, in their opinion, the plaintiffs ought to be willing to accept as its fair price between them. . . .
> This, we think, is very far from being a positive, unconditional, and unequivocal declaration of fixed purpose not to perform the contract in any event or at any time. In view of the consequences sought to be deduced and claimed as a matter of law to follow, the defendants have a right to claim that their expressions, sought to be converted into a renunciation of the contract, shall not be enlarged by construction beyond their strict meaning.[19]

Although Dingley v. Oler was decided before the Supreme Court had fully adopted the doctrine of anticipatory repudiation, the case does reflect a long standing judicial predilection for "saving the contract."[20]

---

17. 117 U.S. 490 (1886).

18. Plaintiff shipped a load of ice to defendant (1879) in return for a promise to deliver a like amount by the end of the next season (September 1880). At the time plaintiff delivered the ice to defendant it was priced at about 50 cents per ton. In the following July, however, the price had climbed to $5.00 a ton.

19. 117 U.S. at 501–502.

20. The alleged repudiation consisted of a written communique from defendant to plaintiff, stating in part:

We must, therefore, decline to ship the ice for you this season, and claim, as our right, to pay you for the ice, in cash, at the price you offered it to other parties here [fifty cents a ton],

Not only must the repudiation be unequivocal, but it must also "substantially impair the value of the contract to the other." [21]   Thus even a clear repudiation of a part of a contract may not be operative as a repudiation and so give rise to 2–610 remedies unless the value of the whole contract is substantially impaired.   Comment 3 to 2–610 characterizes the test as "the same as that in the section on breach in installment contracts  . . ., whether material inconvenience or injustice will result if the aggrieved party is forced to wait and receive an ultimate tender minus the part or aspect repudiated." [22]

A third distinguishable kind of repudiation occurs when a defendant willing to perform finds himself unable to do so.   Perhaps

or give you ice when the market reaches that point.
Id. at 501.

With all due respect intended, the Court could not realistically have foreseen a ninety percent price reduction from July to September such that the market price would be satisfactory to both.   Yet it may be that decisions like this actually spurred the development of Section 2–609.   See, e. g., United States ex rel. Gaunt v. Carl M. Geupal Constr. Co., 423 F.2d 818, 7 UCC Rep. Serv. 446 (7th Cir. 1970) (contractor's refusal to pay for gravel unless measurement occurred with gravel compacted in place at dam site was repudiation of the contract); Aura Orchards v. A. Peltz & Sons, Inc., 27 Agri.Dec. 1546, 6 UCC Rep.Serv. 149 (1968) (buyer's refusal to order shipment of apples was repudiation of the contract); Puget Sound Marina Inc. v. Jorgensen, 3 Wash.App. 476, 475 P.2d 919, 8 UCC Rep.Serv. 478 (1970) (demand by seller for additional $555 for rescue boat was repudiation of $29,500 contract to sell vessel).   For examples of pre-Code cases, see also Gold Mining & Water Co. v. A. B. Swinerton, 23 Cal.2d 19, 142 P.2d 22 (1943) (lessee's failure to begin performance and refusal to have anything more to do with property or lease unless lessor consented to assignment was repudiation of the contract); Rottman v. Endejan, 6 Wis.2d 221, 94 N.W.2d 596 (1959) (buyer's refusal to accept abstract and return $500 down payment was repudiation of the contract).

21.   § 2–610.

22.   Consider section 2–612:

(1) An "installment contract" is one which requires or authorizes the delivery of goods in separate lots to be separately accepted, even though the contract contains a clause "each delivery is a separate contract" or its equivalent.

(2) The buyer may reject any installment which is non-conforming if the non-conformity substantially impairs the value of that installment and cannot be cured or if the non-conformity is a defect in the required documents; but if the non-conformity does not fall within subsection (3) and the seller gives adequate assurance of its cure the buyer must accept that installment.

(3) Whenever non-conformity or default with respect to one or more installments substantially impairs the value of the whole contract there is a breach of the whole.   But the aggrieved party reinstates the contract if he accepts a non-conforming installment without seasonably notifying of cancellation or if he brings an action with respect only to past installments or demands performance as to future installments.

Subsection (3) of 2–612 is most relevant to a consideration of anticipatory repudiation, since when there is a material breach of an installment contract such that it "substantially impairs the value of the whole contract," there will also be an anticipatory repudiation as to the remaining installments.   Thus it is not surprising that the Code draftsmen have elected to use an interchangeable test.

Comments 4, 6, and 7 provide some help (1) to define *beforehand* what kind of nonconformity will and will not be acceptable and (2) to project the result of a battle in court *after* a nonconforming installment has been tendered.

See Graulich Caterer, Inc. v. Hans Holterbosch, Inc., 101 N.J.Super. 61, 243 A.2d 253, 5 UCC Rep.Serv. 440 (App.Div.1968).

out of charity to the earnest but incompetent defendant, courts have been more hesitant to find anticipatory repudiation here than in those cases in which the prospective defendant expressed an unwillingness to perform.[23] But we believe that the aggrieved party's position here is no different than in the situation described above [24] and think he should have all the same rights as a repudiatee there.

Section 2–611(1) recognizes that an anticipatory repudiation may be revocable. Under 2–611(1), the repudiator may retract until his next performance is due.[25] However, he may retract only if the aggrieved party has not (1) cancelled, (2) materially changed his position, or (3) otherwise indicated that he considers the repudiation final.[26] This section is consistent with the approach taken by the leading commentators on pre-Code law.[27] Prior law should help define what is a "material change." For example, pre-Code cases held that bringing suit for anticipatory breach constitutes a material change.[28]

Section 2–611(2) allows the repudiator to retract by "any method which clearly indicates to the aggrieved party that the repudiating party intends to perform. . . ." While a verbal communication would be the most direct method of retracting, the section strives to preserve the contract by allowing any other method that clearly evidences intent to comply with the contract. Thus if a party regains the ability to perform or experiences other relevant changes of circumstance and these facts are communicated to the repudiatee before a material change of position, both pre-Code law and 2–611 favor re-

---

**23.** Professor Corbin notes:

There may be cases in which expressions of inability by one party or an existing appearance of inability on his part to perform will justify the other party in non-performance of his part of the contract or in materially changing his position so as to make performance impossible, without at the same time operating as an anticipatory breach, for which an action for damages could be maintained.

4 A. Corbin, Corbin on Contracts § 974 (1951).

**24.** Id.; 11 S. Williston, Williston on Contracts § 1324 (3d ed. 1968).

**25.** Section 2–611:

(1) Until the repudiating party's next performance is due he can retract his repudiation unless the aggrieved party has since the repudiation cancelled or materially changed his position or otherwise indicated that he considers the repudiation final.

(2) Retraction may be by any method which clearly indicates to the aggrieved party that the repudiating party intends to perform, but must include any assurance justifiably demanded under the provisions of this Article (Section 2–609).

(3) Retraction reinstates the repudiating party's rights under the contract with due excuse and allowance to the aggrieved party for any delay occasioned by the repudiation.

This has led Professor Patterson to question whether a retraction might be given as to any future performance even if the repudiator had committed a "present material breach." 1 N.Y. State Law Revision Comm'n, 1955 Report 676 (1955).

**26.** § 2–611, Comment 1.

**27.** 4 A. Corbin, Corbin on Contracts § 980 (1951); 11 S. Williston, Williston on Contracts § 1335 (3d ed. 1968).

**28.** See, e. g., Quivirian Development Co. v. Poteet, 268 F.2d 433 (8th Cir. 1959).

instating the contract.[29] If the repudiation occurred because of a failure to give adequate assurance of performance (2–609), then 2–611(2) requires that retraction include any assurance so demanded.

### § 6–3   Cover, 2–712

Once "seller fails to make delivery or repudiates or the buyer rightfully rejects or justifiably revokes acceptance . . .," the buyer may resort to the remedies identified in 2–711. Chief among those remedies and the only one that enables him "to obtain the goods" and thus meet his "essential need" is his right to cover embodied in 2–712.[30]

Section 2–712 reads as follows:

(1) After a breach within the preceding section the buyer may "cover" by making in good faith and without unreasonable delay any reasonable purchase of or contract to purchase goods in substitution for those due from the seller.

(2) The buyer may recover from the seller as damages the difference between the cost of cover and the contract price together with any incidental or consequential damages as hereinafter defined (Section 2–715), but less expenses saved in consequence of the seller's breach.

(3) Failure of the buyer to effect cover within this section does not bar him from any other remedy.[31]

In most cases, the operation of 2–712 is simple and easy to understand. After seller breaches and the buyer "covers" under 2–712(1), the buyer can recover the difference between the cost of the substitute goods and the original contract price. The court in Willred Co. v. Westmoreland Metal Manufacturing Co.[32] recognized this basic formula. Plaintiff buyer was faced with a breach of a contract for school furniture under subcontract for the New York Board of Education.[33] The court concluded:

Inasmuch as the defendant had totally breached the contract, the plaintiff was not bound to offer to purchase

---

29. Cf. Restatement of Contracts § 319 (1932):

The effect of repudiation is nullified

(a) where statements constituting such a repudiation are withdrawn by information to that effect given by the repudiator to the injured party before he has brought an action on the breach or has otherwise materially changed his position in reliance on them; or

(b) where facts other than statements constitute such repudiation and these facts have, as the injured party knows, ceased to exist before

action brought or such change of position as is stated in Clause (a).

30. See also In re Vaughan's Estate, 156 Misc. 577, 282 N.Y.S. 214 (Sur.Ct. 1935).

31. Section 2–712 suffered no significant change between the 1949 draft and its present form.

32. 200 F.Supp. 59, 1 UCC Rep.Serv. 181 (E.D.Pa.1961).

33. However, in this particular case the court found existent special circum-

the necessary furniture from the defendant or to have any more dealings with it. The plaintiff, in order to carry out its contract obligations, in good faith and without unreasonable delay contracted . . . for furniture to take the place of that which should have been supplied by the defendant. Having done this and having completed its contract with the New York board, the plaintiff would, upon satisfactory proof, be entitled to damages in the amount of the difference between the costs of its "cover" and the defendant's price to it.[34]

Since 2–712 measures buyer's damages by the difference between his actual cover purchase and the contract price, the formula will often put buyer in the identical economic position that performance would have. This result is a significant departure from the prior law. Under prior law, if an aggrieved buyer made a cover purchase, there was no assurance that the court would measure the market at or near the time when he made his purchase,[35] and accordingly, the court's contract-market differential formula might over or under compensate him. His actual cost of cover and the market price at the time and place of his cover were, at least in theory, irrelevant to the damage suit.[36] If for example, seller repudiated a $20,000 contract for shoes and buyer promptly covered for $24,000, and the market price at this time for performance was $22,000, buyer could recover only $2,000. Except in the rare case in which he could prove that the requisition of substitute goods was in the contemplation of the parties at the time the contract was made, buyer was forced to bear the $2,000 loss.[37]

stances such that the formula was found inapplicable.

34. 200 F.Supp. 59, 66, 1 UCC Rep. Serv. 181, 182 (E.D.Pa.1961).

35. An exception to this proposition was discussed by Professor Honnold, 1 N.Y. State Law Revision Comm'n, 1955 Report 570 (1955). He noted one context where pre-Code decisions found buyer's substitute purchase binding:

If buyer purchases substitute goods for *less* than market price, this repurchase price may be the maximum amount on which damages can be measured.

36. Uniform Sales Act § 67, "Action for Failing to Deliver Goods," reads:

(1) Where the property in the goods has not passed to the buyer, and the seller wrongfully neglects or refuses to deliver the goods, the buyer may maintain an action against the seller for damages for non-delivery.

(2) The measure of damages is the loss directly and naturally resulting in the ordinary course of events, from the seller's breach of contract.

(3) Where there is an available market for the goods in question, the measure of damages, in the absence of special circumstances showing proximate damages of a greater amount, is the difference between the contract price and the market or current price of the goods at the time or times when they ought to have been delivered, or, if no time was fixed, then at the time of the refusal to deliver.

37. The outlandish results produced by the failure of the courts to accord sufficient effect to a purchase of substitute goods were evident in common law times and remained under the Uniform Sales Act. See, e. g., Missouri Furnace Co. v. Cochran, 8 F. 463 (W.D.Pa.1881). Plaintiff contracted to purchase 36,621 tons of coal at $1.20 per ton (to be delivered periodically), but after a delivery of only 3,765 tons,

A few interpretative problems of undetermined importance remain on the periphery of 2-712. The language "but less expenses saved in consequence of the seller's breach" presents an initial interpretative problem when the buyer has covered. This problem will appear when the shipping terms of the cover contract differ from those in the original contract. Assume for example, that a Washington, D. C. buyer contracts to purchase food blenders from a Seattle seller for $10,000, F.O.B. shipping point (Seattle), with shipping costs totaling $500. Further assume a breach by seller, and that buyer covers in Kalamazoo for $12,000, F.O.B. buyer's plant (Washington, D. C.). What are the "expenses saved in consequence of the breach"? Bearing in mind the goal of placing the buyer in the position he would have been in had no breach occurred, one sees that the buyer's cost of putting the blenders in his hands in Washington, D. C. under the original contract was $10,500.[38] Under the substitute contract the analogous cost is $12,000, and the proper recovery is $1,500. Collating the hypothetical figure with the 2-712(2) formula leads to the same result: cost of cover ($12,000) less the contract price ($10,000) plus other damages ($0) less expenses saved ($500 shipping charges from Seattle). $12,000 - 10,000 + 0 - 500 = $1,500.[39]

A second interpretative difficulty lies in defining the phrases "good faith" and "goods in substitution." Good faith will always be a slippery phrase, but there is no reason why it should be more slippery here than elsewhere. Sections 1-201(19) [40] and 1-203 have established a subjective standard for measuring good faith, that is, good faith in fact—the old white heart and empty head standard. In addition, a *merchant* buyer must observe "reasonable commercial standards of fair dealing in the trade" and is therefore subject to both a subjective and an objective test of good faith.[41] Presumably the covering buyer acts in good faith unless he intentionally avoids a less expensive market in favor of a more expensive one. If the cover remedy is to work to the benefit of an aggrieved buyer, the court should give him wide latitude to reject the least expensive cover when there is any reasonable basis for choosing a more ex-

defendant breached. Only two weeks later, plaintiff "covered" by making a substantially similar contract for all of the coal at $4 per ton "which was the market rate for such a forward contract, and rather below the market price of present deliveries. . . ." Under 2-712 damages would have roughly approached $83,000; the court's decision, however, refused to adopt that standard (which was urged by counsel) and instead awarded somewhat more than $22,000. The value the Code would have had to Missouri Furnace was over $60,000! See also Sauer v. McClintic-Marshall Const. Co., 179 Mich. 618, 146 N.W. 422 (1914).

38. $10,000 contract price plus $500 shipping charges.

39. The problem of expenses "saved in consequence of the seller's breach" is discussed more fully in relation to "Buyer's Damages for Nondelivery" (2-713) in Section 6-4 infra.

40. Section 1-201(19) provides, " 'Good faith' means honesty in fact in the conduct or transaction concerned."

41. Section 2-103(1) (b) provides, " 'Good faith' in the case of a merchant means honesty in fact and the observance of reasonable commercial standards of fair dealing in the trade."

pensive cover (for instance, the goods are of better quality or the seller more reliable).

It is a more difficult task to assign substance to the standard of reasonableness in 2–712. Section 2–712 presents two occasions to define reasonableness. Cover must be made without "unreasonable delay," and it must be a "reasonable purchase." Comment 2 to 2–712 suggests:

> The test of proper cover is whether at the time and place the buyer acted in good faith and in a reasonable manner, and it is immaterial that hindsight may later prove that the method of cover used was not the cheapest or most effective.

Thus, the unreasonable delay requirement is not intended to limit the time necessary for the buyer to decide how he may best effect the cover. Section 1–204(2) defines reasonable time as follows:

> What is a reasonable time for taking any action depends on the nature, purpose and circumstances of such action.

The drafters have hardly left us with a solid basis upon which to predict whether a given act was or was not "reasonable;" each new sentence of the comment is like an additional bucket of muck thrown into a quagmire. Of course the draftsmen were not dummies, and their vagueness was doubtless purposeful. One aid to which floundering courts and lawyers may turn is the Code's basic 1–106 remedial injunction: put the plaintiff in the position performance would have. If 2–712 is to be the remedy used by more aggrieved buyers than any other remedy, then the courts must be chary of finding a good faith buyer's acts unreasonable. The courts should not hedge the remedy about with restrictions in the name of "reasonableness" that render it useless or uncertain for the good faith buyer. Indeed, one may argue that the courts should read very little substance into the reasonableness requirement and insist only that the buyer proceed in good faith. A question a lawyer might put to test his client's good faith under 2–712 is this: "How, where, and when would you have procured these goods if you had not been covering and had no prospect of a court recovery from another?" If the client can answer truthfully that he would have spent his own money in the same way, the court should not demand more.

To comply with 2–712, buyer must purchase goods "in substitution for those due from the seller." Comment 2 to 2–712 tells us that the section "envisages . . . goods not identical with those involved but commercially usable as reasonable substitutes under the circumstances of the particular case; and contracts on credit or delivery terms differing from the contract in breach, but again reasonable under the circumstances." The "substitution" requirement poses two problems. First, how does one determine which of several contracts are in substitution when the buyer makes a series of purchases? Second, how does one adjust the damage formula when the cover item is "in substitution" but differs significantly from the contract items (for instance, A.M./F.M. radios in substitution for A.M. radios)?

When the relevant market prices are subject to abrupt and significant variation, a buyer who continually goes into the market for new purchases may have a wide range of possible alternatives for a cover contract. Though it seems unlikely that a buyer in reliance upon the outcome of an always uncertain law suit will spend more than necessary to cover, some buyer somewhere might select the contract that most significantly enhances his damage recovery. For example, if a buyer knows of four potential cover sellers whose prices for substantially identical goods range from $10,000 to $6,000 and if he buys from the seller charging the highest price, a court should deny his cover claim because he did not cover in good faith.[42]

What of the buyer who covers by purchasing goods of superior quality for use as a commercial substitute? Suppose, for example, that seller breaches a sales contract for four-speed food blenders. Desiring to take advantage of the Code's cover provision, buyer procures a substitute contract for more expensive eight-speed food blenders. If comparable four-speed machines were available, it is clear that buyer should not recover the full difference between his cover price and the contract price. Although Comment 2 instructs that the substitute need not be the least expensive cover, nothing in the Code indicates that the buyer is free to pass over an identical substitute and to select his own windfall.[43] Indeed 1–106 aims at matching performance, not more.

If the eight-speed blenders were the only available substitute, then what? One can argue that the buyer should recover the full difference between the price of the superior eight-speed and the contract price. Unlike in the former case, here the buyer has not elected to increase his damage recovery. If the added quality of the cover item will not benefit the buyer in any way, then he should be allowed to claim the full differential from the breaching seller. However, if because of the added quality the seller can prove that the buyer stands to make a greater profit on resale, then the buyer's damage recovery under 2–712 should be reduced sufficiently to put him in the same position as performance would have.

If the aggrieved buyer will himself consume the cover goods as for example by the use of furniture or equipment in a business, the

---

42. Peters, Remedies for Breach of Contracts Relating to the Sale of Goods Under the Uniform Commercial Code: Roadmap for Article Two, 73 Yale L.J. 199, 256 (1963).

43. Obviously if the buyer resells the item of superior quality for an increased subcontract price, his profit is that much larger; hence a windfall. But what if the goods are already under subcontract such that the buyer cannot raise the price and thus increase his profit? Commercial reality indicates that a windfall of value need not always take the form of dollar receipts. Certainly the buyer who resells a higher quality item without accordingly raising the price creates a favorable relationship with the sub-purchaser. In this case the buyer would derive a windfall in the form of goodwill.

problem is more difficult. Should the damage recovery under 2–712 be reduced because the cover machinery which the aggrieved buyer purchased is marginally more efficient? Because the waiting room furniture is slightly more attractive than that contracted for? We think the damage recovery should not be reduced unless the seller comes forward with persuasive evidence that the buyer will reap added profits because of the superior quality of the cover merchandise. To see that the buyer gets his full measure under 2–712 absent powerful evidence by seller, we would urge courts to construe 2–712 as a generous and relatively unfettered remedy for the aggrieved buyer. Of course it is possible that 2–712 will over-compensate an occasional buyer because the seller will be unable to prove that the buyer specially benefited from the added quality of the cover, but it seems equally likely that nonrecoverable legal fees and other costs of litigation will often offset any such benefit and that the more likely and more common consequence of 2–712's application is to leave the buyer short of the economic position that full and timely performance offered.

A final problem of some importance is whether a buyer who has covered may disregard 2–712 and sue for the contract-market differential in 2–713. We discuss that problem in Section 6–4. In sum, the importance of 2–712 cannot be overstated. Not only does the damage formula in 2–712 come close to putting the aggrieved buyer in the same economic position as actual performance, it also enables him to achieve his prime objective, namely that of acquiring his needed goods.[44]

## § 6–4  Contract-Market Damages, 2–713

Section 2–713 is as routine as 2–712 is novel. Section 2–713 gives the buyer the familiar contract-market differential. If businessmen do behave as the Code draftsmen believed that they do, 2–713 will be much less significant and much less used than 2–712. Presumably, the typical aggrieved buyer will persist in his desire to own the goods that he did not acquire from the breaching seller; accordingly he will cover. If our hypotheses are correct about business behavior, 2–713 will come into play only in the aberrational case in which the buyer decides not to cover or finds that he is unable to do so. Section 2–713 provides:

> (1) Subject to the provision of this Article with respect to proof of market price (Section 2–723), the measure of damages for non-delivery or repudiation by the seller is the difference between the market price at the time when the buyer learned of the breach and the contract price together with any incidental and consequential damages provided in this Article (Section 2–715), but less expenses saved in consequence of the seller's breach.

44. § 2–712, Comment 1.

(2) Market price is to be determined as of the place for tender or, in cases of rejection after arrival or revocation of acceptance, as of the place of arrival.[45]

The formula in 2–713 can be expressed as follows:

market price (at the time buyer learned of the breach)
- —  contract price
- —  expense saved
- +  incidental and consequential damages (2–715)

In its abstract form the damage formula is deceptively easy to understand. However, understanding the formula and putting it into operation are two different things. Consider the following questions:

*(1)*  When and where does one measure the market price? Does "tender" occur when goods are given to the carrier or only when the carrier delivers them to the buyer?

*(2)*  Has a buyer "saved expenses" when seller fails to ship and so frees buyer from paying the shipping costs on the contract goods? Or has such a buyer not "saved" these expenses because he will have to pay similar costs on any replacement contract?

*(3)*  What is the time for measuring the market in the special case of an anticipatory repudiation? Does "learned of the breach" mean the time buyer learned of the "repudiation," or the time of tender, or something else?

Before proceeding to these questions, one is well advised to search the section and its history for some principle to guide the trip through the thickets. Surely the Code draftsmen did not by this section intend to "put the buyer in the same position as performance would have." Performance would have given the buyer certain goods for consumption or resale. The consequence of such consumption or resale might have been either a net economic gain for the buyer or a net loss. The contract-market differential itself bears no necessary relation to the change in the buyer's economic status that the breach causes. It is possible that this differential might yield the buyer a handsome sum even though the breach actually saved him money in the long run (as for example when a middleman buyer's resale markets dry up after the breach). It is also quite possible that the buyer's lost profit from resale or consumption would be greater than the contract-market difference. Assume, for example, that seller breaches a $50,000 contract for hot pants. Assume further that the market

---

**45.** A prior draft of section 2–713 appeared in 1949 and 1952 as follows:

(1) The measure of damages for non-delivery is the difference between the price current at the time the buyer learned of the breach and the contract price together with the incidental and consequential damages as provided in this Article (Section 2–715), but less any expense saved in consequence of the seller's breach.

(2) Current price is to be determined as of the place for tender or, in cases of rejection after arrival or revocation of acceptance, as of the place of arrival.

price at the time used for the purposes of measuring 2–713 damages was $55,000 and that 2–713 would have yielded a $5,000 recovery for buyer.  Consider two separate hypothetical cases.  Assume that in each case, upon learning of the breach, the buyer decides not to cover for he believes that the market in hot pants is going cold.  Assume in case 1 that he proves to be correct; had seller delivered, buyer's gross receipts on resale of the contracted for goods would have been only $40,000.  Thus carrying out the contract would have cost him in excess of $10,000.  In such case a $5,000 difference money recovery under 2–713 would put buyer in a better position than performance would have.  Assume in case 2 that buyer also does not cover but assume that his judgment proves to be faulty.  It develops that hot pants are in short supply and can be sold at higher prices than he ever imagined so that his net profit on the contract would have been in excess of $20,000.  In that case the $5,000 recovery would leave him in a substantially worse economic position than performance would have.  So putting the buyer in the same place as performance would have cannot be the purpose of 2–713.

A second but no more happy explanation for the existence of 2–713 is simply that it is an historical anomaly.  Since cover was not a recognized remedy under pre-Code law, it made sense under that law to say that the contract-market formula put buyer in the same position as performance would have *on the assumption that the buyer would purchase substitute goods.*  If things worked right, the market price would approximate the cost of the substitute goods and buyer would be put "in the same position  .  .  .  ."  But under the Code, 2–712 does this job with greater precision, and 2–713 reigns over only those cases in which the buyer does not purchase a substitute.  Perhaps the draftsmen retained 2–713 not out of a belief in its appropriateness, but out of fear that they would be dismissed as iconoclasts had they proposed that the court in noncover cases simply award the buyer "any economic loss proximately caused by seller's breach."

A third, and perhaps the best, explanation of 2–713 is that it is a statutory liquidated damage clause, a breach inhibitor the payout of which need bear no close relation to plaintiff's actual loss.  This explanation conflicts with the policy in 1–106 (only as good a position as performance and no more), but is consistent with the belief that plaintiffs recover too little and too infrequently for the law of contracts to be effective.

Which of these analyses actually explains 2–713's presence in Article Two?  The draftsmen unquestionably intended that 2–713 take a backseat to 2–712 and certainly did not intend to offer an incentive (in the form of a higher damage award) which would influence buyers not to use 2–712.  It appears that the draftsmen intended 2–713's formula to yield approximately the same judgment in noncover cases against the seller as the 2–712 formula would have yielded had the buyer covered.  Comment 1 to 2–713 expresses the idea as follows:

> The general baseline adopted in this section uses as a yard-stick the market in which the buyer would have obtained cover had he sought that relief.

Section 2–713's statutory ancestor is section 67 of the Uniform Sales Act: "Action for Failing to Deliver Goods." [46]  The only important departure in 2–713 from USA § 67 is the choice of the "time when the buyer learned of the breach" as the time for measuring the market.  The Uniform Sales Act, in the absence of special circumstances, used "the time or times when they ought to have been delivered, or if no time was fixed, then at the time of the refusal to deliver." [47]  Except in the anticipatory repudiation cases (see Section 6–7 below) where the "learned of the breach" language contributes to hopeless confusion, this difference in the time when one measures the market is not likely to be significant since the buyer will usually learn of the breach at the time of tender or shortly thereafter.[48]  In fact we expect little if any change in the law as applied by the courts.[49]  Thus in Perkins v. Minford,[50] plaintiff contracted to purchase sugar from the defendant, F.O.B. shipping point (Cuba).  Defendant breached by sending too small a quantity, and plaintiff was unaware of this until receipt of the bill of lading.  By the time of receipt prices had risen sharply.  The court concluded that since the buyer neither knew nor had the means of discovering the breach and so could not protect against a rising market by buying from others:

> special circumstances are present showing proximate damages of a greater amount than those provided for by the general rule.  The time as to when the damages are to be measured is shifted.  It is now the date when the buyer knew or should have known of the default.[51]

The "learned of the breach" language of 2–713 may simply be a codification of the Act's "special circumstances" exception.

The basic operation of 2–713's formula is well illustrated by Deardorff-Jackson Co. v. National Produce Distributors, Inc.,[52] a reparation proceeding under the Perishable Agricultural Commodities Act of 1930.  Defendant entered into a written contract as the exclusive marketing agent for plaintiff's potatoes.  Defendant contracted to purchase fifty carloads of potatoes from the plaintiff, a local grower in Wasco, California.  Only twenty carloads of potatoes

---

**46.**  See note 36 supra.

**47.**  Id.

**48.**  Comment, The Uniform Commercial Code: Changes in the New York Law of Damages, 31 Fordham L.Rev. 749, 758 (1963).

**49.**  1 N.Y. State Law Revision Comm'n, 1955 Report 697 (1955).

**50.**  235 N.Y. 301, 139 N.E. 276 (1923).

**51.**  Id. at 305, 139 N.E. at 277.  A similar case relied on by the Perkins court was Boyd v. L. H. Quinn, 18 Misc. 169, 41 N.Y.S. 391 (1896).

**52.**  26 Agri.Dec. 1309, 4 UCC Rep.Serv. 1164 (1967).

were ever delivered. The court concluded that notice of the breach was first given on June 14, the date the first carload was shipped. The grower brought suit for the price of the potatoes delivered, and the buyer counterclaimed for the damages suffered because he was not able to fulfill his own resale obligations. Acknowledging the applicability of the 2–713 formula, the court took official notice of the prices quoted in the Federal Market News Report for June 14, 1965, for the type of potatoes specified under the contract. The court first ascertained the market value for the undelivered thirty carloads as $5.87½ per 100 pound sack or a total of $84,600. The contract price for the undelivered thirty carloads equalled $39,600. Applying the formula of market price less contract price, the court found damages in the amount of $45,000. However, because the defendant still owed $39,075 for potatoes delivered, his net recovery was $5,925. In this case defendant did not claim any additional incidental or consequential damages (2–715), nor did he claim the benefit of any expenses saved in consequence of the breach.

An initial and at least superficially thorny problem in the 2–713 formula concerns the place of tender—the place where the market is to be measured. Section 2–713 measures the market at "the place for tender or, in cases of rejection after arrival or revocation of acceptance . . . the place of arrival." Thus in all cases where the seller breaches or repudiates before delivery the relevant market will be the place for tender. Nowhere does the Code precisely define place of tender, but a good starting point in a search for a definition is 2–503:[53] "Manner of Seller's Tender of Delivery." Section 2–503 (1) at least half-heartedly defines tender in the "across the counter" sale, but only in the most oblique fashion does it deal with place of tender in the more common commercial contract in which seller ships to buyer via common carrier. Does tender occur when seller delivers goods to the carrier or only when the carrier delivers to buyer? Section 2–503(2) provides:

> Where the case is within the next section respecting shipment tender requires that the seller comply with its provisions.

If the section had gone on to say "and when a seller has complied with 2–504[54] he has tendered," our prayers would be answered. Un-

---

53. § 2–503:

(1) Tender of delivery requires that the seller put and hold conforming goods at the buyer's disposition and give the buyer any notification reasonably necessary to enable him to take delivery. The manner, time and place for tender are determined by the agreement and this Article, and in particular

(a) tender must be at a reasonable hour, and if it is of goods they must

be kept available for the period reasonably necessary to enable the buyer to take possession; but

(b) unless otherwise agreed the buyer must furnish facilities reasonably suited to the receipt of the goods.

54. § 2–504:

Where the seller is required or authorized to send the goods to the buyer and the contract does not require him to deliver them at a particular destina-

fortunately, only by implication does one get the message that a seller who complies with 2–504 has thus tendered. The implicit meaning of 2–503(2) is that a seller who is bound to ship goods to a buyer but not required to deliver them at a particular destination (that is, one who has contracted to ship "F.O.B. seller's plant," not F.O.B. buyer's plant) properly tenders by delivering the goods to the carrier and contracting for proper shipment. It follows that tender in a "destination" contract in which seller undertakes the obligation not just to ship but to deliver "F.O.B. buyer's plant" occurs only upon carrier's tender in buyer's city.[55]

The plausibility of the foregoing analysis is enhanced by the fact that it is consistent with the terms of the analogous risk of loss provisions.[56] Sections 2–509 and 2–319 indicate that risk of

---

tion, then unless otherwise agreed he must

(a) put the goods in the possession of such a carrier and make such a contract for their transportation as may be reasonable having regard to the nature of the goods and other circumstances of the case; and

(b) obtain and promptly deliver or tender in due form any document necessary to enable the buyer to obtain possession of the goods or otherwise required by the agreement or by usage of trade; and

(c) promptly notify the buyer of the shipment.

Failure to notify the buyer under subsection (c) or to make a proper contract under subsection (a) is a ground for rejection only if material delay or loss ensues.

55.  § 2–507:

(1) Tender of delivery is a condition to the buyer's duty to accept the goods and, unless otherwise agreed, to his duty to pay for them. Tender entitles the seller to acceptance of the goods and to payment according to the contract.

(2) Where payment is due and demanded on the delivery to the buyer of goods or documents of title, his right as against the seller to retain or dispose of them is conditional upon his making the payment due.

56.  § 2–509:

(1) Where the contract requires or authorizes the seller to ship the goods by carrier

(a) if it does not require him to deliver them at a particular destination, the risk of loss passes to the

buyer when the goods are duly delivered to the carrier even though the shipment is under reservation (Section 2–505); but

(b) if it does require him to deliver them at a particular destination and the goods are there duly tendered while in the possession of the carrier, the risk of loss passes to the buyer when the goods are there duly so tendered as to enable the buyer to take delivery.

(2) Where the goods are held by a bailee to be delivered without being moved, the risk of loss passes to the buyer

(a) on his receipt of a negotiable document of title covering the goods; or

(b) on acknowledgment by the bailee of the buyer's right to possession of the goods; or

(c) after his receipt of a non-negotiable document of title or other written direction to deliver, as provided in subsection (4)(b) of Section 2–503.

(3) In any case not within subsection (1) or (2), the risk of loss passes to the buyer on his receipt of the goods if the seller is a merchant; otherwise the risk passes to the buyer on tender of delivery.

(4) The provisions of this section are subject to contrary agreement of the parties and to the provisions of this Article on sale on approval (Section 2–327) and on effect of breach on risk of loss (Section 2–510).

§ 2–319:

(1) Unless otherwise agreed the term F.O.B. (which means "free on board") at a named place, even though used

loss in a destination contract passes to the buyer when the goods arrive at the particular destination [57] and in a shipment contract when the seller duly delivers the goods to the carrier.[58]  Consider for example, a shipment contract (F.O.B. shipping point) for pills from seller in Kalamazoo to buyer in East Liverpool.  Section 2–509 (1) (a) and 2–319(1) (a) indicate that the risk of loss passes to the buyer when the pills are delivered to the carrier in Kalamazoo. If the pills are destroyed *en route* and tender occurred when risk of loss passed on delivery to the carrier, buyer must bear the risk and

only in connection with the stated price, is a delivery term under which

(a) when the term is F.O.B. the place of shipment, the seller must at that place ship the goods in the manner provided in this Article (Section 2–504) and bear the expense and risk of putting them into the possession of the carrier; or

(b) when the term is F.O.B. the place of destination, the seller must at his own expense and risk transport the goods to that place and there tender delivery of them in the manner provided in this Article (Section 2–503);

(c) when under either (a) or (b) the term is also F.O.B. vessel, car or other vehicle, the seller must in addition at his own expense and risk load the goods on board.  If the term is F.O.B. vessel the buyer must name the vessel and in an appropriate case the seller must comply with the provisions of this Article on the form of bill of lading (Section 2–323).

(2) Unless otherwise agreed the term F.A.S. vessel (which means ("free alongside") at a named port, even though used only in connection with the stated price, is a delivery term under which the seller must

(a) at his own expense and risk deliver the goods alongside the vessel in the manner usual in that port or on a dock designated and provided by the buyer; and

(b) obtain and tender a receipt for the goods in exchange for which the carrier is under a duty to issue a bill of lading.

(3) Unless otherwise agreed in any case falling within subsection (1) (a) or (c) or subsection (2) the buyer must seasonably give any needed instructions for making delivery, including when the term is F.A.S. or F.O.B. the loading berth of the vessel and in an appropriate case its name and sail-

ing date.  The seller may treat the failure of needed instructions as a failure of cooperation under this Article (Section 2–311).  He may also at his option move the goods in any reasonable manner preparatory to delivery or shipment.

(4) Under the term F.O.B. vessel or F.A.S. unless otherwise agreed the buyer must make payment against tender of the required documents and the seller may not tender nor the buyer demand delivery of the goods in substitution for the documents.

57. § 2–509:

(1) Where the contract requires or authorizes the seller to ship the goods by carrier . . .

(b) if it does require him to deliver them at a particular destination and the goods are there duly tendered while in the possession of the carrier, the risk of loss passes to the buyer when the goods are there duly so tendered as to enable the buyer to take delivery.

§ 2–319:

. . .

(a) when the term is F.O.B. the place of shipment, the seller must at that place ship the goods in the manner provided in this Article (Section 2–504) and bear the expense and risk of putting them into the possession of the carrier . . . .

58. § 2–509:

(1) Where the contract requires or authorizes the seller to ship the goods by carrier

(a) if it does not require him to deliver them at a particular destination, the risk of loss passes to the buyer when the goods are duly delivered to the carrier even though the shipment is under reservation (Section 2–505) . . .

See note 56 supra (§ 2–319).

cannot shift it by responding with a suit for damages for breach, for seller's conforming "tender" in Kalamazoo fulfilled his obligations. If, on the other hand, we were to conclude that tender under 2–503 and 2–504 occurred only on arrival in East Liverpool, then we would have open warfare between 2–509 (buyer bears the risk in shipment) and 2–507 (seller's tender in East Liverpool must conform to the contract). Our conclusion that tender in a "shipment" contract occurs when goods are duly delivered to the carrier and that in a "destination" contract it occurs only upon tender to the buyer by the carrier puts all these sections in harmony.

Our analysis of place of tender in 2–713 is consistent with pre-Code case law. The Uniform Sales Act specified no particular place for the measurement of damages, and many courts relied on Judge Cardozo's holding in Standard Casing Co. v. California Casing Co.[59] where plaintiff-buyer in New York contracted for twenty casks of salted pig guts F.O.B. shipping point from a California seller:

> The damages are to be estimated according to the conditions prevailing at the place where the final act of performance was due from the vendor [California].[60]

What of the case in which seller holds the goods for buyer? The place of tender under the Code would be seller's place of business, but it still may be difficult to determine the time for tender. The pre-Code cases decided under the USA reflect a substantial concern with the elusive concept of property and title. In Sadler Machinery Co. v. Ohio National, Inc.,[61] a machine manufacturer in Upper Sandusky, Ohio, who had contracted to sell equipment to a dealer in Detroit, Michigan, agreed to retain and store the machinery at his plant for a week or two beginning about January 26, 1951. On January 30, 1951, the machinery was destroyed by fire. The court framed the issue as follows: "Did title to the machine pass to the plaintiff prior to the loss?"[62] The court set out USA § 18 and USA § 1[63] and decided that title had passed.[64] Unlike the

**59.** 233 N.Y. 413, 135 N.E. 834 (1922).

**60.** Id. at 419, 135 N.E. at 836.

**61.** 102 F.Supp. 652 (N.D. Ohio 1952), aff'd, 202 F.2d 887 (6th Cir. 1953).

**62.** 102 F.Supp. at 653.

**63.** USA § 18:

(1) Where there is a contract to sell specific or ascertained goods, the property in them is transferred to the buyer at such time as the parties to the contract intend it to be transferred.

(2) For the purpose of ascertaining the intention of the parties, regard shall be had to the terms of the contract, the conduct of the parties, usages of trade and the circumstances of the case.

USA § 19:

. . .

(Rule 5) If the contract to sell requires the seller to deliver the goods to the buyer, or at a particular place, or to pay the freight or cost of transportation to the buyer, or to a particular place, the property does not pass until the goods have been delivered to the buyer or reached the place agreed upon.

**64.** Then relying on USA § 22, the court concluded that risk of loss was also on the buyer.

USA § 22:

Unless otherwise agreed, the goods remain at the seller's risk until the property therein is transferred to the buyer, but when the property therein is transferred to the buyer the goods are

situation where the goods are shipped via a carrier, 2–503 and 2–509 (3) of the Code indicate that where the seller holds goods for the buyer, tender and risk of loss are not inextricably intertwined.[65] Subsection (1) of 2–503 requires the tendering seller to put conforming goods at the buyer's disposition and that the buyer be given reasonable notice. Applying the Code to the *Sadler Machine Co.* facts a court should probably find that Ohio National had put the goods at buyer's disposition, and the several communications passing between the parties served as adequate notice. Thus, under the Code too, tender probably occurred before the fire. (Note, however, that risk probably will have passed only upon receipt and not upon tender in *Ohio National* under the Code.)[66]

A second interpretative problem in 2–713 concerns the meaning of "expenses saved in consequence of the seller's breach."[67] There are at least three common contracts in which this problem may arise with respect to transportation costs: (*1*) an F.O.B. shipment contract under which goods are shipped and eventually rejected, (*2*) an F.O.B. shipment contract under which goods are never shipped, and (*3*) an F.O.B. destination contract. In the first (goods are shipped F.O.B. seller's plant but rejected by buyer before he pays the shipping cost), the 2–713 damage formula measures the market for the con-

---

at the buyer's risk whether delivery has been made or not, except that

(a) where delivery of the goods has been made to the buyer or to a bailee for the buyer, in pursuance of the contract and the property in the goods has been retained by the seller merely to secure performance by the buyer of his obligations under the contract, the goods are at the buyer's risk from the time of such delivery.

(b) Where delivery has been delayed through the fault of either the buyer or seller the goods are at the risk of the party in fault as regards any loss which might not have occurred but for such fault.

**65.** Thus, in the case of a merchant seller, section 2–509(3) and Comment 3 thereto indicate that risk of loss will not pass to the buyer until actual receipt of the goods.

**66.** However, under section 2–509(3) tender and the passage of risk of loss are not synonymous. Section 2–509(3) reads as follows:

In any case not within subsection (1) or (2), the risk of loss passes to the buyer on his receipt of the goods

if the seller is a merchant; otherwise the risk passes to the buyer on tender of delivery.

Thus unless Ohio National is a merchant, risk of loss would have passed to Sadler when Ohio National tendered delivery. However, under 2–104 Ohio National is probably a merchant since it "deals in goods of the kind" and "holds [it]self out as having knowledge or skill peculiar to the practices or goods involved." Because Ohio National is thus a merchant, risk of loss does not pass until the buyer actually receives the goods, and thus under the Code the case would have come out differently.

**67.** § 2–713:

(1) Subject to the provisions of this Article with respect to proof of market price (Section 2–723), the measure of damages for non-delivery or repudiation by the seller is the difference between the market price at the time when the buyer learned of the breach and the contract price together with any incidental consequential damages provided in this Article (Section 2–715), but less expenses saved in consequence of the seller's breach.

tract market differential as of the place of arrival.[68]   Comment 1 to 2–713 states the philosophy as follows:

> . . . as a yardstick the market in which the buyer would have obtained cover had he sought that relief.  So the place for measuring damages is the place of tender (or the place of arrival if the goods are rejected or their acceptance is revoked after reaching their destination). . . .[69]

The assumption is that in cases of rejection after arrival the buyer will eventually or would have covered as of the place of arrival.  In a shipment contract, that is, F.O.B. seller's place of business or shipping point, the buyer would have borne the expenses of shipment.  If, however, the buyer in case of rejection after arrival would turn to a local market for cover, there would be no shipping expenses in the replacement contract.  As a result of the breach the buyer would pay that much less or save that amount "in consequence of the seller's breach."  Therefore the shipping cost should be subtracted from the contract-market differential and any incidental and consequential damages recovered under 2–715.

To illustrate, assume a Chicago seller ships $20,000 of nonconforming goods, F.O.B. seller's plant, to a San Diego buyer who rejects the goods upon their arrival.  Assume that the market value in California is $25,000 at the time buyer learned of the breach and that buyer's shipping expenses would have been $4,000.  Damages under 2–713 should be the market-contract differential, ($25,000–$20,000) less expenses saved ($4,000), or total damages of $1,000.  Note that $1,000 puts buyer in the same position as he would have been in had he covered in San Diego on the date he learned of the breach.  When the goods are never shipped under an F.O.B. shipping point contract, market price is measured as of the place for tender, the seller's place of business.[70]  The assumption, expressed in Comment 1 to 2–713, is that the buyer will search for a replacement contract at the shipping point.[71]  If buyer seeks a replacement at the shipping point, he would incur replacement shipping costs roughly equivalent to those on the original contract.  Thus by comparison with such a replacement contract there would be no expenses "saved" in consequence of the seller's breach because we are assuming that the buyer must pay the expenses for shipment under the new contract as well.

---

68. § 2–713(2):

Market price is to be determined as of the place for tender or, in cases of rejection after arrival or revocation of acceptance, as of the place of arrival.

69. § 2–713, Comment 1.

70. § 2–713.

71. Thus the Code makes contradictory assumptions in the cases where the "shipping market" or the "delivery market" is used to measure market price.  Is the distinction well founded?  Conceding that the shipping market may be the norm, in a case of rejection the buyer may be pressed for time and therefore be unable to return to the usual market.  However, there is little reason to assume that this reason is sufficiently widespread to justify transforming an exception into a rule.

A final case is that of a destination contract (F.O.B. buyer's plant). In this situation the place for tender and the place of arrival will be identical. The buyer bears no shipping cost. Thus there are no shipping expenses to be saved in consequence of the seller's breach.

Assuming that an aggrieved buyer can find the proper time and place at which to measure the market price, what proof of the market is necessary? What is sufficient? Comment 2 to 2–713 suggests one should turn first to the "general market price" for goods of the same kind.[72] Commodity and securities markets of course fit this description. It would also seem that one could usually find a general market for widely sold goods such as new and used cars. For those who cannot find such a market the Code offers 2–723. That section allows reasonable leeway in time, place, and even kinds of substitutes.[73] Comment 3 to 2–713 goes even further; it approves the use of evidence of spot sale prices where there is no available market price. The Code directs the courts to accept virtually any evidence, even that with marginal relevance. Of course, aggrieved buyers and sellers will still argue that some evidence is too uncertain to be received in a court of law. And not all courts will be as fortunate as the *Deardorff-Jackson* court which simply picked the relevant price of potatoes from the Federal Market News Report.

Finally we come to the problem of a buyer who has covered but who seeks to ignore 2–712 and sue for a larger contract-market differential under 2–713. On first reading, it seems that he can disregard 2–712; section 2–711 tells buyers they can "cover" or they can recover damages for nondelivery under 2–713. Commenting on the relationship between 2–712 and 2–713, Professor Peters has argued that an aggrieved buyer who purchases goods "in substitution" may disregard 2–712 and seek recovery under the standard-contract differential of 2–713.[74] However, this interpretation allows a buyer to learn of a breach on September 2 when the market is at $25,000, wait until September 15 to cover, when the market is at $23,000, and then sue under 2–713 for the higher damages of contract-

---

72. § 2–713, Comment 2:

The market or current price to be used in comparison with the contract price under this section is the price for goods of the same kind and in the same branch of trade.

73. § 2–723:

. . . . .

(2) If evidence of a price prevailing at the times or places described in this Article is not readily available the price prevailing within any reasonable time before or after the time described or at any other place which in commercial judgment or under usage of trade would serve as a reasonable sub-

stitute for the one described may be used, making any proper allowance for the cost of transporting the goods to or from such other place.

(3) Evidence of a relevant price prevailing at a time or place other than the one described in this Article offered by one party is not admissible unless and until he has given the other party such notice as the court finds sufficient to prevent unfair surprise.

74. Peters, Remedies for Breach of Contracts Relating to the Sale of Goods Under the Uniform Commercial Code: Roadmap for Article Two, 73 Yale L.J. 199, 260 (1963).

market differential.  Moreover Comment 5 to 2–713 indicates that a buyer who has covered may not use 2–713 (emphasis added):

> The present section provides a remedy which is *completely alternative* to cover under the preceding section and applies only *when and to the extent that the buyer has not covered.*

If the Code's goal is to put the buyer in the same position as though there had been no breach,[75] and if 2–712 will accomplish that goal but 2–713 [76] will do so only by coincidence, why not force the covering buyer to use 2–712?  This setting does not call for punitive damages.  Nor is it analogous to the similar case on the seller's side when an aggrieved seller who resells under 2–706 to one of his customers loses volume and thus needs an additional remedy to put him in the same position as performance would have.  Notwithstanding Professor Peters' arguments concerning the statutory history and her pleas for identical rules on the buyer's and seller's side, both the message of the comment and the policy of the Code properly deny the covering buyer any use of 2–713.[77]

---

75.  Section 1–106(1).  The "same position" would include as badly off as though there had been no breach.  See L. Albert & Son v. Armstrong Rubber Co., 178 F.2d 182 (2d Cir. 1949) (Learned Hand, C. J.).  Buyer was given a set-off, against seller's damages, in the amount of $3,000 buyer spent building the foundation for the "Refiners."  But buyer's set-off was "subject to the seller's privilege to deduct from that amount any sum which upon a further hearing it can prove would have been the buyer's loss upon the contract, had the 'Refiners' been delivered on or before May 1st, 1945." 178 F.2d at 191.  But see Annot., 17 A.L.R.2d 1300, 1334 (1951) and cases cited therein.  See also Professor Palmer's incisive analysis, The Contract Price as a Limit on Restitution for Defendant's Breach, 20 Ohio State L.J. 264 (1959).

76.  Section 2–713(1) states, "[T]he measure of damages for non-delivery or repudiation by the seller is the difference between the market price . . . and the contract price together with any incidental and consequential damages provided in this Article (Section 2–715), but less expenses saved in consequence of the seller's breach."

77.  Section 2–712(3) provides that "failure of the buyer to effect cover within this section does not bar him from

any other remedy."  However, as Comment 3 candidly admits, failing to cover when such is possible can have ramifications.  First, 2–715(2)(a) limits consequential damages from seller's breach to:

any loss resulting from general or particular requirements and needs of which the seller at the time of contracting had reason to know *and which could not reasonably be prevented by cover* or otherwise.  (Emphasis added.)

Thus failing to utilize the cover remedy when a reasonable substitute is available will preclude recovery of consequential damages.  Secondly, recovery may be a determinant of the availability of specific performance which "may be decreed where the goods are unique or in other proper circumstances."  Rejecting uniqueness as the singular requirement for specific relief, Comment 2 explicitly recommends that "inability to cover is strong evidence of 'other proper circumstances.'"  Finally, speaking for itself as to the effect of the possibility of cover on the remedy of replevin, section 2–716(3) provides in part:

The buyer has a right of replevin for goods identified to the contract if after reasonable effort he is unable to effect cover for such goods or the circumstances reasonably indicate that such effort will be unavailing . . . .

## § 6–5   Buyer's Incidental and Consequential Damages

We deal with the question of incidental and consequential damages at length in Chapter 10.   See Sections 10–3 and 10–4.

## § 6–6   Specific Performance

When, in normal circumstances, the seller of five-penny nails defaults on his contract, his buyer will then purchase nails from another supplier and may or may not think it worth the legal fees, time, and grief to sue under 2–712.   If, however, the buyer can readily procure five-penny nails only from the breaching seller, he may try to force the seller to deliver.   If in addition the aggrieved buyer has pre-paid the price to a shaky seller who may not be good for a money judgment, his interest in specific performance will intensify. To accommodate buyers who want the goods and not money, the Code offers sections 2–716 and 2–502.[78]   Section 2–716 provides:

(1) Specific performance may be decreed where the goods are unique or in other proper circumstances.

(2) The decree for specific performance may include such terms and conditions as to payment of the price, damages, or other relief as the court may deem just.

(3) The buyer has a right of replevin for goods identified to the contract if after reasonable effort he is unable to effect cover for such goods or the circumstances reasonably indicate that such effort will be unavailing or if the goods have been shipped under reservation and satisfaction of the security interest in them has been made or tendered.[79]

Of course the Code draftsmen did not write on a *tabula rasa* here but upon a slate already crowded with centuries of judicial and legislative markings.   The most familiar of these markings is the requirement that for a court to grant specific performance, the plaintiff's remedy at law must be inadequate.   Section 68 of the Uniform Sales Act sought to liberalize that requirement by inviting courts to grant specific performance as to "specific or ascertained goods" whenever they "think fit." [80]   However, the pre-Code decisions (both under the USA and general equity powers) generally did not liberalize the availability of specific performance in sale of goods cases.[81]

---

**78.**   § 2–502:

(1) Subject to subsection (2) and even though the goods have not been shipped a buyer who has paid a part or all of the price of goods in which he has a special property under the provisions of the immediately preceding section may on making and keeping good a tender of any unpaid portion of their price recover them from the seller if the seller becomes insolvent within ten days after receipt of the first installment on their price.

(2) If the identification creating his special property has been made by the buyer he acquires the right to recover the goods only if they conform to the contract for sale.

**79.**   At this point the reader should compare section 2–709 and discussion in Sections 7–2 et seq., infra.

**80.**   See also 1 N.Y. State Law Revision Comm'n, 1955 Report 575 (1955).

**81.**   See, e. g., Eastern Rolling Mill Co. v. Michlovitz, 157 Md. 51, 145 A. 378

Like the USA, the Code (2–716(1)) omits any express proviso that the remedy at law be inadequate; moreover it deletes the Uniform Sales Act's requirement that the goods be "specific" and instead authorizes specific performance "where the goods are unique or in other proper circumstances." [82]   Comment 1 to 2–716 reveals the intent of the draftsmen to continue "in general prior policy as to specific performance and injunction against breach," but it also "seeks to further a more liberal attitude than some courts have shown" toward specific performance.[83]   It is still too early to tell whether the Code will be more successful than the USA in liberalizing the availability of specific performance.

An initial lawyer problem under 2–716 concerns the words "unique or in other proper circumstances."   Surely treasured heirlooms remain "unique," but Comment 2 to 2–716 suggests an even broader reach:

> The test  .  .  .   must be made in terms of the total situation which characterizes the contract.  Output and requirements contracts involving a particular or peculiarly available source or market present today the typical commercial specific performance situation.  .  .  .

The courts are thus encouraged to take notice of current market sources and commercial realities in determining whether goods are "unique."

The three decisions thus far under 2–716(1) put little flesh on the bones of "unique."   In the first, McCormick Dray Line, Inc. v. Lovell,[84] the court granted specific performance of a contract for the sale of a trucking business.  The court found that the rights under the certificates issued by the Interstate Commerce Commission and the Public Utility Commission were unique.  In a second case, Hilmor Sales Co. v. Helen Neushaefer Division of Supronics Corp.,[85] the plaintiff sought to enjoin the defendant from disposing of lipstick and nail polish which were the subject of a sale contract.  According to the court the only unique aspect of the contract was the "closeout" price.  Plaintiff could not purchase similar goods at such a favorable

---

(1929); Curtice Brothers Co. v. Catts, 72 N.J.Eq. 831, 66 A. 935 (1907); Manchester Dairy System, Inc. v. Hayward, 82 N.H. 193, 132 A. 12 (1926); Fortner v. Wilson, 202 Okl. 563, 216 P.2d 299 (1950).

**82.** USA § 68:

> Where the seller has broken a contract to deliver specific or ascertained goods, a court having the powers of a court of equity may, if it thinks fit, on the application of the buyer, by its judgment or decree, direct that the contract shall be performed specifically, without giving the seller the option of retaining the goods on payment

of damages.  The judgment or decree may be unconditional, or upon such terms and conditions as to damages, payment of the price and otherwise, as to the court may seem just.

**83.** Yet in the absence of unique goods, the adequacy test may be relevant to determine if this is a case of "other proper circumstances."  Cf. Hilmor Sales Co. v. Helen Neushaefer Division of Supronics Corp., 6 UCC Rep. Serv. 325 (N.Y.Sup.Ct.1969).

**84.** 13 Pa.D. & C.2d 464 (C.P.1957).

**85.** 6 UCC Rep.Serv. 325 (N.Y.Sup.Ct. 1969).

price elsewhere, but he did not claim that replacement was impossible; accordingly the court denied specific relief. The third case, Division of the Triple T Service, Inc. v. Mobile Oil Corp.,[86] also resulted in a denial of plaintiff's claim for injunction. There the plaintiff sought to enjoin the defendant from ending his service station franchise relationship. In a long opinion which contains dictum to the effect that a franchise agreement is analogous to an output contract and therefore an appropriate subject for injunctive relief, the court denied the injunction principally on the ground that the contract contained a clause allowing the franchisor to cancel and that in so doing it did not breach its franchise obligations.

The outcome of all three cases seems correct under the Code, but the direction in which they point is unclear. The analogy in the dictum in the *Mobil Oil* case between an output contract and a franchise seems correct and in the absence of a specific clause authorizing termination, the court could properly have granted the franchisee's request for specific performance of the franchise contract. One certainly can not quarrel with the holding in the *Hilmor* case if the plaintiff showed only that he had a contract at a very favorable price. However, the dictum in that case is disturbing, for it states that it is never appropriate to award specific performance where the "plaintiff can be adequately compensated for any breach . . . by an award of money damages."[87] It is also disturbing that the court (in dictum) requires that the plaintiff "demonstrate that it would be irreparably damaged if the injunction . . . is not granted."[88] If other courts persist in similar resurrection of common law and equity doctrine of this kind, it seems likely that the Code will meet with no more success than the USA did in its attempt to expand the availability of specific relief.

Even if goods are not unique, specific performance may be in order if a buyer can show "other proper circumstances." Comment 2 to 2–716 gives this cryptic phrase some meaning:

> [T]he relief may also be granted "in other proper circumstances" and inability to cover is strong evidence of "other proper circumstances."

Perhaps this phrase was added to preserve the traditional power of an equity court to provide or withhold specific relief at its sound discretion and subject to such traditional defenses in equity as clean hands, laches, etc. The section is troublesome, however, since the perimeters of uniqueness *vis a vis* "other proper circumstances" remain undefined. If "uniqueness" equals "not available elsewhere," then what is left for the category "other proper circumstances"? Your guess is as good as ours.

---

86. 60 Misc.2d 720, 304 N.Y.S.2d 191, 6 UCC Rep.Serv. 1011 (Sup.Ct.1969).

87. 6 UCC Rep.Serv. 325, 325 (N.Y.Sup. Ct.1969).

88. Id.

Sections 2–502 and 2–716(3) give buyer a *right* to goods in seller's hands in certain limited circumstances when the goods have been "identified" to the contract. Unlike the discretionary remedy of specific performance, presumably the court must grant a decree of replevin if the buyer's case fits the narrow limits of 2–502 or the somewhat more generous terms of 2–716(3). Still the principal condition for application to 2–716(3) (cover unavailable) looks suspiciously like "uniqueness" in a new attire.

Section 2–502(1) reads as follows:

> Subject to subsection (2) and even though the goods have not been shipped a buyer who has paid a part or all of the price of goods in which he has a special property under the provisions of the immediately preceding section may on making and keeping good a tender of any unpaid portion of their price recover them from the seller if the seller becomes insolvent within ten days after receipt of the first installment on their price.

Section 2–502 gives a right to specific recovery of goods identified to the contract if the seller becomes insolvent within ten days after receipt of the first installment on their price.[89] Thus in a limited number of cases the Code resolves the perplexing problem whether insolvency alone is a sufficient ground for specific relief.[90]

However, the Code limits this right to reach the goods in several ways. First it limits that right to the situation in which the seller becomes insolvent "within 10 days after receipt of the first installment on their price." The period is short, and the contract goods must be identified within or prior to those ten days. At least in the case of the buyer who advances capital to finance manufacture of his goods, identification will often come too late to aid an aggrieved buyer. When one considers not only the ten-day limitation but also the possibility (if not probability) that buyer's 2–502 rights will be subordinate to the rights of the trustee in bankruptcy under sections 60 and 70 of the Bankruptcy Act and to the rights of secured creditors, the importance of this section diminishes even further.[91]

When 2–502 is unavailable, buyer can fall back on 2–716(3) as a second line of defense. Under this section the buyer may replevy goods identified to the contract when (*1*) cover is or reasonably appears to be foreclosed, or (*2*) goods are shipped under reservation (for instance, shipment under a negotiable bill of lading to seller's order) and satisfaction of the security interest is at least tendered. Of course, the buyer's rights under this section are subject to attack

---

**89.** § 2–502, Comment 1.

**90.** See 5A A. Corbin, Corbin on Contracts § 1156 (1964).

**91.** See Kennedy, The Trustee in Bankruptcy Under the Uniform Commercial Code, 14 Rutgers L.Rev. 518, 556–59 (1960); Shanker, Bankruptcy and Article 2 of the Uniform Commercial Code, 40 J.Nat'l Con.Ref.Bankr. 37, 43–44 (1966); Comment, 79 Harv.L. Rev. 598, 600–607 (1966).

by the trustee in bankruptcy with the same weapons he will use against 2–502.

While one would expect this section to be used most commonly where cover is unavailable, even here the section may be of limited use since if the goods are unique the buyer can get specific performance; if they are not unique, then reaching the goods is unnecessary. However, even if the bare inability to cover proves neither "uniqueness" nor "other proper circumstances," the aggrieved buyer faces a difficult burden to prove that he was "unable to effect cover" for the goods. Not only must the buyer prove that a market did not exist (or at least was inaccessible), he must also convince the court that a breaching seller who is willing to sell to the buyer at a price over the contract price should not be considered an available source for cover. Also, equity is by tradition unwilling to force parties to work together, especially for any sustained period.[92] It may be crucial here to consider the relative bargaining positions of the parties, good faith, changes in market conditions, etc. It is far too early to predict how the courts will resolve these issues, and the wise attorney (like the timid treatise writer) should here be wary of any firm predictions.

## § 6–7   The Buyer's Possible Responses to Repudiation

Above we have discussed buyer's remedies in general and have attempted to define "repudiation." Here we turn to the most difficult interpretative problems that face the buyer who desires a remedy for anticipatory repudiation.

His basic alternatives are indexed in 2–610:

> . . . the aggrieved party may

> (a) for a commercially reasonable time await performance by the repudiating party; or

> (b) resort to any remedy for breach (Section 2–703 or Section 2–711), even though he has notified the repudiating party that he would await the latter's performance and has urged retraction; and

> (c) in either case suspend his own performance. . . .

Section 2–610(b) thus provides a remedy for breach of contract before the time for performance has arrived. Section 2–610(c) follows logically from 2–610(b), for it would be inconsistent to allow one party to sue for breach and at the same time to require him to continue performance. Yet several questions remain under the 2–610 option of treating a repudiation as an immediate breach. When does the breach occur? Are damages measured as of the time for performance, time of repudiation, or some other time?

---

92.   See generally 5A A. Corbin, Corbin on Contracts §§ 1204, 1206 (1964).

The buyer who chooses to treat the repudiation as a breach may "resort to any remedy" (2–610(b)). That is to say he may (1) recover "so much of the price as has been paid" (2–711),[93] (2) cancel [94] (that is, tell the seller to stop work), and (3) seek damages under 2–713 or cover and seek damages under 2–712.[95]

If cover is unavailable (as where the goods are unique), 2–610, 2–711, and 2–716 indicate that specific performance may be available.[96] One significant problem arises with specific relief in the context of anticipatory breach: when should the repudiator perform? Although 2–610(b) directs the aggrieved buyer immediately to "resort to any remedy for breach," the Code doesn't answer this question. The problem, of course, concerns the propriety of accelerating the contractual obligations of the repudiator. Pre-Code law soundly resolved this issue by allowing the repudiatee to bring an immediate action for a decree of specific performance, but it postponed the effectiveness of the decree itself until the date for performance specified in the contract.[97] Section 2–610(b) is susceptible to the same analysis. The aggrieved party will have immediate recourse against the repudiator (as 2–610(b) directs in order to provide relief for an injured party to a contract). However, to avoid undue hardship on the repudiating party, the decree of specific relief should in most circumstances require performance in accordance with the contract and not at an accelerated pace.

A buyer's suit for damages under 2–713 upon an anticipatory repudiation presents perhaps the most grizzly interpretative problem in Article two: when does one measure the market? Does "learned of the breach" mean "learned of the repudiation"? The Code sections

93. Throughout Chapters 6 and 7 we maintain that the plaintiff should never recover more than enough to put him in the same position as performance would have put him (1–106). This may not be precisely true since 2–711 allows a buyer to recover "so much of the price as has been paid" whether or not he recovers other damages. If the buyer has paid $5,000 of the contract price and the contract would have lost him $5,000 or more because his resale market price was lower than the contract price, our theory would say that buyer could not recover damages since that would exceed the value of performance. Nevertheless 2–711 seems to allow buyer to recover the full amount he paid. An old restitution case, Bush v. Canfield, 2 Conn. 485 (1818), specifically rejects the seller's argument that the buyer's potential loss of $3,000 on 2,000 barrels of flour should be deducted from the recovery of a $5,000 down payment made on the contract.

For an illuminating and useful discussion of limitations on damages, see Palmer, The Contract Price as a Limit on Restitution for Defendant's Breach, 20 Ohio State L.J. 264 (1959).

94. Distinguish this true rescission from rescission of anticipatory breach coupled with a right of action on the contract. See, e. g., Baird v. Barton, 163 Cal.App.2d 502, 329 P.2d 492 (3d Dist.1958); Gordon v. Southgate Park Corp., 341 Mass. 534, 170 N.E.2d 691 (1960); Graulich Caterer, Inc. v. Hans Holterbosch, Inc., 101 N.J.Super. 61, 243 A.2d 253, 5 UCC Rep.Serv. 440 (App.Div.1968); Carvage v. Stowell, 115 Vt. 187, 55 A.2d 188 (1947).

95. See Section 6–3 supra (§ 2–712).

96. See Section 6–6 supra (§ 2–716).

97. See, e. g., Brackenbury v. Hodgkin, 116 Me. 399, 102 A. 106 (1917).

whose branches entangle to make an impossible legal ticket are 2–610, 2–711, 2–713, and 2–723.

Consider first 2–713 (emphasis added):

> Subject to the provisions of the Article with respect to proof of market price (Section 2–723), the measure of damages for nondelivery or repudiation by the seller is the difference between the market price at the time when the *buyer learned of the breach* and the contract price. . . .

The most obvious reading of the language of 2–713—the one you would get from your spouse if you presented an anticipatory repudiation case to her—"learned of the breach" is the equivalent of "learned of the repudiation," and therefore damages should be measured at the time the buyer learned of the repudiation.[98]

One learned in the tortuous ways of legal analysis of statutory material and freed by his legal training from the layman's common sense, can think of several other interpretations of the language. The most plausible rival interpretation is to find that the words "time when the buyer learned of the breach" mean "time of performance" in anticipatory repudiation cases. By referring to the commercially reasonable time for awaiting performance which 2–610 (a) offers, one can argue that "learned of the breach" should be interpreted to mean repudiation plus such a "commercially reasonable time." We can offer several persuasive and elegant arguments in support of our first alternative reading, the reading that would interpret the language "time when the buyer learned of the breach" to mean "time of performance" in an anticipatory repudiation case.

In the first place, if they intended to mean repudiation why didn't those able fellows who drafted the Code use the word "repudiation" instead of "breach"? Secondly, if the buyer's damages are to be measured at the time he learned of the breach, then he cannot do what 2–610(a) apparently gives him the right to do, namely await performance for a "commercially reasonable time" without suffering

---

98.  Consider § 2–723(1):

(1) If an action based on anticipatory repudiation comes to trial before the time for performance with respect to some or all of the goods, any damages based on market price (Section 2–708 or Section 2–713) shall be determined according to the price of such goods prevailing at the time when the aggrieved party learned of the repudiation.

This section explicitly applies to any case of anticipatory repudiation coming to trial before the time for performance named in the contract. In that situation the market is to be measured "at the time when the aggrieved party learned of the repudiation." Although the conflicting provisions affecting repudiation might more easily be reconciled by finding that 2–723 applies only to sellers (and thus does not conflict with 2–713, 2–712, etc.), two important facts to the contrary make such an argument untenable: (1) 2–723 in terms refers to 2–713 and thus was probably intended to be used by buyers and (2) 2–713 as well refers specifically to 2–723.

The importance of 2–723 should not be overestimated, however. Unfortunately court dockets have become increasingly longer, and the result is often to force an aggrieved party to wait for several years. Thus it will usually be only the long term installment contract party who can avail himself of 2–723(1).

any loss from what would otherwise have been his appropriate damage claim. Assume, for example, that a buyer of skis learns of a seller's repudiation of the contract on August 2 when the market is $125 per pair. Buyer exercises his right to wait a reasonable time and waits for performance until September 2 (when the market has risen to $150 a pair). Under the "plain meaning" interpretation of 2–713(1) the buyer would be forced to compute his damages based upon the August 2 market price, and he would be deprived of the right to wait that 2–610 apparently offers. (Of course if buyer can and does cover, he will not be affected by the interpretation put on 2–713.)

A third argument which serves to explain the use of the language "learned of the breach" is that the draftsmen intended to deal only with that case in which there had been no anticipatory repudiation but in which the buyer had learned of the breach only after performance had come and gone. It appears that Professor Patterson in his report to the New York Law Revision Commission adopted this interpretation of the language "learned of the breach" and did not consider the possibility that it could also apply to a time prior to the time of tender.

He commented that 2–713 was "apparently a change in New York law; but actually it probably is not a change in the law as applied by New York courts." [99] He was referring to the "special circumstances" exception to section 67 of the Uniform Sales Act which allowed the court in special circumstances to measure the market at a time other than that scheduled for performance. However, the two cases cited [100] for this proposition indicate that the "special circumstances" exception (and thus the Code "learned of the breach" rule) was used to delay the time to measure the market past the date scheduled for performance; the section was not intended to accelerate the time to measure the market in a repudiation case. In Perkins v. Minford,[101] defendant (seller) breached a contract for the sale of sugar by shipping too small a quantity; defendant was unaware of the breach until he received the bill of lading. It was in this setting that the court declared that special circumstances warranted measuring the market at a *later* date:

> The reason is clear. Usually, knowing of the breach of the contract, the buyer may protect himself against the consequences of a rising market by buying from others. But . . . what if the delivery being made at a distance the buyer neither knows nor has means of knowledge that the contract has not been completed until he actually receives the goods or a bill of lading stating the amount shipped to him? . . . The time as to when the damages are meas-

99. 1 N.Y. State Law Revision Comm'n, 1955 Report 698 (1955).

100. Perkins v. Minford, 235 N.Y. 301, 139 N.E. 276 (1923); Boyd v. L. H.

Quinn, 18 Misc. 169, 41 N.Y.S. 391 (App.Term 1896).

101. 235 N.Y. 301, 139 N.E. 276 (1923).

ured is shifted. It is now the date when the buyer knew or should have known of the default.[102]

Similarly in Boyd v. Quinn,[103] the court recognized an extraordinary situation existed where seller breached a contract to ship goods by rail (from Illinois to New York), but buyer was unaware of the breach until he questioned seller and received his refusal. Thus *Boyd* as well as *Perkins* illustrates the intent in 2–713 to delay the time to measure the market after the time for performance has passed in those cases where the buyer fails to learn of the breach at the time it actually occurs.

That the draftsmen intended the "learned of the breach language" to apply only to the post-tender cases and not to mean a barring of the "repudiation" is supported by other and unchallenged statements in the New York Law Revision Commission reports.

When Professor Patterson reviewed 2–610, he indicated:

> The measure of damages for the anticipatory repudiation of a duty to deliver, or to accept, goods under a contract of sale, is to be determined as of the date when performance was due, rather than the date of repudiation, under New York law.[104]

Professor Honnold, when he reviewed 2–723, agreed that the rule at common law and under the USA based "market value on the date for performance prescribed in the contract." [105] If the language of 2–713 was intended to change the New York law on the time of measuring the market in anticipatory repudiation cases, that fact apparently escaped two wily critics, and it was a change accompanied by deafening silence of the draftsmen.

The fourth and most elegant argument against the "plain words" interpretation of 2–713 is that it conflicts with, and would render useless, a part of 2–723(1). Section 2–723(1) reads as follows:

> If an action based on anticipatory repudiation comes to trial before the time for performance with respect to some or all of the goods, any damages based on market price (Section 2–708 or Section 2–713) shall be determined according to the price of such goods prevailing at the time when the aggrieved party learned of the repudiation.

Of course every interpreter of statutes knows the doctrine that one should interpret the statute in such a way as to give some meaning to all of the words. If "learned of the breach" means "learned of the repudiation," then the court would always look to the time when

102.  Id. at 305, 139 N.E. at 277.

103.  18 Misc. 169, 41 N.Y.S. 391 (App. Term 1896).

104.  1 N.Y. State Law Revision Comm'n, 1955 Report 669, 672 (1955). Professor Patterson cites two New York cases to support his position: Segall v. Finlay, 245 N.Y. 61, 156 N.E. 97 (1927); Goldfarb v. Campe Corp., 99 Misc. 475, 164 N.Y.S. 583 (N.Y. City Ct.1917).

105.  1 N.Y. State Law Revision Comm'n, 1955 Report 590 (1955).

the aggrieved party learned of the repudiation to measure damage whether or not the time for performance had passed when the case came to trial.[106]  Thus the "plain meaning" construction makes the portion of 2–723(1) which refers to 2–713 superfluous.  Consequently, the draftsmen in writing section 2–723(1) must have thought "learned of the repudiation" had a different meaning than "learned of the breach."

A final and most persuasive argument in favor of reading "learned of the breach" to mean "time for performance" in anticipatory repudiation cases is the history upon which the Code was built.  Pre-Code common law, the Restatement of Contracts, and the Uniform Sales Act all permitted the buyer in an anticipatory repudiation case to recover the contract-market differential at the date for performance.[107]  Before we permit the draftsmen to upset such uniform and firmly entrenched doctrine, we can rightfully ask for at least a sentence or two of comment and more explicit statutory language than "learned of the breach."

In summary, it appears that the soundest arguments support the interpretation of "learned of the breach" to mean "time of performance" in the anticipatory repudiation case.[108]  We conclude that

---

106.  Note that the draftsmen used "repudiation" in 2–723 and "breach" in 2–713.  Any argument constructed upon the apparently inconsistent use of the two words falters on two counts.  First, "breach" is used in 2–713 to refer to anticipatory repudiation and to failure to perform at the time of tender.  Second, although the pre-Code law relying on Lord Chief Justice Cockburn's opinion in Frost v. Knight, L.R. 7 Ex. 111 (1872), continued the obscure distinction between "repudiation" and "breach" by requiring the repudiatee to manifest an election to treat repudiation as a breach in order to pursue an immediate cause of action, even the pre-Code trend was toward abolishing the attenuated distinctions between repudiation and breach.  See 11 S. Williston, Williston on Contracts §§ 1302–1322 (3d ed. 1968); 4 A. Corbin, Corbin on Contracts § 959 (1951); Restatement of Contracts § 318 (1932).  To this end the Restatement of Contracts states that the various acts described above "constitute an anticipatory repudiation which is a total breach of contract."  It appears that 2–610 continues this idea since after repudiation the buyer is given resort to any remedy for breach.

Cf., Restatement of Contracts § 322 (1932) ("When Statute of Limitations

Begins to Run in Case of Anticipatory Breach").

107.  Restatement of Contracts § 318 (1932); USA §§ 64(3), 67(3).

108.  Note, however, that there are additional possibilities which we have not considered.  One might argue, for example, that language in 2–610 authorizing an aggrieved party to wait only a "reasonable time" and depriving him of damages resulting from his waiting beyond the commercially reasonable time means that the contract-market differential should be measured at the end of such "reasonable time" after the buyer learns of the repudiation.  Such an argument, of course, does more violence to the language of 2–713 than does the one which we have suggested above.  Moreover, it lacks the weight of tradition and rests almost exclusively upon an implication drawn from a comment.  For a discussion of the American courts' rejection of the "election" theory, see 1 N.Y. State Law Revision Comm'n, 1955 Report 673 (1955).

Consider the applicability of the notions of mitigation or avoidable consequences.  11 S. Williston, Williston on Contracts § 1302 (3d ed. 1968); 4 A. Corbin, Corbin on Contracts § 983 (1951).

the time for performance is that most likely intended by the Code draftsmen as the time for measuring damages in anticipatory repudiation; it is one consistent with giving the aggrieved party wide latitude and one supported by the pre-Code case law. For these reasons we think it the best interpretation of 2–713. Until a number of courts speak authoritatively on this topic, each is entitled to his own reading and no interpretation is completely satisfactory.

Even after one has settled upon the proper time for measuring damages, troublesome questions about cover and buyer's other behavior after the repudiation remain. Section 2–610(a) provides that the aggrieved party "may for a commercially reasonable time await performance by the repudiating party." Several difficult questions are:

(1) How long is a commercially reasonable time?

(2) What rights does the aggrieved party lose by waiting too long? Does he lose only the right to cover? The right to have his damages measured at the time of performance? Consequential damages which the defendant proves he could have avoided? Or some combination?

(3) Is there any duty to mitigate while he suspends performance?

There has been even less case law development under the Code in the situation where the buyer exercises his option to await performance "for a commercially reasonable time" [109] than where he immediately resorts to his remedies for breach.[110] Thus the several questions above can be answered only with a limited degree of certainty.

First, how long can the aggrieved party wait without forfeit.[111] The early English decisions apparently allowed the repudiatee to treat the repudiation as inoperative until the time for performance had arrived.[112] Professor Williston found the "continuance of the obligations of the contract upon both sides" to be most objectionable practically:

Under the early law if the promisee, after receiving the repudiation, demands or manifests a willingness to receive performance, his rights are lost.

---

109. § 2–610(a).

110. § 2–610(b).

111. As mentioned above, Comment 1 implies that an aggrieved party is entitled to await performance for a reasonable time and then resort to his remedies for breach. A similar implication arises from section 2–610(b) which allows an action for breach "even though he had notified the repudiating party that he would await the latter's performance. . . ." Presumably if such a notification were given, the buyer will have waited a short time, however minimal it may have been. Comment 4 further supports this view.

112. Hochster v. De la Tour, 2 El. & Bl. 678 (1853); Frost v. Knight, L.R. 7 Ex. 111 (1872).

> Not only can he not thereafter bring an action on the
> repudiation, but he "keeps the contract alive for the benefit
> of the other as well as his own. . . ." [113]

However this rigid application was soon tempered by eliminating
the requirement for tender. Some wanted to retain the requirement that the plaintiff have the ability to perform,[114] some required
the aggrieved party to mitigate his damages, and most allowed the
repudiatee a reasonable time in which to make an election.[115] The
pre-Code cases are in conflict on the question of how long the
repudiatee has to decide what he will do.[116] One can see the basic
remnant surviving in 2–610 that the repudiatee not be forced into
making a hurried decision.

The Code itself consistently disclaims setting specific time
periods, and 2–610 is no exception. Comment 1 simply reiterates that
the test of a reasonable time is to be judged by a commercial standard.
The only other limitation is that the repudiatee pursue his remedy in
good faith.[117] One court directly faced this issue in Aura Orchards v.
A. Peltz & Sons, Inc.[118] where plaintiff contracted on October 12, 1965
for the sale of apples to be stored until receipt of shipping instructions no later than April 15, 1966. Sometime between mid-November
and mid-December, 1965, buyer repudiated. Plaintiff waited until
April, 1966 to resell after which he brought suit for the contract-
market differential, resale expenses, and storage charges. The court
interpreted 2–610 as follows:

> Under 2–610 of the Uniform Commercial Code, complain-
> ant was not required to recognize respondents' anticipatory
> breach of the contract but could wait the time for perform-
> ance by respondents under the contract.[119]

Of course this language is sweeping; it is reminiscent of Lord Cockburn.[120] Yet sweeping as the opinion may be, still the total waiting
period between repudiation and time for performance was only four
or five months. It is difficult to imagine that it is always commercially reasonable to wait until the scheduled time for performance.
First, if that was the draftsmen's intention, it was unnecessary to define the time period as commercially reasonable at all. Additionally,
it would indeed be drastic for a court to decide that waiting until
the time for performance is reasonable in a long term installment

---

113.  11 S. Williston, Williston on Contracts § 1333 (3d ed. 1968).

114.  4 A. Corbin, Corbin on Contracts
§§ 977–78 (1951).

115.  11 S. Williston, Williston on Contracts § 1321 (3d ed. 1968).

116.  Roller v. George H. Leonard &
Co., 229 F. 607 (4th Cir. 1915); Skeele
Coal Co. v. Arnold, 200 F. 393 (2d
Cir. 1912); Roehm v. Horst, 178 U.S.
1 (1900); Paducah Cooperage Co. v.

Arkansas Stave Co., 193 Ky. 774, 237
S.W. 412 (1922).

117.  Comment 4 to section 2–610 explicitly refers to section 1–203.

118.  27 Agri.Dec. 1546, 6 UCC Rep.
Serv. 149 (1968).

119.  Id. at 1553, 6 UCC Rep.Serv. at
152.

120.  Frost v. Knight, L.R. 7 Ex. 111
(1872).

contract where the waiting period may actually be several years. Thus although it is too soon to predict exactly what the courts will decide, some standard other than the mechanical "wait for performance date" should be pursued.

Assuming the aggrieved party elects to await performance for a commercially reasonable time, what rights will be lost by waiting too long?

The Code is silent on this question. However, the Code draftsmen probably intended that an aggrieved party who awaits performance for more than a commercially reasonable time should lose his right to cover.[121] Although 2–610 fails to set definite limits for what will be considered a commercially reasonable time, it does parallel the Code description of the time allowed for "cover" under 2–712. Section 2–712(1) allows the buyer to cover if he proceeds "without unreasonable delay." Comment 2 reveals the intention against limiting:

> the time necessary for him to look around and decide as to how he may best effect cover. The test here is similar to that generally used in this Article as to reasonable time and seasonable action.

Thus the intention is probably that the time periods be roughly equivalent. This analysis is consistent with the philosophy underlying the "cover" option. It is intended to be a shield, that is, a means by which an aggrieved buyer can obtain substituted goods without suffering any loss. The buyer is given a "reasonable time" to cover instead of any specific time period to allow him to find "how he may best effect cover." It is not a sword to be used to punish the seller for breaching.

In addition, consequential damages that the defendant proves the buyer could have avoided will not be allowed when the buyer has delayed too long. If a breaching seller knows that buyer has made two resale contracts in reliance on the breached contract, but the aggrieved buyer waits an unreasonable length of time to cover, then the buyer will not recover the profits on the two resale contracts as consequential damages. Section 2–715(2) (a) allows the buyer to collect only losses "which could reasonably be prevented by cover or otherwise." In this context section 2–610 is but a specific application of 2–715 and 2–712 to an anticipatory repudiation.

Does delaying too long affect the right to have damages measured as of the time for performance? There are no reported cases at this writing, but it seems likely that the damage recovery will not be affected by delaying for more than a commercially reasonable time. First, no real harm is done to the repudiating seller since the contract-market differential is measured at the time for performance. (Contrast the effect of increasing consequential damages by delay as described in the preceding paragraph.) Second, consider

121.   §§ 2–610(b); 2–711; 2–712.

the unappealing nature of the alternatives available. One alternative might be to bar the buyer from any recovery under 2–713 at all, but since the function of 2–713 is probably to serve as a type of statutory liquidated damage clause,[122] total elimination of this remedy seems altogether unwarranted. Another option is to hark back to the time when the buyer learned of the repudiation. Yet the discussion above indicates that this was probably not intended. A third alternative is to measure the market at the end of the "commercially reasonable time." The difficulties of pinpointing this time, however, especially in a rapidly fluctuating market, may far outweigh the advantages of using this time. One should remember, too, that contract-market damages equal actual damages suffered only by the remotest of chances.[123] Perhaps the major purposes of 2–713 in the repudiation context are *not* accurately to compensate for profits and losses, but are instead (*1*) to provide a minimum recovery in all cases and (*2*) to induce the repudiatee to return quickly to the market [124] and then recover the contract-cover differential.[125] Hence to seek an alternative to measuring the market at the time for performance is probably a relatively unimportant exercise.

Both at common law [126] and under section 2–610(c),[127] the repudiatee may at least suspend his own performance. But what of the reverse, that is, can the aggrieved party continue readying himself for performance, must he take affirmative steps to mitigate his damages, or must he just refrain from taking affirmative steps that might further increase his damages?

Even though some pre-Code courts spoke of treating the repudiation as totally inoperative until the time for performance,[128] they also recognized that a repudiatee should not continue with his own performance if doing so would increase his damages.[129] The decisions fail to distinguish between an affirmative duty to cover or resell and the less demanding duty not to take affirmative action increasing damages. Probably the pre-Code courts desired only to prohibit the affirmative acts that would increase damages.[130] The

---

122. See Section 6–3 supra (§ 2–712).

123. Id.

124. §§ 2–610(b); 2–713.

125. But if this was the goal, why allow the option of awaiting performance at all? Is it the remnant of history?

126. 4 A. Corbin, Corbin on Contracts §§ 975, 977–78 (1951).

127. See note 12 supra.

128. Carvage v. Stowell, 115 Vt. 187, 55 A.2d 188 (1947); Bu-Vi Bar Petroleum Corp. v. Krow, 40 F.2d 488

(10th Cir. 1930); Frost v. Knight, L.R. 7 Ex. 111 (1872); Hochster v. De la Tour, 2 El. & Bl. 678 (1853).

129. See, e. g., Mays Mills v. McRae, 187 N.C. 707, 122 S.E. 762 (1924); Roth & Co. v. Taysen, Townsent & Co., 8 Asp.M.Cos. 120 (Queen's Bench 1895).

130. "Cover," of course, is a term new in the Code. What is meant here is whether there is a duty to seek a replacement contract, etc. This is directly influential when considering the position of a seller (manufacturer) confronted with buyer's repudiation and the question of whether or not to complete manufacture.

market-contract differential remedy [131] in the normal breach situation (because the market price is set in time and place) is unaffected by mitigation [132] except with respect to consequential damages.[133] Two Code cases deal with mitigation of incidental damages of repudiatees. In Aura Orchards v. A. Peltz & Sons, Inc.,[134] the seller of apples (under a contract repudiated by the buyer four to five months before the last possible time for performance had arrived) was allowed to await performance until the date specified in the contract. In awarding damages, the court included storage charges of $1,570 and did not mention mitigation. A New York Supreme Court, in E–Z Roll Hardware Mfg. Co. v. H & H Products & Finishing Corp.,[135] was not as generous. A manufacturer (seller) in the process of making 10,000 sets of special folding door hardware received buyer's repudiation after 3,010 sets had been shipped. Seller elected not to complete manufacture and instead brought suit (within a reasonable time) under 2–709(3) and for storage costs as incidental damages.[136] The court refused compensation for storage costs:

> The plaintiff's claim for storage is rejected. To qualify for incidental damages as contemplated by UCC § 2–710, there must be compliance with the statutory provisions (UCC §§ 2–709, 2–706) designed to minimize damages. No such action was taken in this case.[137]

We find these cases impossible to reconcile. We favor *Aura Orchards*.

---

131.  § 2–712.

132.  See Section 6–3 supra (§ 2–712).

133.  Section 2–715(2) limits consequential damages to those "which could not reasonably be prevented by cover."

134.  27 Agri.Dec. 1546, 6 UCC Rep. Serv. 149 (1968).

135.  4 UCC Rep.Serv. 1045 (N.Y.Sup. Ct.1968).

136.  § 2–710.

137.  4 UCC Rep.Serv. 1045, 1048 (N.Y. Sup.Ct.1968).

# CHAPTER 7

# SELLER'S REMEDIES

*Analysis*

**Sec.**
7–1.  Introduction, 2–703.
7–2.  Action for the Price, 2–709.
7–3.  —— Goods Accepted.
7–4.  —— Lost or Damaged Goods.
7–5.  —— Goods Not Reasonably Resalable.
7–6.  Seller's Resale, 2–706.
7–7.  Damages for Nondelivery or Repudiation, 2–708(1).
7–8.  Lost Profits, 2–708(2).
7–9.  —— The Lost Volume Seller.
7–10.  —— Components and Jobber Sellers.
7–11.  —— Other Cases.
7–12.  —— Is 2–708(1) Ever Too Generous?
7–13.  —— The Formula.
7–14.  Seller's Rights and Obligations with Respect to Unidentified and Incomplete Goods, 2–704.
7–15.  Unpaid Seller's Goods-Oriented Remedies on Buyer's Insolvency.

## § 7–1  Introduction, 2–703

Section 2–703 catalogues the seller's principal remedies under the Code.[1]  It lists the following options open to an aggrieved seller:

(a) withhold delivery;

(b) stop delivery by any bailee as hereafter provided (Section 2–705);

(c) proceed under the next section respecting goods still unidentified to the contract;

(d) resell and recover damages as hereafter provided (Section 2–706);

(e) recover damages for non-acceptance (Section 2–708) or in a proper case the price (Section 2–709);

(f) cancel.

In this chapter we will consider four of those options:

(*1*) recovery of the price under 2–709;

(*2*) resale and recovery of damages under 2–706;

(*3*) recovery of damages under 2–708(1) and (2) (Particularly by the lost volume seller); and

(*4*) proceeding under 2–704.

The interpretation of these sections requires consideration of some of the same words we discussed in the foregoing chapter on buyer's rem-

---

1.  See also section 2–721 which reconciles common law remedies for fraud with the remedies under the Code.

207

edies (for instance, "tender"), and we will not repeat that discussion here. Nor will we repeat our discussion of the Code's remedial philosophy embodied in 1–106(1) to the effect that "the aggrieved party" should be put "in as good a position as if the other party had fully performed." Still, as we will demonstrate, some of the interpretive problems presented by the seller's remedy provisions differ significantly from those presented by the buyer's remedy provisions.

## § 7–2    Action for the Price, 2–709

In limited circumstances 2–709 [2] gives an aggrieved seller a right to recover the contract price.[3] He may recover the price:

(*1*) when goods have been "accepted" by the buyer, or

(*2*) when the risk of loss has passed to the buyer and the goods have been lost or damaged within a reasonable time after risk has passed, or

(*3*) when goods have been identified to the contract and the seller is unable to resell them.

It is only by meeting one of these three conditions that the seller can recover the price and any expenses reasonably incurred as a result of the breach.[4]

2.  Prior drafts of section 2–709 differ little from the current version. Section 2–709 reads as follows:

(1) When the buyer fails to pay the price as it becomes due the seller may recover, together with any incidental damages under the next section, the price

(a) of goods accepted or of conforming goods lost or damaged within a commercially reasonable time after risk of their loss has passed to the buyer; and

(b) of goods identified to the contract if the seller is unable after reasonable effort to resell them at a reasonable price or the circumstances reasonably indicate that such effort will be unavailing.

(2) Where the seller sues for the price he must hold for the buyer any goods which have been identified to the contract and are still in his control except that if resale becomes possible he may resell them at any time prior to the collection of the judgment. The net proceeds of any such resale must be credited to the buyer and payment of the judgment entitles him to any goods not resold.

(3) After the buyer has wrongfully rejected or revoked acceptance of the goods or has failed to make a payment due or has repudiated (Section 2–610), a seller who is held not entitled to the price under this section shall nevertheless be awarded damages for nonacceptance under the preceding section.

3.  The action for the price is, of course, the analogue to the buyer's action for specific performance.

A classic example of 2–709 in action is Jacobson v. Donnkenny, Inc., 4 UCC Rep.Serv. 850 (N.Y.Sup.Ct.1967), where the parties contracted for 25,000 pounds of 100% combed cotton at various prices. The seller also contracted to have the cotton dyed to the buyer's specifications, but the buyer later instructed the seller simply to hold the cotton in the dyer's grege. When the buyer breached, the seller brought an action for the price under 2–709(1) (b). The court found that the seller who had purchased yarn and procured manufacture was entitled to the contract price (less what it would have cost for dyeing), because that type of knit was no longer acceptable on the market and the seller was unable to resell after reasonable efforts were made to do so.

4.  § 2–710.

Before considering 2–709 in detail we will outline its general scope and explain the policies which shaped it. The seller can recover the price of goods "accepted," and, with important exceptions, he cannot recover the price of goods not yet accepted. Why the buyer should have to pay the price for accepted goods is not hard to understand. He has possession of them, they have started to depreciate, and any number of things may have happened to them after his acceptance. In such circumstances it would be unfair to limit the seller's recovery to the contract-market differential and thus impose on him the burden of redisposing of the goods in order to make himself whole. Here, the seller ought to get the price, and he does. On the other hand, the Code draftsmen have generally denied the price to a seller of goods not yet accepted because he is usually in the business of selling goods of the kind in question, is likely to have better market contacts and is therefore in a better position to salvage by redisposing of the goods through his normal channels. Although it is easy to think of circumstances in which the buyer has better redisposition opportunities than the seller (for instance, Sears, Roebuck as a buyer), the draftmen's general hypothesis seems accurate.

There are two exceptions to the general rule that seller cannot recover the price of unaccepted goods. First, 2–709(1) (a) permits recovery of the price of "conforming goods lost or damaged within a commercially reasonable time after risk of their loss has passed to the buyer." Here, since the goods are at least damaged, often missing, or destroyed, the seller's presumptively superior resale opportunity is diminished and may be nonexistent. Section 2–709(1) (b) states the second exception to the general rule that the seller cannot recover the price of unaccepted goods. That subsection permits the seller to recover the price if he is "unable after reasonable effort to resell them at a reasonable price or the circumstances reasonably indicate that such effort will be unavailing." By hypothesis, the seller in such case is no better able than the buyer to redispose of the goods. To illustrate: assume Slalom, the operator of a local ski shop, orders one hundred pairs of hand-made wooden skis from seller, Vadel, at a cost of $10,000. Upon arrival of the skis, Slalom refuses to accept because a new fiberglass ski has been introduced which makes wooden skis obsolete. Assuming that the demand for wooden skis has fallen so far that the market no longer exists, Vadel can recover the contract price under 2–709(1) (b), and buyer will be left with the goods.[5] Since there is no market for the goods and seller could not resell, the outcome is consistent with the policy behind 2–709. However, if the availability of fiberglass skis merely reduced the demand for wooden skis, our seller could not resort to the price remedy but would have to content himself with a damage action and would have to redispose of the wooden skis himself to make himself whole.

---

5. § 2–709(2). See note 2 supra.

## § 7–3 Action for the Price—Goods Accepted

Under the first clause of 2–709(1) (a) the buyer is liable for the price of "goods accepted." Acceptance [6] is a term of art in the Code, and both luck and lawyer skill are required to pinpoint the time of acceptance. Some lawyers, particularly those familiar with the Uniform Sales Act, will be tempted to equate "acceptance" with "passage of title" to the goods from seller to buyer. However, under the Code acceptance is unrelated to passage of title; rather, its occurrence is more dependent upon the buyer's acquisition of control and opportunity to inspect.

Needless to say, a principal legal issue in a suit under 2–709(1) (a) will be whether the buyer has accepted under 2–606. For more extensive discussion of "acceptance," see Section 8–2 below. Here we limit our consideration to the relationship between acceptance and rejection and revocation; this relationship is important and complex.[7] Note at the outset that if a buyer has accepted under 2–606, he may not *reject* under 2–602, though he may still be entitled to *revoke* his acceptance under 2–608. At the outset it is also useful to distinguish between possible "substantive" grounds for rejection or revocation (nonconformity as to quality, delay, etc.) and possible "procedural" requirements for a rejection or revocation. Under 2–602(1) and 2–608(2) procedurally effective rejections and revocations generally require timely action and proper notice. First, it is clear that under 2–602 a procedurally effective rejection for which there are substantive grounds forecloses acceptance and eliminates any putative claim by the seller for the price under the first clause of 2–709(1) (a).[8] Likewise under 2–608 a procedurally effective

---

6. Acceptance (defined by section 2–606) was described above as a technical term of art. The Code rejects the Uniform Sales Act's focus on passage of title and instead adopts new standards.

In addition to reviewing the discussion of acceptance in Section 8–2 infra, the reader may compare the pre-Code approach to acceptance by referring to Hall v. Keller, 9 Ariz.App. 584, 455 P.2d 266 (1969) where the court applied the Uniform Sales Act approach in concluding that an action for the price depends on whether the property in the goods has passed to the buyer.

7. The Code draftsmen have described three distinct types of rejection. First, Section 2–606(1) (b) notes that acceptance will occur unless the buyer makes a rejection that is "effective." Second, section 2–703 indexes the seller's various remedies that are to be available when the buyer's rejection is "wrongful." Finally, section 2–711 contemplates the available remedies to

the buyer when his rejection is "rightful."

Revocation of acceptance is also described in three different ways. First, Section 2–608(2) requires that notice be given to the seller in order that the revocation be "effective." Next, the index of remedies suggested by section 2–703 are triggered by a "wrongful" revocation of acceptance. Finally, in two places the Code refers to a "justified" revocation. Comment 5 to section 2–709 defines "goods accepted" as used in section 2–709(1) (a) as "goods as to which there has been no justified revocation of acceptance." And section 2–711 refers to justifiably revoking acceptance as a ground to invoke the various buyer's remedies.

8. § 2–602:

(1) Rejection of goods must be within a reasonable time after their delivery or tender. It is ineffective unless the buyer seasonably notifies the seller.

revocation of acceptance for which there are substantive grounds will bar seller's recovery of the price under the first clause of 2–709(1) (a).[9]

But what of a rejection or revocation that is not "procedurally" effective because it is not timely, or not properly communicated, or the like?  Here 2–606 provides that acceptance occurs and that the buyer is liable for the price under 2–709(1) (a) (subject to a potential set-off for damages because of the nonconformity).  Thus a procedurally effective rejection or revocation for which there are substantive grounds bars acceptance; a rejection or revocation which is not effective (that is, has a procedural flaw) does not bar acceptance, even though the goods are actually nonconforming and the rejection or revocation therefore substantively rightful.

The most troubling case is the one in which the buyer has no substantive basis on which to reject or revoke but he nevertheless effectively rejects or revokes procedurally, that is, he acts in time and properly communicates his rejection or revocation to the seller.[10] All commentators [11] agree that the Code draftsmen contemplated effective *rejections* which might be substantively wrongful and intended that all such rejections forestall acceptance without regard to their substantive wrongfulness.  Writing for the New York Law Revision Commission, Professor Honnold stated:  "Buyer may have the power to make an 'effective' rejection even though his action is a breach of contract and subjects buyer to liability for damages." [12] Professor Honnold's judgment is consistent with the negative implication of 2–606(1) (b) which provides that failure to make an "effective rejection" results in acceptance.  The negative implication of that subsection is that *any* effective rejection bars acceptance. We conclude, therefore, that a procedurally proper (that is, effective)

§ 2–606:

(1) Acceptance of goods occurs when the buyer. . . .

. . .

(b) fails to make an effective rejection (subsection (1) of Section 2–602), but such acceptance does not occur until the buyer has had a reasonable opportunity to inspect them. . . .

See also, Beco Inc. v. Minnechaug Golf Course, Inc., 5 Conn.Cir. 444, 256 A.2d 522, 6 UCC Rep.Serv. 910 (1968) (failure to reject within one month was failure to reject within reasonable time and thus evidence of election to accept).

9.  Comment 5 to Section 2–709 states " 'Goods accepted' by the buyer under subsection (1) (a) include goods as to which there has been no justified revocation of acceptance." Section 2–608(2) further states:

Revocation of acceptance must occur within a reasonable time after the buyer discovers or should have discovered the ground for it and before any substantial change in condition of the goods which is not caused by their own defects.  It is not effective until the buyer notifies the seller of it. . . .

10.  For a more extensive discussion of rejection, revocation and acceptance, see Ch. 8 infra.

11.  See Peters, Remedies for Breach of Contracts Relating to the Sale of Goods Under the Uniform Commercial Code: A Roadmap for Article Two, 73 Yale L.J. 199, 241–42 (1963); R. Nordstom, Handbook on the Law of Sales 544 (1970).  But see Cochran v. Horner, 121 Ga.App. 297, 173 S.E.2d 448, 7 UCC Rep.Serv. 707 (1970).

12.  1 N.Y. State Law Revision Comm'n, 1955 Report 520 (1955).

rejection forestalls acceptance whether or not the rejection is rightful (that is, founded upon a proper substantive basis). This conclusion is consistent with the policy behind 2–709, which normally imposes the burden of redisposing of the goods upon the seller.

Whether the buyer is entitled to make "effective" but wrongful *revocations*, and if so whether they free the buyer from "acceptance" and therefore from his liability for the price under 2–709(1) (a) is unclear. On the one hand, 2–607(2) states that buyer cannot revoke an acceptance he made with knowledge of a nonconformity unless he accepted on the reasonable assumption that the nonconformity would be seasonably cured. It would seem to follow *a fortiori* from this and from the grounds stated in 2–608 that a buyer cannot revoke acceptance of conforming goods. At least one reading of Comment 5 to 2–709 supports the interpretation that a procedurally flawless but substantively wrongful revocation does not undo acceptance.[13] That comment seems to mean that goods accepted remain accepted unless the buyer "justifiably" revokes. On the other hand, 2–709(3) seems to contemplate at least some circumstances in which a buyer who has "wrongfully . . . revoked" will *not* be liable for the price. If only justified revocations free the buyer from his liability under 2–709(1) (a), then there would be no need to mention wrongful revocations in 2–709(3), for one who wrongfully revoked would always be liable for the price as one who "accepted" the goods. Moreover, 2–703 refers to wrongful revocation and rejection in tandem without apparent distinction. Finally, one may argue that there is no reason to distinguish here between rejection and revocation and that if the Code lets a naughty buyer out of his liability for the price when he rejects effectively but wrongfully, then it must do the same for the buyer who revokes "effectively" but wrongfully. This "parallel" construction argument is unpersuasive, however. In almost all sales transactions there is a continuum of control running from the seller's initial ownership and absolute control of the goods to the buyer's ownership, absolute control, and use of the goods at the end. All agree that we must at some point draw the line and say to the buyer, "You are liable for the price, no matter what you do hereafter." Logic does not dictate that this line be drawn after the time for revocation. Indeed, we believe that revocation of acceptance is generally a more drastic remedy than rejection and therefore a remedy that should not be as readily available. It is appropriate to say to a

---

13.  § 2–709; Comment 5:

"Goods accepted" by the buyer under subsection (1) (a) include only goods as to which there has been no justified revocation of acceptance, for such a revocation means that there has been a default by the seller which bars his rights under this section.
. . .

See also Tennessee-Virginia Constr. Co. v. Willingham, 117 Ga.App. 290, 160 S.E.2d 444, 5 UCC Rep.Serv. 106 (1968). Here the purchaser of a tractor retained the machine for two or three months and then returned it. The court found that the burden was on the buyer to justify its revocation of acceptance in order to avoid liability for breach of contract under 2–708. Since the buyer's only evidence in this regard was that the machine was "unsatisfactory," the seller prevailed.

buyer who attempts to revoke acceptance: "All right, you may revoke acceptance, but beware, for if your revocation is found to be substantively wrongful, you will be liable for the full price, and you'd better think twice before you allow those accepted goods to rot in a warehouse or on a railroad siding."   Moreover, to leave the burden on the buyer with respect to goods which might have depreciated, which he might have used to his benefit, and which he might actually have misused or otherwise damaged, is consistent with the policy of 2–709 and with the idea that the buyer should normally have to pay the price of accepted goods.   Despite the language of 2–709(3) and notwithstanding the parallel references to rejection and revocation in 2–703, we would argue that any buyer who accepts goods is liable for the price unless he makes a procedurally effective *and* substantively *rightful* revocation of acceptance; we believe that a procedurally effective but substantively wrongful revocation should not free him from price liability under 2–709(1)(a).

### § 7–4   Action for the Price—Lost or Damaged Goods

Under the second clause of 2–709(1)(a) the seller can also recover the price of "conforming goods lost or damaged within a commercially reasonable time after risk of their loss has passed to the buyer. . . ."[14]   To apply this clause of 2–709(1)(a), a court must resort to Article Two's complex risk of loss provisions (which we have discussed in Chapter 5).   Except for possible difficulty in defining "commercially reasonable," the second clause of 2–709(1)(a) offers few other problems worthy of lawyer concern.   A routine case under the second clause of 2–709(1)(a) is Ninth Street East, Ltd. v. Harrison.[15]   A Los Angeles seller shipped goods F.O.B. Los Angeles to a Connecticut buyer.   After the carrier attempted to deliver the goods to the buyer's place of business (an attempt frustrated by a dispute between the buyer's wife and the carrier's agent) the goods disappeared.   The court found that risk of loss had passed to the buyer in Los Angeles under the F.O.B. term and properly held the buyer liable for the price under the second clause of 2–709(1)(a).

### § 7–5   Action for the Price—Goods Not Reasonably Resalable

Section 2–709(1)(b) also permits the seller to recover the price of goods "identified to the contract" which seller cannot reasonably unload.   Since here the seller can recover the price only as to goods "identified to the contract," he must resort to 2–501 which defines such goods.[16]   In general these are goods already shipped to the buy-

---

14.   Risk of loss is treated more fully in Ch. 5 supra.

15.   5 Conn.Cir. 597, 259 A.2d 772, 7 UCC Rep.Serv. 171 (1968).

16.   § 2–501:

(1) The buyer obtains a special property and an insurable interest in goods by identification of existing goods as goods to which the contract refers even though the goods so identified are nonconforming and he has an option to return or reject them.   Such identification can be made at any time and in any manner explicitly agreed to by the parties.   In the absence of explicit agreement identification occurs

er, labeled as his, or "otherwise designated by the seller as goods to which the contract refers." [17] Next, and more difficult, the seller must show that the goods are not resalable at "a reasonable price" after "reasonable effort" or circumstances that "reasonably indicate" that an effort to resell will be unavailing. Elsewhere we have despaired of interpreting sentences which contain only one "reasonable"; only a misguided soul would attempt to interpret a sentence with three such words in it.

As guideposts for sellers who invoke 2–709(1) (b) we offer three recently decided cases. In two, the courts found that the seller was unable to resell at a reasonable price, but in the third the court rejected that argument. The first case [18] is straightforward enough. There the plaintiff sued for $16,000, the price of several specially manufactured, "tailor-made," rolling steel doors. The plaintiff proved that the doors were not stocked but were "tailor-made" for each job as the contract for it was awarded. The doors in question would have had a scrap value of $630, could not have been adapted to any other job, and would have cost $75 to $100 to deliver to a scrap dealer. Here the court held that buyer is liable for the price. In similar circumstances the Massachusetts Court of Appeals [19] held a buyer liable for the price of a mink jacket of "petite size" that had been further altered to make it even smaller in the neck and shoulders. The court found that the plaintiff had been "ready and willing to sell the coat at any time it received a good offer" but that efforts to resell were unavailing. Accordingly the court held that the seller could recover the price.

In *Bacon Estate* [20] a Pennsylvania court rejected the seller's plea for the price on a contract for a dining room suite, a bedroom suite,

(a) when the contract is made if it is for the sale of goods already existing and identified;

(b) if the contract is for the sale of future goods other than those described in paragraph (c), when goods are shipped, marked or otherwise designated by the seller as goods to which the contract refers;

(c) when the crops are planted or otherwise become growing crops or the young are conceived if the contract is for the sale of unborn young to be born within twelve months after contracting or for the sale of crops to be harvested within twelve months or the next normal harvest season after contracting whichever is longer.

(2) The seller retains an insurable interest in goods so long as title to or any security interest in the goods remains in him and where the identification is by the seller alone he may until default or insolvency, or notifi-

cation to the buyer that the identification is final substitute other goods for those identified.

(3) Nothing in this section impairs any insurable interest recognized under any other statute or rule of law.

17. See Draper v. Minneapolis-Moline, Inc., 100 Ill.App.2d 324, 241 N.E.2d 342, 5 UCC Rep.Serv. 972 (1968) (dealer identified tractor to contract by showing it to buyer in store, and buyer recalled last three digits of tractor's serial number which coincided with number on purchase agreement).

18. Walter Balfour & Co. v. Lizza & Sons, Inc., 6 UCC Rep.Serv. 649 (N.Y. Sup.Ct.1969).

19. Ludwig, Inc. v. Tobey, 28 Mass.App. Dec. 6, 5 UCC Rep.Serv. 832 (1964).

20. 45 Pa.D. & C.2d 733, 5 UCC Rep. Serv. 486 (Orphan's Ct.1968).

two sofas, a cocktail table, and assorted chairs.  Although the court acknowledged that the merchandise might be quite difficult to sell at the prices the deceased buyer had agreed to pay (apparently because of the buyer's bizarre choice of fabric colors), the court found that the plaintiff had not proved his inability to sell the goods at "reasonably marked down prices."

The first of the foregoing cases is soundly decided and largely unremarkable; if the steel doors would fit on defendant's building and no other, the goods are simply not reasonably resalable.  But why the furniture was resalable at a reasonable price yet the mink coat not, is hard to explain.  Neither case offers guidelines about the kind of search for purchasers the seller must undertake, nor about what a "reasonable price" might be in terms of the original price, the resale market, the seller's cost, or any other obective basis.  Indeed, we suspect that the real difference between the cases is the Pennsylvania court's unwillingness to allow a seller to reap the benefits of a decedent's profligacy out of the heirs' legacy.  These two cases may be but the beginning of apparently random interpretations of 2–709(1) (b), interpretations that may turn on factors neither reported in the facts nor identified in the opinions.  Certainly a court should determine what inquiries seller made, at what price he attempted to sell the goods, and how long he placed them on what markets.  Each of these factors is relevant to the reasonableness of the seller's conclusion that the goods could not reasonably be resold; unfortunately none is likely to be decisive.

As a final supplement to our discussion of 2–709(1) (b), consider the case of a seller who receives an anticipatory repudiation from his buyer before he has completed the manufacture of the contract goods.  If the seller chooses not to complete the manufacture, the goods could never be "identified to the contract" under 2–709(1) (b) nor be "accepted" or conforming under 2–709(1) (a); accordingly, he could have no action for the price.[21]  If instead the seller chooses to complete the manufacture after the repudiation, it is conceiv-

---

21.  In E-Z Roll Hardware Mfg. Co. v. H & H Prods. & Finishing Corp., 4 UCC Rep.Serv. 1045 (N.Y.Sup.Ct. 1968), buyer repudiated a contract for the sale of 10,000 sets of folding-door hardware after delivery of about 3,000 sets, and the court found that since the seller had elected to cease manufacture he was foreclosed from an action for the purchase price.  What if seller elects not to complete manufacture of the goods as such, but instead integrates the as yet unfinished goods into another product?  Can he maintain an action for the price under 2–709, subtracting the value of the goods in their alternative use?  No case has yet responded to this question, but the Nebraska Supreme Court faced a similar issue in Chicago Roller Skate Mfg. Co. v. Sokol Mfg. Co., 185 Neb. 515, 177 N.W.2d 25, 7 UCC Rep.Serv. 804 (1970).  There the buyer accepted the contract goods, truck and wheel assemblies for the manufacture of skate boards, but then breached by returning the goods without the seller's consent.  This alone gave rise to an action for the price under 2–709.  However, the seller rebuilt the assemblies for use on roller skates, credited the buyer with reasonable value of the rebuilt material, and brought suit for the balance of the purchase price.  The court allowed recovery, but emphasized that this was not, nor would it allow, a 2–709 action for the price.  The court said the rebuilding was an attempt to mitigate damages "evidencing good faith."

able though unlikely that he may recover the price. As we will see, 2–704 authorizes him to complete manufacture "in the exercise of reasonable commercial judgment for the purpose of avoiding loss." It will require very careful navigation to achieve a finding that his completion was commercially reasonable under 2–704(2) but that the goods, when completed, were not reasonably resalable under 2–709 (1) (b). Of course the two findings are not logically inconsistent, for the one is made at the time of the decision to complete and the other only after the goods have been completed. Conceivably the picture could be rosy at the time of the repudiation but disastrous at the time of the actual completion. It will take a persuasive lawyer to convince a court that it should not measure the 2–704 decision by hindsight when the plaintiff, having completed, finds himself unable to resell.[22]

## § 7–6   Seller's Resale, 2–706

The analogue to the buyer's right to cover under 2–712 is the seller's right to resell under 2–706.[23] This section authorizes an ag-

---

22. For a general discussion of 2–704, see Section 7–14 infra.

23. § 2–706:

(1) Under the conditions stated in Section 2–703 on seller's remedies, the seller may resell the goods concerned or the undelivered balance thereof. Where the resale is made in good faith and in a commercially reasonable manner the seller may recover the difference between the resale price and the contract price together with any incidental damages allowed under the provisions of this Article (Section 2–710), but less expenses saved in consequence of the buyer's breach.

(2) Except as otherwise provided in subsection (3) or unless otherwise agreed resale may be at public or private sale including sale by way of one or more contracts to sell or of identification to an existing contract of the seller. Sale may be as a unit or in parcels and at any time and place and on any terms but every aspect of the sale including the method, manner, time, place and terms must be commercially reasonable. The resale must be reasonably identified as referring to the broken contract, but it is not necessary that the goods be in existence or that any or all of them have been identified to the contract before the breach.

(3) Where the resale is at private sale the seller must give the buyer reasonable notification of his intention to resell.

(4) Where the resale is at public sale

(a) only identified goods can be sold except where there is a recognized market for a public sale of futures in goods of the kind; and

(b) it must be made at a usual place or market for public sale if one is reasonably available and except in the case of goods which are perishable or threaten to decline in value speedily the seller must give the buyer reasonable notice of the time and place of the resale; and

(c) if the goods are not to be within the view of those attending the sale the notification of sale must state the place where the goods are located and provide for their reasonable inspection by prospective bidders; and

(d) the seller may buy.

(5) A purchaser who buys in good faith at a resale takes the goods free of any rights of the original buyer even though the seller fails to comply with one or more of the requirements of this section.

(6) The seller is not accountable to the buyer for any profit made on any resale. A person in the position of a seller (Section 2–707) or a buyer who has rightfully rejected or justifiably revoked acceptance must account for any excess over the amount of his security interest, as hereinafter defined (subsection (3) of Section 2–711).

grieved seller to resell the contract goods and to measure his damages by the difference between the contract price and the resale price. Like the "cover" provision for the buyer, 2–706 is an important Code innovation. If the buyer is solvent, 2–706 will usually put the seller in the same position as performance would have. Resale is not mandatory,[24] and when the seller does resell, he may resell privately or at a public sale. The Code nowhere defines public sale. It is clear enough that an auction sale open to the public is a public sale, but what of a nonauction to which the public may come or an auction sale (such as a dealer's used car auction) from which some of the public is excluded? Comment 4 to 2–706 states that "[b]y 'public' sale is meant a sale by auction," but the courts have yet to work out the precise dividing line between public and private resales. We would classify most sales open only to a limited segment of the public, such as dealer auctions, as public sales on the theory that usually competitive forces are at work at such sales similar to those usually at work at public sales to which all of the public is invited.[25]

If the seller chooses to resell privately, 2–706 sets out three comparatively simple steps for him to follow:

(*1*) identify the resale contract to the broken contract;

(*2*) resell in good faith and in a commercially reasonable manner; and

(*3*) give the buyer reasonable notification of his intention to resell.

However if the seller resells publicly, he must:

(*1*) identify the resale contract to the broken contract;

(*2*) resell in good faith and in a commercially reasonable manner;

(*3*) unless there is a recognized market in goods of the kind in question, resell only identified goods;

(*4*) conduct the resale at the usual place for a public sale, if there is such a place;

(*5*) except in the case of perishable goods or of goods which threaten to decline in value rapidly, give the buyer a reasonable notice of time and place of resale; and

(*6*) keep the goods on view at the time of sale, or provide for reasonable inspection elsewhere where the goods are located and provide for reasonable inspection by prospective bidders.

---

**24.** Although the test of section 2–703 and Comment 1 thereto indicate that resale is not mandatory, our discussion of section 2–708(2) indicates that where a seller has completed goods on hand and brings an action under 2–708(2), the court should treat him as though he had resold. See Section 7–11 infra.

**25.** See the discussion of private and public resale in context of default in Sections 26–9 to 26–10 infra.

Failure to comply deprives the seller of the measure of damages stated in 2–706 and relegates him to the measure provided in 2–708. Even if the seller does not resell properly, any purchaser at the resale who buys in good faith will still take the goods free of any claims of the original buyer.[26]

The application of 2–706 in a simple contract case is not difficult. Assume, for example, that a New York seller sells 1,000 embroidered pot holders at a contract price of $1,000, F.O.B. buyer's plant, to a New York buyer. The buyer breaches and seller resells to another New York party for $900 F.O.B. buyer's plant. The costs of shipping ($60) are the same under both contracts. If seller incurs no additional costs in reselling the pot holders, he will recover $100 (the difference between the resale price and the contract price). If the seller incurs $50 additional resale costs, his recovery is $150 (the difference between the resale price and the contract price together with incidental damages under 2–710). However if the resale contract is F.O.B. seller's plant and the seller thus saves the $60 shipping costs which he would have incurred under the original contract, then the seller's recovery will be only $90, that is, the difference between the resale price and the contract price, plus incidental damages, but less expenses saved as a consequence of buyer's breach.

We deal elsewhere (Section 7–7 below) with the most difficult question under 2–706, the effect of resale upon the seller's 2–708 claim for damages. Does resale foreclose a later claim for damage under 2–708 or may the seller who has resold nevertheless elect a more generous damage recovery under 2–708?

Section 2–706 basically requires that resale be made in a commercially reasonable fashion and that the seller act in good faith.[27] What we have said in Chapter 6 on the comparable 2–712 requirements applies here as well.

In certain circumstances the courts must adjust the resale contract price to put it on a footing comparable to the original contract. If, for example, the original contract called for payment of $20,000 (including interest) in semi-annual installments over three years but the resale contract required total payment of $12,000 in cash, the court could not simply subtract the price received in the second case from the total time price in the first case and get a fair result. The court must adjust for the credit factor in the original contract.[28] The present value of $20,000 to be paid in six semi-annual

---

26. See § 2–706(5).

27. For interpretations of the requirements of section 2–706, see Meadowbrook Nat'l Bank v. Markos, 3 UCC Rep.Serv. 854 (N.Y.Sup.Ct.1966) (advertisement resale of boat not in good faith); In re Greenwood, 3 UCC Rep. Serv. 1139 (Ref.Dec.C.D.Cal.1966) (failure to give notice of resale by

bankrupt or trustee frees purchaser of liability). Cf. Bacon Estate, 45 Pa. D. & C.2d 733, 5 UCC Rep.Serv. 486 (Orphan's Ct.1968).

28. For example, the buyer may have contracted to pay $100,000 a year for five years for an inventory to be placed in the buyer's new store. Upon the buyer's breach the seller enters

payments over three years would be much less than $20,000. The cash resale price should be subtracted from the present value of the $20,000 in order to get the correct damage figure. No case law to date suggests that these problems will be grave; hopefully they will be less grave than analogous problems respecting cover under 2-712.

Section 2-706 differs from 2-712 in one important respect: it lives in the shadow of a large and growing body of case law on resales by secured creditors under 9-504(3). Under 9-504 a seller or creditor who has repossessed collateral and chosen to resell must do so in "a commercially reasonable manner." The same phrase appears in 2-706, and courts will surely look to decisions under 9-504 for guidance in determining what is "commercially reasonable." One should beware of undue reliance upon Article Nine decisions in Article Two cases. In the 9-504 cases we detect a most skeptical judicial attitude about the fairness of "deficiency judgment sales." The ignorant, ill represented, and foolish consumer-debtor calls forth the milk of judicial kindness in these 9-504 cases. If one assumes that the typical 9-504 deficiency judgment case is "GMAC v. Pitiful Wretch" but that the typical 2-706 case is "Sears Roebuck v. General Electric," the courts need not and should not be as finicky about commercial reasonability under 2-706 as they have been under 9-504. Inevitably the debtor under 9-504 is down at the heel or he would not be in default. The same is not necessarily true of the businessman defendant under 2-706.

In the handful of cases under 2-706 to date, the courts have found little difficulty with the section. All four of the reported cases have been before hearing boards of the Department of Agriculture which permitted sellers who resold lettuce, onions, and the like to recover their difference money. Indeed one hearing officer, a Mr. Flavin, appears to be making the law under 2-706 singlehandedly.[29] In six other cases courts have refused to apply 2-706 either as a final matter or on summary judgment on the ground that the seller failed to give notification of his intention to resell.[30] In most of these cases 2-706 worked like a well-oiled machine, and from all appearances the courts all reached appropriate conclusions.

into a proper resale contract for $350,-000 cash. If one assumes that seller complied with the requirements of 2-706, a mechanical application of 2-706 would yield $150,000 damages. However, in our hypothetical, seller expected the use of only $100,000 cumulatively each year for five years. Thus a recovery of $500,000 cash in one year will give him a windfall. Somehow the courts must discount the $150,000 damage figure to reflect the actual contract situation accurately.

29.　See Aura Orchards v. A. Peltz & Sons, Inc., 27 Agri.Dec. 1546, 6 UCC Rep.Serv. 149 (1968); Bruce Church,

Inc. v. Tested Best Foods Div. of Kane-Miller Corp., 28 Agri.Dec. 377, 6 UCC Rep.Serv. 326 (1969); I. Kallish & Sons v. Jarosz Produce Farms, Inc., 26 Agri.Dec. 1285, 4 UCC Rep.Serv. 1168 (1967); Quattlebaum v. Schutt, 27 Agri.Dec. 242, 5 UCC Rep.Serv. 370 (1968).

30.　See Foster v. Colorado Radio Corp., 381 F.2d 222, 4 UCC Rep.Serv. 446 (10th Cir. 1967); In re Greenwood, 3 UCC Rep.Serv. 1139 (Ref.Dec.C.D.Cal. 1966); Portal Galleries, Inc. v. Tomar Prods., Inc., 60 Misc.2d 523, 302 N.Y. S.2d 871, 6 UCC Rep.Serv. 1047 (Sup. Ct.1969); Meadowbrook Nat'l Bank v.

One of the six, Foster v. Colorado Radio Corp., [30a] is somewhat bizarre. There the buyer breached a contract for the sale of the assets of a radio station. The parties had stipulated at trial that the measure of damages would be the difference between the resale price and the contract price. The court concluded that such a formula could not be used as to goods covered by the Code because the seller had not complied with the notice requirement of 2–706. As to the "non-goods" the court awarded the difference between the contract price and the resale price since the assets were outside the scope of Article Two and could therefore be resold without notice to the buyer. We welcome the court's willingness to apply a sensible rule by analogy, but we would criticize its unwillingness to accept the stipulation as a waiver of the notice requirement.

In sum, it appears that courts are willing and ready to apply 2–706 when the proper case presents itself, and *mirable dictu* none of the courts appear disposed to restrict it unduly by narrow definitions of good faith or commercial reasonability.[31]

## § 7–7   Damages for Nonacceptance or Repudiation, 2–708(1)

Section 2–708(1) embodies the seller's right to the traditional contract-market differential recovery. It reads:

> Subject to subsection (2) and to the provisions of this Article with respect to proof of market price (Section 2–723), the measure of damages for non-acceptance or repudiation by the buyer is the difference between the market price at the time and place for tender and the unpaid contract price together with any incidental damages provided in this Article (Section 2–710), but less expenses saved in consequence of the buyer's breach.

The provision is among the least novel and least remarkable of the Code's damage sections,[32] and the principal questions that 2–708(1) leaves unanswered are these: May a seller who has resold under 2–706 elect to use 2–708(1)? May a seller who could not have benefited by completion of the contract and who would get no damages under 2–708(2) (lost profit), nevertheless recover under 2–708(1)?

Markos, 3 UCC Rep.Serv. 854 (N.Y. Sup.Ct.1966); Bacon Estate, 45 Pa.D. & C.2d 733, 5 UCC Rep.Serv. 486 (Orphan's Ct.1968); Wood v. Downing, 243 Ark. 120, 418 S.W.2d 800, 4 UCC Rep.Serv. 733 (1967).

**30a.** 381 F.2d 222, 4 UCC Rep.Serv. 446 (10th Cir. 1967).

**31.** For able and extensive discussion of section 2–706, see Nordstrom, Sellers Damages Following Resale Under Article Two of the Uniform Commercial Code, 65 Mich.L.Rev. 1299 (1967); Peters, Remedies for Breach of Contracts Relating to the Sale of Goods Under the Uniform Commercial Code

—A Roadmap for Article Two, 73 Yale L.J. 199 (1963).

**32.** Section 2–708(1)'s immediate ancestor is Uniform Sales Act § 64, which reads in part as follows:

> (3) Where there is an available market for the goods in question, the measure of damages is, in the absence of special circumstances showing proximate damage of a greater amount, the difference between the contract price and the market or current price at the time or times when the goods ought to have been accepted, or, if no time was fixed for acceptance, then at the time of the refusal to accept.

Before we consider these lawyer questions, we should put 2–708 (1) in perspective.   Here as on the buyer's side,[33] the contract-market differential will seldom be the same as the seller's actual economic loss from breach.   Consider a contract to sell 5,000 pairs of "tire-sole" sandals F.O.B. seller's plant for $5,000.   If it cost the seller $2,000 to manufacture the sandals, his expectation would be a profit of $3,000. Only if the seller resells the sandals at the market price prevailing on the date of tender and the collection of his damages is cost free will 2–708(1) put him in the same economic position as performance would have.[34]   If he resells for less than the market price at the date of tender, his profit on the resale and his damage recovery under 2–708(1) will not equal the $3,000 profit he would have had.[35]   On the other hand if he resells for more than the market price at the time of tender, his resale profit and his 2–708(1) damages will total more than $3,000, and he will get a windfall.[36]   Of course one may view 2–708(1) and its buyer's counterpart, 2–713, as statutory liquidated damage clauses.   For a fuller discussion of that view of 2–708 and 2–713, see the discussion of 2–713 in Chapter 6.

If one understands the formula in 2–713,[37] he can readily cope with 2–708(1).[38]   The market is measured at "the time and place for tender," and the seller is entitled to the difference between the contract price and the market price.   Even a first year law student knows when and where tender has occurred in an "across the counter" sale.   Less clear is the case when the seller ships goods to the buyer, "F.O.B. buyer's plant" or "F.O.B. seller's plant."   In the former case we believe tender occurs at buyer's plant, in the latter at seller's plant.[39]

The aggrieved seller may recover any incidental damages flowing from the breach (2–710),[40] but he must subtract any "expenses saved in consequence of the buyer's breach."

33.   For consideration of the buyer's analogue, section 2–713, see the discussion in Section 6–4 supra.

34.   Resale under 2–706 will put most sellers, except for those with the lost volume problem, back into the same economic position as performance would have.

35.   Compare this outcome with that reached under 2–706 discussed in Section 7–6 supra.

36.   For an argument against this result, see Section 7–12 and note 44 infra.

37.   See Section 6–4 supra.

38.   For judicial consideration of the formula, see Bacon Estate, 45 Pa.D. & C.2d 733, 5 UCC Rep.Serv. 486 (Or-phan's Ct.1968) ;   and Jagger Bros., Inc. v. Technical Textile Co., 202 Pa. Super. 639, 198 A.2d 888, 2 UCC Rep. Serv. 97 (1964).

39.   For a discussion of these matters, see Section 6–4 supra.

40.   See § 2–710:

Incidental damages to an aggrieved seller include any commercially reasonable charges, expenses or commissions incurred in stopping delivery, in the transportation, care and custody of goods after the buyer's breach, in connection with return or resale of the goods or otherwise resulting from the breach.

See also Beco v. Minnechaug Golf Course, Inc., 5 Conn.Cir. 444, 256 A.2d 522, 6 UCC Rep.Serv. 910 (1968).

Although seller's 2–708(1) is an almost identical twin of buyer's 2–713, 2–708(1) varies in one puzzling respect. Under 2–713 the aggrieved buyer measures the market at the time he "learns of the breach." [41] Section 2–713(2) fixes the crucial place as "the place for tender or, in cases of rejection after arrival or revocation of acceptance, as of the place of arrival." Apparently the draftsmen used the "place of rejection" and the time buyer "learned of the breach" to measure the market at the time and place where buyer would be most likely to cover. Section 2–708(1), however, directs the aggrieved seller to measure the market at the time and place for tender, and this is not the time and place where the seller is most likely to resell. The significance of this difference can be illustrated by an example. Suppose that a New York buyer contracts to purchase 5,000 toenail clippers from a Los Angeles seller, F.O.B. seller's plant. Assume the contract price was $5,000. Seller correctly crates and ships his clippers, and two weeks after the shipping date they duly arrive in New York. There the buyer, who has since cornered the market in emery boards, wrongfully rejects the goods and thus breaches the contract. If the market prices are as follows, what is the proper measure of recovery under 2–708(1)?

    (1) Los Angeles market price at the time the goods were shipped, $3,000.

    (2) Los Angeles market price at the time the goods were wrongfully rejected, $2,500.

    (3) New York market price when the goods were shipped and when they were rejected, $2,000.

Since the contract was F.O.B. Los Angeles, tender occurs upon delivery to the carrier. Therefore the seller's damages are measured in the Los Angeles' market on the date of shipment. This is true even though the goods are in New York and the seller did not learn of the breach until well after the time for tender. Why the philosophy exhibited in section 2–713 (to choose the most likely cover market) should not apply to the seller's contract-market differential with respect to the most likely resale market is unclear. In our case the seller will doubtless resell in the New York market. If he fails to qualify for a 2–706 recovery (because, for example, he did not give the buyer notice of the resale), he will then recover $1,000 less under 2–708(1) than he would have recovered if he could have used the New York market at the time he learned of the breach.

A more significant and troublesome question about 2–708(1) is its relationship to the other seller's remedies. May the seller's lawyer select 2–708(1) any time it suits his fancy, irrespective of his client's resale or other behavior? First consider the relationship with 2–706. In circumstances in which he is not a "lost volume" seller, [42] his 2–706

---

41. For discussion of the confusion which the quoted language has caused, see Section 6–4 supra.

42. "Lost volume" occurs when the seller resells to a buyer who would have bought from the seller even if there had been no breach of the original

remedy will put him in precisely the same position as performance would have.  Yet a greedy seller may seek a windfall in the form of a larger 2–708(1) recovery.  Assume, for example, this seller resells goods for $4,000 bearing a contract price of $6,000.  Assume that the contract-market differential under 2–708(1) was $3,000.  In such a case may the seller recover the $3,000 and thus gross $7,000?  Or is he limited to a $2,000 recovery and a $6,000 gross?  The courts could avoid this conflict by fiddling with the "expenses saved in consequence of the buyer's breach" part of the 2–708(1) formula.  However, nothing in the pre-Code law or in the statutory history of the Code suggests that "expenses saved" were intended to include profits made on resale.[43]

Whether the draftsmen intended a seller who has resold to recover more in damages under 2–708(1) than he could under 2–706 is not clear.  We conclude that he should not be permitted to recover more under 2–708(1) than under 2–706, but we admit we are swimming upstream against a heavy current of implication which flows from the comments and the Code history.  Yet 1–106 indicates that a seller who has resold may not invoke 2–708(1).  That section states that Code remedies are to put the aggrieved party in as good a position as performance would have, but no better.  By hypothesis our seller would recover more under 2–708(1) than he "needs" to make himself whole.  Section 1–106 derives faint assistance from the third sentence in Comment 1 to 2–703: "Whether the pursuit of one remedy bars another depends entirely on the facts of the individual case." The comment at least suggests that the seller's use of one remedy may foreclose his use of another.  Yet, the immediately preceding sentence in the same comment says: "This Article rejects any doctrine of election of remedy as a fundamental policy and thus the remedies are essentially cumulative in nature and include all of the available remedies for breach."

Some Code history supports the proposition that a seller who has resold under the provisions of 2–706 may nevertheless sue under 2–708(1).  One writer for the New York Law Revision Commission recommended that section 2–703 be rewritten to make it clear that an aggrieved seller who had resold could use 2–708(1).[44]  In response to that recommendation the Editorial Board deleted the language "so far as any goods have not been resold" from 2–703(e), stating its purpose as being to "make it clear that the aggrieved seller was not required to elect between damages under 2–706 and damages under 2–708."[45]

contract.  The result is the seller's total volume of sales by year's end is reduced by one, and his damages are the profit the seller would have made on that additional sale.  For a more detailed discussion, see Harris, A Radical Restatement of the Law of Seller's Damages: Sales Act and Commercial Code Results Compared, 18 Stan.L. Rev. 66, 80–87 (1965) and Section 7–9 infra.

43. "Expenses saved" are dealt with more fully in connection with Buyer's Remedies.  See Sections 6–4 et seq. supra.

44. 1 N.Y. State Law Revision Comm'n, 1955 Report 550 (1955).

45. The comparable remedies on the buyer's side are sections 2–712 (Cover) and 2–713 (Damages for Non-Delivery

Where does this leave us? Note first that the current Code and comments are equivocal at best; though they may bend in the direction of permitting the seller to choose at will, they stop well short of clearly authorizing this. It is possible that the New York Law Revision Commission had in mind the seller who would not receive a windfall by suing under 2–708(1) and simply wanted to make it clear that a seller who makes a good faith attempt to comply with 2–706 but fails may then resort to 2–708(1). Nothing in their report suggests that they considered the case in which 2–706 recovery would be small because the seller sold at a price very near to the contract price yet the contract-market differential under 2–708 would be large. Despite the powerful arguments of Professor Peters [46] and the broad implications from the statutory history, we conclude that a seller who has resold at the time of trial should not be permitted to recover more under 2–708(1) than he could recover under 2–706. However, we would not cast the burden on the seller who sues under 2–708(1) to prove that 2–706 was less advantageous to him. Rather we would make it the buyer's burden to show that the seller had in fact resold, that this was not a lost volume case, and that 2–708(1) recovery would be greater than 2–706 recovery. Of course it is possible that with this burden so imposed, the seller will in practice have the option to use 2–706 or 2–708 because the buyer will be unable to prove the facts necessary to keep the seller out of 2–708. We acknowledge that possibility, but we think it unlikely at least in all cases in which the recovery at stake makes it worth the lawyer's and the client's time and money to do some discovery.

If the reselling-seller's recovery is to be limited to the difference between his contract price and the resale price, it will be necessary for courts to police seller's disposition and treat certain sales as resales that do not technically qualify for 2–706 treatment. Assume, for example, that buyer breaches a $6,000 contract to purchase 10,000 feet of chicken wire. The market price at the time and place for tender is $4,000, and the contract-market differential under 2–708(1) would be $2,000. However, seller resells the 10,000 feet of chicken wire for $5,800. Should he proceed under 2–706, his recovery would be only $200 (the difference between the $6,000 contract price and the $5,800 resale price). If he purposely fails to give notice of the intended resale and so technically fails to qualify under 2–706, may he then sue under 2–708(1) and recover $2,000 of damages? We should not permit him to do that; rather we should treat his resale as a resale under 2–706 even though he did not comply with all of the terms of 2–706.

or Repudiation). However, the draftsmen clearly indicated their essentially "elective" intention in Comment 3 to section 2–712:

Subsection (3) expresses the policy that cover is not a mandatory remedy for the buyer. The buyer is always free to choose between cover and damages for non-delivery under the next section.

46. See Peters, Remedies for Breach of Contracts, 73 Yale L.J. 199, 260–61 (1963).

If the seller is making many sales of goods of the kind contracted for, courts will also have to be on the watch for the seller who manipulates resales in bad faith in order to apply the lowest possible resale to the broken contract. For example, suppose the seller seeks damages under section 2–706 on a contract to sell a fleet of thirty cars. The unscrupulous seller may resell each of the cars at various prices but ask for damages computed on the basis of the lowest resale price he obtained to maximize damages for the entire fleet.

We will consider the relationship between 2–708(1) and 2–708(2) in Sections 7–11 and 7–12 below. Except for the questions concerning its relationship to 2–706 and 2–708(2), section 2–708(1) deserves comparatively little of the student's or the lawyer's time. It is a contract-market formula that the draftsmen assembled from old and familiar parts.

## § 7–8   Lost Profits, 2–708(2)

Section 2–708(2) says:

> If the measure of damages provided in subsection (1) is inadequate to put the seller in as good a position as performance would have done then the measure of damages is the profit (including reasonable overhead) which the seller would have made from full performance by the buyer, together with any incidental damages provided in this Article (Section 2–710), due allowance for costs reasonably incurred and due credit for payments or proceeds of resale.

This section addresses a group of problems that the draftsmen did not formulate well and presumably did not understand well. In light of Professor Harris' writing [47] on seller's damages it is easy to be critical of the draftsmen's work in 2–708(2). It almost seems as though the draftsmen expended their total supply of energy in the production of one novel and admirable seller's remedy, 2–706. It appears that the draftsmen incorporated the standard contract-market formula in 2–708(1) without questioning it and then proceeded by a series of fits and starts to add 2–708(2). In the pages to follow we will deal with two general questions under 2–708(2). First, what cases does it cover? This is a question of considerable complexity with no certain answer. Second, when it does apply, what do its various parts mean, and what kind of evidence must the plaintiff or the defendant bring forward to satisfy his burden in each case?

---

47. See Harris, A Radical Restatement of the Law of Seller's Damages: Sales Act and Commercial Code Results Compared, 18 Stan.L.Rev. 66 (1965); Harris, A General Theory for Measuring Seller's Damages for Total Breach of Contract, 60 Mich.L.Rev. 577 (1962); Harris, A Radical Restatement of the Law of Seller's Damages: Michigan Results Compared, 61 Mich. L.Rev. 849 (1963); Harris, A Radical Restatement of the Law of Seller's Damages: New York Results Compared, 34 Fordham L.Rev. 23 (1965); Harris & Graham, A Radical Restatement of the Law of Seller's Damages: California Results Compared, 18 Stanford L.Rev. 553 (1965).

## § 7–9   Lost Profits, 2–708(2)—The Lost Volume Seller

Judges in pre-Code cases, writers, and Code draftsmen [48] perceived that a contract-market formula would not even grossly approximate the proper damage recovery for certain sellers. The draftsmen early labeled one such class as those who sell "standard priced" goods.[49] Apparently their theory was that the absence of a contract-market differential must necessarily mean in such cases that some other measure of recovery was needed. At a later stage the draftsmen made room in 2–708(2) for a seller who had ceased manufacture and sold the goods for salvage or who had never purchased the goods.[50] Unfortunately, the draftsmen never identified or articulated any principle to unite these cases. In fact it appears that they did not identify the relevant characteristic of the "standard priced" class. That characteristic is not the "standard pricedness" of the goods the seller is selling but the fact that he will lose one sale when Buyer No. 1 breaches and, if he resells Buyer No. 1's goods to Buyer No. 2, he will still not be made whole by difference-money because he will have lost one sale, one profit, over the course of the year. To illustrate, assume a contract for the sale of a washing machine with a list price of $500. Buyer breaches, and seller resells that washing machine at the same list price the buyer had been willing to pay. However, the resale buyer is one of seller's regular customers who had intended to purchase a washing machine from him anyway. If the seller's total cost per machine was $300, he stood to gain an aggregate profit of

---

**48.** The statutory history begins with the Joint Editorial Committee of the American Law Institute and the National Conference of Commissioners on Uniform State Laws. Their product was a revision of the Uniform Sales Act and became the proposed draft of the Uniform Revised Sales Act (Sales Article of the proposed Commercial Code). Section 110 of the Uniform Revised Sales Act reads as follows:

*Damages for Non-Acceptance.* The measure of damages for non-acceptance is the difference between the unpaid contract price and the price current at the time and place for tender together with any incidental damages under Section 112 but less any expense saved in consequence of the buyer's breach, except that if the foregoing measure of damages is inadequate to put the seller in as good a position as performance would have done then the measure of damages is the profit the seller would have made from full performance by the buyer.

Uniform Revised Sales Act, Proposed Final Draft No. 1 at 58 (1944). Of course, it is the "except . . . if" clause that is of prime concern here. Unfortunately, no notes or comments

to section 110 in the Proposed Final Draft of 1944 explain what kind of "profit" cases the draftsmen meant to accommodate. However, the section is useful if only to note the early belief in inadequacy of the general damage formula which now appears in section 2–708(1).

**49.** In May, 1949, when section 110 became section 2–708 in the 1949 draft of the Uniform Commercial Code, official comments were added. The "except" clause was explained in Comment 2 to 2–708 as follows (emphasis added):

The provision of this section permitting recovery of expected profit where the standard measure of damages is inadequate, together with a new requirement that price actions may be sustained only where resale is impractical, are designed to eliminate the unfair and economically wasteful results arising under the older law when *fixed price articles* were involved. This section permits the recovery of lost profits in all appropriate cases, which would include *all standard priced goods.*

**50.** 1954 Recommendations of the Enlarged Editorial Board to § 2–708 at 14.

$400, that is, $200 profit from each of two sales. Clearly the 2–708 contract-market differential formula is inadequate in this situation since it gives no damages to the seller who has lost a $200 profit because of the breach. In such a case the damage award should be the lost profit, that is, $200, for this will place the seller "in as good a position as performance would have done."

If the seller is in a market in which the demand for the product exceeds the available supply (as for example the car market immediately after World War II), he will lose nothing when one party breaches, and he should recover no damages even if his goods are "standard priced." By the same token when his goods are not standard priced but he loses one sale as a result of one buyer's breach, he needs more than the contract-market differential on the resale to put him in the same economic position as performance would have; he needs the profit on the sale he lost that year. (If in the foregoing example washing machines fluctuated between $450 and $550 and the seller could prove a contract-market difference of $100 or $150, he still would not be made whole by that difference.) Following Professor Harris' nomenclature, we will call this seller the "lost volume" seller.

## § 7–10    Lost Profits, 2–708(2)—Components and Jobber Sellers

In the later stages of the drafting process the draftsmen identified a second class of sellers who deserved special treatment. These are sellers who can be said to lose volume not because they resell completed goods to another regular customer but because they either resell uncompleted goods for scrap or are jobbers who never purchase the contract goods at all. These are Professor Harris' "components" and "jobber" sellers.[51] The "components seller" is one who agrees to manufacture or assemble the contract goods. Regardless whether the seller himself produces all of the necessary components or instead acquires them from a third party, the seller's final task is one of assembly. If the buyer breaches before final assembly and the seller elects to cease manufacture,[52] he can be said to have lost the volume of one sale since no sale of completed goods will occur. Unless the seller substantially completes he cannot pursue an action for the price under 2–709. And while 2–708(1) and 2–706 both refer to market price, those sections imply the use of the finished entity as the subject of the market price. However, our seller can at best tally up the value of the components on hand. Professor Harris has argued that:

> where plaintiff stops production after breach and seeks *components-valued* damages, the court should side with him unless defendant shows that (1) plaintiff knew or should have known this decision would enhance damages and (2) a deci-

---

51. See Harris, A Radical Restatement of the Law of Seller's Damages: Sales Act and Commercial Code Results Compared, 18 Stan.L.Rev. 66, 97–98 (1965) [hereafter cited as Harris].

52. Section 2–704(2) allows an aggrieved seller who has not yet completed the contract goods to cease manufacture in the exercise of reasonable commercial judgment.

sion to complete would not have unreasonably imperiled or harmed plaintiff's other interests.[53]

And previously, Professor Harris had noted:

> To calculate what plaintiff saved or should have saved as a result of the breach, the court must add the total value of the various goods on hand at the time of repudiation that were to be used in plaintiff's performance to the costs of completing performance that were saved because of breach.[54]

The draftsmen apparently had similar intentions, for in December, 1954, the Recommendations of the Enlarged Editorial Board inserted an additional phrase at the end of what was then 2–708 (emphasis added):

> . . . except that if the foregoing measure of damages is inadequate to put the seller in as good a position as performance would have done then the measure of damages is the profit, (including reasonable overhead,) which the seller would have made from full performance by the buyer *with due allowance for costs reasonably incurred and due credit for any resale.*

The additional phrase at the end of section 2–708 was added "to clarify the privilege of the seller to realize junk value when it is manifestly useless to complete the operation of manufacture." [55] Thus the draftsmen indicated a second situation as appropriate for the profit remedy of 2–708, namely the situation where a seller-manufacturer who learns of the buyer's breach while in the process of manufacturing the contract goods.

The "jobber" is yet another kind of seller who can look to 2–708 (2) for recovery of lost profits. By "jobber" we refer to a seller who satisfies two conditions. First, he is a seller who never acquires the contract goods. Second, his decision not to acquire those goods after learning of the breach was not commercially unreasonable under 2–704.[56] In these circumstances the seller's actions for the price or resale are inapplicable. And a recovery of damages under 2–708(1) will place him in the same position as performance only by chance. Since he has no goods on hand to resell, he cannot even resell on the market at the time of tender and so recoup the amount necessary to make him whole by adding such proceeds to his 2–708(1) recovery. Thus the only recovery which grossly approximates the "jobber's" economic loss is a recovery based on lost profits.

Of course the jobber is not functionally different from the components seller, and as Professor Harris notes:

> In this situation a components approach is more appropriate—that is, plaintiff should abandon efforts to acquire

**53.** Harris, supra note 51, at 72 (emphasis in original).

**54.** Harris, supra note 51, at 68.

**55.** 1954 Recommendations of the Enlarged Editorial Board to § 2–708 at 14.

**56.** See Section 7–14 infra.

the goods. Valuation of the yet-to-be-acquired goods should be at cost of acquisition ("components valuation") even if there is only a single component to be valued—the goods themselves.[57]

## § 7–11  Lost Profits, 2–708(2)—Other Cases

If the draftsmen had simply identified the above two classes of plaintiffs and had told us that 2–708(2) should apply to them and to no others, the law would be simple if not necessarily fair. However, the draftsmen left us with the troublesome preamble to 2–708(2): "If the measure of damages provided in subsection (1) is inadequate to put the seller in as good a position as performance would have done then the measure of damages is   .  .  .   [that set out in subsection (2)]." This general principle literally covers a multitude of plaintiffs who are neither lost volume sellers, nor jobbers, nor components sellers. As Professor Peters has pointed out,[58] only by happenstance does the contract-market differential of 2–708(1) put the seller in the same economic position as performance would have. When the seller who sues under 2–708(1) resells the goods at a lower price than the market price on the date of tender, 2–708(1) will always leave him short of the economic position in which performance would have put him. If on the other hand he resells the goods at a higher price than the market price on the date of tender, 2–708(1) makes him more than whole; it gives him a larger profit than performance would have. Since history tells us, and presumably all agree, that the lost volume seller, the components seller (who ceases manufacture and sells for salvage), and the jobber are entitled to enter through the pearly gates to 2–708(2), the question arises: what of the seller who is neither of those and who simply argues that 2–708(1) will not leave him in the same economic condition as would performance? More puzzling yet, what of the defendant buyer who argues that plaintiff seller should be forced to use 2–708(2) because 2–708(1) would put the seller in a *better* economic position than performance would have?

### *2–708(1), Not Enough Compensation*

In answer to the first question we believe that any plaintiff who is hardy enough to prove that the 2–708(1) measure of damages will not put him in the same position performance would have, should be permitted to prove what performance would have done for him and should recover that amount under 2–708(2). We take that position with a healthy respect for the problems it poses for the plaintiff and the court. When one asks a court to put a plaintiff in the same economic position as performance would have done, he is asking it for a much more subtle and difficult judgment than he is when he simply asks the court to find the difference between a contract price and a market price.

57.  Harris, supra note 51, at 77.

58.  Peters, Remedies for Breach of Contracts, 73 Yale L.J. 199, 258–570 (1963).

Before examining the complexities of these cases, we first consider the kinds of cases, apparently now excluded from 2–708(2), which we argue ought to be included in 2–708(2). If the seller has resold to one of his regular customers and so lost volume, he is already within 2–708(2) as a lost volume seller. Moreover if he is a jobber or a manufacturer who incurred no costs, he falls within the Harris jobber category and is included in 2–708(2). Likewise if he is a manufacturer who ceases manufacture in midstream, he is already within the confines of 2–708(2). That leaves only two other cases for inclusion. The first arises when the seller resells a finished product but is unable to prove that he lost volume as a result of the breach. The second is the seller who holds completed goods on hand and unsold at the time of trial. Presumably because the contract-market differential at the time of tender would grossly approximate the damage which these two types of sellers would have suffered if they had resold in the relevant market at or shortly after the breach, standard doctrine would send each of these types of sellers to 2–708(1). These sellers differ, then, from the lost volume seller in that they cannot prove that they lost a profit on one sale during the year. They differ from the jobber or salvage seller in that they have a completed product which they could have sold on the market at or near the time of tender, presumably thereby reducing their damages.

In both cases (completed goods on hand at time of trial; completed goods resold prior to trial) the 2–708(2) formula is easy to apply in a mechanical fashion. The art comes in establishing the figure which the court will allow as "due credit for payments or proceeds of resale." If the seller has resold, the due credit should never be less than the amount for which he has resold (remember he is not a lost volume seller), but conceivably it should be more than that figure if the court finds, for example, that the seller lacked commercial reasonability in waiting as long as he did in the falling market. If the seller still holds the goods at time of sale, the court will still have to determine a figure to include as due credit for a putative resale even though the seller has not yet resold. If the court does not deduct some amount for due credit for resale, 2–708(2) will simply become a back door action for the price, and quite clearly the draftsmen did not intend that result. To sharpen our focus on the problem, consider the following hypothetical case. Assume that Boeing has a contract for the sale of two used 707's at a price of $2 million each. The buyer breaches at a time when the used 707 market is $1.7 million per aircraft (give or take $100,000). After breach seller resells one aircraft for $1.6 million, and at the time of trial Boeing has not sold the other 707. At the time of trial the fair market value of used 707's has fallen to $1.4 million because many more aircraft have come onto the market with the introduction of widebody jets. Note that 2–708(1) will not put Boeing in the same position that performance would have. Under 2–708(1) Boeing will recover $300,000 on each aircraft (the difference between the $2 million contract price and the $1.7 million market price at the time and place for tender).  However, Boeing did not receive the market price of $1.7 million for the aircraft which it resold, and it appears that Boeing will receive $1.4 million or less for the aircraft still on hand.  Consequently, the damages obtained under 2–708(1) will be inadequate to put Boeing in the same economic position as performance would have, that is, performance = $4 million in pocket, but 2–708(1) = $600,000 (damages) + $1.6 million (proceeds of resale) + $1.4 million (probable proceeds of resale) = $3.6 million.

Assume that Boeing's direct cost of purchasing the used aircraft and refurbishing them was $1.3 million per aircraft and that the remaining $700,000 between that figure and the contract price would have been net profit and reimbursement for overhead.  With respect to the aircraft which it resold for $1.6 million, Boeing will argue for a 2–708(2) recovery as follows:

|  |  |  |
|---|---|---|
|  | $   700,000 | (profit plus overhead) |
| plus | 1,300,000 | (costs reasonably incurred) |
| minus | 1,600,000 | (due credit for resale) |
|  | $   400,000 | Damage |

In the second case it will argue for:

|  |  |  |
|---|---|---|
|  | $   700,000 | (profit plus overhead) |
| plus | 1,300,000 | (costs reasonably incurred) |
| minus | 1,400,000 | (due credit for resale) |
|  | $   600,000 | Damage |

Buyer's first line of defense will be to argue that Boeing may not use 2–708(2) since it can show no lost volume and is neither a jobber nor a manufacturer who ceased manufacture.  If the court rejects that argument, the buyer's second line of defense will be to argue that he should be given a greater "due credit" in each case.  He may maintain that Boeing should have resold for $1.7 million at the time of tender and that its failure to do so was a failure of commercial reasonability.  Unless the buyer can show that Boeing's failure to resell was commercially unreasonable, that is, that Boeing knew the market would fall and could have resold but did not, we would reject the buyer's contention and permit Boeing to recover under 2–708(2).  Since Boeing's recovery under 2–708(1) would be $300,000 per aircraft, their use of 2–708(2) would net them an additional $400,000.

Some may argue that this opportunity to receive a more ample recovery under 2–708(2) than would be available under 2–708(1) will encourage the Boeings of this world to forego resale and to lie in the Johnson grass in hopes of a sizable recovery under 2–708(2) and a later lucky resale at a higher price.  As we have said before, we suspect this is not the way businessmen behave.  To forego dollars in the pocket from a reasonably satisfactory resale in hopes of recovering a larger amount through litigation, the outcome of which is unpredictable at best (disastrous, if the court finds no breach), is not the way businessmen behave.  Therefore we consider the problem minimal and would give the courts a somewhat freer rein than they have had heretofore to award the seller his economic benefit. We appreciate that such cases will present novel and difficult questions both to the parties' lawyers and to the judges, but we believe these costs to be outweighed by the benefits to be gained.

### § 7–12   Lost Profits, 2–708(2)—Is 2–708(1) Ever Too Generous?

The other side of the coin, whether the defendant can ever restrict the plaintiff to 2–708(2), is equally interesting. The case might arise when the defendant argues that the seller's direct costs (all saved) would have equalled the contract price and argues therefore that he should recover none of the contract-market differential. We believe that the defendant should be permitted to restrict the plaintiff to 2–708(2) in those circumstances in which 2–708(1) will overcompensate the plaintiff. This position is consistent with the basic damage philosophy of the Code at least insofar as it is stated in 1–106: to put the plaintiff in the same economic position performance would have and not in a better one.[59]

In the case put above the plaintiff of course would have the burden of proving his loss under 2–708(2). Here the placing of the burden is important, perhaps crucial. We argue that the defendant is entitled to restrict the plaintiff to 2–708(2) only when defendant can prove that the measure of damages in 2–708(1) will overcompensate the plaintiff. We well understand that we impose on defendant a heavy burden, for he must find this evidence largely through oral and documentary discovery of the opposing party's employees and business records. However, we believe that it would place an undue burden on plaintiff-seller to require not only that he prove the market under 2–708(1) but that he also prove that 2–708(1) will not overcompensate him.

There is at least one case and several highly respectable arguments against our position. In Jagger Brothers Inc. v. Technical Textile Co.,[60] defendant buyer argued that the proper recovery should be "the difference between the cost of manufacturing and the contract

---

59. An analogous problem in computing damages occurs when a plaintiff sues on a losing contract in the construction industry. Assume that a builder sues for breach of a $50,000 contract. He estimated his profit as $10,000 when he began the project, and he has spent $30,000 toward completing the Gothic riding stable for the local law school. If the cost to finish the project was $10,000, the damages that the builder should receive are his out of pocket expenses plus the profit he would have made ($30,000 + $10,000 = $40,000). But if the cost to finish the project is $25,000, then he would have lost $5,000 ($50,000 (contract price)—$55,000 (cost)) if no breach had occurred. The damages the builder should receive with a losing contract should be limited by the total contract price minus the estimated cost to finish the structure. ($50,000—$25,000 = $25,000) This would leave the builder of the losing contract $5,000 in the red ($30,000 (costs already incurred)—$25,000 (damages awarded)) which is where he would be if the other party had not breached. For more detailed discussion, see H. Jones, E. Farnsworth & W. Young, Cases and Materials on Contracts 669–73 (1965); Patterson, Builder's Measure of Recovery for Breach of Contract, 31 Colum.L. Rev. 1286 (1931).

60. 202 Pa.Super. 639, 640, 198 A.2d 888, 889, 2 UCC Rep.Serv. 97, 98 (1964).

price." The court rejected the buyer's argument and concluded that the trial court had acted properly in allowing the plaintiff to recover the contract-market differential under 2–708(1). The case is not powerful precedent against our position for several reasons. In the first place, there was no showing that the defendant in that case offered to prove that 2–708(1) would overcompensate the plaintiff; he simply argued that the plaintiff should be restricted to 2–708(2). That is not our position. Secondly, there is no showing that the buyer argued the policy of section 1–106, that is, that the aggrieved party should only be put in as good a position as performance would have and not in a better position.

More damaging to the proposition that a seller may be restricted to a 2–708(2) recovery are the arguments from the language and from the statutory history of 2–708(2). In the first place the preamble to 2–708(2) states that it is available when the measure of damage in subsection (1) is "inadequate" to put the seller in as good a position, etc. On its face it does not consider the possibility that the measure in subsection (1) may be more than adequate. Secondly, it is clear from Code history that the plaintiffs foremost in the draftsmen's minds were ones who would not be sufficiently compensated by 2–708(1); [61] we find no mention in the New York Law Revision Commission Reports or elsewhere of the plaintiff who would receive too much from 2–708(1). It is possible that the draftsmen believed that plaintiffs in general are too little rewarded and breachers too little deterred. If that was their philosophy, it is conceivable that they regarded 2–708(1) as a liquidated damage clause available to the plaintiff irrespective of his actual damage. That position of course is inconsistent with the philosophy stated in 1–106. We prefer to stick by Comment 1 to 1–106: " . . . compensatory damages are limited to compensation. They do not include consequential or special damages, or penal damages; and the Act elsewhere makes it clear that damages must be minimized." [62] We are unpersuaded by the need to have a liquidated damage clause; we suspect that damage formulas play an insignificant part in the decisions of businessmen who are deciding whether to break a contract. For that reason we reject breach deterrence as an important factor in choosing damage formulas and would choose that formula which best approximates the actual economic loss.

61. Patterson, 1 N.Y. State Law Revision Comm'n, 1955 Report 694 (1955).

62. Consider the seller's consequential damage problem. Suppose seller has a contract with buyer to distribute his goods. Buyer-distributor breaches the contract, and seller loses profits because it takes him a year to find another distributor in the same market to sell his goods. In some ways the problem resembles an aggravated version of the lost volume problem considered in Section 7–9 supra. So far as we are able to tell, the Code does not contemplate a seller's recovery of consequential damages. (See § 1–106, Comment 1.) However, it seems only fair that in the case posed the seller should receive consequential damages. One possible way to give consequential damages to him is to interpret the "profit" language in 2–708(2) very broadly. Doubtless, though, this stretches 2–708(2) well beyond the intention of the draftsmen.

## § 7-13    Lost Profits, 2-708(2)—The Formula

In explaining how the formula of 2-708(2) actually works we will focus mainly on the two types of sellers traditionally entitled to 2-708(2) treatment: (1) the lost volume seller and (2) the components seller and the jobber. The formula for the third group of sellers, those we have elegantly labeled "Other Cases," has been considered in our discussion above.

Since the statutory history of the Code and in particular Comment 2 to 2-708 indicate that the current 2-708(2) was intended to provide an adequate remedy for the lost volume seller,[63] it is most surprising to find that the 2-708(2) formula will not yield the correct recovery to a lost volume seller. That formula reads as follows:

> If the measure of damages provided in subsection (1) is inadequate to put the seller in as good a position as performance would have done then the measure of damages is the profit (including reasonable overhead) which the seller would have made from full performance by the buyer, together with any incidental damages provided in this Article (Section 2-710), due allowance for costs reasonably incurred and due credit for payments or proceeds of resale.

Assume that Boeing has a contract for the sale of 100 747's during the coming year. TWA who had contracted to buy the third aircraft off the line breaches its contract and Boeing sells that particular plane to Pan Am who had agreed to buy the fourth. Because of the breach Boeing sells only 99 aircraft and loses one $3 million profit (its unit profit and overhead allocation per aircraft):

|  | $2 million | (profit) |
|---|---|---|
| *plus* | 1 million | (overhead) |
| *plus* | 0 | (incidental) |
| *plus* | 0 | (costs reasonably incurred) |
|  |  | (all allocated to Pan Am and so saved) |
| *minus* | 0 | (credit for resale) |
|  | $3 million | Damage |

Ignoring for the moment the problems of defining "reasonable overhead" and the questions relative to "cost reasonably incurred," how does one answer TWA's argument: "You resold the 747 which you had manufactured for us and which you had labeled with our name to Pan Am for the same price which you were going to charge us. Therefore, we have the right under the 2-708(2) formula to 'due credit for payments or proceeds of resale.'" Of course if one gives TWA due credit for the resale, 2-708(2) will produce no damages, and it will misfire in every other lost volume case.

---

63. See Section 7-9 supra.

TWA figures the damages as follows:

|        | $2 million  | (profit)                     |
|--------|-------------|------------------------------|
| *plus*   | 1 million   | (overhead)                   |
| *plus*   | 0           | (incidental)                 |
| *plus*   | 17 million  | (cost reasonably incurred)   |
| *minus*  | 20 million  | (credit for resale)          |
|        | $0          | Damage                       |

How does one meet this problem? Unfortunately there is no explanation for it, and there is no polished solution. As the formula is now written, it simply will not yield the recovery which all right-minded people would agree the lost volume seller should have.

Gross errors of the kind here committed by the draftsmen call for extraordinary solutions. We agree with Professor Harris: courts should simply ignore the "due credit" language in lost volume cases.[64] Only by ignoring that language can they apply 2–708(2) to put the Boeings of this world in the same position as performance would have. What must a lost volume seller prove in order to win under 2–708(2)? First, the seller must prove that he is in fact a lost volume seller. In the words of Professor Harris, "Resale results in loss of volume only if three conditions are met: (1) the person who bought the resold entity would have been solicited by the plaintiff had there been no breach and resale; (2) the solicitation would have been successful; and (3) the plaintiff could have performed that additional contract." [65] Second, the seller must establish "the profit (including a reasonable overhead)." This phrase is likely to be the scene of bloody battles between the accountants of the various parties. One can expect no unanimity among accountants about what is overhead and what is not or about how the overhead is to be allocated to the seller's various contracts. We can give no assistance with those highly practical problems; we hope only to shed some light upon the principles embodied in the phrase. Presumably the Code gives the seller net profit after taxes plus that part of his fixed costs which he would have satisfied out of the proceeds from this contract. Courts should not be hesitant to award more than the plaintiff's net profit; a contract with a theoretical net profit of zero may nevertheless carry a substantial economic benefit to the contracting party. Assume for example, that Boeing owes rent, state and local property taxes, and executive salaries. It will incur all of these costs whether it sells 50 airplanes or 100 airplanes. Any contract whose additional direct costs are less than the contract price will produce some cash flow to pay a share of the property taxes, salaries, and rent. Therefore any such contract offers an economic benefit to Boeing even though there is a zero or negative "net profit" on it. Therefore, it is logical and also consistent with the policy of 1–106 to award the seller

64.  Harris, supra note 51, at 99.       65.  Harris, supra note 51, at 82.

not only his net profit but also that pro rata share of his fixed costs which the broken contract would have satisfied.[66]

The 2–708(2) formula has three remaining parts. It permits the seller to recover "incidental damages" (2–710). Those should offer no difficulty. It authorizes "due credit for payments or proceeds of resale," a phrase which we have said above must be ignored if we are to reach the right outcome in lost volume cases. And it gives the seller "due allowance for costs reasonably incurred." This latter phrase will apparently give the seller in addition to his profit and his overhead an amount equal to what he has expended for performance of the contract that will now be valueless. If, for example, Boeing had made a contract with a supplier for some equipment which TWA wished to have installed in the airplane but which was of no use to Pan Am, and Boeing had to pay a fee to be freed from that contractual obligation, that fee would be a cost reasonably incurred which it could charge against TWA.

The use of the 2–708(2) formula by the components seller can be illustrated by the "junk value, partially manufactured goods" situation, and here the formula set forth in subsection 2 works like a charm. One begins with the "profit," including reasonable overhead. To this add incidental damages as authorized by section 2–710. Then add "costs reasonably incurred" in the manufacturing, less the "payments or proceeds of resale" or salvage. In Chicago Roller Skate Manufacturing Co. v. Sokol Manufacturing Co.,[67] the court handled this problem with great facility although neither party argued the Code correctly. The buyer of wheel assemblies without commercial resale value repudiated his contract. Seller rebuilt the assemblies for use on roller skates and credited the buyer with the reasonable value of the salvaged goods. At trial the seller recovered the balance of the price ($4,285.00). On appeal by the buyer, however, the court recognized that under 2–708(2) the proper recovery should have been lost profits (determined by subtracting the salvage value) of $2,572.00 plus salvage expenses of $3,540.76 for a total of $6,112.76. However, since only the buyer had appealed, the court felt bound to affirm the lower court's finding of damages in the amount of $4,285.00.[68]

---

66. See Vitex Mfg. Corp. v. Caribtex Corp., 377 F.2d 795, 4 UCC Rep.Serv. 182 (3d Cir. 1967) (overhead allowed in recovery of lost profit on contract to process imported cloth; although UCC was not controlling in the Virgin Islands when contract was formed, court specified its opinion based on Code's language).

67. 185 Neb. 515, 177 N.W.2d 25, 7 UCC Rep.Serv. 804 (1970).

68. The components seller might encounter problems under 2–708(2), how-

ever, if the abortive contract would have been a losing one for him. Assume, for example, that a seller has a contract that would cost him $120,000 to complete and that the contract price is $100,000. Buyer breaches when seller has incurred $20,000 in costs, but seller is able to save all additional costs thanks to the breach. Seller then sues buyer under 2–708(2) and seeks to recover the $20,000 as "due allowance for costs reasonably incurred." Buyer responds that the contract would have been a loser (let us assume that there are no fixed

The jobber has no particular problems in using the formula set out in 2–708(2). There can be no resale, because by definition the jobber is without any goods to resell.

Finally, how precise must plaintiff's proof be if he is to recover under section 2–708(2)? Although a number of courts have denied plaintiffs' claims under 2–708(2) because they did not prove their damages, neither these cases nor those that permit recovery treat the precision with which plaintiff must prove his lost profits or treat the possibly successful attacks on plaintiff's proof defendant can mount. By and large these cases are joustings between the plaintiffs' and the defendants' accountants. When the plaintiff has lost, it usually appears from the opinion that he simply offered no proof whatsoever from which the court could determine his damages.[69] But when the plaintiff has offered such proof, the courts have not been unduly finicky.[70] So we await with anticipation the case that

---

costs such as depreciation, taxes, etc.) and that the "profit" term in 2–708(2) should be interpreted as including losses, as negative profits, and that the $20,000 which the seller would have lost had the contract been performed must be subtracted. Thus the buyer argues the damages as he computes them ($0 in this case) will put seller in the same position as performance would have put him. Buyer's argument finds some support from the theory that the damage formula is only meant to put the seller in the position that performance would have and no better. (See § 1–106(1)). For another statement of the problem, see Peters, Remedies for Breach of Contracts Relating to the Sale of Goods Under the Uniform Commercial Code: A Roadmap for Article Two, 73 Yale L.J. 199, 274 (1963).

Reynolds Metals Co. v. Electric Smith Constr. & Equip. Co., 4 Wash. App. 695, 483 P.2d 880 (1971) lends some support to buyer's argument, although the damages were computed under Restatement of Contracts § 333 (1932) rather than under 2–708(2). Electric Smith had a contract to build a bus assembly for a Reynolds aluminum plant at a price of approximately $1.4 million. Reynolds cancelled because of production delays, but the court found that Reynolds had "substantially and materially" contributed to the delay. The damages awarded by the trial court and affirmed by the Washington court of appeals were computed as approximately: $376,000 (net costs incurred by Electric Smith less credit for buyer's payments and resale of materials and equipment) minus $30,000 ($50,000 projected loss

on contract, prorated on an "apportionment of fault" theory). Seller's total award for damages was thus $346,000.

In Stolper Steel Products Corp. v. Behrens Mfg. Co., 10 Wis.2d 478, 103 N.W.2d 683 (1960), buyer cancelled an order for 100 portable water bubblers (drinking fountains) since they were not delivered on schedule. The total contract price was $2,450, but due to various mishaps in production, seller had already incurred $2,972 in costs, including overhead. The trial court had awarded seller $220 in damages which equalled the contract price for the nine bubblers buyer accepted before cancelling the order. On appeal, the Wisconsin Supreme Court held that seller was entitled to reasonable costs incurred (labor and materials) or the contract price for 100 units, whichever was lower (i. e., the $2,450 contract price in this case), which coincidentally equalled the cost incurred reduced by the expected loss on the contract. See note 59 supra.

69. See Royal Store Fixture Co. v. Bucci, 48 Pa.D. & C.2d 696, 7 UCC Rep. Serv. 1193 (Co.Ct.1969) (recovery of lost profits denied for breach of contract to purchase fixtures and refrigeration equipment because no effective proof of cost); Rowland Meledandi, Inc. v. Kohn, 7 UCC Rep.Serv. 34 (N.Y.Civ.Ct. 1969) (failure to prove "amount" of damage barred recovery for breach of contract to purchase a suit).

70. See Anchorage Centennial Dev. Co. v. Van Wormer & Rodrigues, 443 P.2d 596, 5 UCC Rep.Serv. 811 (Alaska 1968) (recovery of lost profits allowed for breach of contract to purchase special-

must even now be brewing somewhere in the court system which will pose a full-fledged disagreement between plaintiff's accountant and defendant's accountant and which will give us some insight into how the courts should and will resolve disputes between the parties over the definitions of profit, overhead, due credit, etc.

So ends the saga of 2–708(2). It is a section of great promise, still largely unfulfilled. It began life as a graft on 2–708(1), bloomed before it was enacted into law, and was finally enacted in such a gnarled mutation that it now barely accommodates some of the cases for which it was originally designed.

## § 7–14  Seller's Rights and Obligations With Respect to Unidentified and Incomplete Goods, 2–704

Some of the most trying moments in a lawyer's practice are likely to occur when his best client, a seller who has received a repudiation, asks what his rights and obligations are with respect to certain uncompleted goods. One can hear the chilling questions of the client who expects and deserves a clear and accurate response: "Am I legally obliged to complete? If I choose not to complete, what damages may I recover? If I complete, can I get my added costs out of the buyer's hide? If I choose to complete, will I lose any rights that I would otherwise have? If I choose not to complete, will I lose any rights I would otherwise have?" Section 2–704 gives some answers, though not necessarily certain ones, to these important practical questions. It reads in full as follows:

> (1) An aggrieved seller under the preceding section may
>
> > (a) identify to the contract conforming goods not already identified if at the time he learned of the breach they are in his possession or control;
> >
> > (b) treat as the subject of resale goods which have demonstrably been intended for the particular contract even though those goods are unfinished.
>
> (2) Where the goods are unfinished an aggrieved seller may in the exercise of reasonable commercial judgment for the purposes of avoiding loss and of effective realization either complete the manufacture and wholly identify the goods to the contract or cease manufacture and resell for scrap or salvage value or proceed in any other reasonable manner.

ly manufactured gold coins for municipal celebration); Distribu-Dor, Inc. v. Karadanis, 11 Cal.App.3d 463, 90 Cal. Rptr. 231, 8 UCC Rep.Serv. 36 (3d Dist. 1970) (lost profit allowed for breach of contract to purchase special mirrors); Detroit Power Screw-Driver Co. v. Ladney, 25 Mich.App. 478, 181 N.W.

2d 828, 8 UCC Rep.Serv. 504 (1970) (costs incurred and expected profit were proved sufficiently to allow recovery under 2–708(2) for breach of contract to purchase machinery, provided seller could show, on remand, that machinery was "specialty item").

Subsection (1) is comparatively free of difficulty. Subsection (1) (a) authorizes identification of the contract goods, and (1) (b) authorizes resale of unfinished goods. Upon such resale the seller will be permitted to recover the difference between the contract price and the resale price less any expenses which he saved because he did not complete. The questions which challenge the lawyer's skill lurk in subsection (2). Let us focus upon the troublesome language: "[S]eller may in the exercise of reasonable commercial judgment . . . either complete the manufacture . . . or cease manufacture and resell for scrap or salvage value. . . ." The quoted language suggests at least three lawyer-questions: (1) By what objective standard does one measure "reasonable commercial judgment," and when does one measure that judgment? (2) If one completes pursuant to a decision which is later found to be commercially unreasonable, what ill consequences will he suffer? (3) Does the section ever oblige one to complete?

The comments give some assistance on the first question. First, they make clear that the burden is on the buyer to prove that seller failed to use reasonable commercial judgment.[71] Second, they point out that the decision is to be measured according "to the facts as they appear at the time he learns of the breach,"[72] not by hindsight after the market has changed in an unforeseen way. Third, the comments offer "damages suffered" as a preliminary litmus test to determine which alternative is the way of reasonable commercial judgment. Hence, if a seller is confronted with a repudiation after very little work under the contract and would, if he then sued, recover a $2,000 profit under 2–708(2), he acts unreasonably if he completes manufacture at a total cost of $10,000 when he knows that the finished goods will bring less than $8,000. By completing with such knowledge he has inflated his damages from $2,000 to an amount greater than $2,000 and, presumptively at least, has acted in a commercially unreasonable manner.

Therefore, the first question which the lawyer should ask himself is what damages the seller may recover from the buyer if he ceases manufacturing at once and sues under 2–708(2) for his lost profit. Next, how do those damages compare with the damages the seller is likely to recover under 2–706 upon completion of the manufacture and the resale of the goods? To make these decisions correctly, one must make not only accurate legal analyses but also careful empirical judgments about the current and future market and about the seller's lost profit. One certainly should preserve all evidence which formed

---

71. § 2–704, Comment 2:

   . . . The burden is on the buyer to show the commercially unreasonable nature of the seller's action in completing manufacture.

72. § 2–704, Comment 2:

   Under this Article the seller is given express power to complete manufacture or procurement of goods for the contract unless the exercise of reasonable commercial judgment as to the facts as they appear at the time he learns of the breach makes it clear that such action will result in a material increase in damages.

the basis for the decision and should document by letter or written memo when and why the decision to complete or not to complete was made.

Additional factors may occasionally complicate the decision about the commercial reasonableness of completion. Suppose the client says the damages on this contract will probably be enhanced by completing, but that he simply cannot afford to cease manufacture, lay off all his skilled employees, and thus lose many of them to other employers? Surely such a seller is making an intelligent and commercially reasonable judgment to complete even though in the narrow context of one contract he is increasing the damages to this particular buyer. In such circumstances we should permit the seller to complete and should not find his action commercially unreasonable.[73]

In summary, the general standard, though not the exclusive one, is to compare: "How much can I recover from the buyer if I stop now?" against "How much can I likely recover if I complete and resell?" If the former is greater than the latter, completion is commercially reasonable. Recall that the burden is on the buyer to show absence of commercial reasonableness and that the test is to be applied at the time of the repudiation, not by hindsight at the time of trial.

Recognizing that section 2–704 gives the seller a right to complete in certain circumstances, does it also oblige him to do so when a commercially reasonable seller would complete? The title to 2–704 speaks of the seller's "right" to complete or cease manufacture, but subsection (2) simply says that the seller may in the exercise of reasonable commercial judgment complete or not complete. The comments, on the other hand, deal principally with the problem of the seller who has completed, and who is faced by the buyer who argues that his completion is commercially unreasonable. Thus one who reads just the Code and its comments is left in considerable doubt about whether the draftsmen intended ever to oblige a seller to complete manufacture; the body of the Code points toward an obligation to complete in some cases, while the comments do not.

To read 2–704 as consistent with the general rules of mitigation, we would interpret it to mean that the seller must exercise commercially reasonable judgment not only when he decides to complete, but also when he decides not to. That is, if it is not commercially reasonable to cease manufacture, we would find that 2–704 obliges him to complete manufacture or suffer the consequences. Although we have found no cases in which a seller ceased manufacture and was later denied recovery of damages he initially suffered on the ground

---

**73.** The court agreed with this proposition in O'Hare v. Peacock Dairies, Inc., 26 Cal.App.2d 345, 79 P.2d 433 (4th Dist. 1938). Plaintiff agreed to sell all of the milk he produced for ten years to the defendant. However, when the market price dropped after four years the defendant breached. Although continuing to produce milk enhanced damages, the court held that plaintiff was not obliged to sell his herd and stop production.

he could have avoided those damages by completing, the general doctrine of mitigation would oblige him to continue manufacture when it was clear that he could minimize his charges by doing so.

Perhaps because the draftsmen thought it self-evident, the Code does not spell out the consequences to a seller of his acting in a commercially unreasonable way under 2-704. It would appear that the consequences under the Code are the same as those under the common law for failure to behave properly in mitigating damages.[74] That is to say, a seller who would be permitted to recover $2,000 if he ceased manufacture but who, in the exercise of commercially unreasonable judgment, completed manufacture and now appears in court with the claim for $5,000, should be limited to a $2,000 recovery. In short, he should get the recovery which he would have had had he behaved in a commercially reasonable way. Of course to preserve the usefulness of 2-704, the courts will have to be careful to place the burden on the buyer and to insist that he come forward with persuasive evidence that the seller acted in a commercially unreasonable way before they foreclose seller from the right to complete or not complete. Otherwise sellers, and particularly their lawyers, will grow even more timid than they are now, and 2-704 may become a dead letter.

### § 7-15  Unpaid Seller's Goods-Oriented Remedies on Buyer's Insolvency

Upon discovery of the buyer's insolvency, a seller who has been selling on credit may, under 2-702(1), refuse further delivery unless the buyer pays in cash. Or, if the seller has already delivered pursuant to a credit sale and thereafter discovers the buyer to be insolvent, the seller may require return of the goods even though the buyer has demands them within ten days of their receipt by the buyer. Indeed, the seller may require return of the goods even though the buyer has had them for more than ten days, provided the buyer misrepresented his solvency in writing within three months before the seller's delivery. However, a seller's rights to reclaim are subject to the rights of a buyer in the ordinary course or other good faith purchaser or lien creditor under the 1962 Official Text of 2-702(3).

There have been few cases under 2-702(1). In one, seller argued that because buyer owed him for goods sold and delivered, he did not have to deliver goods already paid for in a current sale.[75] The court held for the buyer, since each contract was evidenced by a separate agreement without reservation of rights by either party. In another case the court held that the seller could not justify his refusal to deliver under 2-702(1) because he did not plead insolvency of the buyer as his reason for refusing to deliver.[76]

---

74. 11 S. Williston, Williston on Contracts § 1353 at 274-78 (3d ed. 1968); 5 A. Corbin, Corbin on Contracts § 1039 at 241-43 (1964).

75. In re Layton Fabrics, Ltd., 6 UCC Rep.Serv. 142 (N.Y.Sup.Ct.1969).

76. V. I. Sales Corp. v. 3M Business Prods. Sales, Inc., 3 UCC Rep.Serv. 170 (N.Y.Sup.Ct.1966).

Subsections 2–702(2) and (3) have inspired far more litigation and scholarly discussion than 2–702(1). Section 2–702(2) applies to sales on credit and provides in full:

> Where the seller discovers that the buyer has received goods on credit while insolvent he may reclaim the goods upon demand made within ten days after the receipt, but if misrepresentation of solvency has been made to the particular seller in writing within three months before delivery the ten day limitation does not apply. Except as provided in this subsection the seller may not base a right to reclaim goods on the buyer's fraudulent or innocent misrepresentation of solvency or of intent to pay.

Note that 2–702 only applies to credit sales.

In re Helms Veneer Corp.[77] was a case in which seller released logs to the buyer without receiving payment by check as agreed. The seller's demands for payment over several months were of no avail. The court characterized the transaction as a credit sale because the seller had released the logs upon buyer's promise to pay. Another seller in the same case, however, received part payment by check, and the court held his transaction a cash sale.[78] In another case, a referee in bankruptcy found that a credit transaction involves loss of control by seller, inspection after receipt, and buyer's choice of time of payment.[79]

If the buyer does not misrepresent his solvency in writing, seller must seek to reclaim the goods within ten days of buyer's receipt.[80] Actual reclamation within the ten days is very likely not necessary; presumably, the seller needs only to make a demand within that period.[81] Furthermore, an intervening bankruptcy within the ten days of receipt neither prevents demand nor extends the ten days.[82] One referee in bankruptcy decided that the ten day period is computed as under the Bankruptcy Act (where the first day is excluded and the last day included).[83]

What constitutes a written misrepresentation of solvency is not clear from the cases, although courts have held insufficient a purchase order,[84] a check,[85] and a letter indicating that inventory was ex-

77. 287 F.Supp. 840, 5 UCC Rep.Serv. 977 (W.D.Va.1968).

78. The court applied 2–507(2) and 2–511 in its reasoning. Id. at 844–45, 5 UCC Rep.Serv. at 982–83.

79. In re Behring & Behring, 5 UCC Rep.Serv. 600 (Ref.Dec. N.D.Tex.1968).

80. In re Weekly, 9 UCC Rep.Serv. 1164 (Ref.Dec. E.D.Tenn.1971).

81. In re Childress, 6 UCC Rep.Serv. 505 (Ref.Dec.E.D.Tenn.1969). But see In re Behring & Behring, 5 UCC Rep. Serv. 600, 605 (Ref.Dec.N.D.Tex.1968)

(something more than bare demand necessary within ten-day period).

82. In re Childress, 6 UCC Rep.Serv. 505 (Ref.Dec. E.D.Tenn.1969).

83. In re Behring & Behring, 5 UCC Rep.Serv. 600, 606 (Ref.Dec.N.D.Tex. 1968).

84. In re Regency Furniture, Inc., 7 UCC Rep.Serv. 1381 (Ref.Dec.E.D. Tenn.1970).

85. Theo. Hamm Brewing Co. v. First Trust & Sav. Bank, 103 Ill.App.2d 190,

tremely heavy and that buyer could not pay his bills as they matured.[86]  A seller who seeks to reclaim because of a written misrepresentation of solvency probably must show that he relied on it.[87]

May a bank as a secured party of the seller reclaim from the buyer under 2–702(2)?  At least one court held that a bank was not entitled to the seller's remedies under 2–702(2) because the real seller had not, as the bank had argued, assigned his right to reclaim, but had only executed a security agreement.[88]  On the other hand, another court assumed that a bank which held the seller's promissory notes was a "seller" and could exercise 2–702(2) rights.[89]

Subsection (3) of the 1962 Official Text of the Code provides that the seller's right to reclaim goods from a buyer "is subject to the rights of a buyer in ordinary course or other good faith purchaser or lien creditor under this article (2–403)."[90]  Courts have held that a creditor with an "after acquired property" clause in his security agreement acquires the rights of a bona fide purchaser, and thus defeats a seller's right to reclaim, provided that the parties executed the security agreement before the sale.[91]  One court reasoned that a secured party's preexisting claim constitutes value, (1–201(44) (b)), and that under 2–403(1) "a person with voidable title" (the buyer here) "has power to transfer good title to a good faith purchaser for value."[92]

In 1966, the Code's Permanent Editorial Board amended the Code to delete the words "or lien creditor" following "good faith purchaser" in the first sentence of 2–702(3).  The Board was moved to do this because of the decision in In re Kravitz.[93]  There the buyer's creditors filed an involuntary petition in bankruptcy one day before his seller took steps to rescind under 2–702(2).  This seller petitioned to reclaim the goods from the buyer's trustee in bankruptcy, but the goods were sold and the proceeds substituted by stipulation.  Ultimately, the referee denied reclamation, and the District Court and the Court of Appeals affirmed.  The Court of Appeals reasoned

242 N.E.2d 911, 5 UCC Rep.Serv. 1230 (1968).

**86.** In re Units, Inc., 3 UCC Rep.Serv. 46 (Ref.Dec. D.Conn.1965).

**87.** In re Haugnbook Auto Co., 9 UCC Rep.Serv. 954 (Ref.Dec. M.D.Ga.1971), aff'd 9 UCC Rep.Serv. 1095 (M.D.Ga. 1971); Theo. Hamm Brewing Co. v. First Trust & Sav. Bank, 103 Ill.App. 2d 190, 242 N.E.2d 911, 5 UCC Rep. Serv. 1230 (1968).

**88.** In re Hardin, —— F.Supp. ——, 9 UCC Rep.Serv. 1218 (E.D.Wis.1971), appeal pending, —— F.2d ——, —— UCC Rep.Serv. —— (7th Cir. 1972).

**89.** In re Haugnbook Auto Co., 9 UCC Rep.Serv. 954 (Ref.Dec. M.D.Ga.1971),

aff'd, —— F.Supp. ——, 9 UCC Rep. Serv. 1095 (M.D.Ga.1971).

**90.** English v. Ralph Williams Ford, 17 Cal.App.3d 1038, 95 Cal.Rptr. 501, 9 UCC Rep.Serv. 437 (2d Dist.1971).

**91.** In re Hayward Woolen Co., 3 UCC Rep.Serv. 1107 (Ref.Dec. D.Mass.1967); First-Citizen's Bank & Trust Co. v. Academic Archives, Inc., 179 S.E.2d 850, 8 UCC Rep.Serv. 1197 (N.C.Ct.App. 1971).

**92.** In re Hayward Woolen Co., 3 UCC Rep.Serv. 1107 (Ref.Dec. D.Mass.1967).

**93.** 278 F.2d 820, 1 UCC Rep.Serv. 159 (3d Cir.1960).

that (1) under the 1962 Official Text of 2–702(2) the rights of an unpaid seller are "subject to" the rights of a lien creditor, (2) a trustee in bankruptcy is a lien creditor under 9–301(3), (3) the Code does not spell out the rights of a lien creditor against an unpaid seller, (4) the court must accordingly resort to Pennsylvania common law to determine those rights, and (5) under that law [94] the lien creditor and therefore the trustee prevails. Of course, the court *might* have reached the same result on a literal reading of 2–702(3) itself, for that section says the unpaid seller's rights are "subject to" those of a lien creditor. That is, the court might have read 2–702(3) itself as a priority rule. *Kravitz* provoked a great deal of controversy. If a seller's rights of reclamation were subject to those of the trustee in bankruptcy, 2–702(2) would not protect the seller in the many cases in which the buyer's bankruptcy was literally "right around the corner." Professor Hawkland remarked that *Kravitz* was based on the "peculiar" local law of Pennsylvania and that under the law of most states the seller would prevail over a lien creditor and therefore over a trustee in bankruptcy.[95] Professor Braucher thought that the *Kravitz* court could have reached a contrary result [96] and that its decision was a "surprise" to the code draftsmen.[97] He favored the 1966 amendment to 2–702(3) dropping the words "or lien creditor," so that the law would be "as most of us thought it should be . . . [with] the right to reclaim stated in section 2–702 according to the terms of that section, in bankruptcy as well as out." [98]

Some courts have followed *Kravitz* [99] and some commentators have concluded that on a literal reading of the 1962 Official Text of 2–702, a lien creditor does cut off the rights of a seller.[100] But other courts subsequent to *Kravitz* and legislative action in fifteen states [101] dropping the "lien creditor" language in 2–702 indicate that in the future the reclaiming seller will often prevail against a lien creditor or a trustee in bankruptcy. In the case of In re Royalty Homes,[102] for example, the referee confronted the issue head on. The jurisdiction was one that had *not* dropped the "lien creditor" language, yet the referee held that bankruptcy did not cut off the seller's reclamation rights, although he conceded that on a literal reading of the 1962

**94.** Schwartz v. McCloskey, 156 Pa. 258, 263, 27 A. 300, 301 (1893).

**95.** Hawkland, Relative Rights of Lien Creditors and Defrauded Sellers, 67 Com.L.J. 86 (1962).

**96.** Braucher, Reclamation of Goods From a Fraudulent Buyer, 65 Mich.L. Rev. 1281, 1288 (1967).

**97.** Id. at 1296.

**98.** Id. at 1298.

**99.** In re Eastern Supply Co., 1 UCC Rep.Serv. 151 (W.D.Pa.1963), aff'd, 331 F.2d 852 (3d Cir. 1964).

**100.** See, e. g., Ashe, Reclamation Under the Uniform Commercial Code—An Exercise in Futility, 43 J. Nat'l Con. Ref.Bankr. 78 (1969); Shanker, Bankruptcy and Article 2 of the UCC, 40 J. Nat'l Con.Ref.Bankr. 37 (1966).

**101.** Arkansas, California, Connecticut, Illinois, Kansas, Maine, Minnesota, North Dakota, New Jersey, New Mexico, New York, North Carolina, Oklahoma, Wisconsin, and Wyoming. 1 U. L.A. § 2–702 at 423, Supp. 87 (Master ed. 1968).

**102.** 8 UCC Rep.Serv. 61 (Ref.Dec. E.D.Tenn.1970).

Official Text of 2–702(3) the lien creditor might prevail.  This decision and another [103] were based on the same approach as *Kravitz*, and differed in result only because the common law of Kentucky (and of Tennessee) favored the reclaiming seller over a lien creditor.[104] These cases bear out Professor Hawkland's remark that the seller lost in *Kravitz* only because of the "peculiar" local law of Pennsylvania.

A trustee in bankruptcy might argue that the avoidance sections of the Bankruptcy Act empower him to strike down the interest of a reclaiming seller valid under 2–702.[105]  Certainly the federal Bankruptcy Act overrides any conflicting state law.  But it is elementary that many provisions of the federal Bankruptcy Act defer to state law.[106]  Thus, under 70(c), the trustee has no greater rights than a state law lien creditor.  If the lien creditor has no priority rights, then neither does the trustee.  Since the lien creditor would lose to the unpaid seller in most states even under the 1962 Official Text of 2–702(3), the trustee would lose too.  Furthermore, under section 60, courts have refused to hold that the reclaiming seller's interest constitutes a preference.[107]

Some miscellaneous problems concerning 2–702 have arisen. *Evans Products v. Jorgensen* [108] put in issue the possible priority of a secured party with a floating lien over a supplier of raw materials to the debtor.  There, when debtor did not pay cash for veneer that seller supplied, seller accepted plywood in exchange.  Plaintiff secured party sued seller for return of the plywood, claiming a security interest in it.  To defeat the secured party the seller argued that he was a buyer in ordinary course inasmuch as he had exchanged his 2–702 (2) reclamation rights for the plywood.  The court nevertheless held that the exchange was in satisfaction of a debt and therefore seller lost!  *Greater Louisville Auto Auction v. Ogle Buick, Inc.*[109] reveals a significant *casus omissus* in the Code.  Section 2–702 applies only to credit sales.  In the *Ogle* case the unpaid reclaiming sellers had sold for cash.  Yet 2–507(2), a provision similar in some respects to 2–702 (2) but applicable to cash sales, does not spell out the reclamation rights of an unpaid cash seller nor does it spell out his priorities (if any) against purchasers from the buyer or against his other creditors. Yet the court held for the unpaid sellers against a creditor of the buyer, partly on analogy to 2–702(2) and partly on equitable principles.

---

103.  In re Mel Golde Shoes, Inc., 403 F. 2d 658, 5 UCC Rep.Serv. 1147 (6th Cir. 1969).

104.  In In re Mel Golde Shoes, Inc., 403 F.2d 658, 5 UCC Rep.Serv. 1147 (6th Cir. 1969), the court says that its reasoning is supported by the *Kravitz* decision.

105.  See generally King, Reclamation Petition Granted: In Defense of the Defrauded Seller, 44 J. Nat'l Con.Ref. Bankr. 81 (1970).

106.  Id. at 81.

107.  3 Collier, Bankruptcy ¶ 60.18 (14th ed.).

108.  245 Ore. 362, 421 P.2d 978, 3 UCC Rep.Serv. 1099 (1966).

109.  382 S.W.2d 17, 2 UCC Rep.Serv. 344 (Ky.Ct.App.1965).

# CHAPTER 8

# REJECTION, REVOCATION OF ACCEPTANCE, CURE AND ACCEPTANCE

*Analysis*

Sec.
8–1. Introduction.
8–2. Acceptance, 2–606.
8–3. Rejection and Revocation of Acceptance, 2–601, 2–608, 2–612.
8–4. Cure, 2–508.

## § 8–1  Introduction

Section 2–601 and the sections following it comprise a comprehensive system of "goods oriented" remedies, specifically, rejection and revocation of acceptance. The Code draftsmen attempted to bring some order out of that chaotic body of law which had previously passed under the title "rescission," [1] and they also sought to codify the concept of cure for the first time. Although the Code language is different (much more comprehensive and explicit than was the Uniform Sales Act) [2] and although the Code appears to have made im-

1. For a consideration of the ambiguity inherent in the concept of rescission, see the discussion accompanying notes 5–10 infra.

2. The USA language most relevant to the discussion here appeared in section 69, which reads in part as follows:

(1) Where there is a breach of warranty by the seller, the buyer may, at his election * * *

(c) Refuse to accept the goods, if the property therein has not passed, and maintain an action against the seller for damages for the breach of warranty;

(d) Rescind the contract to sell or the sale and refuse to receive the goods or if the goods have already been received, return them or offer to return them to the seller and recover the price on any part thereof which has been paid.

(2) When the buyer has claimed and been granted a remedy in any one of these ways, no other remedy can thereafter be granted.

(3) Where the goods have been delivered to the buyer, he cannot rescind the sale if he knew of the breach of warranty when he accepted the goods, or if he fails to notify the seller within a reason-able time of the election to rescind, or if he fails to return or to offer to return the goods to the seller in substantially as good condition as they were in at the time the property was transferred to the buyer. But if deterioration or injury of the goods is due to the breach of warranty, such deterioration or injury shall not prevent the buyer from returning or offering to return the goods to the seller and rescinding the sale.

(4) Where the buyer is entitled to rescind the sale and elects to do so, the buyer shall cease to be liable for the price upon returning or offering to return the goods. If the price or any part thereof has already been paid, the seller shall be liable to repay so much thereof as has been paid, concurrently with the return of the goods, or immediately after an offer to return the goods in exchange for repayment of the price.

(5) Where the buyer is entitled to rescind the sale and elects to do so, if the seller refuses to accept an offer of the buyer to return the goods, the buyer shall thereafter be deemed to hold the goods as bailee for the seller, but subject to a lien to secure the re-

portant advances in its doctrine of cure, at this writing the extent of change is unclear. It is clear that the provisions on cure and revocation of acceptance have raised nearly as many questions (at least in academic minds) as they have answered.

Rejection and revocation are self-help remedies of substantial significance. Although the Code describes the procedure one must follow in order to make an effective and rightful rejection, the Code nowhere defines the verb "reject." Somewhat simplified, rejection is a combination of the buyer's refusal to keep delivered goods and his notification to the seller that he will not keep them. Revocation of acceptance is a similar refusal on the buyer's part to keep goods, but in this case it is a refusal which comes at a later time in the transaction and after the buyer has "accepted" by allowing the time for rejection to pass or by some act with respect to the goods. As we will see, in certain circumstances a seller who learns of an alleged defect in the goods has the right under 2–508 to "cure" and thus foreclose the buyer's rejection. The right to cure does not, however, limit revocation of acceptance.

At the outset one should understand the significance of a self-help remedy which permits the buyer to return the goods to the seller, (that is, rejection or revocation of acceptance). In such cases the buyer is freed from his obligation to pay the price, and he has a right to recover that part of the price he has already paid.[3] Moreover, except in unusual circumstances, he need not undertake to resell the goods.[4] One should understand the economic difference between the status of the buyer who has rejected and the status of the buyer who has accepted and sued for breach of warranty. The typical buyer who accepts and sues for breach of warranty under 2–714 will recover only for injury proximately resulting from defects in the goods at the time of sale. If, for example, the purchased automobile had a cracked piston that will cost $100 to repair (and the value of the car is so diminished by $100), buyer will recover that $100. On the other

payment of any portion of the price which has been paid, and with the remedies for the enforcement of such lien allowed to an unpaid seller by section 53.

\* \* \*

3. Section 2–711(1) grants the right to a return of money paid (emphasis added):

Where the seller fails to make delivery or repudiates or the buyer rightfully rejects or justifiably revokes acceptance then with respect to any goods involved, and with respect to the whole if the breach goes to the whole contract (Section 2–612), the buyer may *cancel* and whether or not he has done so may *in addition to recovering so much of the price as has been paid*

• • • •

4. Section 2–602(2) (a) provides that after rejection the buyer must avoid "any exercise of ownership" with respect to the goods. Section 2–602(2) (b) requires the buyer in physical possession of rejected goods to "hold them with reasonable care at the seller's disposition for a time sufficient to permit the seller to remove them ;" and section 2–602(2) (c) states "the buyer has no further obligations with regard to goods rightfully rejected." For a discussion of buyer's obligations with respect to rejected goods, see Garfinkel v. Lehman Floor Covering Co., 60 Misc. 2d 72, 302 N.Y.S.2d 167, 6 UCC Rep.Serv. 915 (Dist.Ct.1969) and the discussion accompanying notes 14–19 infra.

hand, if buyer rejects the goods, he is first recompensed for the injuries resulting from the seller's failure to perform his end of the contract (for example, by a suit under 2–713 or 2–712); more important, he escapes the bargain, and he throws any loss resulting from depreciation of the goods back upon the seller. The importance of goods oriented remedies can be illustrated by an example from the commodity market. Assume that the seller delivers 10,000 bushels of potatoes and that 100 of those bushels are rotten. If the buyer accepts the potatoes, he will have a cause of action under 2–714, and he will recover money approximately equivalent to the value of those 100 bushels. If, on the other hand, he rejects the entire delivery and the price of the potatoes has fallen substantially, his rejection may save him several thousands of dollars by allowing him to purchase conforming goods on the market at a much lower price than that which he agreed to pay. Thus rejection lets him out of the bad bargain as well.

A final introductory word should be devoted to that ambiguous action called "rescission." Some use the word rescission to encompass what the Code defines as a rejection or revocation of acceptance;[5] others use it to mean simply the buyer's act in returning the goods;[6] still others use it to cover the buyer's cancellation of the executory terms of the contract;[7] and finally some might call it the buyer's cause of action for fraud,[8] (including presumably the return of the goods, cancellation of the executory portion of the contract and the return of money paid). It is the apparent intention of the draftsmen to restrict the word rescission to a rather limited number of cases, those involving a mistake or in which the seller has committed fraud, duress, or the like. Comment 1 to 2–608 makes the point as follows: "The section no longer speaks of 'rescission,' a term capable of ambiguous application either to transfer of title to the goods or to the contract of sale and susceptible also of confusion with cancellation for cause of an executed or executory portion of the contract."[9] If the

5. See, e. g., Dorne and Margolin Inc. v. Hull Corp., 82 Montg.Co.L.R. 233 (Pa. C.P.1963); Marbelite Co. v. Philadelphia, 208 Pa.Super. 256, 222 A.2d 443, 3 UCC Rep.Serv. 845 (1966); Wilson v. Scampoli, 228 A.2d 848, 4 UCC Rep.Serv. 178 (D.C.Ct.App.1967); Woods v. Van Wallis Trailer Sales Co., 77 N.M. 121, 419 P.2d 964 (1966).

6. See, e. g., Leveridge v. Notaras, 433 P.2d 935, 4 UCC Rep.Serv. 691 (Okla. 1967).

7. Some cases limit "rescission" to cancellation of the executory portion of the contract; others require a full restoration by both parties to the *status quo ante*. See, e. g., Lea v. Young, 168 Wash. 496, 12 P.2d 601 (1932); United States v. Landers, 128 F.Supp. 97 (S.D.N.Y.1953); Youngstown Steel

Products Co. v. State Board of Equalization, 148 Cal.App. 2d 205, 306 P.2d 983 (2d Dist.1957); King v. Oakley, 434 P.2d 868 (Okla.1967).

8. See, e. g., In re Woederhoff Shoe Co., 184 F.Supp. 479 (N.D.Iowa 1960); Mosely v. Johnson, 90 Ga.App. 165, 82 S.E.2d 163 (1954).

9. Section 2–721 states that all of the Article Two remedies are available to a defrauded party to a sales transaction. It continues, "Neither rescission nor a claim for rescission of the contract . . . shall bar or be deemed inconsistent with a claim for damages or other remedy." Although their meaning is not crystal clear, it appears that the draftsmen contemplate a cause of action for fraud in which the buyer would have a right to return

seller has not committed mistake, fraud, or the like, we believe that the Code preempts the field and that the buyer's only rights to return the goods are those stated in Article Two.[10]

## § 8–2 Acceptance, 2–606

"Acceptance" is a term of art which must be sharply distinguished from a variety of other acts which the buyer might commit. Note first that whether the buyer has "accepted" the goods is unrelated to the question whether title has passed from seller to buyer. Secondly, acceptance is only tangentially related to buyer's possession of the goods, and in the usual case the buyer will have had possession of the goods for some time before he has "accepted" them.

Under section 2–606(1), buyer has accepted if he has done any of the acts described therein:

(1) Acceptance of goods occurs when the buyer

> (a) after a reasonable opportunity to inspect the goods signifies to the seller that the goods are conforming or that he will take or retain them in spite of their non-conformity; or

> (b) fails to make an effective rejection (subsection (1) of Section 2–602), but such acceptance does not occur until the buyer has had a reasonable opportunity to inspect them; or

> (c) does any act inconsistent with the seller's ownership; but if such act is wrongful as against the seller it is an acceptance only if ratified by him.

Section 2–607 states the general legal consequences of acceptance. Upon acceptance, (1) the buyer must pay at the contract rate for the goods accepted, (2) he loses his right to reject, (3) time starts to run within which he must complain of breach or be barred from any remedy, and (4) the burden shifts to the buyer to "establish . . .

the goods purchased and get his money back. Presumably this right to return the goods and get his money back is a right to "rescission" which exists outside the Code.

Absent fraud, we believe the draftsmen intended to limit the buyer to the rights specified in the Code. See 1 N. Y. State Law Revision Comm'n, 1955 Report 528 (1955) where Professor Honnold said, "Under the Code 'revocation of acceptance' takes the place of 'rescission.'" In Lawner v. Engelbach, 433 Pa. 311, 315, 249 A.2d 295, 297, 5 UCC Rep.Serv. 1236, 1238 (1969) the court remarked, "[T]he Uniform Commercial Code has largely abandoned

the concept of recission in favor of the concept of revocation of acceptance."

10. But see Sarnecki v. Al Johns Pontiac, 3 UCC Rep.Serv. 1121, 1132 (Pa. C.P.1966) where the court said, "[T]he UCC does not change the already established law of [Pennsylvania] as to a buyer's right to rescind and recover the purchase price."

The courts have been slow to abandon old words, and they have been far from precise in applying the rejection and revocation sections of Article Two. Thus, it comes as no surprise that Code opinions still refer to "rescission" and fail to deal with some

breach." [11]  Apart from the case in which the contract explicitly renders acceptance "final" and so bars all remedies thereafter and the case where the legal consequences of acceptance to the buyer are clearly substantial, it is difficult to calculate the real significance of acceptance.  Absent an explicit contract term so providing, acceptance does not foreclose buyer's suit for breach of warranty.[12]  Theoretically, one needs a more serious complaint to support revocation of acceptance than he needs to support rejection; theoretically, the burden of proving breach may be a difficult one and conceivably the "reasonable time" specified in 2–607(3) may be a short one which promptly cuts off the buyer's rights if he fails to give notice.  Despite these theoretical legal consequences, we are hounded by the fear that it is a rare case when acceptance really has changed the outcome.  The cases decided to date give little support to the proposition that the buyer may freely reject but only rarely revoke acceptance; neither do the cases make plain just what this shifting burden is or how difficult it is to bear.[13]  Thus it is with a somewhat faint sense of purpose that we present the 2–606 cases and the statutory analysis of 2–606 which follow.

Some of the circumstances in which 2–606(1) (a) will apply are easy to identify; others are not.  Certainly when a professional purchaser inspects goods bought for use in his business and then states orally or in writing to the seller that he will take the goods or "retain them in spite of the nonconformity," we have an acceptance.  According to Comment 3 to 2–606, payment is another "circumstance tending to signify acceptance," but it is ambiguous and not, according to the comment, "conclusive."

The cases that have caused interpretive difficulty under 2–606 (1) (a) are those in which a purchaser, usually a consumer, signs a contract which contains a clause to the effect that he has inspected the automobile or other merchandise and found it to be conforming. One case to the contrary notwithstanding,[14] the prevailing view is that

of the intricacies of sections 2–601 et seq.  See, e. g., note 4 supra.

11.  Acceptance will also take the contract out of the statute of frauds.  § 2–201(3) (c).  Furthermore, many government contracts provide that acceptance forecloses the buyer from all remedies for nonlatent defects.  See, e. g., Mazur Bros. & Jaffee Fish Co., 3 UCC Rep.Serv. 419 (VACAB 1965).

12.  Section 2–714 is explicitly designed to recompense one who has accepted defective goods.  A handful of cases contain language which suggests that failure to make a timely rejection cuts off the right to sue for damages for breach of warranty.  See, e. g., Hudspeth Motors, Inc. v. Wilkinson, 238 Ark. 410, 382 S.W.2d 191, 2 UCC

Rep.Serv. 273 (1964); Harry Winston, Inc. v. Robert Simons, Inc., 4 UCC Rep. Serv. 482 (N.Y.Sup.Ct.1967);  Green Chevrolet Co. v. Kemp, 241 Ark. 62, 406 S.W.2d 142, 3 UCC Rep.Serv. 805 (1966).  But see Shreve v. Casto Trailer Sales, Inc., 150 W.Va. 669, 149 S.E. 2d 238, 3 UCC Rep.Serv. 796 (1966).

13.  Miron v. Yonkers Raceway, Inc., 400 F.2d 112, 5 UCC Rep.Serv. 673 (2d Cir. 1968), is a case in which the buyer lost nominally because he did not carry his burden.  There the court found that the burden had shifted to the buyer and found that his proof did not show that the horse in question was defective at the time of sale.

14.  Rozmus    v.    Thompson's    Lincoln- Mercury Co., 209 Pa.Super. 120, 224 A.

one who buys complex goods such as an automobile and signs a contract for purchase after only a short demonstration ride should not be held to have had "a reasonable opportunity to inspect" and therefore not held to have accepted the goods.

The section that will most often produce an acceptance is 2–606 (1) (b) which provides that one has accepted when he "fails to make an effective rejection . . . ." An effective rejection under 2–602 must occur "within a reasonable time after . . . delivery or tender," and there must be seasonable notification of the rejection by the buyer to the seller. The fighting issues in a 2–606(1) (b) case are those discussed below in Section 8–3 on rejection.

The final and most obstreperous provision of 2–606(1) is subsection (c) which provides that a buyer has accepted when he has done "any act inconsistent with the seller's ownership." Assume, for example, that buyer purchases 1400 feet of cast iron pipe. On the day after the purchase he discovers that the sections of pipe are not of uniform length. Thereafter he makes a contract to resell the pipe, and still later, after the resale contract has fallen through for other reasons, he attempts to reject. In such circumstances the attempt to resell at a time when he was aware of the alleged defect in the goods should be regarded as an act inconsistent with the seller's ownership and should constitute an acceptance.

We think it vital to an intelligent interpretation of section 2–606 (1) (c) that one consider the buyer's act in the context of his knowledge and behavior prior to that act. Presumably a given act has a different meaning when it is done by a buyer in ignorance of a defect which he later discovers than it would if the buyer had discovered the defect and had made a purported rejection. Assume, for example, that Judas Construction Company purchases a large truck. No one would regard its use of that truck on the day after purchase and before any defect was discovered as the kind of act encompassed in 2–606(1) (c) despite the fact that any use is theoretically inconsistent with the seller's ownership. One might draw quite a different conclusion if the buyer discovered a defect, attempted unsuccessfully to reject the truck, and then took it back to the job site and used it on a regular basis. To give meaning to 2–606(1) (c), buyer's acts ought to be divided into at least three categories: (1) acts done in ignorance of the defect; (2) acts done with knowledge that the goods are defective, but before any attempt is made to reject; and (3) acts done with knowledge that the goods are defective and after an attempt to reject. We would argue that acts done in ignorance of the defects which buyer should not have discovered are never covered by 2–606(1) (c). The use of the goods and passage of time might constitute an acceptance under 2–606(1) (a) or 2–606(1) (b). But if any use (and all use is theoretically inconsistent with seller's ownership) constitutes an inconsistent act as that term is used in 2–606(1) (c), then there will always be acceptance the minute the buyer uses the goods notwithstanding the fact he has not yet had a "reasonable opportunity to inspect" under 2–606(1) (a) and still has a "reasonable time" to reject under 2–602 (and therefore has not accepted under 2–606(1) (b)). The only reading of 2–606(1) (c) which is consistent with the policy [15] and which leaves any elbow room for the other provisions of 2–606 is to find that use of goods in ignorance of the defective nature of the goods is not "inconsistent" under 2–606(1) (c).

At the other end of the spectrum are acts done after an attempted rejection and with knowledge of the defect. These are acts contemplated by 2–606(1) (c). Comment 4 to 2–606 specifically refers to them as follows: "[A]ny action taken by the buyer, which is inconsistent with his claim that he has rejected the goods, constitutes an acceptance." Any buyer who goes more than a very small step beyond the acts which he is obliged and permitted to take under 2–603 and 2–602 takes a grave risk that he will have accepted the goods.[16] Note however that there may be cases in which continued use is inevitable (for instance, a carpet nailed to the floor), and in such cases use should not be regarded as inconsistent with seller's ownership.[17]

The most difficult case is that in which the buyer uses the goods in his business with the knowledge that they are defective but before he has attempted to reject. Such circumstances will often arise as the buyer and the seller are attempting to work the bug out of a complex piece of machinery. In such circumstances courts should be hesitant to find that the acts are "inconsistent with the seller's ownership." The parties should be encouraged to engage in this kind of bargaining and adjustment, and the buyer should not be made to engage in it at his peril. Thus we conclude that 2–606(1) (c) is designed principally,

2d 782, 3 UCC Rep.Serv. 1025 (1966). See also Green Chevrolet Co. v. Kemp, 241 Ark. 62, 406 S.W.2d 142, 3 UCC Rep.Serv. 805 (1966).

15. One policy of the Code is to encourage the parties to work out their differences and so to minimize losses resulting from defective performance. A rule which makes any use tantamount to acceptance will make the buyer understandably nervous about attempting to use the goods while he works out the bugs with the seller and may so cause him to reject more quickly than he would otherwise.

16. See, e. g., Marbelite Co. v. Philadelphia, 208 Pa.Super. 256, 222 A.2d 443, 3 UCC Rep.Serv. 845 (1966). Some courts have required that a buyer seeking to revoke acceptance avoid acts of dominion over the goods after giving notice of revocation. See, e. g., Hays Merchandise, Inc. v. Dewey, 78 Wash.2d 342, 474 P.2d 270, 8 UCC Rep.Serv. 31 (1970); Bassman v. Manhattan Dodge Sales, 5 UCC Rep.Serv. 128 (N.Y.Sup.Ct.1968).

17. See Garfinkel v. Lehman Floor Covering Co., 60 Misc.2d 72, 302 N.Y.S. 2d 167, 6 UCC Rep.Serv. 915 (Dist.Ct. 1969). Of course one may have trouble drawing a line between those cases where the buyer must use the goods (e. g., a rug) and those where it would be very convenient but not necessary for him to do so (e. g., commuting by "rejected" car rather than by bus). In Minsel v. El Rancho Mobile Home Center, Inc., 32 Mich.App. 10, 188 N.W. 2d 9, 9 UCC Rep.Serv. 448 (1971), the court speaks of rescission, rejection, and revocation of acceptance. It is unclear whether the court finds that the use of a mobile home for six weeks after a letter of "rejection" has been sent constitutes an acceptance. The court holds that buyer has no liability to seller for such use and affirms the judgment of "rescission." It is unclear whether the court is stating that the buyers could revoke acceptance (on the assumption that the use was acceptance) or whether it finds that the use was not acceptance and that the rejection was effective.

perhaps exclusively, for the case in which the buyer has attempted to reject and then has done some act with respect to the goods. Under no circumstances should an act of the buyer in ignorance of the defective nature of the goods be held "inconsistent with the seller's ownership," and we think it only rare and extraordinary that one who has not first attempted to reject should be regarded as having acted in a manner inconsistent with the seller's ownership.

The cases have not painted a consistent pattern here. They have not focused with any consistency upon the status of the buyer's knowledge nor upon the question whether he has attempted to reject. One suspects in fact that the courts are first deciding upon the merits of the buyer's claim and then reasoning backwards to the determination whether there has been an acceptance because of an inconsistent act.[18] Acts which courts have found inconsistent with the seller's ownership are many and varied. They include making payments, taking possession of the goods, use of the goods, repairing, working on them, and dealing with them in other varied ways.[19]

## § 8–3   Rejection and Revocation of Acceptance, 2–601, 2–608, 2–612

Although the circumstances which give rise to the right to revoke acceptance differ somewhat from those which spawn the right to reject, we think it appropriate to consider the two remedies together. Since the lawyer who counsels the buyer will often not know whether his client has "accepted," he will have to measure his client's proposed behavior simultaneously against the standards for rejection (pre-acceptance behavior) and revocation of acceptance (post-acceptance behavior). Sections 2–601 and 2–612 are the basic provisions which confer the right to reject upon a disappointed buyer. Section 2–608 authorizes revocation of acceptance.

Why is it necessary to have both a right of rejection and a right to revoke acceptance? After one has dug through the detail in 2–601 and sections following, detail necessitated in part by the distinction between rejection and revocation, he will have even more doubt about the necessity for the two rights. In general the right to reject is more readily available, and one wishing to exercise that right has fewer procedural and substantive hoops through which to jump. The draftsmen believed, probably wisely, that when one had held goods long enough that "acceptance" had occurred, he should have to make a better case in order to throw the goods back on the seller. A variety of policies support the proposition that a buyer who has had posses-

18. Compare Casey v. Philadelphia Auto Sales Co., 428 Pa. 155, 236 A.2d 800, 4 UCC Rep.Serv. 1012 (1968), with Grandi v. LeSage, 74 N.M. 799, 399 P. 2d 285, 2 UCC Rep.Serv. 455 (1965) and Campbell v. Pollack, 101 R.I. 223, 221 A.2d 615, 3 UCC Rep.Serv. 703 (1966).

19. Regarding payment as evidence of acceptance, see § 2–606, Comment 3. Regarding modifying the goods, see Park County Implement Co. v. Craig, 397 P.2d 800, 2 UCC Rep.Serv. 379 (Wyo.1964). Taking possession of the goods contributed to a finding of acceptance in Campbell v. Pollack, 101 R.I. 223, 221 A.2d 615, 3 UCC Rep. Serv. 703 (1966).

sion for any considerable period of time or has otherwise accepted should only rarely have the right to put the goods back on the seller. In the first place, the longer the buyer has the goods, the higher is the probability that the alleged defect was caused by him or aggravated by his failure properly to maintain the goods. Secondly, the longer the buyer holds the goods, the greater the depreciation. Finally, the longer the buyer holds the goods (if he uses them), the greater the benefit he will have derived from them. All of these factors support a rule which makes it difficult for the buyer who has accepted to throw the goods and the attendant loss from depreciation and market factors back on the seller.

In the following discussion we will first specify the substantive grounds for rejection and revocation. We devote most of the discussion to the two questions which seem most difficult: Was the buyer's rejection or revocation timely? Did the nonconformity in the goods justify the buyer's action? We conclude with a brief discussion of the "procedure"—the substance of the buyer's notice and his duties with respect to rejected goods in his possession or control.

Section 2–601 confers the right to reject as follows:

Subject to the provisions of the Article on breach in install-ment contracts (Section 2–612) and unless otherwise agreed under the sections on contractual limitations of remedy (Sec-tions 2–718 and 2–719), if the goods or the tender of delivery fail in any respect to conform to the contract, the buyer may

(a) reject the whole;   .   .   .

From sections 2–601, 2–508, and 2–612 one can distill at least four conditions which must exist to give the buyer the right to reject: (1) a nonconforming tender; (2) absence of effective cure by seller; (3) absence of acceptance; and (4) absence of a contract term pro-hibiting rejection.

Section 2–608 confers the right to revoke acceptance as follows:

(1) The buyer may revoke his acceptance of a lot or com-mercial unit whose non-conformity substantially im-pairs its value to him if he has accepted it

  (a) on the reasonable assumption that its non-conform-ity would be cured and it has not been seasonably cured; or

  (b) without discovery of such non-conformity if his ac-ceptance was reasonably induced either by the dif-ficulty of discovery before acceptance or by the sell-er's assurances.

(2) Revocation of acceptance must occur within a reason-able time after the buyer discovers or should have dis-covered the ground for it and before any substantial change in condition of the goods which is not caused by

their own defects.  It is not effective until the buyer notifies the seller of it.

The term "revocation of acceptance" is new, and the courts have not taken to it.  What the draftsmen would call revocation of acceptance and would analyze under 2–608, the courts are likely to define as rescission or rejection and to discuss without reference to the provisions of 2–608.[20]  Since revocation of acceptance always occurs after acceptance and may occur long after the seller regarded the transaction as closed, a buyer who might have rejected with ease must in theory at least meet several additional conditions to revoke acceptance.  Section 2–608 of the Code sets up the following conditions for the buyer who wishes to revoke acceptance:  (*1*) a nonconformity which substantially impairs the value of the "lot or commercial unit;"  (*2*) acceptance (*a*) (with discovery of the defect) on the reasonable assumption that the nonconformity would be cured or (*b*) (without discovery) reasonably induced by the difficulty of the discovery or by seller's assurances;  (*3*) revocation within a reasonable time after the nonconformity was discovered or should have been discovered;  and (*4*) revocation before a substantial change occurs in the condition of the goods not caused by their own defects.

The road to rejection is often easy; if the goods or the tender depart in any important respect from the contract, the buyer may reject if he acts with diligence and if the seller does not exercise the right to cure.  Much less easy is the road to revocation for the lawyer who is attempting to advise a client.  First, our lawyer must decide whether the acceptance was made with or without discovery of the defect.  Second, he must consider whether it was made on "the reasonable assumption" of cure or whether it was induced by the "difficulty of discovery" or the "seller's assurances."  Finally, he must determine whether the attempted revocation will occur within a reasonable time after discovery (or time when the buyer should have discovered) and, last of all, whether there has been a substantial deterioration in the goods.  Consider all of the difficult empirical judgments which the lawyer will have to make to give useful advice: When did the acceptance occur? Was the buyer's assumption of cure reasonable?  Was the acceptance "reasonably" induced by the difficulty of discovery or by seller's assurances? Has more than a reasonable time passed since the discovery of the nonconformity? Have the goods undergone a substantial change? Does the nonconformity substantially impair? A search for that rare form of certainty which soothes the student's anxiety and warms the heart of the corporate lawyer will often prove fruitless here.  We can do little more than footnote some of the relevant cases and advise the lawyer dealing with 2–608 to charge a handsome fee.

20.  See, e. g., Sarnecki v. Al Johns Pontiac, 3 UCC Rep.Serv. 1121 (Pa.C.P. 1966).  See also note 4 supra.

At least in theory the standards of nonconformity which authorize rejection in installment contracts, rejection in one shot contracts, and revocation of acceptance are different. In a noninstallment contract the buyer may reject if the goods fail to conform "in any respect." For installment contracts they must be "substantially" nonconforming and for revocation, substantially nonconforming "to him." We counsel a healthy skepticism about practical distinctions among these standards.

Section 2–601 *purportedly* states the perfect tender rule; seller must perform perfectly, for buyer may reject any time "the goods or the tender of delivery fail *in any respect* to conform to the contract." But even before enactment of the Code, the perfect tender rule was in decline.[21] Close examination of the Code reveals that the Code well nigh abolishes the rule. First of all, section 2–601 renders the perfect tender rule inapplicable to installment contracts, and 2–612 permits rejection in such contracts only if "the non-conformity substantially impairs the value of that installment. . . ." Secondly, the seller's right to cure a defective tender, embodied in 2–508 and discussed below, is a further substantial restriction upon the buyer's apparent right to reject for insubstantial defects under 2–601. Additional restrictions upon the perfect tender rule in 2–601 may be found in 2–504 (an improper shipment contract which causes a late delivery is grounds for rejection only if "material delay or loss ensues")[22] and in the Code's general invitations to use trade usage, course of dealing, and course of performance in the interpretation of contracts.[23] If trade usage states that nineteen or twenty-one items are the equivalent of twenty items, a buyer who receives nineteen on a contract calling for twenty cannot complain. Finally, the courts

---

**21.** See E. Peters, Commercial Transactions 33–37 (1971).

**22.** Section 2–504 reads as follows (emphasis added):

Where the seller is required or authorized to send the goods to the buyer and the contract does not require him to deliver them at a particular destination, then unless otherwise agreed he must

(a) put the goods in the possession of such a carrier and make such a contract for their transportation as may be reasonable having regard to the nature of the goods and other circumstances of the case; and

(b) obtain and promptly deliver or tender in due form any document necessary to enable the buyer to obtain possession of the goods or otherwise required by the agreement or by usage of trade; and

(c) promptly notify the buyer of the shipment.

*Failure to notify the buyer under paragraph (c) or to make a proper contract under paragraph (a) is a ground for rejection only if material delay or loss ensues.*

The courts have not yet interpreted the phrase "material delay or loss" used in this section. Professor Honnold has pointed out that no causal relationship between the seller's deviation in shipment and the transit need be shown. See 1 N.Y. State Law Revision Comm'n, 1955 Report 472 (1955). However Comment 6 to section 2–504 ("rejection by the buyer is justified only when the seller's dereliction as to any of the requirements of this section in fact is followed by material delay or damage") and the language of the section certainly lends itself to the inference that there must be a causal relation.

**23.** §§ 2–208; 1–205.

have the power to deny rejection for what they regard as insubstantial defects by manipulating the procedural requirements for rejection. That is, if the court concludes that a buyer ought to be denied his right to reject because he has suffered no damage, the court might arrive at that conclusion by finding that the buyer failed to make an effective rejection (for example, because his notice was not timely).

We conclude, and the cases decided to date suggest, that the foregoing changes have so eroded the perfect tender rule that little is left of it; the law would be little changed if 2–601 gave the right to reject only upon "substantial" nonconformity. Of the two dozen reported Code cases on rejection, none grants rejection on what could fairly be called an insubstantial nonconformity.[24] Of course it is still possible to conceive of cases which are covered by the perfect tender rule, unchanged by any of the sections or doctrine quoted above. Assume, for example, that seller was obliged to deliver $10,000 of goods to buyer's place of business on January 2. Seller delivered on January 3, and buyer suffered no injury. Assume further that this was a single shot contract, that there was no pertinent trade usage, course of performance, or course of dealing, and that buyer promptly rejected. Section 2–504 does not apply, and a late delivery is arguably incurable. In such case 2–601 would give buyer the right to reject. However, even in the case which we have just put, we suspect that a court may find a way to deny the buyer's right to reject ("ten dollars off the price is a cure"), and given the chance of either side on a contingent fee basis, we would choose the seller's. We conclude, therefore, that the perfect tender rule apparently embodied in 2–601 may be worth a bargaining point or two but that the Code as written and as interpreted grants rejection (except in the rarest case) only when the goods or tender of the delivery fail in some substantial respect to conform to the contract.

The basic test in both the installment case and in the case of revocation of acceptance is that the goods be "substantially" nonconforming. The Code gives no guidelines to determine which performances are substantially nonconforming and which are only insubstantially so. The common law concept of "material breach" is at least a first cousin to the concept of "substantial nonconformity," and it offers a fruitful analogy to one who seeks to determine whether the

**24.** See, e. g., Menard & Holmberg Rambler, Inc. v. Shea, 44 Mass.App. Dec. 204, 8 UCC Rep.Serv. 167 (1970) (constant stalling of new car); Commonwealth Bank & Trust Co. v. Keech, 201 Pa.Super. 285, 192 A.2d 133, 1 UCC Rep.Serv. 63 (1963) (failure of seller of car to furnish title certificate); Garfinkel v. Lehman Floor Covering Co., 60 Misc. 2d 72, 302 N.Y.S.2d 167, 6 UCC Rep.Serv. 915 (Dist.Ct.1969) ("unsightly" pressure bands on carpeting); Zabriskie Chevrolet, Inc. v. Smith, 99 N.

J.Super. 441, 240 A.2d 195, 5 UCC Rep. Serv. 30 (Law Div.1968) (defective transmission made car operative only in low gear).

Rejection denied (after offer of cure): Bartus v. Riccardi, 55 Misc.2d 3, 284 N.Y.S.2d 222, 4 UCC Rep.Serv. 845 (Utica City Ct.1967) (tender of new and improved hearing aid instead of model ordered); Appleton State Bank v. Lee, 33 Wis.2d 690, 148 N.W.2d 1 (1967) (tender of functionally identical sewing machine of different brand).

seller's performance substantially nonconforms. Among the factors which the Restatement of Contracts § 275 lists as influential in determining whether the breach has been material are the following:

(1) The extent to which the injured party will obtain the substantial benefit which he could reasonably anticipate;

(2) The extent to which the injured party may be adequately compensated in damages for lack of complete performance;

(3) The extent to which the party failing to perform has already partly performed or made preparations for performance;

(4) The greater or less hardship on the party failing to perform in terminating the contract;

(5) The willful, negligent, or innocent behavior of the party failing to perform; and

(6) The greater or less uncertainty that the party failing to perform will perform the remainder of the contract.

Whether the listed factors will carry the lawyer much farther toward a decision on the substantiality of a breach than his common sense will, we are unsure. For what they are worth, there they are. Since the standard applicable to installment contracts is supposedly different from that on "one-shot" contracts, one needs to be able to identify an installment contract. Section 2–612(1) defines an installment contract as follows:

An "installment contract" is one which requires or authorizes the delivery of goods in separate lots to be separately accepted, even though the contract contains a clause "each delivery is a separate contract" or its equivalent.

Comment 1 to this section explains the intention of the draftsmen to phrase the definition "more broadly in this Article   .   .   . so as to cover installment deliveries tacitly authorized by the circumstances or by the option of either party." Note that section 2–612(2) gives the buyer the right to reject an installment when there is a substantial impairment in the installment that cannot be cured. When the breach of one installment of the contract gives the buyer the right to reject subsequent installments and to cancel executory portions of the contract is quite another question. That question is covered by section 2–612(3) which reads in full as follows:

Whenever non-conformity or default with respect to one or more installments substantially impairs the value of the whole contract there is a breach of the whole. But the aggrieved party reinstates the contract if he accepts a non-conforming installment without seasonably notifying of cancellation or if he brings an action with respect only to past installments or demands performance as to future installments.

When a specific default or nonconformity substantially impairs "the value of the whole" is a most difficult question. In Continental Forest Products v. White Lumber Sales, Inc.,[25] there was an installment contract for the sale of twenty carloads of plywood. The first carload did not conform to the contract in that nine percent of the plywood in the car deviated from the thickness specifications. The trade standard authorized deviations of five percent of the load. The second and third carloads which arrived at buyer's place of business after he had purportedly canceled the contract did conform to the specifications. The court held that the deviation did not substantially impair the value of the whole contract and found moreover that the nonconformity could be cured by an adjustment in the price. The best judicial analysis of the question, "When does a breach of part of an installment contract constitute a breach of the whole?," appears in the pre-Code case, Plotnick v. Pennsylvania Smelting & Refining Co.[26] In that case seller had delivered a carload of lead but had not received his payment. Seller then refused to make further deliveries except for cash and declined the buyer's offer even to pay by sight draft against a bill of lading. In analyzing section 45 of the Uniform Sales Act from the seller's standpoint, Judge Hastie observed:

> First, non-payment for a delivered shipment may make it impossible or unreasonably burdensome from a financial point of view for the seller to supply future installments as promised. Second, buyer's breach of his promise to pay for one installment may create such a reasonable apprehension in the seller's mind concerning payment for future installments that the seller should not be required to take the risk involved in continuing deliveries.[27]

One could apply a similar analysis to the problem which faces the buyer. If the first shipment constitutes a part of a machine that will be delivered in subsequent installments, and if the part is not repairable but is necessary for the operation of the machine, then the failure of the first installment will be a breach of the whole contract. Likewise if the defect in the first shipment is such as to give "reasonable apprehension" in the buyer's mind about the ability or willingness of the seller to complete the other installments, the breach should be regarded as a breach of the whole. Thus the Code has substantially altered the right to reject in installment contract cases. The draftsmen have defined installment contracts broadly, and they have limited rejection to cases of substantial nonconformity.

A buyer who wishes to revoke acceptance under 2–608 must also show "substantial nonconformity." The analogy suggested above to

25. 256 Ore. 466, 474 P.2d 1, 8 UCC Rep. Serv. 178 (1970).

26. 194 F.2d 859 (3d Cir. 1952).

27. Id. at 862.

the law of material breach will be the lawyer's most fruitful source of measurement of substantiality.

However, section 2–608 offers a slightly different standard, for it tells the buyer that he may revoke only if there is substantial impairment of the value "to him." The reference "to him" suggests that the court is to measure the impairment by reference to the particular buyer's particular needs. That suggestion is confirmed by the last clause in the last sentence of Comment 2: "[T]he question is whether the non-conformity is such as will in fact cause a substantial impairment of the value to the buyer though the seller had no advance knowledge as to the buyer's particular circumstances." It was also raised by the New York Law Revision Commission in its examination of 2–608.[28] It is theoretically possible, therefore, for the seller to deliver goods which a garden variety, reasonably prudent buyer would find reasonably satisfactory (though nonconforming in insubstantial details) and yet find that because of his buyer's particular needs, his buyer has a right to revoke acceptance. Why a buyer should be permitted to measure the seller's tender by such subjective standards is not clear. Insofar as we are able to tell, no appellate case [29] has yet squarely faced a situation in which the defect would be such as to cause only an insubstantial impairment on an objective basis. Doubtless it is an unusual case in which one will be unable to convince a court or a jury that the goods are substantially conforming on an objective basis but will be able to convince the court or jury that they are substantially defective to a particular plaintiff. Perhaps we are unduly cynical about the powers of fine discrimination of courts and juries, but we suspect that a single standard of objective "substantial nonconformity" will cover 99.44% of all rejection and revocation cases.

The most persistently litigated yet perpetually confused question in rejection and revocation cases is whether the buyer's action in rejecting or revoking acceptance was timely. Rejection of goods must occur "within a reasonable time after their delivery or tender" (2–602 (1)). Revocation must take place "within a reasonable time after the buyer discovers or should have discovered the ground for it. . . . " (2–608(2)).[30] The policies which support a requirement

28. See N.Y. State Law Revision Comm'n, 1956 Report 391 (1956).

29. In Hays Merchandise, Inc. v. Dewey, 78 Wash.2d 343, 474 P.2d 270, 8 UCC Rep.Serv. 31 (1970), the court addressed itself to the subjective-objective problem. We leave it to the reader to conclude how the court came out: "[I]t is an objective factual determination of the buyer's particular circumstances rather than some unarticulated desires." Id. at 347, 474 P.2d at 272, 8 UCC Rep.Serv. at 34. Cf. Campbell v. Pollack, 101 R.I. 223, 221 A.2d 615, 3 UCC Rep.Serv. 703 (1966).

30. Comment 4 to section 2–608 states that a reasonable time for revocation of acceptance "should extend in most cases beyond the time in which notification of breach must be given, beyond the time for discovery of non-conformity after acceptance and beyond the time for rejection after tender." See also Braginetz v. Foreign Motor Sales, Inc., 76 Dauphin Co. 1 (Pa.C.P.1960). Did the draftsmen intend by this comment to relieve the buyer from giving notice of breach under 2–607(3) (a)? We think not. We believe that they meant to tell us only that one who has complied with

telling the buyer to act with reasonable speed in notifying the seller are not mysterious.  The obvious policies behind the notice provisions are to give the seller an opportunity to cure, to permit seller to assist the buyer in minimizing the buyer's losses, and to return the goods to seller early, before they have substantially depreciated.  If the seller can step in and cure the difficulty and so save the sale and prevent several months' lost profit that the buyer might otherwise suffer, the policy has been fulfilled.  Even if seller's inspection discloses that the goods are defective and he agrees to take them back, the entire loss from the transaction may be minimized by early action, because the seller may be able to resell the goods to another party shortly after the sale at a higher price than the goods would command after they had depreciated over a period of time.

Both the cases and the Code are full of disheartening platitudes on timeliness.  Section 1–204 tells us, "What is a reasonable time for taking any action depends upon the nature, purpose and circumstance of such action;" one hardly needs to read the Code to find that out.  At the risk of peddling a few of our own platitudes, we suggest at least four "circumstances" which will always have relevance to the determination of whether a reasonable time has passed before the buyer took his action to reject or revoke.  Obvious, and indeed explicit in 2–608, is the difficulty of discovery of the defect.  Under 2–608(2) the reasonable time for revocation of acceptance does not run until "the buyer discovers or should have discovered" the ground for the revocation.  That is, if the defect was difficult to discover, the reasonable time would not commence to run until a time later, perhaps substantially later, than it would have commenced with a defect that was easy to find.  Although 2–602 does not make explicit reference to the difficulty of discovery, the comments, the statutory history, and the cases suggest that that factor is equally relevant there.[31]  The nature of the defect, the complexity of the goods, and the sophistication of the buyer may all influence the difficulty of discovery.  Quite clearly one needs more time to discover the defect in an automobile or an airplane than in an ax or a wedge.

Although the cases do not make clear the extent to which the buyer's sophistication is to be considered in determining whether a particular defect was difficult to discover, at least in a gross sense,

the 2–607 notice requirements (notification that the transaction is troublesome) still usually has an additional time to revoke.

31.  In discussing what is a reasonable time for rejection under 2–602(1), Comment 1 to that section states, "The sections of this Article dealing with inspection of goods must be read in connection with the buyer's reasonable time for action under this subsection."  Thus, where inspection requires only a simple micrometer measurement of rolled steel, seven weeks exceeds a reasonable time for rejection.  Michael M. Berlin & Co. v. T. Whiting Mfg., Inc., 5 UCC Rep. Serv. 357 (N.Y.Sup.Ct.1968).  Where an alleged injury to a horse's leg could have been discovered by the inspection customarily made at the time of sale, buyer's attempted rejection twenty-four hours later came too late.  Miron v. Yonkers Raceway, Inc., 400 F.2d 112, 5 UCC Rep.Serv. 673 (2d Cir. 1968).  Cf. Grandi v. LeSage, 74 N.M. 799, 399 P.2d 285, 2 UCC Rep. Serv. 455 (1965).

the buyer's skill should be relevant to this question.  For example, a defect in an automobile may be "more difficult to discover" when the purchaser is a consumer than when the purchaser is the Yellow Cab Company.  We believe it will be a rare case in which a business buyer is given substantial additional time in which to reject because the defect was "difficult to discover," and the courts will be more willing to listen to that argument when it is made by a consumer purchaser of a complex machine.[32]

A second factor which can have a substantial impact upon the determination of reasonable time is the contract itself.  If the contract provides that the buyer must inspect and report all complaints within a specified period of time, the court will give effect to such a contract term under 1–204(1), provided the time so set is not "manifestly unreasonable."  Even if the time appears to be manifestly unreasonable and the court finds that the term is not part of the contract, it may still hold that the term puts the buyer on notice that he must inspect with reasonable promptness.  As one court put it:

> The court attaches no significance to the caveat [about time for rejection] announced in the seller's invoice.  It was unilateral and the court finds it not to be binding upon the purchaser.  Its only probative value was to activate the purchaser to a reasonably timely inspection of the goods purchased.[33]

A third and a highly relevant circumstance is the relative perishability of the goods.  If the goods are potatoes which may rot, a live horse which may injure itself, or shrimp that will spoil, the buyer had better get himself in gear if he wishes to reject or revoke acceptance.[34]

A final factor, sometimes articulated in court opinions, is the course of performance between the parties after the sale but before the formal rejection.  If the principal policy of the rejection notice requirement is to give the seller an opportunity to cure and to permit him to assist in minimizing the buyer's losses, that policy is met if there has been a continuing series of complaints, negotiations, and attempted repairs prior to the formal rejection.  That is so even though the formal notice of rejection comes a considerable time after

---

32.  See, e. g., Lanners v. Whitney, 247 Ore. 223, 428 P.2d 398, 4 UCC Rep. Serv. 369 (1967) (unairworthy condition of airplane difficult to discover; buyer not a mechanic).  Cf. Lawner v. Engelbach, 433 Pa. 311, 249 A.2d 295, 5 UCC Rep.Serv. 1236 (1969) (value of diamond ring difficult to discover without appraisal by expert; buyer was a consumer).  But see Michael M. Berlin & Co. v. T. Whiting Mfg., Inc., 5 UCC Rep.Serv. 357 (N.Y.Sup.Ct.1968) (buyer was a businessman).

33.  Michael M. Berlin & Co. v. T. Whiting Mfg., Inc., 5 UCC Rep.Serv.

357, 359, 360 (N.Y.Sup.Ct.1968).  Cf. § 2–513, Comment 7.  Time limits found manifestly unreasonable in other circumstances: Q. Vandenberg & Sons, N. V. v. Siter, 204 Pa.Super. 392, 204 A.2d 494, 2 UCC Rep.Serv. 383 (C.P.1964); Neville Chemical Co. v. Union Carbide Corp., 422 F.2d 1205, 7 UCC Rep.Serv. 81 (3d Cir. 1970), cert. denied 400 U.S. 826 (1970).

34.  A. C. Carpenter, Inc. v. Boyer Potato Chips, 28 Agri.Dec. 1557, 7 UCC Rep.Serv. 493 (1969) (potatoes: ten days too late); Miron v. Yonkers Raceway, Inc., 400 F.2d 112, 5 UCC Rep.

the sale.  For example, in Irrigation Motor & Pump Co. v. Belcher,[35] the court held that revocation notice sent on July 27 was timely with respect to a machine which was delivered in January of the same year. In that case the buyer had notified the seller of difficulty with the machine shortly after the machine had been installed.  The court pointed out:

> Here, the buyer gave the seller an opportunity to repair the machine and withheld his revocation of acceptance until it became apparent that seller could not or would not perform its contract.  Under the circumstances of this case, the delay in the notice in no way prejudiced the seller and the delay was not unreasonable.[36]

In a similar case, Sarnecki v. Al Johns Pontiac,[37] the court allowed a jury verdict permitting rejection to stand even though the rejection of the automobile did not occur until five months and more than 3,000 miles after the purchase.  A noteworthy fact reported in the opinion without comment is that the buyer first complained about the defect in the automobile only four days after the purchase.  From that time until the rejection five months later there was an almost continuous series of negotiations and repairs.  In such circumstances it came as no surprise that the buyer rejected, and certainly the principal purpose of a timely rejection requirement was fulfilled by the continuous complaints of the buyer.[38]

We realize that this modest accumulation of four factors: (1) difficulty of discovery, (2) contract terms, (3) perishability, and (4) course of dealing between the parties after sale and before rejection, will often take the lawyer only a short distance toward a reliable judgment about whether buyer's rejection or revocation was timely.  However, we despair of doing more than citing a few more cases [39] and acknowledging that we will gratefully bow to any of more powerful

Serv. 673 (2d Cir. 1968) (race horse; twenty-four hours too late); Mazur Bros. & Jaffe Fish Co., 3 UCC Rep. Serv. 419 (VACAB 1965) (shrimp; five days too late).

35.  483 P.2d 980, 9 UCC Rep.Serv. 60 (Colo.Ct.App.1971).

36.  Id. at 982, 9 UCC Rep.Serv. at 63.

37.  3 UCC Rep.Serv. 1121 (Pa.C.P.1966).

38.  The court found that much of the mileage was put on by the seller in his attempt to remedy the defect and left to the jury the question whether "rescission" under "2–601" came within a reasonable time.

39.  Post-Code rejection and revocation cases for which we could find no

other home in this Chapter are the following: American Container Corp. v. Hanley Trucking Corp., 111 N.J. Super. 322, 268 A.2d 313, 7 UCC Rep. Serv. 1301 (Chancery Div.1970); Schneider v. Person, 34 Pa.D. & C.2d 10, 2 UCC Rep.Serv. 37 (C.P.1964); Dorne & Margolin, Inc. v. Hull Corp., 82 Montg.Co.L.R. 233 (Pa.C.P.1963); Warren's Kiddie Shop, Inc. v. Casual Slacks, Inc., 120 Ga.App. 578, 171 S.E. 2d 643, 7 UCC Rep.Serv. 166 (1969); Philip A. Feinberg, Inc. v. Bernstein & Sparber Corp., 8 UCC Rep.Serv. 190 (N.Y.App.Term 1970); Wakerman Leather Co. v. Irvin B. Foster Sportswear Co., 34 App.Div.2d 594, 308 N.Y. S.2d 103, 7 UCC Rep.Serv. 710 (3d Dep't 1970); Sig Hoffman, Inc. v. Victory Spud Service, Inc., 25 Agri.Dec. 1175, 3 UCC Rep.Serv. 977 (1966).

insight or greater wisdom who can distill useful principles from the Code and the decided cases.

A residual substantive question under 2–608 is the meaning of the "assurances" in 2–608(1) (b) :

> [Revocation is permitted if acceptance occurred] without discovery of such non-conformity if his acceptance was reasonably induced either by the difficulty of discovery before acceptance or by the seller's assurances.

It is easy to think of cases in which seller has given reasonable assurances that the difficulties complained of by the buyer would be cured or are "normal" and indicate no real defect. That is almost the unbroken pattern in the purchase of automobiles and other complicated machinery. In such circumstances both parties understand that a complex machine will not work perfectly at once but that it will require a certain amount of adjustment, tuning, and minor repair. The buyer expects the machine to be defective in that sense, but he also expects the seller to cure those defects. Presumably the draftsmen had such "assurances" in mind in 2–608, but how far they meant to go beyond such limited cases is quite unclear. The language about assurances in Comment 3 to 2–608 is not helpful nor are the cases. In one sense all advertising, puffing, and trade talk of the seller are assurances which reasonably induce the buyer to take the goods and use them; if the draftsmen had in mind only more explicit kinds of assurances which go to specific potential problems with the goods, they made a secret of that intent.

Finally, the buyer's lawyer must pay careful attention both to the procedure he must follow in rejecting or revoking and to his client's rights and obligations with respect to rejected goods in his possession or control. A perfectly innocent mis-step here can undo a rejection for which substantive grounds existed, and a post-rejection error can turn an effective rejection into an acceptance. For example, if the seller has delivered goods that are horribly defective and has refused to cure, he has given the buyer all of the substantive basis he needs to reject, yet if the buyer fails to jump through the procedural hoops (giving notice, etc.), buyer's attempted rejection may be found "ineffective," and he will be left with the rights of a buyer who has accepted nonconforming goods.

It is important to distinguish between "wrongful" rejections and "ineffective" rejections. As we use the term (and as we believe the draftsmen intended the term to be used), a rejection of a conforming tender would be a wrongful rejection. Nevertheless if timely notice was sent and if the buyer lived up to his post rejection obligations under section 2–602 and those following, the rejection though "wrongful" would be "effective" and would so preclude his acceptance of the goods and foreclose a consequent liability for the price under 2–709 (1) (a) (first clause). On the other hand a rejection which is procedurally defective (for instance, notice was given too long after tender) will be an "ineffective" rejection, and even if the goods were nonconforming, the parties will be treated as though no rejection has occurred; in such case the buyer will have accepted the goods. For an extensive discussion of these questions and of the comparable questions with respect to revocation of acceptance, see Section 7–3 above.

Both 2–601 and 2–608 make it clear that the buyer need not revoke or reject the entire amount but may accept and keep "any commercial unit or units and reject the rest." Likewise the sections make it clear that the buyer who rejects or revokes acceptance may recover damages for nondelivery under 2–713, or he may cover and collect damages under 2–712. Thus neither rejection nor revocation of acceptance is the end of the line for the buyer; he has not so "elected his remedy."

Section 2–602 provides that a buyer who wishes to reject must "seasonably notify" the seller, and section 2–608(2) contains a similar requirement for one revoking acceptance. Note that under 2–605 a buyer who fails to particularize his objection in connection with rejection may lose his right to rely on "the unstated defect" to justify the rejection or to establish a breach. Needless to say such rejection or revocation notice should be in writing, and it should be carefully drafted. Those who have depended upon nonwritten notice or equivocal notice of rejection have not fared well in the courts.[40]

Sections 2–602, 2–603, and 2–604 also instruct the buyer on proper post-rejection procedure. If the buyer has taken "physical possession" of the goods, he is obliged to hold them for a time sufficient to permit the seller to remove them. The buyer has an obligation to do more than that only if each of the following conditions is met: (1) the seller has no agent or place of business at the market of rejection; (2) the buyer is a merchant, and (3) the goods are in his possession or control. If each of the three foregoing conditions is met, the buyer must follow reasonable instructions of the seller and in the absence of instructions, sell the goods for the seller's account if they are "perishable or threaten to decline in value speedily." [41] The buyer has the same obligations with respect to goods he has revoked (2–608 (3)). As we saw in Section 8–2 above, the buyer should use care not to take acts "inconsistent with the seller's ownership" for fear of accepting goods that he has attempted to reject.

---

40. An unsuccessful attempt to return the goods to the seller was held insufficient notice of rejection in Beco, Inc. v. Minnechaug Golf Course, Inc., 5 Conn.Cir. 444, 256 A.2d 522, 6 UCC Rep.Serv. 910 (1968). Contra, Commonwealth Bank & Trust Co. v. Keech, 201 Pa.Super. 285, 192 A.2d 133, 1 UCC Rep.Serv. 63 (1963). In Julian C. Cohen Salvage Corp. v. E. Elec. Sales, Inc., 205 Pa.Super. 26, 206 A.2d 331, 2 UCC Rep.Serv. 432 (1965), the court required that the notice of rejection be in writing. See also Grossman v. D'Or, 98 Ill.App.2d 198, 240 N.E.2d 266 (1968) (buyer's letters asking for credit and return of unused merchandise did not meet notice requirement of section 2–608); Bomyte v. L-Co Cabinet Corp., 5 UCC Rep.Serv. 1060 (Pa.C.P. 1968) (buyer's letter stating, "we will not be ordering any more material from you," did not accomplish rejection).

41. § 2–603(1).

Fortunately the buyer may look to the goods and their proceeds and to the seller himself for certain of his expenses and damages. Section 2–603(2) specifies that the buyer is entitled to reimbursement from the seller out of the proceeds for reasonable expenses incurred in caring for and selling goods. Section 2–711(3) gives the buyer "a security interest in goods in his possession or control for any payments made on their price and any expenses reasonably incurred in their inspection, receipt, transportation, care and custody. . . ." Note that the security interest does not secure the buyer against his inability to recover damages under 2–713 from the seller.

## § 8–4  Cure, 2–508

Section 2–508, which specifies the seller's right to cure, has no antecedent in the Uniform Sales Act. The section is a sharp potential restriction upon the buyer's right to reject; it is an important section, one which offers many significant but unanswered questions. Although it is a novel legal doctrine, the right to cure is not at all novel in another sense, for it does no more than give legal recognition to a right which many sellers have doubtless had and exercised over the years. Professor Macaulay has informed us that legal sanctions are neither the only nor the most important sanctions an aggrieved party to a contract has,[42] and it seems likely that 2–508 simply recognizes a general pattern of business behavior and adds a legal sanction to those economic and nonlegal sanctions which the parties had and still have.

Once one finds that the seller has a right to cure and that he has exercised it properly, the legal rights of the parties under 2–508 and the other provisions are clear. Upon proper exercise by seller of his right to cure, the buyer loses any right to reject, although he retains his right to sue under 2–714 if he has suffered any injury because the original tender was nonconforming.[43]

Section 2–508(1) gives the seller an unfettered right to cure "within the contract time." That section offers few interpretive difficulties. Beyond the "contract time"—after the time for performance has passed—the seller has the right to cure only if: (1) the seller had reasonable grounds to believe that a nonconforming tender would be acceptable; (2) the seller seasonably notifies the buyer of his intention to cure; and (3) he cures within a "further reasonable time."

Combing through the words of the section and applying them to the wide variety of cases to which they could conceivably apply, one

42. Macaulay, Non-Contractual Relations in Business: A Preliminary Study, 28 Am.Soc.Rev. 55 (1963).

43. Comment 2 to section 2–714 states, "The 'non-conformity' referred to in subsection (1) includes not only breaches of warranties but also any failure of the seller to perform according to his obligations under the contract." See also section 2–715 on buyer's incidental and consequential damages. Thus where the buyer incurs, for example, transportation expenses to return nonconforming goods to the seller, the buyer can recover these expenses from the seller notwithstanding a subsequent cure and acceptance.

can find a host of questions lurking in 2-508(2).[44] Here we will consider only two interpretive difficulties: (1) when does the seller have "reasonable grounds to believe" that tender would have been acceptable; and (2) what constitutes an effective cure? Section 2-508 reads in full as follows:

> (1) Where any tender or delivery by the seller is rejected because non-conforming and the time for performance has not yet expired, the seller may seasonably notify the buyer of his intention to cure and may then within the contract time make a conforming delivery.

> (2) Where the buyer rejects a non-conforming tender which the seller had reasonable grounds to believe would be acceptable with or without money allowance the seller may if he seasonably notifies the buyer have a further reasonable time to substitute a conforming tender.

Comment 2 to 2-508 gives some direction to one's search for meaning of the "reasonable grounds to believe" language; it indicates that:

> such reasonable grounds can lie in prior course of dealing, course of performance or usage of trade as well as in particular circumstances surrounding the making of the contract. The seller is charged with commercial knowledge of any factors in a particular sales situation which require him to comply strictly with his obligations under the contract as, for example, strict conformity of documents in an overseas shipment or the sale of precision parts or chemicals for use in manufacture. Further, if the buyer gives notice either implicitly, as by a prior course of dealing involving rigorous inspections, or expressly, as by the deliberate inclusion of a "no replacement" clause in the contract, the seller is to be held to rigid compliance. If the clause appears in a "form" contract evidence that it is out of line with trade usage or the prior course of dealing and was not called to the seller's attention may be sufficient to show that the seller had reasonable grounds to believe that the tender would be acceptable.

Under the comment an understanding in the trade that a one percent deviation in quantity or a course of performance under which seller has always been permitted to adjust machines after they have been sold or an explicit provision in the contract which authorized or prohibited post-delivery adjustments would have powerful and probably

---

44. E. g., can a seller be legitimately surprised by a sudden demand for strict compliance in a falling market? Or by the terms of the contract to which he has agreed? Or by the non-conformity of his own tender? When *must* the buyer accept a money allow- ance as a cure? See generally Peters, Remedies for Breach of Contracts Relating to the Sale of Goods Under the Uniform Commercial Code: A Roadmap for Article Two, 73 Yale L.J. 199 (1963).

controlling influence on the question of whether the seller had reasonable grounds to believe that his tender would be acceptable with or without money allowance. In Continental Forest Products, Inc. v. White Lumber Sales, Inc.,[45] the court did not explicitly discuss the question whether the seller had reasonable grounds to believe his tender would be acceptable, but it had no difficulty in finding that a seller who gave a price allowance made an effective cure on a shipment of plywood which contained a nine percent deviation from the contract specifications under trade usage which permitted a five percent deviation. The court found that a contract term requiring the buyer to "accept the balance of the shipment as invoiced" meant that the buyer could not reject but was obliged to accept the reduction of price as a method of cure.

The cases decided under 2–508 indicate that the seller has "reasonable grounds" when he delivers what he believes to be a newer and better model than the hearing aid called for in the contract.[46] Likewise the seller may cure when he delivers a sewing machine "not shown to be of lesser quality than that contracted for" but of a different brand than that called for in the contract.[47] Thus, presumably, in absence of special circumstances, when the seller delivers goods which are not identical to those called for in the contract but which are the functional equivalent, he has reasonable cause to believe they will be acceptable. When a retailer receives goods from a wholesaler or a manufacturer and simply sells them off the shelf, he too has reasonable cause to believe that the goods will be acceptable and is so entitled to further reasonable time in which to cure.[48] Thus, for example, a retailer of Sony merchandise who sells a television set without opening the shipping container has reasonable cause to believe that the set will be acceptable and should have the right to cure if the set proves defective. Such reasonable cause will arise from the retailer's past dealings with the manufacturer.

How one generalizes from the foregoing cases and the above quoted comment is not clear. It is apparent, of course, both in the cases and the comments, that the seller can have knowledge of the "defect" and yet have reasonable grounds to believe that the goods will be acceptable. Although the cases do not make it clear, the seller's ignorance of a defect should not *ipso facto* mean that he has reasonable grounds to believe that they would be acceptable. We should burden the seller not only with the knowledge of the goods which he actually possesses but also with that which a reasonable, prudent seller in his shoes should have had. If such imputed knowledge would have deprived him of reasonable grounds to believe that the goods would be acceptable, then we should deny him the right to cure under

45. 256 Ore. 466, 474 P.2d 1, 8 UCC Rep.Serv. 178 (1970).

46. Bartus v. Riccardi, 55 Misc.2d 3, 284 N.Y.S.2d 222, 4 UCC Rep.Serv. 845 (Utica City Ct.1967).

47. Appleton State Bank v. Lee, 33 Wis.2d 690, 148 N.W.2d 1 (1967).

48. Wilson v. Scampoli, 228 A.2d 848, 4 UCC Rep.Serv. 178 (D.C.Ct.App. 1967).

2–508(2). If we did not impute such knowledge to the seller, then any seller could preserve his right to cure simply by convincing the court that he had no actual knowledge that the goods would be unacceptable, irrespective of the fact that any nonnegligent businessman in his shoes would have known that the goods would not have been acceptable. This seems an appropriate stopping point between charging a seller with only his actual knowledge and attributing to him knowledge of the actual status of the goods.

We believe that cure is a remedy which should be carefully cultivated and developed by the courts. To that end we would argue that a buyer should be found to have had reasonable cause to believe that his tender would have been acceptable any time he can convince the court that (*1*) he was ignorant of the defect despite his good faith and prudent business behavior, or (*2*) he had some reason such as prior course of dealing or trade usage which reasonably led him to believe that the goods would be acceptable.

To one ignorant of the cases and unburdened with any consideration of the policy of 2–508, the definition of effective cure is simple. Section 2–508(2) tells us that the seller has a further reasonable time to substitute a "conforming tender." Arguably that is both the most and the least that the seller can and must do: substitute a second and conforming tender.[49] However, if one accepts the proposition that 2–508 is a case of Muhammad coming to the mountain, of the draftsmen accommodating the law to what they believed to be business behavior, then one can argue for the acceptance of other seller's behavior as cure. Price adjustments sufficient to recompense the buyer for deficiency in quantity or quality must certainly be the most common form of businessmen's cure. The seller delivers 995 bushels of potatoes on a contract calling for 1,000, and if 995 are sufficient for the buyer's purposes, should we not permit the seller to cure by offering a reduction in price equal to the value of the five bushels which were not delivered? It would seem that businessmen do and that we should, even though it appears that 2–508(2) does not recognize such behavior as a form of cure. In the first place, it refers to "money allowance" as something which the seller might offer the buyer which would not constitute cure and which if not accepted by the buyer, would require the seller to substitute a fully conforming tender. Secondly, Comment 4 to 2–508 specifies that "trade usage as permitting variations without rejection but with price allowance . . . are not covered by this section." Despite the modest violence it does to the language of 2–508(2), we believe that the buyer who complains of some insubstantial nonconformity which can be recompensed by a reduction in the price should be made to accept such a reduction as cure even if there is no usage in the trade to accept such reductions.[50]

**49.** Professor Honnold takes the position that a curative tender must conform to the contract requirements in all respects other than time. 1 N.Y. State Law Revision Comm'n, 1955 Report 484 (1955).

**50.** In Continental Forest Prods., Inc. v. White Lumber Sales, Inc., 256 Ore. 466, 474 P.2d 1, 8 UCC Rep.Serv. 178 (1971), the court saw and sidestepped the "price as cure" question. The court found that the parties had agreed up-

The second interpretive difficulty in defining "cure" is illustrated by the New Jersey Superior Court case, Zabriskie Chevrolet, Inc., v. Smith.[51] In that case the purchasers had difficulty with the transmission in a new Chevrolet. The seller offered to cure by substituting another transmission which the court described as one "not from the factory and of unknown lineage from another vehicle in [seller's] possession." [52] The court found that the offer of this substitute transmission was an ineffective cure, and it commented as follows about the state of the purchasers' mind, "Once their faith is shaken, the vehicle loses not only its real value in their eyes, but becomes an instrument whose integrity is substantially impaired and whose operation is fraught with apprehension. The attempted cure in the present case is ineffective".[53] Of course one may argue that the court was applying an objective standard and that any reasonable purchaser in the Smiths' shoes would not have accepted the automobile with the substituted transmission. If that is the meaning of the case, the outcome is not revolutionary; it is simply a recognition that "cure" cannot be defined unilaterally but must be defined with respect to the reasonable expectations of both parties. However, it may be that the court was in fact speaking of the state of mind of the particular purchasers before it. If the case means that a cure must satisfy not just the reasonable expectations of the purchaser but the actual expectations of *these* purchasers, the holding is an extraordinary one. Surely the draftsmen did not intend to reopen the subjective-objective contract interpretation question under 2–508, and the case is wrong if it stands for the proposition that the only acceptable cure is one which meets the subjective desires of the particular purchaser in the case in question.

Section 2–508 is an important addition to our law. It substantially restricts the right of the buyer to reject, and it substantially complicates the job of the lawyer who represents the buyer who wishes to reject. Although it raises almost as many problems as it answers, in wise judicial hands it offers the possibility of conforming the law to reasonable expectations and of thwarting the chiseler who seeks to escape from a bad bargain.

on a price reduction as a permissible method of cure and so did not decide whether other methods "may have existed or should be required."

One must remember that there are many defects which cannot be cured by a money allowance. If, for example, the buyer needs the full contract quantity and cannot readily use the cure money to buy the additional quantity, then a price reduction is not an effective cure. Likewise a price reduction does not satisfy the buyer of a red car who receives a green one, nor does it cure a quality defect which makes the goods unusable or unsalable.

51. 99 N.J.Super. 441, 240 A.2d 195, 5 UCC Rep.Serv. 30 (Law Div.1968).

52. Id. at 458, 240 A.2d at 205, 5 UCC Rep.Serv. at 42.

53. Id.

# CHAPTER 9

# WARRANTY

*Analysis*

Sec.
9–1.   Introduction.
9–2.   Express Warranties, 2–313.
9–3.   —— What Words or Symbols?
9–4.   —— When and Where?  Basis of the Bargain.
9–5.   —— Samples and Models.
9–6.   The Implied Warranty of Merchantability, 2–314—Introduction.
9–7.   —— Merchantability Defined.
9–8.   —— Causation.
9–9.   Fitness for Particular Purpose, 2–315.
9–10. The Warranties of Title and Against Infringement, 2–312.
9–11. —— Cause of Action.
9–12. —— Disclaimer.

## § 9–1  Introduction

It is difficult to know how much or how little one should say about warranty liability under the Code.  Others have written books and articles on the topic,[1] and the personal-injury cases in particular tend to present a seamless web running from express warranty through the implied warranty of merchantability to strict tort liability.[2]  Only because our space is limited do we omit strict tort liability, for we well appreciate that such liability is often indistinguishable from liability for breach of the implied warranty of merchantability.  We know that a plaintiff will sometimes be able to state a cause of action on the basis of the same facts under either theory,[3] and in succeeding chapters we point to some of the legal consequences of choosing one or the other theory.[4]

Our discussion in the following pages will deal exclusively with the meaning of four warranty sections, 2–313, 2–314, 2–315, and 2–312 (and two damage sections, 2–714 and 2–715).  The fourth (warranty of title and warranty against infringement) and the third (warranty of fitness for a particular purpose) are least important, and we

---

1.  See, e. g., R. Duesenberg & L. King, Sales and Bulk Transfers Under the Uniform Commercial Code Ch. 5–7 (1969); Ezer, The Impact of the Uniform Commercial Code on the California Law of Sales Warranties, 8 U.C.L.A.L.Rev. 281 (1961).

2.  See, e. g., Seely v. White Motor Co., 63 Cal.2d 9, 403 P.2d 145, 2 UCC Rep. Serv. 915 (1965) (defective truck); Greenman v. Yuba Power Prods., Inc., 59 Cal.2d 57, 377 P.2d 897 (1962) (defective power drill); Jakubowski v. Minnesota Mining & Mfg., 42 N.J. 177,

199 A.2d 826 (1964) (abrasive disc found not to be defective).

3.  See Greeno v. Clark Equipment Co., 237 F.Supp. 427 (N.D.Ind.1965) (defective fork-lift truck caused personal injuries); Putman v. Erie City Mfg. Co., 338 F.2d 911 (5th Cir. 1964); Greenman v. Yuba Power Prods., Inc., 59 Cal.2d 57, 377 P.2d 897 (1962); Restatement, Second, Torts § 402A, comment c at 349 (1965).

4.  See Ch. 11, especially Sections 11–3, 11–7, and 11–8 infra.

deal with them last and least. Most important is the implied warranty of merchantability (2–314) ; next in importance are express warranties (2–313).

At the outset, one should understand how a warranty lawsuit looks to a plaintiff's lawyer and how it differs from a suit against an "insurer" on the one hand and an allegedly negligent defendant on the other. If an insurance company insures against the loss of an arm, all the claimant need do to recover is show the bloody stump. If the same claimant wishes to recover in warranty from the seller of the offending chain saw, he has a much tougher row to hoe. Once the plaintiff has proven his injury, specifically, the loss of his arm, his troubles are just beginning. First, he must prove that the defendant made a warranty, express or implied, under 2–313, 2–314, or 2–315. Second, he must prove that the goods did not comply with the warranty, that is, that they were defective at the time of the sale. Third, he must prove that his injury was caused, "proximately" and in fact, by the defective nature of the goods (and not, for example, by his careless use of the saw). Fourth, he must prove his damages. Finally, the warranty plaintiff must fight off all sorts of affirmative defenses such as disclaimers, statute of limitations, privity, lack of notice, and assumption of the risk.[5]

Although the warranty plaintiff need not prove negligence, warranty liability has much more in common with negligence liability than it does with a life, collision, or health insurer's liability. The two causes of action pose common problems for the plaintiff's lawyer. In both he must prove cause in fact and proximate causation on the part of a specific defendant. And too much should not be made of the fact that in a negligence suit the plaintiff must also prove that the defendant was negligent. Professor Whitford has suggested that the *res ipsa loquitur* doctrine will often carry the plaintiff to the jury and that the jury will find defendant negligent even absent explicit proof of negligence.[6]

Finally, one should distinguish between warranty, particularly express warranty, and fraud or misrepresentation. Typically, only a naughty seller is guilty of misrepresentation or fraud, but a seller can be Simon pure and yet break an express warranty. The former cases usually require at least that the defendant be negligent in making his representation and in some cases that he intentionally state a mistruth. There is no such requirement of evil doing on the part of a warranty defendant. A seller can fully believe that the representations he makes are accurate and yet find himself liable for the breach of an express warranty.

---

5. See Ch. 11 infra.

6. See Whitford, Strict Products Liability and the Automobile Industry;

Much Ado About Nothing, 1968 Wisc. L.Rev. 83.

### § 9–2  Express Warranties, 2–313

Section 2–313, which governs express warranty liability under the Code, reads in full as follows:

(1) Express warranties by the seller are created as follows:

(a) Any affirmation of fact or promise made by the seller to the buyer which relates to the goods and becomes part of the basis of the bargain creates an express warranty that the goods shall conform to the affirmation or promise.

(b) Any description of the goods which is made part of the basis of the bargain creates an express warranty that the goods shall conform to the description.

(c) Any sample or model which is made part of the basis of the bargain creates an express warranty that the whole of the goods shall conform to the sample or model.

(2) It is not necessary to the creation of an express warranty that the seller use formal words such as "warrant" or "guarantee" or that he have a specific intention to make a warranty, but an affirmation merely of the value of the goods or a statement purporting to be merely the seller's opinion or commendation of the goods does not create a warranty.

Before one steps more than ankle deep into this section, he should note several obvious but important facts. First, the section gives a cause of action only against "the seller."[7] If the prospective defendant is a bailor or lessor, one may have a cause of action against him only by analogy to 2–313. Second, the pre-Code requirement that the plaintiff specifically rely on the warranty is gone. In its place is a rather mysterious but much diluted reliance requirement that the warranty be "part of the basis of the bargain  .  .  .  ." Finally, 2–313 implies that the plaintiff must satisfy other requirements: for example, that he prove an injury that resulted from a breach that occurred with the sale.

One who reads a handful of express warranty cases gets the uneasy feeling that he is seeing the same play enacted again and again with different props. Sometimes the question is whether the seller's statement was a "puff" or an express warranty. At other times the question is whether the statement formed part of the "basis of the bargain." Although one may fit the cases into a variety of legal cubby holes—for example, "descriptive" cases, "basis-of-the-bargain" cases, and "puffing" cases—he is left with the concern that sometimes the trial judge or jury approach all cases with a single undifferenti-

---

7. Note that the Code provisions can be and with increasing frequency are extended by analogy to non-sale-of-goods cases. See Farnsworth, Implied Warranties of Quality in Non-Sales Cases, 57 Colum.L.Rev. 653 (1957).

ated question: should the plaintiff recover because the goods did not do what the defendant said they would do? With that warning, we divide our discussion of express warranties into three segments:

(1) What seller's words or symbols constitute an express warranty?

(2) What reliance must buyer-plaintiff show? Where and when?

(3) Samples and models.

### § 9–3 Express Warranties, 2–313—What Words or Symbols?

In many cases, the seller makes an explicit oral or written representation that is unquestionably an "affirmation of fact or promise . . . which relates to the goods . . . ." Such was the case in Rhodes Pharmacal Co. v. Continental Can Co.,[8] in which the seller stated "that the use of rustproof linings in the cans would prevent discoloration and adulteration of the Perform solution."[9] Subsection (2) of 2–313 makes clear that a seller need not use words such as "warrant" or "guarantee." Most courts would instantly agree that a statement as explicit and relevant as that in *Rhodes* was an express warranty.

The "what" difficulty arises largely in two contexts: "puffing" cases and "description" cases. The law recognizes that some seller's statements are only puffing, not express warranties. Thus, 2–313 (2) provides: "[A]n affirmation merely of the value of the goods or a statement purporting to be merely the seller's opinion or commendation of the goods does not create a warranty." But the recognition that some statements are not warranties tells one nothing about where he should draw the line between puff and warranties, and anyone who says he can consistently tell a "puff" from a warranty may be a fool or a liar. A statement that a seller's representation is only a puff and not a warranty is but a conclusory label. Indeed, one who reads a few cases gets the strong impression that the puff or warranty conclusion is only the product of an unobserved and subtle analysis that has to do with the reasonableness of the plaintiff's reliance, the seriousness of the plaintiff's injury, and other similar factors.

Of course, one can single out some factors that suggest that a statement is only an "opinion" as opposed to a warranty. Certainly the specificity of the statement is important: "this is a top-notch car" versus "this truck will give not less than 15.1 miles to the gallon when it is driven at a steady 60 miles per hour." Certainly a written statement is less likely to pass as a puff than is an oral one, and a written statement in the contract of the parties is less likely to pass as a puff than a written statement in an advertisement. It is familiar contract doctrine that the context in which words are spoken influence the

---

8. 72 Ill.App.2d 362, 219 N.E.2d 726, 3 UCC Rep.Serv. 584 (1966).

9. Id. at 364, 219 N.E.2d at 728, 3 UCC Rep.Serv. at 585.

listener's reasonable understanding of them and thus their legal effect.　Professor Honnold [10] has well demonstrated the intractability of the puffing-warranty distinction to generations of students by his juxtaposition of the *Wat Henry Pontiac* [11] case and Frederickson v. Hackney.[12]　In the former, a used car salesman stated that a car was in "A–1 shape" and "mechanically perfect." [13]　In the *Frederickson* case, the seller stated that a bull calf would "put the buyer on the map" and that "his father was the greatest living dairy bull."[14]　When the car broke down and when the bull proved sterile, the buyers sued. While the Oklahoma court found that the used car salesman's statements were express warranties,[15] the Minnesota court was made of sterner stuff: the palaver about the bull was only trade talk, not a warranty of reproductive capacity.[16]　One can dig about in the cases for distinguishing features, but the most persuasive difference is that the plaintiff in *Wat Henry* was a woman who bought the car to make a trip with her seven-month old child in 1944 to visit her husband in the army.　The car broke down *en route*.　Except by reference to the natural compassion one feels for a World War II service wife who is stranded with a seven-month old child, the cases are difficult to distinguish.　It is true that the plaintiff in the *Frederickson* case was a farmer, not just an ignorant consumer; but, on the other hand, oral statements by used-car salesmen are notoriously unreliable, archetypal puffs, some might say.

　　The lesson for a lawyer from these cases and others [17] like them is obvious.　Only a foolish lawyer will be quick to label a seller's statement as puffs or not puffs, and only a reckless one will label a seller's statement at all without carefully examining such factors as the nature of the defect (was it obvious or not) and the buyer's and seller's relative knowledge.　The cases also suggest that the nature of the plaintiff's reliance is not as irrelevant as the Code and cases appear to say it is.　To some courts the puff-warrant question is a backdoor means of examining the nature and reasonableness of the plaintiff's reliance.　For example, in Roscher v. Band Box Cleaners, Inc.,[18] the seller of a plastic telephone attachment stated that he did not think that the telephone company would object to the use of the attachment. In refusing to construe this statement as an express warranty, the court emphasized that the buyer could easily have determined the

10.　E. Farnsworth & J. Honnold, Cases and Materials on Commercial Law 456–60 (1965).

11.　Wat Henry Pontiac Co. v. Bradley, 202 Okl. 82, 210 P.2d 348 (1949).

12.　159 Minn. 234, 198 N.W. 806 (1924).

13.　202 Okl. at 83, 210 P.2d at 350–51.

14.　159 Minn. at 235, 198 N.W. at 806.

15.　202 Okl. at 84, 210 P.2d at 351.

16.　159 Minn. at 235, 198 N.W. at 806.

17.　See Foote v. Wilson, 104 Kan. 191, 178 P. 430 (1919) (representation by seller of stock of goods that goods were salable held to be warranty); Roscher v. Band Box Cleaners, Inc., 90 Ohio App. 71, 103 N.E.2d 404 (1951).

18.　90 Ohio App. 71, 103 N.E.2d 404 (1951).

phone company's true position. This seems tantamount to finding that buyer loses because his reliance was not reasonable.[19]

A related problem involves the degree to which the seller hedges in making an affirmation or promise. For example, in Hupp Corp. v. Metered Washer Service,[20] a buyer discovered that the clothes dryers he had purchased from the seller were defective. The seller then sold the buyer some parts and stated, " '[M]aybe' or 'we think that this might solve your problem.' "[21] Apparently because the language was so uncertain, the Oregon Supreme Court held that this language was not an express warranty that the parts would correct the defects.[22]

A second class of cases that present difficulty for those who seek to determine what words and symbols constitute express warranties are the "description" cases. Section 2–313(1) (b) states the Code rule on descriptions as follows:

> Any description of the goods which is made part of the basis of the bargain creates an express warranty that the goods shall conform to the description.

In a recent application[23] of 2–313(1) (b), the Georgia Court of Appeals found that the description of an aircraft as "Aero Commander, N–2677B, Number 135, FAA, Flyable"[24] was an express warranty that the aircraft complied with Federal Aviation Regulation Part 135, concerning instrument and visual flight. More difficult are those description cases in which the plaintiff argues that a generic title such as "auto" or "haybaler"[25] is an express warranty that the machine described will carry passengers on the highway or bale hay.[26] Comment 4 to 2–313 urges courts to reject a literal reading of blanket disclaimers and to recognize "that the probability is small that a real price is intended to be exchanged for a pseudo obligation." What are the reasonable expectations of a buyer who has paid money and signed a document that disclaims all warranties but promises to deliver a new "automobile?" We believe that the buyer can reasonably believe

---

19. See also Hupp Corp. v. Metered Washer Service, 256 Ore. 245, 472 P.2d 816, 8 UCC Rep.Serv. 42 (1970), discussed in text accompanying notes 20–22 infra.

20. 256 Ore. 245, 472 P.2d 816, 8 UCC Rep.Serv. 42 (1970).

21. Id. at 247, 472 P.2d at 818, 8 UCC Rep.Serv. at 44.

22. Id. at 247, 472 P.2d at 817–18, 8 UCC Rep.Serv. at 44.

23. Hill Aircraft & Leasing Corp. v. Simon, 122 Ga.App. 524, 177 S.E.2d 803, 8 UCC Rep.Serv. 474 (1970).

24. Id. at 526–27, 177 S.E.2d at 805, 8 UCC Rep.Serv. at 475.

25. Moss v. Gardner, 228 Ark. 828, 310 S.W.2d 491 (1958). In applying section 71 of the Uniform Sales Act, the Arkansas court held that the description "hay baler" in a sales contract did not constitute an express warranty that the hay baler could bale hay because express warranties in the contact excluded all other warranties.

26. Of course, such a warranty will not normally promise more than an implied warranty of merchantability would give. However, when defendant has disclaimed all implied warranties, the proof of an express warranty may be crucial to plaintiff's case.

that the word "automobile" is an express warranty that the machine purchased will behave in a certain way, namely, that it will carry him around town for at least a few thousand miles. Finding the meaning of such one-word descriptions is much like defining the meaning of the implied warranty of merchantability in various contexts. (Is a cigarette not merchantable because it causes cancer in some smokers?) Likewise, the court must decide whether the use of the noun "automobile" conveys the meaning that the machine would propel itself about on its four wheels in a certain way or whether that word promises only a machine with the external characteristics of a car. We consider those problems in Section 9-7 below.

## § 9-4   Express Warranties, 2-313—When and Where?   Basis of the Bargain

Under the Uniform Sales Act, the plaintiff in an express warranty case had to prove that he "relied" on the warranty. Section 12 of the Uniform Sales Act provided:

> Any affirmation of fact or any promise by the seller relating to the goods is an express warranty if the natural tendency of such affirmation or promise is to induce the buyer to purchase the goods, and if the buyer purchases the goods relying thereon . . . .

The Code omits any explicit mention of reliance and requires only that the promise or affirmation become "part of the basis of the bargain." The extent to which the law has so been changed is thoroughly unclear. It is possible that the draftsmen did not intend to change the law, or that they intended to remove the reliance requirement in all but the most unusual case, or that they intended simply to give the plaintiff the benefit of a rebuttable presumption of reliance. In his analysis of this section for the New York Law Revision Commission, Professor Honnold has well stated the prior law and the confusion inherent in the basis of the bargain test:

> The extent to which the Code's "basis of the bargain" test would change present law is less than clear. The Comments hardly solve the problem; Comment 3 to 2-313 states by way of explanation:
>
> > In actual practice affirmations of fact made by the seller about the goods during a bargain are regarded as part of the description of those goods; hence no particular reliance on such statements need be shown in order to weave them into the fabric of the agreement. Rather, any fact which is to take such affirmations, once made, out of the agreement requires clear affirmative proof. The issue normally is one of fact.
>
> But what is the issue by which the facts are to be measured? One must suppose that the "basis of the bargain" test has some meaning: this test is made an integral part of the three express warranties in Section 2-313(1) of the

Code. Presumably, buyers must plead and prove that the requirement is met. But the ultimate standards by which buyers will satisfy, or fail to satisfy, this test are not disclosed.

One ground for confusion is the fact that the word "basis" has no generally understood legal or psychological meaning. The term does have a well understood physical meaning, but with connotations of breadth and importance. Thus, Section 2–615(a), in dealing with impossibility of performance, excuses the parties from the contractual obligations on failure of a [sic] "a *basic* assumption" on which the contract was made.

To limit buyer's legal protection to seller's representations and promises which are basic, in the sense employed in Section 2–615, would radically restrict the present scope of buyers' [sic] warranty protection. Such a change undoubtedly was not intended by the draftsmen. Buyer is entitled to legal protection for compliance of the goods with *all* of seller's promises and representations on which buyer relies, even though some may be of relatively small import.

There remains the central question: What is the meaning of "basis of the bargain"? Possibly for lack of any other meaningful standard, courts must employ the test of whether buyer relied on the affirmation or promise, the test presently employed in Section 12 of the Uniform Sales Act.

It might be suggested that the present law should be changed because it is too burdensome to require buyers to prove that they relied on seller's representation or promise. Professor Williston writes:

> There is danger of giving greater effect to the requirement of reliance than it is entitled to. Doubtless the burden of proof is on the buyer to establish this as one of the elements of his case. But the warranty need not be the sole inducement to the buyer to purchase the goods; and as a general rule no evidence of reliance by the buyer is necessary other than the seller's statements were of a kind which naturally would induce the buyer to purchase the goods and that he did purchase the goods.

Serious difficulty with the reliance test in this State has not come to light. There are cases which have employed the reliance test to bar warranty recovery, but it seems unlikely that the draftsmen of the Code would wish to reverse these decisions.

The problem is posed by the facts of Hellman v. Kirschner, 191 N.Y.Supp. 202 (1921). Buyer purchased a used automobile which the memorandum of sale described as a "Cadillac sedan, model 57–V". Buyer sued seller for breach of warranty on the ground that the car was not model 57–V, but was model 57–J. Seller proved that buyer had inspected the car before the purchase so that the actual type and model of the car were then apparent. Judgment for the buyer was reversed on the ground that the trial court's instruction implied that buyer was entitled to receive a model 57–V, regardless of buyer's lack of reliance on the statement of the model number in the sales memorandum.

The same result would follow under the Code, if we assume that the "basis of the bargain" test incorporates the present reliance requirement. But this assumption cannot be made with confidence since (i) "basis of the bargain" does not convey a definite meaning, and (ii) the Code's rejection of the present reliance language might well imply an intent to modify present law.[27]

Comment 3 to 2–313 arguably means that any affirmation is presumed to be part of the basis of the bargain and that the plaintiff need put in no evidence unless the defendant offers evidence of the buyer's nonreliance: "no particular reliance on [a seller's affirmations during a bargain] need be shown . . . . Rather, any fact which is to take such affirmations, once made, out of the agreement requires clear affirmative proof." If a plaintiff is suing on a seller's statement made orally during the negotiation or in writing as part of the contract, a lazy lawyer can likely pass the basis-of-the-bargain test at least initially without any proof of buyer's reliance. We would so define the "presumption" here: even though plaintiff has not put on proof of reliance, defendant's motion for a directed verdict will be denied.[28] A careful lawyer, however, will allege some reliance and offer some proof.

When the plaintiff sues on a representation far removed in time or space from the actual sales negotiation and agreement, what he must prove is totally unclear. Can an advertisement form the basis of the bargain? What of a representation made to plaintiff's doctor, a representation that the plaintiff himself never saw or heard? What of a representation made after the sale has been consummated?

It is clear that an advertisement can be a part of the basis of the bargain,[29] and it is only fair that it be so. However, the language in

---

27. 1 N.Y. State Law Revision Comm'n, 1955 Comm'n 392–93 (1955).

28. Where defendant presents evidence of nonreliance, it is doubtful that plaintiff can get to the jury on proof of seller's affirmation alone. The presumption (that is, the likelihood for a mechanical ruling in plaintiff's favor) arising from proof of seller's affirmation alone is gone. Plaintiff has left only an inference of reliance against which the court, in ruling on a directed verdict motion, will weigh defendant's evidence of nonreliance. Plaintiff may survive the motion if defendant's evidence is weak enough, but we doubt this is the usual case. Plaintiff would be well-advised to bolster his proof of seller's affirmation with evidence of reliance if he wants to create enough doubt in the judge's mind to get to the jury. See C. McCormick, Laws of Evidence §§ 310–11 (1954).

29. See, e. g., Harris v. Belton, 258 Cal.App.2d 595, 65 Cal.Rptr. 808 (1968);

Comment 3, from which some have found a presumption, is limited to "affirmations of fact made by the seller about the goods during a bargain . . . ." In the usual case one would not regard an advertisement as being made "during a bargain," and therefore no statement in an advertisement would normally qualify for the presumption that may be authorized in Comment 3. At minimum a plaintiff in such a case should have to testify that he (or his agent) knew of and relied upon the advertisement in making the purchase. The cases give us no help here.

With the fall of the privity barriers, many plaintiffs have been enabled to sue defendants with whom they had no direct contact. Such suits seem justified when the plaintiff has read the defendant's advertisement. But what of the cases in which the express warranty was made to the plaintiff's employer, his doctor, or his seller? In a recent case, a California appellate court had no difficulty in finding the plaintiff's doctor to be an agent for the purpose of receiving and relying on a manufacturer's warranty that its plastic tubing was suitable for heart catheterization.[30]

Statements made by a seller to the buyer after the sale has been concluded are another bountiful source of reliance dispute.[31] One may argue most persuasively that once a legally binding contract of sale exists, no additional statements of the seller can be made part of the basis of that bargain. Since the buyer has already agreed to the deal, he cannot plead that he relied on the additional statement in making his deal. To that argument one may respond that in the merchandising world a buyer, even one already legally obligated to buy, has greater rights while he is still standing at the seller's counter than he does two weeks later.[32] For example, suppose a camper purchases a sleeping bag, which is advertised as suitable for winter use, and right after handing over his money the seller tells him that it can be used when the temperature goes below zero. The camper relies on that statement and suffers frostbite one night when the temperature reaches two below. If back in the camp store the seller had told the camper that the bag could not be used in sub-zero weather, the camper, as a practical matter, probably could have returned the bag im-

Capital Equip. Enterprise, Inc. v. North Pier Term. Co., 117 Ill.App.2d 264, 254 N.E.2d 542, 7 UCC Rep.Serv. 290 (1969); Neel v. Ford Motor Co., 49 Pa. D. & C.2d 243, 7 UCC Rep.Serv. 1311 (C.P.1970); Cooper Paintings & Coatings, Inc. v. SCM Corp., 457 S.W. 2d 864, 8 UCC Rep.Serv. 159 (Tenn.Ct. App.), cert. denied 8 UCC Rep.Serv. 159 (Tenn.Sup.Ct.1970).

**30.** Putensen v. Clay Adams, Inc., 12 Cal.App.3d 1062, 91 Cal.Rptr. 319, 8 UCC Rep.Serv. 449 (1st Dist.1970).

**31.** See, e. g., Terry v. Moore, 448 P.2d 601 (Wyo.1968), in which a statement by a driller, made after the contract was made and the drilling was completed, that a well would produce a certain output was held not to be an express warranty, because it was not a part of the basis of the bargain.

**32.** For example, section 2–607(2) provides that acceptance of goods precludes their later rejection, and section 2–608(2) provides that "[r]evocation of acceptance must occur within a reasonable time after the buyer discovers or should have discovered grounds for it and before any substantial change in condition of the goods which is not caused by their own defects."

mediately and received a full refund. But after the camper has used the bag in reliance on the seller's statement, the bag will have acquired some holes and a great deal of mud, and the seller will be far less willing to rescind. In these circumstances it would seem reasonable to make the seller's post-sale statement an express warranty.

Comment 7 to 2–313 offers a novel solution to the post-agreement puzzle:

> The precise time when words of description or affirmation are made or samples are shown is not material. The sole question is whether the language or samples or models are fairly to be regarded as part of the contract. If language is used after the closing of the deal (as when the buyer when taking delivery asks and receives an additional assurance), the warranty becomes a modification, and need not be supported by consideration if it is otherwise reasonable and in order (Section 2–209).

If one accepts the analysis of Comment 7, the buyer may have a new bargain, which is based in part upon the modified warranty, when the seller utters a description or affirmation after the time of contracting.

Note, however, that section 2–209 and the modification analysis validate only a handful of all the possible post-deal warranties. First, section 2–209 contemplates an "agreement modifying a contract . . . ." It is far from self-evident that a seller's post-sale words uttered during delivery are an "agreement of modification," and one can hardly attribute that bilateral connotation to an advertisement that is not published until after the sale. Indeed, Comment 7 seems to contemplate only the cases of face-to-face dealings that occur while the deal is still warm. Second, any oral modification of a contract for goods costing more than $500 must somehow meet the statute of frauds under 2–209(3) or constitute a waiver of the statute under 2–209(4). As we point out elsewhere,[33] the statute of frauds and waiver provisions of 2–209 are highly ambiguous, and one might read them as prohibiting oral modification on items costing more than $500.

In our judgment it would be reasonable for a court to find that the "deal" had not been concluded despite the payment of money at least until the buyer had passed the seller's threshold. Until that time (or until some other necessarily arbitrary limit) the buyer, as a matter of empirical fact, will have the power to get the seller to take the goods back and undo the sale. To say that statements made after the payment of the cash but before the expiration of this short period are express warranties recognizes the practical realities even though it does some violence to normal contract doctrine. We would urge a different rule for seller's statements made more than a short period beyond the conclusion of the agreement.

---

33. See Section 1–5 supra.

We find enough vitality and merit in the reliance requirement that we would not find such post-deal representations to be warranties under 2–313 unless they could be proved as modifications under the terms of 2–209.  However, a buyer would not necessarily be deprived of all recourse against his seller on a post-deal statement that misled him but did not qualify as a warranty.  Like any advertiser, the seller might be liable in tort to those he misleads by his advertising.[34]  In most cases we would send the buyer who had relied on a post-sale representation down the tort road.

What the Code does to the pre-Code reliance requirement is quite unclear.  One may argue that the exchange of the "basis of the bargain" language for the old "reliance" language will not change the outcome in any cases.  (Indeed, we can point to none where we are sure the outcome has been changed.)  Others apparently believe that the Code dilutes and perhaps even emasculates the pre-Code reliance requirement.  We favor the former interpretation.  Why should one who has not relied on the seller's statement have the right to sue?  Such a plaintiff is asking for greater protection than he would get under the warranty of merchantability, far more than he bargained for.  We would send him to the implied warranties.

The next twenty years may see the reliance requirement go the way of the Nineteenth Century requirement that a seller intend to warrant; that is, it may disappear altogether.  Whatever the Code or the courts say, we suspect that the requirement that buyers rely on the seller's representation will live on in the juries' minds and will remain an unarticulated but important part of the puffing doctrine.[35]

## § 9–5  Express Warranties, 2–313—Samples and Models

We commonly conceive of warranties as verbal representations, but such a view is much too narrow.  What could be a better representation than the sample or model that is to represent the very thing that the seller is selling?  Section 2–313(1) (c) recognizes these symbolic statements as express warranties:

> Any sample or model which is made part of the basis of the bargain creates an express warranty that the whole of the goods shall conform to the sample or model.

---

34.  For example, Restatement, Second, Torts § 402B (1965), provides a cause of action when a seller makes an innocent misrepresentation in the course of advertising of a material fact concerning the character or quality of an item sold to a consumer who suffers physical harm caused by justifiable reliance on the misrepresentation.

35.  Janssen v. Hook, 1 Ill.App.3d 318, 272 N.E.2d 385, 9 UCC Rep.Serv. 846 (1971), illustrates the continuing vitality of the reliance requirement.  The court found as follows:

The defendant testified that the plaintiff advised him that one of the trucks was in "good condition" when, in fact, it needed extensive repair.  The defendant admitted, however, that he had inspected and worked with the trucks prior to his purchase of them and was aware that they needed repairs.  Under the circumstances, the finding of the trial court that an express warranty, as defined by the Code, had not been made was not against the manifest weight of the evidence.

Id. at 320, 272 N.E.2d at 388, 9 UCC Rep. Serv. at 849.

Much of what we have said above about the basis of the bargain and about the other aspects of express warranty litigation applies equally to sample or model express warranties. We see only two significant, clear questions that have elements unique to samples or models. First, was the item under consideration in fact a "sample" or a "model?" Second, what does the sample or model mean?

We have found no significant post-Code appellate litigation that deals with the question whether an item under consideration by the parties constitutes a sample or model.[36] Comment 6 to 2–313 distinguishes between the two terms as follows:

> This section includes both a "sample" actually drawn from the bulk of goods which is the subject matter of the sale, and a "model" which is offered for inspection when the subject matter is not at hand and which has not been drawn from the bulk of the goods.

The comment then gives some indication of the scope of the definitions of the two terms (emphasis added):

> [T]he facts are often ambiguous when something is shown as *illustrative,* rather than as a straight sample. In general, the presumption is that *any* sample or model just as any affirmation of fact is intended to become a basis of the bargain.

Although it is not free from doubt, the second quoted passage appears to mean that anything illustrative that the seller holds out to the buyer is at least presumptively a sample or model. Surely a buyer can make a plausible argument on the basis of this comment that anything that remotely resembled [37] the goods in question and that was pointed out by the seller [38] constitutes a sample or model and therefore that the burden should be upon the seller to show that the goods considered did not constitute a sample or model.

---

36. Under section 16 of the Uniform Sales Act, it was generally held that the mere fact that a sample was exhibited did not create a warranty that the bulk would conform to the sample. See, e. g., American Canning Co. v. Flat Top Grocery Co., 68 W.Va. 698, 70 S.E. 756 (1911). Thus, if the deal was made in terms that excluded the possibility that the buyer relied on the sample as conforming to the bulk, there was no warranty to that effect. See generally L. Vold, Law of Sales § 88 at 434–35 (2d ed. 1959). One Code case appears to apply the Uniform Sales Act reasoning to 2–313(1) (c). Sylvia Coal Co. v. Mercury Coal & Coke Co., 151 W.Va. 818, 156 S.E.2d 1, 4 UCC Rep.Serv. 650 (1967). See note 39 and acompanying text infra.

37. Cf. Washington Fruit & Produce Co. v. Ted Mirski Co., 24 Agri.Dec.

1559, 3 UCC Rep.Serv. 175 (1965), in which a sizing card containing holes and numbers denoting the diameters of cherries was held not to be a sample or model that was the basis of a contract. Apparently the resemblance of the holes in the card to the offered cherries was too remote.

38. In Neville Chemical Co. v. Union Carbide Corp., 294 F.Supp. 649, 5 UCC Rep.Serv. 1219 (W.D.Pa.1968), a trial court held that a sample and subsequent trial barge shipment of a chemical created an express warranty under section 2–313(1) (c). While the Third Circuit Court of Appeals did not reverse, it treated the case as one involving only negligence and the implied warranty of merchantability under section 2–314. 422 F.2d 1205, 7 UCC Rep.Serv. 81 (3d Cir.), cert. denied 400 U.S. 826 (1970).

Nevertheless, there still should be circumstances in which an item considered by the parties is not a sample or model. For example, when a seller presents a "sample" of coal to a buyer but makes it clear that the coal actually being sold is of inferior quality, it seems reasonable to conclude that the previewed coal is not a sample or model for purposes of 2–313(1) (c).[39] However, a more difficult situation can easily be imagined. Assume that buyer wishes to purchase two tons of coal from seller. Seller sends buyer into the yard where a pile of coal of several thousand tons is located. He makes no representation either oral or written about the nature of the coal, nor does he do anything to indicate that the coal in the pile is a "sample or model." If the two reach a deal and seller delivers coal which differs from that which the buyer inspected in the pile, has seller made and breached an express warranty? We find this a close case, but absent some statement by buyer or seller to indicate that the coal sold was somehow to conform to the coal in the pile, we believe that there would be no express warranty.

In general, we suspect that the presumption embodied in Comment 6 will make the definition of samples and models a much less troublesome one under the Code than it was under the Uniform Sales Act.[40] We suspect that it will be a rare circumstance in which the seller is able to convince a court that an item inspected by him and the buyer or by the buyer at seller's suggestion does not constitute either a sample or model. Of course, the buyer would still have to show that the sample or model was made a part of the basis of the bargain. Thus, even if a court found that the previewed items in the coal and siding cases were in fact samples or models, it could reasonably hold, for the reasons discussed in Section 9–4 above, that the sample or model was not a part of the bargain.[41]

If one decides that the goods inspected are a sample or model made a part of the basis of the bargain, he must still determine exactly what characteristics the goods must display in order to conform to the sample or model. Comment 6 again gives some help and suggests that the kind of meaning that a sample transmits may differ from that which a model transmits:

> If the sample has been drawn from an existing bulk, it must be regarded as describing values of the goods contracted for unless it is accompanied by an unmistakable denial of such responsibility. If, on the other hand, a model of merchan-

---

39. The West Virginia Supreme Court held that these facts did not create an express warranty in Sylvia Coal Co. v. Mercury Coal & Coke Co., 151 W.Va. 818, 156 S.E.2d 1, 4 UCC Rep. Serv. 650 (1967). However, the court appeared to say that the previewed coal was a sample but that the sample did not create an express warranty because it was not a part of the basis of the bargain. Id. at 826–27, 156 S.E. 2d at 7, 4 UCC Rep.Serv. at 656.

40. Because the determination whether an item was a sample under the Uniform Sales Act turned on the intention of the parties and the reliance of the buyer, see note 36 supra, litigation frequently involved difficult questions of fact. See L. Vold, Law of Sales § 88 at 435 (2d ed. 1959).

41. See note 39 and accompanying text supra.

dise not on hand is offered, the mercantile presumption that
it has become a literal description of the subject matter is
not so strong, and particularly so if modification on the
buyer's initiative impairs any feature of the model.

This portion of the comment tells us that when one shows a model,
that is, something not drawn out of an existing bulk, he has more
leeway than when he shows a sample.  Beyond this conclusion the
quoted language begs the fundamental question.  We know that no
sample or model is truly a literal reproduction of the good itself.
Just as no snowflake is the literal reproduction of any other, so no
Ford Torino is the literal reproduction of any other of its particular
species.  In most cases, therefore, it will take at least some expert
testimony about trade usage and understanding to put sufficient
meat on the bones of the sample or model to enable the court or the
jury to make a judgment whether the goods lived up to that sample
or model.[42]

An obvious example of the inherent ambiguity in a sample or
model is given in Washington Fruit & Produce Co. v. Ted Mirski
Co.[43]  In that case, the seller warranted that his cherries would be
"twelve row larger." [44]  The boxes used by the seller were capable
of holding exactly twelve rows of cherries $^{56}\!/_{64}$ inches in diameter.
The seller also sent the buyer a sizing card with a hole, shaped like a
perfect circle $^{56}\!/_{64}$ inches in diameter, punched in it to indicate the
size of the cherries.  The buyer maintained that the warranty was
to the effect that each of the cherries would be at least $^{56}\!/_{64}$ inches in
diameter, but the seller argued that the warranty meant that the
average diameter of the cherries offered would be $^{56}\!/_{64}$ of an inch.
The court agreed with the seller, but in the absence of proof of trade
usage, the buyer's argument was equally plausible.  Although the
court here held that the sizing card was not a sample or a model,[45]
it would have faced the same interpretative problem if it had held
otherwise or if the seller had displayed an actual cherry exactly $^{56}\!/_{64}$
inches in diameter.  Incidentally, the lawyer's job in ferreting out
the meaning of a sample or a model is similar to the work that he
must undertake in finding what is "merchantable" under section
2–314, and we direct him to our discussion of that task in the next
section.

---

42. One might assume that difficult
proof problems would be encountered
in determining whether the taste of
catered food lived up to samples. The
appellate court in Graulich Caterer,
Inc. v. Hans Holterbosch, Inc., 101 N.J.
Super. 61, 243 A.2d 253, 5 UCC Rep.
Serv. 440 (App.Div.1968), apparently
recognized this problem, because it deferred to the original trier of fact's
judgment of the witnesses' demeanor
and credibility.  Similarly, the Massachusetts Supreme Judicial Court, in
Regina Grape Products Co. v. Supreme Wine Co., 357 Mass. 631, 260
N.E.2d 219, 7 UCC Rep.Serv. 1168
(1970), accepted without question an
auditor's report that delivered wine
did not conform in quality or color
to samples supplied.

43. 24 Agri.Dec. 1559, 3 UCC Rep.Serv.
175 (1965).

44. Id. at 1561–62, 3 UCC Rep.Serv. at
176.

45. See note 37 supra.

In summary, the Code has made express warranties out of samples and models and thus strengthened the hand of the buyer somewhat. All other things being equal, we suspect that a buyer is more likely to be victorious in a suit on an express warranty than in a suit on an implied warranty. This is so because an express warranty, once made, is harder to disclaim and because it is easier to prove breach of an explicit express warranty than it is to prove breach against a more general standard of "merchantability" or "fitness for a particular purpose." Beyond that 2–313(1) (c) does little to disturb the pre-Code law, and so far it has produced only a handful of cases, none of which is remarkable.

### § 9–6  The Implied Warranty of Merchantability, 2–314—Introduction

The implied warranty of merchantability in 2–314 is by far the most important warranty in the Code. It is a first cousin to strict tort liability, and "products liability" cases are often tried under the merchantability banner. Section 2–314 is not revolutionary; it is simply a modernized version of the comparable Uniform Sales Act provision.[46]

Although section 2–314 offers a form of "strict liability," the plaintiff is not assured of winning with ease. Except that he need not prove negligence on the part of the defendant, the wise plaintiff's lawyer will regard a 2–314 case as highly similar to a negligence suit. A plaintiff in a merchantability lawsuit must prove that the defendant deviated from the standard of merchantability and that this deviation caused the plaintiff's injury both proximately and in fact. These necessities of proof make the merchantability case a first cousin to a negligence lawsuit. Under 2–314, a plaintiff must prove (*1*) that a merchant sold goods, (*2*) which were not "merchantable" at the time of sale, and (*3*) injury and damages to the plaintiff or his property (*4*) caused proximately and in fact by the defective nature of the goods, and (*5*) notice to seller of injury. The plaintiff can fail on any of the points listed; he can also succumb to any of the affirmative defenses that the defendant may raise, for instance, warranty disclaimed, or notice of breach not timely given, or statute of limitations expired. Recall that a merchantability case is likely to be somewhat more difficult for the plaintiff than an express warranty case, for implied warranties are more easily disclaimed than are express warranties, and proof of breach of an explicit express warranty is likely to be easier than is proof of breach of the standard of merchantability.

Under 2–314, there must be a "contract for [the] sale . . . [of] goods," and the seller must be a "merchant." Some courts have applied the implied warranty of merchantability to nonsale trans-

---

46. USA § 15(2) provided:

Where the goods are bought by description from a seller who deals in goods of that description (whether he be the grower or manufacturer or not), there is an implied warranty that the goods shall be of a merchantable quality.

actions.[47]   For example, the Supreme Court of New Jersey has found that an implied warranty arises on the lease of personal property.[48] However, these cases apply 2–314 by analogy, and not all courts will do this.[49]   On a related front, plaintiffs and defendants have fought forty years of skirmishes over whether the serving of food,[50] the giving of a blood transfusion,[51] and the dressing of hair [52] constitute "sales of goods" that carry implied warranties of merchantability or constitute sales of services that do not carry such warranties.   The second sentence of 2–314(1) has resolved the issue in respect to food:

> Under this section the serving for value of food or drink to be consumed either on the premises or elsewhere is a sale.

Whether under the Code beauty treatments and blood transfusions are essentially sales of goods rather than sales of services remains to be seen.   We doubt that courts are deciding these cases on the basis of distinctions between sales and services.   The courts of various states have recently gone different ways in the blood transfusion cases.[53]   Courts seem hesitant to throw added liability on the

47.   See, e. g., Bachner v. Pearson, 479 P.2d 319, 8 UCC Rep.Serv. 515 (Alas. 1970) (leased airplane); Hertz Commercial Leasing Corp. v. Transportation Credit Clearing House, 59 Misc. 2d 226, 298 N.Y.S.2d 392, 6 UCC Rep. Serv. 132 (Civ.Ct.1969), rev'd on other grounds 64 Misc.2d 910, 316 N.Y.S.2d 585 (App.Term 1970) (lease of equipment).

Comment (2) to 2–313 states:

[T]he warranty sections of this Article are not designed in any way to disturb those lines of case law growth which have recognized that warranties need not be confined to sales contracts or to the direct parties to such a contract . . . .   [T]he matter is left to the case law with the intention that the policies of this Act may offer useful guidance in dealing with further cases as they arise.

This comment has frequently been cited by courts that have extended Article Two warranties to nonsales transactions by analogy.   The arguments in favor of such extension are developed in Farnsworth, Implied Warranties of Quality in Non-Sales Cases, 57 Colum. L.Rev. 653 (1957).

48.   Cintrone v. Hertz Truck Leasing and Rental Service, 45 N.J. 434, 212 A.2d 769 (1965).

49.   See, e. g., Aegis Productions, Inc. v. Arriflex Corp., 25 App.Div.2d 639, 268 N.Y.S.2d 185, 3 UCC Rep.Serv. 298 (1st Dep't 1966) (no implied warranty attaches to the performance of repair

services); Victor v. Barzaleski, 19 Pa. D. & C.2d 698 (C.P.1959) (installation of stoker boiler unit by handy man did not create buyer and seller relationship and therefore no implied warranty of fitness arose under section 2–314 or section 2–315).

50.   Compare Nisky v. Childs Co., 103 N.J.L. 464, 135 A. 805 (1927) (stating the pre-Code majority rule that one serving food to be immediately consumed on premises is not liable under implied warranty), with Heise v. Gillette, 83 Ind.App. 551, 149 N.E. 182 (1925) (stating opposite rule).

51.   Compare Perlmutter v. Beth David Hospital, 308 N.Y. 100, 123 N.E.2d 792 (1954) (blood transfusion is service transaction not subject to implied warranties), with Russell v. Community Blood Bank, Inc., 185 So.2d 749 (Fla. 1966), aff'd as modified 196 So.2d 115 (Fla.1967) (commercial blood banks may be held liable for breach of warranty because transaction is arguably a sale).

52.   Compare Epstein v. Giannattasio, 25 Conn.Supp. 109, 197 A.2d 342, 1 UCC Rep.Serv. 114 (1963) (beauty-parlor treatments do not constitute sales for purposes of Article Two warranty provisions), with Newmark v. Gimbel's, Inc., 54 N.J. 585, 285 A.2d 697, 6 UCC Rep.Serv. 1205 (1969) (Article Two warranty provisions do apply to beauty treatments).

53.   The current trend appears to be to apply the strict tort liability doctrine

backs of hospitals that may be financially hard pressed non-profit institutions. Moreover, it may not be possible to discover defects in blood even by use of the best medical research.[54] Theoretically, the seller's inability to discover defects in the goods he sells is not relevant to a warranty cause of action; however we suspect that court and jury are often influenced by assumptions that the defendant was not at fault. About half the states have provided that those who give blood transfusions do not warrant the merchantability of the blood.[55]

The law here is today in flux. If one takes a longer view, it is apparent that the courts have continuously extended the seller's liability, and the service-sale cases are not likely to be an exception. Beyond the transfusion and hairdresser cases, there are numerous other borderline transactions that have yet to produce appellate litigation. Consider, for example, the doctor who installs a ten-cent interuterine device or the plumber who does forty dollars of work and installs a twenty-cent fixture. Each is certainly a merchant under the definition of 2–104; does each have liability in warranty or only for negligence? To answer this question by asking whether sales or service predominate in the transaction is crude. We suspect that the courts and the legislatures—those deciding who is and who is not strictly liable—have been influenced by a variety of factors not easily articulated as part of the sales-service formula. For example, one might argue that a doctor's task is so complex and so crucial to society's needs that one ought not make him warrant the outcome of each operation or procedure he performs. On the other hand, the doctor has far greater potential for causing injury than most sellers of services, and plaintiffs have had notorious difficulty in proving negligence against doctors. Additionally, one must ask how the legal outcomes would change if merchantability liability were extended to the particular transaction. As we have pointed out, one who warrants merchantability does not insure a specific outcome, and a doctor could perform a "merchantable" appendectomy in the sense that it would pass in the trade as a satisfactory appendectomy, yet the patient might still die from a complication against which the doctor had not warranted. A lawyer could draw a merchantable will that failed to take advantage of the maximum marital

---

to blood transfusion cases. In both Cunningham v. MacNeal Memorial Hospital, 47 Ill.2d 443, 266 N.E.2d 897 (1970), and Hoffman v. Misericordia Hospital, 439 Pa. 501, 267 A.2d 867, 7 UCC Rep.Serv. 897 (1970), the sale-service distinction was regarded as not crucial in determining strict tort liability in blood transfusion cases.

54. See, e. g., Balkowitsch v. Minneapolis War Memorial Blood Bank, Inc., 270 Minn. 151, 159, 132 N.W.2d 805, 811 (1965).

55. See, e. g., Fla.Stat.Ann. § 672.2–316(5) (Supp.1970). According to Note, Strict Liability for Disease Contracted from Blood Transfusion, 66 Nw.L.Rev. 80, 96 (1971), twenty-five states have enacted similar legislation. Query whether provisions written into the Code to free hospitals from warranty liability are also effective to free them from strict tort liability. One suspects that the intent of the draftsmen is to free the seller from all such strict liabilities, and the language should probably be construed to accomplish that purpose.

deduction. It may be, therefore, that the extension of warranty liability to certain transactions would do little or nothing to change the actual legal outcomes. In any event we suspect that the sale-service dichotomy is merely a verbal formula in which results are expressed, results which courts reach upon analysis of a variety of factors. We would urge courts to identify these factors more candidly. We would also remind courts who do wish to impose warranty liability in nonsale cases that they can do so by analogy without indulging the fiction that the transaction at hand is a true sale of goods.

Only rarely will one have occasion to wonder whether a potential defendant is a "merchant." If the seller is not a merchant, he cannot give the warranty under 2–314. Section 2–104(1) defines merchant as follows:

> "Merchant" means a person who deals in goods of the kind or otherwise by his occupation holds himself out as having knowledge or skill peculiar to the practices or goods involved in that transaction or to whom such knowledge or skill may be attributed by his employment of an agent or broker or other intermediary who by his occupation holds himself out as having such knowledge or skill.

The section deserves some explanation. Note first that one can be a merchant by (1) "dealing in goods" or (2) "otherwise by his occupation" holding himself out as having "knowledge or skill peculiar to the practices or goods involved." The first phrase captures the jeweler, the hardware store owner, the haberdasher, and others selling from inventory. The second description, having to do with occupation, knowledge, and skill, includes electricians, plumbers, carpenters, boat builders,[56] and the like. The comment points out that a "bank" or "even universities" through their agents can have the necessary knowledge or skill to make them merchants. Under 2–314, the merchant must be a merchant with respect to "goods of that kind," that is, goods of the kind that are the subject of the transaction in question. Although one court, relying on pre-Code law, has held that a farmer selling soybeans he has raised is not a merchant,[57] one should understand that the 2–104 definition of "merchant" includes a considerably broader class than the man on the street might think.

### § 9–7  The Implied Warranty of Merchantability, 2–314—Merchantability Defined

Most of the elements of the merchantability cause of action are familiar to any tort lawyer; we deal with only two of the elements here. The two questions that give ulcers to plaintiff's and defendants' lawyers are:

(1) How does one define merchantability?

(2) How does one prove causation?

56.  Mercanti v. Pearson, 160 Conn. 468, 280 A.2d 137, 8 UCC Rep.Serv. 969 (1971).

57.  Cook Grains v. Fallis, 239 Ark. 962, 395 S.W.2d 555, 2 UCC Rep.Serv. 1141 (1965).

There are thousands, perhaps tens of thousands, of cases in which the plaintiff's lawyer has had to convince the jury or a judge that the goods his client purchased were not merchantable, not "fit for the ordinary purposes" for which such goods are purchased. The cigarette cases are dramatically illustrative. On the one hand, American Tobacco will argue that its Lucky Strikes are merchantable since they are fit for the ordinary purposes for which such goods are used, namely, smoking. They will admit that their cigarettes would not be merchantable if they contained some foreign object such as a toenail or a mouse's ear, but they will maintain that the goods are merchantable as long as they are essentially identical to other goods that pass in the trade under the label "cigarettes." The plaintiff will argue, on the other hand, that the proper measure of merchantability is whether the cigarette causes cancer, and he will maintain that if the cigarette causes cancer, *ipso facto* it is not suitable for the ordinary purposes for which it is sold, and it is not merchantable. Thus arises the question: to be merchantable must cigarettes be noncancer causing, or is it sufficient that they be like all other cigarettes despite the fact that they might contribute to lung cancer in some users? In Green v. The American Tobacco Co., a fascinating case that must have put the plaintiff's lawyers in bankruptcy and the defendant's lawyers on easy street, just that question was passed upon in some way or other by the Florida Supreme Court,[58] by two trial courts,[59] and by the United States Fifth Circuit Court of Appeals[60] on four different occasions. Ultimately, the Fifth Circuit concluded as follows:

> We are not dealing with an obvious, harmful, foreign body in a product. Neither do we have an exploding or breaking bottle case wherein the defect is so obvious that it warrants no discussion. Instead, we have a product (cigarettes) that is in no way defective. They are exactly like all others of the particular brand and virtually the same as all other brands on the market.[61]

To those who would reject the Fifth Circuit's conclusion out of hand, let us suggest the case of whiskey or butter. One might want to argue that butter is unmerchantable because it contains cholesterol, and cholesterol causes heart disease. Is whiskey or are automobiles not merchantable because they may cause injury or even death when they are used improperly and contribute to injury or death even when they are used properly? Surely we have not seen the last of the cases in which the parties argue about the meaning of "fit for

**58.** 154 So.2d 169 (Fla.1963).

**59.** CCH 1963–65 Product Liability Rep. ¶ 5341 (S.D.Fla.1964) (second trial).

**60.** 304 F.2d 70 (5th Cir.), aff'd on rehearing 304 F.2d 85 (5th Cir. 1962); 325 F.2d 673 (1963), cert. denied 377 U.S. 943 (1964); 391 F.2d 97 (5th Cir. 1968); 409 F.2d 1166, cert. denied 397 U.S. 911 (1969).

**61.** 391 F.2d at 110 (dissenting opinion of Simpson, J., adopted as majority opinion in 409 F.2d 1166).

the ordinary purposes;" the *Green* case will offer interesting study for courts and lawyers who must decide those cases.[62]

Most of the 2–314 cases in which courts found breaches of the warranty of merchantability involved goods that because of defects either did not work properly or were unexpectedly harmful.  Such defects may arise from improper manufacturing,[63] incorrect labeling,[64] or the presence of unexpected objects.[65]  Holowka v. York Farm Bureau Cooperative Association [66] presents the merchantability issue in terms analogous to the cigarette cases.  There a farmer purchased an insecticide called Malathion to rid his alfalfa of boll weevils.  The insecticide succeeded in eliminating the bugs, but it also managed to kill and injure his livestock.  In imposing liability, the court observed, "It would appear to us that the use of a material which as a by-product causes death or injury to property is a classic example of a breach of warranty that the material was safe to use." [67]  Perhaps butter, whiskey, and cigarettes are distinguishable from Malathion only because the injury to butter eaters, whiskey drinkers, and smokers is farther removed in time and probability [68] than the in-

62.  The allergy cases present the analogous question of seller's liability for products that injure some of the people all of the time.  If an appreciable class of buyers (but less than all buyers) are allergic to the product, seller is liable.  See Zirpola v. Adam Hat Stores, Inc., 122 N.J.L. 21, 4 A.2d 73 (1939) (4–5% of population constitutes an appreciable class).  Seller is not liable for a one-in-a-million allergic reaction.  See Ray v. J. C. Penney Co., 274 F.2d 519 (10th Cir. 1959).  See also Case Note, 46 Cornell L.Q. 465 (1960).  See also note 68 infra.

63.  See, e. g., Koellmer v. Chrysler Motors Corp., 6 Conn.Cir. 478, 276 A.2d 807, 8 UCC Rep.Serv. 668 (1970) (truck repeatedly steamed over because of hole in engine block).

64.  See, e. g., Kassab v. Central Soya, 432 Pa. 217, 246 A.2d 848, 5 UCC Rep. Serv. 925 (1968).  See notes 77, 78 and accompanying text supra.

65.  See, e. g., DeGraff v. Myers Foods, Inc., 19 Pa.D. & C.2d 19, 1 UCC Rep. Serv. 110 (C.P.1958) (chicken bone in pot pie).  But see Flippo v. Mode O'Day Frock Shops, 248 Ark. 1, 449 S.W.2d 692, 7 UCC Rep.Serv. 282 (1970) (bite by a spider concealed in trousers was not breach of implied warranty of merchantability because spider was not part of the goods); Webster v. Blue Ship Tea Room, Inc., 347 Mass. 421, 198 N.E.2d 309, 2 UCC Rep.Serv. 161 (1964) ("We should be prepared to

cope with the hazards of fish bones, the occasional presence of which in chowder is, it seems to us, to be anticipated . . . .").

66.  Holowka v. York Farm Bureau Coop. Ass'n, 2 UCC Rep.Serv. 445 (Pa. C.P.1963).

67.  Id. at 448.  Dean Prosser has suggested that inherently dangerous products, such as dynamite, rabies vaccine, and presumably Malathion, should be regarded as defective if sold without adequate warning.  Prosser, The Fall of the Citadel, 50 Minn.L. Rev. 791, 808 (1966).

68.  The "allergy" cases present analogous questions.  In absolving sellers of liability for their buyers' reactions, presumably the courts are making the judgment that society should not bear the cost of allergic reactions, but that it should encourage those who are allergic to choose the products they use with care.  In any event, a defendant can often get off the hook if he is able to show that the injury of which the plaintiff complains is due to some peculiarity shared by an insignificant portion of the population.  See, e. g., Harris v. Belton, 258 Cal.App.2d 595, 65 Cal.Rptr. 808 (1968) (no breach when product could be used safely by 98% of the public, as long as manufacturer advises consumer of possible adverse consequences); Esborg v. Bailey Drug Co., 61 Wash.2d 347, 378 P.2d 298 (1963) (product must be harmful to reasonably foreseeable and appreciable

jury to Malathion users. Since the injury to butter eaters, cigarette smokers, or whiskey drinkers is so remote,[69] the product may be viewed as merchantable. Also, judge and jury may be unsympathetic to cigarette plaintiffs because of traditional distaste for paternalistic laws, a distaste that can be expressed by finding that the product in question was risky but merchantable.

In the usual case the lawyer's job is considerably less dramatic than in the cigarette cases but it is still the same job. He may be called on to convince the jury, for example, that merchantable wine must be of a certain color,[70] that merchantable cherries must be of a certain diameter,[71] or that a merchantable logging chain must be able to pull a certain weight without breaking.[72] In the log chain case, for example, the defendant sold plaintiff a log chain, cut the last link and, at plaintiff's request, inserted a hook and rewelded the link. The chain link broke while it was being used to tow a truck uphill on a dirt road. The truck was considerably damaged. Plaintiff sued defendant on the theory that the chain was not merchantable. How does plaintiff's lawyer prove his case? First he will need testimony from his client and, if possible, from others about the normal purposes for which log chains are used. Second, he will need testimony from his client and also from a metallurgical expert that the log chain in this case was not (at time of sale) capable of withstanding the strain which would normally be experienced in such operations. Typically, expert testimony is required to prove the causal connection between the breach and the injury. But establishing the standards of merchantability is likely to be a joint task shared in part by those expert in the trade but not necessarily technical experts and by the technical experts.

---

numbers of people). But see Crotty v. Shartenberg's-New Haven, Inc., 147 Conn. 460, 162 A.2d 513 (1960) (under pre-Code law there could be breach of warranty of merchantability even though a normal person would not be injured by using product); Zirpola v. Adam Hat Stores, Inc., 122 N.J.L. 21, 4 A.2d 73 (1939) (injury to scalp caused by hatband breached warranty of merchantability even though only small proportion of users could be so injured). The point at which the suffering class becomes so large that their reaction is no longer classified as "allergic" is unclear, and equally unclear is the question why we permit the allergy exception. If a manufacturer sold 1000 products a year and could predict with certainty that one out of 1000 would fail during the year and would likely cause serious injury, he would not be freed from liability to that one injured person because of the low probability of injury. But the same is not true if the low probability of injury is, in part, the result of the special qualities of the user.

**69.** See Section 9–8 infra.

**70.** Regina Grape Products Co. v. Supreme Wine Co., 357 Mass. 631, 260 N.E.2d 219, 7 UCC Rep.Serv. 1168 (1970).

**71.** See Washington Fruit & Produce Co. v. Ted Mirski Co., 24 Agri.Dec. 1559, 3 UCC Rep.Serv. 175 (1965), which dealt only with express warranties under 2–313.

**72.** Robert H. Carr & Sons, Inc. v. Yearsley, 31 Pa.D. & C.2d 262, 1 UCC Rep.Serv. 97 (C.P.1963).

The lawyer is given some slight help in his task of defining merchantability by section 2–314(2):

Goods to be merchantable must be at least such as

(a) pass without objection in the trade under the contract description; and

(b) in the case of fungible goods, are of fair average quality within the description; and

(c) are fit for the ordinary purposes for which such goods are used; and

(d) run, within the variations permitted by the **agreement**, of even kind, quality and quantity within each unit and among all units involved; and

(e) are adequately contained, packaged, and labeled as the agreement may require; and

(f) conform to the promises or affirmations of fact made on the container or label if any.

The first three paragraphs make it clear that if the product conforms to the quality of other brands in the market, it will normally be merchantable. Judge Simpson's dissenting opinion in *Green*, which eventually became the majority opinion,[73] was strongly guided by this no-worse-than-anybody-else ethic.[74] Note that an item can "pass without objection" and yet be considerably short of perfection. For example, if a contract called for "4,000 dozen Bagdad goatskins dry salted," a certain small percentage of the goatskins can be rotted, but if the lot contains "more than 3% of rotted skins," it may be abnormal and therefore not a merchantable lot.[75]

The most widely quoted of the synonyms in subsection (2) is paragraph (c), which provides that goods must be "fit for the ordinary purposes for which such goods are used." However, in most cases, to say that goods are fit for the ordinary purposes does little to advance the analysis; it simply substitutes one synonym for another and does nothing to tell a lawyer whether the protective guards around the sides of a rotary lawn mower are sufficient to make it fit for the ordinary purposes or whether the design is fatally defective and the mower, therefore, unmerchantable.[76] In these pages we cannot hope to summarize the thousands of cases that deal with the

73. Green v. American Tobacco Co., 409 F.2d 1166 (5th Cir. 1969).

74. 391 F.2d at 110.

75. Agoos Kid Co. v. The Blumenthal Import Corp., 282 Mass. 1, 6, 184 N.E. 279, 281 (1933). Note that paragraph 2(f) makes conformity to affirmation on the container or label into an implied warranty. Thus, one who sues on the basis of a statement on the label need not prove that the label was part of the basis of the bargain and thus an express warranty. Rather he can sue under 2–314. Note also that a disclaimer of such warranties must comply with 2–316(2) and (3), not with 2–316(1).

76. In this type of fact situation the Maryland Court of Appeals found no breach of warranty. Myers v. Montgomery Ward & Co., 253 Md. 282, 252 A.2d 855, 6 UCC Rep.Serv. 493 (1969).

question of merchantability; we can only suggest where a frustrated lawyer might look for help in determining whether the goods in his particular case ought to be classified as merchantable or nonmerchantable.

Certainly the first place one should look is to the usage in the trade. In a recent Pennsylvania case,[77] the seller sold some cattle feed that contained the female hormone stilbestrol. It appeared that much of the feed for cattle being fattened for slaughter contained stilbestrol and that stilbestrol causes cattle to grow more rapidly than would otherwise be the case. However, stilbestrol also causes, or at least contributes to, abortions in pregnant cows and sterility in bulls. Unfortunately, plaintiff's cattle were used for breeding rather than slaughter, and he sued. Now a city kid might think that cattle feed is cattle feed and that since stilbestrol was an additive commonly found in cattle feed, the feed was fit for the ordinary purposes for which such goods were used. However, an investigation of the trade usage disclosed that the hormones were normally excluded from the food of breeding cattle [78] and that they were not included in feed unless specifically ordered and disclosed on the feed label.

Comment 7 to 2–314 suggests another source of information about the parties' intention:

> In cases of doubt as to what quality is intended, the price at which a merchant closes a contract is an excellent index of the nature and scope of his obligation under the present section.

If, for example, there is a dispute on the question whether an airplane that is the subject of a sale must be flyable to be merchantable, it would be revealing to find that the agreed price fell precisely within the price range charged for flyable airplanes and twenty to thirty per cent above the price normally charged for nonflyable airplanes. In such a case, the price is an objective manifestation of the intention of the parties to deal over a flyable aircraft.[79]

Obviously, one will also wish to look at the characteristics exhibited by goods of the same class that are manufactured by persons other than the seller in question.[80]

Finally, one should get some idea about merchantability in cases from government standards and regulations which are now published

---

**77.** Kassab v. Central Soya, 432 Pa. 217, 246 A.2d 848, 5 UCC Rep.Serv. 925 (1968).

**78.** Id. at 221, 224, 226, 246 A.2d at 849, 851, 857, 5 UCC Rep.Serv. at 927, 928, 935.

**79.** In Sylvia Coal Co., v. Mercury Coal & Coke Co., 151 W.Va. 818, 156 S.E.2d 1, 4 UCC Rep.Serv. 650 (1967), the court stated that an excellent guide to the nature and scope of the implied warranty of merchantability was the fact that the contract price of coal was one-half the standard price for coal used for the buyer's intended purpose.

**80.** Such a comparison was made in *Green*, 391 F.2d at 110. See also Pritchard v. Liggett & Myers Tobacco Co., 295 F.2d 292, 302 (3d Cir. 1961) (another cigarette case).

by an increasing number of federal and state agencies.[81]  If, for example, a used car lacks shoulder harnesses, which are required under federal law for a car made in that year, that fact is powerful evidence that the car is not merchantable.

A concluding question of burning interest, at least to many plaintiff's lawyers, is how the merchantability standard differs from the comparable strict tort standard "defective condition, unreasonably dangerous. . . ."  The most obvious difference between the two standards is that the strict tort standard is considerably narrower in scope.  It does not purport to reach all defective goods but only those that are not only defective but also "unreasonably dangerous," that is those that have the capacity to cause personal injury or property damage as opposed to those which cause only economic loss.[82]  Apart from that difference, we would find the terms nearly synonymous and would expect a court to hold that any automobile which was not merchantable was also in a defective condition unreasonably dangerous.  The draftsmen of 402A of the Restatement, Second, Torts have, however, added comments which indicate their opinion that cigarettes and similar products are not in a defective condition unreasonably dangerous.  Presumably, these comments caused the plaintiff's lawyers in the cigarette cases to try those cases exclusively as warranty claims.  Notwithstanding the draftsmen's statements, we see no reason why there should be a different rule with respect to an item such as cigarettes under strict tort than under warranty.  Except in these areas which the draftsmen have given rather explicit meaning to 402A by their comments and except for the fact that 402A would not normally apply to economic losses, we believe that the two standards are interchangeable.

In summary, the student and lawyer should understand that "merchantable" is not a synonym for perfect.  Fish chowder containing bones that stick in the buyer's craw may nevertheless be merchantable[83] as may a cigarette that kills[84] and a car that maims.[85]  It is the lawyer's challenging job to define the term "merchantability" in his case in some objective form so that the court or jury can make a determination whether that standard has been breached.

### § 9–8   The Implied Warranty of Merchantability, 2–314—Causation

Plaintiff's proof of causation deserves at least a word in passing.  To prove that the plaintiff died of lung cancer caused by smok-

81.  See, e. g., Woodbury Chem. Co. v. Holgerson, 439 F.2d 1052, 8 UCC Rep. Serv. 999 (10th Cir.1971), in which the existence of federal specifications concerning the effectiveness of weed killers helped create express and implied warranties.

82.  But see Santor v. A & M Karagheusian, Inc., 44 N.J. 52, 207 A.2d 305, 16 A.L.R.3d 670, 2 UCC Rep.Serv. 599 (1965).

83.  See, e. g., Webster v. Blue Ship Tea Room, Inc., 347 Mass. 421, 198 N.E.2d 309, 2 UCC Rep.Serv. 161 (1964).

84.  See, e. g., Green v. American Tobacco Co., 409 F.2d 1166 (5th Cir. 1969), discussed in notes 58–61 and accompanying text supra.

85.  See, e. g., Schneider v. Chrysler Motors Corp., 266 F.Supp. 115 (D.Neb.

ing the defendant's cigarettes or that the plaintiff's scalp rash was caused by the defendant's hair dye will often be a tricky and difficult task. Not only must the plaintiff disclose that the breach of warranty was the cause "in fact," but he must show, in the words of Comment 13 to 2–314, that the "breach of the warranty was the proximate cause of the loss sustained." It takes a better Ouija board than your writers possess to devine "proximate"; we simply wish to alert the lawyer to the fact that he must prove a sufficiently close causal connection to convince the court that it ought to be defined as proximate.

*Post hoc propter hoc* is normally not enough; the plaintiff must show more than that the goods injured the plaintiff in a certain way.[86] However, it is not always necessary that the plaintiff offer expert testimony or explicit proof to disclose the precise chain of causation. One court recently held that a plaintiff stated a claim against a seller of applesauce when she alleged that her children, ages eight and ten, ate the applesauce, complained of its "funny taste," and were then so discomforted that they had to have their stomachs pumped.[87] Likewise, one need not prove exactly how the fuel in the carburetor of a Corvette caught fire and burned the car to a cinder; it is sufficient to prove a continuing source of carburetor trouble and offer an expert to opine that the carburetor probably caused the difficulty.[88] Of course, other courts have required plaintiffs to go to greater lengths to rule out rival plausible hypotheses,[89] and it appears that in most cases the plaintiff will wish to procure expert testimony. However, when the connection between the product and the injury is reasonably obvious even to a layman, expert proof and explicit analysis of the chain of causation should not be necessary.[90]

## § 9–9    Fitness for Particular Purpose, 2–315

Those unfamiliar with the differences between the warranty of merchantability (fitness for the *ordinary* purposes for which such goods are used) and the warranty of fitness for a *particular* purpose

1967), aff'd 401 F.2d 549 (8th Cir. 1968).

86. See Proctor & Gamble Mfg. Co. v. Langley, 422 S.W.2d 773 (Tex.Civ. App.1967) (plaintiff failed to follow instructions when using permanent wave product).

87. Martel v. Duffy-Mott Corp., 15 Mich. App. 67, 166 N.W.2d 541, 6 UCC Rep. Serv. 294 (1968).

88. McCrossin v. Hicks Chevrolet, Inc., 248 A.2d 917 (D.C.Ct.App.1969).

89. See, e. g., Jakubowski v. Minnesota Mining & Mfg., 42 N.J. 177, 199 A.2d 826 (1964). In that case, the court found that there were four possible

causes of the breaking of an abrasive disc, only two of which were attributable to the defendant, and that the plaintiff failed to introduce evidence indicating that one cause was more probable than the others. Stating that the plaintiff had the burden of establishing a probability, not just a possibility, that the disc was unmerchantable, the court dismissed the case.

90. See, e. g., Lucchesi v. H. C. Bohack Co., 8 UCC Rep.Serv. 326 (N.Y.Sup.Ct. 1970) (no further proof needed to hold supermarket liable when pop bottle exploded in shopping basket); Martel v. Duffy-Mott Corp., 15 Mich.App. 67, 166 N.W.2d 541, 6 UCC Rep.Serv. 294 (1968), discussed in text accompanying note 87 supra.

often confuse the two; one can find many opinions in which the judges used the terms "merchantability" and "fitness for a particular purpose" interchangeably. Such confusion under the Code is inexcusable. Sections 2–314 and 2–315 make plain that the warranty of fitness for a particular purpose is narrower, more specific, and more precise. 2–315 reads in full as follows:

> Where the seller at the time of contracting has reason to know any particular purpose for which the goods are required and that the buyer is relying on the seller's skill or judgment to select or furnish suitable goods, there is unless excluded or modified under the next section an implied warranty that the goods shall be fit for such purpose.

Note the conditions that are not required by the implied warranty of merchantability but that must be present if a plaintiff is to recover on the implied warranty of fitness for a particular purpose:

(1) The seller [91] must have reason to know the buyer's particular purpose.

(2) The seller must have reason to know that the buyer is relying on the seller's skill or judgment to furnish appropriate goods.

(3) The buyer must, in fact, rely upon the seller's skill or judgment.

Many goods that are perfectly merchantable will not meet the implied warranty of fitness for a particular purpose. For example, in Kobeckis v. Budzko,[92] a pre-Code case, pork infected with trichinosis was not unmerchantable since cooking of even infected meat renders it safe for human consumption. If the plaintiff, who contracted trichinosis after eating the seller's raw pork, had succeeded in proving that the seller knew he was a sausage maker and that sausage makers customarily taste raw pork, he might nevertheless have made out a cause of action for breach of warranty of fitness for a particular purpose.[93]

The most common circumstance in which one meets the warranty of fitness for a particular purpose is where one businessman buys goods that have to be specially selected or particularly manufactured and assembled for his business. A typical case is Kokomo Opalescent Glass Co. v. Arthur W. Schmidt International, Inc.,[94] in which the

---

91. At least one court has applied the warranty of fitness for a particular purpose to leases of chattels. W. E. Johnson Equip. Co. v. United Airlines, 238 So.2d 98, 8 UCC Rep.Serv. 53 (Fla. 1970).

92. 225 A.2d 418 (Maine 1967).

93. The court, however, emphasized that the seller could not be held liable, because USA § 15(I) only requires that goods "be reasonably fit" for a particular purpose made known to the seller. Since there is no practical manner of determining whether raw pork is free of trichinae, the court concluded that the pork was reasonably fit for consumption, even when raw. 225 A.2d at 422–23.

94. 371 F.2d 208 (7th Cir. 1966). The case was decided under the Uniform Sales Act.

Some courts have applied the warranty of fitness for a particular purpose in

buyer offered to buy a new glass rolling machine if the defendant "thought it could be used in plaintiff's operation." [95] The seller visited the buyer's plant and advised him about the kind of machine to use. Ultimately, the machine did not roll glass of the particular kind that the buyer wished to roll, and the court found that the warranty had been breached. In such cases, the "particular purpose" of the buyer is communicated to the seller in the course of the negotiations and occasionally through the contract itself. The buyer's reliance is disclosed by his request for assistance. Such cases fit neatly within 2–315, and thus most 2–315 cases are businessman versus businessman not businessman versus consumer.

How does one prove that the seller knew or had reason to know of the "buyer's purpose"? Comment 1 to 2–315 states "that the buyer need not bring home to the seller actual knowledge of the particular purpose for which the goods are intended or of his reliance on the seller's skill and judgment, if the circumstances are such that the seller has reason to realize the purpose intended or that reliance exists." As we have said, in most cases the buyer discloses his purpose in the early negotiations, and he may incorporate it into the contract. But the circumstances or form of disclosure must be reasonably explicit. Thus, in Kobeckis v. Budzko,[96] the Maine court found that the fact the buyer had a Polish name was not a sufficient basis to give the seller "reason to know" that the buyer was going to be making Polish sausage and eating the pork raw.

How does one prove a buyer's reliance (or lack of it) on his seller's skill and judgment? If the seller is a manufacturer and the buyer has initiated the contract negotiations by the request for a product that will do certain things, the seller is unlikely to win the reliance argument.[97] There are some circumstances, however, that give the seller some hope of winning the reliance argument. If, for example, the buyer "insists on a particular brand," he is not relying on the seller's skill and judgment, and, in the words of Comment 5, "no warranty results." Moreover, the relative state of the knowledge of the two parties about the product is highly relevant, and in the unusual case in which the buyer is more knowledgeable than the seller, the seller may win on the grounds that the buyer did not rely. In

the consumer context. See, e. g., Filler v. Rayex Corp., 435 F.2d 336, 8 UCC Rep.Serv. 323 (7th Cir. 1970), in which an advertisement display proclaiming that certain flip-type sunglasses were designed for baseball players was sufficient to establish the reliance and notice requirements under 2–315. The plaintiff, a baseball player, recovered damages for the loss of an eye, which was pierced by a splinter of the sunglasses after they were struck by a fly ball and shattered. While the court dealt solely with 2–315, we believe this case might better fit into the merchantability of express warranty categories.

**95.** 371 F.2d at 214.

**96.** 225 A.2d 418, 421 (Maine 1967).

**97.** See, e. g., Beech Aircraft Corp. v. Flexible Tubing Corp., 270 F.Supp. 548 (D.Conn.1967); DeLamar Motor Co. v. White, 249 Ark. 708, 460 S.W.2d 802, 8 UCC Rep.Serv. 437 (1970); Royal Pioneer Paper Box Mfg. Co. v. Louis DeJonge & Co., 179 Pa.Super. 155, 115 A.2d 837 (1955).

Sylvia Coal Co. v. Mercury Coal & Coke Co.,[98] for example, the seller showed that he was simply a coal miner and was ignorant of the process by which one makes coke but that the buyer was an experienced coke maker; the court found that these circumstances did not give rise to justifiable reliance, and it therefore held that there was no warranty under 2–315 despite the fact that the coal was not satisfactory for making coke.[99]

In general, the implied warranty of fitness for a particular purpose is a mature legal doctrine, little changed by the Code. Unlike the warranty of merchantability, it is not beset by the tides and winds of personal-injury lawsuits brought by consumers against manufacturers; its modest place in our jurisprudence has been carefully carved out for it by the draftsmen and the case law.

## § 9–10   The Warranties of Title and Against Infringement, 2–312

Among the warranties that ride along with the contract for the sale of goods is an implied warranty [100] that the seller has good title. In the words of section 2–312, the seller warrants:

    (a) the title conveyed shall be good, and its transfer rightful; and

    (b) the goods shall be delivered free from any security interest or other lien or encumbrance of which the buyer at the time of contracting has no knowledge.

If a seller sells a stolen car or one that is burdened with an unsatisfied perfected security interest, he has almost certainly breached section 2–312 and will be liable in damages to the buyer.[101] We deal with damage and statute of limitations questions below.[102] Here we focus on two questions peculiar to section 2–312:

    (1) What interference by whom with his title or possession must the plaintiff prove in order to have a cause of action under 2–312?

    (2) What language will disclaim and what circumstances will foreclose the warranty of title?

## § 9–11   The Warranties of Title and Against Infringement, 2–312— Cause of Action

If the object of a sale is subject to a valid security interest or a valid claim of title in a third person, clearly the warranty in 2–312

---

98.   151 W.Va. 818, 156 S.E.2d 1, 4 UCC Rep.Serv. 650 (1967).

99.   Id. at 828, 156 S.E.2d at 7, 4 UCC Rep.Serv. at 657.

100.   Comment 6 to section 2–312 states that the warranty of title "is not designated as an 'implied' warranty," but the purpose of the comment is to make clear that the 2–312 warranty is not subject to the disclaimer provision of 2–316. In practical effect, the warranty of title may be regarded as implied since it need not be expressed.

101.   See, e. g., John St. Auto Wrecking v. Motors Ins. Co., 56 Misc.2d 232, 288 N.Y.S.2d 281, 5 UCC Rep.Serv. 112 (Dist.Ct.1968) (stolen car); Kruger v. Bibi, 3 UCC Rep.Serv. 1132 (N.Y.Sup. Ct.1967).

102.   See Sections 10–2 and 11–8 infra.

has been breached, and the seller is liable in damages.[103]  Moreover, the seller need not be a merchant, and he is not saved by his own ignorance of the defect in his title.  Thus, if the plaintiff buyer proves the defective title or the presence of a lien or encumbrance [104] of which he had no *knowledge* at the time of the sale, he will win.

What of the case in which the seller's title is good, but it is subject to a colorable claim of title in the third party or colorable claim of encumbrance on the part of some financier?  Under pre-Code law, such cases would have been governed by the warranty of quiet possession,[105] but in the words of Comment 1 to section 2–312, "The warranty of quiet possession is abolished."  Comment 1 then goes on to tell us that "[d]isturbance of quiet possession, although not mentioned specifically, is one way, among many, in which the breach of the warranty of title may be established."  Thus, the comment appears to preserve the warranty of quiet possession, but it does nothing to resolve the ambiguities inherent in that warranty.  Assume, for example, that a buyer purchases an automobile, that a third party subsequently claims a security interest in the automobile, but that the third party is mistaken and his security interest proves to be in another automobile.  Is it the buyer's or the seller's obligation to incur the expense of defending the suit by the third party?  Put another way, does the seller warrant against claims by third persons that prove to be invalid?

The Code itself says nothing about this issue.  The problem apparently arises rarely, since we are unable to find any pre-Code cases that squarely face the issue.  However, the situation was presented before the United States Supreme Court in a real property context.  In Curtis v. Innerarity,[106] a seller brought suit against a purchaser of real property for interest due on a purchase money mortgage.  The purchaser attempted to set off his expenses incurred in successfully establishing good title against the federal government.  The Court denied any such set-off and stated:

> [T]here was no covenant in this sale, nor is there in this or in any sale, either of real or *personal property*, any implied warranty by the vendor that his vendee shall enjoy it forever free from all unjust or illegal interference  .   .   .   . [107]

Comment 1 to section 2–312, however, suggests that the Code's warranty of title goes beyond what was previously available.  It

---

103.  See note 101 supra.

104.  Comment 1 states that the "knowledge" referred to in 2–312(1) (b) is "actual knowledge as distinct from notice."  Thus, the mere fact that a financing statement is filed does not relieve the seller of his warranty.

105.  See USA § 13(2).  See generally 8 S. Williston, Williston on Contracts §§ 975–80 (3d ed. 1964).

106.  47 U.S. (6 How.) 146 (1848).

107.  Id. at 157 (emphasis added).  See also Eggers v. Mitchem, 240 Iowa 1199, 38 N.W.2d 591 (1949); Jones v. Hood, 46 S.W. 71 (Tex.Civ.App.1898); Hoffman v. Dickson, 65 Wash. 556, 118 P. 737 (1911).

states that a buyer is entitled to "receive a good, clear title transferred to him also in a rightful manner *so that he will not be exposed to a lawsuit in order to protect it.*" (Emphasis added.)  While this language is not required by section 2–312 and is not a logical outgrowth of the pre-Code law, it seems to provide a remedy for the buyer who successfully defends a title suit.  The language of Comment 1 was given effect in American Container Corp. v. Hanley Trucking Corp.[108]  A New Jersey Superior Court found that a buyer of a truck trailer, alleged to have been stolen, could recover from his seller when the truck was seized by the State Police.[109]  The court stated:

> However, I find it unnecessary to rule on these various questions.  I think the relevant one is not whether the semitrailer was properly taken and retained by the State Police, but on whom the burden of contesting the police action should have rested.

> The purchaser of goods warranted as to title has a right to rely on the fact that he will not be required, at some later time, to enter into a contest over the validity of his ownership.  The mere casting of a substantial shadow over his title, regardless of the ultimate outcome, is sufficient to violate a warranty of good title.  The policy advanced here has found expression in the past in cases where courts of equity have refused to order specific performance of contracts for sale of land.[110]

By contrast, a Georgia court has recently found that a third party's invalid attachment of property in the buyer's possession is not a breach of 2–312.[111]  Although it is not clear that the plaintiff in the Georgia case argued the theory of quiet possession, the two cases appear to be in conflict.  In our judgment, the New Jersey rule is better.

However, there is some point at which the third party's claim against the goods becomes so attenuated that we should not regard it as an interference against which the seller has warranted.  The problem lies in defining that point.  While the courts have yet to work out this problem, there are at least two plausible alternatives.  A court might hold a seller liable for expenses incurred in successfully defending against an inferior claim only if the seller knew or had reason to

---

108.  111 N.J.Super. 322, 268 A.2d 313, 7 UCC Rep.Serv. 1301 (Chancery Div. 1970).

109.  Id. at 332, 268 A.2d at 319, 7 UCC Rep.Serv. at 1309.

110.  Id. at 330–31, 268 A.2d at 317–18, 7 UCC Rep.Serv. at 1307.

111.  Cochran v. Horner, 121 Ga.App. 297, 173 S.E.2d 448, 7 UCC Rep.Serv. 707 (1970).  The Oregon Supreme Court reached a similar conclusion under pre-Code law in a case in which

the seller had expressly warranted against all lawful claims.  Price v. The Boot Shop, 75 Ore. 343, 146 P. 1088 (1915).

In Wujnovich v. Colcord, 105 N.H. 451, 202 A.2d 484, 2 UCC Rep.Serv. 238 (1964), a pre-Code case, a buyer failed to recover for breach of warranty of title because he did not prove that the seller did not have good title when he conveyed the car, even though the car was seized on grounds that it was stolen.  The court did not discuss whether the buyer's quiet possession had been disturbed.

know that such a claim was likely to be asserted. Or a court could analogize to the standards used to determine whether title to real property is marketable, specifically, whether the claim is of such a substantial nature to subject the buyer to serious litigation.[112] While this statement of the standard is vague, it at least makes clear that frivolous claims should not give rise to warranty of title liability, and it provides reference to a well-developed body of case law.[113]

Even if courts refuse to read Comment 1 as expanding the warranty of title beyond its pre-Code scope, a buyer faced with an unfounded claim does have a remedy against his seller. At common law and under the Uniform Sales Act, a buyer whose title to purchased personal property was challenged in court could give notice to his seller and request that the seller defend. If the seller then failed to defend and the challenger prevailed, even if by default judgment, the seller would be liable for breach of warranty of title.[114] Sections 2–607(3) (b) and 2–607(5) give the buyer a similar right to offer the litigation to his seller and to hold his seller liable if the seller does not defend.

Section 2–312(3) creates a new warranty "that the goods shall be delivered free of the rightful claim of any third person by way of infringement or the like. . . . " The warranty applies only to merchants dealing regularly in the kind of goods sold. Besides requiring that the seller protect the buyer against patent, trademark, and other similar claims, this section provides that a buyer who furnishes a seller with specifications "must hold the seller harmless" against infringement claims arising from compliance with the specifications. Thus, 2–312(2) is unique in imposing a warranty on the buyer.

Although this section has not yet been litigated, there are two issues that deserve notice. First, the provision only requires that goods "be *delivered* free" (emphasis added) of infringement claims. It could be argued that this language does not protect the buyer against claims arising out of his use or resale of the goods. Although the comments do not help clarify the matter, it has been suggested that the draftsmen probably did not intend such a meaning and that "where the normal, anticipated use of the product infringes a patent, the buyer is entitled to protection."[115] A second question is related to the quiet possession problem involved with the warranty of title. Is the warranty against infringement breached when the buyer incurs litigation expenses in successfully defending against an infringement

---

112. See e. g., Kay v. Carter, 243 La. 1095, 150 So.2d 27 (1963).

113. See, e. g., Wesley v. Eells, 177 U.S. 370 (1900); Clarke v. Title Guaranty Co., 44 Hawaii 261, 353 P.2d 1002 (1960); McCubbin v. Urban, 247 Iowa 862, 77 N.W.2d 36 (1956). See generally 4 American Law of Property § 18.7 (A. Casner ed. 1952).

114. See, e. g., Thomas v. Ferriss, 113 Conn. 539, 155 A. 829 (1931); 8 S. Williston, Williston on Contracts § 980 (3d ed. 1964).

115. Remarks of Professor Pasley in 1 N.Y. State Law Revision Comm'n, 1955 Report 740 (1955).

claim?　One commentator has opined: "A rightful claim is one where the buyer or seller reasonably believes that a third party's infringement charge would probably be upheld by the courts." [116]　In any event, both of these problems will have to be worked out by the courts, which have hardly been inundated with 2–312(3) cases.

### § 9–12　The Warranties of Title and Against Infringement, 2–312—Disclaimer

Unlike the warranties in sections 2–314 and 2–315, the warranty of quiet title is not governed by the disclaimer provision of 2–316. Subsection (2) to 2–312 is the section's own disclaimer provision:

> A warranty under subsection (1) will be excluded or modified only by specific language or by circumstances which give the buyer reason to know that the person selling does not claim title in himself or that he is purporting to sell only such right or title as he or a third person may have.

Comment 5 tells us that "subsection (2) recognizes that sales by sheriffs, executors, foreclosing lienors and persons similarly situated are so out of the ordinary commercial course, that their peculiar character is immediately apparent to the buyer and therefore no personal obligation is imposed upon the seller who is purporting to sell only an unknown or limited right." [117]　Insurance companies, who often purchase the rights of owners of cars that have been stolen from their insured owners and ultimately resell those cars when they are discovered, have argued that they fit within the terms of 2–312(2); that is, that they do not "claim title" in themselves and therefore make no warranty under 2–312.　The only two cases that we have found on the point have rejected that argument and have found that the insurance companies are not "situated like" sheriffs and other similarly situated persons.[118]　Another party who closely resembles the sheriff and executor is the auctioneer.　The Uniform Sales Act expressly excepted auctioneers professing to sell by virtue of authority in fact or in law from the warranty of title,[119] and at common law an auctioneer who disclosed the fact of his agency was not liable for the failure of title of goods auctioned off.[120]　This background plus Comment 5 to section 2–312 should absolve auctioneers from any warranty of title, if they make it clear that they are selling someone else's goods.[121]　However,

---

116.　Dudine, Warranties Against Infringement Under the Uniform Commercial Code, 36 N.Y.S.B.F. 214, 219 (1964).　See also Pasley, supra note 115, at 738–39.

117.　Cf. USA § 13(4).

118.　Spillane v. Liberty Mut. Ins. Co., 65 Misc.2d 290, 317 N.Y.S.2d 203, 8 UCC Rep.Serv. 332 (Civ.Ct.1970); John St. Auto Wrecking v. Motors Ins. Co., 56 Misc.2d 232, 288 N.Y.S.2d 281, 5 UCC Rep.Serv. 112 (Dist.Ct.1968).

119.　USA § 13(4).

120.　See, e. g., Mercer v. Leihy, 139 Mich. 447, 102 N.W 972 (1905) (principal was present at auction); Benton v. Campbell, Parker & Co., Ltd., [1925] 2 K.B. 410, 14 B.R.C. 295, 8 S. Williston, Williston on Contracts § 979 (1964).

121.　In Gaito v. Hoffman, 5 UCC Rep. Serv. 1056, 1058–59 (N.Y.Sup.Ct.1968), the court held that an agent-salesman without interest in the subject

basic principles of agency law do impose on auctioneers a warranty
of their authority to act for a principal,[122] and there is no reason why
an auctioneer should not be held to warrant the title of goods he sells
on his own behalf.

Of course, not only "circumstances" but also "specific language"
can give the buyer reason to know that the person selling does not
claim title or that he is purporting to sell only the right that a third
person may have.[123]  Neither the Code, the comments, nor the cases
tell us exactly what specific language is sufficient to disclaim the
warranty of title.  Certainly one can think of language that would
suffice, for example, "I do not claim title to these goods."  What of
the seller who uses the real property quit-claim language: "Seller
hereby forsakes and quit claims all of his right, title, and interest in
X to buyer."  Is such a statement "specific language" sufficient to
put the buyer on notice that the seller is not claiming title in himself?
Several older cases decided under the common law held such language
sufficient.[124]  In Jones v. Linebaugh,[125] the Michigan Court of Appeals reached a different result.  The buyer in that case offered to
purchase two Bugatti automobiles possessed by the seller.  The seller
explained that he did not have title to the cars, but the buyer asked
him to obtain title.  The seller later said that his attorneys were in
the process of obtaining title for him.  The sale was subsequently
completed, and the buyer received a bill of sale, which provided that
the seller sold and assigned all his "right, title and interest" in the
cars and that to the "best of [his] knowledge there [was] no title in
existence by way of registration with the State of Michigan or with
any other State or with any Nation." [126]  The court followed an old
Michigan case, [127] which it found to be in accord with 2–312(2), and
held that the quoted language was "not precise and free from ambiguity" and then, "as a matter of law, [was] not sufficient to exclude the warranty of title." [128]  We prefer the approach taken in
this case over the older view, which apparently was influenced by

matter of the sale was not liable for
the principal's breach of warranty under 2–312.

**122.** 8 S. Williston, Williston on Contracts § 979 (1964).

**123.** § 2–312(2).

**124.** See, e. g., First Nat'l Bank of
Northampton v. Massachusetts Loan
& Trust Co., 123 Mass. 330 (1877);
Gould v. Bourgeois, 51 N.J.L. 361, 18
A. 64 (1889); Krumbhaar v. Birch,
83 Pa. 426 (1877).  But in Croly v.
Pollard, 71 Mich. 612, 39 N.W. 853
(1888), similar language was held in-
sufficient in light of other circum-
stances.

**125.** 34 Mich.App. 305, 191 N.W.2d 142,
9 UCC Rep.Serv. 1187 (1971).

**126.** Id. at 309, 191 N.W.2d at 144, 9
UCC Rep.Serv. at 1189.

**127.** Croly v. Pollard, 71 Mich. 612, 39
N.W. 853 (1888).  See note 124 supra.

**128.** 34 Mich.App. at 309, 191 N.W.2d
at 144, 9 UCC Rep.Serv. at 1190.  A
dissenting opinion argued that the case
presented "circumstances which give
the buyer reason to know that the
person selling does not claim title in
himself or that he is purporting to
sell only such right or title as he or
a third person may have."  See § 2–
312(2).

real property law, since it accords with the rigid standards for warranty disclaimer in section 2–316.[129]

Like section 2–315, 2–312 is an unremarkable and relatively mature provision. It provides a persistent trickle of litigation, but most of the cases do not offer difficult or novel points of law. To the extent that the doctrine is still growing, that growth concerns two questions: (*1*) what disturbance is sufficient to give the plaintiff a cause of action, and (*2*) what are the damages?

---

**129.** See Ch. 12 infra. But see Menzel v. List, 24 N.Y.2d 91, 246 N.E.2d 742, 298 N.Y.S.2d 979, 6 UCC Rep.Serv. 330, 336 (1969), a non-Code case in which the court suggests in dicta that the sellers of a painting could have avoided liability under the warranty of title by selling "subject to

any existing lawful claims unknown to them at the time of the sale."

The warranty against infringement in section 2–312(3) is applicable "[u]nless otherwise agreed." This phrase does not appear to be as stringent as the "specific language" requirement in 2–312(2).

# CHAPTER 10

# DAMAGES FOR BREACH OF WARRANTY

*Analysis*

Sec.
10–1. Introduction.
10–2. Damages for Breach of Warranty—The Basic Formula, 2–714(1)
      and (2).
10–3. —— Incidental Damages, 2–715(1).
10–4. —— Consequential Damages.

## § 10–1 Introduction

At the outset, we should distinguish the cases treated in Chapter Six on buyer's remedies and Chapter Eight on acceptance, rejection, and revocation from the cases to be covered here. In the former chapters we treated buyer's rights under 2–712 (cover) and 2–713 (contract-market damages) when the seller failed to deliver or when the buyer rightly rejected or revoked his acceptance of delivered goods. In this chapter we will be mostly concerned with cases in which the buyer accepts the goods, does not reject or revoke his acceptance, but sues for damages because the accepted goods are not as warranted. The principal Code section that governs the rights of a buyer who has accepted nonconforming goods is 2–714. We believe that only buyers who have accepted and neither rejected nor revoked can use 2–714. Thus, in our view, sections 2–713 and 2–712 on the one hand and 2–714 on the other are mutually exclusive. Section 2–714 reads in full as follows:

> (1) Where the buyer has accepted goods and given notification (subsection (3) of Section 2–607) he may recover as damages for any nonconformity of tender the loss resulting in the ordinary course of events from the seller's breach as determined in any manner which is reasonable.

> (2) The measure of damages for breach of warranty is the difference at the time and place of acceptance between the value of the goods accepted and the value they would have had if they had been as warranted, unless special circumstances show proximate damages of a different amount.

> (3) In a proper case any incidental and consequential damages under the next section may also be recovered.

In the concluding portions of this chapter, we will consider section 2–715 on buyer's incidental and consequential damages. That discussion will treat not only the buyer who accepts goods and neither rejects nor revokes but also the buyer who has rejected, revoked, or who has never received the goods that the seller promised. In that portion, we offer a taste of that bitter pill from first-year contracts, Hadley v. Baxendale.[1]  We now turn to the basic damages formula under 2–714.

## § 10–2  Damages for Breach of Warranty—The Basic Formula, 2–714(1) and (2)

Section 2–714(1) states the general rule—the buyer may recover any damages "resulting in the ordinary course of events from the seller's breach as determined in any manner which is reasonable. . . ."[2]  But section 2–714(2) states the time honored and most commonly applied formula, namely, that the buyer gets the difference at the time of acceptance between "the value of the goods accepted and the value they would have had if they had been as warranted . . .."[3]  One should first note an important element of damages that the buyer will not recover under 2–714 but that he might recover under 2–713 or 2–712.  That element is the cost of a bad bargain. Assume, for example, that a buyer has agreed to purchase tomatoes for a total price of $5,000 but that the market price is only $4,000 at the time of delivery.  If the buyer accepts the tomatoes despite the fact that they are not as warranted and then sues under 2–714, he will recover the difference between $4,000 (their value had they been as warranted) and their actual value.  If, on the other hand, he rejects the tomatoes, revokes his acceptance, or never receives the tomatoes, he would have an opportunity to cover in the $4,000 market and so escape the $1,000 bad bargain.

Note that the converse is not true.  Section 2–714 does award the buyer the benefit of a good bargain.  Assume in our hypothetical case that the price of tomatoes has risen at the time of delivery such that the agreed upon tomatoes would have had a fair market value of $7,000 had they been as warranted.  Because they are somewhat defective, the tomatoes' actual market value is only $6,500.  Under the formula set out in section 2–714(2), our buyer could recover the difference between the value of the goods accepted ($6,500) and the value they would have had if they had been as warranted ($7,000) and so get the benefit of the good bargain he struck.  Note that our hypo-

---

1.  156 Eng.Rep. 145 (Ex.1854).

2.  See Section 10–3 infra.

3.  Damages for breach of warranty, or any other breach of contract, may be asserted as an affirmative defense to an action brought by the seller for the purchase price.  Section 2–717 provides:

The buyer on notifying the seller of his intention to do so may deduct all or any part of the damages resulting from any breach of the contract from any part of the price still due under the same contract.

In permitting the buyer to deduct damages resulting from a breach, the Code has followed the common law.  See 3 S. Williston, Sales of Goods §§ 605–607 (1948); Uniform Sales Act § 69(1)(a).  The operation of section 2–717 does not require judicial action if the seller is willing to acquiesce in the buyer's deduction.  Section 2–717 can also be used as the basis for a declaratory judgment.  In Pendarvis v. General Motors Corp., 6 UCC Rep. Serv. 457, 459 (N.Y.Sup.Ct.1969), the court held that if a buyer could prove a breach of warranty, he would be entitled to a declaratory judgment that he was not indebted for all or a part of the balance due on an automobile.

thetical case is a deviation from the usual rule discussed below in which the court will accept the market price as the best measurement of the value that the goods would have had if they had been as warranted.

In the following pages we will deal with three lawyer questions, all generally related to the definition of the formula contained in section 2–714(2):

(*1*) By what guidelines does one measure the "value" of the goods accepted and their "value" if they had been as warranted?

(*2*) To what extent is the measurement of value subjective (that is, determined by the particular need of the plaintiff buyer as opposed to the general market measurement)?

(*3*) What are the "special circumstances" that might show proximate damages of a different amount?

*Measure of Value*

The 2–714(2) formula (difference between the value of goods as accepted and the value of goods as warranted) is essentially the same as the pre-Code formula.[4]  A useful objective measurement of the difference in value as is and as warranted is the cost of repair. Thus, if a buyer accepts a truck with a defective radiator, a good measure of the difference between the value of the truck as warranted and its value as delivered is the price of a new radiator less the value of the faulty one.   Cox Motor Car Co. v. Castle [5] provides a larger scale example.  The buyer purchased a new truck under an agreement in which the seller's liability was limited to replacement of defective parts.  The truck continually shimmied, but the dealer refused to do anything about the problem.  Said the court:

> Under those circumstances, we think that the whole truck properly may be considered one big defective part, and the measure of damages would be the cost of replacing the truck with one not defective, which would be the same as the difference in market value.[6]

4. C. McCormick, Law of Damages § 176 at 672 (1935). Cases involving the sale of seeds provide good examples: Klein v. Asgrow Seed Co., 246 Cal.App.2d 87, 54 Cal.Rptr. 609 (3d Dist.1966) (similar formula used under Uniform Sales Act); White v. Miller, 71 N.Y. 118 (1877) (value of crop of Bristol cabbage that would ordinarily have been produced under existing conditions less value of crop actually produced with seeds of inferior quality).

5. 402 S.W.2d 429, 3 UCC Rep.Serv. 397 (Ky.Ct.App.1966).

6. Id. at 431, 3 UCC Rep.Serv. at 399–400. See also Water Works & Indus. Supply Co. v. Wilburn, 437 S.W.2d 951, 5 UCC Rep.Serv. 1169 (Ky.Ct. App.1968).  In Le Blanc v. Newman Comet-Lincoln-Mercury, Inc., 6 Conn. Cir. 367, 273 A.2d 726, 8 UCC Rep. Serv. 833 (1970), the court refused to limit damages for breach of warranty to the fair market value of the cost repair and replacement of defective parts of a new car. A background of numerous unsuccessful repairs and replacements suggested that the car could not be placed in warranted condition.

There are many cases in which the injury will be irreparable, and therefore the costs of repair will not serve as a yardstick of the buyer's damages. In such cases, the court will have to determine by some other measure the value of the goods as warranted and the value of the goods as accepted. The contract price offers strong evidence of the value of the goods as warranted.[7] On goods such as commodities that are traded on an open market, price quotations may be helpful.[8] In such cases, finding the value of defective goods as accepted is likely to be more difficult. In one case involving peaches, the court used the price of a prompt resale as the appropriate measure.[9] In W & W Enterprises, Inc. v. Dennler,[10] the Iowa Supreme Court adopted a more radical solution. It held that the value at the time of delivery of feeder pigs so infected with pneumonia and other diseases that they eventually died was zero. Thus, the court allowed

Since Section 2–714(2) states that it provides the "measure of damages for breach of warranty," that formula applies to breaches of warranty of title. In this respect the Code has changed, or at least made uniform, the previously existing law. See Annot., 13 A.L.R.2d 1372 (1950) (at least four different formulas mentioned in state-by-state analysis). Probably because such breaches frequently were not discovered until long after the sale, at which time the item's value would have greatly depreciated, the courts often required the buyer to compute his damages according to the value of the item at the time of dispossession. C. McCormick, Law of Damages, § 176 at 678 (1935). A unique twist occurred in Menzel v. List, 24 N.Y.2d 91, 246 N.E.2d 742, 6 UCC Rep.Serv. 330 (1969). The buyer purchased a Chagall painting in 1955 for $4,000. In 1962, the painting's true owner, who had lost it during the German invasion of Belgium during World War II, sued the buyer and recovered the painting. The buyer sued his seller in a non-Code case and recovered the full fair market value of the painting as of the date the true owner recovered it, a total of $22,500. The court reasoned that such a recovery was necessary in order to put the buyer in the same position he would have been in had there been no breach.

Section 2–714(2), however, requires that the values used in determining difference money damages are to be measured as of "the time and place of acceptance." A Massachusetts court applied this formula in Miles v. Lyons, 42 Mass.App.Dec. 77, 6 UCC Rep.Serv. 659 (1969). A woman sold furniture, which actually belonged to her estranged husband, for $100 when it was worth $275. The husband recovered the furniture from the buyer, and the buyer then recovered damages of $275 in a suit against the fraudulent seller. See also Gaito v. Hoffman, 5 UCC Rep.Serv. 1056 (N.Y.Sup. Ct.1968) (buyer recovered $1200 he had paid to discharge tax lien on automobile, which presumably was equal to the amount by which the value of the car was reduced by the tax lien on the date of acceptance); John St. Auto Wrecking v. Motor Ins. Co., 56 Misc.2d 232, 288 N.Y.S.2d 281, 5 UCC Rep.Serv. 112 (Dist.Ct.1968) (buyer recovered purchase price, apparently equal market value, he paid to insurance company for stolen car).

7. David Pepper Co. v. Jack Keller Co., 28 Agri.Dec. 474, 6 UCC Rep.Serv. 673 (1969) (sale of unmerchantable peaches); W & W Livestock Enterprises, Inc. v. Dennler, 179 N.W.2d 484, 8 UCC Rep.Serv. 169 (Iowa 1970) (sale of diseased pigs); K & C, Inc. v. Westinghouse Elec. Corp., 437 Pa. 303, 262 A.2d 390, 7 UCC Rep.Serv. 679 (1970) (sale of coin operated dry cleaners). (dicta).

8. See, e. g., Jerome Kantro Co. v. Summers Bros., Inc., 27 Agri.Dec. 129, 5 UCC Rep.Serv. 135 (1968) (lettuce price quotations from Federal Market News Service).

9. David Pepper Co. v. Jack Keller Co., 28 Agri.Dec. 474, 6 UCC Rep.Serv. 673 (1969).

10. 179 N.W.2d 484, 8 UCC Rep.Serv. 169 (Iowa 1970).

the buyer to recover his purchase price, the value of healthy pigs.[11] Such a measure may have been appropriate in that case; however, defective goods will normally have at least scrap value, and it should be a rare case in which the buyer can recover his full price under 2–714(2). For a discussion of the problem of defining "market value" see Section 6–4 above.

In sum, the general application of the 2–714(2) formula offers a variety of difficult factual problems but few questions that are unique or legally difficult. In many cases the court can refer to the cost of repair in order to estimate the difference in value of the goods as warranted and as delivered. In other cases it will have to cast about for the usual and almost invariably unsatisfactory evidence of market value.

### Subjective or Objective?

Occasionally, the value of the goods to the particular buyer may not be the same as their value to a class of buyers in general. For example, a seller might deliver steel of a different gauge than called for in the contract. The value of such steel on the market might be ten per cent lower than the value of the steel for which the contract called, yet this difference in gauge of steel might render it wholly unsuitable for the buyer's purposes; on the other hand, the lesser-gauge steel might be ninety-eight percent effective for the buyer's purposes. When the value of the steel to this buyer (the subjective value) differs from its value to a general class of buyers (the objective value), to what extent does one adjust the formula to take account of the individual needs of the buyer? Professor Peters has suggested that the value of the goods accepted is intended to be "a personalized criterion designed to allow the buyer . . . to show that the goods accepted are less valuable to him than their market price would otherwise indicate." [12] Likewise, one may argue that the other part of the formula, the value of the goods as warranted, should be subjectively measured because the draftsmen failed to use the objective term "market price," the term that they did use in section 2–713(1). As we have indicated,[13] the value of goods as warranted will seldom be in dispute, for the contract price will be a powerful measure of that end of the formula. On the other end, the outcome is not so clear. Section 1–106, which states that the aggrieved party should get only those damages necessary to "put him in as good a position as if the other party had fully performed," suggests that the court should use a subjective measure, at least in those cases in which an objective measure would over-compensate the buyer.[14] The same

11.  Id. at 490, 8 UCC Rep.Serv. at 177.

12.  Peters, Remedies for Breach of Contracts Relating to the Sale of Goods Under the Uniform Commercial Code: A Roadmap for Article Two, 73 Yale L.J. 199, 269 (1963).

13.  See notes 7–8 supra and the accompanying text.

14.  Consider, for example, our case in which the seller delivered steel having a substantially smaller market value, but only a slightly smaller value

section of the Code would seem to argue for the use of a subjective standard in cases in which that standard would increase the buyer's damages, because, by hypothesis in such cases, the buyer needs the additional damages to put him in as good a position as performance would have.

## Special Circumstances

We would arrive at the "subjective" outcome not by bending the word "value" in the formula but by an expansive definition of the last clause in 2–714(2). That clause authorizes a different amount of damages when "special circumstances show proximate damages of a different amount."

Most of the cases to date have used objective criteria for determining market value, and none of the cases discussing special circumstances addresses itself to our problem.[15] Even if one accepts the proposition that special circumstances should be expansively construed, he will have interpretive difficulties in measuring the appropriate amount of buyer's damages. Assume, for example, that a buyer purchases a truck that proves to be subject to a $2,000 tax lien in the State of New York. The buyer operates only in California, and his operations will therefore be unaffected by the presence of the New York lien, which can be enforced only in that state. The seller will argue that this special circumstance renders the $2,000 tax lien irrelevant and that the buyer has suffered no damages because of the lien. Note, however, that the buyer's resale value may be reduced because of the lien. On that basis, we would argue that the buyer should receive some recovery because of the presence of the lien.

Section 2–714(2) carries forward the pre-Code law and measure of damages for accepted goods that are in breach of warranty. In many cases, courts will find a ready measure of damages by using the cost of repair that the buyer has incurred or will incur in order to bring the goods delivered up to snuff. In other cases the courts will have to turn to the familiar but difficult standards for measuring value. In all such cases the courts should give due concern to the particular needs of the buyer.

---

to the particular buyer, than the steel specified in the contract.

15. The courts have generally assumed that the 2–714(2) formula represents the floor of recovery in breach-of-warranty cases. See, e. g., Spada Distrib. Co. v. Belson, 26 Agri.Dec. 888, 4 UCC Rep.Serv. 743 (1967) (when consequential damages ruled out, buyer limited to difference money damages); City Mach. & Mfg. Co. v. A. & A. Mach. Corp., 4 UCC Rep.Serv. 461 (E.D.N.Y.

1967) (in considering special circumstances, the court mentioned only incidental and consequential damages). The Supreme Court of Pennsylvania, in Keystone Diesel Engine Co. v. Irwin, 411 Pa. 222, 191 A.2d 376, 1 UCC Rep.Serv. 184 (1963), interpreted the phrase "special circumstances" as a prerequisite to the recovery of incidental and consequential damages under 2–714(3) and 2–715. See Section 10–4 infra (Hadley v. Baxendale).

## § 10–3  Damages for Breach of Warranty—Incidental Damages, 2–715(1)

In Chapter 6 we discussed the buyer's remedies in regard to goods that he does not retain (because they are never delivered or because he rejects or revokes acceptance). This chapter has thus far dealt only with breaches of warranty involving goods accepted. Since sections 2–712(2) (cover),[16] 2–713 (buyer's damages for nondelivery or repudiation),[17] and 2–714(3),[18] all permit the buyer to recover incidental and consequential damages (the subjects of 2–715), the remainder of the discussion in this chapter is applicable to any kind of seller's breach. Section 2–715(1) provides:

> Incidental damages resulting from the seller's breach include expenses reasonably incurred in inspection, receipt, transportation and care and custody of goods rightfully rejected, any commercially reasonable charges, expenses or commissions in connection with effecting cover and any other reasonable expense incident to the delay or other breach.

What are incidental damages? Note first that they must "result from the seller's breach" and be reasonable expenses "incidental" to the breach. Section 2–715(1) lists many expenses that are included as incidental damages. However, Comment 1 to 2–715 stresses that those listed "are not intended to be exhaustive" but are merely illustrative of the typical kinds of incidental expenses that can be recovered under 2–715: (1) those associated with rightful rejection [19] (for instance, inspection and storage); (2) those associated with a proper revocation of acceptance; [20] and (3) those involved in effecting cover.[21]

The wording of 2–715(1) and the comment thereto indicates that the draftsmen intended to reimburse the buyer for expenses causally related to the breach and to leave damages related to the value of the bargain to the coverage of 2–715(2). For example, in Grandi v. LeSage,[22] the buyer purchased a race horse for breeding purposes. The seller had represented the horse to be a stallion; in fact the horse was a gelding. The buyer revoked acceptance under 2–608 and brought suit to recover the purchase price and incidental damages.[23] The final award included incidental damages for the

---

16. See Section 6–2 supra.

17. See Section 6–4 supra.

18. Section 10–4 infra.

19. See § 2–602.

20. See § 2–608.

21. See § 2–712.

22. 74 N.M. 799, 399 P.2d 285, 2 UCC Rep.Serv. 455 (1965).

23. The case is one of the relatively few contract cases in which a court acknowledged the applicability of punitive damages. The court found that since section 2–711 "permits recovery of damages in an action for rescission, punitive damages may likewise be recovered in such action where the breach is accompanied by fraudulent acts which are wanton, malicious and

care, feeding, and maintenance of the horse for about three months at $1.50 per day.[24]  The Oregon court, in Lanners v. Whitney,[25] granted a similar recovery.  The buyer revoked his acceptance of an airplane that the seller had misrepresented as airworthy.  The court approved the buyer's return of the aircraft and allowed "expenses reasonably incurred as a result of seller's breach, including those incurred in the care and custody of the goods." [26]  Included in the recovery were "the amounts spent in repair on the aircraft on the Chicago trip, amounts spent to preserve the craft after the Chicago trip, including cost of removal of the radio and battery, installation of storage oil, ground insurance and storage charges." [27]  An example of an award of incidental damages in a breach-of-warranty case is Lewis v. Mobil Oil Corp.,[28] in which the seller supplied unsuitable oil to the buyer's hydraulic saw mill system.  The oil caused the system to work improperly for two and one-half years.  The court found that the seller had breached its warranty of fitness for a particular purpose,[29] and it held that the buyer was entitled to incidental damages for amounts spent on excessive quantities of oil used and on repairs and replacement of mechanical parts damaged by the failure of the oil to function as warranted.[30]

A greedy plaintiff might interpret the liberal recovery of incidental damages allowed by the Code as an invitation to seek recovery of expenses remotely connected to the breach.  For example, an aggrieved buyer might purchase a substitute that does not qualify as a cover because its purchase occurred beyond a "reasonable time." [31] If he then sues for contract-market damages under 2–713, can he also recover the charges incurred in finding the substitute on the grounds that they were a "reasonable expense incident to the delay or other breach"?  Comment 1 to 2–715 indicates that such charges should not be recovered, since the expenses were not incurred "in connection with the handling of rightfully rejected goods or goods whose acceptance may be justifiably revoked, or in connection with effecting cover where the breach of the contract lies in nonconformity or nondelivery of the goods." [32]  Moreover, since the substitute was not purchased within a reasonable time, its purchase price should not

intentional."  Id. at 810, 399 P.2d at 293, 2 UCC Rep.Serv. at 463.

24.  Id. at 803, 399 P.2d at 288, 2 UCC Rep.Serv. at 457–58.

25.  247 Ore. 223, 428 P.2d 398, 4 UCC Rep.Serv. 369 (1967).

26.  Id. at 236, 428 P.2d at 404, 4 UCC Rep.Serv. at 379.

27.  Id. at 236–37, 428 P.2d at 404, 4 UCC Rep.Serv. at 379.

28.  438 F.2d 500, 8 UCC Rep.Serv. 625 (8th Cir. 1971).

29.  Id. at 507, 8 UCC Rep.Serv. at 636.

30.  Id. at 508, 8 UCC Rep.Serv. at 636–37.

31.  Section 2–712(1) requires that cover be made "without unreasonable delay."

32.  One might argue that expenses in addition to those "in connection with effecting cover" must have been intended by the language "any other reasonable expense incident to the delay or other breach," but Comment 1 to 2–715 suggests that the draftsmen did not so intend.

be deemed a "reasonable expense." [33]   We are clear that the causal link between the breach and the damages becomes so attenuated at some point that the damages are no longer "incidental to the breach." We decline to predict where one should draw that line in the thousands of fact situations that can present themselves.

## § 10–4   Damages for Breach of Warranty—Consequential Damages

### Hadley v. Baxendale

Most of the law regarding consequential damages can be traced back to the classic English case, Hadley v. Baxendale.[34]   For those readers who somehow missed that crucial day (or week) in first-semester contracts when *Hadley's* depths were plumbed, we briefly restate the facts.   An employee of the plaintiff brought a shaft, which was vital to the operation of the plaintiff's mill, to the defendant-carrier.   The defendants' clerk agreed to carry it to Greenwich, where the shaft was needed in order to serve as a model for producing a replacement.   The defendants neglectfully delayed delivery of the shaft, and the plaintiff sued for lost profits that resulted from the extended incapacity of the mill.   After reviewing these facts, the Court of the Exchequer announced The Rule, knowledge of which has become a *sine qua non* to second-year standing in law school:

> Where two parties have made a contract which one of them has broken, the damages which the other party ought to receive in respect of such breach of contract should be such as may fairly and reasonably be considered either arising naturally, i. e., according to the usual course of things, from such breach of contract itself, or such as may reasonably be supposed to have been in the contemplation of both parties, at the time they made the contract, as the probable result of the breach of it.   Now, if the special circumstances under which the contract was actually made were communicated by the plaintiffs to the defendants, and thus known to both parties, the damages resulting from the breach of such a contract, which they would reasonably contemplate, would be the amount of injury which would ordinarily follow from a breach of contract under these special circumstances so known and communicated.   But, on the other hand, if these special circumstances were wholly unknown to the party breaking the contract, he, at the most, could only be supposed to have had in his contemplation the amount of injury which would arise generally, and in the

---

33.  Another way to limit incidental damages in this situation would be to determine that damages caused by purchasing a substitute that is not a cover are *per se* unreasonable.

34.  156 Eng.Rep. 145 (Ex.1854).

great multitude of cases not affected by any special circumstances, from such a breach of contract.[35]

In regard to the particular facts before it, the court concluded that lost profits due to the inoperation of the mill

> . . . cannot reasonably be considered such a consequence of the breach of contract as could have been fairly and reasonably contemplated by both the parties when they made this contract. For such loss would neither have flowed naturally from the breach of this contract in the great multitude of such cases occurring under ordinary circumstances, nor were the special circumstances, which, perhaps, would have made it a reasonable and natural consequence of such breach of contract, communicated to or known by the defendants.[36]

## The Foreseeability Test

The immediate result of Hadley v. Baxendale was two-fold: (1) the rule placed a limit on the recoveries that juries could grant for breach of contract and thus reduced business risk somewhat,[37] yet at the same time (2) it provided a mechanism by which victims of contract breaches could recover damages peculiar to their special circumstances.[38] The language of the opinion was sufficiently vague that courts in England and America have struggled for more than a century with the question: How much notice of the special circumstances must the breacher have in order to hold him liable for special loss?[39] Is it necessary that the parties actually discuss the

35. Id. at 151.

36. Id.

37. C. McCormick, Law of Damages § 138 at 567 (1935).

38. 11 S. Williston, Williston on Contracts § 1356 at 291 (3d ed. 1968).

39. This interpretive problem may have stemmed from the statement of facts preceding Baron Alderson's opinion which said, "The plaintiff's servant told the [defendant's] clerk that the mill was stopped, and that the shaft must be sent immediately . . . ." 156 Eng.Rep. at 147. Authorities have differed over the effect of that statement. Professor McCormick concluded that the court decided that this information did not constitute notice to the defendant of the plaintiff's special circumstances sufficient to hold the defendant liable for the special loss. C. McCormick, Law of Damages § 140 at 573 (1935). The English courts, however, have now recognized that the Hadley court either rejected or was unaware of such evidence. Victoria Laundry (Windsor) Ltd. v. Newman Indus. Ltd., [1949] 2 K.B. 528, 537.

Obviously, a court's view of the facts in *Hadley* will color its opinion regarding the effect of the rule announced in the case. On the basis of the facts, as reported, it is not surprising Justice Holmes concluded from his reading of Hadley v. Baxendale that "mere notice to a seller of some interests or probable action of the buyer is not enough necessarily and as a matter of law to charge the seller with special damage on that account if he fails to deliver the goods." Globe Ref. Co. v. Landa Cotton Oil Co., 190 U.S. 540, 545 (1903) (breach of contract to sell and deliver crude oil). According to Holmes, the extent of a defendant's liability "should be worked out on terms which it fairly may be presumed he would have assented to if they had been presented to his mind." Id. at 543.

buyer's special circumstances and that the seller consciously assume the risk of consequent loss in case of his breach? Or is it enough that the seller know of the buyer's situation?

The courts have adopted two approaches to this question. The more restrictive or "tacit-agreement" test permits the plaintiff to recover damages arising from special circumstances only if "the defendant fairly may be supposed to have assumed consciously, or to have warranted the plaintiff reasonably to suppose that it assumed, [such liability] when the contract was made." [40] In effect, this test requires the plaintiff to prove that the parties had specifically contemplated that consequential damages might result and that the defendant actually assumed the risk of such damages.[41] The other group of cases, and certainly the recent trend of authority, has rejected this test. As Professor Corbin said:

> All that is necessary, in order to charge the defendant with the particular loss, is that it is one that ordinarily follows the breach of such a contract in the usual course of events, or that reasonable men in the position of the parties would have foreseen as a probable result of breach.[42]

The Code draftsmen agreed with this latter view and stated: "The 'tacit agreement' test for the recovery of consequential damages is rejected." [43] Section 2–715(2) holds the defendant liable for "any loss resulting from general or particular requirements for which the seller at the time of contracting *had reason to know.* . . ." (emphasis added). In other words, "the test is one of reasonable foreseeability of probable consequences." [44] This objective formulation is wholly consistent with the language used by Baron Alderson himself, "[The defendant is liable for such loss] as may *reasonably be supposed* to have been in the contemplation of both parties." [45] The Baron went on to say that if the buyer communicated

---

**40.** Globe Ref. Co. v. Landa Cotton Oil Co., 190 U.S. 540, 544 (1903). See also note 39 supra.

**41.** At one point in *Hadley*, the court suggested that "had the special circumstances been known, the parties might have specially provided for the breach of contract by special terms." 156 Eng.Rep. at 151. That statement, however, is only a suggestion of what the defendant could have done if he had been aware of the special circumstances; it was not intended as a test for foreseeability or as the fundamental rationale for the rule of the case. The tacit-agreement test is discussed and criticized in 5 A. Corbin, Corbin on Contracts §§ 1008–12 (1964); C. McCormick, Law of Damages § 176 (1935); 11 S. Williston, Williston on Contracts § 1357 (3d ed. 1968).

**42.** 5 A. Corbin, Corbin on Contracts § 1010 at 79 (1964).

**43.** § 2–715, Comment 2, cited in Adams v. J. I. Case Co., 125 Ill.App.2d 388, 405, 261 N.E.2d 1, 9, 7 UCC Rep.Serv. 1271, 1278 (1970). But see Keystone Diesel Engine Co. v. Irwin, 411 Pa. 222, 191 A.2d 376, 1 UCC Rep.Serv. 184 (1963).

**44.** Gerwin v. Southeastern Cal. Ass'n of Seventh Day Adventists, 14 Cal. App.3d 209, 221, 92 Cal.Rptr. 111, 118, 8 UCC Rep.Serv. 643, 653 (4th Dist. 1971). *Gerwin* is discussed in text accompanying notes 66–67 infra.

**45.** 156 Eng.Rep. at 151 (emphasis added). See text accompanying note 35 supra. One court has said that section 2–715 "codifies the rule enunciated in Hadley v. Baxendale." Ger-

"special circumstances" to the seller, the loss that would ordinarily follow in such circumstances should be compensable because the parties should reasonably have contemplated it, that is, because such loss would have been foreseeable.  Similarly, under the Code, the seller is liable for consequential damages when he had reason to know of the buyer's general or particular requirements at the time of contracting, regardless of whether he consciously assumed the risk of such loss.[46]

With this knowledge of the common law forebearers of 2–715(2), we turn to judicial interpretations of the section itself.  The courts have been a bit fractious, and the first court to face the question applied the tacit-agreement test.  In Keystone Diesel Engine Co. v. Irvin,[47] the plaintiff sold the defendant a truck engine which failed to work properly.  The defendant performed repair services for which the plaintiff refused to pay, and the plaintiff sued to collect the amount due.  The Pennsylvania Supreme Court upheld the defendant's counterclaim for breach of the implied warranty of merchant-

win v. Southeastern Cal. Ass'n of Seventh Day Adventists, 14 Cal.App. 3d 209, 221, 92 Cal.Rptr. 111, 118, 8 UCC Rep.Serv. 643, 653 (4th Dist. 1971), discussed in text accompanying notes 66–67 infra.

The English courts have recently reaffirmed the objective, reasonable-man standard: "It suffices that, if [the defendant] had considered the question, he would as a *reasonable man* have concluded that the loss in question was liable to result." Victoria Laundry (Windsor) Ltd. v. Newman Indus. Ltd., [1949] 2 K.B. 528, 540 (emphasis added).  For further support of the proposition that Hadley v. Baxendale applies a reasonable-man standard, see Krauss v. Greenbarg, 137 F.2d 569, 571 (3d Cir. 1943).

46.  § 2–715, Comment 3.  The Code therefore rejects the oft-suggested rationale that the rule of Hadley v. Baxendale protects the seller against insuring risks for which, had he been aware of them, he would have demanded a greater compensation.  See 5 A. Corbin, Corbin on Contracts § 1008 at 74 (1964).

Another aspect of *Hadley* should be mentioned. Baron Alderson really talked about two kinds of contract damages: (*1*) those arising naturally or in the *ordinary* course of things from the breach and (*2*) those that ordinarily follow from a breach of contract under *special* circumstances. The latter type of damages could be recovered only if the special circumstances were communicated to the seller.  See text accompanying note 35 supra.  Section 2–715 also recognizes these two forms of damages.  The first category, those arising in the ordinary course of things, is covered in the incidental-damage definition of subsection (1) and the "general requirements" language of subsection (2).  As we have seen, incidental damages include handling and cover charges.  Comment 3 states that "general needs must rarely be made known to charge the seller with knowledge."  In other words, losses resulting from the buyer's general needs arise in the ordinary course of things.  For example, if Amalgamated Aluminum contracted to sell 1000 pans to Harry's Hardware Store, an obvious general need of Harry would be that the pans be in salable condition.  See § 2–715, Comment 6.  If the pans are full of holes, Amalgamated should be responsible for Harry's lost profits from lost sales and for his expenses for storage and handling.  Note that lost resale profits may be fully compensated by difference money damages under 2–714 or contract-market price differential under 2–713; thus, further damages under 2–715(2) may be available.  But if Harry needed the pans in order to fill an unusually lucrative resale contract, Amalgamated would not be responsible for those extra profits unless it had reason to know of that contract.

47.  411 Pa. 222, 191 A.2d 376, 1 UCC Rep.Serv. 184 (1963).

ability of the engine, but refused to award lost profits for the twenty-seven days that the truck could not be used.[48]  The court acknowledged that the seller knew the buyer was a contract carrier, that a failure of the engine to function properly would undoubtedly give rise to lost profits resulting from inability to use the truck, and that damages for such loss could easily be computed; it nevertheless refused to allow the lost profits as damages because there was no evidence that the buyer had put the seller on notice of an intent to hold him liable for lost profits resulting from the inability to use the engine.[49]  Such a result is out of harmony with the language of section 2–715(2) and of Comments 2 and 3.  The opinion reveals that the seller knew or at least had reason to know that the buyer, a contract carrier, needed the engine for propelling one of his trucks and that he should have foreseen that if the engine failed to work there would be a loss of profits.  Under those circumstances, the buyer should have recovered his lost profits.

In Adams v. J. I. Case Co.,[50] the Illinois Court of Appeals hewed closer to the draftmen's intent.  A bulldozer contractor had purchased a crawler loader tractor that proved to be defective, and he alleged that the seller failed to make repairs called for in its warranty.  The court explicitly rejected the *Keystone* reasoning and held that the buyer's allegation that his particular needs and existing contracts were known to the seller sufficed to show special circumstances that justified the recovery of consequential damages in the form of lost profits.[51]  Most other courts that have considered the questions of consequential damages have followed the objective approach used in *Adams* rather than the tacit-agreement approach of *Keystone*.[52]

### Types of Consequential Damages

Finding that one qualifies for consequential damages is only the beginning of the story; one next needs to know what kinds of loss

**48.**  Id. at 225–26, 191 A.2d at 379, 1 UCC Rep.Serv. at 187.

**49.**  Id. at 225–26, 191 A.2d at 379, 1 UCC Rep.Serv. at 186.

**50.**  125 Ill.App.2d 388, 261 N.E.2d 1, 7 UCC Rep.Serv. 1271 (1970).

**51.**  Id. at 406, 261 N.E.2d at 9–10, 7 UCC Rep.Serv. at 1278–79.

**52.**  See, e. g., Lewis v. Mobil Oil Corp., 438 F.2d 500, 8 UCC Rep.Serv. 625 (8th Cir. 1971) (seller of goods to manufacturing enterprise should know that defective goods will disrupt production); Marion Power Shovel Co. v. Huntsman, 246 Ark. 152, 437 S.W.2d 784, 6 UCC Rep.Serv. 100 (1969) (no consequential damages for loss of soybean crop, because seller had no reason to know that buyer bought power-er shovel to prepare land for raising soybeans); Valley Die Cast Corp. v. A. C. W., Inc., 25 Mich.App. 321, 181 N.W.2d 303, 8 UCC Rep.Serv. 488 (1970) (seller should have known that renovation costs for replacing car wash system would be necessary in case original system failed; alternatively, seller had reason to know of buyer's particular purpose).  But see Head & Guild Equip. Co. v. Bond, 470 S.W.2d 909 (Tex.Civ.App. 1971).  In that case, despite the testimony of the defendant's sales manager that he knew that the plaintiff-contractor wanted the subject drag line to dig fish ponds, the court found that the contract to dig fish ponds was not "known to or in contemplation of" the parties; held, plaintiff cannot recover lost profits.

can be recouped as consequential damages. *Hadley, Keystone,* and *Adams* illustrate that the most commonly litigated and doubtless the most often sought after item of consequential damages is lost profits. We have seen that most cases decided under the Code have permitted the recovery of lost profits if such damages are sufficiently foreseeable.[53]  In fact, the recovery of lost profits is becoming commonplace in at least one important area.  The United States Court of Appeals for the Eighth Circuit, applying the Arkansas Code, has recently held:

> Where a seller provides goods to a manufacturing enterprise with knowledge that they are to be used in the manufacturing process, it is reasonable to assume that he should know the defective goods will cause a disruption of production, and loss of profits is a natural consequence of such disruption. Hence, loss of profits should be recoverable under these circumstances.[54]

In the *Lewis* case quoted above, the defendant had supplied the wrong kind of oil for the plaintiff's hydraulic saw mill system.  As a result, the mill did not work properly for two and one-half years.  The court held it was permissible to compute lost profits for that period on the basis of past profits, since the plaintiff had an established business.[55] However, the court denied damages for loss of profits during the two and one-half years *following* correction of the problem.  The plaintiff had argued that he was entitled to such damages because the burden caused by the malfunctioning hydraulic system had so hurt his capital situation that he could not operate at full capacity.  In rejecting that argument, the court said that if there was a market available for the plaintiff's full-capacity production, he could have obtained the necessary financing to see him through the period.[56]

---

**53.**  In addition to *Adams* and the cases cited in note 52 supra, see Birkner v. Purdon, 27 Mich.App. 476, 183 N.W.2d 598, 8 UCC Rep.Serv. 1018 (1970) (delivery of inferior quality Christmas trees).

At least one court has ruled that lost profits cannot be recovered as a matter of law because they are too remote.  Comet Indus., Inc. v. Best Plastic Container Corp., 222 F.Supp. 723 (D.Colo.1963) (Uniform Sales Act case dealing with breaches of warranties regarding sale of plastic farming machine).  Pennsylvania has a stringent foreseeability requirement for loss-of-profits damages.  See notes 47–49 supra and accompanying text.

**54.**  Lewis v. Mobil Oil Corp., 438 F.2d 500, 510, 8 UCC Rep.Serv. 625, 641 (8th Cir. 1971).

**55.**  Id. at 511–12, 8 UCC Rep.Serv. at 642, citing 5 A. Corbin, Corbin on Contracts § 1023 (1964), and 11 S. Willis-

ton, Williston on Contracts § 1346A (3d ed. 1968).  See also Kokomo Opalescent Glass Co. v. Arthur W. Schmidt Int'l, Inc., 371 F.2d 208 (7th Cir. 1966) (quantity of lost production by glass rolling machine determined under Sales Act by average of production in equivalent months in preceding and subsequent years).

**56.**  438 F.2d at 508, 8 UCC Rep.Serv. at 637.

Lost profits have also been recovered outside the manufacturing context. For example, a breach of contract or warranty in the sale of equipment may deprive the buyer of profits that could have been earned by performing services with that equipment. See, e. g., Gerwin v. Southeastern Cal. Ass'n of Seventh Day Adventists, 14 Cal.App.3d 209, 92 Cal.Rptr. 111, 8 UCC Rep.Serv. 643 (4th Dist.1971) (sale of used bar equipment); Seely v. White Motor Co., 63 Cal.2d 9, 45 Cal.Rptr. 17, 403 P.2d 145 (1965) (pre-

Numerous other items besides lost profits have been recovered as consequential damages. These range from legal fees [57] to the cost of feed consumed by pigs that eventually died of a disease contracted before delivery.[58] While repairs might normally be regarded as incidental damages, expenses for repairs that are not necessitated by the breach but are rendered worthless by the breach should be recovered as consquential damages. For example, buyers have recovered money spent on repairing or renovating used cars when they have lost possession because of the seller's breach of warranty of title.[59] Many courts have indicated a willingness to allow any recognizable loss as consequential damages, if such loss can be translated into monetary terms. In one case, an appellate court stated that if the plaintiff could convince a jury that applesauce sold by the defendant and eaten by the plaintiff was inedible, that as a result the plaintiff no longer enjoyed eating it, and that there was a true loss measurable in a dollar amount,[60] then he could recover consequential damages for loss of enjoyment.[61]

Code case involving truck for heavy-duty hauling); Adams v. J. I. Case, 125 Ill.App.2d 388, 261 N.E.2d 1, 7 UCC Rep.Serv. 1271 (1970) (excavating tractor); Valley Die Cast Corp. v. A. C. W., Inc., 25 Mich.App. 321, 181 N.W.2d 303, 8 UCC Rep.Serv. 488 (1970) (car wash system).

Similarly, lost profits can be suffered in the form of lost crops. For example, in Ford Motor Co. v. Taylor, 60 Tenn.App. 271, 446 S.W.2d 521, 6 UCC Rep.Serv. 798 (1969), the court allowed consequential damages for the buyer's deprivation of the use of his tractor caused by breaches of warranties. He did not, however, recover the full amount of his lost profits. Although it did not itemize the lump-sum damages award, the court said it was small enough to reflect deductions for compensations for the buyer's own labor, which he could have used elsewhere, and his saved maintenance expenses, yet large enough to compensate "for a measure of trouble hereafter." 60 Tenn.App. at 293, 446 S.W.2d at 581, 6 UCC Rep.Serv. at 801. The deductions for labor and maintenance apparently represent a recognition by the court that a buyer should only be allowed to recover his *net* profits. See also Gerwin v. Southeastern Cal. Ass'n of Seventh Day Adventists, 14 Cal.App.3d 209, 92 Cal. Rptr. 111, 8 UCC Rep.Serv. 643 (4th Dist.1971).

Finally, lost resale profits can be recovered. Comment 6 establishes a strong presumption that lost resale profits are recoverable whenever goods are sold to a buyer in the business of reselling them. See, e. g., Spada Distrib. Co. v. Belson, 26 Agri.Dec. 888, 4 UCC Rep.Serv. 743 (1967), discussed in notes 69–70 and accompanying text infra.

57.  The recovery of legal fees is probably available in rare circumstances only. C. McCormick, Law of Damages § 176 (1935). See, e. g., Frank R. Jelleff, Inc. v. Pollak Bros., Inc., 171 F.Supp. 467 (D.Ind.1957) (damages of retailer in non-Code action over against manufacturer for breach of warranty); Gaito v. Hoffman, 5 UCC Rep.Serv. 1056 (N.Y.Sup.Ct.1968) (warranty-of-title action).

58.  W & W Livestock Enterprises, Inc. v. Dennler, 179 N.W.2d 484, 8 UCC Rep.Serv. 169 (Iowa 1970). See also 11 S. Williston, Williston on Contracts § 1393, at 450.

59.  Spillane v. Liberty Mut. Ins. Co., 65 Misc.2d 290, 317 N.Y.S.2d 203, 8 UCC Rep.Serv. 332 (Civ.Ct.1970) (plaintiff recovered cost plus value added); John St. Auto Wrecking v. Motor Ins. Co., 56 Misc.2d 232, 288 N.Y.S.2d 281, 5 UCC Rep.Serv. 112 (Dist.Ct.1968) (plaintiff recovered purchase price plus repairs and other expenses incurred in putting car in salable condition).

60.  See text accompanying notes 65–73 infra.

61.  Martel v. Duffy-Mott Corp., 15 Mich.App. 67, 166 N.W.2d 541, 6 UCC Rep.Serv. 294 (1968).

Consequential damages may also arise in the form of liability to third persons incurred as a result of the use or resale of the seller's product. Suppose, for example, that a shipowner buys a bottle of ketchup, which explodes at sea and injures a seaman. Compensation paid the seaman by the shipowner should be recoverable as consequential damages from the seller of the ketchup.[62] Some courts have limited the buyer's recovery in this area to payments made to third persons under legal obligation.[63] But one court held that when evidence showed it was the accepted practice in the aerial insecticide spray business to respray if the first spray was ineffective, the plaintiff could recover the cost of respraying as consequential damages from the seller of substandard weedkiller even if the plaintiff was not legally obligated to respray.[64] This latter holding appears to be the better approach, since it recognizes practical obligations that require a businessman to conform to custom and usage in his trade in order to stay in business.

### Degree of Certainty Required in Measurement of Consequential Damages

To say that certain items can be recovered as consequential damages is not to say that all a plaintiff need do is allege his loss. On the contrary, a defendant has two other defenses available once he has lost the foreseeability battle. First, he can avoid paying consequential damages, especially lost profits, by showing that they are too uncertain or speculative. Comment 4 to section 2–715 indicates the Code's attitude towards the certainty problem:

> The burden of proving the extent of loss incurred by way of consequential damage is on the buyer, but the section on liberal administration of remedies [1–106] rejects any doctrine of certainty which requires almost mathematical precision in the proof of loss. Loss may be determined in any manner which is reasonable under the circumstances.[65]

Nevertheless, it is obvious that a defendant is not liable for one million dollars merely because the plaintiff testifies: "If this ma-

62. In Gambino v. United Fruit Co., 48 F.R.D. 28, 6 UCC Rep.Serv. 1056 (S.D. N.Y.1969), a shipowner was allowed to implead the manufacturer of the ketchup.

63. Neville Chem. Co. v. Union Carbide Corp., 422 F.2d 1205, 7 UCC Rep. Serv. 81 (3d Cir. 1970), cert. denied 400 U.S. 826 (1970) (payments made to customers of producer of resin who purchased defective hydrocarbon oil from seller); Butane Prods. Corp. v. Empire Advertising Serv., Inc., 39 Mass.App.Dec. 92, 5 UCC Rep.Serv. 361 (1967) (credit given customers of lighter distributor).

64. Woodbury Chem. Co. v. Holgerson, 439 F.2d 1052, 8 UCC Rep.Serv. 999 (10th Cir. 1971). For an extensive discussion of the liability of an independent supplier whose product might precipitate a recall by an automobile manufacturer, see B. Stone, Product Recall and Consequential Damages (1971).

65. One pre-Code case held that as long as the fact of damage was established with certainty, uncertainty regarding the amount did not prevent recovery. Pace Corp. v. Jackson, 151 Tex. 179, 284 S.W.2d 340 (1955) (seller failed to supply cigarettes to buyer at price lower than wholesale pursuant to contract).

chine hadn't broken down, I might have made a million dollars last year."   Gerwin v. Southeastern California Association of Seventh Day Adventists,[66] a recent California case, offers some guidance on the degree of certainty necessary for a plaintiff to recover.   The seller breached its contract by failing to deliver used bar equipment to the buyer, who intended to use it for a hotel with restaurant and cocktail lounge.   Because the proposed business was new, the buyer was new to the business, and no evidence of comparable businesses in the area had been presented, the court concluded that future profits had not been established with reasonable certainty.[67]

Of course, there are many situations where lost profits can be computed with considerable certainty.   For example, when a buyer has purchased for resale, his lost profits will equal the amount of profit that he would have realized on resale; that amount may readily be ascertained by reference to a subcontract or the buyer's normal resale mark up.[68]   Thus, in Spada Distributing Co. v. Belson,[69] lost profits on a contract to purchase potatoes for resale were based on the resale market price at the point of delivery.[70]

While most courts will allow a buyer to prove lost profits resulting from an inability to use specific property, no court has yet granted recovery under the Code for lost profits resulting from a loss of customer good will.   The Pennsylvania courts have flatly held

---

**66.**   14 Cal.App.3d 209, 92 Cal.Rptr. 111, 8 UCC Rep.Serv. 643 (4th Dist.1971).

**67.**   Id. at 222, 92 Cal.Rptr. at 119, 8 UCC Rep.Serv. at 655.   See also Earle M. Jorgensen Co. v. Teamer Mfg. Co., 10 Ariz.App. 445, 459 P.2d 533 (1969) (pre-Code case denying recovery of lost profits because buyer could not provide evidence sufficient "to furnish a reasonably certain factual basis for computation" of future profits of new business).

**68.**   Ease of computation may explain why out of 200 cases decided from 1946–1955, plaintiffs recovered lost profits in 75% of the resale cases but in only 50% of the buyer-manufacturer cases.   Comment, Lost Profits as Contract Damages: Problems of Proof and Limitations on Recovery, 65 Yale L.J. 992, 1016 n. 137 (1956).

**69.**   26 Agri.Dec. 888, 4 UCC Rep.Serv. 743 (1967).

In granting a buyer lost profits because he is unable to resell a product, a court must be careful not to overcompensate him.   Assume, for example, that a buyer sues wholesaler for nondelivery of a shipment of fiberglass skiis under section 2–713.   He

might ask for the market-contract differential (assume it is $10,000 — $8,000) plus consequential damages which are lost resale profits.   If he could resell the shipment of skiis at $15,000 but he cannot cover, his lost profits will be $7,000 ($15,000 — $8,000).   Should a court allow a recovery of $9,000 (the market-contract differential plus lost profits)?   First, 2–715(2)(a) requires cover if it is at all reasonable, and that principle would eliminate lost profits in most cases.   Secondly, in the unusual case where cover is impossible the court should award only $7,000 since that amount will put the wholesaler in the same position he would have been in if the manufacturer had sent the skiis.   If a court gives the buyer the market-contract differential of $2,000 under 2–713, then the "loss resulting" from the wholesaler's inability to resell under 2–715(2)(a) is only $5,000.

**70.**   The recovery was thus essentially that allowed by 2–714(2).   The court did not allow the buyer to base his damages on the market price prevailing at the point of resale because the buyer had provided no evidence that the seller had knowledge of the intent to resell.   26 Agri.Dec. at 897, 4 UCC Rep.Serv. at 746.

that such damages are too speculative and therefore not recoverable.[71]  But at least one court has recognized that loss of good will may be a compensable item if the buyer can "establish just what his loss was worth in money damages." [72]  Obviously, such a task is a difficult one, and one court in a non-Code case has said that merely multiplying profits for one year by five (one method used by accountants to compute the value of good will) is not a sufficiently precise measurement.[73]

## *Mitigation*

Section 2–715(2) (a) explicitly imposes a third restriction on the recovery of consequential damages: There can be recovery only for losses "which could not reasonably be prevented by cover or otherwise." [74]  In what circumstances should a court find that the loss could have been prevented?  In Columbia Novelty Co. v. Leslie Dawn, Inc.,[75] the seller brought an action for the price of goods delivered and used by the buyer-manufacturer.  The buyer counterclaimed for consequential damages caused by the defective goods.  The court, in a terse opinion, affirmed a dismissal of the counterclaim, commenting:

> [I]t was undisputed that the defendant, an experienced manufacturer, knew of the defect but used the goods and took a chance that its customers would not complain.  No recovery may be had for damages which could reasonably have been prevented  .  .  .  ." [76]

The mitigation principle has also been applied in the consumer context.  For example, when a consumer used a color television set and left it plugged in all night despite the fact that it had twice previously given off sparks and smoke and that its "instant-on" device had previously turned the set on spontaneously, he could not hold the television dealer for $62,000 worth of damages caused when the television caught fire and burned his house down.[77]  While these

---

71.  Harry Rubin & Sons, Inc. v. Consolidated Pipe Co., 396 Pa. 506, 153 A.2d 472, 1 UCC Rep.Serv. 40 (1959) (failure to deliver plastic "Tee Vee" hoops).  See also Neville Chem. Co. v. Union Carbide Corp., 422 F.2d 1205, 7 UCC Rep.Serv. 81 (3d Cir. 1970), cert. denied 400 U.S. 826 (1970) (breach of express warranty regarding shipment of unsaturated oil).

72.  Butane Prods. Corp. v. Empire Advertising Serv., Inc., 39 Mass.App.Dec. 92, 95, 5 UCC Rep.Serv. 361, 362 (1967).

73.  Sherwin-Williams Co. v. Perry Co., 424 S.W.2d 940 (Tex.Civ.App.1968) (sale of paint for use on diving boards).

74. In Section 6–3 supra, we discussed the duty to cover.  We should note at this point that in the *Seventh Day Adventist* case the buyer's failure to cover did not preclude his recovery of consequential damages, since his financial condition had prevented him from purchasing a substitute item. Gerwin v. Southeastern Cal. Ass'n of Seventh Day Adventists, 14 Cal.App. 3d 209, 92 Cal.Rptr. 111, 8 UCC Rep. Serv. 643 (4th Dist.1971), discussed in the text accompanying notes 66–67 supra.

75.  6 UCC Rep.Serv. 679 (N.Y.App. Term 1969).

76.  Id. at 679.  The opinion was *per curiam* and gave no specific facts.

77.  Erdman v. Johnson Bros. Radio & TV Co., 260 Md. 190, 271 A.2d 744, 8 UCC Rep.Serv. 656 (1970).

cases illustrate the clear-cut situation where a buyer has not acted reasonably to prevent consequential loss, more difficult cases do arise. For example, in Bevard v. Howat Concrete Co.,[78] although preliminary tests by the buyer indicated that purchased concrete might be too weak, it was impossible to ascertain for certain whether the concrete was defective until twenty-eight days after its pouring. Under these circumstances, the District of Columbia Circuit Court of Appeals held that when the buyer immediately used the concrete he did not fail to take action that would reasonably have prevented loss, and thus he was entitled to recover consequential damages.[79]

### Injuries to Person or Property

The color television case also involves the second variety of consequential damages mentioned in 2–715(2). Paragraph (b) allows recovery for "injury to person or property proximately resulting from any breach of warranty." The issues raised by the term "proximately" are discussed in Section 11–7 below; consequently, very little needs to be said about this provision now. We should nevertheless note at this point that an action brought under 2–715(2) (b) has one major advantage over actions brought under paragraph (a): paragraph (b) contains no foreseeability requirement. Thus, a seller is liable for injury to person or property even if he did not know of or have reason to know of the buyer's intended use.

### Conclusion

To sum up what we have said about consequential damages, 2–715 (2) codifies the more liberal reading of Hadley v. Baxendale. Most of the courts have recognized that a seller is liable for all damages resulting from his breach if they arise from circumstances that the seller knew about or had reason to know about, even if he did not consciously assume the risk of such liability. The plaintiff can recover lost profits if the seller had reason to know at the time of contracting that if he breached the contract the plaintiff would be deprived of those profits. But subsection (2) imposes two restrictions on the recovery of consequential damages in addition to the foreseeability requirement: they must be reasonably ascertainable, and the plaintiff cannot recover for losses he reasonably could have prevented. While damages for injuries to person and property may be recovered under 2–715(2) (b) even if they were not foreseeable, the requirement that injuries proximately result from a breach of warranty probably embraces the mitigation restriction.

Section 2–715(2) is remarkably brief in light of its impact; whether or not consequential damages are allowed can mean the difference between a fifty-cent and a million-dollar damages award. For example, if a defective fifty-cent bolt snaps, it may cause the deaths of thirty children riding a school bus or the break-down for

78.  433 F.2d 1202, 7 UCC Rep.Serv. 966      79.  Id. at 1203, 7 UCC Rep.Serv. at
     (D.C.Cir.1970).                              968–69.

several months of a giant generator needed to operate a factory.[80] The consequential damages provisions provide the only Code remedy that can come close to fully compensating plaintiffs in these cases. Because of the brevity and significance of 2–715, it is important to remember that it draws on over a century of common law development, which began with Hadley v. Baxendale. The better-reasoned authority emerging from that background and the intent of the draftsmen declare that the basic test for the recovery of consequential damages is whether the losses were foreseeable (not foreseen) by the seller at the time he entered the contract. The trend of Code cases to date strongly suggests that the courts will construe this foreseeability requirement to the plaintiff's benefit.

**80.** In such circumstances a seller might argue that he should not be held liable for damages vastly disproportionate to the purchase price. He could find some support in pre-Code cases, which held that lost profits greatly out of proportion to the price paid may not be recovered. See, e. g., Hooks Smelting v. Planter's Compress Co., 72 Ark. 275, 79 S.W. 1052 (1904) (tacit consent must be present when damages are ten times as great as possible profit to seller); Flug v. Craft Mfg. Co., 3 Ill.App.2d 56, 120 N.E.2d 666 (1954) ($130,000 in lost profits resulting from defective die cast costing $2,625 not recoverable because such an award would be "unjust" to the seller); Thurner Heat Treating Co. v. Memco, Inc., 252 Wis. 16, 30 N.W.2d 228 (1947) ($2,337 in lost profits resulting from defective heat treating of gears costing $147 is evidence that parties would not have contemplated such damages). These cases reflect a somewhat inhospitable attitude toward the recovery of lost profits (see Farnsworth, Legal Remedies for Breach of Contract, 70 Colum.L.Rev. 1145, 1206–1209 (1970)), and they do seem to be based on a decision that the greatly disproportionate damages were not foreseeable.

The Code cases decided so far have rejected this disproportionality argument. In Ford Motor Co. v. Reid, 250 Ark. 176, 465 S.W.2d 80, 8 UCC Rep. Serv. 985 (1971), the buyer of a $6,100 Lincoln-Continental recovered nearly $90,000 from the manufacturer when a defect in the car set his house on fire. In Lewis v. Mobile Oil Corp., 438 F.2d 500, 8 UCC Rep.Serv. 625 (8th Cir. 1971), the plaintiff recovered lost profits for a two-and-one-half-year period from the supplier of lubricating oil for a hydraulic saw mill system, even though the price of the oil was apparently only a fraction of the total lost profits. Based on these decisions and the language of section 2–715(2), a buyer should be able to recover the full amount of consequential damages that are foreseeable or, in the case of injury to person or property, that proximately resulted from a breach of warranty regardless of the disproportionate relationship between such damages and the price paid.

# CHAPTER 11

# DEFENSES TO WARRANTY ACTIONS

*Analysis*

Sec.
11–1. Introduction.
11–2. Lack of Privity as a Defense to a Warranty Cause of Action.
11–3. Privity—Personal Injury.
11–4. —— Property Damage.
11–5. —— Economic Loss—Loss of the Bargain and Profits.
11–6. —— Express Warranty.
11–7. Defenses Based Upon Plaintiff's Contributory Behavior.
11–8. Statute of Limitations.
11–9. Buyer's Failure to Give Notice as a Defense to Actions for Breach of Warranty.

## § 11–1  Introduction

In this chapter we have collected four leftover parts of warranty theory that fit nowhere else.  They are privity, plaintiff's misbehavior (contributory negligence, assumption of the risk, etc.), statute of limitations, and plaintiff's failure to give timely notice of a broken warranty.  Unfortunately most of the law on these issues tends to be of an ad hoc and ungeneralizable nature, especially as regards contributory negligence and plaintiff's failure to give notice.  In the pages to follow we highlight pitfalls and, where possible, offer answers.  For the most part the legal concepts that we discuss in this chapter are not precise or cut and dried.  Inevitably a lawyer's decision on issues of the kind we consider here calls for a large measure of fact analysis and judgment.  We will try to identify the factors he should consider in making his judgment.

Before turning to the substance of the defenses to be considered here, we will first consider which party has the burden of pleading and the burden of going forward with the evidence on each defense.  In general it is the defendant's burden to plead and to go forward with evidence on the defenses of contributory negligence, assumption of the risk, and the statute of limitations.[1]  The courts generally characterize these defenses as affirmative defenses.[2]  On the other hand courts generally hold that the plaintiff has the burden of pleading and going forward with proof on the issues of privity and

---

1. F. James, Civil Procedure 143–46 (1965).

2. Id. at 145–46. The statute of limitations is an affirmative defense under the federal rules and under most states' procedure.  The federal rules also allow one to raise the statute of limitations by motion to dismiss for failure to state a claim where the complaint shows the statute to have run.  The practice in states varies as to whether the question of statute of limitations can be raised by demurrer. See 3 Fed. Rules Serv. 671–73 (1940).  See also Thalrose v. General Motors Corp., 8 UCC Rep.Serv. 1257 (N.Y.Sup.Ct.1971); Constable v. White Motor Corp., 317 N.Y.S.2d 590, 8 UCC Rep.Serv. 814 (Sup.Ct.1970) (motions for dismissal granted in both cases).

notice.[3]  That is, plaintiff's complaint is demurrable if it fails to allege privity or notice.  In most cases the placing of the burden will have little effect upon the outcome of the law suit, but in some it will be crucial.  For example, if a court were to hold that a corporate defendant may assert the notice defense only by proving that none of its agents ever received notice, in practical effect the notice defense would become unavailable to a large corporate defendant.

## § 11-2  Lack of Privity as a Defense to a Warranty Cause of Action

It may be an impossible task to write briefly but not superficially about the question of privity as it relates to a warranty cause of action under the Code.  An initial difficulty is that of defining the word "privity."  Parties who have contracted with each other are in "privity."  Those who have not contracted are not in privity.  Thus, a woman poisoned by a bottle of beer that her husband purchased from a local merchant is not in privity with the merchant.  Some writers have it that her case is one of "horizontal" non-privity.  A man who buys a lathe from a local hardware store and then chooses to sue the manufacturer of the lathe is not in privity with the manufacturer.  Some writers characterize his case as one of "vertical" non-privity.  The 1962 version of the Code took no position on the question of vertical privity,[4] but in section 2-318 it took a position on the horizontal privity question.[5]  That section extends the seller's warranty against personal injury to any natural person who is in the family or household of his buyer and to any guest in his home provided such party could reasonably be expected to use, consume, or be affected by the goods.  As we will see, non-standard amendments and

3.  See, e. g., L. A. Green Seed Co. v. Williams, 246 Ark. 463, 438 S.W.2d 717, 6 UCC Rep.Serv. 105 (1969) (tomato grower's complaint was defective because it lacked allegation of notice); Faucette v. Lucky Stores, Inc., 219 Cal.App.2d 196, 33 Cal.Rptr. 215 (Dist.1963) (pre-Code case stating buyer has to plead and prove giving of notice); Spring Valley Country Club, Inc. v. Malden Supply Co., 349 Mass. 764, 208 N.E.2d 230, 2 UCC Rep.Serv. 968 (1965) (the complaint in a breach of warranty case failed to state a cause of action because complaint affirmatively showed lack of privity); Donnell & Mudge, Inc. v. Bonita Leather Fashions, Inc., 8 UCC Rep. Serv. 699 (Sup.Ct.1971) (leather skin buyer's burden of proof concerning notice of breach of warranty not sustained by vague, oral complaints of unspecified shortages); Avant Garde, Inc. v. Armtex, Inc., 4 UCC Rep.Serv. 949 (N. Y.Sup.Ct.1967) (complaint concerning faulty garment material failed to state cause of action without allega-tion of notice); Hupp Corp. v. Metered Washer Service, 256 Ore. 245, 472 P.2d 816, 8 UCC Rep.Serv. 42 (1970) (privity must be pleaded in suit to recover economic loss with implied warranty theory); Holowka v. York Farm Bureau Coop. Ass'n., 2 UCC Rep.Serv. 445 (Pa.C.P.1963) (motion for more specific pleading concerning notice of breach of warranty granted).

4.  See § 2-318, Comment 3.  See also Leach v. Wiles, 58 Tenn.App. 286, 429 S.W.2d 823, 5 UCC Rep.Serv. 129 (1968) (section 2-318 does not by implication eliminate need for privity between manufacturer and purchaser). However, Alternatives B and C of the 1966 Official Recommendations for the amendment of section 2-318 do speak to the vertical privity problem by extending a seller's warranty to any natural person "who may reasonably be  .  .  .  affected by the goods."

5.  See § 2-318.

newly proposed Alternative sections 2–318(B) and (C) deal with vertical as well as horizontal privity.

Today, courts are not yet agreed on whether the Code or judge-made doctrines of strict liability control the rights of non-privity plaintiffs. Many courts seem more willing to allow recovery to a non-privity plaintiff when they characterize his cause of action as one in tort than when they characterize it as one in warranty. The most thorough judicial analyses of the warranty vs. tort question appears in the celebrated California case, Seely v. White Motor Co.[6] and in the less celebrated but more informative Oregon case, State ex rel. Western Seed Production Corp. v. Campbell.[7] Justice Traynor, who wrote for the majority in *Seely*, had previously held that a remote purchaser could sue the manufacturer of a lathe which caused the purchaser to suffer personal injury.[8] In *Seely*, a purchaser of a truck sued the manufacturer, White Motor, to recover that part of the price he had paid, his lost profits, and certain damages sustained in an accident involving the truck. The trial court denied the plaintiff any damages arising out of the accident (since he failed to prove causation), but ordered the defendant to return that part of the price the plaintiff had paid and awarded him more than $9,000 in lost profits. The California Supreme Court upheld the lower court, and Justices Traynor and Peters offered lengthy *dicta* on the rights of non-privity plaintiffs in warranty and in strict tort. Justice Traynor stated that a remote purchaser should not recover economic loss (here, lost profits) in strict tort, for no seller undertakes that his goods will meet *all* needs of *all* of his potential purchasers and sub-purchasers. It appears that Justice Traynor would also deny relief to a remote purchaser seeking similar recovery on a theory of implied warranty of merchantability.[9] Justice Peters, concurring and dissenting in *Seely*, thought Justice Traynor was unduly concerned that strict tort might authorize unfair consequential damages against remote sellers. According to Justice Peters, remote sellers are liable in strict tort only for damages flowing from the failure of their goods to conform to the ordinary purposes for which such goods are used. Also, in Justice Peters' world, any plaintiff who is an "ordinary consumer" can sue a remote seller in strict tort but other plaintiffs must resort to the Code.

A comparison of Justice Traynor's opinion with those in the *Campbell* case reveals complexity dear to the hearts and minds of the academic law professor. In *Campbell* Justice Goodwin held that "[w]here the purchaser of an unmerchantable product suffers only loss of profits, his remedy for the breach of warranty is against his immediate seller unless he can predicate liability upon some fault on the part of a remote seller." [10] Put another way, sellers have liability

6.   63 Cal.2d 9, 403 P.2d 145, 2 UCC Rep.Serv. 915 (1965).

7.   250 Ore. 262, 442 P.2d 215 (1968).

8.   Greenman v. Yuba Power Products, Inc., 59 Cal.2d 57, 377 P.2d 897 (1962).

9.   63 Cal.2d at 16–18, 403 P.2d at 150–51.

10.   250 Ore. at 268, 422 P.2d at 218.

to remote buyers only for negligence and not for implied warranty.[11]
Justice O'Connell, a dissenter in *Campbell*, argued that implied warranty liability runs to remote buyers when breach of that warranty causes a loss of profits.   In *Seely* and *Campbell* we have articulate spokesmen for at least three different positions, and possibly four. Presumably all dispense with privity when the plaintiff is a consumer who has suffered a personal injury or property damage.   Justice O'Connell dispenses with privity in nearly all circumstances, but Justice Goodwin and possibly Justice Traynor would require that a plaintiff who seeks lost profits always be in privity with his defendant. Justice Peters would not require "ordinary consumer" plaintiffs to be in privity.   In our efforts to summarize the arguments in these cases, we have doubtless over-generalized somewhat, but the point should be clear: the privity cases are complex and confusing.

The foregoing cases also illustrate some ways in which it is possible to divide fact patterns into manageable packages.   A division into four groupings is consistent with the cases and should be helpful to those who must predict outcomes for their clients.   The first three classifications are by type of injury:

   *(1)*  Personal injury,

   *(2)*  Property damage, and

   *(3)*  Economic loss (loss of bargain, and consequential damage such as loss of profits).

Our fourth classification, cuts across the first three, and involves a plaintiff suing on an express warranty.

## § 11–3  Privity—Personal Injury

Cases in which the plaintiff suffers personal injury are largely beyond the scope of this work.   However, these cases are occasionally tried as warranty actions, and they intersect with the Code in two ways.   First, courts have evolved much of the non-privity case law in such cases, and courts sometimes cite them in cases in which a non-privity plaintiff seeks damages for other kinds of injuries.   Secondly, while 2–318 in its original form had little impact on privity doctrine in personal injury cases, the newly proposed Code Alternatives B and C are likely to have substantial impact.

In most states non-privity personal injury claims can be brought under the rubric of strict tort liability, a liability that finds its most authoritative statement in section 402A of the Restatement, Second, Torts.   That section of the *Restatement* gives a cause of action to the "ultimate user or consumer," and applies even though "the user or consumer has not bought the product from or entered into any contractual relations with the seller" (402A(2) (b)).   The Reporter states in a comment that the American Law Institute does not express

---

11.  Justice O'Connell's dissent in *Campbell* points out that the majority's reasoning would also require privity for express warranties (since privity is necessary for "consentual" transactions and such consent is a "matter for bargaining" and necessary to impose contractual liability).

any opinion as to whether 402A applies to persons other than users or consumers.[12]   Under 402A, therefore, lack of privity is no defense to a cause of action in strict tort where the plaintiff is a user or consumer.   Comments to 402A and cases decided on strict tort theory expand the user and consumer classes greatly.   For example, Comment 1 to section 402A states that the class of consumers may include "the housewife who contracts tularemia while cooking rabbits for her husband . . . also the husband who is opening a bottle of beer for his wife to drink."

Are there cases where lack of privity would be a defense to strict tort liability?   The draftsmen of the *Restatement* are not sure.   However, they suggest some possibilities in Comment *o*: "[c]asual bystanders . . . employees of the retailer, or a passerby injured by an exploding bottle, or a pedestrian hit by an automobile. . . ."   Comment *o* is now several years old, and a number of cases have gone far beyond it and allowed parties to recover who might well not be classified as consumers or users.[13]   Except in the rarest case, it appears lack of privity is no defense against a plaintiff who states a cause of action in strict tort.

The present book is about the Code, and the reader may well ask what the Code has to do with all of this.   Until recently the answer was very little.   The 1962 version of section 2–318 entitled "Third Party Beneficiaries of Warranties Express or Implied" read as follows:

> A seller's warranty whether express or implied extends to any natural person who is in the family or household of his buyer or who is a guest in his home if it is reasonable to expect that such person may use, consume or be affected by the goods and who is injured in person by breach of the warranty.   A seller may not exclude or limit the operation of this section.

This section timidly extended warranty liability to "natural persons" in the "family and household" of the buyer and to his guests, but only where it was reasonable to expect that such persons would use, consume, or be affected by the goods.   The draftsmen carefully included Comment 3 to indicate that 2–318 was not designed to inhibit case law growth on behalf of the plaintiff.[14]   Either on strict tort or war-

---

12.   Restatement, Second, Torts § 402A, Comment o (1965).

13.   See, e. g., Delaney v. Towmotor Corp. 339 F.2d 4 (2d Cir. 1964) (employee of prospective purchaser was injured while trying out forklift truck); Mitchell v. Miller, 26 Conn. Supp. 142, 214 A.2d 694, 2 UCC Rep. Serv. 1152 (1965) (bystander struck by car allowed to sue manufacturer in strict tort).   Contra, Revlon, Inc. v. Murdock, 103 Ga.App. 842, 120 S.E. 2d 912 (1961) (beautician injured in course of employment when nail polish bottle exploded, held not to be ultimate consumer or user).

14.   Comment 3 to 2–318 reads in part:

[T]he section is neutral and is not intended to enlarge or restrict the developing case law on whether the seller's warranties, given to his buyer who resells, extend to the other persons in the distributive chain.

ranty theory, most courts have gone well beyond 2–318, and in a majority of states it stands like the Maginot Line, a carefully and conservatively constructed provision largely irrelevant to the battle ultimately fought.   As part of its 1966 Official Recommendations for Amendment, the Permanent Editorial Board for the Uniform Commercial Code has offered two further optional versions of 2–318:

> *Alternative B*
>
> A seller's warranty whether express or implied extends to any natural person who may reasonably be expected to use, consume or be affected by the goods and who is injured in person by breach of the warranty.   A seller may not exclude or limit the operation of this section.
>
> *Alternative C*
>
> A seller's warranty whether express or implied extends to any person who may reasonably be expected to use, consume or be affected by the goods and who is injured by breach of the warranty.   A seller may not exclude or limit the operation of this section with respect to injury to the person of an individual to whom the warranty extends.

Alternative A is the same as the 1962 official version of section 2–318. At least four jurisdictions have adopted Alternative B.   At least eight states have adopted Alternative C or a similar provision.[15] Four other jurisdictions have adopted an expansive hybrid provision.[16]   These alternatives offer the prospect of expanding liability even beyond that contemplated by 402A.   Note that each of them permits the seller's warranty to run not only to "users and consumers" but also to any party who may "reasonably be expected to . . . be affected by the goods . . . ."   The Editorial Board note to the 1966 amendment indicates that Alternative C was intended to expand the class of beneficiaries, and the use of the "be affected by" phrase is a further conscious restriction of the lack of privity defense.   Thus it could happen that jurisdictions which have enacted Alternatives B or C of 2–318 may offer a wider range of defendants to plaintiffs suing under the Code than to those suing in strict tort.[17]   In any event, 2–318 should be considered by the plain-

---

15.   Alabama, Kansas, Maryland, and Vermont have all enacted Alternative B to 2–318 or a similar provision. Arkansas, Hawaii, North Dakota, Colorado, Delaware, Minnesota, Rhode Island, and Wyoming have enacted Alternative C to 2–318 or a similar provision.

16.   Georgia, Maine, South Carolina, and Virginia have enacted an expansive hybrid of 2–318.   Alaska, Arizona, Connecticut, Washington D. C., Florida, Idaho, Illinois, Indiana, Iowa, Kentucky, Massachusetts, Michigan, Mississippi, Missouri, Montana, Nebraska, Nevada, New Hampshire, New Jersey, New Mexico, New York, North Carolina, Ohio, Oklahoma, Oregon, Pennsylvania, South Dakota, Tennessee, Virgin Islands, Washington, West Virginia, and Wisconsin have the 1962 Official Text version (Alternative A) or a similar provision.   The exceptions are as follows:  California and Utah omit 2–318; Texas' 2–318 merely states that the whole issue is left to the courts.

17.   Mack Trucks, Inc. v. Jet Asphalt & Rock Co., 246 Ark. 101, 437 S.W.2d 459, 6 UCC Rep.Serv. 93 (1969) (suit for breach of implied warranty of fitness of two diesel truck engines; held

tiff's lawyer in states which have enacted Alternatives B or C or any of the other non-standard versions of 2–318.

## § 11–4  Privity—Property Damage

In this discussion we use the terms "property damage" on the one hand and "economic loss" on the other to describe different kinds of damages a plaintiff may suffer.  An action brought to recover damages for inadequate value, costs of repair, and replacement of defective goods or consequent loss of profits is one for "economic loss." Property damage, on the other hand, is the *Restatement's* "physical harm . . . to [user's] property."[18]  If one purchases a new truck and finds that the radiator has to be replaced at a cost of $300, he would suffer an economic loss of at least $300 rather than property damage.  If, in addition, he should lose $1,000 in profits while his truck was out of commission, that too would be an "economic" loss.  Of course, borderline cases can arise that do not fit comfortably in either the property damage or the economic loss category.  Consider a car that throws a rod after a thousand miles of normal use.  Is the loss property damage because the injury occurred suddenly?  Or is the loss an economic one because the suit will be for replacement of the engine?[19]

Many non-privity plaintiffs who today seek recovery for property damage now find themselves in much the same position as those who seek recovery for personal injury.[20]  Although the cases which first struck down the privity doctrine were personal injury cases, and although recovery in those cases was sometimes limited to harm from "intimate body products" (for instance, food and cosmetics), the distinction between property damage and personal injury has now largely disappeared in many states.  Note, however, that Alternatives A

that Arkansas statute similar to Alternative C to 2–318 eliminated defense of lack of privity not only for injury to persons and property but also for economic or commercial losses) ; L. A. Green Seed Co. v. Williams, 246 Ark. 463, 438 S.W.2d 717, 6 UCC Rep.Serv. 105 (1969) (tomato grower might sue distributor of tomato seed for lost profits despite lack of privity, but plaintiff neglected to allege that he gave sufficient notice of breach of warranty) (dictum). See note 3 supra.

**18.**  Restatement, Second, Torts § 402A (1965).

**19.**  See Seely v. White Motor Co., 63 Cal.2d 9, 22–23, 403 P.2d 145, 153–154, 2 UCC Rep.Serv. 925–26 (1965) ; see also Note, Economic Loss in Products Liability Jurisprudence, 66 Colum.L. Rev. 917, 918 (1966).

**20.**  W. Prosser, Handbook of the Law of Torts § 101 at 666–67 (4th ed. 1971). See, e. g., Newton v. Admiral Corp., 280 F.Supp. 202 (D.Colo.1967) ; Rossignol v. Danbury School of Aeronautics, Inc., 154 Conn. 549, 227 A.2d 418, 4 UCC Rep.Serv. 305 (1967) ; Picker X-Ray Corp. v. General Motors Corp., 185 A.2d 919, 1 UCC Rep.Serv. 143 (D.C.Ct.App.1962) ; Suvada v. White Motor Co., 32 Ill.2d 612, 210 N.E.2d 182, 2 UCC Rep.Serv. 762 (1965) ; Hawkeye-Security Ins. Co. v. Ford Motor Co., 174 N.W.2d 672 (Iowa 1970) (the claim settlement paid by plaintiff to third party considered as property loss rather than lost profits or personal injury) ; MacDougall v. Ford Motor Co., 214 Pa.Super. 384, 257 A. 2d 676 (C.P.1969).  Contra, Kenney v. Sears, Roebuck & Co., 355 Mass. 604, 246 N.E.2d 649, 6 UCC Rep.Serv. 313 (1969).

and B of 2–318 retain the distinction. Those two alternatives remove the privity bar only when the plaintiff is "injured in person." Thus one who seeks recovery for property damage or for anything other than personal injury may not rely on either of those alternatives. The "in person" language does not appear in Alternative C of 2–318; under it personal injury and property damage cases are treated alike for the purposes of the privity requirement.

### § 11–5 Privity—Economic Loss—Loss of the Bargain and Profits

Our main focus in the warranty chapters of this book is on the party who seeks to recover either the loss of his bargain under 2–714, or consequential damages (excluding personal injury and property damages) under 2–715, or both. Although at least one court [21] has let a plaintiff recover economic loss on a strict tort theory, most such recoveries are based on warranty theory. Neither Alternative A nor Alternative B of 2–318 lets a plaintiff recover for the loss of bargain or loss of profits against a remote seller. Alternative C applies to persons who are "injured," but it is unclear that the Alternative authorizes recovery for loss of bargain and loss of profits as well. The note of the Code's Permanent Editorial Board accompanying Alternative C states that it reflects "the trend of more recent decisions as indicated by Restatement, Second, Torts § 402A . . . ." [22] This explicit reference to 402A which is itself limited to "physical harm . . . to the ultimate user . . . or to his property" implies that Alternative C is aimed at personal injury and property damage and not at loss of bargain or loss of profit damages.

The courts are split on whether a plaintiff may recover economic loss (loss of bargain and loss of profits) from a seller with whom he did not deal and who made no express warranties to him. The majority deny recovery in these circumstances,[23] but a healthy minority permits recovery.[24] Dean Prosser has argued that plaintiffs should

---

21. See, e. g., Santor v. A & M Karagheusian, Inc., 44 N.J. 52, 207 A.2d 305 (1965) (rug was defective; held *either* strict tort or implied warranty theory available).

22. Permanent Editorial Board for The Uniform Commercial Code, Report No. 3 at 14 (1966).

23. See, e. g., Atlas Aluminum Corp. v. Borden Chemical Corp., 233 F.Supp. 53, 2 UCC Rep.Serv. 154 (E.D.Pa. 1964); Perfecting Serv. Co. v. Products Dev. & Sales Co., 259 N.C. 400, 131 S.E.2d 9 (1963); Poldon Eng'r & Mfg. Co. v. Zell Elec. Mfg. Co., 1 Misc.2d 1016, 156 N.Y.S.2d 169 (N.Y. City Ct.1965); State ex rel. Western Seed Prod. v. Campbell, 250 Ore. 262, 442 P.2d 215, 5 UCC Rep.Serv. 584 (1968); Henry v. John W. Eshelman

and Sons, 99 R.I. 518, 209 A.2d 46, 2 UCC Rep.Serv. 154 (1965); Oliver Corp. v. Green, 54 Tenn.App. 647, 393 S.W.2d 625 (1965); Kyker v. General Motors Corp., 214 Tenn. 521, 381 S.W. 2d 884 (1964). In all of these cases the plaintiffs sought to recover on the theory of breach of implied warranty. They would also have failed had they sought to recover on a strict tort theory. Section 402A of the Restatement, Second, Torts only authorizes recovery for "*physical* harm thereby caused to the ultimate user or consumer, or to his property" (emphasis added).

24. One commentator has suggested that courts are more willing to permit recovery for economic loss under implied warranty where the defective product has caused or has the poten-

not recover their "losses on bargains" from remote sellers, but he apparently believes they should recover loss of profits from such persons.[25] We believe Dean Prosser's distinction is imperfect. We would distinguish between those cases in which the defect is attributable to a remote party (for instance, the manufacturer) and those in which the defect is attributable only to the plaintiff's seller (for instance, the retailer). Illustrative of the former would be an automobile that did not run properly; of the latter, a truck that lived up to all the manufacturer's warranties, but did not comply with an additional express warranty of the retail seller.

In any event, we agree with the majority position that generally non-privity plaintiffs may not recover for economic loss.[26] Under the minority view, the seller's position with respect to remote buyers is perilous, for these buyers may use the goods for unknown purposes from which enormous lost profits might ensue. Since the remote seller cannot predict the purposes for which the goods will be used he faces unknown liability and may not be able to insure himself.[27] Insurers are hesitant to insure against risks they cannot measure.[28] Moreover, here more than in personal injury and property damage cases, it is appropriate to recognize the traditional rights of parties to make their own contract. If a remote seller wishes to sell at a

tial to cause injury to persons or property. See Note, Economic Loss in Product Liability Jurisprudence, 66 Colum.L.Rev. 917, 935 (1966). Recovery for economic loss was allowed by the Michigan Supreme Court under alternate theories of negligence and implied warranty despite lack of privity when the defective cinder blocks, bought and installed by the builder, created a future danger to the entire structure. See Spence v. Three Rivers Builders & Masonry Supply, Inc,. 353 Mich. 120, 90 N.W.2d 873 (1958).

However, in Continental Copper & Steel Indus. v. E. C. "Red" Cornelius, Inc., 104 So.2d 40 (Fla.Ct.App.1958), there was no indication of harm or potential harm to persons or property, and recovery was allowed for replacement costs of defective electric cable. See also Manheim v. Ford Motor Co., 201 So.2d 440 (Fla.1967) (plaintiff could recover damages for loss of bargain in implied warranty action involving his Lincoln Continental). The extent to which the opinion discusses the role of advertising in modern business suggests the court may have regarded the case as one on express warranty. Similarly, in Lang v. General Motors Corp., 136 N.W.2d 805 (N.D.1965), the court emphasized the influence of the manufacturer's national advertising campaign and a trade name in allowing recovery for economic loss on implied warranty. See also note 17 supra.

25.  Prosser, The Fall of the Citadel (Strict Liability to the Consumer), 50 Minn.L.Rev. 791, 822–23 (1966).

26.  156 Eng.Rep. 145, 9 Ex. 341 (1854). Section 2–715(2) (a) incorporates the doctrine of Hadley v. Baxendale.

27.  Most products liability insurance policies do not cover economic loss. This means that not only are lost profits not covered but damage to insured's own products or work project is not covered either. The comprehensive general liability policies, as they are called, only include personal and property damage of others caused by insured's defective product. See Arnold, Products Liability Insurance, 25 Ins. Counsel J. 42, 44–46 (1958); Sorensen, What a Lawyer Ought to Know About Products Liability Insurance Coverage, 12 Trial Lawyers Guide 322 (1968).

28.  See Anderson, Current Problems in Products Liability Law and Products Liability Insurance, 31 Ins. Counsel J. 436, 446 (1964); see generally, Note, Economic Loss in Products Liability Jurisprudence, 66 Colum.L.Rev. 917, 953–58 (1966).

lower price and disclaim his liability for economic loss to sub-purchasers, why should we deny him that right? Why should we design a system that forces him to bear the economic loss of the Seelys or other sub-purchasers? Indeed, by forcing the buyer to bear such losses we may save costly law suits and even some economic losses against which buyers, knowing they have the responsibility, may protect themselves. In short, we believe that a buyer should pick his seller with care and recover any economic loss from that seller and not from parties remote from the transaction.

### § 11–6 Privity—Express Warranty

When the non-privity plaintiff's suit is not based upon 402A or implied warranty, but rather upon the defendant's express representation made to the particular plaintiff in advertising or otherwise, courts generally hold that the plaintiff need not be in privity with the defendant.[29] Usually courts characterize such cases as express warranty cases,[30] though in some jurisdictions they are classed as misrepresentation cases.[31] The misrepresentation may come through the defendant's advertising,[32] through labels attached to the product,[33] or through brochures and literature about the product.[34] The only limitation is that the plaintiff must be a party whom the defendant could expect to act upon the representation.[35] Of course, any such plaintiff must also state the other elements of his cause of action.

It is possible that lack of privity as a defense to a cause of action will be only an historic relic in the year 2000. It is a doctrine in hasty retreat; its current vitality is largely in cases in which plaintiffs seek recompense for economic loss.

### § 11–7 Defenses Based Upon Plaintiff's Contributory Behavior

Whether a plaintiff should be foreclosed from recovery because his own action or inaction or something peculiar to him contributed to his injury is a question that masquerades in many costumes. It ap-

**29.** Prosser, The Fall of the Citadel (Strict Liability to the Consumer), 50 Minn.L.Rev. 791, 835–36 (1966); Putensen v. Clay Adams, Inc., 12 Cal.App.3d 1062, 91 Cal.Rptr. 319, 8 UCC Rep. Serv. 449 (1st Dist.1970); Connolly v. Hagi, 24 Conn.Supp. 198, 188 A.2d 884 (1963).

**30.** Prosser, The Fall of the Citadel (Strict Liability to the Consumer), 50 Minn.L.Rev. 791, 834–35 (1966).

**31.** See Cooper v. R. J. Reynolds Tobacco Co., 234 F.2d 170 (1st Cir. 1956); Ford Motor Co. v. Lonon, 217 Tenn. 400, 398 S.W.2d 240 (1966).

**32.** See, e. g., Pritchard v. Liggett & Myers Tobacco Co., 295 F.2d 292 (3d Cir. 1961); Connolly v. Hagi, 24 Conn. Supp. 198, 188 A.2d 884 (1963).

**33.** See, e. g., Maecherlein v. Sealy Mattress Co., 145 Cal.App.2d 275, 302 P.2d 331 (2d Dist.1956); Wise v. Hayes, 58 Wash.2d 106, 361 P.2d 171 (1961).

**34.** See, e. g., Greenman v. Yuba Power Prods., Inc., 59 Cal.2d 57, 377 P.2d 897 (1963).

**35.** Prosser, The Fall of the Citadel (Strict Liability to the Consumer), 50 Minn.L.Rev. 791, 837 (1966). And plaintiff must rely on the representation, at least in using the product. Id. at 837–38.

pears in the clothing of contributory negligence, assumption of risk, and lack of proximate cause in the standard tort cases. In the vernacular of strict tort liability, it is likely to be called misuse, abnormal use, or hypersensitivity. In each case the question whether something about the plaintiff or his behavior should bar him from recovery may also be part of the larger, ultimate question whether the causal connection between the defendant's act and the plaintiff's injury is sufficiently close to justify liability. It seems to us that courts should view the plaintiff's behavior and his peculiarities only as factors that may sufficiently attenuate the causal connection between defendant's act and plaintiff's injury to bar recovery.

He who rejects our analysis and seeks to follow the ebb and flow of the language of warranty opinions is likely to be misled and confused. Some courts steadfastly maintain that contributory negligence is no defense to a warranty cause of action or to a strict tort cause of action.[36] Others hold that contributory negligence is a defense to a warranty or strict tort cause of action.[37] Some courts which maintain that contributory negligence is no defense nevertheless hold that the defendant may parade the same misconduct of the plaintiff before the jury to show a lack of proximate cause.[38] On the other hand, courts are in unanimous agreement that the egregious form of contributory negligence called "assumption of the risk" bars plaintiff's recovery in strict tort and in warranty.[39] Predictably, one court's assumption of risk may be another's contributory negligence and vice versa.[40] Because of this conflicting nomenclature, it

---

**36.** See, e. g., Dagley v. Armstrong Rubber Co., 344 F.2d 245 (7th Cir. 1965); Kassouf v. Lee Bros., Inc., 209 Cal.App.2d 568, 26 Cal.Rptr. 276 (Dist. 1962) (food); Jacobs Pharmacy Co. v. Gipson, 116 Ga.App. 760, 159 S.E.2d 171, 4 UCC Rep.Serv. 909 (1967); see also W. Prosser, Handbook on the Law of Torts § 79 at 522; § 103 at 670 (4th ed. 1971).

**37.** See, e. g., Nelson v. Anderson, 245 Minn. 445, 72 N.W.2d 861 (1955); Schneider v. Suhrmann, 8 Utah 2d 35, 327 P.2d 822 (1958); see also Prosser, The Fall of the Citadel (Strict Liability to the Consumer), 50 Minn.L. Rev. 791, 838–40 (1966).

**38.** See, e. g., Dallison v. Sears, Roebuck & Co., 313 F.2d 343 (10th Cir. 1962) (instruction to jury that if proximate cause of the plaintiff's injuries was not breach of implied warranty, but was negligence of plaintiff, then that would be a defense); Webster v. Blue Ship Tea Room, Inc., 347 Mass. 421, 198 N.E.2d 309, 2 UCC Rep.Serv. 161 (1964) (boney fish chowder served to resident of Massachusetts who got a bone stuck in her

craw is merchantable and plaintiff had embarked on "gustatory adventure which may entail the removal of some fish bones").

**39.** See, e. g., Bronson v. Club Comanche, Inc., 286 F.Supp. 21, 5 UCC Rep. Serv. 694 (D.V.I.1968); Greeno v. Clark Equip. Co., 237 F.Supp. 427 (N.D.Ind. 1965); Williams v. Brown Mfg. Co., 45 Ill.2d 418, 261 N.E.2d 305 (1970); Cornette v. Searjeant Metal Products, Inc., 258 N.E.2d 652 (Ind.App.1970).

**40.** Compare Cornette v. Searjeant Metal Products, Inc., 258 N.E.2d 652 (Ind.App.1970) (plaintiff knew that punch press might malfunction and therefore she assumed risk that it would injure her), with O. S. Stapley Co. v. Miller, 6 Ariz.App. 122, 430 P. 2d 701 (1967), vac. 103 Ariz. 556, 447 P.2d 248 (sitting on dash of motor boat which is pulling water skiers and not in seat may be contributory negligence and a good defense) and Pizza Inn, Inc. v. Tiffany, 454 S.W.2d 420 (Texas Ct.Civ.App.1970) (plaintiff's attempt to clean dough rolling machine while it was operating may have been negligence yet not a defense since em-

is difficult to identify real differences among courts of different jurisdictions on these questions, and it is beyond the scope of our work to catalogue the cases. It suffices to say that the lawyer must review the relevant cases carefully. Conduct that should be offered to the court as contributory negligence in one jurisdiction may have to be presented as assumption of risk or absence of proximate cause in another.[41] We limit our efforts to a summary of the relevant *Restatement* language and to a brief analysis of the pertinent Code language and comments.

Comment *g* of 402A of Restatement, Second, Torts states the obvious, namely that "subsequent mishandling" which makes a product harmful or defective bars recovery against the seller. In a similar vein Comment *h* warns that for injuries which result from abnormal handling (as where a beverage bottle is knocked against a radiator to remove the cap), or from abnormal preparation for use (as where too much salt is added to food), or from abnormal consumption (as where a child eats too much candy and falls ill), the seller is not liable. Like wise Comment *i* states that goods harmful only if "over-consumed" are not unreasonably dangerous.[42] Comment *j* implies that the seller may reasonably assume that buyers will read directions and warnings on containers. Comment *n* states explicitly:

> [C]ontributory negligence of the plaintiff is not a defense when such negligence consists merely of a failure to discover the defect of the product, or to guard against the possibility of its existence. On the other hand, the form of contributory negligence which consists in voluntarily and unreasonably proceeding to encounter a known danger, and commonly passes under the name of assumption of risk, is a defense under this Section as in other cases of strict liability. If the user or consumer discovers the defect and is aware of the danger, and nevertheless proceeds unreasonably to make use of the product and is injured by it, he is barred from recovery.

So one sees that even the most authoritative statement of strict tort liability suggests numerous forms of plaintiff misconduct that bar his recovery.

ployee who trained plaintiff told him the machine could not hurt him and plaintiff had not assumed risk).

**41.** Courts seem oblivious to the inconsistency between their rejection of plaintiff's misconduct as a defense under one name, and their acceptance of the same conduct as a valid defense under another name. See Jacobs Pharmacy Co. v. Gipson, 116 Ga.App. 760, 159 S.E.2d 171, 4 UCC Rep.Serv. 909 (1967) (there is no defense of contributory negligence, but plaintiff's action can be scrutinized to decide if it is the proximate cause of her injury): Brockett v. Harrell Bros., Inc., 206 Va. 457, 143 S.E.2d 897 (1965) (contributory negligence is not defense, but defendant is not liable for breach of implied warranty if condition of the goods sold (ham) was known, visible, or obvious to plaintiff).

**42.** Comment i of section 402A indicates that the seller will not be liable to the hypersensitive plaintiff.

The Uniform Commercial Code includes only a few words on the relevance of plaintiff's behavior to his right to recover in warranty. These appear in Comment 13 to 2–314, Comment 5 to 2–715, and in section 2–715(2). Section 2–715(2)(b) authorizes recovery for "injury to person or property proximately resulting from any breach of warranty." The crucial word is "proximately," a word that imports into the Code the many pre-Code warranty cases [43] and the many tort cases on proximate cause which courts turn out in every jurisdiction of the United States every year. Comment 5 to 2–715 elaborates:

> Where the injury involved follows the use of goods without discovery of the defect causing the damage, the question of "proximate" cause turns on whether it was reasonable for the buyer to use the goods without such inspection as would have revealed the defects. If it was not reasonable for him to do so, or if he did in fact discover the defect prior to his use, the injury would not proximately result from the breach of warranty.

The draftsmen do not say whether they intend this comment as a definition, as an exclusive statement of the meaning of "proximately," or only as an illustration. In view of the traditional expansiveness of the word and the absence of any language in Comment 5 which purports to make it a definition we regard Comment 5 as only illustrative.

Note that 2–715(2)(b) applies only to injury to persons and property and not to loss of bargain or loss of profits. In the Code scheme, loss of bargain can be recovered under 2–714(2) and loss of profits under 2–715(2)(a). One may ask, therefore, whether a plaintiff who seeks recovery only for loss of bargain or loss of profits must prove proximate causation. Comment 13 to 2–314 indicates that proximate causation is an element of proof at least in all implied warranty cases, whatever the relief sought. In pertinent part it reads as follows:

> In an action based on breach of warranty, it is of course necessary to show not only the existence of the warranty but the fact that the warranty was broken and that the breach of the warranty was the proximate cause of the loss sustained. In such an action an affirmative showing by the seller that the loss resulted from some action or event following his own delivery of the goods can operate as a defense.

The quoted comment is artfully vague about the kinds of conduct that may negate proximate cause. It does reiterate the illustrative case in the comments to 2–715 about buyer's use of goods he knows

---

**43.** Yormack v. Farmers' Co-op. Ass'n, 11 N.J.Super. 416, 78 A.2d 421 (App. Div.1951) (evidence was insufficient to support finding that use of insecticide could have proximately caused the death of chickens); Hanrahan v. Walgreen Co., 243 N.C. 268, 90 S.E. 2d 392 (1955) (evidence was insufficient to show that hair rinse proximately caused damage to plaintiff's scalp).

to be defective. And certainly it also includes misuse and overuse by the plaintiff-buyer. The lawyer may resort to cases for further illustrations.[44]

To the extent the Code draftsmen considered plaintiff misbehavior a defense to warranty actions, they apparently conceived of it in terms of proximate cause. Note, as already indicated, that some courts hold that contributory negligence *as such* is a defense to a warranty cause of action. We reiterate our warning: a careful lawyer must carefully consider the cases in his jurisdiction and dress his facts in the attire of that locale whether that attire be contributory negligence, lack of proximate cause, assumption of risk, misuse, hypersensitivity, or something else.

Finally, it should now be clear that it is a gross distortion to say that contributory misconduct of plaintiff is no defense to a warranty cause of action.

## § 11–8    Statute of Limitations

Section 2–725 contains the basic Article Two statute of limitations. It provides that "[a]n action for breach of any contract for sale must be commenced within four years after the cause of action has accrued." Subsection (2) specifies that a breach of warranty normally occurs when "tender of delivery is made." The application of this statute presents no difficulty to the lawyer or the judge in most cases. Suits for damages for failure to pay or failure to tender accrue on the date that *payment* or *tender* is due.[45] Similarly uncomplicated is the usual businessman's warranty case in which the machine he accepted proved not to work properly, and he sues the seller under 2–714 for the difference in value between the machine as warranted and the machine as delivered. Unless our buyer falls within the exception to 2–725(2),[46] he must sue within four years of delivery of the machine.

Most of the interpretative difficulties in 2–725 arise out of the continuing friction between strict tort liability on the one hand and warranty liability under the Code on the other. The Code statute of limitations does not apply to strict tort cases, only to warranty cases. If the case is strict tort, the appropriate statute will be one

---

**44.** See, e. g., Jacobs Pharmacy Co. v. Gipson, 116 Ga.App. 760, 159 S.E.2d 171, 4 UCC Rep.Serv. 909 (1967) (whether plaintiff's use of drug contrary to instructions on package was proximate cause of her injury was question for the jury); Haralampopoulos v. Capital News Agency, Inc., 70 Ill.App.2d 17, 217 N.E.2d 366, 3 UCC Rep.Serv. 608 (1966) (sale of obscene magazines by plaintiff was proximate cause of loss of his liquor license); Erdman v. Johnson Bros. Radio & Television Co., Inc., 260 Md. 190, 271 A.2d 744, 8 UCC Rep.Serv. 656 (1970)

(use of television set after plaintiffs noticed sparks and heavy smoke issuing from back of the set prevented breach of warranty from being proximate cause of damages); Maiorino v. Weco Products Co., 45 N.J. 570, 214 A.2d 18 (1965) (careless manner by plaintiff removing toothbrush from glass case was proximate cause of his injuries).

**45.** See 4 A. Corbin, Corbin on Contracts § 989 (1951).

**46.** See notes 54–57 infra.

dealing with tort claims. (Tort statutes are typically two years or less in duration.) [47] Significantly, tort statutes do not commence to run until the defect causes an injury,[48] and in some cases, not until the plaintiff has or should have discovered the injury.[49] Depending upon such circumstances as the length of time between the sale and the injury, whether the injury is "latent" or not, and the duration of the appropriate tort statute, a particular cause of action may be barred by 2–725 but not by the tort statute, or it may be barred by the tort statute but not by 2–725. The courts have not drawn a clear line between those cases which are "essentially tort" and those which are "essentially warranty." [50] As we have noted, courts are likely to classify a personal injury case as tort and unlikely to classify an economic loss case as tort. For a further discussion of factors which point toward "tort" and away from "warranty" or vice versa, see our discussion in Section 11–2 above.

Of course, the theory upon which a plaintiff bases his claim may affect the foregoing analysis profoundly. If he invokes negligence theory, quite clearly the tort statute will apply. His own explicit characterization of the case as one in warranty or in strict tort may also affect the court's judgment about which statute of limitations applies. Of course, neither the defendant nor the court is bound by the plaintiff's own characterization of his cause of action, and the court should make up its own mind how to characterize the plaintiff's claim on the basis of the facts. Nevertheless, one suspects that a clever plaintiff's lawyer occasionally avoids a statute of limitations issue altogether by careful choice of theory and careful pleading.

Once a court determines that 2–725 or, alternatively, a tort statute applies, it must still determine when the statute commences to run. Section 2–725(2) is explicit and straightforward on this point:

> A cause of action accrues when the breach occurs, regardless of the aggrieved party's lack of knowledge of the breach. A breach of warranty occurs when tender of delivery is made, except that where a warranty explicitly extends to future performance of the goods and discovery of the breach must await the time of such performance the cause of action accrues when the breach is or should have been discovered.

47.  See, e. g., Ariz.Rev.Stat.Ann. § 12–542 (1956); Ill.Stat.Ann. Ch. 83, § 15 (1966); Mass.Ann.Laws ch. 260, § 2A (1968). See also LoPucki, Statute of Limitations in Warranty, 21 U.Fla.L. Rev. 336–37 (1969).

48.  See, e. g., Tyler v. R. R. Street & Co., 322 F.Supp. 541, 8 UCC Rep.Serv. 1253 (E.D.Va.1971). Contra, Leyen v. Dunn, Tenn.App., 461 S.W.2d 41 (1970). (However special statute of limitations commenced with the injury for defective property improvements, where injury occurred within four years after completion of the improvement.)

49.  See, e. g., the following malpractice suits: Mayer v. Good Samaritan Hospital, 14 Ariz.App. 248, 482 P.2d 497 (1971); Berry v. Branner, 245 Ore. 307, 421 P.2d 996 (1966); Wilkinson v. Harrington, 104 R.I. 224, 243 A.2d 745 (1968).

50.  See the discussion in Annot., 4 A.L.R.3d 821 (1965) and Annot., 37 A.L.R.2d 698 (1954) for an extensive compilation of cases on choosing the proper statute of limitation.

Apart from the case in which the warranty "explicitly extends to future performance," the section is quite clear. The statute normally commences to run upon tender of delivery, and the clock ticks even though the buyer does not know the goods are defective. This outcome contrasts markedly with that under the typical tort statute which does not begin to run until the defect manifests itself by causing some injury. If, for example, a wheel on an automobile were defective, the cause of action would not arise until the wheel caused some injury.[51] Moreover, if the injury is difficult to discover (as when a drug causes a personal injury discoverable only long after the drug is purchased and used), many cases hold that the statute does not begin to run until the plaintiff discovered or reasonably should have discovered the injury.[52]

It is not clear how the tort statute will be applied by those few courts which appear willing to apply strict tort liability in cases which involve no physical or personal injury. For example, in Santor v. A. & M. Karagheusian,[53] the plaintiff sued in strict tort and warranty for the diminution of value of a rug which, after a period, commenced to show unusual lines. In that case there was no accident or sudden event which revealed the defect and "caused injury"; presumably the deterioration of the rug was gradual. In such cases the courts could apply the tort standard for latent defects and find that the statute did not commence to run until the plaintiff should have known of the defect. A better solution would be to hold that strict tort does not apply at all and to hold, instead, that 2–725 governs.

A final interpretative difficulty arises out of the second sentence of 2–725(2) which provides that the statute does not begin to run upon tender of delivery where "a warranty explicitly extends to future performance of the goods and discovery of the breach must await the time of such performance." In such cases 2–725(2) states that the cause of action accrues when "the breach is or should have been discovered." First, it should be clear that this extension of the normal warranty period does not occur in the usual case, even though all warranties in a sense apply to the future performance of goods. The quoted portion of 2–725(2) applies only in a case in which the warranty "explicitly extends to future performance." Presumably such a case would be one in which the seller gave a "life time guaran-

---

51. W. Prosser, Handbook of the Law of Torts § 30 at 144 (4th ed. 1971) (statute of limitations does not run against negligent action until some damage is done). See also Rush v. Pierson Contracting Co., 310 F.Supp. 1389 (E.D.Mich.1970); Williams v. Brown Mfg. Co., 45 Ill.2d 418, 261 N.E.2d 305 (1970). For sample tort statutes, see N.J.Rev.Stat. § 2A:14–2 (1952) (two years for personal injury actions); Pa.Stat.Ann. tit. 12, § 34 (1953) (two years for personal injury).

52. See, e. g., R. J. Reynolds Tobacco Co. v. Hudson, 314 F.2d 776 (5th Cir. 1963); Brush Beryllium Co. v. Meckley, 284 F.2d 797 (6th Cir. 1960); Breaux v. Aetna Cas. & Sur. Co., 272 F.Supp. 668 (E.D.La.1967); Stafford v. Shultz, 42 Cal.2d 767, 270 P.2d 1 (1954).

53. 44 N.J. 52, 207 A.2d 305, 2 UCC Rep.Serv. 599 (1965).

tee" or one in which he, for example, expressly warranted that an automobile would last for 24,000 miles or four years whichever occurred first. If the automobile failed in the 20,000th mile and after three years of driving, the buyer (if he had no notice or knowledge of the defect prior to the failure) would have four years from that date to commence his suit notwithstanding that his suit would then be brought seven years after the sale had occurred. Two recent cases illustrate the difficulty that the courts have had in determining which warranties "explicitly extend."

In Perry v. Augustine [54] the allegedly defective product was a heating system. The seller had warranted the system would "be able to heat at 75° inside at a -20° outside temp." The time of tender was July, 1961. The court decided that the statute did not begin to run as of that date because the warranty explicitly extended to future performance of the goods. The court stated:

> Here the warranty in question relates to what the heating system sold and delivered in June and July 1961, would do in the future, i. e., when it was tested under subzero temperature conditions. Discovery of a breach of that kind of a warranty in this climate would necessarily have to await winter weather.[55]

Whether this warranty in fact extended to the future performance of the goods is unclear. The court's rationale is that *discovery* of breach would have to await the future performance of the goods, and therefore the warranty was explicitly prospective. The reasoning is not persuasive. The same could be said of all warranties, and in the *Perry* case the temperature might never reach -20°.

In Rempe v. General Electric Co.,[56] the court "assumed" that section 2-725 did not govern. The opinion, however, included dictum that were the Code statute of limitations applicable, the case would have fallen within the exception in section 2-725 regarding future warranties. In purchasing the defective product, the plaintiff received a "lifetime" warranty. The court properly found that this warranty was prospective, that is, that it promised performance of the product not merely at the moment of purchase but at some future date as well. The cause of action, therefore, did not accrue until "the breach is or should have been discovered." [57] The court suggested, however, that because of the ambiguity of the warranty (how long is a "lifetime"?), the defendant should have the opportunity to persuade the trier of fact that the warranty had expired more than four years before commencement of the action.

In summary, we can do little more than warn the lawyer not to make hasty judgments about the applicable statute of limitations or about when it will commence to run. Section 2-725 offers a sane and

54. 37 Pa.D. & C.2d 416, 3 UCC Rep. Serv. 735 (C.P.1965).

55. Id. at 418, 3 UCC Rep.Serv. at 737.

56. 28 Conn.Supp. 160, 254 A.2d 577, 6 UCC Rep.Serv. 647 (1969).

57. § 2-725(2).

workable statutory scheme,[58] but it is one the courts will infrequently follow when the plaintiff's blood has been spilled [59] or when the defendant is a remote seller.[60]  To courts, these cases look like tort, not contract, particularly when the tort statute of limitations favors the plaintiff.[61]

## § 11–9    Buyer's Failure to Give Notice as a Defense to Actions for Breach of Warranty

A buyer who accepts nonconforming goods must notify the seller that the goods are nonconforming, "or be barred from any remedy." Section 2–607(3) (a) of the Code provides:

> Where a tender has been accepted
>
> (a) the buyer must within a reasonable time after he discovers or should have discovered any breach notify the seller of breach or be barred from any remedy   .   .   .   .

"Any remedy" within the meaning of section 2–607(3) (a) includes ancillary rights such as the right to revoke acceptance under 2–608 as well as the right to damages.  Of course, if plaintiff's cause of action is in strict tort, 2–607(3) (a) does not apply.

The most vexatious and frequently litigated 2–607(3) (a) question is:  what constitutes a "reasonable time" within which the buyer "should have discovered any breach" and have notified the seller? On reading the cases one is tempted to say that a reasonable time in this context has as many meanings as there are fact patterns in the cases.[62]  Although we are tempted to leave it at that, the situation

---

**58.**  Comment 2 to 2–312 makes clear the draftsmen's opinion that the implied warranty of title and its corollary of quiet possession is breached if at all, at the time of sale.  This result will differ from that reached under the pre-Code law of some states.  See Menzel v. List, 24 N.Y.2d 91, 246 N.E. 2d 742, 6 UCC Rep.Serv. 330 (1969) (warranty of title action brought more than seven years after sale is not too late).  Comment 2 of the 2–312 reads as follows:

Section 2–725 provides that the cause of action accrues when the breach occurs.  Under the provisions of that section the breach of the warranty of good title occurs when tender of delivery is made since the warranty is not one which extends to "future performance of the goods."

**59.**  Abate v. Barkers of Wallingford, Inc., 27 Conn.Supp. 46, 229 A.2d 366, 4 UCC Rep.Serv. 310 (1967).

**60.**  Rosenau v. City of New Brunswick, 51 N.J. 130, 238 A.2d 169, 5 UCC Rep. Serv. 126 (1968).

**61.**  See generally Rapson, Products Liability under Parallel Doctrines: Contrasts Between the Uniform Commercial Code and Strict Liability in Tort, 19 Rutgers L.Rev. 692, 704–707 (1965) (courts incline toward tort statute of limitations where plaintiff is injured more than four years after sale).

**62.**  Notices were held timely in the following cases: Lewis v. Mobil Oil Corp., 438 F.2d 500, 8 UCC Rep. Serv. 625 (8th Cir. 1971), (nonadditive oil was used for two and one-half years before notice of breach given although Mobil dealer was aware that oil was suspect); Larrance Tank Corp. v. Burrough, 476 P.2d 346, 8 UCC Rep.Serv. 337 (Okla.1970) (underground gasoline tank leaked 150 gallons per week for 60 weeks before notice was given); Schneider v. Person, 34 Pa.D. & C.2d 10, 2 UCC Rep.Serv. 37 (C.P.1964) (notice given in six and one-half months about horse suffering from splints).  Contra, Hays Merchandise, Inc. v. Dewey, 78 Wash. 2d 342, 474 P.2d 270, 8 UCC Rep.Serv. 31 (1970) (notice given after two

may not be quite that dismal. A lawyer cognizant of the policies behind the notice requirement may be able to predict how a court will apply "reasonable time," and may be able to argue convincingly that a specific time was or was not reasonable in light of those policies. One can identify at least three policies behind 2–607. The first and most important reason for requiring notice is to enable the seller to make adjustments or replacements or to suggest opportunities for cure to the end of minimizing the buyer's loss and reducing the seller's own liability to the buyer.[63] For example, the purchaser of a truck should tell the seller at once of any defects and procure any necessary replacements and adjustments. He should not allow the truck to sit in his yard for a year and then sue for the profits that he would have made during that year had the truck worked properly. The second policy behind the notice requirement is to afford the seller an opportunity to arm himself for negotiation and litigation. For example, our sources tell us that the Henningsens notified Chrysler so late in their famous case that Chrysler was not even able to find and inspect the automobile in which Mrs. Henningsen was injured.[64] Had Chrysler been able to find the allegedly defective car, it might have been able to present certain defenses or at least have been able to limit the jury's speculation. A final, and less important policy behind the notice requirement is to give the defendant that same kind of mind balm he gets from the statute of limitations. There is some value in allowing a seller, at some point, to close his books on goods sold in the past and to pass on to other things.

In cases resting mostly on the first policy, the courts are not at all hesitant to find that a commercial buyer failed to live up to the notice requirements and thus forfeited his Code remedies.[65] Comment 4 states that in such cases 2–607 defeats "commercial bad faith," and if the court senses that a merchant buyer is lying in the Johnson grass with the thought of increasing his damages, it will not hesitate a moment to cut him off. A case in point is A. C. Carpenter, Inc. v. Boyer Potato Chips.[66] In that case the buyer sent a "breach" letter to the seller eight days after receiving nonconforming potatoes. The seller received the letter four days after it was sent. The hearing officer held that the notice was not timely; twelve days was too long for parties dealing in perishables. The hearing officer might have suspected that the buyer was not acting in good faith, for the buyer did not call the seller although he knew the seller's address and the

months held unreasonable for toys in Christmas season).

**63.** See § 2–607, Comment 4; L. A. Green Seed Co. v. Williams, 246 Ark. 463, 438 S.W.2d 717 (1969).

**64.** Henningsen v. Bloomfield Motors, Inc., 32 N.J. 358, 161 A.2d 69 (1960).

**65.** Notices were held untimely in the following cases: Mazur Brothers v.

Jaffe Fish Co., Inc., VACAB–512, 3 UCC Rep.Serv. 419 (1965) (government waited five days before notifying local supplier of unfit shrimp); General Food Corp. v. Bittinger Co., 31 Pa. D. & C.2d 282, 1 UCC Rep.Serv. 168 (C.P.1963) (corporation waited four months after discovery of defects in corn before notifying seller).

**66.** 28 Agri.Dec. 1557, 7 UCC Rep.Serv. 493 (1969).

telephone number. In G. & D. Poultry Farms, Inc. v. Long Island Butter & Egg Co.,[67] the court found a delay unreasonably long because, in part, the buyer had ordered and paid for additional goods without notifying the seller that the goods were in any way unsatisfactory. In short, a merchant buyer who receives defective goods and who expects to reject, revoke acceptance, or sue under 2–714 and 2–715 should act fast.

The cases which rest mostly on the second policy, that is, the policy affording the seller a fair opportunity to arm himself to defend against a suit arising out of an injury caused by the defect, reflect much greater judicial willingness to permit the buyer to dilly-dally.[68] Indeed, the draftsmen of the comments went out of their way to encourage courts not to close the door too quickly on a "retail consumer," and one suspects that the draftsmen (and many courts) would tolerate an even longer delay on the part of a retail consumer whose blood has been spilled.[69] Comment 4 to 2–607 states that "[a] 'reasonable time' for notification from a retail consumer is to be judged by different standards so that in his case it will be extended, for the rule of requiring notification is [not designed] to deprive a good faith consumer of his remedy." Not only the draftsmen but also the writers and the courts seem to disfavor the lack of notice defense when invoked against an injured consumer. Indeed, one of the oft cited virtues of strict tort theory is that it does not require notice.[70] The defendant's lawyer whose client is sued not by a merchant-buyer but by a consumer, especially by a consumer who suffered personal injury or property damage, should not rely heavily on a lack of notice defense. Here the notice policies collide with a countervailing policy that unsophisticated consumers who suffer real and perhaps grievous injury at the hands of the defendant-seller ought to have an easy road to recovery.

To what extent may the parties to a sales contract legislate for themselves with regard to notice and its timeliness? Section 1–204 (1) validates a contractual time limit within which a buyer must notify his seller, provided that the agreed time period is not "manifestly unreasonable" within the meaning of 1–204(1) and (2). In Q. Van-

---

**67.** 33 App.Div.2d 685, 306 N.Y.S.2d 243, 6 UCC Rep.Serv. 1258 (2d Dep't 1969).

**68.** See, e. g., Pritchard v. Liggett & Myers Tobacco Co., 295 F.2d 292 (3d Cir. 1961) (ten months after his lung was removed cigarette smoker gave notice to cigarette manufacturer; held notice was not untimely under section 49 of Uniform Sales Act); Schneider v. Person, 34 Pa.D. & C.2d 10, 2 UCC Rep.Serv. 37 (C.P.1964) (notice that horse had splints six and one-half months after purchase was timely).

**69.** Bonker v. Ingersoll Prods. Corp., 132 F.Supp. 5 (D.Mass.1955) (notice of bone in can of "Boneless Chicken" given to manufacturer four months after injury was not unreasonable delay under Uniform Sales Act); Downey v. Mahoney, 25 Mass.App.Dec. 196, 4 UCC Rep.Serv. 661 (1962) (notice of unfit pork given 32 days after plaintiff fell ill was held reasonable notice of breach of warranty).

**70.** See W. Prosser, Handbook of the Law of Torts § 97 at 655 (4th ed. 1971) (2–607(3) is a "booby-trap for the unwary").

denberg and Sons, N. V. v. Siter,[71] the goods were tulip bulbs which the seller warranted to be capable of flowering at the time of shipment.  Months after delivery, the buyer discovered they would not flower.  The buyer alleged that the inability of the bulbs to flower was due to a defect existing at the time of delivery.  However, the contract provided that the buyer waived any claim for breach of warranty unless he asserted such claim within eight days after delivery. The buyer argued that such a provision, insofar as it applied to defects which were latent and impossible to discover within the eight-day period, was "manifestly unreasonable" within the meaning of 1–204(1).  The court held that the buyer succeeded in raising a jury question.

Two questions remain.  First, does anyone other than a buyer have a duty to give notice of breach?  Second, must a buyer give notice to any seller other than the one from whom he actually purchased the goods?  Tomczuk v. Town of Cheshire,[72] a personal injury action, raised both questions.  Plaintiff was a playmate of a girl whose parents had purchased a bicycle.  While riding the bicycle, plaintiff sustained injuries allegedly caused by defects in the bicycle. Section 2–318 indicated that plaintiff would have the same rights under the seller's warranties as an actual purchaser would.  The question was whether plaintiff had the same or similar duties under section 2–607.  Comment 5 to 2–607 answers this question affirmatively:

> Under this Article various beneficiaries are given rights for injuries sustained by them because of the seller's breach of warranty.  Such a beneficiary does not fall within the reason of the present section in regard to discovery of defects and the giving of notice within a reasonable time after acceptance, since he has nothing to do with acceptance. However, the reason of this section does extend to requiring the beneficiary to notify the seller that an injury has occurred.  What is said above, with regard to the extended time for reasonable notification from the lay consumer after the injury is also applicable here; but even a beneficiary can be properly held to the use of good faith in notifying, once he has had time to become aware of the legal situation.

The court, however, ignored the above comment and absolved plaintiff of any duty to give notice to the manufacturer.  The court reasoned that the notice requirement applied only to buyers, and since the plaintiff was not a buyer,[73] she had no duty to give notice.  Although it was a moot question in view of the court's position that the requirements of 2–607(3) (a) did not apply to the plaintiff in this case, the court went on to opine that the words "the seller" in 2–607

---

71.  204 Pa.Super. 392, 204 A.2d 494, 2 UCC Rep.Serv. 383 (1964).

72.  26 Conn.Supp. 219, 217 A.2d 71, 3 UCC Rep.Serv. 147 (1965).

73.  See § 2–103(a).

(3) (a) should be read "his immediate seller." In short the court indicated that a consumer need not notify a manufacturer provided the consumer did not purchase directly from him.[74] This may not be unfair to manufacturers when the buyer sues both the retailer and the manufacturer, for the retailer will very likely notify the manufacturer, especially when the retailer is one who (for example, an auto dealer) buys his entire inventory from one manufacturer. On the other hand, when the buyer sues only the manufacturer, we think courts should require the buyer to notify the manufacturer of the defect. The manufacturer may bear responsibility for the buyer's losses and needs the protection of notice at least as much as a retailer. As a matter of logic, there is no reason to distinguish between retailers and manufacturers, insofar as their respective rights to notice are concerned. The retailer's right to notice derives from the fact that the buyer dealt directly with him. When, therefore, the manufacturer is the only defendant, the buyer should have to give him notice.

Finally, what constitutes sufficient notice under 2–607(3) (a)? How explicit must it be? May it be oral? Must it threaten litigation? Quite clearly the drafters intended a loose test; a scribbled note on a bit of toilet paper will do:

> The content of the notification need merely be sufficient to let the seller know that the transaction is still troublesome and must be watched. There is no reason to require that the notification which saves the buyer's rights under this section must include a clear statement of all the objections that will be relied on by the buyer, as under the section covering statements of defects upon rejection (Section 2–605). Nor is there reason for requiring the notification to be a claim for damages or of any threatened litigation or other resort to a remedy. The notification which saves the buyer's rights under this Article need only be such as informs the seller that the transaction is claimed to involve a breach, and thus opens the way for normal settlement through negotiation.[75]

Under this comment, it is difficult to conceive of words which, if put in writing, would not satisfy the notice requirement of 2–607. Indeed, a letter containing anything but the most exaggerated en-

---

74. Cf. Bennett v. Richardson-Merrell, Inc., 231 F.Supp. 150 (E.D.Ill.1964); Ruderman v. Warner-Lambert Pharmaceutical Co., 23 Conn.Supp. 416, 184 A.2d 63 (1962); Piercefield v. Remington Arms Co., 375 Mich. 85, 133 N.W.2d 129, 2 UCC Rep.Serv. 611 (1965). In each of the foregoing cases the courts rejected seller's defense of lack of notice.

But cf. Spada v. Stauffer Chemical Co., 195 F.Supp. 819 (D.Ore.1961) (ultimate users of selective herbicide had to give notice to manufacturer). This holding may, however, no longer be valid. See Wights v. Staff Jennings, Inc., 241 Ore. 301, 405 P.2d 624, 2 UCC Rep.Serv. 1061 (1965), where the Supreme Court of Oregon held that the defense of lack of notice will not bar an action in implied warranty. However, the court emphasized that an implied warranty of merchantability rests upon strict liability in tort.

75. § 2–607, Comment 4.

comiums would seem to tell the seller that the transaction "is still troublesome and must be watched."

Although the question is not free of doubt, it appears that an oral notice will suffice. Section 2–607(3) (a) uses the verb "notify;" that word is defined in 1–201(26) in a way that would permit an oral statement to constitute notice. That other Code sections impose writing requirements by using the word "sent" supports our interpretation of 2–607(3) (a).[76] Moreover, the most authoritative interpretation of 2–607 to date indicates that a variety of acts other than a formal written notice may satisfy 2–607. In Boeing Airplane Co. v. O'Malley,[77] the buyer purchased a helicopter which was delivered on December 1, 1959. The seller did not receive formal notice of dissatisfaction until February, 1961. The court held that certain events well prior to February, 1961 were sufficient to constitute notice to the seller. The first of these was the failure of the helicopter to function properly in the presence of one of the seller's experts. After the demonstration, but before February, 1961, the buyer had informed the seller that the buyer was closing down operations because of inadequacies in the helicopter and was moving the helicopter elsewhere in order to take care of it.

In conclusion, we draw attention to the difference between the notice specified in 2–607(3) (a) and discussed in this chapter and that specified in 2–602(1) and discussed in Chapter 8. The former is a condition to any remedy; the latter is a condition only to the remedy of rejection. The rejection notice should normally come earlier in time, for it must be given a reasonable time after "delivery or tender," whereas the 2–607 notice must be given within a reasonable time after buyer discovers or should have discovered the breach. For reasons discussed in Chapter 8, it is fair and proper that the buyer who seeks to reject should be required to give notice and to act more quickly than one who seeks only to recover damages.[78]

---

**76.** See, e. g., § 9–504(3) (notice must "be sent," i. e., letter or telegram presumably).

**77.** 329 F.2d 585, 2 UCC Rep.Serv. 110 (8th Cir. 1964); Warren's Kiddie Shoppe, Inc. v. Casual Slacks, Inc., 120 Ga.App. 578, 171 S.E.2d 643, 7 UCC Rep.Serv. 166 (1969) (telephone call to the seller's president informing him that because shipment was late price of ordered goods would have to be lowered might be sufficient notification of breach); Bailey v. Jordon Marsh Co., 6 Mass.App.Dec. 17 (1953) (oral notice held sufficient under Uniform Sales Act).

**78.** Miron v. Yonkers Raceway, Inc., 5 UCC Rep.Serv. 76 (S.D.N.Y.1968), aff'd, 400 F.2d 112, 5 UCC Rep.Serv.

673 (2d Cir. 1968) (notification day after auction that race horse was lame was not reasonable for purposes of rejection); Beco, Inc. v. Minnechaug Golf Course, Inc., 5 Conn. Cir. 444, 256 A.2d 522, 6 UCC Rep.Serv. 910 (1968) (returning restaurant equipment after one month did not constitute effective rejection within reasonable time); Menard & Holmberg Rambler, Inc. v. Shea, 44 Mass.App. Dec. 204, 8 UCC Rep.Serv. 167 (Mass. App.1970) (returning car after three days was notification of rejection within reasonable time); Zabriskie Chevrolet, Inc. v. Smith, 99 N.J.Super. 441, 240 A.2d 195, 5 UCC Rep.Serv. 30 (Law Div.1968) (whether notification was reasonable was not questioned when buyer rejected car after driving it home).

# CHAPTER 12

# DISCLAIMERS OF WARRANTY LIABILITY AND MODIFICATION OF BUYER'S REMEDIES

*Analysis*

Sec.

12–1.   Introduction.

12–2.   Disclaimers of Express Warranties, 2–316(1).

12–3.   —— Conflict Within Written Agreement.

12–4.   —— Oral Warranties Made Prior to the Written Agreement.

12–5.   Disclaimers of Implied Warranties—Explicit Disclaimers of Implied Warranties, 2–316(2).

12–6.   —— Other Methods.

12–7.   Cumulation and Conflict of Warranties, 2–317.

12–8.   Modification or Limitation of Remedies, 2–719.

12–9.   —— How to Limit the Buyer's Remedies, 2–719(1).

12–10.  —— Failure of Stipulated Remedy to Achieve Its Essential Purpose, 2–719(2).

12–11.  —— Unconscionable Limitation of Remedy, 2–719(3) and 2–302.

12–12.  —— Use of 2–719(3) to Invalidate an Otherwise Valid Disclaimer.

## § 12–1   Introduction

Now that we have surveyed the buyer's rights and remedies in regard to warranties, it is appropriate to ask what rights the seller has to protect himself against warranty liability.[1]  Freedom of contract affords some protection for the seller who wishes to avoid liability that would otherwise arise from implied warranties or from his own express statements made in the heat of a sales pitch. Section 1–102(3) provides that "[t]he effect of provisions of this Act may be varied by agreement, except as otherwise provided . . . ."[2]  Building on this general principle, 2–316 and 2–719 delineate specific measures that the seller may take to disclaim warranty liability and to limit the buyer's remedies for breach. Also, 2–202, the Code's parol evidence rule, enables the seller under some circumstances to disavow statements made by his salesmen that could be construed as express warranties, a topic we treated in Section 2–12 supra.

The seller does not have unlimited power to avoid liability.  As we will see, appellate courts do not favor disclaimers, particularly when the plaintiff is an injured consumer.  Moreover, the Congress is now making noises that it will soon enact federal limitations on dis-

---

1. Disclaimer of the warranty of title is dealt with in Section 9–12 supra.

2. Comment 2 to section 1–102 declares: "Subsection (3) states affirmatively at the outset that freedom of contract is a principle of the Code . . . . ."

claimers to consumers.[3]  The Code itself hardly leaves the buyer unprotected.  The very Code provisions that purport to enable the seller to escape liability include significant restrictions on the form and substance that disclaimers may take and offer a great deal of leeway for courts to strike down exculpatory clauses.  Moreover, the specter of unconscionability, specifically embodied in 2–719(3) and applicable to all contract terms under 2–302, constantly lurks above consumer transactions, ready to strike down the most artfully drafted disclaimer or limitation-of-remedy clause.

Despite the specificity of 2–316 and 2–719, the effects of these limitations are among the most uncertain in the Code.  This uncertainty is attributable to the availability of 2–302 as a policing device; to the use in 2–315, 2–317 (on cumulation and conflict of warranties) and 2–719 of such discretion-inviting terms as "unreasonable",[4] "consistent",[5] and "circumstances",[6] and to the tendency of many courts in recent years to take a more sympathetic view toward consumers.[7]  Partly because of these sources of uncertainty, the official reporters are filled with cases litigating issues arising in this area.  Since virtually all lawyers in commercial practice inevitably litigate at least a few disclaimer cases, and since students in courses on commercial transactions inevitably encounter at least one such case on their finals, we will discuss the formal Code requirements at length and will indicate how courts now seem to be exercising their almost boundless discretion in this area.

Before proceeding further, however, the reader should note the difference between attempts to disclaim warranty liability and attempts to disclaim strict tort liability.  Section 402A of the Re-

---

3.  Recently the Senate passed the "Magnuson-Moss Act" which, among other things, establishes disclosure requirements and federal standards for written warranties on consumer products.  See 117 Cong.Rec.S.17,887–91 (daily ed. Nov. 8, 1971).  The Act's definition of consumer products (§ 101 (2)) substantially conforms to the definition of consumer goods in UCC § 9–109(1), but it also encompasses fixtures.  Section 108(a) of the Act prohibits disclaimer of implied warranties when the supplier makes a written warranty which states that the products, material, or workmanship is defect-free or will meet a specified level of performance, or undertakes to replace or repair the product.  Section 108(b) further provides that "implied warranties may be limited only as to duration".  Presumably section 108 (b) precludes limitation of damages or remedies for breach of implied warranties.

Noncompliance with the Act is a violation of the Federal Trade Commission Act § 111.  FTC § 110 also provides for private remedies.  Note that the Act does not apply when the goods are other than consumer goods or when no written warranty is given.

4.  "Reasonable" or "unreasonable" appears twice in 2–316 and once in 2–317.

5.  "Consistent" or "inconsistent" appears once in 2–316 and four times in 2–317.

6.  Reference to "circumstances" is made twice in 2–316 and once in 2–719.

7.  This sympathy is perhaps most effectively expressed and implemented in Henningsen v. Bloomfield Motors, Inc., 32 N.J. 358, 161 A.2d 69 (1960).

statement, Second, Torts sets up a special theory of liability for sellers who sell goods for consumer use:

> (1) One who sells any product in a defective condition unreasonably dangerous to the user or consumer or to his property is subject to liability for physical harm thereby caused to the ultimate user or consumer, or to his property, if
>
> > (a) the seller is engaged in the business of selling such a product, and
> >
> > (b) it is expected to and does reach the user or consumer without substantial change in the condition in which it is sold.[8]

Official Comment *m* makes clear that the consumer's rights under this section are not governed by the Code and are "not affected by any disclaimer or other agreement." [9] Thus, at least in theory, Code law on procedures for excluding warranty liability has no bearing on the seller's liability in tort. Indeed some courts (including the California Supreme Court) [10] have explicitly held that a seller cannot disclaim strict tort liability. While other courts adopting strict tort theory might disagree, the lawyer should recognize that strict tort liability arises independently of any contractual relationship and may not be disclaimable.

## § 12–2  Disclaimers of Express Warranties, 2–316(1)

The very idea that a seller may disclaim an express warranty may seem illogical or dishonest. How could a seller legitimately disavow an express representation of his that by definition was "part of the basis of the bargain"? [11] The draftsmen of the 1952 Code apparently did not think a seller could do this, for the 1952 version of 2–316 provided: "If the agreement creates an express warranty, words disclaiming it are inoperative." But the draftsmen later rejected this approach; 2–316(1) now provides:

> Words or conduct relevant to the creation of an express warranty and words or conduct tending to negate or limit warranty shall be construed wherever reasonable as consistent with each other; but subject to the provisions of this Article on parol or extrinsic evidence (Section 2–202) negation or limitation is inoperative to the extent that such construction is unreasonable.

---

8. Restatement, Second, Torts § 402A (1965).

9. Id. § 402A, Comment *m* at 356.

10. Vandermark v. Ford Motor Co., 61 Cal.2d 256, 391 P.2d 168 (1964) (action against automobile manufacturer and dealer for personal injuries re-

sulting from brake failure). See also Haley v. Merit Chevrolet, Inc., 67 Ill. App.2d 19, 214 N.E.2d 347 (1966) (personal injuries resulting from defective tires and steering column of new car).

11. See § 2–313.

As a result,[12] the trier of fact must now determine whether the seller's statement that a used car will get twenty miles to the gallon is consistent with his further statement that the car is sold with no warranties.   In this section we will be concerned with how the courts have resolved this kind of problem in two contexts:

> (1) when both the express warranty and disclaimer are contained in a written agreement; and
>
> (2) when a parol warranty is made before the disclaimer is incorporated into a written contract.

### § 12–3   Disclaimers of Express Warranties, 2–316(1)—Conflict Within Written Agreement

Comment 1 to 2–316 indicates that subsection (1) "seeks to protect a buyer from unexpected and unbargained language of disclaimer by denying effect to such language when inconsistent with language of express warranty . . . ."   Thus if a seller warrants, in a printed form contract for the sale of a used truck, that the engine is free of defects, he cannot escape the obligation implicit in that warranty by pointing to another clause in the contract providing that the seller shall not be liable for any repairs that become necessary as a result of defective parts.   In such case, the inconsistency between the two clauses renders the disclaimer inoperative.[13]

Presumably, conflicting express warranties and disclaimers rarely appear in printed forms, since these forms are usually drafted with meticulous care in order to provide sellers with maximum protection.   The New York courts, however, seem willing to say that the most carefully drafted disclaimers may conflict with express warranties.   In Walsh v. Ford Motor Co.,[14] the plaintiff was injured when the new car he had just purchased went out of control because of defects in the throttle linkage.   The manufacturer's printed warranty was limited to the replacement and repair of defective parts, and it provided: "The warranties herein are expressly In Lieu of any other express or implied warranty, condition or guarantee on this vehicle or any part thereof . . . ." [15]   The court thought these provisions sought both to disclaim *all* warranties and to limit the remedies available for breach of warranty.   The court concluded that

---

12.   One court has concluded that the revision did not affect a major change in the substantive law.   It noted that the new version "modifies the 1952 language, but the spirit of the provision remains the same."   Berk v. Gordon Johnson Co., 232 F.Supp. 682, 688, 2 UCC Rep.Serv. 240, 244 (E.D. Mich.1964) (Uniform Sales Act case that looked to Code to construe contract).

13.   Under the language of Comment 1 to section 2–316, the seller could introduce evidence that the parties had specifically bargained over the disclaimer clause.   If such evidence were convincing, a court could try to find some reasonable construction of the contract that harmonized the two terms.

14.   59 Misc.2d 241, 298 N.Y.S.2d 538, 6 UCC Rep.Serv. 56 (Sup.Ct.1969).

15.   Id. at 242, 298 N.Y.S.2d at 539, 6 UCC Rep.Serv. at 57.

they could not reasonably be reconciled and held the disclaimer inoperative.[16]  In fact the provisions did not conflict, since the disclaimer clause only disclaimed warranties "other" than "[t]he warranties herein" and the contract did make *some* express warranties.[17]  Nevertheless, *Walsh* illustrates that 2–316(1) provides consumer-oriented courts with a powerful tool for striking down disclaimers.

A conflict between express warranties and disclaimer language may also develop when an express warranty is handwritten or typed on a printed form.  For example, one Pennsylvania case [18] involved a contract to convert a heating system from steam to hot water and to replace component parts.  A printed provision disclaimed all liability on the seller's part for damage to person or property, but a typed-in provision stated, "This installation shall be done in a neat and workmanship like [*sic*] manner and guaranteed for one year." [19]  The court held that under these circumstances the warranty would not be defeated by the printed disclaimer unless such an intention were spelled out clearly and certainly.[20]

We hope courts will reach similar conclusions and strike down attempted disclaimers in cases in which the seller includes a description of the article which amounts to a warranty and then attempts to disclaim all express warranties.  Assume, for example, that the sales contract describes machinery to be sold as a "haybaler" and then attempts to disclaim all express warranties.  If the machine failed to bale hay and buyer sued, we would argue that the disclaimer is ineffective.  In our judgment, the description of the machine as a "haybaler" is a warranty that the machine will bale hay and, in the words of 2–316, a negation or limitation ought to be "inoperative" since it is inconsistent with the warranty.

16.  Id. at 242–43, 298 N.Y.S.2d at 540, 6 UCC Rep.Serv. at 57.  The court also held that the attempt of the disclaimer and warranty provision to limit damages for personal injury was unconscionable.  For an opinion reaching a similar result with a sounder factual basis, see Wilson Trading Corp. v. David Ferguson, Ltd., 23 N.Y. 2d 398, 244 N.E.2d 685, 5 UCC Rep. Serv. 1213 (1968) (express warranty of merchantability of yarn with clause disclaiming liability for defects discovered more than ten years after delivery).

17.  59 Misc.2d at 242, 298 N.Y.S.2d at 539, 6 UCC Rep.Serv. at 57.

18.  Henry v. W. S. Reichenbach & Son, Inc., 45 Pa.D. & C.2d 171, 5 UCC Rep. Serv. 985 (C.P.1968).

19.  Id. at 171, 5 UCC Rep.Serv. at 986.

20.  Id. at 172, 5 UCC Rep.Serv. at 986.  See also Berk v. Gordon Johnson Co.,

232 F.Supp. 682, 2 UCC Rep.Serv. 240 (E.D.Mich.1964) (Uniform Sales Act case that looked to Code to construe contract); Leveridge v. Notaras, 433 P.2d 935, 4 UCC Rep.Serv. 691 (Okla. 1967) (printed general disclaimers and handwritten "30 day warranty").  For the proposition that handwritten and typewritten provisions prevail over inconsistent printed provisions, see 3 A. Corbin, Corbin on Contracts § 548 at 181–83 (1960).

In Woodbury Chem. Co. v. Holgerson, 439 F.2d 1052, 8 UCC Rep.Serv. 999 (10th Cir. 1971), the court assumed that a disclaimer printed on the label attached to a container of insecticide did not affect representations on the label regarding the chemical content of the product.  See also Walcott & Steele, Inc. v. Carpenter, 246 Ark. 95, 436 S.W.2d 820, 6 UCC Rep.Serv. 89 (1969), in which an invoice received with a shipment of seed contained a general disclaimer.  Tags attached to the bags of seed specified a germina-

## § 12–4  Disclaimers of Express Warranties, 2–316(1)—Oral Warranties Made Prior to the Written Agreement

Section 2–316(1) makes clear that its provisions "are subject to the provisions of this Article on parol or extrinsic evidence (Section 2–202) . . . ."[21] Section 2–202 provides:

Terms with respect to which the confirmatory memoranda of the parties agree or which are otherwise set forth in a writing intended by the parties as a final expression of their agreement with respect to such terms as are included therein may not be contradicted by evidence of any prior agreement or of a contemporaneous oral agreement but may be explained or supplemented

(a) by course of dealing or usage of trade (Section 1–205) or by course of performance (Section 2–208); and

(b) by evidence of consistent additional terms unless the court finds the writing to have been intended also as a complete and exclusive statement of the terms of the agreement.

According to Comment 2 to 2–316, the reference to the parol evidence rule is intended to protect the seller "against false allegations of oral warranties." However the seller's protection is subject to two important restrictions. First, the written agreement may be contradicted by parol evidence if it was not intended by the parties as a final expression of their agreement. Thus a disclaimer in one incomplete memorandum does not negate an oral warranty previously made by the seller. Second, even if the writing was intended as the final expression of part of the parties' agreement, it may be supplemented with evidence of consistent additional terms if the writing was not intended as a complete and exclusive statement of the terms of the agreement. Thus the courts[22] have considerable discretion in deciding whether to admit evidence of oral warranties.[23]

An effectively worded merger or integration clause can have the same effect as a disclaimer.[24] That is, if a party includes a clause in his contract which states that the written contract is the "complete and exclusive statement of the terms of the agreement," the most likely legal consequence will be to exclude from evidence the proof of any oral warranty. The careful disclaimer draftsman will

---

tion of eighty percent. The court held that the disclaimer did not invalidate the express warranty created by the tags, because they could not reasonably be reconciled.

21. For an extensive discussion of the parol evidence rule, see Ch. 2 supra.

22. As paragraph (b) of section 2–202 expressly stipulates, rulings on parol evidence are for the court.

23. Of course parol evidence is always admissible to show the invalidity of the document itself. 3 A. Corbin, Corbin on Contracts § 578 at 405 (1960).

24. See 1 W. Hawkland, A Transactional Guide to the Uniform Commercial Code 85 (1964); Moye, Exclusion and Modification of Warranty Under the U.C.C.—How to Succeed in Business Without Being Liable for Not Really Trying, 46 Denver L.J. 579 (1969).

not rely exclusively on 2–316 and 2–719 but will also consider 2–202 and the parol evidence rule. Under pre-Code law, a clause providing that the contract "contains the entire agreement of the parties, and that there are no antecedent or extrinsic representations, warranties, or collateral provisions that are not intended to be discharged and nullified" was often effective to exclude evidence of previously made oral warranties.[25] Similar language was given effect in the post-Code case of Green Chevrolet Co. v. Kemp,[26] which involved the sale of a used car. The conditional sales contract provided that it covered all conditions and agreements between the parties. The Arkansas Supreme Court held that 2–202 and the contract provision prevented the introduction of evidence that the salesman made an oral guarantee concerning the mechanical parts.[27]

Note, however, that the mere inclusion of a merger clause does not prevent a court from deciding that the writing is incomplete.[28] For example, a court can take the position that the merger clause is only *evidence* of the parties' intent.[29] Moreover, if other language in the contract conflicts with the merger clause, the court can hold that the writing is incomplete and look to parol evidence for explanation or clarification.[30] In Leveridge v. Notaras,[31] a printed form contract contained both a printed disclaimer clause and the following handwritten notation:

> 30 day warranty
> Repair clutch as needed
> not too [sic] exceed $100.00
> date no later then [sic] Sat.
> Feb. 24, 1963 [32]

The court held that because this notation rendered the document ambiguous, evidence of an oral warranty against latent mechanical defects could be introduced.[33]

---

25. 3 A. Corbin, Corbin on Contracts § 578 at 402–403 (1960). At least two courts have said that 2–202 does not significantly change the pre-Code parol evidence rule. Stern & Co. v. State Loan & Fin. Corp., 238 F.Supp. 901, 2 UCC Rep.Serv. 721 (D.Del.1965) (parol evidence rule does not apply when parties have intended that no one writing contains their whole agreement) (dictum); Green Chevrolet Co. v. Kemp, 241 Ark. 62, 406 S.W. 2d 142, 3 UCC Rep.Serv. 805 (1966) (evidence of oral guarantees concerning used car excluded by inclusion of merger clause in conditional sale contract). But see Comment 1 to 2–202, which makes clear that the Code rejects several pre-Code propositions.

26. 241 Ark. 62, 406 S.W.2d 142, 3 UCC Rep.Serv. 805 (1966).

27. Id. at 64, 406 S.W.2d at 143, 3 UCC Rep.Serv. at 807.

28. For a lengthy discussion on merger clauses in other contexts, see Ch. 2 supra.

29. See, e. g., Holland Furnace Co. v. Heidrich, 7 Pa.D. & C.2d 204 (C.P. 1955) (purchased furnace failed to conform to "parol considerations").

30. See 3 A. Corbin, Corbin on Contracts § 578 at 411 (1960); 4 S. Williston, Williston on Contracts § 643 at 1082 (3d ed. 1961).

31. 433 P.2d 935, 4 UCC Rep.Serv. 691 (Okla.1967).

32. Id. at 937, 4 UCC Rep.Serv. at 692.

33. Id. at 940–41, 4 UCC Rep.Serv. at 694. Note that the oral evidence was

Since any attempt to disclaim an express warranty will encounter considerable judicial scrutiny, the only certain way to avoid liability for express warranties is to avoid making them in the first place. However, the seller can provide himself with some protection against carelessly uttered (or falsely alleged) affirmations of fact by incorporating a carefully drafted merger clause into his contract for sale. We offer the following as an example:

> MERGER CLAUSE: The seller's salesmen may have made oral statements about the merchandise described in this contract. Such statements do not constitute warranties, shall not be relied on by the buyer, and are not part of the contract for sale. The entire contract is embodied in this writing. This writing constitutes the final expression of the parties' agreement, and it is a complete and exclusive statement of the terms of that agreement.

If this clause conspicuously appears in the agreement, a court will have some difficulty in giving effect to oral warranties that the buyer says the seller gave before the written agreement was signed. Moreover, this clause may provide the seller with a powerful bargaining tool during settlement negotiations. For further discussion of merger clauses, see Section 2–12 above.

### § 12–5  Disclaimers of Implied Warranties—Explicit Disclaimers of Implied Warranties, 2–316(2)

Disclaimers most often attempt to negate the implied warranties of merchantability and fitness for a particular purpose. Subsection (2) of 2–316 sets out rather specific requirements in this regard, and subsection (3) describes other circumstances that exclude implied warranties. We will examine both of these provisions in considerable detail, but the reader should bear in mind that a buyer can also assert the doctrine of unconscionability against warranty disclaimers.[34]

Subsection (2) provides:

> Subject to subsection (3), to exclude or modify the implied warranty of merchantability or any part of it the language must mention merchantability and in case of a writing must be conspicuous, and to exclude or modify any implied warranty of fitness the exclusion must be by a writing and conspicuous. Language to exclude all implied warranties of fitness is sufficient if it states, for example, that "There are no warranties which extend beyond the description on the face hereof."

Consider several preliminary points. First this provision applies to attempts to modify (for example by setting a time limit) as well as

---

admitted despite the fact that the written contract contained the following merger clause:

It is agreed that no change, alteration, interlineation, or verbal agreement of any kind shall be effective to change, alter, or amend the printed terms of this agreement.

Id. at 937, 4 UCC Rep.Serv. at 692.

34. See Section 12–11 supra.

to attempts fully to exclude implied warranties. Any written disclaimer must be conspicuous, and the warranty of fitness can be disclaimed only in writing.[35] While the implied warranty of merchantability can be orally excluded or modified, any attempt, written or oral, to disclaim that warranty must specifically mention the word "merchantability." On the other hand general written language is sufficient to exclude the implied warranty of fitness for a particular purpose. There are three questions involving subsection (2) that we will attempt to answer:

(*1*) According to the courts what language satisfies the requirements of 2–316(2)?

(*2*) What does "conspicuous" mean?

(*3*) Is a disclaimer made after the time of contracting valid?

### Required Language

Section 2–316(2) explicitly requires that, subject to subsection (3), any disclaimer of the warranty of merchantability must mention the word "merchantability." Most courts have enforced this requirement,[36] but the First Circuit apparently disregarded it in Roto-Lith, Ltd. v. F. P. Bartlett & Co.[37] and held a disclaimer operative that provided: "Seller hereby expressly excludes any and all warranties, guaranties, or representations whatsoever."[38] Both parties were businessmen, and the quoted language certainly shows the seller's intent to bail out of all warranty responsibility. Nevertheless, one is hard pressed to justify the court's disregard of the plain statutory command,[39] and it is unlikely that courts in the future will follow *Roto-Lith*.

35. Since this particular requirement applies to the "warranty of fitness," it has been suggested that it governs attempted disclaimers of the warranty of fitness for ordinary purposes (See § 2–314(2)(c)) as well as the warranty of fitness for a particular purpose. Note, The Uniform Commercial Code and Greater Consumer Protection Under Warranty Law, 49 Ky.L.J. 240, 255 (1961). In rebuttal, see Moye, Exclusion and Modification of Warranty Under the U.C.C.—How to Succeed in Business Without Being Liable for Not Really Trying, 46 Denver L.J. 579, 601 (1969).

36. See, e. g., Mutual Serv. Inc. v. S. O. S. Plumbing & Sewerage Co., 93 Ill.App.2d 257, 235 N.E.2d 265, 5 UCC Rep.Serv. 365 (1968) (agreement to purchase hammer and bit provided that no other guarantee, written or oral, was authorized); S. F. C. Acceptance Corp. v. Ferree, 39 Pa.D. & C.2d 225, 3 UCC Rep.Serv. 808 (C.P.

1966) (sale of ice making machine and ice and soda vending machines).

37. 297 F.2d 497, 1 UCC Rep.Serv. 73 (1st Cir. 1962).

38. Id. at 499, 1 UCC Rep.Serv. at 75.

39. It is possible that the court thought the disclaimer language satisfied the requirements of 2–316(3)(a), which provides:

Notwithstanding subsection (2)

(a) unless the circumstances indicate otherwise, all implied warranties are excluded by expressions like "as is", "with all faults" or other language which in common understanding calls the buyer's attention to the exclusion of warranties and makes plain that there is no implied warranty; . . .

The court did not articulate such a belief; it merely said that this language was "an appropriate disclaimer of warranties" and cited 2–316. Id. at 500, 1 UCC Rep.Serv. at 77.

Comment 4 states that the implied warranty of fitness for a particular purpose may be excluded by general language. Indeed, one court has held that the following language is sufficient to negate this warranty: "The warranties and guaranties herein set forth are made by us and accepted by you in lieu of all statutory or implied warranties or guaranties, other than title." [40] The Code itself approves for this purpose language that states " 'There are no warranties which extend beyond the description on the face hereof'." [41] The seller's lawyer should remember, however, that under 2–316(1) such language will not negate an *express* warranty that the goods being sold are fit for the buyer's special purpose.[42] Moreover, language that is too general will fail. For example, the mere statement in a written express warranty that "no claim for labor or damages will be allowed" has been held insufficient to exclude the implied warranty of fitness for a particular purpose.[43]

One should have little difficulty drafting a disclaimer clause that contains the language required by 2–316(2). Most ineffective disclaimers fail not because they were improperly worded but because they were inconspicuous or unconscionable. Nevertheless the cost to the seller of sloppy draftsmanship can be great. We suggest language similar to the following, which should be used in conjunction with the merger clause quoted above: [44]

> EXCLUSIONS OF WARRANTIES: The parties agree that the implied warranties of MERCHANTABILITY and fitness for a particular purpose and all other warranties, express or implied, are EXCLUDED from this transaction and shall not apply to the goods sold.

If the seller wants to provide the buyer with some limited protection— for example, he may be willing to repair or replace defective parts— he should spell out the nature of the express warranty in specific terms. The express warranty should be followed by language to the effect:

> The warranty described in this paragraph shall be IN LIEU OF any other warranty, express or implied, including but not limited to, any implied warranty of MERCHANTABILITY or fitness for a particular purpose.[45]

**40.** Thorman v. Polytemp, Inc., 2 UCC Rep.Serv. 772, 774 (N.Y.City Ct.1965) (sale of steam heater to dry cleaning establishment). See also Roto-Lith, Ltd. v. F. P. Bartlett & Co., 297 F.2d 497, 1 UCC Rep.Serv. 73 (1st Cir. 1962), discussed in text accompanying notes 37–39 supra.

**41.** § 2–316(2).

**42.** See, e. g., Berk v. Gordon Johnson Co., 232 F.Supp. 682, 2 UCC Rep.Serv. 240 (E.D.Mich.1964) (Uniform Sales Act case; court looked to Code to construe contract).

**43.** Water Works & Indus. Supply Co. v. Wilburn, 437 S.W.2d 951, 955, 5 UCC Rep.Serv. 1169, 1170–71 (Ky.Ct.App. 1968) (sale of pipe and gaskets for water main).

**44.** See Section 12–4 supra.

**45.** A clause similar to this was held to be properly worded in Koellmer v. Chrysler Motors Corp., 6 Conn.Cir.

While more general language may be sufficient,[46] it is unwise to take chances, since many courts strictly construe disclaimers and resolve doubts against the seller.[47]

### Conspicuousness

Section 2–316(2) also requires that disclaimers of the implied warranties be conspicuous. Section 1–201(10) defines "conspicuous" as follows:

> "Conspicuous": A term or clause is conspicuous when it is so written that a reasonable person against whom it is to operate ought to have noticed it. A printed heading in capitals (as: NON-NEGOTIABLE BILL OF LADING) is conspicuous. Language in the body of a form is "conspicuous" if it is in larger or other contrasting type or color. But in a telegram any stated term is "conspicuous". Whether a term or clause is "conspicuous" or not is for decision by the court.

Comment 10 emphasizes that subsection (10) merely indicates some of the methods of making a term conspicuous and that "the test is whether attention can reasonably be expected to be called to it." Many courts have nevertheless assumed that the capitalization, typeface, and color methods described in 1–201(10) are absolute requirements; this reflects a judgment that terms embedded in a lengthy printed form contract are in reality not conspicuous unless there is something unusual about the way they are printed. At any event, the rule has gradually developed that "[a] provision is not conspicuous when there is only a slight contrast with the balance of the instrument." [48]

---

478, 8 UCC Rep.Serv. 668 (1970). However, it was held ineffective because it was inconspicuous and because it was delivered after the sales contract was formed. See text accompanying notes 48–68 infra.

**46.** See text accompanying notes 36–39 supra.

**47.** See, e. g., Water Works & Indus. Supply Co. v. Wilburn, 437 S.W.2d 951, 5 UCC Rep.Serv. 1169 (Ky.Ct.App. 1968) (disclaimer did not affect implied warranty of fitness for particular purpose); Henningsen v. Bloomfield Motors, Inc., 32 N.J. 358, 391, 161 A.2d 69, 87 (1960) (pre-Code case; courts have adopted "doctrines of strict construction" to protect buyers against disclaimers); Henry v. W. S. Reichenbach & Son, Inc., 45 Pa.D. & C.2d 171, 172, 5 UCC Rep.Serv. 985, 986 (C.P. 1968) (ambiguous disclaimer construed "most strongly against the party who prepared it"); Cooper

Paintings & Coatings, Inc. v. SCM Corp., 457 S.W.2d 864, 8 UCC Rep. Serv. 159 (Tenn.Ct.App.1970) (disclaimer read as applying only to misuse of roofing materials by buyer).

**48.** Greenspun v. American Adhesives, Inc., 320 F.Supp. 442, 444, 8 UCC Rep. Serv. 439, 441 (E.D.Pa.1970). In that case only the first letter of each word was capitalized in the disclaimer heading printed on the label attached to drums of glue, and the heading in the accompanying invoice was printed in capital letters smaller than any other heading on the form. See also DeLamar Motor Co. v. White, 249 Ark. 708, 406 S.W.2d 802, 8 UCC Rep. Serv. 437 (1970) (disclaimer in italic type which was smaller and lighter than much of the rest of the form); Sarnecki v. Al Johns Pontiac, 3 UCC Rep.Serv. 1121 (Pa.C.P.1966) (slight variation in contrasting type was perfunctory attempt to comply with Code).

There has been some indication in the cases that a disclaimer's location is relevant in determining whether it was made conspicuously. For example, in Massey-Ferguson v. Utley [49] a contract for the sale of a combine attachment contained an express warranty, with a heading in capital letters that excluded all implied warranties. The Kentucky Court of Appeals held that because this provision was on the back of the contract form and was referred to by words in only ordinary type on the front, it was not conspicuous.[50] While several other courts adopted a similar rationale,[51] the Kentucky court was quick to emphasize that disclaimers on the reverse side of contract forms are not invalid *per se*. In Childers & Venters, Inc. v. Sowards,[52] the court said that if the draftsmen intended a per se rule, they would have said so since they knew it was customary to print terms on the back sides of form contracts.[53] The court therefore validated a disclaimer appearing on the back side of a contract for the sale of a used truck, since the clause was printed in larger and heavier print than was used on the rest of the form.[54] We think the Kentucky court was correct in concluding that the placement of a disclaimer is but one of the factors to consider in determining its conspicuousness.

Several sellers have attempted to satisfy the conspicuousness requirement by printing only the heading of the combined express warranty and disclaimer clause in capital letters. When these headings have failed to disclose the true nature of the clause, the courts have denied effect to the disclaimer. For example, in the *Utley* case,[55] the disclaimer was contained in a paragraph headed in capital letters as "WARRANTY and AGREEMENT"; the disclaimer language itself was printed in the same type size and face as the rest of the contract. Said the court:

> It is true the *heading* was in large, bold-face type, but there was nothing to suggest that an exclusion was being made; on the contrary, the words of the heading indicated a *making* of warranties rather than a *disclaimer*.[56]

**49.** 439 S.W.2d 57, 6 UCC Rep.Serv. 51 (Ky.Ct.App.1969).

**50.** Id. at 59, 6 UCC Rep.Serv. at 53.

**51.** Hunt v. Perkins Mach. Co., 352 Mass. 535, 226 N.E.2d 228, 4 UCC Rep. Serv. 281 (1967) (disclaimer on reverse side of form was concealed from buyer because form was on pad when he signed it); Dougall v. Brown Bay Boat Works & Sales, Inc., 287 Minn. 290, 178 N.W.2d 217, 7 UCC Rep.Serv. 1160 (1970) (Uniform Sales Act case; disclaimer was contained on inside back cover of owner's manual); Zabriskie Chevrolet, Inc. v. Smith, 99 N.J.Super. 441, 240 A.2d 195, 5 UCC Rep.Serv. 30 (Law Div.1968) (disclaimer in fine print on back of order form); General Elec. Credit Corp. v. Hoey, 7 UCC Rep.Serv. 156 (N.Y.Sup. Ct.1970) (only reason given for disclaimer not being conspicuous was its location on reverse side of form).

**52.** 460 S.W.2d 343, 8 UCC Rep.Serv. 433 (Ky.Ct.App.1970).

**53.** Id. at 344–45, 8 UCC Rep.Serv. at 435.

**54.** Id.

**55.** Massey-Ferguson v. Utley, 439 S.W. 2d 57, 6 UCC Rep.Serv. 51 (Ky.Ct.App. 1969), discussed in notes 49–50 supra.

**56.** Id. at 59, 6 UCC Rep.Serv. at 53. Accord, Mack Trucks, Inc. v. Jet

The *safest* course for a seller to follow is to print all disclaimer language in bold-face capitals of a contrasting color.

The comment says a term is conspicuous if "attention can reasonably be expected to be called to it." A mild controversy has developed whether a consumer's attention must *actually* be called to a disclaimer. A court in New Jersey, where disclaimers have enjoyed little favor,[57] refused to give effect to a disclaimer of warranties concerning a new car, partly because there was no evidence that the disclaimer had actually been brought to the buyer's attention or explained to him in detail.[58] On the other hand, the Kentucky Court of Appeals has held that it is not necessary that the buyer's attention be specifically called to a disclaimer.[59] This latter view appears to be correct since it accords with 1–201(10)'s "reasonable-person" standard, the language of the comment.

Does it matter whether a disclaimer was printed conspicuously if the seller actually points it out to the buyer? Comment 1 to 2–316 indicates that the purpose of the conspicuousness requirement is to "protect the buyer from surprise" and "unexpected and unbargained language of disclaimers." This purpose should be accomplished when the buyer becomes aware in fact of the seller's disclaimer. On the other hand, section 1–201(10) says, "A term or clause is conspicuous when *so written*. . . ." (Emphasis added). This situation is analogous to that described in the preceding paragraph, where the buyer claims the disclaimer was not actually pointed out to him. Both of these arguments would reward the convincing liar who claims that the buyer was—or was not—made aware of the disclaimer. We think the draftsmen intended a rigid adherence to the conspicuousness requirement in order to avoid arguments concerning what the parties said about warranties at the time of the sale.[60]

### Disclaimer Subsequent to Contracting

Frequently the seller does not make a disclaimer until after the contract for sale has been made. For example a buyer might

Asphalt & Rock Co., 246 Ark. 101, 437 S.W.2d 459, 6 UCC Rep.Serv. 93 (1969) (sale of diesel engines). See also Gindy Mfg. Corp. v. Cardinale Trucking Corp., 111 N.J.Super. 383, 268 A. 2d 345, 7 UCC Rep.Serv. 1257 (Law Div.1970) (same rationale used when applying conspicuousness requirement to "as is" clause). See Section 12–6 infra (discussion of 2–316(3) (a)).

57. See Henningsen v. Bloomfield Motors, Inc., 32 N.J. 358, 161 A.2d 69 (1960).

58. Zabriskie Chevrolet, Inc. v. Smith, 99 N.J.Super. 441, 240 A.2d 195, 5 UCC Rep.Serv. 30 (Law Div.1968). The disclaimer also was not "reasonably" conspicuous, since it was in fine print on

the back. See also Peters, Remedies for Breach of Contracts Relating to the Sale of Goods Under the Uniform Commercial Code: A Roadmap to Article Two, 73 Yale L.J. 199, 282 (1966).

59. Childers & Venters, Inc. v. Sowards, 460 S.W.2d 343, 8 UCC Rep.Serv. 433 (Ky.Ct.App.1970). This case is discussed in notes 52–54 and accompanying text supra.

60. If the seller orally explained his inconspicuous written disclaimer and mentioned the word "merchantability," he might nevertheless have established an effective oral disclaimer of the implied warranty of merchantability.

sign a purchase agreement for a new car and the next week sign an installment sales contract that contains a printed disclaimer. This situation appears to be governed by the Code. Section 9–206(2) provides that Article Two governs all secured sales with respect to disclaimers of warranty. Comment 3 to that section makes clear that this provision "prevents a buyer from inadvertently abandoning his warranties by a 'no warranties' term in the security agreement when warranties have already been created under the sales arrangement." Thus, a disclaimer in a security agreement that is executed subsequent to the signing of the sales agreement should not affect either express or implied warranties created on the earlier date.[61]

In the more common situation the buyer is given a disclaimer at the time of delivery of the goods. Such a disclaimer may be printed on a label, in an operator's manual, or on an invoice. According to the prevailing trend of pre-Code law, "[I]f a bargain with even an implied warranty has once arisen, a subsequent disclaimer of warranty when the goods are delivered will not avail the seller."[62] Most

---

**61.** But see Garner v. Tomcavage, 34 Northumb.L.J. 18 (Pa.C.P.1961). In that case, an "as is" clause (see Section 12–6 infra) in an installment sales contract for a hearing aid executed one month after the buyer signed a purchase agreement was held effectively to disclaim all implied warranties. The court did not consider 9–206(2).

**62.** 8 S. Williston, Williston on Contracts § 993A at 610 (3d ed. 1961). See also Klein v. Asgrow Seed Co., 246 Cal.App.2d 87, 54 Cal.Rptr. 609, 3 UCC Rep.Serv. 934 (3d Dist.1966) (disclaimer printed on cans of seed delivered after contract for sale completed held inoperative); Dougall v. Brown Bay Boat Works & Sales, Inc., 287 Minn. 290, 178 N.W.2d 217, 7 UCC Rep.Serv. 1160 (1970) (disclaimer in owner's manual, which was delivered to buyer after time of sale, held ineffective).

A different situation is presented when the seller's acknowledgement of the buyer's order contains a disclaimer clause. In J. A. Maurer, Inc. v. Singer Co., 7 UCC Rep.Serv. 110 (N.Y. Sup.Ct.1970), the plaintiff ordered forty motors from the defendant. Although the purchase order stated that no variations from its terms could be made unless they were agreed to in writing by the plaintiff, the defendant's acknowledgement of the order contained a disclaimer and limitation-of-remedy clause. The New York court looked to Section 2–207 (see Section 1–2 supra) of the Code and

held that the clause became a binding part of the contract since it did not "materially alter" the plaintiff's order. 7 UCC Rep.Serv. at 111. However, the court apparently disregarded 2–207(2)(a), which provides in part:

Between merchants [additional terms proposed in an expression of acceptance of an offer] become part of the contract unless:

    (a) the offer expressly limits acceptance to the terms of the offer . . . .

The plaintiff's order contained such a limitation; therefore, the proposed disclaimer should not have been considered part of the contract. It may also be argued that the court was incorrect in holding that the disclaimer clause did not materially alter the contract. (See the discussion of 2–207(2)(b) in Ch. 1 supra.) At any event, the buyer's attorney should be wary of disclaimers contained in order acknowledgements.

See also Roto-Lith, Ltd. v. F. P. Bartlett & Co., 297 F.2d 497, 1 UCC Rep. Serv. 73 (1st Cir. 1962), in which the court held that the buyer assented to a disclaimer contained in an order acknowledgement, which naturally altered the contract, by accepting and using the ordered goods. This decision has been the butt of a great deal of criticism. See, e. g., Comment, Nonconforming Acceptances Under Section 2–207 of the Uniform Commercial Code: An End to the Battle of the Forms, 30 U.Chi.L.Rev. 540 (1963); Note, Offer: Acceptance

courts have continued to follow this trend when interpreting the Code.[63]  For example, in Koellmer v. Chrysler Motors Corp.[64] a properly worded disclaimer clause was contained in the operator's manual for a new truck.  A Connecticut court held this clause ineffective because the manual was delivered after the sale had been consummated.[65]

The reader will recall that Comment 7 to 2–313 indicated that an express warranty made after the closing of the deal can be made a binding part of the contract so long as the parties comply with the provisions of 2–209 on contract modification.[66]  This analysis should be equally applicable to disclaimers made pursuant to 2–316. Compliance with 2–209 is not easy, for subsection (1) requires that the parties agree to any modifications.  Thus, a warranty booklet stuffed in a glove compartment of a new car would not be binding on a buyer who receives the car three days after signing the sales agreement, unless he agreed to the modification.  Moreover since the contract as modified by the subsequent disclaimer would undoubtedly involve more than 500 dollars, the disclaimer could not be enforced against the buyer unless he signed a writing that complied with the statute of frauds.[67]  At any event, section 2–209 does provide a forgetful seller with a means of disclaiming those warranties that arose when he closed the deal.[68]

Unlimited?  UCC Section 2–207 on the Courts, 57 Nw.U.L.Rev. 477 (1962); Case Note, 76 Harv.L.Rev. 1481 (1963).

63.  See, e. g., Tiger Motor Co. v. McMurtry, 284 Ala. 283, 224 So.2d 638, 6 UCC Rep.Serv. 608 (1969) (disclaimer contained in owner's manual for station wagon); Marion Power Shovel Co. v. Huntsman, 246 Ark. 152, 437 S.W.2d 784, 6 UCC Rep.Serv. 100 (1969) (disclaimer clause contained in operation manual supplied upon delivery of purchased power shovel); Zabriskie Chevrolet, Inc. v. Smith, 99 N.J.Super. 441, 240 A.2d 195, 5 UCC Rep.Serv. 30 (Law Div. 1968) (disclaimer for new car contained in warranty delivered after contract signed); Ford Motor Co. v. Taylor, 446 S.W.2d 521, 6 UCC Rep.Serv. 798 (Tenn.Ct.App.1969) (written warranty for tractor delivered subsequent to sale).

64.  6 Conn.Cir. 478, 8 UCC Rep.Serv. 668 (1970).  A properly worded disclaimer "embedded" in the sales contract was inoperative because it was not conspicuous.  Id. at ——, 8 UCC Rep.Serv. at 672.

65.  Id. at ——, 8 UCC Rep.Serv. at 673. Several courts have invalidated disclaimer clauses on other grounds with-

out considering the fact that the disclaimer was made after contracting. See, e. g., Woodbury Chem. Co. v. Holgerson, 439 F.2d 1052, 8 UCC Rep. Serv. 999 (10th Cir. 1971) (disclaimer printed on label affixed to container of insecticide); Greenspun v. Am. Adhesives, Inc., 320 F.Supp. 442, 8 UCC Rep.Serv. 439 (E.D.Pa.1970) (disclaimer printed on label affixed to goods and in invoice sent following delivery); Walcott & Steele, Inc. v. Carpenter, 246 Ark. 95, 436 S.W.2d 820, 6 UCC Rep.Serv. 89 (1969) (disclaimer clause printed on invoice that accompanied delivery of seeds).

66.  See Ch. 1 supra.

67.  Section 2–209(3) makes the statute of frauds (2–201) applicable to contract modifications.

68.  Presumably a seller could persuade most uninitiated buyers to sign written warranties even after execution of the contract for sale.  For example, he might say: "Please sign this written guarantee which explains our warranty obligations.  Your signing enables us to register your name with the manufacturer and thus entitles you to free replacement and repair of defective parts."  Indeed some appliance manufacturers "require" pur-

## § 12–6  Disclaimers of Implied Warranties—Other Methods

After setting out the relatively specific requirements of subsection (2), the Code draftsmen provide in subsection (3) several alternative and less formal means of disclaiming warranty liability "[n]otwithstanding subsection (2)."  Comment 6 to 2–316 explains:

> The exceptions to the general rule  .  .  .  are common factual situations in which the circumstances surrounding the transaction are in themselves sufficient to call the buyer's attention to the fact that no implied warranties are made or that a certain implied warranty is being excluded.

One must keep in mind that each of the alternative routes depends to some extent on the circumstances surrounding the particular sale in question: these are not absolute rules.  As a result, attempts to disclaim under subsection (3) are always subject to judicial scrutiny.

### "As is" Clauses, 2–316(3) (a)

Perhaps the easiest way for a seller to rid himself of potential warranty liability is to provide in the sales agreement that the buyer takes the goods sold "as is."  Section 2–316(3) (a) reads:

> Notwithstanding subsection (2)
>
> (a) unless the circumstances indicate otherwise, all implied warranties are excluded by expressions like "as is", "with all faults" or other language which in common understanding calls the buyer's attention to the exclusion of warranties and makes plain that there is no implied warranty  .  .  .

Comment 7 tells us that "[s]uch terms in ordinary commercial usage are understood to mean that the buyer takes the entire risk as to the quality of the goods involved."  Thus, if one bottler agrees to sell his used bottling equipment to another bottler "as is, where is," an experienced businessman-buyer cannot hold the seller responsible for any defects in the equipment.[69]  The seller has other magic words available also: paragraph (a) mentions "with all faults" and Comment 7 adds "as they stand."  It is unclear what other shibboleths would work.  One court held that a statement in a sales contract to the effect that the buyer accepts the car "in its present condition" had the same effect as an "as is" clause;[70] yet another court, in a case involving an almost identical transaction, said the terms were not synonymous.[71]

chasers to mail in signed warranty registration cards within a short period after purchase.

**69.**  Crown Cork & Seal Co. v. Hires Bottling Co., 254 F.Supp. 424, 3 UCC Rep.Serv. 609 (N.D.Ill.1966), rev'd on other grounds 371 F.2d 256 (7th Cir. 1967).

**70.**  First Nat'l Bank of Elgin v. Husted, 57 Ill.App.2d 227, 205 N.E.2d 780, 2 UCC Rep.Serv. 777 (1965).

**71.**  Hull-Dobbs, Inc. v. Mallicoat, 57 Tenn.App. 100, 415 S.W.2d 344, 3 UCC Rep.Serv. 1032 (1966).

Subsection 2–316(3) (a) does give the buyer an opportunity to nullify an "as is" clause by showing that "the circumstances indicate otherwise." One such circumstance might be the fact that the buyer is an ordinary consumer without knowledge of the consequences of "as is," "with all faults," or "as they stand." No court has reached this conclusion yet, but the language of subsection (3) (a) and of Comment 7 lends support to it. The subsection itself refers to language "in common understanding." If "common" is read as meaning common to both parties—rather than common in the trade— the buyer's understanding would be highly relevant. Similarly, Comment 7 refers to "ordinary commercial usage," a subject with which a consumer buyer may not be fully familiar. While this construction may go beyond the draftsmen's intent,[72] it could convince a consumer-oriented court.

A New Jersey court has indicated that the use of an "as is" clause in a contract for the sale of new goods may be inoperative. Gindy Manufacturing Corp. v. Cardinale Trucking Corp.[73] involved the sale of twenty-five new semi-trailers. The contract form, which the seller used for the sale of both new and used vehicles, contained an "as is" disclaimer. The court found that under the custom of the trade,[74] "as is" clauses are expected in contracts for the sale of used vehicles but not when new vehicles are involved.[75] It therefore held that under these circumstances the "as is" clause was not a disclaimer.[76]

In any event a buyer's attempt to establish circumstances that indicate that an "as is" clause was not intended as a disclaimer will almost surely be defeated by evidence that the parties bargained over the term. Chamberlain v. Bob Matick Chevrolet, Inc.[77] involved the sale of a used car, which turned out to have a defective master cylinder. The dealer finally agreed to sell the car for $325 "as is," but earlier he had offered to sell it with a guarantee for $350. The court held that in light of these circumstances, and the fact that the seller told the buyer that a sale at the lower price would be at the buyer's risk, the seller had made an effective disclaimer.[78]

**72.** Professor Honnold has taken the position that an "as is" clause should exclude all warranties, even in a contract with a consumer who is unaware of the trade meaning of the term. 1 N.Y. State Law Revision Comm'n, 1955 Report 409 (1955). He conceded that this result may not have been intended by the draftsmen. Id.

**73.** 111 N.J.Super. 383, 268 A.2d 345, 7 UCC Rep.Serv. 1257 (Law Div.1970).

**74.** Comment 7 to 2–316 states, "The terms covered by paragraph (a) are in fact merely a particularization of paragraph (c) which provides for exclusion or modification of implied warranties by usage of trade."

**75.** 111 N.J.Super. at 397, 268 A.2d at 353, 7 UCC Rep.Serv. at 1268.

**76.** Id. at 399, 268 A.2d at 354, 7 UCC Rep.Serv. at 1269. The court suggested that an "as is" clause in a contract for the sale of new goods, if accompanied by a statement that the goods are delivered in good condition, means that the goods are in new and good mechanical condition.

**77.** 4 Conn.Cir. 685, 239 A.2d 42, 4 UCC Rep.Serv. 936 (1967).

**78.** Id. at 696, 239 A.2d at 46, 4 UCC Rep.Serv. at 942. See also Crown Cork & Seal Co. v. Hires Bottling Co., 254 F.Supp. 424, 3 UCC Rep.Serv. 609 (N.D.Ill.1966), rev'd on other grounds

A few pre-Code cases held that an "as is" clause did not operate to negate the seller's obligation to deliver goods as described. For example, in a misrepresentation case one court held the buyer of a 1933 truck "in its present condition" was entitled to rescission upon his discovery that the truck was actually a 1932 model.[79] Would the same result be reached under the Code? Under 2–313(1) (b), any description of the goods that is made part of the basis of the bargain creates an express warranty that the goods conform to that description. Since 2–316(3) (a) provides a means of disclaiming *implied* warranties only; an express warranty based on a description of the truck as a 1933 model would not be disclaimed by an "as is" provision. Moreover, Comment 4 to section 2–313 states that a court cannot give literal effect to a clause that purports to disclaim *all* warranties, express or implied; at the very minimum, the seller cannot disclaim his obligation to deliver goods that conform to their description.

One final question remains in regard to 2–316(3) (a): must disclaimer language under this provision be conspicuous? The Code does not explicitly impose such a requirement. Moreover, Comment 6 suggests that the very fact that an "as is" clause is included should be sufficient to call the buyer's attention to the seller's exclusion of implied warranties.[80] However, a New Jersey court in the *Gindy Manufacturing*[81] case held that the conspicuousness requirement applies to "as is" clauses on the ground that otherwise that requirement's presence in subsection (2) would be useless.[82] It probably violates the intent of the draftsmen to read such a requirement into subsection (3) (a)—after all, they could easily have provided for it expressly. But conspicuousness, should be relevant in determining whether the term was sufficient to call the buyer's attention to the disclaimer and make its meaning plain to him.

371 F.2d 256 (7th Cir. 1967) ("as is" clause insisted on by seller was effective because it had been the subject of bargaining).

**79.** Denenberg v. Jurad, 300 Mass. 488, 15 N.E.2d 660 (1938); accord, Williams v. McClain, 180 Miss. 6, 176 So. 717 (1937) (identical facts involving sale of used car).

**80.** For an argument based on the comments that 2–316(3) (a) does not incorporate a conspicuousness requirement, see Hogan, The Highways and Some of the Byways in the Sales and Bulk Sales Articles of the Uniform Commercial Code, 48 Cornell L.Q. 1, 7–8, 8 n. 29 (1962).

**81.** Gindy Mfg. Corp. v. Cardinale Trucking Corp., 111 N.J.Super. 383,

396, 268 A.2d 345, 353, 7 UCC Rep. Serv. 1257, 1267 (Law Div.1970), discussed in notes 73–76 and accompanying text supra.

**82.** The court indicated that the clause would not have to be conspicuous if it were supported by a course of dealing or usage of trade. Presumably, the clause would not be at all operative if it were not supported by usage of trade, since Comment 7 tells us that the use of an "as is" clause is a method of disclaiming warranties by usage of trade.

The result in *Gindy Mfg.* is supported by Professor Hawkland, 1 W. Hawkland, A Transactional Guide to the Uniform Commercial Code 77 (1964).

*Disclaimer Because of Examination or Opportunity To Examine*

Paragraph (b) provides an alternative method by which a seller may shift the risk of the quality of the goods to his buyer. It provides:

> (3) Notwithstanding subsection (2)
>
>     *    *    *
>
> (b) when the buyer before entering into the contract has examined the goods or the sample or model as fully as he desired or has refused to examine the goods there is no implied warranty with regard to defects which an examination ought in the circumstances to have revealed to him; and . . . .

The draftsmen have provided an unusually long and helpful Comment 8. The gist of (3) (b), according to the comment, is that by demanding that the buyer examine the goods sold, "[t]he seller . . . puts the buyer on notice that he is assuming the risk of defects which the examination ought to reveal." Thus it is not sufficient that the seller merely make the goods available for inspection. Once the seller makes the demand,[83] however he is free of any implied warranty for defects that an examination should have revealed, even if the buyer does not examine the goods.[84] On the other hand even if the seller does not make a demand, he receives the same protection if the buyer voluntarily examines the goods, or a sample or a model [85] as fully as he wishes.[86]

---

83. Paragraph (b), like paragraphs (a) and (c), deals only with excluding implied warranties. The First Circuit Court of Appeals, in General Elec. Co. v. United States Dynamics, Inc., 403 F.2d 933, 5 UCC Rep.Serv. 1053 (1st Cir. 1968), held that the inspection of a model of a gas purifying machine did not negate an express warranty.

84. In Refrigeration Discount Corp. v. Crouse, 2 UCC Rep.Serv. 986 (Pa.C.P. 1965), the buyer had possession of a tractor for one month prior to the sale, and he used it immediately before signing the contract. The court held that this opportunity for examination excluded the implied warranty of merchantability, since the alleged defect was easily discoverable. Section 2–316(3) (b) and Comment 8 thereto make clear that mere opportunity to examine was not envisioned by the draftsmen as a sufficient basis for the exclusion of warranties. The court may have tacitly concluded, however, that the buyer had examined the tractor as much as he desired during the month preceding the sale.

85. While the words "sample or model" are used in connection with an actual examination by the buyer, they are not used in connection with his refusal to examine. This wording would indicate that a disclaimer does not arise by virtue of paragraph (b) when the buyer refuses to examine a sample or model. The comment neither supports nor determines this construction, and no reported cases have yet faced the issue.

86. One court has held that the fact that the buyer acknowledged his examination of a car in the contract for sale is sufficient evidence to preclude implied warranties. First Nat'l Bank of Elgin v. Husted, 57 Ill.App.2d 227, 205 N.E.2d 780, 2 UCC Rep.Serv. 777 (1965).

For rather straight-forward cases involving paragraph (b), see Reeves Soundcraft Corp., 2 UCC Rep.Serv. 210 (Armed Serv. Bd. of Contract Apps. 1964) (buyer examined sample of magnetic tape before entering contract); Willis v. West Ky. Feeder Pig Co., —— Ill.App.2d ——, 265 N.E.2d 899, 8 UCC Rep.Serv. 1010 (1971) (buyer

The comment emphasizes the importance of "[t]he particular buyer's skill and the normal method of examining goods in the circumstances . . . ." The comment then suggests a distinction between professional and nonprofessional buyers. For example, a governmental agency buying magnetic tape [87] or a farmer purchasing feeder pigs [88] will be held to have assumed the risk for any defects that professionals in their respective fields should have discovered upon examination.[89] On the other hand, a layman purchasing an automobile cannot be expected to be able to discover subtle mechanical and design defects. Absent unusual circumstances, we expect that most courts would be reluctant to find that an examination by a consumer has excluded the implied warranties.[90]

While the buyer's examination of the goods sold, or of a model or sample, may lead to an exclusion of implied warranties, it can also lead to the creation of express warranties under 2–313.[91] For example, if the buyer examines a sample or model considered part of the basis of the bargain, an express warranty arises that the goods shall conform to the sample or model.[92] In a pre-Code case the seller urged the buyer to examine surplus rope being sold on an "as is—where is" basis. The court held that when the seller accepted the buyer's offer based on his examination, the seller warranted that the rope would conform to its condition at the time of inspection.[93] Such a result might not be possible under the Code, since nothing in 2–313 provides that examination of goods prior to sale, without more, creates an express warranty that the goods should conform to the condition they were in at the time of the examination.[94] But a

examined pigs, and even rejected three, before acceptance).

87. See, e. g., Reeves Soundcraft Corp., 2 UCC Rep.Serv. 210 (Armed Serv. Bd. of Contract Apps. 1964). See also Sal Metal Prods. Co. v. Rennert, 5 UCC Rep.Serv. 826 (N.Y.Sup.Ct.1968) (buyer held to have examined, and hence to have assumed the risk for ascertainable defects in models of hardware).

88. See, e. g., Willis v. West Ky. Feeder Pig Co., —— Ill.App.2d ——, 265 N. E.2d 899, 8 UCC Rep.Serv. 1010 (1971).

89. The buyer is only held to such defects as can be discovered under the circumstances. Thus, he will not be held to latent defects or defects ascertainable only by testing procedures not possible under the circumstances. See § 2–316, Comment 8.

90. But see First Nat'l Bank of Elgin v. Husted, 57 Ill.App.2d 227, 205 N.E. 2d 780, 2 UCC Rep.Serv. 777 (1965) (buyer's acknowledgement in sales contract that he had examined the used car was held to preclude any implied warranty). In an earlier Illinois case,

an appellate court had recognized the inability of the average consumer to understand complex machines like automobiles. Sutter v. St. Clair Motors, Inc., 44 Ill.App.2d 318, 323–24, 194 N. E.2d 674, 677, 1 UCC Rep.Serv. 125, 129 (1963) (pre-Code). See also Henningsen v. Bloomfield Motors, Inc., 32 N.J. 358, 375, 161 A.2d 69, 78 (Law Div. 1960), in which the court stated that the ordinary consumer "cannot be expected to have the knowledge or capacity or even the opportunity to make adequate inspection of mechanical instrumentalities, like automobiles, and to decide for themselves whether they are reasonably fit for the designed purpose."

91. See Section 9–2 et seq., supra.

92. § 2–313(1) (c).

93. United States v. Blake, 161 F.Supp. 76 (D.N.C.1958).

94. Section 2–313 provides for the creation of express warranties only by affirmation of fact, description of the goods, or exhibitions of samples or models.

few words carelessly tossed out by the seller could be construed, in combination with the examination, to be an express warranty. Comment 8 to 2–316 tells us:

> [I]f the offer of examination is accompanied by words as to their merchantability or specific attributes and the buyer indicates clearly that he is relying on those words rather than on his examination, they give rise to an "express" warranty. . . .

Of course, once the seller creates an express warranty, he must look to subsection (1) of 2–316 to exclude or modify it.

In sum, one should be on the alert that whenever the buyer examines the goods or a sample or model, both the creation of express warranties or the exclusion of implied warranties are possible. The lawyer must carefully scrutinize the facts to determine what effect an examination will have.

### Disclaimer by Other Circumstances, 2–316(3) (c)

Paragraph (c) of 2–316(3) is a "catch-all" provision for miscellaneous methods of excluding or modifying warranties. It provides:

> (3) Notwithstanding subsection (2) . . .
>
> (c) an implied warranty can also be excluded or modified by course of dealing or course of performance or usage of trade.

This provision has little meaning without reference to section 1–205, which defines "course of dealing" and "usage of trade":

> (1) A course of dealing is a sequence of previous conduct between the parties to a particular transaction which is fairly to be regarded as establishing a common basis of understanding for interpreting their expressions and other conduct.
>
> (2) A usage of trade is any practice or method of dealing having such regularity of observance in a place, vocation or trade as to justify an expectation that it will be observed with respect to the transaction in question. The existence and scope of such a usage are to be proved as facts. If it is established that such a usage is embodied in a written trade code or similar writing the interpretation of the writing is for the court.

In addition, section 2–208(1) provides a definition of "course of performance":

> (1) Where the contract for sale involves repeated occasions for performance by either party with knowledge of the nature of the performance and opportunity for objection to it by the other, any course of performance accepted or

acquiesced in without objection shall be relevant to determine the meaning of the agreement.

"Repeated occasions for performance" presumably includes attempts
by the seller to make good on his express warranty.[95] "Course of
performance" and "course of dealing" are closely related to each
other since both arise solely from relationships between the parties.
A usage of trade, on the other hand, develops out of a history of
transactions within a particular business community of which the
parties are members.  To borrow a phrase from labor law,[96] course
of performance and course of dealing represent the "common law"
of the parties, while usage of trade embodies the "common law" of the
parties' trade or trades.

How can a course of dealing or course of performance disclaim
a warranty?  In Country Clubs, Inc. v. Allis-Chalmers Manufacturing Co.,[97] a contract for the sale of electric golf carts contained an
express warranty for repair and replacement of parts and also purported to exclude all other warranties without using the word "merchantability."  The carts developed numerous problems, and the
buyer returned them for repairs.  The seller made the repairs at a
total cost of 12,000 dollars but billed the buyer for 4,663 dollars to
cover parts not within the warranty terms but which in the seller's
opinion needed replacing because of ordinary wear and tear.  The
buyer refused to pay and sued for breach of warranty to recover
damages for the cost of the carts and lost profits.  The court held
that regardless of the language used in the disclaimer, the course
of dealing and the course of performance were sufficient to exclude
implied warranties because the parties had discussed and negotiated
the warranty provisions and the buyer had asserted several claims
under those provisions.[98]  It should also be noted that the buyer
had ordered carts from the seller on two different occasions, so
it was possible to refer to "a sequence of previous conduct between
the parties" that could support a course of dealing.  Nevertheless,
the extent of previous conduct and of course of performance was
rather limited; the result may show judicial willingness to uphold
an imperfectly drafted disclaimer clause in a sales contract between
businessmen dealing at arm's length when their conduct reveals an
intention to be bound by that clause.

It should be easier to determine whether a disclaimer by usage
of trade exists, since a court may refer to other members of the

---

95.  See Country Clubs, Inc. v. Allis
Chalmers Mfg. Co., 430 F.2d 1394, 7
UCC Rep.Serv. 1253 (6th Cir. 1970)
(buyer of golf carts made several
claims under warranty provision of
sales contract).

96.  See United Steelworkers v. Warrior
& Gulf Navigation Co., 363 U.S. 574,
579–80 (1960), which refers to the
"common law of the shop."

97.  430 F.2d 1394, 7 UCC Rep.Serv.
1253 (6th Cir. 1970).

98.  Id. at 1397, 7 UCC Rep.Serv. at
1256.  The court also noted that the
buyer's agent was a businessman and
attorney and that the buyer had referred to the warranty provisions in
the contract when it defended against
the seller's counterclaim.

trade or to trade manuals or trade codes to determine the meaning of words or conduct. Usages of trade are frequently found in agricultural transactions. For example, the Nebraska Supreme Court recently upheld a trial court's determination that when a cattle buyer inspects cattle and cuts out those that do not suit him, there is a usage of trade that his acceptance of others "is irrevocable and without recourse," and thus excludes all implied warranties.[99] Pre-Code law frequently recognized a trade usage of seed sellers that excluded implied warranties and bound the purchaser, even if he did not know about the usage.[100] In Zicari v. Joseph Harris Co.,[101] a recent New York case decided under the Code, a seed seller tried to assert this usage of trade when the exclusionary language printed on its order forms failed to comply with 2–316(2). The seller contended that the alleged usage of trade should be binding on the buyer since other seedsmen in the area used similar exclusionary language and since only one out of 400 customers with damaged crops had complained to the seller. The court, however, concluded that these facts failed to establish "a usage of trade understood by all persons in the seed business and farming." [102]

The court's implication in *Zicari* that a trade usage must be understood by "all persons" in the trade represented by both the buyer and seller limits 2–316(3) (c). The use of the term "all persons" was probably not strictly intended by the court and should be replaced by a concept like "most persons" engaged in the trade. But that a trade usage must be understood by both parties to the transaction deserves more serious attention. Under pre-Code law, a trade usage was not operative against a party who was not a member of the trade unless he actually knew of it or the other party could reasonably believe he knew of it.[103] This view has been carried forward by 1–205(3), which provides that usages of trade "in the vocation or trade in which they are engaged or of which they are or should be aware give particular meaning and supplement or qualify terms of an agreement." In other words, a disclaimer by usage of trade is only binding on members of the trade involved or persons who know or should know about it. Persons who should be aware of a trade usage doubtless include those who regularly deal with members of the relevant trade, and also members of a second trade that commonly deals with members of the relevant trade (for example, farmers should know something of seed selling).[104] We think the

---

99. R. D. Lowrance, Inc. v. Peterson, 185 Neb. 679, 682, 178 N.W.2d 277, 279, 7 UCC Rep.Serv. 1179, 1181 (1970).

100. 8 S. Williston, Williston on Contracts § 993A at 610 (3d ed. 1961).

101. 33 App.Div.2d 17, 304 N.Y.S.2d 918, 6 UCC Rep.Serv. 1246 (4th Dept.1969).

102. Id. at 22, 304 N.Y.S.2d at 923–24, 6 UCC Rep.Serv. at 1250.

103. 3 A. Corbin, Corbin on Contracts § 557 at 248 (1960). See also Restatement of Contracts § 247, Comment *b* (1932); 5 S. Williston, Williston on Contracts § 661 at 113–18 (3d ed. 1961).

104. If the buyer were a member of the seller's trade, he would be charged

court's approach in *Zicari* was correct and that the seller should have the burden of showing that the buyer knew or should have known that a usage in the seller's trade excluded implied warranties.

## § 12–7   Cumulation and Conflict of Warranties, 2–317

Sometimes warranties will conflict with each other. In Section 12–3 we dealt with the common situation where disclaimer language in a printed warranty clause conflicts with an express warranty. Section 2–316(1) instructs us to construe these provisions as consistent unless this would be unreasonable. Section 2–317 embodies a similar policy with regard to conflicts between any warranties, express or implied.

> Warranties whether express or implied shall be construed as consistent with each other and as cumulative, but if such construction is unreasonable the intention of the parties shall determine which warranty is dominant. In ascertaining that intention the following rules apply:
>
> (a) Exact or technical specifications displace an inconsistent sample or model or general language of description.
>
> (b) A sample from an existing bulk displaces inconsistent general language of description.
>
> (c) Express warranties displace inconsistent implied warranties other than an implied warranty of fitness for a particular purpose.

Comment 2 tells us that the purpose of this section is to assist in determining the intent of the parties as to which of two conflicting warranties should prevail. But this kind of determination is made only when the court has first decided (*1*) that it would be

with knowlwedge of that trade's usages.

Comment 9 to 2–316 suggests another method by which warranties may be excluded:

The situation in which the buyer gives precise and complete specifications to the seller is not explicitly covered in this section, but this is a frequent circumstance by which the implied warranties may be excluded.

Sal Metal Products Co. v. Rennert, 5 UCC Rep.Serv. 826 (N.Y.Sup.Ct.1968), involved this type of case. The buyer gave the seller models of moving van hardware items that the seller had contracted to make and sell to the buyer. Since the buyer had provided the specifications, the court held that he had not relied on the seller's skill and judgment and therefore that there could be no warranty of fitness for a particular purpose. 5 UCC Rep. Serv. at 829. While Comment 9 characterizes this situation as one involving warranty exclusion, it also recognizes that the warranty of fitness for a particular purpose normally would not arise in this situation. We think that this latter point is correct and that the inquiry is only confused by introducing the concept of warranty exclusion when the matter could be disposed of under 2–315.

The comment also suggests that the warranty of merchantability could be excluded under 2–317, which deals with cumulation and conflict of warranties. Thus, the situation posed appears not to involve 2–316 at all; it is a problem for 2–315 and 2–317.

unreasonable to construe the warranties as consistent with each other and (2) that the seller is not estopped from denying such consistency. According to Comment 2, equitable estoppel operates against the seller when he has not acted in "perfect good faith" in making inconsistent warranties or when he has led the buyer to believe that all warranties could be performed.

In practice, 2–317 is most often applied when the seller has made an express warranty that operates to exclude or limit the implied warranties. If the express warranty cannot reasonably be read as consistent with the implied warranties, the court must try to ascertain which warranty the parties intended to be dominant. Subsections (a), (b), and (c) list rules to aid this inquiry. While Comment 3 points out that these rules are not intended as absolute, other evidence of the parties' intent in most cases will be lacking. As a result, courts that have concluded that multiple warranties are inconsistent will usually be forced to apply strictly the three rules presented in subsections (a), (b), and (c).

Subsection (c) requires that an express warranty displace inconsistent implied warranties other than the implied warranty of fitness for a particular purpose. Perhaps the most common example of inconsistent express and implied warranties arises in sales of automobiles. Assume, for example, that a new car is sold with the following warranty clause: "This vehicle is warranted to be free of defects for 24,000 miles or twenty-four months, whichever occurs first; this warranty is given in lieu of all other warranties, express or implied." The clause is not conspicuously printed and it does not mention the word "merchantability." On the 26,000th mile the transmission fails as a result of a manufacturing defect. The buyer sues the dealer and manufacturer for breach of the implied warranty of merchantability, but the defendants move for summary judgment on the grounds that under 2–317(c) the express warranty displaced the implied warranty of merchantability. What result should a court reach?

If the court views the language of the express warranty as a whole, it would conclude that this warranty was inconsistent with the implied warranty of merchantability.[105] However, this conclusion would permit the seller to disclaim the warranty of merchantability in certain respects even though he had not complied with the formal requirements of 2–316(2)—(conspicuousness, use of the word "merchantability"). Since the warranty clause really contained both an

105. In Bassman v. Manhattan Dodge Sales, 5 UCC Rep.Serv. 128 (N.Y.Sup. Ct. 1968), the court did not even discuss 2–317 in holding that this kind of express warranty precluded an action for breach of implied warranties. The facts given did not disclose whether the word "merchantability" was used. See also Evans Mfg. Corp. v. Wolosin, 1 UCC Rep.Serv. 193 (Pa.C.P. 1957), in which the following language in a contract for the sale of a dairy and vegetable refrigerator was held sufficient to exclude all other warranties: "This warranty is in lieu of any and all other warranties, stated or inferred, and of all other obligations on the part of the manufacturer." The version of 2–316 then in effect did not require that a disclaimer mention the word "merchantability."

express warranty and a disclaimer, it would be appropriate to treat the two terms separately.[106]  The "24,000 miles or 24 months" express warranty, viewed in isolation from the disclaimer language, and the implied warranty of merchantability may conceivably be construed as cumulative.  For example, the express warranty could be viewed as merely prescribing the procedure for the seller's fulfillment of his general warranty obligations, establishing a conclusive presumption that any part that is discovered to be defective during the warranty period shall be regarded as unmerchantable.  We find this interpretation unpalatable and would argue that the 24,000 mile express warranty displaced any implied warranty on the same item at least as to damage covered by the express warranty.  However, one court, in Koellmer v. Chrysler Motors Corp.,[107] has held that an automobile guarantee against defective parts for five years or 50,000 miles is not inconsistent with the implied warranty of merchantability.  In that case the court separately evaluated the disclaimer language, which was similar to that used in our hypothetical case, in light of 2–316's requirement and held that it was ineffective because it was not conspicuous.[108]  Of course, even though our seller is obligated under the implied warranty, he may be able to avoid liability by persuading the court that a transmission that lasts for 26,000 miles is merchantable.[109]

Section 2–317(c) includes an important exception to its general rule: an express warranty does not displace an inconsistent implied warranty of fitness for a particular purpose.[110]  Professor Honnold has illustrated the reason for this exception.  Suppose a contract for the purchase of a cold-storage room includes an express warranty that the motor is three horsepower and will deliver ten tons of refrigeration.  If the buyer also has an implied warranty of fitness

---

106.  Section 2–313 enumerates the types of express warranties that may be created under the Code.  See Section 9–2 et seq., supra.  Nothing in 2–313 or in the accompanying comments suggests that the term "express warranty" encompasses language that excludes warranties; rather, express warranties are portrayed as affirmative obligations of the seller.  Thus, the use of the term "express warranties" in 2–317(c) should not be construed as incorporating disclaimer language that happens to appear in the same printed paragraph.

107.  6 Conn.Cir. 478, 8 UCC Rep.Serv. 668 (1970).

108.  Id. at ——, 8 UCC Rep.Serv. at 672.  The disclaimer did mention the word "merchantability."

109.  For discussion of merchantability, see Section 9–7 supra.

110.  In Sutter v. St. Clair Motors, Inc., 44 Ill.App.2d 318, 194 N.E.2d 674, 1 UCC Rep.Serv. 125 (1963) (Uniform Sales Act case that interpreted Code), an express warranty on a new car, similar to the one set out in the text, was held not to be inconsistent with the warranty of fitness for a particular purpose.  The facts in that case probably would not support such an implied warranty under 2–315.  See also L. & N. Sales Co. v. Stuski, 188 Pa.Super. 117, 146 A.2d 154, 1 UCC Rep.Serv. 119 (C.P.1958).  In that case, the court found that an express "warranty of marketability," which covered pouring devices for bartenders, was not inconsistent with the warranty of fitness for a particular purpose.  In Stuski, the court recognized that even if the two warranties were inconsistent, the fitness warranty would not be excluded.  188 Pa.Super. at 121, 146 A.2d at 157, 1 UCC Rep.Serv. at 121–22.

for a particular purpose based on the seller's knowledge of his needs and on his reliance on the seller's skill and judgment, that warranty would not be negated by the express warranty.[111]

Subsections (a) and (b) of 2–317 contain two other rules of construction that help resolve conflicts between express warranties. In essence these rules establish a hierarchy based on the specificity of the express warranties. Thus exact or technical specifications are given priority over inconsistent samples, models, or general descriptions, and a sample drawn from an existing bulk prevails over inconsistent general language of description. The scheme of 2–317, as reflected in all three rules, is to give effect to the more specific of conflicting warranties. Presumably, a specific express warranty would have "claimed the attention of the parties in the first instance," and hence, in the absence of contrary evidence, it was probably intended by the parties to be dominant.[112] The guidelines in subsections (a) and (b) for construing inconsistent express warranties should be considered in light of 2–313(1) (b) and (c) (creation of express warranty by description, sample, or model) [113] and 2–316(1) (exclusion or modification of express warranties).[114]

The reader should bear in mind that in practice a court—or jury—has a great deal of discretion in determining whether warranties are inconsistent. A court could reasonably conclude, for example, that a "five years or 50,000 miles" warranty was or was not intended to preempt all implied warranties. For two reasons we believe that courts should exercise some restraint in ruling that multiple warranties are inconsistent. First, 2–316 provides several devices for disclaiming warranties, and the comments to that section indicate a policy of preserving implied warranties unless the seller complies with the prescribed formal requirements. Second, in nearly all cases the seller drafts the sales agreement including the express warranty clause; in those cases it seems reasonable to place the burden of multiple warranties on the seller, since he had the opportunity to resolve any possible inconsistencies. Yet we suspect that the garden variety buyer who buys in reliance on a "5 year 50,000 mile" express warranty does not expect to be able to assert an implied warranty for the damage covered by the express warranty and would in fact tell an empirical researcher that such waranties are "inconsistent."

### § 12–8    Modification or Limitation of Remedies, 2–719

While 2–316 is primarily concerned with the exclusion or modification of warranties, it also tells the seller that he may limit by

---

111.  1 N.Y. State Law Revision Comm'n, 1955 Report 412 (1955).

112.  See § 2–313, Comment 3.

113.  See Section 9–2 et seq. supra.

114.  See Section 12–2 supra.

agreement the buyer's remedies for breach of warranty.   Section 2–316(4) provides:

> Remedies for breach of warranty can be limited in accordance with the provisions of this Article on liquidation or limitation of damages and on contractual modification of remedy (Sections 2–718 and 2–719).

Section 2–719 plays the dominant role in limiting buyer's remedies, and that role may easily be confused with 2–316's exclusion of warranties role.   For example, a tractor dealer may achieve the same effect by disclaiming all warranties except for the repair and replacement of defective parts under 2–316 or by limiting the buyer's damages to the cost of replacing defective parts under 2–719(1). In either case, if the seller has complied with all statutory requirements, the buyer will be barred from recovering such consequential damages as lost crops or injury to property.   However, one route may offer greater chance of court acceptance than another in certain circumstances.   Before we compare 2–719 and 2–316, we will examine 2–719's provisions and the restrictions that operate on it.

### § 12–9   Modification or Limitation of Remedies—How to Limit the Buyer's Remedies, 2–719(1)

Section 2–719(1) provides:

Subject to the provisions of subsections (2) and (3) of this section and of the preceding section on liquidation and limitation of damages,

> (a) the agreement may provide for remedies in addition to or in substitution for those provided in this Article and may limit or alter the measure of damages recoverable under this Article, as by limiting the buyer's remedies to return of the goods and repayment of the price or to repair and replacement of non-conforming goods or parts; and

> (b) resort to a remedy as provided is optional unless the remedy is expressly agreed to be exclusive, in which case it is the sole remedy.

Comment 1 tells us: "Under this section parties are left free to shape their remedies to their particular requirements and reasonable agreements limiting or modifying remedies are to be given effect."   Consistent with this policy of freedom of contract, 2–719 enables the parties to provide for remedies "in addition to or in substitution for" those normally available under the Code.   In actual practice, however, the section is most often invoked to limit the buyer's remedies for breach.   For example, in Dow Corning Corp. v. Capitol Aviation, Inc.[115] a contract for the sale of an executive passenger aircraft in-

---

115.   411 F.2d 622, 6 UCC Rep.Serv. 589 (7th Cir. 1969).

cluded a clause that limited the buyer's remedy for non-delivery to cancellation and refund of deposit. In an unsuccessful action by the buyer for consequential damages,[116] the court held that 2–719(1) (a) authorized the clause even though it was "obvious that this remedy deprives the buyer of the benefit of his bargain . . . ." [117] Section 2–719(3), which explicitly provides that the parties may opt to limit or exclude consequential damages, also supports the *Dow* decision. Comment 3 explains that 2–719(3) enables the parties to allocate "unknown or undeterminable risks." Although any contract term purporting to limit or exclude consequential damages is subject to judicial scrutiny under the unconscionability standard, courts usually uphold such clauses in transactions between experienced businessmen.[118]

One way for a buyer to get around a limitation-of-remedy clause is to show that the remedy stipulated was not expressly agreed to be exclusive. In that case, 2–719(1) (b) requires that the stipulated remedy be regarded as optional. Comment 2 says that "[s]ubsection (1) (b) creates a presumption that clauses prescribing remedies are cumulative rather than exclusive," but the seller can rebut this presumption through good draftsmanship in the original agreement. For example, in Wyatt Industries, Inc. v. Publiker Industries, Inc.,[119] which involved the sale of a pressure vessel for a chemical plant, Judge Carswell [120] held that the following clause was sufficiently explicit to limit the buyer to the stipulated remedy:

> Guarantee: Fabricator warrants the completed work against defective material and workmanship, exclusive of corrosion, for the period of one year from completion thereof. Its liability under this warranty shall be limited to the replacement within the aforesaid time of any defective work or material f. o. b. Fabricator's shop, and Fabricator shall be liable for no other damages or losses . . . .[121]

116. The alleged consequential damages consisted of a judgment suffered by the buyer in favor of his customer. The customer recovered his lost profits among other things. Id. at 623–24, 6 UCC Rep.Serv. at 591.

117. Id. at 626, 6 UCC Rep.Serv. at 594.

118. In *Dow*, for example, the court held that the stipulated remedy was not unconscionable in light of the commercial setting, which involved a transaction between a manufacturer and distributor. Id. at 627, 6 UCC Rep.Serv. at 595. See also K & C, Inc. v. Westinghouse Elec. Corp., 437 Pa. 303, 263 A.2d 390, 7 UCC Rep.Serv. 679 (1970) (sale of coin operated dry cleaners to attorney and experienced businessman); discussion in Section 12–11 supra.

119. 420 F.2d 454, 7 UCC Rep.Serv. 105 (5th Cir. 1969).

120. Judge Homer Thornberry also sat on the unanimous panel. Presumably, the fact that the United States Senate failed to approve their Honors' qualifications does not render this opinion's reasoning suspect.

121. 420 F.2d at 456, 7 UCC Rep.Serv. at 106–107. The parties subsequently modified the guarantee to limit the seller's liability to $25,000. The court held that the buyer was "entitled to recover 'damages,' as well as the cost of repairs, in the maximum amount

The courts are divided over the interpretation of one commonly used clause to the effect that a written express warranty is "expressly in lieu of any and all other warranties, express or implied, and of all other obligation on the part of the seller." An early Pennsylvania case [122] involving the sale of vegetable and dairy refrigeration held this language sufficiently specific to constitute an express agreement that the stipulated remedy be exclusive. However, a more recent Arkansas case, Ford Motor Co. v. Reid,[123] held almost identical language insufficient for the purposes of 2–719(1)(b). The court emphasized that the contract language dealt only with warranties and obligations and not with remedies.[124] It distinguished remedies from obligations as "the rights arising from failure to perform obligations" [125] and concluded that the printed clause did not expressly state that the *remedy* of repair or replacement was exclusive.[126]

The lessons from these three cases are two. First, the identity of the plaintiff and the nature of his injury may make a major difference. The plaintiffs in the first two cases were businessmen who incurred commercial losses. Mr. and Mrs. Reid, on the other hand, were consumers whose house burned down as a result of defective wiring in their new car. Once again, we may have a situation where courts show more sympathy to consumers than to businessmen. A second lesson is that regardless of the type of transaction, a seller attempting to limit his buyer's remedies should do so in the most specific terms possible. For example, in the *Reid* case, the warranty clause should have provided, in addition to the disclaimer language:

> The parties agree that the buyer's sale and exclusive remedy against the seller shall be for the repair or replacement of defective parts as provided herein. The buyer agrees that no other remedy (including, but not limited to, incidental or consequential damages [127] for lost profits, lost sales, injury

---

of $25,000.00 . . . ." Id. at 457, 7 UCC Rep.Serv. at 109.

In Water Works & Indus. Supply Co. v. Wilburn, 437 S.W.2d 951, 5 UCC Rep.Serv. 1169 (Ky.Ct.App.1968), a contract for the sale of pipe and gaskets contained an express warranty with liability limited to replacement cost. The warranty clause contained a statement that "no claim for labor or damages will be allowed." The court held that this language applied only to the express warranty and did not preclude the recovery of consequential damages for breach of the implied warranty of fitness for a particular purpose.

122. Evans Mfg. Corp. v. Wolosin, 1 UCC Rep.Serv. 193 (Pa.C.P.1957).

123. 250 Ark. 176, 465 S.W.2d 80, 8 UCC Rep.Serv. 985 (1971).

124. Id. at 184, 465 S.W.2d at 85, 8 UCC Rep.Serv. at 990.

125. Id. at 184, 465 S.W.2d at 85, 8 UCC Rep.Serv. at 991.

126. Id. at 184, 465 S.W.2d at 85, 8 UCC Rep.Serv. at 991.

127. Section 2–719(3) makes limitation of consequential damages for personal injuries in the case of consumer goods prima facie unconscionable. Theoretically, the seller may overcome this presumption. The seller's chances of accomplishing that feat should be weighed against the possibility that a court would improperly strike the entire limitation-of-remedy clause be-

to person or property, or any other incidental or consequential loss) shall be available to him.

Of course, it is conceivable that a court could find any clause to be too vague or ambiguous, and a court always has the option of refusing to enforce a clause it deems unconscionable. Nevertheless, the more explicit the limitation-of-remedy clause is, the more likely it will be enforced. Moreover, even if an explicit clause would be a loser before an appellate court, it might win the case in negotiations or at the trial level. In sum, a well-drafted remedy limitation clause will in most situations protect the seller against enormous damage judgments. Nevertheless we urge the lawyer to consider the risks of limitation clauses discussed in the rest of this chapter before he picks up his drafting pencil.

### § 12–10    Modification or Limitation of Remedies—Failure of stipulated Remedy to Achieve Its Essential Purpose, 2–719(2)

The basic mechanism provided by 2–719 is not very difficult to understand or apply. However, even if the contract contains a perfectly drafted clause, which explicitly states the exclusive remedy the parties intended for the buyer to have, the buyer can still resort to subsections (2) and (3) to avoid the effect of that clause. If the buyer can establish that the exclusive remedy provided in the contract "fails of its essential purpose" or that the limitation or exclusion of consequential damages is unconscionable, he may disregard those terms of the contract and pursue the remedies to which he would otherwise have recourse. Comment 1 to 2–719 explains the policy behind these subsections:

> [I]t is of the very essence of a sales contract that at least minimum adequate remedies be available. If the parties intend to conclude a contract for sale within this Article they must accept the legal consequence that there be at least a fair quantum of remedy for breach of the obligations or duties outlined in the contract.

The standards provided in this excerpt—"minimum adequate remedies" and "fair quantum of remedy"—are of limited assistance to the attorney drafting a sales agreement and to a court interpreting that agreement. In the remainder of this chapter, we will try to describe more specifically the situations in which these provisions will be applied.

Section 2–719(2) provides:

> Where circumstances cause an exclusive or limited remedy to fail of its essential purpose, remedy may be had as provided in this Act.

cause of the single unconscionable term. The chances of either occurrence are slight, and on balance it is probably wisest to make the clause as comprehensive as possible.

Comment 1 explains that this subsection applies to "an apparently fair and reasonable clause," which "because of circumstances fails in its purpose or operates to deprive either party of the substantial value of the bargain . . . ." Notice that both the statutory language and the comment refer to "its [i. e., the limited or exclusive remedy's] essential purpose . . ." (emphasis added). That is, 2–719(2) should be triggered when the remedy fails of its essential purpose, not of the essential purpose of the Code or of contract law or of justice or of equity. To use the words of Professor Honnold, this provision "is not concerned with arrangements which were oppressive at their inception, but rather with the application of an agreement to novel circumstances not contemplated by the parties."[128]

When are "novel circumstances" presented? A recent federal case applying the Alabama Code, Riley v. Ford Motor Co.,[129] may provide a clue. The plaintiff purchased a new car, which was accompanied by an express warranty limited to repair or replacement of defective parts. The warranty explicitly provided that the seller would not be responsible for consequential loss. During the first few weeks of ownership the buyer discovered at least fourteen major and minor defects in the car, which the dealer and the manufacturer's representative were unable satisfactorily to repair.[130] The jury returned a verdict for the plaintiff in an amount far exceeding the cost of repairs. The Fifth Circuit Court of Appeals held that the jury was not unjustified "in its implicit finding that the warranty operated to deprive the purchaser 'of the substantial value of the bargain.' "[131] In other words, the exclusive remedy of repair and replacement of defective parts failed of its essential purpose because even after numerous attempts to repair, the car did not operate as should a new car free of defects.[132]

Wilson Trading Corp. v. David Ferguson, Ltd.,[133] illustrates another context in which an exclusive remedy can fail of its essential purpose. A contract for the sale of yarn provided: "No claims . . . shall be allowed if made after weaving, knitting, or proc-

128. 1 N.Y. State Law Revision Comm'n, 1955 Report 584 (1955). As we shall see, limitations that are "oppressive" at the outset will face sufficient trouble from 2–302 and 2–719 (3).

129. 442 F.2d 670, 8 UCC Rep.Serv. 1175 (5th Cir. 1971).

130. The plaintiff alleged both breach of warranty and negligent repair. Id. at 671, 8 UCC Rep.Serv. at 1176.

131. Id. at 673, 8 UCC Rep.Serv. at 1178–79.

132. Accord, Jones & McKnight Corp. v. Birdsboro Corp., 320 F.Supp. 39, 8

UCC Rep.Serv. 307 (N.D.Ill.1970) (if buyer could show that seller was unreasonable or wilfully dilatory in making good its exclusive warranty to repair automated machinery, then buyer would not be limited to that remedy). See also Adams v. J. I. Case Co., 125 Ill.App.2d 388, 402, 261 N.E.2d 1, 7, 7 UCC Rep.Serv. 1270, 1276 (1970) (seller breached its exclusive warranty to repair and replace defective parts of crawler loader tractor; held that these circumstances demonstrated that exclusive remedy failed and noted that "[r]epudiation of the obligations of the warranty destroy its benefits").

133. 23 N.Y.2d 398, 244 N.E.2d 685, 5 UCC Rep.Serv. 1213 (1968).

essing, or more than 10 days after receipt of shipment." [134]  It was possible that there were latent defects that would render the yarn unmerchantable and could not reasonably be discovered within the given time period.  If so, said the New York Court of Appeals, the limited remedy would fail of its essential purpose since the buyer would be left with no remedy for those kinds of defects.[135]

In both of these cases it could be argued that the exclusive remedy provided for in the agreement did not fail of its essential purpose.  *Wilson Trading* especially appears to be a case in which the court was concerned with a term oppressive at its inception.  It was not circumstances that left the buyer remediless but rather his own agreement to assume the risk for defects that could not be discovered within ten days.  The stipulated remedy may have been unreasonable or unconscionable (and unenforceable for that reason), but it did not fail to achieve its essential purpose—to indemnify the buyer against latent defects that could have been discovered within ten days.

What the courts in *Wilson Trading* and *Riley* seem to have seized upon is the notion that a sales contract must have "at least minimum adequate remedies." [136]  The buyer in both cases complained in essence that they had no remedy at all under the contract.  The car buyer in *Riley* alleged that the car was worth nothing to him since it could not be repaired, and the yarn purchaser in *Wilson Trading* complained that it was barred from filing claims against the seller once the ten days had passed.  *Riley* appears to fit into the literal scheme of 2–719(2).  In the ordinary course of events, a few repairs and replacements can be expected to put a new car in good working condition.  Thus, under the facts of that case, relatively unusual circumstances caused the exclusive remedy to fail of its essential purpose.  The exclusive remedy in *Wilson Trading*, on the other hand, should have been abrogated, if at all, by those provisions of the Code that deal with inherently oppressive terms.[137]

---

**134.**  Id. at 401, 244 N.E.2d at 686, 5 UCC Rep.Serv. at 1214.

**135.**  Id. at 404, 244 N.E.2d at 688, 5 UCC Rep.Serv. at 1217.  In reaching this conclusion, the court cited 1–204 (1), which provides:

> Whenever this Act requires any action to be taken within a reasonable time, any time which is not manifestly unreasonable may be fixed by agreement.

The purpose of this provision, according to Comment 1, is to enable a court to disregard "a clause which whether by inadvertence or overreaching fixes a time so unreasonable that it amounts to eliminating all remedy under the contract."  See also Neville Chem. Co. v. Union Carbide Corp., 422 F.2d 1205,

7 UCC Rep.Serv. 81 (3d Cir. 1970), cert. denied 400 U.S. 826 (1970) (15-day notice requirement was manifestly unreasonable within the meaning of 1–204(1) if it applied to latent defects that could not be discovered in 15 days).

**136.**  § 2–719, Comment 1.

**137.**  As suggested in note 135 supra, a manifestly unreasonable time period may be disregarded under 1–204(1).  The court in *Wilson Trading* also recognized that the facts of that case presented a question of unconscionability.  23 N.Y.2d at 403–04, 244 N.E. 2d at 687–88, 5 UCC Rep.Serv. at 1216.  Unconscionability is discussed in Section 12–11 supra.

There are probably relatively few situations where a remedy can fail of its essential purpose. Section 2–719(2) will probably be called into action most often in cases like *Riley* when the exclusive remedy involves replacement or repair of defective parts, and the seller because of his negligence in repair or because the goods are beyond repair, is unable to put the goods in warranted condition. Section 2–719 (2) might also apply when the exclusive remedy requires performance of an act by the buyer that is precluded by the seller's breach. For example, suppose an automobile manufacturer makes an exclusive warranty to repair and replace defective parts if such parts are delivered to its plant. If the entire car is destroyed as a result of defective wiring, the buyer would be unable to return the wiring to the manufacturer's plant. The exclusive remedy would therefore fail of its essential purpose.[138]

One other question remains with regard to 2–719(2): When an exclusive remedy is set aside under subsection (2), may the buyer resort to all remedies made available under the Code? In other words, is the buyer in the *Riley* case limited to some form of difference money damages [139] or may he also recover incidental and consequential damages? The seller may argue that the buyer should recover no more damages than he would have, had the exclusive remedy not failed of its essential purpose. The purpose of the new-car warranty was to ensure the buyer of a new car free of defects; it expressly provided that the buyer could not recover consequential loss. Yet the court allowed the buyer to recover the reasonably incurred cost of substitute transportation and suggested that other incidental and consequential damages could be recovered if the plaintiff proved them.[140] In a similar case, the buyer was permitted to prove lost profits.[141] Even though the effect of these rulings is to grant the buyer something he did not bargain for, they are supported by the language of the Code and Comment 1. Subsection (2) states that "remedy may be had as provided in this Act," and Comment 1 tells us that a term that fails in its essential purpose "must give way to the general remedy provision of this Article." Thus, the seller's attorney should take note that a limitation-of-remedy clause that takes too much away from a buyer may give him everything.

Can a seller protect himself against 2–719(2)? He may gain some protection if the agreed limitation-of-remedy clause states what the essential purpose of the exclusive remedy shall be and what shall not be deemed a failure of that essential purpose. For example, sup-

---

138. See W. Hawkland, A Transactional Guide to the Uniform Commercial Code 175 (1964).

139. Section 2–714(2) allows damages for breach of warranty based on the difference of the value of the goods actually accepted and the value the goods would have had if they had been as warranted. See Section 10–2 supra.

140. Riley v. Ford Motor Co., 442 F.2d 670, 674, 8 UCC Rep.Serv. 1175, 1179–80 (5th Cir. 1971).

141. Adams v. J. I. Case Co., 125 Ill. App.2d 388, 261 N.E.2d 1, 7 UCC Rep. Serv. 1270 (1970).

pose an automobile dealer has expressly warranted a new car to be free of defects, has properly disclaimed all other warranties, and has stipulated that the buyer's exclusive remedy shall be the repair or replacement of defective parts by the dealer. The following two sentences might protect him against 2–719(2):

> The sole purpose of the stipulated exclusive remedy shall be to provide the buyer with free repair and replacement of defective parts in the manner provided herein. This exclusive remedy shall not be deemed to have failed of its essential purpose so long as the seller is willing and able to repair or replace defective parts in the prescribed manner.

If the warranty for repair or replacement requires the buyer to return the defective part to the seller, a clause to this effect should be added:

> The buyer shall not be required to deliver a defective part to the seller if:
>
> > (1) the part was destroyed as a result of its defect or of any defect in any part covered in this warranty, *and*
> >
> > (2) the seller is reasonably satisfied that the part was defective at the time of sale.
>
> If both of these conditions are met, the seller shall replace the part in the same manner provided herein as if the buyer had delivered it to the seller's plant.

These suggested clauses *may* prevent a court from disregarding an otherwise valid limitation-of-remedy clause in the situations described. We can say with somewhat more certainty that they will provide the seller's attorney with additional negotiation weapons.

### § 12–11  Modification or Limitation of Remedies—Unconscionable Limitation of Remedy, 2–719(3) and 2–302

Perhaps the most difficult question posed in the entire area of seller's attempts to avoid warranty and contract liability involves the role of the unconscionability concept as a device for policing remedy limitation and disclaimer clauses. We have already discussed the policies behind and operation of the court's power under section 2–302 to refuse to enforce unconscionable contracts and clauses.[142] Section 2–719(3) provides that a court should strike a clause that limits or excludes consequential damages if "the limitation or exclusion is unconscionable." Under this provision, courts have invalidated warranty *disclaimers* that deny the buyer consequential damages. The interrelationship among 2–302, 2–316, and 2–719(3) has thus become complex and confusing.

Part of the confusion undoubtedly arises from a failure to distinguish between disclaimer and exclusionary clauses. A disclaimer

---

142. See Ch. 4 supra.

clause [143] is a device used to exclude or limit the seller's warranties; it attempts to control the seller's liability by reducing the number of situations in which the seller can be in breach. An exclusionary clause, on the other hand, restricts the remedies available to one or both parties once a breach is established. Assume, for example, that a new-car buyer sues for breach of warranty, and the seller raises defenses based on disclaimer and exclusionary clauses. The disclaimer defense denies the existence of any cause of action. The exclusionary-clause defense, on the other hand, denies that the buyer is entitled to the remedy he demands—for example, consequential damages.[144] Because these two types of clauses are easily confused, we will first see how the concept of unconscionability operates on each in isolation. Then we will look at the interrelationships among sections 2–316, 2–719, and 2–302.

### Unconscionable Consequential-Loss Exclusion

2–719(3) states an apparently simple, but vague, rule and corollary:

> Consequential damages may be limited or excluded unless the limitation or exclusion is unconscionable. Limitation of consequential damages for injury to the person in the case of consumer goods is prima facie unconscionable but limitation of damages where the loss is commercial is not.

The first thing to note about subsection (3) is that it is not the buyer's best friend: as the courts have recognized, the subsection explicitly authorizes the contractual exclusion of consequential damages.[145] Moreover, except in cases in which consumer goods cause personal injuries, the buyer carries the burden of proving the unconscionability of the limitation-of-remedy clause.[146] Comment 1 further suggests that a remedy limitation clause should be deleted on the grounds of unconscionability only when it fails to provide a "minimum adequate remedy." Thus, at least in theory, one should not view 2–719(3) as an all powerful weapon against valid remedy limitation language.

Suppose Acme Motors sells a pick-up truck to a consumer, who plans to use it for fishing trips.[147] The printed form sales contract

---

143. While the Code itself does not use the term "disclaimer," the comments refer to it. See §§ 2–316, Comments 1, 3, 5, 8; 2–719, Comment 3.

144. Since an exclusionary clause may reduce the period of limitation for a cause of action (see § 2–725), a defense based on such a clause may, in effect, deny the existence of a cause of action. Note also that an exclusionary clause may apply to all seller breaches, not just to breaches of warranty.

145. K & C, Inc. v. Westinghouse Elec. Corp., 437 Pa. 303, 263 A.2d 390, 7 UCC Rep.Serv. 679 (1970) (sale of coin operated dry cleaner to commercial corporation).

146. The statement "but limitation of damages where the loss is commercial is not" could mean that such a limitation is not prima facie unconscionable or that it is prima facie not unconscionable. The first alternative seems more probable.

147. Under section 9–109(1), the truck would be a consumer good since it

contains a remedy limitation clause which provides that under no circumstances shall the buyer be entitled to consequential damages. The buyer suffers serious injuries when the truck explodes on the way home from the showroom. Unless Acme comes forward with evidence rebutting the presumption of unconscionability of the exclusion clause,[148] the buyer may recover damages for his personal injuries. On the other hand, if the buyer had purchased the truck for delivering groceries from his store, and if the only injuries caused by the explosion were to the truck and to groceries on board, the buyer would have to prove that the exclusionary clause was unconscionable.[149]

Can the buyer ever win in a commercial setting? The New York Court of Appeals said yes in a case in which a contract for the sale of yarn required that all claims against the seller be made within ten days after the sale. The court indicated that the clause might be unconscionable if latent defects could not reasonably be discovered by the buyer, a sweater manufacturer, during the designated time period.[150] Moreover, two courts have held that when an automobile dealer suffers a judgment in favor of a consumer buyer who sustained personal injuries caused by a purchased automobile, a contractual arrangement limiting the manufacturer's liability to the dealer is unconscionable.[151] Nevertheless, findings of unconscionability

was bought "primarily for personal, family or household purposes." 2–103 (3) states that this definition applies to Article Two, and the courts have applied it to 2–719(3). See, e. g., Ford Motor Co. v. Tritt, 244 Ark. 883, 430 S.W.2d 778, 5 UCC Rep.Serv. 312 (1968).

148. The comments to 2–719 contain a cross-reference to section 2–302. Comment 1 to that section suggests that the purpose of the section is to prevent "oppression and unfair surprise." Therefore, it is possible that Acme could rebut the presumption if it could show that the exclusion clause was conspicuously printed, that it was explained to the buyer, that the parties bargained over it, and that the buyer knew that Acme's trucks had a tendency to explode. It's possible, but not likely.

The reader will note that we have failed to cite any cases in which exclusion-of-remedy clauses have been declared unconscionable in the context of personal injuries caused by consumer goods. This absence of authority is attributable to the fact that the personal-injury cases that have thus far invoked 2–719(3) have really dealt with warranty disclaimers. See Section 12–12 infra.

149. Section 3–302(1), which presumably applies to 2–719(3) by virtue of the cross-reference in the comments, requires that the court itself determine unconscionability. A clause excluding consequential damages for injury to the person in the case of goods that are not consumer goods apparently is not prima facie unconscionable. However, the fact of personal injuries should enhance the buyer's case.

150. Wilson Trading Corp. v. David Ferguson, Ltd., 23 N.Y.2d 398, 244 N.E. 2d 685, 5 UCC Rep.Serv. 1213 (1968), discussed in text accompanying notes 133–35 supra.

151. See, e. g., Ford Motor Co. v. Tritt, 244 Ark. 883, 430 S.W.2d 778, 5 UCC Rep.Serv. 312 (1968). See also Sarfati v. M. A. Hittner & Sons, Inc., 35 App.Div.2d 1004, 318 N.Y.S.2d 352, 8 UCC Rep.Serv. 442 (2d Dep't 1970), aff'd. mem. 28 N.Y.2d 808, 270 N.E.2d 729 (1971) (liability of manufacturer of automobile to buyer who suffered personal injury judgment in favor of his lessee). Both of these cases really involved warranty disclaimer clauses rather than remedy exclusion clauses.

should be rare in commercial settings.[152]  An exemplary analysis in this context may be found in K & C, Inc. v. Westinghouse Electric Corp.[153]  An experienced businessman and an attorney formed the plaintiff corporation, which contracted to purchase coin operated dry cleaners from the defendant.  The machines developed difficulties, and the plaintiff sued for consequential damages, even though the sales contracts purported to bar such a remedy.  The court concluded that "it is clear that the exclusion was not unconscionable here, where the buyer was hardly the sheep keeping company with wolves that it would have us believe."[154]  To support this conclusion, the court cited the experience of the plaintiff's owners and the fact that they had carefully studied their investment for six months before making the purchase.

### Unconscionable Disclaimer of Warranty

In the K & C case, the buyer apparently assumed that if he could convince the court that the consequential-loss exclusion clause was unconscionable, he could recover consequential damages.  The contract, however, also excluded all warranties except an express warranty to repair and replace parts.[155]  If the disclaimer clause had been perfectly drafted and complied with all of the requirements under 2–316,[156] would a finding that a consequential-loss exclusion clause was unconscionable entitle the buyer to prove consequential damages?  In other words, does a finding of unconscionability under 2–719(3) invalidate disclaimer language as well as exclusionary language?

Before we answer that question we should first decide whether a warranty disclaimer that meets the 2–316 requirements can be unconscionable.  There are some good reasons for answering this question in the negative.  Most of these have been articulated by Professor Leff in his classic article on unconscionability.[157]  In the first place, 2–316 contains a list of specific formal requirements with which a seller must comply in order to disclaim successfully.  These requirements are intended "to protect a buyer from unexpected and unbargained language of disclaimer,"[158] an intent that coincides with

---

152.  County Asphalt, Inc. v. Lewis Welding & Eng'r Corp., 323 F.Supp. 1300, 8 UCC Rep.Serv. 445 (S.D.N.Y. 1970) (sale of equipment for use in asphalt plants), aff'd 444 F.2d 372 (2d Cir. 1971), cert. denied 404 U.S. 939 (1971).

153.  437 Pa. 303, 263 A.2d 390, 7 UCC Rep.Serv. 679 (1970).

154.  Id. 308, 263 A.2d at 393, 7 UCC Rep.Serv. at 682.  See also Dow Corning Co. v. Capitol Aviation, Inc., 411 F.2d 622, 6 UCC Rep.Serv. 589 (7th Cir. 1969) (sale of executive passenger aircraft).

155.  K & C, Inc. v. Westinghouse Elec. Corp., 437 Pa. 303, 306–07, 263 A.2d 390, 392, 7 UCC Rep.Serv. 679, 681 (1970).

156.  It is not clear whether the disclaimer in K & C, Inc. v. Westinghouse Elec. Corp. was conspicuous, but it definitely did not mention the word "merchantability."  Hence it may be that the parties assumed that the buyer would automatically win if he could get over the 2–719(3) hurdle.

157.  Leff, Unconscionability and the Code—The Emperor's New Clause, 115 U.Pa.L.Rev. 485, 516–28 (1967).

158.  § 2–316, Comment 1.

2–302's purpose of preventing "oppression and unfair surprise." [159] Once a disclaimer has been expressed so conspicuously that a buyer's "attention can reasonably be expected to be called to it," [160] he can hardly complain that he was unfairly surprised or that the disclaimer was unexpected. Moreover, 2–316 makes no reference to 2–302, not even in the cross references listed in the official comment. When several other sections in Article 2—including 2–719(3)—make such reference,[161] it would seem that the draftsmen would have done so in 2–316 if they intended for it to be governed by 2–302. As Professor Leff sums up:

> Here is 2–316 which sets forth clear, specific and anything but easy-to-meet standards for disclaiming warranties. It is a highly detailed section, the comments to which disclose full awareness of the problem at hand. It contains no reference of any kind to section 2–302, although nine other sections of article 2 contain such references. In such circumstances the usually bland assumptions that a disclaimer which meets the requirements of 2–316 might still be strikable as "unconscionable" under 2–302 seems explainable, if at all, as oversight, wishful thinking or (in a rare case) attempted sneakiness.[162]

In the heat of attack Professor Leff has overstated his case somewhat, for one can raise a few unsneaky arguments in favor of the application of 2–302 to disclaimers. First of all, 2–302, by its express terms, applies to "any clause of the contract." There is nothing in that section removing its operation from types of contractual provisions that are dealt with elsewhere in the Code. Similarly, section 2–316 does not state expressly that all disclaimers meeting its requirements are immune from general policing provisions like 2–302 or 1–203 (obligations of good faith). Moreover, the courts have had no difficulty finding that other types of clauses—for example, waiver-of-defense [163] and cross-security [164] clauses—could be unconscionable

---

159. § 2–302, Comment 1.

160. § 1–201(10), Comment 10 (definition of "conspicuous").

161. See Leff, Unconscionability and the Code—The Emperor's New Clause, 115 U.Pa.L.Rev. 485, 523 n. 140 (1967).

162. Id. at 523. The author also argues that if the draftsmen had meant to outlaw all disclaimers they would have said so. Id. at 524. But just because the draftsmen did not manifest an intent to prohibit all disclaimers does not mean they intended to insulate particular disclaimers from the policing of 2–302.

For further support of Leff's view, see 1 N.Y. State Law Revision Comm'n, 1955 Report 586 (1955).

163. See, e. g., Unico v. Owen, 50 N.J. 101, 232 A.2d 405, 4 UCC Rep.Serv. 542 (1967). Waiver-of-defense clauses are explicitly permitted, "[s]ubject to any statute or decision which establishes a different rule for buyers or lessees of consumer goods," by section 9–206(1).

164. Williams v. Walker-Thomas Furniture Co., 350 F.2d 445, 2 UCC Rep. Serv. 955 (D.C.Cir. 1965) (suggestion that a cross-security clause could be unconscionable) (dictum). Cross-security clauses are permitted by section 9–206.

even though they are regulated by provisions in the Code that make no cross-reference to 2–302.

Further support for the argument that 2–302 applies to disclaimers can be found in the comments to 2–302. Comment 1 lists and describes ten cases which are presumably intended to illustrate the underlying basis of the section; in seven of those cases, disclaimers of warranty were denied full effect. It is difficult to reconcile an intent on the part of the draftsmen to immunize disclaimers from the effect of 2–302 with the fact that they used cases in which courts struck down disclaimers to illustrate the concept of unconscionability.[165]

A third argument derives from the fact that even though a disclaimer may be conspicuous and actually understood by the buyer, it may be "oppressive" within the meaning of Comment 1 to 2–302. The comments to 2–316 make clear that the former requirements set out in that section are intended "to protect a buyer from unexpected and unbargained language of disclaimer." [166] Yet the mechanisms provided in 2–316 only serve to make the buyer aware of a disclaimer so that he can attempt to bargain with the seller; those devices do nothing about the situation where the seller insists on imposing a written disclaimer and refuses to bargain over that term. While Comment 1 to 2–302 announces that the principle of unconscionability does not involve "disturbance of allocation of risks because of superior bargaining power," we have seen in the earlier chapter on 2–302 [167] that the courts have seized upon other language in the comments, such as "one-sided" and "oppressive," in order to invalidate harsh clauses that could be attributed to gross disparities in bargaining power. Thus, one can argue that when a seller has such a strong bargaining position that he can impose a perfectly drafted disclaimer, which operates to deprive the buyer of virtually all protection that the law would otherwise provide, and he refuses to bargain at all concerning its scope, then that clause has become "oppressive" and "so one-sided" as to be unconscionable.[168]

This argument was accepted before the enactment of the Code by the Supreme Court of New Jersey. In Henningsen v. Bloomfield Motors, Inc.,[169] the plaintiff suffered personal injuries when a defective steering mechanism in a new car purchased by her husband broke and caused the car to run into a brick wall. The plaintiff sued the manufacturer and its dealer for breach of the implied warranty

---

165. According to Professor Leff, these cases are intended merely to illustrate "the skewing of legal doctrine that may be caused by an emotional pressure to get a more heartwarming particular result." Leff, Unconscionability and the Code—The Emperor's New Clause, 115 U.Pa.L.Rev. 485, 527 (1960). While the cases doubtless do illustrate "manipulative techniques," one would think the comment writer would not have selected the majority of the cases from a substantive area that 2–302 was not supposed to touch.

166. § 2–316, Comment 1 (emphasis added).

167. See Section 4–2 et seq., supra.

168. § 2–302, Comment 1.

169. 32 N.J. 358, 161 A.2d 69 (1960).

of merchantability; the defendants asserted as a defense a rather typical disclaimer clause that was contained in the purchase order. In striking down the disclaimer, the court stressed the "grossly disproportionate bargaining power" of the manufacturer.[170]   This power arose from the fact that the warranty disclaimer was a uniform one used by the "Big Three" automobile manufacturers.   As a result of standardization, a buyer had no choice but to accede to the seller's terms; moreover the various automobile manufacturers had no incentive to provide effective warranties since they did not compete in that area.[171]   The court therefore held that under these circumstances, the attempted disclaimer could not be given effect because it was "inimical to the public good." [172]   While the *Henningsen* opinion never mentions the term "unconscionability," its conclusion that a warranty disclaimer can contravene public policy is precisely the type of conclusion that the Code intends for a court to reach under 2–302.[173]   Therefore, it seems entirely reasonable for a court to apply the reasoning in *Henningsen* when it is it is judging the unconscionability under the Code of a disclaimer that complies with 2–316.[174]

There is no agreement among the commentators or among the courts on the question whether 2–316 preempts the field of warranty disclaimers and so excludes 2–302 from any operation here.   The Supreme Court of Appeals of Virginia in Marshall v. Murray Oldsmobile Co.,[175] appeared to side with those favoring the preemption view.   That pre-Code case involved a disclaimer clause like the one in *Henningsen* [176] in connection with the sale of a new car to a consumer. The court, however, refused to follow the New Jersey court.   In upholding the disclaimer, the court stated:

> [I]f there exist the "overriding reasons of public policy," as claimed by the complainant and as relied upon by the New Jersey court in the *Henningsen* case, those reasons surely would have been known to our legislature when, in 1964, it adopted the Uniform Commercial Code, effective January 1, 1966.   And yet, while providing in Code, § 8.2–315 that there shall be an implied warranty of fitness at-

170.   Id. 404, 161 A.2d at 95.

171.   Id. at 391, 161 A.2d at 87.

172.   Id. at 404, 161 A.2d at 95.   Other courts have adopted the New Jersey court's reasoning in non-Code cases. See, e. g., State Farm Mut. Auto Ins. Co. v. Anderson-Weber, Inc., 252 Iowa 1289, 110 N.W.2d 449 (1961); Browne v. Fenestra, Inc., 375 Mich. 566, 134 N.W.2d 730 (1965) (sale of garage door).

173.   § 2–302, Comment 1.

174.   Indeed, a few Code cases have specifically cited the *Henningsen* case in declaring disclaimers to be unconscionable.   See, e. g., Zabriskie Chevrolet, Inc. v. Smith, 99 N.J.Super. 441, 448, 240 A.2d 195, 199, 5 UCC Rep. Serv. 30, 35 (Law Div.1968); Sarfati v. M. A. Hittner & Sons, Inc., 35 App. Div.2d 1004, 1005, 318 N.Y.S.2d 352, 354, 8 UCC Rep.Serv. 442, 444 (2d Dept. 1971); Walsh v. Ford Motor Co., 59 Misc.2d 241, 242, 298 N.Y.S.2d 538, 540, 6 UCC Rep.Serv. 56, 57 (Sup.Ct.1969).

175.   207 Va. 972, 154 S.E.2d 140, 4 UCC Rep.Serv. 172 (1967).

176.   See notes 169–72 and accompanying text supra.

tached to the sale of goods, the legislature specifically provided in Code, § 8.2–316 how such an implied warranty may be excluded.[177]

While this language suggests that disclaimers drafted in accordance with 2–316 are immune from unconscionability attacks, two other statements tend to cut against that suggestion. First, the court stressed that the Code does not say that "there shall be no exclusion of implied warranties of fitness in the sale of personal property." [178] The fact that the Code does not prohibit all disclaimers does not insulate individual disclaimers from unconscionability attacks. Second, the court observed that rescission was not available because neither "fraud, mistake," nor "disability" was alleged.[179] Since those factors are akin to unconscionability, it is conceivable that the Virginia court might entertain a 2–302 attack on a disclaimer that complies with 2–316.[180]

While there are no reported decisions that explicitly reject the preemption argument, four different courts have strongly indicated that a warranty disclaimer may be unconscionable. A Pennsylvania trial court asserted in a footnote that even if the new-car dealer in the case before it had used the proper forms for his disclaimer, the disclaimer might still be unconscionable under 2–302.[181] The Third Circuit Court of Appeals suggested in dicta that when a disclaimer is manifestly unreasonable, section 1–102(3) [182] "prevents the enforcement of unconscionable sales where, as in this instance, the goods exchanged are found to be totally worthless." [183] While the court did

---

177. 207 Va. at 978, 154 S.E.2d at 144–45, 4 UCC Rep.Serv. at 177.

178. Id. at 979, 154 S.E.2d at 145, 4 UCC Rep.Serv. at 178 (emphasis added).

179. Id. at 979, 154 S.E.2d at 145, 4 UCC Rep.Serv. at 178.

180. Cf. Arrow Transp. Co. v. Fruehauf Corp., 289 F.Supp. 170 (D.Ore.1968). This pre-Code case took place in a commercial setting and involved the sale of tanker trailers. The court upheld a written disclaimer and noted that section 2–316 "provides that the parties are free to contract away any warranties which may be implied by law, the only requirement being that the disclaimer be clearly stated and be conspicuous." Id. at 172–73. However, the court also found, "Nothing here presented would indicate that the language of the disclaimer is in any way unconscionable." Id. at 173.

181. Willman v. American Motor Sales Co., 1 UCC Rep.Serv. 100, 103–104, 104 n. 3 (Pa.C.P.1961) (new car destroyed

by fire while being operated). It was unnecessary for the court to decide the unconscionability issue because it held that the disclaimer failed to use the clear and definite language required by the 1952 version of 2–316.

182. § 1–102(3) provides:

The effect of provisions of this Act may be varied by agreement, except as otherwise provided in this Act and except that the obligations of good faith, diligence, reasonableness and care prescribed by this Act may not be disclaimed by agreement but the parties may by agreement determine the standards by which the performance of such obligations is to be measured if such standards are not manifestly unreasonable.

183. Vlases v. Montgomery Ward & Co., 377 F.2d 846, 850, 4 UCC Rep.Serv. 164, 169 (3d Cir. 1967) (emphasis added) (sale of one-day-old chicks with avion bukosis, a form of bird cancer). The seller apparently had not used sufficiently specific disclaimer language to satisfy the requirements of 2–316.

not cite 2–302, the quoted language demonstrates the court's belief that disclaimers are subject to the general policing provisions of the Code and particularly to the unconscionability standard. A New Jersey appellate court was more explicit when it declared in dicta that the policy enunciated in *Henningsen* that disclaimers of the implied warranty of merchantability are "against public policy now finds statutory support not only in N.J.Stat.Ann. 12A: 2–316(2) but also in N.J.Stat.Ann. 12A: 2–302, N.J.S.A. (unconscionable contract or clause)." [184]

Finally a New York court recently suggested that a disclaimer provision that explicitly excludes the implied warranties of merchantability and fitness for a particular purpose may under some circumstances be unconscionable even though it is conspicuously printed. In Jefferson Credit Corp. v. Marcano,[185] the court refused to enforce an installment contract, that is, it excused the buyers from making futher payments for a used car that was constantly in need of major repairs. The sales contract included a thirty-day warranty and an apparently flawless disclaimer which the Spanish-speaking couple could not fully understand since the terms were printed in English.[186] On three different occasions the dealer led the buyers to believe that the car would be put in good condition, but at the end of the thirty days, he denied all responsibility. The case was filled with juicy unconscionability equities: the dealer's deception in avoiding responsibility under the express warranty; the inability of the buyers to understand English; the fact that the buyers paid out a total of $621.63 for the partial use of a defective used car for six months while both the dealer and the plaintiff-assignee apparently realized reasonable returns; the fact that the assignee sold the re-possessed car to the original dealer seven months after the sale for less than one-fifth of the total charges to the buyer under the install-ment contract; and the fact that the dealer then had to spend $402 to put the car in salable condition.[187] Although the court's judgment for defendant rested upon plaintiff's violation of the resale provi-sions in section 9–504, it relied principally upon the disclaimer and

184. Zabriskie Chevrolet v. Smith, 99 N.J.Super. 441, 448, 240 A.2d 195, 199, 5 UCC Rep.Serv. 30, 35 (Law Div.1968). The attempted disclaimer was not con-spicuous, and it was delivered after the contract for sale was signed. This case is discussed at note 58 and ac-companying text supra.

185. 60 Misc.2d 138, 302 N.Y.S.2d 390, 6 UCC Rep.Serv. 602 (Civ.Ct.1969).

186. It could be argued that a disclaim-er written in English is not conspicu-ous to a buyer who cannot read En-glish, since such a buyer's attention cannot reasonably be expected to be called to it. See the discussion of conspicuousness in Section 12–5 supra.

187. 60 Misc.2d at 139–40, 302 N.Y.S.2d at 392–93, 6 UCC Rep.Serv. at 604–05. The original purchase price for the car was $1395, and the total price, which included tax and credit charges, was $1766.23. The plaintiff-finance company sued for the unpaid balance of $796.60 plus attorney's fees of $119.-49. The dealer received a total of $1169.75 (including the downpayment by the buyers and the amounts re-ceived from the assignee and resale purchaser), and the assignee received $749.88 (including amounts received from the buyers and from the dealer on resale) to cover the $650 it paid the dealer for the contract.

the facts immediately surrounding it in declaring the contract unconscionable:

> It is my opinion that the lack of equality between the bargaining parties, the contract clauses under which the defendants unwittingly and unknowingly waived both the warranty of merchantability and the warranty of fitness for the particular purpose for which the motor vehicle was purchased and the defective condition of the motor vehicle, are sufficient to render the contract unenforceable under the provisions of the Uniform Commercial Code, sec. 2–302 as between [defendants and the dealer-assignor].[188]

Dismal as the prospect is to at least one of your authors, we suspect that the courts have the bit in their teeth and that most are bound and determined to apply 2–302 to warranty disclaimers whether or not those disclaimers comply with 2–316. One of us believes that such courts misread the intention of the draftsmen and that the draftsmen never intended 2–302 to be an overlay on the disclaimer provisions of 2–316. Nevertheless, the lawyer must recognize the judicial hostility to warranty disclaimers, particularly in contracts made with consumers who are injured by the seller's product. Despite the four cases discussed above, which in holding and dicta have applied 2–302 to warranty disclaimer clauses, we believe that a lawyer, at least *in commercial cases*, has a good chance with an argument that 2–316 has preempted the unconscionability doctrine with respect to warranty disclaimers and that a court should not strike down a disclaimer under the provisions of 2–302 if the disclaimer complies with 2–316.

### § 12–12 Modification or Limitation of Remedies—Use of 2–719(3) to Invalidate an Otherwise Valid Disclaimer

Most buyers who have invoked the aid of the courts to nullify properly drafted disclaimers on grounds of unconscionability have not even bothered with 2–302. Rather, they have succeeded in convincing courts that 2–719(3)'s prohibition of unconscionable consequential-loss exclusion clauses prevents a court from upholding *a disclaimer* that denies the plaintiff consequential damages. This route around 2–316 flies in the face of the apparent intention of the draftsmen.[189] Two cases from the Arkansas Supreme Court will illustrate the point.

188. Id. at 142, 302 N.Y.S.2d at 394–95, 6 UCC Rep.Serv. at 606. It should be noted that the buyers in Marcano lacked one key equity—personal injuries.

The court in Marcano also had to overcome a clause in the sales contract in which the buyers waived all defenses against the assignee, a feat which was accomplished by a rather novel interpretation of 9–504.

189. Comment 3 to 2–719 states: "The seller in all cases is free to disclaim warranties in the manner provided in Section 2–316."

In Ford Motor Co. v. Tritt,[190] the plaintiff's husband purchased a new truck which was covered by the manufacturer's express warranty to repair and replace defective parts. The warranty contained the following clause:

> This warranty is expressly in lieu of any other express or implied warranty, including any implied warranty of merchantability or fitness, and of any other obligation on the part of the Dealer.[191]

The buyer was killed when a defective axle caused a wheel to collapse and the truck to turn over.[192] The court had little difficulty holding that it would be unconscionable to allow the printed disclaimer to preclude damages for wrongful death:

> The waiver of the implied warranty of merchantability or fitness certainly does not protect [the dealer] from liability, for to do so would be unconscionable under the Uniform Commercial Code within the meaning of Ark.Stat.Ann. § 85–2–719(3) (Add. 1961) . . . . [193]

A couple of years later, Ford got involved in another Arkansas warranty suit in Ford Motor Co. v. Reid.[194] This time no one was hurt, but a new automobile purchased by the plaintiff caught fire in his garage and burned down his house. The car was sold with a warranty and disclaimer clause almost identical to the one involved in *Tritt*. But since there were no personal injuries, the contractual exclusion of consequential damages was not automatically unconscionable under 2–719(3).[195] So the court took a different tack. It accepted at face value the manufacturer's express warranty regarding defective parts,[196] but it held that the language in the disclaimer did not constitute an express agreement within the meaning of 2–719(1) (b) that repair and replacement would be the exclusive remedy. The court reached this conclusion by emphasizing that the disclaimer

---

190. 244 Ark. 883, 430 S.W.2d 778, 5 UCC Rep.Serv. 312 (1968).

191. Id. at 889, 430 S.W.2d at 781, 5 UCC Rep.Serv. at 315.

192. In the initial opinion, the court held there was no evidence establishing proximate cause. On rehearing, the court held that a proffer of evidence by an expert witness was sufficient to support the verdict in plaintiff's favor. Id. at 890, 430 S.W.2d at 783, 5 UCC Rep.Serv. at 312.

193. Id. at 889, 430 S.W.2d at 781, 5 UCC Rep.Serv. at 315. The court also held that the trial court could properly conclude that the disclaimer was unconscionable as between the dealer and the manufacturer. Id. at 890, 430 S.W.2d at 782, 5 UCC Rep.Serv. at 316.

194. 250 Ark. 176, 465 S.W.2d 80, 8 UCC Rep.Serv. 985 (1971).

195. No defendant in any of the reported cases has yet succeeded in overcoming the prima facie case for unconscionability established by 2–719(3).

196. The court relied on 2–316(1), which directs that disclaimer language be construed whenever reasonable as consistent with express-warranty language, in order to construe a statement in the warranty that "[a]ll the warranties shall be fulfilled by the Selling Dealer" as explaining the seller's obligation rather than as limiting the buyer's rights to other remedies. 250 Ark. at 184, 465 S.W.2d at 84, 8 UCC Rep.Serv. at 990.

clause dealt with "obligations" and "warranties," not "remedies." [197] Thus in the court's opinion there was no language in the contract that prevented the buyer from recovering consequential damages for the seller's breach of its express warranty.

The problem with the *Reid* holding is that it conflicts with the holding in *Tritt*. In the earlier case the court held that the language "This warranty is expressly in lieu of  . . .  any other obligations" was unconscionable because it excluded consequential damages. Then in *Reid* the court held that virtually identical language does *not* exclude consequential damages.[198] How can these two cases be reconciled? *Tritt* could be viewed as standing for the proposition that whenever a disclaimer operates to deny the buyer consequential damages, that disclaimer becomes subject to 2–719(3), which prohibits the unconscionable exclusion of consequential damages. *Reid* can then be seen as merely going a step further and holding that all language of disclaimer is inoperative to exclude consequential damages for breach of warranties unaffected by disclaimer.[199]

This interpretation of *Reid* appears to be reasonable. But the proposition enunciated by *Tritt*—that a disclaimer that has the effect of modifying or excluding consequential damages may be unconscionable under 2–719(3)—is out of line with the scheme of the Code. Comment 3 to 2–719(3) provides (emphasis added):

> Subsection (3) recognizes the validity of clauses limiting or excluding consequential damages but makes it clear that they may not operate in an unconscionable manner. Actually such terms are merely an allocation of unknown or undeterminable risks. *The seller in all cases is free to disclaim warranties in the manner provided in Section 2–316.*

The last sentence seems to be telling the seller, "If you really want to limit your liability, why don't you disclaim all warranties? Then

---

197.  250 Ark. at 184, 465 S.W.2d at 85, 8 UCC Rep.Serv. at 990. Support for this distinction was found in 2–301's definition of "obligation": "The obligation of the seller is to transfer and deliver  . . .  in accordance with the contract." The court might also have quoted from Comment 34 to 1–201(34), which states that remedial rights are "those to which an aggrieved party can resort on his own motion." Together, these two definitions suggest that obligations and remedies are counterparts: when the seller fails to do what he is required to do by the contract, i. e., fails to perform his obligation, the buyer may invoke an appropriate remedy.

The distinction between remedy and obligation is well established in constitutional law. A state may significantly modify or alter contractual remedies without impairing the obligation of contract within the meaning of Article I, Section 10 of the Constitution. See, e. g., Home Bldg. & Loan Ass'n v. Blaisdell, 290 U.S. 398 (1934).

198.  The appellate court was apparently precluded from finding the disclaimer to be an unconscionable exclusion of consequential damages by the failure of the buyer to provide a factual basis for such a holding at the trial. 250 Ark. at 184, 465 S.W.2d at 84, 8 UCC Rep.Serv. at 989 (quoting from the manufacturer's brief).

199.  The buyer in Reid recovered under the manufacturer's express warranty which was unaffected by the disclaimer. Id. at 185, 465 S.W.2d at 85, 8 UCC Rep.Serv. at 991.

you won't have to worry about limiting damages." Note that the sentence appears after the discussion of remedy limitations and after the discussion of the extent to which such clauses are governed by the unconscionability doctrine and that it announces that the seller may disclaim warranties in all cases. These facts strongly indicate that the draftsmen intended for 2–316 to operate independently of 2–719 (3).[200]

This implication is buttressed by Comment 2 to 2–316 (emphasis added):

> .  .  . This Article treats the limitation or avoidance of consequential damages as a matter of limiting remedies for breach, separate from the matter of creation of liability under a warranty. *If no warranty exists, there is of course no problem of limiting remedies for breach of warranty.*[201]

The comment's reasoning is elementary: there can be no consequential damages if there is no breach; there can be no breach of warranty if there is no warranty; there can be no warranty if the seller has disclaimed them pursuant to 2–316. Although a particular disclaimer may be unconscionable under 2–302, it seems clear that the scheme of the Code does not permit a court to disregard that disclaimer on the basis that it operates to exclude consequential damages that could not be excluded under 2–719(3).

Nevertheless, some courts have struck down disclaimers on the grounds such clauses are unconscionable under 2–719(3). The *Tritt* case [202] demonstrates how blithely these courts have ignored the clearly delineated boundaries between 2–316 and 2–719. In Walsh v. Ford Motor Co.,[203] a personal-injury case involving the same disclaimer drafted by the same manufacturer who was sued in *Tritt*, a New York trial court devoted a small amount of discussion to the unconscionability issue. The defendants (manufacturer and dealer) had argued that their disclaimer of warranties was permitted by 2–316. The court conceded that point but ruled against them because they "tendered no factual proof to rebut the plaintiff's showing that under the statute (U.C.C. § 2–719(3)) the exclusion of a cause of action for recovery of damages for personal injuries is *prima facie* unconscionable." [204] This holding, of course, misses the

---

**200.** See also Leff, Unconscionability and the Code—The Emperor's New Clause, 115 U.Pa.L.Rev. 485, 520 (1967).

**201.** Prior to 1957, Comment 2 read:

It is the view of this Article that the desire to limit or avoid consequential damages by excluding all warranties has nothing to do with the creation of liability under a warranty but goes rather to the problem of limiting remedies for its breach. Subsection (3) [now (4)] indicates that this question is in no way affected by the present section but is fully covered in the sections of this Article on limitation of damages and remedy.

**202.** See notes 190–93 and accompanying text supra.

**203.** 59 Misc.2d 241, 298 N.Y.S.2d 538, 6 UCC Rep.Serv. 56 (Sup.Ct.1969).

**204.** Id. at 242, 298 N.Y.S.2d at 540, 6 UCC Rep.Serv. at 57. The Walsh v. Ford Motor Co. opinion was relied on in Sarfati v. M. A. Hittner & Sons, Inc., 35 App.Div.2d 1004, 318 N.Y.S.2d

base because 2–719 deals with limitations of remedies, not causes of action.

Undoubtedly the main reason why courts refuse to follow the literal scheme of the Code is its harshness.[205] If neither 2–302 nor 2–719(3) operate as restrictions on disclaimers drafted pursuant to 2–316,[206] then the seller has the power to thrust on the consumer all risks of personal injury resulting from defects in its products. Even adherents of "strict-construction" concede that such power is not needed in order to keep the wheels of commerce turning.[207] It is not surprising then that courts faced with a consumer plaintiff who has been seriously injured by a large corporate defendant's product are often willing to disregard the literal meaning of the Code. One may nevertheless question the wisdom of twisting a carefully devised statutory scheme, especially when alternative forms of relief, like strict tort, may be available.

It is difficult to sum up the law on disclaimers, exclusion clauses, and unconscionability because the courts have not yet faced enough cases. We can say with confidence that a clause purporting to limit the buyer's damages or remedies is subject to attack as unconscionable under 2–719(3). Such attacks will probably only be successful (with rare exceptions) in consumer settings involving personal injuries. If the seller has made a disclaimer that complies with 2–316, it is not clear at this date whether the buyer can attack it with 2–302. As a matter of statutory construction, one of us thinks disclaimers should be policed solely by 2–316, the other thinks 2–302 should be available at least for consumer buyers. It is clear that some courts will continue to invoke unconscionability as embodied in 2–302 and 2–719(3). In light of the cases decided thus far, we suspect that whenever a consumer's blood is spilled, even wild horses could not stop a sympathetic court from plowing through the most artfully drafted and conspicuously printed disclaimer clause in order to grant relief. On the other hand, when the buyer is a merchant, no court should apply unconscionability of any variety to a disclaimer that complies with 2–316.

352, 8 UCC Rep.Serv. 442 (2d Dep't 1970), to invalidate a disclaimer in an action over against an automobile manufacturer by a lessor, who had suffered a personal-injury judgment in favor of its lessee.

**205.** It has also been argued that it does not make sense to prohibit a seller of consumer goods from excluding consequential damages for personal injuries but to permit him to exclude *all* warranty liability by complying with the formal requirements of 2–316. See R. Dusenberg & C. King, Sales and Bulk Transfers Under the Uniform Commercial Code § 7.03

at 7–47 n. 30 (1969); Peters, Remedies for Breach of Contracts Relating to the Sale of Goods Under the Uniform Commercial Code: A Roadmap to Article Two, 73 Yale L.J. 199, 282–83 (1966). Speidel, The Virginia 'Anti-Privity' Statute: Strict Products Liability Under the Uniform Commercial Code, 51 Va.L.Rev. 804, 838 (1965).

**206.** See notes 157–62 and accompanying text supra.

**207.** See Leff, Unconscionability and the Code—The Emperor's New Clause, 115 U.Pa.L.Rev. 485, 516 (1967).

# CHAPTER 13

## THE NEGOTIABLE INSTRUMENT: PARTY'S CONTRACT LIABILITY; DISCHARGE; AND THE UNDERLYING OBLIGATION

*Analysis*

Sec.
13–1.  Introduction.
13–2.  Signature: Requirement and Form.
13–3.  Some Agency Questions—Principal's Liability for Signature by Agent, 3–403(1), 3–404.
13–4.  —— Personal Liability of the Agent on Instruments Allegedly Signed in a "Representative Capacity".
13–5.  —— Parol Evidence to Show Representative Capacity, 3–403(2) (b).
13–6.  Contractual Liability—Parties to an Instrument.
13–7.  —— Liability of the Maker, 3–413(1).
13–8.  —— Liability of the Acceptor, 3–413, 3–412, 3–411, 3–410, 3–409.
13–9.  —— Liability of the Drawer, 3–413(2).
13–10. —— Liability of the Indorser, 3–414.
13–11. Warranty Liabilities.
13–12. Accommodation Parties, 3–415, 3–416, 3–606, General Liability of Article Three Surety.
13–13. —— Establishing Suretyship Status—Form of Signature and Parol Evidence, 3–415(3), 3–415(4), 3–416.
13–14. —— Suretyship Defenses, 3–606 and Beyond.
13–15. —— Effect of Surety's Consent or Creditor's Reservation of Rights, 3–606(1), 3–606(2).
13–16. —— Relationship Between Surety and Principal, Subrogation, Reimbursement and 3–415(5).
13–17. —— Right of Surety to Assert Principal's Defenses.
13–18. Discharge, 3–601, 3–603, 3–605.
13–19. —— Cancellation and Renunciation, 3–605.
13–20. —— The Underlying Obligation, Suspension, and Discharge, 3–802.
13–21. —— Discharge of a Disputed Obligation by Tender of a Check in "Full Satisfaction", 1–207.
13–22. Lost or Stolen Instruments, 3–804.

## § 13–1  Introduction

The common negotiable instruments, checks and notes, have been with us for centuries. The layman can identify a check and explain its legal significance in a general way, and the general obligation of one who signs a promissory note is acutely familiar to the layman in an age of consumer credit. However, the ignorance of most laymen and that of too many lawyers exceeds their knowledge about important consequences of dealing with negotiable instruments. Scholars, too, are today neglecting Article Three of the Code on commercial paper. This and the four chapters that follow can be no more than a modest effort to help rectify this state of affairs.

In this chapter we will consider the contractual liability of parties to a negotiable instrument and the effects of the transfer and payment of a negotiable instrument upon any underlying obligation between the parties. We will discuss the liability of the maker of a promissory note, of the drawer of checks and drafts, and of indorsers generally. We also will treat the liability of more exotic animals of the forest: accommodation parties and guarantors. Let us consider a simple example. Assume that Seller sells fifty steers to Rich Buyer and fifty steers to Poor Buyer. The contract of sale in each case is "the underlying obligation." At the time of tender Rich Buyer gives Seller his check. On signing it in the lower right hand corner, Rich Buyer becomes the "drawer." Assume that the check is payable to the order of Seller who thus becomes the "payee," and that it is drawn on Rich Buyer's bank, the "drawee." However, Poor Buyer has insufficient money in the bank to pay by check, nor can he pay in cash. Accordingly Poor Buyer gives Seller a note. He too signs in the lower right hand corner and so becomes the "maker" and he too names the Seller as the one to whom payment is to be made and so makes the Seller the "payee." While he has possession of these two documents, Seller is also the "holder" of each of them.

Although courts often use the terms maker and drawer interchangeably, the Code uses the former word to designate the party in the position of Poor Buyer and uses the word "drawer" to designate the party in the position of Rich Buyer (the signer in the lower right hand corner) on a check or other draft. Section 3–413 of the Code sets out the "statutory contract" of each. While our focus in this chapter will be on these stereotyped statutory contracts, we will also consider matters related to the contractual liability of parties to negotiable instruments such as the effect of a signature by the agent and, of course, the effect that the issuance of an instrument and its ultimate payment has upon the underlying obligation. Finally we will examine the various ways in which a party's liability on a check and on the underlying obligation can be discharged. (We will postpone our discussion of noncontractual liabilities of parties to a check (warranty, tort, etc.) until later chapters on lost and stolen instruments.)

One must first understand that a negotiable instrument is a peculiar animal and that many animals calling for the payment of money and others loosely called "commercial paper" are not negotiable instruments and not subject to the rules of Article Three. Since one can be a "holder in due course" only of a negotiable instrument, the question whether an instrument is "negotiable" becomes most acute when one is trying to determine whether a party is a "holder in due course" who cuts off prior claims and defenses. For that reason we reserve intensive discussion of the interpretive difficulties in determining whether or not an instrument is negotiable for Chapter 14 on the holder in due course. For now a brief summary of the requirements of negotiability will suffice. Section 3–104(1) is the basic definition of negotiable instrument; it defines negotiable instruments as follows:

> Any writing to be a negotiable instrument within this Article must
>
> (a) be signed by the maker or drawer; and
>
> (b) contain an unconditional promise or order to pay a sum certain in money and no other promise, order, obligation or power given by the maker or drawer except as authorized by this Article; and
>
> (c) be payable on demand or at a definite time; and
>
> (d) be payable to order or to bearer.

Consider, for example, the typical retail installment sales contract. Will it be a negotiable instrument subject to the rules of Article Three, or will it fail to be a negotiable instrument? Most retail installment sales contracts will fail on two grounds. First, they are not usually payable to "order or to bearer" and thus fail the test in (d). Secondly, they usually include additional promises by the maker or drawer and thus fail the "no other promise" test in subsection (b). However, Sections 3–105 and 3–112 authorize certain additional conditions and promises notwithstanding 3–104. As we will explain in Chapter 14, one cannot safely give an opinion on whether a document is negotiable without examining those two sections in addition to 3–104.

What policy supports Article Three's narrow concept of negotiability? One policy is to put persons who deal with negotiable instruments on notice of their negotiability. Many businessmen and some consumers appreciate the unique legal liabilities associated with negotiable instruments and conduct their affairs accordingly. If the variety of instruments that qualify as negotiable were allowed to proliferate, the expectations of such persons would be frustrated: those who thought they had undertaken one of the stereotyped Article Three liabilities might have quite another liability, and those who expected to be able to assert contract defenses might be denied that right.

## § 13–2   Signature: Requirement and Form

Section 3–401(1) of the Code states the general rule for liability on an instrument: "No person is liable on an instrument unless his signature appears thereon." [1] The rule is as old as the law merchant and stems from the necessity for takers of instruments to tell at a glance whose obligation they hold. Note, however, that the section

---

1. Section 3–404(1) states the exception as follows:

   Any unauthorized signature . . . operates as the signature of the unauthorized signer in favor of any person who in good faith pays the instrument or takes it for value.

   A forger who signs another's name to the instrument is himself liable to one who meets the requirements of this section.

states the rule only for "action upon the instrument" and does not preclude liability ". . . arising apart from the instrument itself".[2] For example, one whose name does not appear on the instrument may nevertheless have liability on the underlying contract. From the outset, the student (and lawyer) must learn to distinguish between an action by a party "on the instrument" and other theories of liability. When a party sues on the instrument, he asserts that the defendant is liable in virtue of his status as a signer of a negotiable instrument.

Comment 2 to 3–401 tells us that a person may make his signature in a variety of ways: "handwritten, typed, printed or made in any other manner." Under this broad view an imaginative plaintiff might argue that pre-printed forms (for instance, checks) with the name of a corporation or individual inscribed on them are "signed" instruments. Before one tears up all his pre-printed checks, he should consider section 1–201(39): " 'Signed' includes any symbol executed or adopted by a party with present intention to authenticate a writing." One would be hard pressed to maintain that a party had "present intention to authenticate" whatever might later be written on a check when he ordered a batch of checks with his name printed on them.[3]

## § 13–3   Some Agency Questions—Principal's Liability for Signature by Agent, 3–403(1), 3–404

Commerce demands and the Code provides that agents may sign negotiable instruments and thus bind their principals. Section 3–403 (1) adopts the general law of agency for commercial paper as follows:

> A signature may be made by an agent or other representative, and his authority to make it may be established as in other cases of representation. No particular form of appointment is necessary to establish such authority.

Comment 1 to 3–403 explains that the power to sign for another may rest upon express, implied or apparent authority. We have neither the space nor the will to deal with the intractable concepts of implied and apparent authority; rather, we focus on the legal consequences of such authority and upon the written symbols by which one indicates such authority on a negotiable instrument.

---

2.  § 3–401, Comment 1. See, e. g., Wenke v. Norton, 120 Ga.App. 70, 169 S.E.2d 663, 6 UCC Rep.Serv. 1070 (1969) (separate agreement); Hamilton Watch Employees Federal Credit Union v. Retallack, 5 UCC Rep.Serv. 739 (Pa.C.P.1967) (separate agreement); First Western Bank & Trust Co. v. Bookasta, 267 Cal.App.2d 910, 73 Cal.Rptr. 657, 5 UCC Rep.Serv. 1181 (2d Dist.1968) (alter ego doctrine); McClung v. Saito, 4 Cal.App.3d 143, 84 Cal.Rptr. 44, 7 UCC Rep.Serv. 517 (2d Dist.1970) (joint venturers liable on underlying obligation); In re Eton Furniture Co., 183 F.Supp. 554 (E.D. Pa.1960), aff'd 286 F.2d 93 (3d Cir. 1961) (underlying obligation).

3.  But see Pollin v. Mindy Mfg. Co., 211 Pa.Super. 87, 236 A.2d 542, 4 UCC Rep.Serv. 827 (1967) (pre-printed form might be sufficient signature) (dictum).

A fundamental canon of agency law provides that the principal is liable for the authorized acts of his agent. However, even the authorized signature of an agent will not bind his principal *on the instrument* unless that signature incorporates the principal's signature or some mark or symbol which meets the requirements of 3–401.[4] Thus the authorized agent who merely signs his own name will not bind his principal (although he does bind himself). Note, however, that if the agent signs the principal's name, the Code creates a presumption that the signature was authorized.[5]

In 3–404(1) the Code states the general rule of agency law on the other side of the coin:

> Any unauthorized signature is wholly inoperative as that of the person whose name is signed unless he ratifies it or is precluded from denying it . . . .

4.  See McCollum v. Steitz, 261 Cal.App. 2d 76, 67 Cal.Rptr. 703, 5 UCC Rep. Serv. 375 (5th Dist.1968) (one partner's signature accompanied by partnership trade name bound other partner on note and parol evidence held admissible to show that trade name "Desert Inn" was intended to bind partnership, not merely to indicate signer's address); Jenkins v. Evans, 31 App.Div.2d 597, 295 N.Y.S.2d 226, 5 UCC Rep.Serv. 1185 (3d Dep't 1968) (proprietor liable on check signed by manager who had authority to write checks on preprinted forms even though signature did not contain the name of defendant's business); Karr v. Baumann, 3 UCC Rep.Serv. 180 (N.Y.Sup.Ct.1966) (signature "Robert Bauman Pres. Central Coffee Shoppe Inc." made note corporate obligation and defense of usury not available to Bauman as accommodation indorser); Modern Free & Accepted Masons of the World v. Cliff M. Averett, Inc., 118 Ga.App. 641, 165 S.E.2d 166, 6 UCC Rep.Serv. 351 (1968) (signature "Modern Free and Accepted Masons of the World, J. B. Baldwin" bound organization on note).

5.  Section 3–307(1) provides:

Unless specifically denied in the pleadings each signature on an instrument is admitted. When the effectiveness of a signature is put in issue * * *

(b) the signature is presumed to be genuine or authorized except where the action is to enforce the obligation of a purported signer who has died or become incompetent before proof is required.

The significance of placing the burden of pleading on the defendant and of giving the plaintiff a presumption that the signature is genuine or authorized is described by the following paragraph in Comment 1 to 3–307:

The question of the burden of establishing the signature arises only when it has been put in issue by specific denial. "Burden of establishing" is defined in the definitions section of this Act (Section 1–201). The burden is on the party claiming under the signature, but he is aided by the presumption that it is genuine or authorized stated in paragraph (b). "Presumption" is also defined in this Act (Section 1–201). It means that until some evidence is introduced which would support a finding that the signature is forged or unauthorized the plaintiff is not required to prove that it is authentic. The presumption rests upon the fact that in ordinary experience forged or unauthorized signatures are very uncommon, and normally any evidence is within the control of the defendant or more accessible to him. He is therefore required to make some sufficient showing of the grounds for his denial before the plaintiff is put to his proof. His evidence need not be sufficient to require a directed verdict in his favor, but it must be enough to support his denial by permitting a finding in his favor. Until he introduces such evidence the presumption requires a finding for the plaintiff. Once such evidence is introduced the burden of establishing the signature by a preponderance of the total evidence is on the plaintiff.

What acts constitute the ratification of an unauthorized signature?[6] Generally, ratification is found when the principal knowingly assents to the unauthorized signature by express statement or conduct.[7] Thus in Rehrig v. Fortunak,[8] a Pennsylvania court held that a wife's retention of benefits from a note constituted ratification of the allegedly unauthorized signature made by her husband.[9] Even if a party does not ratify the unauthorized signature he may still be "precluded from denying it." Comment 4 to 3–404 explains that the section recognizes the possibility of estoppel based on a representation that the signature is genuine or based on negligence of the person whose name is signed. Several Code sections give content to the notion of "preclusion." For example, 3–406 provides that "Any person who by his negligence substantially contributes to . . . the making of an unauthorized signature is precluded from asserting the . . . lack of authority against [certain persons] . . . ." Similarly, 3–405 outlines three situations where "An indorsement by any person in the name of the named payee is effective . . . ." Finally, 4–406 spells out the customer's duty to notify his bank of unauthorized signatures and the penalty for failure to exercise reasonable care and promptness in carrying out that duty. For a discussion of 3–405, 3–406 and 4–406, see Chapter 16 below.

In at least one type of case (discussed more fully in Section 13–5), the Code is unclear on the principal's liability. Assume the agent reveals either his agency status or the name of the principal but not both and later successfully frees himself from personal liability in a suit by an immediate party by proving that he acted in an agency capacity. When the agent is free of liability in such case, is the prin-

6. Section 1–201(43) defines unauthorized signature:

"Unauthorized" signature or indorsement means one made without actual, implied or apparent authority and includes a forgery.

7. Restatement, Second, Agency § 82 (1957) defines ratification:

Ratification is the affirmance by a person of a prior act which did not bind him but which was done or professedly done on his account, whereby the act, as to some or all persons, is given effect as if originally authorized by him.

Restatement, Second, Agency § 83 (1957) states:

Affirmance is either

(a) a manifestation of an election by one on whose account an unauthorized act has been done to treat the act as authorized, or

(b) conduct by him justifiable only if there were such an election.

8. 39 Pa.D. & C.2d 20, 3 UCC Rep.Serv. 636 (C.P.1966). See also Wiest v. First Citizens Nat'l Bank, 3 UCC Rep. Serv. 875 (Pa.C.P.1966) (ratification of employee's forgery when forged check deposited in another account to conceal employee's previous embezzlements); But see Comment 3 to section 3–404 which says, "[Ratification] may be found from the retention of benefits received in the transaction *with knowledge* of the unauthorized signature . . . ." (emphasis added)

9. See also Johnstown School Employees Federal Credit Union v. Mock, 47 Pa.D. & C.2d 703, 7 UCC Rep.Serv. 311 (C.P.1969) (no ratification when wife denied husband's authority to sign for her and so notified the creditors even though she took no further action when notified that confession of judgment had been entered against her).

cipal nonetheless liable although his name does not appear on the instrument and the instrument does not reveal the agency status of the one who signed as his agent? Section 3–401(1) would seem to indicate that the principal is not liable since his signature does not appear on the instrument. Comment 2 to 2–304 reinforces that conclusion and seems to apply even when the agent names the principal: "Even though he [the agent] is authorized the principal is not liable on the instrument, under the provisions (Section 3–401) relating to signatures, unless the instrument names him and clearly shows that the signature is made on his behalf." The rule is clear, yet there is something fundamentally unfair about letting the agent weasel out of the apparent agreement on the note without at least holding the principal liable; in such case the payee is left with a wholly worthless instrument. Yet in the face of 3–401 and Comment 2 to 3–403 we see no way to avoid that conclusion.[10]

## § 13-4   Some Agency Questions—Personal Liability of the Agent on Instruments Allegedly Signed in a "Representative Capacity"

A party who signs a negotiable instrument as the authorized representative [11] of another normally does not expect to assume liability for his principal's obligation. The Code lays down some simple rules for determining when an authorized agent's signature subjects him to personal liability on the instrument. Under 3–403(2) the agent's liability turns almost entirely on the written symbols he uses to disclose his agency status. The typical case involves the officer of a small corporation who signs a corporate note. When the corporation becomes insolvent, the holder seeks to recover from the officer individually. Usually the argument revolves around whether the written symbols in the signature sufficiently disclose that the officer was signing as an agent rather than a principal. Section 3–403(2) provides:

> An authorized representative who signs his own name to an instrument
>
> (a) is personally obligated if the instrument neither names the person represented nor shows that the representative signed in a representative capacity;
>
> (b) except as otherwise established between the immediate parties, is personally obligated if the instrument

---

10. The rule set down in 3–403(2) (authorizing the agent to weasel out by showing his agency status) was based on the New York case of Megowan v. Peterson, 173 N.Y. 1, 65 N.E. 738 (1902). An early and hasty reading of that case by one of your authors convinced him that it stood for the proposition that the principal became liable *ipso facto* upon the agent's freeing himself from liability. Others have rudely disclosed to him that the case cannot be so read.

11. Section 1–201(35) defines representative:

"Representative" includes an agent, an officer of a corporation or association and a trustee, executor or administrator of an estate, or any other person empowered to act for another.

names the person represented but does not show that the representative signed in a representative capacity, or if the instrument does not name the person represented but does show that the representative signed in a representative capacity.

If, under 3–403(2) (a), the agent merely signs his own name, he is personally liable on the instrument, but his principal is not.[12] Even if the person taking the instrument knows that the agent is signing in a representative capacity, the agent cannot introduce parol evidence to show that his signature was made for another.

Section 3–403(2) (b) outlines two additional situations where the agent is personally obligated. First, the agent incurs liability if he signs his name and names his principal, but fails to show representative capacity. Thus a signature in the form "Mr. Scrooge, Bob Cratchett" binds the agent and may bind his principal. Secondly, the agent is bound if his signature indicates representative capacity, but fails to name the principal. Thus, an individual who signs a note "Bob Cratchett, Agent" is personally obligated on the instrument.[13] Since even the most careless agent usually will name his principal, the issue most frequently presented under 3–403(2) (b) is whether the additional words accompanying the signature show "representative capacity." [14] If they do not, the agent will himself be personally liable at least to "nonimmediate" parties. Section 3–403(3) states one form of signature that establishes representative capacity:

> Except as otherwise established the name of an organization preceded or followed by the name and office of an authorized individual is a signature in a representative capacity.

Thus a signature in the form, "InterGlactic Transport Corp., Flash Gordon, Pres." would do. The word "Pres." which appears in combination with the corporate name tells everyone that Flash Gordon is signing as an agent. Section 3–403(3) does not purport to be an exclusive statement of symbols that show representative capacity.[15]

To what extent may one deviate from the form set out above and still sign in a representative capacity? The cases do not give answers

---

12. See United Burner Service, Inc. v. George Peters & Sons, Inc., 5 UCC Rep.Serv. 383 (N.Y.Sup.Ct.1968) (corporate officer liable on note allegedly made for corporation when note neither carried corporation's name nor revealed fact of representation); First Nat'l Bank v. Maidman, 2 UCC Rep. Serv. 1048 (N.Y.Sup.Ct.1965) (purported agent's signature did not bind principal when signature did not designate principal or show representative capacity).

13. See Rushton v. U. M. & M. Credit Corp., 245 Ark. 703, 434 S.W.2d 81, 5

UCC Rep.Serv. 1078 (1968) (signature in form "Joe F. Rushton, M. D., Trustee" did not relieve defendant of personal liability because it did not show for what trust he signed).

14. See note 13 supra and notes 16–28 infra.

15. For instance the section does not cover the case in which the principal is an individual. In such cases Comment 3 to section 3–403 recommends signature in the following form:

Peter Pringle by Arthur Adams, Agent.

for all possible symbols, but they impose personal liability even though the individual signs under a corporate name. Thus in Universal Lightning Rod, Inc. v. Rischall Electric Co., Inc.,[16] and Perez v. Janota,[17] unhappy corporate agents found themselves personally liable when they signed their name and the corporation's name to notes but did not show a corporate title.

In Pollin v. Mindy Mfg. Co.,[18] the court had more compassion for the individual signer. There a check cashing service brought suit against a corporate officer on payroll checks the plaintiff had cashed which were returned for insufficient funds. The trial court held that the officer had obligated himself individually when he failed to indicate his office on the corporate payroll check. On appeal the Pennsylvania Superior Court reversed a summary judgment for plaintiff and entered judgment for the defendant. First, the appellate court noted that the checks were imprinted with the name of the corporation and that persons taking such checks commonly expect them to be signed by officers of the corporation. Secondly, the check itself bore imprinted information that it was a payroll check payable from a special account. Accordingly, the court said that the:

> . . . . instrument of itself would refute any contention
> that the appellant intended to make the instrument his own
> order on the named bank to pay money to the payee. The
> money was payable from the account of the corporation de-
> fendant over which [the individual defendant] had no con-
> trol.[19]

The different outcomes in the *Pollin* case and the two cases above in which the courts found corporation officers liable may reflect differences in business practices with respect to notes and checks. All recent cases known to us [20] in which the court found an officer personally liable involved corporate notes. It is common for creditors of small corporations to demand that major officers personally obligate themselves on corporate notes. Yet it would be most unusual to demand the individual obligation of an officer on corporate checks, and practically unheard of to demand individual liability on payroll checks. The *Pollin* court's emphasis on business expectations is proper and entirely consistent with the spirit of 3–403.[21]

In each case involving the question whether a signature was in "representative capacity" the court must balance the cost to an individual who claims to have signed as an agent against the need for

16.  24 Conn.Sup. 399, 192 A.2d 50, 1
UCC Rep.Serv. 269 (1963).

17.  107 Ill.App.2d 90, 246 N.E.2d 42, 6
UCC Rep.Serv. 357 (1969).

18.  211 Pa.Super. 87, 236 A.2d 542, 4
UCC Rep.Serv. 827 (1967).

19.  Id. at 92–93, 236 A.2d at 545, 4
UCC Rep.Serv. at 830.

20.  See, e. .g., notes 12, 16, 17 supra and
cases cited therein.

21.  Comment 3 to section 3–403 in the
1952 Official Draft of the Code was
particularly explicit in requiring the
courts to take account of business understanding, usage, and practice.

"certainty and definiteness in commercial paper." [22]   When an agent objectively manifests his intent to sign as a representative, he puts subsequent holders of the instrument on notice that the signer does not expect to incur personal liability.   Thus 3–403(3) expressly recognizes that an agent gives such notice when he adds the designation of his office to the signature.   But what if the agent signs for a corporation: "InterGlactic Transport Co. by Flash Gordon"; or signs for an individual: "Flash Gordon, Dr. Zarkhov, Agent"?   The courts may wish to examine such signatures in light of extrinsic factors such as business practice, business expectations, and the like. We believe that courts should find signatures of the type set out above to be representative signatures.   In the first, the preposition "by" discloses the agency relationship and in the other the noun "agent" does that job.

## § 13–5   Some Agency Questions—Parol Evidence to Show Representative Capacity, 3–403(2)(b)

When the plaintiff who sues the agent personally is one who dealt directly with the agent, and the signature either names the principal or indicates representative capacity, section 3–403(2)(b) permits the agent to introduce parol evidence of his agency status to avoid personal liability.[23]   The current version of the Code reverses the 1952 Code which excluded "parol evidence for any purpose except reformation." [24]   Evidently the Code draftsmen believed that anyone permitted to prove his agency by parol should offer as an entry fee some extrinsic evidence that he acted in a representative capacity.   Accordingly, parol evidence is not admissible when the agent merely signs his own name but does not indicate either the fact of representation or the name of his principal.[25]

If the agent's signature indicates representative capacity or recites the name of the principal, what evidence must one offer to ex-

---

22.  See 2 N.Y. State Law Revision Comm'n, 1955 Report 987 (1955) (description of underlying rationale for requirements of 3–403).

23.  Section 3–403(2)(b) provides that an agent who fails to meet its requirements is personally obligated "except as otherwise established between the immediate parties  .  .  .."   Megowan v. Peterson, 173 N.Y. 1, 65 N.E. 738 (1902) involved a suit by the payee against the trustee of an insolvent firm.   On the question whether a collecting bank is an immediate party against whom parol evidence is admissable.   Compare section 4–201 (bank agent or sub-agent of owner of item), with Central Bank of Rochester v. Gleason, 206 App.Div. 28, 200 N.Y.S. 384 (4th Dep't 1923) (parol evidence admissable to show that defendant

signed as corporate officer against plaintiff bank who took note as assignment from transferee of payee with knowledge of facts).

24.  Comment 3 to section 3–403 of the 1952 Code (Official Draft).   The 1952 Code's strict rule against admitting parol evidence received criticism from the New York Law Revision Commission.   2 N.Y. State Law Revision Comm'n, 1955 Report 985–91 (1955). Pursuant to these and other criticisms the draftsmen adopted the present provisions in the 1958 Code.   Recommendations of the Editorial Board for the UCC, 107–108 (1956).

25.  Section 3–403(2)(a) is not modified by the "except as otherwise established" language found in section 3–403(2)(b).

onerate the agent from personal liability? Of course, the agent should first offer any documentary evidence he can muster. Thus one should examine all correspondence between the plaintiff and the defendant-agent and should review the plaintiff's business records. Either may reveal that the plaintiff regarded the obligation as the principal's, not the agent's. However, any corporate by-laws or resolutions which require the agent to sign all corporate obligations would tend to indicate that he did not sign in an individual capacity.[26] Evidence regarding the nature of the transaction would be even more important. If the transaction was of a nature that no reasonable participant could have expected the agent to bear personal liability, that fact would be powerful evidence of agency status. For example, in Chips Distributing Co. v. Smith,[27] a New York court (applying Pennsylvania law) refused to enforce a confession of judgment on a note against the individual signer. The note carried the name of the corporate maker over the signature of its secretary-treasurer, and there was no indication of representative capacity on the note. The court considered the motives for making the note (defendant corporation gave its note to cover a debt and plaintiff corporation discounted it to obtain needed cash) and concluded that the parties must have intended the individual defendant's signature to be representative in character. The court noted, too, that plaintiff's bank had issued the loan payment book to the defendant corporation and that all correspondence was addressed to the corporation, not to the individual signer. In Leahy v. McManus [28] the chairman of the board of directors avoided personal liability on a corporate note executed in favor of another board member when he showed that the note covered funds which went to the corporation and that the payee, during his lifetime, made no demand for payment from the individual defendant, and the board had passed a resolution requiring his extra counter-signature on all corporate obligations.

Thus the lawyer for one who claims he signed only in an agency capacity has many stones to turn. He should inquire into the pertinent business customs and expectations. He should dig out and subpoena correspondence and corporate records. Finally, he should determine the extent to which the agent was himself benefited by the transaction in question [29] (that is, did the money go into the corporate

26. See Uptown Federal Savings & Loan Ass'n v. Collins, 105 Ill.App.2d 459, 245 N.E.2d 521, 6 UCC Rep.Serv. 354 (1969) (organization's requirement that five persons sign debt introduced to show that individuals who added "trustee" after signature intended representative capacity).

27. 48 Misc.2d 1079, 266 N.Y.S.2d 488, 3 UCC Rep.Serv. 177 (Sup.Ct.1966).

28. 237 Md. 450, 206 A.2d 688, 2 UCC Rep.Serv. 523 (Ct.App.1965). Contra, Fanning v. Hembree Oil Co., Inc., 245 Ark. 825, 434 S.W.2d 822, 5 UCC Rep. Serv. 1187 (1968) (evidence supported judgment against individual signer when plaintiff testified he asked for personal note of corporate shareholder).

29. In response to a suit attempting to impose personal liability the agent might hedge his bet by arguing that he

account or into the agent's pocket?). In summary we can distill three imperatives from the language of 3–403(2):

(*1*) always name the principal;

(*2*) always indicate representative capacity;

(*3*) make certain that the other party understands that you are acting as an agent.

To be certain that an agent will receive the blessing of the Code, he should sign in the following manner: "InterGlactic Transport Co. by Flash Gordon, Pres." The ideal form of signature when the principal is an individual is: "Flash Gordon by Dr. Zarkhov, Agent." An agent who so signs will not have to bear his principal's burden. Though it is faint solace to the agent of a bankrupt principal, an authorized agent who is made to pay is entitled to recover the money so paid from his principal on an indemnity theory.[30]

## § 13–6   Contractual Liability—Parties to an Instrument

Once it is established that a defendant signed the instrument or that his agent did so, we must turn to the Code to define his liability. Although this liability is set out in a statute and is in that respect statutory, the Code itself characterizes the liability as contractual (for instance, section 3–413, "Contract of Maker, Drawer and Acceptor"). This liability is in fact contractual in the sense that parties voluntarily incur it and can modify it by agreement. Thus we shall refer to the liability as contractual.

## § 13–7   Contractual Liability—Liability of the Maker, 3–413(1)

The contract liability of the maker of a note is as easy to understand as the words "I promise to pay . . . ." Section 3–413(1) provides that the maker "engages that he will pay the instrument according to its tenor at the time of his engagement or as completed pursuant to Section 3–115 on incomplete instruments."[31] Thus, the

---

signed in a representative capacity and, in the alternative, that he signed as a surety for his principal which entitles him to the special defenses of a surety. For a discussion of the problems of proving suretyship status, see Section 13–13 infra.

In any event, the agent who pays the instrument is entitled to contribution from his principal. Restatement of Restitution § 81 (1937) says:

Unless otherwise agreed, a person who has discharged more than his proportionate share of a duty owed by himself and another as to which, between the two, neither had a prior duty of performance, is entitled to contribution from the other . . .

30. See Restatement, Second, Agency §§ 438–39 (1958); Restatement of Restitution §§ 76–80 (1937).

31. Section 3–115 reads as follows:

(1) When a paper whose contents at the time of signing show that it is intended to become an instrument is signed while still incomplete in any necessary respect it cannot be enforced until completed, but when it is completed in accordance with authority given it is effective as completed.

(2) If the completion is unauthorized the rules as to material alteration apply (Section 3–407), even though the paper was not delivered by the maker or drawer; but the burden of establishing that any completion is unauthorized is on the party so asserting.

maker's liability is unconditional and absolute; he is obliged to pay a time instrument "on the day after maturity" and a demand instrument "upon its date or, if no date is stated, on the date of issuance." [32]

When two or more persons sign a note as makers, one maker will sometimes argue that he is only jointly and not severally liable (that is, that he is obliged to pay only a pro rata share to the holder and not the entire amount of the instrument). The Code deals with this problem in 3–118(e):

> Unless the instrument otherwise specifies two or more persons who sign as maker, acceptor or drawer or indorser and as part of the same transaction are jointly *and* severally liable even though the instrument contains such words as "I promise to pay". (emphasis added)

In Ghitter v. Edge, the court applied this rule of construction.[33] Plaintiff sued one of three co-makers on a note which recited "We promise to pay." Defendant argued that an action could not be brought against him without joinder of the other co-makers and the trial court dismissed plaintiff's petition. The Georgia Court of Appeals held the dismissal improper:

> Appellee [defendant] contends that the use of the words "We promise to pay" in the notes is sufficient specification of the manner in which the makers agreed to be held liable. We can not agree. Such is but an indirect specification by reference to the meaning which the words "we promise" held in the prior law. We understand the Code section to mean that whenever two or more persons sign as maker they are jointly and severally liable unless the instrument in its own language specifies the obligation differently, e. g., "we jointly promise . . ." or "we promise severally . . . ."

> Each of the three makers of the notes sued upon was jointly and severally liable. Therefore an action can be maintained against appellee alone and the fact that the other

---

32. § 3–122(1). In the case of a note payable at a bank the maker's liability is equivalent to a drawer. § 3–121 (Alternative A). However, as a practical matter, the holder's defect in presentment and notice of dishonor is only significant in the situation where the bank has failed. § 3–502(1) (b); County Restaurant & Bar Equip. Co. v. Shaw Mechanical Contractors, Inc., 56 Misc.2d 832, 290 N.Y.S.2d 377, 5 UCC Rep.Serv. 522 (Dist.Ct.1968) (complaint need not allege presentment and notice of dishonor to hold liable maker of note payable at a bank); Mandel v. Sedrish, 3 UCC Rep.Serv. 524 (N.Y. Sup.Ct.1966) (defense alleging defective presentment insufficient because of failure to allege payor bank's insolvency).

33. 118 Ga.App. 750, 165 S.E.2d 598, 5 UCC Rep.Serv. 1253 (1968). Accord, Simpson v. Wages, 119 Ga.App. 324, 167 S.E.2d 213, 6 UCC Rep.Serv. 518 (1969) (holder could bring action against two of three co-makers when instrument stated "we promise to pay"); Valley Bank & Trust Co. v. Roy, 41 Mass.App.Dec. 44, 6 UCC Rep. Serv. 828 (1969).

two makers were not joined or legally accounted for affords no basis for a dismissal of the action.[34]

Note the Court's *dictum* that an instrument which states "we jointly promise" or "we severally promise" falls within the "unless, otherwise" clause of 3–118(e).

When one co-maker pays the instrument he is entitled to contribution from other co-makers. There is a rebuttable presumption that all co-makers are liable (vis-a-vis one another) for an equal proportion of the debt.[35] Even though he is liable for the full amount to a holder, a maker may sue his co-maker, establish that he signed as a surety for the co-maker, and obtain complete reimbursement.[36]

### § 13–8  Contractual Liability—Liability of the Acceptor, 3–413, 3–412, 3–411, 3–410, 3–409

A party who takes a check in payment of a debt expects the bank on which it is drawn to pay it. However, the drawee bank is not, without more, obligated to pay such a party a nickel. In the words of 3–409(1):

> A check or other draft does not of itself operate as an assignment of any funds in the hands of the drawee available for its payment, and the drawee is not liable on the instrument until he accepts it.

Thus, even if the drawee arbitrarily dishonors a check, the payee or holder ordinarily has no cause of action against the drawee bank on the instrument.

Under 3–413(2), the drawer of a draft is only "secondarily" liable. He promises to pay only if the drawee fails to carry out his order, and the holder makes presentment and gives notice of dishonor as required by 3–501 (to be discussed in the upcoming section). Accordingly, a particular payee may demand some assurance that the drawee will carry out that order. Thus, the payee or holder may demand that the drawee "accept" the draft[37] and thus become "pri-

---

**34.** Ghitter v. Edge, 118 Ga.App. 750, 752–53, 165 S.E.2d 598, 600, 5 UCC Rep.Serv. 1253, 1254 (1968).

**35.** See Restatement of Restitution § 85 (1937) which provides:

A person who has discharged more than his proportionate share of a duty owed by himself and another, as to which neither of the two had a prior duty of performance and who is entitled to contribution from the other under the rules stated in Sections 81–84, is entitled to reimbursement limited

(a) to the proportionate amount of his net outlay properly expended . . . .

Comment (e) provides:

Two or more persons engaging in a common enterprise or becoming sureties for a third person share the duty of performance equally, in the absence of an agreement between them providing for different shares . . .

**36.** § 3–415(5). See text accompanying notes 136–139 infra.

**37.** Section 3–410(1) provides:

Acceptance is the drawee's signed engagement to honor the draft as presented. It must be written on the draft, and may consist of his signature alone. It becomes operative when completed by delivery or notification.

marily liable" upon the instrument.[38]　A drawee who "accepts" usually manifests this acceptance by signing vertically across the face of the instrument.[39]　Acceptance of a draft other than a check enlarges the number and nature of parties liable to the holder on the instrument.　In the absence of acceptance, the holder must make presentment and give notice of dishonor before he can even hold the drawer or indorser liable on the instrument.　Acceptance adds the primary independent liability of the drawee.

Certification of a check is a special type of acceptance under 3–411, but unlike acceptance of a draft which merely adds another party to the instrument, certification of a check by a holder discharges the drawer and all prior indorsers.[40]　By inference certification procured by a nonholder (for instance, the drawer) does not operate to discharge him or any other parties.[41]

## § 13–9　Contractual Liability—Liability of the Drawer, 3–413(2)

The drawer of a draft is nominally a "secondary" party on the instrument.[42]　Although the drawer, like the maker, signs the instrument in the lower right-hand corner, his contract is unlike the maker's in that he orders another to make payment and promises to pay only if the order bears no fruit.[43]　Thus, in common experience the holder of a check (according to 3–104(2)(b) a check is a draft "drawn on a bank and payable on demand") looks first to the bank for payment [44] and if it cannot be had there, to the drawer.　The legal basis for this action is the contract of a drawer set out in 3–413(2) as follows:

> The drawer engages that upon dishonor of the draft and any necessary notice of dishonor or protest he will pay the amount of the draft to the holder or to any indorser who

---

38.　Section 3–413(1) says:

> The maker or acceptor engages that he will pay the instrument according to its tenor at the time of his engagement or as completed pursuant to Section 3–115 on incomplete instruments.

39.　Comment 4 to section 3–410 discusses the formalities required for accepting an instrument.

40.　Section 3–411 reads as follows:

> (1) Certification of a check is acceptance.　Where a holder procures certification the drawer and all prior indorsers are discharged.
>
> (2) Unless otherwise agreed a bank has no obligation to certify a check.
>
> (3) A bank may certify a check before returning it for lack of proper indorsement.　If it does so the drawer is discharged.

41.　§ 3–411, Comment 1; 2 N.Y. State Law Revision Comm'n, 1955 Report 1034 (1955).

42.　Section 3–102(1)(d) provides, "Secondary party means a drawer or indorser."

43.　Section 3–104(2) provides, ". . . (a) a "draft" ("bill of exchange") if it is an order: . . ."

44.　The bank has no obligation to the holder to pay a check.　Section 3–409 (1) provides:

> A check or other draft does not of itself operate as an assignment of any funds in the hands of the drawee available for its payment, and the drawee is not liable on the instrument until he accepts it.

The bank's obligation to the drawer is stated in sections 4–401 and 4–402.

See Sections 17–3, 17–4 infra.

takes it up. The drawer may disclaim this liability by drawing without recourse.

Note the two conditions precedent to the drawer's contractual liability: dishonor and notice of dishonor. Part 5 of Article Three details the intricacies of dishonor and the manner of giving notice of dishonor. A lazy lawyer can save considerable effort by referring directly to 3–502. That section states the consequences of failure to meet the requirements of dishonor and necessary notice of dishonor as follows:

> Where without excuse any necessary presentment or notice of dishonor is delayed beyond the time when it is due
>
> .  .  .
>
>> (b) any drawer  .  .  . who because the drawee or payor bank becomes insolvent during the delay is deprived of funds maintained with the drawee or payor bank to cover the instrument may discharge his liability by written assignment to the holder of his rights against the drawee or payor bank in respect of such funds, but such drawer  .  .  . is *not otherwise discharged.* (emphasis added)

The practical effect of the quoted Code section is that the holder's failure to satisfy the conditions of 3–413(2) has legal significance only when the drawee bank has failed. Writing for the New York Law Revision Commission Professor Willcox analyzed section 3–502 (1) (b) as follows:

> Except in the case of the insolvency of a drawee or of a payor bank, occurring during a delay of presentment while such drawee or payor bank had funds to cover the instrument, the Code would *convert a drawer into a primary party,* like a maker or an acceptor. And for drawer, maker and acceptor alike, the Code would create a partial and limited discharge in the case of such an insolvency, available by means of an assignment to the holder of the drawer's, maker's or acceptor's rights against the insolvent estate. (emphasis in original) .  .  .  .

> (It must be borne in mind that this all relates to the one unlikely contingency of the payor's failure during the period of delay—an event so unlikely to occur today at least in the case of a bank payor that Professor Sutherland has characterized the whole matter [unless there be more depositing of funds with non-bankers to meet drafts than we know about] as a "salute to yesterday" i. e., before Federal deposit insurance was established. Sutherland, "Article 3—Logic, Ex-

perience and Negotiable Paper," 1952 Wis.L.Rev. 230, 249–251 [March, 1952]).[45]

As pointed out by Comment 2 to section 3–502:

> The purpose of the rule is to avoid hardship upon the holder through complete discharge, and unjust enrichment of the drawer or other party who normally has received goods or other consideration for the issue of the instrument.

In recognition of this state of affairs at least one court has held that the holder need not even plead dishonor and notice of dishonor in an action against a drawer; rather, the drawer must prove their absence as an affirmative defense.[46] Thus, the conditions of dishonor and notice of dishonor in the drawer's contract as stated in 3–413 turn out to be relatively unimportant.

## § 13–10   Contractual Liability—Liability of the Indorser, 3–414

"Indorsement" is a formal act which passes title to the indorser's transferee [47] and obligates the indorser on the stereotyped contract set forth in 3–414. All indorsements fall into two broad categories, special and blank. A special indorsement ("pay to the order of Joe Jones, John Peterson") makes the instrument into an "order instrument" if it is not already one. A blank indorsement on the other hand ("Joe Jones") makes an instrument into a "bearer instrument." Thus, sections 3–204(1), (2), and (3) provide:

> (1) A special indorsement specifies the person to whom or to whose order it makes the instrument payable. Any instrument specially indorsed becomes payable to the order of the special indorsee and may be further negotiated only by his indorsement.

> (2) An indorsement in blank specifies no particular indorsee and may consist of a mere signature. An instrument payable to order and indorsed in blank becomes payable to bearer and may be negotiated by delivery alone until specially indorsed.

> (3) The holder may convert a blank indorsement into a special indorsement by writing over the signature of the indorser in blank any contract consistent with the character of the indorsement.

---

45. 2 N.Y. State Law Revision Comm'n, 1955 Report 1085 (1955) (emphasis in original).

46. Esslinger's, Inc. v. Stravino Bros., Inc., 28 Lehigh L.J. 494 (Pa.Ct.C.P. 1960) (defective presentment of note payable at bank). The cases cited in note 32, supra, are in accord with this decision.

47. A surety may undertake his obligation by indorsing the instrument. In such cases, section 3–415(4) creates the presumption that an indorsement which shows it is outside the chain of title is made by an accommodation party. See text accompanying notes 106–107 infra.

Note that a special or a blank indorsement may also be a "restrictive indorsement" ("For deposit only, Joe Jones").  In Chapters 14, 15, and 16 we consider the legal consequences that flow from the choice of a particular kind of indorsement.

In the case of an order instrument,[48] transferees (subsequent to the payee) become holders (one of the essential prerequisites for qualifying as a holder in due course under 3–302) only when the instrument is "indorsed" to them.[49]  Although a party need not indorse bearer paper in order to make his transferee a holder, most persons taking a bearer instrument demand an indorsement from the transferor in order to assure themselves of his identity and to gain the benefit of the indorsement contract.[50]  The closest thing to a definition of indorsement is 3–202(2) which reads as follows:

> An indorsement must be written by or on behalf of the holder and on the instrument or on a paper so firmly affixed thereto as to become a part thereof.[51]

Note that indorsement "must be written by or on the behalf of a holder."  Thus in the case of order instruments only the payee or one who signs on his behalf can make the first effective indorsement and negotiate the instrument.[52]  If he fails to do that no subsequent

---

**48.**  Section 3–110 defines an order instrument as follows:

   (1) An instrument is payable to order when by its terms it is payable to the order or assigns of any person therein specified with reasonable certainty, or to him or his order, or when it is conspicuously designated on its face as "exchange" or the like and names a payee.  It may be payable to the order of

   (a) the maker or drawer; or

   (b) the drawee; or

   (c) a payee who is not maker, drawer or drawee; or

   (d) two or more payees together or in the alternative  . . ..

   (2) An instrument not payable to order is not made so payable by such words as "payable upon return of this instrument properly indorsed."

   (3) An instrument made payable both to order and to bearer is payable to order unless the bearer words are handwritten or typewritten.

**49.**  Section 3–202(1) provides:

Negotiation is the transfer of an instrument in such form that the transferee becomes a holder.  If the instrument is payable to order it is nego-

tiated by delivery with any necessary indorsement; if payable to bearer it is negotiated by delivery.

**50.**  The transferor of bearer paper who attempts to avoid liability as an indorser by arguing that he merely signed the instrument as a receipt for the proceeds will not get very far.  Section 3–402 creates the presumption that:

[u]nless the instrument clearly indicates that a signature is made in some other capacity it is an indorsement.

The Comment to 3–402 points out that the location of the signature is sufficient indication of signature in a capacity other than an indorser.

**51.**  See James Talcott, Inc. v. Fred Ratowsky Ass'n, Inc., 2 UCC Rep.Serv. 1134 (Pa.Ct.C.P.1965) (plaintiff failed to qualify as holder because indorsement on paper "clipped" to instrument was not "firmly affixed" to the instrument).

**52.**  Section 1–201(20) defines holder as follows:

"Holder" means a person who is in possession of a document of title or an instrument or an investment security drawn, issued or indorsed to him or to his order or to bearer or in blank.

transferee can qualify as a holder or *a fortiori* as a holder in due course. Thus neither a thief of an order instrument nor any transferee who traces title through the thief will be a holder.[53] Not so with bearer paper; one who takes a bearer instrument from a thief can attain holder status.[54]

One who transfers an instrument may make a special indorsement or indorse the instrument in blank. Section 3–204(1) defines the nature and effect of a special indorsement:

> A special indorsement specifies the person to whom or to whose order it makes the instrument payable. Any instrument specially indorsed becomes payable to the order of the special indorsee and may be further negotiated only by his indorsement.

Thus the recipient of a bearer instrument may convert it into an order instrument by specially indorsing it when he transfers it. Similarly, under 3–204(2), the holder of an order instrument may convert it into a bearer instrument by indorsing it in blank.[55] For example, an instrument which recites "Pay to the order of—John Jones" becomes a bearer instrument when John signs the back "John Jones." Note that a thief's signature in the name of the true owner does not constitute an indorsement (because the thief is not himself a holder) and therefore does not convert order paper into bearer paper.

Under 3–414(1) a party who indorses makes the following contract:

> Unless the indorsement otherwise specifies (as by such words as "without recourse") every indorser engages that upon dishonor and any necessary notice of dishonor and protest he will pay the instrument according to its tenor at the time of his indorsement to the holder or to any subsequent indorser who takes it up, even though the indorser who takes it up was not obligated to do so.

At the time an order instrument is issued or drawn only a payee who has possession can meet the requirements of this section and qualify as a holder.

53. Since the thief of order paper cannot qualify as a holder under section 1–201(20), his indorsement was not made by or on behalf of a holder and his transferee did not become a holder under section 3–202(1). The transferee's indorsement suffers from the same infirmity as the thief's and is likewise ineffective to confer holder status on one who takes from him. For an arcane discussion of sections 1–201(20) and 3–202, see White, Some Petty Complaints About Article Three,

65 Mich.L.Rev. 1315, 1316–21, 1326–29 (1967).

54. The thief in possession of bearer paper probably satisfies the requirements of 1–201(20); in any event his indorsement is unnecessary to confer holder status on his transferee.

55. Section 3–204(2) provides:

An indorsement in blank specifies no particular indorsee and may consist of a mere signature. An instrument payable to order and indorsed in blank becomes payable to bearer and may be negotiated by delivery alone until specially indorsed.

Note that an indorser is also "secondarily" liable: the indorser's contract, like the drawer's, conditions liability upon the occurrence of "dishonor" and "any necessary notice of dishonor and protest." Unlike the conditions to the drawer's contract, these conditions generally have bite; the penalty for noncompliance is complete discharge of the indorser.[56]  One can readily grasp the policy reasons underlying the Code provisons which provide that noncompliance discharges the indorser but does not discharge the drawer unless the drawee bank has failed.  Consider, for example, the position of a drawer who has received goods, services, or cash in return for his promise to pay embodied in his check.  After the check's transfer and before it is paid, the drawer is in a net positive position; he has received goods but he has not yet advanced cash from his account.  Failure of the payee to make timely presentment injures the drawer only if in the interim the drawee has become insolvent and funds on deposit are lost before they could be applied against the instrument.  There the drawer is and ought to be discharged, but if he is otherwise discharged he will get a windfall, that is, he will get goods or services for which he pays nothing.[57]

On the other hand, the ordinary indorser is one who gave up money, goods, or services when he received the instrument.  Of course, he received an equivalent amount when he transferred the check but that leaves him in a net zero position with respect to the transaction.  If he is excused by the holder's delay (or other noncompliance), he does not receive a windfall.  Accordingly the Code requires the holder to act promptly if he hopes to hold the indorser liable.

Article Three, Part 5 defines "dishonor", "presentment," and cognate terms, specifies when presentment is necessary, and tells when one must give notice of dishonor—all in boring and incessant detail. At the risk of oversimplifying, but in the interest of lightening the reader's load, we will outline the pertinent provisions.  Section 3–507 (1) tells us that an instrument is dishonored when the holder makes presentment and payment is refused or cannot be obtained within specified time limits.[58]  Section 3–501(1) provides that unless excused under section 3–511, presentment (that is, a demand for pay-

---

56.  Section 3–502(1) provides:

Where without excuse any necessary presentment or notice of dishonor is delayed beyond the time when it is due

(a) any indorser is discharged; . . .

57.  See §§ 3–502, Comment 2; 3–503, Comment 2.

58.  Section 3–507(1) reads as follows:

An instrument is dishonored when

(a) a necessary or optional presentment is duly made and due acceptance or payment is refused or cannot be obtained within the prescribed time or in case of bank collections the instrument is seasonably returned by the midnight deadline (Section 4–301); or

(b) presentment is excused and the instrument is not duly accepted or paid.

ment)[59] is a condition precedent to holding an indorser liable on the instrument.[60] For instance, presentment and dishonor occur when the holder of a check attempts to cash it at the drawee bank, but payment is refused because the drawer lacks sufficient funds on deposit. The demand for payment is a presentment. The bank's refusal to pay is a dishonor.

Under 3–502(2) the holder must make presentment within the required time limits if he hopes to impose liability on an indorser. Section 3–503 stipulates the time for presentment of various types of instruments and 3–503(1) (e) tells us:

> [W]ith respect to the liability of any secondary party presentment for acceptance or payment of any other instrument is due within a reasonable time after such party becomes liable thereon.[61]

Section 3–503(2) elaborates the meaning of a "reasonable time" and establishes the presumption that seven days after indorsement is a reasonable time in which to present for payment or initiate bank collection "[i]n the case of an uncertified check which is drawn and payable within the United States and which is not a draft drawn by a bank . . . ." Several features of the section erode its seven day requirement. First, the seven day period is only a presumption.[62] If a check has passed through the hands of several indorsers over a period of two weeks, presentment after that time probably would not constitute unreasonable delay.[63] Secondly, all the holder need do

---

**59.** Section 3–504(1) defines presentment:

Presentment is a demand for acceptance or payment made upon the maker, acceptor, drawee or other payor by or on behalf of the holder.

**60.** Section 3–501(1) provides:

Unless excused (Section 3–511) presentment is necessary to charge secondary parties as follows:

\* \* \*

(b) presentment for payment is necessary to charge any indorser;

. . .

Comment 2 to section 3–501 explains:

The words "Necessary to charge" are retained from the original Act. They mean that the necessary proceeding is a condition precedent to any right of action against the drawer or indorser. He is not liable and cannot be sued without the proceedings however long delayed.

**61.** The subsections establish the date that the "party becomes liable thereon" as the benchmark for measuring whether presentment was made in a

reasonable time. This is an unfortunate piece of drafting, because the subsection defines one of the criteria for making presentment (i. e., a condition precedent to the indorser's liability). No doubt the draftsmen intended that reasonable time be measured from the time that the party signed the instrument.

**62.** Section 1–201(31) defines presumption:

"Presumption" or "presumed" means that the trier of fact must find the existence of the fact presumed unless and until evidence is introduced which would support a finding of its nonexistence.

**63.** The draftsmen considered the possibility that a check might remain in circulation more than seven days after the first indorsement. See Uniform Commercial Code, 1953 Official Draft of Text and Comments 121 (Supp. No. 1, 1955) where they expressed the following opinion:

Nominally, under UNIL 71, NY NIL 131, the indorser's liability might continue without presentment for an

within the time is to cash or deposit the check at a bank.[64]   Nevertheless a holder who wants to charge an indorser cannot afford to let any grass grow under his feet.

Section 3–504(2) specifies various ways in which a holder may make presentment.[65]   In the case of a check in the bank collection process, presentment may be made "through a clearing house."   Comment 2 to 3–504 points out that if a clearing house is used presentment occurs when the item reaches the obligor.   However, section 4–204(3) says that "Presentment may be made by a presenting bank at a place where the payor bank has requested that presentment be made."   Thus, presentment may take place at a "centralized book-

---

indefinite time while the check was rapidly passed from hand to hand among successive holders.   Section 3–503(2) (b) sets up a presumptive limit of seven days to the period of an indorser's liability without express provision for a series of rapid negotiations.   The policy of placing this presumptive time limit on the indorser's continued liability must be considered in the light of the fact that circumstances rendering it inapplicable will presumably change the judicial application of the presumption.

**64.**   See 2 N.Y. State Law Revision Comm'n, 1955 Report 1096 (1955). Note that under 3–503(1) (e) and (2) the initiation of bank collection within the two week period arguably is not sufficient.   One may further argue that presentment must be completed within the seven-day period.   One would make such an argument on the basis of 3–503(1) (e) which states that presentment must be made within a reasonable time.   Subsection (2) then defines a reasonable time for presentment and states "the following are presumed to be reasonable periods within which to present for payment or to initiate bank collection: [seven days]."   One might argue that the reference to the initiation of bank collection was wholly unrelated to one's satisfaction of his obligation to present within seven days and that that was just a convenient place to make reference to the reasonable time for the institution of bank collection. The trouble with that argument is that the reference to the initiation of bank collection is within a section titled "Time of Presentment" and within a subsection whose first sentence refers only to presentment.   Moreover, we know of no other place in Article Three or Four in which a presumed time for the initiation of bank collection would be relevant.   Admitting

that the draftsmanship is not perfect, we conclude that one makes a timely presentment of a check with respect to an indorser if he initiates bank collection within seven days after the indorsement.

**65.**   Section 3–504(2) reads as follows:

Presentment may be made

(a) by mail, in which event the time of presentment is determined by the time of receipt of the mail;  or

(b) through a clearing house;  or

(c) at the place of acceptance or payment specified in the instrument or if there be none at the place of business or residence of the party to accept or pay.   If neither the party to accept or pay nor anyone authorized to act for him is present or accessible at such place presentment is excused.

Comment 1 to section 3–504 states:

This section is intended to simplify the rules as to how presentment is made and to make it clear that any demand upon the party to pay is a presentment no matter where or how. Former technical requirements of exhibition of the instrument and the like are not required unless insisted upon by the party to pay (Section 3–505).

The thrust of the comment goes beyond the language of the statute because the latter seems only to contemplate physical presentment of the instrument.   The comment suggests that merely telephoning the party and demanding payment would constitute presentment.   But see Kirby v. Bergfield, 186 Neb. 242, 182 N.W.2d 205, 8 UCC Rep.Serv. 710 (1970) (telephone call to bookkeeping department of drawee bank and inquiry about amount of funds did not constitute presentment for payment).

keeping center and electronic processing centers", when the payor so requests. (Comment 4 to 4–204).

The other event stated in 3–414 as a prerequisite to the indorser's liability is notice of dishonor. Notice of dishonor informs the secondary party that the primary party has defaulted on his obligation and that the secondary party will be called upon to carry out his contract. As in the case of presentment, delay in giving notice of dishonor completely discharges an indorser.[66]

Section 3–508 governs the time and manner of giving notice of dishonor. Section 3–508(2) differentiates between banks and other persons; banks have until their midnight deadline and other persons must give notice "before midnight of the third business day after dishonor or receipt of notice of dishonor." Section 3–508(3) announces liberal rules governing the manner in which notice is given. It specifically provides that notice may be given orally or in writing.[67] Of course, as a general business practice oral notice is ill advised.

In the case of some "international" instruments there is an additional condition to drawer's or indorser's liability, namely, "protest." One must procure "protest" of any dishonor in order to hold the drawer and indorsers of a draft which "on its face appears to be drawn or payable outside of the states and territories of the United States and District of Columbia" (3–501(3)). Protest is a formal certification by a consul, notary, or the like that an instrument has been dishonored.[68]

### Excuse, 3–511

If a lawyer finds himself representing a client who has missed a step in the ritual outlined above, he should not push the panic button until he has consulted 3–511. In many circumstances that section forgives the holder for his delay or failure to comply with the re-

---

**66.** § 3–502(2). See note 56 supra.

**67.** Section 3–508(3) provides:

Notice may be given in any reasonable manner. It may be oral or written and in any terms which identify the instrument and state that it has been dishonored. A misdescription which does not mislead the party notified does not vitiate the notice. Sending the instrument bearing a stamp, ticket or writing stating that acceptance or payment has been refused or sending a notice of debit with respect to the instrument is sufficient.

**68.** Section 3–509 reads in full as follows:

(1) A protest is a certificate of dishonor made under the hand and seal of a United States consul or vice consul or a notary public or other

person authorized to certify dishonor by the law of the place where dishonor occurs. It may be made upon information satisfactory to such person.

(2) The protest must identify the instrument and certify either that due presentment has been made or the reason why it is excused and that the instrument has been dishonored by nonacceptance or nonpayment.

(3) The protest may also certify that notice of dishonor has been given to all parties or to specified parties.

(4) Subject to subsection (5) any necessary protest is due by the time that notice of dishonor is due.

(5) If, before protest is due, an instrument has been noted for protest by the officer to make protest, the protest may be made at any time thereafter as of the date of the noting.

quirements of Part 5, Article Three. As a practical matter 3–511 greatly reduces the harshness of the technical requirements of presentment and notice of dishonor. Not surprisingly it has received the attention of the courts in most of the cases decided under Part 5 of Article Three.[69]

Section 3–511(2) specifies those circumstances which completely excuse presentment or notice of dishonor. The simplest case is one in which the indorser has expressly waived his right to have the instrument presented or to receive notice of dishonor. If the indorser has waived presentment or notice of dishonor, he will have no basis for complaint if there is some defect in the holder's performance of these duties.[70] An express waiver may take any number of forms [71] and might appear on the body of the instrument as well as on the back.[72] Many standard form printed notes contain waivers of notice, protest, and the like. Note that 3–511(5) provides that "[a] waiver of protest is also a waiver of presentment and of notice of dishonor even though protest is not required." [73] An indorser can waive dishonor and notice by implication as well as by express language. Thus in Wiener v. Van Winkle [74] defendant indorsers were found liable despite plaintiff's failure to make presentment because the indorsers impliedly waived presentment when they requested an extension of time for payment.

69. See notes 70–82 infra and cases cited therein.

70. See Fett Dev. Co. v. Garvin, 119 Ga.App. 569, 168 S.E.2d 212, 6 UCC Rep.Serv. 680 (1969) (complaint need not allege presentment and notice of dishonor when waiver incorporated in note); Lizza Asphalt Const. Co. v. Greenvale Const. Co., Inc., 4 UCC Rep. Serv. 954 (N.Y.Sup.Ct.1968) (notice sent to wrong address did not discharge indorser who signed under waiver); Abby Fin. Corp. v. Weydig Auto Supplies Unlimited, Inc., 4 UCC Rep.Serv. 858 (N.Y.Sup.Ct.1967) (indorser not discharged by holder's failure to make presentment and give notice of dishonor when note contained waiver); G.S.H.W. Ass'n v. Tonray Realty Corp., 2 UCC Rep.Serv. 783 (N.Y.Sup.Ct.1965) (indorsers who waived notice of any character remained liable despite plaintiff's failure to give notice).

71. See Held v. Moore, 2 UCC Rep. Serv. 14 (Pa.C.P.1964) where the indorser signed under the following conditions:

For value received the undersigned and each of them hereby forever waives presentment, demand, protest, notice of protest and notice of dishonor of the within note and the undersigned and each of them guarantees the payment of said note at maturity and consents without notice to any and all extension of time or terms of payment made by holder of said note.

Id. at 15.

The court held that the indorser was a guarantor under section 3–416 and thereby waived presentment and notice of dishonor under section 3–416(5).

72. Section 3–511(6) states the different effect of waiver in the body of the note or waiver appearing on the back of the note:

Where a waiver of presentment or notice or protest is embodied in the instrument itself it is binding upon all parties; but where it is written above the signature of an indorser it binds him only.

73. See Gerrity Co. v. Padalino, 51 Misc.2d 928, 273 N.Y.S.2d 994, 3 UCC Rep.Serv. 989 (Sup.Ct.1966) (waiver of protest in body of note).

74. 273 Cal.App.2d 774, 78 Cal.Rptr. 761, 6 UCC Rep.Serv. 819 (2d Dist.1969).

Section 3–511(2) (b) says that requirements of presentment and notice are excused when:

> such party has himself dishonored the instrument or has countermanded payment or otherwise has no reason to expect or right to require that the instrument be accepted or paid  .  .  .  .

When an indorser has played an active role in causing an instrument to be dishonored there is little reason to force the holder to go through the formality of presentment and notice of dishonor.[75]  A problem arises when the indorser played no active role, but had access to facts from which he could infer that the instrument would not be paid.  For instance, does the indorser's knowledge of the maker's insolvency excuse presentment and notice of dishonor?  Both pre-Code cases [76] and post-Code cases [77] hold that mere knowledge of insolvency does not excuse presentment and notice of dishonor.  For example, in Makel Textiles, Inc. v. Dolly Originals, Inc.,[78] the payee of a corporate promissory note sought payment from the corporation's president and another person, both of whom had signed as individual indorsers.  The defendants maintained that they were not liable because plaintiff had not made presentment or given notice of dishonor.  The New York Court responded to the corporation president's argument:

> By virtue of his active participation in the affairs of Dolly Originals, Inc., it is obvious that the defendant Nathan Goldberg well knew that the notes could not be and were not paid from corporate funds.  Under these circumstances the obligation to serve Goldberg with notice of dishonor and non-payment must be deemed unnecessary, at least impliedly, within the meaning of the Uniform Commercial Code.  Plaintiff's failure to present the notes for payment and give the said

---

75.  See General Bronze Corp. v. Barclay Towers, Inc., 4 UCC Rep.Serv. 765 (Sup.Ct.1967) (individual indorsers of corporate note cannot claim discharge for lack of presentment and notice of dishonor when note not paid pursuant to their order);  Franklin Nat'l Bank v. Eurez Const. Corp., 60 Misc.2d 499, 301 N.Y.S.2d 845, 6 UCC Rep.Serv. 634 (Sup.Ct.1969) (accommodation indorser of corporate note not entitled to notice of dishonor when he ordered bank not to honor note).

76.  See W. Britton, Handbook of the Law of Bills and Notes § 188 at 530 (2d ed. 1961).

77.  See Hane v. Exten, 7 UCC Rep.Serv. 35 (Md.Ct.App.1969) (no excuse against corporate officer who indorsed corporate note when payments made during officer's tenure).  But cf. 2 N.Y. State Law Revision Comm'n, 1955 Report 1142–43 (1955) (remarks of Professor Willcox):

> The phrasing of the text 'nor reason to expect *or* right to require  .  .  . that the instrument be accepted or paid' indicates, as suggested above, that the knowledge by the party to be charged of any facts making it probable that the primary party or drawee *will not* pay serves to excuse presentment, notice or protest—including, as a most common example, knowledge of such party's insolvency. (emphasis in original)

78.  4 UCC Rep.Serv. 95 (N.Y.Sup.Ct. 1967).

defendant notice of non-payment could not and did not injure nor prejudice his rights in any way. Formal notice of presentment and dishonor to Mr. Goldberg would be merely a useless gesture of advising him of a fact with which he was most familiar [citing UCC sections 3–511 and 3–507 and several pre-Code cases].[79]

However the other indorser convinced the court that presentment and notice of dishonor were required to hold him liable. The court said:

> As to said defendant Kushner, the record is void of any testimony, or proof of notice of presentment and dishonor as required under the Uniform Commercial Code. Nor is there any evidence of any activity or participation in the affairs of the corporation so as to excuse presentment or notice of dishonor.[80]

The court dismissed the suit against the indorser who did not participate in the corporate affairs and held the corporate president liable.[81]

Under pre-Code law a party's insolvency or bankruptcy did not excuse presentment and notice of dishonor,[82] but 3–511(3) changes that rule:

> Presentment is also entirely excused when
>
> (a) the maker, acceptor or drawee of any instrument except a documentary draft is dead or in insolvency proceedings instituted after the issue of the instrument; or
>
> (b) acceptance or payment is refused but not for want of proper presentment.

Note that an insolvency proceeding, unlike the events described in 3–511(2), does not excuse both presentment and notice of dishonor.[83] Unless the indorser comes under the "or otherwise no reason to expect" language of 3–511(2)(b), the holder must meet the notice requirements in order to hold the indorser liable. This is understandable, for even if the party primarily liable files bankruptcy, it is not

---

79. Id. at 97.

80. Id. at 97.

81. Corporate officers are not the only ones who might be confronted with 3–511(2)(b) arguments. Shareholders may similarly come up against the argument that as to them presentment and notice of dishonor was excused because they are so intimately involved in corporate affairs. See A. J. Armstrong, Inc. v. Janburt Embroidery Corp., 97 N.J.Super. 246, 234 A.2d 737, 4 UCC Rep.Serv. 748 (Law Div.1967) (shareholder in close corporation has sufficient knowledge of

corporation's inability to pay presentment; notice of dishonor excused).

82. See W. Britton, Handbook of the Law of Bills and Notes § 188 at 530 (2d ed. 1961).

83. Despite the fact that presentment is excused, dishonor can occur under section 3–507(1)(b):

An instrument is dishonored when

* * *

(b) presentment is excused and the instrument is not duly accepted or paid.

certain that he will lack sufficient assets to pay the instrument. Moreover, undue delay may make it impossible for the indorser to recover from the bankrupt or other prior parties.

The Code requires that the party making presentment or giving notice of dishonor only exercise "reasonable diligence." If "by reasonable diligence the presentment or protest cannot be made or the notice given", then the party is entirely excused.[84] Comment 5 to 3–511 explains this section as follows (emphasis added):

> The excuse is established only by proof that reasonable diligence has been exercised without success, *or that reasonable diligence would in any case have been unsuccessful.*

The emphasized language of the comment considerably expands the scope of the subsection. The New York Law Revision Commission expressed approval of the broader version indicated by the comment,[85] but we have found no cases on this point.

### *Qualified and Restrictive Indorsements:* *Sections 3–205, 3–206, 3–419*

The clever indorser can subscribe his name under a variety of magic phrases. The Code itself specifies the legal effect of some of these phrases. Some phrases may constitute offers or contract terms of underlying agreements between the parties (for instance, "in full satisfaction of all claims"). Some are only friendly messages ("Kiss my foot"), and more than a few have clouded legal effect.

If an indorser adds the words "without recourse" to his indorsement and so makes a "qualified" indorsement, he does not make the contract embodied in 3–414. That is, he transfers title to the instrument, but he does not promise to pay should the instrument be dishonored upon presentment. (Despite the disclaiming words "without recourse" the indorser makes all the warranties embodied in 3–417 save one.) [86]

Section 3–205 classifies certain indorsements as restrictive:

An indorsement is restrictive which either

(a) is conditional; or

(b) purports to prohibit further transfer of the instrument; or

(c) includes the words "for collection", "for deposit", "pay any bank", or like terms signifying a purpose of deposit or collection; or

(d) otherwise states that it is for the benefit or use of the indorser or of another person.

---

84.  § 3–511(2) (c).

85.  See 2 N.Y. State Law Revision Comm'n, 1955 Report 1144 (1955).

86.  The "without recourse" language dilutes his warranty in 3–417(2) (d) from one of warranting the absence of defense to warranting only "that he has no knowledge of such a defense". 3–417(3).

The most common restrictive indorsement is the "for deposit" type described in 3–205(c) and only that type will be considered here. Section 3–206(3) explains the effect of this type of indorsement:

> Except for an intermediary bank, any transferee under an indorsement which is conditional or includes the words "for collection", "for deposit", "pay any bank", or like terms (sub-paragraphs (a) and (c) of Section 3–205) must pay or apply any value given by him for or on the security of the instrument consistently with the indorsement and to the extent that he does so he becomes a holder for value. In addition such transferee is a holder in due course if he otherwise complies with the requirements of Section 3–302 on what constitutes a holder in due course.

To see the legal consequences of a "for deposit" indorsement assume that Tom Swift receives a $25 check from his grandparents on his twenty-first birthday. Tom indorses the check with the inscription "for deposit only, Tom Swift," and mails the check to his bank. However, the postman steals Tom's check, adds his name below Tom's indorsement and deposits the check in his account in First National Bank. First National forwards the check to Second National who transfers it to the payor bank, Third National, where the check is finally paid. What right of recovery does Tom have against the various banks? Second National is an intermediary bank [87] and under 3–206(3) has no obligation to respect a restrictive indorsement. It is equally clear under pre-Code law and 3–419 that Tom has a cause of action in conversion against First National, the depositary bank.[88] The only proper indorsement immediately following an indorsement "for deposit" should be that of a bank. What are Tom's rights against Third National, the payor bank? Although 3–206(3) does not expressly except a payor bank from liability for failure to pay consistently with "for deposit" indorsements, a payor who pays the transferee of a thief in such circumstances is not liable for conversion. Section 3–206(2) expressly states that a:

> payor bank which is not the depositary bank, is neither given notice nor otherwise affected by a restrictive indorsement of any person except the bank's immediate transferor or the person presenting for payment.

Might one argue that the draftsmen's failure to exclude payor banks in the specific provision dealing with "for deposit" indorsements, 3–206(3), creates an exception to the general rule stated in 3–206 (2)? Any doubts about the effect of 3–206(2) are resolved by 3–419

---

**87.** Section 4–105(c):

"Intermediary bank" means any bank to which an item is transferred in course of collection except the depositary or payor bank.

**88.** See Ch. 15 infra (3–419 and conversion liability).

(4) which provides that nondepositary intermediary banks and payor banks are not liable in conversion for paying an instrument inconsistently with a restrictive indorsement made by one other than their immediate transferor.[89]   Moreover, 4–205(2) is an almost verbatim restatement of 3–206(2).[90]   Intermediary banks and payor banks which are not depositary banks are excepted from 3–206(3) on the ground that the large number of checks they handle makes it impossible for them to scrutinize all prior indorsements.[91]

The sole significant legal consequence, then, of placing "for deposit" above a blank indorsement is to prevent a depositary bank or nonbank taker from a thief from being a holder in due course. Since such depositary bank or other person lacks good title and is not a holder in due course, he is liable in conversion.

## § 13–11  Warranty Liabilities

In addition to the contract liability discussed above most transferors of instruments make the implied warranties embodied in 3–417 or 4–207.   Such transferors may warrant to their transferees and, in some cases to subsequent parties, that they have good title to the instrument, that all signatures are genuine or authorized, and that the instrument has not been altered, etc.   Since warranty liability most often arises in cases in which there has been theft or alteration, we reserve the discussion of the warranty sections to Chapters 15 and 16.   Those chapters deal exclusively with stolen instruments, forged signatures and such matters.   See particularly Section 15–5.

## § 13–12  Accommodation Parties, 3–415, 3–416, 3–606—General Liability of Article Three Surety

One with money to lend, goods to sell or services to render may have doubts about a prospective debtor's ability to pay.   In such cases he is likely to demand more assurance than the debtor's bare promise of payment.   The prospective creditor can reduce his risk by requiring some sort of security.   One form of security is the Article 9 security interest in the debtor's goods.[92]   Another type of security takes the form of joining a third person on the debtor's obligation.

---

89.   Section 3–419(4) provides:

An intermediary bank or payor bank which is not a depositary bank is not liable in conversion solely by reason of the fact that proceeds of an item indorsed restrictively (Sections 3–205 and 3–206) are not paid or applied consistently with the restrictive indorsement of an indorser other than its immediate transferor.

90.   Section 4–205(2) states:

An intermediary bank, or payor bank which is not a depositary bank, is

neither given notice nor otherwise affected by a restrictive indorsement of any person except the bank's immediate transferor.

Section 3–603(1) provides in certain cases that payment inconsistent with a restrictive indorsement does not discharge the party making such payment.

91.   § 3–206, Comment 3.

92.   See Chs. 22–26 infra.

A third party who thus obligates himself to answer for the debt or default of the debtor is called a surety.

Structurally, suretyship is a three party relationship involving the creditor, the principal debtor and the surety.[93] The debtor's obligation as a purchaser of goods or borrower of money is already familiar. So, too, his obligation as a signer of a negotiable instrument. The surety's obligation is somewhat different. In effect the surety undertakes to "back up" the performance of the debtor and he thereby gives the creditor the added assurance of having another party to the obligation.[94] It is common practice for a surety to appear on a note either as a co-maker or as an indorser. Assume for example that a father is going to be the surety on his son's contract to pay for a new car. The father may sign the note as co-maker or he may simply indorse the note. As we will see, in either case he is what the Code calls an "accommodation party" and owes the holder of the note the obligation of a maker, or of an indorser as the case may be (although he will have certain defenses not normally available to makers or indorsers against all but holders in due course without notice of his accommodation status.)

As between the surety and the debtor, it is clear that the debtor has the primary obligation to pay the debt.[95] Since the creditor is entitled to only one performance and the debtor receives the benefit of the transaction, the surety's obligation is undertaken with the expectation that the debtor will meet his commitment to the creditor. Thus if the surety is made to pay his principal's debt, he has the right to recover from the principal.[96] If the creditor releases the principal debtor and so deprives the surety of the right to recover from the principal by being subrogated to the creditor's rights, or if the creditor fails to perfect a security interest in collateral given

---

**93.** Throughout this discussion we most often use the generic terms (surety, debtor, creditor). Occasionally we use specific Code terminology (e. g., accommodation party, guarantor). Note that section 1–201(40) specifies that "[s]urety' includes guarantor." With the exception of an excellent article by Professor Peters, the Article Three surety has received little attention from the commentators. See Peters, Suretyship Under Article 3 of the Uniform Commercial Code, 77 Yale L.J. 833 (1968).

**94.** See L. Simpson, Handbook on the Law of Suretyship §§ 3–17 (1950) (discusses primary and secondary liability of surety and distinguishes liability of surety, guarantor, and indorser).

**95.** See Restatement of Security § 82 (1941):

Suretyship is the relation which exists where one person has undertaken an obligation and another person is also under an obligation or other duty to the obligee, who is entitled to but one performance, and as between the two who are bound, one rather than the other should perform.

* * *

Comment f. When the statement is made that the principal should perform, or that the principal has the principal or primary duty and the surety an accessorial or a secondary duty, it does not mean that the creditor's assertion of his right against the surety must be postponed until some action is taken against the principal. So far as the creditor is concerned, the surety may be the primary obligor. Where principal and surety are bound jointly, from the standpoint of the creditor there is no secondary liability.

**96.** See Section 13–18 infra (§ 3–415 (5)).

by the debtor and so is unable to recover his debt out of the collateral, the surety's burden will be increased. The law assumes that the surety has not assented to such increased burdens. Consequently the law has traditionally held that conduct by the creditor which increases the surety's risk discharges the surety.[97]

In this section we deal with the legal consequences when a surety joins with the debtor on a negotiable instrument.[98] One should not be intimidated by the vocabulary of suretyship law. Under the Code the word "surety" includes all "guarantors"[99] and all "accommodation parties."[100] A "guarantor" differs from an "accommodation party" only because he has added some words to his signature and has so altered (slightly or greatly) the liability he would have had if he had simply put his signature on the instrument as a mine-run accommodation party. Section 3–415(1) defines an accommodation party as "one who signs the instrument in any capacity for the purpose of lending his name to another party to it."[101] Section 3–415

---

**97.** See Section 13–16 infra (§ 3–606).

**98.** One of the vexsome problems raised by the Code provisions governing Article Three suretyship is determining the extent to which the Code incorporates or modifies the pre-existing law of suretyship. The problem principally comes up when the surety wishes to assert a right or defense against the principal debtor or the creditor. See Section 13–18 infra (surety's right of subrogation and reimbursement against creditor); Section 13–19 infra (surety's right to assert defenses of debtor against creditor).

The legislative history of 3–415(1) is not particularly enlightening. Section 3–415(1) (1952 Official Draft) originally provided:

An accommodation party is one who signs the instrument in any capacity as surety for another party to it.

Comment 1 to 3–415 (1952 Official Draft) explained:

The word "surety" is intended to incorporate the entire background of the law of suretyship as applied to negotiable instruments.

The section was criticized as confusing and complicated because it introduced the law of suretyship into negotiable instruments. 1 N.Y. State Law Revision Comm'n, 1954 Report 208–209, 428 (1954). Professors Sutherland, Mentschikoff, and Gilmore responded that the section merely codified prior law and that the obligation of an accommodation party could not be under-

stood as other than a suretyship obligation. 1 Id. at 253, 274, 461 (1954); 2 Id. at 1168 (1954). The original language of the statute and the comment were deleted and the present § 3–415(1) substituted as the result of the debate before the New York Law Revision Commission. Permanent Editorial Board for the Uniform Commercial Code, 1956 Recommendations 113 (1956).

**99.** Section 1–201(40) provides, "'Surety' includes guarantor."

**100.** § 3–415, Comment 1.

**101.** Sureties who undertake their obligation by executing an instrument to which the debtor is not a party cannot claim the advantages of 3–415. See Bank of America Nat'l Trust & Sav. Ass'n v. Superior Court of San Diego City, 4 Cal.App.3d 435, 84 Cal. Rptr. 421, 7 UCC Rep.Serv. 713 (4th Dist.1970) where plaintiff-bank sought and obtained a writ of mandamus ordering grant of summary judgment against the agent of a corporation who in return for a loan to the corporation gave his own note. Defendant claimed status as an accommodation party and alleged defenses under section 3–415 (3). The appellate court concluded that since the corporation was not a party to the note, defendant was not an accommodation party. Although it is unclear what defenses defendant would have raised if he had been permitted to do so, he might have had more success under section 3–606 which permits the surety to claim discharge even when the debtor does

(2) tells us that an accommodation party "is liable in the capacity in which he has signed." Thus an accommodation party may appear on the instrument as a maker, acceptor, drawer or indorser and his liability is governed by the Code sections on the contracts of parties who sign in these capacities.[102] An accommodation maker's basic liability to a holder is identical to that of any other maker, and the rules requiring presentment and notice of dishonor apply to an accommodation indorser in the same manner that they apply to a regular indorser. As we will see, however, surety status of an accommodation party may give him special defenses unavailable to the general run of parties on instruments.[103]

The liability of a party who adds words of guarantee to his signature is governed by 3–416.[104] If a party adds "payment guaranteed" to his signature, section 3–416(1) provides:

> "Payment guaranteed" or equivalent words added to a signature mean that the signer engages that if the instrument is not paid when due he will pay it according to its tenor without resort by the holder to any other party.

Under 3–416(5) an indorser who adds "payment guaranteed" to his signature relinquishes any right to require presentment and notice of dishonor.[105] Thus in the words of the Comment to 3–416, "the liability of the indorser becomes indistinguishable from that of a co-maker." The words "collection guaranteed" added to the signature of a party make a substantial change in the signer's liability. Section 3–416(2) provides that such words forestall liability until the holder has a judgment and unsatisfied execution against the principal debtor.[106] Note, however, that 3–416(2) says the holder satisfies the requirements of 3–416(2) if he shows that proceeding to judgment and execution would be a useless act.

A surety who has signed an instrument is like other parties in that he is generally liable in the capacity in which he signed. Unlike

---

not appear on the instrument. See note 120 infra.

**102.** See text accompanying Sections 13–7 through 13–11 supra.

**103.** See Section 13–16 infra (§ 3–606).

**104.** To obtain a complete picture of the rights of guarantors one must consult section 3–415 as well as section 3–416. Comment 1 to section 3–415 points out that accommodation parties and guarantors are both sureties on the instrument. Presumably sections 3–415(3) and 3–415(5) apply to both accommodation parties and guarantors. Similarly section 3–415(4) defines one form of signature which presumptively will give the signer status as an accommodation party.

**105.** Section 3–416(5) reads:

When words of guaranty are used presentment, notice of dishonor and protest are not necessary to charge the user.

**106.** Section 3–416(2) reads:

"Collection guaranteed" or equivalent words added to a signature mean that the signer engages that if the instrument is not paid when due he will pay it according to its tenor, but only after the holder has reduced his claim against the maker or acceptor to judgment and execution has been returned unsatisfied, or after the maker or acceptor has become insolvent or it is otherwise apparent that it is useless to proceed against him.

other parties the surety may have special defenses, for: (*1*) he is not liable to the party accommodated (3-415(5)) (even if his contract on the instrument would normally make him liable to such person); (*2*) he may be discharged if the holder "releases or agrees not to sue" the party accommodated or extends the time for payment or otherwise "suspends" the right to enforce his obligation against the party accommodated, and (*3*) he may be discharged if the holder "unjustifiably impairs any collateral for the instrument" (for example, fails to perfect a security interest).

A difficult threshold problem that one must face before he considers the surety's defenses is whether the surety will be permitted to prove his suretyship status by parol evidence against the party who is suing him. We now turn to that problem.

### § 13-13  Accommodation Parties—Establishing Suretyship Status— Form of Signature and Parol Evidence, 3-415(3), 3-415(4), 3-416

Three separate issues arise:

(*1*) What symbols on the instrument are sufficient to put one on notice that a signer is an accommodation party?

(*2*) Assuming that the symbols are insufficient to put one on notice, against what plaintiff may a defendant prove his suretyship status by parol evidence and so acquire the benefit of the suretyship defenses?

(*3*) What parol evidence is sufficient to establish suretyship status?

The Code does not answer the first question explicitly. The position of the surety's signature on the instrument and the words he adds to his signature are the strongest indicators of his status. A surety who accommodates another party by signing as an indorser will usually disclose his surety status merely by the relative position of his name on the instrument. Section 3-415(4) of the Code says, "An indorsement which shows that it is not in the chain of title is notice of its accommodation character." Normally one indorses an instrument in order to negotiate it to his transferee.[107] Section 3-415(4) establishes a presumption that an indorsement which shows that it is not made for the purpose of transfer is made as an accommodation for another party. To see how this provision works in the typical case, assume that Rocky has agreed to become an accommodation party for Bullwinkle's note which is payable to Boris. Bullwinkle executes the note as maker with Boris as payee. Rocky indorses the note prior to its delivery to Boris. When Boris negotiates the note to Natasha she has notice under section 3-415(4) that Rocky is an accommodation party. Rocky's signature is outside the chain of title, because it appears above that of the payee

107. See text accompanying notes 48–49 supra (§ 3–202).

who would normally be the first indorser.[108]   Because an indorsement out of the chain shows accommodation status without the need for any words, signature as an indorser is a desirable way for the accommodation party to sign the instrument.

The Code provides some magic words to designate the surety who enters into a contract of guarantee.   Section 3–416 provides that the party who adds "payment guaranteed," "collection guaranteed," or equivalent words to his signature incurs the obligation of a guarantor as defined in that section.[109]   As we have indicated above, "payment guaranteed" will not normally change an accommodation party's contract except to deprive an accommodation indorser of the right to demand presentment, dishonor, *etc.*, as conditions to his liability.    However, "collection guaranteed" will substantially alter a co-maker or indorser's contract.[110]

Presumably then nearly every defendant who is an accommodation party reveals his status by indorsing out of the chain, or by using the words "payment guaranteed" or the like, or by the addition of the title "surety or accommodation party" after his name. The addition of such words to his signature or the position of his name gives any taker notice, and any holder in due course of such an instrument would have notice.

Against what plaintiffs may a defendant prove his suretyship status by parol evidence?   Section 3–415(3) reads:

> As against a holder in due course and without notice of the accommodation oral proof of the accommodation is not admissible to give the accommodation party the benefit of discharges dependent on his character as such.   In other cases the accommodation character may be shown by oral proof.

The only person who can forestall the defendant's use of parol evidence to prove his accommodation status is a holder in due course who takes *without notice* of the accommodation (and presumably his transferees (3–201)).   In all other cases the subsection permits proof of the status by "oral proof."   Why the draftsmen used the adjective "oral" instead of "parol" is unclear.   Presumably written proof extrinsic to the instrument can also be introduced to prove the accommodation status.

What kind of parol evidence is sufficient to prove accommodation status?   According to 3–415(1) the accommodation party must

108.  See Factors & Note Buyers, Inc. v. Green Lane, Inc., 102 N.J.Super. 43, 245 A.2d 223, 5 UCC Rep.Serv. 611 (Law Div.1968) (corporation's secretary who indorsed note above indorsement of payee was liable as accommodation indorser).

109.  Section 3–416(3) provides, "Words of guaranty which do not otherwise

specify guarantee payment."   See Sadler v. Kay, 120 Ga.App. 758, 172 S.E. 2d 202, 7 UCC Rep.Serv. 322 (1969) (party who added "guarantor" to his signature was liable to holder without resort to any other party).

110.  See text accompanying note 105 supra.

show that he signed the instrument for the "purpose of lending his name to another party to it." Since receipt of proceeds from the instrument or other direct benefit would generally be inconsistent with accommodation status, courts focus on that aspect of the transaction.[111] Thus if father and son sign a note for the purchase of a truck and both use it in a partnership business, the father is not simply "lending his name" to the son but is getting a more direct benefit from the truck and is not an accommodation party.[112]

An examination of one or two cases fleshes out our analysis. In Riegler v. Riegler,[113] husband and wife both signed as makers of a note and were subsequently divorced. When the payee secured judgment against both parties the husband sued his ex-wife for contribution. The wife argued that she only signed as an accommodation party and was not liable under 3–415(5). The trial court found for the husband, because the wife had received benefits from the proceeds of the note. On appeal, the Arkansas Supreme Court affirmed on the basis of the wife's testimony that the proceeds of the note were used to build a house in which she had a half interest. MacArthur v. Cannon [114] also involved a dispute between two makers. In that case two corporate officers, who owned one hundred percent of the stock of a corporation, executed a note and deposited the proceeds in the corporation's account to pay corporate debts. After one maker paid the note, he sued the other for contribution. The defendant argued that as an accommodation maker he was not liable to the party accommodated. The trial court found that the defendant's signature was not required for plaintiff to obtain the loan, that the proceeds were used to pay corporate debts including a debt due the plaintiff, and concluded that defendant was not an accommodation maker. On appeal the Connecticut appellate court affirmed. It is unclear whether the appellate court focused on the trial court's finding that plaintiff could have obtained the loan without defendant's signature or applied the "benefit of proceeds" test broadly to include the benefits which a fifty-one percent shareholder and corporate officer receives when the proceeds of an instrument are deposited in the corporate account. In any event the case indicates the necessity for a corporate officer or

---

111. See, e. g., Ridings v. Motor Vessel "Effort," 387 F.2d 888, 4 UCC Rep. Serv. 899 (2d Cir. 1968); Riegler v. Riegler, 244 Ark. 483, 426 S.W.2d 789, 5 UCC Rep.Serv. 150 (1968); Seaboard Finance Co. v. Dorman, 4 Conn.Cir. 154, 227 A.2d 441, 4 UCC Rep.Serv. 86 (1966); MacArthur v. Cannon, 4 Conn.Cir. 208, 229 A.2d 372, 4 UCC Rep.Serv. 199 (1967); James Talcott, Inc. v. Fred Ratowsky Ass'n, Inc., 2 UCC Rep.Serv. 1134 (Pa.C.P.1965); Bank of America Nat'l Trust & Sav. Ass'n v. Superior Ct. of San Diego City, 4 Cal.App.3d 435, 84 Cal.Rptr. 421, 7 UCC Rep.Serv. 713 (4th Dist. 1970) (dictum).

112. Comment 2 to 3–415 points out that the surety may undertake his obligation gratuitously or for compensation without affecting his status as a surety.

113. 244 Ark. 483, 426 S.W.2d 789, 5 UCC Rep.Serv. 150 (1968).

114. 4 Conn.Cir. 208, 229 A.2d 372, 4 UCC Rep.Serv. 199 (1967).

shareholder clearly to indicate his status when he signs an instrument as an accommodation party.[115]

## § 13–14  Accommodation Parties—Suretyship Defenses, 3–606 and Beyond

For reasons mysterious to one of your authors, sureties have been ancient favorites of the courts.  Thus, if the creditor and debtor agreed to any modification in their agreement, the courts would often discharge the surety.  The policy behind such discharges is easy to see in the starkest cases: assume that debtor pays creditor a small sum under the table in return for debtor's release from his obligation on a note.  Creditor then sues the surety, an accommodation maker on the note.  Curbstone equity requires us to discharge the surety in such a case.  But what if there is no collusion and the creditor in good faith makes a binding agreement with debtor to give debtor additional time to pay?  Although 3–606 gives the creditor a way to extend time without releasing the surety (see Section 13–15 below), the general rule remains: a binding extension of time discharges the surety.  One justification for discharge is that *any* such extension increases the surety's risk.  In theory the surety calculated and undertook the probability of debtor default on the original term, but did not undertake the supposedly greater probability of default over a longer period.[116] A related justification for the general rule is that any release or binding extension diminishes the surety's rights by depriving him of subrogation to the creditor's cause of action against the debtor; when creditor releases the debtor, he destroys the creditor's right to sue on the instrument, the right to which the surety hoped to be subrogated.[117]

When one considers that the surety has a right of reimbursement against the debtor (which does not depend upon the creditor's rights against the debtor) and that there is no empirical evidence that most or even many good faith extensions or other modifications in fact increase the risk of nonpayment, one may question the wisdom of the general rule which discharges the surety.  Perhaps doubts about its wisdom prompted the draftsmen to give the creditor an easy way (Section 13–15 below) to modify his contract without releasing the surety.

115.  In *MacArthur*, the court, without citation of authority, observed, "The burden of establishing the defendant's special defense rested upon him."

Id.  A similar statement was made by the Arkansas Supreme Court in *Riegler* where the court cited *MacArthur* and a pre-Code case decided in 1916. Section 3–415(3) does not impose any special burden of proof upon a party claiming accommodation status. Perhaps the *MacArthur* and *Riegler* courts simply meant to say that a party claiming accommodation status must substantiate that claim by a preponderance of the evidence.  The imposition of a higher standard of proof does not find support in the Code. See § 3–307.

116.  See L. Simpson, Handbook on the Law of Suretyship § 73 at 354 (1950); Peters, Suretyship Under Article 3 of the Uniform Commercial Code, 77 Yale L.J. 833, 868–69 (1968).

117.  See L. Simpson, Handbook on the Law of Suretyship § 73 at 352–53 (1950).

At the outset one should understand that an accommodation party's failure to receive dollars in his pocket from the creditor is not a defense. Time and again sureties respond to a holder's suit by arguing, "I am a surety and I did not receive consideration for my contract." This is a losing argument.[118] Section 3–415(2) specifically provides that the surety is liable to a taker (and *a fortiori*, holders and holders in due course) when the instrument is taken for value before it is due.[119] Regardless whether the surety signs gratuitously or receives compensation, his obligation is supported by the consideration which moves from the creditor to the principal debtor.[120]

What, then, will constitute a defense? Although modifications of the debt agreement which arguably discharge the surety can take infinite forms, we devote most of the following discussion to two situations of pre-eminent concern to lawyers: (*1*) extension of time for payment and (*2*) impairment of collateral. Section 3–606(1) provides:

> The holder discharges any party to the instrument to the extent that without such party's consent the holder
>
> (a) without express reservation of rights releases or agrees not to sue any person against whom the party has to the knowledge of the holder a right of recourse or agrees to suspend the right to enforce against such person the instrument or collateral or otherwise discharges such person, except that failure or delay in effecting any required presentment, protest or notice of dishonor with respect to any such person does not discharge any party as to whom presentment, protest or notice of dishonor is effective or unnecessary; or
>
> (b) unjustifiably impairs any collateral for the instrument given by or on behalf of the party or any person against whom he has a right of recourse.

---

**118.** On a surety's defense of lack of consideration rejected, see Fairfield County Trust Co. v. Steinbrecher, 5 Conn.Cir. 405, 255 A.2d 144, 6 UCC Rep.Serv. 682 (1968); Woodhouse, Drake & Carey, Ltd. v. Anderson, 7 UCC Rep.Serv. 214 (N.Y.Sup.Ct. 1970); Berger v. Norad Enterprises, Inc., 6 UCC Rep.Serv. 161 (N.Y.Sup. Ct.1969); First Nat'l City Bank v. Valentine, 61 Misc.2d 554, 306 N.Y.S.2d 227, 7 UCC Rep.Serv. 53 (Sup.Ct.1969); Abby Financial Corp. v. Weydig Auto Supplies Unlimited, Inc., 4 UCC Rep. Serv. 858 (N.Y.Sup.Ct.1967); Shulman v. Steve Lynn, Inc., 2 UCC Rep.Serv. 1046 (N.Y.Sup.Ct.1965).

One should distinguish the argument, "I am a surety and my principal did not receive any consideration." See Section 13–17 infra (surety's inability to assert principal obligor's defenses).

**119.** See Franklin Nat'l Bank v. Eurez Const. Corp., 60 Misc.2d 499, 301 N. Y.S.2d 845, 6 UCC Rep.Serv. 634 (Sup. Ct.1969) (accommodation indorser who did not receive consideration liable to plaintiff bank who failed to qualify as a holder because it lacked indorsement of depositor); Peters, Suretyship Under Article 3 of the Uniform Commercial Code, 77 Yale L.J. 833, 844–48 (1968).

**120.** See § 3–415, Comment 2; L. Simpson, Handbook on the Law of Suretyship § 26 at 75 (1950).

Section 3–606(1) (a) specifies changes in the legal relationship between debtor and creditor that discharge the surety. When, without the surety's consent the holder "releases or agrees not to sue . . . or agrees to suspend the right to enforce . . . the instrument or collateral . . . or otherwise discharges . . ." the principal debtor, the surety is discharged. Note that a surety may claim discharge under 3–606 even though the principal debtor is not a party to the instrument.[121] The subsection does not expressly state that if the creditor grants an extension, the surety is discharged, but the draftsmen intended that result.[122] The surety, then, can claim discharge under 3–606 when, without his consent and without an "express reservation of rights," the creditor and debtor enter into a binding agreement to extend time for payment.

Under section 3–606(1) (b) the surety is also discharged when, without his consent, the creditor "unjustifiably impairs any collateral for the instrument." [123] Often the creditor on a guaranteed obligation will have two kinds of back-up for the debtor's promise, the surety's promise and a security interest in the debtor's collateral. If the creditor handles the collateral carelessly so that its value is

121.  Comment 1 to Section 3–606 says:

> The suretyship defenses here provided are not limited to parties who are "secondarily liable" but are available to any party who is in the position of a surety, having a right of recourse either on the instrument or dehors it, including an accommodation maker or acceptor known to the holder to be so.

When two makers sign a note but neither is an accommodation party, and the holder extends time for one or releases him, what result under section 3–606? On its face, section 3–606 seems to discharge the other co-maker to the extent of half his liability, even though such co-maker is not an accommodation party. This is so because 3–606 "discharges any party to the instrument *to the extent that* without such party's consent the holder . . . releases or agrees not to sue any person against whom the party has to the knowledge of the holder a right of recourse . . . ." If the parties were co-makers to a note and neither was an accommodation party, one co-maker would have a right of recourse by way of contribution against the other party for one-half the note. Thus even though the co-maker is not an accommodation party, he would be discharged to the extent of one-half by 3–606(1) (a). If the draftsmen intended 3–606 to apply only to accommodation parties, they did not say so. The comment quoted above which

speaks of the holder's knowledge of the accommodation status of a maker or acceptor is equally ambiguous. It could mean that only accommodation makers can take the benefit of 3–606. On the other hand it might mean that accommodation makers would have the benefit of 3–606 and so be fully discharged but nonaccommodation makers would be discharged only to the extent of their right to contribution, i. e., one of the two co-makers would be discharged as to only one-half the entire liability on the note.

122.  In his analysis of this section for the New York Law Revision Commission Professor Willcox states, "Covenants to 'suspend the right to enforce' the instrument or collateral would be simply binding contracts to extend time." 2 N.Y. State Law Revision Comm'n, 1955 Report 1177 (1955). This analysis is confirmed by Comment 4 to 3–606 which says:

> This section retains the right of the holder to release one party, or to postpone his time of payment, while expressly reserving rights against others.

123.  Although section 3–606(1) (b) does not contain an explicit requirement that the holder have knowledge of the surety's existence, the adverb "unjustifiably" and the standard of care (reasonableness) probably mean that knowledge is required.

diminished or acts in a way which makes the collateral unavailable to the surety (for example, fails to perfect his security interest), then the surety may claim discharge under 3–606(1)(b). Comment 5 to 3–606 explains that the creditor's conduct in respect to the collateral is measured by the standard of 9–207 (that is, reasonable care).[124] In Shaffer v. Davidson,[125] the principal debtor gave the creditor a chattel mortgage on his automobile. The debtor sold the car to a third party and disappeared. When the creditor sued, the accommodation maker argued that the creditor's failure to perfect the security interest impaired the collateral and discharged her. The trial court set off the value of the auto against the face amount of the note, accrued interest and attorney's fees. On appeal, the creditor argued that "impairment of collateral" in 3–606(1)(b) refers only to diminishment of the value of the physical property subject to the security interest and not to impairment of the security interest itself. The Wyoming Supreme Court rejected his argument and held that the accommodation maker was discharged by the payee's failure to perfect.[126] The court also concluded that since the value of the auto was equal to the principal amount of the debt, the award of interest and attorney's fees was improper.[127]

124. Section 9–207(1) reads as follows:

A secured party must use reasonable care in the custody and preservation of collateral in his possession. In the case of an instrument or chattel paper reasonable care includes taking necessary steps to preserve rights against prior parties unless otherwise agreed.

125. 445 P.2d 13, 5 UCC Rep.Serv. 772 (Wyo.1968); accord, Security Nat'l Bank v. Temarantz, 6 UCC Rep.Serv. 157 (N.Y.Sup.Ct.1969) (accommodation party stated meritorious defense against motion for summary judgment when he claimed impairment of collateral because of plaintiff's failure to perfect security interest). Cf. Buffington v. Nalley Discount Co., 117 Ga.App. 820, 162 S.E.2d 212, 5 UCC Rep.Serv. 624 (1968) (summary judgment against accommodation party affirmed when defendant failed to allege that substitution of one auto for another increased his risk).

126. The court concluded that the definition of collateral in section 9–105 did not apply in Article Three, but it reached the same result by using the common meaning of the word. Shaffer v. Davidson, 445 P.2d 13, 5 UCC Rep.Serv. 772, 775 (Wyo.1968). Several states substitute the word "security" for "collateral" in section 3–601(1)(d), but the Permanent Editori-

al Board for the UCC has rejected this deviation from the uniform statute.

The Board said:

The word should be "collateral." These states failed to observe the difference between the 1956 Recommendations and the 1958 Official Text at this point. Moreover, the word "collateral" is precisely defined in Section 9–105, whereas the word "security" as used is not.

Permanent Editorial Board for the Uniform Commercial Code, Report No. 2 at 68–69 (1965).

127. The court implies that if the value of the collateral had been less than the amount of the debt then the creditor's impairment would only partially discharge the surety. Shaffer v. Davidson, 445 P.2d 13, 5 UCC Rep. Serv. 772, 778 (Wyo.1968); accord, Still v. Citizens Bank, 6 UCC Rep. Serv. 813 (Okla.App.1969) (accommodation party not discharged by creditor's release of valueless second mortgage). See also Buffington v. Nalley Discount Co., 117 Ga.App. 820, 162 S.E.2d 212, 5 UCC Rep.Serv. 624 (1968) (summary judgment for plaintiff affirmed when accommodation party failed to allege that substitution of collateral increased his risk).

Authority for partial discharge of the surety is found in the introductory clause of 3–606(1) which says, "The

## § 13–15  Accommodation Parties—Effect of Surety's Consent or Creditor's Reservation of Rights, 3–606(1), 3–606(2)

The creditor can forestall a surety's claim of discharge under 3–606 in either of two ways.  First, he may procure the surety's express or implied consent to the modification in the relationship with the debtor.  Second, by adding a sentence to the modification agreement to "expressly reserve" his rights against surety, he bars a discharge.  According to Comment 2 to 3–606 the consent may take many forms and come at any time:

> Consent may be given in advance, and is commonly incorporated in the instrument; or it may be given afterward. It requires no consideration, and operates as a waiver of the consenting party's right to claim his own discharge.

An express statement of consent incorporated in the instrument is effective against the surety.[128]  However, under 3–118(f) a consent is presumed to be for "a single extension for not longer than the original period, [unless 'otherwise specified']." [129]  The surety's consent may also take the form of conduct which shows assent to the creditor's action.  For example, in London Leasing Corp. v. Interfina, Inc.,[130] the president of the defendant corporation executed a corporate note and personally indorsed it.  Subsequently, the president, acting solely in his corporate capacity, sought, negotiated, and signed an agreement to extend the time for payment.  When the payee sued the corporate maker and the accommodation indorser, the indorser argued that the extension discharged him under 3–606(1)(a).  Citing pre-Code cases, the court held that the indorser's par-

---

holder discharges any party to the instrument *to the extent that.  . . ."* (emphasis added); § 3–606, Comment 2 (1952 Official Draft); 2 N.Y. State Law Revision Comm'n, 1955 Report 1189–90 (1955).

**128.**  See Abby Financial Corp. v. Weydig Auto Supplies Unlimited, Inc., 4 UCC Rep.Serv. 858 (N.Y.Sup.Ct.1967) (accommodation indorser not discharged by extension of time when note contained clause permitting extension without notice or consent); Rauch v. First Nat'l Bank, 244 Ark. 941, 428 S.W.2d 89, 5 UCC Rep.Serv. 379 (1968) (release of one guarantor did not discharge the other guarantor when agreement contained clause consenting to release).

**129.**  Section 3–118(f) reads:

Unless otherwise specified consent to extension authorizes a single exten-

sion for not longer than the original period.  A consent to extension, expressed in the instrument, is binding on secondary parties and accommodation makers.  A holder may not exercise his option to extend an instrument over the objection of a maker or acceptor or other party who in accordance with Section 3–604 tenders full payment when the instrument is due.

**130.**  53 Misc.2d 657, 279 N.Y.S.2d 209, 4 UCC Rep.Serv. 206 (Sup.Ct.1967); accord, A. J. Armstrong, Inc. v. Janburt Embroidery Corp., 97 N.J.Super. 246, 234 A.2d 737, 4 UCC Rep.Serv. 748 (Law Div.1967) (shareholders who signed as accommodation indorsers and participated in negotiations for extension agreement and signed agreement consented to extension).

ticipation in obtaining the extension constituted consent to the extension:

> As a matter of fact he applied for, negotiated, signed in his corporate capacity and received the agreements extending the time for payment. While mere knowledge and acquiescence is not, in and of itself, sufficient to prevent discharge, the defendant's conduct here far exceeded these limits and under the special circumstances here presented, constituted consent.[131]

The individual indorser was not discharged.

If the creditor wishes to release the debtor or grant him an extension of time to make payments, but cannot obtain the surety's consent to such action, he can preserve his rights against the surety by expressly reserving them.[132]   Section 3–606(2) says:

> By express reservation of rights against a party with a right of recourse the holder preserves
>
> (a) all his rights against such party as of the time when the instrument was originally due; and
>
> (b) the right of the party to pay the instrument as of that time; and
>
> (c) all rights of such party to recourse against others.

To rationalize the reservation rule, one can say that the surety suffers no injury from the creditor's action because the surety can immediately pay the instrument and exercise his right of recourse against the principal debtor.[133]   Of course, the surety cannot exercise his theoretical option to pay and sue if he does not know that the creditor has released or granted the debtor an extension of time for payment and expressly reserved his rights.  Note that 3–606 does not require the creditor to notify the surety of the modification.[134]

The most satisfactory justification for permitting unconsented good faith modifications which do not in fact increase the surety's

---

131. London Leasing Corp. v. Interfina, Inc., 53 Misc.2d 657, 660–661, 279 N.Y.S.2d 209, 213, 4 UCC Rep.Serv. 206, 209 (Sup.Ct.1967).

132. Section 3–606(1)(b) does not authorize the creditor to reserve his rights when he impairs the collateral.

133. See § 3–606(2); L. Simpson, Handbook on the Law of Suretyship § 64 at 302–303 (1950). For a criticism of this alternative as potentially misleading to the principal obligor, see 2 N.Y. State Law Revision Comm'n, 1955 Report 1189 (1955).

134. Section 3–606(3) 1952 Official Text reads as follows:

> An express reservation of rights is not effective as such as against any party whom the holder does not use due diligence to notify within ten days after the reservation.

The section was deleted from the 1958 Official Text in response to criticism expressed before the New York Law Revision Commission. Permanent Editorial Board for the Uniform Commercial Code, 1956 Recommendations 129 (1956). Accordingly, the creditor need not notify the surety when he expressly reserves his rights against him. Parnes v. Celia's, Inc., 99 N.J.

risk is simply that they do not adversely affect the surety, and at least nine times out of ten he would consent anyway.[135]

### § 13–16	Accommodation Parties—Relationship Between Surety and Principal, Subrogation, Reimbursement and 3–415(5)

The legal obligations between the surety and the debtor are not complex.  Since the surety must pay only if the debtor is unable to do so, it is no surprise that the debtor, having paid, has no right to make the surety share his cost even if both are co-makers on a note.  It also follows from the nature of the surety's undertaking that he is entitled to recover from the debtor any payment he is called on to make to the creditor.  If a friend agrees to sign another's note and is ultimately made to pay that note to the creditor, curbstone equity tells us that he should have a cause of action against the person who actually benefited from the creditor's loan.  The surety's traditional rights of recovery [136] are two: subrogation and reimbursement.  The surety's right of subrogation is his equitable right to assert the rights of the creditor against the debtor.[137]  In common parlance the surety upon payment "stands in the shoes"

Super. 179, 4 UCC Rep.Serv. 1159 (N.J. App.Div.1968).  The last sentence in Comment 4 to 3–606 (1962 version) refers to the now departed 1952 notice requirement.

135.  The surety has no basis for complaint against a holder in due course who took the instrument without notice that a prior holder performed an act which would discharge the surety under 3–606.  Section 3–602 provides:

No discharge of any party provided by this Article is effective against a subsequent holder in due course unless he has notice thereof when he takes the instrument.

See Rushton v. U. M. & M. Credit Corp., 245 Ark. 703, 434 S.W.2d 81, 5 UCC Rep.Serv. 1078 (1968) (accommodation party liable to holder in due course despite fact that prior party failed to perfect security interest).

136.  Under general suretyship law the surety has the right prior to payment to compel the principal obligor to pay the creditor and thereby exonerate the surety.  See L. Simpson, Handbook on the Law of Suretyship § 46 (1950).

Restatement of Security § 112 (1941) provides:

Where the surety is under an obligation to the creditor which has matured and which he has undertaken

with the consent of the principal, and the surety, if he performed would be entitled to reimbursement from the principal, the surety has the right to exoneration.

Comment: a.  The principal owes the surety a duty to perform as soon as the performance is due.  It is inequitable for the surety to be compelled to suffer the inconvenience and temporary loss which a payment by him will entail if the principal can satisfy the obligation.  The surety is entitled to equitable relief without alleging any particular reason for fearing that he will not be reimbursed in the event of payment.  The right to such equitable relief is called the right of exoneration.

Since the surety's right of "recourse" under section 3–415(5) only arises after he has paid the instrument, it is clear that the Article Three surety has no right of exoneration on the instrument.  Whether he retains an independent right of exoneration remains to be seen.

137.  See L. Simpson, Handbook on the Law of Suretyship § 47 (1950).  Comment 5 to section 3–415 states:

Under ordinary principles of suretyship the accommodation party who pays is subrogated to the rights of the holder paid, and should have his recourse on the instrument.

of the creditor. That is to say, the surety can assert the rights that the creditor had against the debtor. If, for example, a surety co-maker paid a note in full, he would be "subrogated" to the holder's right to sue his co-maker (debtor) on the note. The surety's right of "reimbursement" does not, however, depend upon the rights of the creditor; rather it rests upon the debtor's express or implied promise to indemnify the surety or upon grounds of unjust enrichment.[138]

Section 3-415(5) recognizes the surety's right of subrogation as follows:

> An accommodation party is not liable to the party accommodated, and if he pays the instrument has a right of recourse on the instrument against such party.

"Recourse on the instrument" means, in the words of Comment 5, that the "accommodation party who pays is subrogated to the rights of the holder paid . . . ."[139] Presumably the surety has the creditor's rights not only on the instrument but also on the underlying obligation. One can arrive at that conclusion either by an expansive reading of the words "recourse on the instrument" or by the application of general suretyship rules to the case under section 1-103.

To this point we have considered only the rights of the surety against his principal after the surety has paid the principal's debt. Occasionally it will be important that the surety has no direct liability to the principal debtor. Subsection five of 3-415 puts it as follows: "An accommodation party is not liable to the party accommodated . . . ." Indeed, a surety has no such liability even though he signs in the capacity which would apparently make him liable to the principal debtor. For example, in Gibbs Oil Co. v. Collentro & Collentro, Inc.,[140] the payee of a promissory note sought to recover from one who had indorsed the note. The defendant had signed as an accommodation indorser to enable the payee to discount the note. The court found that the indorser was not liable to his principal. (For a consideration of the problems of proving suretyship by parol evidence in circumstances in which the relationship of the parties on the instrument would seem to indicate that

138. See L. Simpson, Handbook on the Law of Suretyship, § 48 (1950).

139. See Simpson v. Bilderbeck, Inc., 76 N.M. 667, 417 P.2d 803, 3 UCC Rep. Serv. 737 (1966) (accommodation maker who paid note has right of recourse against debtor).

In light of the "on the instrument" language in 3-415(5) and Comment 5 thereto, one might conclude that reimbursement is unavailable as a remedy for the Article Three surety. However, Professor Peters concludes that the Code did not intend to overturn the pre-Code law allowing a

surety on a negotiable instrument to obtain reimbursement from his principal. Peters, Suretyship Under Article 3 of the Uniform Commercial Code, 77 Yale L.J. 833, 869 n. 151 (1968).

140. 356 Mass. 725, 252 N.E.2d 217, 6 UCC Rep.Serv. 1237 (1969); accord, United Refrigerator Co. v. Applebaum, 410 Pa. 210, 189 A.2d 253, 1 UCC Rep. Serv. 295 (1963) (defendants' allegation that they signed as accommodation parties for plaintiff's benefit stated defense sufficient to deny motion for summary judgment).

the surety is liable to the principal obligor, see the discussion in Section 13–13 above).

## § 13–17  Accommodation Parties—Right of Surety to Assert Principal's Defenses

Suretyship law on the right of a surety to assert defenses of the principal debtor against the creditor has always been opaque, and Article Three renders the law even less clear than it was. Consider the following situation: Father, as an accommodation maker, co-signs little Johnny's note and the two give the note to a car dealer in partial payment for Johnny's new car. If Johnny takes bankruptcy or asserts his infancy, and the car dealer sues Father, what outcome? If the car turns out to be a lemon, and Johnny fails to pay because the car does not work properly, what outcome when the dealer sues Father? If the facts are further complicated because the car dealer transfers the note to bank who is a holder in due course, what outcome? To reduce the problems to manageable size we find it useful first to divide the questions according to the kinds of defenses which the accommodation party wishes to raise and then to examine the problems unique to a lawsuit against one who is an accommodation party on an instrument governed by Article Three.

Common sense and common business understanding tell us that there are certain defenses of the principal (Johnny) which the accommodation party cannot and should not be permitted to raise. In our example, these are the defenses of bankruptcy [141] and incapacity.[142] Whether or not it was made explicit in the negotiation for the car, the father should have realized that he was signing the note to provide a solvent adult back-up in case Johnny took bankruptcy or, more likely, claimed that the contract could not be enforced against him because of his infancy. Having signed with that understanding, the accommodation party should not be permitted to raise the defense of infancy or bankruptcy even though those defenses might be perfectly valid ones in the hands of the principal debtor, Johnny. Except for the case in which a minor has in fact disaffirmed and returned the consideration, it appears that an accommodation party cannot raise either incapacity or bankruptcy as a defense.[143]

On the far side of the continuum are defenses of the principal which the surety has been traditionally and universally entitled to

---

141.  See L. Simpson, Handbook on the Law of Suretyship § 67 at 308–311 (1950); Bankruptcy Act § 16, 11 U.S. C.A. § 34 (1970). The surety may assert the creditor's claims against the debtor in a bankruptcy proceeding. Bankruptcy Act § 57(i), 11 U.S.C.A. § 93(i) (1970).

142.  See L. Simpson, Handbook on the Law of Suretyship § 59 at 286–87 (1950).

143.  See McKee v. Harwood Automotive Company, 204 Ind. 233, 183 N.E. 646 (1932), cited in L. Simpson, Handbook of the Law of Suretyship § 59 at 289 (1950); Restatement of Security § 125 (1941).

raise: failure of consideration [144] (the promised car was never delivered to Johnny) and other similar contractual defenses which would totally free the principal debtor from his obligation.[145] Since the surety is nothing more than a back-up for the principal debtor, his liability should be no greater than the contractual liability of his principal.

Less certain under suretyship law are those cases in which the principal debtor has some obligation to pay but has a counterclaim or setoff. Assume for example that the car proved to be defective to the tune of $500, but that Johnny nevertheless accepted it and had it repaired. In that case he would have had a warranty claim for $500 against the seller and could himself have set that off in the seller's suit for the price. Can Father, the accommodation party, do so as well? Under pre-Code law the courts split. Some permitted him to do so; others did not.[146] We are persuaded by the minority which permitted the father to raise such defenses, but we see nothing in the Code which changes prior law in this respect.

Because the surety in which we are interested is by hypothesis an accommodation party on a negotiable instrument, two additional complications arise. First, what if the plaintiff is a holder in due course? If the plaintiff is a holder in due course, we believe that the accommodation party (even if the instrument reveals that he is an accommodation party) has no greater right to raise defenses than the principal debtor would have.[147] If, therefore, the defense which the accommodation party wishes to assert is a personal defense under 3–305, it is cut off and he loses to the holder in due course. If, on the other hand, the defense is a real defense under 3–305, he should be permitted to raise it.[148]

---

144. See L. Simpson, Handbook of the Law of Suretyship § 60 at 291 (1950); Restatement of Security § 126 (1941).

145. The defenses of the principal might take several forms. On forgery of the principal's signature, see L. Simpson, Handbook of the Law of Suretyship § 54 at 271–73 (1950). On fraud or duress practiced on the principal, see id. at § 56 at 278–83; Restatement of Security § 118 (1941).

146. See L. Simpson, Handbook of the Law of Suretyship § 70 at 319–26 (1950).

147. Of course purported defenses of the *principal* which would be ineffective in the principal's hands will also be ineffective in the surety's hands. Accordingly, individuals who sign as sureties for corporations cannot raise the defense of usury in states where usury is not a defense available to a corporation. See, e. g., Raby v. Com-

mercial Banking Corp., 208 Pa.Super. 52, 220 A.2d 659, 3 UCC Rep.Serv. 489 (1966); E'Town Shopping Center, Inc. v. Lexington Fin. Co., 436 S.W.2d 267, 6 UCC Rep.Serv. 159 (Ky.App.1969); Reynolds v. Service Loan & Fin. Co., 116 Ga.App. 740, 158 S.E.2d 309, 4 UCC Rep.Serv. 1068 (1967); A. J. Armstrong, Inc. v. Janburt Embroidery Corp., 97 N.J.Super. 246, 234 A.2d 737, 4 UCC Rep.Serv. 748 (Law Div. 1967). But see Meadow Brook Nat'l Bank v. Recile, 302 F.Supp. 62, 78–80 (E.D. La.1969) (non-Code case in which the court disapproves of the policy and holds for surety).

148. Section 3–305(2) says a holder in due course takes free from:

all defenses of any party to the instrument with whom the holder has not dealt except

(a) infancy, to the extent that it is a defense to a simple contract; and

(b) such other incapacity, or duress, or illegality of the transaction, as

More puzzling is the problem which the plaintiff-holder may pose (whether or not he is a holder in due course) by pointing to the last sentence in 3–306(d) and arguing that an accommodation party cannot raise *any* defenses of the party accommodated (so-called *jus tertii*). That sentence reads in full as follows:

> The claim of any third person to the instrument is not otherwise available as a defense to any party liable thereon unless the third party himself defends the action for such party.

Of course, if our accommodation party impleads or otherwise somehow brings the principal debtor into the lawsuit, the problem disappears.[149] But assume that the principal debtor is dead or not subject to suit. Does the quoted sentence reverse all of the well settled doctrines which plainly authorize the surety to raise certain of his principal's defenses? We do not believe that the draftsmen intended this. Perhaps the draftsmen did not have accommodation parties in mind when they drafted 3–306(d).[150] Better yet, we might

renders the obligation of the party a nullity; and

(c) such misrepresentation as has induced the party to sign the instrument with neither knowledge nor reasonable opportunity to obtain knowledge of its character or its essential terms; and

(d) discharge in insolvency proceedings; and

(e) any other discharge of which the holder has notice when he takes the instrument.

There are two lines of attack open to a surety who wishes to assert a personal defense of the principal against one that claims the protection of section 3–305(2). First, he may argue that the plaintiff does not qualify as a holder in due course because he had notice of a defense when he took the instrument. §§ 3–302, 3–304. However, notice that a party signing the instrument in accommodation status does not prevent one from becoming a holder in due course. § 3–304(4) (c). Secondly, the surety might argue that plaintiff does not come under the protective umbrella of section 3–305(2), because the wrong-doer has "dealt with" the surety. Accordingly, an "innocent" holder in due course holds the instrument free from the personal defenses of the principal whether they are asserted by the principal or the surety. On the other hand, one who acts improperly either before or after taking the instrument is subject to defenses raised by the surety on be-

half of the principal. This result is consistent with the effect given to conduct of the holder which discharges the surety under 3–606. See text accompanying note 140 supra (§ 3–602).

**149.** The Code provides an alternative to the joinder provisions of the rules of civil procedure. Section 3–803 reads:

Where a defendant is sued for breach of an obligation for which a third person is answerable over under this Article he may give the third person written notice of the litigation, and the person notified may then give similar notice to any other person who is answerable over to him under this Article. If the notice states that the person notified may come in and defend and that if the person notified does not do so he will in any action against him by the person giving the notice be bound by any determination of fact common to the two litigations, then unless after seasonable receipt of the notice the person notified does come in and defend he is so bound.

**150.** Under this theory the surety would argue that the pre-Code cases govern pursuant to the mandate of section 1–103 which provides:

Unless displaced by the particular provisions of this Act, the principles of law and equity, including the law merchant and the law relative to capacity to contract, principal and agent, estoppel, fraud, misrepresentation, duress, coercion, mistake, bankruptcy, or

argue that the accommodation party is in fact asserting his own defense and not that of the principal debtor. That is, his suretyship obligation is based on an implied condition precedent that the creditor will not act in a manner which substantially increases his risk, and the creditor's failure to perform has increased that risk and given the surety his own personal defense.[151] We thank Professor Peters for this argument. We hope and believe that courts will move mountains to avoid reading the last sentence of 3–306(d) in such a way as to flatly bar an accommodation party from asserting any of his principal debtor's defenses against the creditor.

## § 13–18 Discharge, 3–601, 3–603, 3–605

The events which may discharge one's liability on a negotiable instrument are many and varied. They range from the failure of a holder to give an indorser timely notice to the common circumstance in which the principal obligor makes payment to the holder. These various events are listed in 3–601(1) as follows:

The extent of the discharge of any party from liability on an instrument is governed by the sections on

(a) payment or satisfaction (Section 3–603); or

(b) tender of payment (Section 3–604); or

(c) cancellation or renunciation (Section 3–605); or

(d) impairment of right of recourse or of collateral (Section 3–606); or

(e) reacquisition of the instrument by a prior party (Section 3–208); or

(f) fraudulent and material alteration (Section 3–407); or

(g) certification of a check (Section 3–411); or

(h) acceptance varying a draft (Section 3–412); or

(i) unexcused delay in presentment or notice of dishonor or protest (Section 3–502).

Elsewhere we consider the discharges which may result from impairment of the right of recourse (3–606)[152] and unexcused delay

---

other validating or invalidating cause shall supplement its provisions.

151. Professor Peters suggests that the surety, under section 3–306(c), might assert the failure of a condition precedent against a holder. Peters, Suretyship Under Article 3 of the Uniform Commercial Code, 77 Yale L.J. 833, 865–68 (1968).

The problem with this implied condition approach is that it may prove too much. If we accept the notion that the creditor breaches an implied condition precedent every time his conduct increases the risk of debtor's nonperformance, section 3–606 becomes superfluous. Perhaps one might avoid this problem by arguing that there is an implied condition precedent in the surety's obligation that the principal is bound on his contract. See L. Simpson, Handbook of the Law of Suretyship § 55 at 276–77 (1950). However, under this approach one has trouble reconciling the cases which hold that the principal's incapacity to contract or discharge in bankruptcy does not free the surety.

152. See Section 13–14 supra.

(3–501).[153] Here we consider only section 3–603 on payment or satisfaction to a holder and section 3–605 on cancellation or renunciation.

### Discharge by Payment or Satisfaction to Holder: 3–603

In the normal course of events the liability of a party to a negotiable instrument will terminate via discharge under 3–603: [154] a holder of a check presents it to a bank for payment or the holder of a note presents it to the maker for payment; the holder is paid and relinquishes the instrument. By such "payment or satisfaction to the holder," the liability of the maker or drawer is discharged and the transaction at an end.[155] Although 3–603 speaks of "his" payment or satisfaction, it appears that the draftsmen intended the bank's payment to the holder of a check to operate as the drawer's payment.

Section 3–603 provides for discharge when payment or satisfaction is made to a "holder." That word is a term of art, and it is important to know whom it includes and excludes.[156] First, *bona fide* owners who lack possession of the instrument (as where it is lost

---

153. See text accompanying notes 56–54 supra.

154. Section 3–603 reads:

> The liability of any party is discharged to the extent of his payment or satisfaction to the holder even though it is made with knowledge of a claim of another person to the instrument unless prior to such payment or satisfaction the person making the claim either supplies indemnity deemed adequate by the party seeking the discharge or enjoins payment or satisfaction by order of a court of competent jurisdiction in an action in which the adverse claimant and the holder are parties. This subsection does not, however, result in the discharge of the liability
>
> (a) of a party who in bad faith pays or satisfies a holder who acquired the instrument by theft or who (unless having the rights of a holder in due course) holds through one who so acquired it; or
>
> (b) of a party (other than an intermediary bank or a payor bank which is not a depositary bank) who pays or satisfies the holder of an instrument which has been restrictively indorsed in a manner not consistent with the terms of such restrictive indorsement.

155. When the drawer or maker is discharged under section 3–603(b), prior parties (e. g., indorsers) are discharged under section 3–601(3). Section 3–601(3) states:

> The liability of all parties is discharged when any party who has himself no right of action or recourse on the instrument
>
> (a) reacquires the instrument in his own right; or
>
> (b) is discharged under any provision of this Article, except as otherwise provided with respect to discharge for impairment of recourse or of collateral (Section 3–606).

If the maker fails to pick up the note or to mark it paid and it gets back into the hands of a holder in due course, the discharge will be ineffective against such holder in due course and the maker will have to pay twice. The moral of the story is obvious: when one pays a note he should take possession of it or, at the least, mutilate it.

156. Section 1–201(20) defines a holder:

> "Holder" means a person who is in possession of a document of title or an instrument or an investment security drawn, issued or indorsed to him or to his order or to bearer or in blank.

or stolen) are not holders.[157]　However, mere possession is not always enough.　One who has possession of order paper that has not been indorsed to him or drawn to his order will never be a holder. But for a discharge to occur, the person who receives payment need not qualify as a holder in due course.　Thus one who takes an overdue instrument or possesses stolen bearer paper is a holder and comes within 3–603.　The significance of all this becomes evident when one considers the effect of payment of a stolen instrument on the liabilities of the parties.　If the instrument was bearer paper at the time it was stolen, subsequent takers from the thief will be holders and payment to them will discharge liability on the instrument and, under 3–802, discharge the underlying obligation.[158]　If, on the other hand, the stolen instrument was order paper, the thief's signature will not constitute an indorsement and all subsequent takers will not be holders.[159]　Thus, when the drawee or maker pays the presenter, the payor will not have paid a holder, there will be no discharge under 3–603, and the original owner can recover on the stolen instrument under 3–804 (liability on lost and stolen instruments) or on the underlying obligation.[160]　Thus 3–603 is a crucial piece in the stolen instrument puzzle, and one must understand its operation to comprehend the liabilities on a stolen instrument.

Occasional questions arise under 3–603 about the meaning of "payment or satisfaction" in various circumstances.　The case is simple enough if the maker pays greenbacks to the one presenting his note.　If, on the other hand, he trades a check for the note, cancels some other indebtedness, or signs a renewal note, there may be doubt about whether there has been "payment or satisfaction."　In Beneficial Finance v. Lachterman,[161] the co-maker of an $800 note procured a cashier's check payable "to the order of Beneficial [the creditor] for the account of [debtor]."　When the maker presented the check to Beneficial (payee on the note) Beneficial gave the debtor another

---

157.　See Investment Serv. Co. v. Martin Bros. Container & Timber Prods. Corp., 255 Ore. 192, 465 P.2d 868, 7 UCC Rep.Serv. 373 (1970) (depository bank that returned dishonored check to payee could not recover as holder because it lacked possession; 3–804 was unavailable because check not "lost or stolen").

158.　The thief of bearer can qualify as a holder and negotiate the instrument.　See text accompanying notes 47–54 supra (§§ 1–201(2); 3–202).　For a discussion of section 3–802, see Sections 13–20 and 13–22 infra.

159.　For some purposes it may be useful to revise the old fiction that a good-faith indorser who traces his title through a thief in effect "writes a new instrument" and so enables subsequent parties to be "holders" of the new instrument.　This analysis is useful in applying the warranties in section 3–417(2) which run only to "holders."　It is clear on the one hand that the draftsmen intended persons who trace their titles through thieves to have the benefit of those warranties, yet without the fiction discussed above they would fail to be holders and thus would not have the benefit of the warranties in 3–417(2). See E. Peters, Commercial Transactions 1430–31 (1971).

160.　The thief who steals order paper cannot qualify as a holder, and his signature is not an indorsement.　See §§ 1–201(2); 3–202.　For a discussion of 3–804, see Section 13–22 infra.

161.　7 UCC Rep.Serv. 515 (N.Y.Sup.Ct. 1970).

$800 in return for the check and left the note outstanding. Subsequently the debtor failed to pay the note and Beneficial sued the other co-maker on the original note. Defendant co-maker argued that Beneficial's receipt of the check payable to its order for the account of the debtor constituted a satisfaction of the note and that neither it nor the debtor had authority to treat the check as something other than payment on the note. The court agreed and found that the original note had been discharged and the co-maker so freed of his guarantor's liability. Chenowith v. Bank of Dardanelle,[162] an Arkansas case, illustrates the operation of 3–603 in another and somewhat bizarre circumstance. There the depositary bank gave its depositor a credit in his account upon his deposit of several of Chenowith's checks which ultimately bounced. Before it learned that the checks were no good, the depositary bank permitted its depositor to draw on his account, and made a second mistake of returning some of the checks (after they had bounced) to its depositor. Ultimately the bank sued the drawer on the checks (on his drawer's contract). The drawer defended on the ground that he had taken back two of his checks from the depositor-payee in settlement of another account, or put another way, that he had paid the checks to the holder (the depositor) by settling a debt that the depositor owed him and therefore was discharged under 3–603. The court agreed. It found the depositor was a holder of the checks in his possession and there was a discharge. As to the other checks which had bounced but which had not been returned to the depositor, the court found no discharge because the depositor, lacking possession, was not a holder of those checks.

It seems that an infinite variety of acts by makers and drawers can be classified as payment or satisfaction.[163] It would serve no useful purpose for us to attempt to catalogue or classify those acts, and except for trades of old notes for renewal notes we see no recurring fact patterns of a problematic nature. We will discuss the renewal note question below in connection with 3–605.

### § 13–19   Discharge—Cancellation and Renunciation, 3–605

Section 3–605 reads in full as follows:

> (1) The holder of an instrument may even without consideration discharge any party
>
> > (a) in any manner apparent on the face of the instrument or the indorsement, as by intentionally cancelling the instrument or the party's signature by destruction or mutilation, or by striking out the party's signature; or

---

162. 243 Ark. 310, 419 S.W.2d 792, 4 UCC Rep.Serv. 758 (1967).

163. See, e. g., Duilio v. Senechal, 7 UCC Rep.Serv. 222 (Mass.App.Div. 1969) (previously dishonored check satisfied when party returned to payee automobile for which check had been given).

(b) by renouncing his rights by a writing signed and delivered or by surrender of the instrument to the party to be discharged.

(2) Neither cancellation nor renunciation without surrender of the instrument affects the title thereto.

Courts have often had to confront 3-605 when one party transfers old notes for so-called renewal notes.[164] If a co-maker or indorser on the original note fails to sign the renewal note, or a signature thereon is forged, it becomes important to know whether the original note remains effective or is discharged by surrender of the instrument to the original maker.

In such cases the party whose signature legitimately appeared on the original notes but whose name did not appear on the renewal notes inevitably launches a two-pronged defense. First, he argues that the new notes were taken in payment or satisfaction of the old ones under 3-603. To this, the payee usually responds that taking one instrument for another under 3-802 does not discharge the liability on the other instrument but simply suspends it.[165] It is a question of intention whether the taking of the note satisfied the earlier obligation, a question to be determined by all the facts and circumstances (what was the state of the bank's knowledge, what did the bank do with the old notes, etc.).[166]

The omitted party's second line of defense is that the holder renounced his rights and discharged him under 3-605(1) (b) "by surrender of the instrument." The courts have glossed this section by requiring that surrender of the instrument be accompanied by an intent to discharge the party. In American Cement Corp. v. Century Mix, Inc.,[167] plaintiff held notes made by Century and individually indorsed by a corporate officer. When the maker changed banks, plaintiff agreed to surrender the original notes and take new notes on condition that the new notes duplicate the operative terms of the originals. Due to a clerical error the new notes did not have the signature of the individual indorser. Upon the maker's default, plaintiff sought judgment against the maker and the individual indorser. The indorser argued that under 3-401 he was not liable on the new notes because he had not signed them and that the surrender of the original notes discharged him under 3-605(1) (b). The New

---

**164.** See notes 166-67 infra and cases cited therein.

**165.** For a discussion of 3-802, see Section 13-22 infra.

**166.** See Slaughter v. Philadelphia Nat'l Bank, 290 F.Supp. 234, 5 UCC Rep.Serv. 856 (E.D.Pa.1968), rev. on other grds. 417 F.2d 21 (circumstances showed intent of parties that renewal note discharged original debt, and party who did not sign renewal note was entitled to return of collateral). The term "satisfaction" found in 3-603 did not appear in the NIL, and under the pre-Code law the effect of a renewal note on the original debt depended upon whether the original instrument was surrendered. See NIL § 119; W. Britton, Handbook of the Law of Bills and Notes at 641-44 (2d ed. 1961).

**167.** 3 UCC Rep.Serv. 424 (N.Y.Sup.Ct. 1966).

York court held that there was no surrender and discharge of the original notes because the plaintiff-holder did not so intend when he agreed to the exchanged notes; accordingly, the court gave judgment for plaintiff under 3–804. In Citizens Fidelity Bank & Trust v. Stark,[168] the court ruled that a party's fraud in the procurement of a new note foreclosed any argument that payee on the new note had intended to discharge the parties on the old notes. In that case two married couples jointly executed notes to three banks. D, one of the co-signers, contacted a fourth bank, Citizens, and proposed to consolidate the several notes with one note held by Citizens. D delivered the consolidated note to Citizens with his own and the purported signatures of the Starks, the other couple, whereupon Citizens paid off two of the old notes which were stamped "paid" and returned to D. It turned out that the Starks' signatures on the consolidation note were forged. The Starks denied liability to Citizens and sought return of their collateral which had been transferred to Citizens along with the original notes. The trial court held that the Starks were entitled to return of the collateral. The Kentucky Court of Appeals reversed and held that the cancellation and surrender of the instruments did not discharge the Starks' liability on the original notes because those acts were procured by D's fraud and because the Starks did not intend to be bound by a consolidation note since they did not know of D's transaction with Citizens. Accordingly, the court ruled that Citizens was entitled to retain the collateral.

### § 13–20  Discharge—The Underlying Obligation, Suspension, and Discharge, 3–802

Section 3–802 of the Code is a tidying-up provision. It states the legal effects on the underlying obligation when ones takes a negotiable instrument for that obligation, and it states the legal effects on the underlying obligation when the obligation on the instrument is discharged.[169] Recall that the "underlying obligation" is the original obligation between the parties which led to issuance of the negotiable instrument in the first place. In most cases, this obligation will be a contract, perhaps a contract for the sale of goods or services, and if no negotiable instrument were issued, this obligation would alone be enforceable by one party against the other. It is

---

168.  431 S.W.2d 722, 5 UCC Rep.Serv. 1086 (Ky.App.1968).

169.  Section 3–802 reads as follows:

(1) Unless otherwise agreed where an instrument is taken for an underlying obligation

(a) the obligation is pro tanto discharged if a bank is drawer, maker or acceptor of the instrument and there is no recourse on the instrument against the underlying obligor; and

(b) in any other case the obligation is suspended pro tanto until the instrument is due or if it is payable on demand until its presentment. If the instrument is dishonored action may be maintained on either the instrument or the obligation; discharge of the underlying obligor on the instrument also discharges him on the obligation.

(2) The taking in good faith of a check which is not postdated does not of itself so extend the time on the original obligation as to discharge a surety.

the issuance of the instrument that muddies the water with respect to the underlying obligation and presents the questions we discuss below.

Usually, when one takes a negotiable instrument for an underlying obligation the legal effect is not to discharge that obligation but in the words of 3–802(1) (b), merely to suspend it "pro tanto until the instrument is due or if it is payable on demand until its presentment." Only if a bank is the drawer, maker or acceptor of the instrument *and* there is no recourse on the instrument against the underlying obligor does 3–802(1) (a) discharge the underlying obligation. This means that issuance of a check in the usual circumstance does not discharge the obligation but merely suspends it. In a typical check case "suspension" of the underlying obligation is likely to have little practical significance, for the parties contemplate that the check will be presented promptly and that the drawer will pay in a relatively short time. The same is not true if one party gives the other a note due in 90 days or in 120 days. Suspension of the payee's right to sue on the underlying obligation for the period until the note becomes due is significant for both parties and the payee gives up a valuable right to insist on immediate payment and the maker acquires valuable time to get his payment together. The suspension language in 3–802(1) (b) assures maker the time to pay for which he has at least implicitly bargained by arranging for a note due only after a period of time has passed. On the other hand if one procures a cashier's check and does not himself become obligated on that check by indorsing it, transfer of that check will extinguish the underlying obligation since a bank is the drawer and there is no recourse on it against the transferor. Doubtless these rules are consistent with normal business expectations. A cashier's check is a great deal like cash and it is likely that the normal expectation of the parties is to treat the obligation as extinguished when such a check is passed. On the other hand, it is a rare and foolish businessman who treats a personal check as identical to cash. The drawer still has the power to stop payment and many a check is drawn against insufficient funds. In reality, taking a personal check is much like trading one promise for another by the same party.

Note that 3–802(1) (and therefore all of the rules which we have cited in the two foregoing paragraphs) are prefaced by the phrase "[u]nless otherwise agreed". If the parties agree that one of them will take the other's check in satisfaction of a debt, then the underlying obligation is discharged. Occasionally a defendant will argue that the circumstances surrounding the taking of the check evidenced an "agreement otherwise," that is, that the check or note constituted payment of the underlying obligation and so discharged it. What circumstances constitute an agreement is not clear from the cases discussed in Section 13–19 of this book. In those cases, a set of checks is exchanged for a set of notes or a set of notes is renewed by the maker's execution of new notes. In these exchanges the question arises, as we have seen, whether the obligation on the originals in this case the underlying obligation) was discharged as to one who was a party to the first set but not to the second when the creditor took the second.  In the *Slaughter* [170] case (in which one maker on the first set refused to sign the second set) the court found that the second set extinguished the obligation.  Where, on the other hand, one signer was inadvertently omitted from the second set [171] or where the first set was cancelled without knowledge of two of the original signers, and their signatures were forged on the second set, the courts found no intention that the second set be taken in satisfaction of the first.[172]  Suffice it to say that the lawyer should be aware of the possibility of an agreement between the parties that the giving of the instrument extinguishes the underlying obligation.

The second important tidying-up provision in 3–802 is the last clause in subsection (1) (b), "discharge of the underlying obligor on the instrument also discharges him on the obligation".  Assume one owes $500 on an account and gives his creditor a check for $500 in satisfaction of that account.  When the payee presents the check and receives payment at the drawee bank, the drawer's obligation on the check will be discharged under the provisions of 3–603 because the bank has made "payment  .  .  .  to the holder."  As we have seen the giving of the check suspended the underlying obligation, and the last clause in (1) (b) discharges the underlying obligation.  Note that this is the case with respect to the underlying obligation even if the check is bearer paper stolen and then presented by a transferee of a thief.[173]  Good faith payment to the holder discharges the obligation under 3–603.  Section 3–802 in turn discharges the underlying obligation.  Presumably the discharge clause in (1) (b) also discharges the obligor's obligation under 3–804 on the lost or stolen instrument (otherwise the parts of the puzzle do not fit together properly).[174]  That payment on a bearer instrument, even to one who traces title through a thief, discharges the payor's liability is the essence of negotiable paper.  Only because he is discharged by paying one who presents bearer paper will the payor freely pay such person,

170.  Slaughter v. Philadelphia Nat'l Bank, 290 F.Supp. 234, 5 UCC Rep. Serv. 856 (E.D.Pa.1968), rev. on other grds. 417 F.2d 21.

171.  American Cement Corp. v. Century Transit Mix, Inc., 3 UCC Rep.Serv. 424 (N.Y.Sup.Ct.1966).

172.  Citizens Fidelity Bank & Trust Co. v. Stark, 431 S.W.2d 722, 5 UCC Rep.Serv. 1086 (Ky.App.1968).

173.  The thief who steals bearer paper qualifies as a holder under 1–201(20), and therefore his transferee is a holder.  See §§ 1–201(2) ; 3–202.

174.  It would be inconsistent to say, on one hand, that payment to a holder (e. g., the transferee of a thief of bearer paper) discharges the obligor's liability on the instrument and, on the other hand, allow the owner of the stolen instrument another payment under 3–804.  In effect, the holder of bearer paper assumes the risk that it will be stolen, and the thief or his transferee will obtain payment.  When the owner sues under 3–804 before the obligor makes payment to the thief or his transferee, the obligor is protected from double payment by the indemnification provision of 3–804.  Accordingly, in every case where owners of bearer paper sue under 3–804, it is essential that the courts exercise the option to require the plaintiff to post security to protect the obligor from a double claim.

and only because he knows he will be freely paid will the presenter and other transferees freely accept such a document without asking for a title opinion and without a search of each transferor's chain of title.

Most of the cases decided to date under 3–802 are strictly mine-run specimens.[175] D'Agostino Excavators, Inc., v. Hayward-Robinson Co.,[176] has at least gossip value owing to the fact that some crafty or lucky lawyer induced the eminences of the Second Circuit (Friendly, Kaufman, and Lumbard, JJ.) thoroughly to misinterpret the Code discharge provisions. In that case, Hayward, the appellant, gave promissory notes in a face amount of $36,250 to D'Agostino. Later D'Agostino negotiated the notes to third parties at less than their face amount. Hayward, the maker, later "re-acquired" the notes from the third party holders (that is, satisfied his obligations under them) for $18,500. At trial Hayward argued his liability to D'Agostino was so discharged to the extent of the full $36,250. The trial court allowed the jury to determine "as a question of fact the amount which should be credited to Hayward on these notes." Judge Lumbard, sitting as the trial judge, instructed the jury that Hayward should be credited with the full amount "only if the parties intended the notes as payment at the time they were received." On appeal the Second Circuit noted in passing that appellant had not pointed out the provisions of 3–802 to the trial court; nevertheless the court found that 3–802 was consistent with the instructions in fact given to the jury. If (as appears, though not clearly) Hayward in fact satisfied the notes for something less than their face value to their holders, his obligation on the notes was discharged under 3–603. Under 3–802(1)(b) that discharge also discharges him on the underlying obligation. All of this follows irrespective of the intentions of the parties at the time Hayward gave the notes to D'Agostino. If the inference we

175. See, e. g., Balmoral Arms v. Rutkin, 104 N.J.Super. 354, 250 A.2d 50, 6 UCC Rep.Serv. 165 (Chancery Div. 1969) (mortgagee could not foreclose on mortgage for failure to pay interest because checks given as interest payments suspended underlying obligations); In re Hayman, 6 UCC Rep. Serv. 928 (Ref.Dec.W.D.Okla.1969) (acceptance of check which was later dishonored did not extinguish the underlying security interest); Makel Textiles, Inc. v. Dolly Originals, Inc., 4 UCC Rep.Serv. 95 (N.Y.Sup.Ct.1967) (checks given as payments on notes did not discharge indorser's liability on notes when checks were unpaid). See also Meckler v. Highland Falls Sav. & Loan Ass'n, 64 Misc.2d 407, 314 N.Y.S.2d 681, 8 UCC Rep.Serv. 368 (Sup.Ct.1970), where, at the request of its depositor, defendant-savings and loan association drew a check on its own account to the order of plaintiff in payment for services rendered to depositor. When a dispute arose between plaintiff and depositor, defendant stopped payment at depositor's request. Held: summary judgment granted to plaintiff since check was drawn by bank and underlying obligor was not a party to the instrument; it would be unfair to payee to allow stop order, because acceptance of check was pro tanto discharge under 3–804(1)(a). The case might have been more accurately characterized as a suit on the drawer's contract which raised the issue whether the drawer could raise defenses of one not a party to the instrument. See §§ 3–413; 3–306(d).

176. 430 F.2d 1077, 7 UCC Rep.Serv. 1331 (2d Cir. 1970). (The title of the case identifies one party as "Hayward;" the opinion styles it "Heyward." We have chosen the former.)

draw from the opinion, that the maker paid the notes, is not correct, the court's analysis of 3–802 would be inartful but accurate. The only fact at issue in that case would be whether the parties had originally "agreed" to transfer the notes in full satisfaction of the underlying obligation.

The court found that Hayward "was entitled to credit against the payee, D'Agostino, only for the amount it paid to the transferees." That finding makes no sense, for it would mean that the payee on the note, D'Agostino, could have sold the notes for $30,000 and then insisted upon additional payment from Hayward amounting to the difference between $36,000 and the amount Hayward paid (in this case a difference of approximately $18,000). It makes no sense to peg Hayward's obligation by reference to the amount he paid to reacquire the notes for he should have been discharged either under 3–603 (payment) or by virtue of 3–601(3) (a) (one who reacquires the instrument in his own right). In defense of the eminent judges of the Second Circuit and their clerks, all apparently ignorant of Parts 6 and 8 of Article Three, Hayward's lawyer was equally ignorant of those provisions.

### § 13–21   Discharge—Discharge of a Disputed Obligation by Tender of a Check in "Full Satisfaction", 1–207

Offering a check for less than the contract amount, but "in full settlement" inflicts an exquisite form of commercial torture on the payee. If the offer is reasonable it creates a marvelous anxiety in some recipients: "Shall I risk the loss of $9,000 for the additional $1,000 that the bloke really owes me?" In general the law has authorized such drawer behavior by regarding such a check as an offer of accord and satisfaction which the payee accepts if he cashes the check.[177] Traditionally the payee could write all manner of disclaimers over his indorsement without avail; by cashing the check he was held to have accepted the offer on the drawer's terms. Even if he scratched out the drawer's notation or indorsed it under protest he was deemed to have accepted subject to the conditions under which the drawer offered it.[178]

At minimum 1–207 of the Code muddies the waters in this area; it may have changed the course of the former law a full 180 degrees. Section 1–207 reads as follows:

> A party who with explicit reservation of rights performs or promises performance or assents to performance in a manner demanded or offered by the other party does not thereby prejudice the rights reserved. Such words as "without prejudice", "under protest" or the like are sufficient.

Some suggest that since Comment 1 speaks of "continuation of performance along the lines contemplated by the contract," section 1–207

177.  See 6A. Corbin, Corbin on Contracts §§ 1277–78 (2d ed. 1962).

178.  See 6A. Corbin, Corbin on Contracts § 1279 (2d ed. 1962).

may not be applicable to the conditional check situation because an accord and satisfaction is a "new" contract.[179] However, Professors Hogan and Penney have said (emphasis added):

> The Code rule would permit, in Code-covered transactions, the acceptance of a part performance or *payment* tendered in full settlement without requiring the acceptor to gamble with his legal right to demand the balance of the performance or *payment*.[180]

In two Code cases courts have stated in *dictum* that 1–207 applies to the conditional check situation. In Hanna v. Perkins,[181] the buyer tendered a check with the notation "In full for labor and material to date." The seller indorsed the check "Deposited under Protest" and deposited it. Seller sued for the balance of the contract price and buyer moved for summary judgment on the ground of accord and satisfaction. The New York court held for the seller and said that the defendant failed to allege the existence of an honest dispute about the amount due and thus there was no accord and satisfaction. The court cited 1–207 and continued:

> If it were not that this court finds that triable issues of fact are present, this court would deny the motion by holding this particular section of the code would seem to favor plaintiff's overriding indorsement of "Deposited under protest" as a reservation of his right to collect payment of the balance.[182]

Similarly in Baillie Lumber Co. v. Kincaid Carolina Corp.,[183] the North Carolina Court of Appeals found that the attempted accord and satisfaction failed and additionally that the creditor had preserved his right to seek the balance of the account by indorsing the checks, "With reservation of all our rights." In both cases the references to 1–207 were unnecessary because the court first found that there was no accord and satisfaction. Whether one believes that 1–207 restores a much needed balance in the relationship between the debtor and creditor or that it wreaks havoc with an established commercial practice, the section exists. The cases discussed above reveal the courts' belief that the draftsmen meant 1–207 to apply to the case of the conditional check.

In summary the tender of a check in full satisfaction of a disputed amount will still constitute an offer of an accord and satisfaction. If the payee indorses without "protest" or similar reservation, he

179. See Hawkland, The Effect of UCC § 1–207 on the Doctrine of Accord and Satisfaction by Conditional Check, 74 Com.L.J. 329, 331 (1969).

180. N.Y. Annotations to the Uniform Commercial Code and Report of Comm'n on Uniform State Laws, Article 1, 19–20 (1961), cited in Hawkland, The Effect of UCC § 1–207 on the Doctrine of Accord and Satisfaction by Conditional Check, 74 Com.L.J. 329, 332 (1969).

181. 2 UCC Rep.Serv. 1044 (N.Y.City Ct.1965).

182. Id. at 1046.

183. 4 N.C.App. 342, 167 S.E.2d 85, 6 UCC Rep.Serv. 480 (1969).

will be bound by the accord and satisfaction, (at least if there was a *bona fide* dispute and the drawer is offering some concession). We believe that the enactment of 1–207 has substantially changed the outcome when the payee adds words of "protest" to his indorsement.[184] Certainly the post-Code case law indicates that 1–207 authorizes the payee who signs under protest to accept the amount of the check without entering an accord and satisfaction or otherwise forsaking his claim to any additional sum allegedly due him.

### § 13–22   Lost or Stolen Instruments, 3–804

Section 3–804 of the Code reads:

> The owner of an instrument which is lost, whether by destruction, theft or otherwise, may maintain an action in his own name and recover from any party liable thereon upon due proof of his ownership, the facts which prevent his production of the instrument and its terms. The court may require security indemnifying the defendant against loss by reason of further claims on the instrument.

Like section 3–802, section 3–804 is but a miscellaneous tidying-up provision. It gives one a right to sue upon a lost instrument, and saves him from the burdensome task of proving the underlying obligation. It contains an understandable provision which requires the plaintiff in the 3–804 suit to indemnify the defendant against loss which might arise if a holder in due course turned up with the instrument after payment had been made to the non holder-owner under 3–804.[185] It is plain enough that a plaintiff in the 3–804 case by oral testimony or otherwise must prove the terms of the instrument, that he was the owner, and that the instrument was "lost." At least one case intimates that such a plaintiff has an obligation to demand payment within a reasonable time from an indorser if he wishes to sue the indorser.[186] We think that 3–804 dispenses with require-

---

184. Perhaps the debtor can protect himself by tendering his offer upon the express condition that the creditor will not take advantage of his option under 1–207. See Hawkland, The Effect of UCC § 1–207 on the Doctrine of Accord and Satisfaction by Conditional Check, 74 Com.L.J. 329, 342 (1969).

185. One can argue that the maker of such a check is not yet "liable," because the check has not been presented for payment and probably never will be. See White, Some Petty Complaints About Article Three, 65 Mich. L.Rev. 1315, 1333–38 (1967). That argument never was more than an academic quibble, and the courts have not been bothered with it. In several cases courts have granted recoveries under 3–804 on lost checks notwithstanding the fact that the drawer of such checks (who was ultimately held liable) was not theoretically "liable thereon." See Dluge v. Robinson, 204 Pa.Super. 404, 204 A.2d 279, 2 UCC Rep.Serv. 376 (1964) (plaintiffs failed to prove that checks were "lost" or that they were still the owners of same when they sued) (dictum); Chase Manhattan Bank, N.A. v. Concord Util. Corp., 7 UCC Rep.Serv. 52 (N.Y.Civ.Ct.1969); 487 Clinton Ave. Corp. v. Chase Manhattan Bank, N.A., 63 Misc.2d 715, 313 N.Y.S.2d 445, 8 UCC Rep.Serv. 69 (Sup.Ct.1970).

186. Dluge v. Robinson, 204 Pa.Super. 404, 204 A.2d 279, 2 UCC Rep.Serv. 376 (1964).

ments of dishonor and notice of dishonor and that the most one can insist upon if he is an indorser is a demand for payment together with reasonable notice that he may soon become a defendant in a 3–804 suit.

The indemnification requirement contained in the last sentence of 3–804 may cause an occasional problem for the lawyer. The uniform version of 3–804 gives the court discretion whether or not it will ask the plaintiff to provide security. In New York and California the court has no such discretion and must require security from the plaintiff.[187] If the plaintiff is the Chase Manhattan Bank, a contract by it to indemnify the defendant may be sufficient security;[188] if the plaintiff is someone of lesser stature he may be obliged to give a bond although the courts have exercised their discretion to accept other kinds of security. For example, in 487 Clinton Avenue Corp. v. Chase Manhattan Bank,[189] the Chase insisted upon a $40,000 bond to indemnify it against a potential loss arising from a stolen $20,000 check. The plaintiff offered $22,500 in certificates of deposits or a savings deposit at Chase as security. The court found that the plaintiff's offer was sufficient and directed that Chase accept that money and pay interest at its normal rate on the savings or certificate of deposit. This seems an appropriate exercise of the court's discretion. Presumably indemnification under 3–804 must protect the defendant not only against the possibility that a holder in due course may appear and in fact recover from him, but against the possibility that he will incur legal fees in defending against those who claim to be holders in due course but in fact are not holders in due course and therefore lack valid claims against the defendant.

---

187. See Cal.Comm.Code § 3804 (West 1964) (substitutes "shall require a sufficient indemnity bond" for "may require security"); N.Y. U.C.C. § 3–804 (McKinney 1964) (second sentence reads in part: "The court shall require security, in an amount fixed by the court not less than twice the amount allegedly unpaid on the instrument . . . .").

188. See Chase Manhattan Bank, N.A. v. Concord Util. Corp., 7 UCC Rep. Serv. 52 (N.Y.Civ.Ct.1969).

189. 63 Misc.2d 715, 313 N.Y.S.2d 445, 8 UCC Rep.Serv. 69 (Sup.Ct.1970).

# CHAPTER 14

# THE HOLDER IN DUE COURSE

*Analysis*

Sec.
14–1. Introduction.
14–2. Holder in Due Course Defined.
14–3. —— Holder.
14–4. —— Instrument.
14–5. —— Value.
14–6. —— Good Faith and Without Notice.
14–7. The Payee as a Holder in Due Course.
14–8. Judge-Made Limitations on the Holder in Due Course Doctrine—
    Close Connectedness.
14–9. Legislative Limitations on the Holder in Due Course Doctrine.
14–10. Rights of the Holder in Due Course.
14–11. Rights of a Holder Who is Not a Holder in Due Course.

## § 14–1  Introduction

In Chapter 13 we considered the *prima facie* liability of various parties to commercial paper, makers, acceptors, indorsers and drawers, in actions "on the instrument." *Prima facie* liability is one thing; ultimate liability after such parties have asserted their contract and other defenses is quite another. Among such defenses are failure of consideration, the failure of a condition, fraud, and so on. In this branch of the law the legal effectiveness of such defenses varies depending on who the plaintiff is, and the holder in due course qualifies as Super-plaintiff. With some exceptions, the holder in due course is immune to defenses that prior parties to commercial paper might assert.

The holder in due course, is, of course, nothing more than a highly refined species of bona fide purchaser who takes free of most defenses of prior parties to the instrument *and* free of conflicting title claims to the instrument itself.[1] In addition certain other procedural and subsidiary rights attach to the status of holder and holder in due course.[2] As befits the emperor of bona fide purchasers, many questions which still trouble other purchasers (e. g., Is an executory promise value?) have long been settled with respect to holders in due course. Both the legislatures and the courts have long been at work defining and refining the rights and status of the holder in due course. While this abundance of statutory and case law answers many questions, important pitfalls and interpretative difficulties remain.

---

1. § 3–305.

2. For example, where a drawee bank accepts an instrument bearing a forged drawer's signature, such acceptance is final as to a holder in due course. § 3–418. Further, 3–307 states that once signatures are ad-

mitted or established, a holder need only produce the instrument in order to recover unless the defendant carries the burden of establishing a defense. Even so, if the holder qualifies as a holder in due course he overcomes the defense. §§ 3–307(3); 3–305.

It is sometimes said that the holder in due course doctrine is like oil in the wheels of commerce and that those wheels would grind to a quick halt without such lubrication. Consider two examples which illustrate the metaphor. The first is the case of a consumer purchaser of, say, a car, who signs a note payable to the order of his seller. To acquire additional capital, the seller transfers his interest in the note to a wholesaler of credit who buys the note at face value or at discount and leaves the seller free to reinvest the money in his business and presumably to purchase additional items which he can sell to other consumers for the benefit of all concerned. Or consider the depositor who takes a check (payable to his order) to his bank and deposits it in his checking account. Although the depositor probably has no right to do so,[3] his bank will usually allow him to write checks on the uncollected credit represented by the check he deposited. In a pinch, the bank can assert rights as a holder in due course of the check [4] and recover from the drawer of the check even in the face of defenses which the drawer might assert against the bank's depositor. Likewise a purchaser of the consumer note in our first example will have the right if he is a holder in due course to enforce the note against the consumer notwithstanding that the consumer has perfectly valid complaints about the seller-payee's performance.

It is desirable for money to flow from lenders to the hands of sellers to make goods available to consumers. It is presumably also desirable to encourage banks to grant credits to their depositors without first waiting for checks to clear. Some, most notably representatives of banks and other lenders, argue that the immunity that holders in due course enjoy from various defenses affects their willingness to buy paper in the first place. However, it is far from obvious that the lender on the one hand or the bank on the other would change his behavior in a substantial way if denied the status of holder in due course. Particularly in the context of the transfer of consumer notes, debate over the likely consequences of denying holder in due course status has proceeded with great passion and in dead earnest.[5] For now, it is enough to see what a holder in due course is and precisely why his status might be important.

---

3. See § 4–212.

4. That is, to the extent that the bank has been "pinched" by its depositor's withdrawals, it can claim the rights of a holder in due course. § 4–208.

5. See, e. g., Felsenfeld, Some Ruminations About Remedies In Consumer-Credit Transactions, 8 B.C.Ind. & Com. L.Rev. 535 (1967); Rosenthal, Negotiability—Who Needs It?, 71 Colum. L.Rev. 375 (1971).

## § 14–2    Holder in Due Course Defined

A holder in due course must meet five conditions.[6]  He must be
  1. a holder
  2. of a negotiable instrument who took it
  3. for value
  4. in good faith
  5. without notice that it was overdue or had been dis-
     honored or of any defense against or claim to it on
     the part of any person.

Most of litigation under the heading "Holder in Due Course" has
nothing whatever to do with the *rights* of the holder in due course, but
with whether the party to the law suit qualifies as a holder in due
course at all.  Once a party so qualifies, the legal consequences of his
status are relatively clear.  One fails to be a holder in due course if he
fails to satisfy any of the five conditions listed above.  Do not be de-
ceived by the simplicity of the list; several of the conditions listed
are but doors which open onto breath-taking vistas of complex statutory and decisional law.

## § 14–3    Holder in Due Course Defined—Holder

Obviously only a holder can be a holder in due course.  To be
a holder one must meet the two conditions in 1–201(20):

  1. He must have possession

  2. of an instrument "drawn, issued or indorsed to him or
     his to order or to bearer or in blank".

The ambiguity in the word "possession" has caused little trouble.
With rare exceptions, those claiming to be holders seem to have had
physical possession of the instrument in question.[7]  But the second
requirement has posed real interpretive difficulties—particularly in
cases in which an instrument has passed through the hands of a thief
before reaching the hands of the putative holder in due course.  If an

---

6.  Section 3–302 reads:

   (1) A holder in due course is a holder who takes the instrument

   (a) for value; and

   (b) in good faith; and

   (c) without notice that it is overdue or has been dishonored or of
any defense against or claim to it
on the part of any person.

   (2) A payee may be a holder in due
course.

   (3) A holder does not become a
holder in due course of an instrument:

   (a) by purchase of it at judicial sale
or by taking it under legal process;
or

   (b) by acquiring it in taking over
an estate; or

   (c) by purchasing it as part of a
bulk transaction not in regular
course of business of the transferor.

   (4) A purchaser of a limited interest
can be a holder in due course only to
the extent of the interest purchased.

7.  In Investment Serv. Co. v. Martin
Bros. Container & Timber Prods. Corp.,
255 Ore. 192, 465 P.2d 868, 7 UCC
Rep.Serv. 373 (1970).  In this case the
plaintiff was denied recovery because
it did not have possession of the
check at the time it filed the complaint, even though it did have possession at the trial.

instrument is payable to bearer, either because it was issued that way and continued its life as a bearer instrument ("pay to the order of Cash") or because it was indorsed in blank by a holder ("Joe Jones"), the possessor of the instrument will be a holder and, if he meets the other tests, a holder in due course. This is so even though the instrument may have passed through the hands of a thief; the holder in due course is one of the few purchasers in Anglo Saxon jurisprudence who may derive a good title from a chain of title that includes a thief in its links.

However the same rule does not apply to a stolen order instrument ("Pay to the order of Joe Jones"). In order to pass a stolen order instrument, a thief must forge the indorsement of the party to whose order it is drawn. The signature of a thief does not constitute an "indorsement" and for that reason the thief's transferee is not a holder.[8] One concludes that the thief's signature does not constitute an indorsement by reading 3–202(2) as a definition of the word "indorsement". That subsection reads as follows:

> An indorsement must be written by or on behalf of the holder . . .

Of course the thief of an order instrument is not *himself* a holder because the instrument is neither payable to nor indorsed to his order. Since he in turn is not a holder and since 3–202(2) permits indorsement only by those who are holders, the thief lacks power to make an indorsement. Thus at the end of the chain, the thief's transferee is not a holder because the instrument was not "indorsed" to him under 1–201(20) and he, as a nonholder, in turn lacks power to indorse under 3–202(2). No party can ever be a holder of an order instrument stolen prior to indorsement by the owner of the instrument.[9]

## § 14–4 Holder in Due Course Defined—Instrument

Perhaps the least obvious requirement in 3–302 is that the holder in due course take an "instrument". Section 3–102(1)(e) in turn defines the word "instrument" as it is used in Article Three to mean

---

8. Stone & Webster Eng'r Corp. v. First Nat'l Bank & Trust Co., 345 Mass. 1, 184 N.E.2d 358, 1 UCC Rep.Serv. 195 (1962) (forged payee's indorsement). Cf. Northside Bldg. & Inv. Co. v. Finance Co. of America, 119 Ga.App. 131, 166 S.E.2d 608, 6 UCC Rep.Serv. 345 (1969) (no indorsement).

A depositary bank may supply a missing indorsement on an item in the collection process. § 4–205. Having done so it becomes a holder. See Investment Serv. Co. v. Martin Bros. Container & Timber Prods. Corp., 255 Ore. 192, 465 P.2d 868, 7 UCC Rep. Serv. 373 (1970); Bowling Green Inc. v. State St. Bank & Trust Co., 425 F.2d 81, 7 UCC Rep.Serv. 635 (1st Cir., 1970).

9. Note that an indorser who takes subsequent to the thief may under a common law fiction be regarded as having written a new instrument and may thus be regarded as having made subsequent parties "holders" with respect to him. The benefit of the fiction is that it permits such subsequent parties to sue on the warranties which run only to "holders" under 3–417(2). A better result in our judgment would be to find that such persons are not holders but to conclude that the draftsmen nevertheless intended that they have a right to sue under 3–417(2). E. Peters, Commercial Transactions 1430 (1971).

"negotiable instrument" and 3–104(1) defines negotiable instrument as follows:

> Any writing to be a negotiable instrument within this Article must
>
> (a) be signed by the maker or drawer; and
>
> (b) contain an unconditional promise or order to pay a sum certain in money and no other promise, order, obligation or power given by the maker or drawer except as authorized by this Article; and
>
> (c) be payable on demand or at a definite time; and
>
> (d) be payable to order or to bearer.

Two of the four conditions in 3–104(1), namely that the instrument be signed by the maker or the drawer and that the instrument be payable on demand or at a definite time, seemed to have caused little difficulty recently and we devote no space to them. However the two other requirements—that the instrument be payable to order or bearer and that it contain an unconditional promise or order to pay and no other promise—have been continuously litigated and are battlegrounds on which the consumer debtor's and lender's blood will certainly be shed in upcoming cases.

When does a document contain "an unconditional promise or order" and "no other promise, order, obligation or power . . . except as authorized by this Article"? This question arises initially for the creditor's lawyer when the creditor asks him to draft a note that will be at once "negotiable" and also carry a heavy burden of promises and obligations. To the extent possible, the creditor payee wants to have his cake and eat it too; he wants a note that will be negotiable, but he also wants certain specified obligations of the maker to travel as baggage with the note. The starting point for the lawyer's analysis in these cases is with the clause at the end of 3–104 (1) (b) "except as authorized by this Article". Sections 3–105 and 3–112 list a variety of conditions and additional promises that may be placed on an instrument without depriving it of its negotiability.

An initial and persistent problem for the draftsman of a note will be the payee's desire for a reference in the note to separate agreements. One might wish a note to disclose its relationship to a capitalization agreement, to a mortgage or to any of a variety of other contractual obligations. Here the draftsman must tread the line between 3–105(1) (c) and 3–105(2) (a). Those subsections read in full as follows:

Section 3–105(1) (c)

> (1) A promise or order otherwise unconditional is not made conditional by the fact that the instrument
>
> (c) refers to or states that it arises out of a separate agreement for rights as to payment or acceleration; or  .   .   .   .

Section 3-105(2) (a)

> (2) A promise or order is not unconditional if the instrument
>
> > (a) states that it is subject to or governed by any other agreement; or . . . .

Quite clearly any note which says that it is "subject to" or "governed by" a separate agreement is thus rendered nonnegotiable. Likewise it would seem that any other reference which incorporates a separate agreement by a reference deprives a note of its negotiability. The careful draftsman who wishes to preserve negotiability would be wise to use the language of 3-105(1) (c) and specify that the note "arises out of" a certain and separate agreement. In a recent case, D'Andrea v. Feinberg,[10] the court found that a statement on the note that it had been issued "as per contract" was only a reference under 3-105(1) (c) and did not amount to a condition.[11]

A second problem arises with respect to a reference on a note or check to the particular fund out of which it is to be paid. Section 3-105(1) (f), (g) and (h) and 3-105(2) (b) all deal with that question. Again the line between 3-105(1) (f) and 3-105(2) (b) is an exceedingly narrow one. Those subsections read in full as follows:

Section 3-105(1) (f)

> [a promise is not made conditional because it] indicates a particular account to be debited or any other fund or source from which reimbursement is expected

Section 3-105(2) (b)

> [a promise is not unconditional if the instrument] states that it is to be paid only out of a particular fund or source except as provided in this section.

Note that a reference to a fund does not interfere with negotiability if it only indicates or specifies a fund from which reimbursement is "expected"; however, a reference to a fund will deprive an instrument of its negotiability if it states that it is to be paid "only" out of a particular fund. Here the creditor who wishes to preserve negotiability is wise to omit any reference to a fund, for it is difficult to choose language which a court will recognize only as an "indication" and not as a "limitation to" a particular fund under 3-105(2) (b). For example in *dictum* in a recent case, Webb & Sons Inc. v. Hamilton,[12] the court said that a promise to pay "from jobs now under con-

---

10. 45 Misc.2d 270, 256 N.Y.S.2d 504, 2 UCC Rep.Serv. 410 (Sup.Ct.1955).

11. In Federal Factors, Inc. v. Wellbanke, 241 Ark. 44, 406 S.W.2d 712, 3 UCC Rep.Serv. 813 (1966), a trade acceptance containing the sentence, "The transaction which gives rise to

this instrument is the purchase of goods by the acceptor from the drawer," was negotiable because the reference did not indicate the conditional nature of the underlying obligation.

12. 30 App.Div.2d 597, 290 N.Y.S.2d 122, 5 UCC Rep.Serv. 524 (3d Dep't 1968).

struction" rendered the promise conditional and deprived the instrument of its negotiability.[13]

A third kind of provision that many creditors wish to include in a note is a kind of mini-security interest. In the case of loans against pledged stock, for example, it is convenient to have the debtor execute only one document to serve both as a note and as a security agreement under Article Nine. Sections 3–105(1) (e) and 3–112(1) (b) give the draftsmen some hope of success in this:

Section 3–105(1) (e)

> [an instrument is not made conditional by the fact that it] states that it is secured, whether by mortgage, reservation of title or otherwise.

Section 3–112(1) (b)

> [the negotiability of an instrument is not affected by] a statement that collateral has been given to secure obligations either on the instrument or otherwise of an obligor on the instrument or that in the case of default on those obligations the holder may realize on or dispose of the collateral.

Conceivably one could draft a document that would constitute a security agreement under Article Nine yet fit within 3–105(1) (e) and 3–112(1) (b). The latter provision explicitly authorizes the statement that the holder "may realize on or dispose of the collateral" in the case of default; and 3–105(1) (e) authorizes a statement to the effect that the note is secured. Whether a "statement" that a note is secured is different from an agreement granting a security interest in specific collateral is unclear. Comment 5 to 3–105 suggests that 3–105(1) (e) contemplates only the recitation of a security interest and not the embodiment of the actual agreement in the note.[14] Comment 5 states the purpose of 3–105(1) (e) as follows: "It rejects cases which have held that the mere statement that the instrument is secured, by reservation of title or otherwise, carries the implied condition that payment is to be made only if the security agree-

---

13. Comment 9 to § 3–105 points out that 3–105(2) (b) restates part of the comparable NIL provision. Pre-Code cases deciding whether or not language constituted a promise to pay from a peculiar source can be found in F. Buetel, Buetel's Brannan Negotiable Instruments Law § 3–(1) at 252–53 (7th ed. 1948), and Annot., 134 ALR 946, 950 (1946).

Language held not to constitute such a promise includes: ". . . proceeds from resale of said car shall apply on this note . . . ," First Nat'l Bank v. Sullivan, 66 Wash. 375, 119 P. 820 (1911); "The tolls collected under lease dated February 17, 1922, will be credited on the face of this note until paid," Jones v. Green, 173 Ark. 846, 293 S.W. 749 (1927); and "In case of the death of the insured before this note falls due, the amount with interest shall be deducted from the amount of the policy," Union Bank v. Spies, 151 Iowa 178, 130 N.W. 928 (1911).

14. Comment 4 to 3–105 also states:

Again such a recital normally is included only for the purpose of making a record or giving information, and is not intended to condition payment in any way.

ment is fully performed." Section 3–112(1) (b) which explicitly authorizes the statement of the holder's right to "realize" on the collateral, offers greater hope to one who would write a mini-security agreement into a negotiable note. However, one must stretch even 3–112(1) (b) to find that it permits anything more than the most abbreviated terms.[15]

Section 3–112(1) explicitly authorizes certain waivers and other terms. The most important among these are "confession of judgment" clauses.[16] However a recent case indicates that one must carefully draft a confession of judgment clause, if he wishes to come within 3–112(1) (d). In Atlas Credit Corp. v. Leonard [17] a Pennsylvania court found that a confession of judgment clause purporting to allow confession of judgment "at any time" was not within 3–112(1) (d), because (1)(d) authorized confession only "if [the instrument] is not paid when due. . . ." One suspects that this case indicates an adverse judicial attitude toward creditors who attempt to use confession of judgment clauses to take advantage of the doctrine that a holder in due course cuts off prior defenses. It would have been easy for the court to interpret the confession of judgment provision and 3–112(1) (b) to make them compatible.[18]

A final question presented by 3–104(1) (b) concerns the physical scope of "instrument." If, for example, a document is made up of a note on the top and a retail installment sales contract on the bottom and the two are divided by a perforated line, do the two together constitute one document—necessarily not a negotiable document—or can they be separated after signing with the consequence that the note will be a negotiable instrument? Although courts say that it makes no difference that the note is attached to another document, the fact that courts discuss the physical attachment indicates that it plays some role in their decisions.[19]

---

15. Comment 1 to 3–112 reads:

Paragraph (b) of subsection (1) permits a clause authorizing the sale or disposition of collateral given to secure obligations either on the instrument or otherwise of an obligor on the instrument upon any default in those obligations, including a default in payment of an installment or of interest. It is not limited, as was the original Section 5(1), to default at maturity. The reference to obligations of an obligor on the instrument is intended to recognize so-called cross collateral provisions that appear in collateral note forms used by banks and others throughout the United States and to permit the use of these provisions without destroying negotiability. . . .

16. § 3–112(1) (d).

17. 15 Pa.D. & C.2d 292, 1 UCC Rep. Serv. 220 (C.P.1957).

18. Note that Comment 2 to section 3–112 is explicit in stating ". . . that a confession of judgment may be authorized only if the instrument is not paid when due. . . ." The court could have interpreted the term on the note to operate only on the maker's failure to pay rather than making it nonnegotiable.

19. See, e. g., Commercial Credit Corp. v. Orange County Machine Works, 34 Cal.2d 766, 769–80, 214 P.2d 819, 821 (1950) (close connectedness) (dicta); Commercial Credit Co. v. Childs, 199 Ark. 1073, 137 S.W.2d 260 (1940) (court mentioned attachment in showing close connectedness because plaintiff printed documents). Cf. Waterbury Sav. Bank v. Jaroszewski, 4 Conn.Cir. 620,

A second recurring issue under 3–104(1) concerns the meaning of subsection (d) which requires that a negotiable instrument "be payable to order or to bearer." More than any other symbols, the words "order" and "bearer" are supposed to put a party on notice that he is dealing with a negotiable instrument. For this reason, courts under the Code have been slow to recognize substitutes for these symbols. Although the Comments suggest certain words that may be the equivalent of order or bearer, they also indicate the draftsmen's intent to restrict courts' power to sanction substitutes. Comment 5 to 3–104 rejects section 10 of the NIL which authorized a court to find any instrument negotiable that indicates the issuer's intent to conform to the act. The Comment summarizes the draftsmen's intention in 3–104(1) (d): "It does mean that either the language of the section or a clear equivalent must be found, and that in doubtful cases the decision should be against negotiability." Two kinds of cases pose the issue. A party may claim he is a holder in due course of a hybrid instrument which lies somewhere in the border land between negotiable instruments and ordinary contracts, e. g., a money order. In another kind of case, a party claims that a retail installment sales contract or other instrument of clearly recognized legal status constitutes a negotiable instrument.

Comment 2 to 3–111 suggests words equivalent of "pay to bearer." Among these are "pay cash," "pay to the order of cash," "pay bills payable" and "pay to the order of one keg of nails." Likewise comment 5 to 3–104 states that "pay to holder" is the equivalent of "pay to bearer." Thus it appears that any document which directs payment to or to the order of an inanimate object, qualifies as a bearer instrument and satisfies the requirements of 3–104(1) (d).

The most frequent case involves an instrument which states "pay to Jones." Here the courts are called upon to determine what additional words, if any, make "pay to" equivalent to "pay to the order of Jones." In two cases interpreting 3–104, the courts held that instruments which read "payable to" a named person did not comply with the subsection and were not negotiable. One of these cases involved a note; [20] the other a money order.[21] These cases are arguably inconsistent with *dictum* in United States v. First National Bank of Boston,[22] where a federal district judge held that a postal money order which provided "pay to" a named payee met the requirements of 3–104(1) (d). In that case the court relied upon the additional

---

238 A.2d 446, 4 UCC Rep.Serv. 1049 (1967) (although documents were attached court did not discuss; held for plaintiff).

**20.** Northerlin Co. v. Rauch Constr. Co., 4 UCC Rep.Serv. 320 (N.Y.Sup.Ct. 1967).

**21.** Nation-Wide Check Corp. v. Banks, 260 A.2d 367, 7 UCC Rep.Serv. 43 (D.C. Ct.App.1969).

**22.** 263 F.Supp. 298, 4 UCC Rep.Serv. 89 (D.Mass.1967). See also First Nat'l City Bank v. Valentine, 62 Misc.2d 719, 309 N.Y.S.2d 563, 7 UCC Rep. Serv. 821 (Sup.Ct.1970) (payable to plaintiff "or order" sufficient for negotiability).

fact that the money order gave the owner specific authority to make one transfer.

Given the important symbolic nature of the words "order" and "bearer," and the code draftsmen's directive to hold "questionable paper" to be nonnegotiable, we believe the courts should deny negotiable status to such questionable paper. Courts should be even less willing to find negotiability in cases involving not hybrid paper but paper which bears all the characteristics of other well recognized contract forms such as retail installment sales contracts and motor vehicle sales contracts.

### § 14–5 Holder in Due Course Defined—Value

Having determined that the plaintiff is in possession of a document which qualifies as a negotiable instrument, one must still find that he took it "for value in good faith and without notice" in order to find him a holder in due course under 3–302. Section 3–303 defines value as follows:

> A holder takes the instrument for value
>
> (a) to the extent that the agreed consideration has been performed or that he acquires a security interest in or a lien on the instrument otherwise than by legal process; or
>
> (b) when he takes the instrument in payment of or as security for an antecedent claim against any person whether or not the claim is due; or
>
> (c) when he gives a negotiable instrument for it or makes an irrevocable commitment to a third person.

Note first that "value" (as defined by 3–303, 4–208 and 4–209) has a different meaning in Articles Three and Four than it does in the other Code Articles. Under 3–303 an executory promise is not itself value, but under 1–201(44) an executory promise constitutes value.[23] The policy behind denying holder in due course status to one who has only given an executory promise is explained in Comment 3 to 3–303 as follows:

> The underlying reason of policy is that when the purchaser learns of a defense against the instrument or of a defect in the title he is not required to enforce the instrument, but is free to rescind the transaction for breach of the transferor's warranty (Section 3–417). There is thus not the same nec-

---

23. Section 1–201(44) defines value:

. . .

(a) in return for a binding commitment to extend credit or for the extension of immediately available credit whether or not drawn upon and whether or not a charge-back is provided for in the event of difficulties in collection; or

(b) as security for or in total or partial satisfaction of a pre-existing claim; or

(c) by accepting delivery pursuant to a pre-existing contract for purchase; or

(d) generally, in return for any consideration sufficient to support a simple contract.

essity for giving him the status of a holder in due course, cutting off claims and defenses, as where he has actually paid value. A common illustration is the bank credit not drawn upon, which can be and is revoked when a claim or defense appears.

In words of one syllable, the person who has given only a promise is not yet out on the limb and he does not pose the typical bona fide purchaser problem in which two people have committed their assets and the intervening person—always a scalawag of some sort—has disappeared. In that typical case the loss must inevitably fall on one of two innocent parties. Such is not the case when a potential bona fide purchaser has not yet paid the scalawag, but has only promised to do so. Assume for example that the thief has stolen a bearer instrument from Templeton and has made a contract to sell the instrument to Cicero. If Cicero discovers that the thief has no title, he will be free of his obligation to pay, for there will be a failure of consideration and the thief will not be able to deliver what he promised. Thus Cicero has given no "value"; he has not yet irrevocably committed himself to the transaction. The owner from whom the instrument has been stolen is irrevocably committed in the sense that his right to payment will be discharged by a payment of the instrument. It is appropriate for the Code to instruct Cicero that he must not go forward and must return the instrument to the owner.

Note that one can be a holder in due course to the extent of a partial interest in the instrument if, for example, he performs one-half of his obligation. Section 3–303(a) specifically makes one a giver of value "to the extent that the agreed consideration has been performed." [24] The case law under 3–303 is hardly remarkable. A variety of cases have applied 3–303(b) to find that one who takes a check as payment for an antecedent debt gives value for that check and may (if he meets the other criteria) sue on it as a holder in due course.[25] Two courts have had occasion to apply 3–303(c). In one of them,[26] plaintiff bank was suing the maker of certain notes. The

**24.** In O. P. Ganjo, Inc. v. Tri-Urban Realty Co., 108 N.J.Super. 517, 7 UCC Rep.Serv. 302 (Law Div.1970), the plaintiff promised to pay $2,800 for a $3,000 note and had in fact paid $1,-000 of the promised amount. The court held that the plaintiff was a holder in due course only to the extent of $1,000 plus a pro rata share of the $200 discount but not as to the remaining $1,800 which he had promised to pay but had not yet paid. See also, Korzenik v. Supreme Radio, Inc., 347 Mass. 309, 197 N.E.2d 702, 2 UCC Rep.Serv. 133 (1964), in which the plaintiff failed to carry the burden of proving the giving of value where he had taken trade acceptances in return for a promise to perform legal services. In Falls Church Bank v. Wesley Heights Realty, Inc., 256 A.2d 915, 6 UCC Rep.Serv. 1082 (D.C. Ct.App., 1969), the court held that the plaintiff-depositary bank was a holder in due course to the extent of the $140 withdrawn from a checking account subsequent to the time that the check on which the bank was suing was deposited in the account.

**25.** See, e. g., Nicklaus v. Peoples Bank & Trust Co., 258 F.Supp. 482, 3 UCC Rep.Serv. 984 (E.D.Ark.1965), aff'd, 369 F.2d 683 (8th Cir. 1966); Westchester Colprovia Corp. v. Pecora, 4 UCC Rep.Serv. 857 (N.Y.Sup.Ct.1967).

**26.** Ashburn Bank v. Childress, 120 Ga. App. 632, 171 S.E.2d 768, 7 UCC Rep. Serv. 215 (1969).

bank had credited the proceeds of the notes to the checking account of a corporation in which the individual defendant was an officer and stockholder. The court found that this action of the bank constituted an "irrevocable commitment to a third person" and established the bank as a holder in due course entitled to recover from the defendant maker. In Crest Finance Co. v. First State Bank of Westmont,[27] the Illinois Supreme Court found that a party who placed stock certificates in escrow had made an "irrevocable commitment" under 3–303(c). The court pointed out that the party who put the certificates in escrow had placed them beyond his own power and in fact under the control of the buyer. The court in that case could probably have reached the same conclusion under 3–303(a) by finding that the "agreed consideration" had in fact been performed when the other party acquired power to control the possession and ownership of the certificates.

The real battleground on which the "value" issue is being fought is a place far removed from 3–303. It arises under 4–208 and 4–209 time and again in circumstances like these: Scallywag Jones, a shady customer and broke as well, procures a check payable to his order for work to be performed and materials to be delivered. Jones takes the check to his bank, deposits it and so procures a credit in his checking account. Before the check is presented to the payor bank, the drawer finds that Jones will not perform and stops payment on the check. Sometimes at once, sometimes only after the depositary bank has received notice of the infirmity, Jones draws on the credit. Unable to procure reimbursement from Jones, the depositary bank then sues the drawer of the check and maintains that it is a holder in due course. The drawer defends on the ground that bank is not a holder in due course, for bank has not given value or at least had not given value at the time it received notice of a defense. The questions presented by these cases may be stated as follows:

(1) Under what circumstances is the mere granting of a credit the giving of value?

(2) If in some circumstances the granting of a credit is not giving of value, what additional facts must occur for the bank to have given value?

(3) If withdrawal is the crucial point, how does one determine whether specific funds have been withdrawn from a commingled bank account over a period of time when there are several deposits and many withdrawals?

Sections 4–208 and 4–209 at minimum make it clear that when the depositor has withdrawn his money, the bank has given value and has so become a holder in due course if it otherwise qualifies. But one must read 4–208(1)(b) with great care to determine the outcome in a case in which the credit has not been withdrawn. At

27. 37 Ill.2d 243, 226 N.E.2d 369, 4 UCC Rep.Serv. 79 (1967).

first reading that subsection seems to say that any giving of credit gives the bank a security interest which in turn would constitute the giving of value. Such a reading is in direct conflict with Comment 3 to 3–303 quoted above and it would render 4–208(1) (a) superfluous. On close reading one finds that the giving of a credit is itself the giving of value only when the credit is "available for withdrawal *as of right*." Whether a customer has the "right" to withdraw a credit will be determined by his agreement with his bank or, in the absence of such an agreement, by 4–213.[28]

Under 4–213(4) the credit is available "for withdrawal as of right" in the usual case when the bank itself receives final settlement and has reasonable time to learn that settlement is final. The negative implication is that such credit is not available as of "right" before that time. Thus in the absence of a contrary agreement between the depositor and his bank, 4–209, 4–208 and 4–213 mean that the bank which gives its depositor a provisional credit still does not give value until final payment of the item deposited or until the credit is withdrawn or otherwise applied. For the reasons stated in the Comment to 3–303 it makes sense to keep the depositary bank from being a holder in due course until the credit is withdrawn or until the bank is committed to give the credit to its customer. Until that time, the depositary bank can protect itself by debiting the account and can thus put the loss on the evil middle party (in this case the depositor) and avoid the dilemma present in all true bona fide purchase cases.

Perhaps because the question is complex and because the path among the relevant Code sections is by no means clear, the courts have had some difficulty under 4–208, 4–209 et seq. in arriving at the results suggested above. They are in agreement that a depositary bank at least gives value at the time the customer withdraws the funds from his account.[29] The courts also generally agree that giving a mere provisional credit does not constitute the giving of value.[30] The First Circuit in an alternate holding has strayed from the flock and found that a revocable credit not yet drawn on nevertheless gave rise to a security interest which would be regarded as the giving of

---

28. Under the terms of section 4–212 (1), the depositary bank has a right to revoke the settlement and charge back the customer's account, if the bank fails by reason of dishonor or for any other reason to "receive a settlement for the item which is or becomes final."

29. Universal CIT Credit Corp. v. Guaranty Bank & Trust Co., 161 F.Supp. 790, 1 UCC Rep.Serv. 305 (D.Mass.1958) (pre-Code case); Falls Church Bank v. Wesley Heights Realty Inc., 256 A. 2d 915, 6 UCC Rep.Serv. 1082 (D.C.Ct. App.1969); Peoples Bank v. Haar, 421 P.2d 817, 3 UCC Rep.Serv. 1065 (Okla. 1966); Pazol v. Citizens Nat'l Bank,

110 Ga.App. 319, 138 S.E.2d 442, 2 UCC Rep.Serv. 330 (1964).

30. See Sorrells Bros. Packing Co. v. Union State Bank, 144 So.2d 74 (Fla. App.1962) (all the deposit was in fact withdrawn) (dictum); Universal CIT Credit Corp. v. Guaranty Bank & Trust Co., 161 F.Supp. 790, 1 UCC Rep.Serv. 305 (D.Mass.1958) (all the deposit was in fact withdrawn) (dictum); Bank of America v. Dade Fed. Sav. & Loan Ass'n, 154 So.2d 191 (Fla.App.1962) (plaintiff was holder in due course only as to amount withdrawn by its depositor); Annot., 59 ALR2d 1173, 1176 (1958).

value under 4–208(1) (b) and 4–209: In Banco Espanol De Credito v. State Street Bank & Trust Co.,[31] the correspondent bank-plaintiff credited "the amounts specified in the letters of credit against debts" owed it by two beneficiaries under the letter of credit. The plaintiff then forwarded the draft to a Boston bank which was obliged to pay under the letter of credit, and the Boston bank refused to pay on the ground that there was fraud in the transaction. Banco Espanol responded that it was a holder in due course and that fraud could not be raised against it. The District Court, in an opinion affirmed by the First Circuit, found that Banco Espanol had in fact given value, was a holder in due course and was entitled to recover from the Boston bank. The lower court held that the Spanish bank had given value because the credit given was not subject to revocation under the terms of the agreement between the Spanish bank and its Spanish customers. The appellate court affirmed on this ground and on the alternate ground that Banco Espanol gave "value" under 4–208(1) "even if the credit were revocable." [32] In support of that statement the First Circuit cited Waltham Citizens National Bank v. Flett,[33] a 1968 Massachusetts case. In the *Waltham Bank* case the plaintiff, depositary bank, sued on a check deposited with it and for which it had given its customer a credit. According to the opinion the customer had had an $11,000 over-draft at the time the $9,000 check was deposited and the bank caused the customer to draw a check on his own account immediately after the deposit to pay off a note he owed the bank. The bank then lent him an additional $6,000 in return for his new note and credited $5,963 of the new loan proceeds to his checking account. It is unclear what happened to the $11,000 over-draft in the course of this transaction. In no event, however, does the case stand for the proposition that the mere granting of a revocable credit constitutes the giving of value. Rather the $9,000 was immediately withdrawn to pay off a note and to the extent that an additional $6,000 credit was given, it was given for a new note and, implicitly at least, was "available for withdrawal as of right" as the proceeds of a new loan. Moreover to the extent that some or all of the $9,000 was used to obliterate the over-draft, the bank would have given value under 3–303(b) by taking the check in satisfaction of an antecedent indebtedness. Thus the First Circuit's reliance upon Waltham Citizens National Bank v. Flett is misplaced. Note that the First Circuit's misuse of authority should not change the outcome, for there were at least two sound bases for its decision that the Spanish bank had given value. The first is that relied upon by the district court which held that the terms of the agreement between the Spanish customer and the Spanish bank permitted the credit to be drawn upon as of right. Secondly, the credit in the

31.  409 F.2d 711, 6 UCC Rep.Serv. 378 (1st Cir. 1969).

32.  Id. at 714, 6 UCC Rep.Serv. at 383.

33.  353 Mass. 696, 234 N.E.2d 739, 5 UCC Rep.Serv. 186 (1968).

Spanish bank was used to satisfy "debts," and presumably the bank therefore could have qualified under 3–303(b).

A bank may give value prior to the time of final payment in ways other than by granting an absolute right to draw. Another First Circuit case, Bowling Green, Inc. v. State Street Bank & Trust Co.,[34] is illustrative. In that case the State Street Bank & Trust Co. had a perfected security interest in various of the assets and proceeds of the assets of its depositor. The depositor deposited a $15,000 government check and State Street argued that it had become a holder in due course by giving value prior to the time when it found out about its customer's bankruptcy. The First Circuit agreed that State Street had complied with 4–209 and by its security agreement with the debtor had procured a security interest in the check prior to the time of collection, for the check was a 9–306 proceed under the secured transaction between the bank and its customer. The court also relied upon 3–303(b) and 4–208(1) (c).[35]

If in the usual case a bank gives value only when an item is "withdrawn," how does one determine when the withdrawal of the specific item is made from an account consisting of many commingled funds? Assume for example, that customer's account stands at zero at 9:00 a. m.; at 10:00 a. m. he deposits check one in the amount of $2,000 and at 11:00 a. m. check two in the amount of $3,000. On the next day customer draws $2,500 from the account. Thereafter both checks bounce since payment has been stopped on each of them and the bank withdraws the remaining $2,500 from the account. Since its customer has disappeared without a trace, the bank sues the drawer on check one and argues that it is a holder in due course and not subject to whatever defense drawer has against the bank's customer. Drawer of check one argues that bank did not give value, for the credit was never withdrawn. Under the provisions of 4–208 (2) the bank wins: "For the purpose of this section, credits first given are first withdrawn." Since the $2,000 check was the first one deposited, it is presumed to have been the amount first withdrawn under the FIFO rule when the customer took $2,500 out of the account. Therefore bank will have a security interest in that check, will have given value for it and will be able to recover only $500 from the other drawer, for $2000. of the $2,500 which the bank set off is presumed to be attributable to that check.

The first sentence of 4–208(2) reads:

When credit which has been given for several items received at one time or pursuant to a single agreement is with-

34. 425 F.2d 81, 7 UCC Rep.Serv. 635 (1st Cir. 1970).

35. Section 4–208 states:

(1) A bank has a security interest in an item and any accompanying documents or proceeds of either . . .

(c) if it makes an advance on or against the item . . . .

\*   \*   \*

drawn or applied in part the security interest remains upon all the items, any accompanying documents or the proceeds of either.

Presumably under this language, the bank would have a right only to a pro-rata recovery if both checks had been deposited simultaneously. It would be a holder in due course of check one to the extent of $1,000 and a holder in due course of check two to the extent of $1,500. Admittedly the quoted sentence does not specify proration in so many words, but there is no reason to believe that the draftsmen intended by the quoted language to give the bank the right to recover the entire $5,000 when it paid out only $2,500 in reliance upon the two checks.

In the usual case a depositary bank will not have become a holder in due course until an item deposited for collection is drawn upon or otherwise "applied." Different rules apply when the item is not deposited for collection but is taken in payment for an antecedent indebtedness or when the credit is payment for a discounted note. The latter case is presumably covered by 4–208(1) (c) in that the depositor has a legal "right" to withdraw such a credit.

### § 14–6  Holder in Due Course Defined—Good Faith and Without Notice

To be a holder in due course under 3–302, a party must take the instrument in "good faith" and "without notice that it is overdue or has been dishonored or of any defense against or claim to it on the part of any person." We deal with these two provisions together because they appear in the cases and in the flesh as first cousins. The same facts which call a party's "good faith" into question, may also give him "notice of a defense." Note however that the two are not identical. For example, knowledge of a defense would prevent one from being a holder in due course of that instrument but it would not necessarily prevent him from being a holder in due course of other instruments of the same party. If, on the other hand the holder knew that makers had asserted good defenses to their liability against a given payee in 50 out of the last 100 instruments made payable to that payee, the holder might fail to be a holder in due course because he lacked good faith as to that instrument, even though he did not know of a specific defense on any given instrument.

A party can acquire notice of a defense in a variety of ways. He can observe that the instrument is crudely altered; he can see that its date for payment has already passed; he can note that it has been stamped "paid," or he may even have actual knowledge of a contract defense of the drawer or maker. In all such cases a would-be holder in due course does not deserve to take free of such defenses, for he could have refused to take the instrument.

The good faith requirement has been the source of a continuing and ancient dispute. The question has been whether courts are to apply a so-called objective test (i. e., if a reasonably prudent man behaved the way the alleged holder in due course behaved, would he have been in good faith?) or whether the test should be subjective (i. e., irrespective of a reasonable prudent man's reaction to this circumstance, was this alleged holder in due course acting in good faith, however stupid and negligent his behavior might have been?). For a time the English law under the case of Gill v. Cubitt [36] applied the so-called objective test of good faith. Under the NIL the American courts generally applied the subjective test and rejected the doctrine of Gill v. Cubitt.[37] This dispute between the backers of the objective and the subjective test carried through to the early days of the Uniform Commercial Code, and 3–302(1) (b) of the 1952 Code which was enacted in Pennsylvania, required not just that the holder be "in good faith" but "in good faith including observance of the reasonable commercial standards of any business in which the holder may be engaged." [38] Whether the language beginning with the word "including" fully implemented the objective standard was the subject of dispute; some argued before the New York Law Revision Commission that it did so.[39] In apparent response to those concerns, the draftsmen deleted the offending language [40] and left the bare words "in good faith" which appear in the current Code. They stated "the omission is intended to make clear that the doctrine of an objective standard of good faith, exemplified by the case Gill v. Cubitt, is not intended to be incorporated in Article 3." At the conclusion of the scrimmaging among the Code draftsmen and the various proponents of different positions, it was clear that the draftsmen intended to adopt a subjective standard for the good faith test in Article 3. Most of the skirmishing on the notice and good faith front occurs not inside banks upon the transfer of checks but upon the transfer of notes and particularly consumer notes.

Under the provisions of 1–201(25) a person has " 'notice' of a fact" when:

(a) he has actual knowledge of it; or

(b) he has received a notice or notification of it; or

(c) from all the facts and circumstances known to him at the time in question he has reason to know that it exists.

A court's power to find notice when the holder "has reason to know" that something exists on the basis of the "facts and circumstances known to him" introduces at least the flavor of the objec-

---

36.  3 B & C 466, 107 Eng.Rep. 806 (K.B. 1824).

37.  F. Beutel, Beutel's Brannon Negotiable Instruments Law § 56 at 772–74 (7th ed. 1948), lists more than two pages of cases supporting the proposition that "suspicious circumstances sufficient to put a prudent man on inquiry . . . are not sufficient of themselves to prevent recovery.

. . ." Three cases are cited contra. Id.

38.  § 3–302(1) (b) (1952 Official Draft).

39.  See, e. g., 1 N.Y. Law Revision Comm'n, 1954 Report 198, 203 (1954).

40.  Permanent Editorial Board for the Uniform Commercial Code, 1956 Recommendations 102 (1956).

tive-subjective fight. It is a short step from that definition to say that one "knows" what a reasonable prudent man in his circumstances "knows". As we will see, courts vary substantially in their willingness to find notice of claims or defenses on the basis of facts known to holders. Some who are willing to find "notice" may be edging toward objective good faith under a new banner.

The starting point for any analysis of the question of notice is section 3–304. That section, entitled "Notice To Purchaser", lists certain circumstances in which one is deemed to have notice and others which do not of themselves give the purchaser notice of a claim or defense.[41] The section merits careful reading by one trying to determine whether or not his holder took with "notice." [42]

41. Id. at 103.

In an excellent memorandum, Robert S. Pasley summarizes the attack on the "reasonable commercial standard language": "[In determining] . . . subjective honesty, the truth of a claim to honesty may be determined by a jury on evidence of knowledge which the jury believes would have led an honest man to refuse to take the instrument. . . ." This issue arises, he explains, because "objective good faith" and "objective bad faith" are not all inclusive; there is a middle ground between. 2 N.Y. State Law Revision Comm'n, 1955 Report 903–904 (1955).

The policy underlying the objection to the objective good faith standard is most forcefully presented by the banking community through its legal representatives. 1 N.Y. State Law Revision Comm'n, 1954 Report 204 (1954), urges that the wheels of commerce would grind to a halt if an objective standard were adopted and supports this fear with the experiences of England: ". . . the 'reasonable commercial standards' phrase in 3–302 definitely opens the prospect of a return to the doctrine of Gill v. Cubitt which, as has been noted, resulted in such discredit of Bank of England on the European continent and complaints of the mercantile community, as to lead subsequent English courts and the NIL itself to adopt the doctrine of good faith and actual notice."

42. Section 3–304 reads:

(1) The purchaser has notice of a claim or defense if

(a) the instrument is so incomplete, bears such visible evidence of forgery or alteration, or is otherwise

so irregular as to call into question its validity, terms or ownership or to create an ambiguity as to the party to pay; or

(b) the purchaser has notice that the obligation of any party is voidable in whole or in part, or that all parties have been discharged.

(2) The purchaser has notice of a claim against the instrument when he has knowledge that a fiduciary has negotiated the instrument in payment of or as security for his own debt or in any transaction for his own benefit or otherwise in breach of duty.

(3) The purchaser has notice that an instrument is overdue if he has reason to know

(a) that any part of the principal amount is overdue or that there is an uncured default in payment of another instrument of the same series; or

(b) that acceleration of the instrument has been made; or

(c) that he is taking a demand instrument after demand has been made or more than a reasonable length of time after its issue. A reasonable time for a check drawn and payable within the states and territories of the United States and the District of Columbia is presumed to be thirty days.

(4) Knowledge of the following facts does not of itself give the purchaser notice of a defense or claim

(a) that the instrument is antedated or postdated;

(b) that it was issued or negotiated in return for an executory promise or accompanied by a separate agreement, unless the purchaser has notice that a defense or

One may classify the kinds of facts a holder may know and from which a court may be willing to infer notice. The first is direct information from the transferor or the principal obligor about the underlying transaction or some aspect of it. A second kind of information is as to documents transferred to the holder in due course together with the note (e. g., mortgage, retail installment sales contract). Third is information concerning the business practices of the transferor, usually the payee of a note. The fourth and perhaps the most important information is that written on the face of the instrument. The date and figures or statements on the face of the instrument as well as blanks and obvious erasures may give the would be holder in due course a notice of claims or defenses. Doubtless the message on the face of an instrument that most often deprives the holder of holder in due course status is that the instrument is overdue. Under 3–304(3) (c) a check drawn and payable within the United States is "presumed to be" overdue 30 days after the date it bears. Likewise the typical note will show whether the due date has passed. Courts have decided that one has "notice" of the due date on an instrument whether or not he in fact examined the instrument.[43]

claim has arisen from the terms thereof;

(c) that any party has signed for accommodation;

(d) that an incomplete instrument has been completed, unless the purchaser has notice of any improper completion;

(e) that any person negotiating the instrument is or was a fiduciary;

(f) that there has been default in payment of interest on the instrument or in payment of any other instrument, except one of the same series.

(5) The filing or recording of a document does not of itself constitute notice within the provisions of this Article to a person who would otherwise be a holder in due course.

(6) To be effective notice must be received at such time and in such manner as to give a reasonable opportunity to act on it.

43. See Srochi v. Kamensky, 118 Ga. App. 182, 162 S.E.2d 889, 5 UCC Rep.

Serv. 868 (1968) (plaintiffs admitted they knew that note was past due) (dictum); County Trust Co. v. Pascack Valley Bank & Trust Co., 93 N.J. Super. 252, 225 A.2d 605, 3 UCC Rep. Serv. 1062 (App.Div.1966) (dictum). Where due date was altered, taker does not have notice if the alteration was carefully done. Unadilla Nat'l Bank v. McQueer, 27 App.Div.2d 778, 277 N.Y.S.2d 221, 4 UCC Rep.Serv. 98 (3d Dep't 1967).

When a demand note becomes overdue is not clear. Section 3–304(3) (c) states that a demand instrument becomes overdue when "more than a reasonable length of time" has passed since its issue. For a detailed annotation of the cases, see Annot., 10 ALR 3d 1199 (1972). That annotation lists a number of factors which influence the reasonableness of the time: trade or business usage, time for presentment, distance between place of issue and the place of negotiation, and special facts of the case. Id. at 1203. The annotation also points out the Sunday intervening between issue and negotiation tends to lengthen the time, and that the lack of interest on the note tends to shorten it. Id.

Another common message that the face of an instrument bears is that of forgery or alteration.  Section 3–304(1) (a) states the rule with respect to such instruments as follows:

> (1) The purchaser has notice of a claim or defense if
>
> (a) the instrument is so incomplete, bears such visible evidence of forgery or alteration, or is otherwise so irregular as to call into question its validity, terms or ownership or to create an ambiguity as to the party to pay; or  .  .  .  .

Note first that one may be a holder in due course of an instrument notwithstanding that it contains blanks or has obviously been completed in a hand different from that of the maker.  Comment 2 to 3–304 reads in part:  "An instrument may be blank as to some unnecessary particular, may contain minor erasures, or even an obvious change in the date, as where 'January 2, 1948' is changed to 'January 2, 1949', without even exciting suspicion.  Irregularity is properly a question of notice to the purchaser of something wrong, and is so treated here."  Likewise 3–304(4) (d) provides that knowledge that an incomplete instrument has been completed is not notice of a defense or claim unless the would be holder in due course has notice of "improper completion."  Thus in Cook v. Southern Credit Corp.,[44] the Arkansas Supreme Court held that the plaintiff was a holder in due course although he knew the plaintiff had filled in blanks in the note, and in National State Bank of Elizabeth, New Jersey v. Kleinburg,[45] the New York Supreme Court held the fact that "41,000" had been obviously changed to "42,000" did not "excite suspicion" under 3–304 sufficient to put the holder on notice of a defense or claim.  Likewise a printed check that had two signature lines with only one containing a signature did not put the holder on notice.[46]  However, the holder of a note bearing the words "consumer note" took with notice under Massachusetts law that the parties who signed the note did not intend it to be negotiable.[47]  Thus courts will tolerate obvious alterations and find a purchaser to be a holder in due course where extrinsic facts adequately explain the change (as for example, when the drawer of a check puts down 1983 on a check drawn in January of 1984).  Section 3–304(1) (a) gives courts a great deal of discretion.  Presumably they will be more hesitant to hold a party to be a holder in due course when extrinsic facts do not explain erasures and the like.

A second kind of information which may put a purchaser on notice derives from documents transferred concurrently with a negotiable instrument.  For example, in HIMC Investment Co. v. Sicili-

**44.**  247 Ark. 981, 448 S.W.2d 634, 7 UCC Rep.Serv. 220 (1970).

**45.**  4 UCC Rep.Serv. 100 (N.Y.Sup.Ct. 1967).

**46.**  New Waterford Bank v. Morrison Buick, Inc., 38 Pa.D. & C.2d 371, 3 UCC Rep.Serv. 426 (C.P.1965).

**47.**  See Section 14–9 infra.

ano,[48] the court pointed out that certain of the terms on a second mortgage accompanying the note revealed a violation in the New Jersey second mortgage law. When a retail installment sales contract or a mortgage or other such documents accompany a note, such documents may reveal violations of the state usury law, or of the retail installment sales act, or of state or federal disclosure acts. Whether courts will find a purchaser of such documents to be on notice of all facts a lawyer-accountant might thus discover in an hour's work with a calculating machine, remains to be seen. The *HIMC* case suggests at least that holders will have notice of any gross legal defects that such documents reveal.

A third kind of information which may prevent a purchaser from assuming status as a holder in due course, is his knowledge of the business practices of his payee. If the holder's knowledge of a transferor's generally shoddy business practices constitutes "notice of a defense" with respect to every instrument he transfers this would exceed the wildest hopes of those who argued for an objective standard; but the courts show no desire to go that far. However in several cases courts seem to have been influenced by the holder's knowledge of business practices of the transferor. For example in Norman v. World Wide Distributors, Inc.,[49] the court stressed that the purchaser of the note "knew enough of the seller's referral plan to require it to inquire further" and secondly that he knew that the seller had been doing business under three different names during the year in which the note was transferred. Those two facts in addition to a substantial discount led the court to find the purchaser was not a holder in due course. On the other hand the court in O. P. Ganjo, Inc. v. Tri-Urban Realty Co., Inc.,[50] found that knowledge of suspicious circumstances was not enough and specifically affirmed the objective good faith test in the face of grave suspicions on the part of the purchaser about the veracity and credit standing of the sub-contractor who transferred the note. Likewise in Waterbury Savings Bank v. Jaroszewski,[51] a Connecticut court found that knowledge of defects in three or four transactions out of five or six hundred prior transactions, did not constitute notice.[52] Thus what notice of defenses or lack of good faith courts will infer from knowledge of a transferor's shoddy business practices is still unsettled. It is clear that the courts give some weight to this knowledge when it is associated with other in-

**48.** 103 N.J.Super. 27, 246 A.2d 502, 5 UCC Rep.Serv. 846 (Law Div.1968). The court also found facts which suggest a close relationship between plaintiff and lender, although the court did not discuss it at length. See Section 14–8 infra.

**49.** 202 Pa.Super. 53, 195 A.2d 115, 1 UCC Rep.Serv. 234 (1963).

**50.** 108 N.J.Super. 517, 7 UCC Rep.Serv. 302 (Law Div.1970).

**51.** 4 Conn.Cir. 620, 238 A.2d 446, 4 UCC Rep.Serv. 1049 (1967).

**52.** See also Universal CIT Credit Corp. v. Ingel, 347 Mass. 119, 196 N.E.2d 847, 2 UCC Rep.Serv. 82, 3 UCC Rep. Serv. 303 (1964) (seller of aluminum siding sold paper to plaintiff; previous dealing and suspicious circumstances are not knowledge).

formation, but so far no court seems willing to rely exclusively on such knowledge to find that a purchaser has notice of a claim or defense.

In some cases the courts find notice not on the basis of information available to the purchaser, but on the basis of his behavior. Examples are cases in which purchasers discount notes by a very large margin and those in which purchasers actually contact the payees on notes to disclaim any complicity in shoddy business practices of the payee. Illustrative of large discount cases is United States Finance Co. v. Jones,[53] in which the Alabama Supreme Court found that the sale of a note with a face value of $2,575.44 for $1,360 was an important factor indicating that the plaintiff had notice of a defense.[54] In Norman v. World Wide Distributors, Inc.,[55] a representative of the purchaser called the maker of a note and informed him that he as holder had nothing to do with the referral-purchase plan. The court inferred knowledge of the referral plan's illegality from this careful disclaimer of any association with it. Whether the star of the holder in due course is waxing or waning on questions of notice and good faith is difficult to say. It seems that courts are quicker to find notice on the part of a purchaser of a consumer note than they are on the part of a purchaser of a businessman's note.[56]

Finally we should note that for most purposes there need be no connection between the defense or claim which the party on the instrument is attempting to assert and the flaw which allegedly deprives one of holder in due course status. Thus if one takes an overdue note, the maker can assert defenses such as failure of consideration which have nothing to do with time and the fact that the note was overdue.[57] Note that one can be a holder in due course as to part of the instrument. If for example the holder receives notice of a defense at a time when he has paid 50% of the agreed value of an instrument, he will be a holder in due course to that extent under 3–303(a).

---

53. 285 Ala. 105, 229 So.2d 495, 7 UCC Rep.Serv. 204 (1969).

54. In Norman v. Worldwide Distrib., Inc., 202 Pa.Super. 53, 195 A.2d 115, 1 UCC Rep.Serv. 234 (1963), a $200 discount on a $1,000 note due in three days was one factor which led to the defeat of a potential holder in due course. In O. P. Ganjo, Inc. v. Tri-Urban Realty Co., Inc., 108 N.J.Super. 517, 7 UCC Rep.Serv. 302 (Law Div. 1970), a $200 discount on a $3,000 note was not evidence of bad faith.

55. 202 Pa.Super. 53, 195 A.2d 115, 1 UCC Rep.Serv. 234 (1963).

56. For instance, in the two cases noted in footnote 54 supra, one was a consumer's note, and the other was a businessman's note. In *Ganjo* the holder had "suspicions" about the business practices of his transferor and discounted the note by almost seven percent; he was a holder in due course of the businessman's note. In *Norman*, the holder "knew" about the refund plan and other shady practices of his transferor and discounted the note by twenty percent; he was not a holder in due course of a consumer's note.

57. In a few pre-Code cases holders with notice of a defense were regarded as holders in due course with respect to certain other defenses. See W. Britton, Handbook on the Law of Bills and Notes 117 (2d ed. 1961). Whether these cases are good law under the Code, we do not know.

## § 14–7  The Payee as a Holder in Due Course

Section 3–302(2) lays to rest an ancient question as follows: "A payee may be a holder in due course." So stated the rule is deceptively simple, and it leaves two important questions unanswered: (1) What is the legal significance of the fact that a payee can be a holder in due course? (2) Must a payee meet any conditions other than those stated in 3–302 ("value etc.") to be a holder in due course? Turning to the first question, consider 3–305. Because that section permits a party to take free of the defenses only of a "party to the instrument with whom the holder has not dealt," most payees will not take free of the drawer's or maker's defenses even when these payees are holders in due course, for they will have dealt with the drawer or maker.[58] In most cases therefore a payee holder in due course will not enjoy the most significant advantage normally accorded one in his shoes. That is not to say that a payee will always be subject to the drawer or maker's defenses. Comment 2 to 3–302 consists of a series of hypothetical cases in which the payee does not deal with the drawer or maker and thus takes free of defenses. For example, the Comment suggests the case in which A induces B to sign as co-maker by fraud and, without authority from B, delivers the note to P who takes it for value, in good faith and without notice. In that case P would be a holder in due course and would take free of the defense of fraud.

A second way in which the payee's status as a holder in due course might affect his legal rights involves 3–418, the finality doctrine. That doctrine (discussed in Section 16–4) operates on behalf only of holders in due course and those who change their position in reliance upon final payment. Thus one who procures final payment on a check which bears a forged drawer's signature may not rely on the finality doctrine (at least insofar as that doctrine is embodied in 3–418) unless he is a holder in due course or one who has changed his position in reliance upon the final payment. In many cases the payee will not have so changed position and he will wish to claim that he is a holder in due course and thus entitled to 3–418's protection. The legal significance to the payee of acquiring holder in due course status is not likely to be great except on rare occasions.[59]

**58.**  Hall v. Westmoreland, Hall & Bryan, 123 Ga.App. 809, 182 S.E.2d 539, 9 UCC Rep.Serv. 604 (1971). But see Bailey v. Polster, 468 S.W.2d 105, 9 UCC Rep.Serv. 611 (Tex.Civ.App. 1971) (court does not discuss the "dealt with" language, but permits plaintiff to take free of defenses against defendant with whom he dealt).

**59.**  Sani-Serv Division of Burger Chef Systems, Inc. v. Southern Bank, 244 So.2d 509, 8 UCC Rep.Serv. 1046 (Fla. App.1970) shows a third and arguably improper benefit which may flow to a payee because he is a holder in due course. In that case the court found that a bank could not stop payment on a cashier's check when it was presented by a holder in due course. The court's holding is probably a misinterpretation of the Code. However, it is unclear whether the misinterpretation caused an improper outcome. It is possible in that case that the payee would have been held not to have dealt with the bank and, as a holder in due course, would have taken free of the bank's defense under 3–305 and could have sued and re-

Must payees meet any conditions other than those embodied in 3–302 to be holders in due course? Comment 2 to 3–302 deals exclusively with payees who did not themselves deal with the drawer or maker. Can one infer from the draftsmen's choice of such examples that only such persons (i. e. those "once removed") can be payee-holders in due course? Is there an unarticulated condition to 3–302(2)? At least one New York judge seems to have adopted that position [60] and at least one New York case suggests the same.[61] We agree with those courts that apparently find no such condition.[62] In our opinion, any payee who meets the other tests embodied in 3–302(1) is a holder in due course. We suspect that the draftsmen discussed payees once removed in Comment 2 because only such payees can take advantage of 3–305.

## § 14–8   Judge-Made Limitations on the Holder in Due Course Doctrine—Close-Connectedness

An important recent development in holder in due course law is the rejuvenation of the "close connectedness" doctrine. Under that doctrine the purchaser of a negotiable instrument is not a holder in due course if he is too closely connected to his transferor. (The transferor is usually the payee on a note). Courts have applied this doctrine erratically over the past fifty years, but since 1967, it has seen a more certain growth. In that year Judge Francis of the New Jersey Supreme Court (the people who brought you Henningsen v. Bloomfield Motors Inc.[63]) applied the doctrine in Unico v. Owens.[64] In a long opinion, Judge Francis found the payee of a note and his transferee to be so closely connected that the transferee could not be a holder in due course. Though hardly novel, *Unico*, like *Henningsen*

---

covered on the bank-drawer's contract. If the payee had "dealt with" the drawer, the outcome would be improper.

**60.** See Saale v. Interstate Steel Co., Inc., 27 App.Div.2d 1, 5, 275 N.Y.S.2d 532, 536, 3 UCC Rep.Serv. 1140, 1144 (1st Dep't 1966) (dissenting opinion, Rabin, J.), affirmed without opinion, 19 N.Y.2d 933, 228 N.E.2d 397, 4 UCC Rep.Serv. 1053 (1967).

**61.** Mansion Carpets, Inc. v. Marinoff, 24 App.Div.2d 947, 265 N.Y.S.2d 298, 3 UCC Rep.Serv. 68 (1st Dep't 1965).

**62.** See, e. g., Morris v. Durbin, 123 Ga. App. 383, 180 S.E.2d 925, 9 UCC Rep. Serv. 92 (1971) (dictum); Hall v. Westmoreland, Hall & Bryan, 123 Ga. App. 809, 182 S.E.2d 539, 9 UCC Rep. Serv. 604 (1971) (plaintiffs failed to establish they were holders in due course) (dictum); Bailey v. Polster, 468 S.W.2d 105, 9 UCC Rep.Serv. 611 (Tex.Civ.App.1971); Sani-Serv Divi-

sion of Burger Chef Systems, Inc. v. Southern Bank, 244 So.2d 509, 8 UCC Rep.Serv. 1046 (Fla.App.1970) (alternative holding, although plaintiff did not argue it). For further enlightenment on the consequences of whether the payee must meet an additional requirement to be called a holder in due course, see the discussion of discharge and 3–418 in Ch. 16 and text accompanying notes 7–9 infra.

**63.** 32 N.J. 358, 161 A.2d 69 (1960).

**64.** 50 N.J. 101, 232 A.2d 405, 4 UCC Rep.Serv. 542 (1967). The decision is specifically limited to the case where a large part of seller's obligation is executory and does not purport to decide the case of when the seller has fully but defectively performed. How one, on similar facts, can be "close connected" in the case of executory contracts but not "close connected" in the case of delivery of defective goods is unclear.

was seminal. Since *Unico*, the courts in the District of Columbia, Delaware and Ohio have applied the doctrine [65] and parties have asserted it without success in Connecticut, Wisconsin and Massachusetts.[66]

Although the legal consequences of the application of the doctrine are clear enough, namely that plaintiff is not a holder in due course and is therefore subject to defenses of the defendant, the theory upon which that legal conclusion is based and the supporting evidence required for it remain unclear. Some courts seem to proceed upon the theory that sufficiently close connection makes a seller of goods into an agent of the lender. Thus the seller's knowledge of defenses is imputed to his principal, the lender.[67] Other courts imply that the "oneness" of the parties is tantamount to no transfer.[68] Other courts have simply concluded that the lender is not "in good faith." [69] If one can specify the kind of evidence that brings the doctrine into play it is less important to determine whether the theory is lack of good faith, presence of notice, or simply "oneness" of the parties.[70]

---

**65.** See American Plan Corp. v. Woods, 16 Ohio App.2d 1, 240 N.E.2d 886, 5 UCC Rep.Serv. 842 (1968) (plaintiff gave seller forms, established financing charges, investigated each customer, and reserved right to reject any risky note); Calvert Credit Corp. v. Williams, 244 A.2d 494, 5 UCC Rep. Serv. 607 (D.C.App.1968) (plaintiff exerted control of seller, and without plaintiff's agreement to buy the commercial paper, seller would not have started business); Jones v. Approved Bancredit Corp., 256 A.2d 739, 6 UCC Rep.Serv. 1001 (Del.1969) (seller and plaintiffs were wholly owned subsidiaries of third corporation).

**66.** Waterbury Sav. Bank v. Jaroszewski, 4 Conn.Cir. 620, 238 A.2d 446, 4 UCC Rep.Serv. 1049 (1967); Milwaukee Acceptance Corp. v. Dore, 43 Wis.2d 412, 168 N.W.2d 594, 6 UCC Rep.Serv. 1065 (1969) (defendant made note as part of shady deal); Universal CIT Credit Corp. v. Ingel, 347 Mass. 119, 196 N.E.2d 847, 2 UCC Rep. Serv. 82, 3 UCC Rep.Serv. 303 (1964).

The close connectedness doctrine has been with us a long time. See Commercial Credit Co. v. Childs, 199 Ark. 1073, 137 S.W.2d 260 (1940) (plaintiff printed sales contracts for seller with assignments already printed on back and bought paper same day as executed); Commercial Credit Co. v. Orange County Machine Works, 34 Cal.2d 766, 214 P.2d 819 (1950) (plaintiff supplied blank form for note and

was consulted by seller during transaction).

**67.** E. g., American Plan Corp. v. Woods, 16 Ohio App.2d 1, 240 N.E.2d 886, 5 UCC Rep.Serv. 842 (1968); Waterbury Sav. Bank v. Jaroszewski, 4 Conn.Cir.Ct. 620, 238 A.2d 446, 4 UCC Rep.Serv. 1049 (1967); Milwaukee Acceptance Corp. v. Dore, 43 Wis. 2d 412, 168 N.W.2d 594, 6 UCC Rep. Serv. 1065 (1969).

**68.** E. g., Jones v. Approved Bancredit Corp., 256 A.2d 739, 6 UCC Rep.Serv. 1001 (Del.1969); Unico v. Owens, 50 N.J. 101, 232 A.2d 405, 4 UCC Rep. Serv. 542 (1967).

**69.** E. g., Calvert Credit Corp. v. Williams, 244 A.2d 494, 5 UCC Rep.Serv. 607 (D.C.Ct.App., 1968); Universal CIT Credit Corp. v. Ingel, 347 Mass. 119, 196 N.E.2d 847, 2 UCC Rep.Serv. 82, 3 UCC Rep.Serv. 303 (1964).

**70.** Section 3–305(2) states that a holder in due course takes free of personal defenses "of any party to the instrument with whom the holder has *not dealt*." (emphasis added) Thus, if holder is so closely connected with the payee that they are "one," the maker could still assert his personal defenses.

Bowling Green v. State St. Bank & Trust Co., 425 F.2d 81, 7 UCC Rep. Serv. 635 (1st Cir. 1970), seems to indicate that close connectedness is a reversion to the objective standard of

What circumstances constitute "close connection"? The appellate opinions in recently decided cases are a rather cloudy window through which to see the factors that influence courts to find "close connection." One suspects that the relative "rawness" of the deal that the seller gives the defendant consumer is highly relevant even though often unarticulated. The opinions yield no precise formula and although each of them includes discussion of two or more of the following factors, the opinions do not quantify any factors or point to those which are particularly decisive. Here are five factors the courts have emphasized:

(*1*) Drafting by the lender of forms for the seller.

(*2*) Approval or establishment or both of the seller's procedures by the lender (e. g., setting of the interest rate, approval of a referral sales plan).

(*3*) An independent check by the lender on the credit of the debtor or some other direct contact between the lender and the debtor.

(*4*) Heavy reliance by the seller upon the lender (e. g., transfer by seller of all or a substantial part of his paper to one lender).

(*5*) Common or connected ownership or management of seller and lender.

Note first that none of the recent cases in which courts found close connectedness involved all five of the foregoing factors. Connected ownership appeared in only one of the cases, while provision of forms by the lender for the seller may have been present in all. Upon reading the cases one can only speculate on the relative weight of the various factors. For example, although provision of forms was most prevalent, it seems insufficient in and of itself, for it was present in the Connecticut and Massachusetts cases that refused to find close connectedness. Since only the Delaware court explicitly found com-

good faith. In *Bowling Green*, the First Circuit rejected an argument which was apparently based upon the doctrine of close connectedness with the statement that the Massachusetts court had not adopted nor indicated a desire to adopt the objective standard of good faith. Such a characterization greatly overstates the impact of the close connectedness doctrine. It would certainly be possible for the law to find that one is in good faith if he has a white heart and an empty head and yet find that a sufficient connection between the lender and his transferor placed the lender in the shoes of the transferor. There would still be many cases as, for example, when a bank takes a check without the kind of investigation that a rea-

sonable prudent man might make, for the application of the doctrine of subjective good faith even by a court that was a whole-hearted supporter of the close connectedness doctrine. Thus as long as the court does not regard the doctrine as a return to the objective standard of good faith, it makes little difference whether it rationalizes the outcome under the close connectedness as an imputation of notice to the lender, as a finding that the lender is not in good faith, or as a finding under 3–305 that the lender is one who "dealt with" the defendant and therefore will not take free of the defendant's defenses notwithstanding the lender's status as a holder in due course.

mon ownership, it seems that close connectedness can exist without
a prior finding of some ownership inter-relation.[71]

71.  Unico v. Owen, 50 N.J. 101, 114–
116, 232 A.2d 405, 412–13, 4 UCC Rep.
Serv. 542, 551–52 (1967), states the
connections between the seller and the
holder:

Unico was a partnership formed expressly for the purpose of financing
Universal Stereo Corporation, and
Universal agreed to pay all costs up to
a fixed amount in connection with
Unico's formation.  The elaborate contract between them, dated August 24,
1962, recited that Universal was engaged in the merchandising of records and stereophonic sets, and that it
desired to borrow money from time to
time from Unico, "secured by the assignment of accounts receivable, promissory notes, trade acceptances, conditional sales contracts, chattel mortgages, leases, installment contracts, or
other forms of agreement evidencing
liens."  Subject to conditions set out
in the agreement, Unico agreed to lend
Universal up to 35% of the total
amount of the balances of customers'
contracts assigned to Unico subject to
a limit of $50,000, in return for which
Universal submitted to a substantial
degree of control of its entire business
operation by the lender.  As collateral
security for the loans, Universal
agreed to negotiate "to the lender" all
customers' notes listed in a monthly
schedule of new sales contracts, and
to assign all conditional sale contracts connected with the notes, as
well as the right to any monies due
from customers.

Specific credit qualifications for Universal's record album customers were
imposed by Unico; requirements for
the making of the notes and their endorsement were established, and the
sale contracts had to be recorded in
the county recording office.  All such
contracts were required to meet the
standards of the agreement between
lender and borrower, among them being that the customer's installment
payment term would not exceed 36
months and "every term" of the Uni-
co-Universal agreement was to "be
deemed incorporated into all assignments" of record sales contracts delivered as security for the loans.  It
was further agreed that Unico should
have all the rights of Universal under the contracts as if it were the
seller, including the right to enforce

them in its name, and Unico was given
an irrevocable power to enforce such
rights.

In the event of Universal's default on
payment of its loans, Unico was authorized to deal directly with the record buyers with respect to payment of
their notes and to settle with and discharge such customers.  Unico was
empowered to place its representatives on Universal's premises with full
authority to take possession of the
books and records; or otherwise, it
could inspect the records at any time;
and it was given a "special property
interest" in such records.  Financial
statements were required to be submitted by Universal "at least semi-
annually"; and two partners of Unico were to be paid one-quarter of one
per cent interest on the loans as a
management service charge, in addition to the interest to be paid Unico.
Significant also in connection with
the right to oversee Universal's business is a warranty included in the
contract.  It warrants that Universal
owns free and clear "all merchandise
referred to and described in [the
sales] contracts, . . . at the time
of making the sale creating such contracts."  Obviously this was not the
fact, otherwise Universal would not
have discontinued shipping records to
its customers, such as Owen.  If Universal did not have such a store of
records, as warranted, Unico might
well have had reason to suspect its
borrower's financial stability.

This general outline of the Universal-
Unico financing agreement serves as
evidence that Unico not only had a
thorough knowledge of the nature and
method of operation of Universal's
business, but also exercised extensive
control over it.  Moreover, obviously
it had a large, if not decisive, hand
in the fashioning and supplying of
the form of contract and note used by
Universal, and particularly in setting
the terms of the record album sales
agreement, which were designed to
put the buyer-consumer in an unfair
and burdensome legal strait jacket
and to bar any escape no matter what
the default of the seller, while permitting the note-holder, contract-as-
signee to force payment from him by
enveloping itself in the formal status
of holder in due course.  To say the

Important for all of the courts which found close connectedness was the extent of lender control over the seller's business procedures. In *American Plan* the court stressed that the lender "established the carrying charge" and "approved the arrangement." In *Calvert Credit* the lender "approved in advance the referral plan" and in *Unico*, the lender not only specified the credit requirements but had certain rights to examine the books and records of the seller. Finally in several of the cases, the seller was economically dependent on the lender. In *Calvert* the court noted that the seller could not have commenced business without a prior agreement on the part of the lender to purchase his paper, and in *Unico* the court noted that Unico was formed for the exclusive purpose of financing the seller's business.

If we ignore the articulated basis for the foregoing cases, we can classify them in another and more pragmatic way. In each of the four recent cases of close connectedness, the defendant was a consumer who had been "reamed, steamed and dry cleaned" by his seller. In *Calvert* the court states that none of the color televisions sold under the referral sales plan worked. American Plan v. Wood involved fraud in the factum and the sale of a machine under a bait referral plan. Moreover, the machine and others sold under the plan broke down. In *Unico* the consumer was supposed to receive five years worth of records, but received only 12 out of 140 promised albums. The dismal circumstances in which the defendant, Mrs. Jones, found herself in Jones v. Approved Bank Credit would make even the most vicious creditor tearful. Mrs. Jones bought a pre-fabricated house. During its construction an employee of the builder bulldozed it off its foundation. On the ground that the damage to the structure was a "work of God," the builder refused to go forward. Ultimately the county authorities forced Mrs. Jones to fill in the water-filled basement at her expense because it had become an attractive nuisance. Not only did poor Mrs. Jones not receive what she had bargained for, she suffered the cost of filling in the hole as well!

In addition to the egregiousness of the seller's behavior in these cases, one should note that the plaintiff in each of them was a finance company; none involved a bank. A court may be willing to conclude that paper handled by a finance company is more smelly than that transferred to a bank, and may be quicker to infer unproven interrelationships between seller and finance company than between seller and bank.

The question remains, what does the lawyer—whether as counsel for a finance company involved in planning or as counsel for a defendant who wishes to raise a defense against a would be holder in due course—make of all this? At least two things should be clear from the foregoing cases and from the material on legislative change in the holder in due course doctrine that follows. First, the status

relationship between Unico and the business operations of Universal was close, and that Unico was involved therein, is to put it mildly.

of many purchasers who as recently as five years ago would have been gold-plated holders in due course may now be much more questionable. Out of the cases cited above a debtor's lawyer can now construct a close connectedness argument in a wide variety of transactions. Some of the factors courts have pointed to, namely the drafting and provision of forms, the inspection and supervision of the seller's practices and the retention of the right to reject notes, at least of persons known to be bad credit risks, are present in countless transactions. Only the continuing tide of cases can tell whether the courts will stop to evaluate and identify those factors which make for close connectedness or whether they will push on in a frenzy of judicial activism to do away with the holder in due course in all consumer transactions.

So far as we can tell, the holder in due course doctrine is still alive even in consumer transactions in most states. Moreover, counsel for finance companies can take hope from recent Connecticut and Massachusetts cases in which courts have turned aside what appear to be close connectedness arguments. Moreover counsel for finance company and bank can take hope from the fact that courts have recently invoked the close connectedness doctrine exclusively on behalf of consumer debtors who received most shabby treatment. It seems likely that responsible courts even of activist bent, will be slower to find close connectedness when the consumer's complaint is more questionable than it was in these cases.

## § 14–9 Legislative Limitations on the Holder in Due Course Doctrine

In the past ten years, several state legislatures have made consumer notes nonnegotiable. Such is now the law in Massachusetts and in the home improvement industry in Connecticut,[72] and in Utah [73] and Oklahoma [74] which have enacted the Uniform Consumer Credit Code. The Uniform Consumer Credit Code provision prohibits the use of negotiable notes in consumer transactions:

> In a consumer credit sale or consumer lease, other than a sale or lease primarily for an agricultural purpose, the seller or lessor may not take a negotiable instrument other than a check as evidence of the obligation of the buyer or lessee. A holder is not in good faith if he takes a negotiable instrument with notice that it is issued in violation of this section. A holder in due course is not subject to the liabilities set forth in the provisions on the effect of violations on rights of parties (Section 5.202) and the provisions on civil actions by Administrator (Section 6.113).[75]

72. Conn.Gen.Stat.Ann. §§ 42–134 to 42–143 (Supp.1971).

73. Utah Code Ann. § 70B–2.403 (Supp. 1971).

74. Okla.Stat. Tit. 14A, § 2–403 (Supp. 1971).

75. UCCC § 2.403.

Under this provision it is of course possible for one in violation of the law to have a consumer sign a negotiable note and then transfer that note to one ignorant of its origin who would himself become a holder in due course. Some have complained that this offers a substantial avenue for abuse. They are surely wrong. Given that courts are increasingly willing to protect consumers, given that the typical consumer note shows its consumer origin by the name of the payee on the note (i. e., "pay to the order of Singer Sewing Machine"), and finally given the sophisticated knowledge of purchasers of consumer paper, it seems most unlikely that courts will listen with sympathy to the argument of a financier that he purchased a batch of consumer paper thinking it to be non-consumer paper. The recent Massachusetts case, Alcoa Credit Corporation v. Nickerson,[76] bears us out. The court found that a transaction on a note entitled "consumer note" not covered by the Massachusetts consumer statute,[77] nevertheless was an agreement that the note should not be negotiable and the words "consumer note" gave notice to the buyer of the note that it was not intended to be negotiable.

A question inherent in the UCCC and suggested by the *Nickerson* case is this: what transactions are "consumer credit sales or consumer leases" or otherwise fall within the definitions of a consumer transaction? UCCC 2.104 defines consumer credit sale,[78] and that definition together with the definition of consumer lease in UCCC 2.106 [79] is broad enough to capture virtually every bother-

76. 43 Mass.App.Dec. 1, 5 UCC Rep. Serv. 152 (1968).

77. Mass.Gen.Laws Ann. Ch. 255, § 12C (1968).

78. UCCC § 2.104 reads in full:

(1) Except as provided in subsection (2), "consumer credit sale" is a sale of goods, services, or an interest in land in which

(a) credit is granted by a person who regularly engages as a seller in credit transactions of the same kind,

(b) the buyer is a person other than an organization,

(c) the goods, services, or interest in land are purchased primarily for a personal, family, household, or agricultural purpose,

(d) either the debt is payable in installments or a credit service charge is made, and

(e) with respect to a sale of goods or services, the amount financed does not exceed $25,000.

(2) Unless the sale is made subject to this Act by agreement (Section 2.601), "consumer credit sale" does not include

(a) a sale in which the seller allows the buyer to purchase goods or services pursuant to a lender credit card or similar arrangement, or

(b) except as provided with respect to disclosure (Section 2.301) and debtor's remedies (Section 5.201), a sale of an interest in land if the credit service charge does not exceed 10 per cent per year calculated according to the actuarial method on the unpaid balances of the amount financed on the assumption that the debt will be paid according to the agreed terms and will not be paid before the end of the agreed term.

(3) The amount of $25,000 in subsection (1) is subject to change pursuant to the provisions on adjustment of dollar amounts (Section 1–106).

79. UCCC § 2.106 reads in full:

(1) "Consumer lease" means a lease of goods

(a) which a lessor regularly engaged in the business of leasing makes to a person, other than an

some transaction from the sale of a water softener or sewing machine to the repair of a driveway or the installation of house siding.[80]

### § 14–10    Rights of the Holder in Due Course

The legal battles fought under the holder in due course banner are largely ones in which the issue is whether a given party is in fact a holder in due course. Once that issue is determined, the battle is usually over, and the legal consequences usually clear. The most important legal consequences of holder in due course status are described in 3–305:

> To the extent that a holder is a holder in due course he takes the instrument free from
>
> > (1) all claims to it on the part of any person; and
> >
> > (2) all defenses of any party to the instrument with whom the holder has not dealt except
> >
> > > (a) infancy, to the extent that it is a defense to a simple contract; and
> > >
> > > (b) such other incapacity, or duress, or illegality of the transaction, as renders the obligation of the party a nullity; and
> > >
> > > (c) such misrepresentation as has induced the party to sign the instrument with neither knowledge nor reasonable opportunity to obtain knowledge of its character or its essential terms; and
> > >
> > > (d) discharge in insolvency proceedings; and
> > >
> > > (e) any other discharge of which the holder has notice when he takes the instrument.

Note first that the draftsmen used the word "claims" in subsection (1) and the word "defenses" in subsection (2) presumably to distinguish between assertion of rights of ownership on the one hand, and assertion of legal defenses which do not involve ownership on

---

organization, who takes under the lease primarily for a personal, family, household, or agricultural purpose,

(b) in which the amount payable under the lease does not exceed $25,000, and

(c) which is for a term exceeding four months.

(2) "Consumer lease" does not include a lease made pursuant to a lender credit card or similar arrangement.

(3) The amount of $25,000 in subsection (1) is subject to change pursuant to the provisions on adjustment of dollar amounts (Section 1.106).

80. For a discussion analyzing the probable effects of the UCCC's making consumer notes nonnegotiable, see Note, A Case Study of the Impact of Consumer Legislation: The Elimination of Negotiability and the Cooling-Off Period, 78 Yale L.J. 618 (1969). The note presents empirical evidence of the effect of the Connecticut Home Solicitation Sale Act of 1967 which forbade evidencing home solicitation sale contracts with a negotiable instrument.

the other (as for example, lack of consideration, breach of warranty, etc.). By tradition, the defenses that a holder in due course generally takes free of are called "personal defenses" and include: failure or lack of consideration, breach of warranty, unconscionability and garden variety fraud (fraud in the inducement). Recall that a holder in due course does not necessarily take free of all "personal" defenses;[81] rather, he takes free only of the personal defenses of parties with whom he has not dealt. Thus as we have seen, the payee of a note can be a holder in due course and yet, if he dealt with the maker, be subject to all of the maker's defenses.

So called "real defenses"—ones which the holder in due course does not take free of—are listed in 3–305(2). (There is no comparable listing of "personal defenses," a category the Code defines by exclusion.) A frequently litigated pre-Code question still very much with us under 3–305(2) is whether a given fraud involves so called fraud in the factum (a real defense) or fraud in the inducement (a personal defense). Section 3–305(2)(c) is an attempt to codify and make more explicit circumstances under which fraud may be raised as a defense against a holder in due course. Note that subsection (c) can be divided into several conditions, each of which a party must meet to raise a defense against a holder in due course:

(1) There must be a misrepresentation which has induced the signature;

(2) the signer must not have had knowledge of the "character or essential terms" of the instrument, nor

(3) a reasonable opportunity to obtain knowledge.

Thus presumably if an uneducated party signs a document that another misrepresents as a receipt and it turns out to be a note, that party can raise a defense of fraud against a holder in due course at least if he was so ignorant that he could not by reading have determined that it was a note, and if no one else was standing by who could have assisted him in determining its character. But if, for example, an uncle with a high school education was standing by, his presence would offer a "reasonable opportunity" and this might preclude the misrepresentation defense against a holder in due course.

Most cases arise because the defendant was tricked into signing another document different from the one which he read,[82] or

---

81. Under pre-Code law the defenses by which a holder in due course takes free are commonly described as "personal" defenses, and those listed in sections 3–305(2)(a)–(e) are described as "real" defenses.

82. See, e. g., Burchett v. Allied Concord Fin. Corp., 74 N.M. 575, 396 P.2d 186, 2 UCC Rep.Serv. 279 (1964). In that case while consumers were reading a blank contract, a salesman was filling in blanks in another. The consumers signed without reading assuming that the contracts were the same; they weren't. *Held*: consumers not entitled to have notes and mortgages cancelled, since under the circumstances, it was unreasonable to rely on the salesman's good faith and to sign

because he did not read the document he signed at all.[83]   Many cases quote with approval the factors set forth in Comment 7 to 3–305:

> The test of the defense here stated is that of excusable ignorance of the contents of the writing signed.   The party must not only have been in ignorance, but must also have had no reasonable opportunity to obtain knowledge.   In determining what is a reasonable opportunity all relevant factors are to be taken into account, including the age and sex of the party, his intelligence, education and business experience; his ability to read or to understand English, the representations made to him and his reason to rely on them or to have confidence in the person making them; the presence or absence of any third person who might read or explain the instrument to him, or any other possibility of obtaining independent information; and the apparent necessity, or lack of it, for acting without delay.

> Unless the misrepresentation meets this test, the defense is cut off by a holder in due course.

In American Plan Corp. v. Woods,[84] the defendant was conned into a classic "let us install it in your home so we can show your friends" deal.   The salesman urged on her the necessity to act quickly and misrepresented the character of the documents to her.   Although the court noted that she had no business experience, it did not consider her education or her ability to read.   Observing that the misrepresentation "involved the nature and effect of the instruments," the court held she had a "real defense." [85]

Another interpretive problem arises with respect to (2) (b) which allows a defendant to raise the defenses of illegality duress, and incapacity against a holder in due course only when these "render the obligation of the party a nullity  .    .    .   ."   The Code does not clarify how one tests whether these defenses render something a nullity under the state law.   Comment 5 to 3–305 states:

> Such incapacity is largely statutory.   Its existence and effect is left to the law of each state.   If under the local law the effect is to render the obligation of the instrument

the forms without reading them.   See also Moore v. Southern Discount Co., 107 Ga.App. 868, 132 S.E.2d 101, 1 UCC Rep.Serv. 243 (1963) (salesman knocked over lamp to distract defendant and switched larger note for one which defendant read; held: plaintiff was holder in due course).

**83.**   See, e. g., Reading Trust Co. v. Hutchison, 35 Pa.D. & C.2d 790, 2 UCC Rep.Serv. 481 (C.P.1964) (defendant signed without reading form which salesman said was to prove that he made a demonstration; held: plaintiff

prevailed);   First Nat'l Bank v. Anderson, 7 Pa.D. & C.2d 661, 1 UCC Rep.Serv. 238 (C.P.1956) (note signed in blank; held: plaintiff prevailed).

**84.**   American Plan Corp. v. Woods, 16 Ohio App.2d 1, 240 N.E.2d 886, 5 UCC Rep.Serv. 842 (1968).

**85.**   Alternatively, the court held that the plaintiff was not a holder in due course anyway because of its close connections with the seller.   See note 65 supra.

entirely null and void, the defense may be asserted against a holder in due course. If the effect is merely to render the obligation voidable at the election of the obligor, the defense is cut off.

Comment 6, dealing with "duress" (which is also modified by "as renders the obligation of the party a nullity") states: "They are primarily a matter of local concern and local policy. All such matters are therefore left to local law." A leading case in this area is Pacific Nat'l Bank v. Hernreich.[86] There the court refused to let a holder in due course recover on a note that a resident jeweler had given to an unlicensed foreign corporation. Arkansas has a strong statute against unlicensed corporations, and, although the dissent argued that the statute renders the transaction voidable rather than void (nullity), the court thought the statute's policy—to protect Arkansas residents from fly-by-night operations—would be defeated if the shoddy characters could sell notes to a holder in due course. The court consciously weighed these policies of protection and the free flow of commercial paper.[87]

The New York Law Revision Commission [88] reported that the Code did not change New York Law in this area. The Commission interpreted "nullity" on the basis of its local statutes and cases to include usurious loans and gambling debts, and also stated that duress voids an obligation only when it is most extreme, so that virtually no volition is involved. Incapacity had arisen in New York only with respect to coverture, but the Commission noted that other states were divided on whether insanity and intoxication void a contract.

How does the defense of unconscionability fit into 3–305, if at all? Presumably most unconscionability is less reprehensible than fraud in the inducement. A fortiori it would be a personal and not a real defense and a holder in due course would take free of the defense of unconscionability. One might argue that particularly egregious unconscionable conduct amounts to "duress" or that unconscionability is itself a form of illegality. It will take a powerful lawyer to win such arguments; certainly 2–302 "illegality" is not the kind which "renders the obligation a nullity" for it takes action of a court in its own discretion to determine whether an unconscionable contract will be enforced, reformed, or not enforced. It seems unlikely that duress is elastic enough to cover even the most outrageous kind of unconscionable conduct.

86. 240 Ark. 114, 398 S.W.2d 221, 3 UCC Rep.Serv. 152 (1966).

87. See also Universal Acceptance Corp. v. Burks, 7 UCC Rep.Serv. 39 (D.C.Ct.Gen.Sess.1969) (payee-seller's

certificate of incorporation was revoked; note was therefore null).

88. 2 N.Y. State Law Revision Comm'n, 1955 Report 963–64 (1955).

## § 14–11  Rights of a Holder Who Is Not a Holder in Due Course

If one fails to be a holder in due course, his substantive rights are spelled out in 3–306 as follows:

> Unless he has the rights of a holder in due course any person takes the instrument subject to
>
> (a) all valid claims to it on the part of any person;  and
>
> (b) all defenses of any party which would be available in an action on a simple contract;  and
>
> (c) the defenses of want or failure of consideration, non-performance of any condition precedent, nondelivery, or delivery for a special purpose (Section 3–408);  and
>
> (d) the defense that he or a person through whom he holds the instrument acquired it by theft, or that payment or satisfaction to such holder would be inconsistent with the terms of a restrictive indorsement.  The claim of any third person to the instrument is not otherwise available as a defense to any party liable thereon unless the third person himself defends the action for such party.

The section does little more than summarize basic rules of contract law.  However, one should understand that a defendant sued by a holder may have certain claims which he could have asserted against other parties but not against the holder.  For example, the last sentence in subsection (d) precludes the use of most *jus tertii* arguments (except in the case in which the holder traces his title through a thief).  Thus the fact that the holder procured the instrument by fraud from a third party would not be a defense which the defendant could assert.  It is also possible under the law of some states that certain defenses available against a contracting party are not available against his assignee and are therefore not assertable under 3–306(b).  Under the *Restatement* rule,[89] defenses which cannot be asserted against an assignee are limited to those based on facts arising after the obligor has notice of the assignment.[90]  In a de-

---

89.  Restatement of Contracts § 167 (1932).

90.  Restatement of Contracts § 167(1) (1932) reads as follows:

An assignee's right against the obligor is subject to all limitations of the obligee's right, to all absolute and temporary defenses thereto, and to all set-offs and counterclaims of the obligor which would have been available against the obligee had there been no assignment, provided that such defenses and set-offs are based on facts existing at the time of the assignment, or are based on facts arising thereafter prior to knowledge of the assignment by the obligor.

See also the rule set out in UCC § 9–318(1):

Unless an account debtor has made an enforceable agreement not to assert defenses or claims arising out of a sale as provided in Section 9–206 the rights of an assignee are subject to

(a) all the terms of the contract between the account debtor and assignor and any defense or claim arising therefrom;  and

(b) any other defense or claim of the account debtor against the assignor which accrues before the account debtor receives notification of the assignment.

parture from the *Restatement* rule, a lower court in New York has recently found that a nonholder in due course was not subject to certain set-offs which would have been available against the payee on a note. In that case, Goldberg v. Rothman,[91] a husband received a series of notes in payment for his interest in a corporation. Subsequently he transferred the notes to his wife who was not a holder in due course and who sued on them. The defendants argued breach of promise and fraud by the husband, but the court held that such set-offs were not available against a holder not the agent of the husband. The case deviates from the *Restatement* rule, and we find it of doubtful wisdom.

More significant for the holder, *whether he is a holder in due course or not*, are the procedural rights embodied in 3–307. That section reads in full as follows:

> (1) Unless specifically denied in the pleadings each signature on an instrument is admitted. When the effectiveness of a signature is put in issue
>
> (a) the burden of establishing it is on the party claiming under the signature; but
>
> (b) the signature is presumed to be genuine or authorized except where the action is to enforce the obligation of a purported signer who has died or become incompetent before proof is required.
>
> (2) When signatures are admitted or established, production of the instrument entitles a holder to recover on it unless the defendant establishes a defense.
>
> (3) After it is shown that a defense exists a person claiming the rights of a holder in due course has the burden of establishing that he or some person under whom he claims is in all respects a holder in due course.

Note how this section assists the plaintiff holder. First, unless the defendant specifically pleads that his signature is fraudulent or unauthorized, he may not contest the validity of the signature at the trial. Even if the defendant does plead that the signature is forged or unauthorized the plaintiff holder will usually benefit from a presumption that defendant's signature is genuine or authorized. Moreover once the signature is admitted and established, a plaintiff holder need only produce the instrument to prove his case. One who compares these rights of the plaintiff holder with the rights of a contracting party who must depend upon an oral contract or a contract composed of various letters and other scraps of paper, will appreciate the significance of holder status all the more.

91. 9 UCC Rep.Serv. 485 (N.Y.Civ.Ct. 1971).

# CHAPTER 15

# LIABILITIES ASSOCIATED WITH STOLEN (AND LOST) INSTRUMENTS; FORGED SIGNATURES

*Analysis*

Sec.

15–1. Introduction.

15–2. Drawer's Liability on Stolen (and Lost) Instruments, 3–804.

15–3. Drawees Liability to Drawer for Paying Over a Forged Indorsement, 4–401.

15–4. Conversion: Liability of Drawee and Other Banks to the "Owner" of a Stolen Instrument for Cashing or Otherwise Dealing With the Instrument, 3–419.

15–5. Stolen Checks and Notes—Warranty Liability, 4–207, 3–417.

15–6. Conclusion.

## § 15–1  Introduction

The drawer of a check need not be paranoid to fear that his check may be stolen. A thief in the costume of a mailman may steal the check, or the thief may be the drawer's trusted employee, or the thief may simply be a burglar or other intruder. If the stolen check is an order instrument, (that is, one drawn "pay to the order of Cicero" or indorsed "pay to the order of Cicero, Repeunzel"), the thief will have to forge the indorsement of the payee or indorsee in order to pass it along to an innocent party. A greedy thief may even alter the instrument by, for example, moving the decimal point a few places so that a $10.00 check becomes a $1000.00 check. Theft, forgery and alteration of negotiable instruments have generated hundreds of litigated cases during this century.

Whether the thief intervenes between the drawer and the payee or further down the stream, the stolen check will usually move from the thief on down to the drawee bank who might or might not pay (depending upon whether it discovers the wrong-doing). Generally a drawee is not entitled to charge the drawer's account when it pays over a forged drawer's signature or over a forged indorsement or when it pays an altered instrument (except to the extent of its original tenor). But there are exceptions to these rules, and we will discuss the rights of the drawer against his bank in Chapter 17.

To utter what is almost a truism, when the dust settles, the wrongdoer will either be off the scene or insolvent. Yet he will have pocketed the proceeds of the check received from someone or some bank and that party in turn may not be successful in procuring payment from the drawee. In any event the party that has paid money to another for the check but has not received payment on it will be the initial loss bearer. That party will inevitably look for a potential defendant on whom to thrust the loss. We find it useful to divide such plaintiffs into two classes—those who sue "down-stream" and those who sue "up-stream." In what then seemed a flash of intuitive brilliance, the stream metaphor occurred to one of your authors several years ago in his sleep. In theory each check flows as would a stream from the drawer to the payee to the depositary bank and so on down to the drawee bank. Despite considerable friendly and some hostile student criticism of our metaphor, we persist in its use, for we know no better one to describe the check collection process.

In chart form our stream appears as follows:

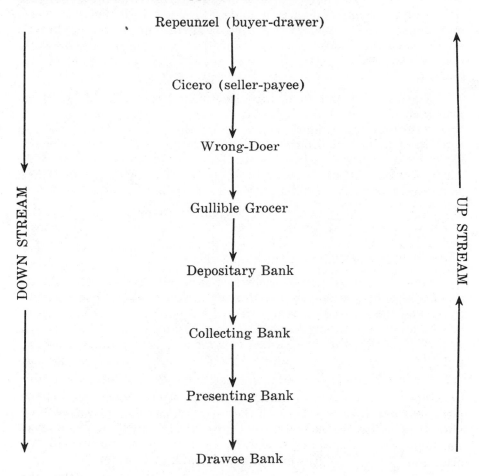

The wrongdoer might appear between Repeunzel and Cicero. Conceivably he could follow Gullible Grocer; there is nothing inevitable about his position on the chart set out above. In the diagram, the first class of potential plaintiffs, those suing downstream, will frequently include the Ciceros of the world and sometimes the Repeunzels, too. As a seller-payee whose check is stolen and ultimately paid over a forged indorsement, Cicero might, for example, sue downstream against the drawee for in effect paying the wrong party. Similarly Repeunzel, the buyer-drawer, might find that the drawee has paid over a forged indorsement in exceptional circumstances where the drawee is entitled to charge the drawer's account (for example, 3–406). In that event Repeunzel would be motivated to become a plaintiff and to try, on some theory, to throw the loss "downstream" on, for example, Gullible Grocer, the party who dealt with the wrongdoer.

The second class of potential plaintiffs sue "upstream." This class consists mostly of drawee banks who make payment and then discover that they have no right to charge the drawer's account. Such drawees commonly try to throw their loss back upstream onto prior banks or onto the party who dealt directly with the wrongdoer. Another familiar inhabitant of the class of "upstream" plaintiffs is a presenting bank (not an agent for collection) to whom the drawee refuses payment and who then seeks reimbursement upstream.

Assume first the following situation: Repeunzel (drawer) issues a check "payable to the order of Cicero"; thief steals the check and forges Cicero's indorsement. Thief then cashes the check at a depositary bank which passes it to a collecting bank which ultimately receives payment from drawee bank. The drawee wrongfully charges the check to Repeunzel's account. The principal law suits that might possibly arise from this case are as follows:

1. *Payee v. drawer* on a stolen instrument (3–804).[1] Under 3–804 the payee may sue upstream against the drawer on a stolen (or lost) instrument, provided he indemnifies the drawer against the possibility of a second claim on the stolen check.

2. *Drawer v. drawee.* The drawer is likely to sue downstream against the drawee only if the drawer issues a second check to the payee and the drawee refuses to recredit the drawer's account (after having paid the first check over a forged indorsement). The drawer's argument is that the drawee has violated (*1*) its statutory duty implicit in 4–401 to pay only checks "properly payable" and (*2*) its contractual obligation to the same effect implicit in the deposit contract.

3. *Payee v. drawee or depositary bank.* Here payee sues downstream as owner of the check on the theory that those who have dealt with the check after the thief are guilty of conversion under 3–419.[2]

4. *Drawer v. collecting bank.* The drawer might sue a collecting bank downstream either on a conversion theory or on the theory that the drawer is somehow a beneficiary of the warranty of title under 4–207(1) (a).[3]

---

1. See § 3–804 set out in the text accompanying note 6 infra.

2. Section 3–419 provides in part:

    (1) An instrument is converted when
    \* \* \*
    \* \* \*

(c) it is paid on a forged indorsement.

See text accompanying note 15 infra.

3. See note 37 and accompanying text infra and cases cited therein.

5. *Drawee v. depositary or other bank.* If the drawee has decided or has been forced to recredit the drawer's account the drawee might then sue back up the stream for breach of the warranty of title unde 4–207(1) (a).[4] In turn, the defendant in the drawee's suit may seek to cast the liability further upstream by suing the party who gave it the check. Thus the drawee may shift the loss upstream onto the presenting bank, the presenting bank onto the collecting bank, the collecting bank onto the depositary bank, the depositary bank onto the forger (a rarity).

One theft sometimes spawns two or three law suits of the foregoing kinds. More often all such suits are impleaded into one case and that case winds up with the payee on one side and the party who took from the thief on the other side. Absent negligence on the part of the owner of a check and irrespective of the sequence of suits or settlements, the loss should normally come to rest upon the first solvent party in the stream after the one who forged the indorsement. Thus in our hypothetical case the depositary bank should ultimately wind up with the loss unless the payee or drawer substantially contributed to the loss by his negligent behavior.[5]

As a student once put it, the material in this chapter and the next one is "for adults only." This material is abstract, difficult and interrelated. We have done our best to make it clear, but we are certain that the student and the neophyte lawyer will have to proceed slowly and back-track frequently.

4. The warranty in section 4–207(1) (a) reads:

Each customer or collecting bank who obtains payments or acceptance of an item and each prior customer and collecting bank warrants to the payor bank or other payor who in good faith pays or accepts the item that

(a) he has a good title to the item or is authorized to obtain payment or acceptance on behalf of one who has a good title;

5. The following is a chart that White put in the body. Summers wanted it removed altogether. White thinks Summers was misguided.

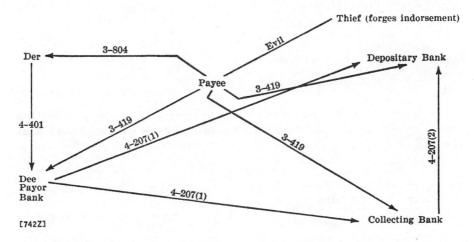

[742Z]

### § 15–2   Drawer's Liability on Stolen (and Lost) Instruments, 3–804

If a thief steals a check from a payee, the payee might turn to his drawer for payment. The payee's acceptance of the drawer's check does not discharge the underlying obligation [6]; *3–802* says that such receipt only suspends that obligation, and 3–804 states that the liability of the drawer persists even after the check is stolen. Section 3–804 reads in full as follows:

> The owner of an instrument which is lost, whether by destruction, theft or otherwise, may maintain an action in his own name and recover from any party liable thereon upon due proof of his ownership, the facts which prevent his production of the instrument and its terms. The court may require security indemnifying the defendant against loss by reason of further claims on the instrument.

A drawer sued under 3–804 can legitimately ask how he protects himself from a double liability. This drawer has already issued one instrument that has been stolen (or lost) and the payee (or other transferee) in his suit under 3–804 now demands in effect that he issue a second one. If a holder in due course should turn up with the stolen check, the drawer would have to pay the holder in due course even if the drawer had in effect issued a second check to the payee (or his transferee). Of course, if the instrument was an order instrument when stolen (that is, one drawn "pay to the order of Cicero" or indorsed "pay to the order of Cicero, Repeunzel"), no subsequent possessor of that instrument could be a holder and therefore no subsequent possessor could be a holder in due course of it. Neither a thief of an order instrument nor a transferee thereof has

---

**6.** The effect of the issuance of a check on the underlying obligation is spelled out in 3–802(1):

Unless otherwise agreed where an instrument is taken for an underlying obligation

> (a) the obligation is pro tanto discharged if a bank is drawer, maker, or acceptor of the instrument and there is no recourse on the instrument against the underlying obligor; and

> (b) in any other case the obligation is suspended pro tanto until the instrument is due or it is payable on demand until its presentment. If the instrument is dishonored action may be maintained on either the instrument or the obligation; discharge of the underlying obligor on the instrument also discharges him on the obligation.

Nor is prior payment to one who took under a forged indorsement a discharge on the instrument, for such person cannot be a holder and accordingly cannot satisfy the discharge provisions of 3–603 which provides, "The liability of any party is discharged to the extent of his payment or satisfaction to the *holder* . . . ." (emphasis added). Thus, the payee can claim that even though the drawee bank has paid the check the drawer's liability was not discharged because the person receiving payment was not a holder. For a discussion of why the presenter is not a holder, see note 7 infra.

However, Professor Allan Farnsworth contends that once the drawee bank has paid the check over a forged indorsement the payee no longer has a cause of action against the drawer, but instead must recover from the drawee under 3–419(1) (c) for payment over a forged indorsement. See letter from Allan Farnsworth to James J. White, Oct. 31, 1967, reprinted in R. Speidel, R. Summers & J. White, Teaching Materials On Commercial Transactions 1024–26 (1969).

power to indorse.[7] Thus the drawer of a stolen order instrument can stop payment or, if the drawee has paid it, can insist that the drawee recredit his account.  If the drawer is sued by one who purports to be a holder in due course taking free of the defects in his title, the drawer can defend on the ground that the plaintiff could not be a holder in due course and is thus subject to the defense of theft under 3–306(d).[8]

However, if the instrument was bearer paper on its face or was converted into bearer paper before it was stolen (e. g., "pay to the order of Cash" or indorsed in blank "Cicero"), then a taker from the thief could be a holder in due course and as such could successfully sue on drawer's contract under 3–413(2), for the defense of theft is not valid against a holder in due course.[9]  Because of this possibility, 3–804 allows a court to require "security indemnifying the defendant against loss by reason of further claims on the instrument."  Section 3–804 as enacted in California and New York directs the court to require such security from the plaintiff.[10]  Presumably such security is to indemnify not only against the possibility that a holder in due course will turn up with the instrument, but also against legal fees and other costs the drawer would incur in showing that a plaintiff is not a holder in due course.  Thus in the recent case Chase Manhattan Bank v. Concord Utilities Corp.,[11] a depositary bank that had credited

---

7.  Section 1–201(20) provides:

"Holder" means a person who is in possession of a document of title or an instrument or an investment security drawn, issued or indorsed to him or his order or to bearer or in blank.

The individual who steals a check made to the order of another person (see § 3–110) cannot qualify as a holder because, even though he "is in possession," the instrument was not "drawn, issued or indorsed to him or his order."  Furthermore the transferee who takes under the thief's forged indorsement cannot qualify as a holder because section 3–202(2) says that "An indorsement must be written by or on behalf of the holder  .  .  .."  Since the thief lacks the status of a holder, he cannot effectively indorse the instrument, and his transferee cannot acquire that status.  The transferee's purported indorsement suffers from the same infirmity that invalidated the thief's indorsement (i. e., the transferee is not a holder) and, thus, no one in the chain of title which begins with the theft of an order instrument can attain the status of holder and consequently claim to be a holder in due course.

8.  Section 3–306 provides:

Unless he has the rights of a holder in due course any person takes the instrument subject to

*  *  *

(d) the defense that he or a person through whom he holds the instrument acquired it by theft  *  *  *

9.  Section 3–305 provides:

To the extent that a holder is a holder in due course he takes the instrument free from

(1) all claims to it on the part of any person;  and

(2) all defenses of any party to the instrument with whom the holder has not dealt except [here the Section lists various "real" defenses which do not include theft of the instrument.]

10.  See Cal. Comm. Code § 3804 (West 1964) which substitutes the words "shall require a sufficient indemnity bond" for "may require security" in the second sentence of 3–804 of the official version of the Code. N.Y. U.C.C. § 3–804 (McKinney 1964) requires plaintiff to post a double indemnity bond.

11.  7 UCC Rep.Serv. 52 (N.Y.Civ.Ct. 1969).

its customer's account with the amount of a check and had then lost the check (apparently without ever presenting it for payment) sued the drawer under 3–804. The court required that the depositary bank put up security equal to twice the amount of the check and gave judgment in favor of the plaintiff-depositary against the drawer for the amount of the check under 3–804.

Of course 3–804 permits the owner of a stolen (or lost) instrument to recover only from the party "liable thereon." The drawer of a stolen (or lost) check can construct a perfectly sound technical argument that he is not "liable" because the conditions of his "liability" under 3–413, namely dishonor and notice, have not been met. The logic of the argument is exceeded only by its lack of merit, for its bite leaves only a shred of 3–804 in existence. The section would apply only to notes and not to checks, but neither the Code nor the comments suggest that the draftsmen intended 3–804 to apply only to notes. One can meet the argument either by saying that dishonor is excused in the case of a stolen (or lost) instrument under 3–511 [12] or by interpreting the term "liable thereon" in a less technical way to include within its ambit a drawer of a check not yet dishonored. No one would deny that the drawer in the *Chase Manhattan* case should pay once for the goods or services he received. As long as the drawer is satisfactorily indemnified against legal costs and against the possibility of having to pay a second time, he cannot complain for having to pay once.[13]

### § 15–3  Drawee's Liability to Drawer for Paying Over a Forged Indorsement, 4–401

In Chapter 17 we will discuss the relationship between the customer and his bank in greater detail. For now it suffices to say that section 4–401 authorizes the drawee bank to charge to its customer's account items "properly payable" and, by negative implication, denies the drawee bank the right to charge amounts not properly payable. Absent the drawer's negligence (for example, drawer did not examine

---

12. Section 3–511(2) provides:

> Presentment or notice or protest as the case may be is entirely excused when * * *
>
> (c) by reasonable diligence the presentment or protest cannot be made or the notice given.

Under 3–511(2) the payee's argument turns on the meaning of "reasonable diligence," and he might argue that no matter what he did he would be unable to make presentment. Accordingly, he would argue that the precondition to the drawer's liability is satisfied because under section 3–507, "An instrument is dishonored when . . . (b) presentment is excused and the instrument is not duly accepted or paid."

The principal difficulty with this method of overcoming the "liable thereon" problem is that many who may have been guilty of negligence themselves and who have failed to use reasonable diligence to present a check, should nevertheless be permitted to recover on the check provided they indemnify the drawer against double liability. Yet if such persons are found to have failed to use reasonable diligence, they will not comply with 3–511 and will not have overcome the "liable thereon" problem.

13. For a tedious discussion of the "liable thereon" question, see White, Some Petty Complaints About Article 3, 65 Mich.L.Rev. 1315, 1337–38 (1967).

cancelled checks and so discover forgeries), the drawee may not charge the drawer's account when it pays a check bearing a forged drawer's signature or a forged indorsement. Section 4–401(2) authorizes a drawee bank acting in good faith to charge its customer's account to the extent of "the original tenor of his altered item" or of the tenor of his completed item (unless the bank knows the completion was improper). The negative implication of this last statement is that the bank may not charge altered items against his account except to the extent of their original tenor. Both pre-Code and post-Code case law support the implication from 4–401, namely that a bank may not charge the customer's account for a check bearing a forged indorsement or an alteration.[14]

## § 15–4    Conversion: Liability of Drawee and Other Banks to the "Owner" of a Stolen Instrument for Cashing or Otherwise Dealing With the Instrument, 3–419

Section 3–419 is a haphazard (critics might even say half-ass) codification of conversion liability. Section 3–419(1)(c) is most relevant and reads as follows:

> (1) An instrument is converted when
>
> . . .
>
> (c) it is paid on a forged indorsement.

The section does not identify the proper plaintiffs nor, except by indirection, the proper defendants. It entirely omits the thief as a possible defendant and it fails to state the theory of the conversion cause of action. Turning to the last problem first, for the purpose of conversion one is best advised to think of a check as if it were goods with the party to whom the check is payable as the "owner." If, for example, Repeunzel makes a check payable to the order of Cicero and gives it to Cicero, Cicero would not only be the holder but also the "owner." After the check is stolen from Cicero he would no longer be the holder (possession is a requisite for holder status), but would continue to be the "owner." Theft would not divest him of title. When a bank or some other party subsequently cashes the check for the thief or for a party who traces his title through the thief, the legal liability of that party is akin to that of a buyer of stolen goods:

14. NIL § 23 provided, "When a signature is forged . . . it is wholly inoperative . . . unless the party . . . is precluded from setting up the forgery or want of authority." Thus with the exception of checks made payable to fictitious or nonexistent persons (NIL § 9(3)), the bank rather than the customer bore the loss when it paid a check bearing a forged indorsement. See, e. g., Russell v. Second Nat'l Bank, 136 N.J.L. 270, 55 A.2d 211 (Err. & App.1941); Wormhoudt Lumber Co. v. Union Bank & Trust Co., 231 Iowa 928, 2 N.W.2d 267 (1942) (bank under contractual duty to determine at its peril genuineness of indorsements unless depositor is negligent). See generally Annot., 146 A.L.R. 840 (1943).

See also Stone & Webster Eng'r Corp. v. First National Bank & Trust, 345 Mass. 1, 184 N.E.2d 358, 1 UCC Rep. Serv. 195 (1962) (section 4–401 retains common-law rule that drawer can insist drawee recredit his account for unauthorized payments).

notwithstanding his good faith, he may be guilty of converting the check by his payment to the thief or to the party who traces title through the thief.

There is nothing complex about the conversion cause of action itself. The thief who steals the check is guilty of conversion whether or not he procures payment on it. Others downstream become liable by cashing or paying the check. The three questions with which we deal in the following pages mainly concern proper parties: (1) May the drawer ever sue in conversion? (Is he an "owner" of his own check?) (2) Of those parties who deal with the stolen check in good faith, which are liable in conversion? (Are depositary or collecting banks who take checks from or through a thief guilty of conversion notwithstanding 3–419(3)?) (3) Are those parties who deal with stolen bearer instruments, and with checks stolen after they have been restrictively indorsed, liable in conversion? Before turning to these three questions, we should note the one case clearly contemplated by 3–419. That case is the one in which a check is stolen from a payee, is passed through several hands and is ultimately paid by drawee over the payee's forged indorsement. Here the payee has a cause of action in conversion against the drawee bank under 3–419.[15] This is the only case 3–419(1)(c) explicitly covers. All other questions we discuss below hover on the periphery of 3–419.

Pre-Code law [16] was divided on whether the drawer may sue in conversion. Assume that the drawer prepares a check, a thief steals it from the drawer, forges the payee's indorsement, and procures payment. The drawer may choose to sue the depositary bank who cashed the check for the thief. The only court recently to consider the drawer's status as a conversion plaintiff is the Massachusetts Supreme Judicial Court which held in Stone & Webster Engineering Corporation v. First National Bank & Trust Company of Greenfield,[17] that a drawer had no cause of action against a collecting bank that had cashed and passed on a check stolen from the drawer. The Court gave both a traditional doctrinal reason for its holding and a more pragmatic one. In the first place it said that the drawer of an undelivered check has no "valuable rights" in such a check: since he

15. See, e. g., Salsman v. National Community Bank, 102 N.J.Super. 482, 246 A.2d 162, 5 UCC Rep.Serv. 779 (1968) (payee recovered from collecting bank when attorney deposited in his own account a check indorsed to order of the estate of payee's deceased husband); Gast v. American Cas. Co., 99 N.J.Super. 538, 240 A.2d 682, 5 UCC Rep.Serv. 155 (1968) (section 3–419 creates absolute right to recover in favor of plaintiff—payee (absent negligence on their part) upon proof that draft was paid on forged indorsement). See generally Annot., 100 A.L.R.2d 671 (1965) and cases cited therein.

16. Recovery permitted: Home Indemnity Co. v. State Bank of Ft. Dodge, 233 Iowa 103, 8 N.W.2d 757 (1943); Franklin Savings Bank v. Internat'l Trust Co., 215 Mass. 231, 102 N.E. 363 (1913). Recovery denied: Trojan Publishing Corp. v. Manufacturers Trust Co., 298 N.Y. 771, 83 N.E. 2d 465 (1948); California Mill Supply Corp. v. Bank of America Nat'l Trust & Sav. Ass'n, 36 Cal.2d 334, 223 P.2d 849 (1950). See generally Annot., 99 A.L.R.2d 637 (1965) and cases cited therein.

17. 345 Mass. 1, 184 N.E.2d 358, 1 UCC Rep.Serv. 195 (1962).

does not have the right of a payee or subsequent holder to present it to the drawee for payment. The "value of . . . [his] rights was limited to the physical paper on which [the checks] were written." The Court also reasoned that allowance of a conversion suit by the drawer against a collecting bank that had paid over a forged indorsement would violate the draftsmen's apparent intention to require the drawer to go against his own bank.

*If* the drawer is guilty of negligence in many such cases, it makes sense to require that he go against his own bank, the drawee, and not against a depositary bank. The drawer's negligence might consist in following sloppy business procedures that enabled his employee to procure the check and forge the indorsement, or his negligence might simply be his failure to examine the returned check or promptly to report the forgery once he had discovered it. If the drawer's negligence is the central issue in most such cases, it makes sense to require the drawee to be the defendant. The drawee is the party who sends out the statements and cancelled checks to the drawer, and can readily prove when they were sent, and when the drawer first gave notice of any forgery. Likewise the drawee is more likely to know of or to find out about the drawer's business procedures than is a bank that has not dealt with the drawer. If the law were to allow the drawer to bring his suit directly against a depositary bank, usually the law would be putting that defendant bank at a considerable disadvantage in proving the defense of negligence. That bank would not know when the cancelled checks were sent to the drawer, nor would it know when the drawer communicated his discovery of the forgery to the drawee, and it would have had no previous contact with the drawer to form the basis for relevant conclusions about the drawer's business behavior. Therefore, it may be appropriate to hold that the drawer has no conversion cause of action against the depositary bank. Certainly the Massachusetts court concluded that the draftsmen intended to place the burden of raising negligence defenses on the drawee bank.[18]

Who are the proper defendants in a conversion suit? Assume that a check is stolen from the payee and is then "cashed" at a depositary bank (the first bank to which an item is transferred for collection 4–105(a)) and passes through various collecting banks ultimately to the drawee who pays. Here, the plaintiff payee might have several potential defendants. First there is the thief, a notoriously unpromising defendant. Second, there is the drawee bank. Third, there is the depositary bank. As we will see, much can be said in favor of the depositary bank as a defendant for it will often be located in the plaintiff's forum, will invariably be solvent, and in many cases should ultimately bear the loss, whatever the outcome of the conversion claim. If the law permits the plaintiff only to sue the drawee, the drawee may in turn have a cause of action against the

---

18. See §§ 3–406; 4–406. See especially § 4–406(5).

depositary bank, and we may end up with two law suits where one would have done.

Section 3–419 covers drawees explicitly: when a drawee pays over a forged indorsement it is liable in conversion. The fighting issue in the cases is whether and in what circumstances the *depositary* bank is liable in conversion. For reasons not too clear to us the draftsmen have attempted to free depositary banks from conversion liability in a substantial number of cases. Subsection (3) of 3–419 deals with the problem as follows:

> Subject to the provisions of this Act concerning restrictive indorsements a representative, including a depositary or collecting bank, who has in good faith and in accordance with the reasonable commercial standards applicable to the business of such representative dealt with an instrument or its proceeds on behalf of one who was not the true owner is not liable in conversion or otherwise to the true owner beyond the amount of any proceeds remaining in his hands.

First we will consider the subsection's apparent meaning; second we will discuss the policies pro and con; and finally we will examine the case law under 3–419(3). In our standard case (thief steals the instrument from payee, forges payee's indorsement and "cashes" the check at a depositary bank), what does the section mean? It renders the depositary bank liable in three cases. First, if the check was indorsed "for deposit only" and the depositary bank cashed it over such an indorsement, the depositary bank is liable in conversion. Second, the depositary bank is also liable in conversion unless it can show that it cashed in good faith and "in accordance with reasonable commercial standards applicable to the business. . . ." Thus if the depositary bank failed to demand identification when reasonable commercial standards called for this, it is liable under 3–419. The third circumstance in which a depositary bank may be liable in conversion arises when the "proceeds" remain in its hands. Assume for example that our thief does not cash the check (that is, take cash in payment) but deposits it in his own account and does not withdraw it. In that circumstance the depositary bank still has "proceeds" and will be liable. To the extent it pays cash over the counter to the thief it has no proceeds.

What policy supports a restriction upon the liability of depositary and other collecting banks? What policy suggests they should have conversion liability? Assume for example that our thief cashes the check at depositary bank, the depositary bank passes it on to a collecting bank which passes it to a second collecting bank which procures payment from the drawee. Neither collecting bank had an opportunity to confront the thief and so prevent the theft. Each acted as a mere conduit between the depositary bank and the drawee bank. One can argue persuasively that neither should be saddled with liability in such a case. But the same argument is not so persuasive with respect to the depositary bank. As we will see, the depositary bank or the other solvent party (for example, Gullible Grocer) who cashed the check for the thief will usually bear the ultimate loss—irrespective of the outcome of the conversion case. That party is the one who dealt with the thief, and he might have prevented the loss by more diligently examining the thief's credentials.

A second policy that offers some support for restricting the liability of depositary and other similarly situated banks is this: One may argue, as the Massachusetts Supreme Judicial Court did, that drawers ought not sue depositary banks in conversion but should sue drawee banks on their deposit contracts and so place the burden of proving negligence defenses upon drawee bank. This policy hardly supports the entirety of 3–419(3), for it applies only when the drawer is plaintiff. Most conversion cases are brought not by drawers but by payees or indorsers. In those cases the negligence of the plaintiff is less likely to be a factor than when the drawer is the plaintiff. Even when the negligence of such a plaintiff is an important factor, the depositary bank may, in a particular case, be as able to show it on behalf of the owner-payee as the drawee bank can. Unlike in the plaintiff-drawer situation, here the drawee does not necessarily have a continuing relationship with the payee.

Critics of 3–419(3) make several points. First they argue that the owner of a check should be permitted to sue the depositary bank or other person who took from the thief because such bank or person will likely bear the ultimate loss, and it is more efficient to have the owner sue the ultimate loss bearer directly than to achieve that result through two law suits.[19] If the one from whom the instrument has been stolen cannot sue the depositary bank who cashed the check for the thief, then he may sue the drawee (as he has a right to do under (1) (c)) or he may sue the drawer (as he has a right to do under 3–804). If he sues the drawer, the drawer will insist that the drawee recredit his account and the drawee will then sue the depositary bank on the warranties of good title a depositary bank gives to the drawee when he passes a check down the collection stream. If our payee-owner sues the drawee directly, the same result follows: drawee pays payee and drawee sues depositary bank on the warranties. (We will discuss the warranties in the next section; for now, let us accept it on faith that a depositary bank who passes a check bearing a forged indorsement to a drawee bank will usually be liable for violation of an implied warranty that it has "title.") In any event the argument stands that a suit by the owner-payee against the depositary bank avoids an additional suit and thus resolves the entire dispute in a more economical manner. However, in these days of impleader, long arm jursidiction, and negotiated settlement, we suspect that a direct suit by the payee-owner against the depositary bank achieves only a modest saving of judicial time. We suspect

19. See Comment, Allocation of Losses From Check Forgeries Under the Law of Negotiable Instruments and the Uniform Commercial Code, 62 Yale L.J. 417, 471 (1953).

that in the usual case in which the payee sues the drawee, the drawee will implead the depositary bank and the suit will actually proceed as one of payee v. depositary bank, with drawee as stake-holder.

A second argument which favors imposing conversion liability on depositary banks and others similarly situated is that these parties are more convenient defendants for aggrieved owners than are drawees. Consider this example. A clerical employee of a doctor steals a number of checks drawn by patients to the doctor's order and forges the doctor's indorsements on those checks. Necessarily the checks are drawn on a variety of different banks but the thief apparently deposits all of them over forged indorsements at one bank. If the payee-owner-doctor were required to sue the drawee in each case, he would have to institute suits in a variety of jurisdictions against a variety of different defendant-drawees. On the other hand if he could sue the single depositary bank, he could save considerable time and effort.

Even in cases involving only one check the depositary bank may be a more convenient defendant than the drawee. Thus the thief who steals the check may cash it at a local depositary bank, but the check may be drawn on a drawee hundreds or thousands of miles away. In that case it will be more convenient for the owner to sue the depositary bank at home. (Of course if the reverse is true, that is, depositary bank is far away and drawee local, the owner may still sue drawee under 3–419).

For reasons that are not clear, 3–419(3) weathered the criticisms set out above and passed the New York Law Revision Commission Examination without much red penciling.[20] Thus in 1962 the Code draftsmen delivered to the courts a section that apparently restricted the conversion liability of depositary and other collecting banks to the comparatively few cases in which the bank (1) held proceeds, or (2) failed to act in good faith or in accordance with reasonable commercial standards, or (3) cashed a check over a restrictive indorsement.

So much for the work of the Code draftsmen. Thereafter, the courts have taken up section 3–419(3), and what they have done to it shouldn't happen to a dog. The courts have ingeniously evaded the restrictions in 3–419(3) and have generally imposed liability on depositary banks in conversion suits by owners of instruments. We have found no cases in which the payee-owner lost. Some courts have simply ignored 3–419(3).[21] Others have found that the depositary bank did not act "in accordance with reasonable commercial standards." [22] In three cases the courts have avoided the question

20. See 2 N.Y. State Law Revision Comm'n, 1955 Report 1082–83 (1955).

21. See, e. g., Harry H. White Lumber Co. v. Crocker-Citizens Nat'l Bank, 253 Cal.App.2d 368, 61 Cal.Rptr. 381, 4 UCC Rep.Serv. 617 (2d Dist.1967).

22. See, e. g., Salsman v. National Community Bank, 102 N.J.Super. 482, 246 A.2d 162, 5 UCC Rep.Serv. 779 (Law Div.1968).

entirely by finding that drawer can sue on the warranties of title given by the depositary bank. (As we will see in the next section, any person who sends a check on for collection impliedly warrants under 3–417 and 4–207 that he has good title to the check. If he traces title through a thief and is not a holder in due course, that warranty will have been breached and he will have liability to those to whom the warranty runs.) In one of the three cases the court found that the drawer could be the assignee of the drawee's cause of action under the warranty [23] and in another the court held the drawer a third-party beneficiary of that warranty.[24] In the third [25] the court found that the collecting bank's warranty of title ran directly to the drawer.[26]

Faithless as the foregoing cases are to the intent of 3–419(3), they are but petty mischief compared to Ervin v. Dauphin Deposit Trust Co.[27] In that case someone, apparently an employee of a doctor, cashed a number of checks payable to the doctor's order over the doctor's forged indorsement at the Dauphin Trust Co. The doctor (payee) sued the Dauphin Trust Co. for conversion. Although the bank had paid the money to the embezzler and thus had no additional assets in its hands as a result of cashing the checks, the court held that the bank had "proceeds" in its hands. Adding insult to injury the court found also that the Code draftsmen did not intend depositary banks to be "representatives" within 3–419(3), even though the relevant words in 3–419(3) are: "including a depositary or collecting bank. . . ." The court reasoned 3–419(3) would cover the banks only if they acted as "representatives" or agents as defined in 1–201 (35).

Perhaps those bankers whose hands were doubtless at work in the drafting of 3–419(3) got what they deserved. If the section be not dead it certainly is mortally wounded; one can only mourn that *Dauphin Trust Co.* inflicted fatal wounds with such little grace and that legislatures will doubtless not give it a decent burial for years to come. Although we deplore that mentality which leads a court to think it is completely free to disregard legislative language, we appreciate the strength of the policy arguments against the restrictions that the bankers presumably wrote into 3–419(3), and if we were in the legislature we would urge its modification.

23. Commonwealth v. National Bank & Trust Co. 46 Pa.D. & C.2d 141, 6 UCC Rep.Serv. 369 (C.P.1968).

24. Allied Concord Fin. Corp. v. Bank of America Nat'l Trust & Sav. Ass'n, 275 Cal.App.2d 1, 80 Cal.Rptr. 622, 6 UCC Rep.Serv. 749 (2d Dist.1969).

25. Insurance Co. of North America v. Atlas Supply Co., 121 Ga.App. 1, 7 UCC Rep.Serv. 526 (1970).

26. Of course, a suit on the warranty is not identical to a conversion cause of action, and the depositary bank might be able to assert defenses against a warranty cause of action which would not be available to him in a conversion cause of action. For example, he might argue that under 4–207(4) there is no warranty cause of action because no claim for breach had been made within a reasonable time after the plaintiff learned of the breach. Still in many, perhaps most, cases a warranty cause of action will reward the owner of the check as fully as a conversion cause of action.

27. 38 Pa.D. & C.2d 473, 3 UCC Rep. Serv. 311 (C.P.1965).

A final situation in which conversion liability arises is only partly dealt with in 3–419 and involves theft of a bearer instrument. For reasons indicated below, a plaintiff is not likely to find a solvent defendant liable in conversion for dealing with a stolen bearer instrument unless that instrument bore a restrictive indorsement at the time of its theft (e. g., "Joe Jones for deposit only"). Assuming that the stolen bearer instrument does not bear a restrictive indorsement, the thief will himself be a holder [28] and whether or not he is a holder he can constitute his transferee a holder simply by transfer.[29] If his transferee then cashes the check and so gives value in good faith and without notice of any defense, that transferee will be a holder in due course under 3–305, free of all claims to the instrument on the part of any person and free of all personal defenses of any prior party. Thus the holder in due course will not be liable in conversion to the true owner. Likewise if the check is passed downstream (depositary bank to collecting bank to drawee bank) and the drawee bank ultimately pays it to a party who is a holder, that payment will discharge the drawer's liability on the check and on the underlying obligation as well.[30] Of course, the owner of the check will have a good cause of action against the thief, but he will have no other cause of action. Moreover his cause of action against the thief is a common law cause of action.[31]

**28.** See Section 14–3 supra.

**29.** See § 3–202(1):

> Negotiation is the transfer of an instrument in such form that the transferee becomes a holder. If the instrument is payable to order it is negotiated by delivery with any necessary indorsement; if payable to bearer it is negotiated by delivery.

**30.** See section 3–603(1) which says, "The liability of any party is discharged to the extent of his payment or satisfaction to the holder . . .," and section 3–802(1) (b) which says ". . . discharge of the underlying obligor on the instrument also discharges him on the obligation."

**31.** See 2 N.Y. State Law Revision Comm'n, 1955 Report 1082 (1955), where the following comments were made in respect to an early version of the Code (Supp. No. 1 to the 1952 Official Draft (1955)):

Section 3–419(1) defines conversion to include:

(a) refusal by a drawee to return an instrument presented to it for acceptance;

(b) refusal by a payor to pay or return an instrument delivered to it for payment; and

(c) payment on a forged indorsement.

Situation (c) is the only one likely to involve subsections (3) or (4), although situation (b) might conceivably involve subsection (4). It is not clear, however, whether subsections (3) and (4) contemplate other situations where liability for common law conversion might arise, or are limited to the three specific instances cited in Section 3–419(1).

It is true that most of the conversion cases in the law of bills and notes have involved forged indorsements. Britton discusses conversion only in connection with forged indorsement. (Britton, Bills and Notes, § 146 (1943).) Still, he states that the general law applies, where not expressly negated by the NIL (Id., p. 682.) The Code includes a similar provision in Section 1–103.

While the point is not a major one it is submitted that any such ambiguity is unfortunate. Section 3–419(1) on its face purports to be all inclusive in defining conversion of an instrument. But subsections (3) and (4) imply the contrary.

If in the foregoing situation a depositary bank takes a check from the thief but does not become a holder in due course, (as for example because the check bore a date more than 30 days prior to the date on which the bank took it), then presumably the bank would be liable in conversion. Note, however, that the Code does not impose such liability and it would have to be common law liability under 1–103.

Suppose a payee indorses a check in blank but indorses it restrictively: [32] Jean Smith takes a check payable to her order, indorses it "Jean Smith for deposit only," the check is then stolen by the mailman, cashed at a depositary bank and ultimately paid by the drawee bank. Here 3–419(4) [33] exempts all of the banks but the depositary bank from liability on the theory that intermediary banks and the drawee bank should not be expected to examine the chain of indorsements, given the volume of checks with which they must deal. In Jean Smith's case, the position of the thief's signature (which would undoubtedly be procured by the depositary bank) immediately beneath the "for deposit only" indorsement should put the depositary on notice of some irregularity for the only indorsements after the "for deposit only" indorsement should be those of *banks*, yet the rear side of the check reading from top to bottom would appear as follows: (*1*) "For deposit only" (*2*) "Jean Smith" (*3*) "Pernicious Thief." (The Jean Smith's of the world put "for deposit only" on their checks only when they send them to banks.) Accordingly, the first clause in 3–419(3) "[s]ubject to the provisions of this Act concerning restrictive indorsements . . ." and section 3–206 (3) together impose conversion liability on the *depositary* bank in such a case. Section 3–206(3) provides in full:

> Except for an intermediary bank, any transferee under an indorsement which is conditional or includes the words "for collection", "for deposit", "pay any bank", or like terms (subparagraphs (a) and (c) of Section 3–205) must pay or apply any value given by him for or on the security of the instrument consistently with the indorsement and to the extent that he does so he becomes a holder for value. In addition such transferee is a holder in due course if he otherwise complies with the requirements of Section 3–302 on what constitutes a holder in due course.

---

32. See § 3–204(2):

An indorsement in blank specifies no particular indorsee and may consist of a mere signature. An instrument payable to order and indorsed in blank becomes payable to bearer and may be negotiated by delivery alone until specially indorsed.

Restrictive indorsement and its effect are governed by sections 3–205 and 3–206.

33. Section 3–419(4) reads as follows:

An intermediary bank or payor bank which is not a depositary bank is not liable in conversion solely by reason of the fact that proceeds of an item indorsed restrictively (Sections 3–205 and 3–206) are not paid or applied consistently with the restrictive indorsement of an indorser other than its immediate transferor.

In Jean Smith's case the depositary bank did not apply the value "consistently with the indorsement," for it should have deposited that money in someone's account; its payment of the money over the counter to the thief or its deposit of the money in the thief's account deviated from the "for deposit only" instructions of Jean Smith—the payee who was first indorser. Thus the principal consequence of a restrictive indorsement is to give a good cause of action against the depositary bank or any other initial taker from the thief.

The current law on conversion of a stolen check is not wholly unclear and confused. Thus it is clear that the payee or later indorsee owner, has a cause of action against the drawee bank who pays over a forged indorsement (3–419(1) (c)). It is clear that such an owner also has a cause of action against the depositary bank if any of the three following conditions are met:

(1) The depositary bank cashed the check over a restrictive indorsement (of the type described in 3–205(a) and (c) and applied the proceeds in a way contrary to that indorsement.

(2) The depositary bank still has the proceeds in its hands.

(3) The depositary bank did not act in accordance with reasonable commercial standards.

Except in the case of restrictive indorsements other collecting banks have the same liability as the depositary bank (3–419(3)).

We summarize the confusion on the questions posed at the outset as follows: (1) The courts are split on whether a drawer may ever sue in conversion. The reasoning in *Stone & Webster* persuades us, and we would generally hold that the drawer is not a proper party plaintiff in a conversion suit. We would tell the drawer to proceed against the drawee on his contract of deposit (a liability discussed more fully in Chapter 17). (2) On what persons are permissible defendants in a conversion cause of action, the Code and the courts agree on certain potential defendants and disagree on others. That is, 3–419 explicitly makes the drawee a proper defendant and makes depositary and collecting banks proper defendants when they do not pay in good faith or in accordance with reasonable commercial standards, and when they have proceeds in their hands. In addition, the Code and the cases find depositary banks liable in conversion for payment on stolen instruments over restrictive indorsements. But at this juncture, the Code and the courts part company. In all cases known to us, the courts have found depositary banks liable to check "owners" in conversion (or on some other basis) when these banks paid checks bearing forged indorsements. The courts have ingeniously evaded the 3–419(3) restrictions on conversion liability. It appears that depositary banks who pay stolen instruments bearing forged indorsements will be liable in conversion to the owners of such checks notwithstanding 3–419(3). (3) On the liabilities that arise upon payment of stolen bearer instruments and checks restrictively indorsed, we summarize as follows: The restrictive indorsement renders a depositary bank liable under 3–419(3) and 3–206.   Section 3–419 does not mention stolen bearer instruments, but we conclude that a party who is neither a holder in due course nor the taker from a holder in due course who cashes or pays a stolen bearer instrument is liable in conversion to the owner of the instrument under the common law via 1–103.   On the other hand if there is a holder in due course in the chain of title of one who pays such a stolen bearer instrument or if the payor is a holder in due course, the payor will take free of the owner's claims and not be guilty of conversion.

### § 15–5   Stolen Checks and Notes—Warranty Liability, 4–207, 3–417

In many cases conversion liability, liability under 3–804, and drawee liability under 4–401 tell only part of the story.   After the drawee recredits the drawer's account for a check improperly paid over a forged indorsement, or after the drawee pays a plaintiff in a conversion action, the drawee will seek recovery from parties up the collection stream between it and the thief.   These parties include the following possibilities: Gullible Grocer who cashes the check for the thief; depositary bank who takes the check from Gullible Grocer or who himself cashes the check; collecting banks who present the check to the drawee or pass it along for others to present it to the drawee.   Each party in this stream between the thief and the drawee bank will normally make an implied warranty of good title directly to the drawee bank.   We should note that under pre-Code law the liability of Gullible Grocer *et al.* was not normally based upon implied warranty but was regarded as quasi-contractual.[34] The theory was that the drawee had paid money by mistake and so had a quasi-contractual right to recover it from the one who had benefited.   Some pre-Code cases involved suits on express warranties [35] of title.   (The indorsement stamp of many banks included the symbols "P.E.G."   These symbols expressly warranted "prior endorsements guaranteed.")   Only rarely did pre-Code courts base liability on an implied warranty.[36]

Today the Code imposes the implied warranty embodied in 4–207(1) (a):

> Each customer or collecting bank who obtains payment
> or acceptance of an item and each prior customer and

---

34.   See, e. g., Canal Bank v. Bank of Albany, 1 Hill 287 (N.Y.Sup.Ct.1841); First Nat'l Bank of Minneapolis v. City Nat'l Bank, 182 Mass. 130, 65 N. E. 24 (1902); W. Britton, Handbook of the Law of Bills and Notes § 139 (2d ed. 1961).

35.   See, e. g. United States v. National City Bank, 28 F.Supp. 144 (S.D.N.Y.

1939); First Nat'l Bank v. North Jersey Trust Co., 18 N.J.Misc. 449, 14 A.2d 765 (1940).   First Nat'l Bank v. First Nat'l Bank, 58 Ohio St. 207, 50 N.E. 723 (1898).

36.   See, e. g., Security Sav. Bank v. First Nat'l Bank, 106 F.2d 542 (6th Cir. 1939); Leather Mfrs. Bank v. Merchants Bank, 128 U.S. 26 (1888).

collecting bank warrants to the payor bank or other payor who in good faith pays or accepts the item that

> (a) he has a good title to the item or is authorized to obtain payment or acceptance on behalf of one who has a good title; . . . .

In nine-tenths of the cases that lawyers will see, "good title" will mean no more than: "this check bears no forged indorsements." [37] Thus a presentor breaks this warranty of good title when he presents an instrument bearing forged indorsements that break the chain of title. Of course, he does not incur warranty liability when he presents a stolen bearer instrument.

Note that the payor bank receives this warranty not only from each collecting bank up the stream, but also from each "customer." The meaning of the word customer in this context is not clear; presumably it includes at least the party who transferred the check to the depositary bank.[38]

Before considering the defenses a collecting bank or a customer may raise in a warranty action under 4–207, let us consider two confusing aspects of that section. First, we may inquire whether 4–207 (1) is necessary, given that 4–207(2) (b) includes an explicit warranty that "all signatures are genuine or authorized"? Secondly, what is the relationship between 3–417 [39] and 4–207—two sections that are almost but not quite identical?

---

**37.** Comment 1 to section 4–207 directs us to the comments to 3–417 for an explanation of its meaning. Comment 3 to 3–417 explains the "good title" language as follows:

Subsection (1) (a) retains the generally accepted rule that the party who accepts or pays does not "admit" the genuineness of indorsements, and may recover from the person presenting the instrument when they turn out to be forged.

See also Insurance Co. of North America v. Atlas Supply Co., 121 Ga.App. 1, 7 UCC Rep.Serv. 526 (1970); First Pennsylvania Banking & Trust Co. v. Montgomery County Bank & Trust Co., 29 Pa.D. & C.2d 596, 1 UCC Rep. Serv. 291 (C.P.1962); County Trust Co. v. Pascack Valley Bank & Trust Co., 93 N.J.Super. 252, 225 A.2d 605, 3 UCC Rep.Serv. 1062 (App.Div.1966).

**38.** The term "customer" is defined in section 4–104(1) (e) as "any person having an account with a bank or for whom a bank has agreed to collect items and includes a bank carrying an account with another bank."

**39.** Section 3–417 provides in full:

(1) Any person who obtains payment or acceptance and any prior transferor warrants to a person who in good faith pays or accepts that

(a) he has a good title to the instrument or is authorized to obtain payment or acceptance on behalf of one who has a good title; and

(b) he has no knowledge that the signature of the maker or drawer is unauthorized, except that this warranty is not given by a holder in due course acting in good faith

(i) to a maker with respect to the maker's own signature; or

(ii) to a drawer with respect to the drawer's own signature, whether or not the drawer is also the drawee; or

(iii) to an acceptor of a draft if the holder in due course took the draft after the acceptance or obtained the acceptance without knowledge that the drawer's signature was unauthorized; and

(c) the instrument has not been materially altered, except that this

A payor bank cannot rely on the warranties embodied in 4–207 (2) (or in 3–417(2)) because those warranties do not run to payors. Although one might argue that the word "transferee" in 4–207(2) includes a payor bank at least in its relationship to the presenting bank, the Code draftsmen quite clearly did not intend the word "transferee" to include a payor. Comment 4 to 4–207 makes that point as follows:

> In this section as in Section 3–417, the (a), (b) and (c) warranties to transferees and collecting banks under subsection (2) are in general similar to the (a), (b) and (c) warranties to payors under subsection (1); but the warranties to payors are less inclusive because of exceptions reflecting the rule of Price v. Neal, 3 Burr. 1345 (1762), and related principles. See Comment to Section 3–417. Thus collecting banks are given not only all the warranties given to payors by subsection (1), without those exceptions, but also the (d) and (e) warranties of subsection (2).

As the Comment indicates, to hold that collecting banks warrant "all signatures" to the payor bank would nullify the rule (discussed in Chapter 16) that imposes liability on drawees for some forgeries of drawer's signatures. According to this rule, some drawees who pay checks bearing forged drawer's signatures (as distinguished from forged indorsements) must bear the ultimate loss and cannot recover upstream from presenters of checks bearing forged signatures of drawers. Thus, the drawee receives only (*1*) the warranty of good title ("no forged indorsements") and (*2*) the warranty in

warranty is not given by a holder in due course acting in good faith

(i) to the maker of a note; or

(ii) to the drawer of a draft whether or not the drawer is also the drawee; or

(iii) to the acceptor of a draft with respect to an alteration made prior to the acceptance if the holder in due course took the draft after the acceptance, even though the acceptance provided "payable as originally drawn" or equivalent terms; or

(iv) to the acceptor of a draft with respect to an alteration made after the acceptance.

(2) Any person who transfers an instrument and receives consideration warrants to his transferee and if the transfer is by indorsement to any subsequent holder who takes the instrument in good faith that

(a) he has a good title to the instrument or is authorized to obtain payment or acceptance on behalf of one who has a good title and the transfer is otherwise rightful; and

(b) all signatures are genuine or authorized; and

(c) the instrument has not been materially altered; and

(d) no defense of any party is good against him; and

(e) he has no knowledge of any insolvency proceeding instituted with respect to the maker or acceptor or the drawer of an unaccepted instrument.

(3) By transferring "without recourse" the transferor limits the obligation stated in subsection (2)(d) to a warranty that he has no knowledge of such a defense.

(4) A selling agent or broker who does not disclose the fact that he is acting only as such gives the warranties provided in this section, but if he makes such disclosure warrants only his good faith and authority.

(1) (b) that the customer at the collecting bank has "no knowledge that the signature, of the maker or drawer, is unauthorized. . . ."

Sections 3–417 and 4–207 are almost identical. However there are some differences of potential significance and when relevant, it will be necessary to determine which of the two sections applies.[40] For most purposes one can base his analysis of the warranty liability on a stolen or altered check on 4–207, but he will have to consult

**40.** The important differences are the following:

(1) 4–207 warranties are given only by "each customer or collecting bank" whereas 3–417 warranties are given by any "person."

(2) 4–207 applies to "items" and 3–417 applies only to "instruments."

(3) 4–207(2) warranties pass to remote transferees whether or not the transferor indorses, but 3–417(2) warranties pass only if the transfer is by indorsement.

(4) 4–207(2) includes what is in effect an indorsement promise whether or not such an indorsement is made: "in addition . . . upon dishonor or any necessary notice of dishonor in protest he will take up the item. . . ."

(5) 4–207(3) limits the amount of damages under the warranty cause of action to the amount of the item.

(6) 4–207(4) frees the defendant unless the plaintiff has made a claim for breach of warranty within a "reasonable time" after he learned of the breach "to the extent of any loss caused by his delay in making the claim."

(7) 3–417(3) defining the meaning of the words "without recourse" specifies that it frees one transferring under such a limited indorsement from the warranty in (2) (d) against defenses unless the transferor knows that there are defenses when he transfers.

(8) 3–417(4) lets an agent off the warranty hook if he discloses his agency status.

The basic rule for resolving conflicts between Article Three and Article Four is the second sentence in 4–102 (1) which reads as follows:

In the event of conflict provisions of this Article govern those of Article 3 . . . .

Most transfers in the bank collection process would be covered by the language in 3–417 as well as the language in 4–207. Clearly the section conflicts in certain respects, as for example in 4–207(2) and 3–417(2) where in one case warranties go to remote transferees without indorsement, and in the other case they go only if there is an indorsement. In such cases 4–207 will govern. Likewise the provisions which appear in 4–207 but do not appear in 3–417 would govern the bank collection process whether or not they are found to be in conflict with the terms of 3–417. If one finds there is a conflict, Article Four governs under 4–102; if one finds there is no conflict, 4–207 simply governs according to its terms. The only possible difficulty arises as to terms which appear in 3–417 but do not appear in 4–207. For example, subsection 4 of 3–417 frees a "selling agent or broker" who discloses his agency from the warranties except to the extent that he warrants his good faith and authority. Could a bank argue that it was such an agent and, since there is no explicitly contrary term in 4–207, that the term is not in conflict with, but merely additional to, the terms in 4–207? We believe not. Absent such a disclosure certainly a transferring bank, even one acting as an agent, would have given the warranty set out in 4–207. Thus the application of the provision in 3–417 would cause a different and "conflicting" legal consequence than would otherwise occur under 4–207. Moreover, the explicit authorization of such disclosure together with the freeing of the agent from warranty liability in 3–417(4) when it is compared with the absence of any such explicit authorization in 4–207 suggests that the draftsmen did not intend a banking institution to have power to get off the warranty hook so readily. Thus terms set out in 3–417 which do not appear in 4–207, but which would change legal consequences under 4–207, should be regarded as "in conflict" and therefore not effective on the 4–207 situation because of 4–102.

3–417 in the case of a stolen note and in the case of checks transferred outside the collection process.[41]

The most common use of the warranties under 4–207 is by the drawee bank who recredits its customer's account and then sues as far up the collection stream as is feasible.[42] Occasions will arise when the party sued will in turn find someone even farther up the collection stream to sue under 4–207(2). Consider for example the case in which a thief forges an indorsement, cashes the check at a depositary bank, and the drawee ultimately pays. When the drawee discovers all this, assume it sues an intermediary bank under 4–207(1)(a) and wins. Intermediary bank may in turn sue depositary bank under 4–207(2)(b) and win because depositary bank broke its warranty that all signatures were genuine.

Besides the payor bank and other banks up the collection stream, who else may be potential plaintiffs under 4–207(1)? The section gives a cause of action to "the payor bank or other payor who in good faith pays or accepts the item. . . ." In several cases under varying theories, drawers of checks on which indorsements have been forged have used 4–207(1) or 3–417(1) to bring suit. In one case the court held that the drawer was a third-party beneficiary of the warranty of title.[43] In another, the Commonwealth of Penn-

---

41. If, for example, a thief stole a check, forged an indorsement and the check was then passed through the hands of two parties before it reached the depositary bank, the liability of the party who took it from the thief would not be under 4–207 but in all probability under 3–417. This is so because such a taker who did not himself deal with the bank would probably not be regarded as a "customer" who gave the warranties under 4–207. Presumably it is a rare check which passes through so many hands before it gets into the collection process at the depositary bank.

Section 3–417(2) runs to the "transferee" and in some cases to "any subsequent holder." We have already learned that one who takes an instrument bearing a forged indorsement cannot be a holder of that instrument. If the Gullible Grocer takes a note bearing a forged indorsement from a thief and passes it by indorsement to several others, the draftsmen apparently intended that a person down the line would have a right to sue Grocer on his warranty under 3–417(2). However, under a standard analysis such a person would not be a holder and would not therefore get the warranty under 3–417(2) (unless he were the immediate transferee of Gullible Grocer). Professor Peters has suggested that one can get around this apparent

limitation by applying the fiction that the one who transfers the note, in effect, establishes a new instrument and that such subsequent persons are "holders" not of the original instrument but of the new instrument written through the indorsement of Gullible Grocer. Whether one applies that fiction or simply attacks the problem head-on by saying that the draftsmen did not intend the word holder to have its usual meaning in this case, we believe that subsequent parties should have a cause of action on the warranty against the Gullible Grocer.

Since the warranties in 4–207(2) run to a transferee and "to any subsequent collecting bank," one need not determine whether such persons would be holders when they took an instrument bearing a forged indorsement.

42. Note that section 4–207 says that the warranty of every party who handles the item is made directly to the payor bank. Thus, Comment 2 provides, "Further, the warranties and engagements run with the item with the result that a collecting bank may sue a remote prior collecting bank or a remote customer and thus avoid multiplicity of suits."

43. Allied Concord Fin. Corp. v. Bank of America Nat'l Trust & Sav. Ass'n, 275 Cal.App.2d 1, 80 Cal.Rptr. 622, 6 UCC Rep.Serv. 749 (2d Dist.1969).

sylvania as a drawer argued successfully that it was an assignee of the drawee's cause of action under 4–207(1) (a).[44] In a third, the Georgia Court of Appeals held that the drawer was "another payor" and permitted recovery on that basis against the depositary bank.[45] For the reasons given in *Stone & Webster* considered earlier, it seems most unlikely that the Code draftsmen intended the drawer to be regarded as "another payor." Apparently the draftsmen intended that the drawer have a suit against his drawee bank for improper payment and that the drawee should bear the burden of raising and arguing any defense such as negligence which would preclude the drawer from asserting forgery or the like. To hold that the warranties in 4–207 flow either directly or under a third-party beneficiary theory to the drawer, is to shift the burden of presenting these defenses to the depositary or other collecting banks[46] who would be likely defendants in such suit. As indicated before, it seems likely that the drawee is in the best position to prove negligence on the drawer's part, that the drawee should therefore be made to do so, and that the drawer has no real complaint if he is limited to a suit against his drawee inasmuch as his own bank is likely to be a convenient defendant located in his own home town.[47] For these reasons we think it unfortunate that some courts have extended the 4–207(1) warranty to the drawer.

## *Alterations*

Warranty theory is used to distribute liabilities upon payment of a materially altered item in the same way it is used to distribute liabilities upon payment of an item bearing a forged indorsement. After the payor bank recredits the account of its customer, it may sue banks up the collection stream (presenting, collecting, depositary) on the warranty embodied in 4–207(1) (c) and the party sued may sue even farther up the stream under 4–207(2) (c) if there be other defendants. There are several exceptions to the alteration warranty made to a payor, but these rarely affect an altered check.[48]

**44.** Commonwealth v. National Bank & Trust Co., 46 Pa.D. & C.2d 141, 6 UCC Rep.Serv. 369 (C.P.1968).

**45.** Insurance Co. of North America v. Atlas Supply Co., 121 Ga.App. 1, 172 S.E.2d 632, 7 UCC Rep.Serv. 526 (1970).

**46.** Section 3–406 permits a "holder in due course" or a "drawee or other payor" to raise the defense of negligence. Depositary banks will have difficulty in fitting themselves within the language of that section when they take a check with a forged indorsement. Nevertheless courts seem inclined to allow them to use it. See, e. g., Gresham State Bank v. O & K Construction Co., 231 Ore. 106, 370 P. 2d 726, 1 UCC Rep.Serv. 276 (1962),

opinion clarified on denial of rehearing, 231 Ore. 106, 372 P.2d 187 (1962). See also Section 16–2 infra.

**47.** Of course, in some situations the drawer will find it more convenient to sue one depositary bank rather than a number of drawee banks. For example, in Commonwealth v. National Bank & Trust Co., 46 Pa.D. & C.2d 141, 6 UCC Rep.Serv. 369 (C.P.1968), a state employee forged indorsements to checks drawn on approximately twenty banks and cashed them all in the defendant bank.

**48.** Section 4–207(1) (c) reads as follows:

the item has not been materially altered, except that this warranty is

## Reasonable Time

There are no Code cases on what is a "reasonable time" for asserting breach of warranty. Note that failure to give timely notice is a defense only "to the extent of any loss caused by the delay."

not given by any customer or collecting bank that is a holder in due course and acts in good faith

    (i) to the maker of a note; or

    (ii) to the drawer of a draft whether or not the drawer is also the drawee; or

    (iii) to the acceptor of an item with respect to an alteration made prior to the acceptance if the holder in due course took the item after the acceptance, even though the acceptance provided "payable as originally drawn" or equivalent terms; or

    (iv) to the acceptor of an item with respect to an alteration made after the acceptance.

Generally the section gives the payor a right to recover from a "customer or collecting bank" when he pays a materially altered item. But since the maker of a note, the drawer of a draft, or the acceptor of an item knows the original tenor of the instrument, subparagraphs (i), (ii), and (iv) prohibit them from asserting the alteration warranty when they make payment in disregard of that knowledge to a holder in due course who acts in good faith.

Subparagraph (iii) prevents an acceptor from recovering on the alteration warranty for an alteration made prior to acceptance even when the terms of the acceptance specify that it will be paid only according to its original tenor. The reasons for this are twofold. First, under 3–413 the acceptor agrees to pay the instrument according to its tenor at the time of acceptance. Secondly, the certification of a check would lose much of its value to subsequent takers if the obligation of the accepting bank was dependent upon the original tenor of the instrument rather than its tenor at the time of acceptance. See, e. g., National City Bank v. National Bank, 300 Ill. 103, 132 N.E. 832 (1921); Wells Fargo Bank & Union Trust Co. v. Bank of Italy, 214 Cal. 156, 4 P.2d 781 (1931). See also § 3–417, Comment 5.

One should not overlook the effect of 3–407 in his analysis of an altered instrument problem. Section 3–407 reads in full:

(1) Any alteration of an instrument is material which changes the contract of any party thereto in any respect, including any such change in

    (a) the number or relations of the parties; or

    (b) an incomplete instrument, by completing it otherwise than as authorized; or

    (c) the writing as signed, by adding to it or by removing any part of it.

(2) As against any person other than a subsequent holder in due course

    (a) alteration by the holder which is both fraudulent and material discharges any party whose contract is thereby changed unless that party assents or is precluded from asserting the defense;

    (b) no other alteration discharges any party and the instrument may be enforced according to its original tenor, or as to incomplete instruments according to the authority given.

(3) A subsequent holder in due course may in all cases enforce the instrument according to its original tenor, and when an incomplete instrument has been completed, he may enforce it as completed.

Section 3–407 provides for the discharge of any party from liability if his contract is changed by a fraudulent and material alteration by *the holder*. This discharge does not apply to a subsequent holder in due course who may enforce the instrument according to its original tenor. A discharge on the instrument has the further consequence of discharging the underlying obligation (§ 3–802(1) (b) ). The only real interpretive difficulty in 3–407 is the question who qualifies as "the holder" in 3–407(2) (a). To illustrate, assume that a thief steals a $1,000 bearer check and alters the amount to $11,000. The thief then cashes the check at a depository bank. Upon

What is a "reasonable time" must await case law development, and lawyers should be hesitant to analogize to 2–607 and the personal injury area. There an injured consumer plaintiff frequently attempts to assert his claim over defendant's argument that the con-

presentment to the payor bank, payment is refused because customer has ordered payment stopped. If the thief is a "holder," and assuming that the depositary bank is not a holder in due course (assume, for example, that the check is overdue (§ 3–304)), the literal application of 3–407 gives the drawer-purchaser perfectly good merchandise for which he did not have to pay; neither the seller nor the depositary bank will have a cause of action against anyone (due to the discharge). This resultant windfall to the drawer-purchaser is undesirable. How, then, can one avoid it?

One possibility is to argue that, at least in the 3–407 context, the draftsmen did not intend a thief of even a bearer instrument to be a holder. Section 3–202(1) can be read to stand for the general proposition that in order to become the holder of a bearer instrument there must be negotiation by *delivery*. Since "delivery" is a voluntary transfer, thieves do not take by delivery; hence a thief is not a holder, and the 3–407 discharge rule would not apply.

The draftsmen of the Code explicitly accepted the common law "spoliation" doctrine, an exception to the general rule that alteration causes discharge. That doctrine was designed to prevent unwarranted discharges and windfalls that could result from such discharges. (See § 3–407, Comment 3(a)). In Walsh v. Hunt, 120 Cal. 46, 53, 52 Pac. 115, 117 (1898), the court gave the following rationale for the spoliation doctrine:

The general rule undoubtedly is, as contended for by appellant, that any material alteration in the contract avoids it, even in the hands of innocent holders, and prevents recovery upon it to any extent. But this rule has application to cases where such alteration has been made by the payee or party seeking to enforce it. By the later authorities the rule does not apply in cases where the alteration is by a stranger to the contract, and it is now the settled doctrine, in this country at least, that such an act by a stranger, without the privity of the grantee or obligee, does not avoid the contract in its entirety, even though

it be without the knowledge or consent of the party to be bound, but amounts to a spoliation merely, which will not prevent a recovery upon the contract in accordance with its original terms, where those terms can be ascertained. And this is obviously upon the principle that the act of a mere interloper without the privity of the parties should not be permitted to defeat a contract to the extent that it would otherwise be valid and binding. . . .

A finding that the thief of a bearer instrument is not a holder for 3–407 purposes (and so does not cause discharge even if he alters the instrument) is consistent with the spoliation doctrine. For a tedious analysis of the foregoing question, see White, Some Petty Complaints About Article Three, 65 Mich.L.Rev. 1315 (1967).

One further interpretation of 3–407 (2)(a) that would avoid a windfall to the drawer-purchaser has been suggested by Professor Roy Steinheimer. He suggests that 3–407(2)(a) could be read to cause discharge only as to claims by the one who made the alteration. The difficulty with such a reading is that it renders 3–407(3) and the introductory phrase, "other than a subsequent holder in due course," of subsection (2) superfluous. See R. Steinheimer, Michigan Negotiable Instruments Law and the Uniform Commercial Code 90 (1960).

There is one final interpretive difficulty involving a potential conflict between 3–407 and 4–401. Assume the same facts as in the preceding paragraphs, except that the payor bank pays the full $11,000 to the depositary bank and that the payor bank does not qualify as a holder in due course (either because payor banks are not holders or because the check is overdue). According to 4–401(2)(a), a payor bank which in good faith makes payment to a holder (here the depositary bank) may charge its customer's account according to the original tenor of his altered item. But what if the drawer-purchaser claims that he is discharged on the instrument because of the alteration by the (holder) thief, and therefore that the payor bank must re-credit his

sumer did not give timely notice; in 4–207 by contrast we have a plaintiff-bank trying to recover money. Needless to say the heart strings of a court are less likely to be twanged by the bank's argument for an extended period in which to make its claim than by the argument of a consumer who has suffered personal injury. In the next chapter we will discuss the defenses that arise when a drawee recredits a negligent drawer's account.

## § 15–6 Conclusion

To return to the hypothetical case with which we began this chapter, consider a check drawn by Repeunzel, payable to the order of Cicero as payee. A thief steals the check from Cicero, forges Cicero's indorsement and transfers it through Gullible Grocer, depositary bank, collecting bank, and presenting bank to drawee bank who ultimately pays. To retrace our steps further, consider the various lawsuits that can arise out of this case:

(1) Cicero's first reaction may be to sue drawer Repeunzel under 3–804 on stolen (or lost) instruments. In our case Cicero should have a good cause of action against Repeunzel.

(2) If payee-Cicero recovers from drawer-Repeunzel, drawer may then wish to sue drawee bank and insist that it recredit drawer's account. This suit will be based upon 4–401 and the plaintiff should win, for the check was not "properly payable" since it bore a forged indorsement.

(3) To consider another alternative, assume that payee-Cicero is a good friend or good customer of the drawer-Repeunzel and would rather not sue him. In such case our payee may choose to sue either the depositary bank or the drawee bank for conversion of the check of which payee is the owner. Our payee will rely upon 3–419 and will have a good cause of action against the drawee and, as we have seen under the decided cases, will probably have a good cause of action against the depositary bank and Gullible Grocer as well.

account because the item was not "properly payable"? A careful analysis of the comments to 3–407 and 4–401 discloses that there is no real conflict between the sections. Comment 4 to 3–407 refers the reader to section 4–401 in the case of a bank's right to charge its customer's account. Comment 2 to 4–401 explicitly deals with the issue (emphasis added):

Subsection (2) parallels the provision which protects a holder in due course against discharge by reason of alteration and permits him to enforce the instrument according to its original tenor. Section 3–407(3). *It adopts the rule of cases extending the same protection to a drawer who pays in good faith.*

One can ask whether the discharge sanction in 3–407 does more harm than good. It is unlikely that a holder bent on theft by alteration will desist from altering the instrument merely because he fears that he will so discharge the drawer or maker's obligation to him. Nor will he be deterred because he may discharge others. Because the likelihood of any salutary inhibition on a would-be alterer is less than the likelihood of a windfall to the drawer-purchaser, it might be better if the discharge provision of 3–407 were removed.

*(4)* If loss rests on the drawee bank after the first lawsuit, either because the drawer caused the drawee to re-credit his account or because the payee-Cicero recovered from the drawee in his conversion suit under 3–419, the drawee will seek to sue "upstream" against those who passed the check down to him and warranted their title. Drawee bank will have a good cause of action under 4–207(1) (a), for neither Gullible Grocer nor any of the banks had good title, yet each warranted he had good title under 4–207. This lawsuit should put the loss ultimately to rest on Gullible Grocer, the first solvent party after the thief.

# CHAPTER 16

# NSF, FORGED DRAWER'S SIGNATURE, AND NEGLIGENCE

*Analysis*

Sec.
16–1.  Introduction.
16–2.  Checks Bearing Forged Drawer's Signature.
16–3.  NSF Checks.
16–4.  Final Payment.
16–5.  Negligence.
16–6.  Negligence, 3–406.
16–7.  Negligence, 4–406.
16–8.  Impostors and Fictitious Payees.
16–9.  Conclusion.

## § 16–1  Introduction

Legal problems presented by a check bearing a forged drawer's signature that a drawee has paid by mistake are often compared with those presented by a check bearing a forged indorsement that a drawee has paid by mistake. In both cases the notorious 18th Century English doctrine of Price v. Neal[1] may impose the loss *initially* on the drawee. But the *ultimate* liability of a drawee who pays a check bearing a forged drawer's signature differs significantly from its *ultimate* liability upon payment of a check bearing a forged indorsement. In the latter case a drawee can sue on warranty theory up the stream of indorsement against those who passed the check bearing the forged indorsement down to the drawee, but in the former case involving a check bearing a forged drawer's signature (or an NSF check) the drawee will almost never have a warranty cause of action and the "final payment" doctrine embodied in 3–418 and 4–213 will often also bar a restitutionary cause of action.

The effect of negligence of one of the parties upon the liabilities associated with forged signatures cuts across the issues considered in this chapter and in the previous chapter. If a party conducts his business in such a manner as to encourage forgeries or if he fails to use diligence in discovering forgeries on his cancelled checks, the Code (§§ 3–406; 4–406; 3–405) estops him from asserting forgery. Of course negligence does not travel without its companion, contributory negligence and if both the customer and his bank are negligent, the two will usually offset one another and re-open the customer's claim on the forgery.

## § 16–2  Checks Bearing Forged Drawer's Signature

Upon considering the drawee's liability on a check bearing a forged drawer's signature, one should use care to distinguish the

---

1.  3 Burr. 1354, 97 Eng.Rep. 871 (K.B. 1762).

519

drawee's liability before it makes final payment from that after it makes final payment. The drawee's status before final payment and absent acceptance is merely that of a party to whom an order has been issued; in the words of 3–409: "A check . . . does not of itself operate as an assignment of any funds in the hands of the drawee . . ., and the drawee is not liable on the instrument until he accepts it." If the drawee's clerk discovers the forgery before final payment and before accepting the check (for example, certifying it) the drawee is not obligated to pay the presenter, for the drawee's contract with the depositor obliges the drawee to pay only over the depositor's authorized signature. Therefore the drawee can and should dishonor. On dishonor the presenter may then seek recovery from his transferor either on the indorsement or on the warranty embodied in 4–207(2).[2]

Suppose, however, that employees of the drawee do not discover the forged signature in advance but make final payment on the check either by posting it to his account or by paying it over the counter. In the absence of drawer's negligence substantially contributing to the forgery, the drawee may not charge the drawer's account, for the drawer did not sign the check (see Chapter 17). If the drawee does charge the drawer's account, the drawer may insist that his account be recredited under 4–401, for the item is not "properly payable." A drawee who has paid in cash or by a credit it cannot revoke, and who cannot take affirmative action against some other party to recover the funds is in an unhappy status. Since it has no cause of action against the drawer, the drawee will usually pursue the presenter or others who transferred the check down the collection stream. With rare exceptions, the drawee will have no warranty cause of action against any of these prior parties. The warranty that all signatures are genuine in 4–207(2) is inviting but the Comments to 4–207 (especially Comment 4) and relevant statutory history[3] make it quite clear that the warranties in 4–207(2) which run to "transferees" do not run to payor banks.[4] Thus the drawee is left to the warranties under 4–207(1), but none of those warranties are broken by the usual transfer of a check bearing a forged signature of a drawer unless the transferor has "knowledge"[5] of the forgery. In a typical case, of course, there will be no such knowledge and neither 4–207(1) (a), (b) or (c) will be broken.

One might argue that a party who presents a check bearing a forged drawer's signature breaks the warranty of "good title" in 4–207(1) (a); however, statutory history and pre-Code cases sug-

2. Under Section 4–207(2) (b) the transferor warrants that "all signatures are genuine or authorized."

3. See 2 N.Y. State Law Revision Comm'n, 1955 Report 1336 (1955).

4. Nor can the payor bank bring itself within the scope of the section as a "collecting bank." Section 4–105(d) says, " 'Collecting bank' means any bank handling the item for collection except the payor bank."

5. Section 1–201(25) says that "[a] person 'knows' or has 'knowledge' of a fact when he has actual knowledge of it."

gest that "good title" does not encompass this case.[6]  A party who presents a check lacks good title to it only if it bears forged indorsements or there is a break in the chain of title (as by theft) after the check has been properly written.  This interpretation is borne out by the 4–207(1) (b) warranty against "knowledge" that the signature of the drawer is unauthorized.  If the presenter breaks the good title warranty anytime the drawer's signature is forged, the 4–207(1) (b) warranty against knowledge of such forgery would be superfluous.  Moreover to hold that a party who presents a check bearing a forged drawer's signature lacks "good title" would obliterate the doctrine of Price v. Neal and wipe 3–418 off the books (that is, Comment 1 to 3–418 summarizes that doctrine as follows: "the drawee who accepts or pays an instrument on which the signature of the drawer is forged is bound  .  .  .  and cannot recover back his payment").  Thus the drawee in most cases has no warranty cause of action against any prior party.  The drawee does not receive 4–207(2) warranties, and the presenter will not normally break the 4–207(1) warranties.

The drawee bank is thus left with a cause of action in restitution for money paid by mistake against the prior parties up the collection stream.[7]  This cause of action enters by way of 1–103;

---

6.  Comment 2 to 4–207 says that the predecessor of that section is the Uniform Negotiable Instruments Law §§ 65, 66.  These sections defined the warranty liability of a person negotiating an instrument by delivery and the liability of a general indorser, respectively.  Further, Comment 1 to § 4–207 tells us that its warranties are identical to those of 3–417.  There Comment 3 makes it clear that the warranties of 3–417(1) (a), and thus § 4–207(1) (a), are applicable only to forged indorsements, not forged drawers' signatures:

Subsection (1) (a) retains the generally accepted rule that the party who accepts or pays does not "admit" the genuineness of indorsements, and may recover from the person presenting the instrument when they turn out to be forged.  The justification for the distinction between forgery of the signature of the drawer and forgery of an indorsement is that the drawee is in a position to verify the drawer's signature by comparison with one in his hands, but has ordinarily no opportunity to verify an indorsement.

7.  See  Restatement  of  Restitution (1936):

§ 28  Mistake Due to Fraud or Misrepresentation

A person who has paid money to another because of a mistake of fact

and who does not obtain what he expected in return is entitled to restitution from the other if the mistake was induced:

(a) by the fraud of the payee, or

(b) by his innocent and material misrepresentation, or

(c) by the fraud or material misrepresentation of a person purporting to act as the payee's agent, or

(d) by the fraud or material misrepresentation of a third person, provided that the payee has notice of fraud or misrepresentation before he has given or promised something of value.

§ 29  In General

A person who, because of a mistake of fact, has paid money to another in the payment or the purchase of a bill of exchange or promissory note, is entitled to restitution in accordance with the rules stated in §§ 6–28, except as modified by the rules stated in §§ 30–38.

§ 30  Forged Signature

The holder of a bill of exchange or promissory note who has received payment thereof from one whose name was forged thereon as a party, or from a drawee on a bill on which the drawer's name was forged, is not thereby under a duty of restitution if

the Code draftsmen overlooked or intentionally omitted it in drafting Article Three. It is based on the theory that the drawee paid the check because of a mistake about the identity of the signer.

The plaintiff-drawee had a rocky road to restitutionary recovery at common law, and the Code has not smoothed that path. The first obstacle was the doctrine of Price v. Neal now embodied in section 3–418:

> Except for recovery of bank payments as provided in the Article on Bank Deposits and Collections (Article 4) and except for liability for breach of warranty on presentment under the preceding section payment or acceptance of any instrument is final in favor of a holder in due course, or a person who has in good faith changed his position in reliance on the payment.

Comment 1 of that section explicitly acknowledges its heritage as follows:

> The section follows the rule of Price v. Neal, 3 Burr. 1354 (1762), under which a drawee who accepts or pays an instrument on which the signature of the drawer is forged is bound on his acceptance and cannot recover back his payment. Although the original Act is silent as to payment, the common law rule has been applied to it by all but a very few jurisdictions.

A variety of policies purportedly justify Price v. Neal; but none is entirely satisfactory. According to Comment 1 to 3–418 the "traditional justification . . . is that the drawee is in a superior position to detect a forgery because he has the maker's signature and is expected to know and to compare it. . . ." But the author of this comment professes greater faith in the policy "to end the transaction on an instrument when it is paid rather than reopen and upset a series of commercial transactions at a later date. . . ." Of course neither of these policies paints a picture consistent with results in forged indorsement cases. If Price v. Neal is founded on the theory that any drawee who fails to discover a forged drawer's signature is negligent and thus is not entitled to recover payment, there should be an exception to the doctrine for those cases in which the signature is so cleverly forged that a banking employee using due care could not discover the forgery. If on the other hand, the rule is premised on the desirability of ending and not reopening commercial transactions, then the same rule should apply to forged

he paid value and received payment without reason to know that the signature was forged.

These doctrines are incorporated in the Code by Section 1–103 which reads as follows:

Unless displaced by the particular provisions of this Act the principles of law and equity, including the law merchant and the law relative to capacity to contract, principal and agent, estoppel, fraud, misrepresentation, duress, coercion, mistake, bankruptcy, or other validating or invalidating cause shall supplement its provisions.

indorsement cases as well as forged drawer cases. We can discern no adequate rationale to explain the difference between the liability of the drawee bank on checks bearing forged indorsements and its liability on those bearing forged drawer's signatures.

Returning to operation of the rule, note the several conditions that must be met before 3–418 blocks the drawee's restitutionary action against a presenter:

(*1*)  There must have been "payment or acceptance" (i. e. final payment as defined in 4–213).

(*2*)  It must have been in favor of (a) a holder in due course or (b) "a person who has in good faith changed his position in reliance on the payment."

Thus if the drawee discovers the forgery while the check is still in the process of posting and before final payment has occurred because of the passage of excess time, the finality doctrine does not apply and the drawee may send the check back under 4–301 or if that fails, sue for restitution. We discuss the meaning of "final payment," Section 16–4 below.

To illustrate the application of 3–418, consider a recent New York case [8] in which the payee of a check bearing a forged drawer's signature asserted the defense of 3–418. In payment for two groups of diamonds Altman took two checks payable to his order over forged drawers' signatures. He held the first group of diamonds until the first check had "cleared," and, by delivering the diamonds, "changed his position in reliance on the payment." Having had a satisfactory experience (or so he thought) with his buyer, he did not wait until the second check cleared before he delivered the second group of diamonds. Upon discovery of the forgeries, the drawee sued to recover the amount of the checks from Altman. The case came up on a motion for summary judgment and the court denied summary judgment since Altman did not change his position in reliance on payment of the second check. Moreover the court found an issue of fact about Altman's "good faith" in taking the second check. The case raises several interesting and important questions. First, may the ordinary payee on a check such as Altman be a "holder in due course" and thus be entitled to the protection of 3–418 even though he does not change his position in reliance upon payment? Secondly, might not some act less than holding the diamonds until the check clears amount to a change of position in reliance? Third, does garden variety negligence on the part of the payee (that is, negligence which would not in and of itself deprive him of a holder in due course status) nevertheless bar him from invoking 3–418?

Section 3–302(2) explicitly provides that a payee may be a holder in due course. Altman's lawyer apparently did not argue that he was a holder in due course, but the New York courts might

8.  First Nat'l City Bank v. Altman, 3 UCC Rep.Serv. 815 (N.Y.Sup.Ct.1966),  aff'd mem. 277 N.Y.S.2d 813 (1st Dep't 1967).

not have agreed even if this had been argued.   Comment 2 to 3–302 lists seven examples in which a payee may be a holder in due course. In each, a third party intervenes between the payee and the drawer or maker against whom holder in due course status is asserted.   Presumably the draftsmen selected these examples because only in such circumstances (that is, where the holder has not dealt with the prior party), may a holder take free of the defenses of such party.[9]   However for 3–418 to operate there is no such requirement of non-dealing. Unless the comments to 3–302 limit the status of a payee as a holder in due course only to those cases in which a third party intervenes, Altman should be entitled to assert that status.   It does appear, though, that at least some New York judges may limit the kinds of payees who can be holders in due course.[10]

The case law is thin on the reliance that brings 3–418 into operation.   Of course, actions such as Altman's on the first check (withholding the delivery of goods until learning of final payment) are sufficient.   Might other behavior such as the manner in which one spends his money after a check has been paid be sufficient? Altman might have argued: "Well, I would not have purchased this new display case if I had not thought this check had been paid." [11] We would hold that such modest reliance is sufficient under 3–418, but then we are not judges.

A final question about the operation of 3–418 concerns the effect of negligence on the part of one who seeks to rely on 3–418. In Altman's case, the drawee apparently argued that Altman should have tried harder to identify his customer and that if he had done

---

9.  See section 3–305(2) which frees a holder in due course from "all defenses of any party to the instrument with whom the holder *has not* dealt except . . . [real defenses]." (emphasis added).

10.  See, e. g., Saale v. Interstate Steel Co., Inc., 27 App.Div.2d 1, 5, 275 N.Y. S.2d 532, 536, 3 UCC Rep.Serv. 1140, 1144 (1st Dep't 1966) (dissenting opinion, Rabin, J.), aff'd 19 N.Y.2d 933, 228 N.E.2d 397, 4 UCC Rep.Serv. 1053 (1967); Merit Bar & Fixture Mfg. Co. v. K. Ranch, Inc., 3 UCC Rep.Serv. 1154 (N.Y. Co.Ct.1967); Mooney v. Leonard C. Adams Co., 4 UCC Rep. Serv. 320 (N.Y.Sup.Ct.1967).  See also Annot., 2 A.L.R.3d 1151 (1965).

11.  The handful of cases decided under the Code sheds no light on the nature of reliance required in 3–418.  Under the common law and the NIL most courts restricted the application of the final payment doctrine to holders in due course and considered change of position by the person receiving payment an immaterial factor in application of the rule of Price v. Neal. See, e. g., Neal v. Coburn, 92 Me. 139, 42 A. 348 (1898).  A few courts required an inquiry into the recipient's change of position.  See Alabama Nat'l Bank v. Rivers, 116 Ala. 1, 22 So. 580 (1897); First State Bank & Trust Co. v. First Nat'l Bank, 314 Ill. 269, 145 N.E. 382 (1924); American Sur. Co. v. Industrial Sav. Bank, 242 Mich. 581, 219 N.W. 689 (1928).  See generally Annot., 12 A.L.R. 1089, 1109 (1921); Annot., 71 A.L.R. 337, 341 (1931); Annot., 121 A.L.R. 1056, 1061 (1939). Note that the 1952 Official Draft of the Code limited application of 3–418 to holders in due course.  The language which broadened its scope to include persons who changed position in reliance on payment was introduced in the 1958 Official Text, but without any change in Comment 3.  See Permanent Editorial Board of the Uniform Commercial Code, 1956 Recommendations 116 (1956).

so, he might not have taken the check.   Comment 4 to 3–418 [12] explicitly deals with this question as follows:

> The section rejects decisions under the original Act permitting recovery on the basis of mere negligence of the holder in taking the instrument.  If such negligence amounts to a lack of good faith as defined in this Act (Section 1–201) or to notice under the rules (Section 3–304) relating to notice to a purchaser of an instrument, the holder is not a holder in due course and is not protected; but otherwise the holder's negligence does not affect the finality of the payment or acceptance.

Since mere failure to ask for sufficient identification does not normally constitute lack of good faith under the Code's subjective test, the *Altman* court apparently strayed from the intention of the draftsmen and fell back on earlier law.[13]

A more imposing obstacle to the drawee's restitutionary recovery than 3–418 is 4–213 and its companion 4–302.  According to those sections a bank which makes final payment or simply holds an item without taking appropriate action to pay or return it becomes "accountable for the amount of the item."  Presumably "accountable for" means that a drawee bank that is making final payment under 4–213, but has not yet disbursed funds, is obligated to disburse those funds.[14]  If on the other hand, such a drawee has disbursed the funds in the course of making final payment under 4–213, the "accountable for" language must mean that the bank has no right to recover the funds so paid.[15]

---

12.   Note that Comment 4 like Comment 3 fails to reflect the broadened scope of 3–418 and refers only to "holders" who lose its protection.

13.   See First Nat'l City Bank v. Altman, 3 UCC Rep.Serv. 815, 816–17 (N. Y.Sup.Ct.1966) where the court says:

However, in all of the circumstances, the court is of the view that the issue of his good faith presents triable issue of fact which precludes summary dismissal of the action based on the first check (see Banca C. I. Trust Co. v. Clarkson, 274 N.Y. 69).  It has been held that the negligence of the purchaser, at the time he acquired title to the instrument, in not making inquiries which, if made, might reveal the fact of forgery, releases the drawee from the rule of Price v. Neal, and enables the drawee to recover from the purchaser the amount paid to him on the instrument (Whitney The Law of Modern Commercial Practices, 2d ed., section 338, p. 504 (1965)).

The juxtaposition of the court's remarks about good faith and its comment about the effect of the purchaser's negligence make it unclear exactly what doctrine the court finally applies to deny the motion for summary judgment.  Perhaps the court thought that the good faith requirement of 3–418 is functionally equivalent to the negligence doctrine under the NIL. However, the Code certainly does not support that view.  See § 1–201(19).

14.   See Comment 7 to Section 4–213 which says, "The term 'accountable' is used as imposing a duty to account which duty is met if and when a settlement for the item satisfactorily clears."

15.   Related liability can arise under 4–302 when a payor who is not also a depositary bank fails to settle for an item by midnight of the banking day of receipt or payor bank (whether or not it is also the depositary bank) fails to "pay or return" by its midnight deadline.

Section 4–213 covers much of the same ground that 3–418 covers.  How does 4–213 apply to cases like *Altman* where the plaintiff seems to stub his toe on 3–418 because he seems not to "change his position in reliance" and may fail to be a holder in due course?  One wonders whether this "accountability" of the drawee bank is only to holders in due course and to those who change their positions in reliance on the bank's action or non-action.  If anybody off the street can claim the protection of 4–213 and its companion 4–302 (even a payor that has not made final payment is "accountable" on checks bearing a forged drawer's signature if it fails to return them within a specified time), then the restrictions embodied in 3–418 which we have already considered in connection with the *Altman* case are relatively unimportant.  Pre-Code law, discussions of the draftsmen and others at the time of Code adoption, and post-Code cases all suggest that a party does not have to be either a holder in due course or one who changes his position in order to claim the protection of 4–213 and 4–302.  Section 4–302 codifies pre-Code cases under section 137 of the NIL.[16]  The Editorial Board of the Code [17] identified its ancestors as State Bank v. Weiss,[18] a New York case, and Wisner v. First National Bank of Gallitzin.[19]  In both cases payees successfully recovered from payor banks who held checks beyond the permitted time.  In the New York case it appears that the payee held his goods until he determined that the check had not been returned as NSF and only then delivered them.  Thus he would have qualified even under the requirements of 3–418 as one who changed position in reliance upon the payor-bank's action or non-action.  However the *Wisner* case revealed no such reliance on the payee's part.  Moreover, while the court in *Wisner* referred in passing to plaintiffs who are "prejudiced" by the bank's failure to act in a timely way, the court did not consider the payee's reliance crucial to the decision.  If the draftsmen did intend 4–302 to codify those cases, change of position in reliance upon the payor's failure to dishonor within the specified period of time cannot be a necessary element, for that element was not present in *Wisner*.

The discussions before the New York Law Revision Commission and the Commission's response to questions and complaints of the New York Clearinghouse Sub-Committee are even more illuminating.  The New York Clearinghouse Subcommittee report clearly identified the issue and pointed out that only a holder in due course receives the protection of 3–418 (the language encompassing

---

**16.**  Section 137 of the NIL reads as follows:

Where a drawee to whom a bill is delivered for acceptance destroys the same, or refuses within twenty-four hours after such delivery, or within such other period as the holder may allow, to return the bill accepted or non-accepted to the holder, he will be deemed to have accepted the same.

**17.**  See Uniform Commercial Code, 1953 Official Draft of Text and Comments 142–43 (Supp. No. 1, 1955).

**18.**  46 Misc. 93, 91 N.Y.S. 276 (Sup.Ct. 1904).

**19.**  220 Pa. 21, 68 A. 955 (1908).

one who changes position in reliance on final payment had not yet been added) but that there appeared to be no such limitations under 4–213.[20]  In response, the Editorial Board's subcommittee acknowledged differences between 3–418 and 4–213 and passed off the problem by citing 4–102(1), which provides that Article Four overrides Article Three.[21]  Although the Code draftsmen in 1956 modified 3–418 to include those who change their position in reliance on final payment, this modification was apparently not intended to meet the criticisms of the New York Law Revision Commission and others about the restrictiveness of 3–418.[22]

**20.**  See Report of Subcommittee on Article 4 to the New York Clearing House Subcommittee on the Proposed Uniform Commercial Code, 1 N.Y. State Law Revision Comm'n, 1954 Report 449–50 (1954), which makes the point as follows (emphasis in original):

(c) The final payment provisions of Article 4 are not consistent with Sec. 3–418, and no good reason is apparent for the fundamental differences.

Sec. 3–418 provides that "Except for recovery of bank payments . . . and except for liability for breach of warranty . . . payment or acceptance of instrument is *final* in favor of a holder in due course."

The five lines of text are followed by 60 lines of comments to the effect that this section gives the payor a right to recover the payment from one who is not a holder in due course or does not hold under one. The basis for recovery is not given in the comments, but presumably it is for payment under mistake and includes overdraft or forgery of drawer's signature.

It seems obvious that "final payment" is used here in a different sense than in Sec. 4–213; but, even so, how can this section reconcile with Sec. 4–302(a) which gives the customer of the depositary bank (whether he is a holder in due course or not) a right to recover from the payor bank the amount of any demand item if that bank returns it after the midnight deadline?

**21.**  See Uniform Commercial Code, 1953 Official Draft of Text and Comments 139 (Supp. No. 1, 1955) where it was said:
The New York Clearing House Sub-Committee contends that the final payment provisions of Article 4 are not consistent with Section 3–418 and that no good reason is apparent for the fundamental differences. *Com-*

*mittee 12, 13.* Of course there are differences between the two rules. Section 3–418 is framed in the background of the Uniform Negotiable Instruments Act and cases arising under it. Section 4–213 is specially drafted to meet the specialized problem of bank collections. If it is wrong to have a difference of approach and language between these two sections then the major portion of existing statutory and case law is also wrong because the same thing applies. The same or stronger criticism can be leveled at differences between NIL Sections 119 through 123 and New York NIL 350–b. Practice and operations under the two sections do not produce problems of inconsistency in view of the rule of Section 4–102(1).

**22.**  See 2 N.Y. State Law Revision Comm'n, 1955 Report 1075 (1955) which said:

Here the question arises, why finality is limited by section 3–418 to finality "in favor of a holder in due course." Obviously, that was what the draftsmen of the Code intended. Professor George E. Palmer doubted the correctness of this approach in "Negotiable Instruments Under the Uniform Commercial Code," 48 Mich.Law Rev. 255 (1950) at page 296. Although he was commenting on an earlier draft, he had the following interesting comments to make on what was then the clause which dealt with Price v. Neal:

It is commonly said that finality of acceptance or payment operates only in favor of a holder in due course, a view which has been vigorously assailed by some writers [referring to Ralph W. Aigler, "The Doctrine of Price v. Neal," 24 Mich.L.Rev. 809 at 823–4 (1926); Britton, Bills and Notes, 632 et seq. (1943)]. After rejection in earlier drafts, [section 512 of Proposed Final Draft No. 2 (1948) which had said that acceptance or payment was to be final "to

With one exception, post-Code cases apply either the Article Four provisions or 3–418 but do not consider the possible conflict between them. The *Altman* case (in which the diamond merchant took a check bearing a forged drawer's signature) appears to be the perfect case for application of 4–213. Altman appeared to be on the verge of losing his claim because he could not qualify on the second check as one who had changed position in reliance, yet the court did not discuss 4–213. On the other hand, other courts have found the payor liable under 4–302, without discussing the status of a plaintiff who claims that the drawee bank was accountable under 4–302.[23]

The Virginia court in Kirby v. First & Merchants National Bank,[24] recognized the possibility of conflict between 3–418 and the Article Four provision. In that case the defendant-payee presented a check to the payor over the counter, took $200 of the check in cash, and had the remaining $2300 credited to her bank account. The court held that the transaction was a payment in cash and that the drawee "finally paid" across the counter. The court found the drawee liable under 4–213. In a footnote [25] the court considered the possibility that one who receives money in bad faith or is guilty

---

the extent that any party has paid for the instrument in good faith"] the latest draft has adopted this view. The holding in due course concept was developed for another purpose and is inapt here at least as applied to payment. Its use means, for example, that results may differ depending upon whether the holder of a check who has received payment took before or after maturity, which usually will be thirty days after issuance under the revision [then section 304; now section 3–504(2)]. Purchase after maturity has a rational bearing on the holder's right to recover free of prior defenses, but it should be irrelevant to the question whether payment is final.

The broader scope of section 3–418 was explained as follows:

The revision follows a New York Commission suggestion to make clear the continued application where appropriate, of a general principle of law.
Editorial Board of the Uniform Commercial Code, 1956 Recommendations 116 (1956). It appears, therefore, that the very difference with which we are concerned was pointed out to the draftsmen in 1954. They answered that the difference was intended and that those who could not claim the protection of 3–418, because they had not changed their position in reliance or because they were not holders in

due course, might nevertheless claim the protection of 4–302 and 4–213.

23. See, e. g., National City Bank v. Motor Contract Co., 119 Ga.App. 208, 166 S.E.2d 742, 6 UCC Rep.Serv. 376 (1969) (payor bank liable for checks returned three days after presentment when Code requires return before midnight deadline to avoid accountability); Farmers Co-operative Livestock Mkt., Inc. v. Second Nat'l Bank, 427 S.W.2d 247 (Ky.Ct.App.1968) (three week delay in returning check meant drawee bank was liable for face amount of instrument); Rock Island Auction Sales, Inc. v. Empire Packing Co., 32 Ill.2d 269, 204 N.E.2d 721, 2 UCC Rep.Serv. 319 (1965) (4–302 not an irrational and therefore not an unconstitutional classification; payor bank liable when it returned an item after midnight deadline. See also, Samples v. Trust Co., 118 Ga.App. 307, 163 S.E.2d 325, 5 UCC Rep.Serv. 998 (1968) (payor bank held liable for an item when it failed to return it before midnight deadline as specified in 4–302). Note, however, that in the latter case the bank had paid the item and the case should have been decided under 4–213.

24. 210 Va. 88, 168 S.E.2d 273, 6 UCC Rep.Serv. 694 (1961).

25. Id. at 91 n. 4, 168 S.E.2d at 275 n. 4, 6 UCC Rep.Serv. at 697 n. 4.

of fraud might not claim under 4–213, but the court pointed out that the drawee did not argue that the payees were not holders in due course or had not changed their position and concluded: "[m]oreover insofar as UCC §§ 3–418 and 4–213 conflict, UCC 4–213 prevails. UCC § 4–102(1)." The synthesis then of pre-Code cases, statutory history, and post-Code cases is that any party not acting in bad faith can claim the protection of 4–302 and 4–213 even though he is not a holder in due course and even though he has not changed position in reliance upon the drawee's action or inaction. Of course this leaves precious little territory for 3–418; presumably it still reigns over notes and other instruments not presented through banking channels. For example, if a draft drawn on a buyer were forged, presented to, and finally paid by the buyer-drawee, 4–213 would not apply because the buyer-drawee would not be a "payor-bank."

In conclusion we may ask whether Price v. Neal is worth the agony it causes lawyers and law students. Not only is there no sound policy ground for the distinction between the outcome in forged indorsement cases and forged drawer cases, one arrives at Price v. Neal only after a good deal of difficult statutory analysis. Most disappointing, one ultimately finds that the rule as set down by the Code draftsmen is unclear in important details.

We conclude that one should not read the holder in due course or reliance requirements from 3–418 into 4–213 and 4–302. Moreover we suggest that when the draftsmen redraft Article Three and Article Four, they consider applying the same rule to both forged indorsement and forged drawer cases. We are unclear whether the finality doctrine ought to apply to forged indorsements and forged drawer cases or whether it should apply to neither, but we believe that the complexity involved in distinguishing the two cases is not justified.

## § 16–3 NSF Checks

Once the drawee pays a check of an "uncollectible" drawer against insufficient funds, the drawee's legal situation will be nearly identical to that when it pays over a forged drawer's signature. All the preceding discussion of warranty and restitutionary theory, and of defenses of the presenting bank under 3–418, 4–302 and 4–213, apply equally to the NSF check case. Of course, an important difference between an NSF case and a forged drawer's case is that in the former the drawee has a good cause of action against its drawer-customer. Under the terms of 4–401(1) the drawee may charge the drawer's account "even though the charge creates an overdraft." Thus the drawee has a cause of action for the overdraft against its depositor, for according to Comment 1 to 4–401: "[T]he draft itself . . . carries an implied promise to reimburse the drawee."

## § 16–4  Final Payment

The time of payment of a check is crucial in determining the foregoing liabilities. Until the drawee pays, it is not liable on the check itself.[26] Thus if it discovers that the drawer's signature is forged before it makes final payment, the drawee can dishonor the check, and the presenter will have no power to make the drawee pay. In that case the presenter may seek to throw the loss back upstream, and it may ultimately come to rest on the one who took the check from the thief. If, however, the drawee has made final payment, in most cases it will not be able to throw the loss back upstream and must bear the loss. Similar results follow in NSF check cases. If the drawee refuses to make final payment, the loss will fall initially on the presenter, and in turn on some party upstream from him. If on the other hand, the drawee has made final payment, the doctrine of 3–418 or 4–213 will come into play, and the drawee will often have to bear the loss itself. The crucial cutoff point—the point at which the drawee becomes bound under 3–418 and the doctrine of Price v. Neal—occurs when the drawee makes final payment under 4–213.[27]

At the outset one should distinguish between NSF and forged drawer cases on the one hand, and priority conflicts over the account on the other. Conflicts of the latter kind arise when one party presents a check at or near the same time another party issues a stop order or garnishees the account or the drawee learns of the drawer's death or petition in bankruptcy. The priority cases are essentially conflicts between two claimants to the proceeds in the account. On the one hand the check holder demands payment; on the other, the depositor's creditor demands the funds through garnishment (for example). Some courts have erroneously analyzed these cases under 4–213 on the theory that the check wins if final payment is made before the other event (for example, garnishment) occurs, but loses if the other event occurs first.[28] The correct analysis is to go to 4–303— a provision similar to but significantly different from 4–213—and to analyze the priority cases there. We discuss the priority cases in Section 17–7.

To pose the problem we face here, consider the following hypothetical case: Payee, Repeunzel, receives two checks, each in the amount of $3,000. Since he is worried about the solvency of one of the drawers, he takes that check to the drawee bank and procures cash for it over the counter. The other check he deposits in his own account in his own bank and the next morning it is delivered to the drawee bank. The drawee takes no action with respect to the second

---

26. See § 3–409.

27. On that rare occasion when the payor receives an item without settling for it, section 4–302(a) imposes accountability on the payor for the item regardless of whether it is properly payable or not, if the payor fails to "pay, or return the item or send notice of dishonor until after its midnight deadline."

28. See West Side Bank v. Marine Nat'l Exch. Bank, 37 Wis.2d 661, 155 N.W.2d 587, 4 UCC Rep.Serv. 1003 (1968). For an extensive discussion of the *West Side Bank* case, see Section 21–8 infra.

check for three days.   Ultimately it develops that both checks were drawn against insufficient funds.   The drawee bank asks its lawyer whether it can now dishonor the checks or send them back to the presenter on some theory.   The answer, as we have seen, is that the drawee probably cannot send them back if it has made final payment. On the facts given the drawee made final payment on the first check when it paid cash across the counter.   It made final payment on the second check by failing to return the check to the one who presented it or to send notice of dishonor to that person before its midnight deadline (or before such longer period as an agreement or clearinghouse rule might give it).

Final payment on the first check occurred under 4–213(1) (a); final payment on the second occurred because of the operation of 4–213(1) (d).   Section 4–213(1) reads in full as follows:

> An item is finally paid by a payor bank when the bank has done any of the following, whichever happens first:
>
> (a)  paid the item in cash; or
>
> (b)  settled for the item without reserving a right to revoke the settlement and without having such right under statute, clearing house rule or agreement; or
>
> (c)  completed the process of posting the item to the indicated account of the drawer, maker or other person to be charged therewith; or
>
> (d)  made a provisional settlement for the item and failed to revoke the settlement in the time and manner permitted by statute, clearing house rule or agreement.
>
> Upon a final payment under subparagraphs (b), (c) or (d) the payor bank shall be accountable for the amount of the item.

Section 4–213(1) (a) is not difficult.   If a party presents the check and receives cash over the counter for it,[29] final payment occurs and

---

29.   In Kirby v. First & Merchants Nat'l Bank, 210 Va. 88, 168 S.E.2d 273, 6 UCC Rep.Serv. 694 (1969), the court held that the payor cashed and thereby made final payment for the entire amount of a $2,500 check when it gave a depositor $200 in cash and $2,300 credit to his account.

We think the case was wrongly decided.   The Supreme Court of Virginia holds in *Kirby* that the bank "paid the check in cash."   They rely on "Currency $2,300" entered on the deposit slip, "Cash for dep." written on the back of the check, and testimony by the bank officer that the bank had, in effect, cashed the check before crediting the deposit in the Kirby account.   We disagree.   Although the court was correct as to the $200 which Mrs. Kirby took December 30, the $2,300 deposit credited to her account January 3 was at best a "provisional settlement" (4–213(1) (d)) and not paid "in cash" (4–213(1) (a)).   The deposit slip was incorrectly filled out by either Mrs. Kirby or the bank's teller.   There is another notation on the slip, "CHECKS 68–728–514 partial," which is a code number describing the origin of the check Mrs. Kirby negotiated.   If Mrs. Kirby had been paid cash and then deposited $2,300 cash in two distinct transactions as the court contends, presumably there would be no need for the bank

the bank is stuck under 3–418 or 4–213 if the presenter qualifies under those sections. Likewise if the bank settled for the item without

to list a code number for the check
they "cashed." The "partial" description of the deposit, along with a computation note subtracting $200 from
$2,500, seems to point to a single split
transaction with the check being partially deposited and partially paid in
cash.

The court concludes that even if the
$2,300 deposit was a provisional set-
tlement, the bank became accountable for the item under 4–301. The
bank failed to comply with 4–301 since
it neither returned the check nor sent
written notice before its midnight
deadline, but only telephoned the Kir-
bys January 5 after the check was
found to be NSF on January 4. The
check was drawn on another branch
of the depositary bank, and the court's
reasoning is enough if one treats the
two branches as one bank for these
purposes. Then the depositary bank
would also be the payor bank and
must send notice of dishonor before
the midnight deadline under 4–301(1).

The court fails to discuss the curious
complications when two branch banks
are involved in the same transaction.
The check was drawn on a Norfolk-
Virginia Beach area branch (drawee-
payor branch), but Mrs. Kirby presented the check at the Princess Anne
Plaza Branch (depositary branch). If
one treats the two branches as separate banks under 4–106 and, assuming
the check was returned by the payor
branch to the depositary branch before the midnight deadline (the facts
are not clear), then the case was
wrongly decided on these grounds as
well. The item would never have been
"paid," for the depositary branch
would have a "reasonable time" under
4–212(1) to charge back the Kirby account. They would no longer be limited by the 4–301 midnight deadline
since they were not the "payor bank"
if they were treated as a separate unit
under 4–106. The depositary branch
took six days after the discovery of
the NSF to charge back the Kirby account on January 10. In view of the
bank officer's phone call to the Kir-
bys on January 5, this elapsed time
could be "reasonable."

The question remains whether the two
branches should be treated as separate banks. Section 4–106 and the
comments thereto give some clues to
the factors involved, but they give no
easy answers. Section 4–106 provides:

A branch or separate office of a
bank [maintaining its own deposit
ledgers] is a separate bank for computing the time within which and determining the place at or to which action may be taken or notices or orders
shall be given under this Article and
under Article 3. (The words in brackets are optional.)

The comments indicate, however, that
branch banks may not be treated as
separate banks for all purposes. Comment 3 to 4–106 says it "seems anomalous for one branch of a bank to have
charged an item to the account of the
drawer and another branch to have
the power to treat the item as dishonored." Comment 4, on the other hand,
says "where the Article provides a
number of time limits for different
types of action by banks, if a branch
functions as a separate bank, it should
have the time limits available to a
separate bank."

Several factors in branch banks might
tend to show they are "separate."
Some branches maintain separate deposit ledgers, although computerized
banks often have central bookkeeping and any branch may "call the
computer" for a report on an account. The method for checking on an
account may be inconvenient or take
longer than the time limits for notification would allow. Some banks may
function with a slow average speed
of payment between branches. Others
send NSF notices and stop orders only
to the branch where the customer
opened the account, regardless of their
bookkeeping system. Many states allow banks to have branches in different cities which might tend to be
more "separate" than branches in the
same city. Branches at the opposite
ends of a large city might, for some
purposes, also be "separate" banks.
The Code does not draw simple guidelines. The distinction is hard to make
and depends on the circumstances of
the particular branches and their operations.

So far no courts have interpreted
4–106. Pre-Code cases such as Dean
v. Eastern Shore Trust Co., 159 Md.
213, 150 A. 797 (1930), where the
branches were in different cities, may
give some glimmerings. See also Note,

reserving a right to revoke or having a right under some other rule, 4–213(1) (b) finalizes payment. In this context "settlement" [30] most commonly means giving the presenter a credit in his account with a third party such as a federal reserve bank. Assume for example that Boston Bank presents a check to Detroit Bank. It may do so through the Chicago Federal Reserve and both banks may have an account at the Chicago Federal Reserve. If that is so, the payor Detroit Bank will settle with the Boston Bank by causing its account to be debited and the Boston's Bank to be credited at the Federal Reserve. In most such cases 4–213(1) (b) would not come into play for it would be uncommon for the payor-bank to settle without reserving or having a right to revoke. Nevertheless it is possible that the payor could settle and neither retain a right to revoke nor have such a right under the Code or under any other rule. The more common case (in which it has such a right to revoke) is governed by subsection 4–213(1) (d). Under that subsection the payor makes final payment when its provisional settlement (for example, with the Chicago Federal Reserve) becomes final because of the passage of time. Section 4–301(1) gives the payor bank until its "midnight deadline" to return the item or send notice of dishonor.[31] If it fails to return the item or send notice of dishonor before its midnight deadline or before any later point in time that it has under an agreement, it will make final payment under 4–213(1) (d). Under 4–104(1) (h) the midnight deadline is "midnight of the next banking day following the banking day on which it receives the relevant item". Thus if a bank receives a check on Wednesday morning and makes a provisional settlement for it (e. g., a credit to the presenter's account in the Federal Reserve), it would have until Thursday midnight to return that item or give notice. It it fails to do so before Thursday midnight it will have made final payment under 4–213(1) (d). Note, however, that it may have additional time because of the clearing

The Stop Order, Branch Banking's Headache—A Computerized Curative, 29 U.Pitt.L.Rev. 287, 292–93, 296–97 (1967). At any rate, we lack sufficient facts to decide whether the Princess Anne Plaza and the Norfolk-Virginia Beach branches were separate banks under 4–106, and we lack the wisdom (or foolhardiness) to do more here than raise the issue.

**30.** Section 4–104(1) (j) provides:

"Settle" means to pay in cash, by clearing house settlement, in a charge or credit or by remittance, or otherwise as instructed. A settlement may be either provisional or final.

As Comment 6 to Section 4–104 explains, settlement may occur in a variety of ways. For example, a payor may settle for an item by debiting and crediting accounts in a local clearing house or by giving credit in one of its own accounts when the presenter is also a customer of the payor.

**31.** Section 4–301(1) reads:

Where an authorized settlement for a demand item (other than a documentary draft) received by a payor bank otherwise than for immediate payment over the counter has been made before midnight of the banking day of receipt the payor bank may revoke the settlement and recover any payment if before it has made final payment (subsection (1) of Section 4–213) and before its midnight deadline it

(a) returns the item; or

(b) sends written notice of dishonor or nonpayment if the item is held for protest or is otherwise unavailable for return.

house rule or other agreement. If for example it settles with a local bank under a clearing house rule which allows three days, it would have that additional time to return the item or give notice before its payment is deemed final under (1) (d). The lawyer who argues that a payor bank has made final payment because it failed to revoke a provisional settlement must first determine when the midnight deadline occurred and then must examine the clearing house rule, the Federal Reserve rules, and any other pertinent agreements to determine whether the midnight deadline is extended in such cases.[32]

The final and most troublesome final payment provision is 4–213(1) (c). That subsection reads as follows:

> An item is finally paid  .  .  .  when the bank has
>
> .  .  .
>
> (c) completed the process of posting the item to the indicated account of the drawer, maker or other person to be charged therewith;  .  .  .

In the usual case in which a payor bank receives a check, it will run the check through the computer; the computer will debit the drawer's account and a clerk will examine the print-out (showing the debit) together with the check. If, by examining the print-out, the clerk finds that the account is not overdrawn and that the check is apparently complete and not forged, the bank will stamp the check paid and will put it in the depositor's file for return to him at the end of the month. Of course all such events may occur well before the provisional settlement under (1) (d) turns into a final settlement. Thus it will often be important to determine whether the "process of posting" has been completed. We would argue that the process has always been completed as soon as the bank's clerk examines the print-out and check and finds both to be in order, and takes some other mechanical step such as stamping the check paid or noting the payment on the account.

Section 4–109 defines the process of posting as follows:

> The "process of posting" means the usual procedure followed by a payor bank in determining to pay an item and in recording the payment including one or more of the following or other steps as determined by the bank:
>
> (a) verification of any signature;

---

32.  See, e. g., West Side Bank v. Marine Nat'l Exch. Bank, 37 Wis.2d 661, 155 N.W.2d 587, 4 UCC Rep.Serv. 1003 (1968) (clearing house rule extended deadline for returning items). Query whether a customer or another person not a party to a clearing house agreement will always be bound by such an agreement. Commonly deposit agreements provide that depositors are bound by such agreements and federal reserve rules. Such deposit agreements are probably enforceable between the bank and depositor, who are parties to the contract, but it is not clear that a depositor's agreement with his own bank amounts to an agreement with a distant bank to be bound by a clearing house rule that prevails there. We have found little discussion of this question in the cases, but we believe it to be a serious one that would merit counsel's attention in a final payment case.

(b) ascertaining that sufficient funds are available;

(c) affixing a "paid" or other stamp;

(d) entering a charge or entry to a customer's account;

(e) correcting or reversing an entry or erroneous action with respect to the item.

Note that the process of posting need not include all of (a) through (e) but only "one or more of the following . . . as determined by the bank." Thus if the bank never verifies any signature, it may have completed the process of posting despite the fact that it failed to verify the signature on the check in question. In each case a lawyer arguing that a bank has or has not made final payment must examine that bank's normal business behavior to determine whether the "steps as determined by the bank" had been taken.

The most troublesome provision of 4–109 is subsection (e) which arguably provides that posting and therefore final payment does not occur until all opportunity of the payor bank for "correcting or reversing an entry or erroneous action" terminates. Thus in the *West Side Bank* case,[33] discussed at length in Section 17–7 below, the bank went through all of its steps: it examined the account in the print-out, examined the check, stamped the check paid and put it in the file. Yet the drawer argued that the bank had not made final payment because it had not completed the process of posting. Drawer argued that posting had not been completed under 4–109(e) because the bank still had an opportunity to reverse errors until its midnight deadline (or such later time as it had under the rules under which it was operating). The Wisconsin Supreme Court was persuaded by that argument and held that the process of posting was not completed until the opportunity for reversing all errors had passed, i. e., until provisional settlement had become final.

The difficulty with the court's analysis is that it reads subsection (1) (c) out of 4–213, for under that analysis there will never be a case in which the process of posting could occur prior to the time when the provisional settlement becomes final under (1) (d). The commentators, including a commentator who was also the draftsman, unanimously agree that the Wisconsin Court erroneously interpreted 4–213 and 4–109.[34] Walter Malcolm, a draftsman of Article 4, states that 4–109(e) (for correcting or reversing an entry or erroneous actions) was put in to accommodate the case in which the bank's computer automatically debited an account for a check that

33. 37 Wis.2d 661, 155 N.W.2d 587, 4 UCC Rep.Serv. 1003 (1968).

34. See Malcolm, Reflections on West Side Bank: A Draftsman's View, 18 Catholic U.L.Rev. 23 (1968); Bailey, UCC Cases: Group No. 6, 14 Prac. Law., May 1968, at 89; Note, Final Payment and the Process of Posting Under the Uniform Commercial Code, 68 Colum.L.Rev. 349 (1968); Comment, Uniform Commercial Code—Article Four—Process of Posting Not Complete Until Midnight Deadline, 20 S.C. L.Rev. 118 (1968); Case Note, 17 Catholic U.L.Rev. 500 (1968).

the bank did not intend to pay (as for example because it was NSF).[35] In such case a bank official typically examines the print-out, decides not to pay the check and has the entry reversed on the next computer run.   The banks wish to avoid any argument in such cases that the original debiting would complete the process of posting and so render them liable as a party who had made final payment.   Mr. Malcolm indicates that the draftsmen did not have in mind the case in which the bank went through the entire process once (that is, debiting, plus inspecting the check and print-out) and then, for whatever reason, decided to change its mind and undo the process.   Thus in any case in which the bank has examined the print-out, looked at the check, marked it paid and put it in the file, we would argue that it had made final payment under 4–213(1) (c) and was so accountable for the item.   Our analysis leaves room for the operation of each of the subsections of 4–213 and for 4–109(e) as well, though it does conflict with the holding in *West Side Bank*.

One can pose a variety of other troublesome problems under 4–213(1) (c).   Assume, for example, that the check runs through the computer, the payor's employee examines the print-out, finds it to be in order, but that examination of the check itself remains.   In such a case one would normally say that the bank had not completed the process of posting, for that process would ordinarily include an examination of the check.   Assume, however, that this particular bank does not ever examine checks drawn for amounts less than $200 and that the check in question was for an amount less than $200. Here we would argue that the process of posting was completed on examination of the computer print-out and the stamping of the check. Surely the latest time in the process when posting ought to be regarded as having been made is the time when the bank has examined the print-out, decided it is in order, has examined the check and decided it is in order and has taken some other action with respect to the account or check to indicate that a decision to pay has been made. Placing the check in the depositor's file (assuming that is not part of the signature checking process) and stamping the check paid are clerical operations and we see no reason why one should have to do all of them to have posting.

In summary if one wishes to argue that a payor bank cannot kick back an NSF check or a check bearing a forged drawer's signature, he should examine (by discovery or otherwise) the acts which occurred in the bowels of bank with respect to that check.   In some cases it will be clear that final payment has been made; the bank may have paid cash over the counter or it may be trying to send the check back several days after it received it and therefore after its provisional settlement has become final.   The most complex cases are those under 4–213(1) (c) and in those cases the lawyer will have

---

35.   Malcolm, Reflections on West Side Bank: A Draftsman's View, 18 Catholic U.L.Rev. 23, 32 (1968).

to examine the bank's normal process and the process which the bank followed with respect to this check. The lawyer's job is further complicated by the fact that one eminent state court has rendered a thoroughly erroneous opinion on the meaning of 4–213(1) (c).

## § 16–5 Negligence

Two Code sections deal with negligence, 3–406 and 4–406. Section 3–406 is the basic negligence provision; it reads in full as follows:

> Any person who by his negligence substantially contributes to a material alteration of the instrument or to the making of an unauthorized signature is precluded from asserting the alteration or lack of authority against a holder in due course or against a drawee or other payor who pays the instrument in good faith and in accordance with the reasonable commercial standards of the drawee's or payor's business.

The section requires that the negligence "substantially" contribute to the alteration or forgery to estop a plaintiff who asserts the alteration or lack of authority. Note too the concluding clause which deprives a negligent drawee or other payor of an estoppel defense. Section 4–406 obliges a customer to check his statement of account and his returned checks and promptly to report any unauthorized signature or alteration to the bank. Upon his failure to do so, the customer may have to bear the losses occasioned by forgery of his signature or alterations. Here too 4–406(3) allows the customer to assert contributory negligence when the bank was itself negligent (as for example, by paying an obviously altered instrument). Section 3–405 is a kind of codified negligence liability. Under its terms a forgery by an impostor or by one authorized to sign for the maker or drawer or by one in the position of a payroll clerk is "effective" with the consequence that loss occasioned by such signatures is thrown on the drawer and not on his bank.

## § 16–6 Negligence, 3–406

The acts sufficient "substantially to contribute" to a material alteration or to the making of an unauthorized signature are limited only by the limits of man's capacity for conducting slovenly business transactions. We cannot hope to catalogue all those limits here, nor even to divide them into useful categories; we seek only to pass on notions from decided cases as guides to lawyer ruminations about whether the acts under consideration constitute negligence. One source of guidance is the nonexclusive list in Comment 7 to 3–406 of acts or omissions which according to the draftsmen constitute negligence. These acts include failure to look after one's signature stamp or automatic signing device, failure to take action to prevent further forgeries after one has found that others have occurred, and mailing of a check to the wrong person.

The cases involve similar but often distinctively elaborate factual webs. In Gresham State Bank v. O. & K. Construction Company,[36] a payee whose indorsement had been forged on a number of checks by its office manager was a two-man construction company. The court found that the company had been negligent in failing to audit its books (an audit would have disclosed defalcations of the office manager) and in failing to make anything more than a cursory comparison of its paid accounts receivable with its receipts. Park State Bank v. Arena Auto Auction, Inc.,[37] involved an Illinois drawer who owed money to Plunkett living in Alabama. The drawer drew a check to the order of Plunkett but the drawer's clerk mailed the check to a man of the same name living in Illinois. The drawer "compounded its vice" by sending a second check to the same incorrect address after discovering that the first one had not reached the proper destination. The court found that the drawer's negligence was sufficient to deprive him of the right to complain of a forged indorsement. In Thompson Maple Products, Inc. v. Citizens National Bank of Corry,[38] a clever non-log hauler simply forged documents indicating that he had delivered logs to the drawer. The drawer's bookkeeper then made checks payable to various parties for these fictitious deliveries and the deceitful non-log hauler forged the indorsements of these fictitious payees. The drawer's negligence consisted (1) of not following its own procedure which required that its employee receiving the logs retain one copy of the document which showed the delivery, and (2) of leaving blank sets of documents readily accessible, and (3) of sending the check back to the purported payees in the hands of the same truckers who had allegedly delivered the logs.

One can extract some ideas from these cases, but even the most theoretically minded would hardly call them principles. First, it may be negligence not to have audits of one's books. Second, it may be negligence not to follow general business practices of organizations of similar size and sophistication. One might suppose it is always a bad business practice in an organization with more than a few employees to have disbursements made by the same employee who also reconciles cancelled checks with the bank statement. Additionally, *Thompson Maple Products* indicates that a party who sets up procedural safe guards and then fails to follow them may be in more hot water than one who has no procedures at all. Of course, what is good for goose is not necessarily good for duck. When the judicial mill turns out more cases, it is likely that we will find that the two employee non-profit corporation that runs the local Red Cross and is governed by a busy volunteer board of directors can safely use more slovenly procedures without being negligent than can a more sizeable for-profit corporation.

36.  231 Ore. 106, 370 P.2d 726 (1962), clarified on denial of rehearing, 231 Ore. 106, 372 P.2d 187, 1 UCC Rep. Serv. 276 (1962).

37.  59 Ill.App.2d 235, 207 N.E.2d 158, 2 UCC Rep.Serv. 903 (1965).

38.  211 Pa.Super. 42, 234 A.2d 32, 4 UCC Rep.Serv. 624 (1967).

On discussing 4–406 below we will treat the contributory negligence of a payor which the drawer or customer may wish to use against a bank that relies on 3–406 or 4–406.

### § 16–7   Negligence, 4–406

Section 4–406 differs from 3–406 in that it deals with the customer's behavior after the fact, after the alteration or the forgery has already taken place. It is also a much narrower provision than 3–406 in that it deals only with the liability between the bank and its customer upon the customer's failure to examine and report "his" unauthorized signature or any alteration. Under this section the customer must:

(1) Examine the statement and items and

(2) promptly notify the bank after discovery of

(3) his unauthorized signature or any alteration.

Upon failure to inspect and report as required, the customer is "precluded" from asserting the unauthorized signature or alteration against the bank, and he is further precluded from asserting an unauthorized signature or alteration by the same wrongdoer on an item paid (1) after the first item and statement were available to the customer for a period of 14 calendar days but (2) before the bank received notification of any such unauthorized signature or alteration. Here as in 3–406 the bank's contributory negligence ("Lack of ordinary care") offsets the customer's own negligence. Although 4–406 is apparently rather straightforward, it poses several modest problems. Subsection (1) does not define the time within which the customer must examine his checks. Presumably under some circumstances he could take several months and still act with "reasonable care and promptness." However if the wrongdoer should repeat his deed and forge or alter a string of the customer's checks, the drawee may properly charge to the customer's account those which it paid 14 calendar days after the first item and statement were made available to the customer. Thus for practical purposes the customer should act within 14 days. The customer's time for examining his checks and statement starts when the bank (1) "sends" or (2) "holds the statement and item pursuant to request" or (3) "otherwise . . . makes the statement available." [39] Under the definition of the word "send" in 1–201(38) the bank sends the items and statement when it puts them in the mail bearing the proper address and postage. If these documents are sent but not delivered to the depositor, they are nevertheless "sent" and the time for the customer's inspection and report starts to run accordingly.

Courts are split on whether the sending of items and statements or "making them available" to a wrongdoing agent engaged in forgery of the customer's signature constitutes a sending or making available

---

39.   See § 4–406, Comment 2.

to the customer himself. In Jackson v. First National Bank of Memphis, Inc.,[40] a remarkable case in which a trusted church employee was cashing checks at the dog track, the Tennessee Court of Appeals in an alternate holding commented:

> In the instant case, the negligence of the depositor relied on by the bank is its failure to examine the checks and report the forgery, thus preventing a repetition thereof. The fallacy of this argument is that the checks were mailed to Cleve Jordan, Financial Secretary of the Church, who was the forger. He was an unfaithful servant, and obviously his knowledge and information on the subject would not be reported by him to the Church, nor imputed to it. He had been a faithful and trusted member of the Church and one of its officers for about twenty years, and, consequently, the Church cannot be held guilty of negligence in employing an unfaithful agent. The contention is made, however, that the Church officials, other than Cleve Jordan, himself, should have called on Jordan for an accounting from time to time, and that the Church was negligent in its failure to perform this duty. The proof shows that the Church did from time to time call on Cleve Jordan for production of the checks and records of the Church, but that he made excuses, said he forgot to bring them, or made other excuses. Under these circumstances, in view of his previous good record and reputation, we cannot say that the Bank carried the burden of showing negligence on the part of the Church.

On the other hand in a New York pre-Code case, the court found that "a 'depositor must be held chargeable with knowledge of all facts that a reasonable and prudent examination of the returned bank statements . . . would have disclosed had it been made by a person on the depositor's behalf who had not participated in the forgeries'." [41] The New York rule seems more sensible. Even under 3–406 it is arguably negligent for any but the smallest business enterprise to allow cancelled checks to return through the hands of the same person who mails checks out in payment. The bank does not control who receives the customer's mail and the law should encourage the customer to establish sound business practices with respect to outgoing checks and returning cancelled checks.[42]

**40.** 55 Tenn.App. 545, 551–52, 403 S.W. 2d 109, 112–13, 3 UCC Rep.Serv. 630, 632 (1966).

**41.** Screenland Magazine Inc. v. National City Bank, 181 Misc. 454, 458, 42 N.Y.S.2d 286, 289 (Sup.Ct.1943). See In re Parry Lines, Inc., 150 F. Supp. 693 (S.D.N.Y.1957); Clarke v. Camden Trust Co., 84 N.J.Super. 304, 201 A.2d 762 (Law Div.1964), aff'd, 89 N.J.Super. 459, 215 A.2d 381 (App.Div. 1965); Huber Glass Co. v. First Nat'l Bank, 29 Wis.2d 106, 138 N.W.2d 157 (1965); Schwabenton v. Security Nat'l Bank, 251 N.C. 655, 111 S.E.2d 856 (1960); Gerber v. Continental Ill. Nat'l Bank & Trust Co., 16 Ill.App.2d 379, 148 N.E.2d 597 (1958). Contra, Union Wholesale Co. v. Bank of Delaware, 190 A.2d 761 (Del.Super.Ct.1963), aff'd, 203 A.2d 109 (Del.1964). See generally Annot., 50 A.L.R.2d 1115, 1131 (1956).

**42.** To whom does the duty of care in 3–406 and 4–406 run? Section 4–406

## § 16–8    Impostors and Fictitious Payees

Like 3–406, section 3–405 is an exception to the general rule that forged indorsements are ineffective to pass title or to authorize a drawee to pay. When these exceptions apply, the forged

clearly contemplates that the drawee bank be permitted to complain that his drawer has been negligent in failing to examine his cancelled checks and his statement. Section 3–406 identifies three specific beneficiaries of the duty of care set out in that section. They are drawee bank, other payors, and holders in due course.

If the suit takes the form which it did in Gresham State Bank v. O. K. Constr. Co., 231 Ore. 106, 370 P.2d 726 (1962), rehearing denied, 231 Ore. 106, 372 P.2d 187, 1 UCC Rep.Serv. 276 (1962), in which the owner-payee sued the store at which the checks were cashed over a forged indorsement, it becomes necessary to determine whether such store or similarly situated collecting bank is also the beneficiary of the duty of care under 3–406. In the cited case, Justice O'Connell was applying pre-Code law, but in dictum he stated that 3–406 would apply. 231 Ore. at 118–19, 370 P.2d at 732. However, his opinion does not discuss the fact that the storekeeper was technically neither the "drawee" bank, nor another "payor," nor a "holder in due course." (He could not qualify as a holder in due course because he took over a forged indorsement and therefore was not a holder under 1–201(20).)

One can envision similar problems in suits in which drawers have been permitted to sue depositary banks upon the theory that such drawers were the beneficiaries of the depositary bank's warranties, or in some cases, on conversion theories. It is clear that the draftsmen intended such depositary banks and others upstream from the drawee to be the beneficiaries under the duty of care in 4–406 because subsection (5) requires the drawee to raise the issue with the drawer and prohibits the drawee from passing the loss upstream when it fails to do so. Subsection (5) reads in full as follows:

If under this section a payor bank has a valid defense against a claim of a customer upon or resulting from payment of an item and waives or fails upon request to assert the defense, the bank may not assert against any collecting bank or other prior party

presenting or transferring the item a claim based upon the unauthorized signature or alteration giving rise to the customer's claim.

It seems equally clear that Justice O'Connell is correct in that, had it occurred to the draftsmen, they would have intended that the depositary banks and others who cash checks over forged indorsements also be the beneficiaries of the 3–406 duty. There is no reason we see which would set them apart from others specifically mentioned in 3–406. Of course, such persons should carry the burden as well as the benefits of 3–406, and they should not be entitled to the estoppel set out there if they themselves are contributorily negligent.

It is quite unclear how a court is to arrive at what seems to be the only sensible solution, namely the application of 3–406 and 4–406 to collecting and depositary banks and to others who handle instruments after there have been forgeries on them. One solution is simply to bend the devil out of the "payor" language and so make it include storekeepers and collecting banks. Such a solution will doubtless give both *Webster* and the draftsmen gas pains (see §§ 3–102(3), 4–105(b)), but it will produce the proper outcome under 3–406. A more honest solution would be simply to apply 3–406 and 4–406 by analogy on the theory that the draftsmen would have intended them to apply but simply failed to consider this case.

It is possible, even likely, that the draftsmen overlooked the need for coverage in the cases cited. Like the Model A, sections 3–406 and 4–406 are well designed to cover the simple life in which drawers sued only drawees (who in turn sued back upstream) and owner-payees sued only drawees and not collecting banks or storekeepers. However as we have seen, the courts have been ingenious in devising ways to permit drawers to sue storekeepers and depositary banks and to permit payee-owners to sue the same persons. It is likely that the draftsmen did not anticipate such lawsuits except in the very narrow area covered by 3–419(3) when the depositary bank failed to use reasonable commercial standards and

indorsement is effective as though it were the indorsement of the owner. One may view 3–405 as a first cousin to 3–406 and 4–406, for it codifies the proposition that certain behavior is negligent and thus renders signatures resulting from that behavior effective against the negligent party. Let us consider two hypothetical cases that illustrate the operation of 3–405. First is the case of Leon Jones who calls on an elderly customer and represents himself as the noted and respectable local real estate dealer Zephyr Zigafuse. Leon, the thief, convinces the potential drawer that he is in fact Zephyr Zigafuse and that the drawer should issue a $5,000 check to him for investment in a specific piece of real estate. The drawer draws a check payable to the order of "Zephyr Zigafuse" and gives it to our friend Leon (who is posing as Zephyr). Leon cashes the check, absconds with the money and a dispute develops between the drawee bank and the drawer. The drawee cites section 3–405(1) (a) and maintains that the signature by Leon, the thief, is effective as Zephyr's signature in these circumstances. He argues that the signature "in the name of a named payee is effective" if an impostor induced the drawer to issue the instrument. Here the drawee will win; the signature is effective. To avoid this loss, all the drawer had to do was to confirm the fact that the person in front of him was Zigafuse. In effect 3–405 conclusively presumes that the drawer was negligent for not requiring identification.

Section 3–405(1) (c) deals with the more common problem of the padded payroll. Assume for example that a trusted employee who makes up the payroll every Friday afternoon, simply adds the name of a fictitious person to the payroll. The treasurer is a busy person and signs fifty or sixty checks (or they are signed automatically) and in due course the check to the fictitious payee comes into the hands of the trusted employee in charge of making up the payroll. That employee signs the name of the fictitious payee as an indorsement and the bank pays. When the facts are discovered, the drawer insists that the bank recredit its account and the bank refuses on the ground of 3–405(1) (c). Bank wins. Apparently the draftsmen believed that an employer should bear losses which result from his employment of a cheating payroll clerk and that employers should carefully choose and supervise persons in such sensitive positions. In addition to the impostor case and the padded payroll case, section 3–405 also covers the garden variety fictitious payee case in which the one signing as drawer or on behalf of the drawer intends the payee to have no interest in the instrument.

Section 3–405 unites several pre-Code doctrines which enjoyed separate pre-Code growth, and significantly changes some pre-Code doctrine. It reads in full:

> (1) An indorsement by any person in the name of a named payee is effective if

still had proceeds in its hands. Of course, the implication in 3–419(3) that there are some circumstances in which an owner-payee has a right to sue a depositary bank, indicates that the draftsmen had in mind at least one case in which they should have seen the potential utility of 3–406.

(a) an impostor by use of the mails or otherwise has induced the maker or drawer to issue the instrument to him or his confederate in the name of the payee; or

(b) a person signing as or on behalf of a maker or drawer intends the payee to have no interest in the instrument; or

(c) an agent or employee of the maker or drawer has supplied him with the name of the payee intending the latter to have no such interest.

(2) Nothing in this section shall affect the criminal or civil liability of the person so indorsing.

If the section applies, it renders a forged indorsement "effective." That is, title to the instrument passes as though there had been no forgery and a good faith transferee of one covered by 3–405 may be a holder in due course and insist upon payment from the parties liable on the instrument. In general 3–405 enlarges "effective" indorsements. Under the former law of some states impostors who had bamboozled drawers and makers by use of the mail but who did not have face to face contact with such drawers did not have power to transfer good title to the instrument. The theory of those cases was that the dominant intent of the drawer was to deal with the named person and not with the physical person who was the thief. Thus, so the argument went, the intent of the drawer was not to give good title to his correspondent (the thief) but only to the person whose name the thief used. In face to face transactions the presumed intent of the drawer was to pass the check to the physical person standing in front of him. Section 3–405 abandons such distinctions. In all such cases it imposes the loss on the party dealing with the impostor, not upon the bank. Likewise 3–405(1) (a) expands the category of those who can sign by allowing a "confederate" of an impostor to procure the check made payable to the order of the impostor.

Subsections (1) (b) and (1) (c) also expand some pre-Code doctrine by including as "fictitious payees" those who are real persons yet not persons whom the thief intended to have an interest in the check. That is, a party who wishes to steal from his employer can draw a check payable to the order of some imaginary person (the arch-type fictitious payee) or he can draw a check payable to the order of a real person but never give the check to that person. Both types of payees are "fictitious payees" under 3–405. In what may be the most important enlargement of the former law, 3–405(1) (c) includes payroll or accounts payable clerks within its scope.[43]

---

43. Comment 4 to 3–405 explains the motivation for including such persons:

The principle followed is that the loss should fall upon the employer as a risk of his business enterprise rather than upon the subsequent holder or drawee. The reasons are that the employer is normally in a better position to prevent such forgeries by reasonable care in the selection or super-

Section 3–405 offers only a small bag of interesting lawyer questions. Most of the action in the courts, and one suspects on the battlefield, has dealt with padded payrolls and padded accounts payable under 3–405(1)(c). Other less important questions about who is and who is not an "impostor" remain unanswered. The first and most difficult lawyer question under 3–405 concerns the scope of 3–405(1)(c). That subsection applies only to "agent[s] or employee[s]" of the employer who have *"supplied* him with the name of the payee *intending* the latter to have no such interest." (Emphasis added.) One should recognize that 3–405 carves an exception into the general rule that the forged signature of a corporate agent is not an effective indorsement. The courts will be left to define the now hazy line between a corporate agent covered in 3–405 (1)(c) as a supplier of the proper intent whose indorsement is "effective" and an agent not covered. Comment 4 to 3–405 identifies at least two kinds of persons who are clearly covered. First is the one who actually prepares the check.[44] The second is the one who "prepare[s] . . . [the] payroll." One can identify a variety of employees on the far side of the line clearly not covered by 3–405. Among those would be an employee whose only contact with the check writing process comes after the checks are prepared. A sorter, messenger or mail clerk would be such a person. As we move to employees less remote from the check writing process, the answers become less clear. Consider, for example, an employee who does not himself physically make up the checks and who does not prepare the names of employees or suppliers to be paid, but only clerks in the accounts payable department and on a grey day submits the name of a fictitious supplier to the accounts payable clerk who then adds that name to the list of checks to be drawn and causes them to be drawn by a third clerk. Is the person back in the accounts payable department covered by 3–405(1)(c)? Certainly one can argue that even a remote employee whose job occasionally calls for him to submit names of persons who are to receive payment is covered by the spirit

---

vision of its employees, or, if he is not, is at least in a better position to cover the loss by fidelity insurance; and that the cost of such insurance is properly an expense of his business rather than of the business of the holder or drawee.

See also, 2 N.Y. State Law Revision Comm'n, 1955 Report 1008 (1955).

The banking industry was sufficiently disturbed by the results under section 9(3) of the NIL that they lobbied for the adoption of the following amendment to that section:

The instrument is payable to bearer when it is payable to the order of a fictitious or non-existing or living person not intended to have any in-

terest in it and such fact was known to the person or other agent who supplies the name of such payee.

The amendment was intended to avoid cases holding that application of the fictitious payee doctrine in padded payroll situations turned upon whether the employee who procured the instrument had the authority to sign the check.

44. Comment 4 to section 3–405 says that paragraph 1(c):

extends the rule of the original Subsection 9(3) to include the padded payroll cases, where the drawer's agent or employee prepares the check for signature or otherwise furnishes the signing officer with name of the payee.

of 3–405(1) (c).  Substantial corporate authority has been delegated to him and he is one whom the corporation should supervise closely. Although the employees covered by 3–405(1) (c) seem not to have been in issue in most of the cases, several courts have found that 3–405(1) (c) covers corporate employees having authority to submit names and procure checks even though the work of those persons be several steps removed from the check writing process.  Thus in May Department Stores Co. v. Pittsburgh National Bank [45] an employee caused checks to be issued to fictitious suppliers, and the court found that the bank was properly freed from recrediting the corporate account because of 3–405.  Likewise in Delmar Bank of University City v. Fidelity & Deposit Co. of Maryland [46] an employee of an insurance company caused checks to be issued to the order of one Becker as a loan against his life insurance policy; these were ultimately paid over Becker's forged indorsement.  The court found that the employee was covered by 3–405(1) (c) and held the indorsements effective.  In *dictum*, federal courts have concluded that 3–405(1) covers a military clerk who added the name of a discharged person to the payroll [47] and a civilian clerk who submitted false travel vouchers.[48] Presumably, any employee no matter how remote from the check writing process who succeeds in adding a name to accounts payable or to the payroll apparently falls within 3–405(1) (c).

A recent New Jersey case, Snug Harbor Realty Co. v. First National Bank of Toms River, New Jersey,[49] dealt with facts that lie on the borderline of 3–405(1) (c).  There a corporate employee, Magee, had the job of initialing invoices to show that work or material represented by the invoices had been done or delivered.  After Magee initialed the invoices, others were to make checks payable to the person who had submitted them and Magee sometimes delivered these checks.  Magee forged the indorsements of a number of actual creditors of the Snug Harbor Realty Co. for a total amount of $27,516.  The lower court directed a verdict for the defendant-drawee because the indorsements were effective under 3–405(1) (c), but in

45.  374 F.2d 109, 4 UCC Rep.Serv. 39 (3d Cir. 1967).

46.  300 F.Supp. 496, 6 UCC Rep.Serv. 1060 (E.D.Mo.1969), rev'd on other grounds 428 F.2d 32 (8th Cir. 1970) (bank's indemnity agreement with surety circumvented limitations of section 3–405 by creating contractual liability).

47.  United States v. Bank of America Nat'l Trust & Sav. Ass'n, 288 F.Supp. 343, 5 UCC Rep.Serv. 991 (N.D.Cal. 1968), aff'd 438 F.2d 1213, 8 UCC Rep.Serv. 962 (9th Cir. 1971).

48.  United States v. Philadelphia Nat'l Bank, 304 F.Supp. 955, 6 UCC Rep. Serv. 1171 (E.D.Pa.1969).  Note, however, that irrespective of their views regarding the application of the rule codified in section 3–405(1) (c) to these situations involving the federal government, the district courts were ruled by the mandate of the Supreme Court in National Metropolitan Bank v. United States, 323 U.S. 454 (1945).  In that case the Court held that in cases involving federal commercial paper, it must apply federal law to protect federal interests.  Thus in both cases the federal government as plaintiff was permitted to recover from the defendant bank.

49.  105 N.J.Super. 572, 253 A.2d 581, 6 UCC Rep.Serv. 689 (App.Div. 1969), aff'd 54 N.J. 95, 253 A.2d 545 (1969).

a decision affirmed by the New Jersey Supreme Court, the Court of Appeals in New Jersey reversed and held that (1) (c) did not apply because "Magee an unfaithful employee of the construction company did not supply to his employer 'the name of the payee intending the latter to have no such interest'. To the contrary the payees are bona fide creditors of the company who had respectively submitted their invoices for work performed or materials furnished." [50]

It is unclear which of three possible grounds the court relied upon in holding 3–405 inapplicable. The court might be saying that 3–405(1) (c) never applies in a case in which the one whose name is submitted has a valid claim against the corporation. Second, it might be saying that Magee was not the kind of employee contemplated by 3–405(1) (c) inasmuch as he was only an "initialer" and not a "supplier". Finally the case might have been decided (though there is no suggestion in the opinion that it was so decided) on the ground that Magee did not have the requisite intent—that he did not intend to steal the check at the time he initialed the invoices but only later when acting as a messenger. If the court's decision rests upon the second proposition, namely, that Magee is not the type of employee contemplated by 3–405(1) (c), the decision is probably wrong and conflicts with earlier decisions discussed above. The intention of 3–405(1) (c) is to impose on drawers losses traceable to acts of employees uniquely in a position to steal from the corporation by causing checks to be issued on the corporation and not upon its bank. Certainly Magee had that power and was no farther removed from the check writing process than was the clerk in the *May Department Store* case or the insurance company employee in the *Delmar Bank* case. The employees properly covered by 3–405(1) (c) may be described as follows: (*1*) those who physically make up the checks, (*2*) those who prepare the list from which checks are made, and (*3*) any other employee with authority to cause a check to be issued by his principal.

There is another possible interpretation of the *Snug Harbor* decision; it may mean that no cases in which a check is drawn to one who has an actual claim against the principal fall within 3–405 (1) (c). Note first that it makes no difference in the application of (1) (c) that the payee is an actual existing person. Such was the case in the *Delmar Bank* case and that is also made plain by Example c in Comment 3 to 3–405 and Example b in Comment 4 to 3–405. The case and the two examples all involve existing persons. But if such an existing person has a legitimate claim against the principal, does that remove his case from 3–405(1) (c)? One might argue that 3–405 should not apply for there is no way that a supervisor or any other person could stop the issuance of the check since it is by hypothesis properly issued for a debt. Perhaps the situation involves nothing more than theft of a properly issued check after its issu-

---

50.  105 N.J.Super. at 574, 253 A.2d at 582, 6 UCC Rep.Serv. at 690.

ance?  On that analysis the loss should eventually fall on the party who took the check from the forger.[51]  On the other hand, if we focus on the kind of employee and his scope of authority, the case is essentially no different from one involving a nonexistent payee or one involving the insertion of an individual's name on a check by a payroll clerk who intends to appropriate it to his own use.  Neither Code nor comments indicate that the presence of an existing claim is relevant to the outcome.  Thus a court faced with this problem must decide whether to allocate the loss to the employer who misplaced his trust in an employee or to the bank who sold its checking account service to the customer partially on the basis of the protection it offers against employee thefts.  We find the policy considerations rather evenly balanced, but are inclined to limit the scope of any provision which frees banks from their traditional obligations to customers.[52]

Section 3–405(1) (a) seems to have caused little difficulty for courts.  In two recent cases a wife used her husband's name to procure loans.  In Franklin National Bank v. Shapiro,[53] the wife procured loans from the bank by mail on the purported signature of herself and her husband.  The depositary bank of the check issued as a disbursement of the loan proceeds successfully defended on the ground that the wife had posed as her husband in the mail transactions and that her signing of his name was effective.  In Philadelphia Title Insurance Co. v. Fidelity-Philadelphia Trust Co.,[54] a man and a woman procured a loan of $15,000.  The man who posed as the woman's husband was in fact not her husband and he did not appear before the agent of the Title Co., but only before a lawyer and real estate agent who were representing the wife.  The court applied the impostor rule even though there was no face-to-face appearance and precluded the Title Insurance Co. from asserting the forgery.

51.  Since under the original version of section 9(3) of the NIL, the crucial factor was the intent and knowledge of the person signing the checks, the courts were not called upon to resolve the issue of the effect of an existing claim by the payee.  Nevertheless one court said:

[W]hether the paper is to be considered as having a fictitious payee depends upon the knowledge or intention of the party against whom it is attempted to assert the rule, and not upon the actual existence or nonexistence of a payee of the same name as that inserted in the instrument: so that, on the one hand, *a real person may be fictitious, and, on the other, a nonexisting person may be real within this rule.*

Soekland v. Storch, 123 Ark. 253, 255, 185 S.W. 262 (1916) (emphasis added).  See also Norton v. City Bank

& Trust Co., 294 F. 839 (4th Cir. 1923).  In Hillman v. Kropp Forge Co., 340 Ill.App. 606, 92 N.E.2d 537 (1950), decided under the Fictitious Payee Amendment to section 9(3) of the NIL (see note 43 supra), the court held that a check naming as payee a person who had previously done business with the drawer was payable to a fictitious payee when drawer's employee fraudulently induced him to issue the check.

52.  But cf. Comment, Allocation of Losses from Check Forgeries Under the Law of Negotiable Instruments and the Uniform Commercial Code, 62 Yale L.J. 417, 444 (1953).

53.  7 UCC Rep.Serv. 317 (N.Y.Sup.Ct. 1970).

54.  419 Pa. 78, 212 A.2d 222, 2 UCC Rep.Serv. 1011 (1965).

The potential application of 3–405(1) (a) which troubled the commentators are discussed in the last paragraph of Comment 2 to 3–405:

> "Impostor" refers to impersonation and does not extend to a false representation that the party is the authorized agent of the payee. The maker or drawer who takes the precaution of making the instrument payable to the principal is entitled to have his indorsement.

Thus it appears that 3–405(1) (a) does not cover one who represents himself as an agent of General Motors and procures a check payable to the order of General Motors; hence, his signature on behalf of General Motors cannot be effective. However, if the party appears on behalf of a third party who is also an impostor and procures the check in the name of that third person, then (1) (a) applies. What then of the case of the one who appears as the agent of a fictitious corporation, say the "South Florida Oil Land Development Corporation," and procures a check payable to the order of this fictitious corporation? Is he covered or not covered by (1) (a)? Apparently there is no imposture for there is no such corporation, yet the drawer acts in an excessively gullible manner here, and the risk ought to be his, not that of the bank. Yet it seems that 3–405(1) (a) does not cover this case since it is like the General Motors situation in which the drawer can insist upon the "principal's indorsement." [55] What if the transferee from the impostor or from the stealing employee is himself negligent? Assume for example that our payroll clerk causes the check to be issued to a fictitious Zephyr Zigafuse and that he does so under circumstances to which 3–405(1) (c) applies. When he cashes the check at the depositary bank, the teller asks for no identification and pays the check in cash over the forged indorsement. Assume further that depositary bank's counsel stipulates that payment without request for identification from one not known to the teller is a clear violation of reasonable commercial standards normally practiced by the bank. If the bank were to argue under 3–406 that the drawer was precluded because of drawer's negligence, the drawer could respond that the bank was itself contributorily negligent and the drawer would win. Section 3–405 is at

---

55. See 2 N.Y. State Law Revision Comm'n, 1955 Report 1007 (1955), where the Commission analyzed this problem as follows:

It is stated in the official Comment that if an impostor poses not as the payee but as an agent or a representative of the payee, the drawer will be entitled to insist on a true signature by the named principal. (Comment 2, par. 2) This would probably not change existing New York law, as indicated above. It is not an impersonation case so much as an agency case. But it should be noted that if FF and G are confederates; and FF, by the use of the mails or otherwise, represents himself as an agent of C and thereby induces D to issue the instrument by mailing it to G, in the name of C, either FF or G could sign "C" as an effective indorsement. This would be true even if D had insisted on making the instrument to C's order rather than to FF's order as a "precaution" (see Comment above). The text (§ 3–405(1) (a)) here seems inconsistent with the Comment.

least a first cousin to 3–406 and 4–406 under which, if both parties are negligent, the bank bears the loss. Should not the same rule follow in 3–405?[56] We think even the negligent customer should be permitted to prove the payor-bank's negligence and, having so proven it, should be able to assert the forged indorsement. Although the logic of this argument may be unassailable, there is nothing either in the Code or in the pre-Code cases that authenticates it. Comment 4 to 3–405 flatly states that the loss should fall upon the employer of an unfaithful employee in a padded payroll case and includes no qualification for the negligence of the payor-bank.

In summary, 3–405 seems a banker's provision intended to narrow the liability of banks and broaden the responsibility of their customers. As a general matter it seems to have worked pretty much as it was intended to, but the precise scope, particularly of 3–405(1)(c), must await further cases on which employees are covered, what intent they must have, and whether 3–405(1)(c) encompasses payees with existing claims. In settling these questions, we believe the courts should be hesitant to expand 3–405 beyond its explicit limits, for 3–405 is an exception to the general obligation of a bank to pay only according to the order of its customer and it is in derogation of one of the main protections customers believe they are buying, namely protection from theft by one who forges the indorsement of the intended payee. Perhaps cases such as *Snug Harbor Realty Co.* which turn the bank's arguments aside with little discussion or analysis can be rationalized, if not justified, on the theory that 3–405 was a banker's provision written by and for them and that it should not be expanded.[57] The lawyer cannot possibly foresee all the forms that a party's negligence might take but he should at least bear in mind a few of the respects in which courts have found parties negligent so that he can test the behavior of his client against those cases. Finally we think it appropriate to regard the impostor and fictitious payee rules of 3–405 to be first cousins of the rules in 3–406 and 4–406,

---

**56.** See Chartered Bank v. American Trust Co., 47 Misc.2d 694, 697–98, 263 N.Y.S.2d 53, 57 (Sup.Ct.1965), decided under the Fictitious Payee Amendment to section 9(3) of the NIL (see note 43 supra), where the court said:

It seems clear that the 1960 amendment shifting the loss to the drawer-employer of a dishonest employee was intended to relieve from responsibility a bank which acted in error but not amounting to bad faith. The amendment could not have been intended to absolve completely from responsibility a bank chargeable in a commercial sense with bad faith and therefore not entitled to the protection it would otherwise receive under the law (cf. Soma v. Handrulis, 277 N.Y. 223, at p. 234, 14 N.E.2d 46, p. 50). Any other interpretation would confer immunity upon banks, while aiding and abetting by means of their gross negligence or willful ignorance dishonest employees to steal from their employers.

Note, however, the court also said that "bad faith is not mere carelessness or negligence." 47 Misc.2d at 697, 263 N.Y.S.2d at 56.

**57.** Representatives of the banking industry appearing before the New York Law Revision Commission uniformly expressed approval of 3–405. See 1 N.Y. State Law Revision Comm'n, 1954 Report 417 (1954) (comments by subcommittee of New York Clearing House Ass'n); 2 id. at 1457 (comments by New York Bar Ass'n).

and would allow a customer to prove a drawee's negligence and, having proved it, to assert the forged indorsement.

### § 16–9  Conclusion

In this chapter and in Chapter 15 we sometimes arbitrarily divided and separately treated different aspects of the same transaction. For example, the negligence of the drawer or payee in contributing to a forgery cannot really be divorced from the liabilities discussed in the immediately preceding Chapter 15 on forged indorsements. Thus this chapter is integrally related to Chapter 15 and to a lesser extent integrally related to the upcoming Chapter 17 on the depositor and his bank. In broad outline, the concepts in the present chapter are complicated but not difficult. On detailed examination, though, at least the problems associated with Price v. Neal and with final payment are devilishly difficult, sometimes impossible. One should at least understand from this chapter that a drawee that pays a check bearing a forged drawer's signature or an NSF check will sometimes have to absorb that loss itself and will often have no cause of action against the party who presented the check. One should also understand the potential conflict between 3–418 and 4–213 and should appreciate the necessity for close examination of actual bank practice in determining whether a drawee has made final payment under 4–213. One should understand, too, that a party's negligence in permitting his name to be forged or in failing to discover forgeries may deprive him of the right to complain about that forgery and may, in effect, make the forgery a valid signature.

# CHAPTER 17

# THE PAYOR BANK AND ITS CUSTOMER

*Analysis*

Sec.
17–1. Introduction.
17–2. The Deposit Contract and Permissible Variation of Code Provisions, 4–103.
17–3. When Bank May Charge Customer's Account, 4–401, 4–404, 4–405.
17–4. The Bank's Liability to Its Customer for Wrongful Dishonor, 4–402.
17–5. The Customer's Right to Stop Payment, 4–403.
17–6. Payor Bank's Liability for Its Failure to Follow a Legitimate Stop Order, 4–403(3); Its Right to Subrogation on Improper Payment, 4–407.
17–7. Priorities in the Customer's Bank Account, 4–303.

## § 17–1  Introduction

The foundation of the relationship between bank and customer is the bank's agreement to pay out the customer's money according to his order. Although one might think of the bank as the bailee of the depositor's money, that would be wrong. The bank has no obligation to keep one depositor's money segregated from another's; rather the law regards the bank's relation to its depositor as a debtor-creditor relation, with the customer as the creditor and the bank as the debtor.[1] That is, in the eyes of the law, the customer has "lent" the amount in his account to bank and bank is obliged to pay it out on order. Generally, the bank must obey the customer's order not only to pay but also not to pay funds on deposit. Most controversies between the customer and his bank arise either when the bank pays a check it ought not to have paid or when the bank fails to pay a check it ought to have paid. Of course "ought" and "ought not" are only legal conclusions which follow when one has answered the questions we discuss in the following pages. In this chapter we will examine in detail when an item is properly payable, what constitutes wrongful dishonor and the extent of liability for a wrongful dishonor. We will also explore uncertainties that revolve around customer stop payment orders and the like. In addition, we will survey the bank's defenses when it has paid an item that it should not have paid. Finally, we will consider the Code provision on priority of a check holder *vis-a-vis* persons who wish to prevent payment and seize the account in satisfaction of their own claim. Since we have already treated the legal effects of the customer's negligence in con-

---

1. The pre-Code cases which describe the customer-bank relationship as one of debtor-creditor are legion. See 5A A. Michie, Banks & Banking ch. 9, § 1 at 1–8 (1950). Cases decided under the Code take the same position. See, e. g., Stone & Webster Eng. Corp. v. First Nat'l Bank & Trust Co., 345 Mass. 1, 5, 184 N.E.2d 358, 360–61, 1 UCC Rep.Serv. 195, 199 (1962).

tributing to and failing to discover forgeries and alterations, here we only refer the reader to Sections 16–5 to 16–7.

Most of the relevant law is in Part 4 of Article Four of the Code (entitled "Relationship Between Payor Bank and Its Customer." It appears that bankers wrote Part 4 of Article Four for bankers. Protection of payor banks is the dominant theme of Part 4; relatively little in Part Four spells out rights of the customer on the bank's default. Two definitions control the scope of Part 4.[2] Subsection 4–104(1) (e) defines a "customer" as:

> . . . any person having an account with a bank or for whom a bank has agreed to collect items and includes a bank carrying an account with another bank . . .

"Customer" may include corporations, partnerships, associations and even other banks.[3] In any litigated dispute our "customer" will also be a "drawer" of a check, a "maker" of a note, or perhaps a "payee" or "indorsee" but these terms suggest liabilities [4] of only tangential concern in this chapter. Here we will call our man "customer" or alternatively "depositor" because those terms express the deposit relationship with the bank, and it is on this relationship that we will focus. In our discussion, "item" will be a key notion. Subsection 4–104(1) (g) defines an "item" as:

> . . . any instrument for the payment of money even though it is not negotiable but does not include money . . .

Personal checks are the most common "items", but the term also includes bank checks, cashier's (teller's) checks, notes and non-negotiable instruments payable at a bank.

## § 17–2     The Deposit Contract and Permissible Variation of Code Provisions, 4–103

We have copied a typical bank-customer deposit agreement in the footnote.[5] For accounts that raise additional legal problems (for

---

2. Section 1–201(4) contains the threshold definition. It says " 'Bank' means any person engaged in the business of banking." Presumably this functional definition encompasses savings and loan associations.

Section 4–105 characterizes banks as "depositary," "payor," "collecting," etc., according to their role in the collection process.

3. Section 1–201(30) provides that " 'Person' includes an individual or an organization . . . ."

See First Nat'l Bank v. Hobbs, 248 Ark. 76, 450 S.W.2d 298, 7 UCC Rep.Serv. 323 (1970) (plaintiff who was instrumental in opening account and who

signed signature card qualified as customer); Loucks v. Albuquerque Nat'l Bank, 76 N.M. 735, 418 P.2d 191, 3 UCC Rep.Serv. 709 (1966) (individual partners not customers and could not recover for personal injury when bank wrongfully dishonored partnership check).

4. We discuss the liability incurred by a maker or drawer under 3–413 in Sections 13–7 and 13–9 supra.

5. The signature card reads as follows (the small print has been enlarged for the reader's enlightenment):

It is mutually agreed by and between the BANK and the depositor as follows:

example, joint,[6] partnership [7] or corporate accounts)[8] the deposit contract will include additional terms.  Some of the clauses of the

All transactions under the account hereby opened shall be subject to the following:

(1) The Bank is hereby authorized to recognize the signature executed herewith in payment of funds.

(2) Credits for all items are subject to final payment in cash or solvent credits.

(3) The depositor waives protest for and notice of the dishonor and/or non-payment of any items deposited. The liability of the depositor, as endorser, shall not be released by the Bank procuring certification of any check deposited.

(4) This Bank shall have a lien on all items handled by it, and on the proceeds thereof, and upon any goods and securities for which such items are drawn, for any advances made by it or other indebtedness, and for any expenses incurred, including court costs and attorney's fees.

(5) Stop payment requests and renewals and revocations thereof must be in writing on a form satisfactory to and served on this Bank. This Bank shall not be liable for unintentional payment through oversight or accident only of a check on which payment has been stopped.

(6) The amounts entered on receipts or in the passbook are taken from the depositor's deposit ticket without verification.  This Bank reserves the right, after examination to correct any mistakes and change any entries which are in error.

(7) All items transmitted for collection to any Federal Reserve Bank shall be governed by the rules and regulations of such bank and of the Federal Reserve Board.

(8) Any item drawn on or payable at this Bank may be charged back to the depositor at or before the end of the second business day following the day of deposit in the event that the item is found not good or not payable for any reason.

(9) This account shall be subject to service charges in effect from time to time at the Bank.

(10) Statements of account together with paid and canceled checks shall be available to the depositor either by mail or delivery at regular monthly intervals, and all objections to any item thereof for any cause or reason whatsoever, whether then known or unknown, not made on or before 15 days after available date for delivery or mailing shall be absolutely barred and waived.

6.  A typical joint account agreement would include these terms:

When signed below, this account becomes a Joint Account payable to either during the lifetime of both or to the survivor.  The bank may make payments from this account upon the orders or receipts of both or either and the bank's records for any payment so made shall be a sufficient acquittance therefor.  Each of the undersigned appoints the other attorney with power to endorse (by rubber stamp or otherwise) for deposit to this account checks, drafts, notes, orders and receipts for the payment of all money belonging or payable to either or both of the undersigned.

7.  A partnership or association account would include the following:

The following represent that they are partners or members of _____ and hereby agree (1) the Bank is designated as its depository for monies, checks or other instruments which may come into the possession of the Partnership/Association. Endorsement may be by any person authorized to sign checks in writing or by stamp without designation of person so endorsing; and (2) until written revocation is received by the Bank, any _____ of the above persons are authorized on behalf of the Partnership/Association to: a) sign checks or other payment orders against the account, b) withdraw or release its property held by the Bank, c) accept instruments of payments at the Bank and d) endorse, negotiate and receive payment of proceeds of any instrument payable to or belonging to the Partnership/Association.

8.  A corporate account requires terms such as these:

This certifies that on _____, 19___, a meeting of the Directors of _____ adopted a resolution (1) designating the

deposit contract merely restate Code law.[9]   Other clauses modify
Code provisions only slightly to emphasize points of particular interest to the bank.[10]   Since a comparatively unfettered and perhaps
zealous bank lawyer usually drafts the deposit agreement, it may
overreach a bit and whether it includes impermissible departures
from Code provisions may be the only important lawyer question that
the deposit agreement poses.   We have concluded that clauses (5)
and (10) in the sample agreement set out in the footnote are objectionable, but we do not imply that different clauses in other deposit
agreements are not also objectionable; we merely use these two as
examples.   In our opinion clauses (5) and (10) of the deposit agreement deprive the customer of substantial rights he would otherwise
have under the Code.   Clause (5) reads in full as follows:

> Stop payment requests and renewals and revocations there-
> of must be in writing on a form satisfactory to and served
> on this Bank.   This Bank shall not be liable for unintentional
> payment through oversight or accident only of a check on
> which payment has been stopped.

First, the payor bank is seeking through Clause (5) to deprive the customer of the right to give oral stop orders, a right he would have
under Part Four of Article Four if the contract were silent.   Secondly, the payor bank is attempting to bind the depositor to a form
"satisfactory" to the bank.   Thirdly, the payor bank is trying to exculpate itself for failure to follow a stop order where that failure
is the result of its "oversight or accident".

Bank as a depository of its funds subject to the standard rules and regulations of the Bank; and (2) authorizing the Bank to accept for credit to the
account of the corporation and/or collection, any and all checks, drafts,
notes and other negotiable instruments
when endorsed in the name of the corporation in writing, by rubber stamp
or otherwise with or without designation of the party making the endorsement; and (3) authorizing the Bank
to pay out funds standing to the credit
of the corporation upon checks,
drafts, notes or other instruments
when signed in the name of the corporation and by _____ of the
above.   Provided further that the
Bank may honor and pay any such
instrument without inquiring as to the
circumstances of issue of the disposition of proceeds including those drawn
to the individual order of officers of
the corporation, any authorized signers
or otherwise.   This resolution shall
remain in full force and effect until
written notice to the contrary is received by the Bank.

9.   Clause (2) restates sections 4–213(2)
and (3).   Clause (7) restates section 4–
103(2).   Clause (8) restates section 4–
212(1).   The Code makes these contract clauses unnecessary unless the
contract drafter intends to alter the
effect of Code provisions.

10.   Clause (3) implements the waiver
of notice of dishonor authorized by 3–
511(2)(a) and thus reduces the bank's
duty under 3–508 and 3–509.   The second sentence of the clause alters the
rules of discharge on certification stated in the second sentence of 3–411(1)
in the instance where the bank, as
holder, procures certification.   Clause
(6) re-emphasizes the effect of 4–109(e)
on final payment under 4–213(1)(c).
Clause (4) states the bank's common
law lien on items handled, a principle
incorporated in large part by 4–208(1)
and extended there to include the entire bank collection process.   This particular contract lien goes beyond 4–208
(1) in attaching "goods and securities
for which such items are drawn."

Clause (10) reads in full as follows:

Statements of account together with paid and canceled checks shall be available to the depositor either by mail or delivery at regular monthly intervals, and all objections to any item thereof for any cause or reason whatsoever, whether then known or unknown, not made on or before 15 days after available date for delivery or mailing shall be absolutely barred and waived.

Through this clause the payor bank is attempting to impose a 15 day statute of limitations in circumstances in which the customer might have as long as three years to make his complaint under 4–406, a section under which he is required only to exercise "reasonable care and promptness." Thus, like Clause (5), Clause (10) also would deprive the customer of substantial rights he would otherwise have under Part Four of Article Four.

Can the payor bank enforce such clauses against the customer? Several Code sections grant considerable leeway for the parties to work out their own bargain.[11] Section 4–103(1)[12] provides:

The effect of the provisions of this Article may be varied by agreement except that no agreement can disclaim a bank's responsibility for its own lack of good faith or failure to exercise ordinary care or can limit the measure of damages for such lack or failure; but the parties may by agreement determine the standards by which such responsibility is to be measured if such standards are not manifestly unreasonable.

Is 4–103 the only restriction on the power of the parties to vary the Code by agreement? For example, could a court hold an agreement at variance with the Code invalid because it was contrary to a public policy? Unconscionable under 2–302? We conclude that other general principles besides those embodied in 4–103 limit the bank's power to alter Part Four's provisions. For example, 4–103 would not itself prohibit a customer and a bank from agreeing that the customer had no right whatsoever to stop payment. Yet we read Comment 2 to 4–403 as a statement of public policy that the customer should have such right: "The position taken by this section is that

---

11. Section 1–102(3) provides a general rule for all Articles of the Code. It reads as follows:

The effect of provisions of this Act may be varied by agreement, except as otherwise provided in this Act and except that the obligations of good faith, diligence, reasonableness and care prescribed by this Act may not be disclaimed by agreement but the parties may by agreement determine the standards by which the performance of such obligations is to be measured if

such standards are not manifestly unreasonable.

12. Note that the customer might find himself bound by agreements to which he is not a party. Section 4–103(2) provides:

Federal Reserve regulations and operating letters, clearing house rules, and the like, have the effect of agreements under subsection (1), whether or not specifically assented to by all parties interested in items handled.

stopping payment is a service which depositors expect and are entitled to receive from banks notwithstanding its difficulty, inconvenience and expense. The inevitable occasional losses through failure to stop should be borne by the banks as a cost of the business of banking." We believe that 1–103 incorporates the standard principle that [13] parties may not depart from legislative statements of public policy, and that the foregoing Comment is not only a statement of such a public policy but an indication that the Code draftsmen did not intend that banks should have the right to eliminate the practice of stopping payment.

Whether the customer can invoke section 2–302 on unconscionability is more doubtful. That section is part of Article Two on sales of goods. Admittedly, courts have frequently applied 2–302 to security transactions but most of those cases also involved sales of goods.[14] It may overstretch the section to apply it to a bank-customer relationship.[15] We conclude that 2–302 can be applied to Article Four transactions only by analogy.

Returning to the two clauses in our deposit agreement, how should a court come out? The first clause (Clause (5)) would deprive the customer of his right to give oral stop orders, would limit the depositor to a written stop order form "satisfactory" to the bank, and would free the bank from liability for payments made "through oversight or accident." One may attack the bank's attempt to free itself of liability for oversight or accident as an effort to evade its responsibility under 4–103 for "failure to exercise ordinary care."[16] Although "accident or oversight" are not identical to negligence, they so closely overlap that we cannot think of a realistic hypothetical case in which the bank would be guilty of oversight or accident but not negligence. We conclude that Clause (5) is invalid under 4–103 (or alternatively, that it would, to be valid, have to be construed so

---

13. Our colleagues who labor in the vineyard previously tended by Professor Williston and Professor Corbin assure us that the text accurately states the law. Nevertheless our search revealed no cases which explicitly dealt with the issue as we find it here. One colleague, wise in the way of peppercorns and broken mill shafts, explained that the proposition is so basic to the law of contracts that only a fool or a knave would litigate the issue. Despite our distrust of disingenuous explanations, we remain convinced that courts should refuse to recognize deposit agreements which deny the right to give oral stop orders. In reaching this conclusion we do not overlook the admonition of sections 1–102(3) and 4–103(1) ("The effect of the provisions of this Article may be varied by agreement. . . ."). We believe the draftsmen did not intend that the parties should avoid specific expressions of policy by utilizing these general rules.

14. See Ch. 4 supra.

15. In David v. Manufacturers Hanover Trust Co., 59 Misc.2d 248, 298 N.Y.S.2d 847, 6 UCC Rep.Serv. 504 (App. Term 1969), rev'g, 4 UCC Rep.Serv. 1145 (N. Y.Civ.Ct.1968), the court refused to apply the doctrine of unconscionability which the lower court had relied upon to strike down a clause in the signature card that waived the right to a jury trial.

16. See 3 UCC Rep.Serv. 115 (Utah Att. Gen. Opinion 1966) (clause which exculpates bank for payment through "inadvertence or accident only" is invalid). Section 4–103(3) provides guidelines for determining what is "ordinary care."

narrowly as to be of no practical effect). On whether Clause (5) can validly change the rule of 4–403(2) ("[a]n oral order is binding upon the bank. . . .") we have slightly more difficulty, but because of the public policy to give customers stop-payment rights,[17] we conclude that the bank cannot validly change that rule of public policy by agreement with its customer.[18] Clause (5) also requires that the customer use a form satisfactory to the bank, and is the least objectionable of all. The bank needs to know check number, payee, date, etc., to be able to stop payment and the use of a standard form can help assure that the bank will always have this information. At least if the form itself does not disclaim liability for negligence or otherwise limit the customer's right to recover for failure to follow the stop order, we would find that the bank can require its own form in those cases in which the customer issues a written stop order.

Clause (10) imposes a fifteen-day statute of limitations on certain customer claims. That is, the customer must inspect his cancelled checks and make any complaints about them (e. g., that there are forgeries) within fifteen days or lose all his rights. We believe that Clause (10) runs afoul of 4–103, for although it is not in form a "disclaimer," in substance it disclaims the bank's ". . . responsibility for its own lack of good faith or failure to exercise ordinary care. . . ." As a practical matter a short statute of limitations can serve as effectively to enable the bank to escape liability as can an outright disclaimer. Accordingly, we would strike down

---

17. In remarks before the New York Law Revision Commission Mr. Malcolm, an Article Four Draftsman, said:

"However, that particular issue [requiring written stop orders] was battled in many forums and on many occasions, in the smaller groups and in the larger groups of the sponsoring organizations, and in September 1951 when the final form of Article 4 was approved, the specific issue was considered by the joint houses of the Institute and the Commissioners and the vote was not to shift to the California rule [requiring written stop orders], and there is the voice of authority so far as I am concerned. That was the policy decision that was made.

1 N.Y. State Law Revision Comm'n, 1954 Report 467 (1954).

The draftsmen responded to criticism of the 1952 Official Draft of section 4–403(2) as follows:

The provision that an oral stop order is binding upon the bank only "until a customer has had reasonable opportunity to send the bank a written confirmation if the bank requests such a confirmation" has been criticized on several grounds, particularly that this language either requires banks to print on signature cards or similar forms standard requests for confirmations of all stop payment orders, or there is likely to be a disputed issue of fact as to whether a written confirmation was requested. The change prescribes a flat fourteen day period in which the customer must confirm in writing an oral stop payment order. *This preserves the right of the customer to give an oral stop payment order but gives some protection to the bank against the uncertainties of oral orders by terminating the binding effect of an oral order unless it is confirmed in writing within fourteen days.*

Uniform Commercial Code, 1952 Official Draft of Text and Comments 36–37 (Supp. No. 1, 1955) (emphasis added).

18. Cf. David v. Manufacturers Hanover Trust Co., 59 Misc.2d 248, 298 N.Y.S.2d 847, 6 UCC Rep.Serv. 504 (App. Term 1969) (clause in signature card waiving jury trial constitutes valid agreement).

a 15 day limitation.   Of course, the bank may argue that Clause (10) only sets a standard by which its responsibility is to be measured and that 4–103 therefore validates the clause.   Our response would be that Clause (10) is "manifestly unreasonable" and that 4–103(1) therefore cannot validate it.

We admit that we have arrived at the foregoing judgments of invalidity in part because the deposit contract is almost always a form drafted by the bank, the clerk who offers the contract to the customer typically has no authority to change it, and the customer usually signs it without negotiation and, indeed, without understanding it.   Furthermore, the bankers who drafted Article Four left precious little to the customer anyway.   Of course, if a sizeable depositor should negotiate Clauses (5) and (10) of a deposit agreement, perhaps the result should differ.

### § 17–3   When Bank May Charge Customer's Account, 4–401, 4–404, 4–405

Section 4–401(1) somewhat obscurely embodies the two most important rules in Part Four of Article Four.   First, the section states that a bank may charge the customer's account for items "properly payable".   Equally important, the section implies that the bank may not charge the customer's account on items not "properly payable".   Section 4–401(1) reads in full:

> As against its customer, a bank may charge against his account any item which is otherwise properly payable from that account even though the charge creates an overdraft.

Whether an item is properly payable is the crunch question in a variety of conflicts between customer and bank.   Translated into practical terms, if a court finds that an item is properly payable, the bank will be entitled to charge the depositor's account; conversely if a court finds that an item is not properly payable, the bank may not charge the customer's account, and if it has done so, it must recredit the account.   Here we will consider the most common "properly payable" issues:

(1)   Are checks bearing alterations, forged indorsements or forged drawer's signatures properly payable?

(2)   Are bearer checks that have been stolen properly payable?

(3)   Are checks dated later than the time of payment properly payable before the stated date?

(4)   Are checks that will create an overdraft properly payable?

(5)   Are stale checks (generally checks presented 6 months or more after date of issue) properly payable?

At the outset, note that 4–104(1) (i) does not satisfactorily define "properly payable." [19]   The draftsman must have assumed that the common law would continue to govern, or that there is need only for rules to cover those things that have been troublesome to banks, as opposed to depositors.   For enlightenment on the meaning of "properly payable," we will turn to the pre-Code law that continues to govern, and to analogous Code provisions, particularly those in Article Three.

### Checks Lacking Necessary Signatures and Altered Checks

An initial question, and an easy one, is whether checks not bearing the customer's signature are "properly payable."   A check may not bear any signature or may bear an unauthorized or forged signature.   Absent customer's ratification or negligence,[20] pre-Code [21] and post-Code [22] cases hold that such checks are not "properly payable" and that the bank must recredit customer's account when it pays such checks.   Section 3–401(1) analogically supports this result, for it states that no person is liable on an instrument unless his signature appears thereon.[23]

Is a check bearing a forged indorsement "properly payable"? The pre-Code case law says no.[24]   That result is consistent with common sense and with Article Three.[25]   In the case of an order [26] instrument, forgery precludes negotiation, so that no subsequent transferee can be a holder under Article Three; [27] accordingly, no payment can be proper since only a holder can make proper presentment and receive payment.[28]

---

19.   Section 4–104(1) (i) provides:

"Properly payable" includes the availability of funds for payment at the time of decision to pay or dishonor  .  .  .  .

20.   See §§ 4–406; 3–406; 3–404, discussed in Sections 16–6 and 16–7 infra.

21.   See, e. g., Morgan v. First Nat'l Bank, 58 N.M. 730, 276 P.2d 504 (1954).

22.   See Wiley v. Manufacturers Hanover Trust Co., 6 UCC Rep.Serv. 1083 (N.Y.Sup.Ct.1969) (customer not entitled to summary judgment on basis of report of handwriting expert in face of bank's claim that signature was authorized).

23.   For a discussion of 3–401(1), see Section 13–2 supra.

24.   See, e. g., Russell v. Second Nat'l Bank, 136 N.J.L. 270, 55 A.2d 211 (Ct. Err. & App.1947); Wormhoudt Lumber Co. v. Union Bank & Trust Co., 231 Iowa 928, 2 N.W.2d 267 (1942).

25.   See Stone & Webster Eng'r Corp. v. First Nat'l Bank & Trust Co., 345 Mass. 1, 184 N.E.2d 358, 1 UCC Rep. Serv. 195 (1962).   For a discussion of the case, see section 15–4 supra.

26.   Since anyone (even a thief or his transferee) in possession of bearer paper qualifies as a holder, his presentment is valid, and payment discharges the drawer's obligation on the check and the underlying obligation. (§§ 1–201(20); 3–603; 3–802(1) (b).)

As a result the loss is thrown back upon the person who lost the check. He can most likely prevent its recurrence.   See White, Some Petty Complaints About Article Three, 65 Mich. L.Rev. 1315 (1967).

27.   See § 3–202.   Note that indorsement is not necessary to negotiate bearer paper.

28.   See § 3–504(1).

In a back-handed way 4–401(2) tells us that altered items are properly payable only to the extent of "their original tenor" but not beyond. Subsection (2) (a) implies as much in stating that the bank may charge the account of its customer according to "the original tenor of his altered item." [29] Thus if the payor pays out $1,000 on what was originally a $100 check, $100 is properly payable and the remaining $900 is not properly payable. The payor must re-credit the $900 to the customer's account. Of course even the $100 payment might not be properly payable for other reasons (for example, the check might bear a forged indorsement). Note too that the check is payable to the full $1,000 if the depositor's negligence substantially contributes to the alteration (see 3–406 and 4–406).

## Post-Dated Checks

Subsection 3–114(2) continues the pre-Code [30] rule that post-dated checks are not properly payable until the date stated on the

---

**29.** Section 4–401(2) protects the payor bank as 3–407(3) does a holder in due course against alteration or unauthorized completion of an item. It reads in full as follows:

A bank which in good faith makes payment to a holder may charge the indicated account of its customer according to

(a) the original tenor of his altered item: or

(b) the tenor of his completed item, even though the bank knows the item has been completed unless the bank has notice that the completion was improper.

The significance of the provision is apparent once one recalls that on such items the customer would otherwise be discharged (§§ 3–407(2); 3–115(2)). Section 4–401(2) is consistent in policy with 3–511 and 3–407 and is a necessary corollary to 3–407. See Ch. 15, note 48, supra. In Newman v. Manufacturers Nat'l Bank, 7 Mich.App. 580, 152 N.W.2d 564, 4 UCC Rep.Serv. 630 (1967), drawer issued two undated checks in 1955 for a debt he later paid by other means. Payee assured him the checks had been destroyed. Eleven years later his bank paid the checks on presentment even though the printed symbols "——— 195—" for the date had been written over with "March 1, 1966." The checks were held properly payable. The court found no issue as to the bank's bad faith or whether it had notice of an improper

completion. One wonders if the customer knew in 1955 how to stop payment on checks.

Section 4–401(2) affects not only the customer's liability but the liability of holders and collecting banks as well. In Franklin Nat'l Bank v. Westbury Trust Co., 65 Misc.2d 604, 318 N.Y.S.2d 656, 8 UCC Rep.Serv. 1299 (Dist.Ct. 1971), collecting bank received an item altered to read $313, presented it to payor bank, and was paid. After the payor bank's customer notified it of the alteration, the payor bank successfully sued the collecting bank on its 4–207(1) (c) warranty. But since the customer was liable to payor bank for the original tenor of the item ($13), the collecting bank was only liable for the $300 difference caused by the alteration.

**30.** See, e. g., Smith v. Maddox-Rucker Banking Co., 8 Ga.App. 288, 68 S.E. 1092 (1910); Montano v. Springfield Gardens Nat'l Bank, 207 Misc. 840, 140 N.Y.S.2d 63 (App.Term 1955) (premature payment and stop order before stated date); Wilson v. McEachern, 9 Ga.App. 584, 71 S.E. 946 (1911) (bank's refusal to pay check before stated date not a dishonor) (dictum). See generally Annot., 76 A.L.R.2d 1301 (1961). The analyst for the New York Law Revision Commission viewed section 3–114(2) as a new statutory formulation which followed existing case law. 2 N.Y. State Law Revision Comm'n, 1955 Report 824 (1955).

check.[31]   However, the practical significance of this rule is limited for the law generally permits the bank to refuse to recredit its customer's account by subrogating itself to the rights of the presenter of the post-dated check (4–407).   We offer three hypotheticals to illustrate the operation of 3–114(2) and its limitations.

Assume that on August 1 a customer who has $100 in his account writes a $95 check post-dated to August 25, and his bank jumps the gun and pays the check on August 15.   In the meantime, customer assumes that the post-dated check will not be cashed by his bank until August 25 and writes a further $75 check that is presented to his bank and dishonored for nonsufficient funds on August 20. The bank's improper payment of the post-dated check led it to dishonor the August 20 check wrongfully.   In one pre-Code case the bank was held liable for the wrongful dishonor.[32]   Nothing in the Code changes that outcome.

To alter the problem, assume that our customer post-dates the check, that the payor pays it before the stated date, and that the drawer-customer does not find out about this until after the stated date.   If the customer would not have stopped payment prior to the stated date, he should have no complaint about the bank's payment— or so it seems to us.[33]   Assume, however, that customer issues a check dated November 20, payor pays the check November 10, and on the 15th customer issues a stop order.   If the bank had not paid until the 20th, it would have received the stop order in time; accordingly there is a causal connection between the customer's predicament and the bank's premature payment.   Even in this type of case, however, the customer will often not have an effective complaint against the bank.   In the first place the bank will claim under 4–407 that it is subrogated to the rights of the party it paid.   If this party was a holder in due course (as for example a depositary bank) the payor as subrogee under 4–407 [34] to the presenter's rights will have a valid defense to its customer's complaint.   At least one court has gone even further and (in our judgment incorrectly) stated that the payor bank was itself a holder in due course of post-dated checks.[35] One might doubt whether a bank or any other party taking a post-dated check can ever be a holder in due course, but the Code and

---

31.   Section 3–114(2) reads as follows:

Where an instrument is antedated or postdated the time when it is payable is determined by the stated date if the instrument is payable on demand or at a fixed period after date.

Nevertheless, the fact that a check is postdated does not impair its negotiability.   § 3–114(1).

32.   See Smith v. Maddox-Rucker Banking Co., 8 Ga.App. 288, 68 S.E. 1092 (1910).

33.   Cf. Roland v. Republic Nat'l Bank, 463 S.W.2d 747, 8 UCC Rep.Serv. 1076 (Tex.Civ.App.1971) (bank had right to reimburse itself when customer failed to make complaint or give stop order before stated date).

34.   For a discussion of 4–407, see Section 17–6 infra.

35.   See Roland v. Republic Nat'l Bank, 463 S.W.2d 747, 8 UCC Rep.Serv. 1076 (Tex.Civ.App.1971) (bank which cashed postdated checks before stated date became holder in due course and in

cases say such a party can be.[36]  The check is said to be tantamount to a note from drawer to payee and, of course, one can be a holder in due course of a note before its stated date.

To summarize, it seems to us that the customer should have no complaint against his bank for its premature payment of a post-dated check unless the customer himself takes steps to stop payment before the stated date and the premature payment causes loss to the customer. Even in such cases the payor bank will be subrogated to the rights of the presenter and if the presenter proves to be a holder in due course, or a holder who could have recovered payment from the drawer in any event, the payor bank may assert those same rights and prevail against its customer.  Thus while post-dated checks may be technically not properly payable, as a practical matter the payor bank will often prevail.

## Overdrafts

Subsection 4–401(1) provides that overdrafts are properly payable on the theory that "the draft authorizes  .  .  .  payment .  .  .  and carries an implied promise [by the drawer] to reimburse the drawee." [37]  A customer who draws an overdraft lacks even a colorable argument that the bank was not authorized to honor the draft or that it exercised improper judgment in doing so.[38]  Indeed some customers may expect the bank to cover certain overdrafts and may be indignant if the bank refuses.  The bank's option to pay or not pay overdrafts is a business decision that turns on factors such as the size of the overdraft, the bank's view of its customer and so forth.  The only limit on the bank's authority to honor an overdraft is that it must be otherwise properly payable.[39]

## Stale Checks

A payor bank has the option to pay or not to pay a stale check. Section 4–404 states in full:

> A bank is under no obligation to a customer having a checking account to pay a check, other than a certified check, which is presented more than six months after its date, but it may charge its customer's account for a payment made thereafter in good faith.

the absence of stop order or complaint was entitled to charge customer's account on stated date).

**36.**  § 3–304(4) (a).  See Briand v. Wild, 110 N.H. 373, 268 A.2d 896, 8 UCC Rep. Serv. 199 (1970); Northern Currency Exch., Inc. v. Strichman, 9 UCC Rep. Serv. 705 (N.Y.Sup.Ct.1971); National Currency Exch., Inc. v. Perkins, 52 Ill.App.2d 215, 201 N.E.2d 668, 2 UCC Rep.Serv. 526 (1964) (pre-Code case).

**37.**  § 4–401, Comment 1.

**38.**  See City Bank v. Tenn, 52 Hawaii 51, 469 P.2d 816, 7 UCC Rep.Serv. 1150 (1970) (bank impliedly authorized to pay overdraft).

**39.**  It is immaterial whether the overdraft occurs on payment or appears after payment by failure of a provisional credit on the customer's account.  See First Nat'l City Bank v. Schneider, 6 UCC Rep.Serv. 930 (N.Y. Sup.Ct.1969) (bank may recover from customer amount of overdraft which results from return of item previously credited to customer's account).

The rule reflects general distrust of checks [40] too long outstanding, yet recognizes that many such checks ought to be honored in the ordinary course of business even though payees do not present them within six months. The bank is free of liability to its customer if it dishonors a stale check or pays it without consulting the drawer, so long as it acts in good faith. A drawer who wants his bank to dishonor a stale check must issue a stop order.

The bank has a right to charge its customer's account on payment of a stale check only if it pays "in good faith." Good faith ranks among the most slippery concepts in the Code.[41] Does it mean that the bank must examine each check to determine if it is stale? For example, does a bank violate 4–404 if it pays a stale check in the normal computer run under circumstances in which no bank employee knew it to be stale? We think not because the bank lacks the requisite dishonesty (1–201(19)). Nevertheless payment under such circumstances arguably constitutes a breach of the bank's obligation to exercise due care.[42]

But what if the bank discovers the check is stale and yet pays? One sentence in the Comments suggests that some such payments may still be in good faith:[43] "[B]ut [bank] is given the option to pay because it may be in a position to know, as in the case of dividend checks, that the drawer wants payment made." This cryptic comment does not explain why a payor bank will be in a position to know that a drawer of dividend checks, more than a drawer of any other check, will wish payment made. Presumably at the time any drawer draws a check, he wishes it to be paid. Perhaps stale dividend checks differ from mine-run checks in that they are commonly presented more than six months after the date of issuance. That is, one might keep a $20 dividend check in his dresser drawer for several months without cashing it whereas he can rarely afford to squirrel away his payroll check in that fashion. If that is not the factor that sets dividend checks apart from others and permits the bank to infer that the drawer still wants payment made six months after issuance, then the comment is completely mysterious to us. Except with respect to types of checks that are routinely presented more than six months after issuance, we conclude that a

40. Note that 4–404 applies only to checks.

41. See Summers, "Good Faith" in General Contract Law and the Sales Provisions of the Uniform Commercial Code, 54 Va.L.Rev. 195 (1968).

42. See Goldberg v. Manufacturer's Trust Co., 199 Misc. 167, 102 N.Y.S.2d 144 (Mun.Ct.1951) (bank liable for payment of 27-month-old check when it failed to consult drawer); cf. W. P. Harlin Constr. Co. v. Continental Bank & Trust Co., 23 Utah 2d 422, 464 P.2d 585 (1970) (bank failed to exercise ordinary care when it paid five month old check for $9,200 which was drawn on unauthorized signature).

43. The Comment to section 4–404 reads in part as follows:

[The bank] is therefore not required to do so, but is given the option to pay because it may be in a position to know, as in the case of dividend checks, that the drawer wants payment made.

bank may not assume that the drawer "wants payment made" and that a bank which knowingly pays such checks will not be in good faith.

One may argue that a stop order which expires at the end of six months still leaves the bank on notice, and that any payment of that check cannot be in good faith. This interpretation is not consistent with the section on stop orders which limits their effective duration to six months.[44] If any payment after six months is in bad faith, then for all intents and purposes the written stop order is good in perpetuity and not for just six months. We reject any interpretation that reads the six month limitation out of 4–403.[45]

Unfettered by case law, we interpret the good faith limitation in 4–404 as follows: We think payments in accordance with the bank's normal custom and in ignorance of the staleness of the check are in good faith. We think 4–404 does not require a bank employee to examine the date of each check, and of course the computer cannot read the date on the check for that number is not printed in magnetic type. If an employee does discover that a check is stale (perhaps because the computer kicks the check out as NSF or as a large item), we think that except in rare cases the bank acts in bad faith if it thereafter pays without first contacting its depositor. The rare cases would be those involving dividend checks and other cases in which payees commonly hold checks for more than six months before cashing them. We cut our conclusions largely out of whole cloth, but they do find support in the Comment to 4–404 on dividend checks and in the banking practice known to us.

There is a special rule for certified checks. The bank must pay these even though they are presented more than six months after issuance. Certified checks represent the bank's obligation, and banks typically charge the customer's account when the check is certified.[46]

### Checks Presented After Customer's Death or Adjudication of His Incompetence—4–404, 4–405

Under 4–405(1) a bank's authority to handle items on its customer's account terminates when the bank learns that he has died or been adjudged incompetent. Section 4–405(1) reads in full as follows:

> A payor or collecting bank's authority to accept, pay or collect an item or to account for proceeds of its collection if otherwise effective is not rendered ineffective by incompetence of a customer of either bank existing at the time the item is issued or its collection is undertaken if the bank does not know of an adjudication of incompetence. Neither death

---

44. For a discussion of 4–403, see Section 17–5 infra.

45. See 2 N.Y. State Law Revision Comm'n, 1954 Report 1427–28 (1954).

46. For a discussion of the bank's obligation under 3–413, see Section 13–8 supra.

nor incompetence of a customer revokes such authority to accept, pay, collect or account until the bank knows of the fact of death or of an adjudication of incompetence and has reasonable opportunity to act on it.

Note that the subsection applies to the relationship between the customer-holder and the collecting bank as well as that of the customer-drawer and payor. Two interesting questions arise. When does the bank have knowledge and what constitutes a reasonable opportunity for the bank to act on that knowledge? With respect to the first question, subsection 1–201(27) states:

> Notice, knowledge or a notice or notification received by an organization is effective for a particular transaction from the time when it is brought to the attention of the individual conducting that transaction, and in any event from the time when it would have been brought to his attention if the organization had exercised due diligence.

It is not sufficient that the janitor have notice or reason to know of the customer's death or adjudication of incompetence. In the context of typical bank office procedure, the head cashier, a branch manager or a head of the accounts department is likely to exert authority over the two places in a bank where payment commonly occurs—teller's windows where items are cashed or the accounts department where items are deposited.[47] We think the bank is charged with knowledge only when the information reaches (or but for bank negligence would have reached) such persons of responsibility in the bank.

Judicial opinions provide little guidance as to what constitutes a reasonable opportunity for the bank to act. In one case the court said that a bank's authority to deal with the proceeds of checks terminated when the bank learned of the payee's death at the beginning of the banking day on which it processed the checks.[48] Per-

---

**47.** Doubtless there are a variety of ways in which a bank can arrest the payment process on a check presented through banking channels. For example, it could instruct the computer to throw out all checks drawn on certain accounts. Or it could assign a clerk to collect data on the death or bankruptcy of its depositors and to intercept checks (after the computer run) drawn on the accounts of dead or bankrupt depositors. If the bank has established any such procedure and the information reaches the person whose responsibility it is to instruct the computer or to intercept such checks but that person fails to act, clearly the bank has "knowledge." Moreover, if the information reaches any bank employee but fails to reach the crucial employee only because of the bank's negligence, the bank also has "knowledge" under 1–201(27). We assume, for example, that information reaching the branch manager of the relevant branch would always give the bank "knowledge" and that information reaching a variety of responsible employees in the central headquarters would also constitute knowledge. Because the titles and responsibilities of such parties vary from bank to bank and place to place, we hesitate to identify by name those whose knowledge should be attributed to the bank.

**48.** See Joseph v. United of America Bank, 266 N.E.2d 438, 8 UCC Rep. Serv. 1098 (Ill.App.1970) (abstract only).

haps even less time suffices where notice of death comes to the branch manager at the branch in which the deceased kept his account.[49]

Subsection (2) of 4–405 states a special rule for checks when a customer dies:

> Even with knowledge a bank may for ten days after the date of death pay or certify checks drawn on or prior to that date unless ordered to stop payment by a person claiming an interest in the account.

This section provides an expeditious means of paying deceased's recent and usually valid obligations and so avoids running the claims through probate. Note that the last clause of 4–405(2) gives a person claiming an interest in the account an implicit right to stop payment. Comments indicate that the bank is under no duty "to determine the validity of the claim or even whether it is 'colorable.' "[50] As a result, once the bank learns of its customer's death, it is likely to obey any stop order without inquiry. In some cases unsecured creditors may want to stop payment of all outstanding checks immediately on the debtor's death; otherwise, their competitors may gain priority by promptly cashing decedent's checks.

### § 17–4 The Bank's Liability to Its Customer for Wrongful Dishonor, 4–402

Section 4–402 was much re-written during the Code's evolution and is the worse for wear:

> A payor bank is liable to its customer for damages proximately caused by the wrongful dishonor of an item. When the dishonor occurs through mistake liability is limited to actual damages proved. If so proximately caused and proved damages may include damages for an arrest or prosecution of the customer or other consequential damages. Whether any consequential damages are proximately caused by the wrongful dishonor is a question of fact to be determined in each case.

In an opinion that reads like a Tale of the Old West (Loucks v. Albuquerque National Bank)[51] the New Mexico Supreme Court passed on the real and imagined effects of a bank's dishonor of a series of checks. Martinez, who owned an auto body shop, borrowed $500 from the bank. Soon afterwards he joined Loucks in partnership, closed his proprietorship account and opened a partnership account. Martinez later fell delinquent on the note. Over his partners' protests, the bank set off the $402 that Martinez owed on his proprietorship note against the partnership account which left a

49. See Comment 4 to section 4–106 which says that for the purpose of receiving knowledge each branch is a separate entity. See also the discussion in Section 16–4, note 29, supra.

50. § 4–405, Comment 4.

51. 76 N.M. 735, 418 P.2d 191, 3 UCC Rep.Serv. 709 (1966).

balance of $3.66 in that account. The partners closed the account and thereafter the bank dishonored ten outstanding checks. Because their checks bounced all over town, Loucks and Martinez allegedly encountered these difficulties: their supplier would deal only in cash; people who had previously accepted their checks now refused to do so; credit previously granted was denied; and a salesman who had sold them a map for one of the rubber checks ripped the map off their wall because they had given him "a bad check for it". The parties also alleged other less tangible injuries, and Loucks complained of an ulcer and was absent from work for awhile. Both believed that the bank had damaged their personal reputations.

Loucks and Martinez sued the bank for:

(1) recovery of the amount set off against the account ($402)

(2) compensatory damages to the partnership for injury to partnership credit and business reputation ($5,000) and for lost profits due to Loucks' absence caused by his ulcer ($1,800)

(3) punitive damages for injury to the partnership ($14,404)

(4) compensatory damages to each partner individually for injury to personal credit and business reputation ($5,000 each)

(5) punitive damages for injury to Loucks and Martinez individually ($60,000 and $10,000 respectively)

(6) compensatory damages for injury to Loucks for an ulcer allegedly caused by the dishonor ($25,000).

At trial plaintiffs recovered the amount set off by the bank, but the court dismissed all other claims. On appeal the New Mexico Supreme Court disallowed all claims for injury to Loucks and Martinez in their individual capacities (that is, compensatory and punitive damages for injury to plaintiff's personal reputation and Loucks' ulcer). The court held that the protection of section 4–402 ran only to customers and that individual partners had no cause of action on a partnership account. The court said the question of compensatory damages for injury to the partnership was one for the jury. On the issue of punitive damages the court ruled that proof of malice or willfulness was necessary to sustain the claim, and concluded that evidence of intemperate remarks by a bank officer when plaintiffs closed the account was not sufficient to warrant submitting that issue to the jury.

The bank's liability for wrongful dishonor is the converse of the bank's liability for paying checks not properly payable. Comment 2 to section 4–402 explains:

"Wrongful dishonor" excludes any permitted or justified dishonor, as where the drawer has no credit extended by the drawee, or where the draft lacks a necessary indorsement or is not properly presented.

Typically wrongful dishonor occurs as the result of bookkeeping errors, a computer error, a charge to the wrong account or the like.[52] It may also occur, as in *Loucks,* when the bank improperly exercises a setoff against the customer's account.[53] The cases suggest that a bank should deal gingerly with setoffs and third party claims.[54] Courts do not recognize purity of heart as a defense when a bank acts erroneously with respect to its customer's account. Even when the bank dishonors an item for legitimate cause, it must act consistently with 4–303 priorities.[55]

Almost all of the interesting lawyer questions under 4–402 have to do with the damages a customer may recover and with proof of those damages. The section requires greater proof for a business plaintiff than formerly, but permits a plaintiff to recover certain damages he could not have recovered under pre-Code law in some states. Under that pre-Code law, a "trader" (businessman)[56] could recover substantial compensation without proof of actual damage on the theory that bouncing his checks generally defamed his business character and injured his business.[57] The rule was one of *per se* liability; that is, a jury could give the plaintiff-trader what he "deserved" even though he proved no injury. Comment 3 states that the section "rejects" the trader rule, but, as we will see, it is perhaps more accurate to say that the section simply narrows that rule.

52. See Bank of Louisville Royal v. Sims, 435 S.W.2d 57, 7 UCC Rep.Serv. 234 (Ky.App.1968) (mistakenly placed ten-day hold on deposit); Skov v. Chase Manhattan Bank, 407 F.2d 1318, 6 UCC Rep.Serv. 170 (3rd Cir. 1969) (dishonor result of mistake).

Note that the damages recoverable for wrongful dishonor under 4–402 are not limited by 4–103(5) which states that damages resulting from "failure to exercise ordinary care" shall not exceed the amount of the item unless bad faith is shown. Section 4–402 contains no such restriction and Comment 4 to section 4–402 specifically states that the customer may recover greater damages under 4–402.

53. See American Fletcher Nat'l Bank & Trust Co. v. Flick, 19 Ind.Dec. 548, 252 N.E.2d 839, 7 UCC Rep.Serv. 224 (Ind.App.1969) (improper setoff).

54. In Pascagoula Nat'l Bank v. Eberlein, 161 Miss. 337, 131 So. 812 (1931), the bank dishonored plaintiff's checks when her husband's creditor garnisheed the account. The court ruled the dishonor wrongful and said that

if the bank had reason to believe that the husband was secreting funds in the account, it should have demanded that the creditor seek a restraining order. In Sumitomo Shoji New York, Inc. v. Chemical Bank New York Trust Co., 47 Misc.2d 741, 746, 263 N.Y.S.2d 354, 2 UCC Rep.Serv. 1088 (Sup.Ct. 1965), affd, 25 App.Div.2d 499, 267 N.Y.S.2d 477 (1st Dep't 1966), the court held the dishonor was not wrongful when creditor served bank with a restraining notice. See generally Annot., 126 A.L.R. 206, 213–15 (1940).

55. For a discussion of 4–303, see Section 17–7, infra.

56. Although the trader rule, as the name suggests, was originally applied only to merchants, it later was extended to any businessman. See Peabody v. Citizens' State Bank, 98 Minn. 302, 108 N.W. 272 (1906) (plaintiff, a farmer who traded horses and cattle, was found to be a "trader").

57. See, e. g., First Nat'l Bank v. N. R. McFall & Co., 144 Ark. 149, 222 S.W. 40 (1920). See generally, Annot. 126 A.L.R. 206, 220–25 (1940).

The draftsmen have also given the plaintiffs something in 4–402. The fourth sentence of 4–402 reads as follows: "Whether any consequential damages are proximately caused by the wrongful dishonor is a question of fact to be determined in each case." Comment 5 tells us that this sentence rejects "decisions holding that as a matter of law the dishonor of a check is not the 'proximate cause' of the arrest and prosecution of the customer . . . ." Presumably a customer whose check bounces is now entitled to recover any damages that he can convince the court or jury were proximately caused by wrongful dishonor of his checks.[58]

We limit the following discussion to two difficult lawyer questions: (*1*) to what extent do remnants of the "trader rule" remain? That is, to what extent may a businessman whose checks have bounced still be awarded substantial damages by a jury despite the fact that he puts on no evidence from which one could reasonably conclude that he has suffered such damages? (*2*) What are the outer limits of actual damages? May one recover for mental distress, etc.?

Despite the statement in Comment 3 that 4–402 rejects the "defamation *per se*" rule, we believe that some remnants of that rule survived enactment of the Code. We believe the rule still applies when the wrongful dishonor results not from mistake or inadvertence but from the willful action of the bank. The wording of the section itself supports our view. The second sentence of 4–402 reads as follows: "When the dishonor occurs *through mistake* liability is limited to actual damages proved." (Emphasis added.) The negative implication is that when wrongful dishonors occur not "through mistake" but willfully, the court may impose damages greater than "actual damages." That the draftsmen may have intended to perpetuate the *per se* liability rule in "willful" cases is also supported by the Code history embodied in a pre-Code statute and decisions under it. That statute and those cases make just the distinction we suggest; namely, that a bank that dishonors a check through inadvertence or mistake is not liable for *per se* defamation of a merchant or trader, and is so liable only if its dishonor is willful or malicious.[59] If the draftsmen wished to abolish the trader rule

---

**58.** See Editorial Board for the Uniform Commercial Code, 1956 Recommendations 159 (1957). Comment 5 to 4–402 reads as follows:

The fourth sentence of the section rejects decisions holding that as a matter of law the dishonor of a check is not the "proximate cause" of the arrest and prosecution of the customer, and leaves to determination in each case as a question of fact whether the dishonor is or may be the "proximate cause".

**59.** A number of states enacted a statute recommended by the American Banking Association. The model statute reads as follows:

An Act to limit the liability of a bank or trust company for non-payment of a check through error. * * *

No bank or trust company doing business in this State shall be liable to a depositor because of the non-payment through mistake or error and without malice of a check which should have been paid unless the depositor shall allege and prove actual damage by reason of such non-payment and in such event the liability shall not exceed the amount of damage so proved.

altogether, they should have chosen stronger language in the face of this pre-Code statutory and case law history. Certainly the reference to "mistake" in the second sentence of 4–401 invites a court to adopt the relevant pre-Code distinction.[60]

See 1 T. Paton, Paton's Digest § 21B:1 at 1117–18 (4th ed. 1940); Woody v. First Nat'l Bank, 194 N.C. 549, 140 S.E. 150 (1927) (statute not applicable when plaintiff alleged dishonor was willful and malicious); Jones v. Citizens Bank, 58 N.M. 48, 265 P.2d 366 (1954) (statute did not prohibit award of exemplary damages when evidence showed bank acted with malice).

**60.** As we read the section's legislative history, neither the third nor the final sentence of 4–402 requires the customer to prove his damages in all cases. The third sentence reads as follows (emphasis added):

*If so proximately caused and proved* damages may include damages for an arrest or prosecution of the customer or other consequential damages.

When one considers the sentence in isolation, he might conclude that the italicized language refers to all consequential damages. However, we think the section's legislative history reveals that the clause italicized above refers only to the case where the wrongful dishonor is the result of mistake. In the 1952 Official Draft, section 4–402 reads as follows:

A payor bank is liable to its customer for wrongful dishonor of an item but where the dishonor occurs through mistake its liability is limited to the actual damages proved including damages for any arrest or prosecution of the customer.

At the hearings of the New York Law Revision Commission, commentators criticized the section on the ground that the word "any" and the phrasing of the comment suggested that the customer need not show a causal connection between the bank's dishonor and his arrest. See 1 N.Y. State Law Revision Comm'n, 1954 Report 318–19, 342, 362 (1954). The evidence demonstrates that the draftsmen did not intend to expand the proof requirement to include willful dishonor when they adopted the changes recommended by the New York Law Revision Commission. In response to criticism the draftsmen revised 4–402 as follows:

A payor bank is liable to its customer for wrongful dishonor of an item but where the dishonor occurs through mistake its liability is limited to the actual damages proved [including damages for any arrest or prosecution of the customer]. *If proximately caused by the dishonor these may include damages for any arrest or prosecution of the customer.*

Reason: The change clarifies present language by avoiding any possible contention that damages for wrongful dishonor automatically include damages for arrest or prosecution, whether or not caused by the dishonor.

Uniform Commercial Code, 1952 Official Draft of Text and Comments 36 (Supp. No. 1, 1955) (brackets and emphasis in original to indicate deletions and additions in language, respectively).

The New York Law Revision Commission's final word on 4–402 was as follows:

1. It was suggested that the Supplement No. 1 revision creates further difficulty in the section, since by inserting a specific requirement of proximate cause as to damages for arrest or prosecution it creates a negative inference that the main provision for recovery of "actual damages proved" is not so limited. It was also suggested that a reference to consequential damages generally is needed to overcome the effect of Section 1–106(1), which provides that consequential damages shall not be had except as specifically provided "in this Act or by other rule of law."

2. Section 4–402 was approved in principle. The following revision was suggested:

A payor bank is liable to its customer for consequential damages proximately caused by wrongful dishonor of an item, including damages for any arrest or prosecution of the customer so caused, but when dishonor occurs through mistake its liability for consequential damages is limited to the actual damages proved. Whether an arrest or prosecution was proximately caused by wrongful dishonor is a question to be determined upon the facts of each case.

N.Y. State Law Revision Comm'n, 1956 Report 430 (1956).

One who believes that the trader rule still applies at least when wrongful dishonor is willful must distinguish mistaken from willful dishonor.   Under pre-Code law, while most jurisdictions applied the trader rule without distinguishing between mistake or willful action,[61] the New York courts recognized the distinction.   In Wildenberger v. Ridgewood National Bank,[62] the bank initially dishonored checks of its customer when his wife filed an adverse claim to the account, and with notice of the first wrongful dishonor the bank dishonored the checks a second time.   At trial the customer, a merchant, recovered nominal damages.   On appeal, Mr. Justice Cardozo, writing for a unanimous court, said:

> We think the plaintiff's damages were to be determined by the jury.   The dishonor of the checks was admittedly a wrong.   .   .   .   The wrong, if willful, charged the bank with liability for the consequences.   In many jurisdictions the liability is the same whether the wrong is willful or merely heedless.   .   .   .   In this state the liability is for nominal damages and no more, if the dishonor of the checks is the result of innocent mistake.   That was the situation in Clark Co. v. Mt. Moris Bank, 85 App.Div. 362, 83 N.Y. Supp. 447, and 181 N.Y. 533, 73 N.E. 1133, where dishonor was due to the blunder of a bookkeeper, who misread the plaintiff's balance.   Sometimes we are told that, to permit the recovery of substantial damages, the wrong must be malicious.   This does not mean, however, that it must be the product of hatred or malevolence.   It is the exclusion of liability for the consequences of accident or mistake.   .   .   . We find nothing of accident or mistake in the defendant's dishonor of these checks.   It dishonored them with full knowledge of the state of the account, setting one risk against another, the risk of adverse claims against the risk of broken contracts.   Here was no heedless act, but one deliberate and willful.[63]

We would adopt Justice Cardozo's test and find the bank guilty of willful dishonor and thus subject to the trader rule any time it dishonored its customer's checks because it had previously reduced his account through its own improper setoff, improper garnishment

The draftsmen responded with the current version of 4–402.   See Editorial Board for the Uniform Commercial Code, 1956 Recommendations 159 (1957).   Compare Comment 3 to section 4–402 (1952 Official Draft), "The merchant or trader is placed upon the same footing as any other drawer, and *in all cases* the damages recoverable are limited to those actually proved." (emphasis added), with Comment 3 to section 4–402 (1958 Official Draft), "The merchant, trader and fiduciary are placed on the same footing as any other drawer and *in all cases of dishonor by mistake* damages recoverable are limited to those actually proved." (emphasis added)

61.   See Woody v. First Nat'l Bank, 194 N.C. 549, 140 S.E. 150 (1927); 1 T. Paton, Paton's Digest § 21A:1 at 1114 (4th ed. 1940).

62.   230 N.Y. 425, 130 N.E. 600 (1921).

63.   Id. at 427–28, 130 N.E. at 600.

or the like. Moreover we would find such reduction "improper" even though the bank acted in a good faith but mistaken belief that the garnishment or setoff was valid. Although such dishonors might be the result of a "mistake" in the sense that the bank official was mistaken about his legal rights, we would classify them as willful for they represent the bank's deliberate judgment to sacrifice the customer's interest to those of some other party. If courts apply the trader rule to cases in which the bank knowingly disobeys its customer's order to protect some other party, banks may become more appropriately loyal to their customers' interests. We well understand that courts would place the bank between a rock and a hard place in cases in which a check competes with a garnishment, for here the bank faces liability to its customer under the trader rule on the one hand and liability, perhaps sizeable, to a garnishing creditor on the other. But bankers are paid to take such risks and should tread carefully with due respect not only for the garnishor but also for their own customer's interest.

If the trader rule survives willful dishonor cases, what of cases in which the bank offers to prove that its customer suffered no substantial injury as a result of the dishonor? Put another way, is the trader rule a conclusive presumption of substantial damage that permits the plaintiff to recover as much as a jury wishes to award (unfettered with mitigation evidence), or rather may the bank offer evidence of no injury and thus reduce the damages that a jury might otherwise award? Both pre-Code law and common sense indicate that the bank should be allowed to show that the customer was not in fact injured by the dishonor.[64] Given that such evidence is often hard to produce and that juries tend to favor customers over bankers, we suspect that mitigation evidence will not dilute the effectiveness of the trader rule as a device for controlling the bank's behavior. However, in the single Code case on this question, the defendant bank effectively limited the plaintiff's damages. In American Fletcher National Bank & Trust Co. v. Flick,[65] the bank exercised a setoff against Flick's account and subsequently dishonored his checks. At trial Flick recovered the amount setoff as well as damages for injury to his credit, business reputation and loss of business. On appeal, the Indiana Court of Appeals determined that the setoff and dishonor were wrongful and then considered defendant's contention that Flick had not shown a causal relation between the dishonor and a decline in his business. The court quoted 4–402 and then, without considering whether the section abolished the trader rule, stated that rule as follows:

> [W]hen a bank wrongfully dishonors its customer's business
> check there arises a presumption that the customer's credit

---

**64.** See First Nat'l Bank v. N. R. McFall & Co., 144 Ark. 149, 222 S.W. 40 (1920); Reeves v. First Nat'l Bank, 20 Cal.App. 508, 129 P. 800 (1st Dist. 1912); Berea Bank & Trust Co. v. Mokwa, 194 Ky. 556, 239 S.W. 1044 (1922); Grenada Bank v. Lester, 126 Miss. 442, 89 So. 2 (1921).

**65.** 252 N.E.2d 839, 7 UCC Rep.Serv. 224 (Ind.App.1969).

and business standing is thereby harmed. The function of this presumption is to remove from the customer the duty of going forward with the evidence on this particular injury or harm and thereby avoid a directed verdict against him if evidence on the issue is not produced. The primary reason for the recognition of this presumption is that a wrongful dishonor renders the existence of *some* harm to the customer's credit and business standing so probable that it makes legal sense to assume the existence of such harm unless and until the adversary comes forward with some evidence to the contrary.[66]   (emphasis original)

Although the court adopted the foregoing "trader" presumption, it ruled that Flick could recover only nominal damages. The court said the presumption applies exclusively to claims for injury to business reputation and Flick failed to show lost income. Furthermore the court said that although Flick's business declined, he did not trace this diminution to the bank's dishonor and did not overcome defendant's evidence that the decline was traceable to other causes. The court contrasted Flick's evidence with that presented in *Loucks'* and noted that Flick did not show that anyone other than the payee knew of the dishonors. Accordingly, the Indiana appellate court affirmed the lower court's award for the amount of the check wrongfully dishonored and reversed that court's award for injury to business reputation and decline of business.

A final question remains. What are the limits on the type of injury for which a customer may recover under 4-402? Certainly courts might take a sympathetic view of customer's claim of financial injury due to wrongful dishonor. For example, in Skov v. Chase Manhattan Bank,[67] the customer contended that the bank's dishonor caused his supplier to stop doing business with him. The trial court awarded customer three years of lost profits and the Third Circuit affirmed. However, as the *Flick* case shows, it may be hard to prove that a dishonor proximately caused a decline in business, a lost deal, or the like.

Courts do not generously receive claims for mental distress and suffering caused by dishonored checks. In Bank of Louisville Royal v. Sims,[68] the customer recovered the cost of a telephone call, two weeks of lost wages, and sums for "illness, harassment, embarrassment and inconvenience." On appeal the Kentucky Court of Appeals struck down the "nerves" award, and the award for lost work time. The court analyzed the case as a breach of contract and said that 4-402 merely codifies Kentucky pre-Code law denying recovery for mental distress. We believe that to label the customer's suit as a

---

**66.**   Id. at 845–46, 7 UCC Rep.Serv. at 231–32 (emphasis in original).

**67.**   407 F.2d 1318, 6 UCC Rep.Serv. 170 (3d Cir. 1969).

**68.**   435 S.W.2d 57, 7 UCC Rep.Serv. 234 (Ky.Ct.App.1968).

contract breach or as a tort adds little.   Comment 2 to 4–402 is in accord:

> The liability of the drawee for dishonor has sometimes been stated as one for breach of contract, sometimes as for negligence or other breach of a tort duty, and sometimes as for defamation.   This section does not attempt to specify a theory. . . .

Might one argue that "actual damages" excludes recovery for mental distress? We think not.   In the first place, the draftsmen went to great efforts to assure that customers can recover for arrest and prosecution.   It is inconsistent to allow recovery for embarrassment and mental distress deriving from arrest and prosecution and to deny similar recovery in other cases.   Moreover, cases under the predecessor to 4–402, the American Banking Association Statute, held that "actual damages" includes damages for mental distress.[69]   Thus we believe the court erroneously decided *Bank of Louisville Royal* and that the Code draftsmen intended to allow recovery for mental distress and other intangible injury.

In conclusion, we owe a word to Templeton Zigafuse, the mine run consumer whose check is wrongfully dishonored.   Of course, if he is arrested and put in jail because his checks bounce, he has the same right to recover as any other party.   Likewise he may recover for any additional loss he suffers because his credit rating falls off, and presumably he may recover for mental distress in those states which permit this.   The pre-Code courts divided on whether nontraders may invoke the trader rule.[70]   We suspect that Templeton Zigafuse will have difficulty showing any damages at all in the usual case, and that courts will not sympathetically receive his arguments that he suffered compensible loss because he had to look at black and white TV rather than the color TV he might have bought with his untarnished credit rating.

## § 17–5   The Customer's Right to Stop Payment, 4–403

A customer may stop payment on "any item payable for his account." [71]   Since stop orders are common only in regard to checks, we consider the relevant rules only in reference to checks.   A stop

---

69.   See Mouse v. Central Sav. & Trust Co., 120 Ohio St. 599, 167 N.E. 868 (1929); accord, Weaver v. Bank of America Nat'l Trust & Sav. Ass'n, 59 Cal.2d 428, 30 Cal.Rptr. 4, 380 P.2d 644 (1963).

70.   Nontrader not entitled to presumption: First Nat'l Bank v. Stewart, 204 Ala. 199, 85 So. 529 (1920); Western Nat'l Bank v. White, 62 Tex.Civ.App. 374, 131 S.W. 828 (1910); Third Nat'l Bank v. Ober, 178 F. 678 (8th Cir. 1910).

Nontrader entitled to presumption: Patterson v. Marine Nat'l Bank, 130 Pa. 419, 18 A. 632 (1889) (bank a quasi-public institution liable for substantial damages for wrongful dishonor); Woody v. Nat'l Bank, 194 N.C. 549, 140 S.E. 150 (1927); Meinhart v. Farmers' State Bank, 124 Kan. 333, 259 P. 698 (1927) (plaintiff introduced some positive evidence of injury).

71.   § 4–403.   By analogy the rule extends to drawees other than banks. § 4–403, Comment 4.

order offers a variety of lawyer problems; here we examine: (1) Who may issue a binding stop order? (2) What form must a stop order take? May it be oral? (3) How are the usual stop order rules altered because a personal check is certified or because the check in question is a cashier's or bank check? (4) What is the bank's liability for failure to follow a binding stop order? (We deal with this last question mostly in the following section for it inevitably turns on the question of subrogation of the bank to the presenter's rights under 4-407).

A drawer promises to pay the holder (3-413), and orders his bank to so pay from his account. The drawer's stop order does not rescind his promise to pay the holder and does not impair the holder's suit on that promise.[72] The drawer's stop order is addressed only to his bank and affects only his relationship with it. Subsection (1) of 4-403 states:

> A customer may by order to his bank stop payment of any item payable for his account but the order must be received at such time and in such manner as to afford the bank a reasonable opportunity to act on it prior to any action by the bank with respect to the item described in Section 4-303.

The right to stop payment is consistent with the concept that "[a] check . . . does not of itself operate as an assignment of any funds in the hands of the drawee [bank] available for its payment and [that] the drawee is not liable on the instrument until he accepts it."[73] Although some post-Code courts have blurred the point,[74] a drawer's stop order is not only effective against holders but also against holders in due course.[75] The presenter's status as a holder in due course can have practical impact where the bank pays over a binding stop order,[76] but it does not impair the *validity* of the drawer's stop order.

### Who May Issue Effective Stop Orders?

Ordinarily only a customer-drawer has the right to stop payment. A payee or indorsee does not have this right.[77] Although some

---

72. See Citizens Nat'l Bank v. Fort Lee Sav. & Loan Ass'n, 89 N.J.Super. 43, 213 A.2d 315, 2 UCC Rep.Serv. 1029 (Law Div.1965) (depositary bank which was holder in due course could enforce check against drawer despite stop order); accord, Peoples Bank v. Haar, 421 P.2d 817, 3 UCC Rep.Serv. 1065 (Okla.1966).

73. § 3-409(1).

74. See Starkey Constr., Inc. v. Elcon, Inc., 248 Ark. 958, 457 S.W.2d 509, 7 UCC Rep.Serv. 923 (1970) (drawer not entitled to stop payment against bank which was holder in due course).

75. Comment 8 to 4-403 explains:

> It has sometimes been said that payment cannot be stopped against a holder in due course, but the statement is inaccurate. The payment can be stopped but the drawer remains liable on the instrument to the holder in due course (Sections 3-305, 3-413) and the drawee, if he pays, becomes subrogated to the rights of the holder in due course against the drawer.

76. For a discussion of the bank's subrogation rights upon payment over a stop order, see Section 17-6 supra.

77. § 4-403, Comment 3.

cases [78] have held otherwise (erroneously we think), a bank drawing a check on its account with another bank is a customer and has the right to stop payment.[79]   On the death or incompetence of the customer, "a person claiming an interest in the account" may also stop payment.[80]   The rights of parties to a joint account to stop payment are unclear.   Where one person's signature alone on a check is valid and binds all parties to the account, that person can order payment stopped.   But can a party to the account who did not draw the check stop payment?   One pre-Code case held that a wife lacked power to stop payment on a check drawn by her husband against an account held by husband and wife as joint tenants.[81]   The Oklahoma Supreme Court reasoned that such power would be inconsistent with the husband's right to draw checks solely on his own signature.   Since in the typical case the signature of any party to a joint account is sufficient for payment and all have some claim to funds in the account, we think the Oklahoma case was wrongly decided.   We believe that the order of any of them ought to suffice.   (If, for example, husband learned that wife had drawn a large check and he wished to frustrate wife's desires, he would be entitled to go to the bank and withdraw all of the funds over his own signature before his wife's check was presented for payment.)   All parties to the account are "customers," and any inference from 4–403(1) affirms that each has power to stop.   Of course, signature card contracts might settle the issue, but they usually do not.[82]

### Form of Stop Orders

Neither 4–403 nor any other part of the Code specifies the form of the stop order.   Presumably prior case holdings [83] that the order

**78.**  See Malphrus v. Home Sav. Bank, 44 Misc.2d 705, 254 N.Y.S.2d 980, 2 UCC Rep.Serv.  373  (Co.Ct.1965); Ruskin v. Central Fed. Sav. & Loan Ass'n, 3 UCC Rep.Serv. 150 (N.Y.Sup. Ct.1966); Meckler v. Highland Falls Sav. & Loan Ass'n, 64 Misc.2d 407, 314 N.Y.S.2d 681, 8 UCC Rep.Serv. 368 (Sup.Ct.1970).

For a more detailed discussion of the drawer bank's right to stop payment on a check drawn on itself or another bank, see text accompanying notes 92– 96 infra.

**79.**  See § 4–104(1) (e); Citizens Nat'l Bank v. Fort Lee Sav. & Loan Ass'n, 89 N.J.Super. 43, 213 A.2d 315, 2 UCC Rep.Serv. 1029 (Law Div.1965) (drawer bank could stop payment but holder in due course entitled to enforce rights on check).

**80.**  See § 4–405(2), discussed in Section 17–4 supra.   Comment 4 to 4–405 reads:

Any surviving relative or other person who claims an interest in the account may give a direction to the bank  .  .  . to stop payment.   The bank has no obligation to determine the validity of the claim or even whether it is "colorable".   But obviously, anyone who has an interest in the estate, including the  .  .  . executor  .  .  . is entitled to claim an interest in the account.

**81.**  See Brown v. Eastman Nat'l Bank, 291 P.2d 828 (Okla.1955).

**82.**  One stop payment form we examined required only an authorized signature and contained language such as "In requesting stop payment *we* agree to hold you harmless.  .  .  ." Yet another one specifically required the signature of the maker or drawer.

**83.**  See Shude v. American State Bank, 263 Mich. 519, 248 N.W. 886 (1933); John H. Mahon Co. v. Huntington

must identify the check with reasonable accuracy are still law. Section 4–403 requires only that "the order must be received . . . in such manner as to afford the bank a reasonable opportunity to act on it. . . ." In the banker's Utopia, stop orders accurately identify the drawer, the payee, the account number, the date and the amount of the check.[84] Printed forms that banks supply also commonly ask the customer to state his reason for stopping payment.[85] We would hold any stop order sufficient that reasonably identifies the account either by the drawer's name or account number and that reasonably identifies the check either by number, by name of the payee or by such information combined with the date and amount of the check. If, for example, the customer had drawn only one check to a given payee and the customer had given the bank his account number and the name of the payee, we would hold the order valid (absent a customer agreement to give more information).

Note that by giving erroneous information a customer may render an otherwise valid stop order invalid. A court should find a stop order valid that names only the account number and the number of the check, but the same court should find a stop order invalid that recites the account and check numbers yet erroneously names the payee. To a certain extent, the validity of stop orders should depend on the procedures that the drawee uses to identify stopped checks and on the reasonableness of such procedures. An incorrect check number is no cause for complaint by a bank that examines checks solely by the name of the payee, but it would be to a bank that hunts for stopped checks principally by reference to check numbers. When the customer gives erroneous information or gives less information than the banker asks for, we urge courts to review the information given to determine whether a reasonably prudent banker with that information should have found the check. Unless the depositor failed to live up to his deposit contract or other agreement with respect to stop orders, any stop order should be sufficient that would enable a reasonably prudent banker using ordinary care to find the stopped check.

---

Nat'l Bank, 62 Ohio App. 261, 23 N.E. 2d 638 (1939).

**84.** The cases provide no guidance on the question of the minimum amount of information the customer must supply. The use of stop payment forms may explain the dearth of case law on this point.

The effect of erroneous information is another matter. However we detect no pattern to the decided cases and therefore simply categorize them according to the outcome. The stop order was held effective despite erroneous information in the following cases: Kentucky-Farmers Bank v. Staton, 314 Ky. 313, 235 S.W.2d 767 (1951) (customer supplied wrong amount but gave correct date, number, and name of payee); Shude v. American State Bank, 263 Mich. 519, 248 N.W. 886 (1933) (incorrect date not significant when bank erroneously placed hold on wrong account). The stop order was held ineffective because customer supplied erroneous information in the following cases: John H. Mahon Co. v. Huntington Nat'l Bank, 62 Ohio App. 261, 23 N.E.2d 638 (1939) (erroneous check number); Mitchell v. Security Bank, 85 Misc. 360, 147 N.Y.S. 470 (App.Term 1914) (wrong date and misdescribed payee).

**85.** See 4 R. Henson & W. Davenport, Uniform Laws Annotated 314–20 (1968).

Subsection 4–403(2) entitles the customer to stop payment orally.[86] Although this provision caused unhappiness in the banking community, the Code draftsmen decided that banks should honor oral as well as written stop orders.[87] As we indicated in Section 17–2 of this book, we read 4–403(2) and comments as a statement of public policy and believe that a bank may not by contract deprive a customer of his right to stop payment orally. For the same reasons, we think courts should invalidate stop order forms that exculpate banks for failure to follow stop orders.

### Certified, Cashier, and Bank Checks

As we have seen, when the customer draws a check he can order payment stopped. However when the customer uses a certified check, a cashier's check or a bank check the matter becomes more complicated. (From a customer's viewpoint the three checks are likely to be functionally identical. One will serve the purpose of the other, and in most cases he will procure a certified, a bank, or a cashier's check to satisfy someone who insists upon a more solid promise than his personal promise.) Complications arise because, on such checks, unlike on ordinary personal checks, the bank incurs contractual liability to the holder. Recall that 3–409 says a drawee is not liable to the holder of a check unless the check is certified.[88] Accordingly, two related questions arise in relation to certified, cashier's, or bank checks: (1) What right does the customer have to compel the bank to stop payment? (2) What are the legal consequences if the bank stops payment?

A bank can incur direct liability to the payee of its customer's check in a variety of ways. First, it can certify the customer's check.[89] Second, it can issue a cashier's check (that is, a check on which it is both the drawer and the drawee).[90] Third, it can issue a bank check (that is, a check on which it is the drawer and the drawee is a second bank). In all three cases the bank incurs direct liability to the payee, either as an acceptor on the check or as a drawer. If the cus-

---

**86.** However several states have enacted a version of 4–403 which requires written stop orders. See, e. g., Cal.Comm.Code § 4–403(1) (West 1964); Tex.Bus. & Com.Code § 4.403 (b) (West 1968).

**87.** See note 17 supra.

**88.** Section 3–409 reads as follows:

(1) A check or other draft does not of itself operate as an assignment of any funds in the hands of the drawee available for its payment, and the drawee is not liable on the instrument until he accepts it.

(2) Nothing in this section shall affect any liability in contract, tort or otherwise arising from any letter of credit or other obligation or representation which is not in acceptance.

**89.** See §§ 3–410; 3–411; 3–413(1). For a discussion of certification and the bank's liability, see Section 13–8 supra.

**90.** See Pennsylvania v. Curtiss Nat'l Bank, 427 F.2d 395, 7 UCC Rep.Serv. 1015 (5th Cir. 1970) (cashier's check held to be bill of exchange drawn by bank upon itself and accepted in advance by act of its issuance); accord, Nat'l Newark & Essex Bank v. Giordano, 111 N.J.Super. 347, 268 A.2d 327, 7 UCC Rep.Serv. 1153 (Law Div. 1970).

tomer orders the bank not to pay the certified check or the cashier's check or asks it to order payment stopped on the bank check, that customer is asking the bank to break its contract under 3–413.   In none of these cases does the customer have a right to insist that his bank dishonor [91] or, in the case of the bank check, the right to order the drawee bank to order payment stopped.   Nevertheless, in deference to a good customer, a bank may voluntarily choose to dishonor a certified check, or a cashier's check and may voluntarily order payment stopped on the bank check.   If the bank voluntarily chooses to dishonor the certified or cashier's check or to order its bank to stop payment on the bank check, the holder will have a cause of action against the bank.[92]   In the case of a certified check on which the *drawer* procured certification, the holder will also have a cause of action on the check against the drawer.[93]   If the holder chooses to sue just the bank on its acceptor's or drawer's liability, the bank probably may not raise defenses available to its customer against the holder.[94]   Before bank accedes to its customer's request, it would be

**91.**   Section 4–303 explicitly states that a stop order "comes too late" if the payor has certified the check.   For a discussion of 4–303, see Section 17–7 supra.

We decline 3–118(a)'s invitation to argue that the customer can compel his bank to stop payment on a cashier's check. Section 3–118(a) reads in part as follows: "A draft drawn on the drawer is effective as a note."   Under section 4–403 the customer may stop payment on notes as well as checks. § 4–403, Comment 4.   Since 4–403 allows customer to stop payment on "any item payable for his account," he might argue that he can stop payment despite the fact that a cashier's check is not payable from his personal account.   Finally customer could argue that 4–403 does not bar his stop order because the cashier's check is a note under 3–118(a) rather than a certified check under 3–411.

Although the argument set out above has superficial appeal, we reject it because it places the bank's reputation at the mercy of the customer.   Moreover, the public treats cashier's checks as the equivalent of cash.   We feel that had the draftsmen intended to overturn public expectations, they would not have chosen the Delphian method outlined above.

**92.**   Section 3–802(1) (a) provides:

Unless otherwise agreed where an instrument is taken for an underlying obligation

(a) the obligation is pro tanto discharged if a bank is drawer, maker or acceptor of the instrument and there is no recourse on the instrument against the underlying obligor
. . .

Accordingly, if the person taking a cashier's check or a bank check wishes to preserve his rights against the customer, he should secure his indorsement.

**93.**   Section 3–411(1) reads:

Certification of a check is acceptance.   Where a holder procures certification the drawer and all prior indorsers are discharged.

Section 3–802(1) (a).   (See note 92 supra.)   If the drawer remains liable on the instrument, the bank's acceptance does not discharge the underlying obligation under section 3–802(1) (a), and section 3–802(1) (b) governs.

Section 3–802(1) (b) provides:

[I]n any other case the obligation is suspended pro tanto until the instrument is due or if it is payable on demand until its presentment.   If the instrument is dishonored action may be maintained on either the instrument or the obligation; discharge of the underlying obligor on the instrument also discharges him on the obligation.

**94.**   The last sentence of section 3–306 (d) prohibits bank from raising certain defenses of its customer against the holder.   The sentence reads as follows: "The *claim* of any third person

well advised to obtain the customer's agreement to join any lawsuit that might result.

Two New York lower courts have disagreed with our analysis with respect to bank checks. In those cases the courts held that one bank that had drawn a check on another bank could not stop payment. In Malphrus v. Home Savings Bank,[95] payee sued the drawer of a bank check that had stopped payment at the request of its depositor. In granting plaintiff's motion for summary judgment the court said that the drawer of a bank check had no right to stop payment because businessmen treat bank checks like cash and the issuance of the bank check discharges the buyer from the underlying obligation under 3–802. We think the case was wrongly decided. In the first place the drawer of a bank check qualifies as a "customer" under 4–104(f) and that status entitles him to issue a stop order under 4–403. Secondly, even if the drawer-bank stops payment, it remains liable to the payee under 3–413(2).[96] Thus even if the buyer-depositor is discharged from the underlying obligation the payee has a solvent bank to sue. Moreover a seller who wishes to retain his rights against the buyer can protect himself by obtaining buyer's indorsement. Under 3–802 issuance of a bank check does not discharge the underlying obligation if the obligor is liable on the instrument.

### § 17–6 Payor Bank's Liability for Its Failure to Follow a Legitimate Stop Order, 4–403(3); Its Right to Subrogation on Improper Payment, 4–407

The payor bank's right to subrogation is inextricably entwined with its liability to its customer for improper payment. To illustrate, consider the following problem: Repeunzel, the buyer of a valuable painting, gives his personal check in the amount of $30,000 to seller, Cicero. Subsequently, Repeunzel has second thoughts about the purchase, properly orders payment stopped, but his bank fails to

---

to the instrument is not otherwise available as a defense to any party liable thereon unless the third person himself defends the action for such party." (Emphasis added.) Examination of Comment 5 to 3–306 and that section's predecessor, NIL § 59, reveals that the prohibition extends only to third party claims of title. Does that mean that bank can raise other defenses of its customer (e g., breach of warranty)? We think not. At common law courts generally rejected defendants' attempts to raise such defenses, and we believe those decisions supplement the Code under section 1–103. See Prouty v. Roberts, 60 Mass. (6 Cush.) 19 (1850) (maker cannot show plaintiff obtained note from payee by fraudulent representations when plaintiff proves legal ti-

tle); Thompson v. Wright, 53 Ga.App. 875, 187 S.E. 311 (1936) (maker cannot raise lack of consideration for transfer by payee against plaintiff-transferee); accord, Gamel v. Hynds, 34 Okla. 388, 125 P. 1115 (1912). See also Bowles v. Oakman, 246 Mich. 674, 225 N.W. 613 (1929) (without participation of defrauded party maker cannot raise indorser's fraud against plaintiff transferee).

**95.** 44 Misc.2d 705, 254 N.Y.S.2d 980, 2 UCC Rep.Serv. 373 (Co.Ct.1965); accord, Ruskin v. Central Fed. Sav. & Loan Ass'n, 3 UCC Rep.Serv. 150 (N.Y. Sup.Ct.1966).

**96.** For a discussion of the drawer's liability, see Section 13–9 supra.

follow the stop order.   Repeunzel instructs his bank to re-credit his account and bank responds as follows:   First, Repeunzel, you have the burden of establishing the fact and the amount of loss resulting from our payment because of 4–403(3) and you have failed to do that.   You have failed because Cicero had a binding contract for the payment of $30,000 from you whether or not we followed your order to stop payment.   Therefore, our failure to follow your orders was not the cause of your loss and in fact no loss "resulted" from that failure.   Secondly, even if you read 4–403(3) more narrowly than we do 4–407 subrogates us to the rights "of any holder in due course on an item against the drawer or maker" and to the rights of the "payee or any other holder" against the drawer or maker. Since payee Cicero had a good claim against you which he could have asserted for $30,000, we are subrogated to that right and can assert it as a defense in any suit you have against us for our failure to follow the stop order.   Furthermore, the check was presented for payment to us not by Cicero but by the depositary bank which was a holder in due course;   therefore, even if you have a defense against Cicero, it is not one you can assert against us for we are subrogated not just to Cicero's rights but also to the rights of the presenting bank who was a holder in due course and who takes free of such defenses.   In such case the payor bank wins;   seller Cicero and buyer Repeunzel get just what they deserve, $30,000, and the painting, respectively.

Of course 4–407 is not coextensive with the liabilities between drawer and payor bank, for it subrogates the payor bank to drawer's claims against other parties as well.   However it comes into play most commonly in the case in which the payor bank asserts the rights of some third party against the customer-drawer.   Section 4–407 reads in full as follows:

> If a payor bank has paid an item over the stop payment order of the drawer or maker or otherwise under circumstances giving a basis for objection by the drawer or maker, to prevent unjust enrichment and only to the extent necessary to prevent loss to the bank by reason of its payment of the item, the payor bank shall be subrogated to the rights
>
> > (a) of any holder in due course on the item against the drawer or maker;  and
> >
> > (b) of the payee or any other holder of the item against the drawer or maker either on the item or under the transaction out of which the item arose;  and
> >
> > (c) of the drawer or maker against the payee or any other holder of the item with respect to the transaction out of which the item arose.

Sections 4–407 and 4–403(3) leave us with several questions concerning the liability of a payor bank to its customer for payment over an effective stop order. First, what does 4–403(3) add to the law? That subsection provides:

> The burden of establishing the fact and amount of loss resulting from the payment of an item contrary to a binding stop payment order is on the customer.

Mr. Malcolm, an Article Four draftsman, tells us that subsection 4–403(3) was inserted as a trade-off for the banks when the draftsmen decided to allow customers to give oral stop orders.[97] We can readily understand the requirement that the customer show that he gave a valid stop order.[98] However the requirement that the customer establish the fact and amount of loss before recovery from bank is more controversial and has a controversial history. One aspect of that controversy revolved around the explanatory comment which appeared in the 1952 version of the Code. The comment reads as follows:

> When a bank pays an item over a stop payment order, such payment automatically involves a charge to the customer's account. Subsection (3) imposes upon the customer the burden of establishing the fact and amount of loss resulting from the payment. Consequently until such burden is maintained either in a court action or to the satisfaction of the bank, the bank is not obligated to recredit the amount of the item to the customer's account and, therefore, is not liable for the dishonor of other items due to insufficient funds caused by the payment contrary to the stop payment order.

---

**97.** Testifying before the New York Law Revision Commission Mr. Malcolm, in an explanation of the decision to permit oral stop orders, said:

However, one interesting thing developed in that particular debate and argument which touches on another criticism that has been made, and that was that after the two houses voted down the bank concept on those two issues, then somebody said from the floor would it not be fair if at least in this situation the burden of proof was placed upon the depositor to establish that there was a stop payment order and the extent of his damages.

Again, without any participation on my part, the actual draftsmen of the Code responded very quickly that they thought that would be a fair proposition, and it was acquiesced in. The policy decision was made, and sub-section (3) was subsequently drafted to meet that policy decision.

Now the criticism is made, that comment 9 to Section 4–403 extends the result of subsection (3) farther than it should go. I am responsible for drafting 9 because I believed it was a logical extension of the rule of subsection (3), but if I am wrong, then some court at some time will say so, and here is an instance where at some time the courts will have to determine whether or not it is a logical extension . . . .

1 N.Y. State Law Revision Comm'n, 1954 Report 467–68 (1954).

**98.** See Dinger v. Market St. Trust Co., 7 Pa.D. & C.2d 674, (C.P.1956) (complaint insufficient because it failed to state specific date and failed to identify bookkeeper receiving stop order).

In hearings before the New York Law Revision Commission several commentators questioned Comment 9;[99] others defended it.[100] Although the Code's Editorial Board affirmed its commitment to Comment 9 in Supplement No. 1,[101] that Comment was deleted from the 1958 Official Text. Presumably this was in response to the New York Law Revision Commission's disapproval.[102]

Is the ghost of Comment 9 yet with us? We are unsure. Consider the following hypothetical: Customer issues a valid stop order and bank pays in disregard of the order. Customer insists that bank re-credit the account and bank refuses on the ground that it is subrogated (4–407) to the rights of the payee who had a good claim against the drawer. Customer then sues bank for the amount of the check, and the court finds that the payee had no good cause of action, that the stop order was valid and permits recovery against the bank. As part of the same cause of action the customer sues for the wrongful dishonor of a series of checks that bank bounced after it had paid the one large check on which the stop order was issued. Assume that the parties stipulate that customer's damages for the dishonor of those checks (if wrongful) are $10,000. Here Comment 9 does its work. Under the rule of Comment 9, bank has no liability for the $10,000 even though its payment over the stop order proved to be improper, for—so the argument goes—it was entitled under Comment 9 to debit the customer's account until the customer established that payment over the stop order was improper. Customer on the other hand will argue that Comment 9 is not the law, that the subsequent dishonors were wrongful and that the bank is liable for such dishonors. What outcome did the draftsmen intend? They seem to have spoken out of both sides of their mouths. Their actions say that Comment 9 is no longer the law, for they removed it from the Code in the face of criticism, yet their words say that Comment 9 lives on. In these circumstances we would find the bank liable. Given that banks apparently had a large hand in drafting these sections, we would resolve ambiguities such as those posed in this case against them. However,

---

99. See 1 N.Y. State Law Revision Comm'n, 1954 Report 320 (1954) (Mr. Robert H. Brome); 1 id. at 444 (Mr. Walter Thomas for the New York Clearing House subcommittee on the UCC).

100. See 1 id. at 468 (1954) (Mr. Walter Malcolm).

101. See Uniform Commercial Code, 1952 Official Draft of Text and Comments 145 (Supp. No. 1 1955).

102. On this point the New York Revision Commission said:

Subsection (3) was disapproved in policy and also on the ground that it is ambiguous in providing that the burden of establishing "the fact and amount of loss" resulting from payment contrary to a stop-order is on the customer, in the absence of provisions under which the customer's recovery is for damages for breach of a duty of care. It was pointed out that where (as in New York) the bank's liability is merely on its debt as represented by the account without debiting the item that should not have been paid, the reference to burden of establishing loss is confusing, and that nothing in Article 4 would change the rule that liability is on the debt, not for breach of a duty of care.

N.Y. State Law Revision Comm'n, 1956 Report 430 (1956).

we confess uncertainty about this conclusion, for it leaves little substance to 4–403(3).

If the bank-customer litigation comes out the other way (by subrogation under 4–407 bank shows that its subrogee—payee or other holder—had a good cause of action against customer), Comment 9 is irrelevant. The bank as subrogor sustains its right to debit the account notwithstanding the stop order. Having sustained this right with respect to the first check, it follows that bank may dishonor checks subsequently presented against insufficient funds. This is so even if Comment 9 is not the law.

Whether one believes that Comment 9 is still the law, the foregoing discussion reveals the importance to the customer of the bank's decision to re-credit or not re-credit after paying over a stop order. The first job for the customer's lawyer should be to convince the bank to re-credit. Even if Comment 9 is the law, the bank cannot refuse to re-credit simply because of the way the customer parts his hair. Comment 9 states that bank has an obligation to re-credit when the customer establishes his loss "to the satisfaction of the bank". We would find that the customer "satisfies" the bank when he produces evidence that would satisfy a reasonably prudent banker exercising ordinary commercial judgment. To reiterate, the customer's lawyer should leave no stone unturned in attempting to get the bank to re-credit. If the bank agrees to re-credit, the customer will have the use of the funds during the ensuing negotiation and litigation with the payee and he may even convince the bank to litigate the issue at bank's expense.

If one rejects Comment 9 and finds that a bank must re-credit pending the outcome of litigation, what is the significance of 4–403 (3)? In Cicci v. Lincoln National Bank & Trust Co.,[103] a New York lower court considered the effect of subsection 4–403(3). A customer sued the bank for payment over a stop order. Lincoln defended on the ground that plaintiff suffered no loss as the result of payment. Citing 4–403(3) the court denied plaintiff's motion for summary judgment. Section 4–303(3) altered the pre-Code law that allowed a plaintiff to recover without alleging damage. Under that section, plaintiff must allege as part of his *prima facie* case that he suffered injury as the result of payment over the stop order. It is not sufficient merely to show that the customer's bank account was reduced by the amount of the check. As we read the *Cicci* case, the customer-drawer must at least allege that if the bank had followed the stop order, the drawer would have had a good defense against a suit by holder. We confess that our reading of 4–403(3) and of the *Cicci* case leaves very little if any scope for 4–403(3).

What Section 4–407 adds to 4–403(3) is not clear. If 4–403(3) means that for the customer to have a cause of action against his

103.   46 Misc.2d 465, 260 N.Y.S.2d 100,
2 UCC Rep.Serv. 1093 (City Ct.1965).

bank, the bank's failure to follow a valid stop order must be the cause of the customer's loss, then 4–407 adds little for it seems simply to restate that rule.   If the holder who received payment would have had a good cause of action against the customer had payment been stopped, then the bank's failure to follow the stop order would not be the cause of the customer's ultimate loss and the customer would lose its action against his bank under 4–403(3).   Section 4–407 would subrogate [104] the bank to the holder's cause of action against the customer-drawer and thus yield the same result in the same circumstances.   We are not certain how 4–403(3) and 4–407 fit together. Section 4–407 reads in full as follows:

> If a payor bank has paid an item over the stop payment order of the drawer or maker or otherwise under circumstances giving a basis for objection by the drawer or maker, to prevent unjust enrichment and only to the extent necessary to prevent loss to the bank by reason of its payment of the item, the payor bank shall be subrogated to the rights
>
> > (a) of any holder in due course on the item against the drawer or maker; and
> >
> > (b) of the payee or any other holder of the item against the drawer or maker either on the item or under the transaction out of which the item arose; and
> >
> > (c) of the drawer or maker against the payee or any other holder of the item with respect to the transaction out of which the item arose.

To see how section 4–407 works assume that Sam Spade agrees to sell a valuable object of art known as the Maltese Falcon to Sidney Greenstreet.   In payment Sid delivers his personal check for $20,000 (the fair market value of the Falcon) drawn on National Bank.   Sid attempts to doublecross Sam and stops payment on the check.   Subsequently Sam presents the check at National which cashes it over the stop order.   Sid demands that National re-credit his account and it refuses.   If Sid sues National for paying over his stop order, National can assert Sam's rights against Sid under subsection 4–407(b). In this case Sam could have enforced the instrument against Sid even if National had obeyed the stop order.[105]   The result is that payment over the stop order caused Sid no loss and he cannot recover from National.

---

**104.**   Comment 5 to section 4–407 makes it clear that the section does not preempt the bank's right to raise the defense of ratification against the customer or to seek restitution.   See Woodmere Cedarhurst Corp. v. Nat'l City Bank, 157 Misc. 660, 284 N.Y.S. 238 (App.Term 1935) (retention of full consideration for check with knowledge of payment constitutes ratification) (dictum); 1 N.Y. State Law Revision Comm'n, 1954 Report 364–68 (1954).

**105.**   Recall that a stop order under § 4–403 does not alter the drawer's liability to a holder.   Thus Sam could enforce the drawer's contract (§ 3–413 (2)) in a suit against Sid.   This assumes, of course, that Sid has no defense which defeats a holder (§ 3–305).

Assume on the other hand that Sam gives Sid a fake "Falcon". In this case Sid has a good defense against Sam (failure of consideration) [106] and the bank's subrogation rights are of no value. Accordingly National is liable for the amount of the loss resulting from payment over the stop order. However the fact that the customer has a legitimate complaint against the payee does not guarantee that he will recover against the bank for payment over a stop order. Suppose that instead of cashing the check at National, Sam deposits it in his account at State Bank and immediately draws checks on the funds deposited. Assume further that State presents Sid's check to National who pays it over the stop order. State qualifies as a holder in due course to the extent that it satisfies 3-302 and allows Sam to draw on the funds represented by Sid's check.[107] Unless he has real defenses, Sid cannot recover against National because 4-407(a) subrogates National to the rights of any holder in due course on the item.[108]

In the case of the fake "Falcon" Sid might persuade his bank to re-credit his account. Comment 3 to 4-407 explains that if the bank reimburses its customer, 4-407(c) authorizes the bank's recovery of that money from the payee or any other holder by asserting the drawer's rights. Note that under 3-418 the fact that the bank has made final payment does not bar the bank's recovery of payment made over a stop order.[109]

Finally consider a case in which bank pays in disregard of a valid stop order to one who is a holder in due course or a holder with a good cause of action against the drawer but who would not have sued the drawer had payment been stopped. Assume for example that the payee (who has received the proceeds of the check) lives in a distant state and would have sold the goods to a third party and forgotten the transaction if payment had been stopped. In such case

---

106. Even if Sam qualifies as a holder in due course (§ 3-302), he has "dealt with" Sid and thus cannot claim the protection of section 3-305. Section 3-306 states the defenses available against one who is not a holder in due course.

107. See §§ 4-209; 4-208(1) (a).

108. In Universal C. I. T. Credit Corp. v. Guaranty Bank & Trust Co., 161 F.Supp. 790, 1 UCC Rep.Serv. 305 (D. Mass.1958), a pre-Code case, Judge Wyzanski examined relevant Code provisions and ruled for defendant-bank on the ground that it was subrogated to a collecting bank which had become a holder in due course to the extent that the collecting bank had allowed its depositor to make withdrawals on plaintiff's check.

109. The introductory clause to 3-418 reads as follows:

Except for recovery of bank payments as provided in the Article on Bank Deposits and Collections (Article 4) . . . .

Since 3-418 only protects a holder in due course or one who in good faith relies upon payment, the bank does not need section 4-407(c) to recover against the thief who steals an order instrument or his transferee. The fact that under 4-407(c) and 3-418 bank can recover mistaken payment only from the payee or a holder means that in cases where a thief steals an order instrument and transfers it to one who relies in good faith on payment the bank cannot utilize 4-407 (c) to recover payment. Nevertheless, bank can recover for breach of warranty on presentment. §§ 3-417; 4-207.

bank can make a solid technical argument that it can utilize its subrogation rights regardless of the inclination of the person presenting the check.[110]   However if the theory behind section 4–407 is that the customer recovers to the extent that the bank's wrongful payment causes him injury,[111] the bank should not have the protection of that section in the case where its action is the cause of his injury.   Customer argues "if you had followed my stop order, my money would never have come into the hands of seller, and seller would have dropped the whole matter.   Because you failed to follow my stop order, he now has the money, and I cannot get it back from him.   Since he would not have come after me for the money you in fact 'caused' my loss."   Although the customer's argument has considerable appeal, we find no place for it in 4–407.   Rather 4–407 flatly grants the bank the right to assert the payee-seller's action for the price in this circumstance and so to free itself from any liability to its customer.   Those who feel compassion for the customer here should recall that the customer is trying to weasel out of a valid obligation to the seller.

The preamble to 4–407 provides that the section comes into play only in those cases where the bank has paid over the customer's stop order or where the customer otherwise has a "basis for objection".   Presumably the bank can invoke 4–407 every time the customer complains about payment of an item that was not "properly payable." [112]   The bank can take advantage of 4–407 subrogation rights "only to the extent necessary to prevent loss to the bank".   Comment 4 explains that the quoted language is intended to prevent the bank from obtaining a double recovery.   If, for example, the bank refused to recredit its customer's account (and therefore was out no money), it would not be subrogated to its customer's claim against the payee.   That bank would seek recovery in such circumstances seems improbable.   For an equally unimportant but substantially more involved discussion of the genealogy of the words "unjust enrichment" in 4–407, see the footnote.[113]

---

110.   Although the draftsmen clearly intended that the bank could resurrect the transaction and assert the payee's or holder's rights against the drawer, the Code does not provide a mechanism for that miracle.   Sections 3–603 and 3–802 discharge the drawer from his liability on the instrument and the underlying obligation when the bank pays the check.   One commentator suggests that the bank's improper payment does not discharge the drawer because it is not "*his* payment or satisfaction."   See J. Clarke, H. Bailey & R. Young, Bank Deposits and Collections 159 (3d ed. 1963).

111.   See Lang v. Chase Manhattan Bank, 6 UCC Rep.Serv. 1259 (N.Y. Sup.Ct.1969) (action by customer against bank; bank's impleader of car dealer, whose breach of warranty was cause of customer's stop order, was proper).

112.   For a discussion of 4–401 and the meaning of "properly payable," see Section 17–3 supra.

113.   The meaning of the phrase "to prevent unjust enrichment" is not entirely clear.   One might construe the preamble as requiring unjust enrichment as a prerequisite to the bank's assertion of its subrogation rights.   See Commercial Ins. Co. v. Scalamandre, 4 UCC Rep.Serv. 956 (N.Y.Civ.Ct. 1967) (payee-defendant's motion for summary judgment granted when plaintiff failed to allege unjust en-

In sum, 4–407 is hardly a remarkable provision. For the most part one can understand its operation after he has studied it a bit and has considered the cases in which the bank will wish to be subrogated to the rights of its customer-drawer or to those of a holder of a check it has improperly paid.

## § 17–7 Priorities in the Customer's Bank Account, 4–303

Since a check is not an assignment of customer's funds but merely represents the customer's order upon his bank to pay a certain sum to the order of a certain person or bearer, the holder is not legally entitled to have the drawee honor the check upon presentment.[114]  Of

richment or that drawer had right to refuse payment). However, under that construction, 4–407 begins to sound like "Catch 22": "The bank must show unjust enrichment before it can assert subrogation rights. The bank can show unjust enrichment only by asserting its subrogation rights." If the draftsmen did not mean that unjust enrichment was a prerequisite to subrogation, then what did they mean?

The geneology of 4–407 reveals that the unjust enrichment language first appears in a comment to the May, 1949 Draft of the Code. Comment 8 to section 3–415 (May 1949 Draft) read in part:

A payment in violation of an effective direction to stop payment is an improper payment, even though it is made by mistake or inadvertence, and it may not be charged to the drawer's account. Any agreement to the contrary is invalid under Subsection (4). The drawee is, however, entitled to subrogation to prevent unjust enrichment.

The phrase "unjust enrichment" first appears in the statutory text in 4–402(4) of the Spring, 1950 Draft which read:

To prevent unjust enrichment a payor bank which has paid an item drawn or made by a customer and which it may not charge to his account may in an action

(a) against the holder who has received payment recover any part of the payment due its customer or any prior party in respect of the transaction in which the customer of the depositary bank acquired the item; and

(b) against its customer recover any amount which would have been due from him on the item if payment had been refused.

The bank has no right to charge the customer's account in respect of such cause of action. The bank may bring either or both such actions but may have only one satisfaction and any right to consequential or punitive damages remains with the customer or holder.

The section quoted above makes it clear that 4–407 was originally drafted on the premise that a bank which paid an item over a stop order could not debit its customer's account. As originally drafted, the section contemplated that the bank would sue the drawer, payee, or holder to recover such payment. In the words of Mr. Leary, the original draftsman of Article Four, "[T]he obvious justification is the prevention of unjust enrichment at the expense of the payor bank who may be deemed to have paid out its own funds." Leary, Check Handling Under Article Four of the UCC, 49 Marq.L.Rev. 331, 367 (1965).

It appears that the draftsmen's viewpoint changed considerably between the Spring, 1951 Draft and the Official Draft promulgated in 1952. The present version of 4–407 repeats the 1952 version. The section contemplates that the bank will use its subrogation rights primarily to defend against a suit by the customer to recover payment. This approach reflects the assumption that a bank who pays over a stop order can legitimately charge its customer's account.

Despite this change in approach, the unjust enrichment language remains. We conclude the phrase at best states the purpose of the section, and at worst it adds meaningless confusion.

114. See § 3–409.

course, the drawee will normally honor. But between the time the check is issued and the time it is presented for payment a variety of things might interfere with the normal payment procedure. For instance, the customer may change his mind and countermand the order (stop payment). Alternatively the drawee may dishonor the check because the customer's creditors have seized the funds in the account to satisfy debts owed them. Section 4–303 provides a rule to settle the rights of the holder of a check demanding payment when certain events intervene to prevent payment from the drawer's account. These events, known to the *cognoscenti* as the "four legals," include: (*1*) knowledge or notice of the customer's death, incompetency or bankruptcy; (*2*) the customer's stop order; (*3*) legal process (for example, garnishment); (*4*) setoff by the payor bank.

The effect of each of the "four legals" is to draw off customer's funds and so prevent normal payment of checks drawn on the customer's account. Elsewhere we have discussed the Code provisions governing the customer's stop orders [115] and the effect of the customer's death or adjudication of incompetency.[116] Setoff and garnishment against an account are actions by the customer's creditors to utilize the funds on deposit to satisfy his debts. In the case of setoff the bank is the creditor. Suppose, for example, that a checking account customer also obtains a loan from the bank to purchase a new car. If the customer defaults on the loan, the bank can repossess the car or it might choose the course of least resistance and apply any funds in the account against his debt.[117] In essence the bank sets off its debt to the customer (the funds in the account) against the debt owed by the customer (the promissory note).

Creditors other than the bank reach funds in the customer's account by means of garnishment. Garnishment may be available to the creditor before judgment; it will almost always be available after judgment.[118] Typically the garnishee process is issued upon the creditor's affidavit and service is made by the sheriff or a party upon the bank.[119] The writ orders the garnishee (bank) to disclose any

---

115. See Section 17–6 supra.

116. See Section 17–3 supra.

117. The bank set off a debt owed by its customer in the following cases: Olsen v. Valley Nat'l Bank, 91 Ill.App. 2d 365, 234 N.E.2d 547, 5 UCC Rep. Serv. 268 (1968); Frank Briscoe Co. v. Suburban Trust Co., 100 N.J.Super. 431, 242 A.2d 54, 5 UCC Rep.Serv. 271 (App.Div.1968); Pines Trailer Corp. v. Roaring Express Co., 127 Ill. App.2d 46, 261 N.E.2d 709, 8 UCC Rep. Serv. 90 (1970).

118. For a discussion of the availability of pre-judgment garnishment or attachment, see S. Riesenfeld, Cases

and Material on Creditors' Remedies and Debtors' Protection 177–83 (1967).

119. For example, Michigan General Court Rule 738.2 states the grounds for issuance of a writ of garnishment. The rule reads as follows:

After an action has been commenced or after any judgment, the clerk of [*sic*] court shall issue a writ of garnishment if the plaintiff or some person on his behalf makes and files in the case an affidavit stating that

(1) the principal defendant is indebted to the plaintiff in a stated amount upon a contract or judgmen over and above all setoffs, and

assets of the debtor in its possession and compels it to hold such assets on pain of personal liability to the creditor.[120]

A customer's bankruptcy disrupts payment of checks because under section 70a of the Bankruptcy Act [121] the trustee takes title to the unencumbered assets of the bankrupt. Thus a trustee might argue under the Bankruptcy Act that bankruptcy froze the customer's account and that regardless of notice the payor was accountable for checks paid after that time.

At this point it should be apparent that each situation involving one of the four legals presents a potential priority dispute between the holder of a check who demands payment and the third party who claims funds in the account. Like priority provisions of Article Nine, section 4–303 sets forth the old rule: first in time, first in right. If the legal arrives at the payor bank *after* the bank has performed one of the steps ("milestones") in the payment process of a check, then the legal cannot interfere with payment of that check. Section 4–303(1) reads as follows:

> Any knowledge, notice or stop-order received by, legal process served upon or setoff exercised by a payor bank, whether or not effective under other rules of law to terminate, suspend or modify the bank's right or duty to pay an item or to charge its customer's account for the item, comes too late to so terminate, suspend or modify such right or duty if the knowledge, notice, stop-order or legal process is received or served and a reasonable time for the bank to act thereon expires or the setoff is exercised after the bank had done any of the following:
>
> (a) accepted or certified the item;
>
> (b) paid the item in cash;
>
> (c) settled for the item without reserving a right to revoke the settlement and without having such right under statute, clearing house rule or agreement;
>
> (d) completed the process of posting the item to the indicated account of the drawer, maker or other person to be charged therewith or otherwise has evidenced by

(2) the deponent knows or has good reason to believe that

(a) a named person has possession or control of property, money, goods, chattels, credits, negotiable instruments, or effects belonging to the principal defendant, or

(b) a named person is indebted to the principal defendant, and stating further whether or not the indebtedness of a named person is on account of labor performed by the principal defendant, and

(3) the plaintiff is justly apprehensive of the loss of his claim against the defendant unless a writ of garnishment is issued and setting forth the facts in support of this claim.

120. See S. Riesenfeld, Cases and Material on Creditors' Remedies and Debtors' Protection 177–83 (1967).

121. Bankruptcy Act § 70(a) (5), 11 U. S.C.A. § 110(a) (5) (1970).

examination of such indicated account and by action its decision to pay the item; or

(e) become accountable for the amount of the item under subsection (1) (d) of Section 4–213 and Section 4–302 dealing with the payor bank's responsibility for late return of items.

Stated briefly, as between one of the four legals and a specific check, the one to get to the bank first is entitled to the funds in the account. Note that the quoted section bears a strong similarity to 4–213. Note too, as we will point out below, it is significantly different from 4–213.

To determine priority in the bank account as between the owner of a check and the conflicting legal, the lawyer must first pinpoint the two relevant events. If any of the events ("milestones") listed in 4–303 has occurred with respect to the check before the effective time of the conflicting legal, the check wins. If, on the other hand, the legal becomes effective before any of the events in 4–303 occur, the legal wins. Thus the lawyer must ask two questions: (1) What was the effective time of the legal; for example, When did garnishment occur? When did bank get notice of bankruptcy? and (2) As of that time had any of the events in 4–303 occurred?

### Timing of the Legals

In the case of stop orders and notice of customer's death or adjudication of incompetency, the Code supplies the criteria for determining the effective time of the legal. Section 1–201(25) defines "notice" and "knowledge" and section 1–201(27) provides, in part:

Notice, knowledge or a notice or notification received by an organization is effective for a particular transaction from the time it is brought to the attention of the individual conducting that transaction, and in any event from the time when it would have been brought to his attention if the organization had exercised due diligence. . . .

Thus in the case where the bank designates a particular person to handle stop orders the legal is effective (at the latest) in a reasonable time after it is communicated to that person. Note too that the time begins to run from the point at which that person should have known about the facts in question and one could certainly argue that knowledge on behalf of certain other responsible but undesignated parties (for example, a branch manager) should also cause the time to run.

Garnishment is a statutory remedy and one must consult local state statutes to determine when the garnishment is effective.[122]

---

122. In some jurisdictions garnishment is effective against indebtedness existing at the time of the garnishee's answer as well as the time of

Some states have statutes specifying the proper procedure for garnishing a bank account,[123] while other state statutes merely provide that garnishment is governed by the same rules that govern service of process.[124] Typically, the latter statutes require only that the party serve a corporate officer.

Section 70(a) of the Bankruptcy Act[125] provides that the trustee in bankruptcy is vested with title to the unencumbered assets of the bankrupt. In Bank of Marin v. England,[126] the trustee

the service of the writ of garnishment. See, e. g., Texas Civ.Prac. Rule 666 which reads in part:

If it appears from the answer of the garnishee that he is not indebted to the defendant, and was not so indebted when the writ of garnishment was served upon him, and that he has not in his possession any effects of the defendant and had not when the writ was served . . . [and] should the answer of the garnishee not be controverted as hereinafter provided, the court shall enter judgment discharging the garnishee. In other jurisdictions garnishment is effective solely as of the time of the service of the writ of garnishment.

See, e. g., Ill.Ann.Stat. ch. 62, § 39(b) (Smith-Hurd 1971) which provides:

The garnishee shall file, on or before the return date, or within the further time that the court for cause may allow, a written answer under oath to the interrogatories, setting forth as of the date of service of the garnishment summons (1) any indebtedness due or to become due to the judgment debtor and (2) any other property in his possession, custody or control (a) belonging to the judgment debtor or (b) in which the judgment debtor has an interest.

See generally S. Riesenfeld, Cases and Materials on Creditors' Remedies and Debtors' Protection 160 n. 2 (1967).

123. For example, the California attachment statute, Cal.Civ.Pro.Code § 542(5) (West Supp.1971), provides in part:

However, debts owing to the defendant by any of the following financial institutions: (a) banks; (b) savings and loan associations; . . . maintaining branch offices, or credits or other personal property whether or not the same is capable of manual delivery, belonging to the defendant and in the possession of or under the control of such financial institution shall

be attached by leaving a copy of the writ and the notice, together with a copy of the complaint if required hereunder, with the manager or other officer of such financial institution at the office or branch thereof at which the account evidencing such indebtedness of the defendant is carried, or at which such financial institution has credits or other personal property belonging to the defendant in its possession or under its control; and no attachment shall be effective as to any debt owing by such financial institution if the account evidencing such indebtedness is carried at an office or branch thereof not so served, or as to any credits or other personal property in its possession or under its control at any office or branch thereof not so served.

124. For example, Michigan General Court Rule 738.4(1) reads as follows:

The writ of garnishment shall be served on the garnishee in the manner provided for the service of summons and complaint in Rule 105. A fee of $1 shall be tendered to the garnishee at the time of such service.

125. Bankruptcy Act § 70(a) (5), 11 U. S.C.A. § 110(a) (5) (1970):

The trustee of the estate of a bankrupt and his successor or successors, if any, upon his or their appointment and qualification, shall in turn be vested by operation of law with the title of the bankrupt as of the date of the filing of the petition initiating a proceeding . . . * * *

(5) property including rights of action, which prior to the filing of the petition he could by any means have transferred or which might have been levied upon and sold under judicial process against him, or otherwise seized, impounded, or sequestered . . . .

126. 385 U.S. 99 (1966).

argued that when the customer filed a voluntary petition in bankruptcy, this froze his bank account so that the payor was liable for any checks paid after that time. The case involved checks drawn before filing of the petition but which were presented for payment after filing. The bank paid the checks without knowledge or notice of its customer's bankruptcy. The district court and the court of appeals ruled that the payor bank and the payee were jointly liable to the trustee. However, the Supreme Court reversed and said that the commencement of bankruptcy proceedings without notice to the payor did not revoke its authority to pay checks drawn on the bankrupt's account. Further, the court read the explicit language of section 70 of the Bankruptcy Act in light of equitable principles to avoid what it called the harsh result of holding the payor liable for checks paid without notice of the customer's bankruptcy. Critics have attacked [127] Justice Douglas' opinion in *Bank of Marin* as contrary to congressional intent. Whatever one thinks of this criticism, the decision makes the federal bankruptcy law and 4–303 consistent. That is, notice of bankruptcy is one of the "notices" with which 4–303 is concerned. The rule in 4–303 is that a check which passes one of the 4–303 milestones before "notice" of bankruptcy takes precedence over the trustee's rights to the account. Had the *Bank of Marin* case come out the other way, the 4–303 rule would have been upset and the trustee would have had a prior claim on the account from the date of filing the petition. As we read *Bank of Marin*, notice of bankruptcy is now like any other notice and one may safely analyze the trustee's rights under 4–303 and deny his claim as to any amounts in the bankrupt's bank account attributable to checks that passed a 4–303 milestone before bank received notice of the bankruptcy.[128]

Note that the "legals" discussed above (notice, stop-order or legal process) do not become effective upon bank's receipt of notice but only after the passage of "a reasonable time for the bank to act" on the notice. In other words if customer telephones a stop-order at 9:00 a. m. and the holder cashes the check over the counter at 9:15 a. m., the check would win because it was cashed before the bank had a reasonable time to act upon the stop-order. Just what constitutes a reasonable time is an open question. Presumably the answer turns on banking practices in the particular community. Our examination of one bank's practices showed that a bank with five to ten branches serving a community of 100,000 expected to be able to notify all tellers and all bookkeeping departments of a stop-order in less than four hours. Where the stop-order indicated that the check had been given to a local payee and was apt to be presented

127. See, e. g., 4A Collier on Bankruptcy ¶ 70.68 at 755 (14th ed. 1971); Holahan & Fisch, Post-Bankruptcy Payment of Checks: Bank of Marin v. England, 28 U.Pitt.L.Rev. 579 (1967).

128. We believe the rationale of the opinion applies equally to the case where the bankrupt draws checks *after* the petition is filed and the payor cashes them without knowledge or notice of the bankruptcy.

immediately, one bank had a special procedure for notifying its tellers within one hour.

A bank has two methods by which it may exercise its right to set-off customer's debt against the funds in his account. It may accomplish the setoff by simply making a bookkeeping entry or by requiring customer to draw checks payable to bank against the account in the amount of the setoff. In either case the setoff is effective when the bank makes the entry or takes the checks.[129] Note that in the case where bank takes customer's checks, subsection 4–303(2) permits bank to charge those checks in "any order convenient to the bank". Presumably this language authorizes bank to pay setoff checks to itself ahead of those payable to others.[130]

### 4–303 Milestones

After establishing the effective time of the legal, the next and more difficult task is to determine whether the competing check has passed one of the milestones in the payment process listed in 4–303. If any of the enumerated events occurs before the legal arrives (or in an appropriate case before the bank has a reasonable opportunity to act upon the legal) the check wins. Some will find the following discussion not up to our usual high standards of clarity and wit; we suggest that those unfamiliar with the general mechanics of the check collection process grit their teeth and hold on.

The events listed in subsection 4–303(1) (a) (certification) and 4–303(1) (b) (cash payment) are everyday events. If the bank has paid the check in cash out of the teller's window, no one would suggest that a subsequent legal could have any effect upon that check.[131] Similarly if the drawee bank has certified the check by signing it or stamping it, the bank has become liable for payment [132] and a subsequent legal directed at the customer's account cannot interfere with the bank's discharge of its obligation.

Two of the criteria listed in 4–303 focus on the payor bank's settlement for the check. Subsection 4–303(1) (c) covers settlement without the right to revoke and subsection 4–303(1) (e) covers

**129.** See Peoples State Bank v. Caterpillar Tractor Co., 213 Ind. 235, 12 N.E.2d 123 (1938); cf. Steinbrecher v. Fairfield County Trust Co., 5 Conn. Cir. 393, 255 A.2d 138, 6 UCC Rep.Serv. 703 (1968).

**130.** See Merchant v. Worley, 79 N.M. 771, 449 P.2d 787, 5 UCC Rep.Serv. 1255 (Ct.App.1969) (dishonor of draft not wrongful when bank set off checks issued to it prior to presentation of draft).

**131.** In Kirby v. First & Merchants Nat'l Bank, 210 Va. 88, 168 S.E.2d 273, 6 UCC Rep.Serv. 694 (1969), the court ruled that the payor had made final payment when it "cashed" a $2,-500 check by giving $200 in cash and a $2300 credit to payee's account. The court concluded on the basis of the deposit slip and a bank officer's testimony that the bank had given the payee $2500 in cash and then accepted a $2300 deposit. We are not persuaded by the majority's opinion. We believe that the dissent's view of the facts reflect the reality of the situation. See Section 16–4 note 29, supra.

**132.** See §§ 3–410; 3–411; 3–413(1), discussed in Section 13–8 supra.

cases in which the payor bank makes provisional settlement but fails to revoke it within a specified time.  Subsection 4–104(1) (j) [133] defines the term "settle" and Comment 6 to that section explains that one may settle for an item in a variety of ways:

> Examples of the various types of settlement contemplated by the term include payments in cash; the efficient but somewhat complicated process of payment through the adjustment and offsetting of balances through clearing houses; debit or credit entries in accounts between banks; the forwarding of various types of remittance instruments, sometimes to cover a particular item but more frequently to cover an entire group of items received on a particular day.

Subsection 4–303(1) (c) provides that a milestone has been passed if the bank has:

> settled for the item without reserving a right to revoke the settlement and without having such right under statute, clearing house rule or agreement

For a variety of reasons it will be most unusual for a bank to settle "without reserving a right to revoke."  When it has such right to revoke either under the Code, under a clearing house rule or under an agreement with the presenter, the check does not win the priority race unless one of the events discussed in 4–303(1) (e) has preceded the legal.  Section 4–303(1) (e) reads as follows:

> [The legal comes too late if the bank has]
>
> (e) become accountable for the amount of the item under subsection (1) (d) of Section 4–213 and Section 4–302 dealing with the payor bank's responsibility for late return of items.

In the interest of clarity if not absolute precision we oversimplify the problem slightly [134] by referring directly to 4–213(1) (d), which

---

133.  Section 4–104(1) (j) reads as follows:

In this Article unless the context otherwise requires * * *

(j) "Settle" means to pay in cash, by clearing house settlement, in a charge or credit or by remittance, or otherwise as instructed.  A settlement may be either provisional or final;

* * *

134.  The analysis of 4–303(1) (e) in the text fails to take into account Section 4–302, which states certain situations where the payor becomes accountable for an item.  Section 4–302(a) reads:

In the absence of a valid defense such as breach of a presentment warranty

(subsection (1) of Section 4–207), settlement effected or the like, if an item is presented on and received by a payor bank the bank is accountable for the amount of a demand item other than a documentary draft whether properly payable or not if the bank, in any case where it is not also the depositary bank, retains the item beyond midnight of the banking day of receipt without settling for it or, regardless of whether it is also the depositary bank, does not pay or return the item or send notice of dishonor until after its midnight deadline . . .

Section 4–302 is likely to come into play only in that rare case where a nondepositary bank (§ 4–105) fails to make settlement by midnight of the

4–303(1) (e) incorporates by reference. It provides that a bank has made final payment when it has "made a provisional settlement for the item and failed to revoke the settlement in the time and manner permitted by statute, clearing house rule or agreement".

To maintain at least a perilous grip on the real-life transactions that underly the operations of 4–303(1) (c) and (e), consider the following hypothetical: On Tuesday morning depositary bank sends a check to payor bank through the Chicago Federal Reserve. Each maintains an account at the Chicago Federal Reserve and the reserve credits the depositary bank with the amount of the check and debits the account of the payor bank in a corresponding amount. Thus payor provisionally settles with the depositary bank. Since the payor has a right to revoke that settlement under 4–301 [135] until its midnight deadline (that is, midnight of the next business day after it receives the item), and may have a right to revoke under a Federal Reserve rule [136] as well, payor will not have passed any of

day of receipt (e. g., depositary bank mails check to payor). Imposition of accountability under 4–302 for payor's failure to meet the midnight deadline is superfluous, because failure to meet the midnight deadline constitutes final payment under 4–213(1) (d) and 4–301. The last sentence in section 4–213(1) states that the payor becomes accountable upon final payment.

135. Section 4–301(1) provides:

(1) Where an authorized settlement for a demand item (other than a documentary draft) received by a payor bank otherwise than for immediate payment over the counter has been made before midnight of the banking day of receipt the payor bank may revoke the settlement and recover any payment if before it has made final payment (subsection (1) of Section 4–213) and before its midnight deadline it

(a) returns the item; or

(b) sends written notice of dishonor or nonpayment if the item is held for protest or is otherwise unavailable for return.

Note that 4–301 is unavailable to a payor which is not also a depositary bank (§ 4–105) unless the payor settles for the item by midnight of the day of receipt.

Section 4–104(1) (h) defines midnight deadline as follows:

"Midnight deadline" with respect to a bank is midnight on its next banking day following the banking day on which it receives the relevant item or notice or from which the time for taking action commences to run, whichever is later.

However, a local clearing house rule might extend the time for return of a check. See West Side Bank v. Marine Nat'l Exchange Bank, 37 Wis.2d 661, 155 N.W.2d 587, 4 UCC Rep.Serv. 1003 (1968) (bank returned check after midnight deadline but within clearing house deadline and before completing process of posting).

136. Regulation J, "Return of Cash Items," 12 C.F.R. § 210.12 (1971), provides in part:

(a) A paying bank which receives a cash item from or through a Federal Reserve bank, otherwise than for immediate payment over the counter, shall, unless it returns such item unpaid before midnight of the banking day of receipt, either pay or remit therefor on the banking day of receipt, or, if acceptable to the Federal Reserve bank concerned, authorize or cause payment or remittance therefor to be made by debit to an account on the books of the Federal Reserve bank not later than the banking day for such Federal Reserve bank on which any other acceptable form of timely payment or remittance would have been received by the Federal Reserve bank in the ordinary course; provided that such paying bank shall have the right to recover any payment or remittance so made if, before it has finally paid the item, it returns the item before midnight of its banking

the milestones under 4–303 on Tuesday morning. The check does not qualify under 4–303(1) (c) because there is still a right to revoke; payor has not yet "become accountable" under 4–303(1) (e) and 4–213(1) (d) until its midnight deadline passes causing the provisional settlement at the Chicago Federal Reserve to become final. When payor's 4–301 right to revoke with the Federal Reserve runs out on Wednesday midnight (and assuming no Federal Reserve rule gives it a longer time to revoke) the bank becomes accountable under 4–213(1) (d) and thus passes the 4–303(1) (e) milestone. Thus any garnishment notice, etc., presented to the payor bank after midnight Wednesday will lose to the check for the check now fits 4–303(1) (e).

We can play out a similar scenario with respect to a settlement made in a local clearing house. In such case presenter and payor will trade checks; each in effect credits the other with the amount of the checks so presented. Under the clearing house rules the parties will only be settling provisionally, and each will have the right to return the checks one or two days later if it develops that they are NSF, subject to stop orders or otherwise not properly payable. In such case (and assuming no compliance with 4–303(1) (d)), the checks will not comply with any of the provisions under 4–303(1) until the time has passed when the payor could no longer return them and undo the credit. This time will be the midnight deadline (or perhaps a day or two beyond under local rules).

The lawyer should consider whether the payor settled without having a right to revoke the settlement, but it will be an unusual case in which the payor settles without such right. If the payor has the right to revoke, either under the Code (for example, 4–301) or clearing house rule or through an agreement with the presenter, the lawyer's job is to cross-examine his client to find the facts with respect to the check in question, examine all pertinent agreements and the Code, and thus determine the last time at which the bank could revoke the settlement it made. That time is the milestone under 4–303(1) (e) against which the lawyer must measure garnishments, notices, etc.

So far we have discussed final settlement and provisional settlement without considering the internal workings of the payor bank. Subsection 4–303(1) (d) is probably the most important criterion in section 4–303 and certainly the most difficult one to pinpoint. It provides in effect that a legal comes too late if the check has already passed through the bulk of the payor's internal payment

day next following the banking day of receipt or takes such other action to recover such payment or remittance within such time and by such means as may be provided by applicable State law; and further provided that the foregoing provisions shall not extend, nor shall the time herein provided for return be extended by, the time for return of unpaid items fixed by the rules and practices of any clearing house through which the item was presented or fixed by the provisions of any special collection agreement pursuant to which it was presented.

procedures when the legal arrives. Subsection 4–303(1) (d) reads as follows (emphasis added):

> [The legal "comes too late" if the payor has]
>
> (d) completed the process of posting the item to the indicated account of the drawer, maker or other person to be charged therewith *or* otherwise has evidenced by examination of such indicated account and by action its decision to pay the item.

The subsection establishes two separate, but related criteria for determining priority: (*1*) completion of the process of posting and (*2*) examination followed by action that evidences a decision to pay. If either has occurred before the legal arrives, the legal loses.

> Section 4–109 defines the "process of posting" as follows:
>
> The "process of posting" means the usual procedure followed by a payor bank in determining to pay an item and in recording the payment including one or more of the following or other steps as determined by the bank:
>
> (a) verification of any signature;
>
> (b) ascertaining that sufficient funds are available;
>
> (c) affixing a "paid" or other stamp;
>
> (d) entering a charge or entry to a customer's account;
>
> (e) correcting or reversing an entry or erroneous action with respect to the item.

The process of posting requirement in 4–303(1) (d) is identical to the requirement in 4–213(1) (c). As we have said above in Section 16–4, we would find that a payor bank has always completed the process of posting when it has examined the computer print-out (showing the status of the account), found it to be in order, examined the check and found it to be in order, and taken some other action with respect to the account that shows the decision has been made (for example, stamping the check "paid"). As we noted above, our interpretation of the meaning of the process of posting differs from that of the Wisconsin Supreme Court.[137] Those who disagree with our interpretation of the "process of posting" language may still find that the check achieved priority under the last two clauses of 4–303(1) (d) because the bank "has evidenced by examination of such indicated account and by action its decision to pay the item . . . ." Assume for example that one concludes (erroneously in our judgment) that the process of posting requires that the midnight deadline pass or that the bank take every conceivable step with respect to the check (for example, stamping, cancelling, and placing in the customer's file), he can still conclude short of the midnight deadline and short of the final filing of the check that the bank has "evidenced by examination" and "by action" its decision to pay the item. If he so finds, the

---

137. See West Side Bank v. Marine Nat'l Exchange Bank, 37 Wis.2d 661,    155 N.W.2d 587, 4 UCC Rep.Serv. 1003 (1968), discussed in Section 16–4 supra.

check wins a priority dispute with any legal that becomes effective after the examination and action.

One post-Code case is directly in point, West Side Bank v. Marine National Exchange Bank.[138]   Although that case presents the archtype 4–303(1) (d) priority dispute, the court did not discuss 4–303(1) (d).   West Side presented a check to Marine through the clearing house on Friday morning.   On the same day Marine put the check through the computer and the computer sorted and coded, stamped the check and charged the drawer's account.   On Monday the bookkeeper received the computer print-out showing sufficient funds in the drawer's account to pay, and cancelled, photographed and placed the check in the drawer's file.   Later on Monday the drawer ordered payment stopped and Marine withdrew the check from the customer's file and returned the check to West Side on Tuesday.   West Side sued Marine on the theory that Marine had completed the process of posting and had thus become accountable for the check before the stop order was given.   Marine argued that subsection 4–109(e) allowed it to reverse any entry whether correct or erroneous and that the process of posting had never been completed until the opportunity for such decision to correct or reverse had passed.   The Wisconsin Supreme Court accepted Marine's literal application of section 4–109(e).   Although the court saw validity in the contrary argument, and conceded that its interpretation of 4–213(1) (c) and (d) would render 4–213 (1) (c) superfluous, the court felt compelled to give effect to the "plain meaning" of the statute.

We believe the court should have found that the payor had completed the process of posting.   We agree with draftsman Malcolm that 4–109(e) was designed for other cases and that the draftsmen intended that the process be completed at the latest when the check is placed in the file to be returned to the depositor.[139]   In our judgment the court made an even more grievous error in analyzing the case under 4–213 and not under 4–303(1) (d).   Had the court analyzed the case under 4–303(1) (d) as a priority dispute, it could have relied on the second part of (1) (d) and held that although the process of posting had not been completed, the payor bank had nevertheless "evidenced by examination and by action" its decision to pay the item long before the stop order was presented.

Comment 3 to 4–303 identifies the *Nineteenth Ward Bank* case [140] as the genesis of the final clause in 4–303(1) (d).   The draftsman explained the process by which the criteria were devised as follows:

> Framed in this background Section 4–303(1) specified the two criteria of priority turning on "payment" of the item. Of these, some consideration was given to specifying only

138.   37 Wis.2d 661, 155 N.W.2d 587, 4 UCC Rep.Serv. 1003 (1968).

139.   See Malcolm, Reflections on West Side Bank: A Draftsman's View, 18 Catholic U.L.Rev. 23, 31–33 (1968).

140.   Nineteenth Ward Bank v. First Nat'l Bank, 184 Mass. 49, 67 N.E. 670 (1903).

posting. However, this language would not be broad enough to cover the factual situation of the *Nineteenth Ward Bank* case itself or practices growing out of it, as for instance so-called "sight posting", where the bookkeeper for the drawer's account examines an item and determines there are sufficient funds in his account to pay it but under the routines of some banks, does not immediately post. Therefore, the final standard or test that the payor bank has "otherwise evidenced by action its decision to pay the item" was added. It is clear, however, that this action *must be closely related to the decision of the appropriate employee that there are sufficient funds to pay the item*, not mere receipting for the item in a passbook or other preliminary acts in no way related to a true decision to pay.[141]

The court in Yandell v. White City Amusement Park, Inc.[142] applied the final clause of subsection 4–303(1) (d). In that case a garnishor served the payor bank with a writ of garnishment on August 1, and the bank responded that it held $246 in defendant's name. Plaintiff claimed that the account contained considerably more than $246. The court found that on July 29 the payor bank received checks drawn on defendant's account for approximately $8,000. Although the checks were not machine posted until August 2, the payor's bookkeeper examined the account to determine whether it contained sufficient funds, made a penciled notation next to the current balance to indicate commitment of that amount, stamped the checks and initialed them on July 29. The court concluded that these acts satisfied the final clause of subsection 4–303(1) (d) and held that the garnishor could not reach the funds covered by those checks.

In conclusion the student and lawyer should not let 4–303 and 4–213 intimidate them. When the holder of a check on the one hand, and a third party on the other (for example, a trustee in bankruptcy, a garnishor or the like) make conflicting claims to funds in a bank account, the lawyer should turn to 4–303. If he bears in mind that the section is simply a priority statute and that he need only check out his facts, he will often find that 4–303 yields a certain and precise answer to priority conflict. Sometimes the lawyer will have to determine when notice to the bank became effective (because of the passage of a reasonable time), but aside from that difficulty he will usually be able to narrow the area of factual dispute to manageable proportions. Of course if his client is not the payor bank and if the bank's interests are in conflict with those of his client, he may have a mean task of digging the appropriate facts out of the bank employees on depositions, but that is a routine, if difficult, problem that lawyers must often face anyway. At minimum we hope courts and lawyers will not follow the lead of the Wisconsin Supreme Court but will turn to the most appropriate statutory provision to govern such disputes: 4–303.

141.   Malcolm, Article 4—A Battle With Complexity, 1952 Wis.L.Rev. 265, 294.

142.   232 F.Supp. 582, 2 UCC Rep.Serv. 205 (D.Mass.1964).

# CHAPTER 18

# LETTERS OF CREDIT

*Analysis*

**Sec.**

18–1. Introduction.

18–2. Legal Nature of the Letter of Credit.

18–3. Relevant Sources of Law and Freedom of Contract.

18–4. Setting up a Valid Irrevocable Letter of Credit Arrangement Pursuant to Article Five; Valid and Invalid Terms; Variation by Agreement; Time the Credit Becomes "Established".

18–5. An Inventory of Ways that a Valid, Irrevocable, and Established Letter of Credit Arrangement May Breakdown or Otherwise Go Astray.

18–6. Actual or Prospective Breakdowns Adversely Affecting the Beneficiary in the First Instance (Herein mainly of issuer's wrongful dishonor).

18–7. Actual or Prospective Breakdowns Adversely Affecting the Customer in the First Instance (Herein mainly of issuer's wrongful honor, and of beneficiary nonperformance of the underlying contract).

18–8. Actual or Prospective Breakdowns Adversely Affecting the Issuer (Herein mainly of wrongful honor).

18–9. Transfer and Assignment of Letters of Credit and Rights Thereunder; Back to Back Credits (Letters of credit as financing devices).

## § 18–1  Introduction

While today letters of credit [1] have important domestic uses,[2] they originated in international trade and continue in wide use there.  To illustrate: American buyer in Newark, New Jersey wants to buy furniture manufactured by Danish seller in Copenhagen.  Buyer sends a proposal to seller in which nothing is said about payment terms.  In reply, seller says that he will not sell on open credit, and buyer responds that he will not pay seller in advance.  Buyer then suggests a "documentary sale" by which buyer would pay "cash against documents," that is, when seller's American agent tenders documents of title covering the goods to buyer, plus a "sight draft" calling on buyer to pay "at sight," buyer would have to pay then and there, even though the goods themselves were still *en route*.

Seller then counters with a proposal that payment be made via a letter of credit.  To understand why seller might counter in this way, it is necessary to delve more deeply into payment via a "documentary sale," for the letter of credit modifies and reinforces that mode of payment.

---

1. Among the leading treatises on letters of credit are H. Gutteridge & M. Megrah, The Law of Bankers' Commercial Credits (4th ed. 1968), B.  Kozalchyk, Commercial Letters of Credit in the Americas (1966), and W. Ward & H. Harfield, Bank Credits and Acceptances (4th ed. 1958).

In the agreed documentary sale the Danish seller would put the goods on board a carrier and receive a negotiable "bill of lading" from the carrier drawn to seller's order. The title to the goods would thus be locked up in this bill of lading (a "document of title") [3], and if the carrier should later deliver the goods to anyone other than the holder of this piece of paper, the carrier would be liable for misdelivery. With the bill of lading in hand seller would then draw a sight draft to his own order showing buyer as drawee and directing buyer to pay the draft "at sight", that is, upon presentment. Seller would thereafter pin the draft to the negotiable bill of lading (and possibly other documents) and mail these papers to his agent (usually a correspondent bank) in New Jersey with instructions to deliver the bill of lading properly indorsed to buyer if and only if buyer properly pays the sight draft.[4] Ordinarily these papers would arrive by air mail well ahead of the goods. Thus a buyer who agrees to pay "cash against documents" may be agreeing to pay "blind," that is, to pay without first inspecting the goods.[5] The theory is that seller makes tender (through his agent) not of goods but of documents, and buyer breaches if he fails to pay the sight draft on presentment of it, a complying bill of lading, and any other specified documents. Of course, the document might not comply; in that event tender would not be proper, and buyer would not be in breach. Assuming proper tender, however, buyer's obligation in a documentary sale is just to pay the draft. And normally he will pay.

Certainly a documentary sale is far less risky to seller than a sale on open credit, for by virtue of the bill of lading through which our Danish seller retains title to and control over the goods, our New Jersey buyer is kept from acquiring the goods without simultaneously paying for them.[6] With cash in hand the seller is not

2. Armstrong, The Letter of Credit as a Lending Device in a Tight Money Market, 22 Bus.Law 1105 (1967); Thompson & Logan, Letters of Credit: Their Use in Domestic Financing, 22 S.C.L.Rev. 381 (1970); Harfield, The Increasing Domestic Use of the Letter of Credit, 4 UCC L.J. 251 (1972); Comment, Recent Extensions in the Use of Commercial Letters of Credit, 66 Yale L.J. 902 (1957). An interesting early study is Llewellyn, Some Advantages of Letters of Credit, 2 U.Chi.J.Bus. 1 (1929). A recent case involving the use of a letter of credit to finance a building contract is The Fair Pavilions, Inc. v. First Nat'l City Bank, 19 N.Y.2d 512, 227 N.E.2d 839, 4 UCC Rep.Serv. 665 (1967) (use of letter of credit to finance construction at New York World's Fair).

3. On documents of title generally, see Chs. 20, 21 infra. Often, the documents required by the terms of a letter of credit in a sales transaction are the same as those required under a C.I.F. contract. See § 2–320.

4. A nonnegotiable document is sometimes used. There are also still other possible variations. See generally Crawford, Analysis and Operation of a CIF Contract, 29 Tulane L.Rev. 396 (1955).

5. In foreign trade, various shorthand symbols are commonly used to state payment (and other) terms. See e. g., "C.I.F." as defined in section 2–320.

6. That is, buyer is prevented from acquiring the goods without first paying for them, provided that (1) seller's correspondent who is to present the draft to buyer for payment insists on payment before releasing the documents and (2) the carrier gives up the goods to buyer only when buyer presents the carrier with the proper documents. If either of these parties fails to act out his proper role, he will incur liability to the seller.

risking the prospect of eventually having to sue buyer in a foreign jurisdiction to force him to pay for the goods. And if buyer is obligated to pay "blind," all (or nearly all) risk that buyer will inspect, find defects, and refuse to pay is eliminated. Moreover, if buyer for some reason refuses to pay the sight draft, seller will still have control over the goods covered by the bill of lading and may thus control the process of redisposing of them.

Yet despite these advantages, the documentary sale is not without limitations—ones which often prompt a party in the position of our Danish furniture seller to want to *reinforce* that arrangement through the introduction of a letter of credit. Where buyer agrees to pay "cash against documents" (pay a sight draft in exchange for the bill of lading), seller still remains exposed to significant risks. First, there is the risk that the New Jersey buyer will be insolvent or otherwise unable to pay when the sight draft is presented to him by seller's American agent for payment. We may call this the "insolvency risk," and when it materializes, seller will usually be .orced to dispose of the goods himself through agents and in a market that may be relatively unknown to him. Moreover, any damage claim he may thereafter assert against buyer for the difference between the resale price and the contract price will be worth little if buyer turns out to be insolvent. Such a claim would have to be litigated in a foreign court with all the uncertainties and expense that this entails.

Another risk may be called the "dishonesty" risk. The buyer might wrongfully refuse to pay against documents upon their presentment. He might, for example, be backing out in order to take advantage of a general decline in the price of goods ordered from seller.

Then there is the "honest-dispute" risk. For example, seller's shipment may be one of a series. The buyer may refuse to pay against documents upon presentment because one of the seller's prior shipments has been nonconforming or because the present shipment arrived prior to presentment in buyer's city and an unauthorized inspection revealed apparent nonconformity.

If seller agrees to a mode of payment whereby buyer is to pay a sight draft in return for documents of title covering the goods, seller will be vulnerable to buyer's insolvency, to his dishonesty, or to a bona fide dispute with him. When such risks materialize, seller may be left unpaid, with the goods in a distant nation (or *en route*), and with a prospect of litigation in a far off and unknown setting. In short a payment arrangement calling for buyer to pay against documents by no means fully protects seller. Seller can better protect himself against the foregoing risks by insisting that buyer's mode of payment also involve the use of a letter of credit issued by a reputable bank. We will see later that there are other risks besides those already enumerated which might cause a seller to insist on a letter of credit from his buyer.[7]

Assume that in the negotiations our Danish furniture seller insists that the New Jersey buyer procure a letter of credit issued by a bank showing seller as "beneficiary" with authority to draw drafts on the issuing bank. What will this involve, and how can it protect against risks that a documentary sale does not protect against? Buyer, having agreed to a mode of payment involving the use of (1) sight draft and documents, plus (2) a letter of credit, will apply at his own bank for the issuance of an irrevocable letter of credit that commits this bank ("issuer") to pay a draft drawn by seller ("beneficiary") upon proper presentment of the draft and any required documents, including the bill of lading.[8] The documents must comply with the conditions stated in the letter of credit. For instance, they must describe the goods in accordance with the description in the letter of credit; they must include any policy of insurance as required by the letter, and so on.[9] But if the presented documents comply then buyer's issuing bank *must* pay, and this is generally true *even if* buyer, thinking he has hot news that a shipment is nonconforming, instructs his bank not to pay drafts presented by seller's agent.[10]

It should be easy to see why a seller might prefer a payment arrangement of this nature over one merely requiring buyer to pay "cash against documents." The insolvency risk is reduced, for banks tend to be far more solvent than buyers. The outright dishonesty risk is much less significant with payor banks than with payor buyers. And while honest disputes may arise over whether documents comply, nonpayment for this reason is less expectable where the party to pay is a bank that has issued a letter of credit than where the party to pay is merely the buyer who has agreed to pay a sight draft against documents. The seller-beneficiary's protection is all the greater when, as will often be the case, the arrangement calls for a bank in the beneficiary's locale to "confirm" the letter of credit. Under the Code, a confirming bank becomes liable to the beneficiary "as though it were the issuer." This is not to say that the letter of credit device is fail-safe from the seller's point of view, and in Section 18–5 we will canvass a number of things that can go wrong. To summarize, drafts drawn by a seller on an issuing bank or a confirming bank committed to pay pursuant to the terms of an irrevocable letter of credit are significantly more certain of payment

---

7.  See Section 18–9 infra.

8.  As we will later see in the text accompanying notes 13–22 infra, there are numerous variations on this pattern.

9.  The documents that the seller (or his correspondent) is called on to present under the terms of a letter of credit may include an invoice, bills of lading,

and an insurance policy. For discussion of these and other documents sometimes used, see Miller, Problems and Patterns of the Letter of Credit, 1959 U.Ill.L.F. 162, 169–80.

10.  There are exceptions to this general duty to pay in the face of nonconformity. See text accompanying notes 103–113 infra.

than drafts drawn on an ordinary buyer committed to pay pursuant to the terms of an ordinary sales contract. Moreover, the issuing bank that pays the draft thereby acquires the documents controlling the goods and these secure any reimbursement claim the bank has against the buyer.[11]

Thus, when our Danish seller obtains a letter of credit naming him as beneficiary with authority to draw drafts on buyer's Newark, New Jersey bank, he will have eliminated or substantially reduced several of the outstanding risks that exist under a mode of payment calling on buyer merely to pay a sight draft in exchange for a bill of lading or other documents. There are other reasons why seller might want a letter of credit. A major one is that seller might himself only be a middle-man, that is, he might not be the manufacturer of the furniture and if so, he would therefore have to procure the furniture from another Dane. This other Dane might, however, lack capital sufficient to enable him to extend credit to seller. And seller himself might not be in a position to pay cash. His right to payment under his sale of goods contract (unearned as yet) is hardly liquid in nature, and its value as collateral to a Danish manufacturer might not be significant, even if that buyer has agreed to pay seller's sight draft "against documents." How might seller, a middleman, raise money to acquire the very goods he has contracted to sell to buyer? With seller named as beneficiary of a letter of credit issued by an American bank he would have an asset that would more readily enable him to procure the goods for shipment to buyer. With letter of credit in hand seller might acquire the goods he needs (*1*) by assigning the entire credit, (*2*) by assigning merely his right to proceeds, or (*3*) by procuring the issuance by a Danish bank of a further letter of credit naming his own supplier as beneficiary. Thus, in the sales field, letters of credit not only have *payment* functions, they have *financing* functions, too.[12] Some scholars refer to the former function as "primary" and to the latter as "secondary." [13]

With the foregoing outlines of a letter of credit transaction in the sales field in mind, basic variations should not be confusing. First, do not think that letters of credit can be used only in international trade to facilitate the purchase and sale of goods. Domestically they may be used to facilitate the purchase and sale of goods or the construction of ships, manufacturing plants, and apartment dwellings, and more.[14] Indeed the simple consumer credit card is a kind of letter of credit arrangement.[15] Second, the issuer of a letter of

---

11. Issuers can readily protect themselves in still other ways, too. They may, for instance, require collateral beyond the documents. Or, they may even require their customers to deposit funds adequate to cover any drafts to be presented.

12. Financing aspects are treated in Section 18–9 infra.

13. See Harfield, Secondary Uses of Commercial Credits, 44 Colum.L.Rev. 899 (1944).

14. See note 2 supra.

15. Davenport, Bank Credit Cards and the Uniform Commercial Code, 85 Banking L.J. 941, 963–77 (1968).

credit need not necessarily be a bank. It may be a finance company, an insurance company, or the like.[16] Third, the draft presented to the issuer might be a "time" draft rather than a sight draft and thus merely call for the issuer formally to "accept" the draft for payment sometime in the future.[17] Fourth, the obligation assumed by the issuer need not necessarily be one conditioned on the presentation of documents such as bills of lading. The document might be a construction certificate certifying that the builder has made such progress as to entitle him to a further payment from the issuer. Indeed the issuer's obligation need not be conditional at all, as in the case of "clean credits" which obligate the issuer to pay upon presentation *merely* of drafts drawn by the named beneficiary.[18] Fifth, the beneficiary may end up with rights not only against the issuer but also against a "confirming party." A bank in Denmark, for example, may not only advise a Danish seller of a credit issued by a Newark, New Jersey bank in his favor, it may also "confirm" that credit and thus become liable to the beneficiary on terms substantially identical to the terms on which the Newark issuing bank is liable.[19] Sixth, if a party in the position of a buyer banks in a small town, its bank may not be in the business of issuing letters of credit. In that event this bank might arrange for a bank in a larger city to issue it, with that bank looking to the local bank for reimbursement, and the local bank looking in turn to its depositor. Seventh, instead of presenting the draft and any documents for payment (through a correspondent), the beneficiary might discount the papers to a bank in the beneficiary's own city, with the transferee thereby becoming a holder in due course of the draft. Letters of credit that permit such transfers are called "negotiation credits"; others that do not are called "straight credits."[20] Eighth, an issuing bank may or may not be entitled to revoke an issued letter of credit, and the beneficiary may or may not be entitled to assign the letter of credit.[21]

The foregoing are only some of the possible variations.[22] We will return to many of them in the remaining sections of this Chapter.

---

16. Article Five on letters of credit was revised to make this possible. Compare, in particular, the 1952 Official Text with the 1962 Official Text of the Code.

17. See generally W. Ward & H. Harfield, Bank Credits and Acceptances, ch. 7 (4th ed. 1958).

18. See American Nat'l Bank & Trust Co. v. Banco Nacional de Nicaragua, 231 Ala. 614, 620, 166 So. 8, 13 (1936).

19. Section 5–107(2) provides that the confirming bank is liable just as if it were an issuer.

20. See W. Ward & H. Harfield, Bank Credits and Acceptances 189–91 (4th ed. 1958) for more on this distinction.

21. These distinctions will be treated in the text accompanying notes 78–79 infra.

22. For others of less significance, see Miller, Problems and Patterns of the Letter of Credit, 1959 U.Ill.L.F. 162.

## § 18–2 Legal Nature of the Letter of Credit

The draftsman of Article Five of the Code on letters of credit has stated that one purpose of the Article was to "set an independent theoretical frame" for this device. Independent of what? Independent of other legal devices, for courts have assimilated letters of credit to a variety of cognate legal devices. This in turn has sometimes led to error. Therefore it is worthwhile to review how an irrevocable letter of credit differs from cognate legal phenomena.[23]

The obligations, particularly those of an issuer to a beneficiary, that arise under a letter of credit are not exclusively contractual in nature,[24] and it is unfortunate that some of the Code comments suggest as much.[25] It is true that the issuer's customer and the beneficiary will ordinarily have a contract, for instance, for the purchase and sale of goods, for the construction of a ship, or the like, and it is also true that the issuer and the customer will ordinarily have a contract between them whereby the customer pays a fee and the issuer issues the letter of credit. But the resulting letter of credit is not itself a contract, and the issuer's obligation to honor drafts drawn by the beneficiary is not, strictly speaking, contractual. The beneficiary does not enter into any agreement with the issuer. Indeed, prior to the moment of issuance of the letter of credit, issuer and beneficiary may be (and often are) wholly unknown to each other. Yet once the letter of credit is established, the issuer becomes obligated to honor drafts drawn by the beneficiary that comply with the terms of the credit.

Is a letter of credit arrangement contractual in that the beneficiary is really a third party beneficiary of the contract between the issuer and its customer? Not quite. A true third party beneficiary's claim is generally subject to all the defenses that the promisor could set up against the promisee if the promisee were plaintiff, including failure of condition, anticipatory breach, certain forms of fraud, and the like.[26] Yet the claim of a beneficiary of a letter of credit is not subject to such defenses.[27] The issuer must honor his drafts even if the issuer's customer has failed to pay agreed fees, has defrauded the issuer, has unequivocally repudiated, and so on.

Similarly, the usual beneficiary of a letter of credit is not an assignee of a contract right, that is, he is not an assignee of a right

---

23. Important books and articles addressed partly to this topic include H. Finkelstein, Legal Aspects of Commercial Letters of Credit (1930); B. Kozalchyk, Commercial Letters of Credit in the Americas ch. 23 (1966); Epps & Chappell, Assimilation of the Letter of Credit By the Common Law, 38 Va. L.Rev. 531 (1952); Thayer, Irrevocable Credits in International Commerce: Their Legal Nature, 36 Colum.L.Rev. 1031 (1936); Trumble, The Law Merchant and the Letter of Credit, 61 Harv.L.Rev. 981 (1948).

24. For an ingenious attempt to force them into a contractual mold, see McCurdy, Commercial Letters of Credit, 35 Harv.L.Rev. 539 (1922).

25. See § 5–114, Comment 1.

26. Restatement of Contracts § 140 (1932).

27. See text accompanying note 113 infra.

of the customer to have the issuer honor drafts.  Indeed the way
most letters of credit are set up, the customer does not, *qua* customer,
acquire a right to have drafts drawn by him honored by the issuer.
Only the beneficiary acquires such a right.  Furthermore, while an
assignee remains subject to all defenses that an obligor could set up
against the assignor,[28] the beneficiary of a letter of credit cannot
be met with defenses the issuer has against the customer.[29]

Nor is a letter of credit a contract of guaranty or suretyship.[30]
A guarantor or surety is often liable only after the beneficiary has
unsuccessfully sought payment from the issuer's customer, that is,
a buyer of goods.  Under a letter of credit, however, the issuer becomes bound *in the first instance* to pay the beneficiary, and the
beneficiary may look immediately to the issuer for payment of drafts
presented.  Again, the beneficiary is not subject to the various
technical and nontechnical defenses that a guarantor or surety may
set up.[31]

Nor is a letter of credit itself a negotiable instrument [32] (although
the draft presented under it may be).[33]  A letter of credit does not
comply with the requisites of a negotiable instrument under section
3–104(1) of the Code.  It is not payable to order or bearer, and it
is typically not unconditional.

In short, a letter of credit is a letter of credit.  As Bishop Butler
once said, "Everything is what it is and not another thing." [34]  Thus,
when a beneficiary sues an issuer for refusal to honor drafts drawn
pursuant to a letter of credit, his theory is not that of breach of contract, nor does he sue "on a negotiable instrument."  Rather, he sues
"on a letter of credit." [35]

## § 18–3   Relevant Sources of Law and Freedom of Contract

Letter of credit transactions may be either "domestic" (between
parties located in the same or different states of the United States)
or "international" (between a party in a state of the United States
and a party in some foreign nation).  The relevant sources of law
vary depending on which type of transaction is involved.

**28.**  Restatement of Contracts § 167 (1932).

**29.**  See text accompanying note 113 in-fra.

**30.**  See generally Campbell, Guaranty and Suretyship Phases of Letters of Credit, 85 U.Pa.L.Rev. 175, 261 (1936).

**31.**  On these defenses, see L. Simpson, Handbook on the Law of Suretyship §§ 52–80 (1950).

**32.**  See generally Turner, Letters of Credit as Negotiable Instruments, 36 Yale L.J. 245 (1926).

**33.**  See generally Farnsworth, Docu-mentary Drafts Under the Uniform Commercial Code, 22 Bus.Law 479 (1967).

**34.**  Somewhere in Bishop Butler's ser-mons.

**35.**  See Bartholomew, Relation Between Banker and Seller Under Irrevocable Letters of Credit, 5 McGill L.J. 89 (1959).

*Domestic Transactions*

Article Five of the Uniform Commercial Code, together with the language of the letter of credit itself (including law incorporated by reference), ordinary trade usage and custom, and applicable extra-Code case law govern domestic letter of credit transactions.[36]   (As we will see, New York has drastically limited the scope of Article Five.) To what kinds of letter of credit transactions does Article Five apply? To what extent are the provisions of Article Five mandatory rather than merely of the gap filler variety?   Does Article Five allow the issuer and its customer much freedom of contract as to the terms of a letter of credit to be issued?   To these questions we now turn.

The principal scope provision of Article Five is section 5–102:

(1) This Article applies

(a) to a credit issued by a bank if the credit requires a documentary draft or a documentary demand for payment; and

(b) to a credit issued by a person other than a bank if the credit requires that the draft or demand for payment be accompanied by a document of title; and

(c) to a credit issued by a bank or other person if the credit is not within subparagraphs (a) or (b) but conspicuously states that it is a letter of credit or is conspicuously so entitled.

(2) Unless the engagement meets the requirements of subsection (1), this Article does not apply to engagements to make advances or to honor drafts or demands for payment, to authorities to pay or purchase, to guarantees or to general agreements.

(3) This Article deals with some but not all of the rules and concepts of letters of credit as such rules or concepts have developed prior to this act or may hereafter develop. The fact that this Article states a rule does not by itself require, imply or negate application of the same or a converse rule to a situation not provided for or to a person not specified by this Article.

It is apparent from the wording of 5–102, from the official comments, and from the evolution of the drafting process [37] that the Code draftsmen intended Article Five to apply to many types of

36.  Annot., 35 A.L.R.3d 1404 (1971).

37.  Professor Rudolph B. Schlesinger of the Cornell Law School prepared a thorough critique of the 1952 official text of Article Five for the New York Law Revision Commission. This appears in 3 N.Y. State Law Revision Comm'n, 1955 Report 1571–1719 (1955) (hereinafter cited as Schlesinger Study). A review of this critique and of subsequent drafts of Article Five makes it clear that the final version was intended to be very broad in scope.

letter of credit transaction besides those involving the sale of goods with an issuer bank obligated to pay drafts on presentment of a bill of lading. The wording is not limited to letters of credit arising out of sale of goods transactions.[38] The issuer need not be a bank but may be "a person other than a bank."[39] The beneficiary need not present a draft but may instead present merely a "demand for payment."[40] A beneficiary may be required to present a document that is not a document of title, for example, a construction certificate.[41] Indeed Article Five may apply even if the beneficiary is not required to present any documents at all as a condition for honor of his draft or demand.[42]

Consistent with the expansive spirit of 5–102 itself, section 5–103 expansively defines terms appearing in 5–102. An issuer is defined as "a bank or other person issuing a credit."[43] A beneficiary is defined as "a person who is entitled under its terms to draw or demand payment."[44] A "credit" is defined in 5–103(1) (a) as follows:

> Credit or letter of credit means an engagement by a bank or other person at the request of a customer and of a kind within the scope of this Article (Section 5–102) that the issuer will honor drafts or other demands for payment upon compliance with the conditions specified in the credit. A credit may be either revocable or irrevocable.

Section 5–103(1) (b) defines the phrase "documentary draft" which appears in a number of succeeding sections. Such a draft is one the "honor of which is conditioned upon the presentation of a document or documents." The term "document" is further defined expansively to mean "any paper including document of title, security, invoice, certificate, notice of default and the like."[45] Thus the word "document" is far broader in meaning than the phrase "document of title."[46]

The provisions of Article Five apply primarily to the *letter of credit* arrangement, not to the contract between the issuer and its customer, nor to the contract between the customer and the beneficiary.[47] Following the basic scope and definitional provisions of Article Five, there are fourteen further sections. A few of these, principally those specifying the formal requisites of creation of a valid letter of credit, cannot be varied by agreement of the parties.[48] The general principle in Article Five, however, is one of freedom of

---

38. See § 5–102, Comment 1.

39. § 5–102(1) (b).

40. § 5–102(1) (a).

41. §§ 5–102(1); 5–102, Comment 1.

42. Id.

43. § 5–103(1) (c).

44. § 5–103(1) (d).

45. § 5–103(1) (b).

46. Compare § 5–103(1) (b) with § 1–201(15).

47. See Section 18–4 infra.

48. These and oher nonvariable provisions will be considered in Section 18–4 infra.

contract. This is made evident in the extensive use of the phrase "unless otherwise agreed" that code draftsmen inserted no fewer than fifteen times in the various substantive provisions of Article Five.[49] A section that includes this phrase is therefore in the nature of a "gap-filler," a provision that supplies a term of the letter of credit arrangement when the parties have left a gap in it (intentionally or unintentionally). Section 5–110(1), for example, states that "unless otherwise specified a credit may be used in portions in the discretion of the beneficiary."

The issuer and customer will often provide in the letter of credit that it shall be governed by certain customs or practices as defined in the Uniform Customs and Practice for Commercial Documentary Credits (the UCP).[50] This may occur in purely domestic as well as in international letter of credit deals.[51] Incorporation by reference in this way can bring a wide range of non-Article Five "custom and law" to bear, and except insofar as there is any conflict between *mandatory* provisions of Article Five and the custom and law incorporated by reference, such incorporation is valid and binding between the parties to the letter of credit.

On their own, courts often read specific customs and practices into particular letter of credit arrangements.[52] It would be natural for courts to apply Article Two's section on course of dealing and usage of trade by *analogy* to the letter of credit context,[53] especially in domestic transactions. Moreover, court decisions must serve as a source of gap-filler law under Article Five as well, for that Article does not include filler provisions for every conceivable gap in a letter of credit arrangement. For example, Article Five is relatively silent on the nature and kinds of documents other than bills of lading that parties to a letter of credit arrangement may call for.

Besides Article Five, the agreement of the parties, customs and usage, and court decisions, there are still other possible sources of law. Thus, Comment 1 to section 5–104 notes that "questions of mistake, waiver or estoppel are left to supplemental principles of law. See Section 1–103." Moreover, Articles Three and Four of the Code apply to rights and liabilities on a documentary draft,[54] and either

---

49. See Works, Unless Otherwise Agreed and Article 5: An Exercise in Freedom of Contract, 11 St. Louis U. L.J. 416 (1967).

50. The origin of the UCP is discussed in Funk, Letters of Credit: U.C.C. Article 5 and the Uniform Customs and Practice, 11 Howard L.J. 88, 93–95 (1965). See also Axworthy, Revision of the Uniform Customs on Documentary Credits, 1971 J.Bus.L. 38; Wheble, Uniform Customs and Practice for Documentary Credits—1971 Revision, 4 Cornell Int'l L.J. 97 (1971); Note, Revised International Rules for Documentary Credits, 65 Harv.L.Rev. 1420 (1952).

51. Domestic uses of letters of credit are explored further in Section 18–9 infra.

52. See, e. g., Dixon, Irmaos & CIA v. Chase Nat'l Bank, 144 F.2d 759 (2d Cir. 1944), cert. denied 324 U.S. 850 (1945).

53. § 1–205.

54. See Ch. 13 supra; Farnsworth, Documentary Drafts Under the Uniform Commercial Code, 22 Bus.Law 479 (1967).

Article Seven or the Federal Bill of Lading Act may apply to documents of title involved in a letter of credit transaction.[55] Article Nine will usually govern any security aspects of letter of credit arrangements.[56]

Applicable Uniform Commercial Code law, including Article Five, is generally uniform from state to state. Hence, ordinarily there can be no statutory choice of law problems when a letter of credit transaction has contacts with more than one state. But there is one exception of great significance. New York is the most important letter of credit jurisdiction in the United States and the only one with an extensive body of pre-Code case law. New York, Alabama, and Missouri did not adopt Article Five's scope provision without modifying it. Instead, these states added a subsection four to section 5–102 which reads as follows: [57]

> Unless otherwise agreed, this Article 5 does not apply to a letter of credit or a credit if by its terms or by agreement, course of dealing or usage of trade such letter of credit or credit is subject in whole or in part to the Uniform Customs and Practice for Commercial Documentary Credits fixed by the Thirteenth or by any subsequent Congress of the International Chamber of Commerce.

The meaning of this amendment is clear in some respects and unclear in others.[58] If the parties state in their letter of credit that it is subject to the Uniform Customs and Practices (UCP), then it is clear that Article Five "does not apply." Also, even though the letter of credit itself does not so state, it may nonetheless be subject to the UCP "by agreement, course of dealing or usage of trade." If the agreement or course of dealing or usage of trade is "tripartite," that is, one encompassing issuer, its customer, and the beneficiary, then the UCP plainly applies if that is what is indicated. But what if the agreement, course of dealing or usage of trade is only between issuer and its customer? Or only between issuer and the beneficiary? Is the other party bound? Section 5–102(4) does not say. In our opinion an understanding between the issuer and its customer should control the beneficiary, but the issuer and the beneficiary should have no power to control the rights of the customer. The customer is the moving party, and it is he who is ultimately liable to the issuer for what the issuer pays out under the letter of credit.

---

55. See Ch. 21 infra; G. Gilmore & C. Black, The Law of Admiralty 87–112 (1957).

56. See Section 18–9 infra.

57. E. g., N.Y. UCC § 5–102(4) (McKinney 1964). On the New York amendment, see Penney, New York Revisits the Code: Some Variations in the New York Enactment of the Uniform Commercial Code, 62 Colum.L.Rev. 992, 1005 (1962).

58. As Henry Harfield has pointed out, the amendment "provides a pinhead upon which the scholarly-minded may provide choreography for innumerable concepts." N.Y. U.C.C. § 5–101 at 647 (McKinney 1964) (practice commentary).

What if the letter of credit or relevant agreement, course of dealing, or usage of trade stipulates both that Article Five applies and that the UCP also applies? Section 5–102(4) permits this, and these two bodies of law are *generally* consistent, (and each covers areas not covered by the other).[59] However, these two bodies of precepts are not wholly consistent, and in cases of conflict, a court will be forced to make a choice between them. Two examples may be cited as illustrative of possible conflicts between the Code and the UCP. First, Article One of the UCP provides that "all credits, therefore, should clearly indicate whether they are revocable or irrevocable. In the absence of such indication, the credit shall be deemed to be revocable even though an expiry date is stipulated." Article Five of the Code is at present silent on this question, but pre-Code New York case law, which construes ambiguous credits as irrevocable and thereby protects the beneficiary, is in conflict with the UCP.[60] This is important, because originally it was thought that courts of other states would follow the New York case law. Now by virtue of the New York amendment to Article Five, it appears that the UCP governs in New York and that the New York case law which would otherwise have dictated a different result has been superseded. A second illustrative conflict is more clean cut. Article Five allows a beneficiary to assign his right to proceeds of the credit even where the credit is designated as nonassignable. The UCP does not permit this.[61] Various other conflicts are also possible.[62]

Of course, even in New York the parties to a letter of credit arrangement can stipulate that Article Five governs.[63] The wording of the New York amendment does not preclude this. Moreover, in some cases it is possible to argue that the language used by the parties to invoke the UCP either fails entirely or fails in part.[64]

Sometimes the express terms of the letter of credit and any relevant agreement will be wholly silent as to the UCP or any other applicable body of law. When this is so, the first issue will be whether relevant course of dealing or usage of trade makes the UCP applicable "in whole or in part." The issue will be one of fact, in light of Code definitions of course of dealing and usage of trade in section 1–205.

Note that the New York amendment only says that when the deal is subjected to the UCP, "Article Five does not apply." This leaves

59.   See, e. g., UCC §§ 5–108; 5–113; 5–115; 5–117; UCP arts. 15–34.

60.   Laudisi v. American Exchange Nat'l Bank, 239 N.Y. 234, 146 N.E. 347 (1924); Ernesto Foglino & Co. v. Webster, 217 App.Div. 282, 216 N.Y.S. 225 (1st Dep't 1926), modified 244 N.Y. 516, 155 N.E. 878 (1926).

61.   Compare UCC § 5–116 with UCP art. 49.

62.   See, e. g., Harfield, Code Treatment of Letters of Credit, 48 Cornell L.Q. 92 (1962).

63.   § 1–102(3).

64.   See Mentschikoff, Letters of Credit: The Need for Uniform Legislation, 23 U.Chi.L.Rev. 571, 572–581 (1956).

intact any pre-Code case law except insofar as it conflicts with the UCP. New York has a vast body of such law.

Given the possible variations at least between New York law and the law of other states, important conflict of laws problems can arise even between parties within the United States. We do not explore those problems here. Note only that under the Code the parties are free to adopt the law of whatever state they agree upon, provided their transaction bears a reasonable relation to that state.[65] Also, a pre-Code tendency to approach conflict of laws problems distributively rather than collectively will probably continue post-Code. That is, in place of one set of choice of law rules for the letter of credit as a whole, separate rules may evolve, for instance, on liabilities of indorsers of documentary drafts, on liabilities of carriers under bills of lading, and on liabilities of issuers of the basic letter of credit itself. While there is now some relevant scholarly literature on the conflict of laws problems in this area,[66] there is almost no case law, and Article Five itself includes no specifically relevant rules.

### International Transactions

Some western nations have a substantial and sophisticated body of law governing letters of credit. This is true of Great Britain, for example.[67] Furthermore, in many international letter of credit transactions, the parties expressly invoke the UCP.[68] Of course, they may also agree to abide by Article Five of the Uniform Commercial Code.

In the absence of any stipulation by the parties, and in the event of a conflict between the law of say, Massachusetts (Article Five), and the law of France, what law governs? One commentator has recently concluded that "no American conflict of laws rules exist which specifically govern the letter of credit." [69] What law there is suggests that, just as in domestic conflict of laws cases, it is likely that in place of one set of choice of law rules for all aspects of the letter of credit arrangement as a whole, courts will evolve different choice of law rules on the liabilities of indorsers of drafts, issuers of bills of lading, issuers of the letter of credit itself, and so on.[70] It would seem that a multiplicity of rules is called for. Given the dearth of cases to go on, we despair of offering any proposals.

---

65. §§ 1–102(3); 1–105(1). See generally Nordstrom, Choice of Law and the Uniform Commercial Code, 24 Ohio St. L.J. 364 (1963); Tuchler, Boundaries to Party Autonomy in the Uniform Commercial Code: A Radical View, 11 St. Louis U.L.J. 180 (1967).

66. Backus, Foreign Loans, Letter of Credit and Conflict of Laws, 73 Banking L.J. 85 (1956); Funk, Letters of Credit: U.C.C. Article 15 and the Uniform Customs and Practice, 11 Howard L.J. 88 (1965); Gewalb, The Law Applicable to International Letters of Credit, 11 Vill.L.Rev. 742 (1966).

67. See H. Gutteridge & M. Megrah, The Law of Bankers' Commercial Credits (4th ed. 1968).

68. See Section 18–3 supra.

69. Gewalb, The Law Applicable to International Letters of Credit, 11 Vill. L.Rev. 742, 753 (1966).

70. See Barrett v. Bank of the Manhattan Co., 218 F.2d 763 (2d Cir. 1954).

Some of the local law of a country may conflict with other law of that country. For example, Article Seven of the Code, on bills of lading, may conflict with a provision of federal law. Ocean bills of lading must comply with the United States Carriage of Goods by Sea Act.[71] Thus, whenever conflicts rules point to American law, federal law on ocean bills of lading would control insofar as there is any conflict between it and Article Seven of the Code.

## § 18–4   Setting up a Valid Irrevocable Letter of Credit Arrangement Pursuant to Article Five; Valid and Invalid Terms; Variation by Agreement; Time the Credit Becomes "Established"

Today revocable letters of credit are uncommon. Beneficiaries want credits to be irrevocable. How is a valid irrevocable letter of credit set up under Article Five? When does it become "established?"

### Validity of Letter of Credit and Its Terms

First, the prospective issuer's customer will ordinarily apply for issuance of the letter of credit by filling out a form supplied by the issuer.[72] This form is a contract and Article Five generally does not dictate the terms of *this contract*, nor does it lay down any formal requirements for the validity of *this contract*. However, Article Five does specify several "formal" requirements for a valid *letter of credit*:

(*1*) The letter must include "an engagement by a bank or other person . . . that the issuer will honor drafts or other demands for payment upon compliance with the conditions (if any) specified in the credit;"[73]

(*2*) If the letter is issued by a bank and does not require a documentary draft or documentary demand for payment or, although requiring neither of these, is issued by a person other than a bank and does not require that the draft or demand be accompanied by a document of title, then the letter must "conspicuously state that it is a letter of credit;"[74]

(*3*) The letter must be in writing;[75] and

(*4*) The letter must be signed by the issuer.[76]

The foregoing are the only formal Code requirements for the issuance of a letter of credit. Observe that no consideration is necessary[77] and that these requirements can all be met under Article Five even though the letter of credit itself is revocable.

71. Act of April 16, 1936, ch. 229, 49 Stat. 1207; 46 U.S.C.A. §§ 1300–1315 (1970).

72. For an illustrative form of application, see B. Kozolchyk, Commercial Letters of Credit in the Americas 674 (1966).

73. § 5–103(1) (a).

74. § 5–102(1) (c).

75. § 5–104(1).

76. Id.

77. § 5–105.

Article Five does not state that letters of credit are presumed to be irrevocable, yet it is a rare beneficiary who will look with delight upon a revocable credit. If the letter of credit is silent, the answer to whether it is irrevocable depends on case law. Thus, for practical purposes, it would appear that a further formal requirement for the issuance of an irrevocable letter of credit is that it expressly state that it is irrevocable.[78]

What of assignability? Section 5–116(1) specifies that if the letter does not expressly state that it is transferrable or assignable, the "right to draw" thereunder is not transferrable or assignable. Thus, if a customer wants a letter under which the right to draw is transferrable or assignable, the letter should expressly so state.[79]

Are there any provisions of Article Five which cannot be varied by the express terms of a letter of credit? To put this question another way, are there any terms that the parties might insert in a letter of credit that would be invalid under Article Five? First, section 5–114(1) provides:

> An issuer must honor a draft or demand for payment which complies with the terms of the relevant credit regardless of whether the goods or documents conform to the underlying contract for sale or other contract between the customer and the beneficiary.

The nonvariability of section 5–114(1) follows from the very nature of an irrevocable letter of credit; one of the basic purposes for which such letters are issued is to eliminate the risk to the beneficiary that the customer will refuse or halt payment because of alleged deficiencies in the beneficiary's performance. (Of course, the parties could choose to issue a revocable credit.) Second, section 5–109(1) provides that "an issuer's obligation to its customer includes good faith . . .," and section 1–102(3) states that obligations of good faith may not be disclaimed. Third, a term stating that a letter of credit is not transferrable or assignable does not, under section 5–116(2), preclude assignment by the beneficiary of his right to proceeds (as distinguished from his right to draw).[80] Fourth, as to remedies against the issuer for wrongful dishonor and the like, it would appear that under section 5–115 an issuer cannot, by terms in the letter of credit, deprive the aggrieved party of any and all remedies. But, the issuer is not precluded from modifying the remedies available under 5–115. Finally, provisions such as 5–106(4) and 5–108(3)(b) which are designed to protect innocent third parties are also presumably not variable.

Beyond the foregoing formal and substantive Article Five provisions, we believe that the parties may by agreement vary any of the

---

**78.** Section 2–325(3) specifies a presumption of irrevocability in the contract for sale between seller and buyer, not in the letter of credit.

**79.** On the importance of such transferrability, see Section 18–9 infra.

**80.** Assignment and transfer will be considered in Section 18–9 infra.

other sections of Article Five.  Indeed, no fewer than fifteen subsections specifically include the phrase "unless otherwise agreed." [81] The general principle of freedom of contract reigns in Article Five.

### Establishment of Credit

Although an irrevocable letter of credit formally complies with Article Five, although all its terms are valid, and although it has in some loose sense been "issued," it does not follow that it has been "established" under section 5–106.  When, and with what consequences, is such a letter of credit "established?"  Section 5–106 provides:

(1) Unless otherwise agreed a credit is established

    (a) as regards the customer as soon as a letter of credit is sent to him or the letter of credit or an authorized written advice of its issuance is sent to the beneficiary; and

    (b) as regards the beneficiary when he receives a letter of credit or an authorized written advice of its issuance.

(2) Unless otherwise agreed once an irrevocable credit is established as regards the customer it can be modified or revoked only with the consent of the customer and once it is established as regards the beneficiary it can be modified or revoked only with his consent.

The foregoing subsections are variable by agreement.  Absent variation, subsection (1) states the time when a letter of credit is "established."  What is the significance of thus establishing a letter of credit?  Section 5–106(2) provides that once an irrevocable credit is established as regards the customer it can be modified or revoked only with the consent of the customer, and once it is established as regards the beneficiary it can be modified or revoked only with his consent.  Comment 1 adds, "The primary purpose of determining the time of establishment of an irrevocable credit is to determine the point at which the issuer is no longer free to take unilateral action with respect to the cancellation of the credit or modification of its terms." [82]

Does 5–106 mean that once an irrevocable letter of credit is established "as regards the beneficiary," the issuer cannot unilaterally cancel the credit for mutual mistake or fraud, as where, for instance, its customer fraudulently induced the establishment of the credit in the first place?  Presumably the language means this, and presumably it applies even where the issuer notifies the beneficiary of cancella-

81.  §§ 5–106(1), (2), (3); 5–107(1), (4); 5–109(1), (2); 5–110(1), (2); 5–111(1), (2); 5–113(2) (a), (b); 5–114(2), (3).

82.  See Association De Azucareros v. United States Nat'l Bank, 423 F.2d

638, 7 UCC Rep.Serv. 531 (9th Cir. 1970) (beneficiary could not be held to have agreed to modification of irrevocable letter of credit).

tion well prior to any reliance by him.[83]  Does the language also mean that once an irrevocable letter of credit is established "as regards the customer" only, the issuer may not unilaterally cancel it for fraud, duress, or mistake, even though he retrieves the letter and thus keeps the customer (or other party) from putting it in the hands of a potentially relying beneficiary?  Surely the language does not mean that.  And if the letter is in the hands of the customer, at the very least, a court should grant the issuer an injunction ordering the customer not to forward the letter to the beneficiary in such cases.[84]

Observe that under 5–106(1) the time when an irrevocable letter of credit becomes "established" differs as regards customer and beneficiary.  Thus, it is established as regards the beneficiary only when he *receives* the letter or a written advice.  Presumably a letter or advice sent air mail could be overtaken by wire or cable and thus kept from ever becoming "established" as regards the beneficiary.

### § 18–5  An Inventory of Ways that a Valid, Irrevocable, and Established Letter of Credit Arrangement May Breakdown or Otherwise Go Astray

Assume that the letter of credit arrangement is validly established and that the underlying transaction between the beneficiary and the customer is a sale of goods.  In the usual case, it will proceed from establishment through performance to discharge *without incident*.  Let us suppose that the beneficiary puts the goods on a carrier headed for the buyer's locale, and receives a negotiable bill of lading from the carrier covering the goods and drawn to the order of the buyer's bank, the issuer of the letter of credit.  The seller will then, in the most common arrangement, draw a draft to be presented to the issuer for payment along with the bill of lading and any other documents required by the terms of the letter of credit as a precondition of the issuer's duty to pay the draft.  The beneficiary will then discount the draft and documents to a local bank (which may or may not be a confirming bank) and this bank will present the papers to the issuer, or the beneficiary may itself send the papers directly to the issuer or through a correspondent bank in the issuer's city.  On receipt, the issuer will carefully review the documents to see if they conform to the conditions of the credit.  Assuming they comply, the issuer will then honor the draft.  In turn, it will charge the customer's account or otherwise procure reimbursement from the customer, or security therefor.  Once satisfied in this respect, the issuer will turn the documents, including the bill of lading properly indorsed, over to the customer.  Armed with the document of title, the customer will thereafter be entitled to demand delivery of the goods from the carrier when they arrive.

The possible breakdowns in the foregoing transaction can be profitably inventoried from the differing points of view of the bene-

---

83.  See text accompanying note 113 infra.

84.  See generally Schlesinger Study, supra note 37, at 1618–30.

ficiary, the customer, and the issuer.  The adversely affected party may or may not be entitled to a remedy, that is, the breakdown may be one for which he bears the risk.  When he does have a remedy, it may take the form of damages, an injunction, a defense, etc.  Also, when he has a remedy, that remedy may not be premised on a letter of credit theory as such.  It may be premised in contract or even in tort.  Remedies for major forms of breakdown and the substantive theories on which they are premised will be discussed in later Sections.

From the beneficiary-seller's point of view, ordinarily the worst that can happen is simply that he will end up having delivered the goods but not having received payment therefor.  Not all breakdowns entail these consequences for the beneficiary, but any one of the following may: insolvency of the issuer or of a transmitting bank; loss or destruction of the draft or documents in transit or while in the possession of others; wrongful refusal of the issuer to honor the draft on presentment; anticipatory repudiation of any and all obligations to honor the draft, and; issuer's rightful dishonor for failure of the beneficiary to send complying documents.

From the buyer-customer's point of view, ordinarily the worst that can happen is simply that he will be out the funds he paid the issuer by way of reimbursement for honor, while ultimately receiving no goods at all or else receiving seriously defective goods.  Not all breakdowns necessarily entail these consequences for the customer, but any of the following may: wrongful honor by the issuer where the documents (and so, too, the goods) fail to conform to the terms of the letter of credit; rightful honor by the issuer where the documents are complying but forged, or shipped goods fail to conform to the documents; wrongful failure of the issuer to turn over the documents to the customer, and; wrongful failure of the carrier to deliver in accordance with the terms of the bill of lading.

From the issuer's point of view, ordinarily the worst that can happen is that the issuer will pay a draft or other demand, but then have a good claim against a solvent party for reimbursement or the like.  Again, not all breakdowns necessarily entail these consequences.  But those that may include: inadvertent but wrongful honor of drafts or other demands for payment; inaction constituting wrongful failure to mitigate damages, and; insolvency of the customer prior to reimbursing the issuer or giving security.

In the next three Sections, we will consider the main breakdowns that adversely affect the beneficiary, adversely affect the customer, and adversely affect the issuer, respectively.

### § 18–6   Actual or Prospective Breakdowns Adversely Affecting the Beneficiary in the First Instance (Herein mainly of issuer's wrongful dishonor)

The most significant breakdown adversely affecting the beneficiary in the first instance is the issuer's wrongful dishonor of the beneficiary's draft.  From the beneficiary's point of view, honor of the draft is the very *raison d'etre* of the irrevocable letter of credit arrangement.  Of course, if the issuer wrongfully dishonors, the beneficiary might still ultimately recover from the customer in an action on the underlying contract of sale,[85] but he might not, and it is mainly to protect against the vagaries of any such proceeding that the beneficiary insists on an irrevocable letter of credit in the first place.

### Wrongful Dishonor

What constitutes wrongful dishonor?  To answer this, it is necessary to consider the issuer's affirmative obligation to honor drafts properly drawn under an irrevocable letter of credit.  The Code's *general principle* is that the "issuer must honor a draft or demand for payment that complies with the terms of the relevant credit." [86]  The issuer who refuses payment wrongfully dishonors unless it can show either (*1*) that the documents presented for payment do not comply with the terms of the relevant credit or (*2*) that the case falls into an exception to the foregoing general principle.

When does a presentment comply with the terms of the relevant credit?  This question is crucial, for the issuer's refusal to pay a complying presentment generally constitutes wrongful dishonor entitling the beneficiary to some remedy.  Most of the letter of credit court cases have arisen over whether a particular presentment complied with the terms of the relevant letter of credit.  When Article Five was being drafted, various individuals urged that it include specific rules on what constitutes compliance with the terms of a letter of credit.[87]  Wisely the draftsmen ignored these urgings.  Section 5–114 (1) merely requires that issuer honor a draft or demand for payment "which complies with the terms of the relevant letter of credit . . . ."  Whether there is compliance in a particular case cannot be soundly dictated in advance by general rules of law, at least if the parties are to have broad freedom of contract to prescribe the particular terms of the letter of credit.  But as an alternative, the Code should have specified whether strict compliance is necessary or whether "substantial performance" will do.  Pre-Code law on this basic choice is in conflict.  Pre-Code New York law, unlike that of some other states, permits the issuer to rightfully dishonor not only for significant non-compliance but also merely for failure to comply strictly.[88]  Presumably the pre-Code law on this general question remains applicable in New York (and elsewhere) via section 1–103 on supplemental general principles.  Of course, the issuer might himself

85.  § 2–301.

86.  § 5–114(1).  See also Annot., 53 A.L.R. 57 (1928).

87.  Schlesinger Study, supra note 37, at 1634.

88.  Compare Lamborn v. Lake Shore Banking & Trust Co., 196 App.Div. 504, 188 N.Y.S. 162 (1st Dep't 1921), aff'd 231 N.Y. 616, 132 N.E. 911 (1921), with Bank of America Nat'l Trust & Savings Ass'n v. Liberty Nat'l Bank & Trust Co., 116 F.Supp. 233 (WD. Okla.1933).  On the "strict" v. "substantial" compliance issue, see also Comment, Letters of Credit Under the Proposed Uniform Commercial Code: An Opportunity Missed, 62 Yale L.J. 227, 243–48 (1953).

insist on a protective clause in the letter of credit.[89] providing that the customer is not entitled to insist on strict compliance as a condition of reimbursement.  But our primary concern here is with the rights of the *beneficiary* for wrongful dishonor.  What would be the effect of a clause in an irrevocable letter of credit empowering the issuer to refuse honor as against the beneficiary if the issuer merely finds the documents "unsatisfactory" to it?  As against the beneficiary, surely the issuer cannot have its cake and eat it too, that is, issue an irrevocable letter of credit and then, via a clause in the credit, reserve in effect a power to revoke the credit.  Section 5–114(1) states that "the issuer is not excused from honor of such a draft or demand by reason of an additional general term that all documents must be satisfactory to the issuer  .  .  .  ."  Comment 1 to this section states, "Attempts by the issuer to reserve a right to dishonor are declared invalid as essentially repugnant to an irrevocable letter of credit."  While the issuer may not insert a mere satisfaction clause in an irrevocable credit, it would appear that he could insert a clause requiring that presented documents "strictly comply" with the terms of the letter of credit.

What are the sources of disputes over whether or not a beneficiary's presentment complies with the terms of the relevant credit?  We will consider four illustrative sources.  First, the terms in a letter of credit that a presentment must satisfy may themselves be vague, ambiguous or otherwise unclearly drafted.  When so, the very standard by which the issuer is to decide upon honor or dishonor is deficient and invites dispute.  A recent case in which a conflict arose partly from this source is Banco Espanol de Credito v. State Street Bank and Trust Co.[90]  There, the terms of the letter of credit called for the issuer to pay against documents, including a certificate of inspection stating that the goods complied with the buyer's "purchase orders."  But, as the court noted, buyer himself sewed "the seeds of dispute by sending to the beneficiary-seller both stock sheets which were really orders and orders which were merely preliminary papers." [91]

Even though the terms of the letter of credit are precise and definite, disputes over compliance can still easily arise.  Thus, in a second type of case, terms are used in the letter of credit that have a meaning in the trade, and doubts may arise as to what that special meaning is.  For example, what does the phrase "clean bill of lading" mean? [92]  Course of dealing or usage of trade may help in such instances.  Also relevant is prior judicial determination.  In a third type of case, the source of dispute lies in shorthand phrases or ab-

**89.**   See the clause quoted in the text accompanying note 121 infra.

**90.**   385 F.2d 230, 4 UCC Rep.Serv. 862 (3d Cir. 1967).

**91.**   Id. at 236, 4 UCC Rep.Serv. at 870. See also Venizelos, S. A. v. Chase Manhattan Bank, 425 F.2d 461, 7 UCC Rep.Serv. 719 (2d Cir. 1970) (unclarity in credit as to terms on which confirmer must honor).

**92.**   See Draper, What is a "Clean Bill of Lading"?—A Problem in Financing International Trade, 37 Cornell L.Q. 56 (1952).

breviations appearing in the documents which do not in so many words repeat the exact language called for by the terms of the letter of credit. The letter of credit might, for example, require a bill of lading specifying "Java White Granulated Sugar," but the bill of lading specifies only "Java White Sugar." [93] In a fourth type of case the terms of the letter of credit call for several documents, all repeating specified language, but the presentment includes a document (for instance, an invoice) that uses general language broad enough to describe what is required but also broad enough to describe other things too. Other documents (for instance, bills of lading) however, repeat the required language exactly.[94] Or, one of these specified documents, possibly an insignificant one, may even be missing.[95] There are still other sources of disputes, too.[96]

Given all these sources of disputes, how do courts resolve them? In particular, is the standard one of strict compliance, or is substantial compliance enough to obligate the issuer to honor? On this simple but important question Article Five says nothing. Thus pre-Code law, most of which is New York case law, remains intact. Professor Schlesinger's summary of this law, written in 1954, remains valid today:

> Existing New York law is clearly to the effect that a strict standard is called for when the beneficiary or a holder of drafts sues the issuing or confirming bank which has rejected the documents, while after honor, when the bank seeks reimbursement from its customer, a reasonable standard is to be applied. The practical effect of this rule is to allow the issuing or confirming bank some leeway for the exercise of honest judgment, especially in times of falling commodity prices when the bank may easily get into a cross-fire of pressures. Its customer, the buyer, may insist that the documents be rejected because of miscrosopic discrepancies, while the seller-beneficiary demands honor and threatens to sue on the credit. The position of the bank in such a case would be unenviable if within the short time allowed it had to guess at its peril whether in a future lawsuit a court will regard the documents as conforming to the documentary requirements which, in language perhaps less than crystal-clear, were formulated by the customer in his application and faithfully repeated by the bank in the letter of credit itself. Frequently, issuers seek to protect themselves against this dilemma by appropriate clauses in the application and in the letter of credit. Even in the absence of such clauses, the New York

93. Lamborn v. Lake Shore Banking & Trust Co., 196 App.Div. 504, 188 N.Y.S. 162 (1st Dep't 1921), aff'd 231 N.Y. 616, 132 N.E. 911 (1926).

94. Laudisi v. American Exch. Nat'l Bank, 239 N.Y. 234, 146 N.E. 347 (1924).

95. Dixon, Irmaos & CIA v. Chase Nat'l Bank, 144 F.2d 759 (2d Cir. 1944), cert. denied 324 U.S. 850 (1945).

96. See generally Miller, Problems and Patterns of the Letter of Credit, 1959 U.Ill.L.F. 162, 169–88.

rule recognizes that the conformity of a given document may be a matter of reasonable doubt. Where such doubt exists, the issuer is not made to act at his peril; so long as he acts within reason, the New York rule confers upon him a measure of discretionary power. If he chooses to insist on strict compliance, the rule protects him against the disappointed beneficiary's damage action. If he honors a draft accompanied by "reasonably" complying documents, the rule preserves his reimbursement claim against the customer.[97]

The New York strict compliance standard can be easily illustrated. It was reaffirmed as recently as 1966 in Marine Midland Grace Trust Co. v. Banco Del Paris, S.A.,[98] a case in which the court upheld the issuer's refusal to honor certain drafts. The issuer justified its refusal partly on the ground that the bills of lading did not, as required by the terms of the letter of credit, state in so many words that the goods were "on board" the trucks. In reply the letter of credit beneficiary's transferee claimed that language in another required document, the inspection certificate, plainly indicated that the goods were "on board." The language recited that "the loading of the 'flasks' was personally supervised by us, verifying that all our seals were intact at loading." [99] Judge McLean dismissed this argument and held that "strictly speaking (and we must speak strictly in this situation), this statement, even if true, does not say that all the goods were actually loaded on board the trucks." [100]

It must not be thought that every instance of alleged noncompliance generates a dispute leading to wrongful dishonor. When doubts arise in the issuer's mind as to whether or not a presentment complies, it is not at all uncommon for the issuer to notify the customer and for the customer, the beneficiary, and the issuer to reach an agreement whereby the customer in effect waives the alleged noncompliance or makes some other adjustment so that the occasion for the beneficiary to assert wrongful dishonor does not arise.[101] Furthermore, it must not be thought that the only way a wrongful dishonor can possibly occur is by express refusal to honor drafts accompanying complying documents. Section 5–112 provides that dishonor may occur as a result of inaction by the issuer following a presentment, and if the documents comply, then generally the dishonor would be wrongful as well.[102]

97. Schlesinger Study, supra note 37, at 1634–35.

98. 261 F.Supp. 884 (S.D.N.Y.1966), noted in 3 Texas Int'l L.F. 359 (1967).

99. 261 F.Supp. at 889.

100. Id.

101. Anglo-South American Trust Co. v. Uhe, 261 N.Y. 150, 184 N.E. 741 (1933); Chairmasters, Inc. v. Public Nat'l Bank, 283 App.Div. 704, 127 N.Y.S.2d 806 (1st Dep't 1954); Schlesinger Study, supra note 37, at 1641–42.

102. For useful discussion of an earlier draft of § 5–112, see Schlesinger Study, supra note 37, at 1677–85.

As stated earlier,[103] the issuer who refuses payment is generally guilty of wrongful dishonor unless it can show either (1) that the documents presented for payment do not appear on their face to comply with the terms of the relevant credit or (2) that the case falls into one of the recognized exceptions excusing honor. We turn now to the exceptions. Section 5–114(2) states:

> Unless otherwise agreed when documents appear on their face to comply with the terms of a credit but a required document does not in fact conform to the warranties made on negotiation or transfer of a document of title (Section 7—507) or of a security (Section 8—306) or is forged or fraudulent or there is fraud in the transaction
>
> (a) the issuer must honor the draft or demand for payment if honor is demanded by a negotiating bank or other holder of the draft or demand which has taken the draft or demand under the credit and under circumstances which would make it a holder in due course (Section 3—302) and in an appropriate case would make it a person to whom a document of title has been duly negotiated (Section 7—502) or a bona fide purchaser of a security (Section 8—302); and
>
> (b) in all other cases as against its customer, an issuer acting in good faith may honor the draft or demand for payment despite notification from the customer of fraud, forgery or other defect not apparent on the face of the documents but a court of appropriate jurisdiction may enjoin such honor.

Observe that subsection (2) (a) does not explicitly state exceptions excusing the issuer from honor. Rather it states exceptions by way of negative implication. Thus it would appear by way of implication (and other argument) that, as against the beneficiary, the issuer may lawfully refuse honor (but is not required to do so), if (1) the required documents do not in fact conform to the warranties made on negotiation or transfer of a document of title (section 7–507) or of a security (section 8–306), or (2) the required document is in fact forged or fraudulent, or (3) there is in fact "fraud in the transaction," provided that the party presenting the draft or demand for payment is the beneficiary or some other party who is not (a) a holder in due course (3–302), or (b) a person to whom a document of title has been duly negotiated (7–502), or (c) a bona fide purchaser of a security (8–302).

The forgery exception codifies pre-Code law.[104] Presumably, a "forged" document is one that includes forged signatures, and a

---

103. See text accompanying note 86 supra.

104. If the issuer discovers the forgery after payment, it is still entitled to reimbursement. Brown v. C.

"fraudulent" document is one that is specious, conjured up out of whole cloth, or one that has been materially altered.[105]  Yet section 5–114 is silent on the meaning of these terms, and pre-Code law is of little help.[106]

What constitutes "fraud in the transaction?"  Again, 5–114 is silent, but apparently this phrase codifies the law of *Sztejn v. Schroder Banking Corp.*[107]  In that case the documents called for bristles, but the goods shipped consisted of fifty cases of rubbish, a fact the issuer learned prior to honor.  The court enjoined honor on the request of the issuer's customer.  The presenter was not a holder in due course (or the like).[108]  Such so-called "fraud in the transaction" must be distinguished from other breaches of the underlying contract between beneficiary and customer which do not justify dishonor.  Thus the *Sztejn* case involved egregious fraud; presumably, ordinary fraud in the inducement (for example, a knowing misrepresentation as to quality) will not qualify as "fraud in the transaction" under 5–114(2).  Certainly, mere breach of warranty by the beneficiary will not justify dishonor under 5–114(2) even when the issuer knows of the breach in advance and the fact of breach is undisputed.[109]  Doubtless this will mean that in some cases the beneficiary may be allowed to profit from its own wrong.[110]

It seems inferable from section 5–114(2) (b) that if the issuer is enjoined from honor in circumstances in which it may choose lawfully not to honor anyway, then *a fortiori* the failure to honor is rightful.  But what if a court enjoins the issuer from honor not in such

Rosenstein Co., 120 Misc. 787, 200 N.Y.S. 491 (Sup.Ct.1923).  It is essential to distinguish between the effect of forgery of drafts and the effect of forgery of documents.  Section 5–114 (2) is addressed only to the latter question.

105. See Williams Ice Cream Co. v. Chase Nat'l Bank, 210 App.Div. 179, 205 N.Y.S. 446 (1st Dep't 1924) (alteration of documents could be fraud). See also Miller, Problems and Patterns of the Letter of Credit, 1959 U. Ill.L.F. 162, 185–87.  One recent lower court case indicates that suspicion of fraudulent dating of shipping documents may be enough to justify a temporary restraining order.  Merchants Corp. v. Chase Manhattan Bank, N. A., 5 UCC Rep.Serv. 196 (N.Y.Sup.Ct. 1968) (court enjoined issuer from honor on showing that issuer had notice that documents were forgeries). Cf. Bank of Taiwan v. Union Nat'l Bank, 1 F.2d 65 (3d Cir. 1924).

106. Schlesinger Study, supra note 37, 1654–77.

107. 177 Misc. 719, 31 N.Y.S.2d 631 (Sup.Ct.1941).

108. If the presenter were a holder in due course (or the like), the result would have been different under section 5–114.  Banco Espanol de Credito v. State Street Bank & Trust Co., 409 F.2d 711, 6 UCC Rep.Serv. 378 (1st Cir. 1969).  For a case similar to Sztejn, see Bank of Montreal v. Recknagel, 109 N.Y. 482, 17 N.E. 217 (1888) (rags for hemp).

109. American Steel Co. v. Irving Nat'l Bank, 266 F. 41 (2d Cir. 1920), aff'd on rehearing 277 F. 1016 (2d Cir. 1921), cert. denied 258 U.S. 617 (1922); O'Meara Co. v. National Park Bank, 239 N.Y. 386, 146 N.E. 636 (1925); Ando International, Ltd. v. Woolmaster Corp., 3 UCC Rep.Serv. 1071 (N.Y. Sup.Ct. 1966) (issuer had accepted drafts before buyer sought injunction because goods were defective; injunction denied).

110. See, e. g., Rosenfeld v. Banco Internacional, 27 App.Div.2d 826, 278 N.Y.S.2d 160, 4 UCC Rep.Serv. 212 (1st Dep't 1967).

circumstances? Surely an issuer acting under court order, even if an invalid order, does not wrongfully dishonor.

So much for the more or less explicit statutory exceptions to the general principle that an issuer wrongfully dishonors as against the beneficiary if it dishonors a presentment that appears on its face to comply with the terms of the credit. Are these the only exceptions? It may be urged that they are, for the statute lists these and no others. Yet one can argue that courts must recognize other exceptions even after enactment of Article Five. Consider, for example, a case in which war breaks out in the beneficiary's country after the beneficiary has shipped the goods by rail and the issuer learns prior to honor that the goods have been destroyed *en route* in circumstances in which the risk of loss is on the beneficiary. Here the issuer should not be guilty of wrongful dishonor in refusing to honor the drafts.[111]

There are two major "non-exceptions" to the general principle that an issuer wrongfully dishonors as against the beneficiary by refusing to honor a presentment that appears on its face to comply with the terms of the credit. First, except in the most extraordinary circumstances such as the war-time destruction case just hypothesized, and except as stated in section 5–114(2)(a) above, it is wrongful for the issuer to dishonor on the ground that the beneficiary has failed to perform its underlying obligations to the issuer's customer. In other words, the issuer generally cannot justify refusal to honor on the ground that its customer is not getting what he bargained for from the beneficiary-seller. Article Five is quite explicit about this. It says the issuer's duty to honor drafts accompanied by documents conforming to the terms of the letter of credit arises "regardless of whether the goods or documents conform to the underlying contract for sale or other contract between the customer and the beneficiary."[112] Accordingly, defenses or claims that the customer has against the beneficiary are generally not grounds for dishonor. Among other things this rules out dishonor for seller's breach of warranty, failure of condition, delay, prospective inability to perform the remainder of an installment contract, insolvency, and so on. *A fortiori* mere customer instructions to the issuer not to honor cannot justify dishonor.

There is a second major "non-exception" to the general principle that an issuer wrongfully dishonors as against the beneficiary if it dishonors a presentment that appears on its face to comply with the terms of the credit. The issuer will have made a contract with his customer to issue the letter of credit. Yet the customer might have fraudulently induced the issuer to enter this contract, the consideration promised by the customer might have failed, or the customer might have gone bankrupt after issue and rendered the issuer's eventual claim for reimbursement highly uncertain or worthless. Even so,

111. For discussion of such a case, see Schlesinger Study, supra note 37, at 1657.

112. § 5–114(1); O'Meara Co. v. National Park Bank, 239 N.Y. 386, 146 N.E. 636 (1925). See generally Annot., 39 A.L.R. 755 (1925).

the issuer may not utilize these and analogous grounds as a justification for refusal to honor. Section 5–114(1) states the issuer's duty to honor in terms that do not cater for any such exception at all.[113] Failure of consideration as a basis for dishonor is also expressly ruled out under section 5–105.

### *Remedies*

Assuming that the issuer wrongfully dishonors, what remedies are available to the beneficiary? Section 5–115 distinguishes between remedies upon wrongful dishonor and remedies upon wrongful cancellation or repudiation of the credit by the issuer: [114]

> (1) When an issuer wrongfully dishonors a draft or demand for payment presented under a credit the person entitled to honor has with respect to any documents the rights of a person in the position of a seller (Section 2—707) and may recover from the issuer the face amount of the draft or demand together with incidental damages under Section 2—710 on seller's incidental damages and interest but less any amount realized by resale or other use or disposition of the subject matter of the transaction. In the event no resale or other utilization is made the documents, goods or other subject matter involved in the transaction must be turned over to the issuer on payment of judgment.

> (2) When an issuer wrongfully cancels or otherwise repudiates a credit before presentment of a draft or demand for payment drawn under it the beneficiary has the rights of a seller after anticipatory repudiation by the buyer under Section 2—610 if he learns of the repudiation in time reasonably to avoid procurement of the required documents. Otherwise the beneficiary has an immediate right of action for wrongful dishonor.

On the issuer's wrongful dishonor or repudiation, the beneficiary has remedies against the documents and against the goods, as well as remedies against the issuer. Against the documents or goods, the beneficiary has the right under section 2–705 of Article Two to withhold or stop delivery on the underlying contract and resell under 5–115(1) and 2–707. In the case of repudiation, he has the right to suspend his performance of the underlying contract under sections 5–115 (2) and 2–610.

Against the issuer, the beneficiary may, in the event of wrongful dishonor, recover the face amount of the draft plus incidental damages and interest, less certain deductions all as specified in section

---

113. Case law is in accord. See, e. g., American Steel Co. v. Irving Nat'l Bank, 266 F. 41, 43 (2d Cir. 1920), aff'd on rehearing 277 F. 1016 (2d Cir. 1921), cert. denied 258 U.S. 617 (1922).

114. Pre-Code law was cognizant of this distinction. See Schlesinger Study, *supra* note 37, at 1702–1703.

5–115(1). The section does not say the beneficiary must take steps to mitigate his losses by reselling the documents, although some pre-Code law so required.[115] If in pursuing his remedies against the documents or the goods, the beneficiary is made whole, he will have no damages against the issuer. And if he mitigates, his damages will be correspondingly reduced.[116] In the event of wrongful cancellation or repudiation the beneficiary has the same damage claim against the issuer as in the case of wrongful dishonor, provided the cancellation or repudiation occurred after the beneficiary procured the required documents.[117] Otherwise the beneficiary has the remedies provided for anticipatory repudiation under Article Two.[118]

The beneficiary may have other "self-help" remedies besides withholding or suspending performance on the underlying contract. On wrongful dishonor the beneficiary may be able to procure honor by offering an indemnity as authorized by section 5–113.[119] In addition, the beneficiary may be able to induce the issuer to honor by getting the issuer's customer to contact the issuer accordingly.

### § 18–7  Actual or Prospective Breakdowns Adversely Affecting the Customer in the First Instance (Herein mainly of issuer's wrongful honor, and of beneficiary nonperformance of the underlying contract)

The issuer might wrongfully honor a draft or demand for payment in circumstances in which the customer has already "put the issuer in funds" or provided the issuer with ample security against which the issuer immediately reimbursed itself. Unlike wrongful

**115.** O'Meara Co. v. National Park Bank, 239 N.Y. 386, 400, 146 N.E. 636 (1925). See also Note, Damages for Breach of Irrevocable Commercial Letters of Credit: The Common Law and the Uniform Commercial Code, 25 U. Chi.L.Rev. 667 (1958).

**116.** De Sousa v. Crocker First Nat'l Bank, 23 F.2d 118, 122 (N.D.Cal.1927), rev'd on other grounds 27 F.2d 462 (9th Cir. 1928).

**117.** § 5–115(2). On what constitutes repudiation, see Foglino & Co. v. Webster, 217 App.Div. 282, 216 N.Y.S. 225 (1st Dep't 1926), modified, 244 N.Y. 516, 155 N.E. 878 (1926); Bril v. Suomen Pankki Finlands Bank, 199 Misc. 11, 97 N.Y.S.2d 22 (Sup.Ct.1950).

**118.** See § 2–610. On what constitutes anticipatory repudiation, see the recent case of Savarin Corp. v. Nat'l Bank of Pakistan, 447 F.2d 727 (2d Cir. 1971).

**119.** Section 5–113 provides in full as follows:

(1) A bank seeking to obtain (whether for itself or another) honor, negotiation or reimbursement under a credit may give an indemnity to induce such honor, negotiation or reimbursement.

(2) An indemnity agreement inducing honor, negotiation or reimbursement

(a) unless otherwise explicitly agreed applies to defects in the documents but not in the goods; and

(b) unless a longer time is explicitly agreed expires at the end of ten business days following receipt of the documents by the ultimate customer unless notice of objection is sent before such expiration date. The ultimate customer may send notice of objection to the person from whom he received the documents and any bank receiving such notice is under a duty to send notice to its transferor before its midnight deadline.

dishonor to the beneficiary, which is usually prejudicial as to him, wrongful *honor* as to the customer may or may not be prejudicial. Where the documents on their face fail to comply with the terms of the credit, yet a mistake was made in copying the description of the goods into the letter of credit from the underlying contract between beneficiary and customer, so that the documents really do conform to the underlying contract, a wrongful honor is not prejudicial. Nor would a wrongful honor be prejudicial where the beneficiary's carrier misdescribed the goods on documents when it issued them so that while the documents failed to comply with the terms of the credit, the actual goods nonetheless conformed to the contract. In this case, the issuer's wrongful honor would not be prejudicial to its customer.

The most common kind of wrongful honor occurs where the issuer honors against noncomplying documents and the noncompliance in the documents actually reflects deficiencies in the beneficiary's performance of the underlying contract. Things are all the worse for the customer if the issuer has already reimbursed itself out of funds supplied by the customer, or from collateral put up by the customer by the time the wrongful honor becomes known.

In these circumstances there are two alternate litigation avenues open to the customer, and one may be far more preferable to the other. The customer may simply sue the beneficiary on the underlying contract for damages (under Article Two of the Code if the underlying deal is a sale of goods). This course is fraught with risks, however. The beneficiary will frequently be in a far-off jurisdiction and possibly not even amenable to service of process locally. Or the beneficiary may be insolvent or otherwise elusive.

As an alternative the customer might sue the issuer, establish the wrongful honor, and recover damages. Unlike the beneficiary's claim for wrongful dishonor against the issuer which is an action on the letter of credit, the customer's action would be for breach of the contract between the issuer and the customer. Because lawyers for issuers [120] greatly influenced the drafting of Article Five, it is remarkably silent on claims by customers for wrongful honor. Section 5–109 reads like a banker's disclaimer or exculpatory clause. It does say that "an issuer must examine the documents with care so as to ascertain that on their face they appear to comply with the terms of the credit  .  .  ." Assuming the issuer fails in this respect and thus wrongfully honors a draft or demand for payment, it still does not follow that the customer will have a good claim against the issuer, for the issuer may have inserted a clause of the following nature in the contract between it and its customer: "That [bank shall not]  .  .  . be responsible for  .  .  . the validity, sufficiency or genuineness of documents or any indorsement  .  .  ." [121] Generally, courts

120. See Schlesinger Study, supra note 37, at 1630.

121. W. Ward & H. Harfield, Bank Credits and Acceptances 207 (4th ed. 1958).

have upheld such clauses.[122]  Certainly there is no hint in Article Five that they are invalid.  It will be interesting to see whether courts will invoke section 1–102(3) to invalidate such clauses:

> The effect of provisions of this Act may be varied by agreement, except as otherwise provided in this Act and except that the obligations of good faith, diligence, reasonableness and care prescribed by this Act may not be disclaimed by agreement but the parties may by agreement determine the standards by which the performance of such obligations is to be measured if such standards are not manifestly unreasonable.

The obligation imposed on issuing banks under section 5–109(2) to examine documents with care is an obligation of "reasonableness and care."  We believe an exculpatory clause of the kind quoted above would be invalid under 1–102(3).

Courts must be wary of the possibility that an issuer's customer is only trying to get out of a bad bargain with the beneficiary.[123]  Issuers are aware of this possibility, and, of course, do not want to be left holding the bag.  Accordingly it is natural for them to draft clauses in their agreements with customers that go far to protect them against liability for wrongful honor.

If the customer does emerge with a valid claim for damages against the issuer for wrongful honor, what is the measure of his damages?  Again Article Five is silent.  The best the customer might hope for would be damages in the entire amount of the wrongfully honored draft.  In a sale of goods this would be the same as a return of the entire purchase price and in most cases would entirely satisfy the customer.  He would not only be made whole, he would also not have to concern himself with disposing of the goods.  Another possibility would be to limit the customer's damages against the issuer to an appropriate share of the loss actually sustained by the customer on his contract with the beneficiary.  Assume the customer was to pay $1000 for goods which in their defective state are worth no more than $500.  The customer might be permitted to recover only $500 from the issuer in such circumstances.  Presumably the issuer would then be subrogated to the customer's claim against the beneficiary.[124]

The foregoing analysis assumes a combination of wrongful honor and beneficiary nonperformance on the underlying contract of sale.  Actually the beneficiary may fail to perform and yet the issuer rightfully honor.  Classic examples are those in which the documents are regular on their face and thus honorable, yet are in fact skillfully forged or there is egregious fraud in the transaction (seller ships cowhair labelled as bristles) [125] that goes undiscovered until after honor.

122.  B. Kozolchyk, Commercial Letters of Credit in the Americas ch. 15 (1966).

123.  Overseas Trading Corp. v. Irving Trust Co., 82 N.Y.S.2d 72 (Sup.Ct.1948).

124.  No specifically applicable authority has been found.

125.  Sztejn v. J. Henry Schroder Banking Corp., 177 Misc. 719, 31 N.Y.S.2d 631 (Sup.Ct.1941).

In these circumstances the customer has no substantive breach of contract claim against the issuer for wrongful honor and is left solely to his breach of contract claim against the beneficiary (or possibly against a carrier).[126]  Is there any way that the letter of credit transaction itself can be set up to help maximize the likelihood that the customer will not be hurt by a wrongful honor?  One device used in sales transactions is worthy of note.  It is possible for the buyer to require that the beneficiary procure a certificate of inspection from an independent and reliable third party who affirms that the goods are as ordered.  The letter of credit would be drafted to require that this certificate be submitted with other documents before the issuer may properly honor an accompanying draft.  Of course, this device is not fail-safe.

Occasionally the customer learns of the beneficiary's impending nonperformance of the underlying contract of sale prior to the time when the issuer is called upon to honor drafts or demands for payment.  Here the customer will want to know whether he can secure an injunction against the issuer's honor of the draft or demand for payment.  The general principle is that this remedy is not available.  There are two quite different explanations for this.  First, it is said that the customer's remedy at law is adequate; he may recover damages against the beneficiary for any breach of the underlying contract.[127]  Second, it is simply in the nature of an irrevocable letter of credit that nonperformance by the beneficiary generally does not empower the issuer to dishonor.[128]

But an injunction is available in exceptional circumstances.  Section 5–114(2) indicates that an injunction will lie for forgery or fraud in the documents or fraud in the transaction, provided that the draft and documents have not passed into the hands of a holder in due course.[129]  The Code is silent, however, on whether a customer can enjoin honor on any other grounds.  One scholar has argued that in other, extraordinary circumstances an injunction should lie.[130]  Can the issuer insert a clause in the contract between itself and its customer providing against resort to the injunction device?  Article Five does not preclude this and presumably such a clause would be valid.  Anti-injunction clauses are not common, however.

Is the beneficiary an indispensable party to a suit by the customer to enjoin honor?  At least in international transactions he is not, for the beneficiary would usually not be subject to the jurisdiction of the court, and thus if he is indispensable, the injunction remedy would seldom be available.[131]  In domestic transactions there still may be

---

**126.**  Statutory law on the carrier's liability appears in UCC §§ 7–301; 7–309 and in The Federal Bill of Lading Act, 49 U.S.C.A. §§ 101, 102 (1970).

**127.**  See § 5–114(2); Schlesinger Study, supra note 37, at 1655.

**128.**  § 5–114(1).

**129.**  See section 5–114(2) quoted in the text following note 103 supra.

**130.**  Schlesinger Study, supra note 37, at 1655–57.

**131.**  Id. at 1667.

jurisdictional problems across state lines. But at least where jurisdiction is no problem, the case for requiring joinder of the beneficiary is strong, for an injunction may in fact violate the rights of the beneficiary.[132] Here the beneficiary will not receive payment, yet the issuer will not be liable for wrongful dishonor either.

### § 18–8  Actual or Prospective Breakdowns Adversely Affecting the Issuer (Herein mainly of wrongful honor)

An issuer that wrongfully honors a draft or other demand for payment is generally not entitled to reimbursement from its customer. Wrongful honor occurs most commonly when the issuer fails to exercise required care and thus pays against noncomplying documents. Recall that wrongful honor does not necessarily occur when the issuer pays against forged or fraudulent documents or when there is fraud in the transaction. The issuer may pay in these circumstances quite innocently.[133]

Assuming wrongful honor, and assuming the issuer may not secure reimbursement from the customer pursuant to the terms of their contract, what relief, if any, might the issuer have? Article Five sets forth one theory on which the issuer might recover the amount paid. Section 5–111(1) states:

> Unless otherwise agreed the beneficiary by transferring or presenting a documentary draft or demand for payment warrants to all interested parties that the necessary conditions of the credit have been complied with. This is in addition to any warranties arising under Articles 3, 4, 7 and 8.

Thus a beneficiary that procures honor by presenting nonconforming documents breaches the foregoing warranty,[134] and the issuer may presumably collect the face amount of the draft as damages. Courts have recognized a second theory of recovery as well, namely, restitution from the beneficiary for money paid by mistake.[135]

The issuer may find that the beneficiary cannot be sued locally, or is insolvent, or is otherwise judgment-proof. Might the issuer recover the money paid from any one else? The beneficiary may have made its presentment through a correspondent. Generally if the correspondent has paid the funds received upon honor over to the beneficiary, the correspondent will not be liable.[136] If the correspondent had become a holder in due course of the draft which the issuer ultimately paid, then the correspondent would not be liable either.[137]

---

132. Id. at 1667–70.

133. Here, the issuer would incur no liability. See §§ 5–109(2); 5–114(1). See also Springs v. Hanover Nat'l Bank, 209 N.Y. 224, 103 N.E. 156 (1913).

134. See § 5–111, Comment.

135. See, e. g., Fitzgerald v. Title Guarantee & Trust Co., 290 N.Y. 376, 49 N.E.2d 489 (1943).

136. See Archibald & Lewis Co. v. Banque de Commerce, 216 App.Div. 322, 329, 214 N.Y.S. 366, 373 (1st Dep't 1926).

137. See § 5–114(2) (a).

Otherwise the correspondent may be liable to the issuer for breach of warranty under section 5–111(2):

> Unless otherwise agreed a negotiating, advising, confirming, collecting or issuing bank presenting or transferring a draft or demand for payment under a credit warrants only the matters warranted by a collecting bank under Article 4 and any such bank transferring a document warrants only the matters warranted by an intermediary under Articles 7 and 8.

In some circumstances an issuer who wrongfully honors should be entitled to recover against its customer on an unjust enrichment theory, even though it would not be entitled to recover on a breach of contract theory. Suppose, for example, that the documents presented do not comply with the terms of the credit, yet the issuer honors the accompanying draft. This would constitute wrongful honor, and by the literal terms of the usual contract between the issuer and its customer, the issuer would not be entitled to reimbursement because the customer's contractual duty to reimburse is conditional upon the issuer's rightful honor. However, if the issuer wrongfully honors a draft accompanied by noncomplying documents, but the goods comply with the underlying contract between the beneficiary and the customer, the issuer should be entitled to reimbursement from the customer on the theory that the issuer's payment to the beneficiary unjustly enriched the customer at the issuer's expense.[138]

## § 18–9    Transfer and Assignment of Letters of Credit and Rights Thereunder; Back to Back Credits (Letters of credit as financing devices)

Heretofore we have treated the letter of credit mainly as a medium for assuring a seller of *payment*. The commercial significance of the letter of credit is not confined to its utility as a payment medium. Indeed the Associate Chief Reporter of the Uniform Commercial Code has stated that the utility of the letter of credit as a *financing device* "is the major reason for its inclusion in the Code."[139] Whether or not this is an overstatement, it is true that many beneficiaries of letters of credit do not themselves have the wherewithal to perform their underlying contracts with the customer who procured the issuance of the letter of credit in the first place. Assume that a Georgia businessman (*1*) has a contract to supply furniture to an Oregon buyer and (*2*) is the named beneficiary of a letter of credit procured by the Oregon buyer and issued through a Georgia bank. Assume further that the beneficiary-seller is not a manufacturer and also does not have the cash required to buy the furniture to fulfill his contract with the Ore-

---

138. No case has been found sustaining this point, but the restitutionary case law on mistaken discharge of another's obligation is analogous. See Restatement of Restitution § 17 (1937).

139. Mentschikoff, How to Handle Letters of Credit, 19 Bus.Law 107, 112 (1963).

gon buyer. The Georgia seller does have an unearned contract right against the Oregon buyer, but since this asset alone is of dubious value,[140] the seller might be unable to borrow against it to acquire the furniture from a Georgia manufacturer for shipment to Oregon. The seller might try to get in touch with the buyer and seek to have him advance the seller necessary money to procure the goods.[141] But buyers don't like to pay in advance. The Georgia seller is, however, a beneficiary of a letter of credit. How might he use this asset to procure the furniture for shipment to Oregon? One possibility may be ruled out right off. The Georgia seller could not merely "negotiate" the letter of credit to his Georgia manufacturer. A letter of credit is not a negotiable instrument.[142] There are three other possible courses of action: [143] (*1*) The beneficiary might transfer his rights and duties under the letter of credit to his supplier; (*2*) The beneficiary might transfer his prospective right to the proceeds of the letter of credit to a financer as security for a loan; or (*3*) The beneficiary might use the letter of credit to procure the issuance of a second letter of credit in favor of his lender or supplier.

### Transfer of Beneficiary's Rights and Duties under Letter of Credit to His Supplier

The Georgia beneficiary's supplier might be willing to step into the beneficiary's shoes. That is, he might be willing to assume both the burdens and the benefits of the seller-beneficiary's status under the letter of credit (as distinguished from his contract for the sale of goods to the Oregon buyer). Thus the supplier would assume the seller-beneficiary's duty to procure and present the necessary documents called for by the terms of the letter of credit and would also acquire the beneficiary's right to draw drafts under the letter of credit and receive payment from the issuer. But our Georgia seller doubtless expects to make a profit from the entire transaction, and to do this he must pay his supplier less for the goods than he is to receive for them under the terms of his own resale contract with the Oregon buyer (and the terms of the letter of credit). Accordingly, the Georgia supplier, under an arrangement whereby he assumes the burdens and the benefits of the seller's letter of credit status, will not realize the whole of these benefits. The contract between seller and supplier will provide that the supplier (transferee beneficiary) must remit to the seller (original beneficiary) the difference between the proceeds

---

**140.** See Gilmore, The Assignee of Contract Rights and His Precarious Security, 74 Yale L.J. 217 (1964).

**141.** On the so-called "red-clause," see W. Ward & H. Harfield, Bank Credits and Acceptances 157–61 (4th ed. 1958).

**142.** See Crawford, Practical Use of Documentary Credit Paper, 30 Tulane L.Rev. 235 (1956).

**143.** The best single overall treatment of this topic in periodical literature is Ufford, Transfer and Assignment of Letters of Credit Under the Uniform Commercial Code, 7 Wayne L.Rev. 263 (1960). See also Schlesinger Study, supra note 37, at 1691–1701; W. Ward & Harfield, Bank Credits and Acceptances ch. 10 (4th ed. 1958).

paid by the issuer to the supplier and the amount owed the supplier by the seller for the goods he bought from the supplier.[144]

Section 5–116(1) is intended to authorize a beneficiary to transfer his benefits and burdens *qua* beneficiary to his own supplier,[145] but the letter of credit must itself provide that it is "transferrable" or "assignable." The express language of Article Five is otherwise silent with respect to this type of financing transaction. Comment 2 appears to say that the original beneficiary (seller) remains liable for the quality of the supplier's performance in procuring and presenting documents to the issuer. Does the original beneficiary remain liable as well to the Oregon buyer on the underlying contract of sale? Absent a novation, it would seem so.[146]

Is a transferee beneficiary (the Georgia supplier) in a financing arrangement of the above kind subject to any defenses or setoffs that the issuer has against the original beneficiary by virtue of the instant or other dealings between them? Article Five is silent on this question.[147] A prospective transferee beneficiary could try to protect himself by seeking an agreement from the issuer not to assert any such defenses or setoffs.[148]

There is also the risk that, after transfer, the original beneficiary may forge documents, draw drafts thereunder, negotiate them to third parties or present them to the issuer, and receive payment. To protect against this risk, the prospective transferee beneficiary can insist on the issuance of an original letter of credit to the initial beneficiary seller (or the amendment of an outstanding letter) which provides that any drafts drawn under it will not be honored by the issuer unless presented by the transferee beneficiary or his correspondent. Alternately, the letter itself could provide that the issuer will not honor any drafts not accompanied by the original letter of credit itself (in addition to the other, usual documents). Or the "notation" credit device could be used.[149]

Beyond the foregoing risks there are still other reasons why the parties might not use a financing device involving a transfer of seller-beneficiary's benefits and burdens to enable him to fulfill his underlying contract with the buyer. For one thing this device entails the risk that the seller's supplier will learn not only the name of the seller's customer, but also his profit margin, and the supplier may

144. Of course, there are many possible variations on such a transaction.

145. § 5–116, Comment 1.

146. At least in general contract law, an assignor (delegator) retains "standby" liability. See Restatement of Contracts § 160(4) (1932).

147. Accord, B. Kozolchyk, Commercial Letters of Credit in the Americas 500 (1966).

148. On problems posed by possible availability of such defenses and setoffs, see also B. Kozolchyk, Letters of Credit in the Americas 498–502, 516–17 (1966); McGowan, Assignability of Letters of Credit, 13 Law & Contemp. Prob. 666 (1948).

149. See § 5–108.

thereafter undertake to deal directly with the customer. It is possible to minimize this risk.[150] Perhaps the principal objection to use of this device comes from the buyers who arrange for the issuance of a transferrable letter of credit in the first place. The Oregon buyer in our example will not stand ready to have the issuer issue a transferrable letter of credit under which the Georgia seller could name just any Tom, Dick, or Harry as transferee beneficiary. And for good reason. By the terms of the usual letter of credit, the issuer's obligation is relatively absolute. If the conditions of the credit are met, the issuer must pay (and will pay), and the buyer will have no recourse against the issuer. Yet compliance with these conditions is not itself a guarantee that the seller (and his transferee) will ultimately perform seller's contract with buyer. The letter of credit beneficiary (transferee, here) only presents documents. These could be skillfully forged. Or, they could cover crates that include not Georgia furniture, but rotten Georgia peaches. Thus the risks to our buyer in dealing with an unknown transferee are substantial. He might just refuse to have a transferrable letter of credit issued in the first place.[151]

### Transfer by Beneficiary Merely of his Rights to Letter of Credit Proceeds as Security for a Loan from His Financer

Let us assume in our Georgia-Oregon furniture sale that the Oregon buyer is unwilling to have a transferrable letter of credit issued and that the Georgia seller desires to borrow money to procure the furniture from his supplier. Assume further that the Georgia seller's financer, a local Georgia bank, is unwilling to take an assignment of the Georgia seller's unearned rights under his furniture sale contract with the Oregon buyer as security for a loan.[152]

The Georgia seller as a beneficiary under a letter of credit could assign his right to the proceeds thereof to his Georgia bank as security for a loan under section 5–116(2). He can do so even where the letter of credit provides that it is not transferrable. With the loan the seller could then pay his own supplier, procure the necessary documents under the letter of credit, and present the same to the issuer, and remit the amount owed to the lending bank. The foregoing arrangement can take other forms, too. For example, the Georgia bank might take an assignment of proceeds from the Georgia seller, but instead of disbursing the loan to the seller, it could notify the seller's supplier that his supplier may draw drafts on the Georgia bank for furniture supplied.[153] Of course, the seller might even as-

150. One method is characterized in Ufford, Transfer and Assignment of Letters of Credit Under the Uniform Commercial Code, 7 Wayne L.Rev. 263, 268 (1960).

151. Schlesinger Study supra, note 37, at 1691–92.

152. See Gilmore, The Assignee of Contract Rights and His Precarious Security, 74 Yale L.J. 217 (1964).

153. But see Ufford, Transfer and Assignment of Letters of Credit Under the Uniform Commercial Code, 7 Wayne L.Rev. 263, 271 (1960).

sign the right to proceeds to his supplier as security for an extension of credit by the supplier himself.

Observe that the beneficiary's mere assignment of his right to proceeds is not a delegation by the beneficiary of his burdens, that is, of his duties to procure proper documents called for by the terms of the letter of credit. Thus the ultimate buyer who arranged the letter of credit in the first place at least does not incur the risk that an unknown party will procure and present forged or fraudulent documents.

What of risks to the assignee financer who lends (our Georgia bank) or extends credit (our Georgia supplier) against an assignment of proceeds from the seller-beneficiary as collateral security? In short how good is this security? First there are risks of assignor double-dealing. After making the assignment the assignor might procure forged documents, negotiate or present them with a properly drawn draft to a third party or to the issuer, and pocket the entire proceeds. Section 5–116(2) allows the assignee to protect himself against assignor double-dealing. By the terms of that section the assignee of proceeds may take possession of the letter of credit and send notice of the assignment (signed by the beneficiary) to the issuer. This notice must reasonably identify the letter of credit involved in the assignment and include a request to pay the assignee. Once these steps are taken, under section 5–116(2) the issuer would remain liable to the assignee if the issuer were duped into paying a double dealing assignor. The language of the section does not in so many words say as much. Yet this appears to be the intent of the subsection and is consistent with cognate Code provisions.[154]

Is there any way to protect the assignee against a double dealing assignor who, after assignment, nonetheless wrongfully negotiates a draft (with forged documents) drawn under the credit to an innocent third party? Here if the issuer is obligated to honor the draft presented by the third party, then it should not also remain obligated to the assignee. And without more, it would appear that the issuer would be so obligated under section 5–114(2) (a). The assignee therefore needs protection against this possibility. One way to provide it is as follows. The letter of credit and drafts can be drawn (or amended) to provide that *no draft* drawn under it is to be honored by the issuer unless accompanied by the letter of credit itself. A third party who bought such drafts and documents from the double dealing assignor would, it appears, not be a party taking "under circumstances which would make it a holder in due course" within subsection 5–114(2). The issuer would, therefore, not be required to honor the drafts even though the documents complied.[155]

154.   Cf. § 9–318(3).

155.   The notation credit device sanctioned by section 5–108 could also be used. See Ufford, Transfer and Assignment of Letters of Credit under the Uniform Commercial Code, 7 Wayne L.Rev. 263, 280–81 (1960).

The prospective assignee can also protect against assignor double dealing whereby the assignor negotiates drafts to an innocent third party with priority under section 5–114(2) by having the original letter of credit issued as a "straight" credit. The purchaser of a draft under a straight credit from the double dealing assignor does not become privy to the issuer's promise to pay, for on a straight credit, the issuer promises only to pay the beneficiary and not those to whom he may transfer drafts drawn under the credit.

So much for risks that the assignor will double deal. How is the assignee protected against creditors of the assignor beneficiary who seek by garnishment or the like to reach the beneficiary's rights under the letter of credit?[156] Provided the assignee has taken the steps specified in section 5–116(2), he will have a perfected security interest with priority over subsequent garnishing creditors under Article Nine.[157] Similarly, such an assignee would also prevail as against a subsequent assignee of the same collateral under the "first to perfect" rule of section 9–312 of the Code.

Could an issuer with a setoff or other defense against the beneficiary (by virtue of a continuing relation between them) effectively set up such a defense against the assignee? Article Five only says that the assignee who complies with 5–116(2) becomes an Article Nine secured party. Section 9–318(1) further suggests that the assignee of proceeds would be subject to such setoffs or other defenses of the issuer. The assignee may be able to protect against this by procuring an agreement directly from the issuer not to assert setoffs or other defenses.[158]

### *Beneficiary's Use of His Rights under Letter of Credit to Procure Issuance of a Second Letter of Credit in Favor of His Lender or Supplier*

So called "back-to-back" letters of credit have been widely used in international trade. In the immediately preceding discussion, we canvassed a variety of risks incurred by the assignee of proceeds (a lender or supplier of the beneficiary) under a non-transferrable letter of credit. A prospective assignee might refuse to become an assignee and insist on being a beneficiary of a second letter of credit procured by the beneficiary of the first ("prime") letter of credit. For example, a Georgia financing institution or the Georgia furniture supplier might demand that the Georgia seller have a second letter of credit issued naming the financer or the supplier as beneficiary. With this status, the Georgia financer or supplier would not incur many of the risks otherwise incurred by a mere assignee of proceeds. Indeed, the Georgia financer or supplier would be assured of payment

---

156. For a case involving just such an attack by an unsecured creditor of the assignor, see Eriksson v. Refiners Export Co., 264 App.Div. 525, 35 N.Y.S.2d 829 (1st Dep't 1942).

157. §§ 9–201; 9–301.

158. See text accompanying notes 147–148 supra.

upon drawing and presenting the drafts (and accompanying documents) called for by the terms of the second letter of credit.

But how could the beneficiary of the "prime" letter of credit, the Georgia seller, induce a Georgia bank to issue a second letter of credit naming his financer or supplier as beneficiary? The prospective issuer of the second credit would likely be willing to issue it on the security of an assignment by the Georgia seller of his right to proceeds under the prime credit. Such an issuer incurs the risks and can have the protections of an assignee already discussed in the preceding subsection.[159] The issuer of the second credit should also see that documents required under the prime credit are procured prior to the time for expiration of the Georgia seller's status as beneficiary of the prime credit. Usually, this poses no problem and the issuer of the second credit simply pays off the beneficiary of the second credit (the seller's financer or supplier) by honoring drafts accompanied by the very documents that the issuer of the second credit will (as assignee of the rights of the beneficiary of the prime credit) forward with further drafts to the issuer of the prime credit for honor.

The illustrative transaction used throughout this section involved a deal between a Georgia furniture seller and an Oregon buyer. The more usual deal would be between a stateside buyer and a foreign seller. But the virtue of a domestic transaction for illustrative purposes is just that it does show how the utility of letters of credit as financing devices is not confined to the international sphere. Moreover, domestic uses of letters of credit for financing purposes are on the increase.

159.  See text accompanying notes 152–158 supra.

# CHAPTER 19

# BULK TRANSFERS

*Analysis*

Sec.
19-1. Introduction.
19-2. Bulk Transfers to Which Article Six of the Code Applies.
19-3. Requirements of Article Six—Ways the Parties to a Bulk Transfer May Fail to Comply.
19-4. "Individual" Remedies of Transferor's Creditors in Event of Non-compliance.
19-5. "Individual" Remedies of Transferor's Creditors in Event of Compliance.
19-6. Conflicts Between Transferor's Creditors and Third Parties—Some Problems of Priority.
19-7. Individual Creditor's Recovery v. Collective Remedies—An Addendum.

## § 19-1  Introduction

Consider a merchant who sells merchandise from stock. He might manufacture the merchandise himself and finance his operations from loans. More often he will buy merchandise ready-made from wholesalers and other suppliers who extend him credit. In either event his creditors usually expect to be paid directly or indirectly from what he realizes upon selling the merchandise to his customers, for usually this is his principal, if not his sole, source of income. It is natural enough, then, for his trade creditors to evince interest in how well his business is going. It is all the more natural for them to evince concern should they hear that he has sold or proposes to sell his entire business or a major part of his inventory all at once.

Yet not every such sale or proposed sale is cause for creditor concern. A merchant might only be changing the form of his business entity. He might be doing business as a sole proprietor or as a co-partner and want merely to convert to corporate status, with no change in substance and thus no adverse impact on creditors. Or a merchant who "sells out" might be wholly solvent and a pillar of strength in the community, financially and otherwise. Here his creditors will have no cause for alarm. Or a merchant might sell out to a transferee even more solvent than he, and who expressly contracts to pay all of the merchant's business debts as they fall due. In these circumstances the transferor's creditors would become third party "creditor-beneficiaries" with enforceable claims against the transferee. Moreover, they would retain whatever rights they had against the transferor (but would be entitled to only one satisfaction). Here too our merchant's creditors have no cause for concern or complaint. Indeed they may well be in a better position than they were prior to the sale.

But suppose the transferor is of doubtful solvency or is disposed to pocket the proceeds of sale and skip the state. Those of his creditors who know the facts will and should be alarmed, for they will be looking to their debtor-merchant's business income for payment. If this income should prove insufficient, they might as a last resort realize considerable payment by levying on the debtor's merchandise. But if the debtor should sell out and squander the proceeds or skip the state, his creditors could no longer look to his business income for payment, for the business would no longer be owned by their debtor, but by his transferee. Moreover in the absence of a statute such as a "bulk sales law," the transferor's creditors would not, in general, be entitled to levy on or otherwise trace the merchandise formerly owned by their debtor into the hands of his transferee.[1] It is a general principle that the *bona fide* purchaser for value of business assets cuts off the rights that the transferor's creditors had prior to the transfer to levy or the like on such assets.[2]

There are exceptions to this general principle. Even in the absence of a "bulk sales law" the transferor's creditors can trace the business assets into the hands of the transferee in limited circumstances. Consider, for example, the "sham" bulk transfer in which the transferor goes through all the legal motions of selling out to a close friend or relative, at a less than fair price, hoping to hang around and reenter the business through the back door. Or consider the transferor who hastily dumps the business on a knowing transferee for less than full value and then skips town, or one who sells for a publicly stated price much lower than the price he actually receives under the table. In such cases the transferor's creditors may have received some prorated payment on their claims, but if and when the true facts eventually come to light, these creditors will want more and will want to levy on or otherwise reach business assets in the hands of the transferee. In the foregoing kinds of cases they will be entitled to reach those assets under some branch of the law of fraudulent conveyances. Thus, for example, sections 4, 7, and 9 of the Uniform Fraudulent Conveyance Act provide:

## § 4. Conveyances by Insolvent

Every conveyance made and every obligation incurred by a person who is or will be thereby rendered insolvent is fraudulent as to creditors without regard to his actual intent if the conveyance is made or the obligation is incurred without a fair consideration.

1. See generally Billig, Bulk Sales Laws: A Study in Economic Adjustment, 77 U.Pa.L.Rev. 72, 101 (1928).

2. Walbrun v. Babbitt, 83 U.S. (16 Wall.) 577 (1872); Hagan v. Walker, 55 U.S. (14 How.) 29 (1852); Gibson v. Stevens, 49 U.S. (8 How.) 384 (1850). See 1 G. Glenn, Fraudulent Conveyances and Preferences §§ 236, 359 (rev. ed. 1940).

## § 7.    Conveyance Made With Intent to Defraud

Every conveyance made and every obligation incurred with actual intent, as distinguished from intent presumed in law, to hinder, delay, or defraud either present or future creditors, is fraudulent as to both present and future creditors.

## § 9.    Rights of Creditors Whose Claims Have Matured

(1) Where a conveyance or obligation is fraudulent as to a creditor, such creditor, when his claim has matured, may, as against any person except a purchaser for fair consideration without knowledge of the fraud at the time of the purchase, or one who has derived title immediately or mediately from such a purchaser,

    (a) Have the conveyance set aside or obligation annulled to the extent necessary to satisfy his claim, or

    (b) Disregard the conveyance and attach or levy execution upon the property conveyed.

(2) A purchaser who without actual fraudulent intent has given less than a fair consideration for the conveyance or obligation, may retain the property or obligation as security for repayment.

Observe that if the transferee of the business can show under section 9 of the Uniform Act that *he* purchased for fair consideration without knowledge of the fraud at the time of the purchase, he will be protected from efforts by the transferor's creditors to reach the assets in his hands. Moreover even if the transferee cannot prove these facts, the transferor's creditors will be out of luck if the transferee has resold to a third party who took in good faith. Generally the rights and remedies of the transferor's creditors under fraudulent conveyance law are of limited scope and do not comprise a very sizeable exception to the general principle that a transferor's creditors may not levy on or otherwise reach the assets sold to the transferee.[3]

A second exception, the so-called "equitable receivership" exception, is similarly narrow. The transferor's creditors generally cannot get a judge to subject transferred assets to a receivership unless they can show that their debtor acted fraudulently or otherwise inequitably.[4] A third exception is even more limited in scope, for it presupposes that the bulk transfer is to one of the transferor's creditors to satisfy an antecedent debt, and a "voidable preference" within

---

3. On the law of fraudulent conveyances as applied to bulk sales, see 1 G. Glenn, Fraudulent Conveyances and Preferences §§ 310–15 (rev. ed. 1940).

4. On the equity receivership as applied to bulk sales, see 4 R. Clark, Law of Receivers §§ 1013, 1111 (3d ed. 1959).

the meaning of section 60 of the Bankruptcy Act at that.[5] Many merchants sell out not to one of their own creditors but to some other party. Moreover the transferee will often pay a consideration not obviously unfair and will often be innocent of any participation in a fraudulent scheme of the transferor. Further it will not always be possible for the transferor's creditors to throw the transferor into bankruptcy.

Thus more commonly than not, the transferor's creditors will (absent a bulk sales law) be unable to reach assets in the hands of the transferee under any of the three exceptions just canvassed, even though the transferor is himself bent on defrauding his creditors. And even when the transferor's creditors do have remedies under one of these exceptions, their remedies will all have a common deficiency. When the transferor's creditors learn of the bulk sale, it will usually be an accomplished fact, and each remedy will be an "after the fact" remedy, that is, one which comes into play after the bulk transfer has been made, after the money, or much of it, may have changed hands, with the transferor thereby having opportunities to skip, squander, or secrete, and the transferee having occasions to resell or to encumber to third parties. Of course, any time the transferor's creditors do learn of an impending bulk sale, they may be able to enjoin it or take some other comparable step. Absent a bulk sales law, they will often not learn of it until after the fact.

Against the foregoing factual and legal background, it is possible to see the need for and the distinctive protection afforded by a bulk sales law. The narrowness and after-the-fact nature of remedies afforded by exceptions to the general principle that a transferor's creditors cannot follow his assets into the transferee's hands leaves these creditors in an unduly vulnerable position. Of course, they might protect themselves by taking security interests in the merchandise they supply, for such security would be good even against a transferee of the business who bought in good faith and for fair value.[6] Some day this may prove sufficient for trade creditors.[7] Today not all creditors can or will protect themselves in this way. What special protection might a bulk sales law offer? This is the central question of the present chapter. A bulk sales law might require the prospective transferee to notify the transferor's creditors of the impending sale sometime in advance, and also require the parties to provide information about the sale on the basis of which these creditors could then seek to protect themselves by levy or the like as indicated. Article Six of the Code on bulk transfers imposes such requirements.[8] Moreover if the transferee should fail to comply with

5. 11 U.S.C.A. § 96 (1970). The transferor's creditors might try to make still other uses of the Bankruptcy Act. See text accompaning notes 102–104, and 109–113 infra.

6. See, e. g., §§ 9–201; 9–301.

7. See especially section 9–312(3) which is a priority provision designed to enable inventory suppliers to take security to protect themselves with ease.

8. The origins of bulk sales legislation in the United States are admirably recounted in Billig, Bulk Sales Law:

requirements of this nature, the resulting bulk transfer could be considered "ineffective against any creditor of the transferor." Among other things this would mean that assets sold to the transferee remain subject to levy and the like by the transferor's creditors even after they have passed into the hands of the transferee. Again Article Six of the Code so provides.[9]

A further possible kind of protection is this: The transferee might be required to see that the relevant part of the proceeds of the sale finds its way into the hands of the transferor's creditors. Article Six includes a provision to this effect [10] but it is optional in nature and only eighteen states have enacted this provision.[11]

In general, then, bulk sales laws are designed not only to protect the transferor's creditors against fraud, these laws are also intended to protect against inadequacy of consideration, even where transferee and transferor alike are innocent of any wrongdoing. Moreover, a bulk sales law such as Article Six not only affords remedies where none existed before (by permitting levy and the like against assets in the hands of a noncomplying transferee), it also affords better remedial possibilities than those already exceptionally available under fraudulent conveyance law, receivership law, or bankruptcy law. These latter are after-the-fact remedies. Bulk sales laws are designed to provide notice to creditors in advance and thus afford the transferor's creditors an opportunity to act before the sale.[12]

## § 19–2  Bulk Transfers to Which Article Six of the Code Applies

Article Six does not apply to all types of bulk transfers that may adversely affect the transferor's creditors. Section 6–102 sets forth the general conditions for the applicability of the Article.[13] Section 6–103 embodies eight "exceptions," that is, eight kinds of transfers which satisfy the general conditions of section 6–102, but to which the Article nonetheless does not apply.

Section 6–102 provides as follows:

> (1) A "bulk transfer" is any transfer in bulk and not in the ordinary course of the transferor's business of a major part of the materials, supplies, merchandise

A Study in Economic Adjustment, 77 U.Pa.L.Rev. 72 (1928). See also section 19–3 infra.

9. §§ 6–104; 6–105; 6–107. Article Six was widely amended upon its enactment in the various states, however. See Bamberger, Article 6 of the UCC: Uniformity Gone Awry, 26 Bus.Law. 329 (1970).

10. § 6–106.

11. Alaska, Florida, Idaho, Kansas, Kentucky, Maryland, Mississippi, Montana, New Jersey, North Dakota, Oklahoma, Pennsylvania, South Dakota, Tennessee, Texas, Utah, Washington, and West Virginia.

12. Billig, Bulk Sales Laws: A Study in Economic Adjustment, 77 U.Pa.L. Rev. 72, 101 (1928).

13. For another recent general discussion of these conditions, see Benett, Bulk Transfers Under the Uniform Commercial Code, 19 U.Kan.L.Rev. 709 (1971).

or other inventory (Section 9–109) of an enterprise subject to this Article.

(2) A transfer of a substantial part of the equipment (Section 9–109) of such an enterprise is a bulk transfer if it is made in connection with a bulk transfer of inventory, but not otherwise.

(3) The enterprises subject to this Article are all those whose principal business is the sale of merchandise from stock, including those who manufacture what they sell.

(4) Except as limited by the following section all bulk transfers of goods located within this state are subject to this Article.

These provisions can be profitably analyzed in terms of the specified kinds of enterprises, kinds of transfers, and kinds of property to which Article Six applies. First, the kinds of enterprises: the relevant language is in subsection (3). "The enterprises subject to this Article are all those whose principal business is the sale of merchandise from stock, including those who manufacture what they sell." According to Comment 2, this excludes "farming, . . . contracting, . . . professional services, cleaning shops, barber shops, pool halls, hotels, restaurants, and the like whose principal business is the sale not of merchandise but of services." The Comment adds: "While some bulk sales risk exists in the excluded businesses, they have in common the fact that unsecured credit is not commonly extended on the faith of a stock of merchandise."

There are now several cases under 6–102(3). Consistent with text and comments of this subsection, courts have excluded the sale of a printing company,[14] a photo-finishing business,[15] a vehicle towing business,[16] a hotel,[17] a small loan company,[18] and a business selling assignments of contracts for the installment and maintenance of vending machines.[19] These businesses are not principally engaged in the sale of merchandise from stock. So far, there is a split of authority over whether restaurants and bars are included.[20] Accord-

14. Markert v. College Offset Press, Inc., 6 Pa.D. & C.2d 519, 1 UCC Rep. Serv. 320 (C.P.1955).

15. Film Marketing Servs., Inc. v. Homer Photo Labs, Inc., 5 UCC Rep. Serv. 201 (Pa.C.P.1966).

16. All Nite Garage, Inc. v. A. A. A. Towing Inc., 85 Nev. 193, 452 P.2d 902, 6 UCC Rep.Serv. 529 (1969).

17. Kane-Miller Corp. v. Tip Tree Corp., 60 Misc.2d 776, 303 N.Y.S.2d 273, 6 UCC Rep.Serv. 721 (Sup.Ct.1969).

18. Credithrift Financial Corp. v. Guggenheim, 232 So.2d 400, 7 UCC Rep. Serv. 728 (Fla.Ct.App.1970).

19. Macke Co. v. Pizza of Gaithersburg, Inc., 259 Md. 479, 270 A.2d 645, 8 UCC Rep.Serv. 372 (1970).

20. Compare Chas. Adler & Son, Inc. v. DiNunzio, 5 UCC Rep.Serv. 743 (Pa. C.P.1967); Zinni v. One Township Line Corp., 36 Pa.D. & C.2d 297, 3 UCC Rep.Serv. 303 (C.P.1965); Brooks v. Lambert, 10 Pa.D. & C.2d 237, 1 UCC Rep.Serv. 316 (C.P.1957); with Silco Automatic Vending Co. v. Howells, 102 N.J.Super. 243, 245 A.2d 765, 5 UCC

ing to the comments, restaurants certainly are not.[21]  Is it the principal business of a bar to sell alcohol from stock?  Presumably, yet do creditors generally extend unsecured credit "on the faith of" this stock?  Presumably not.[22]

What kinds of *transfers* are included?  Section 6–102(1) says, "A bulk transfer is any transfer in bulk and not in the ordinary course of the transferor's business of a major part of the materials, supplies," etc.  What does "major part" require?  At least one court has held under prior similar legislation that it means more than fifty percent.[23]  But fifty percent of what—quantity or value?  Surely the reference must be to value, for this is what is of interest to creditors.  And some pre-Code cases have so held.[24]  We would offer the further *caveat* that transferees should not rely on the fifty percent of value test of "major part."  The statutory words are "major part."  We can easily imagine a court holding that forty-five percent of value constitutes a "major part."

Suppose thirty percent of value is sold on Monday to Ajax and twenty five percent on Tuesday to Acme.  Will a court require Ajax and Acme to comply with Article Six?  It seems that it should, for the impact on creditors is just the same as if only one transferee were involved, and Pre-Code cases have so stated.[25]  Suppose the transferor owns several branch stores of the same business (for instance women's clothing stores) and decides to sell all but one of them.  Will a court hold that Article Six applies, even though the value of goods in one store is far less than fifty percent of what the transferor has in stock in all his stores?  Presumably it will, at least if different creditors supply the different stores.  Again there is some relevant pre-Code law.[26]  What if all the stores except the one to be sold are located out of state?  Applicability of Article Six is here all the more clear, especially in light of section 6–102 which says that "all bulk transfers of goods located within this state are subject to this Article."

But even if fifty percent of value is transferred, the transfer may still not be a bulk transfer under section 6–102(1), for such

---

Rep.Serv. 625 (Ch.Div.1968), aff'd 105 N.J.Super. 511, 253 A.2d 480, 6 UCC Rep.Serv. 531 (1969); Levy v. Paul, 207 Va. 100, 147 S.E.2d 722, 3 UCC Rep.Serv. 412 (1966).

**21.** § 6–102, Comment 2.

**22.** See Brooks v. Lambert, 10 Pa.D. & C. 2d 237, 1 UCC Rep.Serv. 316 (C.P. 1957).

**23.** Zenith Radio Distrib. Corp. v. Mateer, 311 Ill.App. 263, 35 N.E.2d 815 (1941).

**24.** See, e. g., Davis v. Lawrence, Cedarhurst Bank, 204 F.2d 431 (2d Cir. 1953), cert. denied 346 U.S. 877 (1953).

See also Miller, Bulk Sales Laws: Meaning To Be Attached to the Quantitative and Qualitative Requirements Phrases of the Statutes, 1954 Wash.U. L.Q. 283, 284–98.

**25.** See, e. g., Main v. Hall, 41 F.2d 715 (7th Cir. 1930); Sabin v. Horenstein, 260 F. 754 (9th Cir. 1919); Slaughter v. Cooper Corp. No. 2, 20 Tenn.App. 241, 97 S.W.2d 648 (1936). But see Larson v. Judd, 200 Ill.App. 420 (1916).

**26.** See Corrigan v. Miller, 338 Ill.App. 212, 86 N.E.2d 853 (1949).  See also Larson v. Judd, 200 Ill.App. 420 (1916); Annot., 33 A.L.R. 62 (1924).

a transfer may still be in the "ordinary course of the transferor's business." A comparab.e requirement appeared in pre-Code bulk sales acts,[27] and cases interpreting this comparable pre-Code language will remain authoritative under the Code. In one such case, Sternberg v. Rubinstein,[28] the court held that a sale of a large batch of off-season shoes was still in the ordinary course of the transferor's business partly because (1) "in the business of shoe retailing the sale of off-season wares is no rare and irregular occurrence," [29] (2) there was no attempt to defraud creditors (though the transferor did soon go bankrupt), and (3) such resales should not be made burdensome by requiring the transferor's buyers to comply with bulk sales provisions. There was a vigorous dissent, and some cases look the other way.[30]

So much for the kinds of enterprises and kinds of transfers covered. What kinds of property must these transfers involve? Section 6–102(1) refers to "materials, supplies, merchandise or other inventory (Section 9–109) . . . ." Section 9–109(4) defines inventory as follows:

> "inventory" if they are held by a person who holds them for sale or lease or to be furnished under contracts of service or if he has so furnished them, or if they are raw materials, work in process or materials used or consumed in a business. Inventory of a person is not to be classified as his equipment.

Comment 3 to section 6–102 states that transfers of "investment securities, . . . of money, accounts receivable, chattel paper, contract rights, negotiable instruments . . .," and choses in action generally are not covered. Are these forms of property subject to the remedies of the transferor's creditors in event of noncompliance with Article Six, provided property of a kind that Article Six does apply to is transferred? The Code does not say, but the implication appears to be negative.

Besides the forms of property enumerated in section 6–102(1), Article Six also applies to equipment as defined in section 9–109(2), provided that (1) a "substantial part" of the equipment of the business is transferred and (2) this transfer is "in connection with" a bulk transfer of inventory.[31] Presumably the "substantial part" requirement (unlike the "major part" one) is satisfied if the transfer involves significantly less than fifty percent of the equipment of the

---

27. E. g., N.Y.Pers.Prop.Law § 44 (McKinney 1962). See, e. g., Fiske Rubber Co. v. Hayes, 131 Ark. 248, 199 S.W. 96 (1917); Krueger v. Hammond, 123 Kan. 319, 255 P. 30 (1927); Sternberg v. Rubenstein, 305 N.Y. 235, 112 N.E.2d 210 (1953).

28. 305 N.Y. 235, 112 N.E.2d 210 (1953).

29. Id. at 240, 112 N.E.2d at 212.

30. E. g., Jubas v. Sampsell, 185 F.2d 333 (9th Cir. 1950). See Annot., 36 A.L.R.2d 1141 (1954) and cases cited therein.

31. § 6–102(2).

business. But even if all the equipment is transferred, Article Six does not apply unless there is also a bulk transfer of inventory.[32]

It should be noted that certain auction sales fall within the scope of Article Six, but they do so only by virtue of a special provision in the Article [33] and not by virtue of its basic scope provisions.

Section 6–103 specifically exempts several types of transactions that otherwise fall within the Article's scope provisions. First, security transfers are exempt.[34] Ordinarily these take the form of security interests in inventory and equipment under Article Nine. Doubtless such transfers can serve as a vehicle for fraud of the sort bulk sales laws are in part aimed against, as where a debtor borrows from a knowing lender against the security of his entire inventory and then skips town.[35] But to be weighed against this risk are the following considerations. The risk of skipping is not so great as in the outright sale. Article Nine itself requires some public notice of the transfer. And it should not be made overly difficult for businessmen to borrow on a secured basis. If each prospective secured creditor were required to comply with a bulk sales law, this would slow things down and perhaps even halt some loans and credit extensions. These and other considerations moved the draftsmen of Article Six to exempt secured transactions and also transfers in settlement or realization of a security interest.

Second, general assignments for the benefit of all creditors of the transferor, and subsequent transfers by the assignee thereunder, are also exempt.[36] Such assignments are usually a kind of common law liquidation of the transferor's business. And when they are truly for the benefit of all creditors, it is needless to comply with a bulk sales law.[37] Third, certain sales made by judicial or public officers (including judicial sales and sales by trustees in bankruptcy) are also exempt. So too are transfers of property that are exempt from execution.[38]

Fourth, Article Six exempts all transfers to a person maintaining a known place of business in the state who becomes bound to pay the debts of the transferor in full, gives public notice of that fact, and is solvent after becoming so bound.[39] This exemption is applicable in numerous cases, for there are significant business advantages to a transferee who buys a business in this way. He in effect steps into the shoes of his transferor with respect to any good ongoing business relationships developed with suppliers. And a transferee who assumes such debts does not have to dig up as much cash

---

32. See Brooks v. Lambert, 10 Pa.D. & C.2d 237, 1 UCC Rep.Serv. 316 (C.P. 1957).

33. § 6–108.

34. § 6–103(1).

35. See, e. g., In re Rosom Util., Inc., 105 F.2d 132, 134 (2d Cir. 1939).

36. § 6–103(3).

37. See J. MacLachlan, Law of Bankruptcy § 8 (1956).

38. § 6–103(4), (5), (8).

39. § 6–103(6).

at the time of purchase as he would if he were to pay full value to the transferor for all assets acquired in the transfer. This fourth exemption can be easily explained. The main purpose of Article Six is to give the transferor's creditors a reasonable chance to collect their debts; they have this chance when the requirements of this exemption are met.[40] Indeed they may be in a better position after the transfer, for they will then have two parties to look to for collection.

Fifth, certain transfers that merely reflect changes in the form or structure of the business enterprise, without any significant changes in substance, are exempt under section 6–103(7).[41]

## § 19–3   Requirements of Article Six—Ways the Parties to a Bulk Transfer May Fail to Comply

The parties to a bulk transfer may fail to comply [42] with Article Six simply because they fail to perceive its applicability to their transaction. But even if they attempt to comply, they may still fail, and in several possible ways. Putting sales at auction [43] to one side, and assuming the state has not enacted section 6–106 (as most have not), the parties to a bulk transfer must satisfy four basic requirements. First, the transferee must require the transferor to furnish a list of his existing creditors.[44] Presumably those creditors are the ones existing at the time the transferor requests the list. "Creditors" includes all persons who are known to assert claims against the transferor even though such claims are disputed.[45] Besides ordinary trade creditors, the category includes general breach of contract claimants, tort claimants, and tax claimants as well.[46] And it makes no difference that the legality as well as the amount of their claims is disputed; they still must be listed, for the statutory language describing creditors includes the phrase "even though such claims are disputed," a phrase broad enough to cover disputes of all kinds. But when the amount of the claim is known, it must be stated.[47]

---

**40.** § 6–103, Comment 4.

**41.** § 6–103, Comment 5. See also Aluminum Shapes, Inc. v. K-A-Liquidating Co., 290 F.Supp. 356, 5 UCC Rep.Serv. 1194 (W.D.Pa.1968); Annot., 96 A.L.R. 1213 (1935).

**42.** Lamey, How to Handle a Bulk Transfer, 19 Bus.Law. 67 (1963).

**43.** § 6–108.

**44.** § 6–104(1) (a).

**45.** § 6–104(2).

**46.** The principal draftsman of Article Six testified before the New York Law Revision Commission as follows:

It is quite true . . . that the definition of creditors does include contingent claims, etc.—that was deliberate, I think, because no one could quite see any reason for excluding the person who was hit by the company's truck any more than the person who had sold goods on credit to the company before the transfer. At least the sponsoring organizations couldn't see the point in justice at which one could separate the two groups of creditors.

1 N.Y. State Law Revision Comm'n, 1954 Report 655 (1954). Accordingly, it would appear that Aluminum Shapes, Inc. v. K-A Liquidating Co., 290 F. Supp. 356, 5 UCC Rep.Serv. 1194 (W. D.Pa.1968) is erroneous.

**47.** § 6–104(2).

Not only must the creditors' names and the amounts of their claims (when known) be listed, their business addresses must be set forth too.[48] Moreover, the list of creditors with accompanying information must be signed and sworn to, or affirmed by, the transferor or his agent.[49] If falsely sworn to or affirmed, the transferor becomes subject to conviction under local penal statutes for the crime of false swearing, but the transfer is not rendered ineffective.[50]

Section 6–104(3) provides that:

> Responsibility for the completeness and accuracy of the list of creditors rests on the transferor, and the transfer is not rendered ineffective by errors or omissions therein unless the transferee is shown to have had knowledge.

"Knowledge" requires actual knowledge under section 1–201(25), and one case so far is in accord.[51] Thus it appears that if a large segment of inventory is from a single supplier and the transferor proposes to sell this as part of the bulk sale, the transferee has no duty to inquire whether the supplier has been paid even though his name does not appear on the list of creditors furnished by the transferor. This provision may prove unwise.

Suppose the transferee does have knowledge of the existence of a creditor that the transferor omitted from the list. Does this render the entire bulk transfer "ineffective"? Section 6–104(3) is not explicit about this. Presumably so far as the listing requirement goes, the transfer is ineffective only as to the omitted creditor. On this, more in the next section.

As a second requirement, both transferor and transferee are required to prepare a schedule of the property to be transferred "sufficient to identify it."[52] This language is far less specific than that of some prior bulk sales laws. Section 44 of the pre-Code New York Personal Property Law required "a full and detailed inventory, showing the quantity and, so far as possible with the exercise of reasonable diligence, the cost price to the seller, transferor or assignor of each article to be included in the sale." Unlike the requirement of listing creditors, under the Code the transferee as well as the transferor is responsible for preparing the schedule of property to be transferred.[53] And this makes sense, for while it may be too much to require the transferee to know a great deal about who the transferor's creditors are, it is not too much to require him to know what assets he is buying. If the schedule omits some of the property to be transferred, strictly speaking there is noncompliance and the sale is therefore entirely ineffective. But, given the purposes of

48. Id.

49. Id.

50. § 6–104, Comment 3.

51. Silco Automatic Vending Co. v. Howells, 102 N.J.Super. 243, 245 A.2d

765, 5 UCC Rep.Serv. 625 (Ch.Div. 1968), aff'd 105 N.J.Super. 511, 253 A.2d 480, 6 UCC Rep.Serv. 531 (App. Div.1969).

52. § 6–104(1) (b).

53. Id.

Article Six, courts will doubtless balk at declaring a sale ineffective unless the omitted property is of significant value.

Third, the transferee must preserve the list and schedule for six months following the transfer and either permit inspection and copying therefrom at all reasonable hours by any creditor of the transferor or file the list and schedule in a public office such as that of the county clerk in which the business is located or in the office of the Secretary of State.[54]  As with the second requirement above, a failure of literal compliance arguably renders the transfer entirely ineffective.  But again courts will doubtless balk at this result unless the noncompliance is in some way significant.

Fourth, the transferee must give a specified form of notice to those of the transferor's creditors listed by the transferor as above and to all other persons known to the transferee to hold or assert claims against the transferor.[55]  This notice must be delivered personally or "sent" by registered mail or certified mail at least ten days before the transferee takes possession of the goods or pays for them, whichever happens first.[56]  "Sent," in the Code, refers to the time of sending.[57]  A cautious lawyer for the transferee will be certain to send any such mail at least eleven days prior to the foregoing dates.  Some commentators have said that the transferee should not make an earlier downpayment or earnest money payment that might cause the ten day period to run.[58]  The statute does not say that a downpayment or earnest money payment causes the period to run, and we doubt that it does.

What if the transferor's list of creditors shows there are no creditors and the transferee has no actual knowledge of any?  Though Article Six does not say, presumably the parties may dispense with the inventory and with preserving it,[59] and, of course, there are no creditors to notify.  In the usual case the transferor will have creditors, often in abundance.

What must the notice to creditors contain?  Section 6–107 provides as follows

> (1) The notice to creditors (Section 6—105) shall state:
>
> (a) that a bulk transfer is about to be made; and
>
> (b) the names and business addresses of the transferor and transferee, and all other business names and addresses used by the transferor within three years last past so far as known to the transferee; and
>
> (c) whether or not all the debts of the transferor are to be paid in full as they fall due as a result of the

---

54. § 6–104(1) (c).

55. §§ 6–105; 6–107(3).

56. §§ 6–105; 6–107(3).

57. § 1–201(38).

58. R. Duesenberg & L. King, Sales and Bulk Transfers Under the Uniform Commercial Code § 1504[3] (1966).

59. But see 3 N.Y. State Law Revision Comm'n, 1955 Report 1748 (1955).

transaction, and if so, the address to which creditors should send their bills.

(2) If the debts of the transferor are not to be paid in full as they fall due or if the transferee is in doubt on that point then the notice shall state further:

(a) the location and general description of the property to be transferred and the estimated total of the transferor's debts;

(b) the address where the schedule of property and list of creditors (Section 6—104) may be inspected;

(c) whether the transfer is to pay existing debts and if so the amount of such debts and to whom owing;

(d) whether the transfer is for new consideration and if so the amount of such consideration and the time and place of payment; and

(e) if for new consideration the time and place where creditors of the transferor are to file their claims.

(3) The notice in any case shall be delivered personally or sent by registered or certified mail to all the persons shown on the list of creditors furnished by the transferor (Section 6—104) and to all other persons who are known to the transferee to hold or assert claims against the transferor.

It is sometimes said that subsection (1) above specifies a short form of notice and subsection (2) a long form of notice. Again cautious lawyers are likely to advise use of the long form of notice except in unusual cases. This is because it will often not be possible for the transferee to be sufficiently certain that the conditions for use of the short form obtain. That is, he may not think he can rely on assurances of the transferor that the transferor is going to use the purchase money to pay his debts. Or the transferee may not be sufficiently certain that he is aware of just what these debts are. The language of section 6–107(2) seems to refer to all debts of the transferor, including ones not even listed by him and therefore possibly unknown to the transferee.

Failure to comply with the cluster of creditor notification requirements specified in sections 6–105 and 6–107 renders the bulk transfer "ineffective against any creditor." [60] It could be argued that this wording empowers any creditor, including one who himself received proper notice, to treat the bulk transfer as ineffective. In our view this is not the correct interpretation; we would find the transfer ineffective against only those creditors to whom no notice or an improper notice had been sent. On this, more later.

Suppose the parties comply with all four kinds of requirements discussed here. This will make a lot of information available to the

60.  § 6–105.

transferor's creditors. What good will this information do for them? For now, it suffices to say that the information should alert these creditors to any action, nonlegal as well as legal, that they may want to take prior to the date of the bulk sale to protect their interests. But the onus for decision and action is on these creditors.

Some experts in the field,[61] and some pre-Code as well as post-Code legislative bodies [62] have thought that the foregoing notice and information functions of bulk sales laws do not adequately protect creditors of the transferor. Accordingly they have imposed a further requirement on the transferee, namely, that he see that the proceeds he pays for the property find their way into the hands of the transferor's creditors. Section 6–106 of the Code so requires, but it is an optional provision and has been adopted in only eighteen states.[63]

It is notorious that lawyers sometimes advise their clients not to go through the formalities of complying with Article Six. Compliance may be time-consuming and expensive. It may also stir up creditors— even questionable ones—who may try to hold up the sale. Indeed if there is to be compliance, circumstances will often dictate that the parties escrow part of the price to protect against, and pay off, claimants. What risks do the parties run if they consciously fail to comply? In some states it is a crime to fail to comply. Also, conscious noncompliance may constitute concealment under section 6–111 with the result that creditors of the transferor may, at least theoretically, exercise their remedies even years after the transfer occurred.

### § 19–4 Individual Remedies of Transferor's Creditors in Event of Noncompliance

In the absence of a bulk sales law a transferor's creditors are generally not entitled to levy or the like on assets the transferor has sold to a new owner.[64] But with a bulk sales law on the books (Article Six), the general picture changes. For in the event of relevant noncompliance with that law, the transferor's creditors may levy or the like on transferred assets even in the hands of a wholly innocent transferee.[65] Worse than this, in some states this transferee may become personally liable for the value of the assets acquired.[66] This is

---

61. E. g., Weintraub & Levin, Bulk Sales Law and Adequate Protection of Creditors, 65 Harv.L.Rev. 418, 434 (1952).

62. Pennsylvania is the leading example. See note 11 supra.

63. See note 11 supra. Although case law under section 6–106 is not, to date, plentiful, see Darby v. Ewing's Home Furnishings, 278 F.Supp. 917, 5 UCC Rep.Serv. 198 (W.D.Okla.1967); Bomanzi of Lexington, Inc. v. Tafel, 415 S.W.2d 627, 4 UCC Rep.Serv. 588 (Ky.Ct.App.1967).

64. See text accompanying note 1 supra.

65. Not every noncompliance with Article Six presents this problem. The transferor may fail to provide the required list of creditors, for example, but if he does, the transfer is not considered ineffective. § 6–104(3). See Note, Article 6: Rights of an Aggrieved Creditor of a Bulk Transferor, 10 B.C.Ind. & Com.L.Rev. 281 (1968).

66. See, e. g., Darby v. Ewing's Home Furnishings, 278 F.Supp. 917, 5 UCC Rep.Serv. 198 (W.D.Okla.1967); Cornelius v. J. & R. Motor Supply Corp.,

a drastic consequence indeed, for a noncomplying transferee could end up having to pay twice for what he gets.

Article Six does not spell all this out in so many words. Sections 6–104 and 6–105 state that noncomplying transfers are "ineffective," and this is so even if the transferee is acting in unquestioned good faith. Of course, the word "ineffective" is not equivalent in meaning to "void." Several things are true of a noncomplying bulk transfer that could not be true if such a transfer were void as such: the contract of sale remains valid as between the bulk seller and buyer;[67] the transferee can pass good title in the assets transferred to a *bona fide* purchaser;[68] and the transferee's creditors can acquire an interest in the bulk transfer assets in the transferee's hands.[69] Also, any such "defect" that arises by virtue of noncompliance with Article Six can be "cured" simply by paying off the aggrieved creditor.[70] Thus, a noncomplying transfer is not void. Nor is it voidable in the usual sense of that word. If, for example, a creditor of a noncomplying transferor should levy on some of the assets transferred and thereby satisfy his claim, this would not render the entire transfer void as to any remaining assets. The Code draftsmen used the word "ineffective," not "void" or "voidable."

Presumably the effect of *total* noncompliance is merely to preserve those remedies of the transferor that would otherwise be lost upon a complying transfer. The Code comments so indicate.[71] But neither the Code comments nor the text exhaustively specifies what these remedies are. Section 6–111 does speak of the creditor who makes a "levy," and Comment 2 to the section states:

> "Levy", which is not a defined term in the Code, should be read broadly as including not only levies of execution proper but also attachment, garnishment, trustee process, receivership, or whatever proceeding, under the state's practice, is used to apply a debtor's property to payment of his debts.

Also, according to Comment 2 to 6–104, the transferor's creditors may "disregard the transfer and levy on the goods as still belonging to the transferor, or a receiver representing them [the creditors] can take them by whatever procedure the local law provides."[72] And courts have held under the Code that a creditor of the transferor may

468 S.W.2d 781, 9 UCC Rep.Serv. 709 (Ky.Ct.App.1971). See also Annot., 61 A.L.R. 364 (1929).

**67.** See Macy v. Oswald, 198 Pa.Super. 435, 182 A.2d 94, 1 UCC Rep.Serv. 321 (1962) (Article Six exists for benefit of creditors, not for parties to transfer).

**68.** § 6–110(2).

**69.** See, e. g., Schwartz v. A. J. Armstrong Co., 179 F.2d 766 (2d Cir. 1950).

**70.** § 6–104, Comment 2.

**71.** Id.

**72.** § 6–104, Comment 2. On the meaning of "levy," see section 6–111, Comment 2. See also Belber v. H. S. F., 26 Pa.D. & C.2d 796, 1 UCC Rep.Serv. 323 (C.P.1960) (receiver appointed). What if the assets to be seized have been commingled with others of like kind? See L. Vold, Law of Sales 117 (2d ed. 1959).

also enjoin the transferee in a proper case from reselling the goods, or if he has resold them, from disposing of the proceeds.[73]  In sum a totally noncomplying transfer will be ineffective in the sense that transferred assets will still be regarded as belonging to the transferor. As a corollary, the noncomplying transferee may also be held liable for the *value* of the transferred goods where they no longer exist or are no longer in his hands.  At least one Code case so holds.[74]  Thus a transferee may have to pay *twice*.  He does not, however, become personally liable for the transferor's debts.

For remedial purposes we believe that it is necessary to distinguish between cases of total noncompliance with Article Six and cases of substantial but not full compliance.  The latter category includes, for example, cases in which the transferee failed to notify a known creditor under 6–105 or sent defective notices to two or three creditors. In all cases of "substantial compliance" as we use that phrase, the parties overwhelmingly comply with Article Six.  But the remedial question that then arises is this: does the minor noncompliance render the entire bulk sale "ineffective" so that any of the transferor's creditors, even ones as to whom compliance was perfect, may levy or the like on the transferred assets?  As we already indicated in the preceding section of this chapter, we prefer a less drastic interpretation. We would make the punishment fit the crime and treat the transfer ineffective only as against an aggrieved creditor and not against all creditors.  The literal wording in 6–104 and 6–105 is arguably to the contrary.  But we believe this wording can be explained away as addressed to cases of total noncompliance, not to cases of substantial compliance in which only one or a very few creditors are aggrieved. There is strong support for our interpretation in Comment 2 to 6–104 which provides that "any defect can always be cured by paying off the unpaid creditors."  Of course, this comment might be read to require that the transferee must pay off all creditors, but this reading would deprive the word "cure" in the comment of its usual meaning. We have uncovered some pre-Code cases that support our analysis.[75]

What creditors of the transferor have standing to assert remedies available by virtue of noncompliance with Article Six?  Section 6–109 (1) provides:

The creditors of the transferor mentioned in this Article are those holding claims based on transactions or events

73.  See, e. g., General Time Corp. v. Gabor, 3 UCC Rep.Serv. 990 (N.Y.Sup. Ct.1966) (injunction would have been granted if case had fallen squarely in Article Six); Markert v. College Offset Press, Inc., 6 Pa.D. & C.2d 519, 1 UCC Rep.Serv. 320 (C.P.1955) (same).

74.  Darby v. Ewing's Home Furnishings, 278 F.Supp. 917, 5 UCC Rep.Serv. 198 (W.D.Okla.1967).  See also note 66 supra.

75.  C. & E. Marshall Co. v. Leon, 267 Ill.App. 242, 247 (1932) ("rights of a creditor who has been given the required notice are not prejudiced by the fact . . . that another creditor has not received the notice."); Ritter v. Wray, 45 Pa.Super. 440, 449 (1911) ("failure to give notice to one creditor . . . [does not] make the sale fraudulent and voidable as to the creditors who were properly notified.").

occurring before the bulk transfer, but creditors who become such after notice to creditors is given (Sections 6–105 and 6–107) are not entitled to notice.

Section 1–201(12) provides:

> "Creditor" includes a general creditor, a secured creditor, a lien creditor and any representative of creditors, including an assignee for the benefit of creditors, a trustee in bankruptcy, a receiver in equity and an executor or administrator of an insolvent debtor's or assignor's estate.

Thus it appears that parties with contingent and unliquidated claims may have standing even if they are not included on a list of creditors entitled to notice and even if their claims do not arise out of trade but are "involuntary," for example, tort claims.[76] Of course, governmental tax claimants are also "creditors" within the foregoing language.[77]

Any remedies that secured creditors of the transferor may have under Article Nine (or other law) against assets transferred are not affected by Article Six. The same is true of any remedies of creditors under fraudulent conveyance law, receivership law, state anti-preference law, and the Federal Bankruptcy Act.[78]

Within what period of time must a creditor take remedial action in event of noncompliance with Article Six? Section 6–111 provides:

> No action under this Article shall be brought nor levy made more than six months after the date on which the transferee took possession of the goods unless the transfer has been concealed. If the transfer has been concealed, actions may be brought or levies made within six months after its discovery.

Although the foregoing provision is not explicit, it would appear that any remedy available by virtue of noncompliance with Article Six must be pursued within the specified six months period.[79] For example, we have already seen that noncompliance leaves the assets transferred subject to "levy" or the like on the theory that the assets still "belong" to the transferor. Normally, absent a bulk transfer law, they would "belong" to the transferee and not be subject to levy or the like. Accordingly, it would appear that such levy or the like

---

76. Sado v. Sado, 4 UCC Rep.Serv. 213 (N.Y.Sup.Ct.1967) (plaintiff in fraud action a creditor). But see Aluminum Shapes, Inc. v. K-A-Liquidating Co., 290 F.Supp. 356, 5 UCC Rep.Serv. 1194 (W.D.Pa.1968) (ordinary breach of contract claimant not creditor) (dictum).

77. At least pre-Code cases so held. E. g., United States v. Goldblatt Bros., Inc., 128 F.2d 576 (7th Cir. 1942).

78. See text accompanying notes 3–5 supra.

79. See Aluminum Shapes, Inc. v. K-A-Liquidating Co., 290 F.Supp. 356, 5 UCC Rep.Serv. 1194 (W.D.Pa.1968). See generally Annot., 61 A.L.R.2d 935 (1958); Annot., 15 A.L.R.2d 937 (1951).

must occur within six months as specified in section 6–111, absent concealment.[80]

What, however, of remedies the availability of which do not turn on noncompliance with Article Six? Must these, too, be pursued within six months? It would appear not, although Article Six does not say, and no cases so hold. Thus it would appear, for example, that a creditor of a transferor could set aside a bulk transfer as a fraudulent conveyance in a proper case even after six months, if this were within the limitation period specified for fraudulent conveyance proceedings.[81] For as we have already seen, fraudulent conveyance remedies survive bulk transfers whether or not the requirements of Article Six are met.

## § 19–5   "Individual" Remedies of Transferor's Creditors in Event of Compliance

Suppose a creditor of a prospective transferor presents a lawyer with a bulk sales notice just received from the transferor. Assume further that the proposed bulk sale appears on investigation to comply with Article Six. Even if our creditor has a claim that is due, he may not have cause for alarm. The transferor could be wholly solvent and highly likely to pay soon. Or, by the terms of the proposed bulk sale, the transferor and transferee could have provided for an escrow arrangement (or the like) out of which our creditor will be paid in full.[82]

On the other hand, our creditor may have real cause for alarm. Thus, just to take one of the worst cases, our creditor may have acquired information that neither party to the sale is in sound financial condition, that the transferee appears to be paying much less for the assets he is acquiring than they are really worth, and that no special provision at all is being made for the payment of creditors. (Information as to the assets to be sold and the consideration to be paid would appear from the documents which the transferee must make available for inspection pursuant to section 6–104.) Let us assume further that the transferor is known to be making plans to move to another state and not only that our creditor's claim is overdue and rather large, but also that a big part of the assets being sold consists of the very inventory which our unpaid unsecured creditor sold to the transferor on credit two months earlier.

At the outset it is realistic to consider possible nonlegal avenues for assuring that our creditor will be paid. Of course, the effectiveness of some of these nonlegal avenues will depend on the prospective

**80.** See E. J. Trum, Inc. v. Blanchard Parfums, Inc., 33 App.Div.2d 689, 306 N.Y.S.2d 316, 6 UCC Rep.Serv. 1261 (2d Dep't 1969) (complete failure to comply with Article Six held tantamount to concealment).

**81.** For a contrary view, see Comment, Article Six: Rights of an Aggrieved Creditor of a Bulk Transferor, 10 B.C. Ind. & Com.L.Rev. 281, 298 (1969).

**82.** For an example of such an arrangement, see Ross Indus. Chem. Co. v. Smith, 5 Mich.App. 422, 146 N.W.2d 816, 4 UCC Rep.Serv. 42 (1966).

effectiveness of threatened legal action. Article Six itself says almost nothing about such action. The indications are that this area is left to general law outside Article Six. Our creditor might initially seek to get the transferee voluntarily to pay him at or before the date of the closing. Or he might seek similarly to exact a promise of voluntary payment from the transferor immediately on receipt of proceeds from the transferee. If these avenues do not appear promising, the creditor may try to "sober up" the parties with threats of effective legal action to be taken prior to the bulk transfer. Here are the principal possibilities: first the creditor might threaten to levy on at least the inventory he sold the transferor. This would have to be either pursuant to a writ of execution which presupposes that the creditor already has a judgment against the prospective transferor, or pursuant to a writ of attachment, which presupposes that the creditor quickly starts a lawsuit and alleges some specific form of "insecurity." Of course, our creditor may not have a judgment. Indeed, his claim might not even be mature when he receives the bulk sale notice. Also a writ of attachment might not lie because our creditor is unable truthfully to allege a requisite form of insecurity, for example, that the transferor is frittering away his assets, or is secreting them, or is about to leave the jurisdiction so that any judgment ultimately secured might prove worthless.[83]

Aside from threatening to levy or the like, our creditor might also consider threatening an injunction against the transfer or threatening to subject the assets involved to a receivership.[84] Generally since these are "equitable remedies," our creditor would have to allege inadequacy of such law remedies as levy and the like,[85] at least if courts follow the usual principles governing the exercise of equity jurisdiction. And even if inadequacy of law remedies could be alleged and colorably shown, then, as Professor Hawkland has pointed out,[86] these equitable remedies may still be unavailable for the very same kinds of reasons that a writ of attachment may not be available. It will not be enough merely to allege irreparable injury in conclusory terms.[87] To get an injunction against the impending transfer, the case law generally requires our creditor to make out a *prima facie*

---

83. See, e. g., N.Y.Civ.Prac.Law § 6201 (McKinney 1963).

84. Belber v. H. S. F., Inc., 26 Pa.D. & C.2d 796, 1 UCC Rep.Serv. 323 (C.P. 1961) (Code does not preclude equitable remedies).

85. The situation in New York is illustrative. See, e. g., Town of Hempstead v. West 45th St. Associates, Inc., 8 Misc.2d 997, 166 N.Y.S.2d 142 (1957); William L. Blumberg Co. v. Farber, 170 Misc. 930, 11 N.Y.S.2d 427 (1939). See also N.Y.Civ.Prac.Law § 6401(a) (McKinney 1963); Fair Sky, Inc. v. International Ride Corp., 23 App.Div.

2d 633, 257 N.Y.S.2d 351 (1st Dep't 1965), order aff'd without opinion 260 N.Y.S.2d 1023 (1st Dep't 1965); Note, Bulk Transfers: An Analysis of the Changes in New York Law, 11 N.Y.L.F. 112 (1965).

86. Hawkland, Remedies of Bulk Transfer Creditors Where There Has Been Compliance with Article Six, 74 Com.L.J. 257, 260 (1969).

87. Crawford v. Newman, 11 Misc.2d 322, 174 N.Y.S.2d 667 (1958), aff'd memorandum 5 App.Div.2d 859, 174 N.Y.S.2d 881 (1st Dep't 1958).

case that he will suffer irreparable injury if the injunction is not granted.[88]   So, too, if a receivership is not granted.[89]

Third our creditor might be able to secure payment by threatening to throw the transferor into bankruptcy immediately prior to the bulk sale.   Bankruptcy would pass the transferor's assets to his trustee and block their sale to the bulk transferee.   If the conditions exist which permit our creditor (and at least two other creditors) to throw the transferor into bankruptcy, the threat of such action will influence any transferee who is genuinely interested in acquiring the assets to take some action to see that our creditor is taken care of.   Of course, the requisite conditions may not exist.   For our creditor to put the transferor into bankruptcy involuntarily, he would have to show, among other things, that the transferor had committed an "act of bankruptcy" (and it is often not possible to show that).[90]   Or, our creditor might threaten to attack the ultimate transfer under any applicable local state law against preferential transfers by insolvents.[91]

Our creditor might threaten to have the eventual transfer set aside as a fraudulent conveyance.[92]   Generally, though, even fraudulent conveyances cannot be set aside against bulk transferees who buy in good faith and for fair value.   From the information required under Article Six, our creditor will usually be able to tell if the transferee is paying a fair price.   Also if our creditor knows of any fraudulent purpose of the transferor, he can put the transferee on notice of that and thereby keep him from being a good faith purchaser.[93]

Thus our creditor might make some or all of the foregoing kinds of threats of legal action prior to the actual date of the bulk transfer and thereby induce one of the two parties to the transfer either to pay up or to take some action short of that satisfactory to our creditor, for example, give him a good Article Nine security interest in some of the assets, an interest which would survive the bulk transfer.[94]   But then such threats might prove unavailing and our creditor might in

---

88.   Id.

89.   See, e. g., National Union Bank v. Riger, 38 App.Div. 123, 56 N.Y.S. 545 (1st Dep't 1899).

90.   Under section 3 of the Bankruptcy Act, there are six "acts of bankruptcy":   (1) either concealment by the debtor of his property and the like with intent to hinder, or a fraudulent transfer under sections 67 or 70 of the Act;   (2) preferential transfers under section 60;   (3) certain liens permitted or suffered by the debtor;   (4) general assignment for the benefit of creditors;   (5) creation of certain trusteeships or receiverships concerning the debtor's property;   (6) certain admissions of inability to pay debts and willingness to be judged bankrupt. 11 U.S.C.A. § 21 (1970).

91.   See, e. g., Bomanzi of Lexington, Inc. v. Tafel, 415 S.W.2d 627, 4 UCC Rep.Serv. 588 (Ky.Ct.App.1967) (attack under Kentucky statute on preferential transfers).

92.   Under the Uniform Fraudulent Conveyance Act, adopted in twenty-four states, and similar laws, the creditor may also levy pursuant to a writ of attachment without first going into equity for an order to set the conveyance aside.   Uniform Fraudulent Conveyance Act § 9.   A list of these states is provided in Ch. 24, note 119 infra.

93.   1 G. Glenn, Fraudulent Conveyances and Preferences § 313 (rev. ed. 1940).

94.   See §§ 9–201; 9–301.

fact be forced to pursue a legal remedy. He would ordinarily have to act fast at least with respect to some of his possible remedies. This is true of levying on the assets to be transferred, for once the bulk sale occurs this remedy is lost to our creditor, and he then will have only those remedies which survive a transfer in compliance with a bulk sales law.

Of course, after the transfer a creditor might still levy or the like on any assets remaining in the hands of the *transferor*, provided the conditions for levy are present. More often he will seek to go after proceeds of the transfer received by the transferor. This may require garnishment of a bank account, or levy on a check, or garnishment of any unpaid portion of the bulk transferee's obligation to the transferor to pay the price, or the like.[95] And it may even involve arresting the debtor under local procedures.[96]

Our creditor may be able to show that the transferee is really the beneficiary of a preferential transfer voidable under the Bankruptcy Act or under state law. And this he may well be, as where the bulk transfer is really used as a kind of liquidation device for the benefit of some but not all of the transferor's creditors.[97] One value of the notice requirement under Article Six is that it notifies creditors that they have roughly four months to try to have the transferor declared bankrupt and a trustee appointed to avoid the bulk transfer to another creditor as a preference.[98] Our own creditor must be careful not to join in as one of the creditors benefiting from use of a bulk transfer as a kind of liquidation device, for if and when he seeks later to recover the remainder of his claim, he may be met with a valid accord and satisfaction defense.[99]

Or, our creditor may be able to show that the transferee is really a fraudulent conveyee under applicable fraudulent conveyance law. If so, he may be able to reach the transferred assets in the transferee's hands.[100] Thus compliance with a bulk sales law does not necessarily immunize a transferee from attack either as a preferred creditor or as a fraudulent conveyee, provided timely action is taken by our aggrieved creditor.

**95.** See, e. g., M. P. Berglas Mfg. Co. v. Hall Wood Working Co., 87 N.Y.S.2d 178 (Co.Ct.1949). See also N.Y.Civ. Prac.Law § 5232(a) (McKinney Supp. 1971).

**96.** See, e. g., N.Y.Civ.Prac.Law § 6101 (McKinney 1963).

**97.** See Weintraub & Levin, Bulk Sales Law and Adequate Protection of Creditors, 65 Harv.L.Rev. 418, 436–39 (1952).

**98.** See Weintraub & Levin, Bulk Sales Law and Adequate Protection of

Creditors, 65 Harv.L.Rev. 418, 432 (1952).

**99.** Abby Financial Corp. v. Margrove Mfg. Co., 5 UCC Rep.Serv. 1088 (N.Y. Sup.Ct.1968) (plaintiff lost creditor status by certifying check with conditions endorsed on it).

**100.** See text accompanying notes 92–93 supra. A fraudulent conveyance is also reachable by the trustee in bankruptcy. Bankruptcy Act §§ 67(d), 70(e), 11 U.S.C.A. §§ 107(d), 110(e) (1970).

## § 19–6  Conflicts Between Transferor's Creditors and Third Parties— Some Problems of Priority

Article Six does not include a body of priority rules to resolve all the various kinds of conflicts that may arise between unsecured creditors of the transferor and third parties. The Article only sets forth rules for conflicts between the transferor's creditors and purchasers from the transferee. Those rules are stated in section 6–110:

> When the title of a transferee to property is subject to a defect by reason of his non-compliance with the requirements of this Article, then:
>
> (1) a purchaser of any of such property from such transferee who pays no value or who takes with notice of such non-compliance takes subject to such defect, but
>
> (2) a purchaser for value in good faith and without such notice takes free of such defect.

But what of conflicts between the transferor's creditors and creditors of the transferee? It might be thought that after a noncomplying bulk sale, a creditor of the transferee who levies on transferred assets should prevail against creditors of the transferor who subsequently levy or seek to levy.[101] Although 6–110 speaks only of purchasers, and so negatively implies that the transferee's lien creditors do not take free of claims of the transferor's creditors, Article Six does not expressly so provide. Absent any relevant pre-Code case law, courts may well consider the question an open one. There is less reason to protect the transferee's levying creditors than to protect his *bona fide* purchasers from claims of the transferor's creditors. As a matter of comparative equity, the *bona fide* purchaser is by definition unaware of potential claims of creditors of the bulk transferor, but this is not necessarily so of levying creditors of the bulk transferee. Furthermore, as far as leviable assets are concerned, the creditors of the transferee who levy on transferred assets shortly or not long after the transfer will often if not usually be levying on a "windfall" that presumably played no part in their own earlier decisions to extend credit. Yet some creditors of the transferor doubtless extended credit to the transferor partly on the strength of his asset position. It would seem that a first in time rule (as to levy or the like) should not be devised and applied to prefer the transferee's creditors over those of the transferor, provided at least that the transferor's creditors are reasonably diligent in pursuing their remedies in the event of noncompliance. A judge-made priority rule generally favoring the transferor's creditors would be more consistent with Article Six, for this Article is generally intended to protect just those creditors in event of noncompliance. Indeed, Article Six says noncomplying transfers are "ineffective" as to these very creditors.

<hr>

101. This view is favored by Weintraub & Levin, Bulk Sales Law and Adequate Protection of Creditors, 65 Harv. L.Rev. 418, 427–29 (1952).

Similar priority conflicts between the creditors of the transferor and creditors of the transferee may arise even in the event of compliance with the bulk sales act. For example, a creditor in the former class might seek to attack the bulk transfer as a fraudulent conveyance. If timely and if successful in this attack, it is submitted that he, too, should prevail over the transferee's creditors on the foregoing analysis, for the contexts are analogous.

What if the *transferee* in a noncomplying bulk sale becomes bankrupt shortly after the bulk transfer? Will his trustee in bankruptcy acquire rights superior to the rights of the transferor's creditors? Consider a case involving these features. On January 15 the noncomplying bulk transfer occurs. On January 20 our transferor creditor levies on part of the assets transferred. On February 20 the *transferee* takes bankruptcy. His trustee under section 67(a)(1) of the Bankruptcy Act attacks our creditor's lien as one acquired when the bankrupt was insolvent and within four months of the date of bankruptcy. Who prevails? On a literal reading of the Federal Bankruptcy Act,[102] the trustee certainly wins and the transferor's creditors are thus subordinated to those of the transferee even where the former were diligent and "first in time." And there appears to be case support for this result.[103] Yet this support is inconsistent with the various considerations just discussed which favor the transferor's creditors in the event of conflict with those of the transferee. Moreover, it might be argued that under section 67(a)(1) the transferor's trustee can only attack levies on "property" of the transferee and that for this purpose the assets transferred pursuant to a noncomplying bulk transfer do not constitute "property" of the transferee. This argument is also supported by Code comments.[104] Admittedly, this would be an impossible argument to sustain in the case of compliance with Article Six.

### § 19–7 Individual Creditor's Recovery v. Collective Remedies—An Addendum

The general law applicable in the bulk transfer context, which includes much law besides Article Six of the Code, ought not only to afford protection for creditors of the transferor, it ought also to protect their interests equitably. How far does this law permit the in-

---

102. The basic language of section 67 (a)(1) of the Bankruptcy Act reads:

Every lien against the property of a person obtained by attachment, judgment, levy, or other legal or equitable process or proceedings within four months before the filing of a petition initiating a proceeding under this Act by or against such person shall be deemed null and void (a) if at the time when such lien was obtained such person was insolvent or (b) if such lien was sought and permitted in fraud of the provisions of this Act . . . .

11 U.S.C.A. § 107(d)(1) (1970).

103. E. g., Schwartz v. A. J. Armstrong Co., 179 F.2d 766 (2d Cir. 1950). See also In re Dee's, Inc., 311 F.2d 619 (3d Cir. 1962). Cf. City of New York v. Johnson, 137 F.2d 163 (2d Cir. 1943) (contest between nonlien creditor of transferor and transferee bankrupt's trustee).

104. § 6–104, Comment 2.

dividual creditor acting as above to satisfy his entire claim without regard to whether other creditors similarly situated receive similar treatment?   What remedies, if any, does this body of law afford against the grabby creditor whose motto may be, "Grab as Grab Can and Devil Take Hindermost"?   All will agree that these are important questions, especially if it be assumed that the claims of the transferor's creditors exceed the value of his assets, including those he purports to transfer.   We close this chapter with a few speculations on these questions.

Potential inequitable treatment of similarly situated creditors of the transferor exists both prior to and subsequent to the bulk transfer.   Prior thereto a creditor may levy or the like and thus satisfy his entire claim.   Or the prospective bulk transferor may apply oil to a squeaky wheel and pay off in full a creditor threatening to take legal action that might jeopardize the prospective transfer.   Assume that after an event of the foregoing kind, the transferor makes a complying bulk sale of his remaining assets.   The transferor's remaining creditors may receive less than full payment and thus be victims of inequitable treatment.   This is always a risk.   But the risk is enhanced where there is a bulk sale, for the transferor is stripping himself all at once of assets that would otherwise be subject to levy or the like.

After a bulk transfer, there is also potential for inequity, even if the transfer be a complying one.   The transferee may prove to be a fraudulent conveyee, and relevant law may permit a single creditor of the transferor to levy on the assets conveyed and thereby satisfy his entire claim.[105]   Or, the transferee may prove to be an assignee for benefit of creditors, but only for some of the creditors.   In circumstances of scarcity it is not difficult to imagine that some creditors will end up receiving less on their claims than those creditors who grab first by levy pursuant to fraudulent conveyance law or who join for their mutual and preferred benefit in an assignment.[106]

After the transfer the potential for inequity is all the greater any time the bulk transfer fails to comply with Article Six.   Absent 6–106 (3), Article Six openly invites the transferor's creditors, acting alone, to rush in and grab off whatever transferred assets there are in the transferee's hands.[107]   The first may satisfy their entire claims, and the last get nothing.

Assume C is a similarly situated creditor who, by virtue of one or more of the foregoing occurrences has been left wholly unpaid following a bulk transfer.   Assume, too, that his claim is sufficiently sizeable to justify "making a fuss."   What might be done on his behalf to make for a more equitable distribution all around?   First he may

105.  See, e. g., Uniform Fraudulent Conveyance Act § 9.

106.  That an assignment may in fact be preferential is an old story.  See, e. g., Bumb v. Bennett, 51 Cal.2d 294, 333 P.2d 23 (1958).  See generally Weintraub, Levin & Sosnoff, Assignments for the Benefit of Creditors and Competitive Systems of Liquidation, 39 Cornell L.Q. 3 (1953).

107.  See § 6–104, Comment 2.

be able to throw the transferor into involuntary bankruptcy, hoping thereby (1) to have a trustee retrieve all the assets transferred to creditors and to the bulk transferee, and (2) to have this trustee distribute the proceeds of retrieved assets equitably on a prorated basis to the transferor's creditors. At least two kinds of factors may drastically limit the value of this remedy. In the first place our creditor may not have the right to put the transferor in bankruptcy involuntarily. According to one of these requirements, our creditor would have to allege and prove that the transferor committed an "act of bankruptcy," and a bulk sale as such is not an act of bankruptcy.[108] If the transferor made a preferential transfer, permitted a levy on assets, or made a fraudulent conveyance, then the "act of bankruptcy" requirement would be met.

But even if our creditor puts the transferor into bankruptcy and does so in timely fashion shortly after the bulk transfer, the trustee may be unable to retrieve sufficient assets to make bankruptcy a worthwhile avenue for securing significant equality of treatment among the transferor's creditors. The possible "factual" explanations for a trustee's inability to come up with a sizeable estate to distribute are numerous: the transferor bankrupt may have squandered all proceeds of the bulk sale, or paid off certain preferred creditors "under the table," and so on.

But even if the transferor's assets are still around, his trustee in bankruptcy still might not be able to reach them under applicable law. These assets might not be subject to retrieval under the trustee's various avoiding powers. It would not be possible for the trustee to avoid the transfer as a preference under section 60 unless the transferee was a creditor of the transferor, and even then numerous other requirements would have to be met.[109] The trustee might try to avoid the transfer as a fraudulent conveyance under sections 67 and 70, but again the applicable requirements might not be met. Certainly in any case in which the transferee gave fair consideration, the bulk transfer would not constitute a fraudulent conveyance, absent a showing of actual fraudulent intent.[110] Then, too, the bulk transfer can hardly be a voidable lien or the like under section 67.[111] Could the

---

108. See note 90 supra.

109. The requirements of a section 60 voidable preference are (1) a transfer, (2) made or suffered by the bankrupt, (3) of the bankrupt's nonexempt property, (4) within four months of bankruptcy, (5) for or on account of an antecedent debt, (6) to or for the benefit of a creditor, (7) while the debtor was insolvent, (8) the effect of which is to enable the transferee a greater percentage of his debt than some other creditors of the same class, (9) where the transferee had, at the time of the transfer, reasonable cause to believe that the debtor was insolvent. 11 U.S.C. § 96 (1970).

110. See Uniform Fraudulent Conveyance Act §§ 4–9; Bankruptcy Act §§ 67(d), 70(e), 11 U.S.C.A. §§ 107(d), 110 (e) (1970). The language of section 70(e) (1) is set forth in note 112 infra. Pertinent language of section 67(d) appears in note 102 supra.

111. Section 67(a) of the Bankruptcy Act applies only to a "lien against the property of a person obtained by attachment, judgment, levy or as other legal or equitable process or proceedings . . . ." 11 U.S.C.A. § 107(a) (1970).

trustee attack the transfer as a successor to the rights of actual creditors under section 70(e) [112] or in its own right under section 70(c) [113] as a hypothetical lien creditor on the date of bankruptcy? If the bulk transfer complied with the requirements of Article Six, then the theory is that an ordinary judgment or attaching creditor of the transferor could not reach the assets in the transferee's hands. Thus, the trustee could not invoke 70(e). Similarly the trustee could not effectively invoke section 70(c), for that section gives the trustee status as a hypothetical lien creditor on assets of the transferor bankrupt as of the date of bankruptcy, and on that date the transferor had already transferred the assets to the complying bulk transferee.

If the federal bankruptcy law seems to be a tool of limited value to a creditor of a bulk transferor seeking equality of treatment, state law tools are all the more limited in value. In pre-Code days, the most widely used state law device that our creditor might have used to secure some equality of distribution was the receivership for the benefit of all creditors of the transferor.[114] Of course, a receiver might be appointed for all the assets of the transferor or only for those assets transferred in the bulk sale. But if these latter assets were to be subjected to receivership, then the bulk sale itself would have to be one that failed to comply with the bulk sales law, for otherwise the assets transferred would ordinarily become the property of the transferee "free and clear," so to speak.

Consistent with Article Six, could our creditor secure the appointment of a receiver to gather up and distribute equitably assets that were the subject of a noncomplying bulk transfer? Article Six does not say so in so many words, but the comments specifically endorse the receivership device. But what would be the powers of the receiver? In the interest of equity could he force a fleet-footed creditor who earlier had levied on part of the bulk transfer assets to disgorge into the receiver's hands for purposes of equitable distribution? The equitable distribution policy is of great moment in this field. In deciding

---

**112.** Section 70(e) (1) of the Bankruptcy Act provides:

A transfer made or suffered or obligation incurred by a debtor adjudged a bankrupt under this Act which, under any Federal or State law applicable thereto, is fraudulent as against or voidable for any other reason by any creditor of the debtor, having a claim provable under this Act, shall be null and void as against the trustee of such debtor.

11 U.S.C.A. § 110(e) (1) (1970) (emphasis added).

**113.** The pertinent language of section 70(c) of the Bankruptcy Act provides:

The trustee shall have as of the date of bankruptcy the rights and powers of: (1) a creditor who obtained a judgment against the bankrupt upon the date of bankruptcy, whether or not such a creditor exists, (2) a creditor who upon the date of bankruptcy obtained an execution returned unsatisfied against the bankrupt, whether or not such a creditor exists, and (3) a creditor who upon the date of bankruptcy obtained a lien by legal or equitable proceedings upon all property, whether or not coming into possession or control of the court, upon which a creditor of the bankrupt upon a simple contract could have obtained such a lien, whether or not such a creditor exists.

11 U.S.C.A. § 110(c) (1970).

**114.** See 4 R. Clark, Law of Receivers §§ 1013, 1111 (3d ed. 1959).

such a momentous question of first impression, a court should be wary of protecting the first to grab, whether he be a levying creditor, a creditor attacking the transfer as a fraudulent conveyance, or a creditor invoking a state anti-preference law. Of course, in states that have enacted 6–106(3), courts must see that the assets are distributed pro rata.[115]

115. Bomanzi of Lexington, Inc. v. Tafel, 415 S.W.2d 627, 4 UCC Rep. Serv. 588 (Ky.Ct.App.1967) (section 6–106 in force). The court's treatment of this case has been criticized in Comment, Article Six: Rights of an Aggrieved Creditor of a Bulk Transferor, 10 B.C.Ind. & Com.L.Rev. 281 (1969).

# CHAPTER 20

## STORAGE OF GOODS COVERED BY WAREHOUSE RECEIPTS—RIGHTS AND LIABILITIES OF PARTIES, INCLUDING PURCHASERS AND LENDERS

### Analysis

Sec.
20–1. Introduction.
20–2. Scope and Structure of Article Seven.
20–3. Rights of Storer Against Warehouseman.
20–4. Rights of Purchaser of Warehouse Receipts.
20–5. Rights of Pledgee of Warehouse Receipts.

## § 20–1  Introduction

Every year warehousemen receive billions of dollars worth of goods for storage.  Some goods have to be aged or cured.  Others are used seasonally and have to be stockpiled.  Some have to be harvested all at once, yet are consumed over time.  Needs for storage are legion.  Also, a storer can transfer legal title to stored goods merely by transferring the warehouse receipts covering them.  Further, a storer or his transferee can pledge warehouse receipts as security for loans.  Warehousing for purposes of storage and for purposes of financing are today thriving business activities.[1]  To storers and to persons who purchase or lend against warehouse receipts, the ideal warehouseman is one who properly cares for the stored goods and delivers them up as requested.  Various federal[2] and state[3] regulatory laws help assure the reliability of warehousemen through solvency requirements, bonding, and the like.  These regulatory laws are beyond the scope of this chapter.

In this chapter we will treat (1) the rights of a storer against his warehouseman, (2) the rights of a purchaser of warehouse receipts against his seller and the warehouseman, and (3) the rights of a pledgee of warehouse receipts against the warehouseman and others who have dealt with the goods.  Most of the governing law is in Article Seven of the Code, a body of law that superseded the Uniform Warehouse Receipts Act[4] which became law in all states after its promulgation in 1906.  Article Seven is analogous in several basic respects to Article Three of the Code on commercial paper.  Both Articles define the obligations of an "issuer" of paper who, in the one

---

1.  Up to date treatises on the law of warehousemen do not exist.  One work that may be consulted, however, is R. Braucher, Documents of Title under the Uniform Commercial Code (1958).

2.  See, e. g., 7 U.S.C.A. § 241 et seq. (1970).

3.  See, e. g., Cal. Agric. Code § 54631 et seq. (West 1968).

4.  3 U.L.A. § 1 et seq. (1959 ed.)

case, is to deliver goods and who, in the other, is to pay money.[5]   Both Articles also distinguish between paper that is "negotiable" and paper that is not,[6] and provide that certain transferees of the negotiable paper cut off most prior claims of ownership and defenses.   Thus, just as the holder in due course of a negotiable promissory note cuts off prior ownership claims, so the holder of a negotiable warehouse receipt who takes by due negotiation does likewise.[7]   Partly for this reason, a warehouse receipt is called a "document of title." [8]

"Bills of lading" issued by carriers are also dealt with in Article Seven and pose problems similar to those posed by warehouse receipts, but we will treat bills of lading in Chapter twenty-one.[9]

## § 20–2   Scope and Structure of Article Seven

Unlike other major Articles of the Code, Article Seven does not include one basic provision that determines its scope.   Rather its scope is equivalent to that of its particular sections taken as a whole.   Certain key terms recur through most of the sections and the scope of a section often turns on the statutorily defined meaning of one of these terms.   Thus 7–104(1) opens: "A  .  .  .  document of title is negotiable if  .  .  .."   Many of the sections also turn on the defined meanings of such key terms as "warehouse receipt," "issuer," "bailee," "negotiable," and so on.

The phrases "document of title" and "warehouse receipt" are defined in 1–201(15) and 1–201(45) respectively:

> 1–201(15) "Document of title" includes bill of lading, dock warrant, dock receipt, warehouse receipt or order for the delivery of goods, and also any other document which in the regular course of business or financing is treated as adequately evidencing that the person in possession of it is entitled to receive, hold and dispose of the document and the goods it covers.   To be a document of title a document must purport to be issued by or addressed to a bailee and purport to cover goods in the bailee's possession which are either identified or are fungible portions of an identified mass.

> 1–201(45) "Warehouse receipt" means a receipt issued by a person engaged in the business of storing goods for hire.

5.  § 7–104, Comment.

6.  §§ 3–104; 7–104.

7.  §§ 3–305; 7–502.

8.  § 1–201(15).

9.  We treat the liabilities of warehouse-men in this chapter and the liabilities of carriers in the next. The two are often treated together, as in Article Seven of the Code. Yet, we think the differences are just as great as the similarities. Failure to recognize this can, on occasion, lead to spectacular error. See, e. g., Thomas Foods, Inc. v. Pennsylvania R. R. Co., 112 Ohio App. 76, 168 N.E.2d 612 (1960) (carrier's common law liability for loss or damage to goods erroneously stated to be the same as that of a warehouseman).

In addition to ordinary warehouse receipts, many Article Seven sections also apply to "delivery orders." [10]   Generally a warehouse receipt is issued by a warehouseman, usually to the storer, whereas the storer himself issues a delivery order, usually to his own transferee. Yet a delivery order will be addressed to the warehouseman and will order him to deliver goods to the storer's transferee.  The transferee of a delivery order does not acquire rights against the warehouseman unless and until the warehouseman "accepts" the delivery order.  According to Comment 3 to 7–102, "when a delivery order has been accepted by the bailee it is for practical purposes indistinguishable from a warehouse receipt."   (A warehouseman is not supposed to honor a delivery order if he has issued an outstanding *negotiable* warehouse receipt covering the goods;  on this more later.)

To the general proposition that the lawyer determines the scope of Article Seven on a section-by-section basis after ascertaining the meaning of defined terms in each section, there is one major qualification, as set forth in 7–401:

> The obligations imposed by this Article on an issuer apply to a document of title regardless of the fact that
>
> (a) the document may not comply with the requirements of this Article or of any other law or regulation regarding its issue, form or content;  or
>
> (b) the issuer may have violated laws regulating the conduct of his business;  or
>
> (c) the goods covered by the document were owned by the bailee at the time the document was issued;  or
>
> (d) the person issuing the document does not come within the definition of warehouseman if it purports to be a warehouse receipt.

Thus, so-called "irregularities of issue" do not limit the scope of Article Seven so far as the *obligations of an issuer* are concerned, even though a specified key definition, such as "document" or "warehouseman," is not satisfied.  This resolves a conflict of authority in pre-Code case law.[11]  Irregularities of issue may, however, impair the right of a receipt holder to recover against a warehouse bondsman, for many bonds include conditions requiring regularity in all respects.[12]

To what extent may storers and warehousemen, by contract, displace otherwise applicable Code provisions?  We will later treat some specific problems concerning the scope of freedom of contract,[13] but most sections of Article Seven are not variable by agreement.  Article Seven is unlike Article Two on sales and Article Nine on secured

10.   §§ 7–102(1) (d);  7–102, Comment 3.

11.   Boshkoff, The Irregular Issuance of Warehouse Receipts and Article Seven of the Uniform Commercial Code, 65 Mich.L.Rev. 1361 (1967).

12.   Bascom, Articles 7 and 9 of the Uniform Commercial Code—Security Interests in the Warehouseman's Own Receipts Covering Fungibles, 1969 Wash.U.L.Q. 105, 107–10.

13.   See Section 20–2 infra.

transactions where freedom of contract is the rule rather than the exception. The paucity of free contract under Article Seven can be readily explained. The Article deals with two ancient common callings, namely, storage and transport. Nonvariable rules prevent storers and transporters from over-reaching their customers and from discriminating between them. Also, documents of title demand the certainty of nonvariable rules. Hence, some of the rules impose essentially nonvariable duties of care and nonvariable duties with respect to delivery.[14] Another category of rules specifies requirements for the content of warehouse receipts,[15] for their negotiability,[16] and for their due negotiation.[17] Still another category defines the rights of certain transferees of warehouse receipts.[18]

A particular state's version of Article Seven still may not control the case at hand, for relevant conflict of laws principles may dictate the application of another state's version of Article Seven. The Article has been the victim of more than its share of nonuniform amendments.[19] The Code does not lay down any specific conflict of laws principles here, and there is relatively little pre-Code law. The parties may stipulate that the law of any state having an appropriate relation to the transaction shall control.[20]

Even though a given state's version of Article Seven applies under relevant conflict of laws principles, some other law may control in the end. This law might be local non-Code state law, or it might be federal law, depending on the facts. Many states have enacted essentially regulatory statutes applicable to the dealings of warehousemen. As to these, 7–103 is quite explicit: "To the extent that any . . . regulatory statute of this state or tariff, classification or regulation filed or issued pursuant thereto is applicable, the provisions of this article are subject thereto." An illustrative example of a *state* regulatory provision is this California law:[21]

No warehouseman shall begin to operate any business of a warehouseman, as defined in subdivisions (b) or (c) of Section 239, without first having obtained from the commission a certificate declaring that public convenience and necessity require or will require the transaction of business by such warehouseman.

In addition to state regulatory law, federal law (statute, treaty, judicial decision) may also supersede or supplement Article Seven.

---

14. E. g., §§ 7–204; 7–403.

15. E. g., § 7–202.

16. § 7–104.

17. § 7–501.

18. §§ 7–502 to 7–504.

19. These nonuniform amendments are reported in Permanent Editorial Board

for the Uniform Commercial Code, Report No. 1 at 88 (1962); Permanent Editorial Board for the Uniform Commercial Code, Report No. 2 at 121–41 (1965); Permanent Editorial Board for the Uniform Commercial Code, Report No. 3 at 5–7, 96–99 (1966).

20. § 1–105.

21. Cal.Pub.Util. Code § 1051 (West Supp.1971).

The effect of federal law on warehouse receipts is confined mainly to the impact of the United States Warehouse Act,[22] which applies to receipts covering agricultural products stored for interstate or foreign commerce. Most sections of this Act are regulatory, but those sections that specify the content of warehouse receipts and define delivery obligations override Article Seven.

The basic structure of the official text of Article Seven is relatively simple. It includes 40 sections subsumed under six different subdivisions called "Parts":

Part    I.    General

Part    II.    Warehouse Receipts: Special Provisions

Part    III.    Bills of Lading: Special Provisions

Part    IV.    Warehouse Receipts and Bills of Lading: General Obligations

Part    V.    Warehouse Receipts and Bills of Lading: Negotiation and Transfer

Part    VI.    Warehouse Receipts and Bills of Lading: Miscellaneous Provisions

The draftsmen intended originally to consolidate the old Uniform Warehouse Receipts Act and Uniform Bills of Lading Act into one unified statute, but the plan could not be fully executed. The result is that the lawyer must usually look in two places. He must look first in the relevant "special provisions" on warehouse receipts and second in the more general provisions covering *both* warehouse receipts and bills of lading. Sometimes the lawyer must search outside of Article Seven in other Articles of the Code, such as Article Nine which applies to pledges of warehouse receipts.[23]

## § 20–3    Rights of Storer Against Warehouseman

Two related risks that a bailor incurs are that (*1*) the goods will be lost, destroyed, or damaged while in the bailee's hands and (*2*) the bailee will, for whatever reason, not be able to deliver up the goods when demanded. These risks are related in that *one* reason why a bailee may not be able to deliver up the goods is that they were lost or destroyed while they were in his custody. Yet the two risks are independently significant and merit separate consideration. A bailee may be unable to deliver for reasons other than loss or destruction of the goods. Thus, he may have misdelivered earlier. Also, a bailee may be able to deliver the goods, but only in damaged or injured condition. In most of the court cases on the bailee's duties of care and delivery, the plaintiff is the bailor, although the plaintiff can be a transferee, too, depending on whether the bailor has transferred the

---

**22.** Act of Aug. 11, 1916, ch. 313, part C, § 1, 39 Stat. 486, 7 U.S.C.A. §§ 241–43 (1970).

**23.** See e. g., §§ 9–304; 9–305.

documents.  Nor are bailees the only defendants in the cases.  Sometimes the real defendant (or plaintiff) is an insurer.[24]

The further risk that the bailee never received the receipted goods at all, or that the bailee misdescribed them in the receipt because the bailor's information was inaccurate, will not be treated here because the bailor is rarely in a position to complain when these risks materialize.  Rather, it is usually only a third party transferee of the receipt who can complain, for he will assume from the existence of the receipt that the goods also exist and that they exist as described in the receipt.  Accordingly these risks will be treated in Sections 20–4 and 20–5 of this chapter.

## THE RISK THAT WAREHOUSED GOODS WILL BE LOST, DESTROYED, OR DAMAGED

This is a real risk.  Given the number of litigated cases for us all to see, and applying the ancient farm-yard principle that for every mouse seen forty others go unseen, millions of dollars worth of goods are lost, destroyed, or damaged every year while they are in the custody of bailees.  Some losses go entirely unexplained.  Others can be readily traced to fire, flood, hurricane, riot, total neglect, and the like.[25]  Storers are well advised to insure.[26]  Indeed, a strong argument can be made that a warehouseman who fails to insure on behalf of the storer is liable therefor.[27]

What is the legal liability of a warehouseman for the care of stored goods?  Section 21 of the Uniform Warehouse Receipts Act which, prior to the Code, was law in all states, provided that:

> A warehouseman shall be liable for any loss or injury to the goods caused by his failure to exercise such care in regard to them as a reasonably careful owner of similar goods would exercise, but he shall not be liable, in the absence of an agreement to the contrary, for any loss or injury to the goods which could not have been avoided by the exercise of such care.

This "reasonably careful owner" standard was watered down only slightly in 7–204(1) of Article Seven of the Code to that of the "reasonably careful man":

> A warehouseman is liable for damages for loss of or injury to the goods caused by his failure to exercise such care in regard to them as a reasonably careful man would exercise under like circumstances but unless otherwise agreed he is not liable for damages which could not have been avoided by the exercise of such care.

24.  See, e. g., Annot. 27 A.L.R.3d 984 (1969) and cases cited therein.

25.  Annot., 92 A.L.R.2d 1298 (1963); Annot., 60 A.L.R.2d 1097 (1958); Annot., 16 A.L.R. 280 (1922).

26.  See, Conklin, Insurance of Warehousing and Other Bailment Risks, 1957 U.Ill.L.F. 560.

27.  J. Honnold, Cases and Materials on the Law of Sales and Sales Financing 442 (3d ed. 1968).

Under 7-204(4), local state statutes outside the Code may validly impose a higher or different standard on warehousemen. For example, in the state of Tennessee 7-204(4) provides:

> This section does not impair or repeal the law relating to tobacco warehousemen as contained in §§ 43-2101 through 43-2135, Tennessee Code Annotated.[28]

The statute referred to reads in part as follows:

> **Warehouses to be floored and kept in repair.**—The proprietor shall fit up his house with plank floors or skids, upon which to place the tobacco, so that the hogsheads may be at least four (4) inches from the earth; and any proprietor who fails to keep his warehouse in good repair, or to furnish it as in this section provided, shall forfeit two hundred dollars ($200) to the state; and is also liable upon his bond to an action for damages, at the instance of any planter or owner whose tobacco is injured.[29]

There are numerous pre-Code cases on the UWRA section 21 negligence standard,[30] and in the handful of Code cases to date the courts have made use of this pre-Code case law.[31] The Code cases do not significantly embellish the "reasonably careful man" standard. Given that Code section 7-204(1) and its UWRA ancestor expressly impose liability on the warehouseman only for negligence, what is his liability when he simply *cannot explain* loss or damage? Usually, a warehouseman who cannot explain loss or damage was negligent. But, it does not necessarily follow that he was negligent.[32] It is possible for a warehouseman to exercise due care, yet the goods still be lost or damaged unbeknown to the warehouseman. But in both pre-Code and post-Code cases in which the warehouseman could not explain what happened to the goods, the courts tend to impose liability,[33]

---

**28.** Tenn.Code Ann. § 43-2107 (1964).

**29.** Id.

**30.** Uniform Warehouse Receipts Act § 21 provided:

A warehouseman shall be liable for any loss or injury to the goods caused by his failure to exercise such care in regard to them as a reasonably careful owner of similar goods would exercise, but he shall not be liable, in the absence of an agreement to the contrary, for any loss or injury to the goods which could not have been avoided by the exercise of such care.

See Annot., 92 A.L.R.2d 1298 (1963); Annot., 60 A.L.R.2d 1097 (1958).

**31.** See, e. g., Procter & Gamble Distrib. Co. v. Lawrence Am. Field Warehousing Corp., 16 N.Y.2d 344, 358-59,

213 N.E.2d 873, 880-81, 3 UCC Rep. Serv. 157, 166-67 (1965).

**32.** Accord, J. Honnold, Cases and Materials on the Law of Sales and Sales Financing 442 (3d ed. 1968).

**33.** E. g., Bean v. Security Fur Storage Warehouse, Inc., 344 Mass. 674, 184 N.E.2d 64 (1962) (fur coat left with bailee for cleaning and storage inexplicably lost); D. H. Overmyer Co. v. Hirsch Bros. & Co., 459 S.W.2d 598, 8 UCC Rep.Serv. 894 (Ky.1970) (unexplained loss of 900 cases of pickles); Procter & Gamble Distrib. Co. v. Lawrence Am. Field Warehousing Corp., 16 N.Y.2d 344, 213 N.E.2d 873, 3 UCC Rep.Serv. 157 (1965) (unexplained shortage of oil discovered on bailor's demand therefor); Scott v. Lawrence Warehouse Co., 227 Ore. 78, 360 P.2d 610 (1961) (unexplained shortage in

and it may be that in some of these cases the warehouseman was subjected to a higher standard of liability than that of the reasonably careful man.   For example, in the recent case of Proctor & Gamble Distrib. Co. v. Lawrence Am. Field Warehousing Corp.,[34] the New York Court of Appeals may have held the warehouseman absolutely liable without realizing it.   The plaintiff was selling vegetable oils to Allied Crude Vegetable Oil Refining Corp. pursuant to an arrangement whereby the plaintiff shipped oil to defendant's field warehouse for storage pending its resale by Allied.   The defendant issued nonnegotiable warehouse receipts in the plaintiff's name covering the oil.   Allied went bankrupt and failed to pay for the oil.   When the plaintiff claimed the oil from the defendant warehouseman, most of it had disappeared, and the defendant could not explain how.   It appears that some of the oil might have even been stolen before it ever reached the defendant's tanks.   There was no evidence that the defendant did not receive the oil, presumably because the defendant simply did not know what had happened to it.   Yet the Court imposed liability.   Under the circumstances, we believe this is the proper result, but it is far from clear that negligence is the true basis of liability in such a case.   Even the nonnegligent may be quite unable to explain a particular loss.

Unless a court is to impose strict liability (in the teeth of 7–204 (1)), the plaintiff must prove negligence.   In many of the cases negligence cannot be readily proved.   When so, the result often depends on who has the burden of producing evidence and on who has the ultimate risk of nonpersuasion on the issues of negligence and causation.   Assume the plaintiff introduces credible evidence at trial that he deposited undamaged goods with the bailee, that he instructed the bailee to deliver them up, and that the bailee either failed to deliver any goods at all, delivered only a part of them, or delivered some or all of the goods in a damaged state.   Assume the plaintiff then rests without offering evidence on how the loss or damage occurred and without offering evidence on whether the cause of the loss was traceable to the warehouseman's negligence.   Has the plaintiff made out a *prima facie* case sufficient to get him to the jury, or is he subject to nonsuit or directed verdict for failure to offer credible proof of negligence and causation?   If it is held that the plaintiff may rest without offering such proof, it follows that it is the warehouseman who must introduce credible evidence that the loss or damage was not traceable to negligence on his part.   That is, it follows that the warehouseman has the *initial* burden of producing evidence on the issues of negligence and causation.   Assume he meets this burden.   If the plaintiff then introduces credible evidence of negligence and causation, and the jury decides that the proof is in equipoise, who wins will depend on the answer to a further question: which party has the ultimate risk of nonpersuasion on these issues?   This is the more important question, but the resolution of

lumber   inventory   discovered   after fire).

34.  16 N.Y.2d 344, 213 N.E.2d 873, 3 UCC Rep.Serv. 157 (1965).

either the question of who must produce credible evidence in the first place, or the question of who bears the ultimate risk of nonpersuasion, can determine the outcome.

What does Article Seven say on these questions? It says nothing on the burden of production question.[35] But 7–204(1) sets forth the substantive standard of liability, namely, negligence, and 7–403(1) (b) provides that:

> The bailee must deliver the goods to a person entitled . . . unless and to the extent that the bailee establishes . . . damage to or delay, loss or destruction of the goods for which the bailee is not liable [but the burden of establishing negligence in such cases is on the person entitled under the document].

The bracketed language is optional and only thirteen states have enacted it.[36] This language addresses the more important question of who has the ultimate risk of nonpersuasion on the issues of negligence and causation, and it allocates that risk to the plaintiff. This allocation is inconsistent with prior statutory law in section 8 of the UWRA, which provided:

> . . . In case the warehouseman refuses or fails to deliver the goods in compliance with a demand by the holder or depositor so accompanied, the burden shall be upon the warehouseman to establish the existence of a lawful excuse for such refusal.

The bracketed language is also inconsistent with a substantial body of pre-Code case law,[37] although there have been some decisions the other way in the teeth of section 8 of the UWRA.[38] In our view, enactment of the bracketed language is not only a step backward, but also unsound. In the usual case the warehouseman will have far better access to the facts than the plaintiff, and he should have to explain how the loss or damage occurred and why he was not negligently responsible. Admittedly this throws the burden of

---

35. On this question, some courts hold that the plaintiff makes out a *prima facie* case if he introduces credible evidence of delivery and loss. World Products, Inc. v. Central Freight Service, Inc., 222 F.Supp. 849, 2 UCC Rep. Serv. 675 (D.N.J.1963) (plaintiff discharges burden of production by introducing credible evidence of delivery and loss); Atkins v. Racquet Garage Corp., 177 Pa.Super. 94, 110 A.2d 767 (1955) (same); Canty v. Wyatt Storage Corp., 208 Va. 161, 156 S.E.2d 582, 4 UCC Rep.Serv. 778 (1967) (same). See generally Annot., 13 A.L. R.2d 681 (1950).

36. The states that have adopted the bracketed language are Arizona, California, Iowa, Kentucky, Maryland, Nevada, New York, North Carolina, Ohio, Oregon, Pennsylvania, Texas, and Wyoming. 2 U.L.A. § 7–403 at 556 (Master ed. 1968).

37. E. g., George v. Bekins Van & Storage Co., 33 Cal.2d 834, 205 P.2d 1037 (1949); Annot., 13 A.L.R.2d 681 (1950).

38. E. g., Schell v. Miller North Broad Storage Co., 142 Pa.Super. 293, 16 A. 2d 680 (1940), 157 Pa.Super. 101, 42 A.2d 180 (1945), aff'd 353 Pa. 319, 45 A.2d 53 (1946).

"proving a negative" on the defendant,[39] but proving nonnegligence is not necessarily proving a negative in the ordinary sense, for it does not necessarily require the defendant to prove that "raw fact" did not exist, only that he did not fail to exercise due care—a question of judgment.[40]

A majority of states did not enact the bracketed Code language. In these states which party has the ultimate burden of proving negligence and causation? Prior to the Code all states had the UWRA which allocated this burden to the warehouseman. It would be natural for courts that have followed section 8 simply to continue its allocation of burden. Doubtless many such courts will do just this.[41] But also recall that in pre-Code days some courts imposed the ultimate burden on the plaintiff contrary to the express language of section 8 of the UWRA.[42] Any courts so disposed to ignore statutes will, post-Code, find it all the easier to continue imposing the burden on the plaintiff, for, absent its bracketed language, section 7–403(1) of the Code is silent on the entire question. Yet enactment of the Code may serve as an occasion to consider this important question afresh.

Once liability is established, what damages may the plaintiff recover from the warehouseman? A plaintiff might sustain two kinds of damage: direct damage in the form of loss or injury to the goods themselves and consequential damage, such as lost profits. A plaintiff may deposit goods in a warehouse expecting to resell them and, after contracting to resell at a profit, find that he cannot do so because of loss or damage to the goods due to the warehouseman's negligence. Section 7–204(1) of Article Seven allows recovery for "loss of or injury to the goods," language which does not expressly allow recovery for consequential damages in the form of lost profits. Suppose, for example, that the market value of plaintiff's goods is $10,000 at the time they are destroyed and that the plaintiff had contracted to resell them for $12,000. A recovery limited by the language of section 7–204(1) to merely $10,000 would not always make the plaintiff whole. There are no Code cases either way.[43] We think the plaintiff should recover consequential damages in a

---

39. On the criteria for allocation of burden of proof, see generally 9 J. Wigmore, Evidence §§ 2485–88 (3d ed. 1940).

40. Accord, Broude, The Emerging Pattern of Field Warehouse Litigation: Liability for Unexplained Losses and Nonexistent Goods, 47 Nebr.L.Rev. 3, 20–21 (1968). Professor Broude also explodes the fallacy of allocating burden of proof depending on whether the complaint sounds in tort or contract.

41. E. g., George v. Bekins Van & Storage Co., 33 Cal.2d 834, 205 P.2d 1037 (1949).

42. E. g., Schell v. Miller North Broad Storage Co., 142 Pa.Super. 293, 16 A. 2d 680 (1940), 157 Pa.Super. 101, 42 A. 2d 180 (1945), aff'd 353 Pa. 319, 45 A. 2d 53 (1946).

43. But on the analogous problem with respect to carriers, see Lowes Glove Co. v. Acme Fast Freight, Inc., 54 Misc.2d 429, 282 N.Y.S.2d 869 (Sup.Ct. 1967) (no recovery for lost profits though carrier delivered gloves too late for Christmas season).

proper case, and we would cite not only 1–103 and general law allowing recovery of consequential damages, but also 1–106 which provides that remedies are to be liberally administered.

When the plaintiff seeks "direct" damages for "loss of or injury to" the goods, such damages are generally measured in terms
of fair market value.[44] But *when* is this valuation to be made? At
the time of loss or damage? At the time the loss or damage is discovered? At the time the plaintiff demands the goods? At some
other time? Resolution of these questions can be of great importance,
especially as to goods the price of which fluctuates markedly within
a short period. Ordinarily damages are ascertained as of the time
when the relevant duty is broken *and* the loss or injury is thereby
sustained. The 7–204(1) duty of care is "statutory-contractual" in
nature and is violated when the neglectful acts or omissions occur
and cause or help to cause loss or injury to the goods. Thus, on
principle it would appear that damages will generally be the difference between the value of the goods just prior to the loss or injury
and their value immediately afterwards. Often, as in the case of fires
and floods, this will not be problematic, and courts have ascertained
fair market value as of these times in such cases,[45] although they have
not always agreed on the applicable theory.[46]

But what if neither the warehouseman nor the plaintiff can
establish just when the loss or injury to the goods occurred? This
problem arose dramatically in Procter & Gamble Distrib. Co. v.
Lawrence Am. Field Warehousing Corp.[47] No one could establish
just when the bailed salad oil disappeared from the bailee's tanks.
Moreover by the time the bailor discovered its disappearance, the
market price of salad oil had fallen drastically because of publicity
given to various manipulations in the salad oil market. Was the
New York Court of Appeals to ascertain market price, and therefore the bailor's loss, as of the time the disappearance of the oil became known or at some other time? The court reasoned that: [48]

> [T]he circumstances regarding the loss of bailed property
> are more likely to be known by the bailee than by the bailor,
> and, where the time and manner of the loss is unknown,
> it ought not to lie in the power of the bailee to choose the

**44.** § 7–204(1). The measure of damages in the special case of negligent
injury to perishables is treated in
Annot., 32 A.L.R.2d 910 (1953). The
measure of damages in the special
case of negligent injury to personal
articles is considered in Layton v.
Ferguson Moving & Storage Co., 109
Ohio App. 541, 160 N.E.2d 138 (1959).

**45.** E. g., Western Surety Co. v. Redman Rice Mills, Inc., 271 F.2d 885
(8th Cir. 1959); Saporiti v. Austin A.
Chambers Co., 134 Conn. 476, 58 A.2d
387 (1948); Harper Warehouse, Inc.
v. Henry Chanin Corp., 102 Ga.App.

489, 116 S.E.2d 641 (1960); Keating v.
F. H. Peavey Co., 71 N.D. 517, 3 N.W.
2d 104 (1942).

**46.** See generally Broude, The Emerging Pattern of Field Warehouse Litigation: Liability for Unexplained
Losses and Nonexistent Goods, 47
Nebr.L.Rev. 3 (1968).

**47.** 16 N.Y.2d 344, 213 N.E.2d 873, 3
UCC Rep.Serv. 157 (1965).

**48.** Id. at 352, 213 N.E.2d at 877, 3 UCC
Rep.Serv. at 161.

date for determining market value by electing when to notify the bailor that the goods have disappeared and cannot be accounted for. The rule that the loss is to be measured as of the time of the conversion, when the conversion date is known, should not be reshaped to designate the date when the bailor is notified of the conversion if the conversion date is unknown. That would place the bailee in a better legal position by pleading ignorance of the circumstances of the loss than if he knew or revealed the circumstances.

This rule should not be applied to the advantage of the warehouseman and the detriment of the bailor if the warehouseman pleads ignorance of the date on which the property disappeared. In order that a bailee may not be permitted to take advantage of his own wrong where the subject of the bailment has been negligently lost or misappropriated, it follows that the bailor should be awarded damages measured by the highest value of the property between the date when the bailment commenced and the date when the bailor has received notice that the property has been lost.

While this approach finds support in other court decisions,[49] it can allow the plaintiff bailor a windfall, as where the market value of the goods peaks at a time when the bailor had no intention whatever of withdrawing the goods from the warehouse.

Assuming the state has not modified 7–204(2) by regulatory law, that section permits a warehouseman to limit his damage liability by contractual bargain with his bailor:

Damages may be limited by a term in the warehouse receipt or storage agreement limiting the amount of liability in case of loss or damage, and setting forth a specific liability per article or item, or value per unit of weight, beyond which the warehouseman shall not be liable; provided, however, that such liability may on written request of the bailor at the time of signing such storage agreement or within a reasonable time after receipt of the warehouse receipt be increased on part or all of the goods thereunder, in which event increased rates may be charged based on such increased valuation, but that no such increase shall be permitted contrary to a lawful limitation of liability contained in the warehouseman's tariff, if any. No such limitation is effective with respect to the warehouseman's liability for conversion to his own use.

This provision deprives the warehouseman of power to force the bailor to choose between accepting an arbitrary limitation or going

---

**49.** See, e. g., McIntyre v. Whitney, 139 App.Div. 557, 124 N.Y.S. 234 (1st Dep't 1910), aff'd 201 N.Y. 526, 94 N.E. 1096 (1911); Corn Exch. Bank v. Peabody, 111 App.Div. 553, 98 N.Y.S. 78 (1st Dep't 1906).

elsewhere.[50]   If the bailor wishes to pay the increased rates, the warehouseman must assume the increased liability.

One case under 7–204(2) indicates that if the warehouseman is to limit his liability, he must strictly follow the steps specified in the section.   In Modelia, Inc. v. Rose Warehouse, Inc.,[51] the bailor agreed to a limitation of the warehouseman's liability stated in terms of a sum of money for the property designated in particular warehouse receipts, rather than in terms of a specific liability "per article or item, or value per unit of weight," which is the literal language of 7–204(2).   The court agreed with the bailor's contention that the limit was invalid because it was not stated in the form indicated in the statute.[52]

## THE RISK OF THE WAREHOUSEMAN'S MISDELIVERY OR NONDELIVERY

When the person entitled under a warehouse receipt (a storer or his transferee) demands delivery, the warehouseman may be unable to deliver because of a prior misdelivery or for some other reason. Under 7–403(1), this constitutes *prima facie* breach of his basic obligation "to deliver the goods" to a person entitled under the warehouse receipt.   Furthermore, the storer is thereby entitled to recover damages for nondelivery provided (*1*) he satisfies the bailee's lien,[53] (*2*) he surrenders for cancellation or notation any outstanding negotiable document of title validly covering the goods,[54] and (*3*) the warehouseman does not establish a "lawful excuse" for nonperformance of his delivery obligation.

In general, a warehouseman is *absolutely liable* to the receipt-holder for misdelivery.   The pre-Code law was the same.   An early New York case, Strong v. Security Storage & Warehouse Co.,[55] is illustrative.   There the court held a warehouseman absolutely liable for misdelivery of a machine and emphasized that the liability "is an absolute one, and is not dependent upon the exercise of care." [56] The Second Circuit Court of Appeals recently adopted the same view for cases falling within admiralty jurisdiction, relying in part on the Code.[57]   We are not unmindful that section 7–404 of the Code

50.  Warren, The Historical Background of Article 7 of the Code: The Law of Documents of Title, 3 N.Y. State Law Revision Comm'n, 1955 Report 1761, 1790–91 (1955).

51.  5 UCC Rep.Serv. 1004 (N.Y.Sup.Ct. 1968).

52.  But see Dunfee v. Blue Rock Van & Storage, Inc., —— Del. ——, 266 A.2d 187, 7 UCC Rep.Serv. 1344 (1970) ("substantial compliance" with the statutory limitation requirement held sufficient); World Products, Inc. v. Central Freight Service, Inc., 222 F.Supp.

849, 2 UCC Rep.Serv. 675 (D.C.N.J. 1963).

53.  § 7–403(2).

54.  § 7–403(3).

55.  108 Misc. 329, 177 N.Y.S. 591 (N.Y. Sup.Ct.1919).

56.  Id. at 331, 177 N.Y.S. at 593.

57.  David Crystal, Inc. v. Cunard Steam-Ship Co., 339 F.2d 295 (2d Cir. 1964) (Cunard Line and stevedoring firm held absolutely liable for misde-

might be interpreted sometimes to change the rule of absolute liability for misdelivery. That section provides:

> A bailee who in good faith including observance of reasonable commercial standards has received goods and delivered or otherwise disposed of them according to the terms of the document of title or pursuant to this Article is not liable therefor. This rule applies even though the person from whom he received the goods had no authority to procure the document or to dispose of the goods and even though the person to whom he delivered the goods had no authority to receive them.

Consider the following case: True owner stores and takes receipts covering the goods. Employee of true owner skillfully forges duplicate receipts and procures the goods. It might be argued that true owner loses in his action against warehouseman, for warehouseman acted in good faith and used due care. A comment to the section supports this interpretation.[58] We reject it. Warehouseman did not deliver according to the terms of the document. Also if the draftsman had intended to change the well-settled principle of absolute liability for misdelivery, he could have said so explicitly.

The most important class of *nondelivery* cases are those in which the warehouseman is unable to deliver part or all of the goods because of their loss, damage, or destruction. Here, under 7–403(1) and 7–402(1), the general rule is not one of absolute liability, but one of liability for negligence, as we have already seen.[59]

In both the misdelivery and the nondelivery cases, the warehouseman may or may not have a "lawful excuse." These excuses are set forth in 7–403(1):

> The bailee must deliver the goods to a person entitled under the document who complies with subsections (2) and (3), unless and to the extent that the bailee establishes any of the following:
>
> (a) delivery of the goods to a person whose receipt was rightful as against the claimant;
>
> (b) damage to or delay, loss or destruction of the goods for which the bailee is not liable [, but the burden of establishing negligence in such cases is on the person entitled under the document];
>
> Note: *The brackets in (1) (b) indicate that State enactments may differ on this point without serious damage to the principle of uniformity.*

---

livery of shirts procured by forgery of delivery order), cert. denied 380 U.S. 976 (1965).

58. § 7–404, Comment.

59. See text accompanying notes 27–31 supra.

(c) previous sale or other disposition of the goods in lawful enforcement of a lien or on warehouseman's lawful termination of storage;

(d) the exercise by a seller of his right to stop delivery pursuant to the provisions of the Article on Sales (Section 2—705);

(e) a diversion, reconsignment or other disposition pursuant to the provisions of this Article (Section 7—303) or tariff regulating such right;

(f) release, satisfaction or any other fact affording a personal defense against the claimant;

(g) any other lawful excuse.

The above circumstances excuse the warehouseman from delivering to "a person entitled under the document." Section 7–403(4) defines this phrase to mean a "holder in the case of a negotiable document, or the person to whom delivery is to be made by the terms of or pursuant to written instructions under a nonnegotiable document." Ordinarily the "holder" of a negotiable warehouse receipt either will be the original bailor who will also be the owner of the deposited goods, or will be the original bailor's rightful transferee of the receipt. But the holder may be a wrongdoer, too. For example, the definition of holder in section 1–201(20) allows even a thief or a finder of certain documents of title to be a holder. Thus, the "person entitled under the document" to whom the warehouseman must *prima facie* deliver under 7–403(1) is not *necessarily* the original owner of the goods or the receipts, let alone a rightful transferee of the owner's rights.[60]

It should not be surprising that the very first lawful excuse set forth above in section 7–403(1) (a) excuses the warehouseman from delivery to a holder of a warehouse receipt whose claim to the goods is inferior to that of another party. For example, suppose a thief steals goods, warehouses them, and receives negotiable receipts therefor (or a nonnegotiable receipt showing himself entitled to delivery). The warehouseman discovers the theft and delivers the goods to the true owner rather than to the "person entitled under the document." Here the warehouseman has a lawful excuse for such delivery under section 7–403(1) (a), an excuse good even as against a *bona fide* purchaser of the receipt from the thief. When the warehouseman is in doubt about which of two claimants is entitled to the goods, he can institute interpleader proceedings under section 7–603.

But suppose the theft was not discovered until *after* the thief had reappeared, withdrawn the goods from the warehouse, and gone off with them. Would the warehouseman be liable to the true owner

60. § 7–403(4).

for his unauthorized handling of the goods?  Section 7–404 says no, provided its terms are met:

> A bailee who in good faith including observance of reasonable commercial standards has received goods and delivered or otherwise disposed of them according to the terms of the document of title or pursuant to this Article is not liable therefor.  This rule applies even though the person from whom he received the goods had no authority to procure the document or to dispose of the goods and even though the person to whom he delivered the goods had no authority to receive them.

In our view, a warehouseman fails to comply with this section if he ignores facts which put him on inquiry.  He similarly fails to comply if he does not invoke interpleader in the face of adverse claims and delivers to the wrong party.

The second excuse in section 7–403(1) excuses the warehouseman for nondelivery because of damage, loss, etc., for which the bailee is not liable; we have treated that excuse elsewhere.[61]  The third excuse arises from the warehouseman's lawful enforcement of his lien or lawful termination of storage and is straightforward enough.[62]  The fourth and fifth excuses generally do not concern warehousemen.  The sixth excuse is "release, satisfaction or any other fact affording a personal defense against the claimant." [63]  The catch-all seventh excuse ("any other lawful excuse") covers such possibilities as delivery of goods as required by court order, destruction of goods that have become hazardous, and refusal of delivery during pendency of interpleader.[64]

Article Seven is silent on the remedies of a "person entitled under the document."  If the goods exist, this person should be entitled to replevy them if he wishes.  At least he should be entitled to recover their dollar value as well as any foreseeable consequential damages.  Of course, a warehouseman may, in general, set contractual limits on the dollar amount of recovery.[65]

## § 20–4  Rights of Purchaser of Warehouse Receipts

That vast quantities of goods stored in warehouses can be bought and sold simply by buying and selling pieces of paper called warehouse receipts is a great convenience not only to the commodity exchanges, but also to ordinary individuals and corporates bodies.  We will first treat the rights of purchasers of negotiable warehouse receipts and then turn to the rights of purchasers of nonnegotiable receipts.

61.  See Section 20–3 supra.

62.  § 7–403(1) (c).

63.  § 7–403(1) (f).

64.  Braucher, In re Article Seven, 28 Temp.L.Q. 564, 573 (1955).

65.  § 7–204(2).

## PURCHASE OF NEGOTIABLE RECEIPTS

Subsections 7–104(1) and (2) distinguish between negotiable and nonnegotiable documents of title:

(1) A warehouse receipt, bill of lading or other document of title is negotiable

(a) if by its terms the goods are to be delivered to bearer or to the order of a named person; or

(b) where recognized in overseas trade, if it runs to a named person or assigns.

(2) Any other document is non-negotiable. A bill of lading in which it is stated that the goods are consigned to a named person is not made negotiable by a provision that the goods are to be delivered only against a written order signed by the same or another named person.

Section 7–104(1) states that a warehouse receipt is negotiable "if by its terms the goods are to be delivered to bearer or to the order of a named person." Section 7–501 provides:

(1) A negotiable document of title running to the order of a named person is negotiated by his indorsement and delivery. After his indorsement in blank or to bearer any person can negotiate it by delivery alone.

(2) (a) A negotiable document of title is also negotiated by delivery alone when by its original terms it runs to bearer.

(b) When a document running to the order of a named person is delivered to him the effect is the same as if the document had been negotiated.

(3) Negotiation of a negotiable document of title after it has been indorsed to a specified person requires indorsement by the special indorsee as well as delivery.

(4) A negotiable document of title is "duly negotiated" when it is negotiated in the manner stated in this section to a holder who purchases it in good faith without notice of any defense against or claim to it on the part of any person and for value, unless it is established that the negotiation is not in the regular course of business or financing or involves receiving the document in settlement or payment of a money obligation.

(5) Indorsement of a non-negotiable document neither makes it negotiable nor adds to the transferee's rights.

(6) The naming in a negotiable bill of a person to be notified of the arrival of the goods does not limit the negotiability of the bill nor constitute notice to a purchaser thereof of any interest of such person in the goods.

The foregoing statutory language can be divided into several distinct requirements: (*1*) indorsement and/or delivery as specified, (*2*) to a "holder," (*3*) who purchases it, (*4*) for value, (*5*) in good faith without notice of any defense or claim to it on the part of any person, and (*6*) all in the "regular course of business or financing." The Code includes definitions of key terms in 7–501, specifically, holder,[66] purchase,[67] value,[68] good faith,[69] and notice.[70]   Comment 1 to section 7–501 expands on the sixth requirement: "The only holder whose possession appears, commercially, to be in order is almost invariably a person in the trade.   No commercial purpose is secured by allowing a tramp or a professor to duly negotiate. . . ."   Relevant Code case law to date is of little moment.   One case, Cleveland v. McNabb,[71] holds that a transferee for purposes of section 7–501(4) has notice of an outstanding claim (here a land-lord's lien on cotton sold to the transferee) when he has reason to know of it.   This holding merely applies the Code definition of notice.[72]

In general a purchaser of a warehouse receipt who takes by due negotiation (*1*) gets the basic rights of the bailor against the bailee considered in the preceding section, namely, the right to have the bailee take reasonable care of the goods and the right to have him deliver on demand (subject to lawful excuses),[73] and (*2*) gets "title to the document and title to the goods" under 7–502 since transfer of the receipt is recognized in law as the exclusive mode of transferring title not only to the receipt, but also to the goods it covers.

A large part of what is meant by saying that a warehouse receipt is "negotiable" comes down to this: A purchaser of such a *receipt* who takes by "due negotiation" cuts off nearly all outstanding equities and claims of prior parties both to the receipt and to the goods it covers.[74]   Purchase of such a receipt cuts to a minimum the risk that some third party will have a "paramount title" that he can assert.   By contrast, direct purchase of the *goods* themselves does not similarly reduce this risk.   To illustrate, assume that O entrusts goods to W for the purpose of storing them.   W is not a merchant with respect to goods of that kind.   W, contrary to instructions, sells the goods to BFP.   O claims them.   O would prevail.[75]   But if W had warehoused these very same goods and sold negotiable receipts to BFP, O would not prevail; BFP would win.[76]   Many other examples might be cited to show how a purchaser of goods takes greater title

---

66.  § 1–201(20).

67.  § 1–201(32).

68.  § 1–201(44).

69.  § 1–201(19).

70.  § 1–201(27).

71.  312 F.Supp. 155, 7 UCC Rep.Serv. 1226 (W.D.Tenn.1970).

72.  § 1–201(25) (c).   But see the pre-Code case of Grauman v. Jackson, 216 Ark. 362, 225 S.W.2d 678 (1950) and cases cited therein.

73.  § 7–502(1) (d).

74.  § 7–502.

75.  § 2–403.

76.  §§ 7–502; 7–503.

risks than the purchaser of a warehouse receipt who acquires it by due negotiation. Because of this difference, we say that *goods* are not negotiable in our law, whereas warehouse receipts in proper form are negotiable. The legal phenomenon of negotiability empowers transferors to transfer substantially better title than they themselves have. When a party transfers something that the law says is not negotiable, the purchaser generally gets only the title of his transferor plus whatever further title any special rules of law confer.[77]

Of course, negotiability is a matter of degree. As we will soon show, not even the purchaser of a warehouse receipt who takes by due negotiation cuts off all prior claims and equities. And at an earlier day, warehouse receipts were far less negotiable than they now are under the Code. Indeed it was not until the widespread enactment of the Code that a purchaser generally cut off the rights of an owner from whom a thief had stolen a negotiable receipt in bearer form, a problem that arose under the pre-Code law on a number of occasions. The Mississippi Supreme Court[78] as recently as 1966 invoked the old Uniform Warehouse Receipts Act to hold for the original owner over such a transferee. The court stressed that "a trespasser, a finder, or a thief [may] . . . not . . . negotiate a receipt so as to give title to the receipt or other goods represented by it to a subsequent purchaser for value."[79] The Code changes this and makes the receipt more fully negotiable. Section 7–502(2) provides that the transferee who takes by due negotiation gets title to the receipt and title to the goods and states specifically that this title and the rights attendant thereto are not defeated by:

> any stoppage of the goods represented by the document or by surrender of such goods by the bailee, and are not impaired even though the negotiation or any prior negotiation constituted a breach of duty or even though any person has been deprived of possession of the document by misrepresentation, fraud, accident, mistake, duress, loss, theft or conversion, or even though a previous sale or other transfer of the goods or document has been made to a third person.

The import of the proposition that a purchaser of a receipt who takes by due negotiation acquires title to the document and title to the goods can be more fully revealed if we list most of the main types of third parties whose interests are cut off by the purchase:

(*1*) An original owner who was somehow deprived of the receipt in bearer form;[80]

(*2*) Unsecured creditors who had previously attached, levied, or the like, on the receipt;[81]

---

77.  §§ 2–403; 7–504.

78.  St. Paul Fire & Marine Ins. Co. v. Leflore Bank & Trust Co., 254 Miss. 598, 181 So.2d 913 (1966).

79.  Id. at 611, 181 So.2d at 919.

80.  §§ 7–501; 7–502.

81.  Id. See Annot., 40 A.L.R. 969 (1926).

(*3*) Article Nine secured creditors who claim the receipt itself as collateral; [82]

(*4*) A bona fide purchaser of the goods who bought them from the warehouseman; [83]

(*5*) An owner of the goods who entrusted them to the original bailor with actual authority to ship, store, or sell, or with other power of disposition under the Code or other law; [84]

(*6*) An owner who entrusted a receipt covering the goods to the original bailor with the same powers as in (*5*) or with power merely to obtain delivery; [85]

(*7*) An owner or secured party who acquiesced in the procurement by the bailor of a receipt covering the goods; [86]

(*8*) Creditors of the transferor and of the bailee who attached, levied, or the like, on the goods; [87]

(*9*) A secured creditor without a perfected security interest in the goods.[88]

Even so, a purchaser of a receipt who takes by due negotiation from his transferor does not defeat the whole world. There are exceptions to Article Seven's general principle that a purchaser who takes by due negotiation gets "title to the document and title to the goods." First, there is the "forged indorsement" exception. Suppose, for example, that O warehouses goods taking negotiable receipts therefor that either run on their face to the order of a named person or that O himself indorses specially to Z. While they are still in O's hands, the receipts are stolen and then sold by the thief to BFP with the thief forging O's indorsement or the special indorsement of Z. Here BFP would not acquire title to the receipts paramount to the title of O, and O could lawfully retrieve the receipts from BFP.[89] If, at the time of the theft the receipts required on their face delivery to bearer or were indorsed in blank, BFP would prevail.[90] In short if the receipts were in such form as to be transferable by delivery, BFP would generally prevail over O, despite the fact that BFP's transferor (or a prior transferor) came into possession of the document by theft, by conversion, by fraud, by duress, by finding, by mistake, by innocent misrepresentation, or the like.[91] Nor is the transferor's legal power to pass title to a document impaired by the fact that his transfer was unauthorized or out of regular course.[92] The one significant source of impairment under section

---

82.  § 9–309.

83.  §§ 7–501; 7–502.

84.  §§ 7–502; 7–503.

85.  §§ 7–502; 7–503.

86.  §§ 7–502; 7–503.

87.  §§ 7–502; 7–503.

88.  Id. Cf. § 9–309.

89.  Cf. John S. Hale & Co. v. Beley Cotton Co., 154 Tenn. 689, 290 S.W. 994 (1927).

90.  §§ 7–502; 7–503.

91.  § 7–502(2).

92.  Id.

7–501 is simply that the document may be in such form that it cannot be transferred without the indorsement of some party besides the transferor.   The hapless purchaser of a negotiable document bearing a forged indorsement where a genuine indorsement is essential to his title may recover against his transferor for breach of warranty under applicable Code provisions.[93]   Alas, this will not often be a fruitful course of action, for the transferor will usually be gone or insolvent.

The second exception involves theft of the goods.   The well known case of Lineburger Bros. v. Hodge [94] poses the problem.   There, a truck driver who had no authority to haul away cotton nonetheless did so.   He thereafter warehoused it and had negotiable receipts issued in fictitious names.   He then sold the receipts to purchasers who took by the Code equivalent of due negotiation.   The court awarded the cotton to the original owners and noted that "an owner of cotton may not be divested of title by a trespasser or a thief." [95] Sections 7–501, 7–502, and 7–503 of the Code embody the same rule.

There is a third exception involving certain bailees.   Suppose O owns goods which he entrusts to R for repair.   R does not have any further authority, actual or apparent.   R warehouses the goods, and receives negotiable receipts therefor which he then sells to BFP.   O is unaware of the bailment and does not acquiesce in it.   Under section 7–503 of the Code, O's title generally remains paramount to BFP's:

> (1) A document of title confers no right in goods against a person who before issuance of the document had a legal interest or a perfected security interest in them and who neither
>
> > (a) delivered or entrusted them or any document of title covering them to the bailor or his nominee with actual or apparent authority to ship, store or sell or with power to obtain delivery under this Article (Section 7—403) or with power of disposition under this Act (Sections 2—403 and 9—307) or other statute or rule of law; nor
> >
> > (b) acquiesced in the procurement by the bailor or his nominee of any document of title.

However, by negative implication and otherwise, the BFP would prevail against any prior owners or prior secured parties who delivered, entrusted, or acquiesced within 7–503(1) (a) or (b).   The case of United States v. Hext [96] is illustrative.   There, the United States took security in growing cotton and later acquiesced in the borrower's storage and procurement of negotiable warehouse receipts

---

93.  § 7–507.

94.  212 Miss. 204, 54 So.2d 268 (1951).

95.  Id. at 222, 54 So.2d at 271.

96.  444 F.2d 804, 9 UCC Rep.Serv. 321 (5th Cir. 1971).

covering the cotton. Without the assent of the United States, these receipts ultimately found their way into the hands of purchasers who took by due negotiation. The court cited, among other sources, 7–503 (1) (a) and (b) and held for the purchasers.[97]

A very limited fourth exception may be called the "perfected security interest" exception. Where a secured party under Article Nine has a valid, enforceable, and perfected security interest *in the goods,* another party cannot warehouse them and pass paramount title to them to a transferee of negotiable receipts covering the goods,[98] unless the secured party delivered or entrusted the goods (or any document covering them) to that other party or his nominee within the meaning of 7–503(1) (a), or acquiesced within 7–503(1) (b). Of course, ordinarily, such other party will have delivered, entrusted, or acquiesced within 7–503(1). Certain statutory lienors also prevail over our transferee, as indicated by the recent case of Cleveland v. McNabb[99] and Comment 1 to section 7–503.

Further exceptions, quite limited in scope, are set forth in Code sections 7–503(2),[100] 7–503(3),[101] and 7–205.[102] Despite these and the exceptions just discussed, it remains generally true that a purchaser of negotiable documents who takes by due negotiation acquires not only title to the goods, but also paramount title to them. In the overwhelming proportion of potential adverse claim controversies, our purchaser emerges the winner. The general rationale for this is set forth in Comment 1 to 7–503:

> In general it may be said that the title of a purchaser by due negotiation prevails over almost any interest in the goods which existed prior to the procurement of the document of title if the possession of the goods by the person obtaining the document derived from any action by the prior claimant which introduced the goods into the stream of commerce or carried them along that stream.

97. Compare Commercial Nat'l Bank v. Canal-Louisiana Bank & Trust Co., 239 U.S. 520 (1916) with Gazzola v. Lacy Bros. & Kimball, 156 Tenn. 229, 299 S.W. 1039 (1927).

98. § 9–201.

99. 312 F.Supp. 155, 7 UCC Rep.Serv. 1226 (W.D.Tenn.1970).

100. § 7–503(2) provides:

Title to goods based upon an unaccepted delivery order is subject to the rights of any one to whom a negotiable warehouse receipt or bill of lading covering the goods has been duly negotiated. Such a title may be defeated under the next section to the same extent as the rights of the issuer or a transferee from the issuer.

101. § 7–503(3) provides:

Title to goods upon a bill of lading issued to a freight forwarder is subject to the rights of anyone to whom a bill issued by the freight forwarder is duly negotiated but delivery by the carrier in accordance with Part 4 of this Article pursuant to its own bill of lading discharges the carrier's obligations to deliver.

102. § 7–205 provides:

A buyer in the ordinary course of business of fungible goods sold and delivered by a warehouseman who is also in the business of buying and selling such goods takes free of any claim under a warehouse receipt even though it has been duly negotiated.

Besides the risk that one of the foregoing exceptional situations will arise so that our purchaser will therefore prove not to have *paramount title* to the receipt or to the goods, there are still other risks that a purchaser runs even when he takes a receipt by due negotiation. Thus he runs the risk of its loss, its destruction, and its theft, all prior to presenting it to the bailee for delivery of the goods. These events rarely occur, but when they do, section 7–601(1) of the Code authorizes a court to order "delivery of the goods or issuance of a substitute document." The claimant must post judicially approved security "to indemnify any person who may suffer loss as a result of nonsurrender of the document." [103] Of course, if the lost document was negotiable only by indorsement, a finder or a thief could not pass good title to it or to the goods covered. Still, under 7–404 the bailee might be excused from liability to the owner if it delivered over a forged indorsement in good faith "including observance of reasonable commercial standards." In that event the owner would have to chase down the goods or the wrongdoer.

A further risk is that the receipts might prove wholly spurious. That is, they might have been issued by a forger covering nonexistent goods "held" by a nonexistent bailee. Here, the purchaser's recourse would be against his own transferor for breach of his warranty that the documents are genuine,[104] or against the forger, if he can be found. The documents might only be "partially spurious" that is, issued for existent goods in the hands of a bailee but by a party wholly without actual authority to issue them. Unless the bailee is in some way legally responsible for the acts of this party, the bailee will not be liable to the purchaser for nondelivery.[105] Again, the purchaser would have recourse against his transferor for breach of his warranty that the documents are genuine.[106]

Assuming the genuineness and authenticity of the documents themselves, section 7–208 is addressed to their alteration or unauthorized completion:

> Where a blank in a negotiable warehouse receipt has been filled in without authority, a purchaser for value and without notice of the want of authority may treat the insertion as authorized. Any other unauthorized alteration leaves any receipt enforceable against the issuer according to its original tenor.

Another risk is that the warehouseman fraudulently or negligently issued receipts for more goods than he received or that he issued duplicates without marking them. The problem has arisen in several cases. Gould v. City Bank & Trust Co.[107] was a 1954 case in which the warehouseman issued duplicate sets of negotiable receipts

103.  § 7–601(1).

104.  § 7–507.

105.  § 7–102(1) (g).

106.  Id.

107.  213 F.2d 314, (4th Cir. 1954).

covering the same whiskey. One set found its way into the hands of a lending bank and the other into the hands of a purchaser. The court held for the bank, inasmuch as the receipts it held were the first ones issued and there was no basis for an estoppel. Under section 7–402 of Article Seven, the result would be the same at least if the whiskey is not a fungible. Also, 7–402 would permit the losing party to recover against the warehouseman for "damages caused by his overissue or failure to identify a duplicate document."

What if the bailee did not receive the goods at all (the "nonreceipt" risk)? Cases have arisen in which the bailee simply could not prove either that he did or did not receive the goods. In these circumstances the bailee generally loses.[108] But, suppose the bailee can and does prove that he did not receive the goods and for this reason could not deliver them to a purchaser of the negotiable warehouse receipt. This may occur where a defrauder induces an employee of the bailee to issue a receipt for nonexistent goods or to issue a receipt on representations that the goods will be bailed, but they never are. Section 7–203 provides:

> A party to or purchaser for value in good faith of a document of title other than a bill of lading relying in either case upon the description therein of the goods may recover from the issuer damages caused by the non-receipt or misdescription of the goods, except to the extent that the document conspicuously indicates that the issuer does not know whether any part or all of the goods in fact were received or conform to the description, as where the description is in terms of marks or labels or kind, quantity or condition, or the receipt or description is qualified by "contents, condition and quality unknown", "said to contain" or the like, if such indication be true, or the party or purchaser otherwise has notice.

When one reads the above together with the Code definition of issuer, the Code imposes liability for nonreceipt on a warehouseman "for whom an agent or employee purports to act in issuing a document if the agent or employee has real or apparent authority to issue documents, notwithstanding that the issuer received no goods."[109] This is a salutary departure from pre-Code law in such states as Massachusetts which permitted the issuer to escape liability for nonreceipt where the issuer's agent, having authority to issue receipts, issued a receipt for goods not delivered.[110] It should be noted, too, that the warehouseman's liability runs only to "a party or purchaser for value in good faith of a document of title  .  .  .  relying in either case

---

108. See, e. g., Proctor & Gamble Distrib. Co. v. Lawrence Am. Field Warehousing Corp., 16 N.Y.2d 344, 213 N.E. 2d 873, 3 UCC Rep.Serv. 157 (1965). See also text accompanying notes 32–34 supra.

109. § 7–102(1) (g).

110. Rosenberg v. National Dock & Storage Warehouse Co., 218 Mass. 518, 106 N.E. 171 (1914).

upon the description therein." A warehouseman's liability to such parties for nonreceipt cannot be disclaimed,[111] except to the extent that the warehouseman "does not know whether any part or all of the goods in fact were received" and so states "conspicuously" in the receipt.

Our purchaser of negotiable receipts who takes by due negotiation also runs the risk that the receipts "misdescribe" the goods. So-called "misdescription" has given rise to only a few litigated cases. Goods may be misdescribed in the documents as to general contents, type, quality, unit size, quantity, weight, and so on. When a holder of a negotiable document takes it relying on the description and then finds the description significantly erroneous, he will be justifiably aggrieved, as where he buys documents describing the goods as "Brignac Braid Shrimp" [112] and they turn out to be cans filled with water, or he buys documents describing rough rice in the amount of two million odd pounds and the quantity turns out to be one hundred thousand pounds short.[113] Of course, the purchaser can usually reduce such risks by checking the goods before buying, and generally he should do this. These checks will not turn up every discrepancy between documentary description and reality. The legal principles governing liability of warehousemen for misdescription are stated in section 7–203 of the Code already set out in the text above. Generally, protected plaintiffs include only those who part with value in reliance on the accuracy of the description.[114] Since the descriptions placed on the documents are almost always supplied by the storer, warehousemen generally seek to disclaim liability for misdescription. Section 7–203 validates a conspicuous disclaimer that the issuer does not know whether any part of all of the goods in fact "conform to the description." Disclaimers such as "contents, condition and quality unknown," "said to contain," etc., are common in warehouse receipts. When a disclaimer recites true facts, the warehouseman is generally not liable for misdescription. A conspicuously disclaiming warehouseman whose disclaimer is truthful has no general duty to verify the accuracy of a storer's description. But special circumstances may impose such a duty. Cases such as Orange Rice Milling Co. v. Hope Rice Mill [115] are illustrative. There rice had been stored with a warehouseman. Before the receipts were issued, the warehouseman fumigated the rice to kill weevil. This process apparently caused a weight loss, yet the warehouseman did not thereafter re-weigh the rice, but instead issued receipts based on the rice's original railroad freight weights. The depositor sold the receipts to the plaintiffs who sued the warehouseman for the deficiency in quantity. The court held

111.  See §§ 7–203; 7–203, Comment.

112.  General Fin. Co. v. Riverside Warehouse, Inc., 85 So.2d 68 (La.App. 1956).

113.  Orange Rice Milling Co. v. Hope Rice Mill, 189 So.2d 64 (La.App.1966).

114.  But see Pacific Micronesian Line, Inc. v. New Zealand Ins. Co., 397 F.2d 236 (9th Cir. 1968).

115.  Orange Rice Milling Co. v. Hope Rice Mill, 189 So.2d 64 (La.App.1966).

for the plaintiffs on the ground that under these special circumstances the warehouseman had a duty to verify the weights supplied him. The opinion does not state whether the warehouseman sought to disclaim any liability for misdescription as to quantity, but the plaintiff-purchasers were put on guard by language in the depositor-seller's offer of sale that the seller did not "warrant or represent that the grade, variety, weight, and milling yield of the rough rice are as shown on . . . warehouse receipts." [116] Yet the court imposed liability on the warehouseman. We believe the court would very likely have decided the case the same way even if the warehouseman had inserted the standard disclaimer. True, the warehouseman did not know of any discrepancy, but it had every reason to know. Where the warehouseman on his own undertakes to describe the bailed goods in the receipts, 7–203 simply cannot validate a disclaimer, for the issuer takes it on himself to know "whether any part or all of the goods in fact were received or conform to the description." [117]

Warehouse receipts are pieces of paper. They are not equivalent to the goods they cover. Our purchaser may buy perfect receipts perfectly in order, but as we have seen, the goods may be nonexistent or of less quantity. The cautious purchaser will always check first with the bailee. A cognate risk is that the goods will not, upon delivery, prove to be of the quality contracted for. One way to try to protect against this risk is for the purchaser to arrange for an independent third party to inspect the goods in the hands of the warehouseman and issue an inspection certificate to accompany the warehouse receipt into the purchaser's hands so that he does not give value without receiving a satisfactory certificate.[118] Even safeguards of this nature are not fail-safe. The inspector may be negligent, or willing to take a bribe, or the like. When delivered goods prove not to be of contract quality, our purchaser may be entitled to recover against his transferor for breach of warranty under 7–507 and under the warranty provisions of Article Two of the Code.[119] But the warehouseman is generally not responsible for the storer's contract quality. That is, if the storer contracts to sell bailed goods, asserting that they are of a given quality, and the goods in the bailee's hands are not of that quality, the bailee generally incurs no liability to the purchaser when the bailee delivers the nonconforming goods. The bailee may incur liability for having originally issued receipts that misdescribe the goods and enable the transferor to offer documents for sale that represent the bailed goods to be other than they actually were at the time of bailment.[120] Even then, the purchaser may encounter obsta-

---

116.  Id. at 67.

117.  § 7–203.

118.  The buyer's use of such a protective measure is extensively discussed in Banco Espanol de Credito v. State Street Bank & Trust Co., 385 F.2d 230, 4 UCC Rep.Serv. 862 (1st Cir. 1967).

119.  §§ 2–312 to 2–316.

120.  Pekin Warehouse Co. v. Parnell Co., 242 F.2d 166 (8th Cir. 1957); Orange Rice Milling Co. v. Hope Rice Mill, 189 So.2d 64 (La.App.1966).

cles.  For instance, the bailee may have inserted valid disclaimers.[121] Or the bailee may urge that its description was only identificatory in nature and did not go to the quality or condition of the goods.[122]

However to the extent that any deficiency in the goods under the contract between transferor and transferee is traceable to causes for which the bailee is legally liable under 7-204 of the Code (on due care)[123] the bailee will again be liable.  In Section 20-3, we explained that the bailee may fail to deliver for a variety of reasons besides loss or damage to the goods, and the bailee will not always be liable, that is, he might have a lawful excuse or defense against an action for nondelivery.[124]  To put this another way, the good faith purchaser of a negotiable document taking by due negotiation takes subject to certain excuses and defenses that a bailee may lawfully set up.  Of course, just because the bailee has a good excuse or defense, it does not follow that the purchaser is without any possible relief.  He may be able to recover against a prior transferor.[125]

Some purchasers of negotiable documents do not take by "due negotiation" or the like under 7-501 of the Code.  Under section 7-501 a given purchaser could fail to take by "due negotiation" in one or more of five different ways: (*1*) He could fail to acquire a document duly indorsed to him by his transferor; (*2*) though the document was so indorsed, he could fail to become a holder for the reason that a necessary prior indorsement was missing or forged; (*3*) he could fail to give value; (*4*) he could fail to take in good faith and without notice; or (*5*) he could fail to purchase "in the regular course of business."  What is the plight of a purchaser of a negotiable document who does not take by due negotiation?  Unless he is able to remedy the deficiency, as where he is able to compel his transferor to supply a missing indorsement,[126] such a purchaser only acquires, under 7-504 "[t]he title and rights which his transferor had or had actual authority to convey."  This is consistent with general pre-Code law as applied in the famous case of John S. Hale & Co. v. Beley Cotton Co.[127]  The plaintiff sold cotton covered by negotiable receipts to Beley and took a rubber check in return.  Meanwhile Beley transferred some of the receipts to a bank for value without duly negotiating them.  Plaintiff prevailed as against the bank on the ground that the bank got no better title than Beley, and Beley "acquired no title by reason of the fact that its checks given for the cotton were dishonored."[128]

---

121.  For example, "Said to contain" etc., which makes it clear that the bailee should not be relied upon.

122.  See Mannell v. Luckenbach, 26 F. 2d 908 (W.D.Wash.1928).

123.  See Section 20-3 supra.

124.  See text accompanying notes 59-65 supra.

125.  § 7-507.

126.  § 7-506.

127.  154 Tenn. 689, 290 S.W. 994 (1926).

128.  Id. at 699, 290 S.W. at 997.

It should be noted that even though our transferee does not acquire title to the goods or paramount title to the goods by virtue of his failure to take by due negotiation, and even though he does not acquire the direct obligation of the bailee to deliver, he may still have become a "holder" of the document to whom a *bailee* under 7–404 may deliver without incurring legal liability provided this delivery is in "good faith including observance of reasonable commercial standards." [129]

## PURCHASE OF NONNEGOTIABLE WAREHOUSE RECEIPTS

Because a transferor can by due negotiation of receipts convey greater rights to the goods than he himself has, his transferee can cut off such claims to the goods as these: (*1*) a claim by the original owner of the goods who entrusted them to a bailor with power to ship, store, or sell; [130] (*2*) a claim by the original owner from whom the documents (in form negotiable by delivery) had been stolen, or who had been defrauded out of the documents, or the like; [131] (*3*) a claim by an original owner of the goods who entrusted a document covering them to an agent who then, without authority, negotiated them to the transferee; [132] (*4*) a claim by certain kinds of creditors of the original owner; [133] (*5*) a claim by a *bona fide* purchaser of the goods from the bailee [134] or even from the original owner who purported to sell the goods themselves while in the bailee's hands. [135] This list can be extended.

It follows that one basic safeguard against the assertion of paramount claims of right is for a transferee to insist on receiving a negotiable document of title by "due negotiation." Given the value of this safeguard, it is appropriate to inquire why nonnegotiable receipts are so widely used. One answer is that sellers have special reasons for putting nonnegotiable receipts into use. For example, an owner of goods in a warehouse may want to sell them off in small lots. He may not be able to forecast in advance the size of each lot he will succeed in selling. If the warehouseman issues negotiable receipts for lots of a given size, seller will be unable to make sales of a different size to different buyers by use of the receipts to transfer the goods in the designated amounts, for under the terms of a negotiable receipt the warehouseman is obligated to deliver exclusively to the holder thereof and only in the amount designated thereon. [136] Thus, it would be necessary for the seller to return the original receipts and have new ones issued so the sale could go through. Why not have a nonnegotiable receipt issued in the first place under the terms of which the seller may issue and transfer "delivery orders" for specified amounts to particular buyers? This device is more flexible and convenient and

129.  § 7–404.

130.  §§ 7–502; 7–503.

131.  §§ 7–502; 7–503.

132.  §§ 7–502; 7–503.

133.  § 7–602.

134.  § 7–502.

135.  Id.

136.  §§ 7–403(1), (2).

is commonly used. Further, although buyers who acquire delivery orders or nonnegotiable receipts do not acquire the rights of a transferee of a negotiable document, there is usually no reason to be leery of the seller's title. All that is needed is some convenient and reliable means of instructing the bailee to whom he should deliver.

Section 7-104 defines a nonnegotiable document to title by exclusion:

> (1) A warehouse receipt, bill of lading or other document of title is negotiable
>
>     (a) if by its terms the goods are to be delivered to bearer or to the order of a named person; or
>
>     (b) where recognized in overseas trade, if it runs to a named person or assigns.
>
> (2) Any other document is non-negotiable. A bill of lading in which it is stated that the goods are consigned to a named person is not made negotiable by a provision that the goods are to be delivered only against a written order signed by the same or another named person.

The comment to this section states that a document of title is negotiable "only if it satisfies this section." [137] Thus any document of title that does not satisfy this section is nonnegotiable.

What are the rights of a party who acquires a nonnegotiable document of title covering goods he purports to buy? Under the Code the purchaser acquires, as against the transferor, whatever right the transferor had to demand the goods from the bailee.[138] But this does not mean that he thereby acquires even a valid claim for damages against the bailee if the bailee refuses to deliver.[139] Indeed, in some circumstances the transferor may even change his mind after the transfer and give delivery instructions to the bailee inconsistent with the transferee's rights, and if the bailee obeys, the transferee will be left with no rights against the bailee under applicable law.[140]

More important, the transferee of a nonnegotiable document does not, *qua* transferee of the document, acquire title to the goods although he may (and usually will) in the particular instance acquire such title. We have seen that when a good faith purchaser takes a negotiable document of title by due negotiation, the general principle of law is that he thereby acquires title to the goods, for the theory is that title to the goods is "locked up" in title to the document, and the way to move title to the goods is to move the title to the document.[141] (We have also seen that there are exceptions to this principle.) [142] But in the case of a purchaser who acquires a non-

137.  § 7-104, Comment 1.

138.  § 7-504.

139.  Id.

140.  Id.

141.  § 7-502.

142.  See text accompanying notes 88-102 supra.

negotiable document of title, the foregoing general principle of law is not applicable. That is, insofar as such a purchaser does acquire title to the goods, this is not by virtue of the operation of the foregoing general principle. For Article Seven provides simply that the transferee of a nonnegotiable document acquires only the actual title and rights to the goods that his transferor had or had actual authority to convey.[143] Therefore, when the transferee of a nonnegotiable document does acquire title to the goods, this is by virtue of the operation of the Article Seven rule that a transferee at least gets the title of his transferor or the title his transferor had authority to convey, and usually this transferor will be one who had full title.

Generally the transferor of a *negotiable* document has legal power to transfer a far better title to the goods than he himself has. We have already seen numerous respects in which a transferor of a negotiable document might have less than full title to the document or full title to the goods.[144] But his transferee can disregard most such title deficiencies, provided he takes by due negotiation. This is not so for the transferee of a nonnegotiable document. He generally takes subject to any deficiencies in his transferor's title. Under 7–504 he generally acquires no better title to the goods than his transferor had. For example, if his transferor was merely an agent who had transferred the documents in breach of authority, the principal could retrieve the goods from the transferee. Or if the transferor defrauded the owner and thereby acquired the goods, warehoused them, and transferred the nonnegotiable receipts to the transferee, the owner could retrieve the goods from the transferee. In both of these examples if the document were negotiable and the transferee took by due negotiation, the transferee would prevail against the agent's principal [145] and against the defrauded owner.[146]

The foregoing legal state of affairs leads to the oft-noted "anomaly" [147] that the transferee of a nonnegotiable document of title covering goods will sometimes acquire less of a title than he would have if he had dealt directly in the goods themselves in the first place. For example, under section 2–403(1) (d), a good faith purchaser who buys goods from a transferor who defrauded the true owner out of them acquires full title thereto. However, a good faith purchaser of nonnegotiable documents covering these very same goods does not acquire full title, for he acquires only the title of his transferor, and as against the true owner, the transferor did not acquire full title.

So far we have considered the legal position of a purchaser of goods who acquires them by merely acquiring nonnegotiable documents of title covering them. Actually, by taking the additional step

143. § 7–504.

144. See text accompanying notes 88–102 supra.

145. § 7–502(2).

146. Id.

147. Gilmore, The Commercial Doctrine of Good Faith Purchase, 63 Yale L.J. 1057, 1078 (1954).

of notifying the bailee of his interest, the transferee can improve his position somewhat under the Code.  Section 7–504(2) provides:

> In the case of a non-negotiable document, until but not after the bailee receives notification of the transfer, the rights of the transferee may be defeated
>
> (a) by those creditors of the transferor who could treat the sale as void under Section 2–402; or
>
> (b) by a buyer from the transferor in ordinary course of business if the bailee has delivered the goods to the buyer or received notification of his rights; or
>
> (c) as against the bailee by good faith dealings of the bailee with the transferor.

By notifying the bailee, the transferee of a nonnegotiable document of title will cut off the rights of those prior parties described in 7–504(2).  When this occurs, the transferee will acquire a somewhat better title to the goods than his transferor had.  Of course, the prior parties whose rights are thus cut off are by no means exhaustive of all the possible categories of prior parties who might have rights superior to the transferor.  Section 7–504(2) can hardly be characterized as manna from heaven.

The transferee of a nonnegotiable document of title incurs the risk that his transferor did not have full title to the goods.  But even where the transferor doubtless had full title, the transferee still incurs the risk that the transferor may, after transfer, defeat the transferee's interest.  Thus the transferor may sell warehoused goods a second time to another buyer.[148]  (The transferee can protect against this by notifying the bailee of his newly acquired interest immediately prior to acquiring the document.) [149]

### § 20–5   Rights of Pledgee of Warehouse Receipts

One authority has remarked that "perhaps the primary reason for codifying the law of title documents in the uniform acts and certainly the main reason for the United States Warehouse Act was to enhance the value of such documents for use as collateral security for loans." [150]  Today warehouse receipts are widely used as security. A lender relies in the first instance on his borrower's reputation and promise to repay.  Beyond this a lender relies on the goods covered by the receipts, on the warehouseman's reputation and solvency, and on the bonding required of warehousemen under any applicable law. In one common transaction pattern involving the use of warehouse receipts as security, the borrower simply pledges receipts issued by a terminal ("public") warehouse to a bank, a finance company, or a government lending institution.  Ordinarily, the receipts are nego-

148.  § 7–540(2) (b).

149.  § 7–504(2).

150.  See generally R. Braucher, Documents of Title 77–78 (1958).

tiable, and the lender takes them by due negotiation. In another common transaction pattern the parties set up a *field* warehouse on the borrower's premises. The warehouse is run by an independent warehouse company that issues the receipts to be transferred. Ordinarily the receipts are nonnegotiable.

Article Nine of the Code [151] governs the creation and perfection of security interests in documents of title and in goods (except insofar as the security interest arises in favor of a seller of goods under 2–505 of Article Two on sales and he transfers it to his own financier). In the case of negotiable documents the Article Nine theory is that the security interest is "in the document." [152] A security interest in the document automatically carries with it a security interest in the goods covered by the document. An Article Nine security interest in a negotiable document of title is created just as a security interest in any form of collateral is created, namely by taking the steps set forth in 9–203 and 9–204, considered in Chapter 23. However, there are special Article Nine sections on the *perfection* of security interests where documents of title are used. To perfect a security interest in a negotiable document of title, the lender may take possession of it (an authorized mode of perfection under 9–305) or the lender may file with respect to it (an authorized mode of perfection under 9–304 (1)). In limited circumstances temporary perfection is possible under 9–304(4) and (5) without either possession or filing.[153] Generally the secured party should perfect his security in negotiable documents by possession, for under 9–309 certain purchasers of these documents defeat secured parties who perfect only by filing.[154] The mechanics of transfer to the pledgee should be arranged so that he acquires the

---

151. See Ch. 22 of this book infra.

152. § 9–304, Comment 2.

153. §§ 9–304(4), (5) provide:

(4) A security interest in instruments or negotiable documents is perfected without filing or the taking of possession for a period of 21 days from the time it attaches to the extent that it arises for new value given under a written security agreement.

(5) A security interest remains perfected for a period of 21 days without filing where a secured party having a perfected security interest in an instrument, a negotiable document or goods in possession of a bailee other than one who has issued a negotiable document therefor

(a) makes available to the debtor the goods or documents representing the goods for the purpose of ultimate sale or exchange or for the purpose of loading, unloading, storing, shipping, transshipping, manufacturing, processing or otherwise dealing with them in a manner preliminary to their sale or exchange; or

(b) delivers the instrument to the debtor for the purpose of ultimate sale or exchange or of presentation, collection, renewal or registration of transfer.

154. § 9–309 provides in full:

Nothing in this Article limits the rights of a holder in due course of a negotiable instrument (Section 3—302) or a holder to whom a negotiable document of title has been duly negotiated (Section 7—501) or a bona fide purchaser of a security (Section 8—301) and such holders or purchasers take priority over an earlier security interest even though perfected. Filing under this Article does not constitute notice of the security interest to such holders or purchasers.

document by due negotiation and thereby acquires title to the document and title to the goods.[155]

With respect to nonnegotiable documents, the general theory of Article Nine is that the security interest is not in the document, but in the goods. The security interest is created by satisfying the requirements of sections 9–203 and 9–204 just as with any security interest, but, under 9–304(3), it is possible to perfect the interest in three different ways:

> A security interest in goods in the possession of a bailee other than one who has issued a negotiable document therefor is perfected by issuance of a document in the name of the secured party or by the bailee's receipt of notification of the secured party's interest or by filing as to the goods.

## RIGHTS OF PLEDGEE OF NEGOTIABLE RECEIPTS

It might be supposed that a pledgee who (1) takes a negotiable warehouse receipt by due negotiation and (2) takes a valid, enforceable, and perfected Article Nine security interest in the document thereby acquires rights superior to those of any and all possible third parties. After all such a lender is doubly armed, is he not? He gets "title to the document and title to the goods" under 7–502, and he defeats a wide variety of third parties under Article Nine. But a pledgee even of negotiable documents of title is still generally subject to the same risks that an outright purchaser of the documents is subject to. For example, after the transfer it may be discovered that the goods themselves had been stolen and that the true owner can now lawfully assert his title as against the secured lender,[156] or that the document was wholly spurious,[157] or had been altered,[158] or that a necessary indorsement had been forged,[159] or that the bailee never did receive the goods,[160] or that some or all of the goods have now disappeared,[161] or that the goods have been destroyed or damaged,[162] or that the transferor earlier made another transfer to a third party,[163]

155. § 7–502.

156. § 7–503, Comment 1.

157. See, e. g., First Trust & Savings Bank v. Fidelity-Philadelphia Trust Co., 214 F.2d 320 (3d Cir. 1954); Maryland Casualty Co. v. Washington Loan & Banking Co., 167 Ga. 354, 145 S.E. 761 (1928).

158. See, e. g., Saugerties Bank v. Delaware & Hudson Co., 236 N.Y. 425, 141 N.E. 904 (1923).

159. See, e. g., Weaver Cotton Co. v. Batesville Compress Co., 168 Ark. 387, 270 S.W. 509 (1925), annotated in 38 A.L.R. 1200 (1925). See also Annot., 18 A.L.R. 588 (1922).

160. E. g., Central States Corp. v. Trinity Universal Ins. Co., 237 F.2d 875 (10th Cir. 1956).

161. E. g., United States v. New York Terminal Warehouse Co., 233 F.2d 238 (5th Cir. 1956); Kendall Produce Co. v. Terminal Warehouse & Transfer Co., 295 Pa. 450, 145 A. 511 (1929); Edward L. Eyre & Co. v. Hirsch, 36 Wash.2d 439, 218 P.2d 888 (1950).

162. E. g., Scott v. Lawrence Warehouse Co., 227 Ore. 78, 360 P.2d 610 (1961) (nonnegotiable receipts).

163. See e. g., State Street Trust Co. v. Lawrence Mfg. Co., 284 Mass. 355, 187 N.E. 755 (1933).

or that the transferor had sold a second time to another,[164] or that the bailee had misdelivered.[165]  We have already discussed these and other risks that transferees of negotiable documents generally incur.[166]  It will be recalled that when such risks materialize, the transferee may still have recourse against some party for relief.  For example, absent an effective disclaimer, the pledgee can generally recover against the warehouseman for prejudicial nonreceipt or misdescription under 7–203.

Furthermore, a perfected security interest under Article Nine even in negotiable documents duly negotiated to the lender is not a *perfect* interest.  In Chapter 25, we systematically explore the outer limits of the Article Nine secured party's rights.[167]  Only such of these limits as bear distinctively on security in negotiable documents will be considered here.  In all situations to be considered, we will assume that the debtor has defaulted and that when the pledgee of negotiable receipts seeks to realize on his security a third party claims a prior right in the goods.  First, the interest of a pledgee with perfected security in negotiable documents is subject to certain *prior* ownership claims *in the goods* and to claims of *prior* secured parties.[168]  Section 7–503(1) provides:

> A document of title confers no right in goods against a person who before issuance of the document had a legal interest or a perfected security interest in them and who neither
>
> (a) delivered or entrusted them or any document of title covering them to the bailor or his nominee with actual or apparent authority to ship, store or sell or with power to obtain delivery under this Article (Section 7—403) or with power of disposition under this Act (Sections 2—403 and 9—307) or other statute or rule of law; nor
>
> (b) acquiesced in the procurement by the bailor or his nominee of any document of title.

Our pledgee can protect against possible prior perfected security interests *in the goods* simply by checking to see who possesses the goods described in the document and by checking the relevant Article Nine filing records for a financing statement covering the goods.  It is much more difficult for the lender to be certain that there are no prior ownership claims valid under 7–502.[169]  Of course, 7–503 does not

---

164.  § 7–502(2).

165.  § 7–502(1).

166.  See text accompanying notes 88–102 supra.

167.  See also Ch. 24 infra.

168.  For example, an owner of the goods generally does not lose title

through theft.  And generally, the first secured party to file with respect to goods wins under 9–312 of Article Nine.

169.  See Lineburger Bros. v. Hodge, 212 Miss. 204, 54 So.2d 268 (1951); Kendall Produce Co. v. Terminal Warehouse & Transfer Co., 295 Pa. 450, 145 A. 511 (1929).

protect all prior parties with ownership or security claims in the goods against a later pledgee of negotiable documents who takes by due negotiation.  Our pledgee prevails under 7–503 and 7–502 against prior owners and secured parties who deliver, entrust, or acquiesce and who fall within 7–503(1) (a) or (b).[170]

Second, the interest of a pledgee of negotiable documents is also subject to defeat by certain *subsequent* parties.  Suppose the pledgee authorizes the warehouseman to release to the debtor goods covered by the document in which the pledgee has perfected security.  While the goods are in the hands of the debtor, one of his creditors levies on them.  Here the lender would prevail only if, at the time of levy, his perfection had not lapsed under section 9–304(5):

> A security interest remains perfected for a period of 21 days without filing where a secured party having a perfected security interest in an instrument, a negotiable document or goods in possession of a bailee other than one who has issued a negotiable document therefor
>
> (a) makes available to the debtor the goods or documents representing the goods for the purpose of ultimate sale or exchange or for the purpose of loading, unloading, storing, shipping, transshipping, manufacturing, processing or otherwise dealing with them in a manner preliminary to their sale or exchange; or
>
> (b) delivers the instrument to the debtor for the purpose of ultimate sale or exchange or of presentation, collection, renewal or registration of transfer.

Under this section, our pledgee's interest continues to be perfected for twenty-one days and takes priority under section 9–201 against any levy on the goods during that period.  However, under 9–307(1), if the debtor wrongfully sells the temporarily unwarehoused goods to a buyer in the ordinary course of business, this buyer prevails over our pledgee even if the sale occurs within the twenty-one day period.  Moreover, any buyer from the debtor of such temporarily unbailed goods prevails over the pledgee under section 9–306 whenever the pledgee authorizes the warehouseman to return the goods to the debtor for purposes of resale.[171]  As we have already seen, even a pledgee with a perfected Article Nine security interest in negotiable receipts will lose to a subsequent transferee of negotiable documents covering the same goods if our pledgee entrusted or acquiesced under 7–503(1)

170. See Note, Financing Inventory Through Field Warehousing, 69 Yale L.J. 663, 702–705 (1960).

171. § 9–306(2) provides:

Except where this Article otherwise provides, a security interest continues in collateral notwithstanding sale, exchange or other disposition thereof by the debtor unless his action was authorized by the secured party in the security agreement or otherwise, and also continues in any identifiable proceeds including collections received by the debtor.

(a) or (b) and thereby empowered a middleman to procure the goods, rewarehouse them, and transfer the receipts to a subsequent transferee who takes by due negotiation.

Certain other purchasers may also defeat a pledgee who wants to realize on his security. If he perfects merely by filing with respect to the negotiable document, leaving the document in the hands of the debtor, the debtor can then pass superior title to the document to a good faith purchaser who takes by due negotiation under section 9–309.[172] So, too, a buyer in ordinary course who buys the goods themselves from the bailee under section 7–205.[173] The Code does not displace state statutes giving statutory lienors priority over Article Nine secured creditors, including pledgees of negotiable receipts.[174] For example, under such a statute a landlord may defeat a pledgee who has taken security in documents covering crops grown on the land of the landlord.[175]

In limited circumstances a pledgee may lose part of his security in fungible goods covered by negotiable receipts to other parties who also hold interests in fungible goods on deposit that have been commingled with the lender's goods. This risk materializes most commonly in the terminal or public warehousing context where an agricultural fungible such as grain has been deposited. Section 7–207(2) provides:

> Fungible goods so commingled are owned in common by the persons entitled thereto and the warehouseman is severally liable to each owner for that owner's share. Where because of overissue a mass of fungible goods is insufficient to meet all the receipts which the warehouseman has issued against it, the persons entitled include all holders to whom overissued receipts have been duly negotiated.

Generally tenants in common bear pro rata any loss for which the warehouseman is not liable (or is unable to make good when liable). This is a principle of property law, and section 7–207 appears to in-

---

172. § 9–309 provides:

Nothing in this Article limits the rights of a holder in due course of a negotiable instrument (Section 3–302) or a holder to whom a negotiable document of title has been duly negotiated (Section 7–501) or a bona fide purchaser of a security (Section 8–301) and such holders or purchasers take priority over an earlier security interest even though perfected. Filing under this Article does not constitute notice of the security interest to such holders or purchasers.

173. § 7–205 provides:

A buyer in the ordinary course of business of fungible goods sold and de-

livered by a warehouseman who is also in the business of buying and selling such goods takes free of any claim under a warehouse receipt even though it has been duly negotiated.

174. Section 9–104(b) states that "[t]his Article does not apply to a landlord's lien." Section 9–104(c) states that "[t]his Article does not apply to a lien given by statute or other rule of law for services or materials except as provided in Section 9–310 on priority of such liens."

175. Cf. Cleveland v. McNabb, 312 F. Supp. 155, 7 UCC Rep.Serv. 1226 (W.D. Tenn.1970).

corporate it by reference.   There is a cluster of pre-Code cases on the problem.[176]

Besides the foregoing types of claimants who may impair or defeat the rights of negotiable documentary pledgees, there is also the debtor's trustee in bankruptcy.   The various circumstances in which the debtor's trustee can upset an Article Nine security interest are considered in Chapter 24.[177]

### Rights of Transferee of Nonnegotiable Receipts

Where the lender lends against nonnegotiable receipts, his security is more precarious even when it is duly perfected under Article Nine by a filing [178] with respect to the goods themselves.   This transferee takes the receipts subject to all the possible title infirmities and defenses to which a pledgee of negotiable documents is subject, and he also incurs the risk of infirmities in his own transferor's title.   In a pre-Code case, First Nat'l Bank v. Petzoldt,[179] the true owner of alfalfa seed entrusted it to an elevator company for processing and sale. Instead, the company warehoused the seed and had nonnegotiable receipts issued to the bank.   When the true owner learned of this, he claimed title to the seed paramount to the bank and prevailed.   The result would be the same under the Code, for the elevator company did not have title and therefore could not pass title to bank under 7–504.   Moreover, 7–503 does not apply to protect transferees of nonnegotiable documents.[180]

A transferee of nonnegotiable receipts is, like a pledgee of negotiable ones, an Article Nine secured creditor and as such does not take priority over all other third parties.   In particular, he may lose out to a prior Article Nine secured creditor.   The question arose in a celebrated arbitration case, "The Philadelphia Nat'l. Bank (Assignee) vs. Irving R. Boody & Co." [181]   There, the first lender creat-

176.   See, e. g., McDonnell v. Bank of China, 33 F.2d 816 (9th Cir. 1929), cert. denied 280 U.S. 612 (1930); Torgerson v. Quinn-Sheperdson Co., 161 Minn. 380, 201 N.W. 615 (1925); Procter & Gamble Distrib. Co. v. Lawrence Am. Field Warehousing Corp., 16 N.Y. 2d 344, 213 N.E.2d 873, 3 UCC Rep. Serv. 157 (1965); State ex rel. Hermann v. Farmers' Elevator Co., 59 N.D. 679, 231 N.W. 725 (1930); Allen V. Smith, Inc. v. Rosalia Producers, Inc., 36 Wash.2d 680, 219 P.2d 986 (1950).   See generally R. Braucher, Documents of Title 98–101 (1958); Bascom, Articles 7 and 9 of the Uniform Commercial Code—Security Interests in the Warehouseman's Own Receipts Covering Fungibles, 1969 Wash.U.L.Q. 105, 113–30.

177.   See especially Sections 24–2 through 24–9 infra.

178.   § 9–304(3).

179.   262 F.2d 540 (10th Cir. 1958).

180.   Accord, Funk, Trust Receipt vs. Warehouse Receipt—Which Prevails When They Cover the Same Goods?, 19 Bus.Law. 627 (1964); Note, Financing Inventory Through Field Warehousing, 69 Yale L.J. 663 (1960).

181.   1 UCC Rep.Serv. 560 (Arb.Dec. 1963), reprinted in Funk, Trust Receipt vs. Warehouse Receipt—Which Prevails When They Cover the Same Goods?, 19 Bus.Law. 627 (1964).   See, too, Douglas-Guardian Warehouse Corp. v. Esslair Endsley Co., —— F. Supp. ——, 10 UCC Rep.Serv. 176 (W. D.Mich.1971).

ed a perfected Article Nine security interest in the debtor's wool. Thereafter the first lender entrusted the goods to the debtor. Without the authority of the first lender, the debtor later warehoused the goods and had the warehouseman issue nonnegotiable receipts in favor of one Wagman as security for a loan. Neither the warehouseman nor Wagman knew of the prior filed security interest. When the debtor ran into financial trouble, both the first lender and Wagman claimed the wool. In a widely publicized opinion, the arbitrator applied 9–312(5) (b) to hold for the first lender. He reasoned that both parties had perfected security interests in the goods and that since the first lender was the first to perfect, he prevailed. Of course, under 9–309, the transferee, Wagman, would have won had the receipts been negotiable, but here they were nonnegotiable. Counsel for Wagman argued that the first lender loses under 7–503(1) quoted above,[182] and 7–504(1) which reads:

> A transferee of a document, whether negotiable or nonnegotiable, to whom the document has been delivered but not duly negotiated, acquires the title and rights which his transferor had or had actual authority to convey.

The transferee's argument was simply that since the first lender had *entrusted* the goods to the debtor, the debtor's transferee prevailed by the negative implication of 7–503(1). The arbitrator answered this argument as follows: First, 7–503(1) does not purport to protect transferees of nonnegotiable documents, only transferees of negotiable ones. Second, when 7–503(1) does apply, it does not specify what rights the transferee of the entrustee gets. "What they are must be found elsewhere in the Code." [183] In favor of the arbitrator's decision, it may be said that transferees of nonnegotiable receipts should check the files for financing statements covering the goods. Moreover, we think that if the draftsmen of Article Nine had wanted to favor the transferee here, they knew how to do so and did not. That is, they drafted 9–309 to protect the pledgee (and other purchasers) of negotiable receipts. Further, while 7–503(1) is not literally confined to protecting a transferee of the entrustee who takes negotiable documents, the official comments so confine it.[184] And, even if 7–503(1) protects an entrustee's transferee who takes nonnegotiable documents, still his rights are not set forth in 7–503 but in 7–504, and under 7–504, such a transferee only takes such title as his transferor had or had power to convey. Thus, the transferee here would take subject to the first lender's security interest in the goods.

Although the practice is at least theoretically precarious, lenders commonly lend against nonnegotiable receipts issued not only by "terminal" warehouses, but by "field" warehouses as well. We will first briefly explore the nature of field warehousing [185] and show why

---

182. See text supra following note 168.

183. Id. at 567.

184. § 7–503, Comment 1.

185. On field warehousing generally, see especially 1 G. Gilmore, Security

nonnegotiable receipts are used. Imagine huge piles of logs decked up next to a sawmill; thousands of cans of canned goods stockpiled during the canning season in rooms adjacent to the cannery; raw materials stockpiled by a manufacturer in case of strike, war, or other emergency; cheese, tobacco, hides, and other such goods which must "cure," on hand in substantial quantities during the curing period; tons of mechanical parts on the premises awaiting assembly into machines; silos full of farm products; large vats full of oils (or better yet, beer and wines); or large quantities of appliances stored by distributors. Of course, the debtor might bail such goods directly to the lender who, through his own employees positioned on the debtor's premises, could perfect by taking possession. However, most banks, finance companies, and other lenders do not have, and do not want to acquire, the equipment and personnel required to establish "field pledges."

For many goods, "terminal" warehousing is frequently not a viable option. Terminal warehouses exist at towns or railway spurs and store goods for the general public at scheduled fees. A warehouse of this kind may be located too far away; the goods may be too difficult to move any distance; or it may be essential to have the goods on the debtor's premises for processing. Rather than move such goods to a terminal warehouse, the reasonable course is to move a warehouse to the goods, that is, to create a "field" warehouse. Businesses exist to set up these entities and issue receipts for the warehoused goods which in turn may be used as collateral. The relevant papers typically include a lease agreement leasing some of the debtor's premises to the warehouseman (usually for nominal rent), an employment agreement between the warehouseman and a person (usually an employee of the debtor) who is to serve as local warehouseman, and an agreement between debtor and warehouseman covering the terms of storage and release.[186]

Field warehouses, unlike their terminal cousins, exist primarily for financing purposes, not for storage. Accordingly many of them do not look like true warehouses at all. Around a deck of logs there may be only a wire fence with the warehouseman's signs posted on it, or a blocked-off area inside the borrower's plant, access to which is controlled by the warehouseman. Indeed a field warehouse may be no more than a lock on an already existing vat of beer, or a silo door the key to which is kept by the warehouseman (who also keeps records of input and outgo).

According to the theory of Article Nine the security interest of a transferee of nonnegotiable field warehouse receipts is in the goods, not in the nonnegotiable receipts covering them. (For this and other

Interests in Personal Property ch. 6 (1965); Skilton, Field Warehousing As a Financing Service, 1961 Wisc.L. Rev. 221, 403; Note, Financing Inventory Through Field Warehousing, 69 Yale L.J. 663 (1960).

186. 1 G. Gilmore, Security Interests in Personal Property, § 6.2 at 147 (1965).

reasons, therefore, it is not strictly appropriate to speak of "pledging" such documents.) [187]   There must be a security agreement between the borrower and the lender giving the lender security in the goods. Furthermore, to perfect this security against third parties, it is not sufficient for the lender to take possession of the receipts as would be the case in a true pledge.   He must do one of the following three things: (1) have the receipts issued in his name; (2) notify the bailee of the secured party's interest; or (3) have a financing statement filed as to the goods.   A field warehouse can be "revolving" in character.   Thus the lender might lend a stated sum against a specified minimum quantity that the debtor must preserve in a warehouse stockpile to which and from which he continuously adds and takes under the warehouseman's supervision.   Procedures will be designed to preserve the lender's desired collateral-to-loan ratio.   According to one procedure, the lender is issued nonnegotiable receipts in his name and is given a supply of "delivery-orders" which he must sign and will sign to authorize the warehouseman's releases to the debtor as he substitutes other goods for those to be released or pays off a proportionate amount of the loan.

Before a field warehouse arrangement is set up, the typical prospective lender investigates the prospective debtor and the prospective collateral.[188]   This helps explain the lender's willingness to take the theoretically more risky nonnegotiable receipts from the warehouseman.   In deciding to lend in the first place the lender is in part deciding that paramount title risks are minimal or nonexistent under all the circumstances.   Also the field warehouse lender typically does not intend to dispose of the receipts and therefore need not be concerned about their marketability.   Also, if the occasion should arise to rediscount the receipts to the Federal Reserve Bank in the area,[189] the lender can readily procure negotiable receipts.   Considerations of flexibility and convenience also help explain why field warehouse lenders typically take nonnegotiable receipts.   Often the debtor will need to have warehoused goods released to him in lots the sizes of which he cannot forecast in advance.   If an outstanding receipt covering the goods is negotiable and if it does not match the desired lot size, this will prove inconvenient.   The warehouseman cannot rightfully deliver such goods without requiring surrender of the negotiable receipt,[190] yet this receipt will likely be for either a larger or smaller amount than the debtor wants released.   Pursuant to non-negotiable receipts, the lender can issue signed delivery orders authorizing the warehouseman to release goods ad hoc in desired quantities.

The field warehouse lender who acquires nonnegotiable receipts incurs all the risks that a lender against negotiable documents in-

---

187.  See generally Annot., 53 A.L.R.2d 1396 (1957).

188.  American Bankers Ass'n Credit Policy Committee, A Banker's Guide to Warehouse Receipt Financing (1966).

189.  Id.

190.  § 2–403(3).

curs [191] and in addition incurs the additional "title" risks that a party acquiring nonnegotiable documents incurs.[192]    Generally insofar as the debtor's title is defective, so too is the lender's title defective. However by taking the steps required under Article Nine to perfect a security interest *in the goods* covered by the nonnegotiable receipts, the lender achieves the significant protections afforded by Article Nine priority rules.    Among other things, he prevails against subsequent creditors of the debtor who levy on the warehoused goods. Thus, in the case of Lofton v. Mooney [193] a transferee of nonnegotiable receipts issued pursuant to a valid field warehousing arrangement prevailed over sellers who had sold the goods to the debtor and had levied on them to collect their claims.    (The Kentucky Supreme Court did not see that it should have cited relevant Article Nine provisions to sustain the result.)

Provided the lender perfects by filing, he will also have some protection against the possibility that the parties who supply goods to the debtor which the debtor in turn places in the warehouse will not retain superior security interests.    Section 9–312(3) requires that these suppliers notify our lender of their retained security interests for those security interests to be valid.    Thus, the field warehouse lender should not, at least unknowingly, accept collateral already subject to a supplier's prior security interest.    Nonsuppliers who have security interests in the goods already perfected when the debtor re-receives them prevail over the lender, but the lender can protect against these by checking the files.

What are the rights of a transferee of nonnegotiable receipts who files a financing statement covering the goods as against subsequent purchasers of the goods or of documents covering the goods?    Of course, if the transferee authorizes the warehouseman to release the goods to the debtor for resale, the debtor's buyer will prevail.[194] But even if the transferee does not release the goods and the warehouseman wrongfully delivers them to the debtor who then sells them to a "buyer in ordinary course," the buyer will prevail over the transferee under 9–307(1).    Assume that the debtor rewarehouses the goods and sells negotiable receipts to the buyer.    Here our transferee will prevail against the buyer under 7–503(1) unless 7–503(1) (a) or (b) applies.

Our transferee may also find himself in conflict with *subsequent* secured parties.    If he authorizes the warehouseman to release the goods to the debtor, and the debtor then creates a further security interest in the goods, our transferee will still prevail under the first to perfect rule of 9–312(5) (b).    This is also the case if the warehouseman wrongfully releases the goods to the debtor who then creates another security interest in them.    But what if the warehouse-

191.    See text accompanying notes 156–177 supra.

192.    See text accompanying notes 138–148 supra.

193.    452 S.W.2d 617, 7 UCC Rep.Serv. 824 (Ky.Ct.App.1970).

194.    § 9–306.

man wrongfully releases the goods and the debtor rewarehouses them and pledges negotiable receipts to another lender? Again, our transferee of the nonnegotiable receipts will prevail both under Article Nine's first to perfect rule and under 7–503(1) of Article Seven, unless he "acquiesced in the procurement by the bailor or his nominee of any document of title" under 7–503(1) (b).

In cases in which the warehouseman wrongfully releases the goods, he will, of course, be absolutely liable for misdelivery to the extent of the loss he causes.[195] A more difficult question arises when the lender asserts that the warehouseman is liable because the warehouseman failed to discover an outstanding interest in goods offered by the debtor for bailment. If the warehouseman should have known that the debtor was not the owner of the goods, or should have known of a prior security interest in or lien on the goods, then it is arguable that the warehouseman should be liable to the lender for losses sustained by him because of advances made against insufficient collateral. Article Seven does not explicitly impose any such liability, and it does not appear to be customary for field warehousemen to inquire whether the debtor owns goods offered as collateral or even whether the debtor owns these goods free and clear of security interests or liens. Nonetheless Professor Gilmore has argued that in a proper case the field warehouseman should be held liable to the lender for failure to discover or disclose an outstanding interest in goods received for bailment from the debtor.[196] Certainly he is right that "the relationship of the field warehouseman with his depositors is factually at a far remove from that of the common carrier or public warehouseman with those who make use of their services." [197] Accordingly more can be expected of the field warehouseman. While Article Seven of the Code does not in specific terms impose liability on the warehouseman here, the Article does not preclude liability either. Many matters are left to common law under 1–103. The case law to date is inconclusive.[198]

For a field warehousing operation to stand up under Article Nine rules on perfection, the secured lender supposedly must see to it that the warehouseman either has "actual, open and exclusive possession" [199] or that a financing statement covering the goods is duly filed.[200] In pre-Code days, third parties not infrequently attacked field warehouses on the ground that the warehouseman did not have

195. Of course, a warehouseman may have a defense under sections 7–403 or 7–404.

196. 1 G. Gilmore, Security Interests in Personal Property, § 6.6 at 172 (1965).

197. Id.

198. Id. We have reviewed the cases since Professor Gilmore's treatise was published, and they continue to be inconclusive.

199. Pittman v. Union Planter's Nat'l Bank & Trust Co., 118 F.2d 211, 214 (6th Cir. 1941), cert. denied 314 U.S. 632 (1941).

200. §§ 9–302 to 9–305.

required control.   Today these attacks are a rarity,[201] and this is so
for two quite different reasons.   Courts have watered down the requirement of "actual, open and exclusive possession," [202] and parties
today can easily file to perfect anyway.   When there is a filing, warehouseman control over the goods is not necessary for perfection,[203]
however desirable this control may be for purposes of policing or
other reasons.[204]

**201.**   One of the few quite recent cases
we have found is Whitney Nat'l Bank
v. Sandoz, 362 F.2d 605 (5th Cir. 1966)
(non-Code law).

**202.**   See, e. g., Bostian v. Park Nat'l
Bank, 226 F.2d 753 (8th Cir. 1955).

**203.**   §§ 9–302 to 9–304.

**204.**   See generally American Bankers
Ass'n Credit Policy Committee, A
Banker's Guide to Warehouse Receipt
Financing (1966).

# CHAPTER 21

## CARRIAGE OF GOODS COVERED BY BILLS OF LADING—RIGHTS AND LIABILITIES OF PARTIES, INCLUDING PURCHASERS AND LENDERS

*Analysis*

**Sec.**
21–1. Introduction.
21–2. Law Applicable to Carriage of Goods and to Bills of Lading.
21–3. Rights of Shipper Against Carrier.
21–4. Rights of Purchasers of Bills of Lading.
21–5. Rights of Pledgees of Bills of Lading.

## § 21–1  Introduction

Every year billions of dollars worth of goods, raw and manufactured, are exported out of and imported into the United States. Billions upon billions of dollars worth of goods are shipped every year from one place to another within the United States. Nature did not put all raw materials in one place. Processers and manufacturers are located in different places, and ultimate users with reciprocally satisfiable wants often reside at remote distances from each other. Hence the need for transport of goods and the growth of independent businesses such as trucking concerns, railways, ocean carriers, and air carriers. Public carriers [1] thrive thoughout the United States; they not only transport goods; but also issue "bills of lading" to shippers which cover the goods to be transported. Shippers can in turn pass title to these goods merely by transferring the bills of lading (documents of title). Equally important, shippers can also pledge these documents as security for loans.

To the shipper and to a purchaser or pledgee of the bill of lading, the ideal carrier is a person or organization that properly cares for the shipped goods, transports them as agreed, and delivers them up only as directed. Various federal [2] and state [3] regulatory laws help assure the reliability of public carriers and thus also protect shippers and their transferees. These regulatory laws are beyond the scope of this chapter.

In this chapter we will treat (*1*) the rights of a shipper against his carrier and other parties to whom the carrier may deliver the goods, (*2*) the rights of a purchaser of bills of lading as against his

1. On public carriers, see generally D. Powers, A Practical Guide to Bills of Lading (1966).

2. E. g., 7 U.S.C.A. § 241 et seq. (1970). See also 1–3 CCH Fed. Carriers Rep. (1972).

3. E. g., N.Y. Transp. Law § 98, 99 (McKinney Supp.1971).

seller and carriers handling the goods, and (*3*) the rights of a pledgee of bills of lading against the carrier and others who have dealt with the goods.

### § 21–2 Law Applicable to Carriage of Goods and to Bills of Lading

Section 1–201(6) of the Code defines "bill of lading" to mean:

"Bill of lading" means a document evidencing the receipt of goods for shipment issued by a person engaged in the business of transporting or forwarding goods, and includes an airbill. "Airbill" means a document serving for air transportation as a bill of lading does for marine or rail transportation, and includes an air consignment note or air waybill.

Various special types of bills of lading are currently in use. A so-called "through bill" is issued by the first of several connecting carriers, and under it an issuing carrier incurs liabilities for certain loss or damage caused by it or any connecting carrier. A so-called "way bill" includes instructions from one carrier to another. "Air bills" are simply bills of lading issued by air carriers. A "freight-forwarder bill" is issued by a freight forwarder who gathers less than car load lots and consolidates them into carloads. "Destination bills" are issued by carriers at destination to a party acting on behalf of the shipper. "Delivery orders" are issued by a shipper. They are addressed to the carrier and order him to deliver the goods to a named person. Whether a type of bill of lading is also a document of title depends on the relevant statutory definitions. For the Code's purposes, 1–201 (15) defines "document of title" to include:

"Document of title" includes bill of lading, dock warrant, dock receipt, warehouse receipt or order for the delivery of goods, and also any other document which in the regular course of business or financing is treated as adequately evidencing that the person in possession of it is entitled to receive, hold and dispose of the document and the goods it covers. To be a document of title a document must purport to be issued by or addressed to a bailee and purport to cover goods in the bailee's possession which are either identified or are fungible portions of an identified mass.

The rights and liabilities of parties to bills of lading (and related documents) are found principally in three places: Article Seven of the Uniform Commercial Code, the Federal Bills of Lading Act,[4] and the Carmack Amendment to the Interstate Commerce Act.[5] Article Seven of the Code displaced, in relevant part, the Uniform Bills

4. Federal Bills of Lading Act of 1916, ch. 415, §§ 1–44, 39 Stat. 538, 49 U.S.C. §§ 81–124 (1970).

5. Interstate Commerce Act of 1887, ch. 104, Part I, § 20, 24 Stat. 386, as added, June 29, 1906, ch. 3591, § 7, 34 Stat. 593, as amended, 49 U.S.C. § 20 (11) (1970).

of Lading Act which had been law in all states.⁶ Article Seven also applies to warehouse receipts. In Section 20–2 of Chapter Twenty we explored the structure of Article Seven, and we will not repeat that discussion here.

In 1916 Congress enacted the Federal Bills of Lading Act (FBLA) which is substantially identical to the old Uniform Bills of Lading Act. The FBLA includes 44 sections. In the text of this chapter we will refer to it as the "FBLA" and will cite it by reference to its United States Code section numbers (49 U.S.C. §§ 81–124).⁷ Courts have decided hundreds of cases under the FBLA;⁸ its presence and the presence of the Carmack Amendment on the federal statute books and the vast case law under both greatly diminish the significance of Article Seven's provisions on bills of lading. Whenever the FBLA is applicable, it rather than Article Seven controls. The FBLA is applicable to:⁹

> Bills of lading issued by any common carrier for the transportation of goods in any Territory of the United States, or the District of Columbia, or from a place in a State to a place in a foreign country, or from a place in one State to a place in another State, or from a place in one State to a place in the same State through another State or foreign country, shall be governed by this chapter.

Given the broad scope of the FBLA, what is left for Article Seven to govern? That Article applies mainly to (1) bills of lading issued for the transportation of goods from a place within one state to another place in the same state, provided the goods are not to pass through another state or foreign country *en route*, and (2) bills of lading issued for the transportation of goods from a foreign country into the United States. Even then the scope of Article Seven is cut down to the extent that other federal statutes besides the FBLA apply. Of other federal statutory law in this field the "Carmack Amendment" to the Interstate Commerce Act is of greatest importance.¹⁰ That amendment codifies the common law liability of interstate carriers for loss, destruction, or damage to goods,¹¹ imposes this liability on the first of two or more connecting carriers for loss, destruction, or damage caused by any carrier in the chain of carriers transporting

---

**6.** 4 U.L.A. §§ 1 et seq. (1922 ed.)

**7.** For example, we will refer to section one of the FBLA (Federal Bill of Lading Act of 1916, ch. 415, § 1, 39 Stat. 538, 49 U.S.C. § 81 (1970)) as FBLA § 81. Section two of the FBLA (49 U.S.C. § 82 (1970)) will be cited FBLA § 82, and so on.

**8.** See 49 U.S.C.A. §§ 81–124 (1951) and the annotations contained therein; see also The Decennial Digest, Carriers—39–231 (West 1916–1970) and the headnotes contained therein.

**9.** FBLA § 81.

**10.** Interstate Commerce Act of 1887, ch. 104, Part I, § 20, 24 Stat. 386, as added, June 29, 1906, ch. 3591, § 7, 34 Stat. 593, as amended, 49 U.S.C.A. § 20(11) (1970).

**11.** Missouri Pac. R. Co. v. Elmore & Stahl, 377 U.S. 134 (1964) (Court explains common law liability and declares that Carmack Amendment codifies it).

an interstate shipment, and proscribes carriers from using certain contract clauses limiting their liability. The Carmack Amendment covers two full pages in the statute book. The courts have interpreted and applied it in hundreds of cases.[12] There are also various special federal statutes more limited in scope. In 1938, for instance, Congress enacted the Perishable Agricultural Commodities Act.[13] In 1893 and 1936, Congress passed the Harter Act[14] and the Carriage of Goods by Sea Act,[15] respectively; both apply to ocean bills of lading.

Besides federal statutes, Article Seven and relevant case law, the lawyer must often consult regulations and rulings of regulatory bodies, including those of the Interstate Commerce Commission. The I.C.C. has prescribed mandatory forms for bills of lading and has prescribed that "order" bills, which are negotiable because they state "deliver to order or bearer," must be printed on yellow paper and "straight" bills, which are nonnegotiable, on white paper.[16] The I.C.C. has also promulgated numerous rules and regulations that affect the liabilities of interstate carriers.[17]

In this chapter we will consider only the provisions of Article Seven, the FBLA, and the Carmack Amendment.

### § 21-3 Rights of Shipper Against Carrier

When a shipper delivers goods to a carrier, the shipper incurs two related risks: (*1*) that the goods will be lost, destroyed, or damaged while in the carrier's hands and (*2*) that the carrier will not deliver the goods as instructed. In this section we will treat the rights of the shipper (or his transferee) against the carrier when these risks materialize. The further risks that the carrier never received the goods or misdescribed them in the bill of lading will be treated in Sections 21-4 and 21-5 of this chapter on the rights of transferees of the shipper. When these two risks materialize, it is rare that the shipper will be in any position to complain.

### A. THE RISK THAT THE GOODS WILL BE LOST, DESTROYED, OR DAMAGED, WHILE THEY ARE IN THE CARRIER'S CUSTODY

While goods are in the hands of a carrier, they may be lost, destroyed or damaged. The processing and payment (or rejection) of shipper's claims to compensation for loss, etc., is a big task for car-

---

12. See 49 U.S.C.A. § 20(11) (1951) and the extensive annotations contained therein.

13. Perishable Agricultural Commodities Act of 1930, ch. 436, §§ 1-18, 46 Stat. 531, as amended, 7 U.S.C.A. §§ 499a-499s (1970).

14. Act of Feb. 13, 1893, ch. 105, §§ 1-6, 27 Stat. 445, as amended, 46 U.S.C.A. §§ 190-195 (1970).

15. Carriage of Goods by Sea Act of 1936, ch. 229, §§ 1-16, 49 Stat. 1207, as amended, 46 U.S.C.A. §§ 1300-15 (1970).

16. Bills of Lading, 52 ICC 671 (1919); Bills of Lading of Freight Forwarders, 259 ICC 277 (1945).

17. See especially the rules and regulations set forth in 52 ICC 671 et seq. (1919).

riers, so big, in fact, that many carriers have set up separate claim departments and now employ "claim adjusters" whose function is similar to that of insurance adjusters.[18] The defending party is sometimes not the carrier. He may be the shipper's insurer or even the shipper himself, as where his improper loading caused the loss. Who asserts the claims? Most shipments are made pursuant to contracts for sale of the goods involved. If harm comes to the goods in transit, the party who initially seeks compensation will usually be either the shipper-seller or his buyer (depending on which has the "risk of loss" under the terms of the contract for sale). If the contract is silent, 2–509 and 2–510 of the Code on risk of loss will apply. If the risk was on the shipper-seller, he (or his insurer) will usually assert the claim against the carrier. If the risk was on the buyer during the relevant times, he (or his insurer) will usually assert the claim.[19]

Carriers make good defendants. They are almost always solvent, and it is relatively easy to prove a claim against a carrier. However the plaintiff must be wary of liquidated damages provisions which drastically limit the carrier's liability.

## GENERAL RULE OF ABSOLUTE LIABILITY

To understand the liability of a carrier today for loss, etc., of goods in its custody, it is necessary to understand what the common law was on the subject. At common law the carrier was absolutely [20] liable for all loss, damage, or destruction. To this general rule there were exceptions [21] for losses, etc., due to acts of God, acts of public enemies, acts of shippers, acts of public authorities, and the inherent vice or nature of the goods themselves. Today this common law liability of carriers is substantially codified in the Carmack Amendment to the Interstate Commerce Act: [22]

> Any common carrier, railroad, or transportation company subject to the provisions of this chapter receiving property for transportation from a point in one State or Territory or the District of Columbia to a point in another State, Territory, District of Columbia, or from any point in the United States to a point in an adjacent foreign country shall

18. Einhorn & Einhorn, Handling Loss and Damage Claims Against Common Carriers, 6 Prac.Law., Nov. 1960 at 54; O'Brien, Damage Claims Against Air Carriers, 35 ICC Prac.J. 653 (1968); Skulina, Liability of a Carrier for Loss and Damage to Interstate Shipments, 17 Clev.-Mar.L.Rev. 251, 260–64 (1968).

19. See generally Sorkin, Allocation of the Risk of Loss in the Transportation of Freight—The Function of Insurance, 40 Fordham L. Rev. 67 (1971).

20. E. g., Olive Kent Park, Inc. v. Moshassuck Transp. Co., 189 Misc. 864, 71 N.Y.S.2d 15 (Sup.Ct.1947) (carrier liable even though its truck hijacked in broad daylight and the goods stolen without any negligence on the part of the carrier whatsoever).

21. See C. Miller, Law of Freight Loss and Damage Claims (2d ed. 1961). See also Beale, The Carrier's Liability: Its History, 11 Harv.L.Rev. 158 (1897).

22. Interstate Commerce Act of 1887, ch. 104, Part I, § 20, 24 Stat. 386, as added, June 29, 1906, ch. 3591, § 7, 34 Stat. 593, as amended 49 U.S.C. § 20 (11) (1970).

issue a receipt or bill of lading therefor, and shall be liable
to the lawful holder thereof for any loss, damage, or injury
to such property caused by it or by any common carrier,
railroad, or transportation company to which such property
may be delivered or over whose line or lines such property
may pass within the United States or within an adjacent
foreign country when transported on a through bill of lading,
and no contract, receipt, rule, regulation, or other limitation
of any character whatsoever shall exempt such common carrier, railroad, or transportation company from the liability
hereby imposed; and any such common carrier, railroad, or
transportation company so receiving property for transportation from a point in one State, Territory, or the District of
Columbia to a point in another State or Territory, or from a
point in a State or Territory to a point in the District of
Columbia, or from any point in the United States to a point
in an adjacent foreign country, or for transportation wholly
within a Territory, or any common carrier, railroad, or
transportation company delivering said property so received
and transported shall be liable to the lawful holder of said
receipt or bill of lading or to any party entitled to recover
thereon, whether such receipt or bill of lading has been issued or not, for the full actual loss, damage, or injury to such
property.  .   .   .

But what if the goods are not received "for transportation from
a point in one State or Territory or the District of Columbia to a point
in another State, Territory, or District of Columbia" or "from any
point in the United States to a point in an adjacent foreign country"?
In particular what if the goods are received for transportation solely
within the boundaries of a single state? Here 7–309(1) of the Code
applies. Its first sentence requires only that the carrier exercise
that degree of care in relation to the goods which a reasonably careful man would exercise under like circumstances. This sounds like a
radical departure from the general rule of absolute liability at common law and as codified in the Carmack Amendment for interstate
commerce. However the second sentence of 7–309(1) reads:

This subsection does not repeal or change any law or rule of
law which imposes liability on a common carrier for damages
not caused by its negligence.

Since in pre-Code days most states followed the general common law
rule of absolute liability,[23] this continues to be the generally prevailing
rule in cases against carriers to which Article Seven applies. If a
carrier can show that the applicable state law was different, then that
rule will govern.

23.  Missouri Pac. R. Co. v. Elmore &
Stahl, 377 U.S. 134 (1964), rehearing
denied 377 U.S. 984 (1964).

Thus under both federal and state law carriers are generally held to a rule of absolute liability for loss, destruction, or damage of goods bailed to them, a rule that obviously favors shippers. Most courts have allocated the burden of producing evidence and the ultimate burden of proof in ways that also favor the shipper. Justice Stewart recently summarized the prevailing allocations in these terms: [24]

> Accordingly, under federal law, in an action to recover from a carrier for damage to a shipment, the shipper establishes his prima facie case when he shows delivery in good condition, arrival in damaged condition, and the amount of damages. Thereupon, the burden of proof is upon the carrier to show both that it was free from negligence and that the damage to the cargo was due to one of the excepted causes relieving the carrier of liability.

We now turn to the exceptions to the general rule of absolute liability. To escape liability, a carrier must not only produce evidence that fits it into an exception, it must also carry the ultimate burden of proof that facts exist to which an exception applies. The exceptions are generally good law not only under the Carmack Amendment, but also under Article Seven. Yet each has been the subject of its own case law development, and the extent to which each is recognized varies from state to state. Here we treat only the general contours of each exception.

## ACT OF GOD EXCEPTION

The carrier is not liable for goods lost or injured by an "act of God." [25] The courts have been no more successful in defining acts of God than mankind has been in defining God. One theory is that the phrase includes all occurrences due to natural causes without the intervention of any human agency. [26] Some courts call this "inevitable necessity." Another theory limits the exception to violent disturbances of nature such as lightning or earthquake and does not include the gradual and more or less orderly changes in the physical world such as the onset of freezing temperatures. [27]

---

**24.** Id. at 138. See also Note, Effect of a Presumption of Common Carrier Negligence Upon the Burden of Proof, 42 Wash.L.Rev. 273 (1966); Annot., 33 A.L.R.2d 867 (1954); 106 A.L.R. 1156 (1937).

**25.** Missouri Pac. R. Co. v. Elmore & Stahl, 377 U.S. 134 (1964), rehearing denied 377 U.S. 984 (1964).

**26.** See, e. g., Williams v. Grant, 1 Conn. 487 (1816) (the striking of a vessel upon an uncharted rock is act of God); Merritt v. Earle, 29 N.Y. 115 (1864) (not act of God where mast of sunken sloop causing loss was visible to car-

rier's agent and loss might, therefore, have been avoided); Hays v. Kennedy, 41 Pa. 378 (1861).

**27.** See, e. g., Gleeson v. Virginia Midland R. R. Co., 140 U.S. 435 (1891) (landslide on a railway car, caused by an ordinary fall of rain, not an act of God); Fish v. Chapman, 2 Ga. 349 (1847) (act of God is any accident produced by physical causes which are irresistible, such as storms, earthquakes, lightning); Friend v. Woods, 47 Va. (6 Grat.) 189 (1849) (the formation of a bar in the Kanawha river by a rise and an ice gorge on which ship ran aground not an act of God).

If the goods would not have been exposed to the act of God but for the carrier's negligence, the courts are in controversy. If the carrier could have reasonably foreseen and avoided the casualty, the courts agree that the carrier is liable.[28] But if the carrier could not have reasonably foreseen or avoided it, and the carrier's negligence caused only a delay in shipment which exposed the goods to injury, then the courts are divided.[29] One line of cases excuses the carrier's negligent delay on the grounds that it was not a "natural or proximate" cause of the loss or damage even though it was a cause in fact. For other courts it is enough that the carrier's negligent delay is a link in the causal chain; they reject the carrier's claim that his was not the "proximate cause."[30]

An act of God that exempts the carrier from liability must generally be the sole and proximate cause of the loss or injury.[31] We will not here deal with the mumbo jumbo which distinguishes a "proximate cause" from a "mere contributing cause." We presume that the reader is sufficiently familiar with tort law to understand that when a court characterizes a cause as "proximate" or "sole" as opposed to "contributing," the court is usually taking into account the relative culpability of the parties and the magnitude of their contributions to the loss.

## ACT OF PUBLIC ENEMY EXCEPTION

Carriers do not insure against losses caused by pirates[32] or by an organized military or naval force with which the country of the carrier is at war.[33] If actual hostilities exist between the two coun-

28. See, e. g., Baltimore & O. R. R. v. Keedy, 75 Md. 320, 23 A. 643 (1892) (carrier liable because exercise of diligence would have avoided damage by approaching flood); Grier v. St. Louis Merchants' Bridge Terminal Ry., 108 Mo.App. 565, 84 S.W. 158 (1904) (if carrier's negligence permitted property to remain exposed to flood damage, then carrier liable).

29. The carrier can breathe easy if the loss or damage was caused by lightning, earthquake, an unusual snowstorm, a severe gale, or the Johnstown flood of 1889. Generally, boiler explosions, man made fires, most collisions, and explosions of war munitions are not excused under this exception.

30. Proponents of the latter theory sometimes base their argument on the ground that the carrier's negligent delay has the same effect as a wrongful deviation. See generally 1 R. Hutchinson, Carriers 301 (1906).

31. Johnson v. Chicago M. St. P. & Pac. R. R. Co., 400 F.2d 968 (9th Cir. 1968) (carrier liable if his negligence mingled with collapse of railroad tunnel); Green-Wheeler Shoe Co. v. Chicago R. S. & P. Ry., 130 Iowa 123, 106 N.W. 498 (1906) (discussing foreseeability); Continental Paper Bag Co. v. Maine Cent. R. Co., 115 Me. 449, 99 A. 259 (1916) (carrier not liable; his negligence delayed arrival, but flood occurred *after* arrival; the flood, not the delay, was proximate cause); Tobin v. Lake Shore & M. S. Ry. Co., 192 Mich. 549, 159 N.W. 389 (1916).

32. See, e. g., The Steamboat Belfast v. Boon & Co., 41 Ala. 50 (1867) (distinguishing pirates (carrier not liable) from robbers (carrier liable)); Pickering v. Barkley, 82 Eng.Rep. 587 (1655) (pirates).

33. See, e. g., Seligman v. Armijo, 1 N.M. 459 (1870) (U. S. Cavalry destroyed liquor carried by an American wagon master and destined for American Indians).

tries, a formal declaration of war is unnecessary.[34] However, a rebellion or insurrection excuses the carrier only if the uprising assumes the dimensions of a civil war and involves the recognition of belligerent rights by the combatants.[35] Losses caused by robbers have not historically been recognized within this exception. But what of Indians on the warpath, mobs, and strikers? There are a few cases.[36]

The public enemy exception has not been applied in recent years. Professor Dobie has suggested that "[t]his exception becomes of historical rather than practical importance . . . with the spread of peace, and the decline of war through the recognition of its inherent barbarism. . . ."[37] (This naively optimistic explanation was written in 1914.) A better explanation for the exception's decline is the development of modern intelligence and communication systems that enable carriers to keep shipments out of peril. Whatever the reason, the exception has fallen into relative disuse.

## ACT OF SHIPPER EXCEPTION

A common carrier is not liable for loss or damage to goods caused by the fraud or negligence of the shipper.[38] Although the shipper does not always have a positive duty to disclose the value of the goods to the carrier, the courts do not tolerate deception of the carrier about the value of the goods shipped, and courts have found certain losses

---

34. See The Prize Cases, 67 U.S. (2 Black) 635 (1862).

35. See, e. g., The Prize Cases, 67 U.S. (2 Black) 635 (1862) (American Civil War); Mauran v. Alliance Insurance Co., 73 U.S. (6 Wall) 1 (1867) (capture of ship by Confederate forces); See also Forward v. Pittard, 99 Eng.Rep. 953 (1785).

36. See, e. g., Holladay v. Kennard, 79 U.S. (12 Wall) 254 (1870) (American Indians robbing a stagecoach while on the warpath are public enemies); Missouri Pac. Railway Co. v. Nevill, 60 Ark. 375, 30 S.W. 425 (1895) (carrier liable for destruction by uncontrolled mob); Greismer v. Lake Shore & M. S. R. R., 102 N.Y. 563, 7 N.E. 828 (1886) (strikers; carrier not liable so long as he exercised due care in face of strike; carrier not an insurer of prompt delivery); Coggs v. Bernard, 92 Eng.Rep. 107 (1703).

37. A. Dobie, Bailments and Carriers 335 (1914).

38. See, e. g., Payne v. Ralli, 74 F. 563 (S.D.N.Y.1896) (carrier not required to recondition defective bags supplied by shipper); Hutchinson v. Chicago S. & P. M. & O. Ry., 37 Minn. 524, 35 N.W.

433 (1887) (horse killed when shipper left car window open; carrier not liable); Rixford v. Smith, 52 N.H. 355 (1872) (shipper negligently attended to the loading of goods); Currie v. Seaboard Air Line Ry., 156 N.C. 432, 72 S.E. 493 (1911) (carrier not liable if shipper's negligence caused a puncheon of molasses to burst by reason of fermentation); American Lead Pencil Co. v. Nashville C. & St. L. Ry., 124 Tenn. 57, 134 S.W. 613 (1910) (carrier not liable for goods burned by negligence of shipper); Shaacht v. Illinois Cent. R. R., 94 Tenn. 658, 30 S.W. 742 (1895) (shipper delivered set of silverware to carrier in a basket which appeared to contain household goods); Pecos & N. T. Ry. v. Hall, 222 S.W. 170 (Tex.Com.App.1920) (carrier who would not transport cattle passing through quarantine territory unless they were dipped, not liable for damages from dipping them); Gibbon v. Paynton, 98 Eng.Rep. 199 (KB 1769) (shipper concealed money in a bag filled with hay; carrier not liable for loss of money); Jackson Architectural Iron Works v. Hurlbut, 158 N.Y. 34, 52 N.E. 665 (1889) (carrier claims that receiving party's order to unload after dark constituted contributory negligence).

to be caused by the shipper's deception.[39]  If the shipper does not answer the carrier's inquiries as to the shipment's value truthfully or, through ignorance or carelessness, leads the carrier to believe that the goods are of no special value, then he cannot recover an amount greater than the acknowledged value.[40]  The courts have reasoned that since the carrier's compensation, methods of handling the goods, and precautions as to their safety are directly related to the value of the goods, a shipper who deceives the carrier as to their value cannot recover for their loss or damage.[41]

The carrier may also escape liability by showing that the loss or damage was due to faulty instructions that the shipper gave the carrier, or due to the shipper's failure to pack the goods properly, or due to the way the shipper loaded the goods.[42]  However there is authority that even though the shipper packed or loaded, the carrier will still be liable if it knew or should have known that the shipper's packing or loading was deficient and did not correct it.[43]  In one recent case, Super Service Freight Co. v. United States,[44] the Sixth Circuit Court of Appeals ruled on burden of proof.  Shipper's employee negligently packaged an expensive camera in a wooden case designed to support the camera only if the package remained in an upright position.  The employee then incorrectly labeled the box so that the camera was upside down when the exterior labels showed it to be upright.  While it was in carrier's possession, the camera fell and was smashed.  The district judge had "assumed that the shipper had carried its burden of proving delivery to the carrier in good condition, arrival in damaged condition, and damages."[45]  He found that the carrier had then carried its burden of proving that the packaging was defective.  He further found that the shipper had failed in carrying a reshifted burden of proof that "the damage was due to the carrier's negligence in handling rather than to its own negligence in packaging."  In vacating a judgment for the carrier and remanding the case to the district court the Court of Appeals for the Sixth Circuit stated that "once the shipper has proved a *prima facie* case the burden of proof

39.  See, e. g., Magnin v. Dinsmore, 62 N.Y. 35 (1875).

40.  E. g., Beaumont v. Pennsylvania R. R. Co., 284 App.Div. 354, 131 N.Y.S. 2d 652 (1st Dep't 1954) (passenger accepted $400 minimum valuation on baggage; held "estopped" to claim higher value), aff'd 308 N.Y. 920, 127 N.E.2d 80 (1955) cert. denied 350 U.S. 838 (1955).

41.  See, e. g., Michalitschke Bros. & Co. v. Wells, Fargo, 118 Cal. 683, 50 P. 847 (1897) (failure to state value of sealed package); Cole v. Goodwin, 19 Wend. 251 (N.Y.Sup.Ct.1838) (carrier absolved from liability for loss not occasioned by negligence or misconduct where owner is chargeable with fraud in valuing property and valuation affects degree of care necessary to be bestowed); Batson v. Donovan, 4 B. & A. 21, 106 Eng.Rep. 846 (1820) (carrier had given *notice* that he would not be answerable for parcels of value, unless entered and paid for as such).

42.  See, e. g., Association of Maryland Pilots v. Baltimore & O. R. R., 304 F.Supp. 548 (D.Md.1969).

43.  See text accompanying note 157 infra, and cases cited.

44.  350 F.2d 541 (6th Cir. 1965).  See also Annot., 7 A.L.R.3d 723 (1966).

45.  350 F.2d at 542.

shifts to the carrier and remains there." [46]   Thus where the "act of shipper" exception might apply, the carrier is obliged to prove not only that the shipper was negligent, but that the carrier was not negligent or that any negligence of the carrier was not the cause of the loss.

The parties may try to shape the act of shipper exception by inserting clauses in the bill of lading.   For example, where the shipper loads, the carrier may insert a disclaimer to the effect that it did not load, count, or weigh the goods.   Section 101 of the FBLA provides that "if such statement be true, the carrier shall not be liable for damages caused by the improper loading or by the non-receipt or by the misdescription of the goods described in the bill of lading."   Section 7–301 includes a comparable provision.   The effectiveness of these disclaimers remains subject to the general case law principle that the carrier remains responsible if it knew or plainly should have known of deficiencies in the shipper's loading, etc., and did not act to correct them.[47]

## ACT OF PUBLIC AUTHORITY EXCEPTION

When the state seizes or destroys inspected goods or contraband under its police power, the carrier is not liable for their destruction.[48] Since the carrier must give up the shipper's goods when the state requires it, the carrier cannot be held liable in damages in the state's court for obeying the state's mandate.   The carrier must, however, satisfy itself that the officers who seize the goods are properly authorized to do so.[49]

This exception encompasses the taking of goods under public authority (fortifying a levee with bales of cotton) and the seizure of goods by legal process (execution or attachment against the owner).[50] When it is practicable to do so, the carrier must give reasonable notice of such seizure or proceedings to the shipper or owner of the goods so that he can protect his interest.[51]

## INHERENT VICE OR NATURE OF GOODS EXCEPTION

Injury caused by the inherent nature of the goods is the fifth exception to the carrier's general liability.   So long as the carrier is not

---

46.   Id. at 543.

47.   See text accompanying notes 155–160 infra.

48.   See, e. g., Kohn v. Richmond R. R., 37 S.C. 1, 16 S.E. 376 (1891) (dictum); Chicago & E. I. R. R. v. Collins Co., 235 F. 857 (7th Cir. 1916) (carrier not liable if chickens confiscated pursuant to martial law), aff'd 249 U.S. 186 (1918).

49.   E. g., Bennett v. American Express Co., 83 Me. 236, 22 A. 159 (1891) (car-

rier liable for loss occasioned by unlawful seizure of public officer) (dictum); McAllister v. Chicago R. I. & P. R. R., 74 Mo. 351 (1881) (carrier protected by a writ issued under statute which was later declared unconstitutional).

50.   E. g., Stiles v. Davis, 66 U.S. (1 Black) 101 (1861) (attached goods).

51.   See, e. g., Bliven v. Hudson River R. R., 36 N.Y. 403 (1867).

negligent, he is not liable for the decay of fruit, the evaporation of liquids, the bursting of a barrel due to fermentation, the decaying of potatoes which are wet when shipped, leakage in a barrel, or the like.[52] If goods are perishable, the carrier must only exercise the care that an ordinary man would exercise to protect his own property. However if the carrier knows the nature of the shipment and its peculiar susceptibility to decay, the carrier's negligent delay in transport or delivery will render him liable.[53]

## DAMAGES MEASURES AND PARTIES LIABLE

Neither federal statutes nor Article Seven of the Code explicitly set forth measures of damages against carriers that are liable for loss, damage, or destruction of the goods. But, the case law is voluminous.[54] We can only survey the most widely recognized general principles. The most widely *cited* general principle is that the plaintiff is entitled to the difference between what the fair market value of the goods would have been at the time and place of delivery had they arrived intact and their fair market value, if any, in their condition on arrival. The most widely *applied* general principle, however, is simply that the plaintiff should receive such damages as will compensate him for his loss. Sometimes this will be a figure equivalent to the difference between fair market value at destination undamaged and fair market value at destination damaged.[55] Courts also frequently look to the contract price the shipper was to receive from his buyer as an indicator of the fair market value the goods would have had if they had arrived.[56] Further there is authority that if the goods at destination have no market value, the shipper-seller's contract price is the measure of his damages.[57]

The basic measure of recovery in terms of market value differentials, however, can either overcompensate or undercompensate, and most courts stand ready to depart from it in either type of case. It

---

52.  See, e. g., R. E. Funsten Dried Fruit & Nut Co. v. Toledo St. L. & W. Ry., 163 Mo.App. 426, 143 S.W. 839 (1912); Beard v. Illinois Cent. R. R., 79 Iowa 518, 44 N.W. 800 (1890); Evans v. Fitchburg R. R., 111 Mass. 142 (1872).

53.  E. g., Cleburne Peanut & Products Co. v. Missouri K & T Ry. of Texas, 221 S.W. 270 (Tex.Civ.App.1920) (carriers must furnish suitable car whether peanuts are green and uncured or dried and well cured).

54.  The Decennial Digest, Carriers—135 (West 1916–1971) and the headnotes contained therein.

55.  E. g., Reider v. Thompson, 197 F.2d 158 (5th Cir. 1952) (evidence held sufficient to determine difference between market value of sheep skins had they been received in good condition and their market value in their condition on arrival); Federated Dept. Stores, Inc. v. Brinke, 316 F.Supp. 1402 (S.D.Fla.1970) (evidence permitted recovery for damage to electric fans in amount of difference between market value at destination undamaged and salvage value damaged).

56.  E. g., Gore Products, Inc. v. Texas & N. D. R. R. Co., 34 So.2d 418 (La. App.1948) (use of contract resale price; court noted that it was also the prevailing market value).

57.  F. J. McCarty Co. v. Southern Pacific Co., 428 F.2d 690 (7th Cir. 1970) (use of seller's contract resale price in New York where grapes had no market value there). See also Annot., 67 A.L.R. 1427 (1930).

will overcompensate where the plaintiff is a shipper who has contracted to sell the goods to a buyer at a price below the fair market price (of undamaged goods) at destination. Accordingly there is authority that in such a case the plaintiff should only recover the difference between the contract price and the market value of the damaged goods on arrival.[58] Again a market value differential will overcompensate where the shipper is the plaintiff and the carrier can show that (1) shipper's costs of replacement yield a lower figure and (2) shipper can feasibly replace the goods and still realize the profit he contemplated.[59] Similarly courts have held that the plaintiff's actual cost of repair should be used as the measure of recovery at least where (1) plaintiff repaired and (2) the repairs brought the value of the goods up to their pre-damage value.[60] This is not to say there is a duty to repair.[61] Cost of repair alone may undercompensate, however, and a court will in such a case award higher damages.[62] Further, in a proper case, a court will award the rental cost of procuring substitute goods.[63]

Numerous cases have arisen in which the plaintiff claims consequential damages from the carrier. These damages take different forms such as profits lost on a contemplated resale, loss of reputation and good will, damages flowing from loss of use of the goods, and so on. The most widely cited principle governing recovery for consequential damages is the familiar one deriving from the leading case of Hadley v. Baxendale [64] (itself a carrier case); namely that the carrier is generally not liable unless the prospect of such damages was fairly within the contemplation of the parties at the time of contracting.[65] Even then the plaintiff may lose if the carrier can show that the plaintiff could have readily avoided the loss.

58.  E. g., United States v. Northern Pac. Ry. Co., 116 F.Supp. 277 (D.Minn.1953) (court held plaintiff-seller to contract resale price of potatoes much lower than their current market value).

59.  National Distillers Products Corp. v. Companhia Nacional, 107 F.Supp. 65 (E.D.Pa.1952) (no evidence of immediate need to replace or of loss of gross sales; court therefore uses costs to plaintiff of wine lost); Meletio Sea Food Co. v. Gordons Transports, Inc., 191 S.W.2d 983 (Mo.App.1946) (court uses cost to shipper of replacing food tainted with turpentine).

60.  Process Equip. Co. v. Denver Chicago Trucking Co., 275 F.Supp. 698 (D.Mass.1967) (use of cost to shipper of repairing machine damaged in transit); Terminal Transport Co. v. Lamtron Indus., Inc., 233 So.2d 854 (Fla.Ct.App.1970) (use of cost to shipper of repairing furniture damaged in transit). Cf. Fredenburgh v. Allied Van Lines, Inc., 79 N.M. 593, 446 P.2d 868 (1968).

61.  See Herrin Transp. Co. v. Sheldon, 209 S.W.2d 943 (Tex.Civ.App.1948).

62.  Merchant Shippers Ass'n v. Kellogg Express & Draying Co., 28 Cal.2d 594, 170 P.2d 923 (1946) (use of difference between machine's value before damage and its value after repairs plus reasonable costs of making repairs); Spainhour v. Nolind, 97 Ga.App. 362, 103 S.E.2d 154 (1958) (use of diminution in market value of house where damage so extensive as to render repair impracticable).

63.  Cagle v. Carr, 101 Ariz. 225, 418 P.2d 381 (1966) (use of rental costs of substitute backhoe where original hackhoe damaged in transit).

64.  9 Ex. 341, 156 Eng.Rep. 145, 5 Eng. Rul.Cas. 502 (1854).

65.  E. g., F. J. McCarty Co. v. Southern Pacific Co., 428 F.2d 690 (9th Cir. 1970); Hycel, Inc. v. American Airlines, Inc., 328 F.Supp. 190 (S.D.Tex.

Some courts will allow punitive damages in a proper case. Thus in Western Coach Corp. v. Vaughn,[66] the court awarded punitive damages against a carrier for carrying the plaintiff's house trailer in a way that manifested a "reckless indifference" to the rights of the plaintiff.

A special doctrine, applicable at least in those cases where the plaintiff is the consignee, is worthy of note. In Kennedy & Kratzer, Inc. v. Chicago, B. & Q. R. Co.,[67] the court summarized the law as follows: [68]

> The law is well settled that the measure of damages for goods injured in transit is the difference between the fair market value of the goods at the time and place of delivery in their injured or deteriorated condition and the fair market value of such goods if delivered without injury. . . . This rule contemplates that the consignee has accepted delivery of the goods and has not abandoned them to the carrier. If the consignee has rightfully abandoned the goods, he may recover the full value of the shipment less freight. . . .
>
> A consignee may rightfully abandon to the carrier goods damaged in transit to such an extent that they are virtually worthless. . . . But a consignee has no right to abandon a shipment of goods which has been only partially damaged and which retains a substantial value.

The court went on to hold that the plaintiff consignee did not rightfully abandon the potatoes to the carrier, for they had a substantial probable value of $2.25 per sack. On the other hand where the court finds that the damaged goods did not have significant value, the plaintiff may abandon them to the carrier and recover their full market value. Thus in Western Steel Buildings, Inc. v. Universal Carloading & Distrib. Co.,[69] the court allowed the plaintiff full value against a carrier responsible for "totaling" a prefabricated building. The upshot of this cluster of doctrine is that the consignee need not, in a proper case, accept delivery, salvage, and sue the carrier for the difference. Rather the consignee may abandon and sue for the full fair market value. The carrier will not have the burden of redisposition, however, where the goods have a significant resale value. This rule is sound, for carriers are not in the business of selling goods.

1971); St. Louis-San Francisco Ry. Co. v. Kittrell, 208 Okla. 147, 253 P.2d 1076 (1953).

**66.** 9 Ariz.App. 336, 452 P.2d 117 (1969). See Annot., 107 A.L.R. 1446 (1937).

**67.** 106 Ill.App.2d 278, 245 N.E.2d 910 (1969). See also Denver-Chicago

Trucking Co. v. Republic Drug Co., 143 Colo. 461, 306 P.2d 1076 (1957).

**68.** 106 Ill.App.2d at 281, 245 N.E.2d at 912.

**69.** 68 Wash.2d 522, 413 P.2d 954 (1966).

As a general rule under federal and state law, a common carrier may not disclaim his absolute liability. The Carmack Amendment and the common law rules embodied in the Code are statements of public policy that parties cannot alter by contract. However both the Interstate Commerce Act [70] and section 7-309 authorize a common carrier to limit the damages for which he will be liable in certain circumstances. These provisions recognize that carriers are entitled to vary their rates in relation to the value of the shipment and that the carrier's compensation should bear a reasonable relation to the risk and responsibility which the carrier assumes. Under the current federal law, the carrier may apply to the Interstate Commerce Commission for authorization to establish different rates dependant upon the value of the goods carried. Thus he may offer two alternatives to the shipper who wishes, for example, to transport goods worth a thousand dollars. Under one rate the carrier will be liable to the extent of a thousand dollars. Under a lesser rate approved by the Interstate Commerce Commission, the carrier may limit his liability to a certain number of dollars per pound or to some other figure which is less than the full value of the goods shipped. Thus although common carriers are in theory absolutely liable for damage to goods shipped, in fact they often enter into agreements with shippers which limit their liability to a small fraction of actual loss. The shipper and the carrier must agree to any limitation.[71]

We turn now to the liability of an initial carrier for the acts of connecting carriers. By enacting the Carmack Amendment Congress relieved shippers of the burden of determining which of the many carriers handling an interstate shipment had caused damage or loss of his goods.[72] Prior to the passage of the amendment, each

---

**70.** 49 U.S.C.A. § 20(11) (1970) reads in pertinent part as follows:

    . . . provided, however, that the provisions hereof respecting liability for full actual loss, damage or injury, notwithstanding any limitation of liability or recovery or representation or agreement or release as to value, and declaring any such limitation to be unlawful and void, shall not apply . . . to property, except ordinary livestock, received. . . .

**71.** Chandler v. Aero Mayflower Transit Co., 374 F.2d 129 (4th Cir. 1967) (shipper must be given genuine opportunity to choose between a tariff rate which does not limit the carrier's liability and a rate which does). See Beaumont v. Pennsylvania R. R. Co., 284 App.Div. 354, 131 N.Y.S.2d 652 (1st Dep't 1954); see also Annot., 25 A.L.R. 736 (1923).

**72.** See Reider v. Thompson, 339 U.S. 113 (1950), rehearing denied 339 U.S. 936 (1950); see also, Bowden v. Philadelphia, B & W R. R., 28 Del. (5 Boyce) 146, 91 A. 209 (1914); Illinois Cent. R. R. v. A. B. Friedman & Co., 263 Mo.App. 946, 161 S.W.2d 440 (1942). Mr. Justice Lurton, in Atlantic Coast Line v. Riverside Mills, 219 U.S. 186, 197-201 (1910), made these remarks: The English cases beginning with Muschamp v. Lancaster Railway Company, 8 M. & W. 421, decided in 1841, down to Bristol & C. Railway v. Collins, 7 H.L. Cases, 194, have consistently held that the mere receipt of property for transportation to a point beyond the line of the receiving carrier, without any qualifying agreement, justified an inference of an agreement for through transportation and an assumption of full carrier liability by the primary carrier. The ruling is grounded upon considerations of public policy and public convenience, and classes the receipt of goods so designated for a point beyond the carrier line as a holding out

interstate carrier attempted, often successfully, to limit its liability to loss or damage occurring on its particular segment of the through

to the public that the carrier has made its own arrangements for the continuance by a connecting carrier of the transportation after the goods leave its own line. There are American cases which take the same view of the question of evidence thus presented.

Upon the other hand, many American courts have repudiated the English rule which holds the carrier to a contract for transportation over the whole route, in the absence of a contract clearly otherwise, and have adopted the rule that unless the carrier specifically agrees to carry over the whole route, its responsibility, as a carrier, ends with its own line, and that for the continuance of the shipment its liability is only that of a forwarder. The conflict has, therefore, been one as to the evidence from which a contract for through carriage to a place beyond the line of the receiving carrier might be inferred.

In this conflicting condition of the decisions as to the circumstances from which an agreement for through transportation of property designated to a point beyond the receiving carrier's line might be inferred, Congress by the act here involved has declared, in substance, that the act of receiving property for transportation to a point in another State and beyond the line of the receiving carrier shall impose on such receiving carrier the obligation of through transportation with carrier liability throughout. But this uncertainty of the nature and extent of the liability of a carrier receiving goods destined to a point beyond its own line was not all which might well induce the interposition of the regulating power of Congress. Nothing has perhaps contributed more to the wealth and prosperity of the country than the almost universal practice of transportation companies to cooperate in making through routes and joint rates. Through this method a situation has been brought about by which, though independently managed, connecting carriers become in effect one system. This practice has its origin in the mutual interests of such companies and in the necessities of an expanding commerce.

Along with this singleness of rate and continuity of carriage there grew up the practice by receiving carriers, illustrated in this case, of refusing to

make a specific agreement to transport to points beyond its own line, whereby the connecting carrier for the purpose of carriage would become the agent of the primary carrier. The common form of receipt, as the court may judicially know, is one by which the shipper is compelled to make with each carrier in the route over which his package must go a separate agreement limiting the carrier liability of each separate company to its own part of the through route. As a result the shipper could look only to the initial carrier for recompense for loss, damage or delay occurring on its part of the route. If such primary carrier was able to show a delivery to the rails of the next succeeding carrier, although the packages might and usually did continue the journey in the same car in which they had been originally loaded, the shipper must fail in his suit. He might, it is true, then bring his action against the carrier so shown to have next received the shipment. But here, in turn he might be met by proof of safe delivery to a third separate carrier. In short, as the shipper was not himself in possession of the information as to when and where his property had been lost or damaged and had no access to the records of the connecting carriers who in turn had participated in some part of the transportation, he was compelled in many instances to make such settlement as should be proposed.

This burdensome situation of the shipping public in reference to interstate shipments over routes including separate lines of carriers was the matter which Congress undertook to regulate. Thus when this Carmack Amendment was reported by a conference committee, Judge William Richardson, a Congressman from Alabama, speaking for the committee of the matter which it was sought to remedy, among other things, said:

One of the great complaints of the railroads has been—and, I think, a reasonable, just and fair complaint —that when a man made a shipment, say, from Washington, for instance, to San Francisco, Cal., and his shipment was lost in some way, the citizen had to go thousands of miles, probably, to institute his suit. The result was that he had to settle his damages at what he could get.

route. As a result, the shipper could look to the initial carrier for recompense only for loss, damage, or delay occurring on its own line.[73] Moreover the shipper who was lucky enough to locate the carrier on whose line the damage or injury occurred was left to sort through a diversity of state regulations which covered the carrier's liability. The process was confusing and discouraging. Also the shipper often had to incur the inconvenience and expense of travelling to a distant forum to bring suit for his damages.[74] Congress decided that interstate carriers holding themselves out to receive packages for destinations beyond their own terminal should be compelled "as a condition of continuing in that traffic to obligate themselves to carry to the point of destination, using the lines of connecting carriers as their own agency." [75] The amendment reinforced the rights of the shipper by securing "unity of transportation with unity of responsibility." [76]

As a result of the passage of the amendment, the initial carrier could no longer exculpate himself from liability for damage, and the initial and connecting carriers were encouraged to use a high degree of care. Freight forwarders acquired the responsibility for shipment from place of receipt to place of destination whether or not a through bill of lading had been issued. The carrier made liable to the lawful holder of a bill of lading found it more difficult to exploit the unequal balance of bargaining power existing between it and the shipper.

Section 7–302 of the Code is patterned after that part of the Carmack Amendment which subjects the initial carrier to liability for loss or damage caused by connecting carriers.[77]

What have we done? We have made the initial carrier, the carrier that takes and receives the shipment, responsible for the loss of the article in the way of damages. We save the shipper from going to California or some distant place to institute his suit. Why? The reasons for inducing us to do that were that the initial carrier has a through route connection with the secondary carrier, on whose route the loss occurred, and a settlement between them will be an easy matter, while the shipper would be at heavy expense in the institution of a suit. If a judgment is obtained against the initial carrier, no doubt exists but that the secondary carrier would pay it at once. Why? Because the arrangement, the concert, the co-operation, the through route courtesies between them would be broken up if prompt payment were not made. We have done that in conference. Cong.Rec. Pt. 10, p. 9580.

73. Atlantic Coast Line v. Riverside Mills, 219 U.S. 186 (1910).

74. See, e. g., Scott Truck Line, Inc. v. Chicago R. I. & Pac. R. R., 312 F. Supp. 511 (N.D.Ill.1970) (shipper is relieved of obligation to determine where loss occurred and of burden of travel to possibly distant forum to bring suit for his damages); Wald-Green Food Corp. v. Acme Fast Freight, 200 Misc. 679, 103 N.Y.S.2d 768 (Sup.Ct.1951), appeal denied 279 App.Div. 766, 109 N.Y.S.2d 191, reaff'd 200 Misc. 687, 110 N.Y.S.2d 514 (Sup.Ct.1952) (freight forwarder was initial carrier of reconsignment).

75. Atlantic Coast Line R. R. v. Riverside Mills, 219 U.S. 186, 203 (1911).

76. Id.

77. § 7–302 provides:

(1) The issuer of a through bill of lading or other document embodying an undertaking to be performed in part by persons acting as its agents or by connecting carriers is liable to anyone entitled to recover on the document for any breach by such other

## CARRIER'S RIGHT TO THE SHIPPER'S INSURANCE

In an earlier chapter we outlined the subrogation problems that an attorney encounters in risk of loss litigation.[78] Here we will develop one aspect of that problem, namely, the common carrier's right to the shipper's insurance.[79] An example will illustrate the problem: Shipper and common carrier contract to transport goods from Houston to Miami. Shipper also contracts with insurer who agrees to insure the shipment. In this case shipper is in the happy position of having two parties who are strictly liable for the loss. Of course, the fight resolves itself to one between carrier and insurer, and the question becomes who between them should bear the ultimate burden of loss. Some commentators argue that neither should benefit and that each should prorate the loss.[80] Although a sharing would seem to be the reasonable solution, it also seems to have been the one solution that courts have never reached. As one reads back through the cases, one sees a fascinating lawyer competition with first the carrier and then the insurer gaining the upper hand by inserting fancy and fancier clauses in their separate contracts with the shipper.

At the present time we believe the dispute is dead and resolved for all time; the shipper's insurer seems to have the upper hand. The pertinent provision of a typical insurance contract might read as follows:

> It is agreed by the insured that this insurance shall not inure directly or indirectly to the benefit of any carrier, bailee or

persons or by a connecting carrier of its obligation under the document but to the extent that the bill covers an undertaking to be performed overseas or in territory not contiguous to the continental United States or an undertaking including matters other than transportation this liability may be varied by agreement of the parties.

(2) Where goods covered by a through bill of lading or other document embodying an undertaking to be performed in part by persons other than the issuer are received by any such person, he is subject with respect to his own performance while the goods are in his possession to the obligation of the issuer. His obligation is discharged by delivery of the goods to another such person pursuant to the document, and does not include liability for breach by any other such persons or by the issuer.

(3) The issuer of such through bill of lading or other document shall be entitled to recover from the connecting carrier or such other person in possession of the goods when the breach of the obligation under the document occurred, the amount it may be re-

quired to pay to anyone entitled to recover on the document therefor, as may be evidenced by any receipt, judgment, or transcript thereof, and the amount of any expense reasonably incurred by it in defending any action brought by anyone entitled to recover on the document therefor.

78.  See Ch. 5 supra.

79.  See generally Campbell, Non Consensual Suretyship, 45 Yale L.J. 69 (1935); King, Subrogation Under Contracts Insuring Property, 30 Texas L. Rev. 62 (1951); Annot., 27 A.L.R.3d 984 (1969).

80.  Stephen Langmaid suggests that where a carrier is made absolutely liable by law, the courts should treat the insurer and the carrier as concurrent insurers; each would have the right of contribution from the other. Langmaid, Some Recent Problems in the Law of Suretyship and Insurance, 47 Harv.L.Rev. 976, 991–92 (1934). Other commentators support this view. E. g., King, Subrogation Under Contracts Insuring Property, 30 Texas L.Rev. 62, 81 (1931).

other party by stipulation in the bill of lading or otherwise, and any breach of this agreement shall render this policy null and void.

Courts have generally allowed the insurer to limit his policy as above and have enforced his right to render it "null and void" to the extent that it would otherwise inure to the benefit of the carrier.[81]

The carrier is at a disadvantage in his competition with the insurer because the carrier is prohibited by law from restricting his liability in the way in which the insurer has done by contract.[82] The carrier is obliged to bear what is essentially strict liability, and it has not been permitted to limit its liability to situations in which the shipper has no insurance. The best it has been able to put forward under the circumstances is a bill of lading clause similar to the following:

The carrier shall have the benefit of any insurance effected on the goods *so far as this shall not avoid the policies or contracts of insurance,* provided that the carrier reimburse the claimant (shipper) for the premium paid thereon.

In general the courts hold that the quoted clause loses when in competition with the avoidance clause in the insurance contract quoted above.[83]

---

8!. See, e. g., Insurance Co. of North America v. Easton, 73 Tex. 167, 11 S.W. 180 (1889).

82. The carrier first attempted to avoid liability by stipulating in the shipping contract that it was exempt from liability to the shipper for damage to or loss of the goods resulting from its negligence. See, e. g., Inman v. South Carolina Ry., 129 U.S. 128 (1889); Liverpool & G. W. Steam Co. v. Phoenix Insurance Co., 129 U.S. 397 (1889) (parties contract upon an unequal footing; the carrier can take advantage of the shipper, and the social interest requires the utmost care of carriers); Bradley v. Lehigh Valley R. R., 153 F. 350 (2d Cir. 1907); Willock v. Pennsylvania R. R., 166 Pa. 184, 30 A. 948 (1895). This and other devices which required the shipper to take out insurance for its benefit and which, in effect, required the shipper to indemnify the carrier from liability for carrier's own negligence were declared illegal at an early date. Inman v. South Carolina R. R., 129 U.S. 128 (1889); The Hadji, 20 F. 875 (D. N.Y.1884) (held this is merely another method of contracting against liability for negligence).

83. The carrier may get the benefit of the shipper's insurance only if there

is no opposing stipulation in the contract of insurance. Adams v. Hartford Fire Insurance Co., 193 Iowa 1027, 188 N.W. 823 (1922). Contra, Kalle & Co. v. Morton, 156 App.Div. 522, 523, 141 N.Y.S. 374, 375 (1st Dep't 1913) (dictum), aff'd on other grounds 216 N.Y. 655, 110 N.E. 1043 (1915). Whenever the insurer uses a clause of avoidance, the insured may recover from the insurer, and the insurer is effectively subrogated to the shipper's cause of action against the carrier and is relieved of all liability. Thus, the carrier bears the ultimate loss. See Graysonia N. & A. R. Co. v. Newberger Cotton Co., 170 Ark. 1039, 1054, 282 S.W. 975, 981 (1926); Hartford Fire Ins. Co. v. Payne, 199 Iowa 1008, 203 N.W. 4 (1925); Adams v. Hartford Fire Ins. Co., 193 Iowa 1027, 188 N.W. 823 (1922); Dejean v. Louisiana Western R. R., 167 La. 111, 118 So. 822 (1928). See also Luckenback v. W. J. McCahan Sugar Co., 248 U.S. 139 (1918); Inman v. South Carolina R. R., 129 U.S. 128 (1889); The R. A. Turrentine v. American Home Ass'n Co., 279 F.2d 811 (5th Cir. 1960), cert. denied 364 U.S. 914, rehearing denied 364 U.S. 944; The Turet Crown, 297 F. 766, 777 (2d Cir. 1924), aff'd 264 U.S. 591 (1924); Bradley v. Lehigh Valley R. R., 153 F. 350 (2d Cir. 1907); Nebraska Co-op Creameries, Inc. v. Des

Until Congress steps in or a carrier's lawyer comes up with more powerful medicine than has been produced heretofore, the carrier will usually be the loser in competition with the shipper's insurer.  Of course, if the insurance contract does not contain an avoidance clause and particularly if it also lacks a subrogation clause, the carrier may succeed in placing the ultimate responsibility on the insurer, but our understanding is that these circumstances rarely occur.

### B.  THE RISK THAT THE CARRIER WILL FAIL TO DISCHARGE DELIVERY OBLIGATIONS

A further basic risk is that the carrier will fail to discharge its delivery obligations.  The basic delivery obligations of the carrier are generally the same under the FBLA [84] and Article Seven.[85]  We will focus on the FBLA, section 88 of which provides:

> A carrier, in the absence of some lawful excuse, is bound to deliver goods upon a demand made either by the consignee named in the bill for the goods or, if the bill is an order bill, by the holder thereof, if such a demand is accompanied by—
>
> (a) An offer in good faith to satisfy the carrier's lawful lien upon the goods;
>
> (b) Possession of the bill of lading and an offer in good faith to surrender, properly indorsed, the bill which was issued for the goods, if the bill is an order bill; and
>
> (c) A readiness and willingness to sign, when the goods are delivered, an acknowledgment that they have been delivered, if such signature is requested by the carrier.
>
> In case the carrier refuses or fails to deliver the goods, in compliance with a demand by the consignee or holder so accompanied, the burden shall be upon the carrier to establish the existence of a lawful excuse for such refusal or failure.

The carrier may misdeliver, that is, he may deliver to a party not authorized to receive the goods.  Or the carrier may be unable to deliver on demand because of loss or damage to the goods, or the carrier may fail to deliver the goods on time.  There are still other ways a carrier may fail to discharge its delivery obligations.

### MISDELIVERY

Courts applying federal law and courts applying state law both frequently say that a carrier is "absolutely liable" for misdelivery.  Southern Express Co. v. C. L. Ruth & Son [86] is one of the classic cases

Moines Transp. Co., 16 F.Supp. 853 (D.Iowa 1936).

**84.**  FBLA § 88.

**85.**  See § 7–403.

**86.**  183 Ala. 493, 59 So. 538 (Ct.App. 1912).  See Annot., 54 A.L.R. 1330 (1928).

on the subject. There the carrier misdelivered a diamond ring to a party skillfully posing as a known and reputable business firm but who was an impostor. The carrier's employee was not a participant in the fraud and did not appear to have been negligent. Yet the Alabama Court of Appeals held that the carrier was liable in such a case inasmuch as carriers are absolutely liable for misdelivery. We quote the language of the opinion for its emphatic flavor: [87]

> No circumstance of fraud, imposition or mistake will excuse the common carrier from responsibility for a delivery to the wrong person. The law exacts from him absolute certainty that the person to whom the delivery is made is the party rightfully entitled to the goods, and puts upon him the entire risk of mistakes in this respect, no matter from what cause occasioned, however justifiable the delivery may seem to have been, or however satisfactory the circumstances or proof of identity may have been to his mind; and no excuse has ever been allowed for a delivery to a person to whom the goods were not directed or consigned. If, therefore, the person who applies for the goods is not known to the carrier, and he has any doubt as to his being the consignee, he should require the most unquestionable proof of his identity.

In a more common type of misdelivery case, the bill of lading instructs the carrier to deliver to X, "notify Y on arrival." Instead of merely notifying Y, the carrier goes further and delivers to Y. Without fail the courts impose liability on the carrier for resulting loss.[88] A rather specialized form of misdelivery occurs in documentary sale transactions by the terms of which the carrier is to deliver the goods to a purchaser who presents a negotiable bill of lading. Instead the carrier delivers without requiring the purchaser of the goods to hand over the negotiable bill. The carrier is sometimes said to be "absolutely liable," though it is only breaking its contract of carriage with the shipper. Certainly the carrier's breach can cause loss to the shipper; the purchaser might get the goods but never pay. Indeed in a documentary sale where the buyer is to pay "cash against documents," the seller's agent is not supposed to hand the bill of lading over to the purchaser without simultaneously collecting the cash price of the goods in exchange, and the carrier is not supposed to hand over the goods to the purchaser without picking up the bill of lading. If all goes as planned, the purchaser will not get the goods without paying. But things do not go as planned when a carrier delivers without requiring that the purchaser present and surrender the negotiable bill. Of course, it does not follow that this failure is always the cause of any loss to the shipper-seller. In the Supreme Court case of Pere Marquette Ry. v. French & Co.,[89] the shipper-seller entered into a contract for

87. Id.

88. Rountree v. Lydick-Barmann Co., 150 S.W.2d 173 (Tex.Civ.App.1941).

89. 254 U.S. 538 (1921).

a cash sale of a carload of potatoes to be shipped to the buyer. The shipper-seller contracted also with the carrier pursuant to a negotiable bill of lading calling for the carrier to deliver only to the party presenting the bill for surrender. When the bill was sent to the shipper-seller's agent in the buyer's city, the agent handed over the bill without requiring the buyer to pay the cash price of the potatoes. Thereafter the carrier delivered the potatoes to the buyer without demanding the bill. The shipper-seller sued the carrier, contending that the carrier had, by delivering the car upon request without requiring surrender of the bill of lading, become liable for conversion of the potatoes. The Supreme Court, Brandeis, J., did not agree: [90]

> If instead of insisting upon the production and surrender of the bill it chooses to deliver in reliance upon the assurance that the deliveree has it, so far as the duty to the shipper is concerned, the only risk it runs is that the person who says that he has the bill may not have it. If such proves to be the case the carrier is liable for conversion and must, of course, indemnify the shipper for any loss which results. Such liability arises not from the statute but from the obligation which the carrier assumes under the bill of lading. . . . But where delivery is made to a person who has the bill or who has authority from the holder of it, and the cause of the shipper's loss is not the failure to require surrender of the bill but the improper acquisition of it by the deliveree or his improper subsequent conduct, the mere technical failure to require presentation and surrender of the bill will not make the delivery a conversion. . . . Similarly, in the case before us, the failure of the carrier to require production and surrender of the bill of lading did not cause the loss. The same loss would have resulted if the bill had been presented and surrendered. The real cause of the loss was the wrongful surrender of the bill of lading by the Indianapolis bank to Marshall & Kelsey. . . .

The carrier's so-called "absolute liability" for misdelivery can be extracted from the text of sections 88 and 89 of the FBLA, 7–403 of the Code, and the contract of carriage of the parties. We doubt that it clarifies analysis to say that the liability is absolute. After all the contract between shipper and carrier calls on the carrier to deliver to a given party, and when the carrier fails to do this, a breach of contract occurs. The liability of a carrier for misdelivery is no more and no less absolute than the liability of any party for breach of contract. Ordinarily it is no defense for the party who breaks his contract to respond that what he did under the circumstances was reasonable, or even that it was his very best effort.

Although courts generally state that the carrier is absolutely liable for misdelivery, they do recognize a special exception. This

---

90.  Id. at 546–47 (Brandeis, J.).

exception is formulated in various ways by different courts. The court in the Southern Express case formulated it as follows:

> Judge Elliott, after noting the various cases, mentions the only exception to the absolute liability of the carrier for a wrong delivery as, 'if the misdelivery is caused by misdirection or other negligence on the part of the shipper, or if fraud is perpetrated on him by a third person in such a manner that he really parts with the title to the goods to such third person, the carrier, rightfully acting on the faith of appearances which the owner himself has created, and in accordance with his directions, and without negligence, ought not to be held liable to him for delivering the goods to such third person, although the owner was imposed on by him.' 4 Elliott on Railroads (2d Ed.) § 1526a, pp. 257, 258.[91]

## NONDELIVERY

Turning away from misdelivery to nondelivery, under the Carmack Amendment, a carrier is also absolutely liable for nondelivery where the nondelivery is traceable to loss, damage, or destruction of the goods occurring while in the carrier's hands. However as we have already explained, the carrier may be able to escape liability for nondelivery by showing that the case fits in to one of five exceptions to the principle of absolute liability for loss or damage incorporated in the Carmack Amendment.[92] In cases to which the Carmack Amendment does not apply the law of most states is generally the same under section 7–309 of Article Seven.

Misdelivery and nondelivery by reason of loss or damage, then, are the two most common ways in which carriers break their delivery obligations. And under the structure of the FBLA and the structure of 7–403 of the Code, misdelivery, nondelivery, and cognate breaches only constitute *prima facie* breaches. The carrier may still escape liability by proving a "lawful excuse."

These lawful excuses include delivery to a party with paramount title, compliance with authorized changes in delivery instructions, and so forth. We will presently review the main types of excuses that a carrier may set forth. It is first necessary to explain the relevant allocations of burden of proof. Under both federal and state law it appears that the plaintiff must, to make out a *prima facie* case against the carrier for breach *of delivery obligations*, allege and introduce credible proof that (1) the carrier refused or failed to deliver on demand of the holder, the consignee, or any other person entitled under the bill of lading, (2) a good faith offer was made or could have been made on request to satisfy the carrier's lien, and (3) an offer was made or could have been made to sur-

---

91. Southern Express Co. v. C. L. Ruth & Son, 183 Ala. 493, 503–504, 59 So. 538, 541 (Ct.App.1912) (carrier misdelivered diamond ring to imposter).

92. See text accompanying notes 20–53 supra.

render for cancellation or notation any outstanding negotiable bill, properly indorsed.  Once the plaintiff introduces credible proof of the foregoing, it would seem that he need not introduce anything further in order to go to the jury.  Admittedly neither the FBLA nor the Code is explicit about this, but it seems to follow from the structure of FBLA section 88 and the structure of 7–403 of the Code.[93]  In some states it is necessary to consult special case law rules on burden of proof where the carrier fails to deliver by reason of loss, damage, or destruction of the goods.[94]

FBLA section 88 is explicit as to who must prove the existence *of a lawful excuse* for misdelivery, nondelivery, or the like:

> In case the carrier refuses or fails to deliver the goods,
> in compliance with a demand by the consignee or holder so
> accompanied, the burden shall be on the carrier to establish
> the existence of a lawful excuse for such refusal or failure.

Article Seven includes a comparable provision.  But the lawyer should consult local case law for any special rules on the burden of proving a lawful excuse where the nondelivery is by reason of loss, damage, or destruction of the goods in transit and where federal law does not apply.[95]

## LAWFUL EXCUSES FOR MISDELIVERY AND NONDELIVERY

We turn now to the various lawful excuses that the carrier might assert.  Under section 89 of the FBLA and 7–403(1)(a) of the Code, a carrier is excused from liability for misdelivery if it delivers to a party that has paramount title.  It will be recalled that a misdelivery under both the FBLA and Article Seven is simply a delivery to a party other than the person entitled to delivery by the terms of the bill of lading.  But the party so entitled might not be the owner of the goods.  Simply because a party is a consignee in a nonnegotiable bill or the holder of a negotiable bill, it does not follow that he is also the owner of the goods.  Indeed the consignee or holder might even be a thief as where a party steals goods, delivers them to a carrier, and procures a bill naming himself as consignee. When the facts are discovered, the carrier can deliver to the true owner without liability to the consignee or even to an innocent pur-chaser of a negotiable bill who took it by due negotiation from the thief-bailor.  On the other hand suppose the facts are not discovered until after the carrier has redelivered to the thief or his transferee. Here carriers are protected under section 90 of the FBLA and 7–404 and 7–303 of the Code at least when they act in good faith and observe reasonable commercial standards.  But the courts have

**93.**  Accord, R. Braucher, Documents of Title 31 (1958).

**94.**  See text accompanying note 24 supra.

**95.**  See text accompanying note 24 supra.

refused to excuse the carrier under section 90 of the FBLA when the evidence showed that the carrier went ahead and delivered in the face of a plain and unambiguous claim of right asserted by the true owner of the goods.[96]

The carrier is also excused for failure to discharge delivery obligations when the failure occurs because the goods were lost, destroyed, or damaged in circumstances where the carrier is not legally liable for the harm. This is generally true both under federal law and under 7–403(1) (b), although when the Code applies, the circumstances in which the carrier is not liable for such harm are not the same in all states.

The Code in 7–403(1) (d) recognizes a further basic excuse for nondelivery to a consignee, holder or other person entitled under the bill, namely that the shipper-seller properly exercised his right to stop delivery under 2–705 of the Code. To claim this excuse the carrier must show that the shipper-seller had a right of stoppage under 2–705 and that the carrier refused to deliver in response to the seller's exercise of that right. It is important to note that under 2–205(2) (d) the seller loses his right of stoppage if the outstanding bill is negotiable and is negotiated to the buyer. Moreover, under 2–705(3) (d), "if a negotiable document of title has been issued for goods the bailee is not obliged to obey a notification to stop until surrender of the document." But if the carrier chooses to stop, it will be excused, provided the bill has not been negotiated to the buyer. Whether a seller has a right to stop is state law and therefore Code law, but whether a carrier subject to the FBLA can claim an excuse on the ground that it obeyed stoppage instructions is a federal question. The FBLA in section 119 makes it clear that the carrier is not excused where the seller orders stoppage but the bill has been duly negotiated to a good faith purchaser. Presumably, we may infer that the carrier is otherwise excused when it refuses delivery because the shipper-seller has properly exercised a right of stoppage.[97]

A different excuse is set forth in 7–403(1) (e) which specifies that the carrier is not liable for refusal or failure to deliver to the party entitled to delivery under the terms of the bill if the carrier establishes "a diversion, reconsignment or other disposition pursuant to the provision of this Article (section 7–303) or tariff regulating such a right." Section 7–303 provides:

> (1) Unless the bill of lading otherwise provides, the carrier may deliver the goods to a person or destination other than that stated in the bill or may otherwise dispose of the goods on instructions from
>
> (a) the holder of a negotiable bill; or

96. E. g., Atlantic Coast Line R. R. Co. v. Roe, 91 Fla. 762, 109 So. 205 (1926) (party with right of property instructed carrier not to deliver to consignee of straight bill).

97. Kasden v. New York, N. H. & H. R. Co., 104 Conn. 479, 133 A. 573 (1926) (carrier can exercise right of stoppage against good faith purchaser of straight bill).

(b) the consignor on a non-negotiable bill notwithstanding contrary instructions from the consignee; or

(c) the consignee on a non-negotiable bill in the absence of contrary instructions from the consignor, if the goods have arrived at the billed destination or if the consignee is in possession of the bill; or

(d) the consignee on a non-negotiable bill if he is entitled as against the consignor to dispose of them.

(2) Unless such instructions are noted on a negotiable bill of lading, a person to whom the bill is duly negotiated can hold the bailee according to the original terms.

The foregoing provisions excuse the carrier from what would otherwise be an actionable misdelivery or nondelivery. They do not impose a duty on the carrier to undertake diversion or the like. The beauty of 7–303 is that it recognizes the facts of life; people do change their minds, and different people do sometimes give conflicting instructions. Under 7–303 the carrier can determine who is authorized to instruct the carrier to divert or the like. If the carrier follows instructions of the authorized party, then it will be excused from refusal or failure to deliver in accordance with the terms of the bill. In Koreska v. United Cargo Corp.[98] the carrier delivered copying paper to the buyer without taking up or demanding an outstanding negotiable bill of lading. This was a misdelivery constituting a *prima facie* breach of delivery obligations since the carrier who issues a negotiable bill undertakes to deliver to the holder thereof, and the purchaser here was not the holder. Yet the carrier claimed a lawful excuse on the ground that an agent of the seller orally authorized the delivery. The court cited 7–303(1) (a), denied this excuse, and stressed that only the holder of a negotiable bill is "entitled to authorize a diversion or modification." Here the seller was no longer the holder of the bill, rather it was in the hands of the seller's collecting bank.

Doubtless carriers would prefer to operate under 7–303 rather than under a provision like section 89 of the FBLA. Under the FBLA, a carrier who receives modifying or conflicting instructions cannot turn to a provision like 7–303 and determine whom to obey. Rather the carrier will be protected, that is, it will have a lawful excuse, only if it delivers to "a person lawfully entitled to the possession of the goods".[99] As Professor Braucher has noted, "This means that the carrier must either delay action until the conflicting claims are resolved or determine at its peril who is lawfully entitled." [100] If he chooses to delay, he may invoke section 97 of the FBLA and have a

**98.** 23 App.Div.2d 37, 258 N.Y.S.2d 432 (1st Dep't 1965).          (carrier converted household goods by delivering them to plaintiff's wife).

**99.** North American Van Lines, Inc. v. Heller, 371 F.2d 629 (5th Cir. 1967)

**100.** R. Braucher, Documents of Title, 39 (1958).

court decide to whom he should deliver.[101]  Of course, the carrier is not required to invoke section 97.  He may guess, and if he guesses correctly, he will not be liable.  In Turner Lumber & Investment Co. v. Chicago, R. F. & P. Ry. Co.,[102] the seller conditionally retained title to goods covered by a straight bill naming plaintiff–buyer as consignee.  The condition on which title was to pass did not occur (payment for the goods), but the consignee nonetheless sought to assume control of the goods.  The carrier followed the seller's orders and escaped liability to the consignee on the ground that the seller was "a person lawfully entitled to the possession of the goods" under section 89 of the FBLA.

There are other miscellaneous types of excuses that a carrier may invoke:  delivery to a third party pursuant to court order or other legal process, destruction of goods that have become hazardous, refusal of delivery during pendency of interpleader, plaintiff's ratification of an unauthorized delivery, and "release, satisfaction or any other personal defense against the claimant." [103]  There is a substantial body of case law on what constitutes ratification of an unauthorized delivery.[104]  It is enough for our purposes to set forth a clear case of ratification and a clear case of nonratification.  In Harford Metal Products Corp. v. Tidewater Express Lines,[105] the carrier delivered a machine to the buyer without requiring the buyer to surrender a negotiable bill of lading as per an agreement of the parties whereby the buyer was to procure the bill of lading by paying a sight draft. Thereafter the unpaid seller and the buyer agreed on new payment terms.  The court decided that the seller by entering into this new agreement ratified the carrier's wrongful delivery and thus relieved the carrier of liability for conversion.[106]  On the other hand in Griggs v. Stoker Service Co.,[107] the seller merely accepted "payment for part of the goods delivered to the wrong person," and the court concluded that seller's action did not constitute "a waiver of the wrongful delivery of the remainder." [108]

101.  FBLA § 97 provides:

> If more than one person claim the title or possession of goods, the carrier may require all known claimants to interplead, either as a defense to an action brought against him for nondelivery of the goods or as an original suit, whichever is appropriate.

102.  225 Mo.App. 1002, 34 S.W.2d 1009 (1931).

103.  § 7–403(1) (f).

104.  See Annot., 15 A.L.R.2d 807 (1951).

105.  183 Md. 105, 36 A.2d 677 (Ct.App. 1944).

106.  See also A. D. Blowers & Co. v. Canadian Pac. Ry. Co., 155 F. 935 (W.D.Wash.1907) (shipper sought and secured part payment for applies thereby ratifying unauthorized delivery).

107.  229 N.C. 572, 50 S.E.2d 914 (1948). See also Adel Precision Products Corp. v. Grand Trunk R. R. Co., 332 Mich. 519, 51 N.W.2d 922 (1952) (mere request for payment from unauthorized deliveree does not constitute ratification).

108.  229 N.C. at 580, 50 S.E.2d at 920.

## DELAYED DELIVERY

The FBLA, the Carmack Amendment, and Article Seven of the Code are all silent on the excuses available to a carrier when the plaintiff seeks damages flowing from delay which caused no harm to the goods themselves. Section 7–403(1) (b) does say that the carrier is not liable for "delay . . . of the goods for which the bailee is not liable," but the section adds nothing beyond this. We have already surveyed the various lawful excuses available to a carrier for loss, damage, and destruction of the goods while they are in the carrier's custody.[109] Recall that at common law and under federal statute the carrier is absolutely liable for such loss, damage, or destruction and that courts have carved out five exceptions to this principle of liability: (1) act of God; (2) act of public enemy; (3) act of shipper; (4) act of public authority; and (5) inherent vice or nature of goods. But with respect to damages caused by delay (other than damages to the goods themselves), the general principle of liability, at least under federal case law, is different. In the absence of special contract the carrier is only "obligated to transport goods with reasonable diligence and to make delivery of goods within a reasonable time." [110] Thus the carrier's liability for delay is not absolute; rather the carrier is generally liable only for negligent delay. "The carrier is not an insurer of promptness." [111] It follows that the carrier may defend against an action for damages for negligent delay by showing that the delay was "caused by the shipper or by an unavoidable accident or was due to such occurrences as could not have been anticipated in the exercise of reasonable prudence, diligence or care." [112]

## MEASURE OF DAMAGES FOR CARRIER'S FAILURE TO DISCHARGE DELIVERY OBLIGATIONS

Assuming that the plaintiff establishes a *prima facie* case that the carrier broke its delivery obligations, and assuming that the carrier cannot establish a valid defense, what measure of damages applies? Neither the FBLA, the Carmack Amendment, nor Article Seven spell out applicable damages measures. Case law is plentiful however, and it sanctions a variety of damages measures depending on the nature and circumstances of the breach. We have already discuss-

---

**109.** See text accompanying notes 25–53 supra.

**110.** Gold Star Meat Co. v. Union Pac. R. R. Co., 438 F.2d 1270, 1272 (10th Cir. 1971), citing Chicago & A. R. R. Co. v. Kirby, 225 U.S. 155 (1912).

**111.** Leo Lococo's Sons v. Louisville & N. R. R. Co., 259 Ky. 299, 302, 82 S.W. 2d 332, 333 (1935).

**112.** Id. at 303, 82 S.W.2d at 333. See also Coyne Bros. v. Oregon Short Line R. R. Co., 244 Ill.App. 359 (1927) (not liable if delay due to congestion at delivery point for which carrier not responsible); Taylor v. Duluth S. S. & A. Ry. Co., 139 Minn. 216, 166 N.W. 128 (1918) (not liable where delay due to necessity of investigation to determine title as between adverse claimants); Vencill v. Quincy R. R. Co., 132 Mo.App. 722, 112 S.W. 1030 (1908) (not liable if engine breaks down due to factors not reasonably anticipatable); Southern Pac. Co. v. H. Rothstein & Sons, 304 S.W.2d 383 (Tex.Civ.App. 1957) (not liable if reasonably unforeseeable strike causes delay).

ed the shipper's measure of damages when the carrier fails to deliver in whole or in part because of loss, damage, or destruction of the goods while in its custody.[113] The two other most common types of cases are those involving some form of misdelivery and those involving delayed delivery.

Suppose the carrier misdelivers to a party who is neither the consignee in a nonnegotiable bill nor the holder of an outstanding negotiable bill. The party who takes delivery fails to pay for the goods and either keeps them or returns them to the carrier. The shipper-seller sues the carrier. Here the courts generally state that the shipper-seller may recover the fair market value of the goods at the time and place of the misdelivery.[114] Where the seller has a contract of sale with a buyer, what the seller loses is the purchase price of the goods, and a court may permit him to recover this sum even though it is not necessarily the same as the fair market value of the goods.[115] The shipper-seller is not required to mitigate his damages by proceeding first against the misdeliveree, even where it has an undoubtedly valid breach of contract claim against the misdeliveree (a party who will often be the buyer). Rather the shipper-seller may proceed initially and directly against the carrier and recover the fair market value of the goods at the time and place of the misdelivery, subject to any valid limitation of liability clauses in the bill of lading.

Of course, a shipper-seller may choose to retrieve the goods and redispose of them himself. In that event the carrier will only be liable for the difference between their fair market value at the time and place of the wrong and the amount the seller receives from a good faith redisposition.

Another form of misdelivery occurs in the "C.O.D." cases where the carrier delivers without picking up the cash. Here the courts generally state that the shipper may recover damages in the amount the carrier was supposed to have collected (assuming that the carrier does not retrieve and retender the goods back to the shipper).[116] But if the goods are retrieved and retendered to the shipper, he must mitigate damages by reselling them "when he has an opportunity to sell them for the same price he expected to receive from the first sale." [117] Also at least one court has said that the carrier may reduce the seller's damages by showing that no collection could have been made on delivery anyway.[118]

113. See text accompanying notes 54–71 supra.

114. Griggs v. Stoker Service Co., 229 N.C. 572, 50 S.E.2d 914 (1948); Norfolk & W. Ry. Co. v. Aylor, 153 Va. 575, 150 S.E. 252 (1929).

115. E. g., Capitol Packing Co. v. Smith, 270 F.Supp. 36 (D.Mass.1967) (recovery of price where carrier delivered to buyer without picking up order bill).

116. E. g., National Van Lines, Inc. v. Rich Plan Corp., 385 F.2d 800 (5th Cir. 1967). See Annot., 27 A.L.R.3d 1320 (1969).

117. 385 F.2d at 803.

118. See Barnhart v. Henderson, 147 Neb. 689, 24 N.W.2d 854 (1947) (evidence sufficient to find a reasonable probability that carrier could have collected entire price of hogs sold).

Suppose that the carrier's only wrong takes the form of delayed delivery or delayed tender of delivery. What is the measure of damages for this breach? Again the FBLA, the Carmack Amendment and the Code are all silent on this important question. Here too case law is plentiful. First, the carrier does not become liable for the full fair market value of the goods, as in conversion.[119] Rather courts state the general rule to be that the plaintiff may recover the difference between the fair market value of the goods on the date and at the place where they were contracted to arrive and their fair market value on the date of arrival.[120] The Supreme Court has said that this rule "is at best but a convenient means of getting at the loss suffered. It may be discarded and other more accurate means resorted to, if, for special reasons, it is not exact or otherwise not applicable."[121] The Seventh Circuit recently cited this language in a case [122] in which the wholesale market value differential between the date plums should have arrived and the date when they did arrive amounted to seventy-four cents per crate. Since the buyer (A & P stores) planned to resell and did resell the plums at retail at the identical price it would have sold them had they arrived on time, the court concluded that the buyer suffered no damages at all and denied recovery.

In numerous cases plaintiffs have sought not only "direct" damages, but also consequential damages for breach of delivery obligations by carriers. Again statutory law is silent. The most frequently cited general principle of case law is the familiar one that the plaintiff may not recover special damages unless the possibility of their occurrence was fairly within the contemplation of the parties at the time of contracting.[123] We doubt that any such formula can be very revealing, and we offer several illustrative cases instead. Since most goods in transit are being delivered pursuant to a contract of sale, and since many buyers expect to resell these very goods, the question naturally arises whether a carrier that defaults on its delivery obligations incurs any liability to a buyer for profits the buyer would otherwise have realized on the resale. The recent cases will not encourage buyers. In Lowes Glove Co. v. Acme Fast Freight,[124] the plaintiff buyer sought to recover for profits it had expected to realize on the resale of gloves for the Christmas season which the carrier failed to deliver on time. The court denied recovery and said a plaintiff could recover such damages only when he proves that (1) at the time of making the contract of carriage, he already had entered an existing contract of resale, (2) the goods in the hands of the carrier

---

119. Railway Express Agency v. Huntress, 51 A.2d 379 (D.C.Ct.App.1947) (carrier's temporary loss of saxophone not conversion).

120. Gold Star Meat Co. v. Union Pac. R. R. Co., 438 F.2d 1270 (10th Cir. 1971).

121. Illinois Cent. R. R. Co. v. Crail, 281 U.S. 57 (1930).

122. Great Atlantic & Pacific Tea Co. v. Atchison, T. & S. F. Ry. Co., 333 F.2d 705 (7th Cir. 1964).

123. See Annot., 166 A.L.R. 1034 (1947).

124. 54 Misc.2d 429, 282 N.Y.S.2d 869 (Sup.Ct.1967). See also Annot., 42 A.L.R. 711 (1926).

were purchased to fulfill the resale contract, (3) such goods could not otherwise be procured in the market, and (4) the carrier was apprised of these facts at the time the contract was made. These are stringent conditions indeed.[125]

In Texas Instruments, Inc. v. Branch Motor Express Co.,[126] a federal district court allowed the consignor to recover the full value of a machine ruined in transit, but refused to grant special damages. The purchaser of the machine claimed that

> . . . this machine was purchased for adaptation to the task of producing circuit boards which plaintiff was already manufacturing using manual labor. When this machine was found to be damaged on arrival, it took six weeks before another machine could be obtained from the manufacturer. As a result of this delay plaintiff says it lost $3600 paid over a six week period to six employees performing manual operations at $100 a week, whose services would not have been needed if the machine could have been used. Further, plaintiff's witness testified that with the use of the machine plaintiff eventually increased production of circuit boards from $5000 a month to $35,000 a month, of which gross amount 40% was what witness described as "inventoriable profit", a term which he did not further define.[127]

In denying recovery for these special damages, the court stressed their speculative character and emphasized that "it does not appear that the damages claimed would obviously have resulted from any delay due to damage to the machine in transit, and defendant was never given any notice of special damages which might result." [128]

Peyton v. Railway Express Agency.[129] is a case that will sadden professors and other authors with greed in their hearts. There the plaintiff sought special damages in the form of lost royalties on a book manuscript that the carrier was allegedly negligent in failing to deliver to a "reader" who was to pass on it for publication. The manuscript was eventually returned to the plaintiff. The court refused to grant special damages even though the record showed that the plaintiff had fully apprised the carrier of what was involved. The damages were too speculative. There was no assurance that the manuscript would have been favorably received, let alone published. Moreover it would have been difficult to estimate the royalties.

Two other strange and recent cases may be noted. In both the court paid lip service to the principle that a carrier is liable for special damages when those damages are fairly within the parties' contemplation at the time of contracting. In American Synthetic

---

125. See Gardner v. Mid-Continent Grain Co., 168 F.2d 819 (8th Cir. (1948).

126. 308 F.Supp. 1228 (D.Mass.1970).

127. Id. at 1230.

128. Id.

129. 124 F.2d 430 (1941), rev'd on other grounds 316 U.S. 350 (1942).

Rubber Corp. v. Louisville & N. R. Co.,[130] the carrier mistakenly delivered a tank carload of ethylene oxide into storage facilities of the plaintiff in which the plaintiff stored another chemical called butadiene. The court remarked that "resulting damages were extensive," but whether the plaintiff recovered on remand is not known. In Marquette Cement Mfg. Co. v. Louisville & Nashville R. R. Co.,[131] the plaintiff sustained consequential damages when the defendant-carrier mistakenly delivered the wrong type of cement to the plaintiff who unknowingly used it but then had to redo the work. The court denied consequential damages and allowed the plaintiff only the fair market value of the shipment of cement and transportation charges. The court held that the consequential damages (the cost of redoing the work) were not "fairly supposed to have been within the contemplation of the parties at the time the contract was made." [132] We think any lawyer who seeks consequential damages against a carrier should be prepared to lose, no matter what his ingenuity or his client's equity.

To what extent may carriers limit their liability either for direct or consequential damages flowing from failure to discharge their delivery obligations? We have already discussed the power of carriers under the Carmack Amendment to limit their liability for loss, damage, or destruction of goods in its custody.[133] There we saw that carriers are generally entitled to vary their rates in relation to the value of the shipment and that compensation is supposed to bear a reasonable relation to the risk and responsibility that they assume. Do the foregoing principles for effective limitation of carriers' liability for loss or damage to the goods also apply to empower carriers similarly to limit their liability for misdelivery, delivery on improper conditions, delayed delivery, and the like? The case law indicates that, at least in circumstances to which the Carmack Amendment applies, the answer is affirmative.[134] Thus carriers may and often do limit the extent of their liability not only for loss, damage, or destruction of the goods, but also for other damages such as those arising from misdelivery, nondelivery, and delayed delivery.[135]

## § 21–4    Rights of Purchasers of Bills of Lading

When a carrier issues a bill of lading, it will either be negotiable or nonnegotiable. Article Seven and the FBLA distinguish between these types of bills in similar terms. Under Article Seven, a negotia-

---

130.   422 F.2d 462 (6th Cir. 1970).

131.   281 F.Supp. 944 (E.D.Tenn.1967), aff'd 406 F.2d 731 (6th Cir. 1969).

132.   281 F.Supp. at 950.

133.   See text accompanying notes 70–77 infra.

134.   Southeastern Express Co. v. Pastime Amusement Co., 299 U.S. 28 (1936) (delay case); Sorenson-Christian Indus. v. Railway Express Agency, 434 F.2d 867 (4th Cir. 1970) (delay case). Cf. American Synthetic Rubber Corp. v. Louisville N. R. R. Co., 422 F.2d 462 (6th Cir. 1970) (misdelivery case).

135.   The Code position is generally the same. § 7–309(2).

ble bill (an "order" bill) is one that requires the carrier to deliver to bearer or to the order of a named person.[136]   In addition where it is recognized in overseas trade, a bill is negotiable if it "runs to a named person or assigns." [137]   Under section 83 of the FBLA, a bill is negotiable if it states that "the goods are consigned or destined to the order of any person named in such bill."   All those bills that do not satisfy the foregoing Article Seven definitions are nonnegotiable. Section 82 of the FBLA is more explicit.   It says a bill is nonnegotiable (a "straight" bill) if it states that "the goods are consigned or destined to a specified person."

## PURCHASE OF NEGOTIABLE BILLS

The most common type of transaction in which a buyer purchases a negotiable bill occurs when a contract between him and his seller calls for him to pay "cash against documents."   Today this type of transaction is not common in domestic trade.   When a buyer agrees to pay "cash against documents," this ordinarily calls for him to pay a sight draft presented by the seller's agent in exchange for a negotiable bill of lading which entitles the buyer to procure the goods from the carrier and without which the carrier will not deliver to the buyer.   The seller is not obligated to hand over the bill (and thus control over the goods) until the buyer pays the draft, and the buyer does not have to pay in advance but only simultaneously with acquiring the bill (the means to procure the goods from the carrier when they arrive).

What rights does a good faith purchaser of a negotiable bill of lading acquire?   First, he generally gets the same rights against the carrier as the shipper had, including the right to have the carrier care for the goods and the right to have the carrier deliver in accordance with the purchaser's instructions.   Section 112 of the FBLA provides that the transferee gets "the direct obligation of the carrier to hold possession of the goods for him according to the terms of the bill as fully as if the carrier had contracted directly with him." Section 7–502(1) of Article Seven includes a similar provision.   Second, a good faith purchaser of a negotiable bill of lading gets (under section 111 of the FBLA) "such title to the goods as the person negotiating the bill had or had ability to convey to a purchaser in good faith for value.   .   ."   Under section 7–502 of Article Seven, the purchaser gets "title to the document and title to the goods." Third, once the carrier issues a negotiable bill covering the goods, whatever title to the goods that the bill covers can generally be transferred only by appropriately transferring the bill.   Transfer of the bill is generally the exclusive method of moving title to the goods. Under Article Seven for a purchaser of a negotiable bill to acquire the foregoing bundle of rights, he must take by "due negotiation." In the preceding chapter we treated the Article Seven requirements

136.   § 7–104.                         137.   § 7–104(1) (b).

of due negotiation.[138]   Under the FBLA, for the purchaser to acquire the foregoing bundle of rights, he must "give value therefor in good faith, without notice," and take by indorsement or delivery as provided in sections 107 and 108.

Even though the transferee of a negotiable bill acquires the foregoing bundle of rights, he still takes risks.   Under Article Seven these risks are generally the same for transferees of bills of lading as they are for transferees of warehouse receipts.   We will therefore not repeat our earlier discussion of the relevant Article Seven provisions.[139]   We will only survey the applicable FBLA provisions.   One risk that a good faith purchaser of a negotiable bill runs is simply that his bill will be lost, stolen, or destroyed before he uses it to pick up the goods.   Section 94 of the FBLA authorizes a court to order delivery upon proof of the loss, etc., and upon posting a bond. Another risk is that the bill of lading will prove spurious.   The bill may be wholly spurious, as where it is issued by a forger covering non-existent goods in the hands of a nonexistent carrier.   Here section 114(a) of the FBLA gives our purchaser a good claim against his transferor for breach of warranty.   But the bill might be only partially spurious, as where it covers actual goods but was issued by a party without actual authority to issue it.   Here again section 114(d) may give our purchaser a good claim against his transferor.

Assuming that the bill of lading is genuine, it still might be altered prior to purchase.   Section 93 of the FBLA provides:

> Any alteration, addition, or erasure in a bill after its issue without authority from the carrier issuing the same either in writing or noted on the bill, shall be void whatever be the nature and purpose of the change, and the bill shall be enforceable according to its original tenor.

There is always the risk that the goods not only do not now exist, but that they never did exist at all, even when the carrier issued the bill covering them.   A defrauder may induce an employee of the carrier to issue a bill for nonexistent goods.   Or a shipper may induce the carrier to issue a bill on representations that goods will be delivered to the carrier when for some reason they are not.   Section 102 of the FBLA deals with "non-receipt:" [140]

> If a bill of lading has been issued by a carrier or on his behalf by an agent or employee the scope of whose actual or apparent authority includes the receiving of goods and issuing bills of lading therefor for transportation in commerce among the several States and with foreign nations, the carrier shall be liable to (a) the owner of goods covered by a straight bill subject to existing right of stoppage in transitu

---

138.   See Ch. 20 text accompanying notes 66–72, supra.

139.   See Section 20–4 supra.

140.   Compare UCC § 7–301 with FBLA § 102.   See also Annot., 67 A.L.R.2d 1028 (1959); Annot., 130 A.L.R. 1315 (1941); Annot., 74 A.L.R. 1382 (1931).

or (b) the holder of an order bill, who has given value in good faith, relying upon the description therein of the goods, or upon the shipment being made upon the date therein shown, for damages caused by the nonreceipt by the carrier of all or part of the goods upon or prior to the date therein shown, or their failure to correspond with the description thereof in the bill at the time of its issue.

The carrier's liability under the foregoing section runs to "holders of order bills" who actually rely on the representation implicit in the bill that the carrier did receive the goods. The Eighth Circuit applied FBLA section 102 in the famous case of Chicago & N. W. Ry. Co. v. Stephens National Bank.[141] A bank bought and paid for bills covering eggs. Yet the eggs were never loaded, and the carrier never transported the cars named in the bills. The shipper-seller became bankrupt, and the bank found itself out the $5,200 it had paid for the bills. In an action against the carrier, the bank prevailed, even though the carrier had inserted in the bill of lading the words "shipper's load and count," a disclaimer that section 101 of the FBLA specifically validates. The court reasoned:[142]

> The weakness of the carrier's position here, it seems to us, lies in the fact that it issued the bills at a time when the cars were not loaded, when they were not sealed, when the freight was not paid, and when it had received neither the cars nor any order from the shipper to move them. In fact, the bills were issued at a time when all that the carrier had done was to place the cars for loading. There was nothing actually fraudulent in the issuance of these bills by the carrier, and it was following a custom with respect to this shipper which, over a period of eleven years, had caused no loss to anyone. The shipper, however, had no right to receive the bills at the time they were issued, and the carrier, by issuing the bills at the time it did, enabled the shipper to defraud the bank. The representations in the bills as to the contents of the cars, by virtue of the notation "shipper's load and count," were the representations of the shipper. The other representations, however, as to seals, as to prepayment of the freight, and as to the receipt of the cars for transportation, were those of the carrier, and they were not true when made, nor did they ever become true.

> . . . Therefore, if we are correct in our position that these bills were issued at a time and under circumstances when they should not have been issued, and that they contained representations by the carrier which were false, it would follow that the conclusion reached by the court below

141. 75 F.2d 398 (8th Cir. 1935), cert. denied 295 U.S. 738 (1935).

142. 75 F.2d at 401.

that, as between the bank and the carrier, the carrier must bear the loss occasioned by the shipper's fraud, was justified.

This question naturally arises: How was the Eighth Circuit able to get around the "shipper's load and count" disclaimer? It might be argued that this disclaimer is valid only when the shipper actually does do *some* loading and that since he did not here load a single egg, the disclaimer could not come into operation. But the Eighth Circuit specifically rejected any such distinction, saying, "We cannot convince ourselves that if one egg or one case of eggs had been loaded into each of the cars furnished by the carrier to the shipper here, that fact could have affected the result of this case." [143] Thus, "shipper's weight load and count" disclaimers are invalid in such cases (at least in the Eighth Circuit), anything to the contrary in FBLA section 101 notwithstanding.[144] In a case ten years earlier,[145] the Eighth Circuit held a carrier liable to a grain dealer who had bought bills reciting 66,000 pounds of wheat when only 45,590 pounds were in the car. The bills also included disclaimers reciting "in apparent good order" and "weights subject to correction." However the court intimated that if the bills had recited "shipper's weight, load and count," the carrier would not have been liable. Perhaps there is a distinction between eggs and wheat! Or if not this then perhaps carriers can rely on "shipper's weight, load and count" at least where the shipper loads a substantial part of the total (not just an egg or two).[146]

---

143. Id.

144. FBLA § 101 provides:

When package freight or bulk freight is loaded by a shipper and the goods are described in a bill of lading merely by a statement of marks or labels upon them or upon packages containing them, or by a statement that the goods are said to be goods of a certain kind or quantity, or in a certain condition, or it is stated in the bill of lading that packages are said to contain goods of a certain kind or quantity or in a certain condition, or that the contents or condition of the contents of packages are unknown, or words of like purport are contained in the bill of lading, such statements, if true, shall not make liable the carrier issuing the bill of lading, although the goods are not of the kind or quantity or in the condition which the marks or labels upon them indicate, or of the kind or quantity or in the condition they were said to be by the consignor. The carrier may also by inserting in the bill of lading the words "Shipper's weight, load, and count," or other words of like purport, indicate that the goods were loaded by the shipper and the description of

them made by him; and if such statement be true, the carrier shall not be liable for damages caused by the improper loading or by the nonreceipt or by the misdescription of the goods described in the bill of lading: Provided, however, Where the shipper of bulk freight installs and maintains adequate facilities for weighing such freight, and the same are available to the carrier, then the carrier, upon written request of such shipper and when given a reasonable opportunity so to do, shall ascertain the kind and quantity of bulk freight within a reasonable time after such written request, and the carriers shall not in such cases insert in the bill of lading the words "Shipper's weight," or other words of like purport, and if so inserted contrary to the provisions of this section, said words shall be treated as null and void and as if not inserted therein.

145. Chicago & N. W. Ry. Co. v. Bewsher, 6 F.2d 947 (8th Cir. 1925).

146. See People's Sav. Bank v. Pere Marquette Ry. Co., 235 Mich. 399, 209 N.W. 182 (1926) (sixteen sacks where 360 sacks were required).

"Misdescription" in the bill is a vice that can materialize in many forms (some of which overlap with nonreceipt) as for instance mislabeling, misdating, misstating quantity,[147] and so on. Section 102 of the FBLA says that the carrier is liable to relying holders of negotiable bills for failure of the goods to correspond to the description in the bill at the time of issue. A carrier is liable for the fraudulent misdescription of an employee.[148] But what if the employee is merely negligent? The problem is posed nicely in a non-FBLA case that we believe is also good law under the FBLA. In Chicago, R. I. & P. Ry. Co. v. Cleveland,[149] the carrier's employee issued bills describing the goods as "sixty-one bales of cotton" when in fact the bales contained grabbots—oilmill motes composed of small particles of refuse cotton. In a generic sense grabbots are cotton but not in the commercial world. In holding the carrier liable to the receiptholder for the misdescription, the Oklahoma Supreme Court stated:[150]

> In the case at bar the agent for the defendant railway company had special warning and notice that the produce to be shipped was not the ordinary merchantable cotton, but was grabbots, but, notwithstanding such notice, the agent issued the bill for the product as cotton without any qualifying or modifying term or description which would, in any manner, give notice to any person who might deal on the representations contained in the bill. This we think was a failure to exercise ordinary care, and negligence for which the railway company is liable.

In the *Cleveland* case the carrier's employee described the goods in the bills as cotton when he should have known that the goods should not have been labeled "cotton." But the shipper, rather than the carrier, usually supplies the information that the carrier uses to write the description in the bill, and frequently the carrier's employee does not know and has no reason to know of any inaccuracy. Thus, for example, if the shipper sends sealed cartons of "poultry" and the cartons turn out to contain rabbits and eggs, the carrier is not liable.[151] Indeed in such a case a carrier is not liable even if it does not insert the usual disclaimer in the bill "said to contain" or the like. As one court put it:[152]

> It is unnecessary for the carrier to insert in the bill the words, "shipper's weight, load and count," or other words of like import, when it plainly appears that contents are unknown to the carrier and that the words of description are the words of the consignor and are superfluous except for the purposes of identification.

---

147. See Annot., 39 A.L.R.2d 329 (1955).

148. Gleason v. Seaboard Air Line Rw. Co., 278 U.S. 349 (1929) (employee forged bill of lading).

149. 61 Okla. 64, 160 P. 328 (1916).

150. Id.

151. Josephy v. Panhandle & S. F. Ry., 235 N.Y. 306, 139 N.E. 277 (1923). See Annot., 1 A.L.R.3d 736 (1965).

152. 235 N.Y. at 309, 139 N.E. at 278.

But, where it does not plainly appear that the contents are unknown to the carrier, the carrier is wise to insert a disclaimer to the effect that it does not know the contents or that the goods are in apparent good order, or that the shipper loaded, etc., as appropriate.  This puts the purchaser of the bill on notice, and generally the purchaser cannot recover for misdescription against a disclaiming carrier, provided that the disclaimer is truthful (that is, for example, the contents were truly unknown) and further provided that the carrier was not negligent.  It is often said that common carriers generally may not disclaim liability for their own negligence although they may by contract limit the amount of their liability.[153]

The transferor of a bill, *qua transferor*, does not warrant to the transferee either that the carrier received the goods or that the bill properly describes them.[154]

Numerous cases have arisen in which the plaintiff sues the carrier for damages to the goods caused by improper loading.  Of course, if the carrier did the improper loading, it is liable.[155]  Also if the shipper did the improper loading, then the general principle is that the shipper is responsible, and the carrier can set up "shipper's act" as a defense to liability under the Carmack Amendment.[156]  However, there is an important exception to this principle.  Even if the shipper loaded, it is often said that the carrier is still liable for damage caused by improper loading "if the defect is patent." [157]  Courts hold that it is the carrier's duty to reject the goods proposed for shipment or to reload them properly in such cases.  If the carrier does not reject or reload and "sees fit to receive them, he assumes to carry them as they are, and his full common law liability as carrier attaches to the contract of carriage." [158]  We have already seen that this liability under the Carmack Amendment is absolute and that it cannot be disclaimed.[159]  Yet, "shipper's load and count" often appears in the bill of lading.  What this language comes to in such a case is not clear.  If because of the improper loading, the carrier can fit itself into the shipper's act exception, the carrier is not liable anyway, and any disclaimer is superfluous.  On the other hand if the purchaser can show that the carrier ought to have remedied the improper loading, then the carrier will be liable despite any disclaimer clause inserted by the carrier that the shipper loaded.  Thus, the disclaimer would appear

---

153.  See, e. g., Bisso v. Inland Waterways Corp., 349 U.S. 85, 90–91 (1955).

154.  FBLA § 114;  UCC § 7–507.

155.  Carrier Corp v. Furness, Withy & Co., 131 F.Supp. 19 (E.D.Pa.1955) (steel sheets not properly blocked, braced, and chocked).  See Annot., 44 A.L.R.2d 993 (1955); Annot., 149 A.L.R. 644 (1944).

156.  E. g., St. Louis-San Francisco Ry. Co. v. Glow Electric Co., 35 Ohio App.

291, 172 N.E. 425 (1929).  See also text accompanying notes 38–47 supra.

157.  Modern Tool Corp. v. Pennsylvania R. R. Co., 100 F.Supp. 595, 598 (D.N.J. 1951).  See Minneapolis, St. P. & S. S. M. R. R. Co. v. Metal-Matic, Inc., 323 F.2d 903 (8th Cir. 1963).

158.  Northwestern Marble & Tile Co. v. William, 128 Minn. 514, 518, 151 N.W. 419, 420 (1915).

159.  See text accompanying notes 20–23 supra.

to have no legal effect on the carrier's liability for improper loading. However some courts cite the disclaimer to shift to the purchaser the burden of proving the carrier's independent negligence, a burden that the carrier might otherwise have to discharge.[160]

A carrier's liability for loss or damage traceable to improper loading is but an instance of the carrier's absolute liability under the Carmack Amendment for loss or damage to goods in its custody. But we also saw in Section 21–3 that the carrier may fail to deliver for reasons besides loss or damage to the goods and that here again the carrier will not always be liable, that is, it may have a lawful excuse or defense against an action for nondelivery.[161] To put this another way, the good faith purchaser of a negotiable bill takes the bill subject to certain excuses and defenses that a bailee may lawfully set up against a purchaser of the bill covering the goods.

One further risk to a good faith purchaser of a negotiable bill under the FBLA may be called the "paramount title" risk. Generally this purchaser not only gets title but also paramount title. Yet there are exceptions; he does not defeat a true owner of goods from whom they were stolen, no matter how clever the intervening shenanigans.[162] Nor does this purchaser get full title to the goods when he buys a bill bearing a forged endorsement, if a genuine endorsement is necessary to his title.[163] Also, he can lose title under FBLA section 118 if he leaves the negotiable bill in the hands of his own transferor who thereafter wrongfully negotiates it to another good faith purchaser. But under FBLA section 119 our purchaser cuts off a prior seller's lien and a prior seller's right of stoppage in transit. Furthermore, he prevails in the varied circumstances recited in FBLA section 117:

> The validity of the negotiation of a bill is not impaired by the fact that such negotiation was a breach of duty on the part of the person making the negotiation, or by the fact that the owner of the bill was deprived of the possession of the same by fraud, accident, mistake, duress, loss, theft, or conversion if the person to whom the bill was negotiated, or a person to whom the bill was subsequently negotiated gave value therefor in good faith, without notice of the breach of duty, or fraud, accident, mistake, duress, loss, theft, or conversion.

What of clashes between a good faith purchaser of a bill of lading governed by the FBLA and a party claiming a security interest in the goods under Article Nine? Neither the FBLA nor Article Nine confront this question. The Uniform Commercial Code includes provisions on an analogous conflict between a purchaser of a bill governed by Article Seven and a secured creditor under Article Nine.[164] We

---

160. Modern Tool Corp. v. Pennsylvania R. R. Co., 100 F.Supp. 595 (D.N.J. 1951).

161. See text accompanying notes 95–108 supra.

162. FBLA § 89(a).

163. FBLA §§ 83; 109; 112.

164. §§ 7–502; 7–503; 9–201; 9–312.

believe courts will invoke those provisions by analogy to resolve any conflicts between FBLA and Article Nine claimants.

## PURCHASE OF NONNEGOTIABLE BILLS OF LADING

Under FBLA section 82 a nonnegotiable ("straight") bill is one which states that "the goods are consigned or destined to a specified person." A transferee of a straight bill is entitled to notify the carrier and thereby become "the direct obligee of whatever obligations the carrier owed to the transferor of the bill." [165] Also by notifying the carrier the transferee of a straight bill defeats garnishing or levying creditors of the transferor and subsequent purchasers who buy the goods from the transferor.[166] But generally a purchaser of a straight bill gets only the title to the document and the title to the goods that his transferor has or has power to convey.[167] Thus if the transferor has neither title nor power to transfer title, the transferee will not get title to the goods. Also in the language of FBLA section 109, "A straight bill cannot be negotiated free from existing equities, and the indorsement of such a bill gives the transferee no additional right." These "existing equities" may be equities of prior transferors or of the carrier. Section 117 of the FBLA illustratively lists types of equities that a prior transferor may assert, including that he was deprived of the bill by fraud, mistake, duress, loss, or conversion, or that a transfer of the bill was in breach of authority.

In the recent case of G. A. C. Commercial Corp. v. Wilson,[168] the carrier asserted an illustrative "existing equity" under FBLA section 109. There the court refused to permit the consignee of a straight bill to recover where the carrier had not received any goods covered by the bill it had issued. The court's theory was that only an "owner of goods covered by a straight bill can recover and it is not possible for there to be an owner of nonexistent goods." One is tempted to dismiss this as arid conceptualism, but the court also said:

> But the overriding policy considerations in the Act look the other way on the issue of liability. First, "[t]here is nothing in the statute to indicate that the mere omission of the words 'Shipper's weight, load, and count' in and of itself makes the carrier liable for damages to goods improperly loaded. The omission of the statutory words merely serves to shift upon the carrier the burden of proving that the goods were improperly loaded by the shipper, and that the damage ensued from that cause." Modern Tool Corp. v. Pennsylvania R. Co., 100 F.Supp. 595, 596–597 (D.N.J.1951); see U.C.C. § 7–401(4). According to the allegations the true culprits in this case were the shipper and its agents; there is no reason to saddle defendant Norwood with liability sim-

165. FBLA § 112.

166. Id.

167. Id.

168. 271 F.Supp. 242 (S.D.N.Y.1967). See also Martin Jessee Motors, Inc. v. Reading Co., 87 F.Supp. 318 (E.D.Pa. 1949), aff'd 181 F.2d 766 (3d Cir. 1950).

ply because it did not insert the "Shipper's weight, load, and count" language in the bills. In addition, practicality demands loading arrangements such as those here, where the shipper places his goods aboard and seals the railroad car which the carrier has provided. Section 21 of the Act, 49 U.S.C. § 101, anticipates that shippers are expected to do much of the counting and loading on their own sidings or spur tracks. The rapid flow of commerce might well be hindered if the carrier in every instance were charged with ascertaining whether in fact there were goods behind every one of its straight bills.

Moreover, denying security value to a straight bill of lading does not work a hardship upon banks and other commercial institutions. G. A. C., as a knowledgeable lender, is fully aware of the risks inherent in straight bills, and could well have required order bills to protect itself. See Chicago & Northwestern Ry. v. Stevens Nat'l Bank, 75 F.2d 398 (8th Cir. 1935). It nevertheless chose to rely upon straight bills to lend money to the now bankrupt St. Lawrence at a profitable rate of interest. Wiser now, G. A. C. seeks to shift its loss to Norwood, an undoubtedly solvent defendant. The Federal Bills of Lading Act protects against this type of hindsight by requiring the lender to accept this kind of security subject to the defenses between the carrier and the shipper.[169]

Apart from the doctrine of the *Wilson* case, the FBLA liabilities of a carrier to a purchaser of a nonnegotiable bill of lading for nonreceipt, misdescription, and damage caused by improper loading are generally the same as its liabilities to a purchaser of a negotiable bill.[170]

## § 21–5  Rights of Pledgees of Bills of Lading

In today's commercial world at least three types of transactions are familiar in which bills of lading are used to help secure loans, advances, and similar credit. All three involve sales of goods. In two the borrower is the seller who is, in effect, seeking to accelerate receipt of his money from the buyer, while in the other transaction, the borrower is the buyer. Sellers sometimes enter into *cash* deals with far-off buyers. Under the Code, unless otherwise agreed, a cash buyer need not pay until the goods arrive at his locale.[171] This might take weeks; meanwhile, our seller would be unpaid. Is there any way he can accelerate receipt of his money? He might try to get his buyer to pay in advance, but often this will be unavailing. On the eve of shipment, he might try to borrow from his lender against the security of his invoices, but contract rights are notoriously precarious security,

169.  271 F.Supp. at 248.

170.  See text accompanying notes 140–161 supra.

171.  § 2–310.

and the prospective lender might simply refuse to lend. This very same lender will more willingly make an advance to the seller on the eve of shipment if the seller sets things up so that the lender will have a security interest in the goods being sold that he can realize on in the event the buyer on the other end refuses to pay and the financer's recourse against the seller proves unavailing. Not surprisingly, the Code sets forth ways in which sellers can arrange such security. Section 2–505(1) provides as follows:

> (1) Where the seller has identified goods to the contract by or before shipment:
>
> (a) his procurement of a negotiable bill of lading to his own order or otherwise reserves in him a security interest in the goods. His procurement of the bill to the order of a financing agency or of the buyer indicates in addition only the seller's expectation of transferring that interest to the person named.
>
> (b) a non-negotiable bill of lading to himself or his nominee reserves possession of the goods as security but except in a case of conditional delivery (subsection (2) of Section 2—507) a non-negotiable bill of lading naming the buyer as consignee reserves no security interest even though the seller retains possession of the bill of lading.

In one type of arrangement, the seller will procure a negotiable bill of lading to the seller's order covering the goods to be sold, draw a draft on the buyer, and indorse both to its financer. In return, the financer will either buy this bundle of rights outright at a discount or will make an advance to the seller. In either event, the seller will receive on the eve of shipment a credit to his account and will not have to wait to get his money out of the deal. Under 2–506(1) and 2–104 (2), the seller's financer succeeds to the seller's right to have the buyer pay and to the seller's 2–505(1) security interest, a security interest that arises under Article Two, not under Article Nine, and therefore that need not comply with 9–203, 9–204, or 9–303 of Article Nine.

The lender will thereafter send the draft and bill of lading to an agent in the buyer's locale with instructions to hold and present same to the buyer upon arrival of the goods after the buyer has had a reasonable opportunity to inspect them. Since the buyer only agreed to pay cash and did not agree to pay "cash against documents," the seller and his lender must take care not to present the draft and demand payment prior to the arrival of the goods. They must also take care to see that the carrier is instructed to permit inspection on arrival prior to payment.[172] Usually all will go well, and the buyer will pay the lender's agent and thereby in effect "repay" the advance the financer made to the seller on the eve of shipment.

172. §§ 2–310; 2–513.

In a second and less common type of transaction the buyer not merely agrees to pay cash, but further agrees to pay "cash against documents." When so, the lender's agent need not hold the draft until arrival of the goods but may present it upon receipt which will usually be well before the goods arrive.[173] It follows that the buyer is not entitled to withhold payment until the goods arrive for inspection.

Suppose that after the seller ships, the buyer immediately repudiates, or suppose that the buyer simply refuses to pay the buyer's agent on proper presentment of the drafts. Since the goods have been shipped, the lender will be out the amount it credited to the seller's account on the eve of shipment and will be holding the drafts plus the bill of lading. Frequently, the lender will, by the terms of its agreement with the seller, be entitled to debit the seller's account and return the documents to the seller. But what if the lender either does not have this right or its exercise proves unavailing? In these circumstances the lender will be a party with an Article Two security interest in the bill of lading and in the goods the bill covers.[174] The lender can then simply dispose of the bill or the goods and apply the proceeds on the amount advanced. Indeed if the buyer defaults or repudiates while the goods are en route, the lender can even stop the goods in transit under 2–506(1).

Thus a seller may use a bill of lading to help secure advances from its financer both in ordinary cash deals and in deals calling for "cash against documents." Similarly when a buyer induces its lender to issue a letter of credit[175] to the seller as beneficiary, the willingness of the issuer to issue the credit in the first place may depend partly on the fact that it receives bills of lading covering the goods when it honors drafts. If after honoring drafts and thus paying the seller, the issuer finds that the buyer is welching on its agreement to reimburse the issuer, the issuer may be able to realize on the security it has in the form of the bills of lading covering the goods (an Article Nine security interest). Comment 2 to 9–303 makes it plain that the issuer still retains a security interest in the goods under certain circumstances even after it has turned the bill of lading over to the buyer:

> The following example will illustrate the operation of subsection (2): A bank which has issued a letter of credit honors drafts drawn under the credit and receives possession of the negotiable bill of lading covering the goods shipped. Under Sections 9—304(2) and 9—305 the bank now has a perfected security interest in the document and the goods. The bank releases the bill of lading to the debtor for the purpose of procuring the goods from the carrier and selling them. Under Section 9—304(5) the bank continues to have a perfected security interest in the document and goods

---

173. § 2–513.

174. §§ 2–505; 2–506; 2–707.

175. On letters of credit, see Ch. 18 supra.

for 21 days. The bank files before the expiration of the 21 day period. Its security interest now continues perfected for as long as the filing is good. The goods are sold by the debtor. The bank continues to have a security interest in the proceeds of sale to the extent stated in Section 9—306(3).

The lender who makes advances against the security of bills of lading generally runs the same risks as one who makes advances against the security of warehouse receipts, a topic we have explored in Section 20–5. There we saw that Articles Two, Seven, and Nine of the Code govern; the same is true with respect to bills of lading used for security except to the extent that FBLA provisions displace Article Seven. As we have already seen,[176] the FBLA includes provisions on most of the problems that a transferee for security of a federal bill of lading may confront: that the original shipper was a thief, that the carrier never did receive the goods, that the bill itself was wholly spurious or altered in some way, that a necessary endorsement on the bill was forged, that the bill misdescribed the goods, that the bill or the goods was lost or destroyed, that the carrier or a prior transferor acted without actual or apparent authority, that the transferor was, after the transfer, double-dealing in some way, and so on. We have already seen that under the FBLA, just as under Article Seven, a transferee gets better protection against these risks if he takes a negotiable bill by due negotiation than if he takes a nonnegotiable bill.[177]

---

176. See text accompanying notes 139–164 supra.

177. See text accompanying notes 165–170 supra.

# CHAPTER 22

# SCOPE OF ARTICLE NINE

*Analysis*

Sec.
22–1.  Introduction.
22–2.  The Basic Article Nine Scope Provision—9–102(1).
22–3.  —— Security Interest or Lease?
22–4.  —— Consignments as Security Interests (Herein, too, of 2–326).
22–5.  Surety's Subrogation Rights not a Security Interest.
22–6.  Extent Article Nine Applies to Realty Interests.
22–7.  A Note on the 9–104 Exclusions.
22–8   Applicability of Article Nine to Sales of Accounts, Contract Rights and Chattel Paper.
22–9.  Conflict of Laws Problems.
22–10. Applicability of Article Nine to "Security Interests" that Arise Under Article Two on Sales.
22–11. State and Federal Law that Over-Rides Article Nine.

## § 22–1  Introduction

The title to Article Nine reads: "Secured Transactions; Sales of Accounts, Contract Rights and Chattel Paper." This language indicates that the Article applies to two kinds of deals: certain secured transactions and certain sales. But here simplicity endeth. To decide whether the Article governs a transaction, the lawyer must usually turn at least to sections 1–201(37), 9–102, 9–103, and 9–104, each of which bristles with problems. After we present essential historical background, we will in the rest of this chapter analyze and discuss these scope provisions and will take account of the cases applying them.[1]

Although Article Nine is the most innovative of all the Code articles, it did not spring full grown from the forehead of Grant Gilmore or Allison Dunham, or even Karl Llewellyn.[2] The draftsmen drew heavily on a large body of pre-Code personal property security law. In pre-Code days, the lawyer had to work with a variety of security devices, each governed by its own law:

*The pledge.* The debtor, who was called a "pledgor," transferred possession of an asset to the lender, the "pledgee," who retained pos-

---

1. Upon its enactment, Article Nine was also the victim of more amendments than any other Code Article. Partly for this reason, a committee constituted by the Code's Permanent Editorial Board has prepared a completely new version of the Article. We will refer to this new version from time to time in this and the upcoming chapters, even though it is highly unlikely to be adopted anywhere very soon.

2. All three seem to have come upon the idea of a unitary security device at about the same time. 1 G. Gilmore, Security Interests in Personal Property § 9.2 at 290 n. 2 (1965). The most important early general discussion of Article Nine is Gilmore, The Secured Transactions Article of the Commercial Code, 16 Law & Contemp. Prob. 27 (1951).

session of the asset until the debtor paid his debt.  In modern law, the pledgee could sell the collateral on default, and keep sufficient proceeds to satisfy the debt.

*The chattel mortgage.*  The debtor, who was called a "mortgagor" would, by agreement, give the lender, the "mortgagee", a security interest, called a "mortgage," in a specific asset on which the mortgagee could realize upon default.  Usually, debtor retained possession. Eventually, the lender had to "record" his mortgage publicly to perfect it against third parties.  Traditionally, this device was used to borrow against assets the debtor had already acquired.

*The "conditional sale."*  This device was most commonly used to secure a seller's extension of credit to a buyer.  What was "conditional" about it?  The seller was said to retain security title to the asset sold.  The buyer would get full title *if* he paid.  This was the condition.  In some states, differences developed between the remedies of chattel mortgagees and conditional vendors upon default.  For example, in some states, the conditional vendor was required to "elect" between repossessing the goods and suing for the price.  He could not both repossess and sue for any difference between the value of the repossessed goods and the unpaid price.  In some states the conditional vendor, unlike the chattel mortgagee, was not required to "record."

*The "trust receipt."*  Among other things this device was widely used to "floor plan" the inventory of auto dealers.  In the standard transaction there were three parties: the manufacturer, who would not itself extend credit directly to the dealer; the lender, who was called an "entruster" in trust receipt parlance; and the dealer, called the "trustee."  Under history's most difficult statute, the Uniform Trust Receipts Act (which was ultimately adopted in 33 states) the lender-entruster publicly filed notice of intent to engage in trust receipt financing with the dealer.  Usually the manufacturer then shipped goods by carrier in the name of the lender, who paid the manufacturer on behalf of the dealer thereby acquiring a security interest in the goods.  When the goods arrived, the lender released ("entrusted") the goods in the carrier's hands to the dealer, who signed a "trust receipt" acknowledging receipt and the lender-entruster's security interest.  This was one pattern; others evolved.  Observe that in property law parlance, the "trust" receipt device is a misnomer.  But little is in a name.

*The "factor's lien."*  This device was often used to secure loans against inventory already acquired, whether the inventory be raw materials, work in progress, or goods in final manufactured form. As with all the foregoing devices except the pledge, the lender ordinarily did not take possession of the collateral.  Laws varied on whether public notice was required.  There had to be a written agreement for the "lien."  The laws governing the factor's lien device (and also the chattel mortgage and the trust receipt) did not, as they evolved in most states, permit the debtor to agree that his after-acquired property also effectively secured the lender's loan.  The factor's lien did not have to be the lien of a "factor," a selling agent.  But in the early days the lien typically was that of a factor, for the factor was a selling agent who had grown stronger than his principal and had lent him money against the security of inventory.

The foregoing list of pre-Code chattel security devices is not exhaustive.  There were others such as field warehousing, the equipment trust, the corporate indenture, and devices for use of accounts receivable as security.  The laws governing the various kinds of security devices in a particular jurisdiction could and did differ in significant respects.  Some devices were available with respect to some types of collateral but not for others.  The steps required to create a security interest varied from device to device.  So, too, the requirements for perfection and remedies on default.  Some laws included priorities provisions and others did not.  Not all differences between devices could be rationalized; some were wholly without justification.  And there was no reason why the terminology of each type of device had to be retained—no reason for example, to call one form of security a "pledge" and another a "mortgage."  Furthermore, the old plethora of devices failed to meet important new needs, particularly the need for "floating liens"—for convenient, efficient, and continuing security in assets that "turn over" such as inventory and accounts.

In Article Nine of the Uniform Commercial Code, Professors Llewellyn, Gilmore and Dunham introduced a single unitary security device.  Terms such as "pledgor," "mortgagee," "conditional vendee," and "trust receipt" do not appear in the Article.  In place of the plethora of devices, e. g., pledge, chattel mortgage, and conditional sale that this jargon bespeaks, and in place of this jargon itself, Article Nine substitutes one device clothed in one set of terms: "secured party," [3] "debtor," [4] "collateral," [5] and "security interest." [6]  There is no official Code name for the device itself, only names for its components, but the device itself is often called, simply, "the Article Nine security interest."

In place of the various bodies of substantive law governing the various pre-Code security devices, the draftsmen substituted a single body of law in Article Nine.  Only a few of the pre-Code legal distinctions between different pre-Code devices reappear in some form in Article Nine,[7] and they are generally attached either to the different types of collateral,[8] e. g., goods, accounts, etc., recognized in Article Nine, or to functionally different types of security interests recognized in such collateral, e. g., possessory or non-possessory,[9] pur-

3.  § 9–105(1) (i).

4.  § 9–105(1) (d).

5.  § 9–105(1) (c).

6.  § 1–102(37).

7.  The best index to these appears in the lengthy official comment to section 9–102.

8.  Article Nine includes an elaborate set of definitions of the different forms of collateral that may be the subject of a security interest.  §§ 9–105; 9–106; 9–109.

9.  See, e. g., §§ 9–203(1) (a); 9–207.

chase-money or non-purchase-money.[10]   Obviously, such distinctions could not be attached to different Article Nine security "devices," for the Article recognizes only one such device.

In light of the foregoing discussion at least one "scope" problem can be seen to be quite simple and we can quickly put it aside.  Substance controls over form.  If Article Nine otherwise applies, the parties cannot render it inapplicable merely by casting their arrangement in the language of some particular pre-Code security device. Section 9–102(2) [11] provides:

> This Article applies to security interests created by contract including pledge, assignment, chattel mortgage, chattel trust, trust deed, factor's lien, equipment trust, conditional sale, trust receipt, other lien or title retention contract and lease or consignment intended as security.

### § 22–2   The Basic Article Nine Scope Provision—9–102(1)

Section 9–102(1) is the Article's basic scope provision:

> Except as otherwise provided in Section 9—103 on multiple state transactions and in Section 9—104 on excluded transactions, this Article applies so far as concerns any personal property and fixtures within the jurisdiction of this state
>
> (a) to any transaction (regardless of its form) which is intended to create a security interest in personal property or fixtures including goods, documents, instruments, general intangibles, chattel paper, accounts or contract rights; and also
>
> (b) to any sale of accounts, contract rights or chattel paper.

Section 1–201(37) defines "security interest" broadly to mean "an interest in personal property or fixtures which secures the payment of an obligation." [12]   The initial comment to 9–102 adds this further gloss:

> The main purpose  .   .   is to bring all consensual security interests in personal property and fixtures, with the exception of certain types of transactions excluded by Sections 9—103 and 9—104, under this Article, as well as sales of accounts, contract rights and chattel paper whether intended for security or not unless excluded by Section 9—104 (f).

Thus Article Nine applies to consensual security interests (as well as to certain sales).  It follows that the Article does not apply to judg-

---

10. See, e. g., §§ 9–107; 9–301(2); 9–302(1) (d); 9–312(3).

11. See also § 9–102, Comment 1.

12. Actually, the definition is even broader than this phrase implies, as we shall later see.

ment liens,[13] judicial liens,[14] statutory liens and other forms of security that arise by operation of law [15] rather than via agreement of the parties. As if all this were not clear from 9–102 itself, section 9–104(b) and (c) expressly exclude several types of liens that arise by operation of law.[16]

Clear cases of consensual security interests to which Article Nine applies are easy to imagine. Perhaps the simplest are the ordinary pledge [17] and the so called "conditional" sale in which the seller extends credit and reserves a security interest.[18] But the Article also applies to highly sophisticated forms of business finance, including inventory floor planning [19] and accounts receivable financing.[20] The Article also governs the rights of the so-called "financing buyer" [21] who advances money to his seller and acquires an interest in the goods to be supplied which secures the supplier's "alternative" duty either to deliver the goods or repay the advance. Thus an Article Nine security interest need not secure the repayment of money. It can secure the performance of non-monetary obligations, too.

But the definition of security interest in 1–201(37) cannot be taken at face value. Section 1–201(37) defines a "security interest" to mean *any* "interest in personal property or fixtures which secures payment or performance of an obligation," a definition broad enough to include *any* distinctive claim to assets of a debtor that his creditor might assert on default. For example, it might be argued that when one creditor of a debtor agrees to subordinate his claim to that of another creditor, the elevated creditor acquires a security interest. The Code's Permanent Editorial Board was worried enough about this possibility to amend the 1962 Official Text in 1966 to add section 1–209 which provides that a subordination of this kind does not create a security interest. As a second example, suppose a debtor agrees with one of his creditors not to create any security interests in his personalty until he has paid off that creditor. It could be argued that such a "negative pledge" clause creates a security interest in the favored creditor. But Professor Gilmore says "no," for the Article was drafted only to "regulate certain well-known and institutionalized

---

13. A lien against realty of the debtor that arises when a judgment is entered is the prime example. See, e. g., Ohio Rev.Code Ann. § 2329.02 (Page Supp.1970); Ore.Rev.Stat. § 18.350 (1969).

14. The lien of an unsecured creditor who arms himself with a judgment and levies is the prime example. See, e. g., Mich.Stat.Ann. § 19.9501 (Rev. Vol. 1964).

15. Article Nine does include one priority rule dealing with certain liens arising by operation of law. See § 9–310.

16. Section 9–104 of the Code is considered in section 22–7 infra.

17. §§ 9–203(1) (a); 9–305.

18. § 9–107.

19. §§ 9–109(4); 9–204(3); 9–303; 9–306; 9–312.

20. §§ 9–106; 9–204(3); 9–302; 9–303; 9–306; 9–312.

21. Speidel, Advance Payments in Contracts for Sale of Manufactured Goods: A Look at the Uniform Commercial Code, 52 Calif.L.Rev. 281 (1964).

types of financing transactions." [22]    However, Professor Gilmore also wants to stress that such interests may still be valid security interests, even though Article Nine does not control them.    Thus he says: [23]

> It is fair enough to say that a transaction which sets out to be one of those types should conform to the Article 9 rules or fall by the wayside.    But beyond the area of institutionalized transaction, there stretches a no-man's land, in which strange creatures do strange things.    For these strange things there are no rules; it makes no sense to measure them against the rules which professionals have developed for professional transactions.    The best that can be done is to let the courts pick their way from case to case, working out their solutions ad hoc and ad hominem.

To date, the sweeping breadth of 9–102 and 1–201(37) has not generated many problems for courts.    But another threshold scope issue has given rise to a large number of litigated cases.    For various reasons the parties have sometimes put their deals in the form of leases, or in the form of consignments, when these deals in substance constituted security transfers.    In the next two sections we will discuss these cases.    Of course, courts will allow a party to introduce parol evidence to show that a transaction in substance creates a security interest regardless of its form.[24]

### § 22–3    The Basic Article Nine Scope Provision—Security Interest or Lease?

The interest of a true lessor of personalty such as equipment is not an Article Nine security interest.[25]    If a levying creditor of the lessee or his trustee in bankruptcy claims the equipment, Article Nine does not determine the outcome, and the lessor generally prevails under property and contract law even though third parties have no reason to know of his interest.[26]    The Code draftsmen might have required even true lessors to file their interests so that third parties dealing with the lessee would not be misled.    Since the draftsmen did not classify the true lessor's interest as a security interest, they may have concluded that he should not be required to file (a *non sequitur*).

But if the transaction is truly not a lease but an installment sale, and if the "lessor" actually retains "title" to secure an obligation of the "lessee" to buy and pay for the goods, Article Nine applies,[27] and

---

**22.**  1 G. Gilmore, Security Interests in Personal Property § 11.1 at 336–37 (1965).

**23.**  Id. § 11.1 at 337; Note, Security Agreements, Equitable Liens, and the Uniform Commercial Code, 69 Colum. L.Rev. 1280 (1969).

**24.**  1 G. Gilmore, Security Interests in Personal Property § 2.6 (1965).

**25.**  §§ 9–102; 1–201(37).

**26.**  In re National Eng'r & Equip. Co., 256 F. 985 (W.D.Wash.1918) (petitioner, adjudicated a lessor, was entitled to return of his property from trustee or a purchase at the list price).    Accord, McEwen v. Totten, 164 F. 837 (5th Cir. 1908).

**27.**  §§ 9–102; 1–201(37).

the "lessor" must comply with its requirements. If he does not comply with 9–203 he will not be entitled to enforce his interest even as against the debtor. If he does not file a required financing statement, he loses to all third parties who, under Article Nine and other law, take priority over an unperfected security interest, including certain purchasers from the "lessee," [28] certain lien creditors of the "lessee," [29] the "lessee's" trustee in bankruptcy,[30] and others. Since the Code's enactment, various third parties have successfully attacked a "lessor's" interest as an unperfected Code security interest vulnerable under Article Nine priority rules.[31] The "lease v. security interest" issue is one of the most frequently litigated issues under the entire Uniform Commercial Code.[32] Different factors may influence parties to follow the widespread practice of casting what is in substance a secured installment sale into the form of a "lease" providing for "rental" payments. The "lessor" may hope to avoid complying with the Article Nine filing and default provisions. Or the "lessee" may hope to get a larger federal tax deduction by paying "rent" than he would were he to buy outright and take a depreciation allowance as a deduction. Or the "lessee" may hope to avoid a local tax or local regulation that applies to owners but not lessees. If a party wants to think of himself as a lessor and has been advised by his lawyer that he is a lessor, he is not likely to file under Article Nine, and he invites attack. Of course, just because some third party attacks his interest as an unfiled Article Nine security interest, it does not follow that his is such an interest. It may be a true lease.

## TRUE LEASES

If the lessor specifically reserves title, his interest is not necessarily a security interest. The Code so states.[33] And that the lessee has an option to buy is not enough to convert a true lease into a se-

---

28. § 9–307.

29. § 9–301(1) (b).

30. Bankruptcy Act § 70(c), 11 U.S.C.A. § 110(c) (1970); UCC § 9–301(1) (b).

31. In re Dennis Mitchell Indus., Inc., 4 UCC Rep.Serv. 1082 (Ref.Dec.E.D. Pa.1967) (good faith purchaser from trustee in bankruptcy); In re Trans-Continental Indus., Inc., 3 UCC Rep. Serv. 235 (Ref.Dec.N.D.Ga.1965) ("lessee's" trustee in bankruptcy); Stanley v. Fabricators, Inc., 459 P.2d 467, 6 UCC Rep.Serv. 1262 (Alaska 1969) (a lien creditor of "lessee"); Crest Inv. Trust, Inc. v. Atlantic Mobile Corp., 252 Md. 286, 250 A.2d 246, 6 UCC Rep.Serv. 206 (1969) (other secured creditor); United Rental Equip. Co. v. Potts & Callahan Contracting Co., 231 Md. 552, 191 A.2d 570, 1 UCC Rep.Serv. 351 (1963) (good faith pur-

chaser at sheriff's sale); Nickell v. Lambrecht, 29 Mich.App. 191, 185 N.W. 2d 155, 8 UCC Rep.Serv. 1381 (1970) ("lessee's" repairman); In re Merkel, Inc., 46 Misc.2d 270, 259 N.Y.S.2d 514, 2 UCC Rep.Serv. 742 (1955) ("lessee's" assignee for the benefit of creditors).

32. See, e. g., Case Note, 49 Cornell L.Q. 672 (1964). For other general treatment, see also Del Duca, Evolving Standards for Distinguishing a "Bona Fide Lease" From a "Lease Intended as Security"—Impact on Priorities, 75 Com.L.J. 218 (1970); Peden, The Treatment of Equipment Leases as Security Agreements Under the Uniform Commercial Code, 13 William & Mary L.Rev. 110 (1971); Note, Leases as Security: Some Problems of Identification, 8 B.C.Ind. & Com.L. Rev. 764 (1967).

33. § 1–201(37).

cured sale.  The Code so states [34] and the cases so hold.[35]  Parties claiming to be true lessors have won a good share of the cases.[36]  Section 1–201(37) purports to offer guidance:

> "Security interest" means an interest in personal property or fixtures which secures payment or performance of an obligation.  . . .  Unless a lease or consignment is intended as security, reservation of title thereunder is not a "security interest" but a consignment is in any event subject to the provisions on consignment sales (Section 2—326). Whether a lease is intended as security is to be determined by the facts of each case; however, (a) the inclusion of an option to purchase does not of itself make the lease one intended for security, and (b) an agreement that upon compliance with the terms of the lease the lessee shall become or has the option to become the owner of the property for no additional consideration or for a nominal consideration does make the lease one intended for security.

In re Alpha Creamery Co., Inc.[37] aptly illustrates a true lease rather than a security interest.  The Burroughs Corporation successfully reclaimed a typewriter accounting machine from the Creamery's trustee in bankruptcy even though Burroughs had not filed under Article Nine.  Burroughs had entered into an agreement with the Creamery called a "Lease" with a "Purchase Option Rider" whereby Burroughs agreed to let the Creamery use the machine for a period of three years for a payment of $118.00 a month.  The Purchase Option Rider empowered the Creamery to buy the machine during the three year term at the list price of $4,690.00 less a deposit of $234.00 and subject to a credit of 75% of the monthly payments if purchased during the first year or 70% if purchased thereafter.  The Referee found that regardless of whether the option were exercised at the end of the first year, the second year or the third, the optionee would have

34.  § 1–201(37).

35.  E. g., In re Wheatland Elec. Prods. Co., 237 F.Supp. 820, 2 UCC Rep.Serv. 486 (W.D.Pa.1964); Crest Inv. Trust, Inc. v. Atlantic Mobile Corp., 252 Md. 286, 250 A.2d 246, 6 UCC Rep.Serv. 206 (1969).

36.  E. g., Sanders v. Commercial Credit Corp., 398 F.2d 988, 5 UCC Rep.Serv. 631 (5th Cir. 1968); Sanders v. National Acceptance Co., 383 F.2d 606, 4 UCC Rep.Serv. 793 (5th Cir. 1967); In re Atlanta Times, Inc., 259 F.Supp. 820, 3 UCC Rep.Serv. 893 (N.D.Ga. 1966); In re Wheatland Elec. Prods. Co., 237 F.Supp. 820, 2 UCC Rep.Serv. 486 (W.D.Pa.1964); In re Universal Medical Services, Inc., 8 UCC Rep. Serv. 614 (Ref.Dec.E.D.Pa.1970); In ·e Overbrook & Barson's, Inc., 5 UCC

Rep.Serv. 546 (Ref.Dec.E.D.Pa.1968); In re Falco Products Co., 5 UCC Rep. Serv. 264 (Ref.Dec.E.D.Pa.1968); In re Alpha Creamery Co., 4 UCC Rep. Serv. 794 (Ref.Dec.W.D.Mich.1967); First Nat'l Bank & Trust Co. v. Smithloff, 119 Ga.App. 284, 167 S.E.2d 190, 6 UCC Rep.Serv. 400 (1969); Crest Inv. Trust, Inc. v. Atlantic Mobile Corp., 252 Md. 286, 250 A.2d 246, 6 UCC Rep.Serv. 206 (Ct.App.1969); Gibreal Auto Sales, Inc. v. Missouri Valley Mach. Co., 186 Neb. 763, 186 N.W.2d 719, 9 UCC Rep.Serv. 121 (1971); In re Merkel, Inc., 46 Misc. 2d 270, 259 N.Y.S.2d 514, 2 UCC Rep. Serv. 742 (Sup.Ct.1965).

37.  In re Alpha Creamery Co., 4 UCC Rep.Serv. 794 (Ref.Dec.W.D.Mich. 1967).

had to pay an amount at least roughly equivalent to the then fair market value of the machine.[38] In holding that the deal was a true lease, the Referee listed relevant factors "indicating" a true lease: [39]

> The character of a transaction as a true lease is indicated by:

> (a) Provision specifying purchase option price which is approximately the market value at the time of the exercise of the option.

> (b) Rental charges indicating an intention to compensate lessor for loss of value over the term of the lease due to aging, wear and obsolescence.

> (c) Rentals which are not excessive and option purchase price which is not too low.

> (d) Facts showing that the lessee is acquiring no equity in leased article during the term of lease.

>    .    .    .

> In this case the option price was more than nominal, the lessee acquired no equity during the lease term, the option purchase price at the termination of the lease term was approximately an additional 32% of the list price indicating that the parties did not intend that the lease with option to purchase created a security interest in the personal property described in the lease.

## SECURITY INTEREST "LEASES"

We turn now to "leases" that are security interests.[40] Nearly all the cases fall into two categories. In our first category, the deal is in every respect a secured installment sale except that the parties clothe it in lease terminology. The clearest possible such case is one in which the "lessee," by the terms of the "lease" itself, is to become owner of the property at the end of the lease period in exchange for amounts previously paid, called "rentals," which were really nothing more than installments on the purchase price.[41] It makes no differ-

---

**38.** Id. at 795.

**39.** Id. at 798.

**40.** E. g., In re Brothers Coach Corp., 9 UCC Rep.Serv. 502 (E.D.N.Y.1971); In re Walter W. Willis, Inc., 313 F. Supp. 1274, 7 UCC Rep.Serv. 1125 (N.D. Ohio 1970); In re Vaillancourt, 7 UCC Rep.Serv. 748 (Ref.Dec.D.Me.1970); In re Dennis Mitchell Indus., Inc., 4 UCC Rep.Serv. 1082 (Ref.Dec.E.D.Pa.1967); In re Pomona Valley Inn, 4 UCC Rep. Serv. 893 (Ref.Dec.C.D.Cal.1967); In re Washington Processing Co., 3 UCC Rep.Serv. 475 (Ref.Dec.S.D.Cal.1966); In re Transcontinental Indus., Inc., 3 UCC Rep.Serv. 235 (Ref.Dec.N.D.Ga.

1965); In re Royer's Bakery, Inc., 1 UCC Rep.Serv. 342 (Ref.Dec.E.D.Pa. 1963); Stanley v. Fabricators, Inc., 459 P.2d 467, 6 UCC Rep.Serv. 1262 (Alas.1969); General Elec. Credit Corp. v. Bankers Commercial Corp., 244 Ark. 984, 429 S.W.2d 60, 5 UCC Rep.Serv. 532 (1968); United Rental Equip. Co. v. Potts & Callahan Contracting Co., 231 Md. 552, 191 A.2d 570, 1 UCC Rep.Serv. 351 (1963); Nickell v. Lambrecht, 29 Mich.App. 191, 185 N.W.2d 155, 8 UCC Rep.Serv. 1381 (1970).

**41.** In re Dennis Mitchell Indus., Inc., 4 UCC Rep.Serv. 1082 (Ref.Dec.E.D. Pa.1967) ("lessee" to become owner up-

ence that the "lease" period is for a time about equal to the life of the property itself, or is for a much shorter period.[42]   Also, it makes no difference that the periodic payments are about equal to a fair rental or vastly exceed this.   And it makes no difference that the "lessee" has to pay a nominal consideration to exercise the "option."   Frequently, though, the lease period will be relatively short, and the periodic payments therefore much higher than a fair rental charge for such intervals.   In all such cases the lessor is simply a seller or other financer in lessor's clothing who has retained an interest to secure the buyer's promise to buy and pay the required installments on the purchase price.   The case of In re Vaillancourt [43] is a paradigm example of cases falling in this first category.   In this case, Maine Sugar Industries, Inc. unsuccessfully sought to reclaim sugar beet machinery from the trustee of a bankrupt farmer.   Maine Sugar had permitted the farmer to use the machinery pursuant to a "lease" with an "option to purchase" clause.   After paying the various "rentals" called for in the agreement, the farmer would be entitled to exercise his option by paying the further sum of $1.00.   The "lessor," of course, had reserved "title."   The Referee decided that the deal was not a lease but a secured installment sale and in support of that conclusion cited 1–201(37) (b) which provides that "an agreement that upon compliance with the term of the lease the lessee shall become or has the option to become the owner of the property for no additional consideration or for a nominal consideration does make the lease one intended for security."   The Referee opined that $1.00 "is the most nominal of considerations." [44]

In our second category, the transaction is not only clothed in lease language, but bears marks of a true lease.   For example, the lessee must make a sizeable payment to exercise his option to purchase.   Even so, if at the end of the lease term the only sensible course economically for the lessee would be for him to exercise his option, the courts generally hold that the transaction is really a secured installment sale and Article Nine applies.   The Referee in the case of In re Washington Processing Co., Inc. used an "economic realities" test.[45]   At the end of the lease term, the lessee would be entitled to become owner of the machine by paying $1,350.   Yet the fair market value of the machine at that time would be between $7,500 and $10,500.

on making "rentals" payments for time required to pay purchase price); Nickell v. Lambrecht, 29 Mich.App. 191, 185 N.W.2d 155, 8 UCC Rep.Serv. 1381 (1970) (when total "rental" paid, "lessee" automatically becomes owner by terms of the "lease" without paying anything additional).

**42.**   In re Pomona Valley Inc., 4 UCC Rep.Serv. 893 (Ref.Dec.C.D.Cal.1967) (lessor did not truly contemplate return of "leased" equipment since rental period would probably extend beyond its useful life).

**43.**   7 UCC Rep.Serv. 748 (Ref.Dec.D. Me.1970).

**44.**   Id. at 761.   See also Stanley v. Fabricators, Inc., 459 P.2d 467, 6 UCC Rep.Serv. 1262 (Alas.1969) (option exercisible for $40 after paying $77,280).

**45.**   3 UCC Rep.Serv. 475 (Ref.Dec.S.D. Cal.1966).   See also In re Royer's Bakery, Inc., 1 UCC Rep.Serv. 342 (Ref.Dec.E.D.Pa.1963);   General Electric Credit Corp. v. Bankers Commercial Corp., 244 Ark. 984, 429 S.W.2d 60, 5 UCC Rep.Serv. 532 (1968).

Thus, in making his rental payments, the lessee had not merely been paying a sum for the use of the machine but had been "building up an equity" in it. Accordingly, the Referee decided that the lease was really a secured installment sale.

In applying the economic realities test, some courts state that if the amount the lessee must pay to exercise his option is roughly equal to the fair market value of the asset at that time, then the transaction is not a secured sale.[46] This equivalence would indicate that the lessee was not really paying installments on the price, but was instead paying true rent (a sum for wear and tear plus reasonable profit). Other courts have analyzed the problem in terms of percentages: if the option price amounts to 25% or more of the total list price, then the "lease" is not one intended for security.[47] This rule of thumb, too, is consistent with the economic realities test, for if the option price amounts to 25% (or more) of the total list price, then it would appear that the lessee has been paying true rent rather than "building up an equity," and it would not follow that the only sensible course for him would be to exercise the option. Whether in terms of economic realities a "lease" providing for rental payments is really a secured sale calling for installment payments is obviously a question of degree. We have a continuum running from one end where the interests are clearly leases to the other end where the interests are clearly security interests. Although courts sometimes consider other indicia,[48] we do not discern any judicial tendency to characterize a lease as a security interest unless it (a) is no more than a security interest clothed in lease language or (b) is characterizable as a security interest on the foregoing economic analysis. A closing caveat: The lawyer must not conclude that if the "lessee" has no option to purchase at all, his interest cannot be a security interest. We quote Professor Gilmore's example:[49]

> Assume, for example, that a piece of equipment is estimated to have a useful life of three years, at the end of which time

46. E. g., In re Universal Medical Sources, 8 UCC Rep.Serv. 614 (Ref. Dec.E.D.Pa.1970); In re Oak Mfg., Inc., 6 UCC Rep.Serv. 1273 (Ref.Dec. S.D.N.Y.1969); In re Alpha Creamery Co., 4 UCC Rep.Serv. 794 (Ref.Dec. W.D.Mich.1967); In re Washington Processing Co., 3 UCC Rep.Serv. 475 (Ref.Dec.S.D.Cal.1966).

47. In re Wheatland Elec. Prods. Co., 237 F.Supp. 820, 2 UCC Rep.Serv. 486 (W.D.Pa.1964) (option price a minimum of 25% of list price; held: lease); In re Alpha Creamery Co., 4 UCC Rep.Serv. 794 (Ref.Dec.W.D. Mich.1967) (option price 32% of list price; held: lease).

48. For example, a clause providing for "interest" payments tends to make the deal look like a secured sale. See, e. g., In re Royer's Bakery, Inc., 1 UCC Rep.Serv. 342 (Ref.Dec.E.D.Pa. 1963). Also, if a clause gives the lessor the right on default to accelerate all further payments under the lease, the deal looks more like a secured sale. See, e. g., in re Pomona Valley Inn, 4 UCC Rep.Serv. 893 (Ref.Dec.C.D.Cal. 1967). Further, if the lessor is not a true lessor of such goods, but rather is a financer, this makes the deal look more like a secured sale. See, e. g., In re Transcontinental Indus., Inc., 3 UCC Rep.Serv. 235 (Ref.Dec.N.D.Ga. 1965).

49. 1 G. Gilmore, Security Interests in Personal Property § 11.2 at 339 (1965).

it will have little or no remaining value. The "lease" requires the lessee to pay during the three years an amount equivalent to the purchase price (or purchase price less scrap value) and provides that at the end of the term the lessor will retake the goods. On the facts hypothesized, the arrangement should be held to be one "intended for security," despite the absence of any option to purchase.

## § 22–4   The Basic Article Nine Scope Provision—Consignments as Security Interests (Herein, too, of 2–326)

The Code's handling of consignments is fraught with uncertainty, and the score of Code cases on the subject clears up little.[50] Indeed, it is difficult to explain why consignors have litigated so many cases. In all but one or two the consignor could hardly have expected to prevail since he did not comply with Article Nine and did not comply with 2–326 of Article Two.[51] Presumably some lawyers for consignors persist in the erroneous belief that the Code did not alter the rights of consignors. Under Pre-Code law, a consignor could generally retrieve the goods against the consignee's creditors (and trustee) even though, as one judge pointed out, the consignor's interest is a "secret lien against creditors . . . as harmful as an unfiled chattel mortgage or conditional sale." [52] But today Article Nine requires that the consignor file a financing statement for a security consignment,[53] and virtually all goods on consignment, whether for security or not, are subject to claims of the consignee's creditors if the consignor does not comply with the public notice re-

**50.** Mann v. Clark Oil & Ref. Corp., 302 F.Supp. 1376, 6 UCC Rep.Serv. 1253 (E.D.Mo.1969), aff'd 425 F.2d 736, 7 UCC Rep.Serv. 695 (8th Cir. 1970); In re Gross Mfg. & Importing Co., 328 F.Supp. 905, 9 UCC Rep.Serv. 355 (D.N.J.1971); In re Bro. Cliff, Inc., 8 UCC Rep.Serv. 242 (Ref.Dec.W.D. Mich.1970); In re De'Cor Wallcovering Studios, Inc., 8 UCC Rep.Serv. 59 (Ref.Dec.E.D.Wis.1970); In re Louis Burk Co., 6 UCC Rep.Serv. 423 (Ref. Dec.E.D.Pa.1969); In re Bankston, 3 UCC Rep.Serv. 345 (Ref.Dec.N.D.Ga. 1966); In re Levy, 3 UCC Rep.Serv. 291 (Ref.Dec.E.D.Pa.1965); In re Downtown Drugstore, Inc., 3 UCC Rep.Serv. 27 (Ref.Dec.E.D.Pa.1965); In re Sam's Furniture & Appliance Stores, Inc., 1 UCC Rep.Serv. 422 (Ref.Dec.W.D.Pa.1962); In re Griffin, 1 UCC Rep.Serv. 492 (Ref.Dec.W.D.Pa. 1960); Allgeier v. Campisi, 117 Ga. App. 105, 159 S.E.2d 458, 5 UCC Rep. Serv. 93 (1968); Guardian Discount Co. v. Settles, 114 Ga.App. 418, 151 S.E.2d 530, 3 UCC Rep.Serv. 838 (1966); In re Novak, 7 UCC Rep.Serv. 196 (Md.Cir.Ct.Equity 1969); General Elec. Co. v. Pettingell Supply Co., 347

Mass. 631, 199 N.E.2d 326, 2 UCC Rep. Serv. 184 (1964); Vonins, Inc. v. Raff, 101 N.J.Super. 172, 243 A.2d 836, 5 UCC Rep.Serv. 433 (App.Div.1968); In re Mincow Bag Co., 29 App.Div.2d 400, 288 N.Y.S.2d 364, 5 UCC Rep. Serv. 60 (1st Dep't 1968); Manufacturers Acceptance Corp. v. Penning's Sales, Inc., 5 Wash.App. 501, 487 P.2d 1053, 9 UCC Rep.Serv. 797 (1971); Columbia Int'l Corp. v. Kempler, 46 Wis.2d 550, 175 N.W.2d 465, 7 UCC Rep.Serv. 650 (1970).

**51.** The consignor appears to have won in only one case so far. In re Griffin, 1 UCC Rep.Serv. 492 (Ref.Dec.W.D.Pa. 1960) (owners of used furniture complied with 2–326(3) (b)). A strong case can be made that the consignor should have won under 2–326 in In re Novak, 7 UCC Rep.Serv. 196 (Md.Cir. Ct.Equity 1969).

**52.** Liebowitz v. Voiello, 107 F.2d 914, 916 (2d Cir. 1939); see Peek v. Heim, 127 Pa. 500, 17 A. 984 (1889).

**53.** §§ 9–102; 9–302; 1–201(37).

quirements of 2–326(3).[54] Thus the Code draftsmen all but abolished the consignor's "secret lien." In only the rarest arrangement can a consignor retrieve the goods without having publicized his interest pursuant to 2–326 or to Article Nine. In re Mincow Bag Co., Inc.[55] seems to have been such a case. Section 2–326 provides:

> (1) Unless otherwise agreed, if delivered goods may be returned by the buyer even though they conform to the contract, the transaction is

> (a) a "sale on approval" if the goods are delivered primarily for use, and

> (b) a "sale or return" if the goods are delivered primarily for resale.

> (2) Except as provided in subsection (3), goods held on approval are not subject to the claims of the buyer's creditors until acceptance; goods held on sale or return are subject to such claims while in the buyer's possession.

> (3) Where goods are delivered to a person for sale and such person maintains a place of business at which he deals in goods of the kind involved, under a name other than the name of the person making delivery, then with respect to claims of creditors of the person conducting the business the goods are deemed to be on sale or return. The provisions of this subsection are applicable even though an agreement purports to reserve title to the person making delivery until payment or resale or uses such words as "on consignment" or "on memorandum". However, this subsection is not applicable if the person making delivery

> (a) complies with an applicable law providing for a consignor's interest or the like to be evidenced by a sign, or

> (b) establishes that the person conducting the business is generally known by his creditors to be substantially engaged in selling the goods of others, or

> (c) complies with the filing provisions of the Article on Secured Transactions (Article 9).

Section 1–201(37) states flatly that "a consignment is in any event subject to . . . 2–326." The facts of *Mincow Bag* did not fall in 2–326(3) at all, or so the majority thought, for the consignee did not "maintain a place of business at which it dealt in goods of the kind involved." Instead, the consignee was a wholesaler who reconsigned the goods to retailers. All the same, its way of doing business entailed the risk that its own creditors would believe that it owned goods consigned to it especially since the goods bore its name. The dissenting judge recognized this, and therefore insisted that the con-

---

54. §§ 2–326(1), (2).

55. 29 App.Div.2d 400, 288 N.Y.S.2d 364, 5 UCC Rep.Serv. 60 (1st Dep't 1968).

signor should lose, for it had neither complied with 2-326(3) nor with Article Nine. The dissenter sought to force 2-326(3) on the majority despite the linguistic strain this involves. It would have been better for the dissent to have urged that the consignor's interest was intended for security and therefore failed on that ground because of non-compliance with Article Nine. Actually, the majority opinion sanctions a secret security interest, for the consignor was allowed to reacquire and retain the goods.

In all significant Code cases to date except *Mincow*, the consignee was a person who maintained "a place of business at which he deal[t] in goods of the kind involved." Accordingly 2-326(3) and its public notice provisions came into play. Since the consignor had not complied with 2-326(3) (a), (b) or (c), he lost on that ground alone. While we think this the right result, ambiguity lurks in 2-326(2), for it does not really state that the consignor loses. It only says that the goods are "subject to" the claims of the consignee's creditors. It is plausible to argue that what those claims are is defined not by 2-326 at all, but other law.[56] Yet this ambiguity is dwarfed by those that arise when the applicability of Article Nine and the relations between that Article and 2-326 are considered.

Today two separate Code sections provide that Article Nine applies at least to consignments intended for security.[57] An earlier draft of the Code had provided that *all* consignments were Article Nine security interests.[58] For business consignments, the earlier version made more sense, for the typical business consignment (and nearly all consignments are of this variety)[59] is a security device. One familiar with "floor planning," that is, the process whereby a seller or lender finances a retailer by taking a security interest in all of his inventory, should see the parallel between this process and consignment selling. Both are means of financing the retail seller's business with the wholesale seller's capital. That is to say, the manufacturer, wholesaler or lender has his capital tied up in the retailer's inventory and the retailer, who will get a slice of the proceeds, has his own capital thus freed for other purposes. The principal purpose of such consignments is to finance the buyer and to maintain a kind of security interest in the seller. There is at least one other

56. Cf. In re Kravitz, 278 F.2d 820, 1 UCC Rep.Serv. 159 (3d Cir. 1960) (not a consignment case, but involved similar kind of ambiguity).

57. §§ 9-102(2); 1-201(37).

58. ALI & National Conference of Commissioners on Uniform State Laws, Uniform Commercial Code § 1-201(37) (Official Draft 1952):

The reservation by a seller or consignor of property notwithstanding identification of goods to a contract for sale or notwithstanding shipment or delivery is a "security interest".

59. For "consignments" of the nonbusiness variety, see In re Griffin, 1 UCC Rep.Serv. 492 (Ref.Dec.W.D.Pa.1960) (individuals left used furniture with bankrupt for sale on commission); Allgeier v. Campisi, 117 Ga.App. 105, 159 S.E.2d 458, 5 UCC Rep.Serv. 93 (1968) (individual owner of automobile delivered it to dealer for purpose of having dealer secure offers and sell it upon owner's approval).

reason why a manufacturer or other seller might wish to use consignments. He might do so as a means to maintain fixed retail prices. Under the anti-trust laws he may be prevented from establishing fixed prices if he sells the goods to retailers out-right, but if he retains title to them it may be that he can fix their prices without violating the anti-trust laws. Of course, a consignment for retail price maintenance purposes could also be a security interest.[60]

Judges must decide whether Article Nine applies to consignments by deciding whether the parties created a "security interest." [61] In our opinion, courts should hold that a consignment creates a security interest if it is one that is functionally equivalent to a floor plan. To date, the courts have disposed of most of the consignment cases solely under 2–326. In only about a third of all the litigated Code consignment cases [62] did the courts go on to find that the parties also intended to create a security interest. We think this proportion would have been much higher if the parties had always presented the issue to the court. We believe that in more and more of the cases courts will hold that both Article Nine and 2–326 apply to the same consignment. With both 2–326 and Article Nine applicable to the same consignment, all kinds of uncertainty and havoc become possible. First of all, it can make a difference whether a third party attacks the consignor's interest under Article Nine or under 2–326. For example, if the court holds a consignment to be for security, a lien creditor (or trustee) may attack the interest as defectively created under 9–203 or 9–204 and prevail.[63] Or, he may attack the interest as unperfected under 9–303 and will prevail unless he became a lien creditor with knowledge of an unperfected security interest under 9–301(1) (b).[64] But it is certainly arguable that under 2–326 (3) even a lien creditor with knowledge would prevail against a consignor who does not comply with 2–326(3). The Code does not indicate which law controls here. Similarly, a consignor who filed under Article Nine pursuant to 2–326(3) (c) would, without more,

**60.** But see Columbia Int'l Corp. v. Kempler, 46 Wis.2d 550, 175 N.W.2d 465, 7 UCC Rep.Serv. 650 (1970) (court said consignment not a security interest since for price-fixing purposes; we dissent since transaction functionally equivalent to floor plan). See also Hawkland, Consignment Selling Under the Uniform Commercial Code, 67 Com. L.J. 146 (1962).

**61.** §§ 9–102(2); 1–201(37).

**62.** E. g., Mann v. Clark Oil & Ref. Corp., 302 F.Supp. 1376, 6 UCC Rep. Serv. 1253 (E.D.Mo.1969), aff'd 425 F.2d 736, 7 UCC Rep.Serv. 695 (8th Cir. 1970); In re Gross Mfg. & Importing Co., 328 F.Supp. 905, 9 UCC Rep. Serv. 355 (D.N.J.1971); In re De'Cor Wallcovering Studios, Inc., 8 UCC

Rep.Serv. 59 (Ref.Dec.E.D.Wis.1970); In re Louis Burk Co., 6 UCC Rep. Serv. 423 (Ref.Dec.E.D.Pa.1969); In re Sam's Furniture & Appliance Stores, Inc., 1 UCC Rep.Serv. 422 (Ref.Dec.W.D.Pa.1962); Manufacturers Acceptance Corp. v. Penning's Sales, Inc., 5 Wash.App. 501, 487 P.2d 1053, 9 UCC Rep.Serv. 797 (1971).

**63.** In re De'Cor Wallcovering Studios, Inc., 8 UCC Rep.Serv. 59 (Ref.Dec. Wis.1970) (trustee defeated consignor who failed to comply with 9–203).

**64.** Mann v. Clark Oil & Ref. Corp., 302 F.Supp. 1376, 6 UCC Rep.Serv. 1253 (E.D.Mo.1969) (trustee defeated consignor who failed to perfect), aff'd 425 F.2d 736, 7 UCC Rep.Serv. 695 (8th Cir. 1970).

prevail over a prior lender with an Article Nine floating lien in inventory. Yet Article Nine would seem to require the consignor to give notice to the prior lender pursuant to 9–312(3). Again, the Code does not indicate which law controls.[65]

Second, suppose the court decides the consignor has an unperfected Article Nine security interest although the consignor has complied with 2–326(3) (a) or (b). Does the consignor lose under Article Nine or does his compliance with 2–326 save his interest? Given the purposes of Article Nine and of 2–326, one compliance should be enough.[66] Until the Code is cleaned up, we urge that courts hold for the consignor who complies with 2–326(a) or (b) regardless of his failure to comply with Article Nine. Even this leaves us with a third ambiguity. Section 2–326 is hardly replete with priority rules for the various conflicts that can arise between consignor and third parties, while Article Nine incorporates numerous priority rules. While we wait for amendment, courts might try to apply the Article Nine rules by analogy here.[67] A fourth problem is this: In the sphere of overlap between 2–326 and Article Nine, what rules govern "default" procedures? Again 2–326 has no such rules. Might we say that for purposes of "perfection", compliance with 2–326(a) or (b) is enough and then turn back to Article Nine for rules on default?

Most of the foregoing problems have not arisen but we believe they are just around the corner. In several cases, including two of the most recent ones, the consignor discovered he was not only a non-complying consignor under 2–326 but was also the holder of an unperfected Article Nine security interest.[68] If this be possible, then it is certainly also possible that a consignor might awaken to find that he is a *complying* consignor under 2–326 but, alas, the holder of an unperfected Article Nine security interest. Then what?

## § 22–5   Surety's Subrogation Rights Not a Security Interest

Sureties figure in many different types of commercial transactions. In construction contracts, sureties underwrite the performance and payment bonds that the contractor must post. If the contractor defaults, these bonds obligate the surety to complete the contract (or arrange for its completion) and pay off all materialmen and laborers. Obviously, the owner who benefits from all this should not be

---

65. The new version of Article Nine tidies this up and provides that consignor, in effect, must take the steps specified in 9–312(3). See Permanent Editorial Board for the Uniform Commercial Code, Review Committee for Article 9 of the Uniform Commercial Code, Final Report § 9–114 at 57–58 (1971).

66. But see 1 N.Y.State Law Revision Comm'n, 1955 Report 295 (1955).

67. Accord, Hawkland, Uniform Commercial "Code" Methodology, 1962 U. Ill.L.F. 291, 314–18.

68. E. g., In re Gross Mfg. & Importing Co., 328 F.Supp. 905, 9 UCC Rep.Serv. 355 (D.N.J.1971); Mann v. Clark Oil & Ref. Corp., 302 F.Supp. 1376, 6 UCC Rep.Serv. 1253 (E.D.Mo.1969), aff'd 425 F.2d 736, 7 UCC Rep.Serv. 695 (8th Cir. 1970). Cf. Manufacturer's Acceptance Corp. v. Penning's Sales, Inc., 5 Wash.App. 501, 487 P.2d 1053, 9 UCC Rep.Serv. 797 (3d Div.1971).

allowed to keep the monies he would have had to pay to the contractor, absent default. Without more, it would seem that the surety should get these monies. It is true that the surety received premiums for underwriting the bonds, but these premiums are not sufficient to make it worthwhile for a surety to incur the risks of having to complete the job and pay off the materialsmen and laborers. Rather, the willingness of a surety to incur these risks depends mainly on "a compound of its confidence in the contractor and the opportunity to prevent or minimize its ultimate loss by its right to salvage the debacle by its own performance." [69] Accordingly, courts have devised the equitable doctrine of subrogation. The surety who completes, and pays off materialsmen and laborers is said to be "subrogated" to the rights of the defaulting contractor, to the rights of materialsmen and laborers, and even to the rights of the owner himself.[70]

Assume the contractor defaults, the surety completes and pays off materialsmen and laborers, and the surety then invokes subrogation theory to establish its right to the monies in the owner's hands that the owner would have had to pay the contractor absent default. It is most unlikely that the surety will be the only party claiming these monies. Other parties, including banks who financed the contractor up to the time of default will also claim them. Does Article Nine apply to resolve the conflict? [71] The trend now is for courts [72] to hold that since the surety's claim to these monies is not based on a security interest in them, Article Nine does not apply.[73] Article Nine applies only to consensual security interests.[74] The surety's subrogation claim is not consensual, but is based on the "status . . . inhering in a surety." [75] Accordingly, conflicts between the rights of the surety and third parties must be resolved outside Article Nine. And outside Article Nine, sureties are generally prevailing as against banks with perfected Article Nine security interests in monies retained by the owner.[76] It may be objected that this state of affairs sanctions "secret liens" of sureties, and that Article Nine ought to be stretched or amended to cover these cases. But as Justice Braucher

**69.** National Shawmut Bank v. New Amsterdam Cas. Co., 411 F.2d 843, 845, 6 UCC Rep.Serv. 441, 444 (1st Cir. 1969).

**70.** Canter v. Schlager, 267 N.E.2d 492, 496, 8 UCC Rep.Serv. 932, 937 (1971).

**71.** See generally Clark, Suretyship in the Uniform Commercial Code, 46 Texas L.Rev. 453 (1968); Cushman, The Surety's Rights of Equitable Priority to Contract Balance in Relation to the Uniform Commercial Code, 39 Temp.L.Q. 239 (1966); Note, Another Step Toward Confusion in Surety Law, 64 Nw.L.Rev. 582 (1969).

**72.** Most of the cases involve clashes between Article Nine secured creditors and sureties.

**73.** National Shawmut Bank v. New Amsterdam Cas. Co., 411 F.2d 843, 6 UCC Rep.Serv. 441 (1st Cir. 1969); Home Indem. Co. v. United States, 193 Ct.Cl. 266, 8 UCC Rep.Serv. 225 (1970); National Sur. Corp. v. State Nat'l Bank, 454 S.W.2d 354, 7 UCC Rep.Serv. 1232 (Ky.1970); Canter v. Schlager, —— Mass. ——, 267 N.E.2d 492, 8 UCC Rep.Serv. 932 (1971); Jacobs v. Northeastern Corp., 416 Pa. 417, 206 A.2d 49, 2 UCC Rep.Serv. 348 (1965).

**74.** § 9–102.

**75.** National Shawmut Bank v. New Amsterdam Cas. Co., 411 F.2d 843, 846, 6 UCC Rep.Serv. 441, 445 (1969).

**76.** Id.

recently noted, third parties who extend credit or lend to contractors are almost always aware of the presence of a surety standing behind the contractor.[77]  Moreover, conflicts between sureties and third parties do not comprise an Article Nine *casus omissus*.  The issue of Article Nine coverage was fought out at the drafting stage, and the surety companies prevailed in their efforts to remain outside the Article.[78]

## § 22–6   Extent Article Nine Applies to Realty Interests

Even though the parties create what qualifies as a "security interest" within 1–201(37), Article Nine still may not apply, for the collateral may not be "personal property or fixtures." [79]  The collateral may be some form of realty and Article Nine generally does not apply to the "creation or transfer of an interest in or lien on real estate, including a lease or rents thereunder." [80]  This language excludes real estate mortgages and land sale contracts, as well as other forms of security in realty.[81]

But there are several exceptions to the general principle that Article Nine does not apply to realty interests.  First, Article Nine does apply to a security interest in a fixture that has not been incorporated in the manner of lumber, bricks, tile, or the like into a structure that is itself realty.[82]  Of the various forms of Article Nine collateral, only goods can become fixtures.  The Article's coverage of fixtures generates two different and important definitional problems.  When do goods cease being personalty subject to the *general* Article Nine rules and become fixtures subject to certain *special* rules in 9–313?  The Code does not answer this question, and leaves what constitutes a fixture entirely to extra-Code law.[83]  The other definitional problem is this: When are goods incorporated in the manner of lumber, bricks, tile or the like into a structure that is itself realty under local law?  Once so incorporated, they lose "their separateness and become lienable only under real estate law." [84]  Except for the illustrative references to lumber, bricks, and tile, etc., the Code leaves it to the courts to draw this boundary as well.  In State Bank of Albany v. Kahn,[85] the court seems not to have seen the argument that Article Nine does not apply at all to security interests in a concrete swimming pool.  Rather, the court assumed that the Article applies and went on to resolve the conflicting claims under 9–313.  Even though a pool is a fixture for some purposes under local law, Article Nine would not apply to a security interest in a pool that had become

77.  Canter v. Schlager, 267 N.E.2d 492, 8 UCC Rep.Serv. 932 (1971).

78.  Id. at 495, 8 UCC Rep.Serv. at 936.

79.  § 9–102.

80.  § 9–104(j).  See further Section 25–8.

81.  E. g., §§ 8–575; 9–531.

82.  §§ 9–102; 9–313.

83.  § 9–313, Comment 2.

84.  §§ 9–313; 9–313, Comment 2.  In re Foskett, 7 UCC Rep.Serv. 267, 270 (Ref.Dec.W.D.Wis.1970).

85.  58 Misc.2d 655, 296 N.Y.S.2d 391, 6 UCC Rep.Serv. 43 (1969).

part of a structure itself realty under local law. In George v. Commercial Credit Corp.,[86] the court had to apply the language of 9–313 (1) and local law to decide whether a mobile home became so affixed to realty as to lose its separateness and become "lienable" only under real estate law.[87] The court decided that the mobile home did lose its "separateness" and that Article Nine did not govern. The mobile home was attached to the realty via "cinder blocks and a C clamp, . . . [and] connections for electricity, sewage and natural gas were provided." It was therefore subject to a mortgage on the real estate.[88]

Although 9–313(1) is not wholly clear on this, it appears that if the collateral is a fixture but has not become part of a structure that is itself realty under local law, a creditor may create and perfect a valid security interest in it either by complying with the relevant Article Nine rules or by complying with applicable law for creating and perfecting security interests under real estate law. Accordingly, a prospective real estate mortgagor who wants security in fixtures need not comply with two different sets of rules on creation and perfection. The rules in 9–313 control priority conflicts, however.

Crops are also close to realty. According to 2–107 and 9–105(1), crops are goods. To create a security interest in crops the parties must comply with Article Nine rules on creation and perfection. A real estate mortgagee cannot subject crops to his mortgage merely by complying with real estate mortgage law. Crops differ from fixtures in this respect.[89] Article Nine does not, however, purport to govern conflicts between holders of security in crops and all other third parties. In particular, Article Nine does not deal with all possible clashes between holders of security interests in crops and landlord lienors, real estate grantees and the like. Here local law controls.

Standing timber, and oil gas or other minerals as yet unextracted are realty [90] and the Official Text of Article Nine does not govern security interests in such properties.[91] However, the Article does apply to timber when severed and to oil, gas or other minerals when

86.  440 F.2d 551, 8 UCC Rep.Serv. 1315 7th Cir. 1971).

87.  In re Foskett, 7 UCC Rep.Serv. 267, 270 (Ref.Dec.W.D.Wis.1970).

88.  George v. Commercial Credit Corp., 440 F.2d 551, 554, 8 UCC Rep.Serv. 1315, 1318 (7th Cir. 1971).

89.  Accord, Coogan & Clovis, The Uniform Commercial Code and Real Estate Law: Problems for Both the Real Estate Lawyer and the Chattel Se-

curity Lawyer, 38 Ind.L.J. 535, 547–48 (1963).

90.  § 9–204(2) (b).

91.  Numerous nonuniform amendments in the "timber" states change the official text to provide that standing timber to be cut under a conveyance or contract for sale constitutes goods for purposes of Article Nine. See 3 U.L.A. § 9–204 at 104 (Master ed. 1968).

extracted.[92]   And once severance or extraction occurs, security interests in such properties under real estate law automatically terminate.

It appears that Article Nine applies to security interests in "realty paper."   B mortgages his real estate to L.   L pledges B's note and the real estate mortgage to Bank as security for a loan. Article Nine does not apply to the transaction between B and L, but does apply to the transaction between L and Bank.   This seems to be the plain meaning of 9–102(3) : "The application of this Article to a security interest in a secured obligation is not affected by the fact that the obligation is itself secured by a transaction or interest to which this Article does not apply." [93]   One case is in accord.[94]   Yet the statute is not too happily drafted, for 9–104(j) seems to say that the Article does not apply to the transaction between L and his bank.[95]

Article Nine does not apply to landlord's liens arising under statute or case law.[96]   However, several cases have arisen in which the parties have, in effect, sought to create landlord liens by contract.[97] Here, the courts hold that Article Nine applies, and properly so.

The question whether prospective collateral is Article Nine collateral must be distinguished from the question whether an Article Nine security interest can be presently created in the collateral or must await some future event.   Section 9–204 governs this latter question, and will be considered in the next chapter.[98]

## § 22–7   A Note on the 9–104 Exclusions

Even though an interest falls within the 1–201(37) definition of "security interest" and even though it is an interest in "personal property or fixtures," Article Nine still may not apply because of an express exclusion in 9–104 :

This Article does not apply

> (a) to a security interest subject to any statute of the United States such as the Ship Mortgage Act, 1920, to the extent that such statute governs the rights of parties to and third parties affected by transactions in particular types of property;  or
>
> (b) to a landlord's lien;  or

---

92.   § 9–204(2) (b).

93.   See, also, the illustration set forth in section 9–102, Comment 4.

94.   Riebe v. Budget Fin. Corp., 264 Cal. App.2d 576, 70 Cal.Rptr. 654, 5 UCC Rep.Serv. 907 (2d Dist. 1968).   But see Coogan & Kripke, The Outer Fringes of Article 9: Subordination Agreements, Security Interests in Money and Deposits, Negative Pledge Clauses, and Participation Agreements, 79 Harv.L.Rev. 229, 271 (1965).

95.   See 1 G. Gilmore, Security Interests in Personal Property § 10.6 at 311 (1965).

96.   § 9–104(b).

97.   See, e. g., In re Leckie Freeburn Coal Co., 405 F.2d 1043, 6 UCC Rep. Serv. 15 (6th Cir. 1969);   In re King Furniture City, Inc., 240 F.Supp. 453, 2 UCC Rep.Serv. 795 (E.D.Ark.1965).

98.   See Section 23–2 infra.

(c) to a lien given by statute or other rule of law for services or materials except as provided in Section 9—310 on priority of such liens; or

(d) to a transfer of a claim for wages, salary or other compensation of an employee; or

(e) to an equipment trust covering railway rolling stock; or

(f) to a sale of accounts, contract rights or chattel paper as part of a sale of the business out of which they arose, or an assignment of accounts, contract rights or chattel paper which is for the purpose of collection only, or a transfer of a contract right to an assignee who is also to do the performance under the contract; or

(g) to a transfer of an interest or claim in or under any policy of insurance; or

(h) to a right represented by a judgment; or

(i) to any right of set-off; or

(j) except to the extent that provision is made for fixtures in Section 9—313, to the creation or transfer of an interest in or lien on real estate, including a lease or rents thereunder; or

(k) to a transfer in whole or in part of any of the following: any claim arising out of tort; any deposit, savings, passbook or like account maintained with a bank, savings and loan association, credit union or like organization.

We discuss most of these exclusions elsewhere.[99] It will be apparent that several of the exclusions merely reaffirm the basic Article Nine inclusions. Thus (b) and (c) reaffirm that 9–102 applies to consensual security, and (j) reaffirms that 9–102 applies to security interests in personal property and fixtures. One exclusion states only what must be obvious anyway, namely, that applicable federal law supersedes Article Nine.[100] A number of other exclusions simply exclude transactions or interests that are not of a financing nature.[101] But exclusion (e), and exclusion (k) (insofar as it applies to pledges of deposits and accounts) do exclude genuine financing arrangements from Article Nine. Comment Seven to 9–104 explains (k) on the basis that such pledges are "adequately covered by existing law," and Comment Five says the same of exclusion (e).[102]

99. See Chs. 23–26 infra.

100. See Section 22–11 infra.

101. See the exclusions listed in sections 9–104(d), (h), (f), (i).

102. The new draft of Article Nine eliminates this exclusion and applies the Article to railway equipment trusts. Permanent Editorial Board for the Uniform Commercial Code, Review Committee for Article 9 of the Uniform Commercial Code, Final Report § 9–104(e) at 33–34 (1971).

### § 22–8    Applicability of Article Nine to Sales of Accounts, Contract Rights and Chattel Paper

Even though a transaction does not create a "security interest" of the usual kind, Article Nine may still apply to it. Section 9–102(1) (b) says that the Article applies "so far as concerns any personal property . . . within the jurisdiction of this state . . . to any sale of accounts, contract rights or chattel paper." Thus, the Article covers some outright sales, which means that the parties thereto must comply with the creation and perfection requirements of the Article. Although these provisions all apply to "security interests", the 1–201(37) definition of that phrase provides that it includes any interest of a "buyer of accounts, chattel paper, or contract rights which is subject to Article 9." These various forms of collateral are all defined in Article Nine.

An "account" is defined in 9–106 as "any right to payment for goods sold or leased or for services rendered which is not evidenced by an instrument or chattel paper." If the right to payment is evidenced by an "instrument" [103] or "chattel paper," [104] as those terms are defined in Article Nine, then it is simply not an account. Also, if the right to payment is not for goods sold or leased or for services rendered but, say, for the sale of an interest in realty, or for the refund of an overpayment of taxes, or insurance proceeds, or the like, then it is not an account. Moreover, if the right is not yet earned, as where the claimant has only a contract to sell goods or to lease them or to render services, then the claimant's claim is not an account, but a "contract right," as that term is defined in Article Nine. It is not, however, essential that an account be a claim to a payment then due.[105] It is enough that it be earned. Thus before Article Nine can apply to the sale of an account, the account must be an "account" as defined in 9–106, a very special definition indeed.

The Article also applies to certain sales of "contract rights," a phrase defined in 9–106 to mean: "Any right to payment under a contract not yet earned by performance and not evidenced by an instrument or chattel paper." Thus, if the right is evidenced by an instrument or chattel paper, it cannot be a "contract right." And if already earned, the right cannot be a contract right either: it will be either an account or a general intangible. (There is now one exception: certain rights earned under a contract for the use or hire of a vessel are contract rights.) [106] Also, if the right to payment is not a right under a contract, it cannot be a contract right, but must be a general intangible instead, and Article Nine does not apply to outright sales of "general intangibles." [107] "General intangibles" is a catchall category defined in 9–106 to mean: "Any personal property (including things

---

103. § 9–105(1) (g).

104. § 9–105(1) (b). See text following note 108 infra.

105. Matthews v Arctic Tire, Inc., 262 A.2d 831, 7 UCC Rep.Serv. 369 (1970).

106. § 9–106.

107. § 9–102(1) (b).

in action) other than goods, accounts, contract rights, chattel paper, documents and instrument." It includes such intangibles as "goodwill, literary rights . . . copyrights, trademarks and patents . . ." [108]

Article Nine applies to sales of "chattel paper." Section 9–105(1) (b) defines "chattel paper" as follows:

> "Chattel paper" means a writing or writings which evidence both a monetary obligation and a security interest in or a lease of specific goods; a charter or other contract involving the use or hire of a vessel is not chattel paper. When a transaction is evidenced both by such a security agreement or a lease and by an instrument or a series of instruments, the group of writings taken together constitutes chattel paper.

The most common source of "chattel paper" today is the ordinary secured consumer sale: A dealer sells goods to a customer who signs a note or other promise to pay and agrees that the dealer shall retain a purchase money security interest in the goods to secure the customer's obligation to pay the price, usually in installments. The resulting writings that the dealer thereby acquires "evidence both a monetary obligation and a security interest in . . . specific goods" and constitute chattel paper. Even if the promissory note is negotiable, it together with requisite language in it or in an accompanying writing constitutes chattel paper and not an "instrument," still another Code category.[109] Papers evidencing a so-called "bailment lease" also ordinarily constitute chattel paper.[110] One court has held, however, that a negotiable note together with an application for a certificate of title signed by the debtor and reciting that the dealer is "first lienor" is not chattel paper, for the application itself does not create a security interest.[111] It should be noted that chattel paper itself embodies a security interest in goods and at the same time can itself constitute Article Nine collateral when a debtor transfers it to his lender as security.

The dealer may either sell his chattel paper outright or transfer it for security to a floor plan lender. When the dealer sells it outright, Article Nine applies in virtue of 9–102(1) (b). When the dealer pledges it as collateral Article Nine applies in virtue of 9–102 (1) (a). It is important to know whether the Article applies because of a sale transfer or because of a security transfer, for the applicable Article Nine default provisions may differ depending on the nature of the transfer.[112] The same is true also with respect to accounts and contract rights.

108.  § 9–106, Comment.

109.  § 9–105(1) (g).

110.  See, e. g., Associates Discount Corp. v. Old Freeport Bank, 421 Pa. 609, 220 A.2d 621, 3 UCC Rep.Serv. 481 (1966).

111.  In re Harmon, 6 UCC Rep.Serv. 1280 (Ref.Dec.D.Conn.1969).

112.  For instance, compare the two sentences in section 9–504(2).

Article Nine applies to certain sales of accounts, contract rights and chattel paper because of their financing character.[113]   The force of this rationale is most obvious with respect to certain sales of accounts and chattel paper.   Factors, who are essentially lenders, often buy accounts outright and without recourse.   Similarly, floor planners often floor plan dealer inventory partly in exchange for chattel paper which they buy outright and without recourse.   Given these practices, if factors and floor planners who buy accounts and chattel paper are to have priority against other *creditors* of the borrower who might assume that the borrower has not sold or encumbered his accounts or chattel paper, then it is only just that factors and floor planners publicize their claims.   Similarly, if these lenders are to have priority over other purchasers of these very same accounts and chattel paper it is only just that they publicize their claims by filing financing statements.

But not all outright sales of accounts, contract rights and chattel paper are of a financing nature.   Since 9–102(1) (b) applies to all sales of these forms of collateral, it seems overbroad.   Section 9–104 (f) cuts it back somewhat:

> This Article does not apply
>
> .  .  .
>
> > to a sale of accounts, contract rights or chattel paper as part of a sale of the business out of which they arose, or an assignment of accounts, contract rights or chattel paper which is for the purpose of collection only, or a transfer of a contract right to an assignee who is also to do the performance under the contract.

However, this section excludes only three of the various types of non-financing sales and therefore does not seem to go far enough.   Professor Gilmore has written that section 9–104(f) should therefore be read as illustrative and not exhaustive.[114]   For example, a court should not, on his view, apply Article Nine where an assignor sells an isolated account for the purpose of paying off a pre-existing debt, even though 9–102(1) (b) is broad enough to apply and the assignment does not fall within the 9–104(f) exclusions.   If, however, the assignment is part of a pattern of financing between two parties, then the Article would apply.   Thus, on his view, Lyon v. Ty-Wood Corp.[115] is wrongly decided.   The court held that an outright sale of an account did not fall within Article Nine, even though the assignee testified that he took the assignment as security, and the assignor made the assignment pursuant to a pattern of financing.   Certainly the assignor can make an assignment that is pursuant to a pattern of financing even though not contemporaneous with receipt of the

113.   1 G. Gilmore, Security Interests in Personal Property § 10.5 (1965).

114.   Id.

115.   212 Pa.Super. 69, 239 A.2d 819, 5 UCC Rep.Serv. 27 (1968).

loan; Spurlin v. Sloan [116] is erroneous to the extent it suggests the contrary.[117]

On our view, Article Nine applies to all sales of accounts, contract rights and chattel paper that do not fall within the 9–104(f) exclusions. See Section 23–8 infra.

For discussion of the perfection problems that arise because of Article Nine's coverage of certain sales, also see Section 23–8 infra.

### § 22–9    Conflict of Laws Problems

Many personal property security transactions and many outright sales of accounts, contract rights and chattel paper have contacts with more than one state. Although Article Nine is law in 49 states, the District of Columbia and the Virgin Islands, amended versions of the Article have been enacted in the various jurisdictions, and case law interpretations also differ. When a transaction has contacts with states having different Article Nine laws, which law governs? [118] The legal question may concern (1) requirements for creating a security interest, or (2) requirements for perfection, or (3) rights and duties between debtor and creditor (or seller and buyer), or (4) priorities as against third parties, or (5) default and foreclosure. Precisely because Article Nine is law nearly everywhere, the answers of different states to the question in issue will usually not vary. But where the state laws do differ on the question in issue, the forum court will have to apply conflict of laws rules to decide which state's law controls. Article Nine includes several conflict of laws rules. Section 9–102(1) says: "Except as otherwise provided in Section 9–103 on multistate transactions . . . this Article applies so far as concerns any personal property and fixtures within the jurisdiction of this state. . . ." This section is intended as a choice of law rule that the substantive law of the place where the collateral is located (situs) governs "without regard to possible contacts in other jurisdictions." [119] But this general situs rule of 9–102(1) is expressly subject to section 9–103, and that section lays down a large number of specific choice of law rules on questions of creation, perfection and priorities in multistate transactions. Of these, questions of perfection are of greatest practical importance. We discuss the 9–103 perfection rules in Sections 23–17 through 23–21 infra. But 9–103 is not exhaustive, even on choice of law with respect to perfection.[120] Also section 9–103 lays down some rules for choosing be-

116.   368 S.W.2d 314, 1 UCC Rep.Serv. 402 (Ky.1963).

117.   See generally Note, Is a Transfer of Accounts to Satisfy a Pre-Existing Debt an Article Nine Transaction?, 22 Okla.L.Rev. 423 (1969).

118.   See generally Weintraub, Choice of Law in Secured Personal Property Transactions: The Impact of Article

9 of the Uniform Commercial Code, 68 Mich.L.Rev. 684 (1970).

119.   §§ 9–102, Comment 3; 9–103, Comment 1.

120.   For example, it does not lay down any perfection rules with respect to chattel paper, instruments, and documents.

tween conflicting priority rules, but does not provide rules for all possible situations.[121]    Further, the section lays down no rules for choosing between conflicting state laws on default and on such rights between creditor and debtor as those set forth in 9–207.    In all such cases, the courts must turn to the situs rule of 9–102 to select governing law.

The independent significance of 9–102(1) as a situs rule for choosing between conflicting security law is aptly illustrated by the facts of Associates Discount Corp. v. Cary.[122]    Debtor and secured party entered into their car sale agreement in the District of Columbia, a jurisdiction that then permitted repossession and resale without notice to the debtor.    The debtor defaulted, and the secured party repossessed and resold the car in Massachusetts without notice to the debtor.    Local Massachusetts law required notice (9–504 of the Code).    The secured party thereafter sued for a deficiency in New York.    The New York Court looked to Massachusetts law, including its conflict of laws rules, for the applicable rule of decision and concluded that Massachusetts Uniform Commercial Code section 9–102(1) would apply the law of the situs of the car at the time of repossession, namely Massachusetts law.    Since this law required notice, the New York court held the repossession and resale invalid and denied the creditor's claim for a deficiency.

Though in a case of the *Cary* variety, the situs rule of 9–102 controls, only a very few courts have invoked it so far.[123]    Furthermore, scholars of the conflict of laws have attacked the rule as too inflexible.[124]    It is interesting to note that the new draft of Article Nine makes 9–102 "silent on conflict of laws problems," and provides that except for questions of perfection and priorities, the basic conflict provisions in 1–105 of Article One control all conflict questions.[125]    Section 9–103 of the new Article is redrafted to deal solely with questions of perfection and the effects of perfection and of non-perfection (rights of third parties).[126]

---

121.  For example, it does not lay down any rules on the "effect of proper filing" with respect to all forms of collateral falling within section 9–103.

122.  See, e. g., Associates Discount Corp. v. Cary, 47 Misc.2d 369, 262 N.Y.S.2d 646, 2 UCC Rep.Serv. 937 (Sup.Ct.1965) (law of state where collateral repossessed and resold controls necessity for notice of resale).

123.  United States v. Sommerville, 211 F.Supp. 843, 1 UCC Rep.Serv. 8 (W.D. Pa.1962), aff'd on other grounds 324 F.2d 712, 1 UCC Rep.Serv. 11 (3d Cir. 1963); In re Longnecker, 7 UCC Rep.Serv. 264 (Ref.Dec.W.D.Mich.

1969); Associates Discount Corp. v. Cary, 47 Misc.2d 369, 262 N.Y.S.2d 646, 2 UCC Rep.Serv. 937 (Sup.Ct. 1965).

124.  E. g. Weintraub, Choice of Law in Secured Personal Property Transactions: The Impact of Article 9 of the Uniform Commercial Code, 68 Mich. L.Rev. 684 (1970).

125.  Permanent Editorial Board for the Uniform Commercial Code, Review Committee for Article 9 of the Uniform Commercial Code, Final Report 229–30 (1971) (General Comment).

126.  Id. § 9–103 at 21–25.

In the 1962 Official Text, section 1–105 provides as follows:

(1) Except as provided hereafter in this section, when a transaction bears a reasonable relation to this state and also to another state or nation the parties may agree that the law either of this state or of such other state or nation shall govern their rights and duties. Failing such agreement this Act applies to transactions bearing an appropriate relation to this state.

(2) Where one of the following provisions of this Act specifies the applicable law, that provision governs and a contrary agreement is effective only to the extent permitted by the law (including the conflict of laws rules) so specified:

Rights of creditors against sold goods. Section 2—402.

Applicability of the Article on Bank Deposits and Collections. Section 4—102.

Bulk transfers subject to the Article on Bulk Transfers. Section 6—102.

Applicability of the Article on Investment Securities. Section 8—106.

Policy and scope of the Article on Secured Transactions. Sections 9—102 and 9—103.

Even with the 9–102(1) situs rule on the books, section 1–105 may apply to provide a choice of law rule for at least the sales aspects of a secured sale. Consider for example, the case of Skinner v. Tober Foreign Motors, Inc.[127] which involved a secured sale of an airplane and posed the necessity of choosing between Connecticut and Massachusetts law on requirements for a valid oral modification of contracts of sale. The court refused to apply 9–102(1) to determine the governing law and instead invoked 1–105(2). In so doing, the court noted that "neither party contests the validity or perfection of the security interest," and stressed that the issue involved was not an Article Nine issue but rather "the duties of the parties under the primary obligation." [128]

## § 22–10 Applicability of Article Nine to "Security Interests" that Arise under Article Two on Sales

The Code draftsmen have called certain interests that arise under Article Two on sales "security interests" even though they arise by operation of law:[129] (1) the rights of a shipper-seller to exercise control over goods in the hands of a carrier when he ships "under reservation" pursuant to 2–505, (2) the rights of a shipper-seller to

---

127. 345 Mass. 429, 187 N.E.2d 669, 1 UCC Rep.Serv. 1 (1963).

128. Id. at 433, 187 N.E.2d at 671, 1 UCC Rep.Serv. at 4.

129. §§ 9–113; 9–113, Comment 2. See generally Hogan, The Marriage of Sales to Chattel Security in the Uniform Commercial Code: Massachusetts Variety, 38 B.U.L.Rev. 571 (1958).

withhold delivery or stop in transit under 2–702, 2–703, and 2–705, (3) the rights of a financing agent to go against the goods under 2–506 and 2–707, and (4) certain rights of a rejecting buyer under 2–711(3).

The Code draftsmen could have left these rights entirely to Article Two. But they chose to call these rights "security interests" as that phrase is defined in 1–201(37). Without more, this would have rendered the whole of Article Nine applicable to these rights. But the draftsmen did not want this either. Accordingly, they drafted 9–113:

> A security interest arising solely under the Article on Sales (Article 2) is subject to the provisions of this Article except that to the extent that and so long as the debtor does not have or does not lawfully obtain possession of the goods
>
> (a) no security agreement is necessary to make the security interest enforceable; and
>
> (b) no filing is required to perfect the security interest; and
>
> (c) the rights of the secured party on default by the debtor are governed by the Article on Sales (Article 2).

This section keeps Article Nine from playing havoc with Article Two security interests. The Article Two interests are non-consensual. Accordingly, it makes sense to dispense with the necessity of a security agreement and this is what 9–113(a) does. Since the Article Two rights are possessory, their exercise ordinarily cannot prejudice relying third parties. Accordingly, 9–113(b) dispenses with filing. Since Article Two includes its own "default-foreclosure" provisions, section 9–113(c) makes those provisions controlling.

But if and when the debtor lawfully acquires possession of the goods, 9–113 provides that the seller's Article Two security interest terminates unless he complies with Article Nine. Even if the debtor does not acquire possession of the goods, some provisions of Article Nine remain applicable because subsections 9–113(a) (b) and (c), taken together, do not render the whole of Article Nine inapplicable. In particular, 9–113 says nothing of the Article Nine priority rules, and it would appear that the Article Nine priority rules apply here. Consider the following cases: Seller seeks to stop in transit or withhold delivery against the buyer, but the buyer has already resold to a bona fide purchaser. Are the rights of this purchaser governed by Article Nine, by Article Two, or by some other law? Or seller stops or withholds, and a lien-creditor of the buyer seeks to levy on the goods in the seller's hands. Do 9–201 and 9–301 control, or is the solution to be found in Article Two, or in still other law? To date there are no Code cases on these questions. But sections 1–201 (37), 9–102, and 9–113, read together and read literally, require that all such priority clashes be resolved under Article Nine.

## § 22-11  State and Federal Law that Over-Rides Article Nine

Even though Article Nine applies to a transaction, other federal or state law may displace the Article in whole or in part.  Most obvious, valid federal law over-rides Article Nine and 9–104(a) reminds us of this:

> "This Article does not apply  .  .  .  to a security interest subject to any statute of the United States such as the Ship Mortgage Act, 1920, to the extent that such statute governs the rights of parties to and third parties affected by transactions in particular types of property  .  .  ."

The U. S. Congress has enacted a variety of statutes in the security field,[130] but except for federal tax lien statutes [131] nearly all of them are skeletal in nature, and typically leave open such matters as requirements for creation of the interest, priorities, and default rights.  If the federal statute is silent, what law should a court use to fill the gap?  A court must choose either (1) to accept the invitation of the Code drafters in 9–104(a) to flesh out a federal statutory skeleton with Article Nine law, or (2) to flesh it out with common law entirely of the court's own making.  So far, most courts are taking the first course either on the theory that Congress had no power to or did not intend to pre-empt the entire field,[132] or on the theory that while the presence of the statute evinces an intent to pre-empt the entire field, the courts may properly look to Article Nine "by analogy" for the relevant governing rule.[133]

In a group of cases involving the Federal Home Administration as secured party, the courts have applied Article Nine unhesitatingly.[134]  In cases involving the federal Ship Mortgage Act, courts have

---

130.  These statutes are

(1) Truth in Lending Act of 1968, Pub. L.No.90–321, Title I, §§ 125, 128, 129, 82 Stat. 152, 15 U.S.C.A. §§ 1635, 1638, 1639 (1970) (regulatory);

(2) Act of Aug. 23, 1958, Pub.L.No.85–726, Title V, §§ 503, 504, 72 Stat. 772 as amended Act of July 8, 1959, Pub.L. No.86–81, §§ 1–4, 73 Stat. 180, 49 U.S.C.A. §§ 1403, 1404 (1970) (recording of aircraft ownership);

(3) Ship Mortgage Act of 1920, ch. 250, §§ 30, Subsections A–W, 41 Stat. 1000 as amended 46 U.S.C.A. §§ 911–984 (1970);

(4) Interstate Commerce Act of 1887, ch. 104, Part II, § 213 as added Aug. 23, 1958, Pub.L.No.85–728, § 1, 72 Stat. 812, 49 U.S.C.A. § 313 (1970) (recording of security interests in certain motor vehicles);

(5) Interstate Commerce Act of 1887, ch. 104, 24 Stat. 384 as added July 16, 1952, ch. 881, § 20(c), 66 Stat. 724, 49 U.S.C.A. § 20(c) (1970) (recording of railroad equipment trust agreements and other evidence of equipment indebtedness).

131.  Int.Rev.Code of 1970, §§ 6321–25.

132.  See, e. g., State Securities Co. v. Aviation Enterprises, Inc., 355 F.2d 225 (10th Cir. 1966); United States v. Sommerville, 211 F.Supp. 843, 1 UCC Rep.Serv. 8 (W.D.Pa.1962), aff'd on other grounds 324 F.2d 712, 1 UCC Rep.Serv. 11 (3d Cir. 1963).

133.  See, e. g., United States v. Hext, 444 F.2d 804, 9 UCC Rep.Serv. 321 (5th Cir. 1971).

134.  United States v. Sommerville, 211 F.Supp. 843, 1 UCC Rep.Serv. 8 (W.D. Pa.1962), aff'd on other grounds 324 F.2d 712, 1 UCC Rep.Serv. 11 (3d Cir. 1963); United States v. Gleaners and Farmers Cooperative Elevator Co., 314 F.Supp. 1148, 8 UCC Rep.Serv. 16 (N.D.Ind.1970).

resorted to Article Nine to resolve issues not explicitly dealt with in the federal act.[135]  In a further batch of cases involving federal statutes on security interests in airplanes, courts have resorted to Article Nine to fill gaps in the federal statutory scheme.[136]  But a few courts, state as well as federal, have indicated a disposition to make up some federal common law of their own on the theory that federal law "pre-empts the field." [137]  Of course, even if federal law pre-empts the field, a court could still resort to Article Nine by analogy.  The contrary assumption is simply fallacious.

State law, too, may over-ride Article Nine.  Of course, Article Nine generally does not apply anyway to the various state statutory and common law liens that arise by operation of law.[138]  But even where the security interest in personalty is consensual, other state law may govern.  Usually this other state law will govern only a relatively limited aspect of the transaction, with Article Nine remaining applicable to all other aspects.  The prime example is a state "certificate of title" law specifying the mode of perfecting a security interest in a motor vehicle.[139]  Article Nine itself contemplates the existence of such title laws, and expressly gives way to them in regard to filing.[140]  But even though some of these laws also include priority rules, those rules do not control when in conflict with Article Nine unless the legislature specifically so provides.

Many states have statutes regulating secured transactions in personalty, particularly those between businessmen and consumers.[141]

135.  See, e. g., Security Bank v. Levens, 480 P.2d 706, 8 UCC Rep.Serv. 977 (1971).

136.  See, e. g., State Securities Co. v. Aviation Enterprises, Inc., 355 F.2d 225 (10th Cir. 1966); Northern Illinois Corp. v. Bishop Distrib. Co., 284 F.Supp. 121, 5 UCC Rep.Serv. 84 (W.D. Mich.1968); American Airation, Inc. v. Airation Ins. Managers, Inc., 244 Ark. 829, 427 S.W.2d 544, 5 UCC Rep. Serv. 339 (1968); Southern Jersey Airways, Inc. v. National Bank, 108 N.J. Super. 369, 261 A.2d 399, 7 UCC Rep. Serv. 341 (1970); Suburban Trust & Savings Bank v. Campbell, 19 Ohio Misc. 74, 48 O.Op.2d 250, 6 UCC Rep. Serv. 964 (1969).

137.  United States v. United Aircraft Corp. 80 F.Supp. 52 (D.Conn.1948); Dowell v. Beech Acceptance Corp., 3 Cal.3d 544, 476 P.2d 401, 8 UCC Rep. Serv. 274 (1970); International Atlas Services, Inc. v. Twentieth Century Aircraft Co., 251 Cal.App.2d 434, 59 Cal.Rptr. 495, 4 UCC Rep.Serv. 439 (2d Dist.1967); cert. den. 389 U.S. 1038 (1968); Smith v. Eastern Airmotive Corp., 99 N.J.Super. 340, 240 A.2d 17, 4 UCC Rep.Serv. 1117 (1968).

138.  But see § 9–310, which reads as follows:

When a person in the ordinary course of his business furnishes services or materials with respect to goods subject to a security interest, a lien upon goods in the possession of such person given by statute or rule of law for such materials or services takes priority over a perfected security interest unless the lien is statutory and the statute expressly provides otherwise.

See also 2 G. Gilmore, Security Interests in Personal Property §§ 33.1–33.6 (1965).

139.  See, e. g., Mich.Stat.Ann. §§ 9.1917, 9.1922 (Supp.1971); Ohio Rev.Code Ann. § 4505.13 (Page Supp.1970).

140.  § 9–302(3).

141.  See, for instance, the Uniform Consumer Credit Code enacted in Oklahoma, Okla.Stat.Ann. tit. 12A, §§ 1–101 to 9–103 (1963), and in Utah, Utah Code Ann. 70B–1–101 to 70B–9–103 (Supp.1971). See also various "Retail Installment Sales Acts" discussed in Hogan, A Survey of State Retail In-

When these regulatory statutes conflict with Article Nine, doubtless most courts will hold that Article Nine must give way, even if the legislature has not specifically so provided. Often, the regulatory statute will simply add to the requirements of Article Nine, rather than over-ride them. For example, the statute may impose certain duties of disclosure on the creditor.[142] Sometimes, the statute will treat an aspect of the transaction that Article Nine does not cover at all. Usury and small loan controls on interest rates are illustrative.[143]

stallment Sales Legislation, 44 Cornell L.Rev. 38 (1958).

142. See, e. g., Uniform Consumer Credit Code § 2.302.

143. See, e. g., In re Cayer, 6 UCC Rep. Serv. 869 (Ref.Dec.D.Me.1969); Equipment Fin., Inc. v. Grannas, 207 Pa. Super. 363, 218 A.2d 81, 3 UCC Rep. Serv. 253 (1966).

# CHAPTER 23

# CREATION AND PERFECTION OF ENFORCE-ABLE ARTICLE NINE INTERESTS

*Analysis*

Sec.
23–1. Introduction.
23–2. Creation of Valid and Enforceable Article Nine Security Interests —General.
23–3. The Agreement and Signed Writing Requirements, 9–203, 9–204.
23–4. Value and Debtor Rights.
23–5. Perfection in General.
23–6. Automatic Perfection.
23–7. —— Purchase Money Interests in Farm Equipment and Consumer Goods, 9–302(1)(c) and (d).
23–8. —— Certain Accounts and Contract Rights, 9–302(1)(e).
23–9. —— Miscellaneous Automatic Perfection Provisions, 9–304(4) and (5), 9–306.
23–10. Perfection by Possession, 9–305.
23–11. Perfection by Filing—Places to File.
23–12. —— Where to File?
23–13. —— Classifying the Collateral.
23–14. —— Place of Business.
23–15. —— Effect of Filings Made in the Wrong Place, 9–401(2).
23–16. —— What to File? The Financing Statement, 9–402.
23–17. Perfection in Multiple State Transactions, 9–103.
23–18. —— Non-Mobile, Tangible Goods.
23–19. —— Mobile Goods, 9–103(2).
23–20. —— Intangibles, 9–103(1) and (2).
23–21. —— Automobiles and Other Vehicles Covered by Certificates of Title, 9–103(4).
23–22. Conclusion.

## § 23–1 Introduction

Article Nine applies to two kinds of interests: ordinary security interests in personal property and fixtures,[1] and the interests of buyers of certain accounts, contract rights and chattel paper[2] (which the Article also calls "security interests.") The Article lays down special steps that parties must take to create an enforceable security interest. Sections 23–2 through 23–4 of the present chapter are addressed to the steps that parties must take to create an enforceable Article Nine security interest.[3] Once such an interest is created, the secured party can always enforce it, on default, against the debtor,

---

1. § 9–102(1) (a). See Section 22–2 supra.

2. § 9–102(1) (b). See Section 22–8 supra.

3. In particular, see §§ 9–203; 9–204.

provided there are no third party interests superior to the interest of the secured party.

When the holder of a valid and enforceable Article Nine interest seeks to enforce that interest, third parties may then assert claims to the assets involved. If, at the time they initially acquired their interests they also took the *additional* steps required under Article Nine to "perfect," they will defeat *most* such third party claimants. Under the Code a creditor ordinarily perfects by making a public filing or by taking possession of the collateral. In Sections 23–5 through 23–21 we treat the Article Nine perfection requirements. In Chapters 24 and 25 we treat the rights of holders of Article Nine interests, perfected and unperfected, as against third parties. There we will see that even the holder of an unperfected interest defeats a few third parties, and that "perfection" is not really perfect: even holders of perfected security interests lose to some third parties under applicable law.[4]

## § 23–2   Creation of Valid and Enforceable Article Nine Security Interests—General

What steps must the parties take in order to create a valid and enforceable security interest? Sections 9–203 and 9–204 of Article Nine require that the parties take four steps to create a valid and enforceable security interest:

(*1*)  Enter into a security agreement,

(*2*)  Reduce so much of that agreement to a writing as is necessary to satisfy 9–203 (which also requires that the debtor sign this writing), or give possession of the collateral to the creditor,

(*3*)  Have the debtor acquire rights in the collateral,

(*4*)  Have the secured party give value.

All of the foregoing steps may not occur simultaneously, but once all have occurred, a valid Article Nine security interest, enforceable at least against the debtor, comes into existence. We consider each of the foregoing requirements in the up-coming sections.

## § 23–3   The Agreement and Signed Writing Requirements, 9–203, 9–204

When one pledges stock to secure a loan from his banker, he will often sign a note but no security agreement. Since the security arrangement is a pledge, the banker-secured party will take possession of the collateral and no writing is required in that transaction. Creditor's possession satisfies 9–203 and the oral understanding on the security aspects satisfies 9–204's agreement requirement. In far more common secured transactions the debtor has possession of the

4.   See, e. g., § 9–307.

collateral and in that case the secured creditor must comply with 9–203(1) (b) which provides that a security interest is not enforceable unless:

> the debtor has signed a security agreement which contains a description of the collateral and in addition, when the security interest covers crops or oil, gas or minerals to be extracted or timber to be cut, a description of the land concerned.

Here we consider the related requirements of an "agreement" (under 9–204) and a "written agreement" (under 9–203(1) (b)).

The quoted Section is Article Nine's statute of frauds and like other such statutes it requires only that certain terms be in writing: debtor's signature, a description of collateral, and enough additional matters to make the document an "agreement". As we shall see, one of the fighting issues is whether a financing statement that contains no clause "granting" a security interest can be an "agreement". Thus 9–203 presents three issues that have been litigated in a handful of cases:  (1) What will suffice as a debtor's signature?  (2) Is the description adequate? and (3) Does the document contain enough flesh to qualify as an "agreement"?

Looking first at the signature requirement, one notes that the word "signed" is defined in 1–201(39) and "includes any symbol executed or adopted by a party with present intention to authenticate a writing." Thus a handwritten signature is not essential—an authenticated symbol such as a typed or *facsimile* signature will do.[5] While the signature requirement (as with all Article Nine formalities) is therefore to be interpreted and applied in a liberal spirit,[6] formalism is already beginning to creep into the decided cases. For example, the Georgia Court of Appeals [7] and a Referee in Bankruptcy in the Eastern District of Tennessee [8] have both refused to regard a signature on one writing sufficient to authenticate other writings all part of the same overall deal. These cases are doubtless mavericks, and we suspect that the signature requirement will cause difficulty only in the rarest case.

Turning to the second requirement, that the security agreement contain a "description of the collateral", one should first compare the description requirement in 9–203 to the analogous description requirement (for financing statements) in 9–402. The two description requirements are intended to perform different functions and they offer different interpretive questions. The function of 9–203 is that of a statute of frauds; it is designed to minimize disputes between parties to the transaction over whether an agreement exists and over

**5.**  See the discussion of the signature requirement in Section 23–16 infra.

**6.**  See 1 G. Gilmore, Security Interests in Personal Property § 11.4 (1965).

**7.**  Food Serv. Equip. Co. v. First Nat'l Bank, 121 Ga.App. 421, 174 S.E.2d 216, 7 UCC Rep.Serv. 878 (1970).

**8.**  In re Atkins, 9 UCC Rep.Serv. 315 (Ref.Dec.E.D.Tenn.1971).

whether a certain item of collateral is or is not included in the security agreement. The function of the description in 9–402 is to put third parties on notice of the secured creditor's claim. In the view of some, tests for acceptable descriptions under the two sections should differ because the functions of the sections are different; the tests may also differ because 9–402(5) explicitly validates a financing statement although it "contains minor errors which are not seriously misleading." Section 9–203 does not include a similar validating proviso with respect to defects in a security agreement under 9–203.

Unfortunately, the functions of the two sections and the policies behind them lead different readers to opposite conclusions. On the one hand Professor Kripke concludes that the financing statement may contain a very broad and general description but that "[t]he detail required under this section [9–203] in the security agreement is greater than that required under UCC § 9–402 in the financing statement. . . ."[9] On the other hand, Referee Cyr has concluded that the policy behind 9–402 calls for a more specific statement than 9–203 requires:

> Whereas the formal requisites of an enforceable security agreement are in the nature of a statute of frauds provision . . . . [o]n the basis of that comparison it would appear that the description envisioned under [9–402] ought to be a more precise one than that required to evidence compliance with [9–203].[10]

We agree with Referee Cyr's analysis of 9–203 and with Professor Kripke's analysis of 9–402 and would conclude that the standards under 9–203 and 9–402 should not be different and that the courts should validate rather broad descriptions under either of them.

The court's inquiry under 9–203 into whether a "description" of the collateral is adequate inevitably leads into a second section, 9–204. That section requires the parties to "agree" that the interest attach. Presumably the written agreement must contain at least a general description which an objective observer would find to include the collateral in question. If it does not, the court should find that the writing requirement is not met and should not allow parol evidence further to define the type of collateral in fact covered by the security agreement. If the court concludes that the written agreement meets the minimum standards of 9–203, (e. g., creditor hereby receives an interest in debtor's "accounts receivable") and if it further concludes that the written security agreement is not a total integration of the agreement of the parties, it should permit testimony from the debtor or the creditor to prove what specific items of collateral the agreement covers (for example, "we agreed that only the accounts from the Detroit store were included"). As long as the

9. N.Y.U.C.C. § 9–203 at 394 (McKinney 1964) (Practice commentary).

10. In re Thibodeau, 6 UCC Rep.Serv. 873, 875 (Ref.Dec.D.Me.1969).

statute of frauds requirement in 9–203 is met and the written agreement is not a total integration, nothing in 9–204 precludes oral proof of the agreement as to specific collateral.

However a court should not permit such oral testimony to expand the objective meaning of a description contained in a financing statement filed under 9–402. Since the function of that statement is to give notice to third parties, it, more than the description in 9–203, must stand on its own two feet and it cannot be buttressed by oral understandings between the parties.

Most of the courts interpreting 9–203(1) (b) have been comparatively generous to the secured creditor. For example, one court found that a description of the collateral as "passenger and commercial automobiles" was satisfactory; [11] another found that "all inventory used in the production of boats" was adequate.[12] Of course if we are to carry out the draftsmen's intention and permit the secured creditor to claim a perfected security interest in after acquired property, comparatively general descriptions of the collateral must suffice for it would be impossible in most such cases for the secured creditor to describe the collateral with any greater precision at the beginning of the agreement. It will always be possible for a court to find that the collateral in question is not covered by the description given and is not therefore part of the agreed collateral.[13] In our judgment, a minority of courts have been unduly illiberal and have required more "description" than 9–203 and 9–110 contemplate.[14] For a discussion of analogous questions under 9–402, see Section 23–16.

Beyond the debtor's signature or authenticating symbol *and* the required description of the collateral, must the writing include anything further to comply with 9–203(1) (b)? In most cases the writing will include much more, but our question is still an important one to those who represent slovenly creditors, after the fact. For various reasons, secured parties have presented a number of cases to courts in which the writings involved included little or nothing beyond the signature and the description of collateral. These cases fall into three groups. First are those in which the parties have signed a document such as a lease which fully sets out the rights of the putative debtor and creditor. The second are those in which the parties executed a proper financing statement and another document such as a note that makes a sketchy reference to the security agreement. Third

---

11.  Girard Trust Corn Exch. Bank v. Warren Lepley Ford, Inc. (No. 2), 13 Pa.D. & C.2d 119, 1 UCC Rep.Serv. 500 (C.P.1957) (bank financed dealer's wholesale purchase of automobiles).

12.  In re Fibre Glass Boat Corp., 324 F.Supp. 1054, 9 UCC Rep.Serv. 118 (Ref.Dec.S.D.Fla.1971).

13.  See, e. g., In re Laminated Veneers, Inc., 8 UCC Rep.Serv. 602 (Ref.Dec.

E.D.N.Y.1970) ("equipment" not sufficient to describe autos in question).

14.  See, e. g., In re Laminated Veneers, Inc., 8 UCC Rep.Serv. 602 (Ref.Dec. E.D.N.Y.1970); Still Associates, Inc. v. Murphy, 44 Mass.App.Dec. 9, 7 UCC Rep.Serv. 560 (1970) (serial number error that occurred apparently in both security agreement and in financing statement defeated secured creditor).

are the cases in which the only written document that makes any reference to a security agreement is the financing statement. In each of these cases the creditor has attempted to persuade the court that the documents so signed constituted a "security agreement". In the first kind of case, those in which the parties have executed a comprehensive written document that sets out their agreement but an agreement to which Article Nine assigns a different label than the parties did (for example, lease with nominal option = security agreement), the courts have found that the parties complied with 9–203 and that a security interest was created.[15]

A recent North Carolina case is illustrative of the second situation. In Evans v. Everett,[16] the financing statement stated that it "covers the following type of collateral . . . same securing note for advanced money to produce crops for the year 1969." The note in that case stated that it was "secured by Uniform Commercial Code financing statement of North Carolina." The court found that the use of the verb "secure" in the note and in the financing statement was sufficient to qualify the two as a security agreement under 9–203 (1) (b).[17]

No court has yet found that a financing statement standing alone meets the requirements of 9–203(1) (b) as a security agreement. Normally one regards the financing statement as a notice or memorialization of an agreement reached at another time and embodied in another document. The description of the collateral in the financing statement is not likely to be as precise as the parties would normally use for description in the security agreement itself, nor does the typical financing statement contain words which would constitute a "grant"[18] of a security interest. Primarily for the latter reason the courts have unanimously rejected the argument that a financing statement is a "security agreement" sufficient to satisfy the statute of frauds requirement of 9–203(1) (b).[19]

15. See In re Walter W. Willis, Inc., 313 F.Supp. 1274, 7 UCC Rep.Serv. 1125 (N.D. Ohio 1970), aff'd 440 F.2d 995; 8 UCC Rep.Serv. 1330 (6th Cir. 1971).

16. 279 N.C. 352, 183 S.E.2d 109 (1971).

17. Accord, In re Center Auto Parts, 6 UCC Rep.Serv. 398 (Ref.Dec.C.D.Cal. 1968) (note stated it was "secured by a certain financing statement").

18. One will not find the "granting" terminology in the Code. Professor Gilmore has sharply criticized an early case which held that a financing statement could not be a security agreement because it failed to contain the debtor's grant of a security interest.

The § 9–402 provision that a short financing statement may be filed in place of the full security agreement was designed to simplify the operation. The Rhode Island court [in American Card Co. v. H. M. H. Co., 97 R.I. 59, 196 A.2d 150, 1 UCC Rep. Serv. 447 (R.I.1963)] gives it an effect reminiscent of the worst formal requisites holding under the nineteenth century chattel mortgage acts.

1 G. Gilmore, Security Interests in Personal Property § 11.4 at 348 (1965).

19. See, e. g., In re Mann, 8 UCC Rep.Serv. 132 (Ref.Dec.W.D.Va.1970); Needle v. Lasco Indus., Inc., 10 Cal. App.3d 1105, 89 Cal.Rptr. 593, 8 UCC Rep.Serv. 9 (2d Dist. 1970).

Have the courts been too quick to reject the secured creditor's argument here? We are unsure. One can argue that the financing statement should be treated like an Article Two statute of frauds memorandum and that its presence is sufficient evidence that an agreement was made to permit the secured party to flesh out the remainder of the agreement orally.[20] On the other side is the argument that financing statements can be and are filed in cases when the negotiations on a security agreement are still in progress and before any security agreement has been reached. Thus, so the argument goes, the mere presence of a financing statement does not sufficiently indicate that there has been an agreement at all between the parties and a court therefore should not receive oral testimony to flesh out the alleged agreement. We mildly incline toward acceptance of the financing statement as a security agreement and think that the courts have perhaps been too quick to reject the secured creditor's argument.

## § 23–4   Value and Debtor Rights

Two parties may have an agreement for security under 9–204(1) and they may reduce it to writing to the extent necessary to comply

---

**20.** Section 9–105(h) determines that a " 'Security agreement' means an agreement which creates or provides for a security interest." (Emphasis added.) An "agreement" can be found in the parties' "language or by implication from other circumstances . . ." § 1–201(3). The agreement can either "create" a security interest or it can "provide for" a security interest. Presumably when courts suggest that a security agreement must "grant" a security interest, they are focusing on the concept of "create." That focus may be too narrow. The courts confuse a secured transaction with a security agreement. It is clear that Article Nine deals only with a "transaction (regardless of its form) which is intended to create a security interest . . . ." § 9–102(1) (a). Nevertheless, the written security agreement may serve a function other than creation. It is not necessary that a writing *create* the security interest; indeed, pledge interests without any writing create effective security interests under the Code. The purpose of a writing is merely evidentiary:

The requirement of written record minimizes the possibility of future dispute as to the terms of a security agreement and as to what property stands as collateral for the obligation secured. Where the collateral is in the possession of the secured party, the evidentiary need for a written record is much less than where the collateral is in the debtor's possession

. . . Subsection (1) (a), therefore, dispenses with the written agreement . . . if the collateral is in the secured party's possession.

§ 9–203, Comment 3.

Put another way, the document is a precautionary device "in the nature of a Statute of Frauds" intended to reduce some of the problems of parol evidence. § 9–203, Comment 3. Courts should be willing to focus on the "provide for" language of 9–105 (h). Presumably it is not superfluous, not synonymous with "create." Websters Third New International Dictionary (unabridged ed. 1968) gives as the primary definition of "provide": "to take precautionary measures." Such a definition works well with the general intent of 9–203 to protect against parol evidence.

Notice that Comment 4 of 9–203 indicates that a security agreement does not require a special type of document. Even "a bill of sale although absolute in form" may constitute a security agreement. Whether such a document can be a security agreement is a matter of "fact"—not law. If the parties intended to have a secured transaction and used a financing statement (signed by the debtor and describing the collateral) as evidence of their agreement, 9–203 should be satisfied. "Further inquiry from the parties concerned will be necessary to disclose the complete state of affairs." § 9–402, Comment 2.

with 9–203(1) (b). Even so, the security interest they intend to create will not come into being until two additional events occur: the debtor must acquire rights in the collateral, and the secured party must give value. When these events occur, the security interest will "attach" under 9–204(1), and not until it thus "attaches" to specific collateral can the interest come into being. (One of your authors is an ontologist.)

The *time* when a security interest comes into being is of great importance under the Article Nine priority rules and under the Federal Bankruptcy Act, topics to which we turn in later chapters.[21] The *time* when a security interest comes into being is an important baseline for determining priorities.

Section 9–204(1) states:

A security interest cannot attach until there is agreement (subsection (3) of Section 1–201) that it attach and value is given and the debtor has rights in the collateral. It attaches as soon as all of the events in the preceding sentence have taken place unless explicit agreement postpones the time of attaching.

Section 1–201(44) defines value in the following terms:

"Value". Except as otherwise provided with respect to negotiable instruments and bank collections (Sections 3–303, 4–208 and 4–209) a person gives "value" for rights if he acquires them

(a) in return for a binding commitment to extend credit or for the extension of immediately available credit whether or not drawn upon and whether or not a charge-back is provided for in the event of difficulties in collection; or

(b) as security for or in total or partial satisfaction of a pre-existing claim; or

(c) by accepting delivery pursuant to a pre-existing contract for purchase; or

(d) generally, in return for any consideration sufficient to support a simple contract.

The initial harvest of Article Nine cases under this section includes few surprises. Despite the plain language of 1–201(44) (b), several parties have argued that a creditor does not give value if he takes his security interest to secure a pre-existing claim against the debtor. The courts have tossed these parties out on their ears, as well they ought.[22] Also, under 1–201(44) (a) and (d), a creditor's

---

21. See Chs. 24 and 25 infra.

22. See, e. g., In re Platt, 257 F.Supp. 478, 3 UCC Rep.Serv. 719 (E.D.Pa. 1966); Stumbo v. Paul B. Hult Lumber Co., 251 Ore. 20, 444 P.2d 564, 5 UCC Rep.Serv. 753 (1968).

binding executory promise to extend credit or to make a loan constitutes value as of the time when his promise becomes binding.[23] What if a creditor does not make a binding commitment, but later extends credit or lends? Here, he gives value as of the time when he actually extends credit or lends.[24] In view of 1–201(44) (d), which provides that a creditor gives value if he gives "any consideration sufficient to support a simple contract" it would appear that in states following the peppercorn theory of consideration, a creditor can acquire a security interest simply by giving a nominal consideration in exchange.

When the debtor and creditor sit down to create a security interest, the debtor may already have "rights in the collateral." If so, the security interest will thereafter "attach" as soon as the parties so specify and the creditor gives value. But, at the time of the agreement, the debtor may not have rights in the prospective collateral. Indeed Article Nine itself specifies that a debtor cannot, for purposes of the Article, have rights in certain specified forms of collateral until certain future events have occurred. Section 9–204(2) states:

> For the purposes of this section the debtor has no rights
>
> (a) in crops until they are planted or otherwise become growing crops, in the young of livestock until they are conceived;
>
> (b) in fish until caught, in oil, gas or minerals until they are extracted, in timber until it is cut;
>
> (c) in a contract right until the contract has been made;
>
> (d) in an account until it comes into existence.

However, as we have already noted, 9–204(3) sanctions "after-acquired property clauses" so integral to the floating lien: "Except as provided in subsection (4), a security agreement may provide that collateral, whenever acquired, shall secure all obligations covered by the security agreement." Thus the parties may agree that the creditor's security interest floats over existing *and* after-acquired property of the debtor. When does the creditor's interest in the after-acquired property attach? It would seem that it could not attach until the debtor later acquired it, for not until then would it seem that he could have "rights in the collateral". Yet at least for the purposes of the bankruptcy law, several courts have held that where the original security is created in an "entity" such as inventory or accounts and at least some items of collateral are then owned by the debtor, the creditor's interest attaches at the time of the original agreement—even to the after-acquired inventory or accounts. For

**23.** See, e. g., In re United Thrift Stores, Inc., 363 F.2d 11, 3 UCC Rep. Serv. 468 (3d Cir. 1966); Honea v. Laco Auto Leasing, Inc., 80 N.M. 300, 454 P.2d 782, 6 UCC Rep.Serv. 37 (1969).

**24.** Cf. State Bank v. Kahn, 58 Misc.2d 655, 296 N.Y.S.2d 391, 6 UCC Rep. Serv. 43 (Sup.Ct.1969) (not clear from facts whether binding commitment was made prior to actual loan).

reasons well stated by Professor Gilmore we believe the same result almost always follows from either theory:

> "In the case of an after-acquired property arrangement, it is clear that, if A made an April 1 loan against X's machinery and X acquired new machinery on May 1, A would have two security interests, one arising on April 1 and the other on May 1. This follows from the § 9–204(1) provision that a security interest cannot attach until the debtor 'has rights in the collateral.' We may note further, however, that in general A would take priority over competing security interests in the after-acquired machinery not from May 1 (date of attachment and perfection) but from April 1 (date of filing) and also that A would not lose to a lien which attached on April 15: on April 15, the May 1 machinery would not be there for the lien to attach to, and on May 1 the new machinery would automatically be covered by A's security interest. (The lien would of course be effective against X's equity in the machinery.) Thus, although we say that an after-acquired property arrangement gives rise to a series of separate security interests which attach and become perfected as property is acquired, we are not thereby led to the conclusion that the secured party becomes vulnerable to intervening liens or security interests . . . ." [25]

In a rare case the creditor may be subordinated because his debtor does not "acquire rights" in the collateral until after other events have occurred. We conclude that such subordinations are rare because most other claimants would also claim through the debtor (for example, lien creditors) and if the secured creditor's interest attached and became perfected simultaneously with the debtor's acquisition of rights, the worst he could suffer against any competitor who claimed through his debtor is parity; in most cases he would be prior to such parties because they would have to levy or take some other action to "perfect" their interests after the debtor acquired rights.[26]

---

25. See 2 G. Gilmore, Security Interests in Personal Property § 35.6 at 936–37 (1965). See also the discussion in Section 24–5 infra. When the debtor owns none of the collateral at the time of agreement and the entire collateral is to be after-acquired, there is no entity to which the security interest can attach and the security interest will not attach until the debtor has acquired at least one piece of the collateral. Assume, for example, that a secured creditor contemplated lending only against a new line of Maytag washing machines that his debtor intended to purchase. At the time the security agreement was signed the debtor owned no Maytag washing machines but dealt exclusively in RCA merchandise. The security interest would attach only when the debtor had acquired rights in the new washing machines, and it could become perfected only at that time (even if a perfecting act such as filing had previously occurred). As we have said, an interest must attach before it can be perfected, and perfection will often be the base line from which we measure priority in collateral.

26. But see Framingham UAW Credit Union v. Dick Russell Pontiac, Inc., 7 UCC Rep.Serv. 252 (Mass.App.Div.

What kinds of "rights in the collateral" may the debtor acquire that will suffice under 9–204(1)? Obviously full ownership will suffice. But courts have so far intimated that less will do. The contract rights of a debtor-purchaser of goods under Article Two may suffice even though the third party seller has not shipped the goods.[27] Thus a secured creditor of a debtor-purchaser *may* have a security interest in goods still in the hands of the debtor's seller. In one case, however, the court suggested that a debtor purchaser could not acquire "rights in the collateral" until the goods were actually delivered to him.[28] While this seems erroneous, a secured party's rights, qua secured party, against his debtor's seller can generally rise no higher than the rights of the debtor against the seller. Article Nine generally does not purport to cut off the rights and remedies under Article Two of third party sellers who have sold but not delivered goods to debtors that have encumbered their assets to secured parties.[29] Nor does Article Nine purport to cut off ownership claims of third parties: If a debtor encumbers "his asset" and it turns out not to be his asset, the Article Nine secured party is generally out of luck.[30] One possible exception should be noted: If the debtor acquires goods from a third party merely on consignment, he may, under appropriate circumstances, pass a security interest in the goods to his creditor that will cut off the interest of the consignor.[31] That is, a debtor may acquire "rights in the collateral" where the collateral consists merely of consigned goods.

Because of the way 9–203 and 9–204 are drafted, a distinction can be drawn between a valid security interest and an enforceable one.[32] The latter section allows a valid security interest to "attach"

N.D.1969), where the court held § 9–312(5) does not demand parity between simultaneously perfected interests. The court's reasoning is circular and unpersuasive. Under the laws of most states a creditor must levy in order to acquire a lien on personal property. Therefore he could not acquire a lien until the debtor had acquired the property. At some time before the debtor's acquisition of the property he would presumably have "acquired rights," and the security interest would have attached. Thus for most purposes the perfected secured creditor would win.

We are unsure how these rules apply in the rare case in which a debtor, already in bankruptcy, acquires new property. In such cases one could argue that the trustee's rights and the secured creditor's rights attach simultaneously. We venture no opinion on the outcome in that case.

27. See In re Pelletier, 5 UCC Rep. Serv. 327 (Ref.Dec.D.Me.1968). See also, Hogan, Future Goods, Floating Liens, and Foolish Creditors, 17 Stan. L.Rev. 822 (1965).

28. In re Page, 6 UCC Rep.Serv. 250 (Ref.Dec.W.D.Ky.1968). In that case, however, the Referee, had concluded that the debtor acquired rights in the collateral when it was shipped to him.

29. Indeed, such a seller may himself have an Article Two "security interest" perfected without filing under 9–113 that takes priority over the consensual Article Nine interest.

30. This is true in the clear case where the debtor is a thief. Whether the debtor can pass a better title than his seller had depends partly on 2–403.

31. Sussen Rubber Co. v. Hertz, 18 Ohio App.2d 1, 249 N.E.2d 65, 6 UCC Rep. Serv. 769 (1969). See § 2–326.

32. Recchio v. Manufacturers & Traders Trust Co., 35 App.Div.2d 769, 316 N.Y. S.2d 915, 8 UCC Rep.Serv. 565 (4th Dep't 1970). Proposed amendments to 9–203(1) cure this anomaly by incorporating into the

even without a writing. The former, however, provides that if the interest is non-possessory it is not enforceable against the debtor or third parties unless in writing. Thus it is possible for a valid security interest to "attach" yet be unenforceable. If and when the parties do sign a writing, does the interest date from the time of its original attachment or from the time of the writing? No court has yet faced this question, but we see no harm in dating the interest from the time of the attachment. Moreover, some of the Code rules expressly require use of the date of attachment.[33]

## § 23–5   Perfection in General

Perfection is a term of art in Article Nine. We devote the remainder of this chapter to mapping its boundaries and plotting its topography. The legal consequences of perfection are considerable. Indeed, the perfected secured creditor is nearly as far above the unperfected secured creditor on the pecking order as the unperfected secured creditor is above the general creditor. The most crucial legal consequence of perfection is the priority it earns the secured party over a subsequent lien creditor. Of course, the lien creditor par excellence is the trustee in bankruptcy wielding his section 70(c) rights. Thus a secured party who perfects prior to bankruptcy is likely to have the right to snatch the collateral out of the trustee's hands, but an unperfected secured party will invariably have to eat from the general creditors' trough in bankruptcy.[34]

Likewise, perfection or performance of the perfecting act of filing is commonly the date from which priority is measured *vis-a-vis* other perfected secured creditors. Usually, though not invariably, a creditor who perfects his security interests in collateral has a right superior to secured creditors who perfect later than he does and is subordinate to those who perfected prior to his perfection.

By far the most common and most important method of perfection of a security interest under Article Nine is the filing of a financing statement. As we will see, a financing statement is a simple notice which contains only enough information to notify a reader that the creditor named claims an interest in certain categories of collateral belonging to the debtor named. The financing statement is not often the operative document which created the

---

concept of enforceability of a security interest the elements of agreement, value, and rights in the collateral. Thus a security interest will "attach" when all such events, including a writing when necessary, have occurred." Permanent Editorial Board for the Uniform Commercial Code, Review Committee for Article 9, Final Report § 9–203 at 61–62 (1971).

**33.**   See, e. g., § 9–312(5) (c).

**34.**   Of course, the perfection also operates as a "four month" notice in the case of the creditor who sees his debtor slipping toward bankruptcy and who has made a delayed filing on a preexisting debt. In such case the other creditors have four months in which to throw the debtor into bankruptcy and so have the benefit of the secured creditor's collateral by virtue of the trustee's use of § 60. If they wait more than four months, the trustee will not be able to upset the secured creditor's interest under § 60.

security interest between the parties but is merely a publicly filed notice which tells a reader where to hunt for more information. A second method of perfection which *may* be used with respect to certain kinds of collateral and which *must* be used with respect to some kinds of collateral is creditor possession of the collateral—the pledge. Finally, some security interests are automatically perfected under the Code at the time of their creation and without the performance of any additional act by the secured creditor. In such cases the secured creditor has a perfected security interest as soon as he has complied with the provisions of 9–203 and 9–204. The most important of this last group are the nickel and dime cases: purchase money security interests in consumer goods.

There is no mystery about the policies the Code draftsmen had in mind when they proposed the perfection provisions in Article Nine. Quite clearly they believed that one who would be given the rights of a perfected secured creditor should in the normal course of events undertake some action, either filing or possession, which would put a reasonably diligent searcher on notice of the secured party's claim. The draftsmen also wished to increase the certainty that a good faith effort at filing would be successful and that a good faith search would reveal the presence of the secured creditor's claim. As we will see, the draftsmen made sensible compromises with respect to some of these policies in circumstances where it appeared that the cost of public filing would out-weigh the benefits to be gained by such filing.[35]

## § 23–6  Automatic Perfection

Those familiar with "conditional sale contracts" and the conditional sales law will find the automatic perfection provision of Article Nine reassuringly familiar. The most significant type of security interest perfected without filing or the taking of possession is the purchase money security interest in consumer goods,[36] (the conditional sale in new attire). Automatically perfected security interests of lesser importance are purchase money interests in farm equip-

---

35. An interesting question which seems not to have been asked in the preparation of the Code is whether a public filing system is really necessary at all. Empirical data on the point is largely unavailable, but one suspects that some of our assumptions about the diligence with which one searches the files and our conclusions about the protection to which he is entitled if there is no filing may be quite wrong. Of course the opportunity for debtor fraud would be significantly increased if there were no method of filing, and it is possible that debtors who are now kept in line by the filing system would misbehave under a system where there was no filing, but it is far from clear that they would so behave in significant numbers.

36. Three states do not permit automatic perfection of purchase money security interests in consumer goods; Kansas, Maine, and Oklahoma. The official text of section 9–302(1)(d) is omitted in those states' codes.

Three other states have imposed purchase price limitations above which automatic perfection is not allowed: Maryland ($500), Colorado ($250), and Wisconsin ($250).

ment costing less than $2500,[37] certain limited security interests in accounts and contract rights (9–302(1) (e)) and the temporarily perfected security interests in instruments, negotiable documents (9–304 (4) and proceeds (9–306)).

Those parts of 9–302(1) relevant to our discussion read:

A financing statement must be filed to perfect all security interests except the following:

. . .

(b) a security interest temporarily perfected in instruments or documents without delivery under Section 9–304 or in proceeds for a 10 day period under Section 9–306;

(c) a purchase money security interest in farm equipment having a purchase price not in excess of $2500; but filing is required for a fixture under Section 9–313 or for a motor vehicle required to be licensed;

(d) a purchase money security interest in consumer goods; but filing is required for a fixture under Section 9–313 or for a motor vehicle required to be licensed;

(e) an assignment of accounts or contract rights which does not alone or in conjunction with other assignments to the same assignee transfer a significant part of the outstanding accounts or contract rights of the assignor; . . .

The comments [38] make explicit what is only implicit in the body of the Code, namely that the interests in (c), (d) and (e) are automatically perfected upon attachment of the security interest.

## § 23–7   Automatic Perfection—Purchase Money Interests in Farm Equipment and Consumer Goods, 9–302(1)(c) and (d)

One impressed with the carefully constructed Code filing system can properly ask why a significant group of all security transactions need not be filed for perfection. Why should not merchants who wish

---

37. Two states do not permit automatic perfection of purchase money security interests in farm equipment: Kansas and Oklahoma. The official text of section 9–302(1) (c) is omitted in those states' codes.

Fifteen states have imposed $500 purchase price limitations: Colorado, Indiana, Kentucky, Maine, Maryland, Massachusetts, Missouri, New Hampshire, New Jersey, Ohio, Rhode Island, Tennessee, Vermont, Virginia,

and Wisconsin. Iowa has a $1000 limitation.

38. See, e. g., § 9–302, Comments 4, 5: " . . . [T]he security interests described in subsections (1) (c) and (1) (d) are perfected without filing. . . ." "A financing statement must be filed to perfect a security interest in accounts or contract rights, except for the transactions described in subsection (1) (e)."

to claim security interests in furniture, stoves, refrigerators and washing machines be required to make their claims a part of the public record when they seek the preferred status of a perfected creditor? The answers to that question seem partly historical and partly practical. In the first place, sellers of consumer goods and those who lent the purchase price of such goods were accustomed under the pre-Code law of many states to perfected status without filing.[39] If the Code had required filing in all cases, these sellers and lenders might not have supported enactment of the Code. Permitting automatic perfection was no departure from the pre-Code law; in fact it was the continuation of a much cherished and well entrenched practice. Secondly, the expense to the creditor and therefore ultimately to the debtor and to the filing system itself of requiring a filing in each modest sized transaction would be considerable. If the filing fee were $2.00 it would make little sense to file on a $100 or $200 transaction, and if creditors had to file with respect to every small transaction all the courthouses in the country would be bulging at the seams in two years. Further, the benefits to be gained from filing in such transactions are marginal. As Professor Bunn pointed out in the New York Law Revision Commission Reports,[40] creditors are accustomed to perfection of "conditional sales" without filing and will therefore be on their guard when a consumer or a farmer attempts to procure a second loan on an item previously perfected automatically. Moreover, most consumer goods are of comparatively low cost and suffer comparatively rapid depreciation. For those reasons it is unlikely that creditors will often make loans in reliance upon such goods. Even by hindsight the decision to free purchase money security interests in inexpensive farm equipment and consumer goods from the filing requirements of the Code seems sensible.

The cases reported to date on 9-302(1) (c) and (d) expose only a few significant lawyer problems. How does one define a purchase money security interest, and particularly how does one identify that part of a consolidated indebtedness which in fact represents the purchase price of a specific item? How does one define "consumer goods" and "farm equipment"? Can massive and expensive items such as house trailers be consumer goods?

In most circumstances the identification of a purchase money security interest is a simple and straightforward task. If the seller has retained an interest in the goods sold to secure payment of some or all of the price, he has a purchase money security interest whether he calls this agreement with the buyer a "conditional sale contract", a "bailment lease" or the "Jefferson Airplane."[41] Note also that a

---

**39.** Section 9-302, Comment 4: "In many jurisdictions under prior law security interests in consumer goods under conditional sale or bailment lease have not been subject to filing requirements."

**40.** 2 N.Y. State Law Revision Comm'n, 1954 Report 1086, 1089 question 4 (1954).

**41.** Section 9-107(a):

A security interest is a "purchase money security interest" to the extent that it is
(a) taken or retained by the seller of the collateral to secure all or part of its price; . . . .

third party (for example, a bank or finance company) who lends money to a prospective buyer to assist him in the purchase can also qualify as a purchase money lender under 9–107(b). Such a person must make advances or incur an obligation "to enable the debtor to acquire rights in or the use of collateral." [42] He is a purchase money lender only if the money lent is "in fact so used". Elsewhere we will consider the importance of the limitations in 9–107(b); [43] it suffices for now to understand that the third party has a purchase money security interest only if he can show that the money he lent was "in fact" used to acquire an interest in the collateral in question.

The principal interpretive dificulty presented by 9–302(1) (d) arises in cases in which the purchaser-debtor buys a series of hard goods from one seller; the seller takes a security interest in each of the goods sold, and provides in his security agreement that the security interest secures not only the purchase price of those goods but also the purchase price of items previously purchased and, to the extent possible,[44] items subsequently purchased. Under 9–107(a) the seller's security interest in any collateral is a purchase money interest only to the extent that it secures all or part of "its price". "Its" modifies the "collateral" purchased; to the extent collateral secures a debt for the price of other collateral, that interest is not a purchase money interest. The problem for the seller who wishes to sustain his interest as perfected in bankruptcy becomes one of proration of the amount paid on a consolidated account to the various items purchased. Unless the seller is able to satisfy the court that a specified amount of the outstanding indebtedness in fact represents the purchase price of the goods in question, he will lose his status as a purchase money lender, will therefore not be perfected under 9–302(1) (d), and will in most circumstances therefore lose to the trustee in bankruptcy.[45] A recent

---

See, e. g., In re Kretzer, 1 UCC Rep. Serv. 369 (Ref.Dec.E.D.Pa.1955); In re Robertson, 6 UCC Rep.Serv. 266 (Ref.Dec.E.D.Tenn.1969); Lonoke Production Credit Ass'n v. Bohannon, 238 Ark. 206, 379 S.W.2d 17, 2 UCC Rep. Serv. 172 (1964).

**42.**   Section 9–107(b):

A security interest is a "purchase money security interest" to the extent that it is . . .

(b) taken by a person who by making advances or incurring an obligation gives value to enable the debtor to acquire rights in or the use of collateral if such value is in fact so used.

Cf. Rockland Credit Union, Inc. v. Gauthier Motors, Inc., 5 UCC Rep. Serv. 637 (Mass.App.Div.1967).

**43.**   See, text, infra at § 25–5.

**44.**   Section 9–204(4) (b):

No security interest attaches under an after-acquired property clause . . .

(b) to consumer goods other than accessions (Section 9–314) when given as additional security unless the debtor acquires rights in them within ten days after the secured party gives value.

**45.**   If the security interest is unperfected (because the secured party has not filed and is not entitled to automatic perfection), the trustee will have a prior right as a lien creditor under Section 70(c) of the Bankruptcy Act and under section 9–301(1) (b) of the Code.

bankruptcy case, In re Brouse,[46] well illustrates the problem. There the bankrupt had made 13 separate purchases from Gamble-Skogmo, Inc.; in each case Gamble-Skogmo had retained a security interest but had filed no financing statements. The total amount of the indebtedness had been combined and the debtor had made periodic payments against the consolidated indebtedness. The trustee argued that his rights were superior to the seller's because the seller could not prove that any specific part of the outstanding indebtedness was in fact part of the purchase price of the collateral in question. The court agreed with the trustee's argument as to a stereo which had been purchased several years prior to the bankruptcy[47] but rejected the trustee's argument as to a cupboard which had been purchased later and subsequent to the enactment of the Michigan Retail Installment Sales Act. As to the latter item the court found that the seller could pro rate the debtor's payments according to a formula provided in the Retail Installment Sales Act and was thus entitled to a perfected security interest in the cupboard equal to the unpaid balance of the purchase price of the cupboard. The court held that the amount of the price unpaid should be determined according to the formula set out in the Retail Installment Sales Act.

The *Brouse* case has several lessons for lawyers who represent secured sellers. There are two airtight solutions to the problem faced by the seller in *In re Brouse*. The first is to file a financing statement which covers all of the transactions with the debtor. The second is to consolidate only nickel and dime indebtedness and to leave any big ticket items on a separate and unconsolidated account. Of course each of these solutions may be economically impractical and it will then be the lawyer's task as a draftsman to provide some contractual formula for the allocation of the debtor's payments to the various items which he has purchased. Although the *Brouse* case does not state whether the security agreement in that case had a pro ration clause and does not indicate whether a pro ration agreement inconsistent with the Retail Installment Sales Act formula would be given effect, such an agreement should be given effect as long as it is not unfair to the debtor.[48] Here the draftsman should tread very carefully, for the question of pro ration of the purchase price has been a burning issue in the case law, in the Uniform Consumer Credit Code[49] and elsewhere. The pro ration clause was a principal basis

---

**46.** 6 UCC Rep.Serv. 471 (Ref.Dec.W.D. Mich.1969).

**47.** Id. at 474. Accord, In re Simpson, 4 UCC Rep.Serv. 243 (Ref.Dec.W.D. Mich.1966).

**48.** Section 1–102(3) authorizes parties to vary the provisions of the Code by agreement "except as otherwise provided in this Act and except that the obligations of good faith, diligence, reasonableness and care . . . may not be disclaimed. . . ."

**49.** See UCCC § 2.409(1) which reads in full as follows:

If debts arising from two or more consumer credit sales, other than sales primarily for an agricultural purpose or pursuant to a revolving charge account, are secured by cross-collateral (Section 2.408) or consolidated into one debt payable on a single schedule of payments, and the debt is secured by security interests taken with respect to one or more of the sales, payments received by the seller after the taking

for the finding that the security agreement in Williams v. Walker-Thomas Furniture Co.[50] was unconscionable.  There the contract provided in effect that each payment would be pro rated to the various items secured in proportion to the price of each item.  The effect of the clause was to retain a security interest in *all* items purchased until the last penny of the entire debt was paid.  In the *Brouse* case the court adopted a pro ration formula from the Michigan Retail Installment Sales Act identical to the one found so offensive in *Walker-Thomas*.  Nevertheless a careful lawyer will not offer such a clause to his client without some serious warnings about potential unconscionability.  We believe that a wise draftsman will provide for a first-in, first-out method of pro ration.  In such case the debtor's payments on the principal of the debt would be assigned first to the debts first incurred.  Thus, if the debtor made ten one hundred dollar purchases but made only one payment per month on the entire one thousand dollar indebtedness, the collateral purchased with the first one hundred dollars woud be freed from the security interest as soon as the debtor had paid one hundred dollars of principal on the indebtedness.  A FIFO pro ration is blessed by the UCCC [51] and will avoid the difficulty suggested in the *Walker-Thomas* case, for the debtor will free items of collateral from the security interest as he pays.  Such a method of pro ration will serve the creditor's legitimate interest in bankruptcy by leaving the full purchase price of any given item outstanding until all items previously purchased have been paid off.

The second lawyer question presented by 9–302(1) (c) and (d) is the classification of the collateral involved.  Turning first to (1) (d), how does one define consumer goods?  Is a stove designed for home use necessarily a consumer good?  Can a good as large and as expensive as a house trailer be a consumer good?  Section 9–109(1) defines consumer goods as follows: "Goods are 'consumer goods' if they are used or bought for use primarily for personal, family or household purposes . . . . "  Note well, goods are not classified in 9–109 according to their design or intrinsic nature but according to the use to which they are put by the owner of the equity.[52]  It follows

---

of the cross-collateral or the consolidation are deemed, for the purpose of determining the amount of the debt secured by the various security interests, to have been first applied to the payment of the debts raising from the sales first made.  To the extent debts are paid according to this section, security interests in items of property terminate as the debts originally incurred with respect to each item is paid.

**50.**  350 F.2d 445 (D.C.Cir. 1965).

**51.**  UCCC § 2.409.  See note 49 supra.

**52.**  See, e. g., In re Bonnema, 4 UCC Rep.Serv. 894 (Ref.Dec.N.D.Ohio 1967)

(furnishings and appliances used in apartments by landlord to obtain additional rental income held to be equipment and not consumer goods); In re Shepler, 1 UCC Rep.Serv. 431 (Ref.Dec.E.D.Pa.1962) (farm equipment held by dealer for resale held to be "inventory" and not equipment); In re Phillips, 5 UCC Rep.Serv. 1040 (Ref.Dec.E.D.Tenn.1968) (musical instruments bought by professional musician for use in commercial band held to be equipment and not consumer goods); In re Symons, 5 UCC Rep. Serv.  262  (Ref.Dec.E.D.Mich.1967) (same).

For a discussion of the potential difficulty when the buyer's intended

that as the use to which the goods are put changes, either because the owner finds some new task for the goods to perform or because an owner who used the goods for one purpose sells it to another who uses it for a different purpose, the classification of the goods will also change. The last clause of Comment 2 to Section 9–109 puts it as follows: "[A] radio is inventory in the hands of a dealer and consumer goods in the hands of a householder." Only the odd case will present any difficulty in determining whether or not goods are consumer goods covered by 9–302(1) (d). Comments to 9–109 suggest borderline cases such as "a physician's car or a farmer's jeep" but these kinds of cases will not often arise and when such cases do arise it will be the court's task to determine whether or not the use was "primarily" personal, family or household. One faced with such a case might profitably turn to the income tax cases dealing with depreciation for some assistance.[53]

One troublesome fundamental problem in defining consumer goods has popped up in cases involving house trailers. In In re Sprague[54] a secured creditor claimed an automatically perfected security interest in a house trailer; the trustee argued that the trailer was not consumer goods because it was large and expensive and it would not be "consumed" (that is, would not depreciate to an insignificant value) as quickly or as fully as most items which are classified as consumer goods. One's initial reaction to the trustee's argument is to point to the plain words of section 9–109 and to reiterate what we said above, namely that the design, size, weight, shape or cost of the goods are not relevant, but rather that the classification is determined by the use to which the goods are put or intended to be put by the debtor. However, the policy which supports 9–302(1) (d) discloses some merit to the trustee's argument. One of the important reasons which permits us to tolerate the secret lien authorized by 9–302(1) (d) is that most consumer goods are of modest value at the time of purchase and decline rapidly in value as soon as they are taken from the merchant's premises. For those reasons subsequent creditors are not likely to lend in reliance upon such goods and are not therefore likely to be misled by the absence of a public filing. Quite clearly this policy does not fit with house trailers; as Referee Ryan points out, the draftsmen of the Code recognized the substantial residual value in a motor vehicle and excluded it from the automatic perfection provision.[55] Referee Ryan decided the *Sprague* case against

---

use ("bought for" use) differs from his actual use, see discussion in Section 23–13 infra.

53. See, e. g., T. K. Lewis, 9 CCH Tex. Ct.Mem. 32 (1950) (doctor: 75% business); M. G. Sheldon, 50 TC 24 (1968) (anesthesiologist's car: all personal); T. C. St. John, 29 CCH Tax Ct. Mem. 1045, TC Mem. 1970–238 (1970) (industrial physician's car: 90% business); L. Marot, 36 TC 238 (1961)

(electrocardiograph technician on twenty-four hour call: car all personal); Rodgers Dairy Co., 14 TC 66 (Acq.) (1950) (corporate officer's car: 90% business).

54. 4 UCC Rep.Serv. 702 (Ref.Dec.N.D. N.Y.1966).

55. The uniform automatic perfection provision, 9–302(1) (d), excludes motor vehicles. Massachusetts formerly

the secured creditor on two grounds: (1) that the house trailer was not consumer goods, and (2) that it was a motor vehicle and so excluded from 9–302(1) (d)'s automatic perfection provisions. On the appeal of a companion case which also involved a house trailer Judge Foley accepted Referee Ryan's holding that the secured creditor was not perfected but he relied exclusively upon a finding that the house trailer was a motor vehicle under New York law and at least by implication he rejected Referee Ryan's interpretation of the words "consumer goods." [56] Conceding the merit in Referee Ryan's policy argument, and in the absence of any empirical data to indicate that creditors are suffering serious injury as a result of the secret lien authorized in (1) (d), we believe that the courts should stick to the "use" test proposed by 9–109. We fear that the test implicit in Referee Ryan's opinion would produce a long series of *ad hoc* judgments having to do with the useful life, size and value of various goods and would thus introduce substantial uncertainty without appreciable benefit to anyone except for an occasional undeserving and unsecured creditor.[57]

Much of what has been said above concerning 9–302(1) (d) could be repeated with respect to 9–302(1) (c). Section 9–302(1) (c) authorizes automatic perfection of purchase money security interests in inexpensive farm equipment. It presents identical problems with respect to the definition of "purchase money" and similar problems in defining "farm equipment." [58] Section 9–109(2) of the Code defines "equipment" as goods "used or bought for use primarily in business (including farming or a profession) . . . . .," however neither 9–109 nor any other section defines "farm" equipment. Presumably one who milks the cows and slops the hogs will be a "farmer" and will be the owner of a good deal of "farm equipment". But what of the

permitted automatic perfection of motor vehicles. Mass.Gen.Laws Ann. ch. 106, § 9–302(1) (d) (19—) omitted the qualification of "a motor vehicle required to be licensed," and did not have a certificate of title law to qualify under 9–302(3) (b). However, in mid-1972, Massachusetts became a certificate of title state. A few states have omitted the motor vehicle qualifications from 9–302(1) (d), but nonetheless have an applicable certificate of title law pursuant to 9–302(3) (b) which precludes automatic perfection for vehicles covered by the title law.

**56.** In re Vinarsky, 287 F.Supp. 446, 5 UCC Rep.Serv. 1042 (N.D.N.Y.1968), aff'g 4 UCC Rep.Serv. 707 (Ref.Dec. N.D.N.Y.1966). Accord, Albany Discount Corp. v. Mohawk Nat'l Bank, 54 Misc.2d 238, 282 N.Y.S.2d 401, 4 UCC Rep.Serv. 669 (Sup.Ct.1967), aff'd 30 App.Div.2d 919, 292 N.Y.S.2d 300 (3rd Dep't 1968), aff'd 28 N.Y.2d 222, 269 N.E.2d 809 (1971). Cf. In re Ten

Brock, 4 UCC Rep.Serv. 712 (Ref.Dec. W.D.Mich.1966).

**57.** Perhaps Article Nine should be amended to establish a separate category for house trailers or to force them into one collateral classification.

**58.** See, e. g., Mammoth Cave Production Credit Ass'n v. York, 429 S.W.2d 26, 5 UCC Rep.Serv. 11 (Ky.App.1968) (purchase price of farm equipment was $2770; amount financed, due to $975 down payment, was $1795; held: 9–302(1) (c) inapplicable because "purchase price" was "in excess of $2500"); In re LaRose, 7 UCC Rep.Serv. 964 (Ref.Dec.D.Con.1970) ("purchase price" for 9–302(1) (c) is "time sales price," not cash price of goods); Lonoke Production Credit Ass'n v. Bohannon, 238 Ark. 206, 379 S.W.2d 17, 2 UCC Rep.Serv. 172 (1964) (secured transaction designated by parties as chattel mortgage held to be purchase money security interest).

person who owns no farm, and who is engaged in the business of selling services to farmers, that is, the cutting of their hay, the combining of their wheat, etc.? The Texas Court of Civil Appeals [59] recently found that a person who operated a commercial baling and cutting business and who purchased a "haybine" was the owner of "farm equipment" even though he was not a farmer. The decision need not be regarded as a departure from the use test embodied in Section 9–109. One can argue that the court was simply defining farming or farm operations to include some who do farm work but neither own nor rent real property. Moreover it seems likely that the decision is consistent with the draftsmen's intent. Apparently the draftsmen intended in 9–302(1)(c) to accommodate the expectations of farm lenders who were accustomed to receiving perfected security interests without filing.[60] It seems unlikely that such lenders would expect different results if they sold a "haybine" to one who was going to use it in his business of selling services to various farmers than if they sold it to a farmer.

A remaining problem in 9–302(1)(c) and (d) of at least academic interest is the question of what happens to the perfected security interests when consumer goods become equipment or farm equipment becomes non-farm equipment. Such metamorphoses from consumer goods to equipment or from farm equipment to some other kind of collateral will be rare, but the question remains, is the secured creditor in such case still perfected as the holder of a "purchase money security interest in consumer goods or farm equipment"? No section of the Code gives an explicit answer to that question, but 9–401(3) offers a compelling analogy. That subsection provides that a "filing" made in the proper place in accordance with the original "use" of the collateral continues effective even though the use has changed. Thus if one had chosen to perfect a security interest in consumer goods by a local filing, his interest would continue perfected (for four months or indefinitely, depending upon which alternative the state in question had enacted) even though the consumer goods became equipment (and as equipment would normally require a state Capitol filing). This is a sensible rule; presumably the courts will apply it by analogy to the cases covered by 9–302(1)(c) and (d) and will hold that one who procured an automatically perfected security interest continues perfected for at least four months even though the debtor's use and thus the classification of the goods have changed.

### § 23–8   Automatic Perfection—Certain Accounts and Contract Rights, 9–302(1)(e)

Section 9–302(1)(e) of the Code provides that one need not file to perfect "an assignment of accounts or contract rights which

---

59. Citizens Nat'l Bank v. Sperry Rand Corp., 456 S.W.2d 273, 7 UCC Rep. Serv. 961 (Tex.Civ.App.1970). But cf. In re Leiby, 1 UCC Rep.Serv. 428 (E.D.Pa.1962).

60. See text accompanying note 40 supra.

does not alone or in conjunction with other assignments to the same assignee transfer a significant part of the outstanding accounts or contract rights of the assignor  . . . ."  An initial interpretive difficulty leaps out at the reader: what is a "significant part" of the outstanding accounts or contract rights? A second difficulty, often present in the cases which deal with 9–302(1) (e) and closely related to that section but not itself an interpretive problem under 9–302(1) (e), is the question whether there are any assignments or sales of accounts or contract rights which are entirely outside the scope of Article Nine and thus subject to rules of priority and perfection to be found elsewhere.

Turning to the second question first, we believe that all sales or assignments of accounts or contract rights except for those specifically excluded under 9–104(f) [61] are governed by Article Nine and that the line of cases which holds otherwise are misinterpretations of the Code.  Spurlin v. Sloan,[62] a Kentucky case, well illustrates the problem.  There a creditor attached an account receivable in the hands of the Kentucky Department of Highways.  The one entitled to the money from the Kentucky Department of Highways had previously assigned his rights in the account to a third party.  In the priority conflict between the attaching creditor and the prior assignee, the attaching creditor argued that he was a lien creditor under 9–301(1) (b) and thus had rights superior to those of the assignee who, so he argued, was no more than the holder of an unperfected security interest.  The assignee argued, and the court held, that the assignee was not the holder of a security interest as that term is defined in 1–201 (37) and that the entire dispute was beyond the scope of Article Nine and should be resolved under the common law of Kentucky.

We believe the court erred in its failure to give careful consideration to Sections 9–102(1) and 1–201(37).  According to 9–102(1) Article Nine applies not only to "any transaction  . . .  which is intended to create a security interest in  . . .  chattel paper, accounts or contract rights" but also to "*any* sale of accounts, contract rights or chattel paper."  (emphasis added).  The history of Section 9–102(1) (b) makes clear the draftsmen's intentional choice of the language "any sale".  Prior to 1956 the Section read "any financing sale"; the restricting participle "financing" was removed as a result of New York Law Revision Commission criticism, and the draftsmen stated at the time "that the Article, except as otherwise excluded, applies to all sales of such kinds of collateral." [63]

61.  Section 9–104(f) reads in full as follows:

This Article does not apply

. . .

(f) to a sale of accounts, contract rights or chattel paper as part of a sale of the business out of which they arose, or an assignment of accounts, contract rights or chattel paper which is for the purpose of collection only, or a transfer of a contract right to an assignee who is also to do the performance under the contract.  . . .

62.  368 S.W.2d 314, 1 UCC Rep.Serv. 402 (Ky.App.1963).  Accord, Lyon v. Ty-Wood Corp., 212 Pa.Super. 69, 239 A.2d 819, 5 UCC Rep.Serv. 27 (1968).

63.  Editorial Board for the Uniform Commercial Code, 1956 Recommendations 253–54 (1956).

One may argue that the purchaser of an account or contract right may be covered by Article Nine by virtue of the reference in Section 9–102 but that he still is not holder of an "unperfected security interest" under 9–301. This argument is severely damaged if not destroyed by the third sentence of 1–201(37) which states that the term "security interest" . . . "also includes any interest of a buyer of accounts, chattel paper, or contract rights which is subject to Article 9." Thus, the attaching creditor would prevail over the party with an unperfected security interest under 9–301(1) (b).

It seems, therefore, that the only possible escape from the grasp of Article Nine for one who has taken the assignment of an account or contract right is to argue that the word "sale" in 9–102 does not cover all assignments of such rights, but covers only those cases which normally involve professionals who are accustomed to refer to the bulk transfer of accounts as "sales". As far as we are able to determine, there is no basis in the Code for such a distinction between "sales" of accounts on the one hand and "assignments" of them on the other. And, in the interest of certainty, we would hope that the courts would not attempt to construct any such distinction, for it would surely lead to confusion about which cases are within and which are without Article Nine.

A second approach which some courts [64] have taken in seeking to determine which assignments of accounts and contract rights are within Article Nine is to attempt to determine the intention of the parties. This approach is not as egregiously in error as the Kentucky court's approach but we believe that it too is misguided. When a court is faced with the argument by a trustee or some other party that a document which purports to be a lease for example, is in fact a security agreement, 1–201(37) and 9–102(1) (a) direct the court to classify the interest according to the "intent" of the parties. As we read 9–102(1) (b), the draftsmen intended to give the courts no such license with respect to transfers of accounts, contract rights, or chattel paper but provided for coverage of "any sale". We believe that the parties to such transactions would be better served by a rule of certain application, namely that Article Nine applies. The exclusions from Article Nine stated in 9–104(f) (the sale of accounts, contract rights or chattel paper as part of the sale of a business, the sale for collection only, the transfer to an assignee who is also to do the performance under the contract) together with the automatic perfection provision of 9–302(1) (e) allow sufficient elbow room for those who might not expect to be governed by the priority rules of Article Nine in assignment cases.

Returning to the question—what assignments are not of a "significant part" of the outstanding accounts of the assignor, and therefore automatically perfected—one finds two somewhat inconsistent tests for determining whether a given set of accounts is a "significant

---

64.   See, e. g., In re Boughner, 8 UCC Rep.Serv. 144 (Ref.Dec.W.D.Mich.1970).

part". The position of Professor Kripke and Mr. Felsenfeld [65] seems to be that the relative "casualness" of the sale is the overriding consideration. They state that " . . . the Code is intended to govern practical commercial transactions." [66] One infers from that statement that they might permit a nonprofessional assignee to take a comparatively larger share of an assignor's account without requiring him to file under 9–302(1) (e) than they would if the assignee were a bank or another financial institution. This proposition finds support in the Comments to 9–302 which identify "casual or isolated" assignments as those entitled to the benefit of Section 9–302(1) (e). A second approach is to disregard the professional status of the assignee and to ask only what percentage of the total accounts of the assignor were assigned and whether those accounts as percentage of the whole constitute a "significant" part. Although he does not say so in so many words, Referee Nims in In re Boughner [67] appears to reject the Kripke and Felsenfeld analysis and there finds that the transfer by an insurance agent of all of his insurance commissions to a third party, not in the business of lending, was the assignment of a significant part and was therefore not automatically perfected under 9–302(1) (e). Neither the *Boughner* case nor any other gives a clear picture about what percentage would be regarded as "significant" if that were the test. One district court case in Arkansas has found that 16% of the outstanding accounts was not a significant part.[68] The most articulate judicial statement of the Kripke-Felsenfeld proposition is found in Abramson v. Printer's Bindery, Inc.[69] Chief Justice Kickson, writing for the Texas Court, finds that:

> The transfer of the accounts in this case may be characterized as casual or isolated. Certainly there is no evidence that Bindery 'regularly takes assignments of any debtor's account,' to quote the language used in the commentary. The purchase by Bindery in this instance was done at the behest of the auditor, Bumpass. He persuaded Wertz, Bindery's President, to have Bindery purchase the accounts, (1) as a safe investment and (2) to enable a good customer of long standing to meet pressing short term debts. It is undisputed, as we shall point out later in this opinion, that so far as Graphic and its creditors are concerned Bindery paid a fair, adequate consideration for the accounts.[70]

This seems to us an appropriate place to exercise our bias in favor of certainty. If the courts define "significant" in terms of a percentage of the total accounts of the assignor, we can hope for the cases

**65.** Kripke & Felsenfeld, Secured Transactions: A Practical Approach to Article Nine of the Uniform Commercial Code, 17 Rutgers L.Rev. 168 (1962).

**66.** Id. at 190.

**67.** 8 UCC Rep.Serv. 144 (Ref.Dec.W. D.Mich.1970).

**68.** Standard Lumber Co. v. Chamber Frames, Inc., 8 UCC Rep.Serv. 139 (Ref.Dec.E.D.Ark.1970).

**69.** 440 S.W.2d 326, 6 UCC Rep.Serv. 732 (Tex.Civ.App.1969).

**70.** Id. at 328, 6 UCC Rep.Serv. at 735.

to produce a comparatively certain and reliable rule on which creditors and debtors can rely. If, on the other hand, we leave it to the courts to determine which sales are casual and isolated and which are not, we suspect that the process could go on for the rest of this century and part of the next without ever producing a rule on which a lawyer could rely. Since we see no powerful policy at work other than the desire to have the law certain, we hope the courts will follow the lead of Referee Nims and of Judge Harris and define "significant" in terms of a percentage of the assignor's accounts or contract rights.[71]

## § 23–9 —— Miscellaneous Automatic Perfection Provisions, 9–304 (4) and (5), 9–306

To those unfamiliar with the transactions for which 9–304(4) and (5) were designed, those subsections will seem an even more radical departure from the standard Code rules than are the purchase money exceptions discussed above. From the discussions before the New York Law Revision Commission[72] and from the writings of the commentators who participated in the drafting,[73] it appears that these two subsections were designed for short term bank loans, mostly for short term bank loans at the import end of an international sales transaction. Consider an international transaction in which a bank has issued a letter of credit and ultimately pays the seller's agent on the letter of credit when the seller's agent presents a bill of lading and various other documents. Of course the bank has no use for a negotiable bill of lading, but it may wish to maintain a security interest in the goods covered by that bill until its customer (the buyer) pays. At the same time it may be necessary for the customer to present the bill of lading in order to get possession of the goods for processing, resale, or for any one of a number of other legitimate purposes. If the buyer is to resell the goods at once, the parties may contemplate that he will repay the bank's loan with the proceeds of that resale in a few days. In such a letter of credit transaction, 9–304 (5) of the Code preserves a perfected security interest in the bank even though the bank has filed no financing statement and despite the fact that it gives the debtor possession of the negotiable document. Of course the security interest remains perfected for only 21 days and the debtor's purpose must be among those listed in 9–304(5) if the transaction is to qualify for 9–304(5)'s protection. Comment 2 to 9–303 puts it as follows:

> A bank which has issued a letter of credit honors drafts drawn under the credit and receives possession of the negotiable bill of lading covering the goods shipped. Under Sec-

---

71. Several "insignificant" assignments should be combined and should be tested by their cumulative impact. We suspect that even a percentage test will require judicial refinement for the foregoing case and for others as well.

72. 2 N.Y. State Law Revision Comm'n, 1954 Report 1125–26 (1954).

73. See, e. g., 1 G. Gilmore, Security Interests in Personal Property § 14.-6.2 (1965).

tions 9–304(2) and 9–305 the bank now has a perfected security interest in the document and the goods. The bank releases the bill of lading to the debtor for the purpose of procuring the goods from the carrier and selling them. Under Section 9–304(5) the bank continues to have a perfected security interest in the document and goods for 21 days. The bank files before the expiration of the 21 day period. Its security interest now continues perfected for as long as the filing is good.

Section 9–304(4) is aimed mostly at other transactions in which the lender will not receive possession of the instrument or negotiable document before it comes into the hands of the debtor. For example, if a bank complied with the requirements of 9–304(4), that subsection would give the bank a perfected security interest in the debtor's stocks and bonds even though the bank took possession of no certificates. Thus the subsection permits banks to secure and perfect their "day loans" to stock brokers even though they never receive possession of any bonds or stock certificates.

One must jump through several hoops to qualify under either of the two subsections. If a creditor gives new value, under a written security interest covering instruments or negotiable documents, 9–304 (4) of the Code gives him perfected security in such negotiable documents and instruments for twenty-one days from the time the security interest attaches.

Under 9–304(5) a creditor who has (*1*) previously perfected his security interest (that is, by possession or by giving notice to the bailee under 9–304(3)) and (*2*) returned the instruments, goods or documents to the debtor for one of the purposes specified in (5) (a) or (b), has a perfected security interest in instruments, negotiable documents, or goods originally in the possession of a bailee "other than one who has issued a negotiable document therefor" for twenty-one days. The twenty-one day period commences when possession of the goods or paper is given to the debtor. Many transactions will be covered by both subsections. However, in many others only one subsection will apply and it will be useful to know the difference between the two subsections. First, note that the twenty-one day period in subsection (4) runs from the time of attachment. Since the bank's security interest in a letter of credit transaction would attach as soon as it had an agreement, had given value,[74] and the debtor had rights in the collateral, attachment might occur in an international transaction long before the bank received possession of the bill of lading. When it receives possession and transfers possession of the bill of lading to the debtor, a substantial part of its 21 day time period may have run. In such circumstances it would wish to qualify under sub-

---

74. A binding promise to loan is the giving of value. § 1–201(44). Therefore in a letter of credit the final event for attachment of the security interest would be the debtor's acquisition of rights. When a buyer "acquires rights" is unclear, but rights could be and likely would be acquired long before the goods had arrived.

section (5), for there the 21 day period does not commence until the creditor gives possession to the debtor.[75]  Subsection (5) has no "new value" requirement but unlike subsection (4) it does require that the creditor somehow have perfected his security interest before the instrument, document or the goods are given over to the debtor.[76]

Other differences between the subsections are as follows: subsection (4) does not cover goods in the hands of a bailee who has not issued a negotiable document for them (that is, it covers only "negotiable documents and instruments"); the "purpose" tests in subsections (5) (a) and (b) are not found in subsection (4), and there is no requirement in subsection (5) that the security agreement be in writing.  We suspect that most of these differences between subsection (4) and subsection (5) are simply consequences of the fact that each was spawned by different specific problems.  Professor Gilmore has suggested,[77] quite rightly we believe, that the subsections could be combined into one subsection that would handily deal with the problems which both now face.

There are two untidy aspects of subsections (4) and (5) which we note in passing and which could cause difficulty in the future.  First is the question whether and to what extent the subsection (4) security interest carries over to goods in the debtor's possession.  Second is a possible conflict on the duration of perfection between 9–304 (3) and 9–304(5).  Subsection (4) states that the security interest "in instruments or negotiable documents" is perfected  .  .  .  and continues perfected for a period of 21 days from the time it attaches.  What happens when the debtor trades the warehouse receipts for the goods and so extinguishes the receipts?  Assume a situation in which a bank makes a loan against a handful of negotiable warehouse receipts and relies upon the 21 day period in subsection (4) to perfect its security interest.  If on the second of those 21 days the debtor cashes in the warehouse receipts and takes possession of the goods, does the secured creditor's perfected security interest continue in the goods?  If so, does it continue for the remainder of the twenty-one days or does it continue for only ten days under 9–306 as proceeds?  Arguably a secured creditor's only claim arises under 9–306, for subsection (4) purports to give a perfected security interest only in "instruments or negotiable documents".  The wording of subsection (5) casts doubt on that analysis and indicates that at least with respect to

---

**75.**  Subsection (5) does not explicitly state that the twenty-one days commences upon debtor's possession, but there is no other sensible interpretation of that subsection.

**76.**  Note that subsection (5) is all that remains of the common law doctrine which permitted a pledgee temporarily to return the goods to the pledgor without loss of his perfected status.  Since subsection (5) applies only to

goods which are in the possession of a bailee and will never apply in the straight pledge of goods case in which the creditor himself holds the goods and returns them to the debtor, the subsection has preserved precious little of the temporary return doctrine.

**77.**  1 G. Gilmore, Security Interests in Personal Property § 14.6.2 at 460 (1965).

subsection (5) in some circumstances, the security interest is intended to carry over to the goods for the remainder of the twenty-one days.

Of course subsection (5) specifically contemplates the case in which the debtor not only takes possession of the instrument or document but also of the "goods . . . for the purpose of ultimate sale or exchange etc." The quoted reference to goods is placed in parallel with the reference to documents representing the goods and with a reference to delivery of the instrument to the debtor. The inference one draws from this parallel reference is that the draftsmen in subsection (5) at least intended for the secured creditor to have a perfected security interest not in just the instruments but in the goods which come into the possession of the debtor when he cashes in the instruments. If subsection (5) is to accomplish the purpose for which it was apparently designed, it would seem only logical to give the secured creditor a perfected security interest in the goods for the entire twenty-one days notwithstanding the fact that the document covering the goods had been traded for the goods at the warehouse.

To return then to subsection (4), do we read into that section a similar understanding so that the secured creditor will have a perfected security interest in goods traded for negotiable warehouse receipts for the remainder of the twenty-one days? To make the sections parallel, it seems that we should do so. However the absence of a reference to goods and the allusion only to security interests "in instruments or negotiable documents" makes that conclusion somewhat more difficult to reach under subsection (4). We conclude that the draftsmen intended to continue the security interest for twenty-one days notwithstanding the debtor's exchange of a document of title for the goods themselves.

The second bit of untidiness left in subsection 9–304 is the possible conflict between 9–304(3) and 9–304(5). Subsection (3) permits a secured creditor to perfect a security interest with respect to goods in the possession of a bailee who has issued a nonnegotiable document by having the document issued in the secured party's name, by the bailee's receipt of notification of the secured party's interest, or by filing as to the goods. Assume, for example, that a creditor gave possession of the nonnegotiable warehouse receipt to the debtor and perfected his security interest by giving notice of that interest to the warehouseman. He has then complied with one of the three alternatives in 9–304(3) and has a perfected security interest presumably for an indefinite period of time. But how does this case differ from those covered by subsection (5)? It appears that the secured creditor perfected his security interest by giving notice but that he then made "available to the debtor the goods or documents" and so fits precisely within subsection (5). Subsection (5) however, permits perfection only for twenty-one days. After the debtor has possessed the document for twenty-one days, is our creditor rendered unperfected or may he return to 9–304(3) and argue that his notice to the bailee gave him a perfected status for an indefinite period? We are persuaded by Professor Gilmore's argument [78] that subsection (5) governs and that one who does not file and allows his debtor to run loose with such a document should be grateful for the twenty-one days permitted in subsection (5). All in all subsections (4) and (5) seem a rather complex but generally satisfactory solution to a problem of most modest proportions.[79]

Last, and least among the automatic perfection provisions, is 9–306(3). That subsection provides:

> The security interest in proceeds is a continuously perfected security interest if the interest in the original collateral was perfected but it ceases to be a perfected security interest and becomes unperfected ten days after receipt of the proceeds by the debtor unless
>
> (a) a filed financing statement covering the original collateral also covers proceeds; or
>
> (b) the security interest in the proceeds is perfected before the expiration of the ten day period.

If a secured creditor perfects a security interest in inventory, for example, and the inventory then changes into accounts, the creditor automatically retains a perfected security interest in the accounts as proceeds for ten days. The provision contains no mystery and its importance is marginal in view of the fact that almost all standard form financing statements contain a block for the creditor to check and so claim "proceeds" in his financing statement. It is surely a rare creditor who does not so perfect his proceeds interest by filing, and in such case the automatic perfection rule of 9–306(3) is irrelevant.[80]

---

**78.** Id. § 14.6.2 at 459.

**79.** Under the pre-Code common law, the creditor could return goods to the debtor temporarily and not lose his security interest. For example, one holding sheep might permit the debtor to shear the sheep, and during the period in which the debtor had possession, the creditor would remain perfected. Note, that subsections (4) and (5) of 9–304 retain only a sliver of that doctrine, for they apply only in cases of return of instruments or documents or when the goods are returned from the possession of a bailee. Thus, in the case of a straight pledge in which the creditor himself had possession, the creditor could not qualify under either (4) or (5) and would become unperfected upon the return of the sheep to the debtor.

**80.** In the unusual case in which one does not file with respect to proceeds the ten-day interim period can present a cute priority puzzle under 9–312. Presumably proceeds are a new kind of collateral, and if one has not filed with respect to them, his interest attaches and becomes perfected only at the time when the proceeds arise, the time when the debtor first has "rights" in them. Thus if one were to have a priority dispute under 9–312 and one party had filed with respect to proceeds but the other claimed the proceeds under the ten-day provision of 9–306(3), the appropriate section for determining priority would be 9–312 (5) (b) (the order of perfection), and arguably at least, perfection of both interests would be simultaneous. That is, perfection could not occur until the security interest had attached (§ 9–303); the security interests could not attach until the debtor had "rights" in the collateral (namely the proceeds (§ 9–204(1)), those rights in the collateral would arise simultaneously with respect to each of the creditors, the security interest of each would attach simultaneously and would become perfected simultaneously. In such case neither would have priority.

## § 23–10    Perfection by Possession, 9–305

Section 9–305 authorizes the pledge: perfection of a security interest by creditor's possession of the collateral.  It reads in full as follows:

> A security interest in letters of credit and advices of credit (subsection (2) (a) of Section 5–116), goods, instruments, negotiable documents or chattel paper may be perfected by the secured party's taking possession of the collateral.  If such collateral other than goods covered by a negotiable document is held by a bailee, the secured party is deemed to have possession from the time the bailee receives notification of the secured party's interest.  A security interest is perfected by possession from the time possession is taken without relation back and continues only so long as possession is retained, unless otherwise specified in this Article.  The security interest may be otherwise perfected as provided in this Article before or after the period of possession by the secured party.

Why possession has been and continues to be recognized as a permissible method of perfection is not hard to understand.  Particularly in a crude economy where few could read and concepts of ownership in personal property were not sophisticated, possession of personal property was a powerful indication of ownership.  If one did not possess the sheep he claimed as his own, at minimum there was cause for investigation.  Even today in a society which is accustomed to the idea that a possessor may have only a minimal interest in the goods he possesses, there are still many cases in which possession, (particularly by one known to be in the business of lending money) is a perfectly sound indication of a security interest.  Because most lending is now done against collateral such as inventory or equipment which the debtor must possess, the pledge is limited to a few commercial contexts, but its use in those contexts is extensive and flourishing.  Consider for example the bank which lends against stocks and bonds, the pawnbroker who takes in valuables, and the finance company which lends against negotiable documents.

One who reflects for a moment on the nature of the various kinds of collateral covered by Article Nine will appreciate that the pledge is uniquely suited to certain kinds of collateral and quite unsuited to other kinds.  If the creditor's possession (and the debtor's lack of it) is to put third parties on notice, the collateral must be the type which one can see, touch and move.  Also, the collateral must have a physical embodiment that can be recognized as exclusively representing the right.  So it follows that contract rights, accounts, and general intangibles cannot be perfected by possession.[81]  The creditor can col-

---

81.  § 9–305, Comment 1:
  This Section permits a security interest to be perfected by transfer of possession only when the collateral is goods, instruments, documents or chattel paper: that is to say, accounts, contract rights and general intangibles are excluded. . . . A security

lect up the ledger cards, journals, computer print-outs, sales slips and any other items which he believes represent accounts receivable and he will not by those acts have perfected a security interest in the accounts. In the words of Comment 1, "[A]ccounts, contract rights, and general intangibles are excluded." The exclusion of these items is consistent with the pre-Code common law [82] and with the principles stated above. None of them is a physical embodiment which can be and is recognized as exclusively representing the right. One creditor might seize the ledger cards, another a computer print-out and a third the sales slips to secure an interest in accounts. When there is such doubt about the physical embodiment of the right and lack of unanimity in the business world about what if anything embodies that right, possession is not a reliable method of perfection. At the other end of the spectrum are instruments. Instruments in this context include not only negotiable instruments but also stock certificates and bonds.[83] Except for the temporary perfection permitted under 9–304, one can perfect a security interest in instruments *only* by taking possession. Filing does not perfect such an interest. Businessmen and bankers are accustomed to dealing with such pieces of paper without referring to a filing system and as though they were the complete embodiment of the underlying right. Apparently the draftsmen believed that it would unduly hamper the transfer of such instruments if every transferee were obliged to check the filings every time he took such an instrument and concluded therefore that perfection (excluding the 9–304 provision) should be limited to possession. Between accounts, contract rights, and general intangibles on the one hand, and instruments on the other, lie goods, negotiable documents, and chattel paper. Interests in each of those kinds of collateral may be perfected either by possession or by filing.

Before one commences to wrestle the meaning of 9–305 in various situations, he should note in passing that the taking of possession is not only a perfecting act but also one which satisfies the Article Nine

---

interest in accounts, contract rights and general intangibles—property not ordinarily represented by any writing whose delivery operates to transfer the claim—may under this Article be perfected only by filing. . . .

(See § 9–302(1) (e) for a minor exception.)

See, e. g., In re Sanelco, 7 UCC Rep. Serv. 65 (Ref.Dec.M.D.Fla.1969) (security interests in accounts receivable or contract rights cannot be perfected by possession.) (dictum); Levine v. Pascal, 94 Ill.App.2d 43, 236 N.E.2d 425, 5 UCC Rep.Serv. 344 (1968) (beneficial interest in land trust held general intangible and not instrument; therefore possession cannot perfect.); M. Rutkin Elec. Supply Co. v. Burdette Elec., Inc., 98 N.J.Super. 378,

237 A.2d 500, 4 UCC Rep.Serv. 1074 (1967) (accounts receivable cannot be perfected by possession); In re Granite City Cooperative Creamery Ass'n, Inc., 7 UCC Rep.Serv. 1083 (Ref.Dec. D.Vt.1970) (accounts receivable).

**82.** 1 G. Gilmore, Security Interests in Personal Property § 14.1 (1965).

**83.** § 9–105(g):

"Instrument" means a negotiable instrument (defined in Section 3–104), or a security (defined in Section 8–102) or any other writing which evidences a right to the payment of money and is not itself a security agreement or lease and is of a type which is in ordinary course of business transferred by delivery with any necessary indorsement or assignment. . . .

statute of frauds embodied in 9–203(1).  If the creditor takes possession of the collateral he need not have a written security agreement in order to have an effective security interest; possession is sufficient.

The operative language of 9–305 authorizes perfection "by the secured party's taking possession of the collateral."  "Possession" is a notoriously difficult word; there is constructive possession, physical possession, actual possession, mere custody, etc.  Criminal courts face the concept in determining whether or not a defendant has committed larceny; in real property cases the courts must decide whether the deed has been delivered to the possession of the transferee, whether a party has commenced adverse possession, whether possession were sufficient to put some other party on notice of an interest.  In the course of the hundreds of decisions which have dealt with its meaning, the word "possession" has taken on a wonderfully plastic form and has accommodated itself to the needs of the real property law, the law of consignment, insurance and the criminal law.  The draftsmen of the Code were aware of this history and they wisely declined the futile task of defining possession in the Code.  Traditionally, possession of encumbered personal property has been important because of the notice which it gives to prospective creditors.  In societies with no method of perfection other than possession—societies in which possession was more likely to equal ownership than it does in our society—the courts were understandably insistent that the creditor make his possession unmistakable in order that the debtor not mislead other creditors.  We are left, therefore, with several hundred years of cases and with the policy of Article Nine to help us define the word possession.  Fortunately the pledge is now restricted largely to circumstances in which the creditor's possession will be unmistakable (for example, the bank puts debtor's stock certificates in creditor's vault).  There is a small trickle of cases concerning who may possess in the secured party's name and there will continue to be the occasional case in which the field warehouseman's possession will be drawn into question.[84]  Beyond these we find few living "possession" problems in the reported opinions.

In many cases a pledge will be consummated by the secured party's taking possession himself.  In the case of a corporate pledgee of course this possession will be taken by an agent on behalf of the corporation; in other cases the possession may be by a bailee on behalf of the secured party.  The question of who may possess is governed by the second sentence of 9–305: "If such collateral other than goods covered by a negotiable document is held by a bailee, the secured party is deemed to have possession from the time the bailee receives notification of the secured party's interest."  The Comment tells us that "[p]ossession may be by the secured party himself or by an agent on his behalf: it is of course clear, however, that the debtor

---

84.  See, e. g., In re Pennar Paper Co., 2 UCC Rep.Serv. 659 (Ref.Dec.E.D. Pa.1964).

or person controlled by him cannot qualify as such an agent for the secured party." [85]    It follows from the principle which lies behind 9–305 that neither the debtor nor one controlled by him will give adequate notice and protection by his possession.    Occasionally creditors argue that debtors possess on their behalf, but this argument has been uniformly and properly rejected.    Note that possession by a bailee commences when he receives notice of the secured party's interest.    Thus in a California case [86] the court found in dictum that a secured party's interest in certain stock held in escrow would be perfected as of the time the escrow holder received a copy of the letter which set out the secured party's interest.    A more common case will be the one in which the bailee is a warehouseman who has issued a nonnegotiable warehouse receipt.

An occasional case still presents an issue whether a secured party "possessed" the collateral.    For example, in In re Republic Engine & Mfg. Co.,[87] the creditor had purported to possess the collateral by locking the debtor out of the premises where the collateral was located.    Before the creditor had locked the debtor out of the premises, the sheriff had levied execution on a third party's judgment against the same collateral and after the creditor had locked the debtor out, the creditor had given up possession to the sheriff.    The court found alternatively that upon the levy the goods were in the constructive possession of the law and that such possession foreclosed the creditor from possessing under section 9–305 notwithstanding his lock on the door and, secondly, that the creditor's giving up possession to the sheriff subsequent to the lock-out dissolved any perfection which he might have had during the time when the goods were locked up on the premises.

In In re Chapman,[88] two creditors had security interests in one note.    At the time of the bankruptcy of the common debtor the note was in the possession of the junior secured creditor and the trustee argued that the senior creditor's lack of possession caused him to be unperfected.    The court rejected the trustee's argument and found that possession by the junior creditor fulfilled the policy of 9–305 (and arguably at least complied with the letter of it as well).    The Court held that the senior creditor was perfected since the court assumed possession by one secured creditor was effective notice of all security interests known to him.    This rag-tag bunch of cases is generally consistent with the policies behind 9–305 and the re-

85.   § 9–305, Comment 2.

86.   Estate of Hinds, 10 Cal.App.3d 1021, 89 Cal.Rptr. 341, 8 UCC Rep. Serv. 3 (2d Dist.1970).

87.   3 UCC Rep.Serv. 655 (Ref.Dec.N. D.Ohio 1966).   See also In re Pennar Paper Co., 2 UCC Rep.Serv. 659 (Ref. Dec.E.D.Pa.1964 (fieldwarehouse improperly conducted);   In re Granite

City Cooperative Creamery Ass'n, Inc., 7 UCC Rep.Serv. 1083 (Ref.Dec.D.Vt. 1970) (no relation back);   In re Childress, 6 UCC Rep.Serv. 549 (Ref.Dec. E.D.Tenn.1969) (creditor took keys to bankrupt's restaurant premises;   held sufficient possession, but interest found voidable preference).

88.   5 UCC Rep.Serv. 649 (Ref.Dec.W.D. Mich.1968).

quirement of possession; they show little pattern but indicate that any problems which exist in defining possession under 9–305 are not grave.

### § 23–11    Perfection by Filing—Places to File

The early chattel recording systems called typically for a recording in a county or city office.  Since most personal property security transactions were undertaken between local businessmen, it made great sense to maintain the records within easy reach of all concerned.  As more sophisticated credit arrangements developed which involved widely separated businessmen, the rationale for local recordation weakened, and in the 1930's the Uniform Trust Receipts Act provided exclusively for filing of pertinent information on a state-wide level.[89]

Since the Code was to supplant the many independent notice systems for the various pre-Code security devices, it needed to provide a filing device which could satisfy all states.  That seemed an impossible feat, and to encourage unanimous acceptance of the Code the draftsmen offered three alternatives for 9–401(1).  The First Alternative provides the least local filing, and the third provides the most.  Several factors barred unanimous agreement about places of filing.  First, there was honest disagreement about the relative merits of local and state-wide filings:

> . . .  [I]t can be said that most credit inquiries about local businesses, farmers and consumers come from local sources; convenience is served by having the files locally available  . . . .   (Comment 1 to Section 9–401)

However, it is becoming more and more convenient to communicate with a central state office.  With the development of inexpensive computer storage facilities and local information retrieval terminals, the convenience argument will cease to exist.  For creditors who seek information about customers who are not within one local filing unit, a state-wide system is more convenient:

> The more completely the files are centralized on a state-wide basis, the easier and cheaper it becomes to procure credit information; the more the files are scattered in local filing units, the more burdensome and costly.  (Comment 1 to Section 9–401)

Moreover, a state-wide system saves the filer the embarrassment of filing in the wrong city or county.  Where combinations of local and central filing exist, the possibilities for mis-filing are considerable.  The secured party may wrongly classify consumer goods as equipment and so file at the state capitol and not locally or he may classify farm equipment[90] as equipment and file centrally and not

---

89.  1 G. Gilmore, Security Interests in Personal Property § 17.4 (1965).

90.  A creditor can also misfile if he confuses other farm related collateral (viz., farm products or accounts, con-

locally.   The risk of error as to the location of the debtor's residence or place of business is even greater.

A final factor which offsets some of the convenience arguments in favor of central filing was the political interest of some local filing officials.   Apparently they regarded the central filing provisions to be a threat to their positions and opposed them.[91]

Before one analyzes the specific provisions of 9–401 of the Code he should understand that 9–401 is not the only filing system that can apply to personal property.   Section 9–302(3) indicates that Code filing is not required where certain alternative systems for giving public notice are available.   One alternative system is created by federal law and the Code dutifully exempts from 9–401 requirements "a security interest in property subject to a statute of the United States which provides for a national registration or filing . . . ."[92]   This exclusion covers security interests in ships,[93] railroad equipment,[94] copyrights,[95] patents,[96] certain interstate commercial vehicles,[97] and all civil aircraft.[98]   To the extent that the federal statutes do not govern other aspects of the secured transaction, the remaining provisions of Article Nine may control.[99]

tract rights, or general intangibles relating to the sale of farm products) with nonfarm collateral.

**91.**  For an interesting discussion of the compromises which helped create the section 9–401(1) alternatives, see 1 G. Gilmore, Security Interests in Personal Property §§ 17.4 and 18.1–18.3 at 512 n. 6, 517–30 (1965).

**92.**  § 9–302(3) (a).

**93.**  46 U.S.C.A. §§ 911–984 (1970).   The Ship Mortgage Act is the most comprehensive federal statute dealing with secured transactions.   For detailed discussion of the Act, see G. Gilmore & C. Black, The Law of Admirality ch. 9 (1957).

**94.**  49 U.S.C.A. § 20(c) (1970).   Section 20(c) of the Interstate Commerce Act directs the Interstate Commerce Commissioner to establish a filing system for railroad rolling stock.   By its own terms, the federal filing system is an alternative to state systems.   One need not file under state law *if* he files under the federal system.   Section 9–104(e) excludes equipment trusts covering railway rolling stock from Code coverage.   Nevertheless, security arrangements on railway rolling stock which are not equipment trusts are still within Article Nine's scope.

**95.**  17 U.S.C.A. §§ 28, 30 (1970).   State law covers all other questions relating

to a security interest in a copyright. Republic Pictures Corp. v. Security-First Nat'l Bank, 197 F.2d 767 (9th Cir. 1952), rev'g 97 F.Supp. 360 (S.D. Cal.1951).

**96.**  35 U.S.C.A. § 261 (1970).

**97.**  49 U.S.C.A. § 313 (1970).   Certain vehicles holding certificates of public convenience and necessity issued under the Interstate Commerce Act must comply with the federal system.   The federal system is no different than the certificate of title systems used in most states.

**98.**  49 U.S.C.A. § 1403 (1970).   The federal recordation system exclusively applies to aircraft and parts whether or not the aircraft is used or intended to be used interstate.   Thus, the reference to airplanes in section 9–103 (2) is deceptive with respect to perfection and filing.

**99.**  Section 9–104, Comment 1 acknowledges the obvious.   When a problem arises under a federal act which is not covered by the act, a court must decide whether to improvise an answer under federal common law or to follow the law of a particular state. If the federal statute does not contain a needed provision, Article Nine could be looked to for an answer.

If, for example, the federal statute provided only that security interests in goods of a particular kind were by a federal filing, and there was some question about the manner of repossession and resale by the secured creditor, the rights and liabilities of the parties with respect to the repossession and resale should be governed by Part Five of Article Nine.

Section 9–302(3) also exempts from Article Nine filing security interests subject to certain state notice systems. Primarily, this permits security interests in motor vehicles to be perfected by notation upon certificates of title. Of lesser importance is subsection (3)(b)'s deference in filing matters to a state statute providing for central filing of security interests. This was originally conceived to exempt certain types of public utility mortgages from Code filing.[100] However, most states have added a non-uniform provision to the Code dealing with utilities.[101] Few other uses of the provision exist.[102]

A second matter one should consider before he dives into filing questions concerns the general kind of collateral with which he is dealing. For interests in accounts, contract rights and general intangibles, filing under 9–401 is the only method of perfection. Interests in instruments and letters of credit on the other hand may never be perfected by filing. The Code makes no restrictions upon other collateral. Legally all other collateral may be perfected either by filing or a creditor's taking possession, but possession will give greater protection than filing when one is dealing with quasi-negotiable instruments such as chattel paper. If a subsequent party gives value and comes into possession of such quasi-negotiable instruments in good faith, he may defeat the prior perfected security interest under 9–308. Creditor possession will foreclose such a danger.

After he decides that filing is the only or the best method to perfect his interest, the filer must face two basic issues. First, where do I file? To answer this he must classify the collateral according to Code descriptions and may need to determine the debtor's residence or place of business. Second, what do I file?

## § 23–12   Perfection by Filing—Where to File?

The "where to file" question begins with 9–401 of the Code. From the First to the Third Alternative of Subsection (1) of 9–401 the interpretive journey becomes progressively more difficult. One

---

100. 1 G. Gilmore, Security Interests in Personal Property § 19.11 at 549 n. 2 (1965).

101. Usually the provision is added to 9–302 as a new subsection. See, e. g., Ala.Code Ann. Tit. 7A, § 9–302(5) (1966).

102. Central filing statutes are presumably important "in some states for cattle and the like." Review Committee for Article 9, Permanent Editorial Board, Preliminary Draft No. 2, § G–5 Ct. 43 (1970). Professor Gilmore cites an interesting story of a Connecticut central filing statute for oyster mortgages which was recently repealed because it had not been used in twenty-five years. 1 G. Gilmore, Security Interests in Personal Property § 19.11 at 549 n. 2 (1965).

factor is constant in the three alternatives: security interests in fixtures are always filed in the office where a mortgage on the related real estate would be recorded.  Since "fixture" is not defined in the Code, a secured party must interpret his state's case law on fixtures. A better solution to that problem, in the planning stage at least, is to file both locally (as if the goods were a fixture) and centrally (as if equipment).  This application of Peskind's law (file everywhere it could possibly benefit you to do so) will save countless hours of frustrating research with dusty and inconclusive fixture cases when the debtor goes bankrupt.

### First Alternative

Aside from the fixture conundrum, the First Alternative of subsection (1) of 9–401 produces no "where" problems.  One always files for non-fixtures centrally, usually in the office of Secretary of State.  Only the choice of the wrong state would cause misfiling and that error would not be peculiar to a central filing system, but would be a result of misunderstanding sections 9–102 or 9–103. Several additional obstacles are presented by the Second and Third Alternatives.

### Second Alternative

The Second Alternative Subsection (1) of 9–401 requires a local, usually a county, filing as to

(*1*) farm collateral (equipment used in farming operations, farm products, farm accounts, farm contract rights, farm general intangibles),

(*2*) consumer goods

(*3*) crops (note that if the crops are not in the county residence of the debtor the creditor must file both where the crops are located and where the debtor resides).  Comment 3 to 9–401 implicitly and probably correctly identifies the three classifications listed above as "transactions of essentially local interests".  Consumer goods transactions are rather obviously local.  Despite the widely lamented metamorphosis of the Nineteenth Century dirt farmer into a Twentieth Century big businessman with a spread of hundreds or even thousands of acres, it seems likely that most farm lending is still done on only a county-wide basis and that it is a comparatively unusual case in which the farmer is doing business in several counties and is borrowing not from the local bank but from a state-wide finance company or an out of county bank.

Under subsection (c) of the Second Alternative, one files centrally "in all other cases" (that is, other than fixtures, consumer goods or farm related collateral).[103]  Theoretically transactions in these

---

103.  Section 9–401(1), Second Alternative:

(1) The proper place to file in order to perfect a security interest is as follows:

(a) when the collateral is equipment used in farming operations, or farm products, or accounts, contract rights or general intangibles arising from or relating to the sale of farm products by a farmer, or consumer

"other cases" are not usually local and thus do not demand local filing.

### Third Alternative

The Third Alternative is identical to the Second except for subsection (c). Subsection (c) of the Third Alternative reads in full as follows:

> in all other cases, in the office of the [Secretary of State] and in addition, if the debtor has a place of business in only one county of this state, also in the office of ...... of such county, or, if the debtor has no place of business in this state, but resides in the state, also in the office of ...... of the county in which he resides.

That subsection is a significant departure from the other filing provisions of the Code and it appears that it will cause the courts nearly as much trouble as will the other subsections combined. Note first that it departs from the usual Code rule in that it requires a dual filing; [104] the creditor must file not only with the Secretary of State but also in the county in which the debtor has his "place of business", *if he has a place of business in only one county*. As we shall see, the courts have had considerable difficulty in determining what constitutes a "place of business" in the variety of circumstances in which a businessman will have his main base of operation in one county and will have contacts of varying permanence and substance with other counties.

As one might expect, the Second Alternative of subsection (1) has been enacted in more states than have the other two sections. That subsection has been enacted in twenty-seven states; [105] the third in 16,[106] and the first [107] in six states.

goods, then in the office of the . . . in the county of the debtor's residence or if the debtor is not a resident of this state then in the office of the . . . in the county where the goods are kept, and in addition when the collateral is crops in the office of the . . . in the county where the land on which the crops are growing or to be grown is located;

(b) when the collateral is goods which at the time the security interest attaches are or are to become fixtures, then in the office where a mortgage on the real estate concerned would be filed or recorded;

(c) in all other cases, in the office of the [Secretary of State].

**104.** The only other time a dual filing requirement occurs when the collateral is crops is if the crops are located in a county other than that of the debtor's residence.

**105.** Alabama, Alaska, Arizona, California, Colorado, Florida, Idaho, Illinois, Indiana, Iowa, Kansas, Kentucky (with substantial variation), Maine (with substantial variation), Michigan, Minnesota, Montana, New Jersey, New Mexico, North Dakota, Oklahoma, Rhode Island, South Carolina, South Dakota, Tennessee, Texas, Washington and Wisconsin. The variations within Kentucky and Maine do not encompass dual filing, the hallmark of the third alternative. The Virgin Islands have also adopted the second alternative.

**106.** Arkansas, Massachusets, Nebraska (with substantial variation; the dual filing that exists is in more than one

**107.** See note 107 on page 823.

A lawyer who deals with the Second or Third Alternatives of subsection (1) faces a series of pesky interpretive problems. The draftsmen could have solved some of these problems had they seen them on the horizon at the time they were drafting 9–401. For the most part, however, the interpretive difficulties which the cases have presented are traceable to the ambiguity inherent in all words. The most obvious and pervasive problem in 9–401(1) is the definition of the various kinds of collateral. Here more than in any other place in Article Nine the definitions of the various kinds of collateral embodied in 9–109 are crucial. The second problem, subsidiary to the first, is the question whether actual use or intended use controls the definition of the collateral for the purpose of filing. A third difficulty which the draftsmen apparently did not foresee is the question whether residence and place of business is to be determined at the time the security interest attaches or at the time of filing if those times are different. The final point, of interest only in those states which enacted the Third Alternative, is the question what constitutes a "place of business" in 9–401(1) (c), Third Alternative.

At the outset one should distinguish the lawyer's role as a planner and as a litigator. Any lawyer worth his salt who operates as a planner will avoid all of the problems which we will discuss below. Either he will follow Peskind's law and file a financing statement in every conceivable place which could benefit him to do so, or he will buy insurance against the possibility that his client's interest will not be perfected. Either solution will save him. When the client calls for help only after an error has been committed, the debtor has filed bankruptcy, and a nasty trustee has come on stage to argue that the filing was not made in the proper place, then the lawyer must deal with the cases and the questions which we discuss below.

## § 23–13   Perfection by Filing—Classifying the Collateral

The first question, how does one classify collateral, is one which we have discussed above in Section 23–7 with respect to farm equipment and consumer goods. As the Code makes clear and as we have previously pointed out, the intrinsic nature of the goods does not classify them, rather it is the use to which the owner of the equity puts the goods which determines their classification.[108] The potential difficulty recognized by the comment to 9–109 when one uses goods

---

county; there is no local and central dual filing), Mississippi, Missouri, Nevada, New Hampshire, New York, North Carolina, Ohio, Oregon, Pennsylvania, Vermont, Virginia, West Virginia and Wyoming (with substantial variation).

107. Connecticut, Delaware, Georgia, Hawaii, Maryland (with substantial variation), and Utah. The District of Columbia has also adopted a variant of the first alternative.

108. Notice, however, that a filer need not understand all the nice distinctions the Code creates. Basically nonpurchase money security interests in all collateral of farmer debtors and all consumer goods require local filing.

for two purposes (for example, as salesman's business car and as the family car) has not developed into a serious problem.[109]

The problem that has appeared is the question whether the debtor's intended use of the goods or his actual use controls. The definitions of consumer goods and equipment in 9–109 contain the words "are used or *bought for* use" (emphasis added). In those definitions at least the intent of the debtor at the time of purchase is important although the definitions give no indication about which controls if the actual use and the use intended at the time of purchase conflict. The definitions of farm products and inventory contained in 9–109(3) and (4) respectively, make no reference to "bought for" and do not therefore give a statutory basis for consideration of the debtor's intent.

The cases abound in *dictum* on the question whether intended use at the time of purchase or actual use controls, but a search of the cases yields very little by way of holding. Opinions in two of the cases state that the debtor's actual use controls; three other opinions intimate, somewhat equivocally, that the debtor's intention at the time of purchase controls. None of the cases presents a square holding for in none is there a finding that the debtor's use in fact deviated from his intended use. In In re Leiby,[110] for example, the court stated that actual use controlled but it then found not only that the debtor's actual and intended use coincided but that the creditor had knowledge of the intended use. A case with equally mighty *dictum* which points the opposite direction is National Bank of Commerce v. First National Bank & Trust Co.[111] There the court emphasized that the debtor "intended" to use a sports car for business, and held that an "equipment" filing perfected the security interests in the car. However, the opinion does not reveal how the car was in fact used.

How one resolves the intended use versus actual use dispute depends ultimately on whether he values more highly the secured creditor interests or third party creditor interests. A secured creditor would like to rely upon the debtor's statement about his intended use at the time the loan is made. A careful creditor can procure the debtor's written statement about his intended use and can then file

109. The courts hold that the "principal" intended or actual use governs the classification. Where the use is divided equally between consumer and business purposes, there is no "principal" use. Thus, the collateral falls within the catchall "equipment," because even if it is not used "primarily in business," it is "not included in the definitions of inventory, farm products or consumer goods." § 9–109(e). In re D'Arcy, 6 UCC Rep.Serv. 1122 (Ref.Dec.W.D.N.Y.1968) (financing statement filed as though collateral was consumer goods and not equipment; held unperfected.) Accord, In re Brawn, 6 UCC Rep.Serv. 1031 (Ref. Dec.D.Me.1969) (alternative holding).

110. 1 UCC Rep.Serv. 428 (Ref.Dec.E.D. Pa.1962). Cf. In re Rutland Tile Center, Inc., 5 UCC Rep.Serv. 1115 (Ref. Dec.D.Vt.1968).

111. 446 P.2d 277, 5 UCC Rep.Serv. 947 (Okla.1968). Cf. Natick Trust Co. v. Bay State Truck Lease, Inc., 28 Mass. App.Dec. 60, 5 UCC Rep.Serv. 1047 (1963); In re Bell, 6 UCC Rep.Serv. 740 (Ref.Dec.D.Colo.1969).

in the proper place according to that use. On the other hand, third party creditors will surely argue for the actual use test. Consider the situation in which the debtor has warranted to the secured creditor that the goods will not be affixed to the real estate in such a way as to become a fixture. Subsequently, and notwithstanding his warranty, debtor affixes the goods. A later mortgagee lends against the real estate partly in reliance upon the presence of the fixture and in the belief that there is no perfected security interest on the fixture. Whom should we favor? The secured creditor because the debtor intended to use the goods as equipment, or the mortgagee because the goods are in fact a fixture? In this hypothetical case surely the mortgagee who has lent in reliance has a very appealing case, but the question is not that easy. One who reads the bankruptcy cases suspects that typical "third party creditor" is not a mortgagee or any other person who has been misled by the secured creditor's improper filing but is rather an unsecured creditor who happens to claim under a trustee in bankruptcy and may never have heard of a filing system much less have relied upon it. If one views the world as consisting largely of such persons, he would then favor the secured creditor who has made a diligent effort to find the debtor's use and has filed accordingly. If one believes that the universe of third party creditors consists mostly of mortgagees and others who have been misled in fact by the debtor's actual use, he should favor the actual use test. Perhaps we are excessively cynical, but we believe the universe of unsecured creditors is made up mostly of non-relyers, persons who have lent in total disregard of filings. Moreover, we think that to require that the creditor follow his debtor around to determine the debtor's actual use would be inconsistent with the Code policy of easy perfection and no policing. We would hold that the stated intention of the debtor at the time of the loan or purchase governs the filing even though his actual use differs from his stated intention. Doubtless such a rule requires some refinement, as in, for example, cases where the debtor has in fact been using the goods in a way contrary to his stated intention before the secured creditor lends. Surely, too, the creditor should not be permitted to hide behind a stated intention of a debtor where the creditor had knowledge that the stated intention was not the debtor's actual intention. On balance we would find a secured creditor perfected who has filed in reliance upon the stated intention of the debtor about the use of the goods even though the debtor's actual use differed from that statement.

## § 23–14   Perfection by Filing—Place of Business

If, under the third alternative 9–401(1), a debtor has a place of business in only one county within a state, the secured party must file both centrally with the Secretary of State and locally at the single place of business. The Code nowhere defines "place of business" and one can easily appreciate the difficulty courts may have in determining whether a temporary construction site or a little known and seldom used office constitute a "place of business."

One can imagine at least two plausible tests to determine whether or not a debtor's business activity constitutes a place of business. One might simply measure the quantity of business work accomplished at that place: how much revenue is attributable to that place, what is its permanence, how many letters were sent there, how many letters were sent from there, how many employees were there, etc. Another test suggested by the opinions is the test of "notoriety": to what extent do creditors and others know that the debtor in fact was doing business at the place in question.

All three of the courts which have wrestled with this problem seem to have used the notoriety test. In In re McQuaide,[112] the most articulate opinion, the secured party had filed centrally and in the town [113] of the debtor's residence. The debtor also had a place of business in a different town from the one in which he lived. Under the peculiar Vermont version of 9–401(1) (c), Third Alternative, if a debtor has multiple places of business, one must file both centrally and at the debtor's residence. However if the debtor has only one place of business, the creditor must file centrally and at the place of business. The trustee argued that the debtor had only one place of business and the secured party should have filed centrally and at the town of business but not at the debtor's residence. The secured party argued that only central filing was required and, apparently in the alternative, that the debtor's residence constituted a second place of business. At the debtor's residence the debtor's wife, without compensation, helped him keep his business records, and

> An oak table was used as a desk and, as equipment, he had at his house a four drawer file, a fireproof safe, a typewriter, an adding machine and a check-writer, but this was not used. . . . [T]he business check book was kept at home where the checks were written and the business telephone was connected so that it also rang at his house.[114]

The referee appeared unconcerned with the actual quantum of work accomplished at the residence. Instead, he focused on the question whether most people knew of the existence of the residence as a work site. The referee held that the residence was not notorious enough to be a place of business within the Code meaning. Two other cases, by implication or in dictum support the use of this test. In In re John Adams Henry, Inc.,[115] the debtor had central offices in New York County and he also employed salesmen who worked out of their homes in other counties. The trustee in bankruptcy argued that the salesmen's homes could not constitute multiple places of business and therefore the secured party was unperfected because he had not filed in the only county where he had a place of business. The referee

---

112. 5 UCC Rep.Serv. 802 (Ref.Dec.D. Vt.1968).

113. Vermont local filing units are set up on a town and not a county basis.

114. In re McQuaide, 5 UCC Rep.Serv. 802, 804 (Ref.Dec.D.Vt.1968).

115. 5 UCC Rep.Serv. 795 (Ref.Dec.S.D. N.Y.1968) (by implication).

disagreed.  The New York County headquarters were open only from
8:00 a. m. to 5:00 p. m.  Since the salesmen worked around the clock,
they were required to use their homes as places of business and the
salesmen's business cards gave their home phones as their business
phones.  Presumably such an arrangement of salesmen working out
of their homes was commonplace in the fresh fruit, vegetable, and
grocery distributing business.  In In re Falkof [116] the secured party
was unperfected because he filed only with the Secretary of State.
According to the court the debtor's residence could not constitute a
second place of business even if business had been conducted there
because it was not a "known or settled place of business for the transaction of [the debtor's] monied concerns." [117]

We believe the courts should use the notoriety test.[118]  That test
conforms with the basic theory behind local filing.  If no one knows
of the business activities being conducted at a certain location, then it
is misleading to credit-searchers to consider that "secret" location as
a second place of business.  Inherent in a dual filing system is the notion that local credit searchers need not consult central files for
notoriously local debtors.  If only one public place of business exists,
credit searchers will only consult the files at that location.[119]

In the usual case attachment and filing will occur simultaneously
or very nearly so and the debtor will not have time to change his residence or move his place of business between the two events.  Occasionally, however, a security interest will attach and a creditor who is not
diligent will fail to file a financing statement until some days or
months have passed.  More important are the many cases in which a

---

116.  2 UCC Rep.Serv. 731 (Ref.Dec.D.
Mass.1963) (dictum).

117.  Id. at 736 (Falkof had used his
home as a base of his operations only
while he was making arrangements
to begin his new enterprise, before
the secured sale occurred).

118.  Note that this test also rejects the
notion that a creditor can rely upon
statements by the debtor in determining the place of business or residence.
In Section 23–13, supra, we argue that
a secured party should be able to rely
upon a debtor's statement about the
use to which collateral will be put,
even if the actual use differs from
the stated use.  That is so because
section 9–109 authorizes the secured
party to classify consumer goods and
equipment according to the debtor's
"bought for," i. e., intended, use.  The
only way to determine that is by having the debtor represent his intentions.
That is particularly true when the
creditor is making a purchase money
loan and the debtor has not yet begun
to use the goods.  Section 9–401 does

not similarly suggest filing at the
debtor's represented residence or
place of business; it appears to demand filing at the actual residence.
In re Falkof, 2 UCC Rep.Serv. 731
(Ref.Dec.D.Mass.1963) (held in favor
of trustee in bankruptcy); In re Simpson, 4 UCC Rep.Serv. 250 (Ref.Dec.
W.D.Mich.1966).  Prior to August 28,
1964 Michigan's § 9–401 required interests in farm equipment to be filed
at the Secretary of State's office and
locally at the debtor's residence "as
stated in the security agreement."
The provision was changed to require
filing only in the "county of the debt-
or's residence."  The Referee in Simpson reasoned that the new language,
the official Code version, demanded
actual and not represented locations.

It is not too great a burden to force
the secured party to determine actual
locations.  Also, it avoids tempting
debtors to misrepresent their locations
in the hope of defrauding subsequent
creditors.

119.  See § 9–401, Comments 3 and 4.

security interest attaches seriatim to after-acquired property over the life of a revolving loan. In such common financing transactions as loans against inventory and accounts receivable it is conceivable that the filing could be as far removed from the attachment as four or five years.

Certainly in the latter case, that involving after-acquired property, the policy and intent of the Code are clear; time of filing is the time for determining debtor's residence or place of business. The whole idea of the "first to file rule" under 9–312(5) (a) [120] is to permit the secured creditor to examine the files, make a filing and take priority from that date irrespective of the time when the security interest attaches or becomes perfected. Comment 4 to 9–312 reads in part as follows: "The justification for the [first to file] rule lies in the necessity of protecting the filing system—that is, of allowing the secured party who has first filed to make subsequent advances without each time having, as a condition of protection, to check for filings later than his." That seems a clear invitation to the secured creditor to file once—perhaps at a time when there is still no perfection—and then forget about it for five years. It is implicit in such an invitation that debtor's residence and place of doing business must be determined at the time of filing and not the time of attachment. Though some courts have had a hard time finding the implications, we believe that 9–401(3) and Comment 6 to 9–401 also carry the implication that time of filing is the determinative time, not time of attachment.[121]

Three reported opinions deal with the question whether residence and place of business should be determined at the time of attachment or at the time of filing. All are bankruptcy cases decided by referees. One [122] favors time of filing and the other two,[123] in dictum or alternative holdings, find that the time of attachment is the proper time for determining residence and place of business. Of at least passing interest is the fact that the secured creditor lost to the trustee in each

---

**120.** § 9–312(5) (a):

(5) In all cases not governed by other rules stated in this section (including cases of purchase money security interests which do not qualify for the special priorities set forth in subsections (3) and (4) of this section), priority between conflicting security interests in the same collateral shall be determined as follows:

(a) in the order of filing if both are perfected by filing, regardless of which security interest attached first under Section 9–204(1) and whether it attached before or after filing;

**121.** Technically, 9–401(3) and 9–401, Comment 6, beg the "time" question. The answer lies uncomfortably within the meaning of "proper." To make the provision more intelligible we suggest interpreting the provision with the following change:

9–401(3): A filing which is made in the proper place [at the time of filing] in this state continues effective even though the debtor's residence or place of business or the location of the collateral or its use, whichever controlled the original filing, is thereafter changed.

A "proper place" with respect to "a filing" reasonably refers to propriety at the time of the filing.

**122.** In re Golden Kernel, Inc., 5 UCC Rep.Serv. 43 (Ref.Dec.E.D.Pa.1968).

**123.** In re Kane, 1 UCC Rep.Serv. 582 (E.D.Pa.1962) (dictum); In re Pelletier, 5 UCC Rep.Serv. 327 (Ref.Dec. D.Me.1968) (alternative holding).

of the three cases. One more cynical than we might argue that the referees, and particularly Referee Cyr, are simply exercising their bias against secured creditors and in favor of unsecured creditors. We are unpersuaded by Referee Cyr's arguments; [124] it is clear to us that at least in the after-acquired property cases the draftsmen intended that the debtor's status at the time of filing govern and we see no reason why that rule should not be applied generally. If a creditor takes a security interest and does not perfect it by filing until six months after the security interest attaches, will not third party creditors at that point be better served by the secured party's filing in accordance with the status of the debtor at the time of filing than at the time of attachment? Again we favor a rule which will give an explicit message to the secured creditor about what he must do in order to insure his perfection.

## § 23–15    Perfection by Filing—Effect of Filings Made in the Wrong Place, 9–401(2)

All is not lost for the secured creditor who files [125] but fails to file in all of the necessary places. Section 9–401(2) of the Code will save our careless creditor in some cases:

> A filing which is made in good faith [126] in an improper place or not in all of the places required by this section

> [First] is nevertheless effective with regard to any collateral as to which the filing complied with the requirements of this Article and

---

**124.** In re Pelletier, 5 UCC Rep.Serv. 327 (Ref.Dec.D.Me.1968).

**125.** There has been some suggestion that where dual filing is required, both financing statements must be identical. Unusual dictum exists in In re Cohen, 4 UCC Rep.Serv. 22 (Ref. Dec.E.D.Pa.1967). In that case, the local financing statement gave no maturity date; the centrally filed one gave the following: "Indefinite: July 1, 1965, or as renewed or extended." The Referee in Bankruptcy commented:

Article 9–401(1) (c) of the Code, in requiring the filing of financing statements at two separate locations to perfect one security interest, means that essentially identical financing statements must be filed at each location in order to perfect . . . .
By reason of the difference in the maturity dates set forth in the financing statements . . . [the secured party] never held a perfected security interest . . . .

Id. at 26 (emphasis added).

Such a decision is unwarranted. When slightly conflicting dual financing statements exist, the interest intended to be secured should be held perfected at least to the extent of the more restricted language. If a credit searcher has knowledge of the contents of the more expansive financing statement, then no limitation of the interest is warranted vis-a-vis that creditor. See text accompanying notes 165–175 infra.

**126.** The good faith language means merely making an effort to file. No amount of "good faith" can give effect to a completely improperly filed financing statement of which no one has knowledge. See, e. g., In re Throckmorton's, Inc., 4 UCC Rep.Serv. 240 (Ref.Dec.S.D.Ohio 1966); In re Federal Wholesale Meats & Frozen Foods, Inc., 5 UCC Rep.Serv. 639 (Wis. Cir.Ct.1968); In re Lux's Superette, Inc., 206 F.Supp. 368, 1 UCC Rep.Serv. 588 (E.D.Pa.1962).

[Second] is also effective with regard to collateral covered by the financing statement against any person who has knowledge of the contents of such financing statement.

The first part of 9–401(2) is simple. It protects the secured party when he has filed one financing statement to perfect interests in more than one type of collateral and the filing is correct for one but not for all of the types of collateral covered. If for example one made only a central filing which purported to perfect an interest in "equipment and consumer goods" Section 9–401(2) would make clear what any sensible man would infer, namely, that the filing perfects the equipment interest even though it does not perfect the consumer goods interest.

The second part of 9–401(2) deals with an ancient problem: what are the rights of one who stumbles upon a financing statement that has been filed in the wrong place? Clear enough is the case of the searcher who in fact finds a wrongly filed statement; as against him the interest is "effective" (i. e., perfected). It is equally clear that one must have knowledge (actual knowledge 1–201(25)) not just notice to be affected by 9–401(2).

A problem in 9–401(2) destined to devil the courts for some time to come is the meaning of the phrase "knowledge of the contents of such financing statement." When does one have such knowledge? One possible reading of the phrase limits it to the case described above in which a searcher actually lays his eyes on the maverick financing statement. At the other extreme is a reading which would hold that knowledge of a creditor's security interest is knowledge of "the contents of such financing statement." Although we are not certain exactly where the line should be drawn between the two extremes suggested, we are certain that the latter reading is incorrect and that the draftsmen did not intend knowledge of a security interest to equal knowledge of the contents of a financing statement. We have found only one reported opinion which holds squarely that knowledge of a security interest is not knowledge of the contents of a filing statement as that term is used in 9–401(2). In that case, In re Advertising Distributors of America,[127] the court found that knowledge of the creditor's claimed "lien" was not sufficient under 9–401(2). There one party admitted knowledge of the other's claim as follows:

[I] while acting as attorney for the petitioning creditors herein, and prior to the filing of the Petition in Bankruptcy therein, was informed by Chesire, Inc. that Chesire, Inc. claimed a lien upon the collateral that is the subject of this action.[128]

127. 2 UCC Rep.Serv. 548 (Ref.Dec.E. D.Ohio 1965), aff'd 3 UCC Rep.Serv. 225 (N.D.Ohio 1965). See also In re Smith, 205 F.Supp. 27, 1 UCC Rep. Serv. 476 (E.D.Pa.1962) (dictum).

128. 3 UCC Rep.Serv. 225, 229 (Ref. Dec.N.D.Ohio 1965).

In rejecting the argument that knowledge of a "lien" was sufficient, the court said, "This stipulation does not identify the document on which Chesire [the secured party] relied for its claim of a lien, nor does it reveal that . . . [the receiver] . . . had knowledge of the contents of said document."[129]

Unfortunately the world is not as tidy as the analysis of Judge Kalbfleisch in In re Advertising Distributors of America would indicate. Two bankruptcy cases contain a good deal of loose talk to the effect that knowledge of the security interest is sufficient to qualify under 9–401(2).[130] The opinions in each of these cases contain interchangeable discussion of sections 9–301 and 9–401. Of course, to the extent that the courts find that knowledge on the part of the lien creditor subordinates him to an unperfected secured creditor under 9–301, they are correct. Following that tack, one can argue that each of those two cases is really a 9–301 case; that the reference to knowledge of the security interest is really a reference to 9–301, and that the discussion of 9–401 is only dictum. We prefer so to classify them as 9–301 cases, for the loose language about knowledge of "the substance of the transaction" and of the "reclaimant's security interest"[131] are fundamental misinterpretations of 9–401(2) if the courts in fact intended them as interpretations of 9–401(2) and not of 9–301.

One should understand the legal significance of expanding the 9–401(2) language to include any creditor who has "knowledge of a prior interest." Such an outcome will render the party with knowledge subject to the prior interest even though it is not correctly filed and will subordinate the second party to the first interest even though the second party was the first to perfect.

A number of factors in addition to the In re Advertising case make us confident that mere knowledge of a creditor's security interest is not "knowledge of the contents of such financing statement" as that term is used in 9–401(2). First there is the history of the provision as revealed by the prior law and by the comments. As we pointed out above, the question of the effectiveness of a mortgage or a deed or a chattel mortgage which is recorded out of place has been with us for years. The second sentence of Comment 5 to 9–401 tells us that the draftsmen at least had those cases in mind when they were preparing subsection (2): "The subsection rejects the occasional decisions that an improperly filed record is ineffective to give notice even to a person who knows of it." Prior versions of 9–401(2) made knowledge of "the filing" sufficient. In our judgment the change in 1956 to the current requirement of knowledge of the "contents" of the financing statement inclines slightly toward the "lay your eyes on the document" end of the spectrum. A third factor which supports our conclusion

---

129.  Id. at 229.

130.  In re Buschmann, 4 UCC Rep.Serv. 260 (Ref.Dec.E.D.Wis.1967); In re Komfo Prods. Corp., 247 F.Supp. 229, 2 UCC Rep.Serv. 1107 (E.D.Pa.1965).

131.  In re Komfo Prods. Corp., 247 F.Supp. 229, 236, 2 UCC Rep.Serv. 1107, 1113 (E.D.Pa.1965). The court failed to say whether it was talking about 9–301 or 9–401.

is the words chosen by the draftsmen.  Section 9–301(1) (b) shows us that the draftsmen knew how to describe "knowledge of a security interest" when that was what they meant to say.  The sophisticated and able draftsmen of Article Nine are entitled to the benefit of our presumption that the language in 9–301(1) (b) "knowledge of the security interest" has a different meaning from the language of 9–401(2), "knowledge of the contents of such financing statement."

Fourth, a broad interpretation of 9–401(2) which would allow knowledge of the security interest to be tantamount to filing, would conflict with the pure race aspect of 9–312(5).  Recall that 9–312(5) gives priority to the first to file or the first to perfect as the case may be, irrespective of the status of his knowledge—the one who wins the race to the courthouse takes priority even though he knows of a prior interest.  The irrelevance of the knowledge is made clear by Example 1 contained in Comment 4 to 9–312, and a broad reading of 9–401(2) would conflict with that policy contained in 9–312.  If one reads 9–401(2) as broadly as some courts have suggested, any claimant who had knowledge of a prior security interest (as to which there could have been an improper filing) could be unseated and subordinated because of that knowledge.  Such an outcome would be a long step toward making 9–312 into a notice race statute—that is, into a statute in which one had not only to file first but also to be without knowledge of the other prior party's interest; for reasons discussed more fully in Chapter 25, we believe that the pure race aspect of 9–312 should be preserved.

Finally, one should read 9–401(2) narrowly for policy reasons.  We see no reason why the one who has filed in the wrong place should be given greater rights than one who, perhaps through no negligence of his own, has failed to file when a third creditor gets knowledge of the security interest of each of them.  If 9–401(2) were read as broadly as the two cases quoted above imply so that knowledge of the security interest equals knowledge of the contents, one who files in the wrong place will have substantially greater rights, in our opinion quite undeserved, than the one who does not file at all; and he will have such rights even though no one stumbles across the financing statement.  We therefore reject the dicta in the *Buschmann* and *Komfo* cases, and in accordance with In re Advertising Distributors of America conclude that knowledge of a security interest is not knowledge of the contents of the financing statement.

The question remains, however, whether 9–401(2) covers cases in which the third party has done more than learn of the security interest, but less than feast his eyes on the improperly filed financing statement.  What of the case in which the secured party sends a copy of the financing statement to the third party?  What of the case in which the third party receives a letter stating that the creditor filed a financing statement covering certain kinds of collateral?  What of the case in which the improper filer tells the third party that he has filed a financing statement (but does not tell him where it is filed)?

We have no goldplated answers to these questions and we suspect that whatever we say, the courts will draw the line on a case by case basis. However, we do hope they read 9–401(2) circumspectly. We believe it was designed mainly for the somewhat abberational case in which a searcher actually stumbles across an improperly filed financing statement. If the courts expand the provision too far beyond that case, they will destroy the "pure race" aspect of 9–312 by giving a colorable argument for priority to many who have not properly filed.

### § 23–16  Perfection by Filing—What to File?  The Financing Statement, 9–402

The history of secured transactions is one of development of new security devices to handle progressively more sophisticated commercial transactions. As we have seen, the pre-Code law recognized many independent security devices. Although the reach of these devices overlapped substantially, each device more or less catered to a specific type of commercial transaction. Article Nine seeks to merge all the independent security devices into one all-encompassing device.[132] The draftsmen also adopted the concept of notice filing, an idea first introduced by the Uniform Trust Receipts Act. Something should be on public file simply to alert credit-searchers that a certain security agreement may exist. If the credit-searcher is interested, he can contact one of the parties to determine the details of the arrangement. The filing simply puts the searcher on "notice" and instructs him where to look for more information.

Under the Code the document filed for public notice is called a financing statement. Its formal requisites for most collateral are as follows:

A financing statement is sufficient if it is

(1) signed by the debtor,

(2) signed by the secured party,

(3) gives an address of the secured party from which information concerning the security interest may be obtained,

(4) gives a mailing address of the debtor and

(5) contains a statement indicating the types, or describing the items, of collateral  .   .   .   .[133]

132. Section 9–101, Comment: "The aim of this Article is to provide a simple and unified structure within which the immense variety of present-day secured financing transactions can go forward with less cost and with greater certainty."

133. Additionally, "When the financing statement covers crops growing or to be grown or goods which are or are to become fixtures, the statement must also contain a description of the real estate concerned." § 9–402(1).

Although a short financing statement is all that is required to be filed under Article Nine, the security agreement itself may still be used as a financing statement:

> A copy of the security agreement is sufficient as a financing statement if it contains the [Section 9–401(1)] information and is signed by both parties.[134]

Ordinarily a security agreement must contain the debtor's signature and ". . . a description of the collateral . . ."[135] but it would not necessarily contain the secured party's signature nor the addresses of the parties. Thus, if one adds the secured party's signature and both addresses to a mine run security agreement, it will suffice as a financing statement. A security agreement may constitute a financing statement, but according to present case law, the converse is not true. See Section 23–3.

In the following pages we discuss the swelling body of case law on the question whether the document which the secured creditor has filed is a sufficient financing statement under 9–402. This body of case law is of interest to the planner, for he should read the cases and warn his clients of the pits into which others have fallen. (For example, does one list the debtor's DBA name or his actual name?) Since the policies which support the various requisites of a financing statement are not identical, the courts should properly permit more deviation from some than from others. We divide our discussion below according to the various kinds of information which one must give on a financing statement. The basic lawyer question in each of the cases below is this: does the purported financing statement in question deviate so far from the requirements of 9–402 that it should not be accepted as an effective financing statement?

### 9–402(5)

The starting point for the analysis in each of the cases below, whatever the alleged defect in the financing statement, is subsection (5) of 9–402 which reads in full as follows:

> A financing statement substantially complying with the requirements of this section is effective even though it contains minor errors which are not seriously misleading.

Comment 5 describes the policy which caused the draftsmen to include subsection (5) and it gives further guidance to the courts: "Subsection (5) is in line with the policy of this Article to simplify formal requisites and filing requirements and is designed to discourage the fanatical and impossibly refined reading of such statutory requirements in which courts have occasionally indulged themselves." Although the message has not reached a few courts, the

---

134. § 9–402(1).

135. Additionally, "when the security interest covers crops or oil, gas or minerals to be extracted or timber to be cut, a description of the land concerned [is necessary]." § 9–203(1)(b).

draftsmen are saying as plainly as they can that certain defects do not void a financing statement; they are rejecting and attempting to change much of pre-Code case law.

It will come as no surprise that errors which are regarded as minor and not seriously misleading in Pennsylvania are treated as major and misleading in Maine. That is an inescapable consequence of our federalist system and the lawyer must learn to live with it. However, there is a more general interpretive difficulty with 9–402(5); the question is whether 9–402(5) contains two conditions or only one which the draftsmen have stated twice. That is, are errors "not seriously misleading" *ipso facto* "minor errors"? Or can an error which is not seriously misleading still be "major" and thus render a financing statement ineffective? Assume, for example, that the debtor failed to sign a financing statement but that his name and address is clearly set out on the financing statement and the financing statement is properly indexed. Under such circumstances the omission is not seriously misleading but the complete omission of one of the five conditions might still be called a major error. Although we are unsure of the wisdom of the draftsmen's judgment,[136] we think it likely that they intended two conditions and that subsection (5) does not save a financing statement which contains major but not misleading errors.

### Signatures

We have found no case construing the official version of 9–402 in which a court found a financing statement to be effective despite the absence of the signature of the debtor. If the debtor's signature is omitted the financing statement is ineffective. However, New York and Indiana have nonuniform provisions which permit financing statements without the debtor's signature if the debtor has authorized such a procedure.[137]

Presumably the policy which calls for a debtor's signature is the fear that some nasty creditor will cast a shadow over all of the debtor's property by filing a financing statement. If such a creditor would not go to the length of forging the debtor's signature, the signature requirement is some protection against such overreaching. Whether such underhanded creditors run loose in any numbers in the commercial jungle is open to question, but the argument about overreaching at least gives a plausible basis for the requirement of a debtor's signature.

Why the creditor must also sign is unclear. Commentators unanimously maintain that the creditor's signature is an unneces-

---

**136.** See, e. g., text accompanying notes 157–64, infra, where we suggest that courts under certain circumstances ought to tolerate total omission of some 9–402(1) conditions.

**137.** Ind.Ann.Stat. § 19–9–402(2) (c) (Smith-Hurd 1964); N.Y.U.C.C. § 9–402(2) (c) (McKinney 1964). Accord, Beneficial Fin. Co. v. Kurland Cadillac-Oldsmobile, Inc., 32 App.Div.2d 643, 300 N.Y.S.2d 884, 6 UCC Rep. Serv. 539 (2d Dep't 1969); Bank of North America v. Bank of Nutley, 94 N.J.Super. 220, 227 A.2d 535, 4 UCC Rep.Serv. 56 (Law Div.1967).

sary technicality, adds nothing to the veracity of the statement, and is unlikely to assist the searcher in uncovering information. Courts, however, are divided on the effect of omitting the creditor's signature.[138] The Permanent Editorial Board has proposed an amendment to the Code which would remove the requirement of the creditor's signature on the financing statement.[139]

The fighting issue in the "signature" cases is whether imperfect attempts at a signature constitute a "signature." Section 1–201(39) defines "signed" to include "any symbol executed or adopted by a party with present intention to authenticate a writing". Comment 39 to 1–201 embellishes upon the language of the Code as follows:

> The inclusion of authentication in the definition of "signed" is to make clear that as the term is used in this Act a complete signature is not necessary. Authentication may be printed, stamped or written; it may be by initials or by thumbprint. It may be on any part of the document and in appropriate cases may be found in a billhead or letterhead. No catalog of possible authentications can be complete and the court must use common sense and commercial experience in passing upon these matters. The question always is whether the symbol was executed or adopted by the party with present intention to authenticate the writing.

There is no reason to believe that 9–402(1) contemplates any more stringent a requirement than 1–201(39) specifies.[140] Nevertheless, a few courts have argued to the contrary. The court in In re Carlstrom[141] was impressed by the "deterrent effect" on a party actually signing. It held that a financing statement is not sufficient if it contains merely "a signature" of a party.

> A construction more consonant with the context language and rationale of § 9–402 is that the financing statement must bear a symbol affixed by the secured party or its authorized representative which is susceptible of evidentiary connection to the signatory. Insofar as § 1–201(39) serves to elevate "any symbol" to the status of a sufficient signature without regard to its evidentiary value it must be held to be inconsistent with the context of § 9–402 and hence inapplicable.[142]

138. Alloway v. Stuart, 385 S.W.2d 41 (Ky.App.1964) (value as precedent may be slight; the court suggested its decision would be different after the Code had been in operation a reasonable time); Strevell-Paterson Fin. Co. v. May, 77 N.M. 331, 422 P.2d 366, 3 UCC Rep.Serv. 1094 (1967) (forceful dictum). Contra, In re Carlstrom, 3 UCC Rep.Serv. 766 (Ref.Dec.D.Me. 1966) (dictum).

139. Permanent Editorial Board for the Uniform Commercial Code, Review Committee for Article 9, Preliminary Draft No. 2 § 9–402(1) at 93–94 (1970).

140. Only Kansas and Missouri had added nonuniform language in 9–402 attempting to explain what "signed" encompasses.

141. 3 UCC Rep.Serv. 766 (Ref.Dec.D. Me.1966).

142. Id. at 772–73.

In re Kane [143] went another unreasonable step further:

> Signatures in the modern world of commerce appear in many forms. There are stampings of signature facsimiles, printed facsimiles, photo-facsimiles, and other chemical and mechanical reproductions, to mention a few. As I construe the Code however, the provision "signed by the debtor and secured party" appearing in Section 9–402 of the Code means an actual signature manually produced by a writing instrument in the hand of the signer in direct contact with the document being executed.

Judicial imposition of such extraordinary requirements smacks of the "fanatical" interpretation of statutory language that the Code drafters hoped to bury. Hopefully future decisions will follow the more enlightened views of the Second Circuit in Benedict v. Lebowitz,[144] where the court held that a typed corporate name was a sufficient signature.

### Names

Section 9–402(1) requires a debtor and creditor to "sign" a financing statement, but does not specifically require that the debtor's or the secured party's "name" appear on the financing statement.[145] Usually, of course, the debtor's and creditor's names will appear as their signatures. It is likely that the name of each will also appear as part of the "address" that 9–402 requires. If the name in the signature and that given in the address differ, if either is misspelled, or if either is not the true business name of the debtor or creditor, the creditor is in trouble, and he may be unperfected. Note that the model form set out in 9–402(3) explicitly refers to "name of debtor and name of secured party". To the extent that the name is a part of the address which one needs in order to make contact with the debtor or creditor, its inclusion is important and because the indexing officer must index the financing statement under the name of the debtor, its inclusion is necessary. Virtually all of the "name" cases are those in which the debtor's name has been misspelled or in which the wrong name was included for the debtor (for example, an informal DBA name when the debtor technically and legally did business under another name). We can pigeon-hole the cases to date in three general categories: (1) those in which the filing officer correctly indexed the financing statement under the proper debtor's

---

143. 1 UCC Rep.Serv. 582, 586–87 (Ref. Dec.E.D.Pa.1962).

144. 346 F.2d 120 (2d Cir. 1965). Accord, In re Horvath, 1 UCC Rep.Serv. 624 (Ref.Dec.D.Conn.1963); In re State Discount Furniture, Inc., 2 UCC Rep.Serv. 20 (Ref.Dec.D.Conn.1964); Plemens v. Didde-Glaser, Inc., 244 Md. 556, 224 A.2d 464, 3 UCC Rep.Serv. 1017 (1966) (financing statement was manually signed by corporate treasurer but not as corporate signature and only as personal signature; held minor error.)

145. Only two states have added this requirement to 9–402(1). Arizona and California provisions demand the parties' signatures, names, and mailing addresses. Arizona requires the names to be typed or printed.

name despite errors in the financing statement; (*2*) those in which the filing officer incorrectly indexed the financing statement which contained the debtor's correct name and also a misspelled or otherwise incorrect name (as, for eaxmple, when the signature was correct but the name in the address was incorrect); and (*3*) those in which the filing officer incorrectly indexed a financing statement which did not contain the debtor's correct name either as part of the address or as the signature.

The courts have held that a correctly indexed financing statement is effective despite the fact that the debtor's name appears incorrectly at least once on the financing statement.[146] In all such cases the principal function of the debtor's name requirement, namely indexing, has been fulfilled. If the filing officer correctly indexed, the odds are 99 out of 100 that a reasonably prudent searcher will find a possible security interest. Of course correct indexing under the debtor's name will not cure omission of or defects in the secured party's name.

When the debtor's correct name is disclosed by the signature but his name is misspelled or otherwise incorrect as part of the address and the filing officer improperly indexes the statement, the courts split. In In re Vaughan,[147] a bankruptcy case applying Michigan law, the financing statement contained the typewritten name of the debtor as "Vaught" and "Voughn." The signature was legible and the court found that the filing officer should have indexed according to the signature. The court reasoned that since the filing officer was obliged to rely upon the signature, the misfiling did not result from the secured party's negligence and he was perfected. All courts do not agree that a legible debtor's signature fulfills the "name" requirement. In re Raymond F. Sargent, Inc.[148] specifically challenged the wisdom of In re Vaughan. The *Sargent* court reasoned that the debtor's unsigned name was necessary; that it is the filing officer's guide for indexing:

> There is no express requirement in § 9–402(1) that the financing statement reflect the "name" of the debtor, although § 9–402(3) would seem to indicate clearly that the Code contemplates the name of the debtor as an integral part of the debtor's mailing address, which is expressly required.
> . . . One of the primary purposes served by reflecting

---

146. See, e. g., National Cash Register Co. v. Firestone & Co., 346 Mass. 255, 191 N.E.2d 471, 1 UCC Rep.Serv. 460 (1963) (proper indexing under the debtor's actual name, but incorrect D.B.A. name also appeared on financing statement; held perfected); In re Raymond F. Sargent, Inc., 8 UCC Rep.Serv. 583, 587 (Ref.Dec.D.Me. 1970) (dictum).

147. 4 UCC Rep.Serv. 61 (Ref.Dec.W.D. Mich.1967). Accord, In re Kulesza, 4 UCC Rep.Serv. 66 (Ref.Dec.W.D.Mich. 1967). See National Cash Register Co. v. Valley Nat'l Bank, 5 UCC Rep.Serv. 396 (N.Y.Sup.Ct.1968); Bank of North America v. Bank of Nutley, 94 N.J. Super. 220, 227 A.2d 535, 4 UCC Rep. Serv. 56 (1967).

148. 8 UCC Rep.Serv. 583, 588 (Ref.Dec. D.Me.1970).

the debtor's mailing address, including the debtor's name, is to enable the filing officer to perform his ministerial indexing duty in accordance with the terms of 11 MRSA § 9–403(4), upon which public access to the Uniform Commercial Code files is dependent.[149] (Footnotes omitted).

In part because we suspect that few general creditors are misled by the misfilings which may occur as a result of the misspellings and misplaced names, we are persuaded by Referee Nims' decision in *Vaughan*.

Our final classification of cases includes those in which the debtor's correct name nowhere appears on the financing statement, either because the parties use an unregistered, fictitious name (for example, Platt Fur Co. for Henry Platt), or because they are not careful in setting out the exact business name (for example, Excel Department Stores instead of Excel Stores, Inc.). Inevitably such cases lead to improper indexing but most of the courts have been willing to tolerate incorrect names and incorrect indexings as effective under 9–402(5) when in their judgment the inaccuracies were not "seriously misleading." We believe this to be the proper approach and encourage the courts to focus here on whether a reasonably diligent searcher would be likely to discover a financing statement indexed under the incorrect name. Of course a variety of empirical facts would affect the probability that such a searcher would find the name. Among other things, one should know: Was the initial word in the incorrect name the same as the initial word in the correct name (for example, Platt Fur Co. v. Platt, Henry)? Was the filing made in Los Angeles county, with several million residents, or was the filing made in a county in North Dakota with only a few thousand residents? Does the name used sound the same as the real name? We believe that a recent federal court case in Pennsylvania shows an appropriate sensitivity to the problem. In that case the financing statement listed the debtor as "Platt Fur Co." That name was an unregistered, fictitious name for the business of Henry Platt. Henry Platt also used the fictitious name of Kenwell Fur Novelty Co.

> The use of Kenwell as the debtor would clearly have left [the secured party] without a perfected security interest. However, the name Platt Fur Co. is sufficiently related to the name of the debtor, Henry Platt, to require those who search the records to make further investigation . . . [T]he name was "not seriously misleading," the criterion for effectiveness under section 9–402(5).[150]

149. Id. at 586.

150. In re Platt, 257 F.Supp. 478, 482, 3 UCC Rep.Serv. 719, 723 (E.D.Pa. 1966), vacating on other grounds, 3 UCC Rep.Serv. 275 (Ref.Dec.E.D.Pa. 1966). Accord, Beneficial Fin. Co. v. Kurland Cadillac-Oldsmobile, Inc., 57 Misc.2d 806, 293 N.Y.S.2d 647 (App. Term 1968), aff'd on other grounds 32 App.Div.2d 643, 300 N.Y.S.2d 884, 6 UCC Rep.Serv. 539 (2d Dep't 1969).

In In re Excel Stores, Inc.[151] the financing statement indicated that the corporate name was "Excel Department Stores." That was the name used for indexing. The correct name was "Excel Stores, Inc." The Second Circuit, reversing both the District Court and the referee, held for the secured party:

> Nor can it be doubted that any creditor of Excel or other interested person searching the record would come to the Excel Department Store at the Shopping Center of Pawcatuck, find Machado's name [the treasurer of Excel who had signed the financing statement in question] and be put on notice that a lien against Excel might be outstanding and that communication with Machado might be appropriate. This is precisely all that the Code requires.[152]

In the recent opinion of In re Raymond F. Sargent, Inc.,[153] Referee Cyr held that the debtor's exact name must appear at least somewhere on the financing statement. Two of his earlier decisions indicate that even where the debtor's exact name appears at a place other than the official "Debtor's name box", the security interest is unperfected in Maine unless the filing officer in fact correctly indexes the statement.[154] The financing statement in *Sargent* gave the debtor's name as "Raymond F. Sargent Co., Inc.". The inclusion of "Co." was a fatal error.[155] The referee wholly misconstrues the

151. 341 F.2d 961, 2 UCC Rep.Serv. 316 (2d Cir. 1965).

152. Id. at 963.

153. 8 UCC Rep.Serv. 583 (Ref.Dec.D. Me.1970). It is interesting to note that the referee discussed or mentioned virtually all case law in this area, with the exception of In re Excel Stores, Inc., 341 F.2d 961 (2d Cir. 1965), a highly relevant case decided by an eminent federal court in direct conflict with Referee Cyr.

154. In re Brawn, 6 UCC Rep.Serv. 1031 (Ref.Dec.D.Me.1969); In re Brawn, 7 UCC Rep.Serv. 565 (Ref.Dec. D.Me.1970).

155. Whether a court insists upon absolute accuracy might properly depend upon the nature of the retrieval system in use in the jurisdiction in question. Referee Cyr suggested that a "computer programmed to search out financing statements *indexed under the exact name listed*' on the call slip, would not spew forth the financing statement under consideration." 8 UCC Rep.Serv. at 589. (Emphasis in original). Nevertheless, with advancing computer technology, it would not be unreasonable for the computer to select a range of possibly conforming financing statements. The computer retrieval could be based upon the debtor's name or address with built in tolerances for letter transposition, fragmentary first or middle names, etc. After mentioning a computer system, which the court admitted did not exist in Maine, the Referee reasoned:

> In the case at bar, where no search was actually made, the court's dilemma concerns the selection of one of these hypothetical approaches—either that which presumes a "bare bones" automation-like compliance with controlling statutory and administrative filing procedures, or that which would clothe the indexing officer and the clerk who processes the call slip with a measure of curative discretion which tends to prevent the notice system from misfiring as a result of the secured party's error in the designation of the debtor's name on the financing statement.
>
> When courts attempt to buttress the position of the errant secured party by hypothesizing so convenient and judicious an exercise of discretion on the part of a ministerial officer, they risk elimination of the congressionally intended protection of third persons. . . .

Id. at 589.

function of 9–402(5); he engages in precisely the type of "fanatical and impossibly refined reading of . . . statutory requirements" that 9–402(5) was designed to discourage:

> A financing statement substantially complying with the requirements of this section is effective even though it contains minor errors which are not seriously misleading.

Comment 5 to 9–402 gives "as an example of the sort of reasoning which this subsection rejects," General Motors Acceptance Corporation v. Haley.[156] The case is directly in point. In that case the debtor's actual name was "E. R. Millen Company, Inc.", but the financing statement omitted "Inc.". The court held the secured party unperfected because of that error. Thus, the Code specifically intended to avoid this sort of slavishness to technical accuracy.

In summary, inclusion of a debtor's name on a financing statement facilitates correct indexing of the financing statement. When the statement is correctly indexed, the few cases decided to date find that the presence of an incorrect name on the statement does not render it ineffective. Where the indexing is not precisely correct, some courts look to the signature and find the statement effective if the signature correctly states the debtor's name; other courts do not agree that the signature is the primary identification of the debtor's name and may find the financing statement ineffective even though the signature is correct. When the debtor's correct name nowhere appears on the financing statement and the officer necessarily indexes it incorrectly, courts generally examine the name used and weigh the probabilities that indexing under that name will mislead a searcher.

Most of the foregoing discussion and nearly all of the "name" cases deal with errors in the *debtor's* name. Because the statement is not indexed under the secured party's name, our system can tolerate even greater deviation in a secured party's name than in the debtor's name. As long as a reasonably prudent searcher can correctly identify the secured party from the information on the financing statement, we believe that the secured party's name is sufficient.

### Addresses

Mistakes in that part of the address which do not involve the party's name have caused much less difficulty for the courts than has the name controversy above. Where the financing statement contains any sort of an address by which a credit searcher can contact the party in question, courts hold the financing statement effective.[157] Total

---

156. 329 Mass. 559, 109 N.E.2d 143 (1952).

For similar cases, see Coogan, Public Notice Under the Uniform Commercial Code and Other Recent Chattel Security Laws, Including "Notice Filing," 47 Iowa L.Rev. 289, 289 nn. 5, 82, 86 (1962); Case Note, 50 Cornell L.Q. 128, 130 n. 29 (1964).

157. In re Raymond F. Sargent, Inc., 8 UCC Rep.Serv. 583 (Ref.Dec.D.Me.

omission of an address appears the only real issue of dispute.  Case law is evenly divided as to whether such omission constitutes a minor error if it does not seriously mislead anyone.  Two cases indicate that omission of the debtor's or the secured party's address causes a financing statement to be ineffective against third parties.[158]  Several other cases suggest in dicta that they would follow that result.[159]  On the other hand two cases have held that omission of addresses is not necessarily a fatal error.  Both cases treat the problem as a question of fact; that is, the omission will be fatal only if, under the facts of the case, it effectively precludes the notice function of the statement.  In In re French [160] the filing officer properly indexed the statement and the court refused to "create a windfall for the general creditors solely because of this slight dereliction  .  .  .  [t]he failure to include the addresses would, at most, have inconvenienced a creditor [under the existing circumstances]." [161]  In a similar case,

---

1970) (address used street name "Ellworth" instead of "Ellsworth;" held perfected); Silver v. Gulf City Body & Trailer Works, 8 UCC Rep.Serv. 1 (5th Cir. 1970) (address was simply post office box number in given city; held to be sufficient mailing address); Architectural Cabinet, Inc., v. Manley, 3 UCC Rep.Serv. 263 (Pa.Ct.C.P.1966) (street address might suffice where city could have been ascertained by comment elsewhere on financing statement indicating where equipment-collateral was to be installed); In re Bengtson, 3 UCC Rep.Serv. 283 (Ref. Dec.D.Conn.1965) ("Coca-Cola Bottling Co., East Hartford, Conn."; held to be a sufficient address in that only one such bottling company operated in East Hartford).  Later cases suggest that the decision would have been proper even if there were more than one such bottling company.  See Silver v. Gulf City Body & Trailer Works, 432 F.2d 992, 8 UCC Rep.Serv. 1, 3 (5th Cir. 1970); In re Bennett, 6 UCC Rep.Serv. 551, 554 (Ref.Dec.W.D. Mich.1969) (party's old address considered sufficient; party still had limited connections with address); In re Simpson, 4 UCC Rep.Serv. 250 (Ref.Dec.W.D.Mich.1966) (party's old address considered sufficient; party had no present ties with old address). In the last case, the Michigan referee commented:

The requirement is that the financing statement "gives *a* mailing address of the debtor."  There is no requirement that *the* mailing address be given .  .  ..  Unless there is some other defect, the financing statement would give notice and either inquiry of the

creditor or at debtor's former address should have disclosed bankrupt's current residence.  Since an inquiring interested party would probably know of debtor's address, the legislature did not intend the debtor's address be essential to the perfecting of the instrument.

4 UCC Rep.Serv. at 252 (emphasis in original).

158.  In re Smith, 1 UCC Rep.Serv. 589 (Ref.Dec.E.D.Pa.1961) (dictum) debtor's address was omitted.  Note, however, that the financing statement was never filed—the Secretary of the Commonwealth refused to file it without the debtor's address.  See Strevell-Paterson Fin. Co. v. May, 77 N.M. 331, 422 P.2d 366, 3 UCC Rep.Serv. 1094 (1967) (secured party's address was omitted).  *Strevell-Paterson* appears to treat the omission and consequent unperfection as a matter of law.

159.  See also In re Childress, 6 UCC Rep.Serv. 549, 550 (E.D.Tenn.1969). There the financing statement was ineffective because it wasn't filed until after bankruptcy.  The court commented it would have been ineffective anyway because it lacked the parties' addresses.  Cf. In re Raymond F. Sargent, Inc., 8 UCC Rep.Serv. 583 (Ref.Dec.D.Me.1970).

160.  317 F.Supp. 1226, 8 UCC Rep.Serv. 580 (E.D.Tenn.1970).

161.  Id. at 1228, 8 UCC Rep.Serv. at 581.

Rooney v. Mason,[162] the Tenth Circuit affirmed a District Court's decision that the omission of both addresses was a minor error:

> The Wyoming Courts might reasonably hold that a creditor examining the records is put on notice to make further inquiry upon seeing the notice of agreement. Further, the fact that the addresses of both parties were readily available and known by virtually all creditors could reasonably be found sufficient to make unnecessary the listing of the addresses of the parties. Therefore, it was not clearly erroneous for the trial judge to find that appellees' security interest was perfected and that the transfer of property was not a preference.[163]

Several other courts have intimated that Rooney v. Mason may be desirable law.[164] We agree.

### Descriptions

No reported case suggests that total omission of a description of collateral is tolerable. Nor do we believe it should be. The theory of notice filing permits a credit searcher to determine from the financing statement itself whether certain types of goods may be encumbered. If the financing statement suggests they are, then he must make further inquiry to find the complete state of affairs. He cannot rely on the premise that goods described in a financing statement are in fact encumbered. Nevertheless, he should be permitted to conclude the converse: collateral not listed is not encumbered.

All the pertinent reported cases deal with the question whether a given description substantially complies with 9–402(1) requirements. The cases deal mostly with two kinds of errors. The first is the case in which the description on the financing statement arguably does not describe the collateral which the secured party claims. If the secured party lists "accounts" on his financing statement and claims the debtor's contract rights in bankruptcy he will be held unperfected as to the contract rights because the description on the financing statement does not include them. Other cases are those in which the description on the financing statement is so broad that it gives insufficient information to the searcher and casts an unfairly broad shadow over the debtor's property. Such a case would be one in which the creditor filed as to "tangible property".

Apart from the case in which the creditor's description contains the incorrect serial number, the outcomes have usually gone against the secured parties when they are met with the argument that their

162. 394 F.2d 250, 5 UCC Rep.Serv. 308 (10th Cir. 1968).

163. Id. at 253.

164. In re Bennett, 6 UCC Rep.Serv. 551 (Ref.Dec.W.D.Mich.1969); Silver v. Gulf City Body & Trailer Works, 432 F.2d 992, 8 UCC Rep.Serv. 1 (5th Cir. 1970) (Ala.); In re Simpson, 4 UCC Rep.Serv. 250, 252 (Ref.Dec.W.D. Mich.1966) ("the legislature did not intend the debtor's address be essential to the perfecting of the instrument") (dictum).

description does not cover the collateral in question.[165]  For example, "premises" does not describe inventory or accounts receivable [166] and the description of a bankrupt's right to his tax refund (a general intangible under Article Nine according to the court) is not covered by a financing statement which claims only accounts receivable.[167]

The problems created by very broad descriptions are obvious. The broader the description allowed the greater the difficulty for a credit searcher to get any meaningful assistance from the financing statement alone.  Too broad a description may be as unhelpful as no description.  Also, permitting very broad descriptions increases the likelihood of creditor overreaching.  If the financing statement describes all debtor's collateral (regardless of the extent of present security interests), the first to file rule ostensibly permits that secured party to have priority over most subsequent creditors when he does reach a security agreement on the remaining collateral.  Nonetheless, nearly all courts permit broad descriptions with respect to shifting and after-acquired collateral, and we applaud this permissiveness. The floating lien with its after-acquired property clause requires broad descriptions.  Consider, for example, the reasoning of Girard Trust Corn Exchange Bank v. Warren Lepley Ford, Inc.: [168]

> Under the business practice of automobile dealer financing, a specific description of each vehicle as it was financed would be an unrealistic and unreasonable requirement. The only description feasible is a general description.

Courts have permitted as sufficient descriptions even the broad Code classifications of "accounts receivable" and "inventory".  The secured party in Industrial Packaging Products Co. v. Fort Pitt Packaging International, Inc.[169] described the collateral as "accounts receivable."  The court reasoned:

> It is difficult under the circumstances to imagine how the description could be more complete without filing new and amended descriptions each time a new account receivable falls within the purview of the financing statement.  No-

---

165. See, e. g., In re Esquire Produce Co., Inc., 5 UCC Rep.Serv. 257 (Ref. Dec.E.D.N.Y.1968);   National Dime Bank v. Cleveland Bros. Equip. Co., 20 Pa.D. & C.2d 511 (C.P.1959).

166. In re Weiner's Men's Apparel, Inc., 8 UCC Rep.Serv. 104 (Ref.Dec.S.D.N.Y. 1970).

167. In re Certified Packaging, Inc., 8 UCC Rep.Serv. 95 (Ref.Dec.D.Utah 1970). Cf. United States v. Antenna Systems, Inc., 251 F.Supp. 1013, 3 UCC Rep.Serv. 258 (D.N.H.1966);  In re Levine, 6 UCC Rep.Serv. 238 (D.Conn. 1969).  See also In re Richards, 1 UCC Rep.Serv. 620 (D.Conn.1963) ("Radios,

Television Sets, Stereo Hi-Fi record players, band Transceivers" held insufficient to describe "3 sets A 20 A crystals, 1 EC 1 Linear Amp # 4549, 4 12 V Mobil Units with Ch. 11, Citizens Band Transceiver");  Annawan Mills, Inc. v. Northeastern Fibers Co., 26 Mass.App.Dec. 115, 4 UCC Rep.Serv. 787 (1963) ("[C]otton waste and proceeds" held insufficient to describe cotton linters;  trade usage indicated there was a difference).

168. 13 Pa.D. & C.2d 119, 128, 1 UCC Rep.Serv. 500, 506 (C.P.1957).

169. 399 Pa. 643, 161 A.2d 19 (1960).

where in the Uniform Commercial Code is such a requirement set forth.[170]

Where the word "inventory" alone described collateral, a court held the financing statement effective:

> Certainly one who sells to a retailer must be aware of the character of his goods and the disposition contemplated by the buyer and that the goods sold would become inventory as defined in the code and subject to a security agreement declaring a security interest in future inventory.[171]

When the agreement between the parties contemplates only a one-shot arrangement and not a revolving loan against inventory or other after-acquired property, an occasional court has rejected the financing statement description because it was too broad. Even in these cases, however, most courts permit exceptionally broad descriptions.[172] In cases in which courts struck down a financing statement because the description was too broad, it appears that the courts are stimulated by the belief that the creditor was in fact reaching for more than he had bargained for.[173] Where there is no such overreaching, the courts have been more generous to creditors. In one case the court accepted the 9–109 classification, "consumer goods," as a sufficient description for household goods, two rifles and a shotgun.[174] Two other courts have not been bothered by the arguably overinclusive descriptions in the financing statements.[175]

By and large the courts have followed the draftsmen's mandates in interpreting the description requirements of 9–402. Of course Section 9–110 instructs as follows: "For the purposes of this Article any description of personal property or real estate is sufficient

---

170. Id. at 648, 161 A.2d at 21.

171. Thomson v. O. M. Scott Credit Corp., 28 Pa. D. & C.2d 85, 92 (Ct.C.P. 1962) (same document used as security agreement and financing statement).

172. See, e. g., In re Stephens, 8 UCC Rep.Serv. 597 (Ref.Dec.W.D.Okla. 1970); In re Trumble, 5 UCC Rep. Serv. 543 (Ref.Dec.W.D.Mich.1968).

173. Coin-o-Matic Service Co. v. Rhode Island Hospital Trust Co., 3 UCC Rep. Serv. 1112 (R.I.Super.Ct.1966); Mammoth Cave Production Credit Ass'n. v. York, 429 S.W.2d 26, 5 UCC Rep.Serv. 11 (Ky.Ct.App.1968).

174. In re Trumble, 5 UCC Rep.Serv. 543 (Ref.Dec.W.D.Mich.1968). Contra, In re Bell, 6 UCC Rep.Serv. 740 (Ref. Dec.D.Colo.1969). The reasoning of Referee Hilliard in In re Bell is un-

persuasive. He premises his conclusion on the consideration "that, used in a financing statement, 'consumer goods' is a term so broad it means any consumable, movable goods whatsoever. It more nearly approaches a description of all personalty than a description of types or items of goods . . . ." 6 UCC Rep.Serv. at 743.

175. In re J.C.M. Cooperative, Inc., 8 UCC Rep.Serv. 247 (Ref.Dec.W.D.Mich. 1970) ("[a]ll tangible personal property" held not too broad; referee discusses security agreement mostly, but sufficiency of financing statement also at issue); In re Stephens, 8 UCC Rep. Serv. 597 (Ref.Dec.W.D.Okla.1970) ("[p]assenger automobiles" was not too broad to prevent perfection of interest in one specific automobile where debtor owned more than one).

whether or not it is specific if it reasonably identifies what is described." Courts have been true to that direction; we hope that they continue to be so.

### § 23–17   Perfection in Multiple State Transactions, 9–103

At the outset one should understand the limited function of 9–102 and 9–103. To conceive of them as choice of law provisions which tell whether one must comply with the Georgia chattel mortgage and have his signature notarized or with the Mississippi conditional sale law and have his signature witnessed in order to have a valid security interest is to misconceive the practical operation of 9–102 and 9–103. Because the Code has been enacted in all the states but Louisiana, the statutory requirements for a valid security interest are substantially identical in all of the states. No longer need one concern himself with such questions because if he complies with 9–203 and 9–204, he will have a valid security interest no matter what law applies,[176] and if he fails to comply with those, his security interest will be invalid no matter what law applies. But a major function of 9–102(1) and 9–103 is to tell the creditor where he must file in order to perfect his security interest.[177] If the goods are located in Cleveland but the chief place of business of the debtor is Detroit, does one file in Columbus, in Lansing or somewhere else? What if the goods are moved from Cleveland to Detroit? These are the questions that 9–102 and 9–103 answer.

One can best divide the lawyer problems under 9–102 and 9–103 according to the kind of collateral involved:

    (1) Nonmobile collateral (lathes, printing presses, washing machines, air conditioners, etc.)

    (2) Mobile goods (rolling stock, airplanes, road building equipment) and intangibles (accounts, contract rights, general intangibles)

    (3) Vehicles covered by certificates of title.

The first category, goods that are not mobile except insofar as all goods are mobile, are governed by 9–102(1) and, when they are moved from one state to another, by 9–103(3). Mobile goods and intangibles are governed by 9–103(2) and 9–103(1). Vehicles covered by certificates of title are governed—most imperfectly—by 9–103(4).

**176.** A few unfortunate exceptions exist. For example, a handful of states have enacted stricter variations for sections 9–110 and 9–203 than exist under the official provisions. See, generally Weintraub, Choice of Law in Secured Personal Property Transactions: The Impact of Article 9 of the Uniform Commercial Code, 68 Mich. L.Rev. 684, 700–701 (1970).

**177.** The proposed 1971 amendments to 9–102 and 9–103 explicitly recognize the limited nature of the choice of law function.

## § 23–18   Perfection in Multiple State Transactions—Non-mobile, Tangible Goods

Except for intangibles, goods "normally used in more than one jurisdiction" [178] and goods covered by certificates of title, the place of perfection is governed by 9–102(1).  That subsection reads in part as follows:

> Except as otherwise provided in Section 9–103 on multiple state transactions and in Section 9–104 on excluded transactions, this Article applies so far as concerns any personal property and fixtures within the jurisdiction of this state
>
> .   .   .

The quoted section is an inartful way of saying that one files in Ohio to perfect goods which are located in Ohio, and he files in California to perfect goods located in California, etc.  Comment 3 to 9–102 states the proposition more clearly:

> In general this Article adopts the position implicit in prior law, that the law of the state where the collateral is located should be the governing law, without regard to possible contacts in other jurisdictions.

Thus, if a Delaware corporation's chief place of business is in Detroit, and it owns a series of printing presses located in Cleveland, Ohio, one perfects a security interest in those printing presses by filing in Ohio, and it is irrelevant that the debtor is incorporated in Delaware or that its chief place of business is outside Ohio.

Section 9–102 also governs the perfection of semi-intangibles— instruments, documents and chattel paper.[179]  Thus, if one wishes to perfect a security interest in chattel paper or a document by filing, he must file in the state in which the paper is physically located. Given the ease with which such collateral can be moved, such perfection is precarious indeed.

### Movement of Nonmobile, Tangible Collateral

If Article Nine contained only the provision of 9–102 which applies local law to "any personal property   .   .   .   within the juris-

---

178.  § 9–103(2).

179.  Although semi-intangibles such as chattel paper would seem to call for a special rule because of the ease with which they can be moved from state to state, the 1962 version of the Code provides none.  Such collateral does not fit within any of the special rules of 9–103 which are discussed below, and accordingly, they are left to be governed by 9–102.

The 1971 Recommendations include the following special provisions for chattel paper, Proposed § 9–103(4):

The rules stated for goods in subsection (1) apply to a possessory security interest in chattel paper.  The rules stated for accounts in subsection (3) apply to a non-possessory security interest in chattel paper, but the security interest may not be perfected by notification to the account debtor.

Under the quoted section, one would file as to chattel paper where "the debtor is located," i. e., his place of business or, if he has more than one place of business, his chief executive office.

diction of this state    .    .    .", movement of semi-tangibles or non-mobile goods from a state in which a secured party had filed to another state would render the secured party's interest instantly unperfected. The interest would be unperfected in the second state because its version of 9–401 would direct a filing somewhere within the second state and the fact that the secured creditors had filed elsewhere would be irrelevant.

Such instantaneous loss of perfection seemed too harsh to the draftsmen. By 9–103(3) they have given the secured creditor a fighting chance to remain perfected even though his debtor moves the collateral. The pertinent provision of 9–103(3) reads as follows:

> .    .    . If the security interest was already perfected under the law of the jurisdiction where the property was when the security interest attached and before being brought into this state, the security interest continues perfected in this state for four months and also thereafter if within the four month period it is perfected in this state.    .    .    .

Thus, the creditor has four months from the time the goods cross the state line to file a financing statement in the proper place at their new location. If he does so, his interest is continuously perfected, and he will maintain his relative priority. If he fails to perfect within the four month period, he will become unperfected at the end of that time, and a later perfection will not relate back.[180]

The quoted provision of 9–103(3) presents but does not answer one puzzling lawyer question: if the creditor fails to perfect within the four month period and some competing subordinate interest arises within that period, what is the relative priority of the interests after the four months? Assume, for example, that goods are moved from Ohio to Indiana and that the secured creditor who perfected in Ohio does nothing to perfect in Indiana either within or after the four month period. Before the expiration of the four months, the debtor goes bankrupt. At the date of bankruptcy the secured creditor is perfected and so superior to the trustee's rights under 70c. At the end of four months when the secured creditor's interest becomes unperfected, does it become subordinate to the trustee's rights or are their relative rights frozen as of the date of the initial conflict? The creditor will argue that the rights of the trustee in bankruptcy were frozen at the time of the filing of the petition. On the other hand, the trustee will acknowledge that his lien under 70(c) was subordinate to the security interest at the time bankruptcy was filed, but he will argue that it became the senior interest upon the expiration of the four month period—the time when the secured creditor became unperfected. Any competitor whose interest arises during the four

180. Section 9–103(3) provides in pertinent part:

The security interest may also be perfected in this state after the expira-
tion of the four month period; in such case perfection dates from the time of perfection in this state.    .    .    .

month period presents the same issue.   He may be a purchaser, another secured creditor or a lien creditor.

Comment 7 to 9–103 supports the conclusion that the rights are not normally frozen when they arise within the four month period and that at the expiration of the four month period, the secured creditor who has failed to file in the second state will find himself subordinated to any who would have priority over an unperfected security interest.[181]   Thus, under our analysis, a buyer (who did not qualify under 9–307 and who, therefore, would be subordinate to a perfected security interest) would hold a junior interest within the four month period but that interest would mature into one superior to the secured creditor's interest if the secured creditor failed to perfect within the four month period.   Likewise, we would argue that one who becomes a lien creditor within the four month period would be junior at that time but would succeed to a senior position at the expiration of the four month period, provided that the out-of-state secured creditor had not perfected within that period and that the lien creditor had not received notice of his interest before the expiration of the four month period.[182]

There is only one flaw in our eminently reasonable argument; the cases are in unanimous disagreement with it.[183]   The courts apparently do not appreciate the argument for the proposition that priorities are redetermined at the end of four months.   The cases seem to us to deviate from the intent of the draftsmen,[184] but they are the cases, and they are unanimous.   Because it is not clear that the losing parties effectively presented our arguments in those cases, we would hope that they do not foreclose the issue and that courts might still

181.   See Comment 7 to 9–103 which reads in pertinent part:

The four month period is long enough for a secured party to discover in most cases that the collateral has been removed and to file in this state; thereafter, if he has not done so, his interest, although originally perfected in the state where it attached, is subject to defeat here by those persons who take priority over an unperfected security interest (see Section 9–301).   Under Section 9–312(5) the holder of a perfected conflicting security interest is such a person even though during the four month period the conflicting interest was junior.   Compare the situation arising under Section 9–403(2) when a filing lapses.

182.   There may be circumstances in which a court would properly find the rights frozen within the four-month period.   If, for example, a secured creditor appeared to assert his claim within the four-month period in a bankruptcy action, it would seem idle to require that he then file.   Likewise,

if a secured creditor sued a buyer of the collateral for conversion in a case in which the defendant buyer had bought and resold the collateral before the expiration of the four months, the rights should be determined without regard to the fact that the secured creditor's interest later became unperfected.

183.   Utah Farm Production Credit Ass'n v. Dinner, 302 F.Supp. 897, 6 UCC Rep.Serv. 937 (D.Colo.1969) (by implication); In re Moore, 7 UCC Rep. Serv. 578 (Ref.Dec.D.Me.1969); First Nat'l Bank of Bay Shore v. Stamper, 93 N.J.Super. 150, 163, 225 A.2d 162, 169, 3 UCC Rep.Serv. 949, 960 (1966); Churchill Motors, Inc. v. A. C. Lohman, Inc., 16 App.Div.2d 560, 566–67, 229 N.Y.S.2d 570, 577, 1 UCC Rep. Serv. 371, 376 (1962).   Cf. Associate Discount Corp. v. Woods, 5 UCC Rep. Serv. 1268 (Mass.App.Div.1968).

184.   We have inferred the draftsmen's intent from Comment 7 to 9–103 and Comment 3 to 9–403.

feel free to examine the question afresh.[185]    The weight of academic opinion is on our side.[186]

The second sentence of 9–103(3) presents an additional problem of modest consequence.    That sentence reads in full as follows:

> However, if the parties to the transaction understood at the time that the security interest attached that the property would be kept in this state and it was brought into this state within 30 days after the security interest attached for purposes other than transportation through this state, then the validity of the security interest in this state is to be determined by the law of this state.

The sentence tells only that the "validity" of a security interest is determined by the law of the state into which the goods are brought; it does not speak of the "perfection." If the omission of any reference to perfection is intentional, and the sentence governs only "validity," the sentence is now unimportant. The cases have not answered this question, but some have suggested that the omission is a drafting oversight and that the sentence should be read as though it governed not only validity but also perfection.

Assuming arguendo that the sentence should be read as though it said "then the validity [and perfection] of the security interest in

---

185.    Although the proposed 1971 Revisions to 9–103 incline in the direction of our argument, they do not entirely resolve the question.    The pertinent 1971 provision is 9–103(1) (d) (i) which reads in full as follows:

[I]f the action is not taken before the expiration of the period of perfection in the other jurisdiction or the end of four months after the collateral is brought into this state, whichever period first expires, the security interest becomes unperfected at the end of that period and is thereafter deemed to have been unperfected as against a person who became a purchaser after removal.

Permanent Editorial Board for the Uniform Commercial Code, Review Committee for Article 9, Final Report § 9–103 at 19–25 (1971).

The section would apparently elevate a "purchaser" who bought within the four-month period.    A second secured creditor who takes and perfects a security interest within the four-month period would meet the Code definition of purchasing and would presumably be a "purchaser" protected by the quoted provision.    However, a lien creditor and a trustee in bankruptcy (at least insofar as he claims under 70(c)) are not purchasers for their in-

terests do not arise by a "voluntary transaction" (§ 1–201(32)) and would presumably not be covered by the quoted section.    Because he does not rely as heavily, the lien creditor is usually regarded as a lesser form of humanity than is the secured creditor who puts out new money; however, it is not clear why he should be discriminated against in this case.

From the words they chose, it appears that the draftsmen of the 1971 amendments intentionally discriminated against lien creditors.    Comment 7 to proposed 9–103 tells one to "compare . . . 9–403(2)."    Section 9–403(2) in turn states "[i]f the security interest becomes unperfected upon lapse, it is deemed to have been unperfected as against a person who became a purchaser or lien creditor before lapse."    The explicit reference to "lien creditor" in 9–403 and the omission of any such reference in 9–103 suggests that the draftsmen intend different results and that they did not intend to include lien creditors within the ambit of "purchasers" in 9–103.

186.    See, e. g., Vernon, Recorded Chattel Security Interests in the Conflict of Laws, 47 Iowa L.Rev. 346, 377–78 (1962).

this state is to be determined by the law of this state," what result? Under such a reading, a secured creditor who takes a security interest in goods to be moved to a new state within thirty days need not concern himself with filing in the first state but is perfected by a filing in the second state provided, of course, the goods come into the second within thirty days after the security interest has attached. Within that thirty day period he would have a perfected security interest in state one even though there would be nothing on file in state one to reveal the security interest. That seems an unfortunate state of affairs.

On the other hand, if one reads the sentence to apply only to validity and to leave the other 9–103(3) perfection rules unchanged, the secured creditor who files in state one will be protected not only for the thirty or fewer days that the collateral is in state one but also for four months in state two. Such a reading gives the debtor up to four months to mislead creditors in state two. Thus, on policy grounds it seems six of one and half a dozen of the other. One reading of the sentence exposes innocent and diligent creditors in state one to subordination; the other reading exposes the same class in state two.

We are persuaded by Professor Gilmore's argument that the first reading is the intended one and that the draftsmen probably omitted the word perfection by oversight. Professor Gilmore argues [187] that prospective creditors would be more often misled by a rule that permits four months perfection without filing in the second state than they would by a rule that permits up to thirty days perfection in state one without filing. His argument proceeds on the assumption that the case most commonly covered by the thirty-day rule is a purchase money loan in which a debtor in state two buys goods from a seller in state one, and one of buyer's creditors in state two takes a security interest in the goods.[188]

So much for 9–103(3). The provision sets out a sensible and workable four month rule that represents a compromise between the interests of the secured creditor who needs some time to follow his travelling debtor and the interests of third persons in the states to which the collateral is moved. When the secured creditor fails to perfect within four months in the new state and within that period com-

187. 1 G. Gilmore, Security Interests in Personal Property § 22.9 at 629–30 (1965). For other comment on the thirty-day rule, see, e. g., H. Taylor, Jr., Section 9–103(3) of the UCC: Ambiguities, Unanswered Questions and Suggestions for Statutory Revision, 35 Tenn.L.Rev. 235 (1968); Comment, Section 9–103 and the Interstate Movement of Goods, 9 B.C.Ind. & Com.L. Rev. 72, 78–82 (1967).

188. By the newly proposed section 9–103(1) (c) set out below, the 1971 Committee has adopted Professor Gilmore's approach:

If the parties to a transaction creating a purchase money security interest in goods in one jurisdiction understand at the time that the security interests attaches that the goods will be kept in another jurisdiction, then the law of the other jurisdiction governs the perfection and the effect of perfection or nonperfection of the security interest from the time it attaches until thirty days after the debtor receives possession of the goods and thereafter if the goods are taken to the other jurisdiction before the end of the thirty-day period.

petes with an interest arising that would be superior to an unperfected interest, we would find that the junior interest becomes senior to the secured creditor's interest upon the expiration of the four months. To date, the cases hold otherwise.

## § 23–19  Perfection in Multiple State Transactions—Mobile Goods, 9–103(2)

In a sense, of course, almost all goods are mobile; here we use the term to describe only goods "normally used in more than one jurisdiction (such as automotive equipment, rolling stock, airplanes, road building equipment, commercial harvesting equipment, construction machinery and the like)  . . . ." [189]  Under 9–103(2) the law of the "chief place of business" of the debtor governs both the validity and perfection of the security in such goods.  Thus, if the debtor's chief place of business is in Tennessee, it makes no difference that the goods are always located in Tennessee or that they are never located in Tennessee.

The principal interpretive difficulty in 9–103(2) is how precisely to define mobile goods.  First, goods are governed by 9–103(2) only if they are "classified as equipment or classified as inventory by reason of their being leased by the debtor to others."  That qualifying phrase will exclude all consumer goods (including such mobile goods as automobiles) and all inventory which is held for sale rather than lease.  Thus, Mrs. Jones' automobile [190] and the John Deere dealer's inventory are not governed by 9–103(2), and in such circumstance one follows 9–102 and perfects at the location of the goods.  Secondly, subsection (2) applies even though the goods never cross a state line.  It is sufficient if the goods are those "normally used" in more

---

**189.**  Section 9–103(2) reads in full:

If the chief place of business of a debtor is in this state, this Article governs the validity and perfection of a security interest and the possibility and effect of proper filing with regard to general intangibles or with regard to goods of a type which are normally used in more than one jurisdiction (such as automotive equipment, rolling stock, airplanes, road building equipment, commercial harvesting equipment, construction machinery and the like) if such goods are classified as equipment or classified as inventory by reason of their being leased by the debtor to others.  Otherwise, the law (including the conflict of laws rules) of the jurisdiction where such chief place of business is located shall govern.  If the chief place of business is located in a jurisdiction which does not provide for perfection of the security interest by filing or recording in that juris-

diction, then the security interest may be perfected by filing in this state. [For the purpose of determining the validity and perfection of a security interest in an airplane, the chief place of business of a debtor who is a foreign air carrier under the Federal Aviation Act of 1958, as amended, is the designated office of the agent upon whom service of process may be made on behalf of the debtor.]

For a case finding that a "traxcavator" (roadbuilding machinery) is mobile equipment governed by 9–103(2), see Foley Machinery Co. v. John T. Brady Co., 7 UCC Rep.Serv. 872 (N.Y. Sup.Ct.1970).

**190.**  Whatever their Article Nine classification (equipment or consumer goods), most automobiles and other vehicles will be exempted from 9–103(2), since they will be covered by certificates of title under 9–103(4).  See Section 23–21 infra.

than one state; a particular debtor's actual use is not relevant.[191] Moreover, even if the practice in one county of Oklahoma were to buy commercial harvesting equipment and to use it locally only, that practice should not override the nationwide or regional use and alter the meaning of "normal;" the goods would still be "normally" used in more than one jurisdiction.

In most cases the debtor's chief place of business will not be difficult to discover (emphasis added):

> "Chief place of business" does not mean the place of incorporation; it means the place from which in fact the debtor *manages* the main part of his business operations. That is the place where persons dealing with the debtor would normally look for credit information    .[192]

A recent Maryland decision has found the debtor's chief place of business to be where it "conducts its greatest volume of business activity."[193] Obviously a wise lawyer faced with ambiguity about the meaning of chief place of business in a particular place will follow Peskind's law and file in each jurisdiction that could conceivably be the chief place of business.

In the uncommon case in which the debtor's chief place of business changes to a new state, the creditor must refile in the new state in order to remain perfected. Neither the Code nor the case law indicates whether the debtor has any grace period or whether he must file at once. Unless the courts apply pre-Code comity rules or apply subsection (3)'s four month rule by analogy, the secured party will become unperfected immediately upon the change of the debtor's chief

---

**191.** Comment 4 to 9–103 makes this point as follows:

Notice that the rule of subsection (2) applies to goods of a type "normally used" in more than one jurisdiction; there is no requirement that particular goods be in fact used out of state. Thus if an enterprise whose chief place of business is in State X keeps in this state goods of the type covered by subsection (2), this rule of the subsection applies even though the goods never cross a state line. The definitions of "equipment" and "inventory" (Section 9–109) should be consulted.

In In re Dennis Mitchell Indus., Inc., 419 F.2d 349, 6 UCC Rep.Serv. 573 (3d Cir. 1969), rev'g 280 F.Supp. 433, 4 UCC Rep.Serv. 1113 (E.D.Pa.1968), the court found that hydraulic cutting machines transported *interstate* were not subsection (2) collateral. It commented as follows:

[W]e think the approach adopted by the district court, however equitable

in intent, places too great a strain on the meaning of "goods of a type which are normally used in more than one jurisdiction." While the enumeration of certain types of goods in § 9–103(2) is not intended to be all inclusive, it seems clear that the test for mobile goods turns on the type of goods involved and not on their actual use in or transportation between more than one jurisdiction. To say that goods fall within that section simply because they may be and are easily transported from state to state overlooks the nature of the test for mobile goods and the particular problem § 9–103(2) was intended to resolve.

Id. at 358, 6 UCC Rep.Serv. at 586.

**192.** § 9–103, Comment 3.

**193.** Tatelbaum v. Commerce Inv. Co., 7 UCC Rep.Serv. 406, 410 (Md.Ct.App. 1970).

place of business; such a result seems unduly harsh, and we could counsel the application of the four month rule by analogy.[194]

### § 23–20  Perfection in Multiple State Transactions—Intangibles, 9–103(1) and (2)

Intangible collateral presents a somewhat different problem from that of mobile goods. It is not the movement of intangibles that renders them unamenable to the usual 9–102 rule, but the fact that intangibles have no clearly identifiable situs. Assume, for example, that a consumer who resides in Madison, Wisconsin, buys a fur coat on credit from a Minneapolis department store and that the department store uses the consumer's account as collateral to secure a debt to Minneapolis bank. Assume further that the Minneapolis department store keeps most of its books and records at its headquarters in Chicago. Is the account situated at the ultimate debtor's residence at Madison, Wisconsin, or where some of the records are kept in Chicago, or where the transaction arose in Minneapolis? Section 9–103 (1) relieves one of the burden of answering that question. It provides that one should perfect at the place "where the assignor of accounts or contract rights keeps his records concerning them. . . ." Our creditor should file in Illinois.[195]

Section 9–103(2) provides a slightly different rule with respect to general intangibles. One perfects with respect to general intangibles in the state of the chief place of business of the debtor. Whether rightly or wrongly, the draftsmen have concluded that the place where the records are kept in the former situation and the chief place of business in the latter is the place where a prospective creditor is most likely to check the files.

---

**194.** Under the terms of section 9–103 (3) (e) of the 1971 proposals, a creditor would remain perfected in most cases for four months after the debtor had moved his place of business:

A security interest perfected under the law of the jurisdiction of the location of the debtor is perfected until the expiration of four months after a change of the debtor's location to another jurisdiction, or until perfection would have ceased by the law of the first jurisdiction, whichever period first expires. Unless perfected in the new jurisdiction before the end of that period, it becomes unperfected thereafter and is deemed to have been unperfected as against a person who became a purchaser after the change. Permanent Editorial Board for the Uniform Commercial Code, Review Committee for Article 9, Final Report § 9–103 at 19–25 (1971).

**195.** If the debtor corporation has widespread operations and maintains, for example, a computer center with certain records at one location and other records pertaining to accounts at a second location, the creditor may still have difficulty in determining where the assignor "keeps his records concerning" the accounts. The 1971 proposals would alter the rule to provide for filing not where the records are kept but at the place of business of the debtor. The new proposals also alleviate any problems one might have in determining where the "chief place of business" is:

A debtor shall be deemed located at his place of business if he has one, at his chief executive office if he has more than one place of business, otherwise at his residence. If, however, the debtor is a foreign air carrier under the Federal Aviation Act of 1958, as amended, it shall be deemed located at the designated office of the agent upon whom service of process may be made on behalf of the foreign air carrier.

§ 9–103(3) (d) of the 1971 proposals.

## § 23–21    Perfection in Multiple State Transactions—Automobiles and Other Vehicles Covered by Certificates of Title, 9–103(4)

The interstate travels of private automobiles and other vehicles covered by certificates of title are typically governed [196] by 9–103(4) which reads in full as follows:

> Notwithstanding subsection (2) and (3), if personal property is covered by a certificate of title issued under a statute of this state or any other jurisdiction which requires indication on a certificate of title of any security interest in the property as a condition of perfection, then the perfection is governed by the law of the jurisdiction which issued the certificate.

Before considering the various combinations of interstate movement which involve at least one certificate of title state, one should understand the rule in the unusual case in which neither of the competing states has a certificate of title law. In that case the perfection will be governed by 9–103(2) or 9–103(3). Even if one should find certain automobiles not to be mobile goods, most private autos will be excluded from subsection (2) because they are consumer goods and not equipment or inventory which is leased. Illustratively, a salesman's car or a Hertz rent-a-car will be mobile goods governed by subsection (2).[197] If there is no certificate of title law in the picture, one must closely examine the debtor's use to determine whether the vehicle in question is equipment or leased inventory and so governed by subsection (2) or whether it is not such collateral and is, therefore, governed by subsection (3).

---

196. Unfortunately some states also have certificate of title provisions that do not refer to 9–103 but set forth a provision which could dispose of interstate movement problems. A question exists as to whether 9–103 or the title act provision will be used. The states most likely to be affected are: Arkansas, Colorado, Florida, Georgia, Illinois, Maryland, Minnesota, Mississippi, Missouri, New Hampshire, New Mexico, New York, Rhode Island, South Carolina, and Vermont. Colorado's title act provision is specifically deferred to by its commercial code. Colo.Rev.Stat.Ann. § 155–9–103 (1965). Cf. Doenges-Glass, Inc. v. General Motors Acceptance Corp., 28 Colo.App. 283, 472 P.2d 761, 7 UCC Rep.Serv. 957 (1970) although court discussed title act provision, no mention of 9–103 was made. Cases from at least two other states suggest that their title act provisions pre-empt the Code. In re Jackson, 268 F.Supp. 434 (E.D.Mo.1967) aff'd sub nom., Zuke v. Merchantile Trust Co. Nat'l Ass'n., 385 F.2d 775 (8th Cir. 1967) (Mo.); Green v. King Edward Employees' Fed. Credit Union, 373 F.2d 613 (5th Cir. 1967) (Ga.); Cf., GMAC v. Whisnant, 387 F.2d 774, 4 UCC Rep.Serv. 1016 (5th Cir. 1968) (Ga.).

197. Despite the statement in Comment 4 to 9–103 that "there is no requirement that particular goods be in fact used out of state," one could make an argument that certain classes of vehicles are not "normally used" in more than one state. Is it permissible to break vehicles into subclassifications such as intra-city panel trucks and then to conclude that some classes are not "normally used" in more than one jurisdiction? We think not. We would argue that any vehicle capable of being licensed and used on the streets should be classified as one normally used in more than one jurisdiction. We see little benefit and much mischief in allowing a creditor or a trustee to argue that a certain classification of vehicle is not normally used in more than one jurisdiction.

All of the remaining situations involve 9–103(4); they can be divided into three categories:

(*1*) Movement from a certificate of title jurisdiction to a noncertificate of title jurisdiction.

(*2*) Movement from a noncertificate of title jurisdiction to a certificate of title jurisdiction.

(*3*) Movement between two certificate of title jurisdictions.[198]

Although the question is not free from doubt, it is our judgment that all the certificate of title statutes except Oklahoma's have the conditions necessary to bring 9–103(4) into play.[199]

### *Certificate—Noncertificate*

If a security interest is perfected by notation on a certificate of title and the vehicle is moved to a noncertificate of title state, 9–103 (4) continues the perfection indefinitely.[200]  The secured party's knowledge of the movement is irrelevant.[201]  Of course, under such

---

**198.** Only two states have no certificate of title legislation. They are Alabama and Maine. At least one author would include Kentucky as a noncertificate of title state. Note, Interstate Movement of Motor Vehicles Subject to Security Interests: A Case for Repealing UCC § 9–103(4) 54 Cornell L. Rev. 610 (1969). It is more appropriate to consider Kentucky as a state having a certificate of title law which is not an exclusive means of perfection. This near unanimity among the states is a recent development. Four states have adopted certificate of title laws that became effective in mid-1972: Maine, Massachusetts, New York, and Rhode Island.

**199.** Subsection (4) is triggered only when a certificate of title has been issued in a jurisdiction "under a statute . . . which requires indication on a certificate of title of any security interest in the property as a condition of perfection . . . ." Thus if one reads the language "requires . . . as a condition" to include a case in which one of several conditions is the indication on a certificate of title, then even those jurisdictions such as Michigan, which require not only notation but also a UCC filing, would be covered by subsection (4). Also, if one reads the language "a statute" to mean a statutory scheme that includes sections 9–302(3) (b) and (4), despite the more limited definition of "a statute" in 9–302(3) (b) itself, then even those states with incomplete title laws, such

as Pennsylvania and Indiana, are included. We believe that subsection (4) should be broadly read and would exclude only Oklahoma. Under Oklahoma law, even though indication on a certificate of title is required for a few interests, the title notation is never a condition of perfection. In that state a UCC filing alone constitutes perfection. Indeed, security interests not existing at the time of a transfer in ownership cannot be noted on a certificate. To permit Oklahoma to trigger 9–103(4) would be to permit continuous perfection of security interests perfected in Oklahoma by filing and without being noted on a certificate.

**200.** See In re White, 266 F.Supp. 863, 865, 4 UCC Rep.Serv. 421, 423 (N.D. N.Y.1967); In re Moore, 7 UCC Rep. Serv. 578, 598 (D.Me.1969) (dictum because neither state required notation on the certificate of title); In re Fougere, 5 UCC Rep.Serv. 410 (D.Me. 1968). It seems only fair to find that perfection would lapse in the second state no later than the time when it would have lapsed in the first state.

**201.** For criticism of the Code's failure to impose a reasonable reperfection requirement after a secured party learns of the movement, see Weintraub, Choice of Law in Secured Personal Property Transactions: The Impact of Article 9 of the Uniform Commercial Code, 68 Mich.L.Rev. 684, 714–15 (1970).

circumstances the potential for misleading buyers and creditors in the second state is considerable. This potential for mischief in the new state may lead courts to read some reasonable limitation into the apparently unlimited period of perfection when a car moves from a certificate state to a noncertificate state. It would not be unreasonable, for example, for a court to hold that the perfection lapses at the end of four months or when a new license and registration is procured in the new state, whichever occurs later.[202]

### *Noncertificate—Certificate*

When the automobile moves from a noncertificate of title state to a state which issues a certificate, the courts have split on the applicability of 9–103(4). About half the courts have decided that subsection (4) was not intended to apply when the first jurisdiction had no applicable certificate of title law.[203] These courts have relied primarily on the alleged policy of subsection (4) to avoid duplication of certificate of title notation. Where the first state does not require

**202.** For criticism of the rule which permits continuous perfection for a long period of time under subsection (4), see Note, Interstate Movement of Motor Vehicles Subject to Security Interests: A Case for Repealing UCC § 9–103(4), 54 Cornell L.Rev. 610, 621–22 (1969).

Proposed 9–103(2) (b) provides a similar limitation. First, as soon as the certificate of title is surrendered the secured party becomes unperfected. Second, if the certificate of title remains extant (i. e., there is no surrender), then the secured party will remain perfected until the vehicle is reregistered in any jurisdiction or until four months elapses, whichever is later. When this period of perfection expires, the vehicle is considered no longer covered by a certificate. Therefore the status of those acquiring interests in the vehicle while there was continuous perfection is determined under proposed 9–103(1) (d) with its "purchaser" limitations.

**203.** A recent example of this reasoning is found in Phil Phillips Ford, Inc. v. St. Paul Fire & Marine Ins. Co., 7 UCC Rep.Serv. 952 (Tex.Civ.App. 1970), aff'd on other grounds, 8 UCC Rep.Serv. 1331 (1971). (In its affirmation, the Supreme Court of Texas rejected the view here stated.) The issue was whether an innocent purchaser, who relied on a clean, fraudulently procured Texas certificate of title, should have priority over the original secured party who properly perfected by filing in Oklahoma. The Texas Appeals Court quoted the 1956

Recommendation of the Editorial Board for the Uniform Commercial Code:

> Subsection (4) is new to avoid the possible necessity of duplicating perfection in the case of vehicles subject to a certificate of title law requiring compliance therewith to perfect security interests. The certificate of title law requirements are adopted as the test for perfection.

Id. at 955.

Then the court held:

> This note by the draftsmen makes clear that this subsection does not have any application to an automobile [coming from a noncertificate of title state to a certificate of title state].

Id.

The court held for the secured party under 9–103(3), since the innocent purchaser acquired his interest prior to the four-month period. Accord, First Nat'l Bank of Bay Shore v. Stamper, 93 N.J.Super. 150, 225 A.2d 162, 3 UCC Rep.Serv. 949 (1966); Churchill Motors, Inc. v. A. C. Lohman, Inc., 16 App.Div. 2d 560, 299 N.Y.S.2d 570, 1 UCC Rep.Serv. 371 (4th Dep't 1962); In re Scannell, 3 UCC Rep.Serv. 884 (Ref.Dec.D.Conn.1966).

At least one commentator agrees with these decisions. Note, Interstate Movement of Motor Vehicles Subject to Security Interests: A Case for Repealing UCC § 9–103(4), 54 Cornell L.Rev. 610, 619 (1969). For conflicting views, see note 204 infra.

the security interest to be noted upon the certificate, no duplication can occur, therefore, so the argument goes, subsection (4) is inapplicable. These courts apply subsection (3) so that the secured party is continuously perfected for four months, despite the existence of a clean local certificate which could mislead local creditors and buyers.

In our judgment the conflicting view which applies subsection (4) is better law.[204] Such a policy recognizes the certificate of title in the new state as the exclusive means of perfection and minimizes the possibility of misleading lenders and purchasers in the new state.[205]

### *Certificate of Title—Certificate of Title*

When a vehicle is moved from one certificate of title jurisdiction to another, there are two difficulties. First, does perfection under the old state's law continue in the second state even though no new

---

**204.** The language of 9–103(4) speaks of personal property "covered by a certificate of title issued under a statute of *this state or* any other jurisdiction. . . ." (Emphasis added). If subsection (4) does not apply to a vehicle coming from a jurisdiction without a title law into a state with a title law, then the language, *"this state or,"* is superfluous in this case and clearly misleading.

Among the courts arguing that subsection (4) is applicable in this circumstance are Phil Phillips Ford, Inc. v. St. Paul Fire & Marine Ins. Co., 465 S.W.2d 933, 8 UCC Rep.Serv. 1331 (Tex.1971), aff'g on other grounds, 454 S.W.2d 465, 7 UCC Rep.Serv. 952 (Tex.Civ.App.1970); GMAC v. Manheim Auto Auction, 25 Pa.D. & C.2d 179, 1 UCC Rep.Serv. 388 (C.P.1961); and In re Friedman, 4 UCC Rep.Serv. 890 (Ref.Dec.D.Conn.1967) (dictum). The latter court commented:

The real purpose and meaning of this subsection (4) is so hazy that one commentator has characterized it as "an example of blunderous draftsmanship" (Bender's Uniform Commercial Code Service, Reporter-Digest Case Annotations, sec. 9–103, p. 2–928). And the editorial Recommendations for the enactment of this subsection (4) serves only to compound the confusion (See Bender's, supra). Id. at 891.

[T]he basic concept is one of supremacy of an extant certificate of title over other methods of reflecting ownership of and security interests in vehicles. . . . [Subsection (4)] embraces the concept that when a certificate of title clashes with other methods of establishing security in-

terests in vehicles, the certificate of title shall prevail.

Id. at 892.

At least the following commentators support this view: Comment, Section 9–103 and the Interstate Movement of Goods, 9 B.C.Ind. & Com.L.Rev. 72, 92 n. 77 (1967); Comment, Uniform Commercial Code—Perfection of Security Interests in Multi-State Transactions when Property is Covered by a Certificate of Title, 47 B.U. L.Rev. 430, 437 (1967).

**205.** The proposed amendments to 9–103 recognize the need to protect those parties who honestly rely on the new state's certificate and are as a group presumed dummies. To this end, proposed 9–103(2) (c), which governs the movement problems between a non-certificate of title state and a certificate of title state, offers different rules for different affected parties. Thus the original secured party's interest is subordinated to the interest of a non-professional "buyer" who relies in good faith on the local, clean certificate and to the extent he has given value. Proposed § 9–103(2) (d). Professionals whose business it is to buy such vehicles, local creditors (since they are typically professionals), and all other "non-buyers," such as lien creditors, are not given this favored treatment. Their rights are governed by the same four-month provision which operates in movement problems between two noncertificate of title states. Proposed § 9–103(1) (d). Permanent Editorial Board for the UCC, Review Committee for Article 9, Final Report (1971).

certificate has been issued and the debtor is violating the new state's law by having failed to procure a new certificate within a specified period of time? Case law is virtually unanimous; subsection (4) applies, and the law of the old state, that is, the state "which issued the certificate" governs. Thus, the secured party remains perfected.[206] This rule has the virtue of certainty; it protects the secured creditor's interest and as long as no new certificate is outstanding, it offers no substantial possibility for the debtor to mislead subsequent creditors since the only certificate outstanding will disclose the secured creditor's security interest.

The second problem arises when certificates of title have been issued in both states. Subsection (4) does not contemplate this occurrence; it speaks only of the jurisdiction "which issued *the* certificate." One can best understand these decisions by dividing them into three types: (*1*) Those involving neither fraud nor theft; (*2*) Those in which local buyers or creditors have been defrauded by misrepresentations that the vehicle was unencumbered, but where the vehicle has not been stolen;[207] and (*3*) Those in which the vehicle has

---

**206.** GMAC v. Whisnant, 387 F.2d 774, 4 UCC Rep.Serv. 1016 (5th Cir. 1968); In re Friedman, 4 UCC Rep.Serv. 890 (Ref.Dec.D.Conn.1967); In re Worsley, 4 UCC Rep.Serv. 1180 (Ref.Dec.E.D. Mich.1967); In re Price, 5 UCC Rep. Serv. 415 (Ref.Dec.W.D.Mich.1968); In re Caraway, 4 UCC Rep.Serv. 1099 (Ref.Dec.W.D.Mich.1968); In re Smith, 311 F.Supp. 900, 7 UCC Rep.Serv. 948 (W.D.Va.1970) rev'g 6 UCC Rep.Serv. 860 (Ref.Dec.W.D.Va.1969), aff'd sub nom. Callaghan v. Commercial Credit Corp., 437 F.2d 898, 8 UCC Rep.Serv. 901 (4th Cir. 1971); Streule v. Gulf Fin. Corp., 265 A.2d 298, 7 UCC Rep. Serv. 734 (D.C.Ct.App.1970).

At least one commentator and one court (reversed on appeal) reasoned that subsection (4) should apply but that the law of the second state should govern. Thus, the interest would be unperfected, and the secured party would lose whatever priority he would otherwise have. See Comment, Security Interests in Motor Vehicles Under the UCC: A New Chassis for Certificate of Title Legislation, 70 Yale L.J. 995, 1015 (1961); In re Smith, 6 UCC Rep.Serv. 860 (Ref.Dec. W.D.Va.1969), rev'd, 311 F.Supp. 900, 7 UCC Rep.Serv. 948 (W.D.Va.1970).

All other courts have favored using the law of the first state. This is the most reasonable interpretation of subsection (4)'s language. The provision permits the law of the state which "*issued* the certificate" to govern. It focuses on the issuance of a certificate rather than on the mere requisite of getting one. Absent the issuance of a second certificate, the issued certificate will probably permit continuous perfection until its effectiveness lapses.

**207.** Only where the vehicle has moved from one certificate state to another have the courts drawn a distinction between the fraud and no fraud cases. In dictum or by implication, courts interpreting 9–103(3) in automobile cases have considered fraud irrelevant. Casterline v. GMAC, 195 Pa. Super. 344, 171 A.2d 813, 1 UCC Rep. Serv. 380 (1961); First Nat'l Bank of Bay Shore v. Stamper, 93 N.J.Super. 150, 225 A.2d 162, 3 UCC Rep.Serv. 949 (Law Div.1966); Churchill Motors Inc. v. A. C. Lohman, Inc., 16 App. Div.2d 560, 299 N.Y.S.2d 570, 1 UCC Rep.Serv. 371 (4th Dep't 1962); Phil Phillips Ford, Inc. v. St. Paul Fire & Marine Ins. Co., 454 S.W.2d 465, 7 UCC Rep.Serv. 952 (Cir.App. Tex.1970), aff'd on other grounds, 465 S.W.2d 933, 8 UCC Rep.Serv. 1331 (Tex.1971). Although the last three cases cited dealt with movement from noncertificate of title states to certificate of title states, they interpreted 9–103(3) for their decisions. There is little reason to believe they would reach an opposite conclusion regarding fraud under 9–103(4). As to movement from noncertificate to certificate states, see also Doenges-Glass, Inc. v. GMAC, 28 Colo.App. 283, 472 P.2d 761, 7 UCC Rep.Serv. 957 (1970) (implication); GMAC v. Manheim Auto

been stolen.  Cases in the second group arise most frequently when the owner of the equity (debtor) procures a new certificate that does not reveal the security interest.  In the third group some third party has usually stolen the car from the debtor.

When there is neither fraud nor theft, courts unanimously hold that 9–103(4) applies and that the law of the state that issued the last certificate governs.[208]  Typically in these cases the creditor has failed somehow to perfect in the second state and so loses to the trustee in bankruptcy.  For example, in In re Edwards [209] the creditor perfected its security interest by causing its interest to be noted on a Wisconsin certificate of title.  Debtor then brought the automobile to Michigan and procured a Michigan certificate of title.  The Michigan certificate showed the creditor's security interest, but the creditor failed to comply with the Michigan hybrid which requires not only a notation but also a Code filing.  In the debtor's bankruptcy the referee held that the creditor was not perfected.

With the "fraud absent theft" cases, courts are in disagreement not only as to whether the law of the state issuing the last certificate will govern, but also as to whether Article Nine controls at all.  A majority of the decisions maintain that the fraudulently procured clean certificate (that is, the *last* certificate) controls.[210]  The original

Auction, 25 Pa.D. & C.2d 179, 1 UCC Rep.Serv. 388 (C.P.1961).

As to fraud being irrelevant under 9–103(4) where movement is from a certificate to a noncertificate jurisdiction, see In re Fougere, 5 UCC Rep. Serv. 410 (Ref.Dec.D.Me.1968) (implication).

**208.**  In re Edwards, 6 UCC Rep.Serv. 1124 (Ref.Dec.E.D.Mich.1969); In re Schoeller, 4 UCC Rep.Serv. 1093 (Ref. Dec.D.Conn.1968).  Cf. In re Singleton, 2 UCC Rep.Serv. 195 (Ref.Dec. E.D.Ky.1963).

**209.**  6 UCC Rep.Serv. 1124 (Ref.Dec. E.D.Mich.1969).

**210.**  See Doenges-Glass, Inc. v. GMAC, 28 Colo.App. 283, 287, 472 P.2d 761, 763, 7 UCC Rep.Serv. 957, 960 (1970) ("The law still favors the rule of comity, and only if a certificate of title is issued and delivered to the buyer [in this state] will this rule be disregarded.") (dictum); Merchants-Produce Bank v. Mack Trucks, Inc., 411 F.2d 1174 (8th Cir. 1969); Northeast Nat'l Bank v. Central Plaza Bank & Trust Co., 209 So.2d 255 (Fla.App.1968) (Implication: facts did not deal with interstate movement.  All events occurred within Florida.  The court permitted a second secured party,

whose interest was noted on a duplicate certificate of title fraudulently procured by Owner, to be prior to the first secured party.  Although the court considered fraud irrelevant, the first secured party had not properly noted his interest on the certificate he retained.  The court may be suggesting that the *first properly noted certificate* will have priority, regardless of fraud.); Ferraro v. Pacific Finance Corp., 8 Cal.App.3d 339, 87 Cal.Rptr. 226 (1970) (dictum; facts did not deal with interstate movement).

Ohio law is presently in confusion.  An infamous pre-UCC case, Commercial Credit Corp. v. Pottmeyer, 176 Ohio St. 1, 197 N.E.2d 343 (1964), held in a 4 to 3 opinion that a clean fraudulently procured Ohio certificate of title would defeat Innocent Secured Party's interest and permit Innocent Purchaser to be victorious.  The court is unusually direct:

In Kelley Kar Co. v. Finkler, supra (155 Ohio St. 541, 545, 99 N.E.2d 665, 667), Judge Middleton described the reason for enactment of the Certificate of Title Act, as follows:

"Because of their mobility and frequent change of ownership it was obviously necessary to create an instrument evidencing title which would

secured party is consequently subordinated to local parties who have been defrauded.   Nevertheless only one of these cases has intimated that 9–103(4) is the applicable law.[211]   The others rely on their state's common law.   We believe that subsection (4) should control and the last issued certificate should be determinative, as it is a "neither fraud nor theft" case.[212]   Indeed, there is a more compelling reason

more adequately protect innocent purchasers of motor vehicles."

Id. at 7–8, 197 N.E.2d at 348.

That a principal purpose of the Ohio Certificate of Title Act is to protect Ohio bona fide purchasers against wrongdoers is also made clear by our decision in Mutual Finance Co. v. Kozoil (1961), 172 Ohio St. 275, 175 N.E.2d 88. . . .

Id. at 11, 197 N.E.2d at 350.

The dissenting opinion apparently relies upon Sections 4505.02 and 4505.-17, Revised Code, because of the assumption that the registrar may, without having his determination reviewed by any court, finally determine that a previously issued certificate of title should be cancelled.   Obviously, the ruling of the registrar, that a certificate has been "improperly issued," would not be immune from judicial review.   See State ex rel. City Loan & Savings Co. v. Taggart, Recorder (1938), 134 Ohio St. 374, 378, 17 N.E. 2d 758.   The words "improperly issued" in those two sections are not defined, and there is nothing in either section requiring or even suggesting the conclusion that a certificate issued to a bona fide purchaser should be considered as "improperly issued."

Id. at 8, 197 N.E.2d at 348.

*Pottmeyer* may no longer be good law in Ohio.   In dictum *Pottmeyer* decided that outright "theft" variation cases should be treated the same.

In a subsequent Ohio Supreme Court case which dealt specifically with theft, the court held that an innocent purchaser could not defeat the original interests in the car (contrary to the *Pottmeyer* dictum).   Hardware Mut. Cas. Co. v. Gall, 15 Ohio St.2d 261, 240 N.E.2d 502 (1968) (5 to 2 decision).   In reaching its decision, the *Gall* court was forced to overrule two unnecessarily broad paragraphs from the *Pottmeyer* syllabus.

Two Ohio lower courts have since interpreted the effect of Hardware Mut. Cas. Co. v. Gall on *Pottmeyer*.   Poland Chevrolet Co. v. Shelly Smith & Sons,

21 Ohio Misc. 30, 254 N.E.2d 728 (1969) held that the *Gall* decision was limited to the outright theft variation and that *Pottmeyer*-type thinking was still good law concerning fraudulent misrepresentation absent theft. Contra: GMAC v. Birkett L. Williams Co., 17 Ohio Misc. 219, 243 N.E.2d 882 (1969).   The *Birkett* case held that *Gall* obliterates *Pottmeyer*:

It is now the law of Ohio that in a controversy between two innocent parties with reference to a motor vehicle that, absent any question of estoppel, an apparently valid Ohio Certificate of Title will *not* provide protection against the claim of a person whose ownership of the car or whose interest in the car, was affected by the fraudulent misrepresentations of a swindler or a thief.

A person cannot now be divested of his rights in a motor vehicle by a thief or the fraudulent misrepresentations of a swindler.

\* \* \*

The title and rights are as valid as any one from whom they stem. Caveat emptor!

Id. at 231–32, 243 N.E.2d at 889–90.

211.   In re Schoeller, 4 UCC Rep.Serv. 1093 (Ref.Dec.D., 1968) (dictum).

212.   But see 1 G. Gilmore, Security Interests in Personal Property § 22.7 at 623 (1965):

Section 9–103(4) is not helpful in the multiple certificate cases, at least if fraud is assumed.   It says merely that, if a certificate has been issued "under a statute of this state or any other jurisdiction," then "perfection is governed by the law of the jurisdiction which issued the certificate." This may work perfectly well in the nonfraudulent case where a proper State A certificate is succeeded by a proper State B certificate (both bearing notations of the security interest): State B becomes the perfection state on issuance of the new certificate. But the rule of § 9–103(4) seems to leave the fraud cases about where

to have such a policy to protect local parties who are defrauded than to protect trustees in bankruptcy.[213] A substantial minority of cases maintain that an original secured party may not be denied his perfected status by fraudulent schemes.[214] All these courts have ignored the Code and decided on the basis of particular certificate of title provisions or traditional concepts of comity.

Different policy issues are presented if the car has been stolen, and the holder of the last certificate of title traces through a thief. Section 9–103(4) was apparently not designed to deal with that problem, and the courts are nearly unanimous in finding that the subsequent party is not protected by his clean certificate of title if he traces his title through a thief.[215]

## § 23–22   Conclusion

Although the Code greatly eases the job of both the filer and the searcher and brings some measure of consistency to the laws of creation and perfection throughout the country, there are still many ways in which a secured creditor can fail to become perfected. Doubtless, the most common is the simple failure to file anything at all. Also common are the problems that arise when the goods move from one

they have been under pre-Code law: that is, in chaos. . . . Decision therefore will have to be based on the relevant title act and the case law under it. That is to say, even in Code states we will have the automobile litigation with us for a while yet. (footnote omitted)

213. Proposed amendment 9–103(2) (d) would protect nonprofessional buyers who rely on local clean certificates. Other purchasers and lien creditors would not be so favored. There appears no question but that the proposed changes in 9–103 are meant to cover fraud cases as well as those in which there are no evil doings. See, e. g., Proposed § 9–103, Comments 4(b), (e). Permanent Editorial Board for the UCC, Review Committee for Article 9, Final Report 79–80 (1971).

214. GMAC v. Birkett L. Williams Co., 17 Ohio Misc. 219, 243 N.E.2d 882 (C.P.1969); Hardware Mut. Cas. Co. v. Gall, 15 Ohio St.2d 261, 240 N.E.2d 502 (1968) (dictum: holding limited to theft.) City of Cars, Inc. v. GMAC, 175 So.2d 63 (Fla.App.1965) (recent changes in Florida's certificate of title law may produce different outcome); Vannoy Chevrolet Co. v. Baum, 260 Iowa 1011, 151 N.W.2d 515 (1967) (implication: facts did not deal with interstate movement). Yousey v. Bogle, 457 S.W.2d 595 (Tex.Civ.App.1970)

(implication: fact did not deal with interstate movement; held: forged certificate will not pass title).

215. Hardware Mut. Cas. Co. v. Gall, 15 Ohio St.2d 261, 240 N.E.2d 502 (1968); Poland Chevrolet Co. v. Shelly Smith & Sons, 21 Ohio Misc. 30, 254 N.E.2d 728 (D.P.1969); GMAC v. Birkett L. Williams Co., 17 Ohio Misc. 219, 243 N.E.2d 882 (C.P.Ohio 1969); Bill Dreiling Motor Co. v. The Travelers Indem. Co., 482 P.2d 999 (Colo.App. 1971) (dictum: not a secured transaction problem); Schrier v. Home Indem. Co., 273 A.2d 248 (D.C.App.1971) (dictum: not a secured transaction problem). In discussing 2–403, the court reasoned:

In the context of the commercial code . . . the principle of voidable title refers to persons who have been entrusted with the possession of the goods they sell by consignors, creditors with unrecorded security interests and certain other kinds of bailors. . . . But a possessor of stolen goods, no matter how innocently acquired, can never convey good title. 273 A.2d at 250.

But cf: Ferraro v. Pacific Fin. Corp., 8 Cal.App.3rd 339, 87 Cal.Rptr. 226 (1970) (possible implication that theft is irrelevant); Federal Ins. Co. v. Mercer, 237 So.2d 243 (Fla.App.1970).

state to another or when the debtor's place of business changes. Other frequent causes of creditor unperfection arise from his filing a document which is incomplete or incorrect, from a lapse after five years of his financing statement, from his misclassification of the collateral and his consequent failure to file or his consequent filing in the wrong place. Finally, he can be unperfected because he did not have possession of the collateral when he thought he did or because he complied with the Code when he should have complied with the federal law, with the certificate of title law or with some other analogous law. To avoid such difficulties, we reiterate Peskind's law: When in doubt about your perfection take all possible steps (including the procurance of insurance [216] and multiple filing) that could help.

---

**216.** One can now procure insurance in some transactions against any loss which might result because of a failure to perfect. Some lenders against automobiles find it less expensive to purchase this insurance than to make any attempt to perfect their security interests. If for example a dealer has a right to charge the lender $10.00 for making an application for the certificate of title and noting his lien on that application, the lender may find it cheaper to insure against any loss resulting from nonperfection. For example, in Michigan the dealer has a right to charge the lender $10.00 for noting the security interest on the certificate, but the lender can purchase insurance against loss resulting from nonperfection for only $2.00 per transaction.

Whether such insurance is available for larger transactions we are unsure. We would suppose that insurance for such larger transactions would take the form not of absolute protection of one who did not attempt to perfect but only protection against errors or omissions in an attempt to perfect. Banks routinely carry such insurance against errors and omissions in their other practices. We are unsure whether these insurance contracts cover errors or omissions in perfection as well.

# CHAPTER 24

# THE BANKRUPTCY TRUSTEE VS. THE ARTICLE NINE CLAIMANT

*Analysis*

Sec.
24–1. Introduction.
24–2. Failure to Create Security Valid and Enforceable Against the Debtor—Trustee's Rights Under Section 70(a) and 70(c).
24–3. Lack of Perfection as of Date of Bankruptcy—Trustee's Rights Under 70(c).
24–4. Delayed Perfection—Trustee's Possible Right to Avoid as Preferential Under Section 60.
24–5. "Floating Liens"—Trustee's Possible Right to Avoid as Preferential Under Section 60.
24–6. Security Interests in "Proceeds"—Trustee's Possible Right to Avoid as Preferential or as Otherwise Invalid.
24–7. Debtor's Payments to Secured Creditor—Trustee's Possible Right to Avoid as Preferential Under Section 60.
24–8. Some Extraordinary and Bizarre Avoidances Under Sections 67 (a) and 70(e).
24–9. The Article Nine Security Transfer as a "Fraudulent Conveyance" Under Sections 70(e) or 67(d).
24–10. Attacks by the Trustee on the Underlying Debt Itself.

## § 24–1  Introduction

Bankruptcy is, of course, a remedy provided by the federal Bankruptcy Act,[1] not the Code.  The Act requires that the bankrupt turn his remaining assets (except "exempt" ones) over to a "trustee" to be sold and applied on the claims of unsecured creditors.  In return, the bankrupt gets a "discharge" from most of his debts which constitutes a defense to any action by a pre-bankruptcy creditor to collect a debt covered by the discharge.[2]  Bankruptcy stops preferential dismemberment of the debtor's estate, for once bankruptcy occurs unsecured creditors cannot grab remaining assets of the debtor, even through levy.  Bankruptcy also empowers the trustee to retrieve certain assets that the debtor preferentially transferred on the eve of bankruptcy.  Of course, once bankruptcy occurs and the trustee takes control of the bankrupt's remaining assets, the bankrupt can no longer dissipate or secrete them.  In the end, the bankrupt's unsecured creditors are supposed to receive a prorata dividend from what the trustee is able to salvage.[3]  Often, this "dividend" amounts to relatively little.

A debtor's petition in bankruptcy triggers a formal meeting of his creditors at which the "trustee" in bankruptcy is usually appoint-

---

1.  Bankruptcy Act of July 1, 1898, ch. 541, 30 Stat. 544, as amended, 11 U. S.C.A. § 1 et seq. (1970) (hereinafter cited as B.A.).

2.  See B.A. §§ 14–17, 11 U.S.C.A. §§ 32–35 (1970).

3.  B.A. § 65, 11 U.S.C.A. § 105 (1970).

ed.[4] The trustee is a creature of federal law and constitutes a new kind of third party (different from those earlier considered) who may defeat certain Article Nine secured creditors. Since it is the trustee's job to gather up the bankrupt debtor's estate, reduce it to cash, and distribute the proceeds prorata to the bankrupt's unsecured creditors, (after paying expenses and certain priority claims such as wages),[5] the trustee has every incentive to try to show that a claimed Article Nine security interest is ineffective. When the trustee prevails, he enhances the size of the potential prorata bankruptcy distribution to unsecured creditors.[6] But the trustee will not always prevail. Indeed the acid test of the quality of an Article Nine security interest is its capacity to survive trustee attack. Our chief purpose in this chapter is to review and analyze the doctrines which determine when a bankruptcy trustee prevails over an Article Nine secured creditor. Most clashes between these parties are fought out in the first instance in a "court of bankruptcy," a branch of the federal district court;[7] the presiding officer in a bankruptcy court is called a Referee in Bankruptcy,[8] and he almost always sits without a jury. He applies a blend of federal and state law to the facts as he finds them. An appeal lies to the federal district court, then to a Circuit Court of Appeals, and finally to the United States Supreme Court. An appeal is exceptional, and the law applied in bankruptcy tends to be what the Referee says it is. To date bankruptcy Referees alone have decided the overwhelming majority of reported cases involving clashes between trustees and Article Nine claimants.

The trustee is a kind of assignee of the debtor (and more). The trustee steps into the legal shoes of the debtor, becomes owner of the debtor's assets, and acquires the various defenses the debtor might assert against parties he previously dealt with, including Article Nine claimants.[9] Thus the trustee may claim that an Article Nine security interest is invalid because the parties did not comply with 9–203 and 9–204 or other law and therefore did not effectively create an Article Nine security interest in the first place. The Bankruptcy Act not only makes the trustee an assignee of the debtor's property rights and defenses under sections 70(a) and 70(c); it also provides that the trustee prevails over unperfected security interests under 70(c) and 9–301(1) (b), gives the trustee power to avoid interests of secured creditors who delay perfection and thus receive preferences under section 60, subrogates the trustee to the priority and avoidance rights of certain unsecured creditors under sections 67(a), 70(e), and state law, and more.

The federal Bankruptcy Act might have provided that *all* security interests, vulnerable or not under state law, are simply invalid in the

---

4. B.A. § 2(a) (17), 11 U.S.C.A. § 11(a) (17) (1970).

5. B.A. § 47, 11 U.S.C.A. § 75 (1970).

6. B.A. §§ 70(a), 70(c), 11 U.S.C.A. §§ 110(a), 110(c) (1970).

7. B.A. § 1(10), 11 U.S.C.A. § 1(10) (1970).

8. B.A. § 39, 11 U.S.C.A. § 67 (1970).

9. B.A. § 70, 11 U.S.C.A. § 110 (1970).

event of bankruptcy. But our system goes in for security interests, and generally holds that an Article Nine security interest that is valid against the debtor and third parties in the absence of bankruptcy is also valid against the debtor's trustee in bankruptcy. Generally, the trustee has no greater right to invalidate an Article Nine security interest than an actual unsecured creditor has, absent bankruptcy. We will see that there are exceptions to this general principle. We now turn to the specific forms of vulnerability to which Article Nine security may be subject in bankruptcy proceedings under applicable federal and state law.[10]

### § 24–2    Failure to Create Security Valid and Enforceable Against the Debtor—Trustee's Rights Under Section 70(a) and 70(c)

The debtor's trustee in bankruptcy suceeds to the property rights of the debtor under Bankruptcy Act section 70(a),[11] and according to section 70(c), "may have the benefit of all defenses available to the bankrupt as against third persons." In attempting to create a valid and enforceable Article Nine security interest, the debtor and creditor may simply fail to comply with sections 9–203 and 9–204 of the Code. In the preceding chapter we considered cases in which the parties did not comply with these sections. When this occurs and the debtor becomes bankrupt, the trustee simply succeeds to property rights of the debtor; he thus takes any "collateral" in which the debtor ineffectively sought to create security.[12] Of course, the Article Nine claimant might force the trustee to establish the invalidity of the security in an adversarial proceeding, but that is another matter.

Even though security is valid and enforceable as against the debtor under Article Nine, it still may not be enforceable even as against the debtor under other state law. Thus it is elementary that one party to a consensual transaction may rescind for fraud, for mutual mistake, for duress or for undue influence.[13] The trustee succeeds to powers of rescission that the debtor has against a secured creditor upon bankruptcy.[14] The trustee similarly succeeds to any defenses or rights that the debtor may have against the secured creditor under the growing doctrine of unconscionability.[15] There is already one case

10. Bankruptcy procedure will not be treated here. For a useful recent summary as such procedure affects Article Nine secured creditors, see Kennedy, The Secured Lender in Bankruptcy, 4 U.C.C.L.J. 13, 27–33 (1971).

11. Section 70(a) of the Bankruptcy Act reads in pertinent part as follows:

The trustee of the estate of a bankrupt and his successor or successors, if any, upon his or their appointment and qualification, shall in turn be vested by operation of law with the title of the bankrupt as of the date of the filing of the petition. . . .

12. See Section 23–2 et seq. supra on ineffective creation of security.

13. Restatement of Contracts §§ 470–511 (1932).

14. B.A. § 70(c), 11 U.S.C.A. § 110(c) (1970).

15. See generally, Symposium, Unconscionability, 31 U.Pitt.L.Rev. 333 (1970); Symposium, Round Table Discussion of Unconscionability, 31 U. Pitt.L.Rev. 547 (1970). Cf. § 2–302.

indicating that a cross-security clause may be unconscionable,[16] and another case indicating that a security agreement giving a creditor excessive power to call the shots in the debtor's affairs may be unconscionable.[17]

It should also be noted that there is a growing body of regulatory laws governing the extension of secured credit to consumers.[18] Trustees succeed to the defensive posture of bankrupt parties under these laws.[19]

### § 24–3    Lack of Perfection as of Date of Bankruptcy—Trustee's Rights Under 70(c)

Far and away the most common and the most simple clash is between the bankruptcy trustee and the Article Nine claimant who either fails to perfect at all or lets his perfection lapse. The resolution of this conflict is also simple. The trustee wins under a blend of federal and state law. Part of section 70(c) states:

> The trustee shall have as of the date of bankruptcy the rights and powers of: (1) a creditor who obtained a judgment against the bankrupt upon the date of bankruptcy, whether or not such a creditor exists, (2) a creditor who upon the date of bankruptcy obtained an execution returned unsatisfied against the bankrupt, whether or not such a creditor exists, and (3) a creditor who upon the date of bankruptcy obtained a lien by legal or equitable proceedings upon all property, whether or not coming into possession or control of the court, upon which a creditor of the bankrupt upon a simple contract could have obtained such a lien, whether or not such a creditor exists.

Thus the trustee gets all the rights under state law of a hypothetical creditor with a lien on all property of the debtor. The relevant state law is Article Nine, and the relevant provision of Article Nine is 9–301(1) (b), doubtless the most important provision in the entire Article to bankruptcy trustees. Section 9–301(1) (b) states:

> (1) Except as otherwise provided in subsection (2), an unperfected security interest is subordinate to the rights of
>
> . . .
>
>      (b) a person who becomes a lien creditor without knowledge of the security interest and before it is perfected;

By the terms of 70(c), the trustee has the rights of a hypothetical lien creditor under 9–301(1) (b), and accordingly prevails over Article

**16.** Williams v. Walker-Thomas Furniture Co., 350 F.2d 445, 2 UCC Rep. Serv. 955 (D.C.Cir.1965).

**17.** In re Elkins-Dell Mfg. Co., 253 F. Supp. 864, 3 UCC Rep.Serv. 386 (E.D. Pa.1966).

**18.** See, e. g., The Uniform Consumer Credit Code, 9 U.L.A. 63–323 (Master ed. 1970); Consumer Credit Protection Act, 15 U.S.C.A. § 1601 et seq., 18 U.S.C.A. § 891 et seq. (1970).

**19.** B.A. § 70(e), 11 U.S.C.A. § 110(e) (1970).

Nine claimants whose interests are unperfected as of bankruptcy. Article Nine's perfection requirement reflects a Code policy against secret security. It furthers this policy to allow lien creditors to strike down secret security absent bankruptcy. It similarly furthers this policy to permit trustees to strike down secret security.

Before the trustee can prevail under 70(c) and 9–301, must he first identify at least one actual creditor of the bankrupt who could have prevailed against the secured creditor if he had acquired a lien? Suppose, for example, that at bankruptcy all the bankrupt's creditors had notice of the unperfected security interest. Absent bankruptcy, not one of these could have prevailed over the secured creditor by acquiring a lien, for 9–301(1) (b) gives priority only to a lien creditor who becomes such without notice of the unperfected security interest before it is perfected. If the trustee were, strictly speaking, a subrogee of the rights of a state law lien creditor with a lien as of the date of bankruptcy, it would seem to follow that the trustee would lose to the unperfected secured party if all state law creditors had notice of the secured party's interest as of bankruptcy. This issue has yet to be definitively resolved. The language in 9–301(3) (which favors the secured party in such a case) cannot be determinative, for 9–301 is state law, and the issue concerns the proper interpretation of a federal statute. The case law to date indicates that the trustee would prevail.[20]

The trustee's rights under 70(c) turn partly on the meaning of "unperfected" in 9–301(1) (b), a state law statute. As we saw in Chapter 23, perfection under Article Nine generally requires that the secured party either file or take possession of the collateral.[21] Absent one or the other, the interest will not be perfected unless it is one of those exceptional interests automatically perfected upon its creation.[22] Article Nine flatly (but exceptionally) sanctions some "secret security." Purchase money security interests in consumer goods are illustrative.[23] Here the secured party is usually the seller. Obviously a seller cannot retain possession of the goods if his buyer is to "consume" them. The Code draftsmen thought it would clutter the records and do little good to require sellers to file their security interests in consumer goods.[24] Accordingly, Article Nine provides that such

---

**20.** See, e. g., In re Babcock Box Co., 200 F.Supp. 80, 1 UCC Rep.Serv. 479 (D.Mass.1961); In re Buschman, 4 UCC Rep.Serv. 260 (Ref.Dec.E.D.Wis.1967). Accord, 2 G. Gilmore, Security Interests in Personal Property § 45.3.2 at 1296 (1965); Kennedy, The Secured Lender in Bankruptcy, 4 U.C.C.L.J. 13, 22 (1971).

**21.** §§ 9–302; 9–303; 9–305.

**22.** See, e. g., § 9–302(1) (d).

**23.** The Code defines such an interest in § 9–107 as follows:

A security interest is a "purchase money security interest" to the extent that it is

(a) taken or retained by the seller of the collateral to secure all or part of its price; or

(b) taken by a person who by making advances or incurring an obligation gives value to enable the debtor to acquire rights in or the use of collateral if such value is in fact so used.

**24.** 1 G. Gilmore, Security Interests in Personal Property § 19.4 at 534–36 (1965).

interests are automatically perfected when created [25] and are there-fore not vulnerable under section 70(c) of the Bankruptcy Act and section 9–301(1) (b) of the Code.  However, Professor Countryman has recently argued that the trustee of a bankrupt buyer prevails over holders of such automatically perfected interests.  He does not argue that nonpossessory and unfiled interests are vulnerable under section 70(c) but rather that they fall as "equitable liens" under section 60(a) (6) of the Bankruptcy Act and section 9–307(2) of Article Nine.[26] We do not find his argument convincing, and we find nothing in the Bankruptcy Act that indicates its draftsmen were out to get all secret security.  No cases to date support Professor Countryman.[27]

The case law involves many varieties of perfection failures and perfection lapses.  The secured party may try but fail to perfect by possession.  Obviously the debtor cannot himself possess the collateral as agent for the creditor.[28]  This would frustrate the general anti-secret security policy [29] of Article Nine.  To satisfy 9–305, the secured creditor (or a third party agent) must possess the collateral.  Where the secured party seeks to perfect by filing, he may simply fail to file [30] or fail to file a financing statement that complies with the requisites specified in 9–402; [31] or not file in enough places; [32] or file in the wrong place; [33] or let his filing lapse, as where he inadvertently removes the filing [34] or takes the collateral into another state so that his original filing lapses after four months; [35] or his filing may run out after the basic five year period.[36]  In these and still other ways, the interest of an Article Nine secured creditor may be "unperfected" at bankruptcy within the meaning of 9–301(1) (b) and therefore vulnerable to the trustee under 70(c).

As we have seen, Article Nine also governs the interest of *buyers* of certain intangibles: accounts, contract rights, and chattel paper.[37] If the buyer does not perfect his interest and the seller goes bankrupt, what are the rights of the trustee?  As of bankruptcy, the third party

25.  §§ 9–302, 9–303.

26.  Countryman, Code Security Interests in Bankruptcy, 75 Com.L.J. 269, 270–71 (1971).

27.  Indeed, the cases are flatly against him.  See, e. g., In re Robertson, 6 UCC Rep.Serv. 266 (Ref.Dec.E.D.Tenn. 1969).

28.  In re North American Builders, Inc., 320 F.Supp. 1229, 8 UCC Rep. Serv. 1132 (D.Neb.1970); In re Black Watch Farms, Inc., 9 UCC Rep.Serv. 151 (Ref.Dec.S.D.N.Y.1971).

29.  See, e. g., In re Republic Engine & Mfg. Co., 3 UCC Rep.Serv. 655 (Ref. Dec.N.D.Ohio 1966); Estate of Hinds, 10 Cal.App.3d 1021, 89 Cal.Rptr. 341, 8 UCC Rep.Serv. 3 (1970).

30.  See, e. g., Gray v. Raper, 115 Ga. App. 600, 155 S.E.2d 670, 4 UCC Rep. Serv. 351 (1967).

31.  See, e. g., In re Osborn, 6 UCC Rep. Serv.  227  (Ref.Dec.W.D.Mich.1969).

32.  See, e. g., In re Goettner, 2 UCC Rep.Serv. 653 (Ref.Dec.E.D.Pa.1964).

33.  See, e. g., In re Falkof, 2 UCC Rep. Serv. 731 (Ref.Dec.D.Mass.1963).

34.  See, e. g., In re Burns, 4 UCC Rep. Serv.  604  (Ref.Dec.D.Conn.1967).

35.  See, e. g., In re Welker, 2 UCC Rep. Serv. 169 (Ref.Dec.W.D.Pa.1964).

36.  See, e. g., In re Cohen, 4 UCC Rep. Serv. 22 (Ref.Dec.E.D.Pa.1967).

37.  § 9–102(1) (b).

obligor might have made no payments at all to the unperfected assignee-buyer. If so, the trustee can invoke 70(c) and 9–301(1) (b) to prevail.[38] But what if the obligor has already made payments to the buyer? Here, it would seem that the trustee cannot use 70(c), but rather must rely on section 60 to recover the payments. At least one court has so held.[39]

There are two exceptions to the general rule that the trustee prevails under 70(c) and 9–301 over the interest of any kind of Article Nine claimant unperfected as of bankruptcy. First, if the interest is in the debtor's exempt property, the trustee does not prevail, for exempt property does not become part of the bankrupt's estate anyway.[40] Second, if the interest is unperfected at bankruptcy, is of the kind that falls in 9–301(2), and is perfected after bankruptcy but within the grace period specified in 9–301(2), the Article Nine claimant will prevail, at least so far as 70(c) and 9–301 are concerned.[41]

In closing this section it is important to stress what 70(c) does not do for the trustee. In an earlier day trustees admiringly referred to 70(c) as their "strong arm" clause. And 70(c) was once an arm with bulging muscle indeed. Consider the following case for example. On February 1, 1970, S acquires an unperfected security interest in D's equipment. On February 13, S perfects. Between February 1 and February 13, no creditor of D came into existence. A year and a half later, D files bankruptcy. Could the trustee "strong arm" S on the theory that between February 1 and February 13 a lien creditor *might have* come into being who would have had priority over S under 9–301(1) (b) and that the trustee is a subrogee to the right of such a hypothetical lien creditor? At one time, the answer appears to have been yes.[42] Today, the answer is no.[43] Whereas in an earlier day, 70(c) made the trustee something of a Charles Atlas, his strength nowadays lies somewhere between that of Charlie and that of a ninety-seven pound weakling. Under section 70(c) of the Bankruptcy Act, the trustee gets the rights of a hypothetical lien creditor *as of the date of bankruptcy* (usually time of filing the petition), not as of any prior date that such a creditor could have prevailed had he existed. Thus in the foregoing hypothetical case, the trustee would not prevail under section 70(c) and state law, for as of the date of bankruptcy S had perfected.[44] Still the trustee might prevail in such delayed perfection

**38.** In re Boughner, 8 UCC Rep.Serv. 144 (Ref.Dec.W.D.Mich.1970).

**39.** Id. Cf. In re Gross Mfg. & Imp. Co., 328 F.Supp. 905, 9 UCC Rep.Serv. 355 (D.N.J.1971).

**40.** In re Rade, 205 F.Supp. 336 (D. Colo.1962); Sears Roebuck & Co. v. Schulein, 282 F.2d 267 (9th Cir. 1960).

**41.** Accord, Kennedy, The Secured Lender in Bankruptcy, 4 U.C.C.L.J. 13, 34 (1971).

**42.** Cf. Constance v. Harvey, 215 F.2d 571 (2d Cir. 1954), cert. denied 348 U.S. 913 (1955).

**43.** Cf. Lewis v. Manufacturers Nat'l Bank, 364 U.S. 603 (1961).

**44.** In re Plonta, 311 F.2d 44 (6th Cir. 1962).

cases under some other section of the Federal Bankruptcy Act (and state law), a topic we take up in the next section.

A much more important and possibly less obvious limitation on 70(c) is that it avails the trustee not one whit in all those cases in which the Article Nine claimant's interest is actually perfected as of bankruptcy. Thus, if an Article Nine secured creditor files his interest within forty-seven seconds of bankruptcy, his interest is entirely immune to successful trustee attack under 70(c). Here if the trustee is to prevail, he must invoke 60(a), 67(a), or 70(e) of the Bankruptcy Act, the scope of which we will treat in upcoming sections of this chapter. Although 70(c), 60(a), and 70(e) overlap in scope, they are far from co-extensive. For example, students almost never get it straight that under 70(c) the trustee need not find an actual 9–301(1)(b) lien creditor to subrogate to in order to prevail; rather, the trustee under 70(c) simply has the rights of an hypothetical 9–301 (1)(b) lien creditor. On the other hand, for the trustee to prevail under 70(e), he must find an actual state law creditor with rights superior to those of the Article Nine claimant. This point bears stressing, and we will stress it again.

## § 24–4   Delayed Perfection—Trustee's Possible Right to Avoid as Preferential Under Section 60

Even though the interest of an Article Nine claimant is perfected as of bankruptcy, that interest is not necessarily invulnerable. The trustee has weaponry besides 70(c). In some circumstances he can use section 60 or 67(a), or 70(e) to bring down the Article Nine interest.

Section 60 provides in essential part:

60(a)(1) A preference is a transfer, as defined in this act, of any of the property of a debtor to or for the benefit of a creditor for or on account of an antecedent debt, made or suffered by such debtor while insolvent and within four months before the filing by or against him of the petition initiating a proceeding under this Act, the effect of which transfer will be to enable such creditor to obtain a greater percentage of his debt than some other creditor of the same class. . . .

60(b) Any such preference may be avoided by the trustee if the creditor receiving it or to be benefited thereby or his agent acting with reference thereto has, at the time when the transfer is made, reasonable cause to believe that the debtor is insolvent. . . .

Now, assume that debtor owes ten unsecured creditors $1,000 each. He thus has liabilities of $10,000. He also has nonexempt assets worth $1,000. On January 10, Debtor gives C, one of the pre-existing ten creditors, a valid, enforceable, and perfected security interest. On February 1 debtor takes bankruptcy. As against the trustee, can C foreclose his security or can the trustee invalidate the security as a preference? The trustee can invalidate it as a preference if at the time of receiving the transfer C had reasonable cause to believe debtor to be insolvent. The same would be true even if the parties had created the security interest at the time C lent money to debtor, provided debtor delayed his perfection to some later time inside four months of bankruptcy. In this type of case the delayed perfection constitutes a "transfer for an antecedent debt." [45]

Before analyzing the specific elements of a voidable preference under section 60 of the Bankruptcy Act, we will explore the two main policy rationales for that section. The result in the foregoing example aptly illustrates the primary rationale for the section. If C were allowed to walk off with the $1,000, C would "obtain a greater percentage of his debt than some other creditor of the same class." [46] C would get $1,000, or one hundred percent of his debt paid. The other nine creditors would get nothing. Yet they were all in the same boat with C. All ten were similarly situated as unsecured creditors of debtor when debtor made his transfer to C. Accordingly it would seem that each should get the same percentage of his debt paid off out of the debtor's $1,000 in assets. Each should get ten percent or something near $100; C should not receive $1,000 or one hundred percent, and the other nine nothing. Hence the draftsmen of section 60 gave the trustee power to take the $1,000 away from C and to divide it up prorata (after priority payments). Note that as between debtor and C, C has done nothing untoward. A creditor is entitled to payment; a debtor ought to pay his creditor in full. Section 60 does not, as such, condemn this. The section comes into play when the equities of *other* creditors are taken into account. A voidable preference, if it is a "wrong," is not a wrong as between debtor and C, but a wrong against other creditors.

The result indicated in the foregoing example also illustrates a secondary rationale for section 60 of the Bankruptcy Act. The section embodies and implements an anti-secret security policy as well. Recall that in our example, although the Article Nine claimant had perfected as of the date of bankruptcy, his perfection did not occur until January 10, twenty-one days before the date of bankruptcy. If the Article Nine claimant were permitted to perfect on the eve of bankruptcy and walk off with the collateral, this would reward secrecy and defeat other creditors who had themselves justifiably assumed that the collateral was free and clear. In some cases it would also sanction collusion, for debtors are not beyond telling friends who might perfect that bankruptcy is just around the corner. Accordingly, the trustee's use of section 60 furthers not only an anti-preference policy, but also an anti-secret security policy as well.

In a number of cases to date trustees have invoked section 60 to defeat Article Nine claimants who delayed perfecting their interests

45. B.A. § 60(a) (2), 11 U.S.C.A. § 96(a) (2) (1970).    46. B.A. § 60(a) (1), 11 U.S.C.A. § 96(a) (1) (1970).

until within four months of bankruptcy.[47]  In several additional cases the trustee presumably would have prevailed under section 60 but he seems to have overlooked this possibility entirely.[48]  For the trustee to prevail under section 60, he must establish the nine elements of a "voidable preference":

(1)  A transfer

(2)  made or suffered by the bankrupt

(3)  of the bankrupt's nonexempt property

(4)  for or on account of an antecedent debt

(5)  within four months of bankruptcy

(6)  to or for the benefit of a creditor

(7)  while the debtor was insolvent

(8)  the effect of which is to enable the transferee to obtain a greater percentage of his debt than some other creditors of the same class

(9)  where the transferee had, at the time of the transfer, reasonable cause to believe that the debtor is insolvent.

The first of the foregoing requirements is that the debtor must have made a "transfer" of his property to the Article Nine claimant.  Section 1(30) of the Bankruptcy Act defines "transfer" as follows:

> "Transfer" shall include the sale and every other and different mode, direct or indirect, of disposing of or of parting with property or with an interest therein or with the possession thereof or of fixing a lien upon property or upon an interest therein, absolutely or conditionally, voluntarily or involuntarily, by or without judicial proceedings, as a conveyance, sale, assignment, payment, pledge, mortgage, lien, encumbrance, gift, security, or otherwise; the retention of a security title to property delivered to a debtor shall be deemed a transfer suffered by such debtor;

From this definition it is plain that "transfer" includes security transfers.  Property must be property "of the debtor."  But the time of transfer under 60 is not necessarily the time when the Article Nine interest is actually created under 9–204 and 9–203.  As we will see, the time of transfer may be later for purposes of section 60.  Second, the transfer must be one "made or suffered" by the bankrupt.  This

---

**47.**  See, e. g., In re Childress, 6 UCC Rep.Serv. 549 (Ref.Dec.E.D.Tenn. 1969); In re Bye, 5 UCC Rep.Serv. 656 (Ref.Dec.D.Minn.1968).

**48.**  See, e. g., In re Komfo Products Corp., 247 F.Supp. 229, 2 UCC Rep. Serv. 1107 (E.D.Pa.1965); In re Regency Furniture, Inc., 7 UCC Rep.Serv. 1384 (Ref.Dec.E.D.Tenn.1970); In re Music Art Center, 7 UCC Rep.Serv. 604 (Ref.Dec.E.D.Pa.1970); In re Robertson, 6 UCC Rep.Serv. 266 (Ref.Dec. E.D.Tenn.1969); In re Kirchen, 5 UCC Rep.Serv. 284 (Ref.Dec.E.D.Mich. 1967); In re Buschmann, 4 UCC Rep. Serv. 260 (Ref.Dec.E.D.Wis.1967); In re Weeks, 2 UCC Rep.Serv. 870 (Ref. Dec.W.D.Mich.1964).

language includes such involuntary transfers by the bankrupt as repossession by an Article Nine security party. Third, the transfer must be of nonexempt property of the debtor. The trustee has no legitimate interest in collecting the debtor's exempt assets, for the debtor's creditors are not entitled to the proceeds of such assets anyway.[49]

Fourth, the transfer must be for or on account of an antecedent debt. This antecedency test is generally met in any case in which the secured party both creates and perfects his security interest after having given value to the debtor. But what if the secured party creates his interest contemporaneously with giving value, yet delays his perfection until a later time? Here the secured party might argue that his "transfer" occurred at the time that he gave value and that the antecedency test is therefore not met. He would lose this argument. Section 60 includes an elaborate set of rules on the time of transfer in cases of delayed perfection. Generally, these rules postpone the time of transfer to that point in time when the secured party actually perfects, even though he may have created his interest much earlier and contemporaneously with giving value.[50] Postponement of this nature automatically assures that the antecedency test will be met. There are two major exceptions to the principle that in cases of delayed perfection the federal bankruptcy act postpones the time of transfer until the date of perfection under state law. One exception has to do with the "floating lien" and after acquired property; we discuss that in Section 24–5. The other exception is this: section 60 provides that where perfection under state law occurs within 21 days of the creation of the security interest, the time of transfer occurs at the date the interest was created so that the transfer is not for an antecedent debt.[51] It might be suggested that only Code purchase money lenders have grace periods, and further that all such periods are only for ten days.[52] We would reject both of these suggestions.[53]

---

**49.** See note 40 supra.

**50.** B.A. § 60(a) (2), 11 U.S.C.A. § 96(a) (2) (1970) provides:

   For the purposes of subdivisions a and b of this section, a transfer of property other than real property shall be deemed to have been made or suffered at the time when it became so far perfected that no subsequent lien upon such property obtainable by legal or equitable proceedings on a simple contract could become superior to the rights of the transferee. A transfer of real property shall be deemed to have been made or suffered when it became so far perfected that no subsequent bona fide purchase from the debtor could create rights in such property superior to the rights of the transferee. If any transfer of real property is not so perfected against a bona fide purchase, or if any transfer of other property is not so perfected against such liens by legal or equitable proceedings prior to the filing of a petition initiating a proceeding under this Act, it shall be deemed to have been made immediately before the filing of the petition.

See also B.A. § 60(a) (6)–(8), 11 U.S.C.A. § 96(a) (6)–(8) (1970).

**51.** B.A. § 60(a) (7), 11 U.S.C.A. § 96(a) (7) (1970).

**52.** §§ 9–301(2); 9–312(4).

**53.** We base this on the literal wording of B.A. § 60(a) (7), 11 U.S.C.A. § 96(a) (7) (1970). Professor Gilmore is in accord. 2 G. Gilmore, Security Interests in Personal Property § 45.8 (1965).

The fifth requirement of a voidable preference is that the transfer for or on account of an antecedent debt occur within four months of bankruptcy. This requirement is not that the antecedent debt be one that arose inside the four months, but rather that the transfer occur within this period. Obviously the antecedent debt may have arisen either without or within the four months. The postponement doctrines we have just discussed are also relevant to the fifth requirement, for the effect of these doctrines is often to postpone the time of transfer in delayed perfection cases to some later point inside the four month period.

A sixth requirement is that the transfer must be to or for the benefit of a creditor. Given the breadth of the definition of "creditor" in section 1(11) of the Bankruptcy Act, an Article Nine secured creditor is plainly a creditor for purposes of section 60. The seventh requirement is that the transfer must have been made or suffered while the debtor was in fact "insolvent," as that term is defined in section 1(19) (liabilities in excess of assets). Factual disputes under this requirement are common.

As an eighth requirement, the trustee must show that the transfer would enable the Article Nine claimant to obtain a greater percentage of his debt than some other creditor of the "same class." This is a puzzling requirement. Presumably those creditors who, in the absence of preferential transfers, would receive the same percentage on their claims out of the bankrupt's estate are creditors of the "same class." If, apart from the eighth requirement, an Article Nine claimant's security is good against the trustee, then that claimant does not fall (with respect to that part of his claim that is secured) into the unsecured creditor class. Indeed, for purposes of distribution, his security does not even become a part of the "bankrupt's estate." Accordingly, if his security is good, it would appear that the trustee could never prove the eighth requirement against him.[54] On the other hand, if the security is not good, apart from the eighth requirement, it may be that the trustee does have an additional hurdle here. For if the security is not otherwise good, then the secured creditor would fall into the unsecured creditor class and the question under the eighth requirement would be whether any transfer he received enabled him to receive a larger percentage of his claim than other unsecured creditors. Given the piddling size of bankruptcy dividends these days, the trustee would almost always be able to show that the "invalid" Article Nine claimant had received a larger percentage than others of his class.

The ninth and final requirement is that at the time of transfer the Article Nine secured creditor must have had reasonable cause to believe that the debtor was insolvent. This requirement is also puzzling. If the primary rationale of section 60 is to assure a more

---

**54.** See Dean v. Planters Nat'l Bank, 176 F.Supp. 909 (E.D.Ark.1959); Russell's Trustee v. Mayfield Lumber Co., 158 Ky. 219, 164 S.W. 783 (1914). See generally, Note, "Class"—The Forgotten Element of Section 60(a) (1) of the Bankruptcy Act, 11 Ariz.L.Rev. 360 (1969).

equitable distribution of the debtor's estate than that achieved through ad hoc payments by the debtor prior to bankruptcy, it would seem that section 60 should dispense with this requirement as irrelevant to its basic rationale.[55] This ninth requirement can easily cause trouble for the trustee. The question is one of "fact" and is sometimes tried before a jury. Moreover, the trustee has the burden of proof.[56]

To prevail over the dilatory perfector, the trustee must establish all of the foregoing nine requirements of a voidable preference. If he fails on any one of them, he will not prevail. For example, if a debtor borrows money on the very eve of bankruptcy, and his creditor contemporaneously acquires a security interest that is valid, enforceable, and perfected under Article Nine, this security cannot be a voidable preference. For one thing, it does not satisfy the antecedency requirement. Any avenue of attack clogged with nine requirements is certain to be of no avail to the trustee in many cases. In a later section of this chapter we will see that the trustee has still other possible weapons to use against the dilatory perfector (principally sections 67(a) and 70(e)).[57]

## § 24–5  "Floating Liens"—Trustee's Possible Right to Avoid as Preferential Under Section 60

There is now a batch of notorious cases in which the trustee attacked Article Nine "floating liens" in the bankrupt's inventory, accounts, or both.[58] In nearly all the cases the trustee claimed that the floating lien, though valid under Article Nine and state law, was nonetheless a voidable preference under section 60 of the Bankruptcy Act. The trustee almost always won before the Referee and always lost on appeal, on one or more of four different legal theories.[59] The issues posed in these cases have aroused far more excitement recently than any others in commercial law, if consumerism be put to one

55. Accord, V. Countryman & A. Kaufman, Cases and Materials on Commercial Law 196–97 (1971).

56. See, e. g., In re Marke Furniture, Inc., C.C.H. Bankruptcy L.Rep. §§ 62, 605 (Ref.Dec.N.D.Ohio 1967). See also Dinkelspiel v. Weaver, 116 F.Supp. 455 (W.D.Ark.1953).

57. See section 24–8 infra.

58. Grain Merchants of Indiana, Inc. v. Union Bank & Savings Co., 408 F.2d 209, 6 UCC Rep.Serv. 1 (7th Cir. 1969), cert. denied 396 U.S. 827 (1969); In re King-Porter Co., 446 F.2d 722, 9 UCC Rep.Serv. 339 (5th Cir. 1971); DuBay v. Williams, 417 F.2d 1277, 6 UCC Rep.Serv. 885 (9th Cir. 1969); In re

White, 283 F.Supp. 208, 4 UCC Rep. Serv. 972 (S.D.Ohio 1967); Rosenberg v. Rudnick, 262 F.Supp. 635, 4 UCC Rep.Serv. 8 (D.Mass.1967).

59. On the substitution theory, see especially Grain Merchants of Indiana, Inc. v. Union Bank & Sav. Co., 408 F.2d 209, 6 UCC Rep.Serv. 1 (7th Cir. 1969), cert. denied 396 U.S. 827 (1969). On the entity theory, see especially DuBay v. Williams, 417 F.2d 1277, 6 UCC Rep.Serv. 885 (9th Cir. 1969). On the relation back theory, see especially Rosenberg v. Rudnick, 262 F. Supp. 635, 4 UCC Rep.Serv. 8 (D.Mass. 1967). On the 9–108 theory, see especially In re White, 283 F.Supp. 208, 4 UCC Rep.Serv. 972 (S.D.Ohio 1967).

side.  New federal legislation is being prepared [60] and there has been a great flurry of scholarly ruminations on the subject.[61]

But first what is a "floating lien"? [62]  We may envision a lender who finances part or all of the operations of a dealer.  If at the time of the lender's original loan, he takes security only in the dealer's existing inventory or accounts, then as this inventory is sold off or the accounts collected, the lender's total security will diminish.  If the dealer does not repay concurrently with the sell off or collection, the lender will find himself wholly unsecured at some point.  If the dealer does repay concurrently (and ratably), the diminution in security will not alarm the lender.  But often the dealer will need a continuing loan or "line of credit," and at a relatively high level.  In these circumstances the lender will want to be continuously secured.  Section 9–204(4) of Article Nine allows him to achieve that end by taking security not only in inventory or accounts of the debtor in existence at the time of the original loan, but also in his after-acquired inventory or accounts.  Moreover, one filing is sufficient to perfect as to all.  This kind of security interest has been dubbed a "floating lien," since it "floats over" existing and after-acquired collateral.

One may divide floating liens into two classes: the "one-shot-loan" type and the "revolving loan" type.  In the one-shot loan arrangement the lender lends, say $100,000, to the dealer and takes a floating lien in the dealer's existing and after-acquired inventory, accounts, or both worth $125,000.  The parties contemplate that the full $100,000 balance will remain continuously outstanding.  If anything goes wrong, the lender may realize on the inventory or accounts to the extent necessary to satisfy his claim in full.  The big difference between the one-shot loan type and the revolving loan type is simply that in the one-shot loan, the lender makes one large loan at the beginning and none thereafter.  But in the revolving loan arrangement, the lender may receive proceeds of the collateral (i. e. payments on accounts) daily or weekly.  He will credit such proceeds against the loan and so reduce it.  Then periodically (weekly or perhaps more often in a computer operation) he will make additional advances (loans) against new accounts or inventory.  At least to the extent the new accounts finance such new advances, there can be no transfer for an antecedent debt and so no voidable preference.[63]

---

60.  See Kohn, Preferential Transfers on the Eve of Bankruptcy, 2 Prospectus 259 (1968).  Those who labor long without reward in law review vineyards should take heart from Mr. Kohn's success.  He was still a third year law student at the Michigan Law School when his article was prominently cited in *Grain Merchants*, note 64 infra.

61.  Among the best are Friedman, The Bankruptcy Preference Challenge to After Acquired Property Clauses Under the Code, 108 U.Pa.L.Rev. 194

(1959) and Hogan, Games Lawyers Play with the Bankruptcy Preference Challenge to Accounts and Inventory Financing, 53 Cornell L.Rev. 553 (1968).  At last count, there were over twenty articles in the law journals on the subject.

62.  This phrase does not appear in Article Nine of the Code.

63.  What if a lender has been lending up to eighty percent of the face amount on the new accounts and on the eve of bankruptcy reduces this to

When trustees have attacked floating liens, they have based their attacks almost entirely on section 60. Although not the first of the cases, Grain Merchants of Indiana v. Union Bank & Savings Co.[64] is aptly illustrative. The Union Bank had created a floating lien in September of 1965 on the grain company's inventory and accounts receivable "now or hereafter received" to secure loans in varying amounts. At that time the bank also filed. On September 20, 1966, the bank extended new value. After this date and prior to October 27, 1966, when the grain company took bankruptcy, the bank appropriated $45,324.97 from the grain company consisting of collections on accounts receivable that came into existence after September 20, 1966. The trustee contended that the bank had thus received a voidable preference and argued as follows: (1) Article Nine itself says that a security interest cannot arise in accounts until the debtor acquires rights in the collateral, (2) the debtor did not acquire rights in the accounts until they came into existence, which was after September 20, (3) the post-September 20 attachment of the bank's security interest to these accounts (and to proceeds thereof) under the after acquired property clause therefore constituted a transfer for an antecedent debt, and (4) the other elements of a voidable preference were present. The Referee in bankruptcy agreed and ordered the bank to turn over the money.[65] The district court set aside the turnover order [66] and the Seventh Circuit affirmed in an elaborate opinion by Judge Cummings. The judge considered all of the various legal theories on which it is possible to say that an Article Nine floating lien is not a preference. First he answered the trustee's above four point argument by stressing that in order for a security transfer to occur, section 60(a) only requires that the secured creditor's interest be so far perfected that a hypothetical lien creditor could not prevail over him under 9–301(1) (b). The judge said "we are presented with a situation where as soon as an account receivable comes into existence and is sought to be attached by a lien creditor, it has already become subject to a perfected security interest—here, that of the Bank." [67] On the *literal* language of section 60 and Article Nine, this theory seems airtight. One might fancy that a lien creditor's interest could come into existence at the very moment that the account came into existence, but even this possibility would not help the trustee for it is not enough for him to show that the lien creditor would share equally with the Article Nine creditor. Under 60(a) (2) the trustee must

forty percent in order to improve his position on past unpaid loans? Presumably the transfers of the new accounts would be preferential to the extent of forty percent. See Kripke, Haydock, Kirsch & Moore, Inventory and Receivables Financing Under the Uniform Commercial Code and the Bankruptcy Act, 87 Banking L.J. 579, 620–21 (1970).

64. Grain Merchants of Indiana, Inc. v. Union Bank & Sav. Co., 408 F.2d 209, 6 UCC Rep.Serv. (7th Cir. 1969), cert. denied 396 U.S. 827 (1969).

65. Id. at 211, 6 UCC Rep.Serv. at 3.

66. In re Grain Merchants of Indiana, Inc., 286 F.Supp. 597, 5 UCC Rep.Serv. 884 (N.D.Ind.1968).

67. Grain Merchants of Indiana, Inc. v. Union Bank & Sav. Co., 408 F.2d 209, 213, 6 UCC Rep.Serv. 1, 6 (7th Cir. 1969), cert. denied 396 U.S. 827 (1969).

show that the lien creditor's rights would be "superior to the rights of the transferee." Moreover, Judge Cummings' analysis is consistent with the evident purpose of 60(a) (2). The bank here did not have a secret security interest. Any hypothetical lien creditor would have been on notice of the bank's claim by virtue of the bank's earlier filing. "Accordingly, it does not distort the Congressional purpose to conclude that the 'so far perfected' language of section 60(a) (2) . . . was satisfied at the time of the September 1965 filing of the financing statements." [68]

Second, Judge Cummings invoked the so-called "entity" theory to save the bank's interest. He concluded that the transfers of the individual accounts did not take place between September 20 and October 27, 1966, but occurred earlier at the time when "the interest in the accounts receivable as an entity was created and the financing statements were duly filing in September 1965." [69] Thus, according to Judge Cummings, the trustee misconceived the situation: he atomized the security when he should have viewed it collectively as an entity. In our opinion this argument is more in the nature of a conceptualization than an argument. Any force it has depends on the independent reasons that can be given for viewing the collateral as an entity. Moreover, the entity theory is intrinsically limited in scope. Strictly applied, the creditor cannot use it to save a floating lien to the extent that the collateral dips during the four month period below the level he claims at bankruptcy.

The third theory on which Judge Cummings relied is the so-called "substitution" theory. It is not a section 60 preference for a secured creditor to receive new collateral in exchange for old of equivalent value, for there is no depletion of the estate. We quote the Judge's analysis at length:

> Here, as existing accounts receivable were collected by Grain Merchants and deposited to its accounts at the Bank, the funds from previously collected accounts were made available to the debtor, enabling it to continue in business and obtain new accounts receivable. During the critical period from September 20 when the Bank last extended value until September 30 when Grain Merchants ceased doing business, the debtor's withdrawals appear generally to have been in line with the deposits from new accounts receivable. See Appendix to this opinion. Our study of this record shows that at the end of each of the four months preceding bankruptcy, there was an excess of collateral over secured debt, indicating that collateral was regularly transferred in substitution for other collateral without diminishing the bankruptcy assets available for creditors. Here the newly aris-

---

**68.** 408 F.2d at 215, 6 UCC Rep.Serv. at 8. But for a contrary view, see Countryman, Code Security Interests in Bankruptcy, 75 Com.L.J. 269, 277 (1970).

**69.** 408 F.2d at 216, 6 UCC Rep.Serv. at 10.

ing accounts receivable may be considered as having been taken in exchange for the release of rights in earlier accounts and for a present consideration. Since the relative positions of the Bank and the debtor were unaltered by the exchanges, the debtor's other creditors cannot be considered harmed by the transactions with the Bank. . . .

As previously observed under Section 9–205 of the Commercial Code, it was unnecessary for the Bank to assume dominion over individual accounts receivable. Therefore, it is no longer appropriate to apply strict timing or value rules so long as at all relevant times the total pool of collateral, as here, exceeded the total debt.[70]

Judge Cummings considered two further theories but did not rely on either. Section 9–108 reveals that the Code draftsmen envisioned the possibility that trustees would attack floating liens as preferential:

Where a secured party makes an advance, incurs an obligation, releases a perfected security interest, or otherwise gives new value which is to be secured in whole or in part by after-acquired property his security interest in the after-acquired collateral shall be deemed to be taken for new value and not as security for an antecedent debt if the debtor acquires his rights in such collateral either in the ordinary course of his business or under a contract of purchase made pursuant to the security agreement within a reasonable time after new value is given.

Judge Cummings remarked that 9–108 "codifies" the substitution doctrine but stated that he need not rely on 9–108 for that point.[71] The Code's Permanent Editorial Board put forward a further theory in its *amicus* brief: that the accounts involved were proceeds of a valid and perfected Article Nine interest in inventory. Judge Cummings refused to consider this theory since no one had advanced it below.[72] Section 9–306(2) and (3) provide in effect that accounts are proceeds of inventory and continue the secured creditor's interest in those proceeds.

Throughout the court's opinion in *Grain Merchants* there are references to business practices which help justify the court's decision. The opinion notes that the parties here could have observed procedures whereby the bank would have advanced new money in exchange for each new account or specifically released rights in old collateral in exchange for new. The trustee conceded that if the parties had followed these procedures "no attack under the preference section of the Bankruptcy Act would have been possible."[73] But the court

70. Id. at 217, 6 UCC Rep.Serv. at 12.          72. Id.

71. Id. at 218, 6 UCC Rep.Serv. at 13–14.          73. Id. at 216, 6 UCC Rep.Serv. at 11.

noted that a great many lenders today make loans secured by a revolving pool of accounts or inventory without observing procedures of the foregoing kind. Doubtless lenders do things in this way because they do not see any good business reasons to follow such procedures in their own cases. The law should not put them to unnecessary trouble and expense. "Good business practice should be good business law." [74] At least where the total collateral outstanding at all times exceeded the debt owed, we believe that it should make no difference to the result that some or all of the individual items of collateral were not specifically and contemporaneously exchanged for new value.

Although the Supreme Court of the United States denied *certiorari* in *Grain Merchants* and although the various Circuits that have passed on the validity of floating liens in bankruptcy have uniformly held for the secured creditor,[75] some questions remain unanswered. Trustees have been rightly concerned over the abuse-potential of floating liens, and revised drafts of section 60 are being prepared to deal with possible abuses.[76] Here we consider one illustrative possibility. Assume that the floating lienor lends $100,000 and contemporaneously takes security in existing inventory or accounts then worth $125,000. Inside the four month period the floating lienor discovers that the borrower is insolvent and that he has sold down his inventory and collected his accounts to the point where remaining inventory and accounts only have a value of $10,000. The floating lienor then demands that the borrower forego paying all other debts as they fall due until the borrower has re-built his inventory and accounts back up to a value of $125,000. The borrower obeys, and at bankruptcy has rebuilt substantially. If it be assumed that no good business reason explains the wild fluctuation in the size of the collateral, then we would say that the floating lienor's interest is substantially preferential in nature. Here the vice lies in the build up of inventory or accounts occurring out of the ordinary course of the borrower's business which in our view disqualifies the floating lienor for fully secured status. It is noteworthy that even the drafters of Article Nine recognized in 9–108 that non-ordinary course transfers should be vulnerable as preferential.

No case has arisen that poses the above problem, nor are many such cases likely to arise, for only the rare debtor can long forestall bankruptcy after he ceases paying all creditors save one or two. Yet when and if the problem does arise, a court will not be able to use *Grain Merchants* doctrine to avoid the floating lien involved, for that doctrine affords no means of distinguishing betwen the non-preferential floating lien involved in that case and the preferential floating lien involved in our hypotetical problem. Recall that the *Grain Merchants* court (and other courts) have indicated that the floating lienor prevails provided he filed his financing statement outside the

---

**74.** Id.

**75.** See text accompanying notes 58–59 supra and cases there cited.

**76.** See Kohn, Preferential Transfers on the Eve of Bankruptcy, 2 Prospectus 259 (1968).

four month period.[77]  On this analysis the floating lienor would also prevail in our hypothetical problem involving the wildly fluctuating inventory.  However, we believe that *Grain Merchants* should not be read to sanction the floating lienor's claim in our problem.  The two types of situations can be distinguished on their facts.  There is no substitution in our hypothetical problem.  Moreover it is not enough to say that the floating lienor gave adequate advance notice.  The dominant policy of section 60 is not an anti-secret security policy anyway; it is an anti-preference policy.  Unlike in *Grain Merchants*, the floating lienor in our problem receives a classic preference if his claim is allowed to stand.  Inside the four month period he let himself become unsecured and then induced his debtor to prefer him rather than other creditors by feeding his floating lien.  In sum we believe as matters now stand courts can readily deal with our hypothetical problem.  Indeed, they could not only distinguish *Grain Merchants*, but could also invoke 9–108.

The National Bankruptcy Conference recently adopted a proposed redraft of section 60 that takes care of our hypothetical problem.[78] In crude generalities the draft provides that the floating lienor's claim is invalid to the extent that the floating lienor "improves his position" inside the four month period.[79]  Upon adopting this proposal, the Conference also recognized its element of overkill.  Thus under the proposal the floating lienor might be deprived of improvements in his position that arose from such events as the transformation of inventory from worthless work-in-process to finished goods, the carrying of inventory from off-season to its seasonal selling peak, or the conversion of inventory into more valuable cash and receivables.  Assuming that the floating lienor improved his position in such ways and assuming that in so doing he did not over-reach or act unfairly toward other creditors, then he should prevail.  Or so thought some members of the Conference.  Accordingly, the Conference has agreed to reconsider this possibility of overkill at its next annual meeting.[80]

It remains to consider cases in which the floating lienor did not perfect under Article Nine until inside the four month period.  The case of In re King-Porter Co., Inc.[81] is the most puzzling of these. There the Fifth Circuit relied on *Grain Merchants*, but the facts in *King-Porter* were importantly different.  The case involved the activities of a manufacturer of air conditioners, a distributor and a dealer.  Inside the four month period the manufacturer sold and delivered 112 units to the dealer on unsecured credit.  If the manufacturer had later taken a security interest in the units to secure this claim, it would have been a transfer for an antecedent debt voidable as a preference (assuming the other elements of a preference were

77. National Bankruptcy Conference, Report of the Committee on Coordination of the Bankruptcy Act and the Uniform Commercial Code (unpublished mimeograph 1970).

78. Id.

79. Id.

80. Id.

81. In re King-Porter Co., 446 F.2d 722, 9 UCC Rep.Serv. 339 (5th Cir. 1971).

met).  But about eighteen days later, the manufacturer assigned his unsecured claim to the distributor who in other transactions with the dealer had previously set up a floating lien on the dealer's inventory. Distributor's security interest had automatically attached to the 112 units when the dealer acquired them from the manufacturer and distributor's interest obviously constituted good security for any new value that the distributor gave to the dealer.  Could this security also secure the antecedent debt that the dealer owed the manufacturer and which the manufacturer assigned to the distributor?  In becoming an assignee of this claim the distributor had given new value, but not to the dealer.  The Fifth Circuit upheld the floating lienor's contention that his security also secured the claim that he acquired by assignment from the manufacturer.  The court's decision in *King-Porter* seems to come down to no more than this: A party (here the manufacturer) can convert what would have been a preferential security transfer if made to him into a non-preferential transfer merely by assigning his own claim to another party who has a security interest in assets of the common debtor (here the dealer).  If this be what the case stands for, it should not be the law.  The Bankruptcy Act simply does not provide that an assignee of an unsecured claim can (without giving new value to the debtor) convert that claim into a secured claim good in bankruptcy.  Such a practice would frustrate the Act's anti-preference policy.  It would permit a creditor to inflate his rights *vis a vis* the debtor's other creditors on the eve of bankruptcy without making any corresponding contribution to the debtor's estate.  Section 60 is aimed precisely at this evil, and on the facts of *King-Porter* the distributor should lose.  Indeed, we believe that the manufacturer should lose as well if the trustee were to claim that he received a preference.

### § 24–6  Security Interests in "Proceeds"—Trustee's Possible Right to Avoid as Preferential or as Otherwise Invalid

"Floating lienors" commonly have security interests in "proceeds" of the inventory or accounts which comprise their "original" collateral.[82]  Other types of lenders sometimes take security in proceeds, too.  Proceeds are a special type of Article Nine after-acquired collateral.  Section 9–306(1) defines proceeds to mean whatever is received when collateral or proceeds are "sold, exchanged, collected or otherwise disposed of."  Thus "proceeds" includes not only money, checks, bank accounts and the like, but also properties (such as goods) which frequently serve as original collateral, for such properties can also be received when collateral is "sold, exchanged, collected or otherwise disposed of."

---

82.  On this topic, too, there has been no dearth of law review articles.  See, e. g., Epstein, "Proceeding" Under the Uniform Commercial Code, 30 Ohio St.L.J. 787 (1969); Gillombardo, The Treatment of Uniform Commercial Code Proceeds in Bankruptcy: A Proposed Redraft of Section 9–306, 38 Cincinnati L.Rev. 1 (1969); Henson, "Proceeds" Under the Uniform Commercial Code, 65 Colum.L.Rev. 232 (1965); Weiss, Original Collateral and Proceeds: A Code Puzzle, 42 N.Y.U. L.Rev. 785 (1967).

At bankruptcy many debtors either have proceeds among their assets or recently have paid proceeds over to a creditor. When an Article Nine secured creditor and the debtor's trustee in bankruptcy both claim the right to such proceeds, who prevails? This is the principal question of this section and we have divided our discussion of it into two parts.

## IDENTIFIABLE PROCEEDS UNDER 9–306(4) (a), (b) AND (c)

In pre-Code days the law was that a secured creditor with a perfected security interest in proceeds which he could *identify* as proceeds of his original collateral would prevail over the trustee.[83] This should not be news to anyone. On principle the law ought to treat proceeds collateral and original collateral in the same fashion. If the law considered security interests in original collateral good against the trustee, then it should do likewise with respect to proceeds collateral, at least if the secured creditor could identify the proceeds as his. And so it was, in and out of bankruptcy. In pre-Code days courts evolved rules for the identification of proceeds. A recent judicial opinion indicates the character of some of these rules:[84]

> In Pennsylvania, prior to 1954, the effective date of the Uniform Commercial Code, the rules for tracing property were judicially established. (See: Erie Trust Company's Case (No. 1), 326 Pa. 198 (1937) for review of Penn. case law.) In the case of Farmers & Mechanics National Bank v. King, 57 Pa. 202 (1868) Justice Strong had declared that equity would follow a fund through a number of transmutations and preserve it for the owner so long as it could be identified. Earmarking was unnecessary, so long as the property or money proceeds could be traced into a substitute. Deposit of the money into an account would not operate to destroy its ownership. In the case of Webb v. Newhall, 274 Pa. 135, it was declared that it was not so much the existence of a trust relation that entitled one to recover, but the ability to trace and identify the fund as his property that controlled. (See also: Lifter v. The Earle Co., 72 Pa. Super. 173.) In the case of the Landsdowne Bank & Trust Co.'s Case, 323 Pa. 380, 388 (1936) it was held that no mere change of form could divest the funds of a trust so long as they could be traced and identified. The transmutation of a check, the subject of a trust, into a credit to one's bank account, could be identified as the new res to which the trust might attach; and where the balance in the account did not fall below the amounts of the checks so received and deposited the "lowest balance doctrine" became applicable.

---

83. 2 G. Gilmore, Security Interests in Personal Property § 45.9 (1965).

84. In re C. E. Pontz & Son, Inc., 2 UCC Rep.Serv. 1131 (E.D.Pa.1965), aff'd mem. 359 F.2d 436, 3 UCC Rep. Serv. 450 (3d Cir. 1966).

Outside of bankruptcy 9–306(2) and (3) appear to continue the secured creditor's pre-Code rights to identifiable proceeds pretty much as before.[85]   But upon bankruptcy, is his perfected interest in proceeds co-extensive with what he would have had under pre-Code law? In pre-Code days secured creditors were entitled in bankruptcy to all identifiable proceeds that were subject to their valid and perfected security interests.   Section 9–306(4) does not *expressly* give the Article Nine secured creditor as much:

> (4) In the event of insolvency proceedings instituted by or against a debtor, a secured party with a perfected security interest in proceeds has a perfected security interest
>
> (a) in identifiable non-cash proceeds;
>
> (b) in identifiable cash proceeds in the form of money which is not commingled with other money or deposited in a bank account prior to the insolvency proceedings;
>
> (c) in identifiable cash proceeds in the form of checks and the like which are not deposited in a bank account prior to the insolvency proceedings; and
>
> (d) in all cash and bank accounts of the debtor, if other cash proceeds have been commingled or deposited in a bank account, but the perfected security interest under this paragraph (d) is
>
> (i) subject to any right of set-off; and
>
> (ii) limited to an amount not greater than the amount of any cash proceeds received by the debtor within ten days before the institution of the insolvency proceedings and commingled or deposited in a bank account prior to the insolvency proceedings less the amount of cash proceeds received by the debtor and paid over to the secured party during the ten day period.

The Article Nine secured creditor does prevail over the trustee as to (*1*) identifiable non-cash proceeds,[86] (*2*) identifiable cash proceeds in the form of money not commingled with other money or deposited in a bank account prior to bankruptcy and (*3*) identifiable cash proceeds in the form of checks and the like which were not deposited in a bank account prior to the bankruptcy proceedings.[87] However except insofar as 9–306(4) (d) applies, the secured credi-

---

85.   See, e. g., Girard Trust Corn Exch. Bank v. Warren Lepley Ford, Inc., 25 Pa.D. & C.2d 395, 1 UCC Rep.Serv. 531 (C.P.1958) (secured creditor allowed to trace proceeds from automobile inventory to chattel paper, to deposit accounts, and back to automobile inventory again).   See also Paramount Financial Co. v. Cleveland's Peppermint Lounge, Inc., 3 UCC Rep.Serv. 991 (Ohio C.P.1965); Associates Discount Corp. v. Old Freeport Bank, 421 Pa. 609, 220 A.2d 621, 3 UCC Rep.Serv. 481 (1966).

86.   § 9–306(4) (a).

87.   § 9–306(4) (b) and (c).

tor is not entitled to *all* identifiable cash proceeds.  By the express language of 9–306(4) (b) he is not entitled to identifiable cash proceeds in the form of money commingled with other money or deposited in a bank account that contains other funds.  And by the language of 9–306(4) (c) he does not seem to be entitled to identifiable cash proceeds in the form of checks and the like deposited in an *unsegregated* bank account.  Note that a bank account is not a cash proceed; it is a debt owed by the bank to the depositor.  Thus a secured creditor has a right to a *segregated* account (one containing only his proceeds) because of 9–306(4) (a).  We are mindful of ways to torture the language of 9–306(4) (b) and (c) to expand the secured creditor's rights to make them more nearly equivalent to his pre-Code rights to identifiable proceeds.[88]  We only offer a summary of the literal language.

## PROCEEDS UNDER 9–306(4) (d) (IDENTIFIABLE AND NON-IDENTIFIABLE)

Of course, if the secured creditor gets less under 9–306(4) (b) and (c) than under prior law, that would seem to mean that the trustee gets more.  But whether or not the trustee really gets more and the secured creditor less depends on the operation of 9–306(4) (d) which purports to give the secured creditor certain other proceeds upon the debtor's insolvency, proceeds which might or might not actually have been identifiable on pre-Code analysis.  It might be that 9–306(4) (d) generally gives secured creditors enough of these other proceeds to make up for what they lose in rights to identifiable proceeds under 9–306(4) (b) and (c).[89]  But it should be obvious that a particular secured creditor might get far less under 9–306(4) (d) than he would if he were permitted simply to claim all proceeds he could actually identify as his regardless of the limitations in 9–306(4) (b) and (c).

Professor Gilmore has recommended three steps to determine the amount of 9–306(4) (d) proceeds that a particular creditor is entitled to:[90]

1.  Ascertain the amount of cash proceeds that the debtor received during the ten days before bankruptcy,

2.  Deduct the amount of any proceeds that the debtor secured and paid over to the secured creditor during the ten days preceding bankruptcy,

3.  Deduct from the amount ascertained in step 1 the amount of any set off that the depositary bank has.

**88.**  See, e. g., Epstein, "Proceeding" Under the Uniform Commercial Code, 30 Ohio St.L.J. 787, 793–96 (1969).

**89.**  One court has observed that the secured party's right to commingled or deposited cash received under section 9–306(4) (d) is exclusive and that the creditor therefore cannot claim a greater sum than section 9–306(4) (d) allows even though he can identify that greater sum as cash proceeds of the collateral.  Howarth v. Universal C.I.T. Credit Corp., 203 F.Supp. 279, 1 UCC Rep.Serv. 515 (W.D.Pa.1962).

**90.**  2 G. Gilmore, Security Interests in Personal Property § 45.9 at 1338 (1965).

The resulting figure represents the maximum amount of proceeds that the Article Nine secured creditor can claim under 9–306(4) (d). If 9–306(4) (d) operates to give the secured creditor no more by way of proceeds than he could have claimed under pre-Code law giving him *all* identifiable proceeds, we see no basis for the trustee to object. Yet commentators have so far theorized at length on the possible invalidity in bankruptcy of 9–306(4) (d).[91] To date no post-Code cases resolve this question of validity. One court has simply assumed that 9–306(4) (d) is valid in bankruptcy.[92]

One of the attacks that the trustee might make on 9–306(4) (d) is that it is a voidable preference: that the interest does not arise until the moment of bankruptcy and is therefor a transfer for an antecedent debt, a transfer occurring at a time when the creditor is likely to have reason to know of the debtor's insolvency. The secured creditor can argue in reply that 9–306(4) (d) merely substitutes by operation of law certain proceeds for other proceeds which the secured creditor could have claimed. To the extent the facts of the case support this argument, it should defeat the trustee. A truly substitutional transfer cannot constitute a preference, for it does not deplete the bankrupt's estate.[93]

The trustee may urge that the 9–306(4) (d) proceeds interest is invalid under 70(c): a hypothetical lien creditor at the date of bankruptcy could have acquired a superior lien on these proceeds under 9–301(1) (b). Here the trustee would simply be wrong on his law (assuming that the proceeds are in fact identifiable as proceeds of original collateral in which our secured party had a perfected security interest under 9–306(2) and (3)). The hypothetical lien creditor at the moment of bankruptcy would be levying on rights of the debtor already subject to a continuously *perfected* security interest in identifiable proceeds. Section 9–301(1) (b) could not come into play.[94]

Some commentators have argued that the trustee could strike down a 9–306(4) (d) proceeds interest as a statutory lien under section 67(c).[95] But 67(c) applies only to interests that arise by operation of law. In our view the secured party who initially acquires his

---

**91.** See note 82 supra.

**92.** Howarth v. Universal C.I.T. Credit Corp., 203 F.Supp. 279, 1 UCC Rep. Serv. 515 (W.D.Pa.1962). See also In re C. E. Pontz & Son, Inc., 2 UCC Rep.Serv. 1131 (E.D.Pa.1965) (no evidence that secured creditor had any rights under section 9–306(4), aff'd mem. 359 F.2d 436, 3 UCC Rep.Serv. 450 (3d Cir. 1966); In re Security Aluminum Co., 9 UCC Rep.Serv. 47 (Ref.Dec.E.D.Mich.1971) (issue as to validity of section 9–306(4) (d) expressly deferred); In re Gibson, 6 UCC Rep.Serv. 1193 (Ref.Dec.W.D.Okla.1969) (section 9–306(4) (d) applied, but its validity not in issue); Morrison

Steel Co. v. Gurtman, 113 N.J.Super. 474, 274 A.2d 306, 8 UCC Rep.Serv. 1203 (App.Div.1971) (section 9–306(4) (d) applied, but its validity not in issue).

**93.** See First Nat'l Bank v. Julian, 383 F.2d 329 (8th Cir. 1967); In re Baumgartner, 55 F.2d 1041 (7th Cir. 1931).

**94.** For a viewpoint in accord, see Henson, "Proceeds" Under the Uniform Commercial Code, 65 Colum.L.Rev. 232, 247 (1965).

**95.** See, e. g., Countryman, Code Security Interests in Bankruptcy, 75 Com.L.J. 269, 274 (1970).

interest in identifiable proceeds under 9–306(2) and (3), acquires by contract, not by operation of law. The fact that upon bankruptcy 9–306(4) (b) and (c) cut this interest back and substitute something else under 9–306(4) (d) should not convert that interest into a non-consensual one, at least insofar as 9–306(4) (d) in the particular case gives the secured party no more than what he would otherwise have had under pre-Code law in identifiable proceeds.

If a court should decide that 9–306(4) (d) is invalid in bank-ruptcy, it would not necessarily follow that the trustee would prevail. We believe that the secured creditor would be entitled to revive his pre-Code common law rights to identifiable proceeds and prevail as to those.

### § 24–7   Debtor's Payments to Secured Creditor—Trustee's Possible Right to Avoid as Preferential Under Section 60

Within the four months prior to bankruptcy, a debtor will usually make a number of payments to his creditors. The trustee can avoid payments to unsecured creditors as preferences (provided the re-cipients had reasonable cause to believe the debtor to be insolvent at the time of the payments). But what if the payments were made to an Article Nine secured creditor? If the trustee is entitled to in-validate the security under some provision of the Bankruptcy Act, he may also avoid the payments as preferential (assuming the creditor had reasonable cause to believe the debtor insolvent), for it is just as if the payments were made to an unsecured creditor.[96] Suppose, how-ever, that the Article Nine security interest is invulnerable to trustee attack. Assume that the debtor paid the secured creditor's claim ($50,000) in full within four months of bankruptcy, and that the average value of his collateral during the four months before bank-ruptcy was $50,000. Here courts have held that a $50,000 payment to him during four months before bankruptcy is not preferential, since there was no diminution in the debtor's estate by virtue of the payments. The secured creditor had a good claim against assets of the debtor equivalent to the amount of payments received by him,[97] and that collateral will now be available for other creditors.

But suppose that the average value of the collateral during the four months before bankruptcy was only $40,000. Here we think the trustee could successfully attack the $50,000 payments as preferential to the extent of $10,000.[98] After all, the secured creditor was par-tially unsecured all along, and the $10,000 transfer depleted the debtor's estate by that amount. Suppose that as of the date of bank-ruptcy the collateral took a sudden jump in value and was on that date worth $50,000. Would this save the $10,000 from being preferential? Here the transfer does not deplete the estate, and at least technically

---

96. See, e. g., Douglass v. Pugh, 287 F.2d 500 (6th Cir. 1961).

97. See, e. g., Small v. Williams, 313 F.2d 39, 44 (4th Cir. 1963).

98. Id. See also W. Collier, The Bank-ruptcy Manual 642–43 (1971).

there can be no preference.[99]   In such a case courts should not permit the trustee to avoid the payment to any extent.

## § 24–8   Some Extraordinary and Bizarre Avoidances Under Sections 67(a) and 70(e)

Occasionally the trustee will be able to use sections 67(a) and 70 (e) to bring down an Article Nine secured creditor although the trustee could not bring this same creditor down under sections 70(c) or 60.   Suppose that on February 2, Jake, a creditor with a $500 claim, levies on a $3,000 compressor owned by Bart and in which Adam has an unperfected security interest to secure a $3,000 claim.   The next day, Adam perfects his interest.   One month later, and prior to a judicial sale of the compressor, Bart takes bankruptcy.   The trustee, Jake and Adam all claim the compressor.   Assume that Adam had no cause to believe that Bart was insolvent.   Hence, the trustee could not defeat Adam under 60.   It should be plain that he could not defeat Adam under 70(c) either, for Adam had perfected as of bankruptcy.   But let us consider the trustee's rights under 67(a), which provides in pertinent part:

(1) Every lien against the property of a person obtained by attachment, judgment, levy, or other legal or equitable process or proceedings within four months before the filing of a petition initiating a proceeding under this Act by or against such person shall be deemed null and void (a) if at the time when such lien was obtained such person was insolvent or (b) if such lien was sought and permitted in fraud of the provisions of this Act: *Provided, however,* That if such person is not finally adjudged a bankrupt in any proceeding under this Act and if no arrangement or plan is proposed and confirmed, such lien shall be deemed reinstated with the same effect as if it had not been nullified and voided.   .   .   .

(3) The property affected by any lien deemed null and void under the provisions of paragraphs (1) and (2) of this subdivision a shall be discharged from such lien, and such property and any of the indemnifying property transferred to or for the benefit of a surety shall pass to the trustee or debtor, as the case may be, except that the court may on due notice order any such lien to be preserved for the benefit of the estate, and the court may direct such conveyance as may be proper or adequate to evidence the title thereto of the trustee or debtor, as the case may be: *Provided, however,* That the title of a bona-fide purchaser of such property shall be valid, but if such title is acquired otherwise than at a judicial sale held to enforce such lien, it shall be valid only to the extent of the present consideration paid for such property.

99.   B.A. § 60(a) (1), 11 U.S.C.A. § 96(a) (1) (1970).

In our example, Jake, the lien creditor, would have priority over Adam, the Article Nine secured creditor, under 9–301(1) (b). And the trustee could avoid Jake's lien and preserve it for the benefit of the estate under 67(a) (1) and 67(a) (3). Accordingly the trustee can subrogate to Jake's priority over Adam and himself take priority over Adam. But to what extent? To $500 only (the amount of Jake's claim) or to the full $3,000 (the amount of Adam's claim)? As we read 67(a), the trustee would prevail only to the extent of $500 on strict subrogation theory.

Section 70(e), however, provides in pertinent part:

> (1) A transfer made or suffered or obligation incurred by a debtor adjudged a bankrupt under this Act which, under any Federal or State law applicable thereto, is fraudulent as against or voidable for any other reason by any creditor of the debtor, having a claim provable under this Act, shall be null and void as against the trustee of such debtor.

Could the trustee subrogate himself to Jake's lien creditor status under 70(e) plus 9–301(1) (b) and avoid Adam's security *in toto* ($3,-000) and not just *pro tanto* ($500)? Certainly 70(e) plus 9–301(1) (b) would permit the trustee to avoid the security to the extent of $500 on strict subrogation theory. But there is also a well known Supreme Court case, Moore v. Bay,[100] in which Justice Holmes interpreted 70 (e) to allow the trustee to avoid *in toto* and not merely to the extent of the claim of the creditor to whose rights the trustee is subrogated under 70(e). Is Moore v. Bay alive here today? The courts have not definitively resolved this question and scholarly opinion is divided.[101] Professor Kennedy [102] has recently argued that Moore v. Bay is no longer the law here. He contends that Congress in re-drafting 67(a) after Moore v. Bay evinced an intent to abrogate the doctrine to the extent that it allows the trustee to subrogate beyond the actual rights of an actual creditor with a voidable lien who has priority over a secured creditor. We find Professor Kennedy's arguments persuasive, and agree with him that in such a case the trustee is "bound by the limits" of the voidable lien creditor's claim unless the trustee "otherwise has a right of recovery under section 70(e)," as where he can show that he subrogates to the rights of state law creditors who could avoid the security *in toto* as a fraudulent conveyance.[103]

Whether or not Professor Kennedy is right in proclaiming a Congressional intent to abrogate Moore v. Bay, he is surely right in his view that the trustee may use 70(e) to subrogate to the rights of a lien creditor only when that creditor's lien is one that the trustee

100.   284 U.S. 4 (1931).

101. See Kennedy, The Trustee as a Secured Creditor Under the Uniform Commercial Code, 65 Mich.L.Rev. 1419, 1435 (1967).

102. Kennedy, The Trustee as a Secured Creditor Under the Uniform Commercial Code, 65 Mich.L.Rev. 1419, 1434–39 (1967).

103.   Id. at 1439.

could avoid under B.A. § 67(a).[104]   Yet the courts have not yet definitively resolved this question either, and again, scholarly opinion is divided.[105]   As fundamental as these questions are, it must seem strange that they are still open.   We doubt that the entire legal world anxiously awaits their resolution.   Actually 67(a) and 70(e) are today much less useful to the trustee than they were in pre-Code days. Many pre-Code versions of the 9–301(1) (b) priority rule did not require that the creditor in Jake's position be a lien creditor to take priority over the unperfected security interest of Adam.   It was enough for Jake merely to extend credit while Adam's interest was unperfected.[106]   Section 9–301(1) (b) not only requires the Jakes of the world to be lien creditors, it also requires that they acquire their liens without knowledge of the unperfected interest.   It is therefore much less common, post-Code, that the trustee will find an actual creditor with priority to whose rights he may subrogate.

Some bankruptcy buffs appear to argue that under 70(e) the trustee could be subrogated not only to any avoidance or priority rights of actual 9–301(1) (b) lien creditors, but also to the priority rights of Article Nine secured creditors over other secured creditors.[107]   Consider this example:   On January 1, 1971, C1 acquires a valid and enforceable (as against the debtor) Article Nine security interest in D's equipment, but does not then perfect.   C1's claim is for $5,000; the equipment is worth $15,000.   On January 2, C2 lends $10,000 against the equipment, taking a valid, enforceable, and perfected Article Nine security interest therein.   February 15, C1 perfects.   A year later, D takes bankruptcy.   Assume that 70(e) is the only possible section of the Bankruptcy Act under which D's trustee might proceed.   D's trustee seeks to take priority over C1's security under 70(e) by claiming that he succeeds to C2's priority under 9–312 (5) (a) over C1's interest.   Thus the trustee would leave C2's interest intact to the extent of $10,000, but would rake in C1's $5,000 interest for distribution to the general creditors he represents.   Some bankruptcy buffs think the trustee has this power under 70(e),[108] and 70(e) read very literally indeed may permit this.   Also one recent case tends to support this reading.[109]   But other bankruptcy buffs say that 70(e) should not be so read, and we agree.[110]   For several reasons the trustee should not be viewed as a subrogee of Article Nine secured creditors unless he has an independent basis on which

---

104.   Id. at 1440.

105.   For the view that the lien need not be one that the trustee could avoid under section 67(a) of the Bankruptcy Act, see S. Riesenfeld, Cases and Materials on Creditor's Remedies and Debtor's Protection 516 (1967).

106.   See, e. g., the law applied in In re Plonta, 311 F.2d 44 (6th Cir. 1962).

107.   E. g., 4A Collier on Bankruptcy § 70.90 at 1034 (14th ed. 1967).

108.   Ibid.

109.   E. g., In re Smith, 326 F.Supp. 1311, 9 UCC Rep. Serv. 549 (D.Minn., 1971).

110.   The most thorough and insightful discussion is in Kennedy, The Trustee in Bankruptcy as a Secured Creditor Under the Uniform Commercial Code, 65 Mich.L.Rev. 1419 (1967).

to defeat (e. g. as a preference) the claim of the secured creditor whose rights he seeks to invoke. First, section 70(e) is subrogational in nature, yet the trustee here seeks to invoke the priority rights of C2, a party whose interest the trustee cannot defeat, for we are assuming that C2's interest is itself immune to attack under the various sections of the Bankruptcy Act. Furthermore we are assuming that no creditor that the trustee "represents" could upset C1's interest under state law. Thus the trustee's argument departs radically (far more so than Moore v. Bay) [111] from the subrogational nature of 70(e) itself. Second, the secured creditor in question, C1, has not done anything that would make his interest vulnerable on our traditional notions. He did not have a secret lien, and he did not wait for the ship to start sinking to assert his interest. Third, the Bankruptcy Act differentiates between secured creditors and unsecured creditors. Secured creditors whose interests are good are supposed to prevail in bankruptcy. Equality of treatment for them with unsecured creditors is not equity. Yet on the trustee's argument, C1 would be forced to share with D's other unsecured creditors even though his interest was perfected as of bankruptcy and otherwise wholly immune to trustee attack. Fourth, the trustee's argument leads to the highly anomalous consequence that all Article Nine security junior to other Article Nine security becomes vulnerable (to the extent junior) inside bankruptcy, regardless of whether the trustee could independently defeat it under 60, 67(d), 70(c) or otherwise under 70(e). Fifth, if the prime purpose of 70(e) is to give creditors of the estate the rights they would have had but for bankruptcy, then the trustee should lose. None of the creditors could have prevailed against C1 outside of bankruptcy. Finally, not even the trustee's good friend Professor Countryman has argued (so far as we know) in support of the trustee here.[112]

## § 24-9    The Article Nine Security Transfer as a "Fraudulent Conveyance" Under Sections 70(e) or 67(d)

When the trustee cannot prevail under other provisions of the Bankruptcy Act, he might still be able to avoid an Article Nine security transfer as a "fraudulent conveyance" under 70(e) or 67(d). Indeed the trustee may invoke these provisions and relevant state law not only to attack a security transfer as fraudulent but also to attack the underlying debt as fraudulent.[113] But putting attacks on the debt itself to one side, it appears that there is not yet a single post-Code case in which the trustee has successfully invoked fraudulent conveyance law against an Article Nine secured creditor.[114] We

111.   284 U.S. 4 (1931).

112.   Countryman, Code Security Interests in Bankruptcy, 75 Com.L.J. 269 (1970).

113.   See Section 24-10 infra.

114.   However, there are instances of successful attack just prior to Code enactment. See, e. g., In re Process—Manz Press, Inc., 236 F.Supp. 333 (N.D.Ill.1964) rev'd on other grounds, 369 F.2d 513 (7th Cir. 1966), cert. den. 386 U.S. 957 (1967) (Illinois law; Code not effective until seven months

find this surprising, for the pre-Code cases are abundant,[115] and we cannot believe that fraud went out when Article Nine came in.

Under either 70(e) or 67(d), the theory is that the trustee is a subrogee of the rights of the creditor or creditors whom the bankrupt wronged in making the fraudulent security transfer. Thus if such creditors no longer exist or were paid off at bankruptcy,[116] or have no claims "provable in bankruptcy," [117] the trustee is powerless to attack the transfer as fraudulent as to them and therefore powerless to attack the transfer as "fraudulent" at all. The trustee may seek to attack via 70(e) plus state law such as the Uniform Fraudulent Conveyance Act, or he may launch his attack under 67(d).[118] We will consider each possibility in turn. Section 70(e) provides:

> (1) A transfer made or suffered or obligation incurred by a debtor adjudged a bankrupt under this Act which, under any Federal or State law applicable thereto, is fraudulent as against or voidable for any other reason by any creditor of the debtor, having a claim provable under this Act, shall be null and void as against the trustee of such debtor.

Under this provision the trustee succeeds to the rights of the wronged creditor or creditors under applicable state "fraudulent" conveyance law. The trustee must establish that, but for the debtor's bankruptcy, the wronged creditor or creditors could have shown that the security transfer was a "fraudulent" conveyance. In states where the Uniform Fraudulent Conveyance Act is in force, [119] the trustee may establish that the transfer is fraudulent by showing that it falls into section 4, 5, 6, 7, or 8 below:

> Section 4. *Conveyances by Insolvent.* Every conveyance made and every obligation incurred by a person who is or will be thereby rendered insolvent is fraudulent as to creditors without regard to his actual intent if the conveyance is made or the obligation is incurred without a fair consideration.

later). In re Farmers Federation Cooperative, Inc., 242 F.Supp. 400 (W.D. N.C.1965) (North Carolina law; Code not yet effective for one and one-half years).

115. See Uniform Fraudulent Conveyance Act, 7 U.L.A. 426–600 (Master ed. 1970) and the numerous cases cited therein. See also 11 U.S.C.A. §§ 107, 110 (1953) and the numerous cases cited therein.

116. 4A Collier on Bankruptcy § 70.90 (14th ed. 1967) and the numerous cases cited therein.

117. B.A. §§ 63, 70(e) (1), 11 U.S.C.A. §§ 103a, 110(e) (1) (1970).

118. For an extended argument that the trustee has a third basic alternative under Bankruptcy Act § 70(a) (4), see Miller, Fraudulent Conveyances— Some Reflections on Section 70(a) (4) of the Bankruptcy Act, 48 B.U.L.Rev. 222 (1968).

119. Arizona, California, Delaware, Idaho, Maryland, Massachusetts, Michigan, Minnesota, Montana, Nevada, New Hampshire, New Jersey, New Mexico, New York, North Dakota, Ohio, Oklahoma, Pennsylvania, South Dakota, Tennessee, Utah, Washington, Wisconsin, and Wyoming. See 7 U. L.A. 423 (Master ed. 1970).

Section 5. *Conveyances by Persons in Business.* Every conveyance made without fair consideration when the person making it is engaged or is about to engage in a business or transaction for which the property remaining in his hands after the conveyance is an unreasonably small capital, is fraudulent as to creditors and as to other persons who become creditors during the continuance of such business or transaction without regard to his actual intent.

Section 6. *Conveyances by a Person About to Incur Debts.* Every conveyance made and every obligation incurred without fair consideration when the person making the conveyance or entering into the obligation intends or believes that he will incur debts beyond his ability to pay as they mature, is fraudulent as to both present and future creditors.

Section 7. *Conveyance Made With Intent to Defraud.* Every conveyance made and every obligation incurred with actual intent, as distinguished from intent presumed in law, to hinder, delay, or defraud either present or future creditors, is fraudulent as to both present and future creditors.

Section 8. *Conveyance of Partnership Property.* Every conveyance of partnership property and every partnership obligation incurred when the partnership is or will be thereby rendered insolvent, is fraudulent as to partnership creditors, if the conveyance is made or obligation is incurred,

(a) To a partner, whether with or without a promise by him to pay partnership debts, or

(b) To a person not a partner without fair consideration to the partnership as distinguished from consideration to the individual partners.

Most of the pre-Code cases in which the trustee or other plaintiffs successfully attacked security interests in personalty as fraudulent conveyances are cases of actual fraud under section 7 of the UFCA (or other local counterpart). For example, in the leading case of In Re Rasmussen's Estate [120] the court found facts that clearly fall within section 7. There, the debtor, who was insolvent, created otherwise valid security in all his personalty to secure several relatively small claims compared to the value of the security. The debtor himself had confided that the purpose of his arrangement was to lead other creditors to believe that his assets were fully encumbered so that they would not dismember him. The secured parties were employees of the debtor and were aware of his fraudulent purpose. The court held that the security interests were entirely void. The

---

120. In re Rasmussen's Estate, 238 Wis. 334, 298 N.W. 172 (1941). See Annot., 138 A.L.R. 1051 (1952).

prevailing party was not a trustee in bankruptcy but an administrator of the debtor's estate acting on behalf of creditors. In most states that have considered the question,[121] this case should be good law today for the trustee, too, under 70(e).[122] And, as we will demonstrate, a trustee may attack an Article Nine security transfer on section 7 grounds besides fraudulent excessiveness of the security; the *Rasmussen* case is merely illustrative.[123] Moreover, it should be apparent that security of the type involved in *Rasmussen* might not be vulnerable under section 60, 70(c) or other provisions of the Bankruptcy Act.

May the trustee avoid *in toto* or is his power of avoidance (and preservation) limited to the amount of the claims of those state law creditors or creditor he represents? Suppose, for example, that under state law the security transfer is a fraudulent conveyance only as against three creditors whom the trustee represents and whose claims total $1,000, while the security is worth $5,000 and secures a $5,000 debt. Under 70(e) may the trustee avoid the transfer *in toto* or only to extent of $1,000? According to the doctrine of Moore v. Bay,[124] the trustee may avoid the fraudulent security transfer in the amount of $5,000, that is, *in toto* and not merely *pro-tanto*.[125] Moreover, the recovery falls into the estate for distribution to all unsecured creditors, not just those specifically wronged.[126] Both of these departures from strict subrogational theory have been much criticized.[127]

In sum, at least where the Article Nine secured creditor is a fraudulent conveyee guilty of *actual fraud* under UFCA section 7 (or like law), the trustee may avoid his security *in toto* and not just *pro-tanto*. However, the story is very different where the Article Nine secured creditor is a fraudulent conveyee under sections 4, 5, 6 or 8 but is not guilty of "actual fraudulent intent." Here, he may "retain the property . . . as security for repayment" under section 9(2) of the UFCA (or like law). Section 9(2) is therefore a drastic inroad on the trustee's subrogational powers under 70(e) for he generally cannot avoid security transfers that are "fraudulent" only in the sense that they fall in UFCA 4, 5, 6 or 8 (or like law). Rather, he can generally avoid only those in which the secured creditor is guilty of "actual fraudulent intent." The pre-Code case law on the

---

121. See Annot., 138 A.L.R. 1051 (1952).

122. See generally 4A Collier on Bankruptcy § 70.71 (14th ed. 1967).

123. For four further illustrative types of cases, see text accompanying notes 129–32 infra.

124. 284 U.S. 4 (1931). See also text accompanying note 100 supra.

125. 4A Collier on Bankruptcy § 70.95 (4) (14th ed. 1967) and the numerous cases cited therein.

126. Cf. American Trust Co. v. New York Credit Men's Adjust. Bureau, Inc., 207 F.2d 685 (2d Cir. 1953); In re Moore, 11 F.2d 62 (4th Cir. 1926); In re Delcon Corp., 194 F.Supp. 111 (S.D.Cal.1961).

127. See, for example, the general critique in 4A Collier on Bankruptcy § 70.95(4) (14th ed. 1967).

meaning of this phrase is voluminous.[128] Below we offer only an illustrative listing, not an exhaustive catalogue, and in each illustrative case we assume that the trustee could not avoid the transfer under non-fraudulent conveyance law.

(1) To ward off D's creditors, C and D together conjure up a fictitious debt (in whole or in part) and secure it with an interest in D's personalty. Courts have permitted D's trustee to avoid C's security entirely, even where the debt was only partially fictitious.[129]

(2) Though C actually lends D money and creates a valid security interest, C agrees with D not to file a financing statement for a time because D fears this would dry up his credit. Later, after D was unable to weather the storm, C files. Still later D becomes bankrupt. Again, courts have permitted the trustee to avoid C's security in its entirety.[130]

(3) C is a major stock-holder of D(1) corp. C has lent money to D(1). C fears a levy by L on D(1)'s most valuable assets. D(1) creates security in these assets in C and C shortly thereafter forecloses, buying in the assets. C and the other shareholders of D(1) then form corporation D(2) and C transfers the assets to D(2) which continues the business. Later, L seeks to levy and finds no assets in D(1)'s hands. Thereafter, D(1) becomes bankrupt. Has C wronged L? A creditor may not so manipulate matters that another creditor is foreclosed of his rights while the debtor and conniving creditor retain their original positions. Accordingly, the trustee may resort to fraudulent conveyance law to avoid the security in part or in whole.[131]

(4) D owes C a genuine debt but D creates security in collateral worth substantially more than the amount D owes C. Other creditors of D threaten to levy. D defaults and C forecloses, buying in at the sale at a sum equivalent to the debt D owes C. Thereafter C secretly remits money to D representing the excess value of the security. D becomes bankrupt nonetheless. Again C has committed a wrong against a creditor or creditors of L. Perhaps his security should be considered void and of no effect at all at anytime past? Or at least to the extent of L's claim? Again if other law will not avail the trustee he may turn to fraudulent conveyance law and prevail.[132]

---

128. See the annotations in 7 U.L.A. 504–61 (Master ed. 1970) (Uniform Fraudulent Conveyance Act § 7). See also the annotations in 11 U.S.C.A. § 110 nn. 1431–1570 (1953) and the cases cited in Annot., 79 A.L.R. 132 (1932).

129. Cf. Jones v. Third Nat'l Bank, 13 F.2d 86 (8th Cir. 1926). Compare M. & N. Freight Lines, Inc. v. Kimbel Lines, Inc., 180 Tenn. 1, 170 S.W.2d 186 (1943), with In re American Metal Products, 276 F.2d 701 (2d Cir. 1960).

130. Cf. Rankin v. Cox, 71 F.2d 56 (8th Cir. 1934). See 4A Collier on Bankruptcy § 70.73 (14th ed. 1967).

131. Cf. Lipson v. H. M. R. Enterprises, Inc., 16 Misc.2d 447, 183 N.Y.S.2d 160 (1959). Compare Ever-Ready Label Corp. v. Stuyvesant Photo E. Corp., 36 N.Y.S.2d 468 (1942), with Wiseman v. United Dairies, 324 Mich. 473, 32 N.W. 2d 174 (1949).

132. Cf. Buffum v. Barceloux Co., 289 U.S. 227 (1933). Compare, also, In re Peacock Food Markets, 108 F.2d 453 (7th Cir. 1939).

Earlier we indicated that the trustee might seek to attack an allegedly fraudulent security transfer under 67(d).[133]  Some states do not have the Uniform Fraudulent Conveyance Act or any developed body of fraudulent conveyance law.  For this and other reasons Congress has, in 67(d), enacted the main features of the UFCA, and the trustee may therefore proceed under 67(d) to attack a fraudulent conveyance.  The trustee may not, however, do this entirely in his own right.  Like 70(e) the theory of 67(d) is also subrogational, though to a lesser extent.  The trustee must be able to identify an actual creditor or creditors of the bankrupt with respect to whom the security transfer would have been a fraudulent conveyance under 67(d).[134]  These creditors must have "provable claims," which the trustee "represents." [135]

Some judicial and scholarly opinion holds that the trustee may under 67(d) avoid a transfer not just *pro-tanto* but *in toto* as under 70(e).[136]  Section 67(d)(6) provides, too, that a secured party who "without fraudulent intent" gave a consideration "less than fair" may nonetheless retain the property interest transferred to him as "security for repayment," a proviso comparable to UFCA (9)(2).[137]  However, to qualify for the 67(d)(6) immunity from avoidance, the secured creditor must not only have taken the security without fraudulent intent, but also have taken it in "good faith." [138]

## § 24–10  Attacks by the Trustee on the Underlying Debt Itself

In preceding sections of this chapter, we have usually portrayed the trustee attacking the security itself or attacking payments by the debtor to the secured creditor.  But do not forget that a trustee may focus on the debt itself, and attack its actuality, its legality or its size.  Generally the trustee who shows that the bankrupt owes no enforceable debt or less of a debt than assumed is just as well off as the trustee who shows that the security for the assumed indebtedness is unenforceable or not fully enforceable.

If the trustee can show that the debt is a sham—a fraud conjured up out of whole cloth—this alone will be enough to scuttle the secured creditor no matter what the validity of his "security" interest.  The legal literature is littered with cases in which the trustee sought to show that an alleged debt was a make-believe or otherwise nonexistent.  Usually the trustee proceeds here under a branch of fraud-

---

133.  For an argument that section 70(a)(4) of the Bankruptcy Act offers a third basic avenue of attack, see Miller, Fraudulent Conveyances—Some Reflections on Section 70(a)(4) of the Bankruptcy Act, 48 B.U.L.Rev. 222 (1968).

134.  B.A. § 67(d)(2), 11 U.S.C.A. § 107(d)(2) (1970).

135.  B.A. §§ 63, 67(d)(6), 11 U.S.C.A. §§ 103a, 107(d)(6) (1970).

136.  See 4 Collier on Bankruptcy § 67.49 (14th ed. 1967).

137.  In re Peoria Braumeister, 138 F.2d 520 (7th Cir. 1943).

138.  B.A. § 67(d)(1)(e), 11 U.S.C.A. § 107(d)(1)(e) (1970).

ulent conveyance law.[139]  Even though the debt be actual, it may still not be legally enforceable even though the security interest "securing" it be otherwise valid and enforceable.  Thus the debt may be barred by the statute of limitations.  It may be unenforceable because of creditor fraud, duress, undue influence, or some other factor rendering the entire transaction voidable.  The trustee succeeds under 70(c) to "all defenses available to the bankrupt as against third persons."  Further, the debt may be unenforceable because the interest provided is usurious.  Indeed, there is a recent flock of cases to the effect that a usurious debt is a fraudulent conveyance.[140]

Even though the debt be real, and be legal, it may be overstated or otherwise inflated.  To the extent the trustee can show this, the more likely it will be that he can show that the debtor has an "equity" in the collateral to which the trustee succeeds as successor to "property" of the debtor.[141]  Again, there are numerous cases in which the trustee has sought to cut down the size of an indebtedness allegedly owed a secured creditor.

**139.**  See, e. g., Duberstein v. Werner, 256 F.Supp. 515 (E.D.N.Y.1966); Gayle v. Jones, 74 F.Supp. 262 (W.D.La. 1947).

**140.**  See generally, Broude, Toward a New Fraudulent Conveyance: The Trustee in Bankruptcy and the Usurious Lender, 63 N.W.U.L.Rev. 331

(1968).  It is often held that the lender can evade the usury laws by using a corporation. See, e. g., Werger v. Haines Corp. 302 N.Y. 930, 100 N.E.2d 189 (1951).

**141.**  B.A. § 70(a), 11 U.S.C.A. § 110(a) (1970).

# CHAPTER 25

# PRIORITY CONFLICTS: MAINLY 9–307—9–313

*Analysis*

Sec.
25–1.  Introduction.
25–2.  Rights of the Secured Creditor vis-a-vis Unsecured Creditors With and Without Judicial Liens, 9–201, 9–301.
25–3.  Basic Priorities—Among Secured Creditors, 9–312.
25–4.  —— First in Time, First in Right, 9–312(5).
25–5.  —— Second in Time, First in Right, Purchase Money Security Interests, 9–312(3) and (4).
25–6.  —— Security Interests in Crops, 9–312(2).
25–7.  Priorities in Fixtures Between Real Estate Claimants and Secured Creditors, 9–313.
25–8.  Fixtures—What is a Fixture?
25–9.  —— The Routine 9–313 Cases.
25–10.  —— Some Interpretative Snarls in 9–313.
25–11.  —— Proposed Changes in 9–313.
25–12.  Priority of Purchasers of Goods, 9–307.
25–13.  —— 9–307(1) and Buyers in the Ordinary Course of Business.
25–14.  —— Consumer Purchasers of Consumer Goods—9–307(2).
25–15.  —— Relationship Between 2–403 and 9–307.
25–16.  —— Special Problems Involving Vehicles, Aircraft and Non-Code Recording Acts.
25–17.  Purchases of Chattel Paper and Non-negotiable Instruments, 9–308.
25–18.  Purchasers of Instruments and Documents, 9–309.

## § 25–1  Introduction

In this chapter the reader will relish those delicious academic morsels so dear to the hearts and minds of commercial law teachers: personal property priority conflicts. Here we will deal with sections 9–307 through 9–313, but not with the more common priority conflicts governed by 9–301 that arise between the trustee in bankruptcy and the secured creditor. Chapter 24 deals with the rights of the trustee *vis-a-vis* the secured creditor. Because sections 9–307 through 9–313 are intricate, interrelated, and logical, we suspect that they get more consideration in the law school curriculum than they deserve. Certainly our hunt for cases on those sections was not terribly productive; rarely do appellate courts consider these sections; even 9–312 has faced few court tests. In the material which follows we will move from the most to the least important questions and will focus on 9–312, the basic provision on conflicting security in the same personalty, and on 9–313 dealing with conflicting security in fixtures. In addition we will consider, in a rather general way, the impact of the proposed 1971 Article Nine Amendments. Those amendments would change the wording of the sections considerably and would clear up certain ambiguities which now exist, but they would make

899

few fundamental changes in the priority system currently embodied in the Code.

Article Nine has no corner on the priority conflicts market. Some of the most ancient priority rules are set down in American real property law; others appear in Article Four of the Code (4–303— priority with respect to a bank account claimed by two parties), Article Seven (7–502 et seq.—priority with respect to goods that are twice sold), etc. In this chapter we will deal exclusively with cases in which at least one of the claimants is an Article Nine secured creditor claiming a prior interest in personal property. His opponent may be a buyer claiming that he took free of the security interest; he may be another secured creditor; or he may be a lender against real property claiming an incidental interest in personal property on that real property. The usual outcome in a priority conflict under the Code is that the winning party satisfies himself *in full* out of the collateral before the subordinate party satisfies himself to *any* extent. Thus, if one secured creditor with a $100,000 claim in collateral is prior to another secured creditor who has a $50,000 claim, the prior secured creditor satisfies his entire $100,000 claim out of the collateral before a single dollar goes to the other secured creditor. If the collateral produces less than $100,000 the prior secured creditor takes all and the other gets nothing.

At the outset, the reader should note the operation of the "shelter" principle in this branch of law.[1] That common law principle enters the Code via 1–103 and 2–403 and provides that a buyer gets as good a title as his seller had. Assume, for example, that a secured creditor had a perfected security interest in inventory and that his security agreement provided that buyers from his debtor did not take free of the interest. Buyer 1 purchases goods and takes free of the interest under the provisions of 9–307(1), despite the term in the security agreement. Buyer 1 then resells the goods to Buyer 2. Buyer 2, as we shall see, would not qualify under subsection (1) of 9–307 because he did not buy from one in the business of selling goods, and he would not qualify under subsection (2) because the creditor had filed a financing statement covering the goods. Nevertheless, he takes free of the financier's security interest *because his seller took free,* and he succeeds to the title of his seller. In other words he is "sheltered" by his seller's title. The shelter principle is stated in the Code explicitly in section 3–201 with respect to commercial paper and in section 2–403(1) with respect to the sale of goods. If one concludes that 2–403 does not protect against a security interest, he may reach

---

1. See J. Cribbet, Principles of the Law of Property 222 (1962), 3 J. Pomeroy, A Treatise on Equity Jurisprudence §§ 754–754(b) (5th ed. 1941). However, the *bona fide* purchaser's power of disposition is subject to one exception according to traditional equity doctrines. The B.F.P's title will not "shelter" a former owner who had notice of the defense or who was a party to fraud affecting the former conveyance, and who re-purchases the property from the B.F.P. 3 J. Pomeroy, A Treatise on Equity Jurisprudence § 754(b).

the same result by adopting the common law shelter principle under the provisions of 1–103.

## § 25–2   Rights of the Secured Creditor vis-a-vis Unsecured Creditors With and Without Judicial Liens, 9–201, 9–301

Section 9–201 states the basic right of the secured creditor vis-a-vis other competitors. The first sentence of that section reads as follows:

> Except as otherwise provided by this Act a security agreement is effective according to its terms between the parties, against purchasers of the collateral and against creditors.

The sentence means what it says, and the secured creditor, even an unperfected secured creditor, has greater rights in his collateral than any other creditor unless Article Nine provides otherwise. Of course, an unsecured creditor without a lien has no claim on any specific collateral, and 9–201 gives a secured creditor a prior right over any such unsecured creditor without a lien. In Chapter 24 we have discussed priority conflicts between a perfected or unperfected secured creditor and the debtor's trustee in bankruptcy as a lien creditor. Here we will treat (somewhat repetitively) conflicts between a secured creditor and a lien creditor who is not a trustee in bankruptcy. Section 9–301 governs, and provides in general that an unperfected secured creditor loses to a lien creditor and, by negative implication, that a perfected secured creditor beats a lien creditor. Section 9–301(1) reads in part as follows:

> (1) Except as otherwise provided in subsection (2), an unperfected security interest is subordinate to the rights of
>
> (a) persons entitled to priority under Section 9–312;
>
> (b) a person who becomes a lien creditor without knowledge of the security interest and before it is perfected;
>
> (c) in the case of goods, instruments, documents, and chattel paper, a person who is not a secured party and who is a transferee in bulk or other buyer not in ordinary course of business to the extent that he gives value and receives delivery of the collateral without knowledge of the security interest and before it is perfected;
>
> (d) in the case of accounts, contract rights, and general intangibles, a person who is not a secured party and who is a transferee to the extent that he gives value without knowledge of the security interest and before it is perfected.

The most important provision is (1)(b) which renders an unperfected secured creditor subordinate to the rights of one who "becomes a lien creditor without knowledge of the security interest and before it is perfected. . . ." Thus, if a bank takes a security interest in debtor's equipment but fails to file a financing statement or to take possession, and an unsecured creditor levies against the property and so procures a judicial lien on it, the unsecured creditor will have a prior right unless he had "knowledge" of the security interest when he procured his lien. Note under subsection (2) of 9–301 that a secured creditor with a purchase money interest has ten days after the collateral comes into possession of the debtor to file a financing statement, and if he does so, he takes priority over the rights of "a transferee in bulk or of a lien creditor which arise between the time the security interest attaches and the time of filing."

Also important but of less significance is 9–301(1) (c):

> . . . An unperfected security interest is subordinate to the rights of . . .
>
> (c) in the case of goods, instruments, documents, and chattel paper, a person who is not a secured party and who is a transferee in bulk or other buyer not in ordinary course of business to the extent that he gives value and receives delivery of the collateral without knowledge of the security interest and before it is perfected. . . .

This subsection, of course, gives priority to good faith bulk purchasers and other buyers over unperfected secured creditors. Note that such buyers must take without knowledge of the security interest and must give value. The subsection excludes buyers in the ordinary course of inventory presumably on the assumption that they will always be superior to an unperfected security interest since they are generally superior even to perfected security interests under the terms of 9–307. Although not mentioned in 9–301(1) (c), presumably such ordinary course buyers as those who buy farm products but who are not superior to a prior perfected security interest under 9–307 are nevertheless superior to an unperfected security interest by analogy to 9–301(1) (c). We believe that the omission of such persons from 9–301(1) (c) was unintended and that they take priority *a fortiori* since 9–301(1) (c) grants superiority over unperfected secured creditors to other less meritorious claimants.

In general, therefore, the secured creditor has claims on the collateral superior to an unsecured creditor who has no lien. If he is secured but unperfected, he will usually be subordinate to lien creditors and to all buyers who give value and take without knowledge. For more detailed discussion of 9–301 and the rights of the lien creditor in the bankruptcy context, see Section 24–3.

## § 25–3    Basic Priorities—Among Secured Creditors, 9–312

Section 9–312 in general and subsection 9–312(5) in particular are supposed to answer the lawyer's dreams:

(1) The rules of priority stated in the following sections shall govern where applicable: Section 4—208 with respect to the security interest of collecting banks in items being collected, accompanying documents and proceeds; Section 9—301 on certain priorities; Section 9—304 on goods covered by documents; Section 9—306 on proceeds and repossession; Section 9—307 on buyers of goods; Section 9—308 on possessory against nonpossessory interests in chattel paper or non-negotiable instruments; Section 9—309 on security interests in negotiable instruments, documents or securities; Section 9—310 on priorities between perfected security interests and liens by operation of law; Section 9—313 on security interests in fixtures as against interests in real estate; Section 9—314 on security interests in accessions as against interest in goods; Section 9—315 on conflicting security interests where goods lose their identity or become part of a product; and Section 9—316 on contractual subordination.

(2) A perfected security interest in crops for new value given to enable the debtor to produce the crops during the production season and given not more than three months before the crops become growing crops by planting or otherwise takes priority over an earlier perfected security interest to the extent that such earlier interest secures obligations due more than six months before the crops become growing crops by planting or otherwise, even though the person giving new value had knowledge of the earlier security interest.

(3) A purchase money security interest in inventory collateral has priority over a conflicting security interest in the same collateral if

(a) the purchase money security interest is perfected at the time the debtor receives possession of the collateral; and

(b) any secured party whose security interest is known to the holder of the purchase money security interest or who, prior to the date of the filing made by the holder of the purchase money security interest, had filed a financing statement covering the same items or type of inventory, has received notification of the purchase money security interest before the debtor receives possession of the collateral covered by the purchase money security interest; and

(c) such notification states that the person giving the notice has or expects to acquire a purchase money security interest in inventory of the debtor, describing such inventory by item or type.

(4) A purchase money security interest in collateral other than inventory has priority over a conflicting security interest in the same collateral if the purchase money security interest is perfected at the time the debtor receives possession of the collateral or within ten days thereafter.

(5) In all cases not governed by other rules stated in this section (including cases of purchase money security interests which do not qualify for the special priorities set forth in subsections (3) and (4) of this section), priority between conflicting security interests in the same collateral shall be determined as follows:

(a) in the order of filing if both are perfected by filing, regardless of which security interest attached first under Section 9—204(1) and whether it attached before or after filing;

(b) in the order of perfection unless both are perfected by filing, regardless of which security interest attached first under Section 9—204(1) and, in the case of a filed security interest, whether it attached before or after filing; and

(c) in order of attachment under Section 9—204(1) so long as neither is perfected.

(6) For the purpose of the priority rules of the immediately preceding subsection, a continuously perfected security interest shall be treated at all times as if perfected by filing if it was originally so perfected and it shall be treated at all times as if perfected otherwise than by filing if it was originally perfected otherwise than by filing.

Here under one roof are clear and certain rules to determine priority among most conflicting security interests in personal property. Section 9–312 replaces a multitude of unclear and inconsistent state laws.[2] Because the section is law in 49 states, it eliminates most

---

2. An issue that may arise during a limited time after the adoption of the Code concerns the relation of pre-Code security interests to the "Article 9 security interests." Before enacting the Code most states had several security devices in personal property, the more common of which were the pledge, the chattel mortgage, the conditional sale, the factor's lien, and the trust receipt. The draftsmen dealt with this problem in section 10–102(2). It reads:

Transactions validly entered into before the effective date specified in Section 10–101 and the rights, duties and interests flowing from them remain valid thereafter and may be terminated, completed, consummated or enforced as required or permitted by any statute or other law amended or repealed by this Act as though such repeal or amendment had not occurred.

At least three courts have decided that a perfected pre-Code security interest will retain priority provided that it remains continuously perfected after the effective date. In General Elec. Credit Corp. v. R. A. Heintz Constr.

choice of law problems. Because it determines priority for nearly all types of personal property collateral, it avoids former difficulties in choosing the law within a state which would govern a given priority dispute.[3] The face of 9–312 is deceptively formidable. One should first understand that the section is like a will with several specific bequests of $10,000, and a million dollar residuary clause. Subsection (5) is the million dollar residuary clause, and it governs more priority disputes than all of the other subsections combined. Subsection (1) is but an elaborate cross reference provision; subsection (2) merits only a passing glance from the city lawyer; and subsections (3) and (4) are purchase money priority provisions. Because we regard it most important, we start with subsection (5).

## § 25–4   Basic Priorities—First in Time, First in Right, 9–312(5)

First in time, first in right—that general rule runs like a gold thread through virtually all priority schemes, and 9–312(5) is no exception. However 9–312(5) is uniquely precise. The pre-Code law amply displayed, and the Code draftsmen well appreciated the ambiguity inherent in the "first in time" slogan; namely, first what? Does the one who makes the first loan have priority? Or is it the first to file? Or the one who first procures the debtor's signature on a security agreement?

Particularly in the context of multiple advance lending (for example, "lines of credit" secured by inventory or accounts receivable) the pre-Code law was in conflict. Some rules gave the lender priority from the time he filed or did some other perfecting act; other rules measured the priority only from the time of the advance,

---

Co., 302 F.Supp. 958, 6 UCC Rep.Serv. 1137 (D.Ore.1969), the holder of a pre-Code chattel mortgage on trucks filed by recording in the appropriate county prior to the effective date of the Code and was thus superior to the rights of a perfected party secured under Article Nine. (However, the rights of a buyer who purchased the mortgaged goods from the debtor six months after the effective date of the Code were determined by the UCC and not pre-Code law.) A similar result was obtained in August v. Poznanski, 383 Mich. 151, 174 N.W.2d 807, 7 UCC Rep.Serv. 739 (1970), where the court decided that possession of mortgaged chattels by the mortgagee one month before the effective date of the Code entitled it to priority over an unrecorded chattel mortgage as well as the mortgagor's trustee in bankruptcy under sections 9–301, 9–302, 9–305, and 9–312. However, in Albany Discount Corp. v. Mohawk Nat'l, 54 Misc.2d 238, 282 N.Y.S.2d 401, 4 UCC Rep.Serv. 669 (Sup.Ct.1967), modified 30 App.Div.

2d 623, 290 N.Y.S.2d 576, aff'd, 30 App.Div.2d 919, 292 N.Y.S.2d 300, aff'd, 28 N.Y.2d 222, 269 N.E.2d 809, 321 N.Y.S.2d 94, the court noted that a perfected pre-Code purchase money security interest continued perfected past the effective date of the Code in New York (September 27, 1964). But when that original filing lapsed in May, 1965, the secured party failed to renew such that a subsequent Code perfected security interest (February, 1966) was allowed priority under the Code.

3. Thus the courts need not grapple with the problem of determining whether, for example, the rules for a chattel mortgage or the rules for conditional sales within the state will apply. The Code eliminates the issue by providing for a single device replacing the assorted pre-Code security interests. Of course, the problem of determining whether a security interest was created still remains.

the time the loan was actually made. As we will see, the Code draftsmen chose the former approach and they stated the rules in 9–312(5)
with precision:

> In all cases not governed by other rules stated in this sec-
> tion (including cases of purchase money security interests
> which do not qualify for the special priorities set forth in
> subsections (3) and (4) of this section), priority between
> conflicting security interests in the same collateral shall be
> determined as follows:
>
> > (a) in the order of filing if both are perfected by filing,
> > regardless of which security interest attached first un-
> > der Section 9—204(1) and whether it attached before or
> > after filing;
> >
> > (b) in the order of perfection unless both are perfected
> > by filing, regardless of which security interest attached
> > first under Section 9—204(1) and, in the case of a filed
> > security interest, whether it attached before or after
> > filing; and
> >
> > (c) in the order of attachment under Section 9—204(1)
> > so long as neither is perfected.

Note first that the subsection is a pure race statute. That is,
the one who wins the "race" to the court house to file is superior
without regard to the state of his knowledge. The section nowhere
requires that the victor be without knowledge of his competitor's
claim. Example three in Comment four illustrates the irrelevance
of knowledge under the subsection.[4] One justification for such a rule
is the certainty it affords. Under 9–312(5) no disappointed secured
creditor can trump up facts from which a compassionate court might
find knowledge on the part of the competitor. If the competitor
filed first or perfected first, as the case may be, that's the end of it;
he wins even if he knew of the other party's prior but unperfected
claim.[5]

---

4. § 9–312(5), Comment 4, Example 3:

A has a temporarily perfected (21 day)
security interest, unfiled, in a negotiable document in the debtor's possession under Section 9–304(4) or (5).
On the fifth day B files and thus
perfects a security interest in the same
document. On the tenth day A files.
A has priority, whether or not he
knows of B's interest when he files.

The result follows from subsection
(6) which classifies security interests
according to the manner of their initial perfection. The case therefore
falls under subsection (5) (b) and not
under (5) (a); A prevails because his
interest was first perfected although
B was first to file.

5. A rather extreme example appears
in First Nat'l Bank & Trust Co. v.
Atlas Credit Corp., 417 F.2d 1081, 6
UCC Rep.Serv. 1223 (10th Cir. 1969).
The bank loaned money and filed a
financing statement in 1963 but failed
to execute a security agreement. Subsequently a finance company made an
advance, executed a security agreement, and filed a financing statement
in 1964. In 1965 the Bank made a
secured loan and finally executed a
security agreement. Despite knowledge of the intervening perfected security interest taken by the finance
company, the court concluded that the
first to file rule gave priority to the
bank. Accord, In re Smith, 326 F.
Supp. 1311, 9 UCC Rep.Serv. 549 (D.

Because the draftsmen chose to permit perfection by possession and by other non-filing acts, they could not simply give priority to the first to file. However they went as far as possible in that direction and 9–312(5) (a) is the result: the first to file wins if both perfect by filing. Since filing is a public act the timing of which can be proved with accuracy from public records, it is the most certain and satisfactory of the measuring points for priority.

One should understand that the draftsmen meant "filing": not more and not less. Assume for example that an unscrupulous debtor is simultaneously negotiating with two creditors; one files long before he agrees to lend, and then the other lends and files. At that point the second has a perfected security interest under 9–204 et seq. but the first creditor has no interest at all, for he has neither lent nor agreed to do so. But assume that the first creditor then signs an agreement, lends and so becomes a perfected secured creditor. Who wins and why? Although the first creditor was the second to become perfected (recall "perfection" requires "attachment" and attachment requires that the creditor give value) he filed first and he wins. The second creditor has no meritorious complaint, for he could have checked the files and so saved himself.[6] And the rule is a convenient one for lenders who plan to make a series of advances. Comment four to 9–312 puts it as follows:

> The justification for the rule lies in the necessity of protecting the filing system—that is, of allowing the secured party who has first filed to make subsequent advances without each time having, as a condition of protection, to check for filings later than his.

Note that the lender's priority as to all advances dates back to the time of filing.[7]

The courts and the writers have discovered only two blemishes on (5) (a)'s countenance. One has clear if modest practical significance; the other problem appears largely if not totally academic. The first concerns whether a creditor enjoys priority from the time of his first filing under (5) (a) if his security agreement con-

---

Minn.1971); Bloom v. Hilty, 427 Pa. 463, 234 A.2d 860, 4 UCC Rep.Serv. 821 (1967).

**6.** First Nat'l Bank & Trust Co. v. Atlas Credit Corp., 417 F.2d 1081, 6 UCC Rep.Serv. 1223 (10th Cir. 1969).

Of course, the financing statement will perfect an interest only in the listed collateral. A federal district court in In re Mann, 318 F.Supp. 32, 8 UCC Rep.Serv. 132 (W.D.Va.1970) limited the priority in this way. A bank filed a financing statement and then executed various trust mortgages. Sub-

sequently the Small Business Administration perfected a security interest in similar collateral. The court limited the bank's priority to the collateral described in the trust receipts rather than applying an expansive interpretation that would have given priority to all the collateral described in the financing statement.

**7.** See Coogan, Article 9 of the Uniform Commercial Code: Priorities Among Secured Creditors and the "Floating Lien," 72 Harv.L.Rev. 838, 857–61 (1959).

templates not a series of advances but rather a one-shot deal.[8]  In Coin-O-Matic Service Co. v. Rhode Island Hospital Trust Co.[9] the Rhode Island superior court held that a second loan did not take its priority from the time the original financing statement was filed where the original security agreement did not provide for future advances.  The case now stands as a minority of one; other courts have held that priority on later advances dates from the first filing even though the original agreement contemplated only one loan.[10] The Rhode Island court apparently feared that a creditor could unduly restrict a debtor's power to borrow if the creditor's rights as to all advances dated from his original filing.  We reject the Coin-O-Matic holding for three reasons.  First, it provides little protection against overreaching, for a creditor can avoid the holding simply by including a future advance clause in his security agreement.  Second, we suspect that the Coin-O-Matic court misunderstands commercial practice.  We suspect that it is a rare banker who will lend against the same collateral which secures a prior loan; in our experience the commercial practice is for the second lender to pay off the first and so take a first priority as to all of the collateral.  Finally, Coin-O-Matic conflicts with the most obvious and we think intended meaning of 9–312(5) (a); if the draftsmen had wished to qualify the rule as the Coin-O-Matic court did, they could have done so.  In summary it appears that Coin-O-Matic may have been aberrational, for other courts have not followed it.  A cautious lawyer can protect himself even in Rhode Island by providing for subsequent advances in his security agreement.[11]

The second and largely academic but truly intriguing problem of 9–312(5) (a) was first raised by Professor Henson.[12]  The basic issue is whether 9–306 or 9–312(5) governs certain priority disputes. The following hypothetical case poses problem: Bank lends against debtor's accounts receivable and files a financing statement.  Later

8.  Where the security agreement contemplates a series of advances all courts have held that the first to file rule of 9–312(5) (a) gives priority from the filing and none has suggested any other rule.

9.  3 UCC Rep.Serv. 1112 (R.I.Super.Ct. 1966).

10.  Household Fin. Corp. v. Bank Commissioner of Maryland, 248 Md. 233, 235 A.2d 732, 4 UCC Rep.Serv. 809 (1967) (termination of old financing statement and filing new one would unduly disrupt priorities); In re Merriman, 4 UCC Rep.Serv. 234 (Ref.Dec. S.D.Ohio 1967) (secured party remains continuously perfected); In re Rivet, 299 F.Supp. 374, 6 UCC Rep.Serv. 460 (Ref.Dec.E.D.Mich.1969) (secured party continuously perfected despite several refinancings).

11.  The Rhode Island court explicitly limits its decision to the situation where the security agreement did not, in terms, provide for future advances. Thus the court says that "a single financing statement in connection with a security agreement when no provision is made for future advances is not an umbrella for future advances based upon new security agreements, notwithstanding the fact that involved is the same collateral." 3 UCC Rep. Serv. at 1120.  The court had similarly noted that "a lender can protect against the situation involved herein by providing in the original security agreement for future advances." Id. at 1117.

12.  Henson, "Proceeds" Under the Uniform Commercial Code, 65 Colum.L. Rev. 232, 239 (1965).

Finance Company lends against debtor's "inventory and proceeds." Of course Finance Company's "proceeds" are Bank's "accounts receivable" and we have a priority conflict. Bank will argue that both perfected by filing and that it wins under 9–312(5) (a) as first to file. Finance company responds that 9–306(3) governs and gives it the same priority in the proceeds it had in inventory, namely first priority. Moreover Finance Company will point to the reference to 9–306 in 9–312(1) and will argue that the reference subordinates 9–312(5) (a) to 9–306. The Bank will respond first that 9–306(3) is only a perfection and not a priority provision and secondly that the 9–312(1) reference to 9–306 applies only to 9–306(5), a subsection which does govern priority in some cases.

Who wins? For several reasons we are persuaded that 9–312(5) governs and that the first to file is victorious. First, we believe that the words of 9–306(3) and 9–312(5) point to 9–312 as controlling. Clearly the latter is a priority provision; no words in the former show it to be anything but a statement that a certain interest is perfected. Second, finding that 9–312(5) governs the priority dispute would be consistent with the policies stated in the comments of 9–312(5), namely that of permitting a lender to check the files once, file a financing statement and make successive loans without further reference to the filing system. If 9–306 governed the priority, such a lender against accounts would be in constant danger of being unseated by one who filed after him. A final reason for favoring 9–312 as the solution to the problem is that such an outcome facilitates accounts lending, a type of lending which is apparently of greater importance and of more commercial significance than is lending against inventory.[13]

Apart from the two blemishes discussed above, 9–312(5) (a), the first to file rule, seems a thoroughly satisfactory and workable general rule. If both of the parties perfected by filing, subsection (5) (a) usually establishes the priority, and we pass on to (5) (b) only when one interest is not perfected or when one interest has been perfected by a method other than filing. Such cases can arise in the case of a purchase money interest in consumer goods (perfected without filing or any other act) [14] or in the case of perfection by possession under 9–305 [15] or in several of the other cases specified in 9–304. In all such cases the parties take priority "in order of perfection."

---

13. See Weiss, Original Collateral and Proceeds a Code Puzzle, 42 N.Y.U.L. Rev. 785 (1967). See further, text accompanying note 44 infra.

14. § 9–302(1) (d).

15. In Foley Machinery Co. v. John T. Brady Co., Inc., 62 Misc.2d 777, 310 N.Y.S.2d 49, 7 UCC Rep.Serv. 872 (Sup.Ct.1970), plaintiff sold a "traxcavator," executed a security agreement, and filed. The equipment was later moved from New Jersey to a construction site in New York, where a subcontract was executed creating a security interest in the machinery on behalf of the general contractor. On default of the subcontract, the general contractor took possession of the traxcavator and so perfected his interest. The court properly resolved the priority conflict in favor of the party who had filed; that filing antedated the possession by the second secured party.

Because the nonfiling perfecting act may be a secret one, a court's job in a (5) (b) case is somewhat more difficult that in the (5) (a) case. To that end it is perhaps useful to recall the implication in 9–303 that no security interest is perfected until it has "attached." Of course no security interest attaches under 9–204 until there is agreement, the creditor has given value, and the debtor has rights in the collateral. The consequence of the rule stated in the two foregoing sentences is that one may file a financing statement but not be "perfected" until long after the filing. Thus, for example, if Bank filed a financing statement which covered all of Johnny's household goods, Johnny subsequently purchased certain household goods and only after that time Bank made a loan against the household goods, the seller (if he retained the security interest at the time of sale) would have a prior right under 9–312(5) (b) because his interest would have been perfected at the time of the sale, but the Bank's would not have been perfected until it gave value at the time of making the loan. Of course the seller in that case could also claim under 9–312(4) as a purchase money lender.[16]

Although some have argued that a lender who perfects other than by filing (e. g. taking possession of stock) and then makes a series of advances does not take priority as to all of the advances from the date he first took possession and first lent (i. e. first perfection), we believe that such loans should not be treated as a series of new security interests, individually perfected, but as one expanding security interest first perfected when all of the conditions of 9–204 and 9–305 were met as to the first advance. In our judgment the priority of later advances relates back to the time of perfection of the first, and we believe this is so whether the advances were obligatory or not.[17] If one regards each subsequent advance as a new security interest, and lender was under no obligation to make such new advance, then the creditor would not have given "value" as to that specific advance until he had, in fact, made the loan, and he would not be perfected until that time. Such a result would be an unwarranted departure from the rule clearly set down in the same circumstances under (5) (a) (namely, priority as to later advances relates back to the time of first filing).

If one exercises his imagination, he can devise a number of intriguing and thoroughly unimportant questions about 9–312(5) (b). Consider, for example, the case in which creditor one files a financing statement as to "inventory" but not as to proceeds. Subsequently, a second creditor files a financing statement as to "accounts receivable." Some of the inventory is sold; accounts arise, and both parties claim the accounts. The second creditor claims under his financing

---

16. See the discussion of purchase money interests section 25–5 infra.

17. Professor Gilmore agrees with this treatment. 2 G. Gilmore, Security Interests in Personal Property § 35.7 (1965) (hereinafter cited as Gilmore).

However, a contrary view is held by Coogan, Article 9 of the Uniform Commercial Code: Priorities Among Secured Creditors and the "Floating Lien," 72 Harv.L.Rev. 838, 852, 867–68 (1959).

statement, and the first creditor claims under the automatic ten-day perfection provision contained in 9–306(3) (b). Thus, we have a priority dispute between two parties, one of whom has filed as to the collateral and the other has not. The case is governed, therefore, by 9–312(5) (b), and who has priority? The answer, or so it seems to us, is that neither has priority. The time of perfection for each was simultaneous, namely the point in time at which the debtor acquired "rights" in the collateral. That time, undoubtedly, was the time of sale of the inventory when the accounts receivable came into existence. Let that hypothetical case be a reminder that one who would deal effectively with 9–312(5) (b) must often consider 9–204 and the perfection provisions in Part 3 of Article Nine. Finally one should understand that (5) (b) will control the many cases in which only one of the two contestants has a perfected security interest. By hypothesis he has perfected first and wins under (5) (b) against one who has never perfected.

The cleanup provision in 9–312(5) is subsection (c) which gives priority "in order of attachment" when neither is perfected. Subsection (c) should be little used, and it poses no complications with which we have not already dealt.

One should not leave 9–312(5) without a passing comment on 9–312(6). That subsection reads in full as follows:

> For the purpose of the priority rules of the immediately preceding subsection, a continuously perfected security interest shall be treated at all times as if perfected by filing if it was originally so perfected and it shall be treated at all times as if perfected otherwise than by filing if it was originally perfected otherwise than by filing.

Since the method of perfection will in some cases determine whether a court uses subsection (a) or subsection (b) of 9–312(5), one needs a rule to tell him which subsection to use in a case in which the secured party has perfected his security interest in two different ways at different times. Subsection (6), of course, is the rule, and it tells us that one looks to the method "originally" used to perfect.

In a document dated April 25, 1971, the Review Committee for Article Nine of the Permanent Editorial Board for the Uniform Commercial Code submitted its final report on proposals for change in Article Nine. Included in the report were a series of suggested amendments to 9–312. These amendments do not cause fundamental change in 9–312; mostly they address the pesky ambiguities in 9–312 we have discussed above.[18]

18. The first recommendation merely simplifies subsection (1) of 9–312. It reads:

The rules of priority stated in other sections of this Part and in the following sections shall govern when applicable: Section 4–208 with respect to the security interests of collecting banks in items being collected, accompanying documents and proceeds; Section 9–103 on security interests related to other jurisdictions; Section 9–114 on consignments.

Permanent Editorial Board for the Uniform Commercial Code, Review Committee for Article 9, Final Report 110

To resolve the largely academic question about priority in the case in which one creditor's interest in proceeds is perfected automatically for ten days and another's is perfected by filing, the case in which one could argue that no one was perfected until the proceeds arose and the debtor had rights in the collateral, the draftsmen have proposed a new subsection (6).[19] This subsection will provide that filing or perfection as to collateral is also to be regarded (for the purposes of subsection (5)) as the date of filing or perfection as to proceeds.[20]

The new subsection (5) (a) does the work of the current (5) (a) and (b). It reads in full as follows:

> Conflicting security interests rank according to priority in time of filing or perfection. Priority dates from the time a filing is first made covering the collateral or the time the security interest is first perfected, whichever is earlier, provided there is no period thereafter when there is neither filing nor perfection.

The new subsection has the virtue of producing a consistent result in at least one case in which the current (5) (a) and (5) (b) produce different results for no apparent reason. Under the current rules, the first to file beats all subsequent filers irrespective of the time of perfection, but if he files and does not perfect and a second creditor perfects by means other than filing, under the current (5) (b), the second in time will have the first right. Under the new (5) (a), the first to file will be victorious not only over those who claim by filing after him but also over those who perfect by means other than filing, and he will be superior even if he perfects after his competitor.

(1971) (hereinafter cited as Review Committee for Article 9).

19. Newly Recommended § 9–312(6) reads as follows:

For the purposes of subsection (5) a date of filing or perfection as to collateral is also a date of filing or perfection as to proceeds.

Id. at 113.

20. However, the Reasons for Change indicate that this principle is subject to the limitations in the proposed 9–306(3). It reads:

The security interest in proceeds is a continuously perfected security interest if the interest in the original collateral was perfected but it ceases to be a perfected security interest and becomes unperfected ten days after receipt of the proceeds by the debtor unless

(a) a filed financing statement covers the original collateral and the proceeds are collateral in which a security interest may be perfected by filing in the office or offices where the financing statement has been filed and, if the proceeds are acquired with cash proceeds, the description of collateral in the financing statement indicates the types of property constituting the proceeds; or

(b) a filed financing statement covers the original collateral and the proceeds are identifiable cash proceeds; or

(c) the security interest in the proceeds is perfected before the expiration of the ten-day period.

Except as provided in this section, a security interest in proceeds can be perfected only by the methods or under the circumstances permitted in this Article for original collateral of the same type.

Id. at 95–96.

By new subsection (7),[21] the draftsmen have made explicit what was implicit to all reasonable men under the old 9-312(5), namely, that future advances made while the security interest is perfected by filing or by the taking of possession relate back to the original date of filing or taking of possession. The subsection also sets up a rule for the unusual case in which the secured party making the subsequent advance is temporarily perfected without filing or possession. Such a creditor does not benefit from the relation back rule unless his subsequent advances are made pursuant to a "commitment."

One should note that the proposed amendments to Article Nine will cause a substantial change in the relative priority between one who makes subsequent advances and a lien creditor who intervenes between two of those advances.[22]

We believe that the proposed amendments to 9-312 can be fairly characterized as cosmetic changes. We suspect that some of the problems they address exist only in the minds of nervous corporate counsel and of law review writers.

### § 25-5   Basic Priorities—Second in Time, First in Right, Purchase Money Security Interests, 9-312(3) and (4)

A party claiming a purchase money security interest will often be the seller of a product who has retained a security interest in it, but he may also be a financier who has lent the money for debtor's purchase of the collateral. "Purchase money security interests" enjoy a priority (provided they comply with the pertinent terms of the priority statute) over certain interests which preceded them in time. Why this special priority? First and least persuasive, purchase money lenders enjoyed special priority under pre-Code property law.[23] Secondly, one can argue that a seller should not be obliged to check the filings with respect to his purchaser in order to sustain his priority as to goods he himself owns and proposes to sell. As we shall see, the strength of this argument is somewhat diminished by the fact that a purchase money lender against inventory must, in fact, make

---

21. Newly Recommended § 9-312(7) reads:

> If future advances are made while a security interest is perfected by filing or the taking of possession, the security interest has the same priority for the purposes of subsection (5) with respect to the future advances as it does with respect to the first advance. If a commitment is made before or while the security interest is so perfected, the security interest has the same priority with respect to advances made pursuant thereto. In other cases a perfected security interest has priority from the date the advance is made.

Id. at 113.

22. Newly Recommended § 9-301(4) provides:

> A person who becomes a lien creditor while a security interest is perfected takes subject to the security interest only to the extent that it secures advances made before he becomes a lien creditor or within 45 days thereafter or made without knowledge of the lien or pursuant to a commitment entered into without knowledge of the lien.

Id. at 78.

23. See 3 N.Y. State Law Revision Comm'n, 1955 Report 2062 (1955).

such inspection to qualify for the special priority given him under 9–312(3). Finally, and most persuasive, is the argument that the debtor needs some protection from a creditor who has filed a financing statement with respect to his goods, but who is unwilling to advance additional funds. If such a debtor can find a lender willing to finance a new line of merchandise, the purchase money provisions enable him to give that new lender a first claim on the new merchandise notwithstanding a prior filing by another creditor. Thus, the purchase money provisions give the debtor somewhat greater bargaining power and at least theoretically enlarge his ability to get credit.

The threshold question under subsections three and four of 9–312 concerns the meaning of "purchase money security interest." That phrase is defined by 9–107 which reads in full as follows:

A security interest is a "purchase money security interest" to the extent that it is

(a) taken or retained by the seller of the collateral to secure all or part of its price; or

(b) taken by a person who by making advances or incurring an obligation gives value to enable the debtor to acquire rights in or the use of collateral if such value is in fact so used.

The secured parties described in subsection (a) are familiar: a seller of a refrigerator who retains the security interest for part of the price, a seller of an automobile who retains a security interest to secure the price, and so on; in short, the 9–107(a) secured party is the old conditional vendor, a seller who has, in effect, made a loan by selling goods on credit. Although the Code does not define the word "seller," we anticipate no trouble for courts in applying subsection (a).[24] Note that trouble can arise if the seller sells a variety of items to the buyer under a cross-collateral provision whereby the price of one item is secured, not only by that item, but by other items as well (see Section 4–2). Under 9–107(a) and under the cases the seller does not have a purchase money interest to the extent his debt is secured by goods other than those he sold.[25]

Subsection (b) of 9–107 describes a less familiar but equally important transaction in which a lender agrees to lend money to a debtor so that he may, for example, buy a new line of merchandise or purchase some new equipment. To insure that the pearly gates leading to a purchase money lender's Valhalla are not open too wide, the Code draftsmen have drafted 9–107(b) rather narrowly. First, the lender must have given "value" by making advances or incurring an

---

**24.** See 2 Gilmore 941.

**25.** Similarly, a purchase money security interest taken to secure only a part of the purchase price will receive priority to that extent. For example, the court in In re Laue, 8 UCC Rep.

Serv. 420 (D.R.I.1970), decided that $200 advanced by a finance company for a down payment on an automobile was a valid basis for a purchase money security interest for that amount even though the total value of the automobile was nearly $3,000.

obligation. Comment 2 tells us that this requirement excludes from the purchase money category "any security interest taken as security for or in satisfaction of a pre-existing claim or antecedent debt." Second, the value must have been "to enable the debtor to acquire rights in or the use of collateral," and third, such value must have been "in fact so used." How, for example, does a creditor prove after the fact how the debtor really used the dollars made available to him? How, moreover, does one prove that the value was given for the purpose of enabling the debtor to acquire rights in specific collateral? Before we turn to difficult problems, consider how a planner might carry out such a transaction to avoid trouble. If he is wise, he will arrange to make his loan in the form of a check payable directly to the seller of the goods. If his debtor will not permit that, he may disburse the loan proceeds in the form of a check payable jointly to the order of the debtor and the seller of the goods. In either case the cancelled check will evidence the purpose for which the loan was intended and the way in which it was, in fact, used.

Turning first to the "enabling" requirement, consider two cases Professor Gilmore poses.[26] One is the case in which a debtor acquires goods on unsecured credit from the seller and, thereafter, borrows the price from a third party who claims a purchase money security interest in the goods. In the second case, the buyer pays the price of the goods but shortly thereafter borrows the amount of the price from a secured party. Can a creditor satisfy the "enabling" requirement when the debtor acquires the goods first and then procures the loan? Professor Gilmore argues that

> . . . [A] court could reasonably find that the secured party had acquired a purchase-money interest. If the loan transaction appears to be closely allied to the purchase transaction, that should suffice. The evident intent of paragraph (b) is to free the purchase-money concept from artificial limitations; rigid adherence to particular formalities in sequences should not be required.[27]

So much for the problems lurking in the enabling requirement.

If our lender is not careful and cannot produce a cancelled check which shows that his loan in fact passed into the hands of the seller of the goods, how does he prove that the loan was "in fact so used"? No cases to date tell us whether the lender must trace the dollars into the hands of the seller, or indicate whether he can make use of fictional tracing methods (e. g., first in, first out; last in, first out). At minimum the statutory history of 9–107 tells us that the lender had better come up with proof of how the debtor used the loan proceeds.

The 1952 official draft of 9–107 included three subsections. The third of these provided that a security interest would be a purchase money security interest if taken by a person who made advances or

26.　2 Gilmore 782.　　　　　27.　Id. at 782.

incurred an obligation not more than 10 days before or after the debtor received possession of the collateral and for the purpose of enabling the debtor to pay for or acquire rights in or the use of collateral even though the value given was not in fact used to pay the price. The last sentence of the 1952 official comment (1) reads:

> To eliminate difficulties of tracing, a conclusive presumption is established that money advanced to a buyer ten days before or after receipt of the collateral is a purchase money loan whether or not such money was in fact used to pay the price if the purpose of the advance was to enable the debtor to acquire the collateral.

In 1955 the Editorial Board deleted subsection (c).[28] Their reasons were as follows:

> "The Subcommittee on Article 9 and the Editorial Board has concluded that subparagraph (c) extends the purchase money concept too far. In addition, the subparagraph creates very difficult problems in the determination of priorities between conflicting security interests since it makes priorities in affected cases depend upon the accident of whose money, as between competing secured parties, was actually used."

The deletion of old subsection (c) should inspire skepticism in the mind of a court faced with a lender who claims to qualify under 9–107(b). Whether the courts will accept the old tracing methods remains to be seen. In many cases in which loan proceeds pass through the checking account of the debtor on which the purchase check was drawn, the lender will be able to produce evidence to show that at least some part of the loan proceeds went into the purchase price. Failing that (as in the case in which the debtor's checking account always contained more than enough money to purchase the goods in question) the creditor will have to hope that he can persuade a court to accept his FIFO [29] or LIFO or other tracing arguments.

### The Purchase Money Security Interest in Inventory

Section 9–312(3) states a special rule for purchase money interest in inventory. That subsection reads in full as follows:

A purchase money security interest in inventory collateral has priority over a conflicting security interest in the same collateral if

> (a) the purchase money security interest is perfected at the time the debtor receives possession of the collateral; and

---

28. Editorial Board for the Uniform Commercial Code 1956 Recommendations 262.

29. Cf. § 4–208(2).

(b) any secured party whose security interest is known to the holder of the purchase money security interest or who, prior to the date of the filing made by the holder of the purchase money security interest, had filed a financing statement covering the same items or type of inventory, has received notification of the purchase money security interest before the debtor receives possession of the collateral covered by the purchase money security interest; and

(c) such notification states that the person giving the notice has or expects to acquire a purchase money security interest in inventory of the debtor, describing such inventory by item or type.

If a party jumps through all the hoops listed above, a feat of some consequence, he takes "priority over a conflicting security interest in the same collateral. . . . " The subsection offers a variety of interpretive difficulties for the lawyer. First, what is inventory? Second, when has one "received notification"? Third, must the notification be in writing? Fourth, how often must one notify? Is once enough even though there will be a series of transactions between the purchase money lender and the debtor? A final question and the one with which we start our analysis is more fundamental: Why the notice requirement at all? Comment 3 to 9–312 explains:

The reason for the additional requirement of notification is that typically the arrangement between an inventory secured party and his debtor will require the secured party to make periodic advances against incoming inventory or periodic releases of old inventory as new inventory is received. A fraudulent debtor may apply to the secured party for advances even though he has already given a security interest in the inventory to another secured party. The notification requirement protects the inventory financer in such a situation: if he has received notification, he will presumably not make an advance; if he has not received notification (or if the other interest does not qualify as a purchase money interest), any advance he may make will have priority.

Returning to the questions posed above, what is inventory? Section 9–109(4) provides that goods are inventory

[I]f they are held by a person who holds them for sale or lease or to be furnished under contracts of service or if he has so furnished them, or if they are raw materials, work in process or materials used or consumed in a business. Inventory of a person is not to be classified as his equipment.

This definition departs from commonly held ideas about inventory in that it includes materials and work in process and also items held for lease. Thus, presumably, all of Hertz' rental cars are inventory, not equipment. A person who wishes to claim purchase money status should study 9–109(4) and the developing case law under it. If he is in doubt about the nature of the collateral, he should comply with 9–312(3), for any secured party who meets the stringent tests of 9–312(3) will also comply with 9–312(4) and be entitled to priority under that provision if a court ultimately determines that his collateral was not inventory.

If a creditor contemplates a series of purchase money transactions, how often must he send notice? Professor Gilmore argues persuasively that one notification is sufficient not only for the "immediate transaction but any other transactions subsequently entered into." [30]  Generally, one notice should serve the purpose of 9–312(3) by putting the prior lender on his guard against any subsequent claims of the debtor about his free and clear ownership of assets subsequently acquired. But difficult cases can arise. For example, should a notice under 9–312(3) be effective for a purchase money loan made more than five years after the notice is given? A financing statement would not be effective for more than five years,[31] and we see no reason why a notice should have a longer life than a financing statement. Secondly, what of the case in which a purchase money lender gives notice of his intention to lend but in fact makes no loans or sales to the debtor for two or three years? One can argue persuasively that if the immediate transaction contemplated at the time the notice is given falls through, and there is then a substantial gap between the notice and the first sale or loan by the purchase money lender, then he should be obliged to give a second notice.

May the notice be oral or must it be written? Of course no sensible businessman would intentionally rely upon an oral notification, he will give written notification under 9–312(3). If our purchase money lender does not dot his "i's" and cross his "t's," but simply makes a phone call to the prior lender, what result? Neither 9–312(3) nor subsections 25 or 26 of 1–201 state that the notification must be in writing. However, the phrase in 9–312(3) (c) "such notification states" certainly presents the image of a written notification. We conclude that 9–312(3) permits oral notification, but we would expect a court to be slow to rely upon an uncorroborated statement of the purchase money lender.[32]

### The Purchase Money Security Interest in Non-Inventory Collateral, 9–312(4)

Section 9–312(4) provides for the priority of a purchase money security interest in collateral other than inventory. It reads:

A purchase money security interest in collateral other than inventory has priority over a conflicting security inter-

30.  2 Gilmore 788–89.

31.  § 9–403(2).

32.  See G. A. C. Credit Corp. v. Small Business Administration, 323 F.Supp. 795 (W.D.Mo.1971) (notification by telephone sufficient to comply with 9–312).

est in the same collateral if the purchase money security interest is perfected at the time the debtor receives possession of the collateral or within ten days thereafter.

Much of what has been said above regarding the purchase money security interest in inventory collateral applies equally to subsection (4), and we will not repeat ourselves. However, 9–312(4) differs from 9–312(3) on time for perfection and notice. A purchase money security interest in collateral other than inventory must be "perfected at the time the debtor receives possession of the collateral or within ten days." Recall that a similar interest in inventory must be perfected at the time the debtor receives possession of the collateral. The Official 1952 Draft allowed a ten day grace period for perfection to all purchase money security interests.[33] In 1954 the Enlarged Editorial Board deleted the ten day period for both interests.[34] In 1958 however, a new Board reinserted the ten day period for the purchase money security interest in collateral other than inventory.[35] The Board believed that "the change . . . conforms to the business practice of filing after delivery in cases of purchase money security interests in collateral other than inventory." This ten day time period parallels a similar time for perfection in 9–301(2).[36] Thus 9–312(4) and 9–301(2) combine to assure the purchase money lender (secured by collateral other than inventory) who files within ten days of debtor's receipt of the collateral a priority over those with conflicting security interests, and over lien creditors.[37]

Unlike 9–312(3), section 9–312(4) does not impose a notice requirement.[38] Comment 3 explains this:

Since an arrangement for periodic advances against incoming property is unusual outside the inventory field, no notification requirement is included in subsection (4).

**33.** § 9–312(4) (1952 Official Draft) provides:

A purchase money security interest has priority over a conflicting interest in the same collateral which is claimed under an after-acquired property clause if the purchase money security interest is perfected at the time the debtor receives the collateral or within ten days thereafter . . . .

**34.** Supplement No. 1 to the 1952 Official Draft of Text and Comments of the UCC, 1952 Recommendation of the Enlarged Editorial Board for Amendments of Text, 75 (1955).

**35.** The 1958 draft of 9–312(4) is identical to the current draft.

**36.** See the discussion of 9–301(2) in Section 25–2 supra.

**37.** Numerous cases illustrate the priority often extended to purchase money security interests. See, e. g., Brodie Hotel Supply Co. v. United States, 431 F.2d 1316, 8 UCC Rep.Serv. 113 (9th Cir. 1970) (purchase money security interest in restaurant equipment).

**38.** Of course, knowledge by a purchase money lender that another claims a security interest in after-acquired property of the kind covered by the purchase money interest will not disturb the priority granted by 9–312(4). In Noble Co. v. Mack Financial Corp., 264 A.2d 325, 7 UCC Rep.Serv. 842 (1970), the debtor traded two trucks subject to a security interest to defendant in partial payment for two new trucks. Defendant apparently reserved and filed to protect a purchase money security interest. The prior secured party claimed an interest in

Thus under 9–312(4), one who, for example, sells equipment, retains a security interest to secure some or all of the price, and files a financing statement within ten days after the debtor "receives possession" takes priority over conflicting security interests without giving the notice required of those who claim purchase money interests in inventory under subsection (3).

Finally, what rule governs priority if the purchase money lender fails to comply with subsections (3) or (4) or if each of two lenders does comply with (3) or (4)? The former case is clearly governed by subsection (5),[39] and we believe the latter is governed by (5) as well. The first sentence of subsection (5) states that it includes "cases of purchase money security interests which do not qualify for the special priorities set forth in subsections (3) and (4). . . ." If one does not meet one of the conditions in (3) or (4), he "does not qualify," but is the same true if he *and* his competitor do meet the tests of (3) or (4)? We believe so. If Bank lends the downpayment, seller lends the rest and each file within ten days, both (and therefore neither) are "entitled to the special priority" in subsection (4). Although one might argue that such creditors should share pro rata and neither receive priority, we believe that the proper rule is to go to the subsection (5) residuary clause and award priority to the winner there.[40]

Two of our questions about purchase money interests in inventory (9–312(3)) will be resolved by the 1971 Permanent Editorial Board proposals for amending section 9–312(3).[41] The new sub-

---

the new trucks as proceeds, but such interest was found subordinate under 9–312(4).

**39.** Mammoth Cave Production Credit Ass'n v. York, 429 S.W.2d 26, 5 UCC Rep.Serv. 11 (Ky.1968) (lender acquired security interest in "all farm equipment" and "all property similar to that listed;" subsequently another lender acquired purchase money interest in tractor but did not file within ten days; held: 9–312(5) governs the priority).

**40.** In Framingham U. A. W. Credit Union v. Dick Russell Pontiac, Inc., 41 Mass.App.Dec. 146, 7 UCC Rep.Serv. 252 (1969), a credit union that had advanced funds for the purchase of an automobile and the automobile dealer who sold the product under a conditional sales contract were found to have purchase money security interests in the automobile. In Massachusetts no filing is necessary to perfect a purchase money interest in an automobile. Thus the dealer had priority under 9–312(5) (b), because his interest attached and was thus simultaneously

perfected with the sale, whereas the credit union's interest failed to attach until the moment the debtor acquired title.

**41.** Newly Recommended § 9–312(3) reads:

A perfected purchase money security interest in inventory has priority over a conflicting security interest in the same inventory and also has priority in identifiable cash proceeds received on or before the delivery of the inventory to a buyer if

(a) the purchase money security interest is perfected at the time the debtor receives possession of the inventory; and

(b) the purchase money secured party gives notification in writing to the holder of the conflicting security interest if the holder had filed a financing statement covering the same types of inventory (i) before the date of the filing made by the purchase money secured party, or (ii) before the beginning of the 21 day period where the purchase money security interest is tempo-

section requires that notice of intent to take a purchase money security interest be in writing.[42] Secondly, the subsection provides that the notice is good for five years.[43] That is to say, the purchase money lender need give a written notice to a given creditor only once; he may then make unlimited purchase money loans within the next five years in conformity with 9–312(3) although he gives only one notice.

The new draft also resolves the "Henson" problem discussed above.[44] When one creditor takes a security interest in accounts receivable, and subsequently another creditor lends against inventory and proceeds, some have argued that the second lender achieves priority over the first not only as to the inventory but also as to the proceeds. The new subsection (3) gives the purchase money lender priority in his inventory and in "identifiable cash proceeds received on or before the delivery of the inventory to a buyer. . . ." By negative implication the subsection subordinates the purchase money lender as to account proceeds. Under the newly proposed 9–312, the conflict between the account lender and the purchase money lender against inventory would be resolved under 9–312(5), and the first to file or perfect would win; thus, the purchase money lender is deprived of any special priority.

When the collateral is not inventory, the new subsection (4) gives a different result.[45] That subsection gives the purchase money lender priority not only as to the collateral but also as to "its proceeds." In their reasons for change, the draftsmen describe this difference as follows:

> Here, where it is not ordinarily expected that the collateral will be sold and that proceeds will result, it seems appropriate to give the party having a purchase money security in-

rarily perfected without filing or possession (subsection (5) of Section 9–304); and

(c) the holder of the conflicting security interest receives the notification within five years before the debtor receives possession of the inventory; and

(d) the notification states that the person giving the notice has or expects to acquire a purchase money security interest in inventory of the debtor, describing such inventory by item or type.

Review Committee for Article 9, 111–12.

42. Note that this amendment would change the result reached in G. A. C. Credit Corp. v. Small Business Administration, 323 F.Supp. 795, 8 UCC Rep. Serv. 952 (W.D.Mo.1971.)

43. The Reasons for Change indicate that "five years has been chosen by analogy to the duration of a financing statement." See Review Committee for Article 9, 113.

44. See text acompanying notes 11–13 supra.

45. Newly Recommended § 9–312(4) reads:

A purchase money security interest in collateral other than inventory has priority over a conflicting security interest in the same collateral or its proceeds if the purchase money security interest is perfected at the time the debtor receives possession of the collateral or within ten days thereafter.

Review Committee for Article 9, 112.

terest in the original collateral an equivalent priority in its proceeds.[46]

It is not clear to us why it "seems appropriate" to arrive at the result, but there it is: the purchase money lender against inventory cannot extend his special priority into most of his proceeds; the purchase money lender against non-inventory collateral can extend his special priority.

## § 25–6  Basic Priorities—Security Interests in Crops, 9–312(2)

Crops are one of the important intersections between real property security law and personal property security law.  The landlord may claim a lien on the crops; many, perhaps most, real property mortgages claim rents, profits, and crops and, of course, a variety of lenders may take security interests under Article Nine in crops.  The complexity of the problem is equal to that presented with respect to fixtures and dealt with in 9–313.  As we will see in the pages to follow, the draftsmen endeavored to codify priority disputes with respect to fixtures; apparently they lacked the will or the courage to tackle the analogous crop problem.  Artice Nine as a whole and 9–312(2) in particular have compounded the confusion under the pre-Code law with respect to crops, and except in a few instances provide no certain priority rules.[47]

Subsection 9–312(2) gives priority to perfected[48] security interests in crops in a limited circumstance in which:

(1) The creditor gave "new value"[49]

---

**46.**  Review Committee for Article 9, 114.

**47.**  See 2 Gilmore §§ 32.2, 32.3.

**48.**  A security interest cannot be perfected until it has attached (§ 9–303), and section 9–204 prescribes some specific rules for the attachment of a security interest in crops.  First, 9–204 (2) (a) provides that the debtor has no right (and therefore the security agreement cannot attach) "in crops until they are planted or otherwise become growing crops."  Thus even if a security agreement is signed and a loan made on January 1, a security interest cannot attach until the crops are planted, i. e., when the debtor acquires rights in the collateral.  Subsection (4) adds another limitation:

(4) No security interest attaches under an after-acquired property clause

(a) to crops which become such more than one year after the security agreement is executed except that a security interest in crops which is given in conjunction with a

lease or a land purchase or improvement transaction evidenced by a contract, mortgage or deed of trust may if so agreed attach to crops to be grown on the land concerned during the period of such real estate transaction. . . .

This subsection is aimed at invalidating long-term security interests in future crops, and it succeeds by simply providing that if the collateral (crops) does not "arise" in one year or less after the execution of the security agreement, the security interest itself will not "attach."  An exception is made when the interest in crops is given in conjunction with certain real estate transactions.  Section 9–204, Comment 6 points out the draftsmen's intention to continue the pattern of many state statutes in the drafting of 9–204(4) (a).

**49.**  The term, "new value," is explained in Comment 2 to section 9–108:

In this Section and in other sections of this Article the term "new value" is used but is left without statutory

(*2*) To enable the debtor to produce the crops during the production season,[50] and

(*3*) The value was given not more than "three months before the crops became growing crops by planting or otherwise."

The scope of this provision is carved down almost to insignificance by the last clause in it which provides that the security interest which meets the three tests above enjoys priority only over interests which secure "obligations due more than six months before the crops become growing crops. . . ." That is, subsection (2) entitles one to priority only over obligations more than six months overdue at the time the crops in question become growing crops.

Where the Code leaves other priority disputes is an open question. Professor Gilmore points out that under the pre-Code law a lender against crops would often, though not invariably, have priority over a prior real estate mortage even though the mortgage claimed the crops.[51] If such claims to crops embodied in real estate mortgages are to be regarded as security interests governed by the priority rules in 9–312, then that outcome will generally be reversed under the Code, for 9–312(5) will normally give priority to the first to file, namely to the real estate mortgagee. Professor Gilmore does not consider whether a clause on rents, profits and crops in a real estate mortgage creates a "security interest" governed by 9–312(5) and not by non-Code common law. Nothing in the definition of security interest in 1–201(37) prevents such a real estate mortgagee's claims from being classified as a security interest, but nothing in 1–201(37) intimates that the draftsmen intended such an interest to be regarded as a security interest. Doubtless courts in states like Iowa which regarded such interests under the pre-Code law as chattel mortgages will now regard such interests as security interests governed by Article Nine. In such states crop lenders will be obliged to obtain subordination agreements from prior mortgagees and landlords in order to be assured of priority. In other states which classify land mortgagees' claims against crops as something other than security interests, presumably priority disputes will be governed by non-Article Nine law, and the pre-existing common law rules will govern.

We well understand that we have not answered many questions that a real estate lawyer or a crop lender's lawyer can legitimately ask. In view of the confusion in Article Nine itself and the diversity of

---

definition. The several illustrations of "new value" given in the text of this Section (making an advance, incurring an obligation, releasing a perfected security interest) as well as the "purchase money security interest" definition in Section 9–107 indicate the nature of the concept. In other situations it is left to the courts to distinguish between "new" and "old" value, between present considerations and antecedent debt.

50. Presumably "the production season" means the season immediately following the loan.

51. 2 Gilmore § 32.3.

state common law rules on crop mortgages, we think it impossible to do justice to these questions in the space available.[52]

## § 25–7  Priorities in Fixtures Between Real Estate Claimants and Secured Creditors, 9–313

In general Article Nine does not deal with real estate security. The single most important exception to that rule is 9–313. That section governs the conflict between personal property interests in fixtures on the one hand and real property interests in fixtures on the other. This confluence of personal property and real property law has produced turbulent waters, waters upon which section 9–313 sails only with difficulty.[53]

Typical of the priority conflicts that we consider here are those which arise when a real estate mortgagee claims not only the real estate but also all "appurtenances, fixtures, buildings, equipment" (and so on in a list as long as his lawyer can devise). After the mortgage is on the property, the debtor purchases a furnace or a lathe or some other item which becomes a fixture on the real property subject to the real estate mortgage under state real property law. Of course, this single transaction comes in a dozen variants depending upon when the interests attached and when they were perfected. Section 9–313 purports to deal with most of the possible conflicts between the real and personal property claimants; as we shall see, it sometimes fails.[54] If the collateral in question is not a fixture but remains personal property despite its attachment to the real estate, priority is determined under 9–312, not 9–313.

## § 25–8  Fixtures—What Is a Fixture?

Wisely, we think, the draftsmen did not define the word "fixture." In the first sentence of 9–313(1) the draftsmen state that the rules of the section "do not apply to goods incorporated into a

---

**52.**  See 2 Gilmore §§ 32.1–32.5; Note, Secured Interests in Growing and Future-Growing Crops Under the Uniform Commercial Code, 49 Iowa L.Rev. 1269 (1964); Note, Agricultural Financing Under the UCC, 12 Ariz.L. Rev. 391 (1970); UCC Symposium Uniform Commercial Code, 22 U.Miami L. Rev. 1 (1967).

**53.**  Section 9–313 has suffered grievous injury at the hands of some state legislatures. California has completely omitted 9–313 from its version of the Code. Cal.Comm.Code (West 1964). Iowa likewise eliminates the section from the Iowa Code. Iowa Code Ann. § 554.9313 (1957). Ohio has reversed the order of priorities established in the uniform version of 9–313. Ohio Rev.Code § 1309.32 (1963). For more detailed discussion of Article Nine and

fixtures, see 2 Gilmore §§ 30.1–30.6; Coogan, Security Interests in Fixtures Under the Uniform Commercial Code, 75 Harv.L.Rev. 1319 (1962); Kripke, Fixtures Under the Uniform Commercial Code, 64 Colum.L.Rev. 44 (1964); Shanker, An Integrated Financing System for Purchase Money Collateral: A Proposed Solution to the Fixture Problem Under Section 9–313 of the UCC, 73 Yale L.J. 788 (1964).

**54.**  The problems encountered since enactment of 9–313 have prompted a redrafting of that section. See Review Comm'n for Article 9 of the UCC, Preliminary Draft No. 1 (1968) and Preliminary Draft No. 2 (1970) (hereinafter cited as Preliminary Draft No. 1 and Preliminary Draft No. 2); Review Committee for Article 9. See Section 25–11 infra.

structure in the manner of lumber, bricks, tile, cement, glass, metal work and the like and no security interest in them exists under this Article. . . ." Although Professor Gilmore has argued persuasively that the quoted language is not really a definition of a fixture,[55] it reads very much like a definition of the boundary between "pure" real property and fixtures. If one conceives "fixtures" as a central gray area which lies on a continuum from pure goods to pure real property, a definition of a fixture must have two aspects: It must distinguish the fixture from goods so fully incorporated as to become real property (a house) on the one side, and on the other side of the continuum it must distinguish the fixture from goods not sufficiently incorporated to become a fixture. Of course, the quoted phrase does nothing to define the boundary between fixtures and goods which have not been fully enough incorporated to be defined even as fixtures. It appears therefore that the "brick" classification consists of goods which have passed through and completely beyond the middle ground of fixtures and become so fully "incorporated" that they are not subject to the priority rules in 9–313, not subject to personal property security interests under Article Nine, and not under any circumstances subject to removal under 9–313(5). We do not share Professor Gilmore's concern that the line between such fully incorporated goods and fixtures will become a hard one to draw;[56] we suspect that the other line, that between goods and fixtures, the one to which 9–313 does not address itself, will prove more difficult for the courts to draw.

We do not propose to undertake a case-by-case analysis of the common law of fixtures. We seek only to outline the general principles in broad terms. Most courts start from the proposition that the status of goods as a fixture depends upon the intention of the parties.[57] Of course, "objective manifestations of intention" are the windows through which we view actual intent. One searching for such manifestations might ask:[58] What did the parties say in their agreement? How did they attach the goods to the realty? What is the relation between the parties? How is the operation of the goods related to the use of the real property? The search for objective manifestation is even more important if one wishes to bind a subsequent third party (such as a mortgagee) by the intention of the two prior parties. Although the courts pay lip service to the proposition that they are merely determining the parties' intent, and although they will occasionally hoist one party on the petard of his written agreement which specifies that goods are or are not to be regarded

---

**55.** 2 Gilmore § 30.2 at 812–14.

**56.** But cf. Dry Dock Sav. Bank v. DeGeorgio, 6 UCC Rep.Serv. 1278 (N.Y.Sup.Ct.1969) (trial required to determine whether security interest in aluminum siding is superior to prior real estate mortgage).

**57.** 5 American Law of Property § 19.3 at 16–19 (1952).

**58.** The factors mentioned in the text were first enunciated in the leading case on fixtures, Teaff v. Hewitt, 1 Ohio St. 511 (1853), which is discussed in 5 American Law of Property § 19.3 at 16–19 (1952).

as a fixture,[59] for a majority of the courts the answer to the question "What is a fixture?" ultimately depends upon the manifestation of intent. For most courts intent is most clearly manifested by the firmness with which the goods are affixed to the real estate and the amount of sweat that removal would entail.

The American Law of Property puts the matter as follows (emphasis added):

> In the United States, whether a given chattel becomes a fixture is said to depend on intention, but whether it is the unilateral intention of the annexor at the time of annexation, or the bilateral intention of the parties to some transaction relating to the chattel or to the land, and whether it is the actual intention, or the manifested intention, or the imputed intention, is not always clear.

> Part of the confusion comes from the various meanings ascribed to the term "fixture." Under the modern cases no more precise definition is possible than this: a fixture is a former chattel which, while retaining its separate physical identity, *is so connected with the realty that a disinterested observer would consider it a part thereof.*[60]

Some courts still recognize the institutional or integrated industrial plant doctrine under which all goods in a plant somehow associated with the operation of the real property (but not necessarily affixed at all) are considered "fixtures" because they are necessary to the functioning of the plant itself.[61] We do not attempt to inject order into this chaotic body of law. We wish only to alert the lawyer that there is more than one line of authority, and that he must examine the cases in his own state with care if he is to arrive at a reasonable guess about what is and what is not a fixture.

---

**59.** Cain v. Country Club Delicatessen, Inc., 25 Conn.Super. 327, 203 A.2d 441, 2 UCC Rep.Serv. 247 (1964) (rights of parties governed by conditional sales agreement which provided that equipment remained personalty).

**60.** 5 American Law of Property § 19.1 at 3–4 (1952).

**61.** For a full discussion of the institutional doctrine, see 5 American Law of Property § 19.4 (1952); Coogan, Fixtures—Uniformity in Words or in Fact?, 113 U.Pa.L.Rev. 1186, 1197–1206 (1965). If one lets his imagination fly, he can easily devise objective standards for determining what is and what is not a fixture. An excellent candidate for a certain rule is the half-inch formula. Under this formula anything which could be moved more than a half inch by one blow with a hammer weighing not more than five pounds and swung by a man weighing not more than 250 pounds would not be a fixture. Another formula might be the screwdriver-crescent-wrench-one-hour rule. Under such a rule anything affixed to the realty would be regarded as a fixture unless one man with a screwdriver and a crescent wrench could loosen it from the floor or wall within one hour. Of course, even our objective standards would meet difficulty in real life (would the item remain a fixture if after removal by the screwdriver and wrench there was no door large enough to allow it to exit from the building?).

## § 25-9   Fixtures—The Routine 9-313 Cases

One should first understand that neither 9-313 nor any other part of Article Nine purports to preempt the field with respect to creation or perfection of security interests in fixtures. The last sentence of 9-313(1) makes this point explicitly: "This Act does not prevent creation of an encumbrance upon fixtures or real estate pursuant to the law applicable to real estate." Therefore, if the real estate law of a particular state defines some object as a fixture and provides that a real estate mortgage attaches to such fixture,[62] the Code recognizes such an interest, and 9-313 only determines its priority vis-a-vis personal property interests. So beware; the lawyer who answers a 9-313 problem should first do his real property homework.

Section 9-313 is the most important part of the machinery the draftsmen devised to accommodate real and personal property security interests. Insofar as it is applicable, it should preempt the field with respect to priority conflicts as to fixtures. Section 9-401 is also relevant here and requires that a fixture claimant file his financing statement in the same place where the mortgage on the relevant real property would be recorded. The theory, of course, is to give notice of the fixture claimant's interest to subsequent real property claimants.

The structure of 9-313 differs considerably from that of 9-312 but its priority rules are similar to those in 9-312. Subsection 9-313 (2) is principally a purchase money security interest provision, a fact not made explicit in 9-313.[63] With certain exceptions, that subsection gives priority to all "security interests which attach to goods before they become fixtures  .  .  .   over the claims of all persons who have an interest in the real estate.  .  .  ." Put another way, purchase money security interests (which attach prior to affixation)[64] in a fixture have priority over *prior* real estate interests even if the purchase money interest is not perfected. What may seem to be a radical departure from other rules about perfection and priority is merely a codification of the traditional preferred status of a purchase money secured creditor. Under the terms of subsection (4), subsequent real estate claimants (who may have lent or purchased in reliance on the fixture) will often defeat the purchase money lender if he fails promptly to perfect. Those who take a security interest in a

---

**62.** See, e. g., In re Foskett, 7 UCC Rep.Serv. 267 (Ref.Dec.W.D.Wis.1969), in which the seller of a mobile home who took a real estate mortgage was held to have priority over the trustee in bankruptcy as to the mobile home which was subsequently affixed to the land.

**63.** 2 Gilmore § 30.6 at 821–22.

Section 9-313(2) reads:

A security interest which attaches to goods before they become fixtures takes priority as to the goods over the claims of all persons who have an interest in the real estate except as stated in subsection (4).

**64.** In considering fixture questions, one must distinguish "attachment and attached" from "installation and installed" or "affixation and affixed." "Attachment" refers to the requirements set forth in 9-204 for the creation of an enforceable security interest; "installation" and "affixation" refer to the physical act of joining personalty to real estate in such a way as to make the personalty a fixture.

fixture after it is affixed (that is, nonpurchase money lender) take last and least under subsection (3).[65]

### Resolution of Conflicting Interests

We divide Article Nine fixture security claimants into four categories to measure their priority against real estate claimants. The most important criteria for dividing the sheep from the goats are (*1*) time the security interest attaches (in relation to installation of the fixture and to time the real property interests arise) and (*2*) time of perfection relative to the time other interests arise.

### Attached and Perfected Before Installation, 9–313(2) and (4)

This fellow is the crown prince of fixture security holders; except for the specious but colorable claim of certain construction mortgagees [66] (a construction mortgagee is one who takes a mortgage on real property and agrees to advance money during the course of construction on the property), our crown prince has a right superior to all others. Because his security interest attached before the goods became fixtures, he takes priority under 9–313(2) over all interests in the real estate except as provided in 9–313(4). Because he is perfected, none of those listed in 9–313(4) can defeat him. He will defeat subsequent purchasers, other creditors, and, absent a voidable preference or such, the trustee in bankruptcy.

### Attached Before Installation; Never Perfected, 9–313(2) and (4)

This secured creditor, almost always a purchase money lender, is usually a winner. Under subsection (2) he takes priority over all interest in the real estate except those listed in subsection (4). Basically, his interest is superior to all prior interests in the real estate—persons who have not relied on his fixtures for security.[67] However,

---

**65.** Section 9–313(3) provides:

A security interest which attaches to goods after they become fixtures is valid against all persons subsequently acquiring interests in the real estate except as stated in subsection (4) but is valid against any person with an interest in the real estate at the time the security interest attaches to the goods who has not in writing consented to the security interest or disclaimed an interest in the goods as fixtures.

**66.** Professor Gilmore points out that a construction mortgagee who typically makes a series of progress payments at various stages of completion might argue for priority over a fixture lender to the extent that payments are made after the goods are affixed to the realty. 2 Gilmore § 30.6 at 830, 31. The basis for the mortgagee's argument is found in 9–313(4)

which confers priority upon the subsequent advances made by a prior mortgagee when the advance is "made or *contracted for* without knowledge of the security interest and before it is perfected." (Emphasis added). However, under this theory the subsequent advances of the construction mortgagee would have priority over the fixture interest even if they were made after perfection by the fixture lender and with knowledge of his interest in Professor Gilmore's words ". . . the result of giving 'contracted for' the broadest possible reading would be to reverse the scheme of priorities which § 9–313 and Article 9 as a whole seem to accept." Id. at 832.

2 Gilmore, § 30.6 at 829–32.

**67.** See House v. Long, 244 Ark. 718, 426 S.W.2d 814, 5 UCC Rep.Serv. 236 (1968).

he should and will lose to the three classes of real estate interest holders listed in subsection (4) who may have relied on the fixtures as part of the realty.  These interests are

    (a) subsequent purchasers for value of any interest in the real estate,

    (b) subsequent judicial lienors, and

    (c) prior encumbrancers who make subsequent advances.

The last sentence of subsection (4) clears up a disputed point by defining the purchaser at a foreclosure sale as a "subsequent purchaser within this section" unless he is the encumbrancer purchasing at his own sale.  Failing to perfect will likely subordinate this secured creditor only to later real estate interests and, of course, to that ubiquitous devil, the trustee in bankruptcy.

### Attached After Installation; Perfected, 9–313(3)

The two foregoing chaps are likely purchase money lenders, sellers who claim an interest before installation.  The real life identity of our third man (whose interest attaches after installation) has never been fully revealed; rumor has it he is alive and well in Pennsylvania.[68]  By hypothesis his interest attaches only after the fixture has been purchased and installed.  Therefore he is not normally a purchase money lender.  Whatever the identity of this mysterious fellow who claims fixtures *after* installation, 9–313(3) gives him a low priority.  He loses to prior real estate interests unless they subordinate to him in writing.  He beats only interests which arise after he has perfected.

One class of purchase money lenders who may be reduced to 9–313(3) status are those who fail to procure a security agreement from the debtor before the goods are affixed.  If seller sells goods that are to become a fixture to buyer under an oral security agreement but does not reduce that agreement to writing until after the goods have become affixed, it is unclear whether 9–313(2) or 9–313(3) governs.  Because all of the requirements listed in 9–204 (agreement, debtor rights in the collateral, and creditor's giving value) have been met in such case upon the sale, technically the security interest has "attached" under 9–204.  Because there is no writing, however, the security interest is not "enforceable against the debtor or third parties"

---

68.  Professor Gilmore says:

"Mr. Homer Kripke sees some merit in the post-affixation interest validated by § 9–313(3).  The author is indebted to Mr. Kripke for the following comment: "This post-affixation interest was put in at the request of Pennsylvania lawyers and they had a real reason.  The Pennsylvania concepts of when a chattel becomes real estate have the result of making a lot of machinery and equipment real estate in Pennsylvania, although no reliance was placed on them in the real estate financing.  Secondary real estate financing on them is unavailable through banks and insurance companies which cannot take second mortgages, while normal chattel financing is available through this concept of post-affixation chattel financing on what has become real estate.""

2 Gilmore § 30.3 at 810 n. 6.

until the writing is signed after the affixation.[69]  Is it possible that
the draftsmen intended that a security interest could be "attached"
yet not "enforceable"?  It seems that they did, and if one follows that
policy, the seller in the case posed would be a purchase money seller
and have the priority set out in 9–313(2) for one whose security interest attached before the goods became fixtures.  The one reported
case which passes close to this question does not tell whether there
was an oral security agreement.[70]  It treats the creditor as a 9–313(3)
creditor whose interest attaches to the goods after they became fixtures and contains no discussion about the possibility that the creditor might qualify under 9–313(2).

### Attached After Installation; Never Perfected

This poor bloke has priority only over subsequent claimants who
somehow fail to qualify under subsection 9–313(4).  One class subordinate to him consists of subsequent takers who took with knowledge of his security interest.

### Rights on Default

If a secured creditor has priority over the claims "of all persons
who have interests in real estate," 9–313(5) authorizes him (on default and subject to the provisions of Part 5 of Article Nine) to

> remove his collateral from the real estate, but he must re-
> imburse any encumbrancer or owner of the real estate who
> is not the debtor and who has not otherwise agreed for the
> cost of repair of any physical injury but not for any diminu-
> tion in value of the real estate caused by the absence of the
> goods removed or by any necessity for replacing them.  A
> person entitled to reimbursement may refuse permission to
> remove until the secured creditor gives adequate security for
> the performance of this obligation.

---

**69.**  Section 9–203(1) provides:

Subject to the provisions of Section
4–208 on the security interest of a
collecting bank and Section 9–113 on
a security interest arising under the
Article on Sales, a security interest
is not enforceable against the debtor
or third parties unless

  (a) the collateral is in the possession of the secured party; or

  (b) the debtor has signed a security
  agreement which contains a description of the collateral and in addition, when the security interest covers crops or oil, gas or minerals to
  be extracted or timber to be cut, a
  description of the land concerned.
  In describing collateral, the word
  "proceeds" is sufficient without fur-

ther description to cover proceeds of
any character.

**70.**  Sunshine v. Sanray Floor Covering
Corp., 64 Misc.2d 780, 315 N.Y.S.2d 937,
8 UCC Rep.Serv. 738 (Sup.Ct.1970)
where a prior real estate mortgagee
whose mortgage claimed fixtures
achieved priority over a later purchase money lender against certain
air-conditioning and heating equipment.  According to the facts given in
the opinion, the seller of the heating
equipment delivered and installed it in
October or November of 1966 but did
not receive a written security agreement until January 1967.  The court
did not discuss the possibility that the
debtor had orally agreed to give a
security interest in the goods at the
time of sale.

As Comment 5 to 9–313 points out, the quoted subsection is an "important departure" from prior law, for it permits removal even if "material injury" will occur.  Under the Code a secured creditor entitled to priority may in all cases remove his fixture, and he is liable to other parties, if at all, only for "the repair of any physical injury" but not for reduction in the economic value of the property because of the absence of the fixture.  Thus, one who removes an air conditioner may have to pay $20 to repair the hole that is left, but he is not liable to the owner of the property for the economic loss which the owner suffers because the un-air-conditioned premises cannot be rented.

If the cost of removing the fixture and repairing the physical injury which results from its removal is greater than its value on the used market, a secured creditor who must pay these costs under the Code will forgo his repossession right and presumably cast his lot with the real estate mortgagee.  Since "goods incorporated into a structure" such as lumber, bricks, etc. are excluded from the definition of fixture by 9–313(1), subsection (5) confers no right on the secured creditor to remove such items nor, presumably, may he maintain a security interest in such items unless his security agreement qualifies as a mortgage or other real estate lien under non-Code state law.

The reference in subsection (5) to the "provisions of part 5" means that the creditor who would repossess must do so without "breach of the peace" if he proceeds by self-help under 9–503 and that after he gains possession of the collateral he may proceed under 9–505 or 9–504 as he would if the collateral had been goods all along.[71]

Section 9–313(5) does not deal with the case in which the secured creditor is subordinate to one or more of the real estate claimants.  If a land mortgage has priority, may the holder of a security interest in a fixture remove that fixture and sell it subject to the mortgagee's interest?  The negative implication of subsection (5) (which authorizes his removal when he has a priority over the "claims of all") is that he does *not* have a right to remove when he is subordinate to one or more real property interests.  A subordinate fixture lender will usually have to wait for the mortgagee to foreclose and then take the scraps off the table after the mortgagee is fully satisfied.

## § 25–10    Fixtures—Some Interpretative Snarls in 9–313

It was inevitable that the attempt to codify fixture priority law in one section would fall short of the mark.  Although no large body of appellate case law has arisen out of 9–313 disputes, writers and lawyers have found the section ambiguous in certain key areas and have questioned the wisdom of the rules which it sets down in other areas.[72]  As a result of this dissatisfaction with 9–313, the Review

---

71.  See Section 26–11, infra, for a discussion of the rights and duties of a secured creditor who repossesses collateral.

72.  See note 52, supra, and the authorities cited therein.

Committee for Article Nine of the Code has proposed three draft amendments of 9–313. This effort reached culmination with the issuance of the Review Committee's final report which, among other things, substantially revises 9–313.[73] Until the proposed revision of 9–313 is enacted, we must live with the current version of 9–313, and we turn first to ambiguities inherent in it.

### Subsequent?

The general policies embodied in 9–313(2) and (4) are clear enough and we have outlined them above. That is, one who fails to perfect his fixture interests at once may well take priority over "prior" interests under subsection (2) but be subordinate to "subsequent" interests under subsection (4). A prior claimant must have made his loan or purchased his interest before he knew of the fixture and without reliance upon it. Therefore he should have a lower priority than one who made a loan or purchase subsequently and conceivably in reliance upon the fixture. All this is clear enough except for one crucial fact; the Code does not identify the event, the point in time, to which one must be "subsequent."

Since the only subsequent parties who are entitled to priority under subsection (4) are those who take "*before*" the security interest is perfected, the event marking the time at which "subsquentness" begins cannot be perfection of the fixture interest. That leaves two alternatives:

(*1*) the time at which the security interest of the fixture holder attaches (almost always the time the sale is made between the seller of the fixture and the debtor) or

(*2*) the time at which the fixture is installed on the premises.

Professor Gilmore has argued that no mortgagee can reasonably rely on a fixture as security until it has been installed on the property. Thus, he would define as "subsequent" (and therefore entitled to priority under subsection (4)) only those who purchased, made an advance, or obtained a lien after installation. If such person purchased, obtained a lien, or made an advance after the debtor had purchased an interest in the soon-to-be fixture but before the fixture was installed on the property, Professor Gilmore would find them "prior," thereby exclude them from 9–313(4) and subordinate them to the seller's unperfected interest.[74]

---

73. See Preliminary Draft No. 1; Preliminary Draft No. 2; Review Committee for Article 9. Preliminary Draft No. 2 and Final Review Committee Report for Article 9 are substantially the same. The Review Committee rejected Preliminary Draft No. 1 as being too complex.

74. 2 Gilmore § 30.6 at 824–28.

Accord House v. Long, 244 Ark. 718, 426 S.W.2d 814, 5 UCC Rep.Serv. 236 (1968) (significant time for determining priority of unperfected fixture lender vis-a-vis construction mortgagee and materialmen's liens held to be date goods were affixed to realty and thereby became fixtures).

Professor Gilmore's arguments persuade us and we find his choice of "installation" more consistent with the reasonable expectations of the seller of fixture collateral than the other interpretation. It seems likely that sellers of fixture collateral feel no pressing need to file before the goods are installed. If a person who purchased, obtained a lien, or made an advance after attachment but before installation were given priority as a "subsequent" purchaser or creditor under 9–313(4), it would mean a secured seller of the fixture collateral would have to file before or simultaneously with his sale. He could not wait for installation, nor would he even enjoy the 10-day grace period which purchase money sellers of non-fixture goods enjoy under 9–312(4).

### Fixtures Owned by a Tenant, Construction Contractor or the Like

If the owner of the fixture is not also the owner of the fee to the real estate on which the fixture is installed, two kinds of problems arise and 9–313 does not deal with either effectively. The first arises principally when a tenant is the debtor, and concerns the effect of a landlord and tenant agreement upon an ultimate priority conflict between the fixture lender and the landlord or another who claims through the landlord. Second, what are the consequences of filing (in the debtor's name) as to a fixture owned by a debtor who has no record interest in the real estate? It is most improbable that one who searches the real estate records and the fixture filings under the name of the owner of the real property will find a financing statement indexed under the name of a contractor or other non-owner.

Turning first to the tenant's case, assume the following facts. Giving a security interest to his seller, tenant purchases and installs a large air-conditioning unit in a place of business which he rents. Under the terms of his lease, tenant has a right to remove the air-conditioning unit when he leaves the premises. Assume further that the landlord procures a loan and gives a real property mortgage to Bank. If the seller of the fixture never files, may he rely upon the tenant's lease right to remove the air conditioner, or is he subordinated to the mortgagee's interest because the mortgagee is a subsequent purchaser under 9–313(4)? Professor Kripke argues that the fixture seller should be able to ride on the tenant's coat tails and should win a priority contest with the mortgagee.[75] We agree. Mortgagees are big boys; they can be expected to understand leases and to know that certain tenants commonly install fixtures and retain a right to remove them. If they wish to guard against that possibility, they can lend a little less money or can insist that landlords to whom they lend use leases which deny the tenant the right of removal.

---

**75.** Kripke, Fixtures Under the Uniform Commercial Code, 64 Colum.L. Rev. 44, 66 (1964). See In re Peterman, 3 UCC Rep.Serv. 370 (N.Y.Sup.Ct.1966) (seller's creditors could remove and sell air-conditioner subject to judgment and order to levy since buyer was a tenant and lease provided that fixtures were to remain personal property of the tenant).

Of course, the shoe can also be put on the other foot. Suppose the tenant has no right to remove the fixture under the lease or under the landlord-tenant law of the jurisdiction in question, but the fixture seller perfects his security interest by filing a financing statement under the tenant's name. We are uncertain about the appropriate outcome here. On the one hand we see the need to give the fixture lender a method of protecting himself, and the language of the Code seems quite plain and unambiguous in its offer of protection under 9–313(2) and (4). The only Code analogy which supports the landlord's claim is to treat him like a personal property lender against after-acquired property who has first filed. But as we have seen, that analogy has not been carried forward in 9–313, for the construction mortgagee (who more than anyone else in 9–313 resembles the lender against after-acquired property of 9–312) does not achieve priority over a purchase money fixture lender who perfects at once.[76] On balance we conclude the seller of the fixture should be preferred over the landlord and those claiming under him and would simply make the landlord and those claiming under him realize that they cannot rely upon fixtures later added, even if they have a right to such fixtures as against the tenant himself.

As we have pointed out, the theory of the filing requirements with respect to fixtures (filing in the place where a mortgage on the pertinent real property would be recorded) is to give notice of fixture interests to real property searchers.[77] When the tenant who may have no interest of record in the real property or a construction contractor who will almost certainly have no interest in the real property is the debtor, and the financing statement is indexed under the name of the tenant or the construction company, one searching the real property records is not likely to find such financing statement. Of course, a diligent searcher and a wise mortgagee will inquire into the nature of the leases with important tenants on business property and can certainly be expected to search the files with respect to such important tenants. However, the same is not true of construction companies or less important tenants. Although the Code is quite clear in granting perfected status to one who files in the debtor's name, the draftsmen probably did not foresee the questions posed by a non-record owner debtor. Lawyers should simply beware; it is not sufficient to search the files under the name of the owner of the equity in the real property if it is conceivable that there is another party who might be the owner of the equity in fixtures attached to the property.

A final question which can arise in the landlord-tenant context is partly an Article 9 scope question and partly a 9–313 question: Does 9–313 govern priority conflicts between landlord liens and security interests in fixtures? One starts his analysis with 9–104 and appears to find both the beginning and the end of his problems in 9–104(b) which reads as follows: "This Article does not apply (b) to

---

76. See 2 Gilmore § 30.6 at 831–32.       77. See § 9–401.

a landlord's lien; . . . ." However, a reading of 9–104(j) and the negative implication in 9–104(j) leave one less certain: "This Article does not apply . . . (j) except to the extent that provision is made for fixtures in Section 9–313, to the creation or transfer of an interest in or lien on real estate, including the lease or rents thereunder; . . . ." Is it possible that subsection (b) means only that a landlord's lien is not subject to the creation, attachment, perfection, and realization provisions in Article Nine, but that a landlord claiming such a lien is nevertheless a "person who has an interest in the real estate" whose priority is therefore governed by 9–313(2), (3), and (4)? To treat a landlord's lien as so governed by 9–313 is consistent with the treatment Article Nine gives to other real estate interests. Mortgages, of course, are not subject to any of the other provisions of Article Nine, but their priority *vis-a-vis* fixture lenders is determined under 9–313. Why should the landlord's lien be excluded? Why not integrate him into this systematic provision for fixture priority? We believe the priority of the landlord's lien is governed by 9–313, but we have found no case which applies 9–313. One interesting Pennsylvania case makes at least a passing reference to 9–313.[78] In that case Brunswick, a seller of bowling alley equipment engaged in a priority dispute with the landlord of Brunswick's debtor. Brunswick ultimately won before the Supreme Court of Pennsylvania, but the majority resolved the case exclusively under the Bankruptcy Act and the common law of Pennsylvania and did not refer to Article Nine.

## § 25–11    Fixtures—Proposed Changes in 9–313

Professor Kripke and his comrades on the Article Nine Review Committee have done radical surgery on 9–313.[79] They have attempt-

---

78. Brunswick Corp. v. Ciaffoni, 432 Pa. 442, 248 A.2d 39 (1968), cert. den. 394 U.S. 997 (1969).

79. The final revised version of 9–313 reads as follows:

(1) In this section and in the provisions of Part 4 of this Article referring to fixture filing, unless the context otherwise requires

(a) Goods are "fixtures" when they become so related to particular real estate that an interest in them arises under real estate law.

(b) A "fixture filing" is the filing in the office where a mortgage on the real estate would be filed or recorded of a financing statement covering goods which are or are to become fixtures and which conforms to the requirements of subsection (5) of Section 9–402.

(c) A mortgage is a "construction mortgage" to the extent that it secures an obligation incurred for the construction of an improvement on land including the acquisition cost of the land, if the recorded writing so indicates.

(2) A security interest under this Article may be created in goods which are fixtures or may continue in goods which become fixtures, but no security interest exists under this Article in ordinary building materials incorporated into an improvement on land.

(3) This Article does not prevent creation of an encumbrance upon fixtures pursuant to real estate law.

(4) A perfected security interest in fixtures has priority over the conflicting interest of an encumbrancer or owner of the real estate where

(a) the security interest is a purchase money security interest, the interest of the encumbrancer or owner arises before the goods become fixtures, the security interest

ed to resolve each of the problems discussed above and others as well. Among the most significant changes the new draft makes are the following:

> (1) It gives priority to a construction mortgagee (recorded before goods become fixtures) as to goods which become fixtures before the completion of construction. That is to say, in the common case in which a mortgagee is making advances periodically, the mortgagee will normally have a priority as to fixtures which are installed before the completion of construction even though the fixture lender has perfected his interest. That provision will reverse the priorities which arise in the same circumstances under the current 9–313. It apparently represents a judgment that construction mortgagees are entitled to greater protection than are fixture lenders when both are essentially purchase money lenders. In its Reasons for Change, the Permanent Editorial

is perfected by a fixture filing before the goods become fixtures or within ten days thereafter, and the debtor has an interest of record in the real estate; or

(b) the security interest is perfected by a fixture filing before the interest of the encumbrancer or owner is of record, the security interest has priority over any conflicting interest of a predecessor in title of the encumbrancer or owner, and the debtor has an interest of record in the real estate; or

(c) the fixtures are readily removable factory or office machines or readily removable replacements of domestic appliances which are consumer goods, and before the goods become fixtures the security interest is perfected by any method permitted by this Article; or

(d) the conflicting interest is a lien on the real estate obtained by legal or equitable proceedings after the security interest was perfected by any method permitted by this Article.

(5) A security interest in fixtures, whether or not perfected, has priority over the conflicting interest of an encumbrancer or owner of the real estate where

(a) the encumbrancer or owner has consented in writing to the security interest or has disclaimed an interest in the goods as fixtures; or

(b) the debtor has a right to remove the goods as against the encumbrancer or owner. If the debtor's

right terminates, the priority of the security interest continues for a reasonable time.

(6) Notwithstanding paragraph (a) of subsection (4) but otherwise subject to subsections (4) and (5), a security interest in fixtures is subordinate to a construction mortgage recorded before the goods become fixtures if the goods become fixtures before the completion of the construction. To the extent that it is given to refinance a construction mortgage, a mortgage has this priority to the same extent as the construction mortgage.

(7) In cases not within the preceding subsections, a security interest in fixtures is subordinate to the conflicting interest of an encumbrancer or owner of the related real estate who is not the debtor.

(8) [5] When the secured party has priority over all owners and encumbrancers of the real estate, he may, on default, subject to the provisions of Part 5, remove his collateral from the real estate but he must reimburse any encumbrancer or owner of the real estate who is not the debtor and who has not otherwise agreed for the cost of repair of any physical injury, but not for any diminution in value of the real estate caused by the absence of the goods removed or by any necessity of replacing them. A person entitled to reimbursement may refuse permission to remove until the secured party gives adequate security for the performance of this obligation.

Review Committee for Article 9, 122–26.

Board comes perilously close to admitting that this change is a capitulation to the real property interests who apparently have more clout than their personal property cousins:

> In other states the word "fixture" had come to mean that a former chattel had become real estate for all purposes and that any chattel rights therein were lost. For lawyers trained in such states the Code provisions seemed to be extreme. Some sections of the real estate bar began attempting with some success to have 9–313 amended to bring it closer to the pre-Code law in their states. In some states, such as California and Iowa, section 9–313 simply was not enacted.[80]

(2) Subsection (5) grants priority to a fixture lender over a real estate interest when the owner of the fixture is a tenant who has a right to remove the goods. The fixture lender has the tenant's right to remove whether or not he has perfected his security interest.

(3) Subsections (4) (a) and (4) (b) restate the general priority rules. Under (4) (a) purchase money security interests in fixtures which attach before the goods become fixtures take priority over the prior real estate interests only if the fixture lender perfects before the goods become fixtures or within 10 days after they become fixtures. The general rule stated in (4) (b) gives a perfected fixture lender priority over interests that are recorded subsequent to his perfection. The most significant change which these rules offer from the current 9–313(2) is the requirement that a purchase money lender perfect his interest in order to prevail over prior real estate interests. Under the current 9–313(2), a fixture lender need not do so in order to prevail over such interests.

(4) The new section institutes the concept of a "fixture filing," a filing in the office where a mortgage on the real estate would be filed and recorded. The section calls for such filing to entitle the fixture lender to priority over competing real estate "reliance" interests such as subsequent purchasers and mortgagees, but it authorizes priority over subsequent lien creditors without the necessity for a fixture filing and grants priority over such lienors to one who has perfected "by any method permitted by this Article". (Presumably a "method" permitted by the Article is a filing as though the goods were equipment, not fixtures). The new subsection deals with the problem of the construction contractor or other party who has no interest of record in the real estate by explicitly denying priority to the fixture lender in some such circumstances (see, e. g., (4) (a) and (4) (b)).

---

80. Id. at 126.

The foregoing is only a simplified consideration of the most significant proposed changes in 9–313. In states in which the new 9–313 is enacted, commercial and real property lawyers must scrutinize it carefully.

## § 25–12    Priority of Purchasers of Goods, 9–307

The golden rule of Article Nine is stated in 9–201:

> Except as otherwise provided by this Act a security agreement is effective according to its terms between the parties, against purchasers of the collateral and against creditors.

That idea is reiterated in 9–306(2) set out below. Thus, in the inevitable conflicts which arise between two innocent parties, the one a perfected secured creditor who has not authorized his debtor to sell and the other a subsequent buyer from the debtor, the perfected secured creditor is usually the winner.

However, there are some cases in which the buyer is the winner, and we wish to examine a few of those in this section. Note first that if the secured creditor has failed to perfect his security interest, he will normally be subordinate to a subsequent buyer's interest under the provisions of 9–301(1) (c) and (d).[81] There are some situations in which it would be manifestly unfair to uphold even a secured creditor's perfected security interest against the rights of a subsequent buyer. Consider the case of Mrs. Jones who buys a washing machine from Big George's Appliance Store. Assume further that Bank has filed a financing statement which covers all of Big George's inventory and that the security interest is not discharged by sale. In such circumstances is it reasonable to expect Mrs. Jones to search the files, to ask Bank for a subordination, and if that is not reasonable, is it fair to permit Bank to assert its security interest in the washing machine after Mrs. Jones has paid full value? Of course, it is neither reasonable to expect her to investigate nor fair to subordinate her interest. Thus, we have 9–307(1) which renders the Bank's security interest subordinate to her interest as purchaser. Apart from the case of the purchaser out of inventory, only one case seems to have bothered the draftsmen. It arises when secured creditor perfects a purchase money security interest in goods sold without filing a financing statement or taking possession. The provisions of 9–302(1) (d) provide that a purchase money security interest in consumer goods is perfected upon attachment even though the creditor does not file or take possession of the collateral. In such a case a

---

81.  Section 9–301(1) provides:

Except as otherwise provided in subsection (2), an unperfected security interest is subordinate to the rights of . . .

  (c) in the case of goods . . . a person who is not a secured par-

ty and who is a transferee in bulk or other buyer not in ordinary course of business to the extent that he gives value and receives delivery of the collateral without knowledge of the security interest and before it is perfected . . .

buyer would have no way of knowing that there was a perfected security interest in the goods he wished to purchase, for there would be no filing and no possession to put him on notice. In such circumstances the buyer will usually take free of the security interest under the provisions of 9–307(2).

Sections 9–201 and 9–306(2) are the starting point for an analysis of the conflict between a secured creditor on the one hand and a subsequent purchaser from the debtor on the other. Section 9–306 (2) provides:

> Except where this Article otherwise provides, a security interest continues in collateral notwithstanding sale, exchange or other disposition thereof by the debtor unless his action was authorized by the secured party in the security agreement or otherwise . . . .

Thus, the lawyer's first task is to examine the security agreement, the course of dealing, and the usage of the trade between the secured party an. the debtor to determine whether the debtor is authorized to sell the goods free of the security interest. If he is, then the purchaser holds the goods free of the security interest, and the secured creditor's interest is cut off by his agreement.[82] Of course, this is the usual case in which the floor planner of inventory expects his debtor to sell the goods free of the security interest and has no interest in chasing them into the hands of consumers.[83] If the security agreement is silent or explicitly prohibits the sale of the collateral or provides that any sale must be subject to the security interest, the lawyer must turn to section 9–307.[84]

82. Universal C. I. T. Credit Corp. v. Middlesboro Motor Sales, Inc., 424 S.W.2d 409, 4 UCC Rep.Serv. 1126 (Ky.App.1968) (security agreement authorized sale of automobiles in ordinary course of trade); First Fin. Co. v. Akathiotis, 110 Ill.App.2d 377, 249 N.E.2d 663, 6 UCC Rep.Serv. 946 (1969) (buyer took free of security interest when secured party was assignee of sales contract and security agreement mentioned sales contract).

83. The "or otherwise" language in 9–306(2) gives the courts leeway to recognize the business expectations of the parties. See Pieper v. First Nat'l Bank, 453 S.W.2d 926, 7 UCC Rep. Serv. 858 (Mo.1970) (bank which had been notified that collateral was placed for sale and had accepted part of the proceeds of sale could not enforce security interest against purchaser).

Comment 3 to section 9–306 suggests:

A claim to proceeds in a filed financing statement might be considered as impliedly authorizing sale or other disposition of the collateral, depending upon the circumstances of the parties, the nature of the collateral, the course of dealing of the parties and the usage of trade (See Section 1–205).

However, at least one court has refused to accept the Code's invitation to find such authorization when a farmer-debtor sold crops subject to a security interest. Vermilion County Production Credit Ass'n v. Izzard, 111 Ill.App.2d 190, 249 N.E.2d 352, 6 UCC Rep.Serv. 940 (1969). See Overland Nat'l Bank v. Aurora Co-operative Elevator Co., 184 Neb. 843, 172 N.W. 2d 786, 7 UCC Rep.Serv. 11 (1969) (dictum). The secured party can avoid this problem by simply claiming proceeds and inserting a clause prohibiting sale of the collateral in the security agreement.

84. Comment 2 to 9–307 explains:

The limitations which this Section imposes on the persons who may take free of a security interest apply of

## § 25–13  Priority of Purchasers of Goods—9–307(1) and Buyers in the Ordinary Course of Business

Subsection (1) of 9–307 is designed principally for Mrs. Jones' case, the case of one who gives new value to purchase out of the seller's inventory.  That subsection reads in full as follows:

> A buyer in ordinary course of business (subsection (9) of Section 9—201) other than a person buying farm products from a person engaged in farming operations takes free of a security interest created by his seller even though the security interest is perfected and even though the buyer knows of its existence.

If one dissects the subsection, he can find five or six conditions a buyer must meet to take free of a prior perfected security interest:

> *(1)* He must be a buyer in the ordinary course
>
> *(2)* who does not buy in bulk and does not take his interest as security for or in total or partial satisfaction of a pre-existing debt (that is, he must give some form of "new" value)
>
> *(3)* who buys from one in the business of selling goods of that kind (that is, cars from a car dealer, i. e. inventory);
>
> *(4)* who buys in good faith and without knowledge that his purchase is in violation of others' ownership rights or security interests, and
>
> *(5)* does not buy farm products from a person engaged in farming operations, and
>
> *(6)* the competing security interest must be one "created by his seller".

Note that several of the foregoing conditions are really embodied in subsection (9) of 1–201 which defines the words "buyer in the ordinary course of business." [85]  The requirement that the buyer buy out of inventory and the new value and good faith requirements enter 9–307 via 1–201.  Let us turn to some of the interpretative difficulties.  Only rarely will it be difficult to tell

course only to unauthorized sales by the debtor.  If the secured party has authorized the sale in the security agreement or otherwise, the buyer takes free without regard to the limitations of this Section.

Section 9–307 is not the sole exception to the general rule of 9–306(2).  For instance, 9–504(4) protects a purchaser of repossessed goods.

**85.**  Section 1–201(9) reads in full as follows:

"Buyer in ordinary course of business" means a person who in good faith and without knowledge that the sale to him is in violation of the ownership rights or security interest of a third party in the goods buys in ordinary course from a person in the business of selling goods of that kind but does not include a pawnbroker.  "Buying" may be for cash or by exchange of other property or on secured or unsecured credit and includes receiving goods or documents of title under a pre-existing contract for sale but does not include a transfer in bulk or as security for or in total or partial satisfaction of a money debt.

whether the seller was "in the business of selling goods of that kind." The jeweler sells jewels, a haberdasher sells clothes, an automobile dealer sells automobiles, an appliance dealer sells appliances, etc. But what of a buyer who purchases an automobile from a seller who is in the business of renting automobiles? In Hempstead Bank v. Andy's Car Rental System, Inc.,[86] the plaintiff bank (secured creditor) sued a wholesale automobile dealer for conversion. The automobile dealer had purchased used cars from the car rental company, and the cars were subject to a perfected security interest of the bank. The buyer claimed that he was a buyer in the ordinary course of business who took free under 9–307(1). He correctly pointed out that the cars were classified for the purposes of Article Nine as inventory in the hands of the car rental company under 9–109(4) and comment 3 to 9–109. The court rejected the buyer's argument. Despite the fact that the automobiles were inventory in the hands of the car rental company, the court found that the car rental company was not in the business of "selling goods of that kind." Accordingly, the court ruled that the buyer was not a buyer in the ordinary course of business and ordered a new trial to determine whether the secured party had authorized the sale free of its security interest under 9–306(2). The case seems a reasonable interpretation of 9–307(1). One who buys from a seller whose principal business is renting or using goods should be on notice that he may be subject to a security interest and that the secured creditor will not necessarily contemplate that buyers take free.[87] We suspect that as an empirical fact such buyers are more likely to check the filings and that it is a reasonable allocation of the risks between the innocent secured creditor and the innocent purchaser to allow the secured creditor to win in such cases.

That the buyer must purchase in "good faith" and "without knowledge that the sale is in violation of the security interest of a third party" may cause uncertainty. Exactly what the good faith requirement adds is unclear.[88] Also, the requirement that the buyer have no knowledge may seem to conflict with the words of 9–307(1) which permits the buyer to take free even though he "knows of [the security interest's] existence." On careful reading the two requirements do not conflict. The buyer fails to qualify under 9–307 only if he knows that the sale is "in violation" of the security

---

86. 35 App.Div.2d 35, 312 N.Y.S.2d 317, 7 UCC Rep.Serv. 932 (2d Dep't 1970).

87. But cf. McFadden v. Mercantile-Safe Deposit & Trust Co., 260 Md. 601, 273 A.2d 198, 8 UCC Rep.Serv. 766 (Md.App.1971), (franchisor who sold ice cream trucks as part of franchising operation was in business of selling goods of that kind).

88. Section 1–201(19) defines good faith as follows, " 'Good faith' means honesty in fact in the conduct or transaction concerned." See Sherrock v. Commercial Credit Corp., 277 A.2d 708, 9 UCC Rep.Serv. 294 (Del.Sup.1971) (merchant must comply with reasonable commercial standards to be in good faith (2–103(1) (b)); car dealer who pays an advance and does not pick up his purchased cars at once from his seller is not following reasonable commercial standards and is not therefore a buyer in ordinary course).

interest.[89]   Presumably, in the usual case in which a lender takes a security interest in inventory, he intends the debtor to be able to sell free and clear.   Thus, it is perfectly consistent for a buyer [90] to know of a security interest but to believe that the sale to him is not in violation of that interest.   Comment 2 to 9–307 explains the matter as follows:

> Reading the two provisions together, it results that the buyer takes free if he merely knows that there is a security interest which covers the goods but takes subject if he knows, in addition, that the sale is in violation of some term in the security agreement not waived by the words or conduct of the secured party.

A final requirement of 9–307(1) likely to cause courts difficult moments is that the security interest of which the buyer takes free be "created by his seller."   In the usual case in which the buyer purchases an automobile from a dealer's inventory, the dealer created the security interest in his lender.   But what of the case in which Mrs. Jones purchases a new automobile and gives a security interest to a lender; then Mrs. Jones sells the automobile to automobile dealer number 2 who in turn sells the automobile to Mr. Smith.   Ultimately, Mrs. Jones' lender attempts to recover the automobile from Mr. Smith. Because the security interest was not created by Mr. Smith's seller, Mr. Smith is not qualified for the coverage under 9–307(1), and his interest will be subordinate to the security interest created by Mrs. Jones.[91]   The language and the intention of the Code seem clear

---

**89.**   O. M. Scott Credit Corp. v. Apex, Inc., 97 R.I. 442, 198 A.2d 673, 2 UCC Rep.Serv. 92 (1964) (buyer could not qualify as buyer in ordinary course of business when he knew sale violated terms of security agreement).

**90.**   The Code does not define the word "buyer." In the absence of such definition, one might argue that attaching creditors and others who take goods in satisfaction of preexisting debts qualify as buyers. Because 1–201(9) explicitly excludes such persons from the larger term, "buyers in the ordinary course," one need not concern himself with the question whether they are "buyers." Neither attaching creditors nor those who take goods as security for or in satisfaction of a debt qualify under 9–307(1). Evans Prods. Co. v. Jorgensen, 245 Ore. 362, 421 P.2d 978, 3 UCC Rep.Serv. 1099 (1966) (supplier who took plywood manufacturer's finished product in lieu of debt was not buyer in ordinary course of business). But see Toyomenka, Inc. v. Mount Hope Finishing Co., 432 F.2d 722, 728, 8 UCC Rep.Serv. 21 (4th Cir. 1970) (trans-

feree did not extend credit for goods but credited an overdue account); General Elec. Credit Corp. v. R. A. Heintz Constr. Co., 302 F.Supp. 958, 963, 6 UCC Rep.Serv. 1137, 1143–44 (D.Ore.1967) (only part of purchase price was cancellation of dealer's preexisting debt to buyer); Western Penn. Production Credit Ass'n v. Sustrick, 8 UCC Rep.Serv. 567 (Pa. C.P.1970) (creditor who purchased at executor's sale and paid difference between debt and value of goods not buyer in ordinary course); Stephenson Fin. Co. v. P. L. Bruce & Co., 254 S.C. 249, 174 S.E.2d 750, 7 UCC Rep. Serv. 944 (1970) (buyer who took autos in exchange for insolvent dealer's worthless checks was not buyer in ordinary course of business; buyer also had knowledge, however, that transfer violated secured creditor's rights) (dictum).

**91.**   National Shawmut Bank v. Jones, 108 N.H. 386, 236 A.2d 484, 4 UCC Rep.Serv. 1021 (1967) (buyer in ordinary course of auto holds it subject to perfected security interest created by dealer's transferor); General Mo-

enough.   The difficulty is that the policy of 9–307 would seem to cover Mr. Smith.   That is, he is neither more nor less than a garden variety purchaser who pays cash and buys out of the inventory of a dealer. Of course, he will have a cause of action against his seller for the breach of warranty of title but we do not understand why the draftsmen excluded him from 9–307(1).

### § 25–14   Priority of Purchasers of Goods—Consumer Purchasers of Consumer Goods, 9–307(2)

Viewed from afar, 9–307(2) is like a mirage; it appears to apply in many circumstances to permit buyers to take free of prior perfected security interests.   In fact it is a provision of narrow scope that deals almost exclusively with a relatively insignificant transaction, one in which one consumer sells used goods to another consumer. Subsection 9–307(2) reads in full as follows:

> In the case of consumer goods and in the case of farm equipment having an original purchase price not in excess of $2500 (other than fixtures, see Section 9—313), a buyer takes free of a security interest even though perfected if he buys without knowledge of the security interest, for value and for his own personal, family or household purposes or his own farming operations unless prior to the purchase the secured party has filed a financing statement covering such goods.

The requirements of the subsection may be subdivided:

(1) In seller's hands the goods are either consumer goods or farm equipment having an original purchase price of $2500 or less

(2) The buyer must have no knowledge of the security interest

(3) The buyer must buy for value and for his own family or household purposes or for his own farming operation (i. e., goods must usually be consumer goods in his hands)

(4) There is no filed financing statement covering the goods.

Mostly the subsection is designed to cover those cases in which a secured creditor has taken a purchase money interest under 9–302 (1) (d) and perfected it without filing.   Consider the parties not covered by 9–307(2).   First of all, no one who qualifies under 9–307 (1) can qualify under 9–307(2), for under subsection (1) the goods must be inventory in the seller's hands and under (2) they must be consumer goods in the seller's hands.   Secondly, if the secured creditor has filed a financing statement, no subsequent party can claim a superior interest under 9–307(2).   Third, no wholesaler or business

tors Acceptance Corp. v. Troville, 43 Mass.App.Dec. 96, 6 UCC Rep.Serv. 409 (1969); Muir v. Jefferson Credit Corp., 108 N.J.Super. 586, 262 A.2d 33, 7 UCC Rep.Serv. 273 (Law Div.1970).

buyer (except for farmers) can claim under 9–307(2) because his use will not be personal, household, etc. This requirement excludes trustees in bankruptcy as well as dealers in goods.[92]

Perhaps a word is in order to explain how we arrived at the conclusion that the goods must be consumer goods in the seller's hands. We find that requirement in the prepositional phrase which introduces 9–307(2): "in the case of consumer goods  . . . ." That phrase must refer to the status of the goods in the hands of the seller or it would be redundant, for the next to the last clause in the sentence ("and for his own personal, family or household purposes") refers to the status of the goods in the buyer's hands. Thus, to give meaning to the introductory phrase, one must find that it refers to the status of the goods in the seller's hands. This interpretation is also supported by earlier drafts of the Code in which subsection (1) was introduced by the phrase "In the case of inventory," an apparent reference to the status of the goods in the seller's hands under subsection (1).[93] That reference was ultimately removed on the ground that it was superfluous because a buyer in the ordinary course is defined as one who must buy out of inventory.[94] Finally, our interpretation is supported by the bulk of the judicial and scholarly opinion on the subsection.[95] For the foregoing reasons, we conclude that the section applies only to the sales "by amateurs to amateurs." [96]

### § 25–15  Priority of Purchasers of Goods—Relationship Between 2–403 and 9–307

Section 2–403 is the Article Two analogue to 9–307. It, like 9–307, is a bona fide purchase provision designed to protect good

---

**92.** A trustee in bankruptcy is not a buyer under 9–307(2). In re Kretzer, 1 UCC Rep.Serv. 369 (Ref.Dec.E.D.Pa. 1955); In re Lucacos, 1 UCC Rep.Serv. 553, (Ref.Dec.E.D.Pa.1957); In re Ten Brock, 4 UCC Rep.Serv. 712 (Ref. Dec.W.D.Mich.1966).

A dealer cannot claim protection of 9–307(2). See United Gas Improvement Co. v. McFalls, 18 Pa.D. & C.2d 713, 1 UCC Rep.Serv. 508 (C.P.1959); Mahaley v. Colonial Trading Co., 6 UCC Rep.Serv. 746 (Pa.C.P.1969); Muir v. Jefferson Credit Corp., 108 N.J.Super. 586, 262 A.2d 33, 7 UCC Rep.Serv. 273 (Law Div.1970).

**93.** § 9–307 (1952 Official Draft).

**94.** Editorial Board for the Uniform Commercial Code, 1956 Recommendations 284 (1956).

**95.** For example, in Everett Nat'l Bank v. Deschuiteneer, 109 N.H. 112, 244 A.2d 196, 5 UCC Rep.Serv. 561 (1968),

defendant purchased an automobile from a purported dealer. The dealer had allegedly purchased it from the debtor who had in turn given a security interest to the plaintiff. The plaintiff, the original financier, was attempting to enforce his security interest against the defendant purchaser who claimed the protection of 9–307 (2). The New Hampshire Supreme Court found that 9–307(2) would not protect the buyer in such circumstance since his seller was purportedly a dealer. Accord, New England Merchants Nat'l Bank v. Auto Owners Fin. Co., Inc., 355 Mass. 487, 245 N.E. 2d 437, 6 UCC Rep.Serv. 58 (1969); National Shawmut Bank v. Jones, 108 N.H. 386, 236 A.2d 484, 4 UCC Rep. Serv. 1021 (1967) (dictum); Muir v. Jefferson Credit Corp., 108 N.J.Super. 586, 262 A.2d 33, 7 UCC Rep.Serv. 273 (Law Div.1970). See also 2 Gilmore § 26.12 at 716.

**96.** See 2 Gilmore § 26.12 at 716.

faith purchasers from certain prior interests.[97]  In certain respects, 2–403 is more generous to subsequent purchasers than is 9–307.  So the question: May a subsequent purchaser disappointed under 9–307 fall back on 2–403 and argue that it renders him superior to a prior security interest?  We believe the answer is no, and we think that the cases holding to the contrary are in error.[98]  We find the New Hampshire court's interpretation to be persuasive: In National Shawmut Bank v. Jones,[99] the court held that the buyer did not qualify for the preferred treatment of 9–307(1) because the competing security interest had not been "created by his seller."  Buyer also argued that he took free from the security interest under 2–403.  The court rejected that argument and found that 2–403 did not apply in part on the basis of the restrictive language in 9–306(2) referring to Article Nine (emphasis added):

> Except where this *Article* otherwise provides, a security interest continues in collateral notwithstanding sale, exchange, etc.[100]

In addition the court pointed to 2–403(4) which at least intimates that the dispute between purchasers and secured creditors should be governed by Article Nine:

> The rights of other purchasers of goods and of lien creditors are governed by the Articles on Secured Transactions (Article 9) . . . . [101]

The outcome of the *Jones*' case is also supported by comment 2 to 2–403.  In pertinent part that comment provides:

> As to entrusting by a secured party, subsection (2) is limited by the more specific provisions of Section 9–307(1), which

---

**97.**  Section 2–403(2) reads:

Any entrusting of possession of goods to a merchant who deals in goods of that kind gives him power to transfer all rights of the entruster to a buyer in ordinary course of business.

**98.**  In several cases courts have suggested that 9–307 and 2–403 may be used interchangeably.  See Sterling Acceptance Co. v. Grimes, 194 Pa. Super. 503, 168 A.2d 600, 1 UCC Rep. Serv. 487 (1961); Kapral v. Hanover Nat'l Bank, 1 UCC Rep.Serv. 542 (Pa. C.P.1962); Charles S. Martin Distrib. Co. v. Banks, 111 Ga.App. 538, 142 S.E.2d 309, 2 UCC Rep.Serv. 900 (1965); Makransky v. Long Island Reo Truck Co., 58 Misc.2d 338, 295 N.Y.S.2d 240, 5 UCC Rep.Serv. 1204 (Sup.Ct. 1968).

**99.**  108 N.H. 386, 236 A.2d 484, 4 UCC Rep.Serv. 1021 (1967).

**100.**  Section 9–201 provides in part:

Except as otherwise provided by this Act a security agreement is effective according to its terms between the parties, against purchasers of the collateral and against creditors. . . .

Although one might view the section's reference to the entire "Act" as authority for applying 2–403 to disputes between secured creditors and purchasers of collateral, we conclude that the draftsmen intended the more specific provision of 9–306 to govern the general statement of 9–201.

**101.**  However, 2–403(4) is ambiguous. One could read the reference to "other purchasers" to mean that only those who do not qualify as buyers in the ordinary course of business under 2–403(2) are relegated to Article Nine. See § 2–403, Comment 4.

deny protection to a person buying farm products from a person engaged in farming operations.

Thus, we conclude that the draftsmen intended that priority disputes between secured creditors and subsequent purchasers be governed exclusively by Article Nine and that they did not intend that such purchasers invoke the more generous provisions of 2–403.

Note that there could be a case in which both 2–403 and 9–307 come into play. Assume, for example, that secured creditor takes a perfected security interest in a lathe. Debtor in turn delivers the lathe to Joe's Machine Shop for repairs. Joe is also a merchant who deals in lathes, and in a weak moment he sells the lathe to a buyer in the ordinary course of business. We now have a three-cornered dispute: buyer in the ordinary course v. debtor (as to debtor's equity) and buyer in the ordinary course v. secured creditor (as to the security interest). The first dispute should be governed by 2–403 and the second dispute by 9–201, 9–306(2), and 9–307. In the hypothetical we have posed, the buyer will take free of the debtor's equity (for he is the buyer of an "entrusted" chattel under 2–403(2)) but he will not take free of the secured creditor's interest (for his seller did not "create" the security interest and he so fails to fit within 9–307(1)).

Why the draftsmen were more protective of the secured creditor's interest in 9–307 than of an owner's equity in 2–403, we cannot say. Perhaps they concluded that the owner deserves less protection since he has the power to select the merchant to whom he will entrust the goods, and the secured creditor has no such control; perhaps it was nothing more sinister than an oversight; or perhaps we see the lender's hand at work in the drafting. In any event courts should use care to limit their consideration to Article Nine in those circumstances in which a buyer is competing with a secured creditor.

### § 25–16  Priority of Purchasers of Goods—Special Problems Involving Vehicles, Aircraft and Non-Code Recording Acts

The problem of the relationship between the Code and motor vehicle certificate of title legislation keeps cropping up like a broken spring in an old couch. Elsewhere at excessive length we have discussed the difficulties of perfecting and maintaining a perfected security interest in automobiles.[102] Here we give mercifully brief consideration to the question that arises when a secured party who has recorded his security interest on a certificate of title claims that certificate of title law governs his rights against a purchaser of the auto who claims that 9–307 governs. We also consider the corresponding problem which arises in respect to aircraft under the Federal Aviation Act.[103]

Consider the situation in which the creditor takes a security interest in an automobile held for sale by a car dealer. Normally,

---

102. See Section 23–21 supra.         103. 49 U.S.C.A. §§ 1403–1406 (1970).

no certificate of title is outstanding until a car is first sold at retail. Accordingly, any conflict between the secured party and the first retail purchaser of an automobile will usually be governed exclusively by the Code. In Sterling Acceptance Co. v. Grimes,[104] the creditor's security interest was noted on a special dealer's certificate of title. Nevertheless, the Pennsylvania court held that section 9–307 governed and that the rights of the purchaser were superior to those of the secured party. The court rejected the secured party's contention that 9–302(3) (b) removed the case from Article Nine; it found that the cited section referred only to the filing provisions of Article Nine. Associates Discount Corp. v. Rattan Chevrolet, Inc.[105] also involved a dispute between a purchaser of collateral and a secured party. The secured party claimed a superior interest in the auto under a provision of the Texas certificate of title act which provides that sale of a motor vehicle "shall not affect the rights of any mortgagee as against all third parties." The Texas Supreme Court ruled that the certificate of title act and the Code must be construed *in pari materia* and that the quoted section must give way to the rule expressed in 9–307.

Because certificates will have been issued for them, used cars are more likely to present a direct conflict between certificate of title acts and the Code. Assume, for example, that a secured creditor perfected his security interest in dealer's used cars by properly recording his security interest pursuant to the local certificate of title act. In such case does a buyer from the dealer take free under 9–307(1)? Correria v. Orlando Bank and Trust Co.[106] is the most pertinent case. There the dealer's creditor held the certificates of title but apparently took no steps to note its security interest in the autos. When a purchaser was unable to obtain license plates without the certificate of title, he sued the bank for delivery of the certificate. The Florida Court of Appeals had no trouble in rejecting the bank's claim that the rights in the auto were governed by the Florida certificate of title act. The court relied upon 2–403 and 9–307(1) and held that the purchaser's rights were superior to those of the secured party. However, dicta in *Grimes* [107] suggest that the purchaser of a used car might not receive the benefit of section 9–307 because he knows that a certificate of title has been issued and expects to receive it at the time of sale.

Although we have found no case which squarely holds that the rights of a purchaser of a used car from a dealer are superior to those of a secured party who has recorded his security interest under a certificate of title act, the trend favors the purchaser. In this situation the purchaser's position is supported by sound technical and policy

104.  194 Pa.Super. 503, 168 A.2d 600, 1 UCC Rep.Serv. 487 (1961). Accord Kapral v. Hanover Nat'l Bank, 1 UCC Rep.Serv. 542 (Pa.C.P.1962).

105.  462 S.W.2d 546, 8 UCC Rep.Serv. 117 (Tex.Sup.Ct.1970).

106.  235 So.2d 20, 7 UCC Rep.Serv. 937 (Fla.App.1970).

107.  194 Pa.Super. 503, 168 A.2d 600, 1 UCC Rep.Serv. 487 (1961). Contra Kapral v. Hanover Nat'l Bank, 1 UCC Rep.Serv. 542 (Pa.C.P.1962) (dictum).

arguments. In the first place the misconduct of the dealers in these cases is normally more susceptible to control by the secured party than by a purchaser who has neither the leverage nor the opportunity to exercise control over a dealer. Secondly, the purchaser in such cases falls squarely within the class of persons section 9–307(1) is designed to protect. Moreover, section 9–302(3) does not render the whole of Article Nine inapplicable. It merely excludes some transactions from the Code's filing system.

We turn briefly to clashes between the Code and the federal law on aircraft. There is no dispute that the provisions of the Federal Aviation Act govern perfection of security interests in aircraft.[108] Whether the conflict between a purchaser and a prior secured party is governed by Article Nine or by federal statutory and common law is up in the air. One may argue that section 1403(d) of the Federal Aviation Act provides its own rule:

> Each conveyance or other instrument recorded by means of or under the system provided for in subsection (a) or (b) of this section shall from the time of its filing for recordation be valid as to all persons without further or other recordation. . . .

On the other hand, one may argue that Congress preempted the field only with respect to perfection of security interests and intended to leave priority conflicts between the purchasers and secured parties to state law. The courts have split on this question.[109]

While we are open to persuasion to the contrary, we incline to the view that the Federal Aviation Act does not govern such priority disputes and that 9–307 controls.[110] Although some aircraft are sufficiently expensive that one might expect buyers to conduct title searches and so exclude those buyers from 9–307(1)'s protection, we see little harm in giving the purchaser the protection of that section.

In summary, we believe that courts should use 9–307 in virtually all cases to resolve disputes between a secured party and a subsequent purchaser of an automobile or aircraft. Such a solution will promote uniformity and will yield a workable and well conceived rule for these cases. Although both the certificate of title acts and the federal act have provisions which arguably govern this priority conflict, neither indicates that its draftsmen considered the unique policy issues involved.

---

108. See Annot., 22 A.L.R.3d 1270, 1275–76 (1968) and the cases cited therein.

109. Compare Northern Ill. Corp. v. Bishop Distrib. Co., 284 F.Supp. 121 (W.D.Mich.1968) (state law governs priorities in aircraft), with Dowell v. Beech Acceptance Corp., 3 Cal.3d 544, 476 P.2d 401, 8 UCC Rep.Serv. 274 (1970), cert. denied 40 U.S.L.W. 3162 (U.S. Oct. 12, 1971) (state law is preempted).

110. See 1 Gilmore, § 13.5 at 427. Compare § 9–104, Comment 1, with Review Committee for Article 9, 238–39.

### § 25–17  Purchasers of Chattel Paper and Non-negotiable Instruments, 9–308

Chattel paper and non-negotiable instruments lie somewhere on the spectrum between the negotiable instrument on the one hand and the account on the other; for the former possession is everything, for the latter it is nothing. Indeed 9–309 and the holder in due course provisions of Article Three often elevate the possessor (holder in due course) to first in right even though he is second in time.[111] In similar circumstances 9–308 gives priority to a much more limited class of persons whose claims are second in time but who have possession of the chattel paper or non-negotiable instrument. What is chattel paper and how does the 9–308 priority conflict arise? Chattel paper is conditional sale contracts, security agreements, leases of personal property, bailment leasees and, in the terms of 9–105, any other "writing . . . which evidence[s] both a monetary obligation and a security interest in or a lease of specific goods."[112] To set the stage for the priority conflict, assume that Bank floor plans dealer's inventory of automobiles, that is, Bank takes a security interest in all of the automobiles of the dealer and claims proceeds as well. Dealer sells a new automobile to a consumer who signs a security agreement under which he promises to pay $2,500 to automobile dealer. Dealer then sells the security agreement to finance company who pays him $2,300 as the discounted value of the "paper." Finally, dealer goes bankrupt or disappears. Bank claims the security agreement as proceeds of its collateral (the new car); finance company claims the security agreement as the collateral which it has just purchased. Who wins? In our hypothetical case finance company will probably win because it has complied with the conditions of 9–308:[113]

(1) Given new value

(2) Taken possession of the chattel paper

(3) In the ordinary course of his business

(4) Without knowledge that the specific paper or instrument is subject to a security interest.

---

111. See § 9–309, discussed in Section 25–18 infra.

112. § 9–105(1) (b). Comment 4 gives several illustrations of chattel paper. Even leases which do not qualify as security agreements are still chattel paper: "Thus, if the dealer enters into a straight lease of the tractor to the farmer (not intended as security), and then arranges to borrow money on the security of the lease, the lease is chattel paper." § 9–105, Comment 4.

113. Section 9–308 reads as follows:

A purchaser of chattel paper or a non-negotiable instrument who gives new value and takes possession of it in the ordinary course of his business and without knowledge that the specific paper or instrument is subject to a security interest has priority over a security interest which is perfected under Section 9–304 (permissive filing and temporary perfection). A purchaser of chattel paper who gives new value and takes possession of it in the ordinary course of his business has priority over a security interest in chattel paper which is claimed merely as proceeds of inventory subject to a security interest (Section 9–306), even though he knows that the specific paper is subject to the security interest.

In effect, the draftsmen have judged that businessmen and lenders should be permitted to purchase chattel paper without having first to examine the files—at least in cases in which they put out new money, take possession and conduct the transaction in the ordinary course of their business. The section thus accommodates the business expectation of quasi-negotiability—the expectation by businessmen that one who "buys" such paper in ignorance of others' claims and takes possession of it has a first claim to the paper.

The conditions the purchaser must meet to qualify under 9–308 are not difficult to define in the normal circumstance. It is simple enough to define possession in the case of chattel paper or non-negotiable instruments; "knowledge" is well defined in 1–201(27) and (25) and in the usual case, the lender will make a new advance or pay by check and so give "new value." The Code nowhere defines "new value," and there may be borderline cases in which it will be difficult to determine whether the purchaser of the chattel paper gave new value. Section 9–108 lists several forms of new value: making an advance, incurring an obligation or releasing a perfected security interest. Beyond those examples the courts are on their own.

The second sentence of 9–308 covers an even more limited class of purchasers than does the first sentence. One who buys under the second sentence will have priority "even though he knows that the specific paper is subject to the security interest." That is to say, the buyer under the second sentence may know of another claimant's interest and still be prior to him. One qualifies there only if he not only gives new value and takes possession in the ordinary course of his business but does so of chattel paper "which is claimed *merely as proceeds of inventory* subject to a security interest . . . ." (Emphasis added.) Before we examine the crucial words "merely as proceeds of inventory subject to a security interest," consider the significance of the differences between the two sentences. Comment 2 to 9–308 points out that one who is lending directly against chattel paper or non-negotiable instruments (not claiming merely as proceeds) but who does not wish to take possession of them may protect himself from a later 9–308 claimant "by stamping or noting on the paper the fact that it has been assigned to him." By so stamping or noting the paper, he gives a subsequent purchaser "knowledge" and so deprives him of the priority which the first sentence of 9–308 would otherwise give. Such a procedure facilitates the widespread practice of lending against paper such as that arising on the sale of furniture and appliances under an indirect collection system. Under such a procedure the seller retains possession of the paper and makes the collections for the lender.[114]

What of the cases in which the first lender claims merely as proceeds? In such a case a later party may prove to be superior to the

---

114. Professor Gilmore so describes the history and purpose of 9–308. 2 Gilmore § 25.5 at 668–69.

proceeds claimant even though such later party had knowledge.   Presumably, the later party is favored on the assumption that chattel paper is his main course but merely the frosting on the cake for the mere proceeds claimant.   But how does one distinguish a mere proceeds claimant from any other?   Surely the financing statement which the original lender filed is not determinative of the question.   Assume, for example, that a lender files as to furniture store's inventory of furniture and "proceeds" but that lender's officer in charge of the loan states that his principal reliance in deciding to make the loan was upon the chattel paper, not upon the inventory?   At that point is his claim in the chattel paper "merely as proceeds?"   Or does he now have a claim of greater magnitude?   In the words of Comment 2, has he "given value against the paper"?   We are unsure;   our inclination is to allow the lending officer to testify and to find his more than a "merely as proceeds" interest if he convinces the court that he, in fact, placed substantial reliance on the chattel paper in making his loan.

For a review of the foregoing principles, consider Associates Discount Corp. v. Old Freeport Bank,[115] a 1966 case that aptly illustrates the operation of 9–308.   There the bank had security interest in the automobiles of the dealer.   Dealer sold one automobile to a buyer for a cash down payment and caused the buyer to execute a "bailment lease," that is, a security agreement, under which the buyer promised to pay approximately $2,000 in installments for the automobile.   This lease was sold to plaintiff, a discounter, for $1,775.   Dealer turned that amount over to the bank with instructions to the bank that it should transfer the "dealer title" to the discounter.   The bank refused to surrender the title to the car.   It forced the buyer to execute a second agreement under the terms of which the buyer was obliged to pay the bank, not the discounter.   The bank argued that the amount which it had received from the dealer had been properly credited against other obligations of the dealer.   The court rejected the bank's argument;   it found that the buyer took free of the bank's security interest because of 9–307 and that the bank retained a proceeds claim to the chattel paper under 9–306.   However, the court found that the discounter had a prior claim to the chattel paper under 9–308 and so took free of the bank's interest.

Apart from the difficulty in defining the phrase "merely as proceeds," section 9–308 poses no significant lawyer questions.   One anomaly in 9–308 (which will be cured by the revision to 9–308 proposed in 1971) [116] is its differential treatment of a knowing subse-

---

115.   421 Pa. 609, 220 A.2d 621, 3 UCC Rep.Serv. 481 (1966).

116.   Section 9–308 of the 1971 Recommendations reads:

A purchaser of chattel paper or an instrument who gives new value and takes possession of it in the ordinary course of his business has priority over a security interest in the chattel paper or instrument

(a) which is perfected under Section 9–304 (permissive filing and temporary perfection) or under Section 9–306 (perfection as to proceeds) if he acts without knowledge that the specific paper or instrument is subject to a security interest;   or

quent taker of chattel paper and a knowing subsequent taker of negotiable paper. Under the second sentence of 9–308, one who takes chattel paper for new value, etc. and with knowledge of another's proceeds claim to that paper will defeat the prior claimant. If in similar circumstances the subsequent party took a negotiable instrument, he would have to look to 9–309 and the holder in due course doctrine for priority over the prior party. But his knowledge of the proceeds interest would prevent his becoming a holder in due course of the instrument, and he would be subordinate. Of course, this outcome is anomalous because it makes chattel paper more "negotiable" than a negotiable instrument in the same circumstances. The 1971 draft includes negotiable instruments in 9–308, and so permits a taker who qualifies under 9–308 to defeat a prior proceeds claim even though he is not a holder in due course.

### § 25–18  Purchasers of Instruments and Documents, 9–309

Section 9–309 is a straightforward but important provision that governs the interface between Article Nine on the one hand and Articles Three, Seven and Eight on the other hand. It reads in full as follows:

> Nothing in this Article limits the rights of a holder in due course of a negotiable instrument (Section 3–302) or a holder to whom a negotiable document of title has been duly negotiated (Section 7–501) or a bona fide purchaser of a security (Section 8–301) and such holders or purchasers take priority over an earlier security interest even though perfected. Filing under this Article does not constitute notice of the security interest to such holders or purchasers.

The comments tell us that the section simply carries forward the pre-Code law; its purpose is to make clear that a secured party's Article Nine claim is subordinate to the claim of one who qualifies as a holder in due course, one to whom a negotiable document has been duly negotiated, or a bona fide purchaser of a security as the case may be. Assume, for example, that a secured party takes a security interest in various negotiable warehouse receipts and that he perfects the security interest by filing. Foolishly, he leaves the debtor in possession of the warehouse receipts, and the debtor duly negotiates them to a third party. In the absence of 9–309, we would have an irreconcilable conflict between the secured creditor on the one hand who would claim a perfectly valid and perfected security interest under Article Nine [117] and the one to whom the warehouse receipts have been

---

(b) which is claimed merely as proceeds of inventory subject to a security interest (Section 9–306) even though he knows that the specific paper or instrument is subject to the security interest.

Review Committee for Article 9, 104–105.

117. Absent 9–309, the secured creditor could point to 9–201 (which gives him priority over all competitors unless another provision subordinates him) and to 9–312 (which would date his priority against other secured creditors from the date of his filing).

duly negotiated who would claim all the rights due to one in his shoes under 7–501, *etc.*[118]  Section 9–309 resolves the conflict by giving priority to the third party to whom the warehouse receipts have been duly negotiated.  An identical problem is presented when a prior lender claims a proceeds (9–306) interest in negotiable instruments that arise on the sale of his collateral, and the debtor transfers the instrument to a holder in due course.  By virtue of 9–309 and Article Three, the holder in due course will be victorious in such a case.

Out of an excess of caution the draftsmen in the last sentence of 9–309 have told us that an Article Nine filing does not "constitute notice of the security interest to such holders or purchasers."  That is to say, filing is not constructive notice of a third party's claim of title which would prohibit a subsequent taker from becoming a holder in due course, bona fide purchaser, or one to whom there has been due negotiation.

---

118.  Under 7–502, the due "negotiatee" receives "title to the document" and "title to the goods," and 7–502(2) nails down his supremacy over prior claimants in no uncertain terms:

Subject to the following section, title and rights so acquired are not defeated by any stoppage of the goods represented by the document or by surrender of such goods by the bailee, and are not impaired even though the negotiation or any prior negotiation constituted a breach of duty or even though any person has been deprived of possession of the document by misrepresentation, fraud, accident, mistake, duress, loss, theft or conversion, or even though a previous sale or other transfer of the goods or document has been made to a third person.

# CHAPTER 26

# DEFAULT AND ITS CONSEQUENCES

*Analysis*

Sec.
26-1. Introduction.
26-2. Defining "Default".
26-3. —— Acceleration Clauses.
26-4. Creditor's Alternatives Upon Default.
26-5. Repossession.
26-6. —— Self-Help.
26-7. —— Judicial Action.
26-8. Strict Foreclosure.
26-9. Resale of Repossessed Collateral.
26-10. —— The Notice Requirement.
26-11. —— Commercially Reasonable.
26-12. Consequences of Creditor Misbehavior.
26-13. Creditor Misbehavior—Criminal or Tort Liability.
26-14. —— Liability Under the UCC, § 9-507(1).
26-15. —— Denial of a Deficiency.

## § 26-1  Introduction

Default, often occurring in conjunction with the debtor's bankruptcy, is the event which calls the lawyer's work to task. Here his advice and draftsmanship receive the "acid test." Here, in repossessing and realizing on the collateral, the secured party must tread a narrow path to satisfy his claim and yet avoid tort and statutory liability. Moreover, default and its consequences are uniquely lawyer concerns. The bank vice-president who makes the loan does not contemplate a default, nor does the debtor. If anyone injects the unspeakable possibility of default into the loan negotiations it will be the lawyer, and, of course, it will fall to him to sue for any deficiency.

Part Five of Article Nine defines the rights and remedies of the secured party and his debtor. Within certain limitations the parties may supplement or vary Part Five by their security agreement.[1]

---

1. Section 9-501(3) limits the parties' freedom of contract as follows:

   To the extent that they give rights to the debtor and impose duties on the secured party, the rules stated in the subsections referred to below may not be waived or varied except as provided with respect to compulsory disposition of collateral (subsection (1) of Section 9-505) and with respect to redemption of collateral (Section 9-506) but the parties may by agreement determine the standards by which the fulfillment of these rights and duties is to be measured if such standards are not manifestly unreasonable:

   (a) subsection (2) of Section 9-502 and subsection (2) of Section 9-504 insofar as they require accounting for surplus proceeds of collateral;

   (b) subsection (3) of Section 9-504 and subsection (1) of Section 9-505 which deal with disposition of collateral;

   (c) subsection (2) of Section 9-505 which deals with acceptance of collateral as discharge of obligation;

   (d) Section 9-506 which deals with redemption of collateral; and

   (e) subsection (1) of Section 9-507 which deals with the secured party's

The crunch provisions of Part Five give the secured party the right to take possession of the collateral upon the debtor's default and dispose of it in satisfaction of his claim, all without setting foot in court in most cases.[2] But in so doing, the creditor must comply with 9–504

liability for failure to comply with this Part.

2. For a discussion of Article Nine's repossession provisions, see § 26–5, infra.

The decision of the Supreme Court in Sniadach v. Family Fin. Corp., 395 U.S. 337 (1969) raises questions about the constitutionality of § 9–503 and kindred statutes which authorize prejudgment seizure of property by creditors. See Note, 68 Mich.L.Rev. 986 (1970). Briefly, *Sniadach* held that prejudgment garnishment of wages deprives the debtor of due process of law. Subsequently debtors have asked the courts to introduce the trappings of due process into other modes of creditor relief. See Fuentes v. Faircloth, 317 F.Supp. 954 (S.D.Fla.1970) (upholding replevin statute), prob. juris. noted, 401 U.S. 906 (1971); Epps v. Cortese, 326 F.Supp. 127 (E. D.Pa.1971) (upholding replevin statute), prob. juris. noted, 402 U.S. 994 (1971); Laprease v. Raymours Furniture Co., 315 F.Supp. 716 (N.D.N.Y.1970) (striking down replevin statute as violative of due process and the 4th Amend.); Dorsey v. Community Stores Corp., 52 F.R.D. 13 (E.D.Wis.1971) (stayed decision on replevin statute pending outcome of *Fuentes*, supra); Jernigan v. Economy Exterminating Co., 327 F. Supp. 24 (N.D.Ga.1971) (upholding prejudgment seizure of auto pursuant to bail trover statute); Wheeler v. Adams Co., 322 F.Supp. 645 (D.Md. 1971) (refused to issue injunction staying replevin action in state court). See also Blair v. Pitchess, 96 Cal. Rptr. 42, 486 P.2d 1242 (1971) (striking down claim and delivery statute on the grounds it violates 4th Amend. and deprived debtor of due process).

Two federal courts have considered and rejected arguments that repossession pursuant to § 9–503 unconstitutionally deprives the debtor of due process. In Brunswick Corp. v. J. & P., Inc., 424 F.2d 100 (10th Cir. 1970), the court responded to *Sniadach* as follows:

"Furthermore, we find no merit in appellants' additional contention that under the recent Supreme Court case of Sniadach v. Family Finance Corp., 395 U.S. 337, 89 S.Ct. 1820, 23 L.Ed.

2d 349 (1969) they have been the victims of a taking of property without the procedural due process required by the Fourteenth Amendment. Sniadach expressly was a unique case involving, 'a specialized type of property presenting distinct problems in our economic system.' That case involved wage garnishment without notice or hearing prior to judgment on a promissory note. It is not in the least comparable to the case here on appeal involving enforcement of a security interest. Appellants have contractually agreed that upon default, their creditor Brunswick ' * * * may take immediate possession of said property [collateral] and for this purpose the Seller may enter the premises where said property may be and remove the same without notice or demand, and with or without legal process; thereupon all the rights and interests of the Buyer to and in said property shall terminate.' Appellants admit that they were in default on the conditional sale, so they cannot now be heard to object to the default procedures they agreed to simply because Brunswick did utilize the legal process of replevin under bond."

The court appears to rely on the fact that the debtor waived any objection to repossession by its contract and upon the fact that collateral is sufficiently different from wages to call for a different rule.

In McCormick v. First Nat'l Bank, 322 F.Supp. 604, 9 UCC Rep.Serv. 137 (S.D.Fla.1971), the court rejected the debtor's argument on the ground that it lacked jurisdiction because the claim involved property rights and the repossession was not under color of state law because the contract authorized repossession without regard to state law. However in Valkeburg v. AUCO Thrift Co., No. 243237 (Cal.Super.Ct., Santa Clara County, Sept. 30, 1971), the court relied on *Sniadach* and enjoined the secured party's repossession on the ground that such action violated procedural due process.

We agree with the 10th Circuit's analysis and would sustain 9–503 against constitutional attack. See further text accompanying notes 67a, 67b, 67c infra.

or 9–505 and if he deviates, the Code affords a remedy to the debtor and others having an interest in the collateral.[3] The principal legal problems of Part Five of Article Nine concern the propriety of the secured party's conduct in repossessing and reselling the collateral and the debtor's remedies for illegal or improper acts by the secured party. Although the creditor may, on default, resort to other methods to satisfy his claim, (strict foreclosure under 9–505 and judgment and execution on the debt under 9–501(1)) here we will focus on his right to resell the collateral because resale is the usual method of realization.

## § 26–2   Defining "Default"

"Default" triggers the secured creditor's rights under Part Five of Article Nine.[4] But what is "default?" Article Nine does not define the word; instead it leaves this to the parties and to any scraps of common law lying around.[5] Apart from the modest limitations imposed by the unconscionability doctrine and the requirement of good faith, default is "whatever the security agreement says it is."[6] Security agreements often include default clauses as long as the creditor's arm and as broad as his counsel's imagination. A provision which stipulates that debtor's non-payment constitutes default is only the starting point for a well-drawn default clause. A default clause should also take into account the possibility that the debtor will suffer financial reverses (i. e., bankruptcy or assignment for benefit of creditors). When the collateral is goods, the default clause commonly includes provisions on the loss, damage, destruction or removal of the goods and a debtor's covenant to maintain insurance on them. Of course, the content of these clauses varies with the facts of each transaction and with the foresight of the lawyers doing the drafting.[7] In

---

3.   For a discussion of debtor's remedies against a misbehaving creditor, see Section 26–12 infra.

4.   §§ 9–503 to 9–505.

5.   The Uniform Consumer Credit Code (UCCC) does not attempt to define default because with some exceptions it relies upon the provisions of UCC Article Nine, Part 5, to determine rights and remedies upon default. See UCCC § 5.103, Comment 1. See also The National Consumer Law Center, Conference on the Uniform Consumer Credit Code 98 (1969). The authors felt that the UCCC provided inadequate protection for consumers and therefore defined default as the failure without justification under any provision of law of the consumer to pay:

(a) three successive installments within the period of time allowable by the Act, or

(b) any remaining balance within three months after the due date of the final installment, or

(c) any amount resulting from the total of the unpaid delinquent installments constituting 30% of the amount financed.

6.   2 G. Gilmore, Security Interests in Personal Property § 43.3 at 1193 (1965). See Borochoff Properties, Inc. v. Howard Lumber Co., 115 Ga.App. 691, 155 S.E.2d 651, 4 UCC Rep.Serv. 229 (1967) (parties' contract defines default).

7.   See 5 R. Henson & W. Davenport, 5 U.L.A. (Forms and Materials), Form 9:1105, at 259 (Master ed. 1968) for a

each case the careful lawyer will study the transaction at hand and insert provisions necessary to protect the secured creditor against those risks which might adversely affect his interest in the collateral.

The case of Whisenhunt v. Allen Parker Co. demonstrates the importance of thoughtful planning in the drafting stage.[8] There the secured party took possession of the collateral immediately upon death of the debtor. Although the security agreement specified that the creditor could take possession upon default, it did not define default. The administrator of the debtor's estate claimed, *inter alia*, that repossession was improper because no payments were due at the time of the decedent's death. The court held that the death of the debtor did not automatically constitute a default. It concluded that use of the term "default" without further elaboration, meant that default would occur only when the debtor failed to meet his obligation to make payments on the debt. Thus, the lawyer must carefully consider those contingencies which may seriously affect his client's security and see that the security agreement specifies them as events of default.[9]

model clause in a security agreement covering accounts receivable:

The occurrence of any one or more of the following events shall constitute a default by Borrower hereunder:

(a) the failure of Borrower to pay on demand the principal of any note evidencing a loan hereunder, or to pay the interest thereon punctually when due;

(b) the failure of Borrower to keep, observe or perform any provisions of this agreement required hereunder to be kept, observed or performed by it;

(c) default by Borrower in the observance or performance of any other of Borrower's Liabilities to Bank;

(d) the making or furnishing by Borrower to Bank of any representation, warranty or certificate in connection with this agreement which is materially false;

(e) the making of an assignment by Borrower for the benefit of its creditors;

(f) the commencement of proceedings in bankruptcy or for reorganization of Borrower or for the readjustment of any of its debts under the Bankruptcy Act or under any other law, whether state or federal, now or hereafter existing for the relief of debtors; or

(g) the appointment of a receiver or trustee for Borrower or for any substantial part of its assets; or the institution of any proceedings for the dissolution, or the full or partial liquidation of Borrower.

If Borrower shall be in default under this agreement, Bank shall have the right to declare payment of any and all notes of Borrower issued hereunder and all other of Borrower's Liabilities to Bank to be due and payable forthwith, and thereupon to avail itself of such other rights with respect to any then outstanding notes evidencing loans hereunder and any and all Accounts and any other Collateral therefore, which are provided for herein, in said notes and in any separate assignments of Collateral. In addition, Bank shall have all rights with respect thereto which are provided for in the Uniform Commercial Code of —— (regardless of whether such Code has been enacted in the jurisdiction where rights or remedies are asserted), including the right to require Borrower to assemble any Collateral for Borrower's Liabilities to Bank, and to make it available to Bank at a place reasonably convenient to both parties. The parties hereto hereby declare that all Accounts transferred to Bank hereunder are transferred in fact to secure loans and are not, in fact, sold to Bank regardless of whether any assignment thereof which is separate from this agreement, is in form absolute.

8.   119 Ga.App. 813, 168 S.E.2d 827, 6 UCC Rep.Serv. 969 (1969).

9.   Even though a true default has occurred, the debtor may argue that the

## § 26–3  Defining "Default"—Acceleration Clauses

Security agreements almost universally provide that under certain circumstances the secured party may accelerate the maturity of the debt and cause all payments to become immediately due and payable.  Typically, such clauses give the creditor the right to accelerate the debt upon the occurrence of any default on the part of the debtor.  Creditors usually insert acceleration clauses to avoid an expensive series of law suits for each installment payment as it becomes due.  The creditor may also wish to have the leverage that an acceleration clause gives him.  Courts uniformly uphold and enforce acceleration clauses.[10]

An "insecurity clause" (one type of acceleration clause) provides that the creditor may accelerate the maturity of the entire debt whenever he "deems himself insecure."  The need for an insecurity clause is less clear than the need for a general acceleration clause and it can present a temptation for the trigger-happy creditor.[11]  Nevertheless, courts have generally upheld insecurity clauses.[12]  Some courts read them to permit acceleration at the creditor's whim,[13] while others

secured party has by his previous failure to require literal compliance with the terms of the security agreement waived his right to exact a penalty for a specific deviation.  Article Nine Part 5, does not authorize such claim, but Section 1–103 says general principles of law are applicable to all transactions under the Code.  See Varela v. Wells Fargo Bank, 15 Cal.App.3d 741, 93 Cal.Rptr. 428, 8 UCC Rep. Serv. 1106 (3d Dist.1971) (secured creditor estopped from repossession when errors in recording payments misled debtor).  However, in Universal CIT Credit Corp. v. Middlesboro Motor Sales, Inc., 424 S.W.2d 409, 411, 4 UCC Rep.Serv. 1126, 1129 (Ky.App. 1968), the Court recognized as effective a clause in the security agreement which stipulated that "waiver of any default is not waiver of any subsequent default."

**10.**  See, e. g., General Motors Acceptance Corp. v. Shuey, 243 Ky. 74, 47 S.W.2d 968 (1932).  But note the line of cases following Street v. Commercial Credit Co., 35 Ariz. 479, 281 P. 46 (1929) applying Uniform Conditional Sales Act § 18 and holding that a secured party may not require a debtor to pay the entire balance due to redeem the collateral after default irrespective of an acceleration clause in the security agreement.  See 83 A.L.R. 959, 976 (1933) and the cases cited therein; 99 A.L.R. 1288, 1301 (1935) and the cases cited therein.  However, these cases are overruled by §

9–506 (which says that "debtor  .  . may . . . redeem . . . by tendering fulfillment of all obligations secured by the collateral") and the accompanying comment (which says "if the agreement contains a clause accelerating the entire balance due on default in one installment, the entire balance would have to be tendered").

**11.**  Mistrust of such clauses is manifested in various retail installment sales acts which prohibit or restrict the operation of insecurity clauses. See, e. g., Mich.Comp.Laws Ann. § 14.-45, .865 (1967): "No retail installment contract or retail charge agreement shall contain any provisions by which a) in the absence of buyer's default in the performance of any of his obligations, the holder may accelerate the maturity of any part or all of the amount owing thereunder."  N.Y.Pers. Prop.Law § 403(3) (b) (McKinney 1962) prohibits a clause by which "[i]n the absence of buyer's default, the holder may, arbitrarily and without reasonable cause, accelerate the maturity of any part on all of the amount owing thereunder."

**12.**  See, e. g., Boice v. Boice, 27 Minn. 371, 7 N.W. 687 (1880); Boak v. Brewer, 5 Misc.2d 924, 160 N.Y.S.2d 146 (Sup.Ct.1957); Cline v. Libby, 46 Wis. 123, 49 N.W. 832 (1879).

**13.**  One of the strongest statements of this approach appears in Werner v.

deny acceleration unless a reasonable, prudent creditor would consider himself insecure.[14] Section 1–208 expressly authorizes the use of insecurity clauses as follows:

> A term providing that one party or his successor in interest may accelerate payment or performance or require collateral or additional collateral "at will" or "when he deems himself insecure" or in words of similar import shall be construed to mean that he shall have power to do so only if he in good faith believes that the prospect of payment or performance is impaired. The burden of establishing lack of good faith is on the party against whom the power has been exercised.

Since 1–208 requires only that the secured party act in "good faith," ("honesty in fact")[15] the Code standard seems to lie somewhere between a strict objective test (reasonable prudent man) and a thoroughly subjective one (whim). The draftsmen apparently intended an objective standard. Professor Gilmore explicitly rejects the subjective standard and says 1–208 means that the "creditor has the right to accelerate if under all the circumstances a reasonable man, motivated by good faith, would have done so."[16]

To date it is unclear whether the courts will follow Professor Gilmore, and the practical differences between an "objective" and a "subjective" test are even less clear. Two decided cases illustrate the difficulties inherent in formulating the Code's standard of "good faith". In the first case, Fort Knox National Bank v. Gustafson,[17] the Kentucky Court of Appeals speaks almost exclusively in "subjective" language, but it would almost certainly have decided the same way under an objective test. The debtor was eight months behind on rent payments and had consulted an attorney about the possibility

Bergman, 28 Kan. 60 (1882), where the court said:

The only question at all material in such a case is, whether the mortgagee does in fact so feel (insecure); and if the mortgagee claims that he has such a feeling, and afterward on the trial testifies that at the time he took possession of the property he had such feeling, and if upon the facts of the case it is possible at all to believe that any person, however timid and fearful he might be, might have had such a feeling, then it should be held that the mortgagee had a right to take possession of the property.

Id. at 65. Accord, American State Bank v. Holding, 189 Kan. 641, 371 P.2d 167 (1962); City Loan & Sav. Co. v. Sheban, 65 Ohio App. 7, 29 N.E.2d 171 (1937).

14. The court in Commercial Credit Co. v. Cain, 190 Miss. 866, 1 So.2d 776 (1941), said that the creditor is justified in exercising his rights under an insecurity clause under "circumstances of presently apparent danger as would furnish probable cause for the belief that the security is unsafe when viewed in good faith by a man of reasonable prudence." Id. at 871, 1 So.2d at 777. Accord, Monson v. Pickett, 253 Minn. 550, 93 N.W.2d 537 (1958); Goggins v. Bookout, 141 Mont. 449, 378 P.2d 212 (1963); Boak v. Brewer, 5 Misc.2d 924, 160 N.Y.S.2d 146 (Sup.Ct.1957). See generally Annot., 125 A.L.R. 313 (1940) and the cases cited therein.

15. § 1–201(19).

16. 2 G. Gilmore, Security Interests in Personal Property § 43.4 at 1197 (1965).

17. 385 S.W.2d 196, 2 UCC Rep.Serv. 336 (Ky.App.1964).

of filing in bankruptcy. However, he had also arranged with the secured party for a pay-off settlement and introduced evidence at trial that another agency had notified the secured party that funds were available for paying off the debt. The appellate court reversed the trial court and concluded that the creditor was sufficiently justified in accelerating the debt that the trial court should direct a verdict in his favor: "It must be remembered that here we are dealing with the 'good faith' *belief* of the bank—that is, its state of mind." [18]  (emphasis in original)

In the second case, Sheppard Federal Credit Union v. Palmer,[19] the Court of Appeals for the 5th Circuit paid homage to the objective nature of the 1–208 test, but reversed a lower court decision in favor of the debtor and remanded with an instruction to the trial court to impose the burden of proving bad faith upon the debtor. In that case an Air Force lieutenant obtained a loan from the base credit union to purchase an automobile. When he told the creditor of his intent to resign from the Air Force, the creditor repossessed the car under a clause which said he could repossess at any time he "shall . . . deem . . . said security unsafe or insecure . . . ." [20] The repossession was accomplished over the debtor's protestations that he had made all the payments promptly and could easily obtain higher wages outside of the Air Force because of his training as a registered nurse. In fact he did obtain a better paying job and continued to make the payments after repossession. He then sued the secured party and sought punitive as well as compensatory damages on the ground that the creditor repossessed "maliciously." The trial court instructed the jury that the debtor was "entitled to damages unless Credit Union proves by a preponderance of the evidence that it had reasonable grounds to believe . . . the debt involved herein or said security was unsafe or insecure. . . ." [21] Although the Court of Appeals, quoting Professor Gilmore, acknowledged that the Code enacts an objective test, it reversed because the trial judge had erroneously imposed the burden of proof upon the secured party. On the good faith test, the court remarked:

> . . . the Credit Union's determination that it was insecure was certainly erroneous; it could hardly have asked for a more conscientious and responsible debtor. However, it takes more than mere error to show unreasonableness or bad faith, not to mention malice.[22]

The above two cases indicate that the objective v. subjective dispute may not be very important. In the *Gustafson* case, it appears that the court would have reached the same result irrespective of the test applied. Presumably a creditor does not act in bad faith on either

18.  Id. at 200, 2 UCC Rep.Serv. at 341.

19.  408 F.2d 1369, 6 UCC Rep.Serv. 30 (5th Cir. 1969).

20.  Id. at 1370, 6 UCC Rep.Serv. at 31.

21.  Id. at 1371, 6 UCC Rep.Serv. at 31.

22.  Id. at 1373, 6 UCC Rep.Serv. at 34.

version of the test when he repossesses from a debtor in default who has gone so far as to consult a lawyer about the possibility of filing for bankruptcy.   Again while in *Palmer* the Court of Appeals explicitly applied an objective standard—one supposedly more favorable to the debtor—it openly invited the court below on remand to find the creditor in good faith, even though the debtor had not defaulted on his payments, held a responsible position in the armed forces and, because of his technical training, could easily obtain a high paying civilian job.   He was, as the court suggests, the very model debtor.

In the final analysis the operational effect of the standard applied must be measured by the results reached rather than the incantations of priests.   An examination of pre-Code cases reveals that although many courts required "good faith" or "reasonable grounds" or both for insecurity, in only a handful did the courts decide that acceleration was unreasonable, and thus improper.[23]   Thus, it appears that the courts, both before and after enactment of the Code are loath to find acceleration of a debt under an "insecurity clause" to be unreasonable.

Even the most reasonable creditor might justifiably consider himself insecure when the debtor's financial condition changes radically or the debtor endangers the collateral through his own misconduct or lack of care.   However, if the good faith limitation of 1–208 is to have any real effect, the courts will have to apply a more stringent standard than in the past.[24]   Certainly the Fifth Circuit's view in the *Palmer* case imposes no real restraint upon the secured party.   Hopefully, other courts will require more serious debtor misbehavior than in *Palmer* to justify acceleration.

## § 26–4   Creditor's Alternatives Upon Default

Part Five of Article Nine carries forward the main outlines of prior law.   Prior uniform laws, like the Code, permitted the secured creditor to take possession and resell, or retain the collateral in satisfaction of the debt.[25]   Likewise prior law permitted any creditor to

**23.**   See Moore v. Wimmer, 77 Cal.App. 2d 199, 174 P.2d 640 (4th Dist.1946); Thomas v. Beirne, 94 Colo. 429, 30 P. 2d 863 (1934); Burris v. Commercial Credit Corp., 15 Ill.App.2d 458, 146 N.E.2d 218 (1957); Rector-Wilhelmy Co. v. Nissen, 35 Neb. 716, 53 N.W. 670 (1892); Parks v. Phillips, 71 Nev. 313, 289 P.2d 1053 (1955); Cook v. CIT Corp., 191 S.C. 440, 4 S.E.2d 801 (1939).   See also Universal CIT Credit Corp. v. Johnson, 41 Ala.App. 148, 127 So.2d 642 (1960); Jacksonville Tractor Co. v. Nasworthy, 114 So.2d 463 (Fla. App.1959); Watson v. Cudney, 144 Ill. App. 624 (1908); Hendrickson v. Grengs, 237 Minn. 196, 54 N.W.2d 105 (1952); Oppenheimer v. Moore, 107 App.Div. 301, 95 N.Y.S. 138 (2d Dep't 1905); Darling v. Hunt, 46 App.Div. 631, 61 N.Y.S. 278 (4th Dep't 1899).

See generally Annot., 125 A.L.R. 313 (1940) and the cases cited therein.

**24.**   Note that the introductory clause to the definitions contained in 1–201 in part provide "unless the context otherwise requires."   One might argue that in the context of 1–208 "good faith" should be construed to prevent a creditor from arbitrary acceleration of the debt.   This construction would temper the subjective test of 1–201 (19) and bring 1–208 in line with reasonable business practices.

**25.**   See Uniform Conditional Sales Act § 16–26;   Uniform Trust Receipts Act § 6.

obtain judgment on the debt and levy against the debtor's property. The Code did draw together the various remedies existing under disparate bodies of pre-Code law applicable to the various pre-Code security devices, and did provide flexible procedures for the secured party to resell the collateral in satisfaction of the debt. Generally, the resale provisions of Part Five of Article Nine follow the less restrictive provisions of the Uniform Trust Receipts Acts, not the definite and formalized procedures required by the Uniform Conditional Sales Act.[26] The basic policies of these resale provisions, as expressed by the draftsmen, are two-fold: to allow realization on the collateral with minimum resort to judicial proceedings, and to encourage higher yields upon disposition by allowing private as well as public sale of the collateral.[27]

Consider the specific alternatives available to the creditor when the debtor defaults. Upon default the secured creditor will usually first seek a working arrangement or plan of compromise with the defaulting debtor. The possibility of repossession may provide considerable incentive for the debtor to agree to an amicable arrangement. Under the Code the creditor may choose between two basic methods of getting his money out of a balky debtor. First, he can seize the goods subject to his security interest and either keep them in satisfaction of the debt or resell them and apply the proceeds to the debt. Often a resale will result in a deficiency for which the debtor is usually liable.[28] Alternatively, the creditor can ignore his security

---

**26.** Comment 1 to § 9–504, points this out as follows:

The Uniform Trust Receipts Act provides that an entruster in possession after default holds the collateral with the rights and duties of a pledgee, and, in particular, that he may sell such collateral at public or private sale with a right to claim deficiency and a duty to account for any surplus. The Uniform Conditional Sales Act insisted on a sale at public auction with elaborate provisions for the giving of notice of sale. This section follows the more liberal provisions of the Trust Receipts Act. Although public sale is recognized, it is hoped that private sale will be encouraged where, as is frequently the case private sale through commercial channels will result in higher realization on collateral for the benefit of all parties. The only restriction placed on the secured party's method of disposition is that it must be commercially reasonable.

For extensive comparisons of Article Nine, Part 5, with prior law, see Project, California Chattel Security & Article 9 of the UCC, 8 U.C.L.A.L. Rev. 806, 951 (1961); Comment, Remedies on Default Under the Proposed

Uniform Commercial Code as Compared to Remedies Under Conditional Sales, 39 Marq.L.Rev. 246 (1955–56); 3 N.Y.State Law Revision Comm'n, 1955 Report 2092–2096 (1955).

**27.** Gilmore, Article 9 of the Uniform Commercial Code—Part V Default, in 7 Conference on Personal Finance Law Quarterly Report 4, 7 (1952).

**28.** A deficiency, as the name implies, is the amount by which the sum obtained from resale of the collateral fails to satisfy the debt outstanding at the time of default. Thus if the net proceeds from resale of a repossessed automobile are $900 and the amount still owed by the debtor is $1400, then the deficiency is $1400 less $900 or $500.

Note, however, that 9–504(1) stipulates that

[t]he proceeds of disposition shall be applied in the order following to

(a) the reasonable expenses of retaking, holding, preparing for sale, selling and the like and, to the extent provided for in the agreement and not prohibited by law, the rea-

interest and obtain a judgment on the underlying obligation and proceed by execution and levy.

Section 9-501(1) provides that: "He may reduce his claim to judgment, foreclose or otherwise enforce the security interest by any available judicial procedure." The Code does not say what the creditor must do to obtain judgment and execution on the debt; state statutes and common law of ancient vintage specify these steps, and they vary somewhat from state to state. Generally, the creditor must first commence suit and obtain a judgment for the debt owed.[29] After judgment the clerk of the court will, on request, issue a "writ of execution" (or the like). This writ recites that a judgment has been obtained and directs the sheriff or other appropriate officer to seize the property of the debtor and sell it to satisfy the judgment debt. With the writ in hand, the officer will levy against the debtor's property at his home or place of business (i. e., exercise dominion over it such that it is safely preserved for satisfaction of the debt). Finally, after giving public notice, the officer will sell the property at a public auction to the highest bidder and then turn proceeds necessary to satisfy the debt over to the creditor. The surplus, if any, goes to the debtor. An attractive alternative to levy is garnishment of the debtor's most liquid asset—his wages. Although the Truth-in-Lending Act severely limits the amount one can reach by garnishment,[30] wages remain an inviting asset for satisfaction of the debtor's obligation.

sonable attorney's fees and legal expenses incurred by the secured party;

(b) the satisfaction of indebtedness secured by the security interest under which the disposition is made;

See Shuchman, Profit on Default: An Archival Study of Automobile Repossession and Resale, 22 Stan.L.Rev. 20 (1969), for an examination of the amount realized on resale and the resulting deficiency in specific cases of automobile repossession.

29. In many cases the creditor will wish to assure that he will have some assets of the debtor against which to execute judgment, and he will attach the debtor's property before judgment. Attachment will normally be available only in limited sorts of circumstances. See, e. g. Mich.Comp.Laws Ann. § 600.4001 (1968) which authorizes attachment in the following situations:

(1) that the defendant has absconded or is about to abscond from the state or is concealed therein to the injury of his creditors;

(2) that the defendant has assigned, disposed of, or concealed any of his property with intent to defraud his creditors;

(3) that the defendant is about to assign, dispose of, or conceal any of his property with intent to defraud his creditors;

(4) that the defendant has removed or is about to remove any of his property from the state with intent to defraud his creditors;

(5) that the defendant has fraudulently contracted the debt or fraudulently incurred the obligation respecting which the suit is brought;

(6) that the defendant is not a resident of the state and has not resided therein for 3 months immediately preceding;

(7) that the defendant is a foreign corporation.

The procedure is initiated by filing a complaint and affidavit stating the grounds for attachment. The court clerk issues a writ of attachment which is executed by the sheriff against the debtor's nonexempt property. The debtor may reclaim the attached property by posting a bond.

30. The Consumer Credit Protection Act, 15 U.S.C.A. § 1673 (1970), restricts the amount which may be garnished in any work week to the lesser of (1)

Why would a secured party ever go through all this rigmarole to get his money when he could on his own repossess the collateral and sell it under 9–504? In the first place, extra-judicial repossession may only be accomplished when it can be carried out without breach of the peace.[31]  In addition, if the value of the collateral has so diminished that the proceeds from resale would be clearly insufficient to satisfy the debt, then it may be to the secured creditor's advantage to proceed by judgment and execution because in that way he can reach assets in addition to the collateral.  Also, by obtaining a judgment and levying against all the debtor's non-exempt property, the secured creditor can eliminate the two-step process of first selling the collateral and then suing for a deficiency.  Moreover, since officers of the court administer the entire procedure of judgment and execution on a debt, the creditor eliminates the risk of an improperly conducted repossession or resale under 9–504.  Finally, 9–501(5) allows the creditor to purchase the collateral at the sheriff's sale; something he cannot usually do in a private sale under 9–504(3).  In spite of all these seeming advantages, it will still be rare that a suit on the debt with its attendant court delay, search for non-exempt assets and sheriff's sale will offer a more promising avenue than seizure and sale of the collateral under 9–504.

Under pre-Code law, courts often held that the secured creditor who sued on the debt irrevocably elected to seek his sole remedy by that method.  Thus, the courts thought that a suit on the debt was inconsistent with a subsequent claim by the seller-creditor that he retained title to the goods under a conditional sales contract.[32]  The election of remedy issue arose early under the Code, and the Third Circuit held that the creditor could first recover in an action on the under-

---

twenty-five percent of the consumer's disposable income (i. e. take-home pay) or (2) his disposable earnings minus 30 times the federal minimum wage. Note that id. § 1675 authorizes the Secretary of Labor to exempt a state from application of the foregoing section when the state law provides essentially the same or greater protection to the consumer.

See also Sniadach v. Family Fin. Corp., 395 U.S. 337 (1969), where the Supreme Court held unconstitutional a Wisconsin statute which permitted the prejudgment garnishment of the debtor's wages. The Court ruled that the procedure under the statute violated the debtor's due process rights, because it permitted the creditor to deprive him of his wages without prior notice and without a hearing.

31.  Section 9–503 says, "In taking possession a secured party may proceed without judicial process if this can be done without breach of the peace . . . ."  For a discussion of the

meaning of the term "breach of the peace," see Section 26–5 infra.

32.  See cases collected in Annot. 113 A.L.R. 653 (1938) and the cases cited therein.  The Uniform Conditional Sales Act § 24 modified the traditional view by providing:

After the retaking of possession as provided in Section 16 the buyer shall be liable for the price only after a resale and only to the extent provided in Section 22.  Neither the bringing of an action by the seller for the recovery of the whole or any part of the price, nor the recovery of judgment in such action, nor the collection of a portion of the price, shall be deemed inconsistent with a later retaking of the goods as provided in Section 16, but such right of retaking shall not be exercised by the seller after he has collected the entire price, or after he has claimed a lien upon the goods, or attached them, or levied upon them as the goods of the buyer.

lying obligation and if that proved unsuccessful, later enforce the security agreement.[33]

The current version of the Code deals with the election of remedy problem as follows in 9-501(5):

> When a secured party has reduced his claim to judgment the lien of any levy which may be made upon his collateral by virtue of any execution based upon the judgment shall relate back to the date of the perfection of the security interest in such collateral. A judicial sale, pursuant to such execution, is a foreclosure of the security interest by judicial procedure within the meaning of this section, and the secured party may purchase at the sale and thereafter hold the collateral free of any other requirements of this Article.

Moreover 9-501(1) also provides that: "The rights and remedies referred to in this subsection are cumulative." The remedies may be "cumulative," but at some point the secured creditor must choose which remedy he will utilize and pursue that route to fruition.[34] In other words, a secured creditor may first attempt to enforce his rights by one method and if that proves unsuccessful follow another one, but he should not be permitted to harass the debtor by simultaneously pursuing two or more of the several avenues of attack open to him. Neither case law nor the language of 9-501 authorizes a "double-barreled" attack upon the debtor.[35]

---

**33.** In re Adrian Research & Chem. Co. v. Kirkpatrick, 269 F.2d 734 (3d Cir. 1959), involved a secured party who issued execution on a judgment and levied against debtor's property and then attempted to reclaim the goods covered by the security agreement when the debtor went to bankruptcy. The Third Circuit applied an early version of the Code and reversed the district court's determination that judgment and attempted execution on the debt was inconsistent with a later claim under the security agreement.

**34.** In Michigan Nat'l. Bank v. Marston, 29 Mich.App. 99, 185 N.W.2d 47, 8 UCC Rep.Serv. 1375 (1970), the court allowed a secured creditor to bring an action on the debt despite the fact that the creditor held the automobile's certificate of title. The court ruled that possession of the certificate did not constitute an election of remedy because the automobile was in the physical control of a garageman who held it subject to a mechanic's lien and disposition of the auto after payment of the garageman would have increased the amount owed by the debtor.

**35.** Might the secured creditor pursue judicial or nonjudicial remedies other than an action on the debt or repossession of the collateral? In Monroe Capital Corp. v. Pom-Pom Lunch & Restaurant, Inc., 4 UCC Rep.Serv. 511 (N.Y.Sup.Ct.1967) the creditor argued unsuccessfully that the second sentence of 9-501(1) which says that the secured creditor "may reduce his claim to judgment, foreclose or otherwise enforce the security interest by any available judicial procedure," meant that he could protect his interest under the security agreement by nullifying the sale of the debtor's restaurant business and enjoining the escrowee from distributing the proceeds of the sale. The New York court said that as a secured creditor the plaintiff could seek either "(1) to reduce its claim to judgment, or (2) foreclose its interest by any available procedure." Id. at 512. However, in Olsen v. Valley Nat'l Bank, 91 Ill.App.2d 365, 234 N.E.2d 547, 5 UCC Rep.Serv. 268 (1968), the Illinois court took a more liberal view of the secured creditor's options. It affirmed the trial court's dismissal of plaintiff-debtor's suit against the bank which, upon debtor's default, had accelerated the

## § 26–5   Repossession

If, after default, the secured creditor chooses to satisfy the debt by means of strict foreclosure or by resale of the collateral, he must first repossess it.  His right to repossess the collateral is the secured creditor's ultimate weapon against a defaulting debtor; in some instances the threat of repossession alone will be sufficient to persuade a misguided debtor to mend his ways ("If you don't pay up, I'll exercise my right to repossess your favorite hunting dog in whom I have a security interest.")  The secured party's alternatives of self-help and judicial action are provided in section 9–503 as follows:

> Unless otherwise agreed a secured party has on default the right to take possession of the collateral.  In taking possession a secured party may proceed without judicial process if this can be done without breach of the peace or may proceed by action.  If the security agreement so provides the secured party may require the debtor to assemble the collateral and make it available to the secured party at a place to be designated by the secured party which is reasonably convenient to both parties.  Without removal a secured party may render equipment unusable, and may dispose of collateral on the debtor's premises under section 9–504.

## § 26–6   Repossession—Self-Help

The quoted section authorizes a secured party to take possession of his collateral upon the default of the debtor, and to do so "without judicial process if this can be done without breach of the peace   ."  The negative implication of this sentence is that the creditor may not employ self-help techniques if doing so would result in a "breach of the peace."  The mode of repossession is important after the fact because the creditor's commission of a breach of the peace may expose him to tort liability and to liability under 9–507, and it may deprive him of his right to a deficiency judgment.  Thus, both the creditor's and the debtor's lawyers will give careful attention to the circumstances of repossession—one with an eye to avoiding potential liability and the other with an eye to discovering a fatal departure from "peaceful" repossession.

The meaning of the phrase "breach of the peace" has been the subject of countless judicial opinions.[36]  The draftsmen knowingly chose this wellworn phrase,[37] and did not define it anew.  According-

debt and debited his checking account as a set-off for the full amount of the debt.

We submit that the New York court took a much too restrictive view of the potential remedies available to a secured creditor, because it makes little sense to deny a creditor an otherwise available remedy, simply because he had the good sense and foresight to secure his debt with collateral.  See § 1–106.

36.  See, e. g., notes 38–46 infra.  See also Annot., 99 A.L.R.2d 358 (1965) and the cases cited therein.

37.  See also Uniform Conditional Sales Act § 16;  Uniform Trust Receipts Act § 6.  UCC § 9–503, Comments.

ly the numerous pre-Code cases are still good law. To determine if a breach of the peace has occurred, courts inquire mainly into: (*1*) whether there was entry by the creditor upon the debtor's premises; and (*2*) whether the debtor or one acting on his behalf consented to the entry and repossession.

In general, the creditor may not enter the debtor's home or garage without permission, but he can probably take a car from the debtor's driveway without incurring liability. The debtor's consent, freely given, legitimates any entry; conversely, the debtor's physical objection bars repossession even from a public street. This crude two-factor formula of creditor entry and debtor response must, of course, be refined by at least a consideration of third party response, the type of premises entered and possible creditor deceit in procuring consent.

Perhaps the most articulate and forceful statement of the general rule that entry into the debtor's residence in his absence is a breach of the peace is found in Girard v. Anderson.[38] There the creditor repossessed a piano from the debtor's home in the latter's absence. The debtor maintained that the house had been locked; the creditor testified that his agents entered through an unlocked door. Despite the presence of a clause in the sale contract purporting to authorize forcible entries, the court found that the entry, even according to the creditor's testimony, was a breach of the peace.

The great majority of cases dealing with entry into debtor's residence [39] are in agreement with *Girard*. However, in Cherno v. Bank of Babylon,[40] the New York Court of Appeals arguably departed from this general rule in interpreting 9–503. There, the creditor, without authority from the debtor, procured a key to the debtor's business premises, opened the door and removed the collateral. The court held that there was no breach of the peace despite the unauthorized entry. It pointed out that the debtor's landlord, who was present during at least part of the festivities, did no more than call the police and ask that the creditor's employees leave the key when they were finished.

The *Cherno* case can be distinguished from most entry cases on several grounds. In the first place, it arose in the context of a contest among the creditors of the original debtor, not between the secured creditor and his debtor. The plaintiff, assignee for the benefit of the creditors of the original debtor, was suing in "conversion . .

---

**38.**  219 Iowa 142, 257 N.W. 400 (1934).

**39.**  See, e. g., Evers-Jordan Furniture Co. v. Hartzog, 237 Ala. 407, 187 So. 491 (1939); Renaire Corp. v. Vaughn, 142 A.2d 148 (D.C.Ct.App.1958); Hileman v. Harter Bank & Trust Co., 174 Ohio St. 95, 186 N.E.2d 853 (1962); M. J. Rose Co. v. Lowery, 33 Ohio App. 488, 169 N.E. 716 (1929); Childers v.

Judson Mills Store Co., 189 S.C. 224, 200 S.E. 770 (1939); Lark v. Cooper Furniture Co., 114 S.C. 37, 102 S.E. 786 (1920). But see Singer Sewing Mach. Co. v. Hayes, 22 Ala.App. 250, 114 So. 428 (1927).

**40.**  54 Misc.2d 277, 282 N.Y.S.2d 114 (Sup.Ct.1967), aff'd 29 App.Div.2d 767, 288 N.Y.S.2d 862 (2d Dep't 1968).

for punitive damages and . . . for violation of the Penal Law," [41] rather than defending a suit for a deficiency judgment. The decision may mean only that the court was not motivated to reallocate the loss among the various creditors by allowing one to sue another for conversion. Had the plaintiff been an outraged debtor, the court might have found a breach of the peace.

Second, the *Cherno* case involved entry upon the debtor's business premises, not upon his residential property. Since the law has traditionally recognized the sanctity of a man's home, *Cherno* may not extend to entry into the debtor's residence. If the purpose of the breach of the peace limitation is to avoid forcing the debtor into a confrontation in his role as family protector, the distinction between home and office is probably valid.[42] Furthermore, even if the distinction is not recognized, *Cherno* may represent only a minority view. In a recent Texas case, which did not discuss 9–503, a creditor's unauthorized entry into a Gulf Oil station, on facts much like those in *Cherno*, was held to be a breach of the peace.[43]

Thus, the great majority of courts find unauthorized entries into the debtor's residence to be breaches of the peace, and many find entry into his place of business or garage [44] to be such a breach. As one moves away from the residential threshold to the yard, the driveway, and finally the public street, however, the debtor's argument becomes progressively more tenuous.[45] We have found no case which holds that the repossession of an automobile from a driveway or a public street (absent other circumstances, such as the debtor's objec-

**41.** 54 Misc.2d at 278, 282 N.Y.S.2d at 116–17.

**42.** In fairness one should note that the *Cherno* opinion does not recognize any such distinction and, in fact, implicitly rejects it by stating that its holding is in conflict with Girard v. Anderson, 219 Iowa 142, 257 N.W. 400 (1934).

**43.** Gulf Oil Corp. v. Smithey, 426 S.W. 2d 262 (Tex.Civ.App.1968). See also Soulios v. Mills Novelty Co., 198 S.C. 355, 17 S.E.2d 869 (1941).

**44.** If the garage doors are closed or locked, a breach of the peace is almost certain to be found. See Dominick v. Rea, 226 Mich. 594, 198 N.W. 184 (1924); Wilson Motor Co. v. Dunn, 129 Okla. 211, 264 P. 194 (1928); Voltz v. General Motors Acceptance Corp., 332 Pa. 141, 2 A.2d 697 (1938); A. B. Lewis Co. v. Robinson, 339 S.W. 2d 731 (Tex.Civ.App.1960). But if the garage doors are open and the creditor enters and tows the car away, at least one case, C. I. T. Corp. v. Short, 273 Ky. 190, 115 S.W.2d 899 (1938), has

held that he is not liable for unlawful repossession (at least not for punitive damages). Cf. Kroeger v. Ogsden, 429 P.2d 781 (Okla.1967) (repossession of airplane from open hangar owned by debtor held not unlawful repossession).

**45.** If the repossession is from the real property of a third person, it is probably lawful in the absence of some special circumstance. In Martin v. Cook, 237 Miss. 267, 114 So.2d 669 (1959) the unscrewing of a small panel to gain entry into a truck in order to repossess it from the property of a third person was held not to be a breach of the peace, and the repossession was found to be lawful. See Commercial Credit Co. v. Spence, 185 Miss. 293, 184 So. 439 (1938) (window broken while repossessing car from hotel lot; repossession held unlawful). See also Rutledge v. Universal C. I. T. Credit Corp., 218 Ark. 510, 237 S.W.2d 469 (1951) (repossession from service station held to be lawful); Furches Motor Co. v. Anderson, 216 Miss. 40, 61 So.2d 674 (1952) (repossession from automobile lot held to be lawful).

tion) constitutes a breach of the peace, and many cases uphold such a repossession.[46]

### Consent of The Debtor or A Third Person to Repossession

If the debtor voluntarily and contemporaneously consents to a repossession it cannot be a breach of the peace.[47]  If a creditor's agent obtains consent by fraud (flashing a counterfeit policeman's badge) or if the consent is given by a mechanic at the garage, or by the debtor's wife or child, the "consent" may not free the creditor from liability.  But in F. A. North & Co. v. Williams,[48] the repossessor entered the debtor's residence by posing as a piano tuner, and the repossession was held lawful.  In Barham v. Standridge,[49] however, a seller-garageman who procured possession by promising that he would repair the car and return it was not as fortunate.  Yet in N. J. Scott Excavating & Wrecking, Inc. v. Rosencrantz,[50] under similar circumstances, the New Hampshire court noting, that the secured party had played no role in the seller-dealer's obtaining possession of the collateral and that there was no evidence of subterfuge, held that a dealer who repossessed at the direction of the secured party was not liable for conversion.

**46.** Driveway cases: Dearman v. Williams, 235 Miss. 360, 109 So.2d 316 (1959); Gill v. Mercantile Trust Co., 347 S.W.2d 420 (Mo.App.1961); Ikovich v. Silver Bow Motor Car Co., 117 Mont. 268, 157 P.2d 785 (1945); Rea v. Universal C. I. T. Credit Corp., 257 N.C. 639, 127 S.E.2d 225 (1962); Gregory v. First Nat'l Bank, 241 Ore. 397, 406 P.2d 156 (1965); Morrison v. Galyon Motor Co., 16 Tenn.App. 394, 64 S.W.2d 851 (1932); Pioneer Fin. & Thrift Corp. v. Adams, 426 S.W.2d 317 (Tex.Civ.App.1968).

Public street cases: King v. General Motors Acceptance Corp., 140 F.Supp. 259 (M.D.N.C.1956); McWaters v. Gardner, 37 Ala.App. 418, 69 So.2d 724 (1954); General Motors Acceptance Corp. v. Shuey, 243 Ky. 74, 47 S.W.2d 968 (1932); General Motors Acceptance Corp. v. Vincent, 183 Okla. 547, 83 P.2d 539 (1938); Malone v. Darr, 178 Okla. 443, 62 P.2d 1254 (1936); First Nat'l Bank & Trust Co. v. Winter, 176 Okla. 400, 55 P.2d 1029 (1936); Leedy v. General Motors Acceptance Corp., 173 Okla. 445, 48 P.2d 1074 (1935); Haydon v. Newman, 162 S.W.2d 1041 (Tex.Civ.App.1942). See also Annot., 146 A.L.R. 1331 (1943) and the cases cited therein. But even though the creditor may not be liable for unlawful repossession of the car, he may be liable for conversion of personal property within the repos-

sessed car.  See Sanders v. General Motors Acceptance Corp., 180 S.C. 138, 185 S.E. 180 (1936).

**47.** In most of the following cases, the creditor introduced evidence of consent, and the court held that the debtor failed to carry the burden of proof that the repossession was against his consent: Klett v. Security Acceptance Co., 38 Cal.2d 770, 242 P.2d 873 (1952) (furniture from store); Besner v. Smith, 178 A.2d 924 (D.C.Ct. App.1962) (television set from house); Johnson v. Modern Furniture & Appliance Co., 76 So.2d 338 (La.App.1954) (furniture from house); White v. Southern Mercantile Co., 162 So. 229 (La.App.1935) (furniture from house); Sims v. Horton, 43 Wash.2d 907, 264 P.2d 879 (1953) (car from street).

Courts will sometimes strain, however, to find that consent was not freely given and is therefore invalid. See; e. g., Dorsey v. Central Fin. Co., 65 So.2d 137 (La.App.1953).

**48.** 120 Pa. 109, 13 A. 723 (1888).

**49.** 201 Ark. 1143, 148 S.W.2d 648 (1941); accord, Franklin v. Spratt, 174 Ark. 268, 295 S.W. 26 (1927).

**50.** 107 N.H. 422, 223 A.2d 522, 3 UCC Rep.Serv. 964 (1966).

The courts are very sensitive to fraudulent or unauthorized use of the policemen's badge by a repossessing creditor. In Rhodes-Carroll Furniture Co. v. Webb,[51] the court found a creditor, who had gained entrance by telling the debtor's wife that he was a policeman, liable for trespass. Similarly, in Stone Machinery Co. v. Kessler,[52] the Washington Court of Appeals concluded that a repossessing creditor had breached the peace when he repossessed with the unauthorized aid of a uniformed sheriff. The court reasoned that the mere presence of the sheriff with his uniform and side-arm "amounted to constructive force, intimidation and oppression constituting a breach of the peace."[53] One can explain some of the inconsistencies in these cases by the magnitude of the fraud and propensity of it to foreclose willing consent. Other policies (such as the desire to penalize those who pose as policemen) may also explain some of the decisions.

Turning to the power of a third party to give consent, one might anticipate, first, that the validity of such consent would depend upon the third party's apparent authority to speak for the debtor and, second, that the consenter's age and familial relation to the debtor would be highly relevant to the apparent authority question. To a considerable extent, the cases substantiate these expectations for they hold that neither the consent of the debtor's tenant nor that of his infant daughter can legitimate an entry which would otherwise constitute a breach of the peace.[54] The courts, however, have divided on whether an adult closely related to the debtor can give effective consent. In Bing v. General Motors Acceptance Corp.,[55] a South Carolina federal court found that the debtor had no cause of action for wrongful repossession after his sister had authorized the repossession of his car from the driveway. Similarly, in Austin v. General Motors Acceptance Corp.,[56] a wife's consent to the repossession of a car from a garage was held sufficient to absolve the creditor from liability. However, since neither case involved an entry into the debtor's residence, they do not authorize a third party to invite a repossessing creditor into the debtor's home. In the *Bing* case, the court's statements about consent are arguably dicta, for the creditor would probably have repossessed the car from the driveway even without consent.

The effect of a clause in the security agreement purporting to authorize non-judicial repossession is unclear. When such a clause seeks to permit the creditor to stomp down the door and burst into the debtor's parlor at any hour of the day or night, the courts do not hesitate to grant relief to the debtor. In Hileman v. Harter Bank &

51. 230 Ala. 251, 160 So. 247 (1935).

52. 1 Wash.App. 750, 463 P.2d 651, 7 UCC Rep.Serv. 135 (1970).

53. Id. at 754, 463 P.2d at 655, 7 UCC Rep.Serv. at 140.

54. Luthy v. Philip Werlein Co., 163 La. 752, 112 So. 709 (1927) (daughter);

McDaniel v. Lieberman, 157 So. 834 (La.App.1934) (tenant).

55. 237 F.Supp. 911 (E.D.S.C.1965); see also Carter v. Mintz & Goldblum, 8 So.2d 709 (La.App.1942) (wife's consent ineffective).

56. 239 Miss. 699, 125 So.2d 79 (1960).

Trust Co.[57] the creditor's representatives entered the debtor's home through a window, and the court brushed aside a repossession clause:

> "These acts of the bank's employees, if not consented to, would have constituted the offense of breaking and entering. Even with prior consent, they are such acts as are likely to produce violence and to provoke or incite others to break the peace. Hileman's immediate armed reaction, although not condoned, was an entirely natural one.
>
> The insertion in a mortgage of a clause whereby a mortgagor purportedly consents in advance to a breaking and entering is an attempt to confer upon a mortgagee an extraordinary privilege not enjoyed by an absolute owner and is not needed for the reasonable protection of the mortgagee's investment. The existence of the privilege is a threat to the peace and contrary to public policy. A contractual provision purporting to authorize a breaking is, therefore, void." [58]

Yet such clauses may sanction more refined creditor conduct. In a Nineteenth Century case, F. A. North & Co. v. Williams,[59] such a clause exonerated an entry obtained by fraud. Other courts have approvingly referred to such clauses.[60] It is impossible to say whether these references only helped rationalize predetermined conclusions, or whether they played a determinative role in the decisions. Surely they are entitled to little weight. The breach of the peace rule in section 9–503 answers not only to the needs of the debtor, but also to those of his wife and children, and to the public policy against fist-fights and shoot-outs. Such a rule should not be varied merely because of a prior agreement between a creditor and a debtor.[61]

---

57. 174 Ohio St. 95, 186 N.E.2d 853 (1962); accord Girard v. Anderson, 219 Iowa 142, 257 N.W. 400 (1934). The clause in Hileman reads as follows:

In the event of any default in the payment of any installment when due on said note . . . then mortgagee may at its option and without notice, elect to treat the entire balance remaining unpaid . . . immediately due and payable; whereupon mortgagor agrees to deliver the chattel(s) to the mortgagee and mortgagee may, upon the failure of the mortgagor so to do, with or without the aid of legal process, make use of such force as may be necessary to enter upon, with or without breaking into any premises where the chattel(s) may be found and take possession thereof and sell and dispose of the same according to law, together with mortgagor's equity of redemption . . . .

174 Ohio St. at 96, 186 N.E.2d at 854.

58. 174 Ohio St. at 97, 186 N.E.2d at 854–55.

59. 120 Pa. 109, 13 A. 723 (1888).

60. See, e. g., Besner v. Smith, 178 A.2d 924 (D.C.Mun.Ct.App.1962); Furches Motor Co. v. Anderson, 216 Miss. 40, 61 So.2d 674 (1952); Commercial Credit Co. v. Cain, 190 Miss. 866, 1 So.2d 776 (1941); Cherno v. Bank of Babylon, 54 Misc.2d 277, 282 N.Y.S.2d 114 (Sup.Ct.1967), aff'd 29 App.Div.2d 767, 288 N.Y.S.2d 862 (2d Dep't 1968).

61. It is consistent with the underlying policy to find, on the one hand, that a consent given contemporaneously with the repossession is effective and, on the other hand, that one given weeks or months before in a clause in the security agreement is ineffective. In the former case, the debtor fully appreciates the consequences of his consent and has no time in which to change his mind. That is not so in the latter case. For these reasons, the contemporaneous consent affords substantial protection against violence, while an earlier written consent does not. Since the goal of the breach of

*Debtor and Third Party Opposition to Repossession*

When the creditor repossesses in disregard of the debtor's unequivocal oral protest, most courts find the creditor guilty of a breach of the peace.[62] However, other courts require something more than an exchange of words before they will conclude that the confrontation between creditor and debtor constituted a breach of the peace. In Owens v. First American National Bank [63] the debtor testified that he argued and pleaded with the creditor to prevent repossession of an automobile. He finally acquiesced with the statement that "I never argue with a white man." [64] After reviewing the conflicting testimony, the Tennessee Court of Appeals concluded that no breach of the peace had occurred. A rule that an oral protest is sufficient to foreclose non-judicial repossession is wise because it does not beckon the repossessing creditor to the brink of violence. Speaking of the debtor's wife, one court has put the policy as follows:

> "It would have availed her nothing to have measured her strength with that of the two employees of the defendant. The plaintiff's evidence shows that she was intimidated by

the peace doctrine is to prevent violence, not to protect contract expectations, the distinction is appropriate.

**62.** Crews & Green v. Parker, 192 Ala. 383, 68 So. 287 (1916) (furniture from debtor's restaurant); Manhattan Credit Co. v. Brewer, 232 Ark. 976, 341 S. W.2d 765 (1961) (car from driveway); Wilson v. Kuykendall, 112 Miss. 486, 73 So. 344 (1916) (mules from barn); Cecil Baber Elec. Co. v. Greer, 183 Okla. 541, 83 P.2d 598 (1938) (refrigerator from "premises"); Ben Cooper Motor Co. v. Amey, 143 Okla. 75, 287 P. 1017 (1930) (car from garage); Lark v. Cooper Furniture Co., 114 S.C. 37, 102 S.E. 786 (1919) (furniture from home); Morrison v. Galyon Motor Co., 16 Tenn.App. 394, 64 S.W.2d 851 (1932) (truck from yard) (dictum). Contra, Fulton Inv. Co. v. Fraser, 76 Colo. 125, 230 P. 600 (1924) (wheat from granary); J. I. Case Threshing Mach. Co. v. Barney, 54 Okla. 686, 154 P. 674 (1916) (machine from debtor's premises); Westerman v. Oregon Automobile Credit Corp., 168 Ore. 216, 122 P.2d 435 (1942) (car from street).

Some courts require affirmative consent from the debtor before a repossession will be found lawful. If the debtor neither consents to nor opposes the repossession, the court will find the repossession unlawful. See Price v. General Motors Acceptance Corp., 95 So.2d 834 (La.App.1957); Carey v.

Interstate Bond & Mortgage Co., 4 Wash.2d 632, 104 P.2d 579 (1940). Contra, Rutledge v. Universal C. I. T. Credit Corp., 218 Ark. 510, 237 S.W.2d 469 (1951).

If, in addition to an oral protest, the debtor offers passive physical resistance, such as refusing to leave the car as it is towed away, the creditor is liable for any injuries caused to the debtor during the repossession. Burgin v. Universal Credit Co., 2 Wash.2d 364, 98 P.2d 291 (1940).

If the creditor attempts to overcome the oral protest of the debtor by trickery, by threats, or by intimidation, he is liable for wrongful repossession. See American Discount Co. v. Wyckroff, 29 Ala.App. 82, 191 So. 790 (1939); Kensinger Acceptance Corp. v. Davis, 223 Ark. 942, 269 S.W.2d 792 (1954); Levy v. Andress-Hanna, Inc., 96 So.2d 373 (La.App.1957); Firebaugh v. Gunther, 106 Okla. 131, 233 P. 460 (1925); Ray v. Navarre, 47 Okla. 438, 147 P. 1019 (1915) (debtor intimidated when creditor accompanied by armed deputy sheriff).

**63.** 6 UCC Rep.Serv. 427 (1968); Harris Truck & Trailer Sales v. Foote, 58 Tenn.App. 710, 436 S.W.2d 460, 5 UCC Rep.Serv. 569 (1968) (violence or threat of violence required to find breach of peace).

**64.** 6 UCC Rep.Serv. at 429.

the superior force arrayed against her.   In order to constitute coercion, it is not always necessary to apply physical force. The highway robber says to his victim, 'Stand and deliver'. And the victim obeys the command and surrenders his purse, yet no physical force is employed, but, notwithstanding, in the eye of the law, he was forced to give up his property. The conduct of the defendant and its agents differs only in degree from that of the highwayman, for in each instance it was 'stand and deliver'.   The defendant was enforcing its contract with a high hand; and was inviting a breach of peace when it invaded plaintiff's home after having been notified not to do so." [65]

Similar sentiments were expressed in a recent Ohio decision, Morris v. First National Bank & Trust Co.,[66] which involved the repossession of a power mower.   There the debtor had refused to permit repossession and had ordered the secured party's agents off his property. Later three men returned, confronted the debtor's son (who objected to their presence on the property but did not make any attempt to prevent repossession) and seized the mower.   In an action by the debtor for conversion and trespass, the Ohio Supreme Court concluded that a breach of the peace had occurred.   The court noted that conduct insufficient to constitute assault, might, nonetheless, be a breach of the peace under 9–503.

Not all courts agree with these views, and several have held that *third parties* must do more than protest orally to turn the creditor's otherwise permissible action into a breach of the peace.[67]   These cases do not explain why a third party's protest is different from the debtor's.   Perhaps these cases are part of the minority which finds that mere oral protest, by whomever made, cannot be a breach of the peace. Or the cases may reflect a view that words spoken by an owner are often swiftly followed by violent action, whereas words spoken by a third party are not.

Thus, the courts generally have reached sound conclusions in defining "breach of the peace."   In the absence of consent, entry into a debtor's house is not permitted.   For the most part courts ignore clauses purporting to authorize a repossession which results in

---

**65.**   Bordeaux v. Hartman Furniture & Carpet Co., 115 Mo.App. 556, 563, 91 S.W. 1020, 1021 (1905).

**66.**   21 Ohio St.2d 25, 254 N.E.2d 683, 7 UCC Rep.Serv. 131 (1970).

**67.**   Third party's protest insufficient: Commercial Credit Co. v. Cain, 190 Miss. 866, 1 So.2d 776 (1941) (debtor's husband protested repossession of car from public street); Willis v. Whittle, 82 S.C. 500, 64 S.E. 410 (1909) (debtor's mother protested repossession of horse from barn); Singer Sewing

Mach. Co. v. Rios, 96 Tex. 174, 71 S.W. 275 (1903) (debtor's employee protested repossession of machine from tailor shop).

Third party's protest rendered repossession a breach of peace: Freeman v. General Motors Acceptance Corp., 205 N.C. 257, 171 S.E. 63 (1933) (wife protested repossession of automobile from driveway or street).   See also Morrison v. Galyon Motor Co., 16 Tenn. App. 394, 64 S.W.2d 851 (1932) (dictum).

a breach of the peace, and they will not usually permit a creditor to repossess in the face of unequivocal oral protests. Conversely, courts do permit the repossession of cars from private driveways and public streets.

It has been our sad fate to witness a minor eruption of constitutional case law just as this book goes to press. In Fuentes v. Shevin [67a] the U. S. Supreme Court has outlawed the usual application of the replevin statutes of most of our states. In Adams v. Egley [67b] and Bank of America v.[67c] Oller two U. S. district courts in California have considered the constitutionality of the right of self-help repossession embodied in 9–503. One court has found 9–503 to be unconstitutional as a denial of due process; the other court upheld the statute on the ground that self-help repossession did not involve state action. At this writing the Court of Appeals for the 9th Circuit is considering these cases.

We have neither the time nor the inclination to consider all of the ramifications of these cases here. Suffice it to say that *Fuentes* will probably require the amendment of most of the replevin statutes in the country to provide the defendant with an opportunity to be heard before his goods are seized by the sheriff or other court officer. It will remain for later cases to spell out the exceptions to the rule set down in the *Fuentes* case and to spell out the exact scope of the case.

More troublesome are the California cases. We hope that the Court of Appeals and ultimately the Supreme Court will side with the District Court in Northern California and find that self-help repossession is not a violation of the Constitution. We suspect that the only persons who will benefit from a finding that 9–503 is unconstitutional are lawyers. If 9–503 is unconstitutional, creditors will have to resort to court process in almost every repossession. Especially after *Fuentes* that process will be considerably more expensive and time consuming than the current self-help repossession method. We suspect that the individual debtor or the debtor class will ultimately bear the costs of filing suit, serving papers, and hiring a lawyer. To what end do debtors shoulder this new cost? Will this invocation of the state process protect the debtors from an invasion of his privacy? From undeserved deficiency judgments? We suspect that it will not. Indeed we suspect that the sheriff or other person who is attempting to seize the goods under color of law will be more aggressive than the private repossessor. The sheriff can enter the house, can use "reasonable force" (shove the debtor's wife aside) and in general proceed without the fear of tort liability and without the inhibition of a breach of peace standard. So we fear that a removal of the self-help repossession would increase, not reduce, the disruption of the debtor's privacy.

67a.  —— U.S. ——, 92 S.Ct. 1983 (1972).    67c.  342 F.Supp. 21 (N.D.Cal.1972).

67b.  338 F.Supp. 614 (S.D.Cal.1972).

Will the opportunity for hearing cause debtors who now do not assert their defenses to assert them and so avoid unwarranted deficiency judgments? Again we are skeptical. We suspect that a hearing system will produce mostly defaults and that it will be only the rare debtor, the sport, who comes forward with a defense when he learns of the prospective repossession. Moreover we fear that the barring of self-help repossession and the requirement that the creditor go to court to repossess may encourage creditors to seek additional deficiency judgments. Because of the expenses involved in starting suit and the low probability of return, many creditors now content themselves with the collateral and seek no deficiency judgment. If they must file suit to repossess, we fear that creditors may simply wait around and take a default. Once he has paid an attorney's fee, an entry and service fee, and filed a complaint, why shouldn't a creditor hang on for a default deficiency? We may be excessively cynical but we see little good and much bad about the abolition of self-help repossession.

### § 26–7    Repossession—Judicial Action

A secured party, wishing to repossess by judicial action, has several means available. For instance, he can bring an action in replevin (originally a common-law action, now largely codified). In other jurisdictions he can proceed under the statutory successor to replevin, an action of claim and delivery. Naturally, repossession by judicial action is more costly than repossession by self-help. In addition to attorney's fees, such costs normally include the cost of posting a bond and fees for the sheriff who actually repossesses the goods. Section 9–504(1) makes the debtor liable for such costs. If the debtor will not part with the goods without a fight and the debtor is good for the costs of repossession, the secured creditor is well advised to proceed by judicial action. Irrespective of its name, the secured party's cause of action in repossessing rests on his right to possess the collateral under 9–503. Under a typical replevin or claim and delivery statute,[68] after the plaintiff files a complaint and an affidavit and posts the required bond, the sheriff may seize the property. Unless the defendant objects within a specified period, the property may

---

**68.** The following is a description of the Michigan Procedure:

The plaintiff files a complaint to recover possession of personal property and causes summons and a copy of the complaint to be served upon the defendant. The plaintiff's affidavit claiming delivery of the property and his bond are then presented to the sheriff of the county where the property is located. Copies of the affidavit and bond must be served upon the defendant. They may be served personally with the summons or served thereafter under GCR 1963, 107. If satisfied as to the sufficiency of the bond, the sheriff seizes the property and holds it for at least five days. Within that five-day period, the defendant may either object to the sufficiency of the sureties or file and serve bond for redelivery of the property. The sheriff then delivers the property to the appropriate party. Thereafter defendant answers the complaint, counterclaiming if appropriate, the sheriff files the affidavit and bond or bonds and his return, and the case proceeds to trial and judgment.

Mich.Comp.Laws Ann. § 600.2920, Comment at 712 (1968).

be delivered to the plaintiff pending final judgment. At common law the plaintiff in a replevin action sought only to recover the property *in specie*, however, under the modern form of the action and under some claim and delivery statutes the plaintiff may recover the property or its value.[69]

The creditor's suit against the debtor for possession of the collateral is relatively simple. However, the situation becomes more complex when the collateral has been transferred to a third party. Assuming that such transfer constitutes a default, then under the mandate of 9–201 and 9–306(2) the security agreement is enforceable against third persons unless one of many exceptions comes into play.[70] If the purchaser cannot bring himself under one of the exceptions to 9–201 and 9–306, then under the provisions of 9–503 the secured party has a superior right to possession of the collateral. In that case the secured party can successfully pursue a suit for conversion or seek to replevy the collateral.[71] The secured party's rights against a purchaser of the collateral were succinctly stated in Beneficial Finance Co. v. Colonial Trading Co.[72] where the secured party brought an action in assumpsit against the purchaser of collateral from a defaulting debtor. The court said (emphasis in original)[73]:

> "Where a debtor sells collateral subject to a perfected security agreement, the secured party may proceed 1) against the debtor a) to collect the debt on the original instrument, or b) to assert his rights under the security agreement against any identifiable proceeds *in the hands of the debtor*, or 2) against the purchaser a) by repossession of the purchased goods in person or by an action in replevin or b) by an action *in trespass for conversion of the collateral*. However, once the purchaser has himself resold the goods, the

---

69. Naturally, if the secured creditor seeks to recover the value of the collateral, his recovery will be limited by the amount of his security interest. See Brandywine Lanes, Inc. v. Pittsburgh Nat'l Bank, 437 Pa. 499, 264 A. 2d 377, 7 UCC Rep.Serv. 969 (1970).

70. Section 9–201 says in part: "Except as otherwise provided by this Act a security agreement is effective according to its terms between the parties, against purchasers of the collateral and against creditors." The primary exceptions which might come into play in this area are those for buyers of goods (§ 9–307), purchasers of chattel paper and nonnegotiable instruments (§ 9–308), persons with service or material liens (§ 9–310) or transfers authorized in the security agreement (§ 9–306(2)). These provisions are examined in detail at Sections 25–12 et seq., supra.

71. Conversion actions were brought in the following cases: Clarke Floor Mach. Div. of Studebaker Corp. v. Gordon, 7 UCC Rep.Serv. 363 (Md.Super. Ct.1970); Still Ass'n v. Murphy, 267 N.E.2d 217, 8 UCC Rep.Serv. 929 (1971); Prime Business Co. v. Drinkwater, 350 Mass. 642, 216 N.E.2d 105, 3 UCC Rep.Serv. 441 (1966); Strevell-Paterson Fin. Co. v. May, 77 N.M. 331, 422 P.2d 366, 3 UCC Rep.Serv. 1094 (1967).

In Platte Valley Bank v. Kracl, 185 Neb. 168, 174 N.W.2d 724, 7 UCC Rep. Serv. 538 (1970), the court approved an action in replevin against a third party.

72. 43 Pa.D. & C.2d 131, 4 UCC Rep. Serv. 672 (C.P.1967).

73. Id. at 132, 4 UCC Rep.Serv. at 673.

secured party has no right of action in *assumpsit* against the *purchaser*, either for the original debt or for the proceeds of resale."

Purchasers are not the only third persons who might gain possession of the collateral. What happens if an unsecured creditor obtains a judgment and levies against the collateral? [74] Under most security agreements this would constitute a default, and the secured party's right to possess would automatically accrue under 9–503. However 9–311 provides:

> The debtor's rights in collateral may be voluntarily or involuntarily transferred (by way of sale, creation of a security interest, attachment, levy, garnishment or other judicial process) notwithstanding a provision in the security agreement prohibiting any transfer or making the transfer constitute a default.

When both a levying creditor and the secured creditor seek to sell the same collateral, who controls the sale? Some courts allow the secured creditor to vacate the levy and take over foreclosure [75] while other courts take the position that the sheriff may sell the collateral subject to secured creditor's interest.[76] We believe that courts should not deny the secured party the important right to control the method of disposition of collateral merely because 9–311 states that the *"debtor's* rights" may be transferred.

## § 26–8    Strict Foreclosure

Upon default and repossession, the secured creditor may wish to avoid the headache of resale and therefore accept the collateral in complete satisfaction of the debt under 9–502(2). By so doing he foregoes any right to a deficiency. This alternative of "strict foreclosure" was known to the common law and was available under the Uniform Conditional Sales Act.[77] Sometimes the secured creditor will find strict foreclosure an attractive alternative to sale and suit for a deficiency. Presumably, when the value of the collateral is roughly equivalent to the amount of the outstanding debt, the secured creditor will choose strict foreclosure.[78] Strict foreclosure has certain

74. For a discussion of disputes between the secured creditor and the trustee in bankruptcy, see Ch. 24 supra.

75. See William Iselin & Co. v. Burgess & Leigh, Ltd., 52 Misc.2d 821, 276 N.Y.S.2d 659, 3 UCC Rep.Serv. 1168 (Sup.Ct.1967); Harrison Music Co. v. Drake, 43 Pa.D. & C.2d 637, 5 UCC Rep.Serv. 417 (C.P.1967).

76. See Altec Lansing v. Friedman Sound, Inc., 204 So.2d 740, 4 UCC

Rep.Serv. 1078 (Fla.App.1967); First Nat'l Bank v. Sheriff, 34 Wis.2d 535, 149 N.W.2d 548, 4 UCC Rep.Serv. 348 (1967); Op. Att'y Gen. Okla. No. 66–245, 3 UCC Rep.Serv. 1004 (1966).

77. See Uniform Conditional Sales Act § 23.

78. See Shuchman, Profit on Default: An Archival Study of Automobile Repossession and Resale, 22 Stan.L.Rev. 20, 53–56 (1969), where the author concludes that, at least for automo-

advantages over resale of the collateral or an action on the debt. In the first place, it may be accomplished with a modicum of effort on the part of the secured party. More important the secured creditor who strictly forecloses knows that the debtor or other parties cannot later plague him about the fairness of a resale price under 9–504. Section 9–505(2) authorizes strict foreclosure:

> In any other case involving consumer goods or any other collateral a secured party in possession may, after default, propose to retain the collateral in satisfaction of the obligation. Written notice of such proposal shall be sent to the debtor and except in the case of consumer goods to any other secured party who has a security interest in collateral and who has duly filed a financing statement indexed in the name of the debtor in this state or is known by the secured party in possession to have a security interest in it. If the debtor or other person entitled to receive notification objects in writing within thirty days from the receipt of the notification or if any other secured party objects in writing within thirty days after the secured party obtains possession the secured party must dispose of the collateral under Section 9–504. In the absence of such written objection the secured party may retain the collateral in satisfaction of the debtor's obligation.

Thus, section 9–505(2) presents an uncomplicated blue-print for strict foreclosure on default. First, the secured creditor must take possession of the collateral after default.[79] Secondly, he is required to send a written notice stating his intention to retain the collateral in satisfaction of the debtor's obligation. Both the debtor and any other secured parties who have filed with respect to the collateral or who are known by the foreclosing party to have an interest in the collateral are entitled to receive such notice. Finally, the foreclosing secured creditor must await the passage of thirty days without an objection from the debtor or any other interested parties. Failure to enter an objection discharges the debtor's obligation and entitles the secured party to keep the collateral. However, if the debtor or one of the other interested parties enters a written objection during the thirty days following receipt of notice, then the secured party must dispose of the collateral under 9–504. Furthermore, when the collateral is consumer goods and the debtor has paid 60 percent of the price, the secured creditor may not use strict foreclosure unless the debtor *after default* signs a statement renouncing his right to require the collateral resold in compliance with section 9–504.[80] This provi-

biles, secured creditors would be adequately protected if they were limited to strict foreclosure upon default.

**79.** See § 9–503. See also Section 26–6 supra.

**80.** Section 9–505(1) provides:

If the debtor has paid sixty per cent of the cash price in the case of a purchase money security interest in consumer goods or sixty per cent of the loan in the case of another security interest in consumer goods, and has

sion is based upon the supposition that a debtor who has paid 60 percent of the purchase price has built up equity in the goods and that resale would result in a surplus.[81]  Hence the secured creditor may not strictly foreclose unless the debtor expressly renounces his right to demand resale.

Although the procedure for accomplishing strict foreclosure is relatively simple, it still includes pitfalls for the unwary secured creditor.  For instance, three sorts of persons are entitled to written notice of the secured party's intention to retain the collateral.  First, of course, is the debtor.  Secondly, the secured party must notify other secured parties who have filed in "this state" as to the collateral.  Thus, presumably one must search the filing of the state where the collateral is located.  Finally, the secured party must notify all secured parties "known" to him who have security interests in the collateral.  What secured parties are "known" to a large institution is an open question [82] and the possibility exists that some slighted secured party will turn up and claim under 9–507 because he did not receive notice.[83]

Another potential problem for the secured party lies in the duration of the period when another party is entitled to object to strict foreclosure.  Section 9–505 stipulates that the parties entitled to notice have thirty days [84] "from the *receipt* of the notification" to object; thereafter the right of redemption and other rights are cut off.  A wise secured party will give notice by registered or certified mail so that he can prove "receipt."

Failure to give notice renders strict foreclosure invalid at least as to those entitled to receive notice who did not receive it.  *In re Sports Autos Inc.*[85] involved a secured party who was also the president and sole shareholder of the debtor corporation.  Without giving notice to the corporation or other secured creditors, he repossessed collateral worth approximately $90,000 more than the debt it secured and then set up essentially the same business under a different name.

not signed after default a statement renouncing or modifying his rights under this Part a secured party who has taken possession of collateral must dispose of it under section 9–504 and if he fails to do so within ninety days after he takes possession the debtor at his option may recover in conversion or under section 9–507(1) on secured party's liability.

81.  See 2 G. Gilmore, Security Interest in Personal Property § 44.3 at 1222 (1965).

82.  This apparently stringent requirement is alleviated somewhat by the provisions of 1–201(27) which provide that an organization has knowledge when the information is communicated to the person conducting the transaction or when due diligence is

exercised in making such communication.

83.  The burden of notification is eased considerably by the proposed changes to 9–505(2).  Under the revised version, the secured party in possession is required to notify only those secured parties who have given him written notice of their security interest.  See Permanent Editorial Board for the Uniform Commercial Code, Review Committee for Article 9, § 9–505 at 179 (1971).

84.  Under the revised version of the UCC, this period would be reduced to 21 days.  Id.

85.  6 UCC Rep.Serv. 991 (Ref.Dec.W.D. Pa.1969).

When the debtor's other creditors filed a petition for an involuntary declaration of bankruptcy, the Referee concluded that the secured party's failure to give notice deprived him of his right to retain the property.[86]

In some cases debtors have attempted to force strict foreclosure upon an unwilling secured creditor. In Northern Financial Corp. v. Chatwood Coffee Shop, Inc.,[87] the debtor argued that the creditor had taken the asset in strict foreclosure under 9–505 notwithstanding the fact that the secured creditor had never served a proposal to retain the collateral in discharge of the debt. The secured creditor had procured the collateral by purchase at a sheriff's sale on a judgment obtained by a third party. The court denied the secured party's motion for summary judgment and found that the debtor's claim of strict foreclosure presented a triable issue of fact. The court made the following statement about the effect of section 9–505(2):

> . . . the plaintiff's failure to serve a proposal to retain the collateral in full satisfaction of the debt pursuant to section 9–505(2) of the Uniform Commercial Code is not a bar to the defendants' claiming that plaintiff actually adopted such course of conduct with respect to that property. This type of notice serves only to relieve a secured creditor from being required to dispose of the property in accordance with section 9–504 of the Uniform Commercial Code.[88]

Under similar circumstances other courts have found the secured party's repossession and delay in reselling the collateral to amount to accord and satisfaction—all to the same end that the creditor has no right to deficiency.[89]

Although 9–501(3) stops just short of stating that the debtor cannot contract away his right to insist upon a resale of the collateral, certainly that is the meaning of 9–501(3) (d) and (c).[90] An agreement, which would bind the debtor to strict foreclosure and bar him from insisting upon resale, would certainly constitute a waiver under 9–501(3) of the "debtor's rights," and it is difficult to see how one could accomplish the effect of a waiver by establishing "standards . . . [which are] not manifestly unreasonable." The debtor cannot contract away his hope, however faint, that a resale will produce more than the amount of the indebtedness and entitle him to a surplus.

---

**86.** We have found no case where the debtor had the audacity to argue that the creditor's failure to give notice to other secured creditors made the disposition improper.

**87.** 4 UCC Rep.Serv. 674, (N.Y.Sup.Ct. 1967).

**88.** Id. at 675. But cf. Priggen Steel Bldg. Co. v. Parsons, 350 Mass. 62, 213 N.E.2d 252, 3 UCC Rep.Serv. 89 (1966) (no strict foreclosure because creditor did not give notice of intent of same).

**89.** See text accompanying notes 164–71 infra. See especially Barnes v. Reliable Tractor Co., 117 Ga.App. 777, 161 S.E.2d 918, 5 UCC Rep.Serv. 422 (1968).

**90.** Section 9–501(3) is set out in note 1 supra.

## § 26–9   Resale of Repossessed Collateral

Repossession and resale of the collateral is the usual method adopted by a secured creditor to satisfy the debtor's obligation upon default.   Ordinarily the secured party has little desire to keep the collateral as permitted by 9–505(2), and ordinarily he sees little advantage in obtaining a judgment on the debt and levying against the debtor's property.   Accordingly, 9–504 which governs resale of the collateral is the real "guts" of Part Five of Article Nine.   The striking feature of the resale provisions is the great latitude they grant to the secured party.   He may   ".   .   . sell, lease or otherwise dispose of any or all of the collateral in its then condition or following any commercially reasonable preparation or processing." [91]   Additionally, 9–504(3) provides that: "Disposition of the collateral may be by way of one or more contracts.   Sale or other disposition may be as a unit or in parcels and at any time and place and on any terms   .   .   .   ." [92]   These liberal rules for disposition of the collateral were enacted to encourage the secured party to seek the most advantageous resale price and thus reduce the possibility and amount of any deficiency.[93]

---

91.   Section 9–504(1) reads in full as follows:

(1) A secured party after default may sell, lease or otherwise dispose of any or all of the collateral in its then condition or following any commercially reasonable preparation or processing. Any sale of goods is subject to the Article on Sales (Article 2). The proceeds of disposition shall be applied in the order following to

(a) the reasonable expenses of retaking, holding, preparing for sale, selling and the like and, to the extent provided for in the agreement and not prohibited by law, the reasonable attorneys' fees and legal expenses incurred by the secured party;

(b) the satisfaction of indebtedness secured by the security interest under which the disposition is made;

(c) the satisfaction of indebtedness secured by any subordinate security interest in the collateral if written notification of demand therefor is received before distribution of the proceeds is completed. If requested by the secured party, the holder of a subordinate security interest must seasonably furnish reasonable proof of his interest, and unless he does so, the secured party need not comply with his demand.

92.   Section 9–504(3) provides:

Disposition of the collateral may be by public or private proceedings and may be made by way of one or more contracts. Sale or other disposition may be as a unit or in parcels and at any time and place and on any terms but every aspect of the disposition including the method, manner, time, place and terms must be commercially reasonable. Unless collateral is perishable or threatens to decline speedily in value or is of a type customarily sold on a recognized market, reasonable notification of the time after which any private sale or other intended disposition is to be made shall be sent by the secured party to the debtor, and except in the case of consumer goods to any other person who has a security interest in the collateral and who has duly filed a financing statement indexed in the name of the debtor in this state or who is known by the secured party to have a security interest in the collateral. The secured party may buy at any public sale and if the collateral is of a type customarily sold in a recognized market or is of a type which is the subject of widely distributed standard price quotations he may buy at private sale.

93.   See § 9–504, Comment 1; Gilmore, Article 9 of the Uniform Commercial Code—Part V Default, 7 Conference on Personal Finance Law Quarterly Report 4 (1952).

However, 9–504 does impose two requirements upon the reselling creditor: (1) the creditor must send notice; and (2) every aspect of the sale including the: method, manner, time, place, and terms must be "commercially reasonable." The notice requirement is easy to understand and to apply; it is inspired by the forlorn hope that the debtor, if he is notified, will either acquire enough money to redeem the collateral or send his friends to bid for it.[94] The second condition is both more important and more difficult to define in operational terms. Its importance lies in the fact that the amount of the deficiency judgment will be inversely proportional to the sales price; if the price is high, the amount of the judgment will be low, and vice versa. The "method, manner, time, place and terms" tests are really proxies for "insufficient price," and their importance lies almost exclusively in the extent they protect against an unfairly low price.

The price that the secured creditor receives from sale of the collateral is of crucial importance for the debtor because any deficiency is determined by deducting the proceeds of sale from the outstanding debt. A study of repossession and resale of 83 automobiles under the Connecticut Retail Installment Sales Financing Act exposes opportunity for abuse.[95] In that study Professor Shuchman found that repossession is typically followed by two resales. In the cases he studied, the first resale from the repossessing financier to a car dealer yielded an average of fifty-one percent of the *Red Book* retail price of the car on the date of repossession.[96] The debtor's deficiency was determined on the basis of this resale. Professor Shuchman found that the dealer-purchaser at the first sale then resold the car at a price that averaged 92 percent of the *Red Book* retail price.[97] The author concluded that present procedures (including those in the Code) permitting recovery of a deficiency provide little incentive for the repossessing secured creditor to exert his best efforts to obtain the highest possible price from resale. Accordingly, Professor Shuchman suggests the elimination of deficiencies, and he would limit secured creditors to strict foreclosure of the collateral upon a consumer debtor's default.[98]

Professor Shuchman's desire to do away with all deficiencies is understandable, but we would suggest that an additional study or two be accomplished before the legislatures undertake that step. In the first place, Professor Shuchman did not study a sample representative of all cars repossessed and resold. His sample comes exclusively from cases in which a claim for deficiency has already been filed. In many cases in which cars are repossessed and resold, perhaps in the large majority, no claim for deficiency is filed. Apparently, Professor Shuchman did not have an opportunity to inspect the cars actually

---

94. See § 9–504, Comment 5.

95. See Shuchman, Profit on Default: An Archival Study of Automobile Repossession and Resale, 22 Stan.L.Rev. 20 (1969).

96. Id. at 31.

97. Id. at 32.

98. Id. at 53–56.

in his sample, and it is possible that the low prices procured for them were in part attributable to their sad state at the time of repossession. Of course, the sizable amount they brought on the second resale suggests that any depreciation in their value at the time of first resale was not permanent. Finally, of course, it is not clear that the financiers and dealers in Hartford are representative of those elsewhere. In sum we find Professor Shuchman's article persuasive and well done, but would like to see more evidence.

### § 26–10   Resale of Repossessed Collateral—The Notice Requirement

In ascertaining the meaning of the language of 9–504(3), one may not safely rely upon pre-Code cases. Here the Code departs from old formulae;[99] it specifies no advertising requirements, requires no publication, states no requisite number of days prior to sale for giving notice, and does not require that the notice be sent by registered mail or conform to any specific form. In this section, therefore, the lawyer's search for meaning must concentrate on the Code, its comments, and on the post-Code cases. Section 9–504(3) requires that

> Unless collateral is perishable or threatens to decline speedily in value or is of a type customarily sold on a recognized market, reasonable notification of the time and place of any public sale or reasonable notification of the time after which any private sale or other intended disposition is to be made shall be *sent* by the secured party to the debtor,  . . . .
> (emphasis added)

The principal question in nearly every notice case is whether the secured party has taken the "reasonable steps"[100] necessary to inform the debtor and other interested parties about the nature and conduct of the resale so that they can protect their interests.

However, when the interests of the debtor would be better served by a quick resale or the fair market value can be established with certainty in the market place, notice need not be sent. Thus, the secured party is excused from giving notice of resale when the "collateral is perishable or threatens to decline speedily in value." Understandably, the time consumed in giving notice might have disastrous consequences on the price realized when the value of the collateral is subject to a sharp decline or the collateral is about to rot for want of refrigeration or other proper storage. Under such conditions the debtor will be better off in most instances if the secured party sells quickly and tells him about it later.

The other exception to the notice requirement occurs when the collateral is "customarily sold on a recognized market." Here the no-

---

**99.** For comparison see Uniform Conditional Sales Act §§ 18, 20–22.

**100.** Section 1–201(26) states:

A person "notifies" or "gives" a notice or notification to another by taking such steps as may be reasonably required to inform the other in ordinary course whether or not such other actually comes to know of it.

tion is that the debtor does need the protection afforded by notice because the price set by independent market forces is presumptively "commercially reasonable." Certainly, the New York Stock Exchange and the bond and commodity markets are "recognized markets." Such places are arenas of pure competition in the classical sense of the term. The forces of supply and demand determine price and the valuation of goods and such market places are relatively free from human connivance and manipulation. On the other hand, the exception to the notice requirement for sales on recognized markets does not encompass the sellers of hard goods. Used cars (and, a fortiori, other kinds of hard goods whose used market is even more uncertain) have been found to be items not "customarily sold on a recognized market." [101] Any transaction which involves haggling over price or competitive bidding should not be considered as one conducted on a recognized market, and the secured party is properly relieved of his obligation to give notice of resale only when neutral market forces rather than negotiations between buyer and seller determine price.

If the transaction does not fall within one of the above mentioned exceptions, then the selling creditor must give notice and four types of potential problems arise: (*1*) the notice may never have been sent; (*2*) if the notice was sent, it may not have contained the correct information; and (*3*) it may not have been timely sent; and (*4*) the creditor may be unable to prove that it was properly sent.

The secured creditor can satisfy the notice requirement merely by sending notification; it is not necessary that the debtor receive it.[102] If the mailman loses the notice or the debtor's wife throws it in the wastebasket, that is the debtor's tough luck; he bears such risks under the Code. For example, in Steelman v. Associates Discount Corp.[103] the notice sent to the debtor by certified mail was received by

**101.** Norton v. National Bank of Commerce, 240 Ark. 143, 398 S.W.2d 538, 3 UCC Rep.Serv. 119 (1966); Nelson v. Monarch Inv. Plan, Inc., 452 S.W.2d 375, 7 UCC Rep.Serv. 394 (Ky.App. 1970); One Twenty Credit Union v. Darcy, 40 Mass.App.Dec. 64, 5 UCC Rep.Serv. 792 (1968); Abbott Motors, Inc. v. Ralston, 28 Mass.App.Dec. 35, 5 UCC Rep.Serv. 788 (1964); Alliance Discount Corp. v. Shaw, 195 Pa.Super. 601, 171 A.2d 548, 1 UCC Rep.Serv. 644 (1961); Family Fin. Corp. v. Scott, 24 Pa.D. & C.2d 587, 1 UCC Rep.Serv. 647 (C.P.1961); see 2 G. Gilmore, Security Interests in Personal Property § 44.5 at 1236 (1965); contra, Third Nat'l Bank & Trust Co. v. Stagnaro, 25 Mass.App.Dec. 58, 4 UCC Rep.Serv. 675 (1962).

**102.** Section 1–201(38) reads as follows:

"Send" in connection with any writing or notice means to deposit in the mail or deliver for transmission by any other usual means of communication with postage or cost of transmission provided for and properly addressed and in the case of an instrument to an address specified thereon or otherwise agreed, or if there be none to any address reasonable under the circumstances. The receipt of any writing or notice within the time at which it would have arrived if properly sent has the effect of a proper sending.

See Hawkins v. General Motors Acceptance Corp., 250 Md. 146, 242 A.2d 120, 5 UCC Rep.Serv. 556 (1968) (merely sending notice sufficient). In Edmonson v. Air Serv. Co., 123 Ga.App. 263, 180 S.E.2d 589, 8 UCC Rep.Serv. 916 (1971), the court ruled that a letter sent by certified mail with insufficient postage did not satisfy the notice requirement of section 9–504.

**103.** 121 Ga.App. 649, 175 S.E.2d 62, 7 UCC Rep.Serv. 697 (1970). See Hud-

the debtor's sister-in-law who had a similar name and lived on the same rural mail route as the debtor. The Georgia Court of Appeals held as a matter of law that the notice was sufficient to satisfy the requirement that reasonable notice be sent to the debtor.

Although several cases and an attorney general's opinion have suggested that oral notice is sufficient,[104] these findings are almost certainly contrary to the draftsmen's intent. Section 9–504 requires that the secured party "send" notice and 1–201(38) tells us that:

> "Send" in connection with any writing or notice means to deposit in the mail or deliver for transmission by any other usual means of communication with postage or cost of transmission properly provided for and properly addressed
> .   .   .   .

It is most difficult to fit an oral message into the quoted language. Rather the subsection seems to contemplate mail or telegraphic notice. Of course, no secured party will intentionally use only oral notices and the question of the propriety of oral notice is likely to arise only when the secured creditor has failed to comply with his usual procedure for some reason.

Section 9–504 stipulates that the secured party must send notice to the "debtor," but the Code use of that term may encompass a variety of people. The term "debtor" is defined in 9–105(1)(d) to include a person "who owes payment or other performance of the obligation secured." Thus, two creditors failed to recover a deficiency because they did not send notice to an indorser of the debtor's note;[105] another creditor had a judgment in his favor reversed and remanded for the same reason.[106] Of course, debtors are not the only persons entitled to notice. The secured creditor who wishes to comply with 9–504 must send notice to other secured creditors who have an interest in the collateral and who have "duly filed a financing state-

---

speth Motors, Inc. v. Wilkinson, 238 Ark. 410, 382 S.W.2d 191, 2 UCC Rep. Serv. 273 (1964).

**104.** A. J. Armstrong Co. v. Janburt Embroidery Corp., 97 N.J.Super. 246, 234 A.2d 737, 4 UCC Rep.Serv. 748 (Law Div.1967) (oral notice to president held sufficient notice to debtor corporation).

An opinion by the Attorney General of Maryland, 50 Op.Att'y Gen.Md. 28 (1965) and dictum in Barker v. Horn, 245 Ark. 315, 432 S.W.2d 21, 5 UCC Rep.Serv. 793 (1968), suggest that oral notification might be sufficient. The sending requirement of 9–504(3) indicates, however, that the notice must in all cases be written. Contra, Foun-

dation Discounts, Inc. v. Serna, 81 N.M. 474, 468 P.2d 875, 7 UCC Rep. Serv. 854 (1970).

**105.** Third Nat'l Bank & Trust Co. v. Stagnaro, 25 Mass.App.Dec. 58, 4 UCC Rep.Serv. 675 (1962) (indorser of note); T & W Ice Cream, Inc. v. Carriage Barn, Inc., 107 N.J.Super. 328, 258 A.2d 162, 6 UCC Rep.Serv. 1230 (Law Div.1969) (accommodation party), *distinguishing*, A. J. Armstrong Co. v. Janburt Embroidery Corp., 97 N.J.Super. 246, 234 A.2d 737, 4 UCC Rep. Serv. 748 (Law Div.1967).

**106.** Norton v. National Bank of Commerce, 240 Ark. 143, 398 S.W.2d 538, 3 UCC Rep.Serv. 119 (1966).

ment indexed in the name of the debtor in this state or who is known by the second party to have a security interest in the collateral." [107]

Even if the secured party gives notice to debtor and all others entitled to it his "notice" may not contain the correct message. Note that notice of a public sale must contain different information from that announcing an intent to sell privately.[108] In the latter case, the notice need only state "the time after which" the collateral is to be sold; in the case of a public sale, it must state "the time and place" at which the sale will occur.[109] A creditor who uses his private sale form for a public sale violates 9–504(3).

An important factor in determining whether the notice was "reasonable" is the length of time by which it precedes the date of resale. Comment 5 to 9–504 states:

> [A]t a minimum [the notice] must be sent in such time that persons entitled to receive it will have sufficient time to take appropriate steps to protect their interests by taking part in the sale or other disposition if they so desire.

This ought to mean that the notice be sent at such a time and in such a way that the creditor would reasonably expect it to arrive in the debtor's hands in time to give him several business days in which to arrange alternative financing. A responsible creditor will recognize that the debtor needs time to seek out and negotiate for credit. The few cases which have been decided on this point support this proposition. In Associate Discount Corp. v. Forcier [110] the secured party repossessed an automobile and gave the debtor notice on November 23 that the auto would be sold at private sale "after December 2." The New York Court held that the notice was reasonable and granted the creditor's motion for a summary judgment in a suit for the deficiency. In Atlas Construction Co. v. Dravo-Doyle Co.[111] a registered letter notifying the debtor that the secured party would resell a repossessed crane was considered timely notice when it was sent eight days before

---

**107.** Under a proposed revision to 9–504(3), the secured party in possession would be required to give notice as follows:

In other cases notification shall be sent to any other secured party from whom the secured party has received (before sending his notification to the debtor or before the debtor's renunciation of his rights) written notice of a claim of an interest in the collateral.

Permanent Editorial Board for the Uniform Commercial Code, Review Committee for Article 9, Final Report § 9–504 at 173–175 (1971).

**108.** The distinction between public and private sale is discussed in text accompanying notes 127–34 infra.

**109.** § 9–504(3).

**110.** 5 UCC Rep.Serv. 294 (N.Y.Sup. Ct.1968); see also Hudspeth Motors, Inc. v. Wilkinson, 238 Ark. 410, 382 S.W.2d 191, 2 UCC Rep.Serv. 273 (1964) ("more than a week's notice" held enough time); Motor Contract Co. v. Sawyer, 123 Ga.App. 207, 180 S.E.2d 282, 8 UCC Rep.Serv. 1122 (1971) (ten days held sufficient). In Conti Causeway Ford v. Jarossy, 8 UCC Rep.Serv. 1348 (N.J.Dist.Ct.1971), the court ruled that the secured creditor failed to satisfy 9–504 when notice was mailed to the debtor in Florida two days prior to the time public sale was held in New Jersey.

**111.** 3 UCC Rep.Serv. 124 (Pa.C.P.1965).

the sale took place.   However, in Ennis v. Atlas Finance Co.[112] the Georgia Court of Appeals said that the reasonableness of two days notice for the private sale of an automobile was a question for the jury.   These cases suggest that a repossessor of even high priced items such as cranes will be in compliance with section 9–504 if he gives at least a week's notice.   Surely, the wise creditor who is going to resell an expensive piece of equipment repossessed from a business debtor will wish to give notice more than a week in advance of sale.

In special circumstances some courts may be willing to require more than a mere "sending" on the part of the creditor.   In Mallicoat v. Volunteer Finance & Loan Corp.,[113] the creditor sent a notice to the debtor informing him of the pending sale.   The notice was returned to the creditor undelivered, nevertheless he sold the repossessed automobile.   The court found that the creditor had failed properly to notify the debtor inasmuch as it knew that the debtor was in its own locale and knew that he had not received its notice, and yet had made no additional attempt, by telephone or otherwise, to contact the debtor. Nothing in the Code specifically requires a second contact when the creditor learns that the first has failed, but under similar circumstances the well-advised creditor will want to follow up on any notices which come back unopened.

### § 26–11   Resale of Repossessed Collateral—Commercially Reasonable

Section 9–504 specifies that every aspect of a sale of a repossessed item, "including the method, manner, time, place and terms must be commercially reasonable;" it does not state that a sale can be overturned because the sale price is too low.   Presumably, the price is one of the "terms of sale."   Whether or not this is so need not be answered because each of the enumerated factors is logically important only to the extent that it contributes to an insufficient price.   If the sale price is sufficient, the debtor has suffered no injury and normally will have no basis for complaint.   (Of course, in the rare cases in which the debtor seeks to redeem he will have suffered injury notwithstanding a fair price if the manner of disposition prevents his redemption or other arrangement for bids.)   The first sentence of 9–507(2)—which was undoubtedly inserted to allay creditors' fears that courts would focus on the sale price—gives a backhanded recognition to the importance of the price:

> The fact that a better price could have been obtained by a sale at a different time, or in a different method than that selected by the secured party, is not of itself sufficient to establish that the sale was not made in a commercially reasonable manner.

112.  120 Ga.App. 849, 172 S.E.2d 482, 7 UCC Rep.Serv. 399 (1969);  see also Baber v. Williams Ford Co., 239 Ark. 1054, 396 S.W.2d 302, 3 UCC Rep.Serv. 83 (1965), purporting to distinguish Hudspeth Motors, Inc. v. Wilkinson, 238 Ark. 410, 382 S.W.2d 191, 2 UCC Rep.Serv. 273 (1964).

113.  57 Tenn.App. 106, 415 S.W.2d 347, 3 UCC Rep.Serv. 1035 (1966).

Some of the recent cases explicitly recognize the primacy of resale price. In Mercantile Financial Corp. v. Miller [114] the guarantor of a note moved to reopen a default judgment which had been entered against him. He claimed that the sale of the collateral was not commercially reasonable because the secured party had sold collateral which allegedly had a fair market value of $750,000 for $19,000. The federal district court granted the motion and made the following comment about the importance of price in determining commercial reasonableness:

> Although § 9–507(2) clearly provides that a discrepancy between a price received by a creditor disposing of assets pursuant to § 9–504 and an isolated price later shown to have been obtainable, is not alone sufficient to grant a debtor affirmative relief under § 9–507(1), certainly such a discrepancy, if substantial, is relevant to a determination of whether a challenged sale was "commercially reasonable". (citing cases) The evidence here established that the price received for the goods sold by the plaintiff [secured party] was substantially less than both the price originally paid for them by G. F. & M. and the price which the purchaser of the assets subsequently received for them on resale, i. e., approximately $57,000.00. This evidence strongly suggested that the plaintiff did not obtain the fair market value for these goods at the time of the sale, and the plaintiff did not rebut this inference.[115]

Careful examination of other cases in which the courts hasten to punish creditors for failure to give notice suggests that the insufficiency of the resale price may be the real, though inarticulated, reason for the outcomes.[116] Notwithstanding the statement in 9–507(2) that low resale price alone is not enough, the crucial issue which one gleans from the "method, manner and time" language and from the several

---

114. 292 F.Supp. 797, 7 UCC Rep.Serv. 402 (E.D.Pa.1968).

115. Id. at 801, 7 UCC Rep.Serv. at 405. See California Airmotive, Corp. v. Jones, 415 F.2d 554, 6 UCC Rep.Serv. 1007 (6th Cir. 1969); Jefferson Credit Corp. v. Marcano, 60 Misc.2d 138, 302 N.Y.S.2d 390, 6 UCC Rep.Serv. 602 (1969); Family Fin. Corp. v. Scott, 24 Pa.D. & C.2d 587, 1 UCC Rep.Serv. 647 (C.P.1961); Atlas Constr. Co. v. Dravo-Doyle, 3 UCC Rep.Serv. 124 (Pa.C.P. 1965).

116. Although courts frequently rely on lack of notice, they seldom mention any causal connection between the debtor's injury and his failure to receive notice; there is no suggestion that he would have redeemed or have been otherwise moved to action by receipt of a notice. Hidden among the facts are some interesting data on the resale prices. See, e. g., Norton v. National Bank of Commerce, 240 Ark. 143, 398 S.W.2d 538, 3 UCC Rep.Serv. 119 (1966) (car purchased for more than $350 in September and resold for $75 in January); Baber v. Williams Ford Co., 239 Ark. 1054, 396 S.W.2d 302, 3 UCC Rep.Serv. 83 (1965) (car purchased in August for at least $882, including interest but not including downpayment, and resold, apparently in December, for $210); Braswell v. American Nat'l Bank, 117 Ga. App. 699, 161 S.E.2d 420, 5 UCC Rep. Serv. 420 (1968) (car purchased for $2,195, excluding interest but including downpayment, and resold, apparently after only a few months, for $850).

cases interpreting 9–504(3) is just that—was the price sufficient? The debtor who asks a court to ignore 9–507(2) probably expects too much, but the cases suggest that given an unusually low resale price little more is needed for the courts to find the sale commercially unreasonable. Other thorny questions remain: by what margin must the fair market value exceed the resale price? What kind of evidence is needed to establish a disparity in price? What is the appropriate market (retail, wholesale) against which to measure the resale price? Who has the burden of going forward—debtor or creditor?

Of the handful of post-Code cases shedding light on these issues, Atlas Construction Co v. Dravo-Doyle Co.[117] is most helpful. In that case the court upheld a jury verdict which found the sale to be commercially unreasonable. The seller of a crane repossessed it and sold it to the single bidder at the resale for $19,500. At the trial, the debtor showed that the "Green Guide Handbook" listed a price for comparable equipment of $25,310. In addition, the debtor produced a witness who testified that he would have paid between $25,000 and $28,000 for the crane at the time of the resale. In reaching its result, the court relied upon the two foregoing pieces of evidence concerning the price and also pointed out that the creditor contacted only one potential purchaser.

The case suggests several kinds of evidence that may be used to establish the adequacy or insufficiency of the resale price. First, it is one of several reported cases in which courts have accepted price handbooks as evidence of the value of the collateral.[118] Even when such handbooks are only considered a guide to valuation, they will provide the attorney with a rough standard by which to measure the sufficiency of the price received. Second, the debtor was able to produce an expert to testify concerning the fair market value. Expert testimony, of course, is the most common method of establishing value in the courtroom. Thus, testimony by qualified salesmen, independent appraisers or other dealers may be introduced by either party to support his claims about the fair market value of the collateral.[119] Another factor which should not be overlooked is the price received by the purchaser if there was a second resale of the collateral. As in-

117. 3 UCC Rep.Serv. 124 (Pa.C.P.1965). See also Goodin v. Farmers Tractor & Equip. Co., 249 Ark. 30, 458 S.W.2d 419, 8 UCC Rep.Serv. 230 (1970) (creditor diligence in arranging sale can outweigh low price; secured creditor placed six newspaper advertisements and mailed two personal invitations to public sale).

118. See also Family Fin. Corp. v. Scott, 24 Pa.D. & C.2d 587, 1 UCC Rep.Serv. 647 (C.P.1961). In Alliance Discount Corp. v. Shaw, 195 Pa.Super. 601, 171 A.2d 548 (1961), and in Ekman v. Mountain Motors, Inc., 364 P. 2d 998 (Wyo.1961), the courts admitted the book but said it was only a guide. Whether the creditor objected to the introduction of such handbooks on the ground that they were hearsay does not appear.

119. See Weaver v. O'Meara Motor Co., 452 P.2d 87, 6 UCC Rep.Serv. 415 (Alaska 1969); Carter v. Ryburn Ford Sales, Inc., 248 Ark. 236, 451 S.W.2d 199, 7 UCC Rep.Serv. 386 (1970); Frontier Inv. Corp. v. Belleville Nat'l Sav. Bank, 119 Ill.App.2d 2, 254 N.E. 2d 295, 7 UCC Rep.Serv. 243 (1969); Ennis v. Atlas Fin. Co., 120 Ga.App. 849, 172 S.E.2d 482, 7 UCC Rep.Serv. 399 (1969).

dicated by Mercantile Finance Corp. v. Miller,[120] (goods sold by secured creditor for $19,000 and resold for $57,000) if the price received on the subsequent resale was substantially greater than the amount credited to the debtor by the secured party, the courts will give favorable consideration to the debtor's claim that the price received by the secured party was insufficient.

None of the opinions discussing 9–504(3) provide much guidance for determining whether the resale price should be measured against the wholesale or retail market.[121]  In California Airmotive Corp. v. Jones [122] the secured party repossessed and resold for $31,000 an airplane which had been sold to the debtor for $100,000 a year earlier. In response to the debtor's claim that the price was insufficient and the sale commercially unreasonable, the creditor pointed out that the wholesale value of the plane was only $40,000 when sold to the debtor and that the resale was of a wholesale nature.  The Sixth Circuit vacated the district court's grant of summary judgment for the secured party and said, "We are not certain that if the $31,000 private resale price was a wholesale price that it would, as a matter of law, constitute a commercially reasonable disposal of the aircraft since the obligation was created by a retail sale." [123]  Nonetheless Comment 2 to 9–507 strongly suggests that the wholesale market is the appropriate measure, at least in the case in which the creditor does not maintain retail facilities:

> One recognized method of disposing of repossessed collateral is for the secured party to sell the collateral to or through a dealer—a method which in the long run may realize better average returns since the secured party does not usually maintain his own facilities for making such sales.

However, it is quite unclear whether either the debtor or the creditor's interest would be served by requiring resale on the retail market.  It is axiomatic that retail sales will bring a higher price than sales in the wholesale market, but retail marketing and advertising expenses

---

120.   292 F.Supp. 797, 7 UCC Rep.Serv. 402 (E.D.Pa.1968).   Accord, Ennis v. Atlas Fin. Co., 120 Ga.App. 849, 172 S.E.2d 482, 7 UCC Rep.Serv. 399 (1969) (secured party purchased auto for $1610 and dealer resold for $2472); Jefferson Credit Corp. v. Marcano, 60 Misc.2d 138, 302 N.Y.S.2d 390, 6 UCC Rep.Serv. 602 (Civ.Ct.1969) (auto sold for $348 and after repairs costing $402 was resold for $1050).   See also Shuchman, Profit on Default—An Archival Study of Automobile Repossession and Resale, 22 Stan.L.Rev. 20 (1969).

121.  In Baber v. Williams Ford Co., 239 Ark. 1054, 396 S.W.2d 302, 3 UCC Rep.Serv. 83 (1965), the court mentioned that the resale had been at wholesale.  Evidently the debtor did

not contend that a wholesale resale was improper.  But note the reference in both the body of and comments to 9–507 that the sale must conform to "reasonable commercial practice among dealers in the type of property sold. . . ."  If most of the financiers of the type of collateral in question sell at retail or if the creditor is also a retail seller, a persuasive argument may be made that the retail market is the proper measure.

122.   415 F.2d 554, 6 UCC Rep.Serv. 1007 (6th Cir. 1969).

123.  Id. at 556, 6 UCC Rep.Serv. at 1010.

will also exceed those of the wholesale market.  For instance, a bank who attempts large scale resales of repossessed automobiles on the retail market may incur substantial additional expenses which it may seek to add to the deficiency under 9–504(1) (a).  Even one who normally sells at retail could argue that one of the costs of selling repossessed autos on his lot is the profit he loses because he has so lost the opportunity to sell another car to the customer who bought the repossessed one.[124]

By how much must the fair market value of the collateral exceed the resale price before the resale can be attacked as commercially unreasonable?  In *Dravo-Doyle*,[125] the debtor's evidence indicated that the resale price was equal to approximately 75 percent of the fair market value.  In Family Finance v. Scott,[126] the fact that the automobile in question had been sold at half its apparent fair market value caused the court to open a deficiency judgment entered by confession. It would be foolish to suggest that these few cases have established an unchangeable pattern and that, consequently, any time the resale is less than 75 percent of the apparent fair market value the sale is commercially unreasonable.  In such cases the creditor should arm himself with memoranda and photographs to substantiate the "poorer than average" nature of the collateral.  Undoubtedly the court's ultimate judgment on the insufficiency of the sale price will be affected by its impression of the creditor's good faith and diligence as evidenced by all of his post-default behavior and particularly by the care with which he sent the notice and by the extent of his solicitation of bidders.

Price is important, but resales may fail the test of "commercial reasonableness" in other ways also.  In this regard we have already discussed the notice requirement.  In addition, no sale may have taken place or the sale may not have been properly conducted.[127]  Some creditors have been ensnared by the "no sale" rule of 9–504(5) which provides that transfer of collateral to "A person who is liable to a secured party under a guaranty, indorsement, repurchase agreement or the like  . . .  is not a sale or disposition of the collateral under this Article."  For instance, in Jefferson Credit Corp. v. Marcano [128] the finance company-assignee of the debtor's obligation attempted to recover the deficiency remaining after selling the collateral to the dealer-assignor who had guaranteed payment of the debt.  The defendant denied liability and relied upon the unconscionability provision of Article Two (2–302).  He argued that the conditional sales

124.  Compare the outcome under section 2–708(2) which permits the seller to recover as damages the profit lost when the buyer fails to perform as promised.

125.  Atlas Constr. Co. v. Dravo-Doyle Corp., 3 UCC Rep.Serv. 124 (Pa.C.P. 1965).

126.  24 Pa.D. & C.2d 587, 1 UCC Rep. Serv. 647 (C.P.1961).

127.  For instance in Cox Motor Car Co. v. Castle, 402 S.W.2d 429, 3 UCC Rep. Serv. 397 (Ky.App.1966), the secured party attempted to recover a deficiency without introducing evidence of a resale and without establishing that the proceeds of resale were insufficient to meet the outstanding debt. He was unsuccessful.

128.  60 Misc.2d 138, 302 N.Y.S.2d 390, 6 UCC Rep.Serv. 602 (Civ.Ct.1969).

contract was unenforceable. In support of this contention the debtor pointed to the fact that the contract which contained clauses waiving warranties of merchantability and fitness of purpose and a clause waiving defenses against the assignee was printed in English while the Spanish-speaking debtor was so unschooled in English that he needed an interpreter to testify in court. The New York Court agreed that the contract was unconscionable, but did not confront the issue of whether unconscionability under 2–302 is a valid defense against enforcement of a security interest under Article Nine.[129] Instead it relied upon 9–504(5) and said that the transfer to the dealer did not constitute the prerequisite sale and, accordingly, held that the finance company could not recover the purported deficiency.

Although 9–504 authorizes resale of collateral by either public or private sale, the Code only hints at the distinction between the two methods. Nevertheless, it is important to know the difference because the method chosen determines the form of notice the secured party must give the debtor [130] and may also affect the rights of the purchaser.[131] Moreover, the secured party may purchase the collateral at a public resale, but he is permitted to purchase at a private resale only when the collateral is "customarily sold on a recognized market" or the subject of widespread price quotations. Thus, purchase by the secured party at a private sale may be a violation of Part Five of Article Nine.[132]

If the secured party wishes to sell the collateral at a public sale, must he literally invite the general public to attend? Under pre-Code law, the consensus was that "public sale" meant a sale open to the general public. Neither the cases discussing 9–504 nor the commentators provide any guidance on this issue.[133] However, the dismal experience of sheriff's sales—indisputably public—has shown that sales on the courthouse steps do not bring high prices. Very likely

129. Note that Article Nine unlike Article Two, does not contain a provision governing unconscionable contracts. Presumably, 2–302 will apply to those security agreements which arise from the sale of goods. However, in other cases the debtor will have to rely upon the good faith requirement contained in 1–103.

130. Section 9–504(3) specifies the different requirements as follows:

. . . reasonable notification of the time and place of any public sale or reasonable notification of the time after which any private sale or other intended disposition is to be made shall be sent by the secured party to the debtor . . . .

131. Section 9–504(4) spells out the difference for the purchaser as follows: The purchaser takes free of all such rights and interests even though the secured party fails to comply with the requirements of this Part or of any judicial proceedings

(a) in the case of a public sale if the purchaser has no knowledge of any defects in the sale and if he does not buy in collusion with the secured party, other bidders or the person conducting the sale; or

(b) in any other case, if the purchaser acts in good faith.

132. See Carter v. Ryburn Ford Sales, Inc., 248 Ark. 236, 451 S.W.2d 199, 7 UCC Rep.Serv. 386 (1970).

133. See 2 G. Gilmore, Security Interests in Personal Property § 44.6 at 1242 (1965); Hogan, The Secured Party and Default Proceedings Under the UCC, 47 Minn.L.Rev. 205, 226 (1962).

resale of repossessed collateral at a regularly scheduled dealer's auction would produce more and higher bids than the traditional sheriff's sale. In the interest of providing an orderly market for repossessed collateral obtaining higher prices in the long run, it may be to the debtor's advantage to allow the secured party to resell the collateral at a dealer's auction where the general public is not admitted.[134] Since the secured party can purchase the collateral at a public sale, the primary consideration is the existence of bona fide competitive bidding—whether at a sale attended by the general public or one more restricted in potential bidders. Requiring literal compliance with the term "public sale" would be inconsistent with the Code's attempt to provide flexible and liberal methods of disposition. Here, as elsewhere, the secured party's conduct should be judged by how well it succeeds in realizing a maximum resale price.

Another issue upon which the Code provides little guidance is the proper conduct of the resale. Must a public sale be by auction or are sealed bids permissible? Comment 1 to 9–504 directs attention to 2–706 as a guide for determining when a resale is commercially reasonable. There we find in comment 4 that "By public sale is meant a sale by auction." It seems unwise to require a public sale by auction if the same or a higher price can be obtained by the submission of sealed bids. As far as the other aspects of a public sale are concerned, some notion of the potential problem areas may be gleaned from several cases decided under the Code. One factor of great importance is the manner in which the sale is publicized and bids are solicited. For example, in California Airmotive Corp. v. Jones,[135] the Sixth Circuit noted that one of the factors affecting its decision to vacate summary judgment entered in favor of the creditor was the fact that while notice of the sale had been published in a trade publication and other potential bidders had been personally contacted, the secured party had given out the wrong location as the place of resale. In that case only two persons made bids. Similarly, in Mercantile Financial Corp. v. Miller [136] the court mentioned that the resale had taken place in the early evening, had received minimal publicity, and was carried out with knowledge that the sole bid would come from a person unfamiliar with local market conditions. Apparently, in both of these cases the resale was conducted by auction.

The importance of the solicitation of bidders in private sales is suggested in *Dravo-Doyle*.[137] There, although the creditor's territory covered parts of Pennsylvania, Ohio, Maryland and West Virginia, it made "no effort to contact" anyone other than the ultimate purchaser. Although Article Nine does not require a specific number of bidders, every single-bid sale invites scrutiny. It may well be that

134. See Shuchman, Profit on Default: An Archival Study of Automobile Repossession and Resale, 22 Stan.L.Rev. 20, 43–46 (1969).

135. 415 F.2d 554, 6 UCC Rep. 1007 (6th Cir. 1969).

136. 292 F.Supp. 797, 7 UCC Rep.Serv. 402 (E.D.Pa.1968).

137. 3 UCC Rep.Serv. 124 (Pa.C.P.1965).

multiple invitations to bid are a prerequisite of a commercially reasonable sale.

If the collateral is very expensive and the debtor is litigious, it may serve the creditor's interest to procure a judicial approval of the sale. Section 9–507(2) provides: "A disposition which has been approved in any judicial proceeding or by any bona fide creditors' committee or representative of creditors shall conclusively be deemed to be commercially reasonable." Unless the stakes are very high, the secured party will not wish to expend the time and money to get prior approval for his resale of the collateral. However, if he desires a stamp of approval he will have to meet the same standard as his fellow creditors.[138]

Finally, it is important to know who has the burden of proving or disapproving commercial reasonableness—the debtor or the creditor. In Mallicoat v. Volunteer Finance & Loan Corp.,[139] plaintiff-creditor called its loan manager as its sole witness. The loan manager testified that the car in question had been sold for $150 at the public sale and that the sale had been advertised on posters. On cross-examination, he could not say where or when the posters had been posted, and he apparently did not testify about the fair market value of the car.

Holding that the creditor had the burden of proving a commercially reasonable resale, the court found that the loan manager's testimony was not sufficient:

> Since the proof incident to advertisement and sale was peculiarly within the knowledge of Volunteer Finance, the burden was upon it to show a compliance with the Act   . .
> The testimony of Mr. Austin   . . .   that the property was disposed of at a public sale, standing alone, was not sufficient to carry this burden.[140]

Judge McAmis cites the conventional doctrine that the burden should be upon the creditor since he had the knowledge. This conclusion is supported by the equally conventional learning that the burden is upon the moving party. Here, as usual, the creditor was the plaintiff seeking a deficiency judgment. When one moves from evidence of the actual conduct of the advertising and sale by the creditor, however, the *Mallicoat* opinion is less informative. Although the general status of the market is more likely to be within the knowledge of the creditor than that of the debtor, it is not "exclusively" or even "peculiarly" within his knowledge. Moreover, the court does not state whether the creditor must show some external evidence of the

138.  See Old Colony Trust Co. v. Penrose Indus. Corp., 280 F.Supp. 698, 4 UCC Rep.Serv. 977 (E.D.Pa.), aff'd 398 F.2d 310, 5 UCC Rep.Serv. 565 (3d Cir. 1968); Frontier Inv. Corp. v. Belleville Nat'l Sav. Bank, 119 Ill.App.2d 2, 254 N.E.2d 295, 7 UCC Rep.Serv. 243 (1969).

139.  57 Tenn.App. 106, 415 S.W.2d 347, 3 UCC Rep.Serv. 1035 (1966).

140.  Id. at 114, 415 S.W.2d at 351, 3 UCC Rep.Serv. at 1040 (1966).

market value of the sold collateral to carry his burden of proving that the sale was commercially reasonable.[141]

The secured party may have done everything right all along the way; nevertheless it may be impossible or extremely difficult to prove it in the courtroom.  If the creditor is meticulous, he will have retained a business record in the form of a copy of the notice of resale with the initials of the sending employee;  he will alternatively have made a ledger entry of the sending of the notice.  Upon laying the proper foundation, he will be able to submit either of these as business records.  Not all creditors are meticulous, and months after the event, the creditor may be unable to muster sufficient admissible evidence to prove his case.  For example, in Barker v. Horn,[142] the creditor seems to have sent a notice of sale, but he thoroughly bungled its introduction into evidence:

> On cross-examination, [debtor] denied that he received a letter from T. E. Martin on September 9, 1966 by registered mail  .  .  .  .  He denied that his signature appeared on a card exhibited to him.  If this was a return receipt for registered mail, it was never introduced.  [Creditor] stated that T. E. Martin was his attorney and apparently sought to testify that he had a copy of a notice Martin had sent.  The copy was not introduced when objection was made on account of lack of personal knowledge by the witness.  Thus, there was no evidence upon which to base any finding that notice was given.[143]

## § 26–12  Consequences of Creditor Misbehavior

A creditor's misbehavior in repossessing or reselling collateral can bring upon him a variety of unpleasant consequences.  Some of these have only marginal importance; others will be important in virtually every transaction which culminates in a default.  They may be classified as follows: (1) criminal liability under state and federal laws; (2) tort liability for improper collection behavior; (3) statutory liability under 9–507 for loss caused by deviation from the provisions of Part Five of Article Nine; (4) statutory liability under 9–507 as a penalty for the improper repossession or resale of consumer goods; and (5) denial of a deficiency judgment.

## § 26–13  Creditor Misbehavior—Criminal or Tort Liability

The possibility of criminal liability arising from an unduly vigorous repossession merits only a passing word.  If, for example, a

---

141.  It is clear in several jurisdictions, however, that the burden of proof falls squarely upon the secured party if it is found that he violated the provisions of Article Nine, Part 5, during the course of repossession and resale of the collateral.  See text accompanying notes 178–83 infra.

142.  245 Ark. 315, 432 S.W.2d 21, 5 UCC Rep.Serv. 793 (1968).

143.  Id. at 316, 432 S.W.2d at 22, 5 UCC Rep.Serv. at 794.

repossessing creditor drags the debtor's wife from her automobile by the hair, or if he enters the debtor's house by removing a screen door, he will probably be guilty of a crime under state law.  If debtor's lawyer can then find a prosecutor willing to prosecute such crimes, he will have a useful device to inhibit such behavior.  If the debt collector threatens violence, but does not commit a battery or an assault, he may still be guilty of an "extortionate" collection practice.  The federal Consumer Credit Protection Act [144] defines such practices as follows:

> An extortionate means is any means which involves the use, or an express or implicit threat of use, of violence or other criminal means to cause harm to the person, reputation, or property of any person.[145]

Although the extortionate practice provisions were designed principally to inhibit Mafia activities, they are broad enough to cover the activities of all creditors.  Even if one is unable to interest the United States attorney in prosecuting, the Act's provisions may still assist the debtor's lawyer in arguing that such behavior is or ought to be regarded as tortious.[146]

The creditor's potential tort liability is of greater importance both to the creditor's lawyer and to the debtor's lawyer than are possible criminal sanctions.  Even if the secured party repossesses and disposes of the collateral without violating the specific provisions of Part Five of Article Nine, he is not exculpated from any tortious conduct which may have occurred in the process.  The secured party's potential liability is limited only by the nature and number of tort actions available in the applicable jurisdiction: the creditor may have entered the house without permission (trespass); he may have threatened the debtor's wife and child (assault); he may have shoved one of them (battery); or he may have taken some valuable diamonds when he repossessed the car (conversion).  Moreover, the collection activity, as a whole, may constitute an intentional infliction of emotional injury or an invasion of the debtor's privacy.[147]

For instance, in Southern Industrial Savings Bank v. Greens [148] the secured party peacefully repossessed an automobile which the debtor claimed contained valuables and cash worth $5,600.  The Florida Appeals Court noted that a secured party who repossesses without judicial action subjects himself to liability for any tortious conduct. Applying common law doctrine, the court concluded that he became

---

144.  15 U.S.C.A. §§ 1601–77 (1970); 18 Id. §§ 891–96.

145.  18 Id. § 891(7).

146.  It is not unusual for a court to consult statutes for a standard of conduct in tort cases.  See W. Prosser, The Law of Torts § 35 (3d ed. 1964) and the cases cited therein.

147.  See S. Riesenfeld, Cases and Materials on Creditors' Remedies and Debtors' Protection 268 (1967); CCH Poverty Law Reporter ¶ 3545 (1968); Annot., 22 A.L.R.2d 1227 (1952) (assault); Annot., 99 A.L.R.2d 358 (1965); Annot., 19 A.L.R.3d 1318 (1968) (right of privacy).

148.  224 So.2d 416 (Fla.App.1969).

a constructive or involuntary bailee of the goods and affirmed the trial court's judgment that the secured party was liable for their loss. However, under similar circumstances in Grucella v. General Motors Corp.[149] the secured party avoided liability for camera equipment allegedly left in the debtor's auto because his agent had the foresight to examine the auto before repossession and was able to testify that there was nothing in the car when he repossessed it.

Conduct by the secured party or his agents in blatant disregard of the rights of the debtor and others may result in liability for punitive as well as compensatory damages. For instance in Franklin Investment Co. v. Homburg,[150] the secured party, without giving notice and with knowledge of the purchaser's good faith claim to title, repossessed an automobile from an individual who had purchased it out of the debtor's inventory. Noting that a purchaser from inventory takes the goods free from a security interest in such inventory,[151] the District of Columbia Court of Appeals affirmed the trial court's award of punitive damages.

## § 26–14   Creditor Misbehavior—Liability under the UCC, 9–507(1)

In addition to the common law liability discussed above, the Code in 9–507 also provides statutory relief when the secured party deviates from the provisions of Part Five of Article Nine. Section 9–507(1) reads in its entirety as follows:

> If it is established that the secured party is not proceeding in accordance with the provisions of this Part disposition may be ordered or restrained on appropriate terms and conditions. If the disposition has occurred the debtor or any person entitled to notification or whose security interest has been made known to the secured party prior to the disposition has a right to recover from the secured party any loss caused by a failure to comply with the provisions of this Part. If the collateral is consumer goods, the debtor has a right to recover in any event an amount not less than the credit service charge plus ten per cent of the principal amount of the debt or the time price differential plus ten per cent of the cash price.

Generally, the section provides two modes of relief when the secured party fails to comply with Part Five of Article Nine. First, the section authorizes the courts to exercise control over dispositions which would be commercially unreasonable. Secondly, the section specifies that the secured party is liable for any loss caused by his non-compliance with the provisions of Part Five, Article Nine.

149.   10 Pa.D. & C.2d 65 (Dist.Ct.1956).

150.   252 A.2d 95, 6 UCC Rep.Serv. 60 (D.C.Ct.App.1969).

151.   See § 9–307. See also Klingbiel v. Commercial Credit Corp., 439 F.2d 1303, 8 UCC Rep.Serv. 1099 (7th Cir. 1971) (amount of punitive damages sustained).

Since the section covers all violations of Part Five, it entitles the aggrieved party to recovery not just for an improper resale, but also for an improper repossession or strict foreclosure under 9–505.[152]

If the secured party resells the collateral in a commercially unreasonable manner, then the logical benchmark by which to measure the debtor's loss is the difference between the amount actually realized on resale and the amount which would have been obtained had there been compliance with the Code's requirements.[153]   However, it is now all but indisputable that compensatory damages are an insufficient deterrent to creditor misbehavior in nickel and dime consumer transactions where such damages will amount to very little in most cases. It is not surprising, therefore, that the draftsmen installed a statutory penalty in 9–507 to up the ante for those who would abuse the consumer:

> If the collateral is consumer goods, the debtor has a right to recover in any event, an amount not less than the credit service charge plus ten per cent of the principal amount of the debt or the time price differential plus ten per cent of the cash price.

The sentence is a penalty—a "minimum recovery" the comment [154] calls it—and the consumer is entitled to it even if he has not suffered a penny's loss.   Whether the prospect of such a penalty will be sufficient to forestall creditor misbehavior is impossible to predict.[155] Given the fact that the penalty is computed on the basis of the original principal amount and includes the total interest charge, however, a debtor may recover a sum substantially in excess of his actual loss.[156]

---

**152.**   Note that the second sentence of 9–507 reads, in part (emphasis added): *"If the disposition has occurred* the debtor  .  .  .  has a right to recover from the secured party any loss caused by a failure to comply with the provisions of this Part."  The "if" clause can be read as a condition so that a creditor might argue that resale of the collateral is a condition precedent to liability under 9–507 and, for instance, that a debtor has no damage remedy for the creditor's violation of the Code when he repossesses and retains the collateral under 9–505(2). However, Comment 2 to 9–505 says that if the secured party violates the requirements of that section he "is liable in conversion or alternatively may incur the liabilities set out in Section 9–507."   Thus we conclude that the section is intended to grant a statutory damage remedy for any violation of Article Nine, Part 5.

**153.**   See A to Z Rental, Inc. v. Wilson, 413 F.2d 899 (10th Cir. 1969) ; T & W Ice Cream, Inc. v. Carriage Barn, Inc., 107 N.J.Super. 328, 258 A.2d 162, 6 UCC Rep.Serv. 1230 (1969).  See also 2 G. Gilmore, Security Interests in Personal Property § 44.9.2 at 1258 (1965).

**154.**   § 9–507, Comment 1.

**155.**   In some cases the Consumer Credit Protection Act and the proposed Uniform Consumer Credit Code provide for penalties equal to twice the amount of the credit service charge plus costs plus attorneys' fees for any successful action.   Consumer Credit Protection Act § 130, 15 U.S.C. § 1640 (1970);   Uniform Consumer Credit Code § 5.203 (Rev. Final Draft 1968).

**156.**   The one reported case in which the penalty was computed, Atlas Credit Corp. v. Dolbow, 193 Pa.Super. 649, 165 A.2d 704, 1 UCC Rep.Serv. 5 (1960), illustrates the difficulties of computation.   There, the debtor purchased a boat which the court characterized as consumer goods.   The "cash price" was $5,980.00 or $5,480.00 (depending upon whether the downpayment is included in the calculation of the "cash price").

For example, an automobile loan of $2,000 financed at $6 per hundred over a period of three years would produce a penalty of $560.[157] Because the interest cost will constitute such a large part of the total cost of installment purchases with terms of three years or more, the penalty may be sufficient in those cases at least to wipe out a deficiency.[158]

The debtor paid $500.00 down and executed a 60-month purchase agreement with monthly payments of $158.53. This totaled $9,511.80 (60 x $158.53). Debtor asked for only $3,598.21 and received a verdict for $3,000. However, because the penalty is figured on the cash price, debtor in such a case should have recovered either $4,579.80 or $4,629.80. The computation would be ten percent of the cash price ($5,480.00 x .10=$548.00) or $5,980.00 x .10=$598.00) plus the time-price differential of ($9,511.80 – $5,480.00=$4,031.80). Professor Gilmore recognized that Dolbow was wrong, but apparently he miscalculated the time-price differential. See 2 G. Gilmore, Security Interests in Personal Property § 44.9.3 at 1260 n. 2 (1965).

Whether one should include the downpayment in the "cash price" is not clear. Arguing for inclusion is the usual meaning as revealed in the usual retail installment form, e. g.:

(1) Cash Sale Price
    Cash Price      $_____
    Taxes      $_____
    Installation Costs      $_____
    _____      $_____      $_____

(2) Down Payment:
    Cash      $_____
    Trade-in      $_____      $_____

(3) Difference (Item (1) less Item (2))      $_____

(4) Official Fees
    _____      $_____
    _____      $_____      $_____

(5) Insurance Costs
    Type      Terms
    Credit Life      _____      $_____
    _____      _____      $_____

(6) Principal Balance      $_____

(7) Time Price Differential      $_____

(8) Time Balance (sum of Items (6) and (7))      $_____

(9) Time Sales Price (sum of Items (2) and (8))      $_____

Time Balance is payable in _____ consecutive monthly installments of $_____ each, all payable on the same day of each month. The first installment is due _____ _____, 19__ or one month from the date of this contract if not otherwise specified.

---

Arguing against including the downpayment in the "cash price" is the possibility that such inclusion would produce different penalties in the same transaction depending upon whether the original lender were the seller or a third party creditor. (In the latter case the penalty would be ten percent of the loan principal, a figure which would not include any part of the downpayment).

157. The computation in this example would be as follows: $200 (ten percent of the principal amount) plus $360 (the credit service charge which equals $6 x 20 (hundreds) x 3 (years)=$560 (the penalty)).

158. See the *Dolbow* example in note 153 supra, where the total amount due was $9,511.80 after the downpayment and where the penalty would have been $4,629.80.

## § 26–15    Creditor Misbehavior—Denial of a Deficiency

The final and potentially most significant consequence of a creditor's misbehavior is that it may cause him completely to lose his right to a deficiency judgment. Whether denial of a deficiency judgment to a misbehaving creditor is consistent with or permissible under Article Nine is the subject of dispute. Professor Gilmore states that the draftsmen of Article Nine did not consider this question.[159] The creditor can surely argue that, since 9–507 is a comprehensive codification of a debtor's remedies and since that section is silent as to denial of a deficiency judgment, such a denial is not a permissible remedy. The statement in 9–201 that the creditor has all the rights that his agreement with the debtor gives him (except when the Code specifically provides otherwise) bolsters this argument.[160]

The debtor, however, can respond first by pointing to the Code's incorporation of the general rules of common law and equity ("a court's denial of a deficiency is only the exercise of its traditional equitable powers").[161] Second, he can point to the case law under the Uniform Conditional Sales Act,[162] where courts dealing with a similar statute denied deficiencies to misbehaving creditors.[163] Debtor can also argue that Part Five's silence in the face of this prior case law indicates that the Code leaves courts free to reach this result.

The premier case in the line of authority which denies any deficiency to a secured creditor who violates Part Five, Article Nine is Skeels v. Universal CIT Credit Corp.[164] There Judge Willson held as follows:

> "It seems to this Court, however, that to permit a recovery by a security holder of a loss in disposing of collateral when no notice has been given, permits a continuation of the evil which the Commercial Code sought to correct . . . In

---

**159.** 2 G. Gilmore, Security Interests In Personal Property § 44.9.4 at 1264 (1965).

**160.** Note too that the Code specifically authorizes deficiencies in 9–502(2) and 9–504(2). A counter-argument is that the 9–201 rights are always subject to general equitable principles.

**161.** § 1–103.

**162.** Uniform Conditional Sales Act § 22 (1922) provided:

If the proceeds of the resale are not sufficient to defray the expenses thereof . . . and the balance due upon the purchase price, the seller may recover the deficiency from the buyer, or from anyone who has succeeded to the obligations of the buyer.

Section 25 of the same act provided further:

If the seller fails to comply with the [resale] provisions [of the Act] . . . the buyer may recover from the seller his actual damages, if any, and in no event less than one-fourth of the sum of all payments which have been made under the contract, with interest.

**163.** See, e. g., United Sec. Corp. v. Tomlin, 198 A.2d 179 (Del.Super. 1964); Commercial Credit Corp. v. Swiderski, 195 A.2d 546 (Del.Super. 1963), motion for rehearing denied, 196 A.2d 214 (Del.Super.1963).

**164.** 222 F.Supp. 696, 1 UCC Rep.Serv. 639 (W.D.Pa.1963), modified on other grounds, 335 F.2d 846, 2 UCC Rep. Serv. 256 (3d Cir. 1964).

my view it must be held that a security holder who sells without notice may not look to the debtor for any loss." [165]

Other courts which have taken this stance likewise seem to feel that compliance with the provisions of Part Five, Article Nine is a condition precedent to recovery of a deficiency.[166]

In denying deficiencies several courts have demonstrated what creditors must regard as treacherous ingenuity. Some of these courts merely assert that a misbehaving creditor should not, and therefore does not, have the right to a deficiency; others have constructed elaborate, if somewhat fictional, justifications for denial. The doctrine of denying deficiency judgments has experienced its most visible and extensive growth in the Georgia Court of Appeals, which has faced the issue four times since 1966. In the first case, Moody v. Nides Finance Co.,[167] the debtor's sister-in-law drove in the encumbered car to the finance company office to make a payment which was overdue. She gave the finance company's agent the keys to the car for a road test to "see whether we have our money's worth in it." After the drive, the loan manager simply informed her, "[W]e are going to keep it." [168] The finance company later sold the car at a private sale without giving notice to the debtor. In reversing the trial court's decision for the creditor, the Georgia Court of Appeals found that the taking of the car in the circumstances described amounted to an accord and satisfaction of the debtor's liability. It appears from the opinion that this novel argument had not occurred to the debtor's lawyer, and he had not pleaded it. As an after-thought the court states that it would "likely have reached the same result by applying UCC provisions." [169]

In the second Georgia case, Johnson v. Commercial Credit Corp.,[170] the debtor voluntarily turned in the car after he had made six payments. Although the seller urged him to keep the car by advising, "You can't afford to turn it in . . . . It's worth more than you owe on it . . . ., he nevertheless assured the debtor, "It's entirely up to you if you want to turn it in." [171] Here the defendant debtor, presumably aware of the *Moody* case, pleaded accord and satisfaction and won in the appellate court.

**165.** 222 F.Supp. at 702, 1 UCC Rep. Serv. at 643–44.

**166.** See One Twenty Credit Union v. Darcy, 40 Mass.App.Dec. 64, 5 UCC Rep.Serv. 792 (1968); In re Bro Cliff, Inc., 8 UCC Rep.Serv. 1144 (Ref.Dec. W.D.Minn.1971); Associates Discount Corp. v. Cary, 47 Misc.2d 369, 262 N.Y. S.2d 646 (Civ.Ct.1965); Foundation Discounts Inc. v. Serna, 81 N.M. 474, 468 P.2d 875, 7 UCC Rep.Serv. 854 (1970). Cf. Morris Plan Co. v. Johnson, 271 N.E.2d 404, 9 UCC Rep.Serv. 728 (1971).

**167.** 115 Ga.App. 859, 156 S.E.2d 310, 4 UCC Rep.Serv. 508 (1967).

**168.** Id. at 860, 156 S.E.2d at 311, 4 UCC Rep.Serv. at 509.

**169.** Id. at 861, 156 S.E.2d at 312, 4 UCC Rep.Serv. at 511.

**170.** 117 Ga.App. 131, 159 S.E.2d 290, 4 UCC Rep.Serv. 1183 (1968).

**171.** Id. at 131, S.E.2d at 291, 4 UCC Rep.Serv. at 1184.

In the third Georgia case, Braswell v. American National Bank,[172] plaintiff-creditor moved for summary judgment on his allegation of repossession and resale of the automobile. The defendant answered that plaintiff had not given him notice of the sale. The trial court granted the plaintiff-creditor's motion, and the Court of Appeals reversed. The appellate court this time did not find an accord and satisfaction; instead, it rested its decision on the proposition that failure to allege and prove proper notice under 9–504 precluded plaintiff-creditor from recovering a deficiency under the Code. The court went on to make the somewhat startling assertion that "the majority of the courts in this country" agreed with its position.[173]

These cases make instructive reading for any lawyer who practices before a court which has not yet dealt with the deficiency question. The Georgia court, like a skater testing March ice, showed great hesitance to base its decision on the UCC, and in both *Moody* and *Johnson* it ultimately preferred to use the barest kind of fiction to enable it to stand on familiar common law doctrine.[174] Having tested the ice in *Moody*, however, the court was finally willing to rest its conclusion exclusively on the Code in *Braswell*.

In Arkansas, the evolution of antideficiency law has followed quite a different course. In Baber v. Williams Ford Co.,[175] the Arkansas Supreme Court dealt with a question of the sufficiency of a notice of resale. Finding that the notice issue was a question for the jury to decide, the court remanded the case for a new trial. In the course of its discussion, the court indicated that if the secured party were "to hold the debtor . . . liable for any deficiency, . . . [it] must give the debtor 'reasonable notice.' "[176] The same court in Norton v. National Bank of Commerce [177] took a different approach in reversing and remanding to the lower court:

"Upon the issue of Norton's damages simple considerations of fair play cast a burden of proof upon the bank. It was

172. 117 Ga.App. 699, 161 S.E.2d 420, 5 UCC Rep.Serv. 420 (1968).

173. Id. at 701, 161 S.E.2d at 422, 5 UCC Rep.Serv. at 422. In the fourth Georgia case, Bradford v. Lindsey Chevrolet Co., 117 Ga.App. 781, 161 S.E.2d 904, 5 UCC Rep.Serv. 558 (1968), the court backslid a bit. There, the Georgia Court of Appeals held that a creditor who had repossessed but made no sale for more than fifty days, who made no demand for payment until suit, and who still possessed the auto at the time of judgment had rescinded and forfeited any right to a deficiency judgment. The court cited *Moody* and *Braswell* and stated that the result would be the same under the Code. Id. at 782–83, 161 S.E.2d at 906, 5 UCC Rep.Serv. at 560. Since the creditor had not disposed of the collateral, and therefore had not quali-

fied for a deficiency judgment under any reading of the Code, the court was correct about the outcome under the Code.

174. Accord and satisfaction is normally founded on the agreement of both parties that one is accepting something in satisfaction of the other's liability. See generally S. Williston, Law of Contracts § 1838 (rev. ed. 1938). The creditors' "agreement" in *Moody* and *Johnson* almost certainly exists only in the court's mind.

175. 239 Ark. 1054, 396 S.W.2d 302, 3 UCC Rep.Serv. 83 (1965).

176. Id. at 1057, 396 S.W.2d at 304, 3 UCC Rep.Serv. at 86.

177. 240 Ark. 143, 398 S.W.2d 538, 3 UCC Rep.Serv. 119 (1966).

the bank which wrongfully disposed of the car without notice to the debtors. Thus it was the bank's action which made it at least difficult, if not impossible, for Norton to prove the extent of his loss with reasonable certainty. A chattel such as a car may well be a thousand miles away before the debtor learns of its sale without notice. It would be manifestly unfair for the creditor to derive an advantage from its own misconduct. We think the just solution is to indulge the presumption in the first instance that the collateral was worth at least the amount of the debt, thereby shifting to the creditor the burden of proving the amount that should reasonably have been obtained through a sale conducted according to law." [178]

In Universal CIT Credit Co. v. Rone,[179] the Arkansas Court elaborated upon its statement in *Norton* that when the secured party fails to comply with Part Five of Article Nine, then the collateral is presumptively worth at least the amount of the debt. In the *Rone* case the debtor claimed that he did not receive notice of the resale and further testified that the collateral (a car and pickup truck) was worth approximately $1400. The secured party had sold the collateral for $325 and introduced the testimony of the purchaser of the car that he considered the amount he paid to be the fair market value. The secured party appealed from a jury verdict denying the recovery of the claimed deficiency. The Arkansas Court explained the secured party's burden as follows:

Appellant also had the burden of showing the amount of the deficiency it was entitled to recover. Carter v. Ryburn Ford Sales supra. Whenever the value of the collateral is an issue in an action to recover a deficiency, there is a presumption that it was worth at least the amount of the debt, and the secured party has the burden of proving the amount that should have been obtained through a sale conducted according to law. Barker v. Horn, 245 Ark. 315, 432 S.W.2d 21. It is only where the sale is conducted according to the requirements of the Code that the amount received or bid at a sale of collateral is evidence of its true value in an action to recover a deficiency.[180]

178. Id. at 149–50, 398 S.W.2d at 542, 3 UCC Rep.Serv. at 124. In Carter v. Ryburn Ford Sales, Inc., 248 Ark. 236, 451 S.W.2d 199, 7 UCC Rep.Serv. 386 (1970), the Arkansas court clarified its position and held that the fact the secured party had violated 9–504(3) by purchasing the collateral at a private sale "did not *ipso facto* relieve the debtor from his obligation for any deficiency." Id. at 243, 451 S.W.2d at 203, 7 UCC Rep.Serv. at 390. The court reversed a directed verdict which had been entered in favor of the debtor and remanded the

case to the trial court. In Barker v. Horn, 245 Ark. 315, 432 S.W.2d 21, 5 UCC Rep.Serv. 793 (1968), the Arkansas court reiterated the doctrine that the collateral should be presumed to have a value equal to the debt, but did not remand the case for a new trial. Instead, the court reversed and dismissed the creditor's claim.

179. 248 Ark. 665, 453 S.W.2d 37, 7 UCC Rep.Serv. 847 (1970).

180. Id. at 669, 453 S.W.2d at 39–40, 7 UCC Rep.Serv. at 850–51.

Notwithstanding this statement of the law, the court reversed and remanded the case for a new trial because the jury was improperly instructed about the measure of damages caused by the secured party's failure to give the required notice. The court said that the instruction did not reflect the possibility that the secured party can still recover a deficiency if the amount of the claimed deficiency exceeded the reasonable value of the collateral.

The rules of the game established by the Arkansas Supreme Court seem fairly clear. First, the secured party brings suit for a deficiency. The debtor responds by claiming that his opponent violated the provisions of Part Five of Article Nine in some way. If the court finds that the secured party committed a foul, it penalizes him by indulging in the presumption that the value of the collateral is equal to the outstanding debt. However, the secured party can still recover a deficiency if he can convince the court that the reasonable value of the collateral was less than the outstanding debt. However, the Arkansas cases omit one crucial fact: How much and what kind of evidence must creditor introduce to meet his burden of proof successfully?

Courts in other jurisdictions have followed the leads of the Arkansas court and indulged in the same presumption. These cases also provide some insight into the type of evidence required to rebut the presumption. For example, in T & W Ice Cream, Inc. v. Carriage Barn, Inc.,[181] the secured party who had failed to give the debtor notice of resale testified that he had contacted a nondealer to get an estimate of the value of the collateral. The New Jersey court noted that the person contacted was not brought into court. Accordingly, the court held that the secured party failed to satisfy his burden of proof and ordered judgment in favor of the debtor. However, in Weaver v. O'Meara Motor Co.,[182] the secured party overcame the presumption, carried his burden of proof and successfully recovered a deficiency. In that case the secured party repossessed and resold four dump trucks without giving notice to the debtor. At trial the secured party introduced the testimony of three individuals that they had solicited offers and bids from a four-state area. In addition, the depositions of two appraisers were introduced into evidence. The Alaska Supreme Court held that the evidence introduced by the secured party satisfied his burden of proof and showed that the resale was commercially reasonable. The secured creditor in the *Weaver* case did what any conscientious creditor should do—he obtained an appraisal of the collateral and then proceeded to make a good faith effort to sell it at the best possible price. Under such circumstances he justly deserved to recover the deficiency.

A third line of cases allows the secured creditor to recover the deficiency subject only to reduction for any damages suffered by

181. 107 N.J.Super. 328, 258 A.2d 162, 6 UCC Rep.Serv. 1230 (Law Div.1969).

182. 452 P.2d 87, 6 UCC Rep.Serv. 415 (Alas.1969).

the debtor. For example, in Abbott Motors, Inc. v. Ralston,[183] the court said that violation of the provisions of Part Five did not excuse the debtor from paying a deficiency, but that he was entitled to a set-off for any loss suffered as a result of it (presumably, the damages would be the difference between the fair market value of the collateral as established by the debtor and the actual resale price.) In a later Pennsylvania case, Mercantile Financial Corp. v. Miller,[184] another federal district court in that state (ignoring the *Skeels* case) determined that because the secured party made a commercially unreasonable sale the debtor was entitled to have a default judgment reopened. But the court did not deny recovery of the deficiency. It said that the sole purpose for reopening the judgment was to establish the fair market value of the collateral. The Court further stated that burden of proving the fair market value fell upon the *debtor*:

> "Moreover, in order to have the judgment altered in his favor, Miller (debtor) still must establish by a preponderance of the evidence what the fair market value of these assets was on the date of sale. By granting Miller's motion we do not suggest that he in fact is entitled to any greater credit arising from the disposition of this collateral than he had already received." [185]

Thus, we see that the judicial response to the misbehaving creditor who seeks a deficiency judgment spans the spectrum of possible results.[186] On one end of the scale, Skeels v. Universal CIT Credit Corp. in Pennsylvania and *Braswell* in Georgia stand clearly and unequivocally for the proposition that a creditor who violates the provisions of Part Five loses his right to a deficiency. The decisions in the other Georgia cases are more equivocal, but they also arrive at the

---

**183.** 28 Mass.App.Dec. 35, 5 UCC Rep. Serv. 788 (1964). See also Mallicoat v. Volunteer Fin. & Loan Corp., 57 Tenn.App. 106, 415 S.W.2d 347, 3 UCC Rep.Serv. 1035 (1966), modified on rehearing, 4 UCC Rep.Serv. 49 (1967). Note, however, that the Abbott case was not followed in One Twenty Credit Union v. Darcy, 40 Mass.App.Dec. 64, 5 UCC Rep.Serv. 792 (1968).

**184.** 292 F.Supp. 797, 7 UCC Rep.Serv. 402 (E.D.Pa.1968). See also Alliance Discount v. Shaw, 195 Pa.Super. 601, 171 A.2d 548, 1 UCC Rep.Serv. 644 (1961).

**185.** 292 F.Supp. at 801, 7 UCC Rep. Serv. at 406.

**186.** In Nelson v. Monarch Inv. Plan, 452 S.W.2d 375, 7 UCC Rep.Serv. 394 (Ky.App.1970), where the debtor voluntarily returned an automobile and said that he wanted it resold, the secured party suffered no penalty even though he sold the collateral without giving notice to the debtor. The Kentucky Court of Appeals found that the debtor's actions manifested an intent to relinquish his right to notice and concluded that he had waived it. In reaching this conclusion, the court noted that the record showed no evidence of lack of good faith, unfairness, or fraud, and more importantly it mentioned that nothing in the record indicated that the secured party would have realized a higher price had he given notice.

In Mutual Fin. Co. v. Politzer, 21 Ohio St.2d 177, 256 N.E.2d 606, 7 UCC Rep. Serv. 747 (1970), the Ohio Supreme Court held that guarantors were estopped from asserting lack of notice as an affirmative defense in a deficiency suit when they signed a post-repossession agreement which induced the secured party to resell without giving proper notice.

same result.   Other cases simply allow the deficiency subject to whatever set-off the debtor can prove as a result of the improper sale.

In Arkansas and the jurisdictions which have followed its lead, the courts have attempted to stake out a middle ground.   Upon a showing of creditor non-compliance with Part Five, the debtor gets the benefit of a presumption that the collateral was worth the amount of the outstanding debt at the time of default.   Accordingly, the debtor is freed from any deficiency unless the creditor proves that the collateral had a lower value.   Whether the procedural arrangements adopted by the Arkansas court make any difference in the trial court is hard to say from reading appellate opinions.   Conceivably, courts will make a creditor working against a presumption come up with more evidence than just the testimony of his credit manager, and possibly he will be unable to produce such testimony in some cases. Absent clearer guidelines in the appellate opinions, we are skeptical that the "presumption" against the creditor will cause any real change.

The problems of the consumer-debtor in the contexts of deficiency suits may be removed from the courts soon.   Several states have already enacted statutes which preclude or restrict the secured party's right to obtain a deficiency judgment against a consumer.[187] Washington has incorporated the following language in its version of 9–501(1):

> Notwithstanding any other provision of this Code in the case of a purchase money security interest in consumer goods taken or retained by the seller of such collateral to secure all or part of its price, the debtor shall not be liable for any deficiency after the secured party has disposed of such collateral under RCW 62A.9–504 or has retained such collateral in satisfaction of the debt under subsection (s) of RCW 62.9–505.[188]

In addition, the UCCC prohibits the secured creditor from recovering a deficiency when he repossesses consumer goods which had a cash sale price of $1,000 or less.[189]

187.   See, e. g., Cal.Civ.Code § 1812.5 (West Supp.1971); Ill.Rev.Stat. ch. 121½, §§ 526, 580 (Supp.1971).

188.   Wash.Rev.Code § 62A.9–501(1) (1967).

189.   Uniform Consumer Credit Code § 5–103:

Restrictions on Deficiency Judgments in Consumer Credit Sales

(1) This section applies to a consumer credit sale of goods or services.

(2) If the seller repossesses or voluntarily accepts surrender of goods which were the subject of the sale and in which he has a security interest and the cash price of the goods repossessed or surrendered was $1000 or less, the buyer is not personally liable to the seller for the unpaid balance of the debt arising from the sale of the goods, and the seller is not obligated to resell the collateral.

(3) If the seller repossesses or voluntarily accepts surrender of goods which were not the subject of the sale but in which he has a security interest to secure a debt arising from a sale of goods or services or a combined sale of goods and services and the cash price of the sale was $1000 or less, the buyer is not personally liable to the seller for the

The consequences of abolition of deficiencies are now much disputed. Some argue that such denial will cut the bottom stratum of debtors out of the legitimate credit market entirely and will restrict the amount of credit available to others. Others dispute the predictions about the market impact. It seems probable that the abolition of deficiencies, particularly in the automobile market, would tend to restrict the availability of credit, and it is for the legislatures to balance that presumably negative market impact against the positive factor of eliminating an opportunity for abuse of the debtor by commercially unreasonable resales.

unpaid balance of the debt arising from the sale.

(4) For the purpose of determining the unpaid balance of consolidated debts or debts pursuant to revolving charge accounts, the allocation of payments to a debt shall be determined in the same manner as provided for determining the amount of debt secured by various security interests (Section 2–409).

(5) The buyer may be liable in damages to the seller if the buyer has wrongfully damaged the collateral or if, after default and demand, the buyer has wrongfully failed to make the collateral available to the seller.

(6) If the seller elects to bring an action against the buyer for a debt arising from a consumer credit sale of goods or services, when under this section he would not be entitled to a deficiency judgment if he repossessed the collateral, and obtains judgment

(a) he may not repossess the collateral, and

(b) the collateral is not subject to a levy or sale on execution or similar proceedings pursuant to the judgment.

(7) The amounts of $1000 in subsection (2) and (3) are subject to change pursuant to the provisions on adjustment of dollar amounts (Section 1.106).

*

# TABLE OF CASES

## References are to Pages

## A

A. Alport & Sons, Inc. v. Hotel Evans, Inc., 17

Abate v. Barkers of Wallingford, Inc., 343

Abbott Motors, Inc. v. Ralston, 984, 1005

Abby Financial Corp. v. Margrove Mfg. Co., 660

Abby Financial Corp. v. Weydig Auto Supplies Unlimited, Inc., 420, 433, 436

A. B. Lewis Co. v. Robinson, 968

Abramson v. Printer's Bindery, Inc., 808

A. C. Carpenter, Inc. v. Boyer Potato Chips, 262, 344

Adams v. Egley, 974

Adams v. Hartford Fire Ins. Co., 728

Adams v. J. I. Case Co., 316, 318, 320, 380, 382

A. D. Blowers & Co. v. Canadian Pac. Ry. Co., 736

Adel Precision Products Corp. v. Grand Trunk R. R. Co., 736

Adrian Research & Chem. Co. v. Kirkpatrick, 965

Advertising Distributors of America, In re, 830

Aegis Productions, Inc. v. Arriflex Corp., 287

Agoos Kid Co. v. The Blumenthal Import Corp., 293

Air Transport Mfg. Co. v. Employers' Liab. Assurance Corp., 165

A. J. Armstrong, Inc. v. Janburt Embroidery Corp., 422, 436, 441, 985

Alabama Farm Bureau Mut. Ins. Serv., Inc. v. Nixon, 151

Alabama Nat'l Bank v. Rivers, 524

Albany Discount Corp. v. Mohawk Nat'l Bank, 804, 905

Alexandra Restaurant, Inc. v. New Hampshire Ins. Co., 153

Allen v. Wolf River Lumber Co., 171

Allen V. Smith, Inc. v. Rosalia Producers, Inc., 703

Allgeier v. Campisi, 765, 767

Alliance Discount Corp. v. Shaw, 984, 989, 1005

Allied Concord Fin. Corp. v. Bank of America Nat'l Trust & Sav. Ass'n, 505, 513

All Nite Garage, Inc. v. A. A. A. Towing, Inc., 645

Alloway v. Stuart, 836

Alpha Creamery Co., In re, 761, 764

Altec Lansing v. Friedman Sound, Inc., 977

Aluminum Shapes, Inc. v. K-A-Liquidating Co., 649, 656

American Airation, Inc. v. Airation Ins. Managers, Inc., 783

American Auto. Ins. Co. v. Republic Indem. Co. of America, 164

American Canning Co. v. Flat Top Grocery Co., 283

American Car & Foundry Co. v. East Jordan Furnace Co., 102

American Card Co. v. H. M. H. Co., 790

American Cement Corp. v. Century Transit Mix, Inc., 447, 450

American Container Corp. v. Hanley Trucking Corp., 263, 301

American Discount Co. v. Wyckroff, 972

American Equitable Assurance Co. v. Newman, 155

American Fletcher Nat'l Bank & Trust Co. v. Flick, 568, 572

American Home Improvement, Inc. v. MacIver, 120, 128, 130

American Lead Pencil Co. v. Nashville C. & St. L. Ry., 718

American Metal Products, In re, 896

American Nat'l Bank & Trust Co. v. Banco Nacional de Nicaragua, 606

American Parts Co. v. American Arbitration Ass'n, 31

American Plan Corp. v. Woods, 480, 488

American State Bank v. Holding, 959

American Steel Co. v. Irving Nat'l Bank, 625, 627

American Sur. Co. v. Industrial Sav. Bank, 524

American Synthetic Rubber Corp. v. Louisville N. R. R. Co., 741

American Trading Co. v. National Fibre & Installation Co., 106

American Trust Co. v. New York Credit Men's Adjust. Bureau, Inc., 895

Anaheim Sugar Co. v. T. W. Jenkins & Co., 106, 107

Anchorage Centennial Dev. Co. v. Van Wormer & Rodrigues, 237

Anchor Cas. Co. v. Bird Island Produce, Inc., 69

Ando International, Ltd. v. Woolmaster Corp., 625

Andrews Coal Co. v. Board of Directors, 107

Angerosa v. White Co., 78

Anglo-South American Trust Co. v. Uhe, 623

Annawan Mills, Inc. v. Northeastern Fibers Co., 844

Antenna Systems, Inc., United States v., 844

Appleton State Bank v. Lee, 257, 268

Archibald & Lewis Co. v. Banque de Commerce, 632

Architectural Cabinet, Inc. v. Manley, 842

Arcuri v. Weiss, 54, 61

Arditi v. Massachusetts Bonding & Ins. Co., 165

Arrow Transp. Co. v. Fruehauf Corp., 390

Asahel Wheeler Co. v. Mendleson, 106

Asburn Bank v. Childress, 466

Asco Mining Co. v. Gross Contracting & Mining Co., 38, 114, 115

Associate Discount Corp. v. Forcier, 986

Associate Discount Corp. v. Woods, 849

Associated Hardware Supply Co. v. Big Wheel Distributing Co., 58, 74, 75, 100

Associates Discount Corp. v. Cary, 779, 1001

Associates Discount Corp. v. Old Freeport Bank, 776, 885, 951

Associates Discount Corp. v. Rattan Chevrolet, Inc., 947

Association De Azucareros v. United States Nat'l Bank, 617

Association of Maryland Pilots v. Baltimore & O. R. R., 719

Atkins, In re, 787

Atkins v. Racquet Garage Corp., 675

Atlanta Times, Inc., In re, 761

Atlantic Coast Line v. Riverside Mills, 724, 726

Atlantic Coast Line R. R. Co. v. Roe, 734

Atlantic Mut. Ins. Co. v. Cooney, 155

Atlas Aluminum Corp. v. Borden Chemical Corp., 333

Atlas Construction Co. v. Dravo-Doyle Co., 986, 988, 989, 991, 993

Atlas Credit Corp. v. Dolbow, 998

Atlas Credit Corp. v. Leonard, 463

A to Z Rental, Inc. v. Wilson, 998

August v. Poznanski, 905

Aura Orchards v. A. Peltz & Sons, Inc., 173, 206, 219

Austin v. General Motors Acceptance Corp., 970

Automatic Sprinkler Corp. of America v. Robinson-Slagle Lumber Co., 155

Avant Garde, Inc. v. Armtex, Inc., 327

# B

Babcock Box Co., In re, 868

Baber v. Williams Ford Co., 987, 988, 990, 1002

Bachner v. Pearson, 287

Bacon Estate, 214, 218, 220, 221

Bailey v. Jordon Marsh Co., 348

Bailey v. Polster, 478, 479

Baillie Lumber Co. v. Kincaid Carolina Corp., 16, 453

Baird v. Barton, 197

Balkowitsch v. Minneapolis War Memorial Blood Bank, Inc., 288

Balmoral Arms v. Rutkin, 451

Baltimore & O. R. R. Co. v. Carter, 147

Baltimore & O. R. R. Co. v. Keedy, 717

Banca C. I. Trust Co. v. Clarkson, 525

Banco Espanol de Credito v. State Street Bank & Trust Co., 469, 621, 625, 692

Bank of America v. Dade Fed. Sav. & Loan Ass'n, 468

Bank of America v. Oller, 974

Bank of America Nat'l Trust & Savings Ass'n v. Liberty Nat'l Bank & Trust Co., 620

Bank of America Nat'l Trust & Sav. Ass'n v. Superior Court of San Diego City, 427, 431

Bank of America Nat'l Trust & Sav. Ass'n, United States v., 545

Bank of Louisville Royal v. Sims, 568, 573

Bank of Marin v. England, 592

Bank of Montreal v. Recknagel, 625

Bank of North America v. Bank of Nutley, 835, 838

Bank of Taiwan v. Union Nat'l Bank, 625

Bankston, In re, 765

Barclay Knitwear Co., In re, 26

Barham v. Standridge, 969

Barker v. Horn, 985, 995, 1003

Barnes v. Reliable Tractor Co., 980

Barnhart v. Henderson, 738

Barrett v. Bank of the Manhattan Co., 614

Bartus v. Riccardi, 257, 268

Bassman v. Manhattan Dodge Sales, 252, 373

Batson v. Donovan, 719

Baumgartner, In re, 887

Bean v. Security Fur Storage Warehouse, Inc., 673

Beard v. Illinois Cent. R. R., 721

Beattie v. American Auto Ins. Co., 165

Beaumont v. Pennsylvania R. R. Co., 719, 724

Beco, Inc. v. Minnechaug Golf Course, Inc., 211, 221, 265, 348

Beech Aircraft Corp. v. Flexible Tubing Corp., 298

Behring v. Behring, In re, 242

Bekkevold v. Potts, 157

Belber v. H. S. F., 654, 658

Belfast, Steamboat The v. Boon & Co., 717

Bell, In re, 824, 845

Ben Cooper Motor Co. v. Amey, 972

Benedict v. Lebowitz, 837

Beneficial Finance Co. v. Colonial Trading Co., 976

Beneficial Finance Co. v. Kurland Cadillac-Oldsmobile, Inc., 835, 839

Beneficial Finance Co. v. Lachterman, 445

Bengston, In re, 842

Bennett, In re, 842, 843

Bennett v. American Express Co., 720

Bennett v. Richardson-Merrell, Inc., 347

Benton v. Campbell, Parker & Co., Ltd., 303

Berea Bank & Trust Co. v. Mokwa, 572

Berger v. Lane, 41

Berger v. Norad Enterprises, Inc., 433

Berk v. Gordon Johnson Co., 79, 352, 353, 358

Berry v. Branner, 340

Besner v. Smith, 969, 971

Best Foods, Inc. v. Mitsubishi Shoji Kaisha, Ltd., 92

Beter v. Helman, 57

Bevard v. Howat Concrete Co., 324

Bill Dreiling Motor Co. v. The Travelers Indem. Co., 862

Bing v. General Motors Acceptance Corp., 970

Birkner v. Purdon, 319

Bisso v. Inland Waterways Corp., 747

Black Watch Farms, Inc., In re, 869

Blair v. Pitchess, 955

Blake, United States v., 368

Bliven v. Hudson River R. R., 720

Bloom v. Hilty, 907

Bloomingdale Milling Co., In re, 15

Blowers v. First Nat'l Bank, 58, 59

Boak v. Brewer, 958, 959

Boeing Airplane Co. v. O'Malley, 348

Boice v. Boice, 958

Boise Dodge, Inc. v. Clark, 87

Bomanzi of Lexington, Inc. v. Tafel, 653, 659, 666

Bomyte v. L-Co Cabinet Corp., 265

Bonker v. Ingersoll Prods. Corp., 345

Bonnema, In re, 802

Bordeaux v. Hartman Furniture & Carpet Co., 973

Borochoff Properties, Inc. v. Howard Lumber Co., 956

Bostian v. Park Nat'l Bank, 709

Boughner, In re, 807, 808, 870

Bowden v. Philadelphia, B & W R. R., 724

Bowling Green, Inc. v. State St. Bank & Trust Co., 459, 470, 480

Boyd v. L. H. Quinn, 183, 199, 200

Brackenbury v. Hodgkin, 197

Bradford v. Lindsey Chevrolet Co., 1002

Bradley v. Lehigh Valley R. R., 728

Brady v. Welsh, 155

Braginetz v. Foreign Motor Sales, Inc., 260

Brandywine Lanes, Inc. v. Pittsburgh Nat'l Bank, 976

Braswell v. American Nat'l Bank, 988, 1002

Braund, Inc. v. White, 76

Brawn, In re, 824, 840

Breaux v. Aetna Cas. & Sur. Co., 341

Briand v. Wild, 562

Bril v. Suomen Pnakki Finlands Bank, 628

Bristol & C. Railway v. Collins, 724

Brockett v. Harrell Bros., Inc., 337

Brodie Hotel Supply Co. v. United States, 919

Bronson v. Club Comanche, Inc., 336

Brooks v. Lambert, 645, 646, 648

Brothers Cliff, Inc., In re, 765, 1001

Brothers Coach Corp., In re, 762

Brouse, In re, 801

Brown v. C. Rosenstein Co., 624

Brown v. Eastman Nat'l Bank, 576

Brown v. Lee, 45

Browne v. Fenestra, Inc., 389

Brownell v. Board of Education, 151

Bruce Church, Inc. v. Tested Best Foods Div. of Kane-Miller Corp., 219

Brunswick Corp. v. Ciaffoni, 935

Brunswick Corp. v. J. & P., Inc., 955

Brush Beryllium Co. v. Meckley, 341

Buffington v. Nalley Discount Co., 435

Buffum v. Barceloux Co., 896

Bumb v. Bennett, 663

Burchett v. Allied Concord Finance Corp., 487

Burgin v. Universal Credit Co., 972

Burns, In re, 869

Burris v. Commercial Credit Corp., 961

Buschmann, In re, 831, 868, 873

Bush v. Canfield, 197

Butane Products Corp. v. Empire Advertising Serv., Inc., 321, 323

Bu-Vi Bar Petroleum Corp. v. Krow, 205

Bye, In re, 873

## C

Cagle v. Carr, 722

Cain v. Country Club Delicatessen, Inc., 926

California Airmotive Corp. v. Jones, 988, 990, 993

California Mill Supply Corp. v. Bank of America Nat'l Trust & Sav. Ass'n, 500

Callaghan v. Commercial Credit Corp., 859

Calvert Credit Corp. v. Williams, 480

Campanelli v. Conservas Altamira, S.A., 26

Campbell v. Pollack, 253, 260

Campbell, State ex rel. Western Seed Prod. v., 333

Canal Bank v. Bank of Albany, 509

C. & E. Marshall Co. v. Leon, 655

Canter v. Schlager, 770, 771

Canty v. Wyatt Storage Corp., 675

Capital Equip. Enterprise, Inc. v. North Pier Term. Co., 280

Capitol Packing Co. v. Smith, 738

Caraway, In re, 859

Carey v. Interstate Bond & Mortgage Co., 972

Carl M. Geupal Constr. Co., United States ex rel. Gaunt, 173

Carlstrom, In re, 836

Carpenter v. Providence Washington Ins. Co., 151

Carrier Corp. v. Furness, Withy & Co., 747

Carter v. Mintz & Goldblum, 970

Carter v. Ryburn Ford Sales, Inc., 989, 992, 1003

Carvage v. Stowell, 197, 205

Casey v. Philadelphia Auto Sales Co., 253

Casterline v. GMAC, 859

Cayer, In re, 784

Cecil Baber Elec. Co. v. Greer, 972

Center Auto Parts, In re, 790

Central Bank of Rochester v. Gleason, 406

Central Budget Corp. v. Sanchez, 118, 121

Central States Corp. v. Trinity Universal Ins. Co., 699

C. E. Pontz & Son, Inc., In re, 884, 887

Certified Packaging, Inc., In re, 844

Chairmasters, Inc. v. Public Nat'l Bank, 623

Chamberlain v. Bob Matick Chevrolet, Inc., 365

Champlin v. Transport Motor Co., 80

Champlin Refining Co. v. Gasoline Products Co., 81

Chandler v. Aero Mayflower Transit Co., 724

Chapman, In re, 817

Charles Adler & Son, Inc. v. DiNunzio, 645

Charles S. Martin Distrib. Co. v. Banks, 945

Chartered Bank v. American Trust Co., 549

Chase Manhattan Bank, N. A. v. Concord Util. Corp., 454, 455, 497

Chenowith v. Bank of Dardanelle, 446

Cherno v. Bank of Babylon, 967, 968, 971

Chicago & A. R. R. Co. v. Kirby, 737

Chicago & E. I. R. R. v. Collins Co., 720

Chicago & N. W. Ry. Co. v. Bewsher, 745

Chicago & N. W. Ry. Co. v. Stephens Nat'l Bank, 744

Chicago & N. W. Ry. Co. v. Stevens Nat'l Bank, 750

Chicago, R. I. & P. Ry. Co. v. Cleveland, 746

Chicago Roller Skate Mfg. Co. v. Sokol Mfg. Co., 215, 236

Chicago, St. L. & N. O. R. R. Co. v. Pullman So. Car. Co., 155

Child v. Godalphin, 44

Childers v. Judson Mills Store Co., 967

Childers & Venters, Inc. v. Sowards, 360, 361

Childress, In re, 242, 817, 842, 873

Chips Distributing Co. v. Smith, 407

Chrysler Credit Corp. v. Sharp, 15

Churchill Motors, Inc. v. A. C. Lohman, Inc., 849, 857, 859

Cicci v. Lincoln Nat'l Bank & Trust Co., 584

Cintrone v. Hertz Truck Leasing and Rental Service, 287

C. I. T. Corp. v. Jonnet, 39, 46

C. I. T. Corp. v. Short, 968

Citizens Fidelity Bank & Trust v. Stark, 448, 450

Citizens Mut. Auto. Ins. Co. v. Liberty Mut. Ins. Co., 164

Citizens Nat'l Bank v. Fort Lee Sav. & Loan Ass'n, 575, 576

Citizens Nat'l Bank v. Sperry Rand Corp., 805

City Bank v. Tenn, 562

City Loan & Sav. Co. v. Sheban, 959

City Mach. & Mfg. Co. v. A. & A. Mach. Corp., 311

City of Cars, Inc. v. GMAC, 862

City of. See under name of city.

Ciunci v. Wella Corp., 75

Clarke v. Camden Trust Co., 540

Clarke v. Title Guaranty Co., 302

Clarke Floor Mach. Div. of Studebaker Corp. v. Gordon, 976

Clark Grave Vault Co. v. Mealtime Foods, Inc., 59

Cleburne Peanut & Products Co. v. Missouri K & T Ry. of Texas, 721

Cleveland v. McNabb, 684, 688, 702

Cline v. Libby, 958

Cochran v. Horner, 211, 301

Coggs v. Bernard, 718

Cohen, In re, 829, 869

Coin-o-Matic Service Co. v. Rhode Island Hospital Trust Co., 845, 908

Cole v. Goodwin, 719

Columbia Int'l Corp. v. Kempler, 765, 768

Columbus Milk Producers' Co-op. v. Department of Agriculture, 100, 101

Comet Indus., Inc. v. Best Plastic Container Corp., 319

Commercial Credit Co. v. Cain, 959, 971, 973

Commercial Credit Co. v. Childs, 463, 480

Commercial Credit Co. v. Spence, 968

Commercial Credit Corp. v. Orange County Machine Works, 463, 480

Commercial Credit Corp. v. Pottmeyer, 860

Commercial Credit Corp. v. Swiderski, 1000

Commercial Ins. Co. v. Scalamandre, 587

Commercial Nat'l Bank v. Canal-Louisiana Bank & Trust Co., 688

Commercial Union Fire Ins. Co. v. Kelly, 155

Commonwealth v. National Bank & Trust Co., 505, 514

Commonwealth Bank & Trust Co. v. Keech, 257, 265

Conner v. May, 51, 67, 72

Connolly v. Hagi, 335

Consolidated Bottling Co. v. Jaco Equip. Corp., 90

Consolidated Shippers, Inc. v. Pacific Employers Ins. Co., 164

Constable v. White Motor Corp., 326

Constance v. Harvey, 870

Construction Aggregates Corp. v. Hewitt Robins, Inc., 31

Conte v. Styli, 317

Conti Causeway Ford v. Jarossy, 986

Continental Cas. Co. v. Curtis Publishing Co., 165

Continental Cas. Co. v. Weekes, 165

Continental Copper & Steel Indus. v. E. C. "Red" Cornelius, Inc., 334

Continental Forest Products, Inc. v. White Lumber Sales, Inc., 259, 268, 269

Continental Paper Bag Co. v. Maine Cent. R. Co., 717

Cook v. CIT Corp., 961

Cook v. Southern Credit Corp., 475

Cook Grains, Inc. v. Fallis, 48, 289

Cooper v. R. J. Reynolds Tobacco Co., 335

Cooper Paintings & Coatings, Inc. v. SCM Corp., 280, 359

Cornelius v. J. & R. Motor Supply Corp., 653

Cornette v. Searjeant Metal Products, Inc., 336

Corn Exch. Bank v. Peabody, 678

Corn Products Refining Co. v. Fasola, 170

Coronis Associates v. Gordon Construction Co., 34

Correria v. Orlando Bank and Trust Co., 947

Corrigan v. Miller, 646

Cosmopolitan Mut. Ins. Co. v. Continental Cas. Co., 165

Coson v. Roehl, 78

Country Clubs, Inc. v. Allis Chalmers Mfg. Co., 370

County Asphalt, Inc. v. Lewis Welding & Eng'r Corp., 386

County Restaurant & Bar Equip. Co. v. Shaw Mechanical Contractors, Inc., 409

County Trust Co. v. Pascack Valley Bank & Trust Co., 474, 510

Courtin v. Sharp, 144, 146

Cox Motor Car Co. v. Castle, 308, 991

Coyne Bros. v. Oregon Short Line R. R. Co., 737

Cragin Prods. Co. v. Fitch, 108

Crawford v. Newman, 658

Credithrift Financial Corp. v. Guggenheim, 645

Crest Finance Co. v. First State Bank of Westmont, 467

Crest Inv. Trust, Inc. v. Atlantic Mobile Corp., 760, 761

Crews & Green v. Parker, 972

Croly v. Pollard, 304

Crotty v. Shartenberg's-New Haven, Inc., 292

Crown Cork & Seal Co. v. Hires Bottling Co., 364, 365

Cunningham v. MacNeal Memorial Hospital, 288

Currie v. Seaboard Air Line Ry., 718

Curtice Brothers Co. v. Catts, 193

Curtis v. Innerarity, 300

## D

Dagley v. Armstrong Rubber Co., 336

D'Agostino Excavators, Inc. v. Hayward-Robinson Co., 451

Dallison v. Sears, Roebuck & Co., 336

D'Andrea v. Feinberg, 461

Darby v. Ewing's Home Furnishings, 653, 655

D'Arcy, In re, 824

Darling v. Hunt, 961

David v. Manufacturers Hanover Trust Co., 556, 557

David Crystal, Inc. v. Cunard Steam-Ship Co., 679

David Pepper Co. v. Jack Keller Co., 309

Davis v. Jacoby, 35

Davis v. Lawrence, Cedarhurst Bank, 646

Dean v. Eastern Shore Trust Co., 532

Dean v. Planters Nat'l Bank, 875

Deardoff-Jackson Co. v. National Produce Distributors, Inc., 183

Dearman v. Williams, 969

Decker Steel Co. v. Exchange Nat'l Bank, 73, 88

De'Cor Wallcovering Studios, Inc., In re, 765, 768

Dees', Inc., In re, 662

DeGraff v. Myers Foods, Inc., 291

Deitch v. Shamash, 137

Dejean v. Louisiana Western R. R., 728

DeLamar Motor Co. v. White, 298, 359

Delaney v. Towmotor Corp., 330

Delcon Corp., In re, 895

Delmar Bank of University City v. Fidelity & Deposit Co. of Maryland, 545

DeMars v. Musser-Sauntry Land, Logging & Mfg. Co., 41

Denenberg v. Jurad, 366

Denkin v. Sterner, 115, 125

Dennis Mitchell Indus., Inc., In re, 760, 762, 853

Denver-Chicago Trucking Co. v. Republic Drug Co., 723

De Sousa v. Crocker First Nat'l Bank, 628

Detroit Power Screw-Driver Co. v. Ladney, 238

D. H. Overmyer Co. v. Hirsch Bros. & Co., 673

Diamond Alkali Co. v. P. C. Tomson & Co., 108

Dietzel v. Patron's Mut. Fire Ins. Co., 162

Dinger v. Market St. Trust Co., 582

Dingley v. Oler, 172

Dinkelspiel v. Weaver, 876

Distribu-Dor, Inc. v. Karadanis, 238

District Motor Co. v. Rodill, 132

Division of Triple T Service, Inc. v. Mobil Oil Corp., 73, 114, 194

Dixon, Irmaos & CIA v. Chase Nat'l Bank, 611, 622

Dluge v. Robinson, 454

D. M. Picton & Co. v. United States, 154

Doenges-Glass, Inc. v. GMAC, 855, 859, 860

Dominick v. Rea, 968

Donnell & Mudge, Inc. v. Bonita Leather Fashions, Inc., 327

Dorne & Margolin, Inc. v. Hull Corp., 263

Dorsey v. Central Fin. Co., 969

Dorsey v. Community Stores Corp., 955

Dougall v. Brown Bay Boat Works & Sales, Inc., 360, 362

Douglas-Guardian Warehouse Corp. v. Esslair Endsley Co., 703

Douglass v. Pugh, 888

Dow Corning Corp. v. Capitol Aviation, Inc., 376, 386

Dowell v. Beech Acceptance Corp., 783, 948

Downey v. Mahoney, 345

Downtown Drugstore, Inc., In re, 765

Draper v. Minneapolis-Moline, Inc., 214

Dry Dock Sav. Bank v. DeGeorgio, 925

DuBay v. Williams, 876

Duberstein v. Werner, 898

Duilio v. Senechal, 446

Dunfee v. Blue Rock Van & Storage, Inc., 679

## E

Earle M. Jorgensen Co. v. Teamer Mfg. Co., 322

Earl of Chesterfield v. Janssen, 114, 130

Eastern Restaurant Equip. Co. v. Tecci, 155

Eastern Rolling Mill Co. v. Michlovitz, 192

Eastern Supply Co., In re, 244

Edmonson v. Air Serv. Co., 984

Edward L. Eyre & Co. v. Hirsch, 699

Edwards, In re, 860

E. F. Lynch, Inc. v. Piccirilli, 116

Eggers v. Mitchem, 300

Ehrenworth v. George F. Stuhmer & Co., 107

80th Division Veterans' Ass'n v. Johnson, 78

E. J. Trum, Inc. v. Blanchard Parfums, Inc., 657

Ekman v. Mountain Motors, Inc. 989

Electric Regulator Corp. v. Sterling Extruder Corp., 90, 137, 141, 142

Electronics Corp. of America v. Lear Jet Corp., 115, 126

Elkins-Dell Mfg. Co., In re, 114, 116, 867

Ellis v. Bell Aerospace Corp., 137, 146

Emco Mills v. Isbrandtsen Co., 87

Employer's Liab. Assurance Corp. v. Fireman's Fund Ins. Group, 164

Employer's Mut. Liab. Ins. Co. v. Griffin Constr. Co., 150

English v. Ralph Williams Ford, 243

Ennis v. Atlas Finance Co., 987, 989, 990

Epps v. Cortese, 955

Epstein v. Giannattasio, 287

Equipment Fin., Inc. v. Grannas, 784

Erdman v. Johnson Bros. Radio & TV Co., 323, 339

Eriksson v. Refiners Export Co., 638

Ernesto Foglino & Co. v. Webster, 613

Ervin v. Dauphin Deposit Trust Co., 505

Esborg v. Bailey Drug Co., 291

Esquire Produce Co., In re, 844

Esslinger's, Inc. v. Stravino Bros., Inc., 413

Estes v. Curtiss Aeroplane & Motor Corp., 171

Eton Furniture Co., In re, 400

E'Town Shopping Center, Inc. v. Lexington Fin. Co., 441

Evans v. Everett, 9, 790

Evans v. Fitchburg R. R., 721

Evans Mfg. Corp. v. Wolosin, 373, 378

Evans Products Co. v. Jorgensen, 245, 942

Ever-Ready Label Corp. v. Stuyvesant Photo E. Corp., 896

Evers-Jordan Furniture Co. v. Hartzog, 967

Everett Nat'l Bank v. Deschuiteneer, 944

Excel Stores, Inc., In re, 840

E-Z Roll Hardware Mfg. Co. v. H & H Products & Finishing Corp., 206, 215

## F

Factors & Note Buyers, Inc. v. Green Lane, Inc., 430

Fairfield County Trust Co. v. Steinbrecher, 433

Fairfield Lease Corp. v. George Umbrella Co., 114

Fairfield Lease Corp. v. Marsi Dress Corp., 114

Fairfield Lease Corp. v. Umberto, 114

Fair Pavilions, Inc. v. First Nat'l City Bank, 602

Falco Products Co., In re. 761

Falkof, In re, 827, 869

Falls Church Bank v. Wesley Heights Realty, Inc., 466, 468

Family Fin. Corp. v. Scott, 984, 988, 989, 991

Fanning v. Hembree Oil Co., 407

F. A. North & Co. v. Williams, 969, 971

Farmers Co-operative Livestock Mkt., Inc. v. Second Nat'l Bank, 528

Farmers' Elevator Co., State ex rel. Hermann v., 703

Farmers Federation Cooperative, Inc., In re, 893

Faucette v. Lucky Stores, Inc., 327

Federal Factors, Inc. v. Wellbanke, 461

Federal Ins. Co. v. Mercer, 862

Federal Wholesale Meats & Frozen Foods, Inc., In re, 829

Federated Dept. Stores, Inc. v. Brinke, 721

Ferraro v. Pacific Finance Corp., 860, 862

Fett Development Co. v. Garvin, 420

F. H. Vahlsing, Inc. v. Hartford Fire Ins. Co., 155

Fibre Glass Boat Corp., In re, 789

Fields v. Western Millers Mut. Fire Ins. Co., 151

Filler v. Rayex Corp., 298

Film Marketing Servs., Inc. v. Homer Photo Labs, Inc., 645

Firebaugh v. Gunther, 972

First-Citizen's Bank & Trust Co. v. Academic Archives, Inc., 243

First Fin. Co. v. Akathiotis, 939

First Nat'l Bank v. Anderson, 488

First Nat'l Bank v. First Nat'l Bank, 509

First Nat'l Bank v. Hobbs, 552

First Nat'l Bank v. Julian, 887

First Nat'l Bank v. Maidman, 404

First Nat'l Bank v. North Jersey Trust Co., 509

First Nat'l Bank v. N. R. McFall & Co., 568, 572

First Nat'l Bank v. Petzoldt, 703

First Nat'l Bank v. Schneider, 562

First Nat'l Bank v. Sheriff, 977

First Nat'l Bank v. Stewart, 574

First Nat'l Bank v. Sullivan, 462

First Nat'l Bank & Trust Co. v. Atlas Credit Corp., 906, 907

First Nat'l Bank & Trust Co. v. Smithloff, 761

First Nat'l Bank & Trust Co. v. Winter, 969

First Nat'l Bank of Bay Shore v. Stamper, 849, 857, 859

First National Bank of Boston, United States v., 464

First Nat'l Bank of Elgin v. Husted, 364, 367, 368

First Nat'l Bank of Minneapolis v. City Nat'l Bank, 509

First Nat'l Bank of Northampton v. Massachusetts Loan & Trust Co., 304

First Nat'l City Bank v. Altman, 523, 525

First Nat'l City Bank v. Valentine, 433, 464

First Pennsylvania Banking & Trust Co. v. Montgomery County Bank & Trust Co., 510

First State Bank & Trust Co. v. First Nat'l Bank, 524

First Trust & Savings Bank v. Fidelity-Philadelphia Trust Co., 699

First Western Bank & Trust Co. v. Bookasta, 400

Fish v. Chapman, 716

Fiske Rubber Co. v. Hayes, 647

Fitzgerald v. Title Guarantee & Trust Co., 632

F. J. McCarty Co. v. Southern Pacific Co., 721, 722

Flippo v. Mode O'Day Frock Shops, 291

Flugg v. Craft Mfg. Co., 325

Foglino & Co. v. Webster, 628

Foley Machinery Co. v. John T. Brady Co., 852, 909

Food Serv. Equip. Co. v. First Nat'l Bank, 787

Foote v. Wilson, 275

Ford Motor Co. v. Lonon, 335

Ford Motor Co. v. Reid, 325, 378, 393

Ford Motor Co. v. Taylor, 320, 363

Ford Motor Co. v. Tritt, 385, 393

Fort Knox Nat'l Bank v. Gustafson, 959

Fortner v. Wilson, 193

Fort Wayne Corrugated Paper Co. v. Anchor Hocking Glass Corp., 107

Forward v. Pittard, 718

Foskett, In re, 771, 772, 927

Foster v. Colorado Radio Corp., 45, 219, 220

Fougere, In re, 856, 860

Foundation Discounts, Inc. v. Serna, 985, 1001

487 Clinton Ave. Corp. v. Chase Manhattan Bank, 454, 455

Framingham UAW Credit Union v. Dick Russell Pontiac, Inc., 794, 920

Frank Briscoe Co. v. Suburban Trust Co., 589

Frank Le Roux, Inc. v. Burns, 111

Franklin v. Spratt, 969

Franklin Investment Co. v. Homburg, 997

Franklin Nat'l Bank v. Eurez Const. Corp., 421, 433

Franklin Nat'l Bank v. Shapiro, 547

Franklin Nat'l Bank v. Westbury Trust Co., 560

Franklin Savings Bank v. Internat'l Trust Co., 500

Frank R. Jelleff, Inc. v. Pollak Bros., Inc., 320

Fredenburgh v. Allied Van Lines, Inc., 722

Frederickson v. Hackney, 275

Freeman v. General Motors Acceptance Corp., 973

French, In re, 842

Friedman, In re, 858, 859

Friend v. Woods, 716

Frontier Inv. Corp. v. Belleville Nat'l Sav. Bank, 989, 994

Frost v. Knight, 169, 201, 202, 203, 205

Frostifresh Corp. v. Reynoso, 118, 120, 131

Fuentes v. Faircloth, 955

Fuentes v. Shevin, 974

Fulton Inv. Co. v. Fraser, 972

Furches Motor Co. v. Anderson, 968, 971

Future Mfg. Cooperative, Inc., In re, 152, 154, 155, 156, 157

# G

G. A. C. Commercial Corp. v. Wilson, 749

G. A. C. Credit Corp. v. Small Business Administration, 918, 921

Gaito v. Hoffman, 303, 320

Gambino v. United Fruit Co., 321

Gamel v. Hynds, 580

G. & D. Poultry Farms, Inc. v. Long Island Butter & Egg Co., 345

Gard v. Razanskas, 155

Gardner v. Mid-Continent Grain Co., 740

Garfinkel v. Lehman Floor Covering Co., 247, 252, 257

Garner v. Tomcavage, 362

Garrison v. Piatt, 58, 61

Gast v. American Cas. Co., 500

Gateway Co. v. Charlotte Theatres, 37

Gaunt, United States ex rel. v. Carl M. Geupal Constr. Co., 173

Gayle v. Jones, 898

Gazzola v. Lacy Bros. & Kimball, 688

General Bronze Corp. v. Barclay Towers, Inc., 421

General Elec. Co. v. Pettingell Supply Co., 765

General Elec. Co. v. United States Dynamics, Inc., 367

General Elec. Credit Corp. v. Bankers Commercial Corp., 762, 763

General Elec. Credit Corp. v. Hoey, 360

General Elec. Credit Corp. v. R. A. Heintz Constr. Co., 904, 942

General Equip. Mfrs. v. Bible Press, Inc., 69, 76

General Finance Co. v. Riverside Warehouse, Inc., 691

General Food Corp. v. Bittinger Co., 344

General Ins. Co. of America v. Western Fire & Cas. Co., 165

General Motors Acceptance Corp. v. Haley, 841

General Motors Acceptance Corp. v. Shuey, 958, 969

General Motors Acceptance Corp. v. Thomas, 122

General Motors Acceptance Corp. v. Troville, 943

General Motors Acceptance Corp. v. Vincent, 969

General Overseas Corp. v. Republic Pictures Int'l Corp., 61

General Time Corp. v. Gabor, 655

George v. Bekins Van & Storage Co., 675, 676

George v. Commercial Credit Corp., 772

Gerber v. Continental Ill. Nat'l Bank & Trust Co., 540

Gerrity Co. v. Padalino, 420

Gersham State Bank v. O. K. Constr. Co., 541

Gerwin v. Southeastern Cal. Ass'n of Seventh Day Adventists, 316, 317, 319, 320, 322, 323

Ghitter v. Edge, 409, 410

Gibbon v. Paynton, 718

Gibbs Oil Co. v. Collentro & Collentro, Inc., 439

Gibreal Auto Sales, Inc. v. Missouri Valley Mach. Co., 761

Gibson, In re, 887

Gibson v. Stevens, 641

Gill v. Cubitt, 472

Gill v. Mercantile Trust Co., 969

Gillingham v. Phelps, 136

Gimbel Bros., Inc. v. Swift, 127

Gindy Mfg. Corp. v. Cardinale Trucking Corp., 361, 365, 366

Girard v. Anderson, 967, 968, 971

Girard Trust Corn Exch. Bank v. Warren Lepley Ford, Inc., 110, 789, 844, 885

Gleaners and Farmers Cooperative Elevator Co., United States v., 782

Gleason v. Seaboard Air Line Rw. Co., 746

Gleeson v. Virginia Midland R. R. Co., 716

Globe Ref. Co. v. Landa Cotton Oil Co., 315, 316

GMAC v. Birkett L. Williams Co., 861, 862

GMAC v. Manheim Auto Auction, 858, 859

GMAC v. Whisnant, 855, 859

Goettner, In re, 869

Goggins v. Bookout, 959

Goldberg v. Manufacturer's Trust Co., 563

Goldblatt Bros., Inc., United States v., 656

Golden Kernel, Inc., In re, 828

Goldfarb v. Campe Corp., 200

Gold Mining & Water Co. v. A. B. Swinerton, 173

Gold Star Meat Co. v. Union Pac. R. R. Co., 737, 739

Goodin v. Farmers Tractor & Equip. Co., 989

Gordon v. Southgate Park Corp., 197

Gore Products, Inc. v. Texas & N. D. R. R. Co., 721

Gould v. Bourgeois, 304

Gould v. City Bank & Trust Co., 689

Grain Merchants of Indiana, Inc., In re, 878

Grain Merchants of Indiana, Inc. v. Union Bank & Sav. Co., 876, 878

Grandi v. LeSage, 253, 261, 312

Granite City Cooperative Creamery Ass'n, Inc., In re, 815, 817

Granite Worsted Mills, Inc. v. Aaronson Cowen, Ltd., 115

Graulich Caterer, Inc. v. Hans Holterbosch, Inc., 15, 173, 197, 285

Grauman v. Jackson, 684

Gray v. Raper, 869

Graysonia N. & A. R. Co. v. Newberger Cotton Co., 728

Great Atlantic & Pacific Tea Co. v. Atchison, T. & S. F. Ry. Co., 739

Greater Louisville Auto Action v. Ogle Buick, Inc., 245

Green v. American Tobacco Co., 290, 293, 295

Green v. King Edward Employees' Fed. Credit Union, 855

Green Chevrolet Co. v. Kemp, 250, 252, 355

Greenman v. Yuba Power Prods., Inc., 271, 328, 335

Greeno v. Clark Equipment Co., 271, 336

Green Seed Co. v. Williams, 344
Greenspun v. American Adhesives, Inc., 359, 363
Green-Wheeler Shoe Co. v. Chicago R. S. & P. Ry., 717
Greenwood, In re, 218, 219
Gregory v. First Nat'l Bank, 969
Greismer v. Lake Shore & M. S. R. R., 718
Grenada Bank v. Lester, 572
Gresham State Bank v. O & K Construction Co., 514, 538
Grier v. St. Louis Merchants' Bridge Terminal Ry., 717
Griffin, In re, 765, 767
Griggs v. Stoker Service Co., 736, 738
Grossman v. D'Or, 265
Gross Mfg. & Importing Co., In re, 765, 768, 769, 870
Groves v. Warren, 136, 138
Grucella v. General Motors Corp., 997
Gruschus v. C. R. Davis Contracting Co., 105
G. S. H. W. Ass'n v. Tonray Realty Corp., 420
Guardian Discount Co. v. Settles, 765
Gulf Oil Corp. v. Smithey, 968

# H

Hackett v. Cash, 151
Hadji, The, 728
Hadley v. Baxendale, 311, 314, 722
Hagan v. Walker, 641
Haken v. Scheffler, 58, 90
Haley v. Dorchester Mut. Ins. Co., 165
Haley v. Merit Chevrolet, Inc., 351
Hall v. Keller, 210
Hall v. Westmoreland, Hall & Bryan, 478, 479
Hamilton Watch Employees Federal Credit Union v. Retallack, 400
Hane v. Exten, 421
Hanrahan v. Walgreen Co., 338
Haralampopoulos v. Capital News Agency, Inc., 339
Hardin, In re, 243
Hardware Mut. Cas. Co. v. Gall, 861, 862
Harford Metal Products Corp. v. Tidewater Express Lines, 736
Harmon, In re, 776
Harper Warehouse, Inc. v. Henry Chanin Corp., 677
Harris v. Belton, 279, 291
Harris Truck & Trailer Sales v. Foote, 972
Harrison Music Co. v. Drake, 977
Harry H. White Lumber Co. v. Crocker-Citizens Nat'l Bank, 504
Harry Rubin & Sons v. Consolidated Pipe Co., 55, 323
Harry Winston, Inc. v. Robert Simons, Inc., 49, 250
Harry Winston, Inc. v. Waldfogel, 59
Hartford Fire Ins. Co. v. Payne, 155, 161, 728

Hartford Steam Boiler Insp. & Ins. Co. v. Cochran Oil Mill & Ginnery Co., 164
Haugnbook Auto Co., In re, 243
Hawkeye-Security Ins. Co. v. Ford Motor Co., 332
Hawkins v. General Motors Acceptance Corp., 984
Haydon v. Newman, 969
Hayman, In re, 451
Hays v. Kennedy, 716
Hays Merchandise, Inc. v. Dewey, 252, 260, 343
Hayward Woolen Co., In re, 243
Head & Guild Equip. Co. v. Bond, 318
Heise v. Gillette, 287
Held v. Moore, 420
Helena Light & R. Co. v. Northern Pac. R. Co., 107, 108
Helms Veneer Corp., In re, 98, 242
Hempstead Bank v. Andy's Car Rental System, Inc., 941
Hempstead, Town of v. West 45th St. Associates, Inc., 658
Hendrickson v. Grengs, 961
Henningsen v. Bloomfield Motors, Inc., 119, 344, 350, 359, 361, 368, 388, 479
Henry v. John W. Eshelman and Sons, 333
Henry v. W. S. Reichenbach & Son, Inc., 353, 359
Herrin Transp. Co. v. Sheldon, 722
Hertz Commercial Leasing Corp. v. Transportation Credit Clearing House, 71, 287
Hext, United States v., 687, 782
Hileman v. Harter Bank & Trust Co., 967, 971
Hill Aircraft & Leasing Corp. v. Simon, 276
Hillman v. Kropp Forge Co., 547
Hilmor Sales Co. v. Helen Neushaefer Division of Supronics Corp., 193
HIMC Investment Co. v. Siciliano, 476
Hinds, Estate of, 817, 869
Hinson v. British Am. Assurance Co., 162
HML Corp. v. General Foods Corp., 108
Hochster v. De la Tour, 169, 202, 205
Hoffman v. Dickson, 300
Hoffman v. Misericordia Hospital, 288
Hoffman v. Red Owl Stores, Inc., 34
Holladay v. Kennard, 718
Holland Furnace Co. v. Heidrich, 355
Holland Furnace Co. v. Williams, 78, 79
Hollywood Wholesale Elec. Co. v. Jack Baskin, Inc., 100
Holowka v. York Farm Bureau Cooperative Ass'n, 291, 327
Home Bldg. & Loan Ass'n v. Blaisdell, 394
Home Indemnity Co. v. State Bank of Ft. Dodge, 500
Home Indemnity Co. v. United States, 770
Home Ins. Co. v. Bishop, 154, 155
Honea v. Laco Auto Leasing, Inc., 793
Hooks Smelting v. Planter's Compress Co., 325

Horvath, In re, 837
House v. Long, 928, 932
Household Fin. Corp. v. Bank Commissioner of Maryland, 908
Howarth v. Universal C. I. T. Credit Corp., 886, 887
Huber Glass Co. v. First Nat'l Bank, 540
Hudspeth Motors, Inc. v. Wilkinson, 250, 985, 986, 987
Hull-Dobbs, Inc. v. Mallicoat, 69, 71, 72, 364
Hult Chevrolet, Inc. v. Meier, 125
Hunt v. Perkins Mach. Co., 360
Hunt Foods & Indus., Inc. v. Doliner, 17, 70, 74
Hupp Corp. v. Metered Washer Service, 276, 327
Hutchinson v. Chicago S. & P. M. & O. Ry., 718
Hycel, Inc. v. American Airlines, Inc., 722

# I

I. Kallish & Sons v. Jarosz Produce Farms, Inc., 219
Ikovich v. Silver Bow Motor Car Co., 969
Illinois Cent. R. R. v. A. B. Friedman & Co., 724
Illinois Cent. R. R. Co. v. Crail, 739
Inman v. South Carolina R. R., 728
Insurance Co. of North America v. Atlas Supply Co., 505, 510, 514
Insurance Co. of North America v. Easton, 728
Insurance Co. of Texas v. Employers Liab. Assurance Co., 164
International Atlas Services, Inc. v. Twentieth Century Aircraft Co., 783
Interstate Ice & Power Corp. v. United States Fire Ins. Co., 155
Interstate Plywood Sales Co. v. Interstate Container Corp., 102, 104
Investment Serv. Co. v. Martin Bros. Container & Timber Prods. Corp., 445, 458, 459
Irrigation Motor & Pump Co. v. Belcher, 263
Irving Tier Co. v. Griffin, 60
ITM, Inc., State ex rel. Lefkowitz v., 120, 122, 130

# J

Jackson, In re, 855
Jackson v. First National Bank of Memphis, 540
Jackson Architectural Iron Works v. Hurlbut, 718
Jacksonville Tractor Co. v. Nasworthy, 961
Jacobs v. Northeastern Corp., 770
Jacobs Pharmacy Co. v. Gipson, 336, 337, 339
Jacobson v. Donnkenny, Inc., 208

Jagger Bros., Inc. v. Technical Textile Co., 221, 232
Jakubowski v. Minnesota Mining & Mfg., 271, 296
J. A. Maurer, Inc. v. Singer Co., 362
James v. Morgan, 131
James Baird Co. v. Gimbel Bros., 34
James B. Berry's Sons Co. v. Monark Gasoline & Oil Co., 170
James Talcott, Inc. v. Fred Ratowsky Ass'n, Inc., 414, 431
Janssen v. Hook, 282
J. C. M. Cooperative, Inc., In re, 845
Jefferson Credit Corp. v. Marcano, 118, 126, 128, 130, 391, 988, 990, 991
Jenkins v. Evans, 401
Jernigan v. Economy Exterminating Co., 955
Jerome Kantro Co. v. Summers Bros., Inc., 309
J. I. Case Threshing Mach. Co. v. Barney, 972
John Adams Henry, Inc., In re, 826
John H. Mahon Co. v. Huntington Nat'l Bank, 576, 577
John H. Wickersham Eng'r & Constr., Inc. v. Arbutus Steel Co., 54
John St. Auto Wrecking v. Motors Ins. Co., 299, 303, 309, 320
John S. Hale & Co. v. Beley Cotton Co., 686, 693
Johnson v. Chicago M. St. P. & Pac. R. R. Co., 717
Johnson v. Commercial Credit Corp., 1001
Johnson v. Modern Furniture & Appliance Co., 969
Johnston Pie Co. v. Acme Egg & Poultry Co., 105, 107
Johnstown School Employees Federal Credit Union v. Mock, 402
Jones v. Approved Bancredit Corp., 480
Jones v. Citizens Bank, 570
Jones v. Green, 462
Jones v. Hood, 300
Jones v. Linebaugh, 304
Jones v. Star Credit Corp., 120, 122, 124, 131
Jones v. Third Nat'l Bank, 896
Jones & McKnight Corp. v. Birdsboro Corp., 380
Joseph v. United of America Bank, 565
Josephy v. Panhandle & S. F. Ry., 746
Jubas v. Sampsell, 647
Julian C. Cohen Salvage Corp. v. Eastern Elec. Sales Co., 59, 265
J. W. Knapp v. Sinas, 95

# K

Kabro Constr. Corp. v. Carire, 118, 130
Kalle & Co. v. Morton, 728
K & C, Inc. v. Westinghouse Elec. Corp., 309, 377, 384, 386
Kane, In re, 828, 837
Kane-Miller Corp. v. Tip Tree Corp., 645
Kapral v. Hanover Nat'l Bank, 945, 947

Karr v. Baumann, 401

Kasden v. New York, N. H. & H. R. Co., 734

Kassab v. Central Soya, 291, 294

Kassouf v. Lee Bros., Inc., 336

Kay v. Carter, 302

Keating v. F. H. Peavey Co., 677

Kelley Kar Co. v. Finkler, 860

Kendall Produce Co. v. Terminal Warehouse & Transfer Co., 699, 700

Kennedy & Kratzer, Inc. v. Chicago, B. & Q. R. Co., 723

Kenney v. Sears, Roebuck & Co., 332

Kensinger Acceptance Corp. v. Davis, 972

Kentucky-Farmers Bank v. Staton, 577

Kernochan v. New York Bowery Fire Ins. Co., 152

Keystone Diesel Engine Co. v. Irwin, 311, 316, 317

King v. General Motor Acceptance Corp., 969

King v. Oakley, 248

King Furniture City, Inc., In re, 773

King-Porter Co., In re, 876, 882

Kirby v. Bergfield, 418

Kirby v. First & Merchants National Bank, 528, 531, 594

Kirchen, In re, 873

Klein v. Asgrow Seed Co., 308, 362

Klett v. Security Acceptance Co., 969

Klingbiel v. Commercial Credit Corp., 997

Knight v. Calvert Fire Ins. Co., 150

Knutson Shipbuilding Corp. v. Rogers Construction Corp., 39

Kobeckis v. Budzko, 297, 298

Koellmer v. Chrysler Motors Corp., 291, 358, 363, 374

Kohn v. Richmond R. R., 720

Kokomo Opalescent Glass Co. v. Arthur W. Schmidt International, Inc., 297, 319

Komfo Prods. Corp., In re, 831, 873

Koreska v. United Cargo Corp., 735

Korzenik v. Supreme Radio, Inc., 466

Krauss v. Greenbarg, 317

Kravitz, In re, 243, 767

Kretzer, In re, 800, 944

Kroeger v. Ogsden, 968

Krueger v. Hammond, 647

Kruger v. Bibi, 299

Krumbhaar v. Birch, 304

Kulesza, In re, 838

Kutner-Goldstein Co. v. Workman, 89

Kyker v. General Motors Corp., 333

## L

L. A. Green Seed Co. v. Williams, 327, 332

L. Albert & Son v. Armstrong Rubber Co., 191

Lamberta v. Smiling Jim Potato Co., 100

Lamborn v. Lake Shore Banking & Trust Co., 620, 622

Lamb-Weston, Inc. v. Oregon Auto Ins. Co., 164

Laminated Veneers, Inc., In re, 789

Landers, United States v., 248

Landisi v. American Exch. Nat'l Bank, 622

L. & N. Sales Co. v. Stuski, 374

Lang v. Chase Manhattan Bank, 587

Lang v. General Motors Corp., 334

Lanners v. Whitney, 262, 313

Laprease v. Raymours Furniture Co., 955

Lark v. Cooper Furniture Co., 967, 972

LaRose, In re, 804

Larrance Tank Corp. v. Burrough, 343

Larson v. Judd, 646

Laudisi v. American Exchange Nat'l Bank, 613

Laue, In re, 914

Lawner v. Engelbach, 249, 262

Layton v. Ferguson Moving & Storage Co. 677

Layton Fabrics, Ltd., In re, 241

Lea v. Young, 248

Leach v. Wiles, 327

Leahy v. McManus, 407

Leather Mfrs. Bank v. Merchants Bank, 509

Le Blanc v. Newman Comet-Lincoln-Mercury, Inc., 308

Leckie Freeburn Coal Co., In re, 773

Leedy v. General Motors Acceptance Corp., 969

Leiby, In re, 805, 824

Leo Lococo's Sons v. Louisville & N. R. R. Co., 737

Leveridge v. Notaras, 248, 353, 355

Levine, In re, 844

Levine v. Pascal, 815

Levy, In re, 765

Levy v. Andress-Hanna, Inc., 972

Levy v. Paul, 646

Lewis, T. K., 803

Lewis v. Manufacturers Nat'l Bank, 870

Lewis v. Mobil Oil Corp., 313, 318, 319, 325, 343

Leyen v. Dunn, 340

Liebowitz v. Voiello, 765

Lineburger Bros. v. Hodge, 687, 700

Lipson v. H. M. R. Enterprises, Inc., 896

Liverpool & G. W. Steam Co. v. Phoenix Insurance Co., 728

Liverpool Steam Co. v. Phoenix Ins. Co., 150

Lizza Asphalt Const. Co. v. Greenvale Const. Co., 420

Lockwood v. Smigel, 58

Lockwood-Conditionaire Corp. v. Education Audio Visual, Inc., 170

Lofton v. Mooney, 707

London Leasing Corp. v. Interfina, Inc., 436, 437

Longnecker, In re, 779

Lonoke Production Credit Ass'n v. Bohannon, 800, 804

Lopez v. Henry Isaacs, Inc., 92

Lott v. Delmar, 136, 138

Loucks v. Alburquerque Nat'l Bank, 552, 566

Loudenback Fertilizer Co. v. Tennessee Phosphate Co., 107

Louis Burk Co., In re, 765, 768

Lowes Glove Co. v. Acme Fast Freight, Inc., 676, 739

Lucacos, In re, 944

Lucas v. Garrett, 154, 162

Lucchesi v. H. C. Bohack Co., 296

Luckenbach v. W. J. McCahan Sugar Co., 161, 728

Ludwig, Inc. v. Tobey, 214

Luther Williams, Jr., Inc. v. Johnson, 71

Luthy v. Philip Werlein Co., 970

Lux's Superette, Inc., In re, 829

Lyon v. Ty-Wood Corp., 777, 806

# M

McAllister v. Chicago R. I. & P. R. R., 720

MacArthur v. Cannon, 431

McClung v. Saito, 400

McCollum v. Steitz, 401

McCormick v. First Nat'l Bank, 955

McCormick Dray Line, Inc. v. Lovell, 193

McCrossin v. Hicks Chevrolet, Inc., 296

McCubbin v. Urban, 302

McDaniel v. Lieberman, 970

McDonnell v. Bank of China, 703

MacDougall v. Ford Motor Co., 332

McDown v. Wilson, 72

McEwen v. Totten, 759

McFadden v. Mercantile-Safe Deposit & Trust Co., 941

McFarland v. Chicago Express, Inc., 164

McIntyre v. Whitney, 678

Macke Co. v. Pizza of Gaithersburg, Inc., 645

McKee v. Harwood Automotive Company, 440

McKnight v. Bellamy, 147

Mack Trucks, Inc. v. Jet Asphalt & Rock Co., 331, 360

McQuaide, In re, 826

McWaters v. Gardner, 969

Macy v. Oswald, 654

Madeirense Do Brasil, S.A. v. Stulman-Emrick Lumber Co., 92, 142

Maecherlein v. Sealy Mattress Co., 335

Magnin v. Dinsmore, 719

Mahaley v. Colonial Trading Co., 944

Main v. Hall, 646

Maiorino v. Weco Products Co., 339

Makel Textiles, Inc. v. Dolly Originals, Inc., 421, 451

Makransky v. Long Island Reo Truck Co., 945

Mallicoat v. Volunteer Finance & Loan Corp., 987, 994, 1005

Malone v. Darr, 969

Malphrus v. Home Sav. Bank, 576, 580

Mammoth Cave Production Credit Ass'n v. York, 804, 845, 920

Manchester Dairy System, Inc. v. Hayward, 193

Mandel v. Sedrish, 409

M. & N. Freight Lines, Inc. v. Kimbel Lines, Inc., 896

Manhattan Credit Co. v. Brewer, 972

Manheim v. Ford Motor Co., 334

Mann, In re, 790, 907

Mann v. Clark Oil & Ref. Corp., 765, 768, 769

Mannell v. Luckenbach, 693

Mansion Carpets, Inc. v. Marinoff, 479

Manufacturers Acceptance Corp. v. Penning's Sales, Inc., 765, 768, 769

Marbelite Co. v. Philadelphia, 248, 252

Marcalus Mfg. Co., In re, 24

Marine Midland Grace Trust Co. v. Banco Del Paris, S.A., 623

Marion Power Shovel Co. v. Huntsman, 318, 363

Marke Furniture, Inc., In re, 876

Markert v. College Offset Press, Inc., 645, 655

Marot, L., 803

Marquette Cement Mfg. Co. v. Louisville & Nashville R. R. Co., 741

Marshall v. Murray Oldsmobile Co., 389

Martel v. Duffy-Mott Corp., 296, 320

Martin v. Cook, 968

Martin Jessee Motors, Inc. v. Reading Co., 749

Marx v. American Malting Co., 106

Maryland Cas. Co. v. Washington Loan & Banking Co., 699

Massachusetts Gas & Elec. Light Supply Corp. v. V-M Corp., 105, 106

Massey-Ferguson v. Utley, 360

Matthews v. Arctic Tire, Inc., 775

Mauran v. Alliance Insurance Co., 718

May Department Stores Co. v. Pittsburgh Nat'l Bank, 545

Mayer v. Good Samaritan Hospital, 340

Mays Mills v. McRae, 205

Mazur Bros. v. Jaffee Fish Co., 250, 263, 344

Meadowbrook Nat'l Bank v. Markos, 218, 220

Meadow Brook Nat'l Bank v. Recile, 441

Meckler v. Highland Falls Sav. & Loan Ass'n, 451, 576

Megowan v. Peterson, 403, 406

Meinhart v. Farmers' State Bank, 574

Meletio Sea Food Co. v. Gordons Transports, Inc., 722

Mel Golde Shoes, Inc., In re, 245

Menard & Holmberg Rambler, Inc. v. Shea, 257, 348

Mendelson-Zeller Co. v. Joseph Wedner & Son Co., 89

Menzel v. List, 305, 309, 343

Mercanti v. Pearson, 289

Mercantile Financial Corp. v. Miller, 988, 990, 993, 1005

Mercer v. Leihy, 303

Merchant v. Worley, 594

Merchant Shippers Ass'n v. Kellogg Express & Draying Co., 722

Merchants Corp. v. Chase Manhattan Bank, N.A., 625

Merchants-Produce Bank v. Mack Trucks, Inc., 860

Merit Bar & Fixture Mfg. Co. v. K. Ranch, Inc., 524

Merkel, Inc., In re, 760, 761

Merriman, In re, 908

Merritt v. Earle, 716

Metal Products Co. v. Rennert, 372

Meyer Koulish Co. v. Cannon, 155

Michael M. Berlin & Co. v. T. Whiting Mfg., Inc., 261, 262

Michael Schiavone & Sons, Inc. v. Securalloy Co., 68, 75, 85

Michalitschke Bros. & Co. v. Wells, Fargo, 719

Michigan Nat'l Bank v. Marston, 965

Midland Lumber & Coal Co. v. Bean, 87

Midway Motors v. Pernworth, 136

Miles v. Lyons, 309

Milford Finance Corp. v. Lucas, 128

Miller v. Newark Fire Ins. Co., 154

Miller v. Preitz, 13

Milwaukee Acceptance Corp. v. Dore, 480

Mincow Bag Co., In re, 765, 766

Minneapolis, St. P. & S. S. M. R. R. Co. v. Metal-Matic, Inc., 747

Minsel v. El Rancho Mobile Home Center, Inc., 15, 16, 252

Miron v. Yonkers Raceway, Inc., 250, 261, 262, 348

Missouri Furnace Co. v. Cochran, 176

Missouri Pac. R. Co. v. Elmore & Stahl, 712, 715, 716

Missouri Pac. Railway Co. v. Nevill, 718

Mitchell v. Miller, 330

Mitchell v. Security Bank, 577

Mitsubishi Goshi Kaisha v. J. Aron & Co., 94

M. J. Rose Co. v. Lowery, 967

Modern Free & Accepted Masons of the World v. Cliff M. Averett, Inc., 401

Modern Tool Corp. v. Pennsylvania R. R. Co., 747, 748

Monroe v. Bankers Life & Cas. Co., 132

Monroe Capital Corp. v. Pom-Pom Lunch & Restaurant, Inc., 965

Monson v. Pickett, 959

Montano v. Springfield Gardens Nat'l Bank, 560

Moody v. Nides Finance Co., 1001

Mooney v. Leonard C. Adams Co., 524

Moore, In re, 849, 856, 895

Moore v. American Molasses Co., 106

Moore v. Bay, 890, 892

Moore v. Southern Discount Co., 488

Moore v. Wimmer, 961

Morgan v. First Nat'l Bank, 559

Morris v. Durbin, 479

Morris v. First Nat'l Bank & Trust Co., 973

Morrison v. Galyon Motor Co., 969, 972, 973

Morrison Steel Co. v. Gurtman, 887

Morris Plan Co. v. Johnson, 1001

Mort Co., In re, 98

Mosekian v. Davis Canning Co., 59, 60

Mosely v. Johnson, 248

Moss v. Gardner, 276

Motor Contract Co. v. Sawyer, 986

Motors Ins. Corp. v. Safeco Ins. Co., 58

Mountain States Mut. Cas. Co. v. American Cas. Co., 165

Mouse v. Central Sav. & Trust Co., 574

M. P. Berglas Mfg. Co. v. Hall Wood Working Co., 660

M. Rutkin Elec. Supply Co. v. Burdette Elec., Inc., 815

Muir v. Jefferson Credit Corp., 943, 944

Muschamp v. Lancaster Railway Co., 724

Music Art Center, In re, 873

Mutual Finance Co. v. Kozoil, 861

Mutual Fin. Co. v. Politzer, 1005

Mutual Serv. Inc. v. S. O. S. Plumbing & Sewerage Co., 357

M. W. Kellogg Co. v. Standard Steel Fabricating Co., 108

Myers v. Montgomery Ward & Co., 293

## N

Natick Trust Co. v. Bay State Truck Lease, Inc., 824

National Bank & Trust Co., Commonwealth v., 505, 514

National Bank of Commerce v. First Nat'l Bank & Trust Co., 824

National Cash Register Co. v. Firestone & Co., 838

National Cash Register Co. v. Valley Nat'l Bank, 838

National City Bank v. Motor Contract Co., 528

National City Bank v. National Bank, 515

National City Bank, United States v., 509

National Currency Exch., Inc. v. Perkins, 562

National Dime Bank v. Cleveland Bros. Equip. Co., 844

National Distillers Products Corp. v. Companhia Nacional, 722

National Eng'r & Equip. Co., In re, 759

National Fire Ins. Co. v. Morgan, 155

National Historic Shrines Foundation, Inc. v. Dali, 44

National Metropolitan Bank v. United States, 545

National Newark & Essex Bank v. Giordano, 578

National Shawmut Bank v. Jones, 942, 944, 945

National Shawmut Bank v. New Amsterdam Cas. Co., 770

National State Bank of Elizabeth, New Jersey v. Kleinburg, 475

National Sur. Corp. v. State Nat'l Bank, 770

National Union Bank v. Riger, 659

National Van Lines, Inc. v. Rich Plan Corp., 738

Nation-Wide Check Corp. v. Banks, 464

Neal v. Coburn, 524

Nebraska Co-op Creameries, Inc. v. Des Moines Transp. Co., 728

Needle v. Lasco Indus., Inc., 790

Neel v. Ford Motor Co., 280

Nelson v. Anderson, 336

Nelson v. Monarch Inv. Plan, Inc., 984, 1005

Nettles v. Imperial Distribs., Inc., 72

Neville Chemical Co. v. Union Carbide Corp., 262, 283, 321, 323, 381

New Amsterdam Cas. Co. v. Certain Underwriters at Lloyds', 165

New England Merchants Nat'l Bank v. Auto Owners Fin. Co., 944

Newman v. Manufacturers Nat'l Bank, 560

Newmark v. Gimbel's, Inc., 287

Newton v. Admiral Corp., 332

New Waterford Bank v. Morrison Buick, Inc., 475

New York, City of v. Johnson, 662

New York Cent. Iron Works Co. v. United States Radiator Co., 106, 107

New York Terminal Warehouse Co., United States v., 699

Niagra Fire Ins. Co. v. D. Heenan & Co., 162

Nickell v. Lambrecht, 760, 762, 763

Nicklaus v. Peoples Bank & Trust Co., 466

Nineteenth Ward Bank v. First Nat'l Bank, 599

Ninth St. E., Ltd. v. Harrison, 90, 91, 137, 141, 213

Nisky v. Childs Co., 287

N. J. Scott Excavating & Wrecking, Inc. v. Rosencrantz, 969

Nobbe v. Equity Fire Ins. Co., 155

Noble Co. v. Mack Financial Corp., 919

Norfolk & W. Ry. Co. v. Aylor, 738

Norman v. World Wide Distributers, Inc., 476, 477

North American Builders, Inc., In re, 869

North American Van Lines, Inc. v. Heller, 735

Northeast Nat'l Bank v. Central Plaza Bank & Trust Co., 860

Northerlin Co. v. Rauch Const. Co., 464

Northern Currency Exch., Inc. v. Strichman, 562

Northern Financial Corp. v. Chatwood Coffee Shop, Inc., 980

Northern Illinois Corp. v. Bishop Distrib. Co., 783, 948

Northern Pac. Ry. Co., United States v., 722

Northside Bldg. & Inv. Co. v. Finance Co. of America, 459

Northwestern Marble & Tile Co. v. William, 747

Norton v. City Bank & Trust Co., 547

Norton v. National Bank of Commerce, 984, 985, 988, 1002

Novak, In re, 765

## O

Oak Mfg., Inc., In re, 764

Ogden v. East River Ins. Co., 162, 165

O'Hare v. Peacock Dairies, Inc., 240

Oil Base, Inc. v. Transport Indem. Co., 164

Old Colony Trust Co. v. Penrose Indus. Corp., 994

Olive Kent Park, Inc. v. Moshassuck Transp. Co., 714

Oliver Corp. v. Green, 333

Olsen v. Valley Nat'l Bank, 589, 965

O'Meara Co. v. National Park Bank, 625, 626, 628

O. M. Scott, Credit Corp. v. Apex, Inc., 942

One Twenty Credit Union v. Darcy, 984, 1001, 1005

O. P. Ganjo, Inc. v. Tri-Urban Realty Co., 466, 476, 477

Oppenheimer v. Moore, 961

Orange Rice Milling Co. v. Hope Rice Mill, 691, 692

Oregon Auto Ins. Co. v. United States Fidelity & Guar. Co., 165.

Osborn, In re, 869

O. S. Stapley Co. v. Miller, 336

Oswald v. Allen, 49, 61

Overbrook & Barson's, Inc., In re, 761

Overland Nat'l Bank v. Aurora Co-operative Elevator Co., 939

Overseas Trading Corp. v. Irving Trust Co., 630

Owens v. First American Nat'l Bank, 972

Ozier v. Haines, 60

## P

Pace Corp. v. Jackson, 321

Pacific Micronesian Line, Inc. v. New Zealand Ins. Co., 691

Pacific Nat'l Bank v. Henreich, 489

Packaging Products Co. v. Fort Pitt Packaging International, Inc., 844

Paducah Cooperage Co. v. Arkansas Stave Co., 203

Page, In re, 795

Page v. Sun Ins. Office, 165

Paine v. Meller, 151

Paragon Homes, Inc. v. Carter, 127, 131

Paragon Homes of Midwest, Inc. v. Crace, 127

Paragon Homes of New England, Inc. v. Langlois, 127

Paramount Financial Co. v. Cleveland's Peppermint Lounge, Inc., 885

Parish & Parish Mining Co. v. Serodino, Inc., 136

Park County Implement Co. v. Craig, 253

Parks v. Phillips, 961

Park State Bank v. Arena Auto Auction, Inc., 538

Parnes v. Celia's, Inc., 437

Parry Lines, Inc., In re, 540

Particle Reduction Board Corp., 57

Pascagoula Nat'l Bank v. Eberlein, 568

Patterson v. Marine Nat'l Bank, 574

Patterson v. Walker-Thomas Furniture Co., 123, 128

Payne v. Ralli, 718

Pazol v. Citizens Nat'l Bank, 468

Peabody v. Citizens' State Bank, 568

Peacock Food Markets, In re, 896

Pearl Assur. Co. v. Hartford Fire Ins. Co., 165

Pearson v. National Budgeting Sys., Inc., 133

Pecos & N. T. Ry. v. Hall, 718

Peek v. Heim, 765

Peerless Cas. Co. v. Continental Cas Co., 165

Pekin Warehouse Co. v. Parnell Co., 692

Pelletier, In re, 795, 828, 829

Pendarvis v. General Motors Corp., 307

Pennar Paper Co., In re, 816, 817

Pennsylvania v. Curtiss Nat'l Bank, 578

Peoples Bank v. Haar, 468, 575

People's Sav. Bank v. Pere Marquette Ry. Co., 745

Peoples State Bank v. Caterpillar Tractor Co., 594

Peoria Braumeister, In re, 897

Pere Marquette Ry. v. French & Co., 730

Perez v. Janota, 405

Perfecting Serv. Co. v. Products Dev. & Sales Co., 333

Perkins v. Minford, 183, 199

Perlmutter v. Beth David Hospital, 287

Perry v. Augustine, 342

Peterman, In re, 933

Peyton v. Railway Express Agency, 740

Philadelphia Nat'l Bank, United States v., 545

Phoenix Die Casting Co. v. Manufacturers & Traders Trust Co., 13

Phoenix Ins. Co. v. Copeland, 163

Philadelphia Nat'l Bank, United States v., 545

Philadelphia Title Ins. Co. v. Fidelity-Philadelphia Trust Co., 547

Philip A. Feinberg, Inc. v. Bernstein & Sparber Corp., 263

Phillips, In re, 802

Phil Phillips Ford, Inc. v. St. Paul Fire & Marine Ins. Co., 857, 858, 859

Pickering v. Barkley, 717

Picker X-Ray Corp. v. General Motors Corp., 332

Pieper v. First Nat'l Bank, 939

Piercefield v. Remington Arms Co., 347

Pines Trailer Corp. v. Roaring Express Co., 589

Pinnel's Case, 40

Pioneer Fin. & Thrift Corp. v. Adams, 969

Piper v. Fosher, 48

Pittman v. Union Planter's Nat'l Bank & Trust Co., 708

Pizza Inn, Inc. v. Tiffany, 336

Platt, In re, 792, 839

Platte Valley Bank v. Kracl, 976

Plemens v. Didde-Glaser, Inc., 837

Plonta, In re, 870, 891

Plotnick v. Pennsylvania Smelting & Refining Co., 259

Poel v. Brunswick Balke-Collender Co., 24

Poland Chevrolet Co. v. Shelly Smith & Sons, 861, 862

Poldon Eng'r & Mfg. Co. v. Zell Elec. Mfg. Co., 333

Polka v. May, 60

Pollin v. Mindy Mfg. Co., 400, 405

Pomona Valley Inn, In re, 762, 763, 764

Portal Gallaries, Inc. v. Tomar Products, Inc., 148, 219

President and Directors of Manhattan Co. v. Monogram Associates, Inc., 78

Price, In re, 859

Price v. General Motors Acceptance Corp., 972

Price v. Neal, 519

Price v. The Boot Shop, 301

Priggen Steel Bldg. Co. v. Parsons, 980

Prime Business Co. v. Drinkwater, 976

Pritchard v. Liggett & Myers Tobacco Co., 294, 335, 345

Prize Cases, The, 718

Process Equip. Co. v. Denver Chicago Trucking Co., 722

Process-Manz Press, Inc., In re, 892

Procter & Gamble Distrib. Co. v. Lawrence Am. Field Warehousing Corp., 673, 674, 677, 690, 703

Proctor & Gamble Mfg. Co. v. Langley, 296

Productions Unlimited, Inc., Appeal of, 170

Prouty v. Roberts, 580

Provident Tradesmen's Bank & Trust Co. v. Pemberton, 74, 85

Puget Sound Marina, Inc. v. Jorgensen, 173

Pulkrabek v. Banker's Mortg. Corp., 142

Putensen v. Clay Adams, Inc., 280, 335

Putman v. Erie City Mfg. Co., 271

## Q

Quattlebaum v. Schutt, 219

Quivirian Development Co. v. Poteet, 174

Q. Vandenberg & Sons, N. V. v. Siter, 262, 346

## R

Raby v. Commercial Banking Corp., 441

Rade, In re, 870

Railway Express Agency v. Huntress, 739

Rankin v. Cox, 896

Rasmussen's Estate, In re, 894

R. A. Turrentine, The v. American Home Ass'n Co., 728

Rauch v. First Nat'l Bank, 436

Ray v. J. C. Penney Co., 291

Ray v. Navarre, 972

Raymond F. Sargent, Inc., In re, 838, 840, 841, 842

R. D. Lowrance, Inc. v. Peterson, 371

Rea v. Universal C. I. T. Credit Corp., 969

Reading Trust Co. v. Hutchison, 488

Recchio v. Manufacturers & Traders Trust Co., 795

Rector-Wilhelmy Co. v. Nissen, 961

Reeves v. First Nat'l Bank, 572

Reeves Soundcraft Corp., 368

Refrigeration Discount Corp. v. Crouse, 367

R. E. Funsten Dried Fruit & Nut Co. v. Toledo St. L. & W. Ry., 721

Regency Furniture, Inc., In re, 242, 873

Regina Grape Products Co. v. Supreme Wine Co., 285, 292

Rehrig v. Fortunak, 402

Reich v. Helen Harper, Inc. 51

Reider v. Thompson, 721, 724

Reliance Cooperage Corp. v. Treat, 168

Rempe v. General Electric Co., 342

Renaire Corp. v. Vaughn, 967

Rennie & Laughlin, Inc. v. Chrysler Corp., 39

Republic Engine & Mfg. Co., In re, 869

Republic Pictures Corp. v. Security-First Nat'l Bank, 819

Revlon, Inc. v. Murdock, 330

Reynolds v. Service Loan & Finance Co., 441

Reynolds Metals Co. v. Electric Smith Constr. & Equip. Co., 237

Rhodes-Carroll Furiture Co. v. Webb, 970

Rhodes Pharmacal Co. v. Continental Can Co., 274

Richards, In re, 844

Ridings v. Motor Vessel "Effort", 431

Riebe v. Budget Fin. Corp., 773

Riegler v. Riegler, 431

Riley v. Ford Motor Co., 380, 382

Ritter v. Wray, 655

Rivet, In re, 908

Rixford v. Smith, 718

R. J. Reynolds Tobacco Co. v. Hudson, 341

Robert H. Carr & Sons, Inc. v. Yearsley, 292

Robertson, In re, 800, 869, 873

Robinson v. Jefferson Credit Corp., 127

Rock Island Auction Sales, Inc. v. Empire Packing Co., 528

Rockland Credit Union, Inc. v. Gauthier Motors, Inc., 800

Rock-Ola Mfg. Corp. v. Leopold, 169

Rodgers Dairy Co., 803

Roe v. Flamegas Indus. Corp., 59

Roehm v. Horst, 203

Roland v. Republic Nat'l Bank, 561

Roller v. George H. Leonard & Co., 203

Romani v. Harris, 51

Romine v. Savannah Steel Co., 105, 109

Rooney v. Mason, 15, 843

Roscher v. Band Box Cleaners, Inc., 275

Rosenau v. City of New Brunswick, 343

Rosenberg v. National Dock & Storage Warehouse Co., 690

Rosenberg v. Rudnick, 876

Rosenberg Bros. & Co. v. F. S. Buffum Co., 92

Rosenfeld v. Banco Internacional, 625

Rosom Util., Inc., In re, 648

Rossignol v. Danbury School of Aeronautics, Inc., 332

Ross Indus. Chem. Co. v. Smith, 657

Rossotti Lithograph Corp. v. Townsend, 114

Roth & Co. v. Taysen, Townsent & Co., 205

Roto-Lith, Ltd. v. F. P. Bartlett & Co., 9, 26, 357, 358, 362

Rottman v. Endejan, 173

Roundtree v. Lydick-Barmann Co., 730

Rowland Meledandi, Inc. v. Kohn, 237

Royal Paper Box Co. v. E. R. Apt. Shoe Co., 108

Royal Pioneer Paper Box Mfg. Co. v. Louis DeJonge & Co., 298

Royal Store Fixture Co. v. Bucci, 99, 237

Royal Zenith Corp. v. Citizens Publications, Inc., 155

Royalty Homes, In re, 244

Royer's Bakery, Inc., In re, 762, 763, 764

Rozmus v. Thompson's Lincoln-Mercury Co., 250

Ruderman v. Warner-Lambert Pharmaceutical Co., 347

Rush v. Pierson Contracting Co., 341

Rushton v. U. M. & M. Credit Corp., 404, 438

Ruskin v. Central Fed. Sav. & Loan Ass'n, 576, 580

Russell v. Community Blood Bank, Inc., 287, 499, 559

Russell's Trustee v. Mayfield Lumber Co., 875

Rutland Tile Center, Inc., In re, 824

Rutledge v. Universal C. I. T. Credit Corp., 968, 972

## S

Saale v. Interstate Steel Co., 479, 524

Sabin v. Horenstein, 646

Sadler v. Kay, 430

Sadler Machinery Co. v. Ohio National, Inc., 187

Sado v. Sado, 656

Safe Deposit & Trust Co. v. Diamond Coal & Coke Co., 50

St. John, T. C., 803

St. Louis-San Francisco Ry. Co. v. Glow Elec. Co., 747

St. Louis-San Francisco Ry. Co. v. Kittrell, 723

St. Paul Fire & Marine Ins. Co. v. Le-flore Bank & Trust Co., 685

Sal Metal Prods. Co. v. Rennert, 368

Salsman v. National Community Bank, 500, 504

Samples v. Trust Co., 528

Sam's Furniture & Appliance Stores, Inc., In re, 765, 768

Sanders v. Commercial Credit Corp., 761

Sanders v. General Motors Acceptance Corp., 969

Sanders v. National Acceptance Co., 761

Sandlin v. First Nat'l Bank, 137

Sanelco, In re, 815

Sani-Serv Division of Burger Chef Systems, Inc. v. Southern Bank, 478, 479

Santor v. A & M Karagheusian, Inc., 295, 333, 341

Santos v. Mid-Continent Refrigerator Co., 78

Saporiti v. Austin A. Chambers Co., 677

Sarfati v. M. A. Hittner & Sons, Inc., 385, 389, 395

Sarnecki v. Al Johns Pontiac, 249, 255, 263, 359

Sauer v. McClintic-Marshall Const. Co., 177

Saugerties Bank v. Delaware & Hudson Co., 699

Savarin Corp. v. Nat'l Bank of Pakistan, 628

Scannell, In re, 857

Schell v. Miller North Broad Storage Co., 675, 676

Schenning v. Devere & Schloegel Lumber Co., 147

Schmaelzle v. London & L. Fire Ins. Co., 165

Schneider v. Chrysler Motors Corp., 295

Schneider v. Person, 263, 343, 345

Schneider v. Suhrmann, 336

Schoeller, In re, 860, 861

Schrier v. Home Indem. Co., 862

Schwabenton v. Security Nat'l Bank, 540

Schwartz v. A. J. Armstrong Co., 654, 662

Schwartz v. McCloskey, 244

Scott v. Lawrence Warehouse Co., 673, 699

Scott Truck Line, Inc. v. Chicago R. I. & Pac. R. R., 726

Screenland Magazine Inc. v. National City Bank, 540

Seaboard Finance Co. v. Dorman, 431

Sears Roebuck & Co. v. Schulein, 870

Security Aluminum Co., In re, 887

Security Bank v. Levens, 783

Security Nat'l Bank v. Temarantz, 435

Security Sav. Bank v. First Nat'l Bank, 509

Seed Production Corp. v. Campbell, 328

Seely v. White Motor Co., 271, 319, 328, 332

Segall v. Finlay, 200

Seligman v. Armijo, 717

S. F. C. Acceptance Corp. v. Ferree, 357

Shaacht v. Illinois Cent. R. R., 718

Shaffer v. Davidson, 435

Sheesley v. Bisbee Linseed Co., 106

Sheldon, M. G., 803

Shepler, In re, 802

Sheppard Federal Credit Union v. Palmer, 960

Sherman Mach. & Iron Works v. Carey, Lombard & Co., 106

Sherrock v. Commercial Credit Corp., 941

Sherwin-Williams Co. v. Perry Co., 323

Shilling v. Campbell, 147

Shreve v. Casto Trailer Sales, Inc., 250

Shude v. American State Bank, 576, 577

Shulman v. Steve Lynn, Inc., 433

Sig Hoffman, Inc. v. Victory Spud Service, Inc., 263

Silco Automatic Vending Co. v. Howells, 645, 650

Silver v. Gulf City Body & Trailer Works, 842, 843

Simons v. American Dry Ginger Ale Co., 104

Simpson, In re, 801, 827, 842, 843

Simpson v. Bilderbeck, Inc., 439

Simpson v. Wages, 409

Sims v. Horton, 969

Singer Sewing Mach. Co. v. Hayes, 967

Singer Sewing Mach. Co. v. Rios, 973

Singleton, In re, 860

Sinkoff Beverage Co. v. Jos. Schlitz Brewing Co., 114, 116

Skeele Coal Co. v. Arnold, 203

Skeels v. Universal CIT Credit Corp., 1000

Skinner v. Tober Foreign Motors, Inc., 41, 780

Skov v. Chase Manhattan Bank, 568, 573

Slaughter v. Cooper Corp. No. 2, 646

Slaughter v. Philadelphia Nat'l Bank, 447, 450

Small v. Williams, 888

Smith, In re, 830, 842, 859, 891, 906

Smith v. Donk Bros. Coal & Coke Co., 106

Smith v. Eastern Airmotive Corp., 783

Smith v. Maddox-Rucker Banking Co., 560, 561

Smith v. Wilson, 85

Sniadach v. Family Fin. Corp., 955, 964

Snug Harbor Realty Co. v. First Nat'l Bank of Toms River, New Jersey, 545

Soekland v. Storch, 547

Soma v. Handrulis, 549

Sommerville, United States v., 779, 782

Sorenson-Christian Indus. v. Railway Express Agency, 741

Sorrells Bros. Packing Co. v. Union State Bank, 468

Soulios v. Mills Novelty Co., 968

Southeastern Enameling Corp. v. General Bronze Corp., 26

Southeastern Express Co. v. Pastime Amusement Co., 741

Southern Express Co. v. C. L. Ruth & Son, 729, 732

Southern Industrial Sav. Bank v. Greens, 996

Southern Jersey Airways, Inc. v. National Bank, 783

Southern Pac. Co. v. H. Rothstein & Sons, 737

Southern Pac. Milling Co. v. Billiwhack Stock Farm, Ltd., 89

Southern Sur. Co. v. Commercial Cas. Ins. Co., 162

Southwest Engineering Co. v. Martin Tractor Co., 95

Southwest Natural Gas Co. v. Oklahoma Portland Cement Co., 107, 108

Spada v. Stauffer Chemical Co., 347

Spada Distrib. Co. v. Belson, 311, 320

Spainhour v. Nolind, 722

Spence v. Three Rivers Builders & Masonry Supply, Inc., 334

Spiering v. Fairmont Foods Co., 61

Spillane v. Liberty Mut. Ins. Co., 303, 320

Sports Autos, Inc., In re, 979

Sprague, In re, 803

Springs v. Hanover Nat'l Bank, 632

Spring Valley Country Club, Inc. v. Malden Supply Co., 327

Spurlin v. Sloan, 778, 806

Srochi v. Kamensky, 474

Stafford v. Shultz, 341

Standard Accident Ins. Co. v. Pellecchia, 152

Standard Casing Co. v. California Casing Co., 187

Standard Lumber Co. v. Chamber Frames, Inc., 808

Stanley v. Fabricators, Inc., 760, 762, 763

Starkey Constr., Inc. v. Elcon, Inc., 575

Starr v. Freeport Dodge, Inc., 58

State Bank v. Kahn, 793

State Bank v. Weiss, 526

State Bank of Albany v. Kahn, 771

State Discount Furniture, Inc., In re, 837

State ex rel. City Loan & Savings Co. v. Taggart, 861

State ex rel. Hermann v. Farmers' Elevator Co., 703

State ex rel. Lefkowitz v. ITM, Inc., 120, 122, 130

State ex rel. Western Seed Prod. v. Campbell, 333

State Farm Mut. Auto Ins. Co. v. Anderson-Weber, Inc., 389

State Securities Co. v. Aviation Enterprises, Inc., 782, 783

State Street Trust Co. v. Lawrence Mfg. Co., 699

Steelman v. Associates Discount Corp., 984

Steinbrecher v. Fairfield County Trust Co., 594

Stephens, In re, 845

Stephenson v. Ketchikan Spruce Mills, Inc., 81

Stephenson Finance Co. v. P. L. Bruce & Co., 942

Sterling Acceptance Co. v. Grimes, 945, 947

Stern & Co. v. State Loan & Finance Corp., 69, 355

Sternberg v. Rubenstein, 647

Stiles v. Davis, 720

Still v. Citizens Bank, 435

Still Associates, Inc. v. Murphy, 789

Still Ass'n v. Murphy, 976

Stolper Steel Products Corp. v. Behrens Mfg. Co., 237

Stone v. Krylon, Inc., 45

Stone & Webster Eng'r Corp. v. First Nat'l Bank & Trust Co., 459, 499, 500, 551, 559

Stone Machinery Co. v. Kessler, 970

Street v. Commercial Credit Co., 958

Streule v. Gulf Fin. Corp., 859

Strevell-Paterson Fin. Co. v. May, 836, 842, 976

Strong v. Security Storage & Warehouse Co., 679

Stumbo v. Paul B. Hult Lumber Co., 792

Suburban Trust & Savings Bank v. Campbell, 783

Sugg v. Hartford Fire Ins. Co., 163

Sumitomo Shoji New York, Inc. v. Chemical Bank New York Trust Co., 568

Sun Printing & Publishing Ass'n v. Remington Paper & Power Co., 101

Sunshine v. Sanray Floor Covering Corp., 930

Super-Cold Southwest Co. v. Willis, 78, 79

Super Service Freight Co. v. United States, 719

Sussen Rubber Co. v. Hertz, 795

Sutter v. St. Clair Motors, Inc., 368, 374

Suvada v. White Motor Co., 332

Sylvan Crest Sand & Gravel Co. v. United States, 104

Sylvia Coal Co. v. Mercury Coal & Coke Co., 283, 284, 294, 299

Symonds v. Adler Restaurant Equip. Co., 68

Symons, In re, 802

Sztejn v. Schroder Banking Corp., 625, 630

## T

Taggart, State ex rel. City Loan & Sav. Co. v., 861

T & W Ice Cream, Inc. v. Carriage Barn, Inc., 985, 998, 1004

Tatelbaum v. Commerce Inv. Co., 853

Taylor v. Duluth S. S. & A. Ry. Co., 737

Teaff v. Hewitt, 925

Ten Brock, In re, 804, 944

Tennessee-Virginia Constr. Co. v. Willingham, 212

Terminal Transport Co. v. Lamtron Indus., Inc., 722

Terry v. Moore, 280

Texas Indus. v. Brown, 108

Texas Instruments, Inc. v. Branch Motor Express Co., 740

Texas Motor Coaches v. A. C. F. Motors Co., 110

Thalrose v. General Motors Corp., 326

Theo. Hamm Brewing Co. v. First Trust & Sav. Bank, 242, 243

Thibodeau, In re, 788

Third Nat'l Bank v. Ober, 574

Third Nat'l Bank & Trust Co. v. Stagnaro, 984, 985

Thomas v. Beirne, 961

Thomas v. Ferriss, 302

Thomas Foods, Inc. v. Pennsylvania R. R. Co., 668

Thompson v. Wright, 580

Thompson Maple Products, Inc. v. Citizens Nat'l Bank of Corry, 538

Thomson v. O. M. Scott Credit Corp., 845

Thorman v. Polytemp, Inc., 78, 358

Throckmorton's, Inc., In re, 829

Thurner Heat Treating Co. v. Memco, Inc., 325

Tiger Motor Co. v. McMurtry, 363

Tobin v. Lake Shore & M. S. Ry. Co., 717

Toker v. Perl, 121, 122, 124, 130

Toker v. Westerman, 121, 122, 128

Tomczuk v. Town of Cheshire, 346

Tomlinson Lumber Sales, Inc. v. J. D. Harrold Co., 87

Torgerson v. Quinn-Sheperdson Co., 703

Town of. See under name of town.

Toyomenka, Inc. v. Mount Hope Finishing Co., 942

Trafalgar Square, Ltd. v. Reeves Bros., Inc., 26

Transatlantic Financing Corp. v. United States, 17

Trans-Continental Indus., Inc., In re, 760, 762, 764

Trinity Universal Ins. Co. v. Moore, 150

Trojan Publishing Corp. v. Manufacturers Trust Co., 500

Trumble, In re, 845

Turet Crown, The, 728

Turner Lumber & Investment Co. v. Chicago, R. F. & P. Ry. Co., 736

Twin City Fire Ins. Co. v. Walter B. Hannah, 155

Tyler v. R. R. Street & Co., 340

### U

UHR v. 3361, Inc., 13

Unadilla Nat'l Bank v. McQueer, 474

Unico v. Owen, 127, 131, 133, 387, 479, 480, 482

Union Bank v. Spies, 462

Union Wholesale Co. v. Bank of Delaware, 540

United Aircraft Corp., United States v., 783

United Burner Service, Inc. v. George Peters & Sons, Inc., 404

United Gas Improvement Co. v. McFalls, 944

United Refrigerator Co. v. Applebaum, 439

United Rental Equip. Co. v. Potts & Callahan Contracting Co., 760, 762

United Sec. Corp. v. Tomlin, 1000

United Serv. Auto Ass'n v. Russom, 165

United States v. Antenna Systems, Inc., 844

United States v. Bank of America Nat'l Trust & Sav. Ass'n, 545

United States v. Blake, 368

United States v. First Nat'l Bank of Boston, 464

United States v. Gleaners and Farmers Coop. Elevator Co., 782

United States v. Goldblatt Bros., Inc., 656

United States v. Hext, 687, 782

United States v. Landers, 248

United States v. National City Bank, 509

United States v. Northern Pac. Ry. Co., 722

United States v. Philadelphia Nat'l Bank, 545

United States v. New York Terminal Warehouse Co., 699

United States v. Sommerville, 779, 782

United States v. United Aircraft Corp., 783

United States ex rel. Gaunt v. Carl M. Geupal Constr. Co., 173

United States Fidelity & Guaranty Co. v. Slifkin, 155, 158, 164, 166

United States Finance Co. v. Jones, 477

United States Leasing Corp. v. Franklin Plaza Apartments, Inc., 115

United Steelworkers v. Warrior & Gulf Navigation Co., 370

United Thrift Stores, Inc., In re, 793

Units, Inc., In re, 243

Universal Acceptance Corp. v. Burks, 489

Universal CIT Credit Corp. v. Guaranty Bank & Trust Co., 468, 586

Universal CIT Credit Corp. v. Ingel, 476, 480

Universal CIT Credit Corp. v. Johnson, 961

Universal CIT Credit Corp. v. Middlesboro Motor Sales, Inc., 939, 958

Universal CIT Credit Corp. v. Rone, 1003

Universal Lightning Rod, Inc. v. Rischall Electric Co., 405

Universal Medical Services, Inc., In re, 761

Universal Medical Sources, In re, 764

Universal Oil Products Co. v. S. C. M. Corp., 26, 36

Upchurch, In re Estate of, 39, 81

Uptown Federal Sav. & Loan Ass'n v. Collins, 407

Uptown Variety, In re, 15
Utah Farm Production Credit Ass'n v. Dinner, 849

# V

Valkeburg v. AUCO Thrift Co., 955
Valley Bank & Trust Co. v. Roy, 409
Valley Die Cast Corp. v. A. C. W., Inc., 318, 320
Valley Nat'l Bank v. Babylon Chrysler-Plymouth, Inc., 85
Vandermark v. Ford Motor Co., 351
Vannoy Chevrolet Co. v. Baum, 862
Varela v. Wells Fargo Bank, 958
Vaughan, In re, 838
Vaughan's Estate, In re, 175
Vencill v. Quincy R. R. Co., 737
Venizelos, S. A. v. Chase Manhattan Bank, 621
Vermilion County Production Credit Ass'n v. Izzard, 939
Victor v. Barzaleski, 287
Victoria Laundry (Windsor) Ltd. v. Newman Indus. Ltd., 315, 317
Villancourt, In re, 762, 763
Vinarsky, In re, 804
V. I. Sales Corp. v. 3M Business Prods. Sales, Inc., 241
Vitex Mfg. Corp. v. Caribtex Corp., 236
Vitromar Piece Dye Works v. Lawrence of London, 17
Vlases v. Montgomery Ward & Co., 390
Voltz v. General Motors Acceptance Corp., 968
Vonins, Inc. v. Raff, 765

# W

Waddell v. Road Transp. & Gen. Ins. Co., 163
Wade v. Chariot Trailer Co., 157
Wakerman Leather Co. v. Irvin B. Foster Sportswear Co., 263
Walbrun v. Babbitt, 641
Walcott & Steele, Inc. v. Carpenter, 353, 363
Wald-Green Food Corp. v. Acme Fast Freight, 726
Walker v. Sheldon, 132
Walsh v. Ford Motor Co., 352, 389, 395
Walsh v. Hunt, 516
Walter Balfour & Co. v. Lizza & Sons, Inc., 214
Walter W. Willis, Inc., In re, 762, 790
Waltham Citizens Nat'l Bank v. Flett, 469
W & W Livestock Enterprises, Inc. v. Dennler, 309, 320
Warren's Kiddie Shoppe, Inc. v. Casual Slacks, Inc., 73, 85, 263, 348
Washington Fruit & Produce Co. v. Ted Mirski Co., 283, 285, 292
Washington Processing Co., In re, 762, 764
Waterbury Sav. Bank v. Jaroszewski, 463, 476, 480

Water Works & Indus. Supply Co. v. Wilburn, 308, 358, 359, 378
Wat. Henry Pontiac Co. v. Bradley, 275
Watson v. Cudney, 961
Watts v. Carter & Sons, Inc., 24
Weaver v. Bank of American Nat'l Trust & Sav. Ass'n, 574
Weaver v. O'Meara Motor Co., 989, 1004
Weaver Cotton Co. v. Batesville Compress Co., 699
Webb & Sons Inc. v. Hamilton, 461
Webster v. Blue Ship Tea Room, Inc., 291, 295, 336
Weekly, In re, 242
Weeks, In re, 873
Weiner's Men's Apparel, Inc., In re, 844
Weiss v. Wolin, 58
W. E. Johnson Equip. Co. v. United Airlines, 297
Welker, In re, 869
Wells v. Alexandre, 108
Wells Fargo Bank & Union Trust Co. v. Bank of Italy, 515
Wenke v. Norton, 400
Werger v. Haines Corp., 898
Werner v. Bergman, 958
Wesley v. Eells, 302
Westchester Colprovia Corp. v. Pecora, 466
Wester v. Casein Co., 171
Westerman v. Oregon Automobile Credit Corp., 972
Western Coach Corp. v. Vaughn, 723
Western Nat'l Bank v. White, 574
Western Penn. Production Credit Ass'n v. Sustrick, 942
Western Steel Buildings, Inc. v. Universal Carloading & Distrib. Co., 723
Western Surety Co. v. Redman Rice Mills, Inc., 677
West Side Bank v. Marine Nat'l Exch. Bank, 530, 534, 596, 598, 599
Whately v. Tetrault, 137, 144
Wheatland Elec. Prods. Co., In re, 761, 764
Wheeler v. Adams Co., 955
Whirlpool Corp. v. Regis Leasing Corp., 67, 72, 73
Whisenhunt v. Allen Parker Co., 957
White, In re, 856, 876
White v. Miller, 308
White v. Southern Mercantile Co., 969
Whitney Nat'l Bank v. Sandoz, 709
Wiener v. Van Winkle, 420
Wiest v. First Citizens Nat'l Bank, 402
Wights v. Staff Jennings, Inc., 347
Wildenberger v. Ridgewood National Bank, 571
Wiley v. Manufacturers Hanover Trust Co., 559
Wilkinson v. Harrington, 340
William F. Wilke, Inc. v. Cummins Diesel Engines, Inc., 148, 418
William Iselin & Co. v. Burgess & Leigh, Ltd., 977
William L. Blumberg Co. v. Farber, 658

Williams v. Brown Mfg. Co., 336, 341

Williams v. Grant, 716

Williams v. Lilley, 151

Williams v. McClain, 366

Williams v. Walker-Thomas Furniture Co., 117, 387, 802, 867

Williams Ice Cream Co. v. Chase Nat'l Bank, 625

Williamson v. Martz, 58

Willis v. West Ky. Feeder Pig Co., 367, 368

Willis v. Whittle, 973

Willman v. American Motor Sales Co., 390

Willock v. Pennsylvania R. R., 728

Willred Co. v. Westmoreland Metal Mfg. Co., 175, 176

Wilson v. Kuykendall, 972

Wilson v. McEachern, 560

Wilson v. Scampoli, 248, 268

Wilson Motor Co. v. Dunn, 968

Wilson Trading Corp. v. David Ferguson, Ltd., 353, 380, 385

Wise v. Hayes, 335

Wiseman v. United Dairies, 896

Wisner v. First Nat'l Bank of Gallitzin, 526

W. M. McElwain Co. v. Fisher, 105

Woederhoff Shoe Co., In re, 248

Wood v. Downing, 220

Woodbury Chem. Co. v. Holgerson, 295, 321, 353, 363

Woodhouse, Drake & Carey, Ltd. v. Anderson, 433

Woodmere Cedarhurst Corp. v. Nat'l City Bank, 585

Woodrich Constr. Co. v. Indemnity Ins. Co. of North America, 165

Woods v. Van Wallis Trailer Sales Co., 248

Woody v. First Nat'l Bank, 570, 571

Woody v. Nat'l Bank, 574

World Products, Inc. v. Central Freight Service, Inc., 675, 679

Wormhoudt Lumber Co. v. Union Bank & Trust Co., 499, 559

Worsley, In re, 859

W. P. Harlin Constr. Co. v. Continental Bank & Trust Co., 563

Wright v. Bank of California, N. A., 12

Wrightstone, Inc. v. Motter, 170

Wujnovich v. Colcord, 301

Wyatt Industries, Inc. v. Publiker Industries, Inc., 377

## Y

Yandell v. White City Amusement Park, Inc., 600

Yormack v. Farmers' Co-op. Ass'n, 338

Youngstown Steel Products Co. v. State Board of Equalization, 248

Yousey v. Bogle, 862

## Z

Zabriskie Chevrolet, Inc. v. Smith, 257, 270, 348, 360, 361, 363, 389, 391

Zenith Radio Distrib. Corp. v. Mateer, 646

Zicari v. Joseph Harris Co., 371

Zinni v. One Township Line Corp., 12, 645

Zirpola v. Adam Hat Stores, Inc., 291, 292

Zuke v. Merchantile Trust Co. Nat'l Ass'n, 855

Zurich Gen. Accident & Liab. Ins. Co. v. Clamor, 165

*

# TABLE OF STATUTES

## UNIFORM COMMERCIAL CODE

| Sec. | This Work Page |
|------|----------------|
| 1–101 | 2 |
| | 20 |
| 1–102 | 15 |
| | 16 |
| | 109 |
| | 110 |
| 1–102, Comment 1 | 45 |
| 1–102, Comment 2 | 109 |
| | 349 |
| 1–102, Comment 3 | 109 |
| 1–102(1) | 19 |
| 1–102(1)(a) | 807 |
| 1–102(2) | 14 |
| 1–102(3) | 20 |
| | 82 |
| | 83 |
| | 109 |
| | 111 |
| | 349 |
| | 390 |
| | 555 |
| | 556 |
| | 613 |
| | 614 |
| | 616 |
| | 630 |
| | 801 |
| 1–102(3)(g) | 10 |
| 1–102(4) | 20 |
| | 83 |
| 1–102(37) | 756 |
| 1–103 | 6 |
| | 20 |
| | 22 |
| | 31 |
| | 34 |
| | 36 |
| | 39 |
| | 48 |
| | 60 |
| | 75 |
| | 80 |
| | 133 |
| | 439 |
| | 442 |
| | 506 |
| | 507 |
| | 509 |
| | 521 |
| | 522 |
| | 556 |
| | 580 |
| | 620 |
| | 677 |
| | 708 |
| | 900 |

## UNIFORM COMMERCIAL CODE

| Sec. | This Work Page |
|------|----------------|
| 1–103 (Cont'd) | 901 |
| | 992 |
| | 1000 |
| 1–104 | 20 |
| 1–105 | 8 |
| | 20 |
| | 85 |
| | 670 |
| | 779 |
| | 780 |
| 1–105(1) | 614 |
| 1–105(2) | 109 |
| | 780 |
| 1–106 | 15 |
| | 16 |
| | 19 |
| | 133 |
| | 178 |
| | 179 |
| | 182 |
| | 223 |
| | 233 |
| | 235 |
| | 485 |
| | 677 |
| | 966 |
| 1–106, Comment 1 | 233 |
| 1–106(1) | 133 |
| | 191 |
| | 208 |
| | 237 |
| 1–107 | 20 |
| | 22 |
| | 85 |
| 1–108 | 20 |
| 1–109 | 20 |
| 1–201 | 20 |
| | 46 |
| | 401 |
| | 961 |
| 1–201, Comment 1 | 53 |
| 1–201, Comment 39 | 51 |
| 1–201(2) | 445 |
| | 450 |
| 1–201(3) | 22 |
| | 70 |
| | 791 |
| 1–201(4) | 552 |
| 1–201(6) | 711 |
| 1–201(9) | 940 |
| | 942 |
| 1–201(10) | 12 |
| | 359 |
| | 361 |
| 1–201(10), Comment 10 | 387 |
| 1–201(11) | 22 |

**UNIFORM COMMERCIAL CODE**

| Sec. | This Work Page |
|------|------|
| 1–201(12) | 656 |
| 1–201(15) | 610 |
|  | 668 |
|  | 711 |
| 1–201(19) | 113 |
|  | 177 |
|  | 525 |
|  | 563 |
|  | 684 |
|  | 941 |
|  | 959 |
|  | 961 |
| 1–201(20) | 414 |
|  | 415 |
|  | 444 |
|  | 450 |
|  | 458 |
|  | 459 |
|  | 497 |
|  | 541 |
|  | 559 |
|  | 681 |
|  | 684 |
| 1–201(25) | 472 |
|  | 520 |
|  | 591 |
|  | 650 |
|  | 830 |
|  | 918 |
|  | 950 |
| 1–201(25)(c) | 684 |
| 1–201(26) | 348 |
|  | 918 |
|  | 983 |
| 1–201(27) | 565 |
|  | 591 |
|  | 684 |
|  | 979 |
| 1–201(30) | 552 |
| 1–201(31) | 417 |
| 1–201(32) | 684 |
|  | 850 |
| 1–201(34), Comment 34 | 394 |
| 1–201(35) | 403 |
|  | 505 |
| 1–201(37) | 754 |
|  | 757 |
|  | 758 |
|  | 759 |
|  | 761 |
|  | 765 |
|  | 766 |
|  | 767 |
|  | 768 |
|  | 771 |
|  | 773 |
|  | 775 |
|  | 781 |
|  | 806 |
|  | 807 |
|  | 923 |
| 1–201(37)(b) | 763 |

**UNIFORM COMMERCIAL CODE**

| Sec. | This Work Page |
|------|------|
| 1–201(38) | 539 |
|  | 651 |
|  | 984 |
|  | 985 |
| 1–201(39) | 51 |
|  | 400 |
|  | 787 |
|  | 836 |
| 1–201(40) | 426 |
|  | 427 |
| 1–201(42) | 70 |
| 1–201(43) | 402 |
| 1–201(44) | 465 |
|  | 684 |
|  | 792 |
|  | 810 |
| 1–201(44)(a) | 792 |
| 1–201(44)(b) | 243 |
|  | 792 |
| 1–201(44)(d) | 792 |
|  | 793 |
| 1–201(45) | 668 |
| 1–202 | 20 |
| 1–203 | 15 |
|  | 20 |
|  | 36 |
|  | 40 |
|  | 41 |
|  | 48 |
|  | 60 |
|  | 80 |
|  | 110 |
|  | 113 |
|  | 177 |
|  | 203 |
|  | 387 |
| 1–204 | 20 |
|  | 261 |
| 1–204(1) | 109 |
|  | 262 |
|  | 345 |
|  | 346 |
|  | 381 |
| 1–204(2) | 89 |
|  | 178 |
|  | 345 |
| 1–205 | 20 |
|  | 22 |
|  | 66 |
|  | 87 |
|  | 256 |
|  | 369 |
|  | 611 |
|  | 613 |
|  | 939 |
| 1–205, Comment 4 | 83 |
|  | 85 |
| 1–205, Comment 5 | 87 |
| 1–205, Comment 7 | 87 |
| 1–205(1) | 84 |
|  | 86 |

## UNIFORM COMMERCIAL CODE

| Sec. | This Work Page |
|---|---|
| 1–205(2) | 84 |
| | 86 |
| | 87 |
| 1–205(3) | 84 |
| | 85 |
| | 371 |
| 1–205(4) | 86 |
| 1–205(6) | 88 |
| 1–206 | 20 |
| | 46 |
| 1–207 | 16 |
| | 18 |
| | 20 |
| | 452 |
| | 453 |
| | 454 |
| 1–207(37) | 760 |
| 1–208 | 20 |
| | 125 |
| | 959 |
| | 960 |
| | 961 |
| 1–209 | 20 |
| | 758 |
| 2–102 | 21 |
| 2–103(1)(b) | 177 |
| | 941 |
| 2–103(1)(c) | 146 |
| 2–103(3) | 385 |
| 2–103(a) | 346 |
| 2–104 | 48 |
| | 145 |
| | 188 |
| | 288 |
| | 289 |
| 2–104(1) | 289 |
| 2–104(2) | 751 |
| 2–105 | 21 |
| 2–105(1) | 45 |
| 2–106 | 21 |
| 2–106(1) | 45 |
| 2–107 | 21 |
| | 772 |
| 2–107(1) | 45 |
| 2–107(2) | 45 |
| 2–201 | 15 |
| | 22 |
| | 38 |
| | 39 |
| | 44 |
| | 45 |
| | 46 |
| | 47 |
| | 49 |
| | 51 |
| | 53 |
| | 54 |
| | 60 |
| | 61 |
| | 62 |
| | 109 |
| | 363 |

## UNIFORM COMMERCIAL CODE

| Sec. | This Work Page |
|---|---|
| 2–201 to 2–210 | 6 |
| 2–201, Comment 1 | 38 |
| | 51 |
| 2–201, Comment 4 | 49 |
| 2–201, Comment 7 | 57 |
| 2–201(1) | 44 |
| | 46 |
| | 47 |
| | 48 |
| | 49 |
| | 51 |
| | 53 |
| | 54 |
| | 55 |
| | 56 |
| | 57 |
| | 58 |
| 2–201(2) | 47 |
| | 48 |
| | 54 |
| | 55 |
| | 57 |
| 2–201(3) | 55 |
| | 59 |
| 2–201(3)(a) | 48 |
| | 50 |
| | 56 |
| | 57 |
| 2–201(3)(b) | 48 |
| | 50 |
| | 56 |
| | 57 |
| | 61 |
| | 65 |
| 2–201(3)(c) | 48 |
| | 50 |
| | 56 |
| | 58 |
| | 59 |
| | 62 |
| | 250 |
| 2–202 | 17 |
| | 23 |
| | 66 |
| | 67 |
| | 68 |
| | 69 |
| | 70 |
| | 71 |
| | 72 |
| | 73 |
| | 75 |
| | 76 |
| | 85 |
| | 88 |
| | 349 |
| | 354 |
| | 355 |
| 2–202, Comment 1 | 355 |
| 2–202, Comment 2 | 73 |
| | 85 |

## UNIFORM COMMERCIAL CODE

| Sec. | This Work Page |
|------|------|
| 2–202, Comment 3 | 67 |
| | 69 |
| | 73 |
| 2–202(b) | 67 |
| | 74 |
| | 354 |
| 2–204 | 15 |
| | 21 |
| | 22 |
| | 30 |
| | 85 |
| | 88 |
| 2–204(1) | 15 |
| | 37 |
| 2–204(3) | 99 |
| | 101 |
| | 104 |
| 2–205 | 21 |
| | 22 |
| | 33 |
| | 34 |
| 2–205(2)(d) | 734 |
| 2–206 | 2 |
| | 21 |
| | 35 |
| | 58 |
| | 59 |
| | 85 |
| | 109 |
| 2–206 to 2–209 | 15 |
| 2–206(1) | 22 |
| 2–206(1)(a) | 34 |
| | 35 |
| 2–206(1)(b) | 35 |
| | 36 |
| 2–206, Comment 3 | 35 |
| 2–206(2) | 35 |
| 2–207 | 23 |
| | 24 |
| | 25 |
| | 26 |
| | 30 |
| | 32 |
| | 35 |
| | 36 |
| | 362 |
| | 363 |
| 2–207, Comment 1 | 30 |
| | 36 |
| 2–207, Comment 6 | 27 |
| 2–207, Comment 7 | 29 |
| 2–207(1) | 22 |
| | 24 |
| | 26 |
| | 27 |
| | 30 |
| | 31 |
| | 32 |
| | 36 |
| 2–207(2) | 26 |
| | 27 |
| | 28 |

## UNIFORM COMMERCIAL CODE

| Sec. | This Work Page |
|------|------|
| 2–207(2) (Cont'd) | 30 |
| | 31 |
| | 36 |
| 2–207(2)(a) | 362 |
| 2–207(2)(b) | 362 |
| 2–207(3) | 22 |
| | 29 |
| | 30 |
| | 32 |
| | 85 |
| 2–208 | 22 |
| | 66 |
| | 256 |
| 2–208, Comment 1 | 86 |
| 2–208(1) | 84 |
| | 85 |
| | 86 |
| | 369 |
| 2–208(1), Comment 4 | 84 |
| 2–208(2) | 86 |
| 2–208(3) | 84 |
| | 85 |
| 2–209 | 36 |
| | 37 |
| | 39 |
| | 40 |
| | 85 |
| | 129 |
| | 281 |
| | 282 |
| | 363 |
| 2–209(1) | 22 |
| | 37 |
| | 38 |
| | 39 |
| | 40 |
| 2–209, Comment 2 | 41 |
| 2–209(2) | 38 |
| 2–209(3) | 38 |
| | 39 |
| | 46 |
| | 281 |
| | 363 |
| 2–209(4) | 38 |
| | 39 |
| | 46 |
| | 281 |
| 2–209(5) | 38 |
| | 39 |
| 2–210(1) | 109 |
| | 110 |
| 2–301 | 89 |
| | 91 |
| | 97 |
| | 394 |
| | 620 |
| 2–302 | 6 |
| | 36 |
| | 40 |
| | 41 |
| | 80 |
| | 87 |

**UNIFORM COMMERCIAL CODE**

| Sec. | This Work Page |
|---|---|
| 2–302 (Cont'd) | 106 |
| | 109 |
| | 110 |
| | 113 |
| | 114 |
| | 115 |
| | 117 |
| | 119 |
| | 120 |
| | 122 |
| | 123 |
| | 124 |
| | 125 |
| | 126 |
| | 127 |
| | 128 |
| | 130 |
| | 131 |
| | 133 |
| | 350 |
| | 380 |
| | 383 |
| | 384 |
| | 385 |
| | 387 |
| | 388 |
| | 389 |
| | 390 |
| | 391 |
| | 392 |
| | 395 |
| | 396 |
| | 489 |
| | 555 |
| | 556 |
| | 866 |
| | 991 |
| | 992 |
| 2–302, Comment 1 | 116 |
| | 385 |
| | 387 |
| | 388 |
| | 389 |
| 2–302(1) | 115 |
| | 385 |
| 2–302(2) | 124 |
| 2–304, Comment 2 | 403 |
| 2–305 | 88 |
| | 99 |
| | 100 |
| | 101 |
| | 102 |
| | 103 |
| | 109 |
| 2–305, Comment 4 | 102 |
| | 103 |
| 2–305(1) | 101 |
| 2–305(1)(a) | 100 |
| 2–305(1)(b) | 100 |
| 2–305(1)(c) | 98 |
| | 100 |
| | 102 |

**UNIFORM COMMERCIAL CODE**

| Sec. | This Work Page |
|---|---|
| 2–305(2) | 100 |
| | 101 |
| 2–305(3) | 100 |
| 2–306 | 88 |
| | 106 |
| 2–306, Comment 1 | 104 |
| 2–306, Comment 2 | 108 |
| 2–306(1) | 104 |
| | 105 |
| | 106 |
| | 108 |
| | 109 |
| 2–306(2) | 109 |
| 2–307 | 109 |
| 2–308 | 83 |
| | 88 |
| | 90 |
| | 109 |
| 2–308, Comment 3 | 94 |
| 2–308(b) | 90 |
| 2–308(c) | 94 |
| 2–309 | 88 |
| | 109 |
| 2–309, Comment 5 | 89 |
| 2–309, Comment 6 | 89 |
| 2–309(1) | 89 |
| | 94 |
| 2–309(1), Comment 5 | 90 |
| 2–309(1), Comment 6 | 90 |
| 2–310 | 88 |
| | 92 |
| | 95 |
| | 109 |
| | 750 |
| | 751 |
| 2–310, Comment 1 | 96 |
| 2–310, Comment 2 | 93 |
| | 96 |
| 2–310, Comment 3 | 94 |
| 2–310(a) | 94 |
| | 95 |
| | 96 |
| 2–310(a), Comment 4 | 97 |
| 2–310(b) | 92 |
| | 93 |
| | 97 |
| 2–310(c) | 94 |
| | 97 |
| 2–311 | 109 |
| 2–311(1) | 89 |
| 2–311(2) | 89 |
| 2–312 | 271 |
| | 299 |
| | 301 |
| | 303 |
| | 304 |
| | 305 |
| 2–312 to 2–316 | 692 |
| 2–312, Comment 1 | 300 |
| 2–312, Comment 2 | 12 |
| | 343 |
| 2–312, Comment 5 | 303 |

**UNIFORM COMMERCIAL CODE**

| Sec. | This Work Page |
|---|---|
| 2–312, Comment 6 | 299 |
| 2–312(1)(b) | 300 |
| 2–312(2) | 302 |
| | 303 |
| | 304 |
| | 305 |
| 2–312(3) | 302 |
| | 303 |
| | 305 |
| 2–313 | 271 |
| | 272 |
| | 273 |
| | 274 |
| | 277 |
| | 282 |
| | 292 |
| | 351 |
| | 368 |
| | 374 |
| 2–313, Comment 2 | 287 |
| 2–313, Comment 3 | 279 |
| | 280 |
| | 375 |
| 2–313, Comment 4 | 276 |
| | 366 |
| 2–313, Comment 6 | 283 |
| | 284 |
| 2–313, Comment 7 | 281 |
| | 363 |
| 2–313(1)(b) | 276 |
| | 366 |
| | 375 |
| 2–313(1)(c) | 282 |
| | 283 |
| | 284 |
| | 286 |
| | 368 |
| | 375 |
| 2–313(2) | 274 |
| 2–314 | 83 |
| | 86 |
| | 271 |
| | 272 |
| | 283 |
| | 285 |
| | 286 |
| | 287 |
| | 289 |
| | 291 |
| | 293 |
| | 295 |
| | 297 |
| | 303 |
| 2–314, Comment 7 | 294 |
| 2–314, Comment 13 | 296 |
| | 338 |
| 2–314(1) | 287 |
| 2–314(2) | 293 |
| 2–314(2)(c) | 357 |
| 2–314(3) | 85 |

**UNIFORM COMMERCIAL CODE**

| Sec. | This Work Page |
|---|---|
| 2–315 | 271 |
| | 272 |
| | 287 |
| | 296 |
| | 297 |
| | 298 |
| | 299 |
| | 303 |
| | 305 |
| | 350 |
| | 372 |
| | 374 |
| 2–315, Comment 1 | 298 |
| 2–316 | 12 |
| | 71 |
| | 125 |
| | 126 |
| | 127 |
| | 129 |
| | 299 |
| | 303 |
| | 305 |
| | 349 |
| | 350 |
| | 351 |
| | 353 |
| | 355 |
| | 357 |
| | 363 |
| | 372 |
| | 373 |
| | 374 |
| | 375 |
| | 376 |
| | 383 |
| | 384 |
| | 386 |
| | 387 |
| | 388 |
| | 389 |
| | 390 |
| | 392 |
| | 394 |
| | 395 |
| | 396 |
| 2–316, Comment 1 | 352 |
| | 361 |
| | 384 |
| | 386 |
| | 388 |
| 2–316, Comment 2 | 354 |
| | 395 |
| 2–316, Comment 3 | 384 |
| 2–316, Comment 5 | 384 |
| 2–316, Comment 6 | 364 |
| 2–316, Comment 7 | 364 |
| | 365 |
| | 366 |
| 2–316, Comment 8 | 368 |
| | 369 |
| | 384 |
| 2–316, Comment 9 | 372 |

## UNIFORM COMMERCIAL CODE

| Sec. | This Work Page |
|---|---|
| 2–316(1) | 293 |
| | 351 |
| | 352 |
| | 353 |
| | 354 |
| | 358 |
| | 369 |
| | 372 |
| | 375 |
| | 393 |
| 2–316(2) | 83 |
| | 293 |
| | 356 |
| | 357 |
| | 358 |
| | 359 |
| | 364 |
| | 366 |
| | 371 |
| | 373 |
| 2–316(3) | 83 |
| | 293 |
| 2–316(3)(a) | 357 |
| | 361 |
| | 364 |
| | 365 |
| | 366 |
| 2–316(3)(b), Comment 8 | 367 |
| 2–316(3)(c) | 86 |
| | 367 |
| | 369 |
| | 371 |
| 2–316(4) | 376 |
| 2–317 | 350 |
| | 372 |
| | 373 |
| | 375 |
| 2–317, Comment 2 | 373 |
| 2–317, Comment 3 | 373 |
| 2–317(a) | 373 |
| | 375 |
| 2–317(b) | 373 |
| | 375 |
| 2–317(c) | 373 |
| | 374 |
| 2–318 | 7 |
| | 12 |
| | 109 |
| | 327 |
| | 329 |
| | 330 |
| | 331 |
| | 332 |
| | 333 |
| | 346 |
| 2–318, Comment 3 | 12 |
| | 327 |
| | 330 |
| 2–319 | 88 |
| | 140 |
| | 141 |
| | 185 |

## UNIFORM COMMERCIAL CODE

| Sec. | This Work Page |
|---|---|
| 2–319 (Cont'd) | 186 |
| 2–319(1) | 140 |
| 2–319(1)(a) | 93 |
| | 140 |
| | 141 |
| | 186 |
| 2–319(1)(a) | 141 |
| 2–319(1)(b) | 140 |
| | 141 |
| 2–320 | 88 |
| | 140 |
| | 141 |
| | 602 |
| 2–321–322 | 88 |
| 2–325(3) | 616 |
| 2–326 | 765 |
| | 766 |
| | 767 |
| | 768 |
| | 769 |
| | 795 |
| 2–326(1) | 766 |
| 2–326(2) | 766 |
| | 767 |
| 2–326(3) | 766 |
| | 767 |
| | 768 |
| 2–326(3)(a) | 767 |
| | 769 |
| 2–326(3)(b) | 765 |
| | 767 |
| | 769 |
| 2–326(3)(c) | 767 |
| | 768 |
| 2–401 | 15 |
| 2–401, Comment 1 | 15 |
| 2–402 | 8 |
| 2–403 | 6 |
| | 110 |
| | 684 |
| | 685 |
| | 795 |
| | 862 |
| | 900 |
| | 944 |
| | 945 |
| | 946 |
| | 947 |
| 2–403, Comment 2 | 945 |
| 2–403, Comment 4 | 945 |
| 2–403(1) | 243 |
| | 900 |
| 2–403(1)(d) | 696 |
| 2–403(2) | 945 |
| | 946 |
| 2–403(3) | 706 |
| 2–403(4) | 945 |
| 2–409 | 1007 |
| 2–501 | 147 |
| | 168 |
| | 213 |

## UNIFORM COMMERCIAL CODE

| Sec. | This Work Page |
|---|---|
| 2–502 | 110 |
| | 168 |
| | 192 |
| | 195 |
| | 196 |
| 2–502, Comment 1 | 195 |
| 2–502(1) | 195 |
| 2–502(2) | 168 |
| 2–503 | 88 |
| | 91 |
| | 93 |
| | 109 |
| | 184 |
| | 187 |
| | 188 |
| 2–503, Comment 5 | 90 |
| | 142 |
| 2–503(1) | 89 |
| | 91 |
| | 94 |
| | 184 |
| | 188 |
| 2–503(1)(a) | 95 |
| 2–503(1)(b) | 97 |
| 2–503(2) | 92 |
| | 94 |
| | 184 |
| | 185 |
| 2–503(3) | 94 |
| 2–503(4)(b) | 144 |
| 2–503(5), Comment 5 | 93 |
| 2–503(5)(a) | 94 |
| 2–503(5)(b) | 94 |
| 2–504 | 15 |
| | 83 |
| | 91 |
| | 92 |
| | 93 |
| | 94 |
| | 95 |
| | 96 |
| | 109 |
| | 140 |
| | 148 |
| | 184 |
| | 185 |
| | 187 |
| | 256 |
| | 257 |
| 2–504, Comment 1 | 141 |
| 2–504(a) | 90 |
| | 141 |
| 2–504(b) | 93 |
| | 94 |
| | 141 |
| 2–504(c) | 141 |
| 2–505 | 93 |
| | 97 |
| | 698 |
| | 752 |
| | 780 |

## UNIFORM COMMERCIAL CODE

| Sec. | This Work Page |
|---|---|
| 2–505(1) | 97 |
| | 751 |
| 2–505(2) | 92 |
| 2–506 | 752 |
| | 781 |
| 2–506(1) | 751 |
| | 752 |
| 2–507 | 92 |
| | 97 |
| | 109 |
| | 185 |
| | 187 |
| 2–507, Comment 2 | 95 |
| 2–507, Comment 3 | 98 |
| 2–507(1) | 91 |
| | 95 |
| 2–507(2) | 98 |
| | 242 |
| | 245 |
| 2–508 | 15 |
| | 92 |
| | 247 |
| | 254 |
| | 256 |
| | 266 |
| | 267 |
| | 268 |
| | 269 |
| | 270 |
| 2–508, Comment 2 | 267 |
| 2–508, Comment 4 | 269 |
| 2–508(1) | 266 |
| 2–508(2) | 267 |
| | 269 |
| 2–509 | 88 |
| | 109 |
| | 135 |
| | 137 |
| | 138 |
| | 139 |
| | 140 |
| | 141 |
| | 142 |
| | 146 |
| | 147 |
| | 148 |
| | 149 |
| | 150 |
| | 185 |
| | 186 |
| | 187 |
| | 714 |
| 2–509, Comment 3 | 138 |
| 2–509(1) | 139 |
| | 140 |
| | 143 |
| | 144 |
| | 145 |
| | 149 |
| 2–509(1)(a) | 90 |
| | 91 |
| | 141 |

### UNIFORM COMMERCIAL CODE

| Sec. | This Work Page |
|---|---|
| 2–509(1)(a) (Cont'd) | 186 |
| 2–509(1)(b) | 90 |
| | 92 |
| | 141 |
| 2–509(2) | 144 |
| | 145 |
| 2–509(2)(b) | 145 |
| 2–509(2)(c) | 144 |
| 2–509(3) | 137 |
| | 143 |
| | 144 |
| | 145 |
| | 149 |
| | 188 |
| 2–509(3) Comment 3 | 188 |
| 2–509(4) | 90 |
| | 135 |
| | 143 |
| | 146 |
| 2–510 | 135 |
| | 137 |
| | 138 |
| | 139 |
| | 140 |
| | 146 |
| | 147 |
| | 148 |
| | 149 |
| | 150 |
| | 153 |
| | 160 |
| | 714 |
| 2–510, Comment 3 | 159 |
| | 160 |
| 2–510(1) | 147 |
| | 148 |
| 2–510(2) | 149 |
| | 157 |
| | 158 |
| | 159 |
| | 160 |
| 2–510(3) | 147 |
| | 149 |
| | 157 |
| | 158 |
| | 159 |
| | 160 |
| 2–511 | 88 |
| | 97 |
| | 109 |
| | 242 |
| 2–511(1) | 94 |
| 2–511(2) | 97 |
| | 98 |
| 2–511(3) | 97 |
| | 98 |
| 2–513 | 88 |
| | 92 |
| | 93 |
| | 96 |
| | 751 |
| | 752 |

### UNIFORM COMMERCIAL CODE

| Sec. | This Work Page |
|---|---|
| 2–513, Comment 5 | 97 |
| 2–513, Comment 7 | 262 |
| 2–513(1) | 92 |
| 2–513(3) | 97 |
| 2–513(3)(b) | 94 |
| 2–601 | 15 |
| | 92 |
| | 168 |
| | 246 |
| | 253 |
| | 254 |
| | 256 |
| | 257 |
| | 265 |
| 2–601 et seq. | 250 |
| 2–602 | 15 |
| | 210 |
| | 211 |
| | 252 |
| | 261 |
| | 264 |
| | 265 |
| | 312 |
| 2–602, Comment 3 | 89 |
| | 91 |
| 2–602(1) | 210 |
| | 260 |
| | 348 |
| 2–602(1), Comment 1 | 261 |
| 2–602(2)(a) | 16 |
| | 247 |
| 2–602(2)(b) | 247 |
| 2–602(2)(c) | 247 |
| 2–603 | 252 |
| | 265 |
| 2–603(1) | 265 |
| 2–603(2) | 266 |
| 2–604 | 265 |
| 2–605 | 265 |
| 2–606 | 56 |
| | 210 |
| | 211 |
| | 249 |
| | 250 |
| | 251 |
| | 252 |
| 2–606, Comment 3 | 250 |
| | 253 |
| 2–606, Comment 4 | 252 |
| 2–606(1) | 47 |
| | 249 |
| | 251 |
| 2–606(1)(a) | 250 |
| | 251 |
| | 252 |
| 2–606(1)(b) | 210 |
| | 211 |
| | 251 |
| | 252 |
| 2–606(1)(c) | 251 |
| | 252 |

## UNIFORM COMMERCIAL CODE

| Sec. | This Work Page |
|------|------|
| 2–607 | 12 |
| | 17 |
| | 110 |
| | 249 |
| | 261 |
| | 344 |
| | 346 |
| | 347 |
| | 348 |
| | 516 |
| 2–607, Comment 4 | 344 |
| | 345 |
| | 347 |
| 2–607, Comment 5 | 346 |
| 2–607(2) | 212 |
| 2–607(3) | 110 |
| | 250 |
| | 345 |
| 2–607(3)(a) | 109 |
| | 110 |
| | 260 |
| | 343 |
| | 346 |
| | 347 |
| | 348 |
| 2–607(3)(b) | 302 |
| 2–607(4) | 109 |
| 2–607(5) | 302 |
| 2–608 | 15 |
| | 168 |
| | 210 |
| | 212 |
| | 253 |
| | 254 |
| | 255 |
| | 259 |
| | 260 |
| | 261 |
| | 264 |
| | 265 |
| | 312 |
| | 343 |
| 2–608, Comment 1 | 248 |
| 2–608, Comment 2 | 260 |
| 2–608, Comment 3 | 264 |
| 2–608, Comment 4 | 260 |
| 2–608(1)(b) | 264 |
| 2–608(2) | 149 |
| | 210 |
| | 211 |
| | 260 |
| | 261 |
| | 265 |
| | 280 |
| 2–608(3) | 265 |
| 2–609 | 169 |
| | 170 |
| | 173 |
| | 175 |
| 2–609, Comment 4 | 170 |
| 2–609(1) | 110 |
| | 169 |

## UNIFORM COMMERCIAL CODE

| Sec. | This Work Page |
|------|------|
| 2–609(2) | 169 |
| 2–609(4) | 169 |
| 2–610 | 89 |
| | 170 |
| | 173 |
| | 196 |
| | 197 |
| | 198 |
| | 199 |
| | 200 |
| | 201 |
| | 203 |
| | 204 |
| | 208 |
| | 627 |
| | 628 |
| 2–610, Comment 1 | 171 |
| | 172 |
| 2–610, Comment 2 | 171 |
| 2–610, Comment 3 | 173 |
| 2–610, Comment 4 | 203 |
| 2–610(a) | 198 |
| | 202 |
| 2–610(b) | 196 |
| | 197 |
| | 202 |
| | 204 |
| | 205 |
| 2–610(c) | 196 |
| | 205 |
| 2–611 | 174 |
| 2–611, Comment 1 | 174 |
| 2–611(1) | 174 |
| 2–611(2) | 174 |
| | 175 |
| 2–612 | 15 |
| | 92 |
| | 148 |
| | 173 |
| | 253 |
| | 254 |
| | 256 |
| 2–612, Comment 4 | 173 |
| 2–612, Comment 6 | 173 |
| 2–612, Comment 7 | 173 |
| 2–612(1) | 258 |
| 2–612(2) | 258 |
| 2–612(3) | 89 |
| | 91 |
| | 97 |
| | 173 |
| | 258 |
| 2–613 | 134 |
| 2–613, Comment 1 | 135 |
| 2–614 | 95 |
| 2–614(1) | 17 |
| 2–615 | 95 |
| | 106 |
| 2–615(a) | 17 |
| 2–697(2) | 280 |

## UNIFORM COMMERCIAL CODE

| Sec. | This Work Page |
|------|------|
| 2–702 | 98 |
|  | 110 |
|  | 242 |
|  | 244 |
|  | 245 |
|  | 781 |
| 2–702(1) | 241 |
|  | 242 |
| 2–702(2) | 242 |
|  | 243 |
|  | 244 |
|  | 245 |
| 2–702(3) | 241 |
|  | 242 |
|  | 243 |
|  | 244 |
|  | 245 |
| 2–703 | 207 |
|  | 210 |
|  | 212 |
|  | 213 |
|  | 216 |
|  | 217 |
|  | 223 |
|  | 781 |
| 2–703, Comment 1 | 223 |
| 2–704 | 207 |
|  | 216 |
|  | 228 |
|  | 238 |
|  | 240 |
|  | 241 |
| 2–704, Comment 2 | 239 |
| 2–704(1) | 239 |
| 2–704(1)(a) | 239 |
| 2–704(1)(b) | 239 |
| 2–704(2) | 216 |
|  | 227 |
|  | 238 |
|  | 240 |
| 2–705 | 207 |
|  | 627 |
|  | 734 |
|  | 781 |
| 2–705(3)(d) | 734 |
| 2–706 | 191 |
|  | 206 |
|  | 207 |
|  | 216 |
|  | 217 |
|  | 218 |
|  | 219 |
|  | 220 |
|  | 221 |
|  | 222 |
|  | 223 |
|  | 224 |
|  | 225 |
|  | 227 |
|  | 239 |
|  | 993 |

## UNIFORM COMMERCIAL CODE

| Sec. | This Work Page |
|------|------|
| 2–706, Comment 4 | 217 |
|  | 993 |
| 2–706(5) | 218 |
| 2–707 | 216 |
|  | 627 |
|  | 752 |
|  | 781 |
| 2–708 | 198 |
|  | 200 |
|  | 207 |
|  | 212 |
|  | 218 |
|  | 221 |
|  | 224 |
|  | 226 |
|  | 227 |
|  | 228 |
| 2–708, Comment 2 | 226 |
| 2–708(1) | 207 |
|  | 220 |
|  | 221 |
|  | 222 |
|  | 223 |
|  | 224 |
|  | 225 |
|  | 226 |
|  | 227 |
|  | 228 |
|  | 229 |
|  | 230 |
|  | 231 |
|  | 232 |
|  | 233 |
|  | 238 |
| 2–708(2) | 207 |
|  | 217 |
|  | 220 |
|  | 225 |
|  | 226 |
|  | 227 |
|  | 228 |
|  | 229 |
|  | 230 |
|  | 231 |
|  | 232 |
|  | 233 |
|  | 234 |
|  | 235 |
|  | 236 |
|  | 237 |
|  | 238 |
|  | 239 |
|  | 991 |
| 2–709 | 110 |
|  | 111 |
|  | 134 |
|  | 148 |
|  | 192 |
|  | 206 |
|  | 207 |
|  | 208 |
|  | 209 |

## UNIFORM COMMERCIAL CODE

| Sec. | This Work Page |
|---|---|
| 2–709 (Cont'd) | 210 |
| | 212 |
| | 213 |
| | 215 |
| | 227 |
| 2–709, Comment 5 | 211 |
| | 212 |
| 2–709(1)(a) | 148 |
| | 209 |
| | 210 |
| | 211 |
| | 212 |
| | 213 |
| | 215 |
| | 264 |
| 2–709(1)(b) | 208 |
| | 209 |
| | 213 |
| | 214 |
| | 215 |
| | 216 |
| 2–709(2) | 209 |
| | 236 |
| 2–709(3) | 206 |
| | 212 |
| | 213 |
| 2–710 | 206 |
| | 208 |
| | 216 |
| | 218 |
| | 220 |
| | 221 |
| | 234 |
| | 236 |
| 2–711 | 167 |
| | 175 |
| | 190 |
| | 197 |
| | 198 |
| | 204 |
| | 210 |
| | 312 |
| 2–711(1) | 247 |
| 2–711(3) | 216 |
| | 266 |
| | 781 |
| 2–712 | 167 |
| | 175 |
| | 176 |
| | 177 |
| | 178 |
| | 179 |
| | 180 |
| | 182 |
| | 190 |
| | 191 |
| | 192 |
| | 197 |
| | 198 |
| | 204 |
| | 205 |
| | 206 |

## UNIFORM COMMERCIAL CODE

| Sec. | This Work Page |
|---|---|
| 2–712 (Cont'd) | 216 |
| | 218 |
| | 219 |
| | 223 |
| | 224 |
| | 248 |
| | 265 |
| | 306 |
| | 307 |
| | 312 |
| 2–712, Comment 1 | 180 |
| 2–712, Comment 2 | 178 |
| 2–712(1) | 175 |
| | 204 |
| | 313 |
| 2–712(2) | 177 |
| | 312 |
| 2–712(3) | 191 |
| 2–713 | 167 |
| | 177 |
| | 180 |
| | 182 |
| | 183 |
| | 184 |
| | 187 |
| | 188 |
| | 189 |
| | 190 |
| | 191 |
| | 197 |
| | 198 |
| | 199 |
| | 200 |
| | 201 |
| | 202 |
| | 205 |
| | 221 |
| | 222 |
| | 223 |
| | 248 |
| | 265 |
| | 266 |
| | 306 |
| | 307 |
| | 312 |
| | 313 |
| | 317 |
| | 322 |
| 2–713, Comment 1 | 183 |
| | 189 |
| 2–713, Comment 2 | 190 |
| 2–713, Comment 3 | 190 |
| 2–713, Comment 5 | 191 |
| 2–713(1) | 191 |
| | 199 |
| | 310 |
| 2–713(2) | 189 |
| | 222 |
| 2–714 | 152 |
| | 168 |
| | 247 |
| | 248 |

## UNIFORM COMMERCIAL CODE

| Sec. | This Work Page |
|---|---|
| 2–714 (Cont'd) | 250 |
| | 266 |
| | 271 |
| | 306 |
| | 307 |
| | 317 |
| | 333 |
| | 339 |
| | 345 |
| 2–714, Comment 2 | 266 |
| 2–714(1) | 307 |
| 2–714(2) | 307 |
| | 308 |
| | 309 |
| | 310 |
| | 311 |
| | 322 |
| | 338 |
| | 382 |
| 2–714(3) | 311 |
| | 312 |
| 2–715 | 184 |
| | 189 |
| | 204 |
| | 266 |
| | 271 |
| | 306 |
| | 311 |
| | 312 |
| | 316 |
| | 317 |
| | 325 |
| | 333 |
| | 338 |
| | 345 |
| 2–715, Comment 1 | 312 |
| | 313 |
| 2–715, Comment 2 | 316 |
| 2–715, Comment 3 | 317 |
| 2–715, Comment 4 | 321 |
| 2–715, Comment 5 | 338 |
| 2–715, Comment 6 | 317 |
| 2–715(1) | 312 |
| 2–715(2) | 206 |
| | 316 |
| | 317 |
| | 318 |
| | 324 |
| | 325 |
| | 338 |
| 2–715(2), Comment 2 | 318 |
| 2–715(2), Comment 3 | 318 |
| 2–715(2)(a) | 191 |
| | 204 |
| | 322 |
| | 323 |
| | 324 |
| | 338 |
| 2–715(2)(b) | 324 |
| | 338 |
| 2–716 | 168 |
| | 192 |

## UNIFORM COMMERCIAL CODE

| Sec. | This Work Page |
|---|---|
| 2–716 (Cont'd) | 193 |
| | 197 |
| 2–716, Comment 1 | 193 |
| 2–716, Comment 2 | 193 |
| | 194 |
| 2–716(1) | 193 |
| 2–716(3) | 191 |
| | 195 |
| 2–717 | 96 |
| | 307 |
| 2–718 | 111 |
| | 125 |
| | 130 |
| | 254 |
| | 376 |
| 2–718(1) | 109 |
| | 125 |
| 2–719 | 111 |
| | 254 |
| | 349 |
| | 350 |
| | 355 |
| | 375 |
| | 376 |
| | 379 |
| | 384 |
| | 385 |
| | 395 |
| | 396 |
| 2–719, Comment 1 | 379 |
| | 381 |
| 2–719, Comment 2 | 377 |
| 2–719, Comment 3 | 377 |
| | 384 |
| | 392 |
| 2–719(1) | 376 |
| | 377 |
| 2–719(1)(a) | 377 |
| 2–719(1)(b) | 377 |
| | 378 |
| | 393 |
| 2–719(2) | 376 |
| | 379 |
| | 380 |
| | 381 |
| | 382 |
| | 383 |
| 2–719(3) | 109 |
| | 125 |
| | 350 |
| | 376 |
| | 377 |
| | 378 |
| | 379 |
| | 380 |
| | 383 |
| | 384 |
| | 385 |
| | 386 |
| | 387 |
| | 392 |
| | 393 |
| | 394 |

## UNIFORM COMMERCIAL CODE

| Sec. | This Work Page |
|---|---|
| 2–719(3) (Cont'd) | 395 |
| | 396 |
| 2–719(3), Comment 3 | 394 |
| 2–721 | 207 |
| | 248 |
| 2–723 | 190 |
| | 198 |
| | 200 |
| | 201 |
| | 220 |
| 2–723(1) | 198 |
| | 200 |
| | 201 |
| 2–725 | 339 |
| | 340 |
| | 341 |
| | 342 |
| | 343 |
| | 384 |
| 2–725(2) | 339 |
| | 340 |
| | 341 |
| | 342 |
| 3–102(1)(d) | 411 |
| 3–102(1)(e) | 459 |
| 3–102(3) | 541 |
| 3–104 | 399 |
| | 464 |
| | 668 |
| | 815 |
| 3–104, Comment 5 | 464 |
| 3–104(1) | 398 |
| | 460 |
| | 464 |
| | 608 |
| 3–104(1)(b) | 460 |
| | 463 |
| 3–104(1)(d) | 464 |
| 3–104(2) | 411 |
| 3–104(2)(b) | 411 |
| 3–105 | 399 |
| | 460 |
| 3–105, Comment 4 | 462 |
| 3–105, Comment 5 | 462 |
| 3–105, Comment 9 | 462 |
| 3–105(1)(c) | 460 |
| | 461 |
| 3–105(1)(e) | 462 |
| 3–105(1)(f) | 461 |
| 3–105(1)(g) | 461 |
| 3–105(1)(h) | 461 |
| 3–105(2)(a) | 460 |
| | 461 |
| 3–105(2)(b) | 461 |
| | 462 |
| 3–110 | 414 |
| | 497 |
| 3–111, Comment 2 | 464 |
| 3–112 | 399 |
| | 460 |
| 3–112, Comment 1 | 463 |
| 3–112, Comment 2 | 463 |

## UNIFORM COMMERCIAL CODE

| Sec. | This Work Page |
|---|---|
| 3–112(1) | 463 |
| 3–112(1)(b) | 462 |
| | 463 |
| 3–112(1)(d) | 463 |
| 3–114(1) | 561 |
| 3–114(2) | 560 |
| | 561 |
| 3–115 | 408 |
| | 411 |
| 3–115(2) | 560 |
| 3–118(a) | 579 |
| 3–118(e) | 409 |
| | 410 |
| 3–118(f) | 436 |
| 3–122(1) | 409 |
| 3–201 | 430 |
| | 900 |
| 3–202 | 415 |
| | 429 |
| | 445 |
| | 450 |
| | 559 |
| 3–202(1) | 414 |
| | 415 |
| | 506 |
| | 516 |
| 3–202(2) | 414 |
| | 459 |
| | 497 |
| 3–204(1) | 413 |
| | 415 |
| 3–204(2) | 413 |
| | 415 |
| | 507 |
| 3–204(3) | 413 |
| 3–205 | 423 |
| | 425 |
| | 507 |
| 3–205(a) | 508 |
| 3–205(c) | 424 |
| 3–206 | 423 |
| | 425 |
| | 507 |
| | 509 |
| 3–206, Comment 3 | 425 |
| 3–206(2) | 424 |
| | 425 |
| 3–206(3) | 424 |
| | 425 |
| | 507 |
| | 766 |
| 3–208 | 443 |
| 3–302 | 414 |
| | 442 |
| | 458 |
| | 459 |
| | 465 |
| | 471 |
| | 478 |
| | 479 |
| | 524 |

## UNIFORM COMMERCIAL CODE

| Sec. | This Work Page |
|---|---|
| 3–302 (Cont'd) | 586 |
| | 624 |
| 3–302, Comment 2 | 478 |
| | 479 |
| | 524 |
| 3–302(1) | 479 |
| 3–302(1)(b) | 472 |
| 3–302(2) | 478 |
| | 479 |
| | 523 |
| 3–303 | 465 |
| | 466 |
| | 467 |
| | 468 |
| 3–303, Comment 3 | 465 |
| | 468 |
| 3–303(a) | 466 |
| | 467 |
| | 477 |
| 3–303(b) | 466 |
| | 469 |
| | 470 |
| 3–303(c) | 466 |
| | 467 |
| 3–304 | 442 |
| | 473 |
| | 475 |
| | 516 |
| 3–304, Comment 2 | 475 |
| 3–304(1)(a) | 475 |
| 3–304(3)(c) | 474 |
| 3–304(4)(a) | 562 |
| 3–304(4)(c) | 442 |
| 3–304(4)(d) | 475 |
| 3–305 | 441 |
| | 456 |
| | 478 |
| | 479 |
| | 481 |
| | 486 |
| | 489 |
| | 497 |
| | 506 |
| | 575 |
| | 585 |
| | 586 |
| | 668 |
| 3–305, Comment 5 | 488 |
| 3–305, Comment 7 | 488 |
| 3–305(2) | 441 |
| | 442 |
| | 480 |
| | 487 |
| | 524 |
| 3–305(2)(a)–(e) | 487 |
| 3–305(2)(b) | 488 |
| 3–305(2)(c) | 487 |
| 3–306 | 490 |
| | 497 |
| | 586 |
| 3–306, Comment 5 | 580 |
| 3–306(b) | 490 |

## UNIFORM COMMERCIAL CODE

| Sec. | This Work Page |
|---|---|
| 3–306(c) | 443 |
| 3–306(d) | 442 |
| | 443 |
| | 451 |
| | 497 |
| | 579 |
| 3–307 | 432 |
| | 456 |
| | 491 |
| 3–307, Comment 1 | 401 |
| 3–307(1) | 401 |
| 3–307(3) | 456 |
| 3–326 | 765 |
| 3–401 | 401 |
| | 403 |
| | 447 |
| 3–401, Comment 1 | 400 |
| 3–401, Comment 2 | 400 |
| 3–401(1) | 399 |
| | 403 |
| | 559 |
| 3–402 | 414 |
| 3–403 | 405 |
| | 406 |
| 3–403, Comment 1 | 400 |
| 3–403, Comment 2 | 403 |
| 3–403, Comment 3 | 404 |
| | 405 |
| | 406 |
| 3–403(1) | 400 |
| 3–403(2) | 403 |
| | 408 |
| 3–403(2)(a) | 404 |
| | 406 |
| 3–403(2)(b) | 404 |
| | 406 |
| 3–403(3) | 404 |
| | 406 |
| 3–404 | 400 |
| | 559 |
| 3–404, Comment 3 | 402 |
| 3–404, Comment 4 | 402 |
| 3–404(1) | 401 |
| 3–405 | 402 |
| | 519 |
| | 537 |
| | 541 |
| | 542 |
| | 543 |
| | 544 |
| | 545 |
| | 546 |
| | 549 |
| 3–405, Comment 2 | 548 |
| 3–405, Comment 3 | 546 |
| 3–405, Comment 4 | 12 |
| | 543 |
| | 544 |
| | 546 |
| | 549 |
| 3–405(1) | 545 |

## UNIFORM COMMERCIAL CODE

| Sec. | This Work Page |
|---|---|
| 3–405(1)(a) | 542 |
| | 543 |
| | 547 |
| | 548 |
| 3–405(1)(b) | 543 |
| 3–405(1)(c) | 542 |
| | 543 |
| | 544 |
| | 545 |
| | 546 |
| | 548 |
| | 549 |
| 3–406 | 402 |
| | 494 |
| | 501 |
| | 514 |
| | 519 |
| | 537 |
| | 539 |
| | 540 |
| | 541 |
| | 542 |
| | 548 |
| | 549 |
| | 559 |
| | 560 |
| 3–406, Comment 7 | 537 |
| 3–407 | 408 |
| | 443 |
| | 515 |
| | 516 |
| | 517 |
| | 560 |
| 3–407, Comment 4 | 517 |
| 3–407(2) | 560 |
| 3–407(2)(a) | 515 |
| | 516 |
| 3–407(3) | 516 |
| | 517 |
| | 560 |
| 3–408 | 490 |
| 3–409 | 520 |
| | 530 |
| | 578 |
| | 588 |
| 3–409(1) | 410 |
| | 411 |
| | 575 |
| 3–410 | 410 |
| | 578 |
| | 594 |
| 3–410, Comment 4 | 411 |
| 3–410(1) | 410 |
| 3–411 | 410 |
| | 411 |
| | 443 |
| | 578 |
| | 579 |
| | 594 |
| 3–411, Comment 1 | 411 |
| 3–411(1) | 554 |
| | 579 |

## UNIFORM COMMERCIAL CODE

| Sec. | This Work Page |
|---|---|
| 3–412 | 410 |
| | 443 |
| 3–413 | 398 |
| | 408 |
| | 410 |
| | 451 |
| | 498 |
| | 515 |
| | 552 |
| | 564 |
| | 575 |
| | 579 |
| 3–413(1) | 408 |
| | 411 |
| | 578 |
| | 594 |
| 3–413(2) | 410 |
| | 411 |
| | 412 |
| | 497 |
| | 580 |
| | 585 |
| 3–414 | 17 |
| | 413 |
| | 419 |
| | 423 |
| 3–414(1) | 415 |
| 3–415 | 17 |
| | 425 |
| | 427 |
| | 428 |
| | 439 |
| 3–415, Comment 1 | 427 |
| | 428 |
| 3–415, Comment 2 | 431 |
| | 433 |
| 3–415, Comment 5 | 438 |
| 3–415, Comment 8 | 588 |
| 3–415(1) | 427 |
| | 430 |
| 3–415(2) | 427 |
| 3–415(3) | 427 |
| | 428 |
| | 429 |
| | 430 |
| | 432 |
| 3–415(4) | 413 |
| | 428 |
| | 429 |
| 3–415(5) | 410 |
| | 426 |
| | 428 |
| | 429 |
| | 431 |
| | 438 |
| | 439 |
| 3–415(5), Comment 5 | 439 |
| 3–416 | 420 |
| | 425 |
| | 428 |
| | 429 |
| | 430 |

## UNIFORM COMMERCIAL CODE

| Sec. | This Work Page |
|---|---|
| 3–416(1) | 428 |
| 3–416(2) | 428 |
| 3–416(3) | 430 |
| 3–416(5) | 420 |
| | 428 |
| 3–417 | 423 |
| | 425 |
| | 505 |
| | 509 |
| | 510 |
| | 512 |
| | 513 |
| | 521 |
| | 586 |
| 3–417, Comment 3 | 510 |
| 3–417, Comment 5 | 515 |
| 3–417(1) | 513 |
| 3–417(1)(a) | 521 |
| 3–417(1)(b) | 512 |
| 3–417(2) | 445 |
| | 459 |
| | 511 |
| | 512 |
| | 513 |
| 3–417(2)(d) | 423 |
| | 512 |
| 3–417(3) | 423 |
| | 512 |
| 3–417(4) | 512 |
| 3–418 | 456 |
| | 478 |
| | 479 |
| | 519 |
| | 521 |
| | 522 |
| | 523 |
| | 524 |
| | 525 |
| | 526 |
| | 527 |
| | 528 |
| | 529 |
| | 530 |
| | 532 |
| | 550 |
| | 586 |
| 3–418, Comment 1 | 521 |
| | 522 |
| 3–418, Comment 4 | 525 |
| 3–419 | 423 |
| | 424 |
| | 494 |
| | 499 |
| | 500 |
| | 502 |
| | 504 |
| | 506 |
| | 508 |
| | 509 |
| | 517 |
| | 518 |
| 3–419(1) | 506 |

## UNIFORM COMMERCIAL CODE

| Sec. | This Work Page |
|---|---|
| 3–419(1)(c) | 496 |
| | 499 |
| | 500 |
| | 503 |
| | 508 |
| 3–419(3) | 500 |
| | 502 |
| | 503 |
| | 504 |
| | 505 |
| | 506 |
| | 507 |
| | 508 |
| | 509 |
| | 541 |
| | 542 |
| 3–419(4) | 424 |
| | 425 |
| | 506 |
| | 507 |
| 3–501 | 410 |
| | 444 |
| 3–501, Comment 2 | 417 |
| 3–501(1) | 416 |
| | 417 |
| 3–501(3) | 419 |
| 3–502 | 412 |
| | 443 |
| 3–502, Comment 2 | 413 |
| | 416 |
| 3–502(1) | 416 |
| 3–502(1)(b) | 409 |
| | 412 |
| 3–502(2) | 417 |
| | 419 |
| 3–503 | 417 |
| 3–503, Comment 2 | 416 |
| 3–503(1)(e) | 417 |
| | 418 |
| 3–503(2) | 417 |
| | 418 |
| 3–503(2)(b) | 418 |
| 3–504, Comment 1 | 418 |
| 3–504, Comment 2 | 418 |
| 3–504(1) | 417 |
| | 559 |
| 3–504(2) | 418 |
| 3–507(1) | 416 |
| 3–507(1)(b) | 422 |
| 3–508 | 419 |
| | 554 |
| 3–508(2) | 419 |
| 3–508(3) | 419 |
| 3–509 | 419 |
| | 554 |
| 3–511 | 416 |
| | 419 |
| | 420 |
| | 498 |
| | 560 |
| 3–511, Comment 5 | 423 |

## UNIFORM COMMERCIAL CODE

| Sec. | This Work Page |
|------|------|
| 3–511(2) | 420 |
|  | 422 |
|  | 498 |
| 3–511(2)(a) | 554 |
| 3–511(2)(b) | 421 |
|  | 422 |
| 3–511(2)(c) | 423 |
| 3–511(3) | 422 |
| 3–511(5) | 420 |
| 3–511(6) | 420 |
| 3–511(b) | 17 |
| 3–601 | 443 |
| 3–601(1) | 443 |
| 3–601(1)(d) | 435 |
| 3–601(3) | 444 |
| 3–601(3)(a) | 452 |
| 3–602 | 438 |
|  | 442 |
| 3–603 | 443 |
|  | 444 |
|  | 445 |
|  | 446 |
|  | 447 |
|  | 450 |
|  | 451 |
|  | 452 |
|  | 496 |
|  | 559 |
|  | 587 |
| 3–603(1) | 425 |
|  | 506 |
| 3–603(b) | 444 |
| 3–604 | 436 |
|  | 443 |
| 3–605 | 446 |
|  | 443 |
|  | 444 |
|  | 447 |
| 3–605(1)(b) | 447 |
| 3–606 | 425 |
|  | 427 |
|  | 428 |
|  | 432 |
|  | 434 |
|  | 437 |
|  | 438 |
|  | 442 |
|  | 443 |
| 3–606, Comment 1 | 434 |
| 3–606, Comment 2 | 436 |
| 3–606, Comment 4 | 434 |
|  | 438 |
| 3–606, Comment 5 | 435 |
| 3–606(1) | 433 |
|  | 435 |
|  | 436 |
| 3–606(1)(a) | 434 |
|  | 436 |
| 3–606(1)(b) | 434 |
|  | 435 |
|  | 437 |

## UNIFORM COMMERCIAL CODE

| Sec. | This Work Page |
|------|------|
| 3–606(2) | 436 |
|  | 437 |
| 3–606(3) | 437 |
| 3–802 | 445 |
|  | 447 |
|  | 448 |
|  | 450 |
|  | 451 |
|  | 452 |
|  | 454 |
|  | 496 |
|  | 580 |
|  | 587 |
| 3–802(1) | 449 |
|  | 496 |
| 3–802(1)(a) | 449 |
|  | 579 |
| 3–802(1)(b) | 449 |
|  | 450 |
|  | 451 |
|  | 506 |
|  | 515 |
|  | 559 |
|  | 579 |
| 3–803 | 442 |
| 3–804 | 445 |
|  | 448 |
|  | 450 |
|  | 454 |
|  | 455 |
|  | 494 |
|  | 496 |
|  | 497 |
|  | 498 |
|  | 503 |
|  | 509 |
|  | 517 |
| 3–804(1)(a) | 451 |
| 4–102 | 8 |
|  | 512 |
| 4–102(1) | 512 |
|  | 527 |
| 4–103 | 552 |
|  | 555 |
|  | 556 |
|  | 557 |
|  | 558 |
| 4–103(1) | 555 |
|  | 556 |
|  | 558 |
| 4–103(2) | 554 |
|  | 555 |
| 4–103(3) | 556 |
| 4–103(5) | 568 |
| 4–104, Comment 6 | 533 |
| 4–104(1)(e) | 510 |
|  | 552 |
|  | 576 |
| 4–104(f) | 580 |
| 4–104(1)(g) | 552 |
| 4–104(1)(h) | 533 |
|  | 596 |

| UNIFORM COMMERCIAL CODE | | UNIFORM COMMERCIAL CODE | |
|---|---|---|---|
| **Sec.** | **This Work Page** | **Sec.** | **This Work Page** |
| 4–104(1)(i) | 559 | 4–207(2) | 511 |
| 4–104(1)(j) | 533 | | 512 |
| | 595 | | 513 |
| 4–105 | 552 | | 520 |
| | 595 | | 521 |
| | 596 | 4–207(2)(b) | 510 |
| 4–105(a) | 501 | | 513 |
| 4–105(b) | 541 | | 520 |
| 4–105(c) | 424 | 4–207(2)(c) | 514 |
| 4–105(d) | 520 | 4–207(3) | 512 |
| 4–106 | 532 | 4–207(4) | 505 |
| | 533 | | 512 |
| 4–106, Comment 3 | 532 | 4–208 | 457 |
| 4–106, Comment 4 | 532 | | 465 |
| 4–109 | 534 | | 467 |
| | 535 | | 468 |
| | 598 | | 470 |
| 4–109(a)–(e) | 535 | | 911 |
| 4–109(e) | 535 | 4–208(1) | 469 |
| | 536 | | 554 |
| | 554 | 4–208(1)(a) | 468 |
| | 599 | | 586 |
| 4–201 | 406 | 4–208(1)(b) | 467 |
| 4–204, Comment 4 | 419 | | 469 |
| 4–204(3) | 418 | 4–208(1)(c) | 470 |
| 4–205 | 459 | | 471 |
| 4–205(2) | 425 | 4–208(2) | 470 |
| 4–207 | 425 | | 916 |
| | 505 | 4–209 | 465 |
| | 509 | | 467 |
| | 510 | | 468 |
| | 512 | | 469 |
| | 513 | | 470 |
| | 514 | | 586 |
| | 517 | 4–209 et seq. | 468 |
| | 518 | 4–212 | 457 |
| | 586 | 4–212(1) | 468 |
| 4–207, Comment 1 | 510 | | 532 |
| | 521 | | 554 |
| 4–207, Comment 2 | 513 | 4–213 | 468 |
| | 521 | | 519 |
| 4–207, Comment 4 | 511 | | 523 |
| | 520 | | 525 |
| 4–207(1) | 510 | | 526 |
| | 513 | | 527 |
| | 514 | | 528 |
| | 520 | | 529 |
| | 521 | | 530 |
| | 595 | | 532 |
| 4–207(1)(a) | 494 | | 535 |
| | 495 | | 536 |
| | 509 | | 550 |
| | 513 | | 591 |
| | 514 | | 599 |
| | 518 | | 600 |
| | 520 | 4–213, Comment 7 | 525 |
| | 521 | 4–213(1) | 531 |
| 4–207(1)(b) | 520 | | 533 |
| | 521 | | 596 |
| 4–207(1)(c) | 514 | 4–213(1)(a) | 531 |
| | 520 | 4–213(1)(b) | 533 |
| | 560 | | |

## UNIFORM COMMERCIAL CODE

| Sec. | This Work Page |
|---|---|
| 4–213(1)(c) | 534 |
| | 535 |
| | 536 |
| | 537 |
| | 554 |
| | 598 |
| | 599 |
| 4–213(1)(d) | 531 |
| | 533 |
| | 534 |
| | 535 |
| | 595 |
| | 596 |
| | 597 |
| | 599 |
| 4–213(2) | 554 |
| 4–213(3) | 554 |
| 4–213(4) | 468 |
| 4–301 | 416 |
| | 523 |
| | 532 |
| | 596 |
| | 597 |
| 4–301(1) | 532 |
| | 533 |
| | 596 |
| 4–302 | 525 |
| | 526 |
| | 528 |
| | 529 |
| | 595 |
| | 596 |
| 4–302(a) | 527 |
| | 530 |
| | 595 |
| 4–303 | 530 |
| | 568 |
| | 579 |
| | 588 |
| | 589 |
| | 590 |
| | 591 |
| | 593 |
| | 594 |
| | 597 |
| | 600 |
| | 900 |
| 4–303, Comment 3 | 599 |
| 4–303(1) | 590 |
| | 597 |
| 4–303(1)(a) | 594 |
| 4–303(1)(b) | 594 |
| 4–303(1)(c) | 594 |
| | 595 |
| | 596 |
| | 597 |
| 4–303(1)(d) | 597 |
| | 598 |
| | 599 |
| | 600 |

## UNIFORM COMMERCIAL CODE

| Sec. | This Work Page |
|---|---|
| 4–303(1)(e) | 594 |
| | 595 |
| | 596 |
| | 597 |
| 4–303(2) | 594 |
| 4–401 | 411 |
| | 498 |
| | 499 |
| | 509 |
| | 516 |
| | 517 |
| | 520 |
| | 558 |
| | 570 |
| | 587 |
| 4–401, Comment 1 | 529 |
| | 562 |
| 4–401, Comment 2 | 517 |
| 4–401(1) | 529 |
| | 558 |
| | 562 |
| 4–401(2) | 499 |
| | 560 |
| 4–401(2)(a) | 516 |
| | 560 |
| 4–402 | 411 |
| | 566 |
| | 567 |
| | 568 |
| | 569 |
| | 570 |
| | 571 |
| | 572 |
| | 573 |
| 4–402, Comment 2 | 567 |
| | 574 |
| 4–402, Comment 3 | 568 |
| | 569 |
| | 571 |
| 4–402, Comment 4 | 568 |
| 4–402, Comment 5 | 569 |
| 4–402(4) | 588 |
| 4–403 | 564 |
| | 568 |
| | 574 |
| | 576 |
| | 577 |
| | 578 |
| | 580 |
| | 585 |
| 4–403, Comment 2 | 555 |
| 4–403, Comment 3 | 575 |
| 4–403, Comment 4 | 574 |
| | 579 |
| 4–403, Comment 8 | 575 |
| 4–403, Comment 9 | 582 |
| | 583 |
| | 584 |
| 4–403(1) | 575 |
| | 576 |
| | 578 |

## UNIFORM COMMERCIAL CODE

| Sec. | This Work Page |
|---|---|
| 4–403(2) | 557 |
|  | 578 |
| 4–403(3) | 580 |
|  | 581 |
|  | 582 |
|  | 584 |
|  | 585 |
| 4–404 | 558 |
|  | 562 |
|  | 563 |
|  | 564 |
| 4–405 | 558 |
|  | 564 |
| 4–405, Comment 4 | 566 |
|  | 576 |
| 4–405(1) | 564 |
| 4–405(2) | 566 |
|  | 576 |
| 4–406 | 402 |
|  | 501 |
|  | 519 |
|  | 537 |
|  | 539 |
|  | 540 |
|  | 541 |
|  | 542 |
|  | 549 |
|  | 555 |
|  | 559 |
|  | 560 |
| 4–406, Comment 2 | 539 |
| 4–406(1) | 539 |
| 4–406(3) | 537 |
| 4–406(5) | 501 |
|  | 541 |
| 4–407 | 561 |
|  | 575 |
|  | 580 |
|  | 581 |
|  | 583 |
|  | 584 |
|  | 585 |
|  | 587 |
|  | 588 |
| 4–407, Comment 3 | 586 |
| 4–407, Comment 5 | 585 |
| 4–407(a) | 586 |
| 4–407(b) | 585 |
| 4–407(c) | 586 |
| 4–409 | 410 |
| 5–101 | 612 |
| 5–101 to 5–117 | 19 |
| 5–102 | 609 |
|  | 610 |
|  | 612 |
| 5–102, Comment 1 | 610 |
| 5–102(1) | 610 |
| 5–102(1)(a) | 610 |
| 5–102(1)(b) | 610 |
| 5–102(1)(c) | 615 |
| 5–102(4) | 612 |
|  | 613 |

## UNIFORM COMMERCIAL CODE

| Sec. | This Work Page |
|---|---|
| 5–103 | 610 |
| 5–103(1)(a) | 610 |
|  | 615 |
| 5–103(1)(b) | 610 |
| 5–103(1)(c) | 610 |
| 5–103(1)(d) | 610 |
| 5–104 | 15 |
| 5–104, Comment 1 | 611 |
| 5–104(1) | 46 |
|  | 615 |
| 5–104(2) | 46 |
| 5–105 | 15 |
|  | 627 |
| 5–106 | 617 |
| 5–106, Comment 1 | 617 |
| 5–106(1) | 617 |
|  | 618 |
| 5–106(2) | 617 |
| 5–106(3) | 617 |
| 5–106(4) | 616 |
| 5–107(1) | 617 |
| 5–107(2) | 606 |
| 5–107(4) | 617 |
| 5–108 | 613 |
|  | 635 |
|  | 637 |
| 5–108(3)(b) | 616 |
| 5–109 | 629 |
| 5–109(1) | 616 |
|  | 617 |
| 5–109(2) | 617 |
|  | 632 |
| 5–110(1) | 611 |
|  | 617 |
| 5–110(2) | 617 |
| 5–111, Comment | 632 |
| 5–111(1) | 617 |
|  | 632 |
| 5–111(2) | 617 |
|  | 633 |
| 5–112 | 623 |
| 5–113 | 613 |
|  | 628 |
| 5–113(2)(a) | 617 |
| 5–113(2)(b) | 617 |
| 5–114 | 625 |
| 5–114, Comment 1 | 607 |
|  | 621 |
| 5–114(1) | 616 |
|  | 620 |
|  | 621 |
|  | 626 |
|  | 627 |
|  | 631 |
|  | 632 |
| 5–114(2) | 617 |
|  | 624 |
|  | 625 |
|  | 631 |
|  | 637 |
|  | 638 |

## UNIFORM COMMERCIAL CODE

| Sec. | This Work Page |
|---|---|
| 5–114(2)(a) | 624 |
| | 626 |
| | 632 |
| | 637 |
| 5–114(2)(b) | 625 |
| 5–114(3) | 617 |
| 5–115 | 613 |
| | 616 |
| | 627 |
| 5–115(1) | 627 |
| | 628 |
| 5–115(2) | 627 |
| | 628 |
| 5–116 | 613 |
| 5–116, Comment 1 | 635 |
| 5–116(1) | 616 |
| | 635 |
| 5–116(2) | 616 |
| | 636 |
| | 637 |
| | 638 |
| 5–117 | 613 |
| 6–102 | 8 |
| | 644 |
| | 646 |
| 6–102, Comment 2 | 12 |
| | 645 |
| | 646 |
| 6–102, Comment 3 | 647 |
| 6–102(1) | 646 |
| | 647 |
| 6–102(2) | 647 |
| 6–102(3) | 645 |
| 6–103 | 644 |
| | 648 |
| 6–103, Comment 4 | 649 |
| 6–103, Comment 5 | 649 |
| 6–103(1) | 648 |
| 6–103(3) | 648 |
| 6–103(4) | 648 |
| 6–103(5) | 648 |
| 6–103(6) | 648 |
| 6–103(7) | 649 |
| 6–103(8) | 648 |
| 6–104 | 644 |
| | 654 |
| | 655 |
| | 657 |
| 6–104, Comment 2 | 654 |
| | 655 |
| | 662 |
| | 663 |
| 6–104, Comment 3 | 650 |
| 6–104(1)(a) | 649 |
| 6–104(1)(b) | 650 |
| 6–104(1)(c) | 651 |
| 6–104(2) | 649 |
| 6–104(3) | 650 |
| | 653 |
| 6–105 | 644 |
| | 651 |
| | 652 |

## UNIFORM COMMERCIAL CODE

| Sec. | This Work Page |
|---|---|
| 6–105 (Cont'd) | 654 |
| | 655 |
| 6–106 | 7 |
| | 644 |
| | 649 |
| | 653 |
| | 666 |
| 6–106(3) | 666 |
| 6–107 | 644 |
| | 651 |
| | 652 |
| 6–107(2) | 652 |
| 6–107(3) | 651 |
| 6–108 | 648 |
| | 649 |
| 6–109(1) | 655 |
| 6–110 | 661 |
| 6–110(2) | 654 |
| 6–111 | 653 |
| | 654 |
| | 656 |
| | 657 |
| 6–111, Comment 2 | 654 |
| 7–102, Comment 3 | 669 |
| 7–102(1)(a) | 144 |
| 7–102(1)(d) | 669 |
| 7–102(1)(g) | 689 |
| | 690 |
| 7–103 | 670 |
| 7–104 | 668 |
| | 670 |
| | 695 |
| | 742 |
| 7–104, Comment | 668 |
| 7–104, Comment 1 | 695 |
| 7–104(1) | 668 |
| | 683 |
| 7–104(1)(b) | 742 |
| 7–104(2) | 683 |
| 7–202 | 670 |
| 7–203 | 690 |
| | 691 |
| | 692 |
| | 700 |
| 7–203, Comment | 691 |
| 7–204 | 670 |
| | 693 |
| 7–204(1) | 672 |
| | 673 |
| | 674 |
| | 675 |
| | 676 |
| | 677 |
| 7–204(2) | 678 |
| | 679 |
| | 682 |
| 7–204(4) | 673 |
| 7–205 | 688 |
| | 702 |
| 7–207 | 702 |
| 7–207(2) | 702 |
| 7–208 | 689 |

### UNIFORM COMMERCIAL CODE

|  | This Work |
|---|---|
| Sec. | Page |
| 7–301 | 631 |
|  | 720 |
|  | 743 |
| 7–302 | 726 |
| 7–303 | 733 |
|  | 734 |
|  | 735 |
| 7–303(1) | 93 |
| 7–303(1)(a) | 97 |
|  | 735 |
| 7–303(1)(b) | 97 |
| 7–309 | 631 |
|  | 724 |
|  | 732 |
| 7–309(1) | 715 |
| 7–309(2) | 741 |
| 7–401 | 669 |
| 7–402 | 690 |
| 7–402(1) | 680 |
| 7–403 | 670 |
|  | 675 |
|  | 708 |
|  | 729 |
|  | 732 |
|  | 733 |
| 7–403(1) | 93 |
|  | 97 |
|  | 676 |
|  | 679 |
|  | 680 |
|  | 681 |
|  | 682 |
|  | 694 |
| 7–403(1)(a) | 681 |
|  | 733 |
| 7–403(1)(b) | 7 |
|  | 675 |
|  | 734 |
|  | 737 |
| 7–403(1)(c) | 682 |
| 7–403(1)(d) | 734 |
| 7–403(1)(e) | 734 |
| 7–403(1)(f) | 682 |
|  | 736 |
| 7–403(2) | 679 |
|  | 694 |
| 7–403(3) | 679 |
| 7–403(4) | 681 |
| 7–404 | 679 |
|  | 682 |
|  | 689 |
|  | 694 |
|  | 708 |
|  | 733 |
| 7–404, Comment | 680 |
| 7–501 | 670 |
|  | 683 |
|  | 684 |
|  | 685 |
|  | 686 |
|  | 687 |

### UNIFORM COMMERCIAL CODE

|  | This Work |
|---|---|
| Sec. | Page |
| 7–501 (Cont'd) | 693 |
|  | 953 |
| 7–501, Comment 1 | 684 |
| 7–501(4) | 684 |
| 7–502 | 624 |
|  | 668 |
|  | 684 |
|  | 685 |
|  | 686 |
|  | 687 |
|  | 694 |
|  | 695 |
|  | 699 |
|  | 700 |
|  | 701 |
|  | 742 |
|  | 748 |
|  | 953 |
| 7–502 et seq. | 900 |
| 7–502 to 7–504 | 670 |
| 7–502(1) | 700 |
|  | 742 |
| 7–502(1)(d) | 684 |
| 7–502(2) | 685 |
|  | 686 |
|  | 696 |
|  | 700 |
|  | 953 |
| 7–503 | 684 |
|  | 686 |
|  | 687 |
|  | 694 |
|  | 700 |
|  | 701 |
|  | 703 |
|  | 704 |
|  | 748 |
| 7–503, Comment 1 | 688 |
|  | 699 |
|  | 704 |
| 7–503(1) | 688 |
|  | 700 |
|  | 704 |
|  | 707 |
|  | 708 |
| 7–503(1)(a) | 687 |
|  | 688 |
|  | 701 |
|  | 707 |
| 7–503(1)(b) | 687 |
|  | 688 |
|  | 701 |
|  | 702 |
|  | 707 |
|  | 708 |
| 7–503(2) | 688 |
| 7–503(3) | 688 |
| 7–504 | 685 |
|  | 693 |
|  | 695 |
|  | 696 |

## UNIFORM COMMERCIAL CODE

| Sec. | This Work Page |
|---|---|
| 7–504 (Cont'd) | 703 |
| | 704 |
| 7–504(1) | 704 |
| 7–504(2) | 697 |
| 7–506 | 693 |
| 7–507 | 624 |
| | 687 |
| | 689 |
| | 692 |
| | 693 |
| | 747 |
| 7–540(2)(b) | 697 |
| 7–601(1) | 689 |
| 7–602 | 694 |
| 7–603 | 681 |
| 8–102 | 815 |
| 8–106 | 8 |
| 8–302 | 624 |
| 8–306 | 624 |
| 8–319 | 45 |
| | 46 |
| | 58 |
| 8–575 | 771 |
| 9–101, Comment | 833 |
| 9–102 | 8 |
| | 754 |
| | 756 |
| | 757 |
| | 758 |
| | 759 |
| | 765 |
| | 770 |
| | 771 |
| | 774 |
| | 779 |
| | 781 |
| | 807 |
| | 821 |
| | 846 |
| | 847 |
| | 852 |
| | 854 |
| 9–102, Comment 1 | 757 |
| 9–102, Comment 3 | 778 |
| | 847 |
| 9–102, Comment 4 | 773 |
| 9–102(1) | 757 |
| | 778 |
| | 779 |
| | 780 |
| | 806 |
| | 846 |
| | 847 |
| 9–102(1)(a) | 776 |
| | 785 |
| | 791 |
| 9–102(1)(b) | 775 |
| | 776 |
| | 777 |
| | 785 |
| | 806 |

## UNIFORM COMMERCIAL CODE

| Sec. | This Work Page |
|---|---|
| 9–102(1)(b) (Cont'd) | 807 |
| | 869 |
| 9–102(2) | 757 |
| | 767 |
| | 768 |
| 9–102(3) | 773 |
| 9–103 | 8 |
| | 754 |
| | 778 |
| | 779 |
| | 821 |
| | 846 |
| | 847 |
| | 850 |
| | 851 |
| | 854 |
| | 855 |
| | 858 |
| | 862 |
| | 911 |
| 9–103, Comment 1 | 778 |
| 9–103, Comment 3 | 853 |
| 9–103, Comment 4 | 853 |
| | 855 |
| 9–103, Comment 7 | 849 |
| | 850 |
| 9–103(1) | 846 |
| | 854 |
| 9–103(1)(c) | 851 |
| 9–103(1)(d) | 857 |
| | 858 |
| 9–103(1)(d)(i) | 850 |
| 9–103(2) | 819 |
| | 846 |
| | 847 |
| | 852 |
| | 853 |
| | 854 |
| | 855 |
| 9–103(2)(b) | 857 |
| 9–103(2)(c) | 858 |
| 9–103(2)(d) | 858 |
| | 862 |
| 9–103(3) | 846 |
| | 848 |
| | 850 |
| | 851 |
| | 855 |
| | 857 |
| | 858 |
| | 859 |
| 9–103(3)(d) | 854 |
| 9–103(3)(e) | 854 |
| 9–103(4) | 846 |
| | 847 |
| | 852 |
| | 855 |
| | 856 |
| | 857 |
| | 858 |
| | 859 |
| | 860 |

## UNIFORM COMMERCIAL CODE

| Sec. | This Work Page |
|------|------|
| 9–103(4) (Cont'd) | 861 |
|  | 862 |
| 9–104 | 754 |
|  | 758 |
|  | 773 |
|  | 934 |
| 9–104 to 9–105 | 952 |
| 9–104, Comment 1 | 819 |
|  | 948 |
| 9–104, Comment 7 | 774 |
| 9–104(a) | 774 |
|  | 782 |
|  | 819 |
| 9–104(b) | 702 |
|  | 758 |
|  | 773 |
|  | 934 |
| 9–104(c) | 758 |
| 9–104(d) | 774 |
| 9–104(f) | 774 |
|  | 777 |
|  | 778 |
|  | 806 |
|  | 807 |
| 9–104(h) | 774 |
| 9–104(i) | 774 |
| 9–104(j) | 771 |
|  | 773 |
|  | 935 |
| 9–105 | 435 |
|  | 756 |
|  | 949 |
| 9–105, Comment 4 | 949 |
| 9–105(1) | 772 |
| 9–105(1)(b) | 775 |
|  | 776 |
|  | 949 |
| 9–105(1)(c) | 756 |
| 9–105(1)(d) | 756 |
|  | 985 |
| 9–105(1)(g) | 775 |
|  | 776 |
| 9–105(1)(i) | 756 |
| 9–105(g) | 815 |
| 9–105(h) | 791 |
| 9–106 | 756 |
|  | 758 |
|  | 775 |
| 9–106, Comment | 776 |
| 9–107 | 757 |
|  | 758 |
|  | 868 |
|  | 914 |
|  | 915 |
|  | 923 |
| 9–107, Comment 2 | 915 |
| 9–107(a) | 799 |
|  | 800 |
|  | 914 |
| 9–107(b) | 800 |
|  | 914 |
|  | 916 |

## UNIFORM COMMERCIAL CODE

| Sec. | This Work Page |
|------|------|
| 9–108 | 876 |
|  | 880 |
|  | 881 |
|  | 882 |
|  | 950 |
| 9–108, Comment 2 | 922 |
| 9–109 | 756 |
|  | 803 |
|  | 804 |
|  | 805 |
|  | 823 |
|  | 824 |
|  | 845 |
|  | 853 |
| 9–109, Comment 2 | 803 |
| 9–109, Comment 3 | 941 |
| 9–109(1) | 350 |
|  | 384 |
| 9–109(2) | 647 |
|  | 804 |
| 9–109(3) | 824 |
| 9–109(4) | 647 |
|  | 758 |
|  | 824 |
|  | 917 |
|  | 918 |
|  | 941 |
| 9–109(e) | 824 |
| 9–110 | 15 |
|  | 789 |
|  | 845 |
|  | 846 |
| 9–113 | 780 |
|  | 781 |
|  | 795 |
| 9–113, Comment 2 | 780 |
| 9–113(a) | 781 |
| 9–113(b) | 781 |
| 9–113(c) | 781 |
| 9–114 | 769 |
|  | 911 |
| 9–201 | 638 |
|  | 643 |
|  | 659 |
|  | 688 |
|  | 701 |
|  | 748 |
|  | 781 |
|  | 901 |
|  | 938 |
|  | 939 |
|  | 945 |
|  | 946 |
|  | 952 |
|  | 976 |
|  | 1000 |
| 1–201(27) | 950 |
| 9–203 | 15 |
|  | 46 |
|  | 698 |
|  | 699 |
|  | 751 |

## UNIFORM COMMERCIAL CODE

| Sec. | This Work Page |
|---|---|
| 9–203 (Cont'd) | 760 |
| | 768 |
| | 785 |
| | 786 |
| | 787 |
| | 788 |
| | 789 |
| | 790 |
| | 791 |
| | 795 |
| | 796 |
| | 797 |
| | 846 |
| | 865 |
| | 866 |
| | 873 |
| 9–203, Comment 3 | 791 |
| 9–203, Comment 4 | 791 |
| 9–203(1) | 795 |
| | 816 |
| | 930 |
| 9–203(1)(a) | 756 |
| | 758 |
| 9–203(1)(b) | 787 |
| | 789 |
| | 790 |
| | 792 |
| | 834 |
| 9–204 | 15 |
| | 698 |
| | 699 |
| | 751 |
| | 768 |
| | 772 |
| | 773 |
| | 785 |
| | 786 |
| | 787 |
| | 788 |
| | 789 |
| | 795 |
| | 797 |
| | 846 |
| | 865 |
| | 866 |
| | 873 |
| | 910 |
| | 911 |
| | 922 |
| | 927 |
| | 929 |
| 9–204 et seq. | 907 |
| 9–204, Comment 6 | 922 |
| 9–204(1) | 791 |
| | 792 |
| | 795 |
| | 813 |
| 9–204(2) | 793 |
| 9–204(2)(a) | 922 |
| 9–204(2)(b) | 772 |
| | 773 |

## UNIFORM COMMERCIAL CODE

| Sec. | This Work Page |
|---|---|
| 9–204(3) | 758 |
| | 793 |
| 9–204(4) | 877 |
| 9–204(4)(b) | 800 |
| 9–205 | 880 |
| 9–206 | 387 |
| | 490 |
| 9–206(1) | 125 |
| | 127 |
| | 133 |
| | 387 |
| 9–206(2) | 362 |
| 9–206(2), Comment 3 | 362 |
| 9–207 | 160 |
| | 161 |
| | 435 |
| | 756 |
| | 779 |
| 9–207(1) | 435 |
| 9–207(2) | 160 |
| | 161 |
| 9–207(2)(b) | 160 |
| 9–301 | 638 |
| | 643 |
| | 659 |
| | 781 |
| | 807 |
| | 831 |
| | 849 |
| | 868 |
| | 870 |
| | 899 |
| | 901 |
| | 902 |
| | 905 |
| 9–301(1) | 901 |
| | 938 |
| 9–301(1)(b) | 760 |
| | 768 |
| | 800 |
| | 806 |
| | 807 |
| | 832 |
| | 865 |
| | 867 |
| | 868 |
| | 869 |
| | 870 |
| | 871 |
| | 878 |
| | 887 |
| | 890 |
| | 891 |
| | 901 |
| 9–301(1)(c) | 902 |
| | 938 |
| 9–301(1)(d) | 938 |
| 9–301(1)(e) | 808 |
| 9–301(2) | 757 |
| | 870 |
| | 874 |

## UNIFORM COMMERCIAL CODE

| Sec. | This Work Page |
|---|---|
| 9–301(2) (Cont'd) | 902 |
| | 919 |
| 9–301(3) | 244 |
| | 868 |
| 9–301(4) | 913 |
| 9–302 | 758 |
| | 765 |
| | 808 |
| | 868 |
| | 869 |
| | 905 |
| 9–302 to 9–304 | 709 |
| 9–302 to 9–305 | 708 |
| 9–302, Comment 4 | 798 |
| | 799 |
| 9–302, Comment 5 | 798 |
| 9–302(1) | 798 |
| 9–302(1)(c) | 798 |
| | 799 |
| | 802 |
| | 804 |
| | 805 |
| 9–302(1)(d) | 757 |
| | 797 |
| | 798 |
| | 799 |
| | 800 |
| | 802 |
| | 803 |
| | 804 |
| | 805 |
| | 868 |
| | 909 |
| | 938 |
| | 943 |
| 9–302(1)(e) | 798 |
| | 805 |
| | 806 |
| | 807 |
| | 815 |
| 9–302(2), Comment 2 | 12 |
| 9–302(3) | 783 |
| | 819 |
| | 820 |
| | 948 |
| 9–302(3)(a) | 819 |
| 9–302(3)(b) | 804 |
| | 820 |
| | 856 |
| | 947 |
| 9–302(4) | 856 |
| 9–302(5) | 820 |
| 9–303 | 751 |
| | 758 |
| | 813 |
| | 868 |
| | 869 |
| | 910 |
| | 922 |
| 9–303, Comment 2 | 752 |
| | 809 |

## UNIFORM COMMERCIAL CODE

| Sec. | This Work Page |
|---|---|
| 9–304 | 671 |
| | 812 |
| | 815 |
| | 909 |
| 9–304, Comment 2 | 698 |
| 9–304(1) | 698 |
| 9–304(3) | 699 |
| | 703 |
| | 810 |
| | 811 |
| | 812 |
| 9–304(4) | 698 |
| | 798 |
| | 809 |
| | 810 |
| | 811 |
| | 813 |
| | 906 |
| 9–304(5) | 12 |
| | 698 |
| | 701 |
| | 809 |
| | 810 |
| | 811 |
| | 812 |
| | 813 |
| | 906 |
| 9–304(5)(a) | 810 |
| | 811 |
| | 906 |
| 9–304(5)(b) | 810 |
| | 811 |
| | 906 |
| 9–304(6) | 906 |
| 9–305 | 671 |
| | 698 |
| | 758 |
| | 814 |
| | 816 |
| | 817 |
| | 818 |
| | 868 |
| | 869 |
| | 905 |
| | 909 |
| | 910 |
| 9–305, Comment 1 | 814 |
| 9–305, Comment 2 | 817 |
| 9–306 | 470 |
| | 701 |
| | 707 |
| | 758 |
| | 798 |
| | 809 |
| | 811 |
| | 883 |
| | 908 |
| | 909 |
| | 945 |
| | 951 |
| | 953 |
| | 976 |

**UNIFORM COMMERCIAL CODE**

| Sec. | This Work Page |
|---|---|
| 9–306, Comment 3 | 939 |
| 9–306(1) | 883 |
| 9–306(2) | 701 |
| | 880 |
| | 885 |
| | 887 |
| | 888 |
| | 938 |
| | 939 |
| | 940 |
| | 941 |
| | 945 |
| | 946 |
| | 976 |
| 9–306(3) | 813 |
| | 880 |
| | 885 |
| | 887 |
| | 888 |
| | 909 |
| | 912 |
| 9–306(3)(b) | 911 |
| 9–306(4) | 885 |
| | 887 |
| 9–306(4)(a) | 884 |
| | 885 |
| | 886 |
| 9–306(4)(b) | 884 |
| | 885 |
| | 886 |
| | 888 |
| 9–306(4)(c) | 884 |
| | 885 |
| | 886 |
| | 888 |
| 9–306(4)(d) | 885 |
| | 886 |
| | 887 |
| | 888 |
| 9–306(5) | 909 |
| 9–307 | 760 |
| | 786 |
| | 849 |
| | 902 |
| | 938 |
| | 939 |
| | 940 |
| | 943 |
| | 944 |
| | 945 |
| | 946 |
| | 947 |
| | 948 |
| | 951 |
| | 976 |
| | 997 |
| 9–307 through 9–313 | 899 |
| 9–307, Comment 2 | 939 |
| | 942 |
| 9–307(1) | 701 |
| | 707 |
| | 900 |

**UNIFORM COMMERCIAL CODE**

| Sec. | This Work Page |
|---|---|
| 9–307(1) (Cont'd) | 938 |
| | 940 |
| | 941 |
| | 942 |
| | 943 |
| | 945 |
| | 946 |
| | 947 |
| | 948 |
| 9–307(2) | 869 |
| | 900 |
| | 939 |
| | 943 |
| | 944 |
| 9–308 | 820 |
| | 949 |
| | 950 |
| | 951 |
| | 952 |
| | 976 |
| 9–308, Comment 2 | 950 |
| | 951 |
| 9–309 | 686 |
| | 698 |
| | 702 |
| | 704 |
| | 949 |
| | 952 |
| | 953 |
| 9–310 | 758 |
| | 783 |
| | 976 |
| 9–311 | 977 |
| 9–312 | 638 |
| | 700 |
| | 748 |
| | 758 |
| | 813 |
| | 832 |
| | 833 |
| | 899 |
| | 903 |
| | 904 |
| | 905 |
| | 907 |
| | 909 |
| | 911 |
| | 913 |
| | 914 |
| | 918 |
| | 921 |
| | 923 |
| | 924 |
| | 927 |
| | 934 |
| | 952 |
| 9–312, Comment 3 | 917 |
| | 919 |
| 9–312, Comment 4 | 828 |
| | 832 |

## UNIFORM COMMERCIAL CODE

| Sec. | This Work Page |
|---|---|
| 9–312(1) | 905 |
| | 909 |
| | 911 |
| 9–312(2) | 905 |
| | 922 |
| 9–312(3) | 643 |
| | 707 |
| | 757 |
| | 769 |
| | 905 |
| | 913 |
| | 914 |
| | 916 |
| | 918 |
| | 919 |
| | 920 |
| | 921 |
| 9–312(3)(c) | 918 |
| 9–312(4) | 874 |
| | 905 |
| | 910 |
| | 913 |
| | 918 |
| | 919 |
| | 920 |
| | 921 |
| | 933 |
| 9–312(5) | 795 |
| | 832 |
| | 849 |
| | 903 |
| | 905 |
| | 906 |
| | 908 |
| | 911 |
| | 912 |
| | 913 |
| | 920 |
| | 921 |
| | 923 |
| 9–312(5), Comment 4, Example 3 | 906 |
| 9–312(5)(a) | 828 |
| | 891 |
| | 907 |
| | 908 |
| | 909 |
| | 910 |
| | 911 |
| | 912 |
| 9–312(5)(a) to 9–306 | 909 |
| 9–312(5)(b) | 704 |
| | 707 |
| | 813 |
| | 909 |
| | 910 |
| | 911 |
| | 912 |
| | 920 |
| 9–312(5)(c) | 796 |
| | 911 |
| 9–312(6) | 911 |
| | 912 |

## UNIFORM COMMERCIAL CODE

| Sec. | This Work Page |
|---|---|
| 9–312(7) | 913 |
| 9–313 | 771 |
| | 772 |
| | 899 |
| | 922 |
| | 924 |
| | 925 |
| | 927 |
| | 931 |
| | 932 |
| | 933 |
| | 934 |
| | 938 |
| 9–313, Comment 2 | 771 |
| 9–313, Comment 5 | 931 |
| 9–313(1) | 772 |
| | 924 |
| | 927 |
| | 931 |
| 9–313(2) | 927 |
| | 928 |
| | 929 |
| | 930 |
| | 932 |
| | 934 |
| | 935 |
| 9–313(3) | 928 |
| | 929 |
| | 930 |
| | 935 |
| 9–313(4) | 927 |
| | 928 |
| | 929 |
| | 930 |
| | 932 |
| | 933 |
| | 934 |
| | 935 |
| 9–313(5) | 925 |
| | 930 |
| | 931 |
| 9–314 | 800 |
| 9–318(1) | 490 |
| | 638 |
| 9–318(3) | 637 |
| 9–401 | 7 |
| | 819 |
| | 820 |
| | 823 |
| | 827 |
| | 831 |
| | 848 |
| | 927 |
| | 934 |
| 9–401, Comment 3 | 821 |
| | 827 |
| 9–401, Comment 4 | 827 |
| 9–401, Comment 5 | 831 |
| 9–401, Comment 6 | 828 |
| 9–401(1) | 818 |
| | 819 |
| | 820 |

### UNIFORM COMMERCIAL CODE

| Sec. | This Work Page |
|---|---|
| 9–401(1) (Cont'd) | 821 |
| | 823 |
| | 825 |
| | 834 |
| 9–401(1)(c) | 823 |
| | 826 |
| | 829 |
| 9–401(2) | 829 |
| | 830 |
| | 831 |
| | 832 |
| | 833 |
| 9–401(3) | 805 |
| | 828 |
| 9–402 | 15 |
| | 787 |
| | 788 |
| | 789 |
| | 790 |
| | 833 |
| | 834 |
| | 836 |
| | 837 |
| | 845 |
| | 869 |
| 9–402, Comment 2 | 791 |
| 9–402(1) | 833 |
| | 834 |
| | 835 |
| | 836 |
| | 837 |
| | 843 |
| 9–402(3) | 837 |
| 9–402(5) | 15 |
| | 788 |
| | 834 |
| | 835 |
| | 839 |
| | 841 |
| 9–403 | 850 |
| 9–403(2) | 849 |
| | 850 |
| | 918 |
| 9–403, Comment 3 | 849 |
| 9–405, Comment 5 | 841 |
| 9–501 | 965 |
| 9–501(1) | 956 |
| | 963 |
| | 965 |
| | 1006 |
| 9–501(3) | 6 |
| | 954 |
| | 980 |
| 9–501(3)(c) | 980 |
| 9–501(3)(d) | 980 |
| 9–501(5) | 964 |
| | 965 |
| 9–502(2) | 977 |
| | 1000 |
| 9–503 | 931 |
| | 955 |
| | 964 |

### UNIFORM COMMERCIAL CODE

| Sec. | This Work Page |
|---|---|
| 9–503 (Cont'd) | 966 |
| | 967 |
| | 968 |
| | 973 |
| | 974 |
| | 975 |
| | 977 |
| | 978 |
| 9–503 to 9–505 | 956 |
| 9–503, Comment | 966 |
| 9–503(1)(a) | 701 |
| 9–504 | 219 |
| | 391 |
| | 779 |
| | 931 |
| | 955 |
| | 964 |
| | 978 |
| | 979 |
| | 981 |
| | 982 |
| | 985 |
| | 986 |
| | 987 |
| | 992 |
| | 1002 |
| 9–504, Comment 1 | 962 |
| | 981 |
| | 993 |
| 9–504, Comment 5 | 982 |
| | 986 |
| 9–504(1) | 962 |
| | 975 |
| | 981 |
| 9–504(1)(a) | 991 |
| 9–504(2) | 776 |
| | 1000 |
| 9–504(3) | 219 |
| | 348 |
| | 964 |
| | 981 |
| | 983 |
| | 985 |
| | 986 |
| | 989 |
| | 990 |
| | 992 |
| | 1003 |
| 9–504(4) | 940 |
| | 992 |
| 9–504(5) | 126 |
| | 991 |
| | 992 |
| 9–505 | 931 |
| | 956 |
| | 979 |
| | 980 |
| | 998 |
| 9–505(1) | 978 |
| 9–505(2) | 978 |
| | 979 |
| | 980 |
| | 981 |

## UNIFORM COMMERCIAL CODE

| Sec. | This Work Page |
|---|---|
| 9–506 | 958 |
| 9–507 | 966 |
| | 979 |
| | 990 |
| | 995 |
| | 997 |
| | 998 |
| | 1000 |
| 9–507, Comment 1 | 998 |
| 9–507, Comment 2 | 990 |
| 9–507(1) | 979 |
| | 997 |
| 9–507(2) | 987 |
| | 988 |
| | 989 |
| | 994 |
| 9–531 | 771 |
| 10–101 | 904 |
| 10–102(2) | 904 |

## UNIFORM COMMERCIAL CODE
### (Proposed Alternative)

| Sec. | This Work Page |
|---|---|
| 2–318(A) | 331 |
| | 332 |
| | 333 |
| 2–318(B) | 328 |
| | 329 |
| | 331 |
| | 332 |
| | 333 |
| 2–318(C) | 328 |
| | 329 |
| | 331 |
| | 332 |
| | 333 |
| 3–121(A) | 409 |
| 9–103, Comment 4(b) | 862 |
| 9–103, Comment 4(e) | 862 |

*

# INDEX

References are to Pages

**ACCELERATION CLAUSES**
Generally, 958, 961.
Good faith, 959–961.
Insecurity clause, 958–961.

**ACCEPTANCE OF GOODS**
Generally, 249–253.
Act inconsistent with seller's ownership, 251–253.
Action for the price, 208–216.
Breach of warranty, 96.
Consequences, 249–250.
Damages, breach of warranty, chapter 10.
Installment contract, 257–259.
Nonconforming goods
Damages, Chapter ten.
Notice required for remedy, 343, 348.
"Reasonable opportunity to inspect," 249–253.
Rejection, 210–213.
Attempted, 251–253.
Ineffective, 251.
Revocation, 210–213.
Statute of frauds, exception, 48, 62.
Title, unrelated to, 249.

**ACCESSIONS**
See After-Acquired Property; Fixtures.

**ACCOMMODATION PARTIES**
See also Suretyship.
Generally, 425–443.
Consent, express or implied, 436–438.
Defenses, 432–435, 440–443.
Definition, 427.
Discharge, 429, 432–438, 443–454.
Establishing suretyship status, 429–432.
Liability, generally, 425–429.
Liability to principal debtor, 426–427, 439–440.
Reimbursement, 438–439.
Reservation of rights, 436, 437.
Signature and symbols, 429–430.
Subrogation, 438–439.

**ACCORD AND SATISFACTION**
Checks, "full satisfaction", 452–454.
Repossession of collateral, 977–980.

**ACCOUNTS**
Automatic perfection, 805–809.
Priority conflicts, 530, 588–600.
Proceeds, 921.
Sale of, 775–778.

**ADEQUATE ASSURANCE OF DUE PERFORMANCE**
Generally, 169–170.

**AFTER-ACQUIRED PROPERTY**
See also Fixtures; Floating Lien.
"Factor's lien", 755.

**AGENCY**
Close-connectedness, holder in due course, 480.
Personal liability, 403–406.
Principal's liability for signature, 400–403.
"Representative capacity," 403–406, 408.

**AGREED REMEDIES**
Generally, 375–396.
Buyer's, 376–386, 392–396.
Consequence of judicial nonacceptance, 382–383.
Disclaimer of warranty compared, 383–384, 392–396.
Drafting, 383.
Exclusionary clause, definition, 384.
Exclusiveness requirement, 377, 379.
Express warranty as limitation, 378–379.
"Fails of its essential purpose", 379–383.
Minimum adequate remedies, 379–382.
Notice requirements, 345–346.
Unconscionable, 377, 379, 383–386, 392–396.

**AGREEMENT WAIVING DEFENSES**
Unconscionable, 125, 127.

**ALTERATION OF INSTRUMENTS**
See also Bill of Lading; Documents of Title; Warehouse Receipts.
Drawer/maker negligent, 537–540.
Notice of defenses, 475.
Payor bank liability, to drawer, 499.
Properly payable, 560.
Warranty liability, 512, 514.

**ANTECEDENT DEBT**
See also Bankruptcy; Voidable Preference.
Purchase money security interest, 915.
Value, holder in due course, 465–466.

**ANTICIPATORY REPUDIATION**
See also Repudiation.
Generally, 168–175.

**ANTICIPATORY REPUDIATION—** Cont'd

Adequate assurance of due performance, 169–170.

Buyer's alternative responses, 196–206.

Retraction, 174–175.

Seller's rights respecting uncompleted goods, 238–241.

**ARTICLE ONE, U.C.C.**

See also Scope of Articles.

Generally, "Introduction", 14–17, 19–20.

**ARTICLE TWO, U.C.C.**

See also Sale of Goods.

Chapter one.

Chapter two.

Chapter three.

Chapter four.

Chapter five.

Chapter six.

Chapter seven.

Chapter eight.

Chapter nine.

Chapter ten.

Chapter eleven.

Chapter twelve.

**ARTICLE THREE, U.C.C.**

Chapter thirteen.

Chapter fourteen.

Chapter fifteen.

Chapter sixteen.

**ARTICLE FOUR, U.C.C.**

Chapter fifteen.

Chapter sixteen.

Chapter seventeen.

**ARTICLE FIVE, U.C.C.**

See also Letter of Credit; Scope of Articles.

Chapter eighteen.

**ARTICLE SIX, U.C.C.**

See also Bulk Sales; Scope of Articles.

Chapter nineteen.

Chapter twenty.

**ARTICLE SEVEN, U.C.C.**

See also Bill of Lading; Scope of Articles; Warehouse Receipts.

Chapter twenty-one.

**ARTICLE NINE, U.C.C.**

See also Scope of Articles; Security Interest.

Chapter twenty-two.

Chapter twenty-three.

Chapter twenty-four.

Chapter twenty-five.

Chapter twenty-six.

**ARTISAN'S LIENS**

See Statutory Liens.

**ASSIGNEE**

Letters of credit, 633–639.

**ASSIGNEE—**Cont'd

Trustee as assignee of debtor, 865–866.

Unsecured claim in bankruptcy, 882–883.

**ASSUMPTION OF RISK**

Defense,

Warranty action, 335–337, 338–339.

Products liability, Chapter ten.

Strict tort liability, 335–337.

**ATTACHMENT**

See also Perfection by Filing.

Bankruptcy, 889–892.

Debtor rights and value, 791–796.

Fixtures, 927–938.

Priority disputes, 911.

**AUTOMOBILES**

See Motor Vehicles.

**BAILEE**

See also Warehouseman.

Liability,

For lost or injured goods, 672–679.

To purchasers of warehouse receipts, 682–697.

Rights of storer against warehouseman, 671–682.

Risk of loss of goods, 144–145.

Warehouseman's liability, "lawful excuse", 680–682.

**BANKER'S LIEN**

See also Set-Off.

**BANKRUPTCY**

Account priority conflicts, 590, 592–593.

Actual fraud, 895.

Antecedent debt, 871–876.

Bulk sales, 659–660, 662, 664–665.

Exempt property, 870.

Floating liens, 876–883.

Fraudulent conveyance, 892–897.

Insolvent seller, buyer's right to specific performance, 195.

Judgment creditor, 889.

Lien creditor, actual, 889–892.

Notice of dishonor not excused, 422–423.

Preferential payments, 888–889.

Preferential transfers, 871–876.

Presentment not excused, 422–423.

Rights of trustee against seller to insolvent buyer, 243–245.

Rule of Moore v. Bay, 890–891, 895.

Security interest in bank accounts, 885–886.

Security interests in fixtures, 929.

Security interests in proceeds, 883–888.

Sham debts, 897–898.

Statute of limitations, 898.

"Strong arm" clause, 870.

Trustee versus secured creditor, 864–898.

Uniform Fraudulent Conveyance Act, 893–897.

Usury laws, 898.

Voidable preference, elements, 873–876.

## BANKS

See also Payor Banks.

Customer, defined, 552.

Debtor of customer, 551.

Deposit contract, 552–558.

Duty to exercise ordinary care, 555, 556, 557–558.

Good faith duty, 555, 557–558.

Item defined, 552.

Relationship to customer, generally, 551–600.

Security interest in bank accounts, 885–886.

Value, holder in due course, 467–471.

## BASIS OF MARGIN

See also Express Warranty.

Advertisements, 279–281, 282.

Evidence, 279–286.

Express warranty requirement, 273, 276, 277–282, 283, 284.

Proof, burden of, 278–279, 282.

## "BATTLE OF THE FORMS"

See also Contract Formation; Offer and Acceptance.

Contract formation with conflicting terms, 23–33.

Nonconforming acceptance, 35–36.

## BILL OF LADING

See also Carrier.

Generally, 601–603, 710–711.

Cash against documents, 742, 752.

Defined, 711.

"Documentary sales", 93–94.

Federal commercial law, 710–713, 714–716, 724–726, 729, 731–737, 739, 741–750, 753.

Improper loading, 747–748.

Misdescription, 746–747.

Negotiable bill,
    Generally, 742–749.
    Defined, 741–742.

Non-negotiable bill,
    Generally, 749–750.
    Defined, 742, 749.

Order bill, defined, 742.

Paramount title, 748.

Rights and liabilities of parties, applicable law, 711–713.

Rights of pledgees, 750–753.

Risk of loss, limitation on subrogation, 161.

Shippers load and count, 744–748.

Straight bill, defined, 742, 749.

Tender of delivery, 93–94.

## BONA FIDE PURCHASER

See also Good Faith Purchaser.

Holder in due course, 456.

## BONDS

Stolen instrument cases, 455.

## BREACH OF CONTRACT

See also Anticipatory Repudiation; Damages; Remedies.

## BREACH OF CONTRACT—Cont'd

Adequate assurance of due performance, 169–170.

Anticipatory repudiation, 168–175.

Breach of warranty damages, Chapter ten.

Buyer's responses to repudiation, 196–206.

Damaged goods, Chapters eight and nine.

Deterrence by 2–708(2), p. 233.

Learned of breach formula, 197–202.

Limitation of buyer's remedies, 376–379.

Nondelivery, 168.

Reasonable time, waiting for repudiator's performance, 202–206.

Risk of loss consequences, 146–150.

Tender of delivery requirement, 89–90, 91, 93–95.

## BREACH OF PEACE

Debtor's consent to repossession, 969–970.

Opposition to repossession, 972–975.

Repossession of collateral, 964, 966–975.

## BULK SALES

Bankruptcy law, 659–660, 662, 664–665.

Creditors versus third parties, 661–662.

Defined, 644–645.

Equitable receivership, 642.

Equitable remedies, 658–659.

Failure to comply, 653–657.

Good faith purchasers, 642, 661–662.

Individual creditors' remedies,
    Noncompliance with Article Six, pp. 653–657.
    Nonlegal avenues, 657–659.
    Versus collective recovery, 662–666.

Introduction, 640–644.

Priorities, 902.

Requirements of Article Six,
    Inspection of list and schedule, 651.
    List of creditors, 649–650.
    Notice to creditors, 643–644, 651–653.
    Schedule of property, 650–651.

Scope of Article 6,
    Specific exceptions, 647–649.
    Types of enterprises, 645–646.
    Types of property, 647–648.
    Types of transfers, 644–645, 646–647.

Statute of limitations, 656–657.

Uniform Fraudulent Conveyance Act, 641–642.

Voidable preference, 642–643.

## BURDEN OF PROOF

Amount of loss, stop-order paid, 582–583.

Basis of bargain, 278–279, 282.

Buyer proves breach after acceptance, 249–250.

Commercially reasonable completion, 240, 241.

Complete agreement embodied in writing, 67, 68.

Consequential damages, 321.

Contract terms, 88.

**BURDEN OF PROOF**—Cont'd
Defenses to warranty actions, 326–327.
Deficiency judgment, 1002–1005, 1006.
Implied warranty of fitness, 298–299.
Implied warranty of merchantability, 286, 290, 292, 295–296.
Insecurity clauses, 959–961.
Limitation-of-remedy clause, 384, 385.
Negligence by drawer, 501, 514.
Requirements contract, good faith, 108.
Resale of repossessed collateral, commercially reasonable, 994–995.
Rights of shipper against carrier, 716, 719–720, 749.
Seller's election of remedies, 224.
Seller's remedies, 2–708(1), overcompensate, 232, 233.
Signatures, instruments, 491.
Statute of frauds, 60.
Stolen instruments, underlying obligation, 454–455.
Trade usage, disclaimer cases, 371–372.
Unconscionability, excessive price, 123–124.
Warehouseman's liability, 674–675.
Warranty, personal injury, 272.

**BUYER IN ORDINARY COURSE OF BUSINESS**
Defined, 940–943.
Inventory, 902.
Priorities, 940–948.
Seller "subject to" under 2–702, p. 243.

**BUYER OF GOODS**
See also Bill of Lading; Bulk Sales; Warehouse Receipts.
Priority disputes, 938–948.
Requirements contract, buyer going out of business, 108.

**BUYER'S REMEDIES**
See also Damages; Rejection of Goods; Remedies; Revocation of Acceptance; Seller's Remedies.
Generally, Chapter six.
Alternative responses to repudiation, 196–206.
Contract-market differential, 180–191.
Cover, 175–180.
Good faith, 177–178.
Expenses saved, 188–189.
Incidental damages, 312–314.
Learned of breach, 183–184, 197–202.
Limitation, 376–386, 392–396.
Market price, proof of, 190.
Modification, 375–396.
Mutual exclusivity, 306.
Notice necessary, 343, 348.
Rejection, generally, chapter 8.
Replevin, 195–196.
Revocation of acceptance, generally, Chapter eight.
Self-help, 246–247.
Specific performance, 192–196.
Warranty of title breach, 302.

**CANCELLATION OF CONTRACT**
See Rescission.

**CARRIER**
See also Bill of Lading.
Carrier's right to shipper's insurance, 727–729.
Damages measure, 721–726.
Defined, risk of loss context, 143–144.
Limitation, 724–726.
Multiple carriers, 724–726.
Rights of shipper against, delivery obligations,
Absolute liability, 729–730, 731–732, 737.
Exception, 731–732.
Damage measures, 737–741.
Limitation, 741.
Delayed delivery, 737.
Lawful excuses,
Generally, 732, 733–736, 737.
Consignee as thief, 733–734.
Diversion of goods, 734–736.
Lost, destroyed or damaged, carrier not liable, 734.
Miscellaneous, 736.
Non-negligent, 737.
Stoppage in transit, 734.
Misdelivery, 729–732.
Non-delivery, 732–733.
Rights of shipper against, lost, destroyed or damaged goods,
Absolute liability, 714–716, 724.
Act of God exception, 716–717.
Act of public authority exception, 720.
Act of public enemy exception, 717–718.
Act of shipper exception, 718–720.
Inherent vice or nature of goods exception, 720–721.

**CASH SALE**
Analogy to credit sales, 245.
Presumed terms for sale of goods, 95.
Seller's right to require, 241.

**CASUALTY TO GOODS**
See Carrier; Risk of Loss.

**CERTIFICATE OF TITLE ACTS**
See Registration of Motor Vehicle Title.

**CHATTEL MORTGAGE**
Definition of, 755.

**CHATTEL PAPER**
Perfection in multiple state transactions, 847, 852.
Purchases of, 949–952.
Sale of, 775–778.

**CHECK COLLECTIONS**
See Checks; Payor Banks.

**CHECKS**
"Accountable for", 525–529.
Altered, warranty liability, 512, 514.

**CHECKS**—Cont'd
Bank, 578–580.
Cancelled, drawer duty to examine, 539–540.
Cashiers, 578–580.
Certified, 564, 578–580.
Conditioned cashing rule, 41.
Conversion, 499–509.
Discharge, generally, 443–454.
Dishonored, seller's right to goods, 97–98.
Drawer's liability, 496–495.
Final payment, 522, 523–525, 530–537.
"Full satisfaction", 452–454.
Introduction, 397–399.
Introduction to liability, 492–495.
Non-sufficient funds, 529, 530.
Payment, conditioned tender, 97–98.
Potential lawsuits, 494–495, 517–518.
"Properly payable", 558–566.
Stolen and lost, 492–518.
Stop-payment orders, 574–588.
Suspends underlying obligation, 449–450.
Warranty suits, 509–517.

**CHOICE OF LAW**
Article seven, UCC, 670–671.
Article nine problem, 778–780.
Letters of credit, 612–615.
Situs of collateral, 778–780.
Unconscionable contract clause example, 125.

**CLASSIFICATION OF PROPERTY**
Changes in classification, 805.
Consumer goods, 802–804.
Farm equipment, 804–805.
Filing financing statement, 820–825.
Financing statement, 843–846.
Intangibles, 854.
Mobile goods, 852–854.
Multiple state transactions, 846, 847, 852–855.
Non-mobile tangible property, 847–852.

**CODIFICATION OF LAW**
Case law construes UCC, 9.
Letters of credit, 620.
Prior drafts of UCC, 9–10.

**COLLATERAL**
See also Default; Security Interest.
Accommodation party, effect of impairment, 433, 434–435.
Deficiency judgment, 1000–1007.
Resale of repossessed collateral, 981–995.

**COMMON LAW**
Anticipatory repudiation, 170–172.
Case law construes UCC, 9.
Close-connectedness doctrine, 479.
Consequential damages, 314–317.
Conversion, bearer paper, 506–507, 509.
Defining unconscionability, 116.
Disclaimer of warranty, trade usage, 370–372.
Estoppel exception, statute of frauds, 59–60.

**COMMON LAW**—Cont'd
Final payment, "accountable for", 526.
Good faith, holder in due course, 471–472.
Letters of credit, 609, 611, 613, 620–623.
Pre-code security devices, 754–756.
"Properly payable", 559.
Requirements contracts, 105–106.
Restitution,
    Oral agreement, 62–63.
    Payor bank, 521.
Rights of shipper against carrier, 714–716, 739–741.
Sales law altered by UCC, 22.
Seller's remedies on buyer's insolvency, 243–245.
Statute of frauds exceptions, 48–49, 59–60.
Strict tort liability, 328–329.
Supplements UCC, 5–6.
Warehouseman's standard of care, 672–674.
Warranty of title disclaimer, 303–305.
    Quiet possession, 300–302.
Wrongful dishonor, 568.

**CONDITIONAL SALE**
Definition of, 755.
Purchase money security interests, 797–805.

**CONSIGNMENT**
See also Carrier.
As security interests, 765–769.
Notice to prior lender, 769.
Risk of loss, subrogation, 158.
Sale or return, 766–768.

**CONSTRUCTION CONTRACTS**
Promissory estoppel, 33–34.

**CONSUMER GOODS**
Certificate of title, 855.
Chattel paper, 776.
Damages for creditor misbehavior, 997–999.
Definition of, 802–804.
House trailers, 803–804.
Priority of purchasers over secured creditors, 943–944.
Purchase money security interest, 797–805.
Strict foreclosure, 977–980.
Where to file, 821.

**CONSUMER PROTECTION**
See also Truth in Lending; Unconscionability; Uniform Consumer Credit Code.
Close-connectedness, 483–486.
Deficiency judgment sales, 219.
Disclaimer,
    Strict tort liability, 350–351.
    Warranty, 349–350, 352–353, 365, 368, 392, 396.
Ghetto merchants, higher prices, 122–123.
Legislative limitations on holder in due course, 484–486.

**CONSUMER PROTECTION**—Cont'd

Limitation of buyer's remedies, 378, 384, 392, 396.

Notice, time requirement relaxed, 345.

Personal injury, 329–333.

Rejection, reasonable time, 261–262.

Unconscionability,
    Injunctive relief, 130–131.
    Punitive damages, 132–133.
    Sales contracts for home appliance, examples, 120–122.

**CONTRACT FORMATION**

    See also Freedom of Contract; Offer and Acceptance.

Generally, Chapters one, two, three.

Basic principles, 21–23.

Common law altered by UCC, 22.

Firm offers, 33–34.

Indefinite quantity terms, 103–109.

Methods of acceptance, 34–36.

Open price term, 98–100.

Oral agreements, 30–31.
    Enforcing, 61–63.

Statute of frauds requirements Chapter two.

Terms,
    Express agreement, 82–83.
    Interpretation of, 84–86.
    Limitations, 109–111.
    Mandatory under code, 109–111.
    Modified by performance, 84–88.
    Supplied by Article Two, 88–109.
    Supplied by course of performance, 84–88.
    Supplied by trade usage, 84–88.

Warranty term, express or implied, 71–72.

Writing, evidence of terms, 65–67.

Writing requirement see Chapter two.

**CONTRACT MODIFICATION**

    See also Modification of Contract.

Generally, 36–42.

Consideration not required, 37–38.

Course of performance, 84–88.

Oral modification, 38–39.

Pre-existing duty rule relaxed, 37–38.

Statute of frauds, 46–47.
    Requirements, 38.

Unconscionable, 39–41.

Waiver, 39.

**CONTRACT RIGHTS**

    See also Breach of Contract; Remedies.

Automatic perfection, 805–809.

Inspection of goods, 92–93.

Instruments liability, 408–425.
    Acceptor, 410–411.
    Drawer, 411–413.
    Indorser, 413–425.
    Maker, 408–410.

Negotiable instruments, introduction, 398.

Sale of, 775–778.

Third parties protected, 110–111.

**CONTRIBUTION**

Co-makers of notes, 410.

Insurance,
    "Other clauses", 163–166.
    Risk of loss, sale of goods, 161–166.

**CONVERSION**

Bailed goods, 678.

Repossession by judicial action, 975–977.

Restrictive indorsements, 424–425.

Stolen and lost instruments, 499–509.
    Bearer paper, 506–507, 509.
    Collecting bank defendant, 502–505.
    Depositary bank defendant, 501–505, 507–508.
    Drawee defendants, 501–502, 508.
    Drawer suit, 500–501.
    Drawer versus collecting bank, 494.
    Restrictive indorsement, 507–508.
    Summary, 508–509.
    Theory, 499–500.

**COURSE OF DEALING**

Admissibility, 73–75, 86–87.

Contracts terms supplied by, 84–88.

Cure, 267–268.

Definition, 84, 369.

Disclaimer of implied warranty, 369–370.

Rejection, restriction, 256.

**COURSE OF PERFORMANCE**

Admissibility, 73–75, 86–87.

Contract terms supplied by, 84–88.

Cure, 267–268.

Defined, 84, 369–370.

Disclaimer of implied warranty, 369–370.

Modifying contract terms, 84–88.

Rejection,
    Reasonable time, 262–263.
    Restriction, 256.

**COVER**

Generally, 175–180.

Commercially reasonable, 177–178.

**COVERAGE OF ARTICLES**

See Scope of Articles.

**CREDITOR'S RIGHTS**

    See also Bulk Sales; Repossession; Secured Party's Remedies.

Against a purchaser of the collateral, 976–977.

Creditor defined, 656.

Creditor misbehavior, 995–1007.

Garnishment of wages, 963.

Judgment and execution, 963.

Judgment lien, 758.

Replevin, 974–977.

Repossession, 955–956, 966–977.

Rights in default, 954–956, 958–995.

Sheriff's sale, 964.

**CROPS**

Attachment of security interest, 793.

Priorities among secured creditors, 903, 922–924.

Where to file, 821.

**CURE**

Generally, 266–270.
Conditions, 266, 267.
Conforming tender, 269–270.
Consequences, 266.
Definition, 269–270.
Effective, 269–270.
Price, adjustment of, 259, 268, 269.
"Reasonable grounds to believe", 267–269.
Rejection, restriction, 256.

**DAMAGES**

See also Buyer's Remedies; Liquidated Damages; Remedies; Seller's Remedies.
Basic formula, 232, 233, 310–311.
Breach of warranty, Chapter ten.
Accepted-warranted differential, 307–311.
Formula, 307–311.
Measure of value, 308–310.
Special circumstances, 311.
Standard of measurement of value, 310–311.
Subjective-objective test of value, 310–311.
Buyer's remedies, 175–192.
Mutually exclusive, 306.
Commercially reasonable completion of goods, 238–241.
Computing with open price term, 99–100.
Consequential, 314–325.
Cover, 204.
Foreseeability test, 315–318.
Hadley v. Baxendale, 314–315, 316–317.
"Injury to person or property", 324.
Liability to third persons, 321.
Limitation of, 125, 376–377, 383–386, 392–396.
Lost profits, 317–318, 319, 321–323.
Mitigation, 204, 205–206, 323–324.
"Reason to know", 316–318.
Repair expenses, 320.
Required certainty, 321–323.
Summary, 324–325.
Tacit agreement test rejected, 316–318.
Types, 318–321.
Contract-market differential, 180–191, 220–225.
Expenses saved, 188–190, 221.
Improper resale of repossessed collateral, 997–999.
Incidental, 312–314.
Mitigation, 205–206.
Indefinite quantity term, 104.
Learned of the breach, 197–202.
Liability to third persons, 321.
Lost profits, 225–238, 317–318, 319, 321–323.
No privity defense, 333–335.
Market-contract differential, 180–191, 220–225.

**DAMAGES**—Cont'd

Market price, time to measure, 197–202.
Measure of rights of shipper against carrier, 721–726, 737–741.
Mitigation, 205–206.
Uncompleted goods, 240–241.
Modification, generally, 375–396.
Non-delivery, 220–225.
Proof of market price, 190.
Repair expenses, 320.
Repudiation, 220–225.
Resale of goods, 216–220.
Seller's,
Action for lost profits, 225–238.
Buyer insolvent, 241–245.
Lost profits formula, 234–238.
Tender of delivery, time and place, 184–188.
Time of performance, market price, 197–202.
Time to measure, 197–202.
Unconscionable contracts, 130–133.
Unconscionable limitation of, 377, 379, 383–386, 392–396.
Warehouseman's liability,
Consequential damages, 676–677.
Fair market value, 677–678.
Limitation by contract, 678–679.
Wrongful dishonor, 568–574.

**DEBTOR'S REMEDIES**

See also Federal Commercial Law; Unconscionability.
Creditor misbehavior,
Criminal liability, 995–996.
Liability under UCC, 997–999.
Tort liability, 996–997.
Denial of deficiency, 1000–1007.
Waiver, 980–981.

**DEFAULT**

Acceleration clauses, 958–961.
Creditor misbehavior, 995–1007.
Defined, 956–961.
Denial of deficiency, 1000–1007.
Fixtures, removal of, 930–931.
Repossession, 955–956, 961–962, 966–977.
Sale of pledged collateral, 754–755.
Transfer of the collateral, 977.

**DEFECTIVE GOODS**

See also Risk of Loss.
Action for the price, 213.
Damages after acceptance, Chapter ten.
Risk of loss, 146–150.
Term supplied by code, 91–92.
Tender of delivery, 96.
Value of, 309–310.

**DEFICIENCY JUDGMENT**

Burden of proof, 1002–1005, 1006.
Denial of, 1000–1007.
Precluded by breach of peace, 966.
Resale of repossessed cars, 982.

**DELIVERY TERMS**

Cash sale presumed by code, 95.

**DELIVERY TERMS—Cont'd**
Payment by check, conditional tender, 97–98.

Payment for goods, 95–98.

Supplied by code, 88–95.

**DEPOSITOR**
Deposit contract, 552–558.

**DESCRIPTION**
See Financing Statement; Security Agreement.

**DESTINATION CONTRACT**
Breach of tender requirements, 91.

Defined, 88, 90.

Distinguished from shipment contract, 90, 140–143.

Risk of loss, 140–141.

Tender of documents, 94.

**DISCHARGE**
Generally, 443–454.

Accommodation party, 429, 432–438.

Cancellation, 446–448.

"Full satisfaction", 452–454.

Payment, 444–446, 450–451.

Renunciation, 446–448.

Satisfaction to holder, 444–446, 450–451.

Stolen instrument, 444–445.

Suspension, 448–452.

Underlying obligation, 448–452.

**DISCLAIMER OF WARRANTY**
Generally, 349–375.

At time of delivery, 362–363.

Cumulation, 372–375.

Defense, 272, 286.

Definition, 383–384.

Drafting, 358, 359.

Express warranty, 351–356.
Conflict within written agreement, 352–353.

Merger clause, 354–356.

Oral warranties, 354–356.

Implied warranty, 356–375.
"As is" clauses, 364–366.

Conspicuousness, 359–361, 366.

Course of dealing, 369–370.

Course of performance, 369–370.

Disclaimer subsequent to contracting, 361–363.

Examination, 367–369.

Explicit disclaimer, 356–363.

Required language, 357–359.

Trade usage, 369–372.

Inconsistent, 372–375.

Limitation-of-remedy, compared, 383–384, 392–396.

Parol evidence rule, 354–355.

Preemption by 2–316, pp. 386–392, 394–396.

Security agreement, disclaimers in, 362.

Uncertainty of availability, 350.

Unconscionable, 125–127, 350, 356–358, 383–384, 386–396.

**DISCLAIMER OF WARRANTY—Cont'd**
Warranty against infringement, 303–305.

Warranty of title, 303–305.

Warranty versus strict tort, 350–351.

**DISHONOR**
Definition, 416.

Drawer liability prerequisite, 411–413.

Holder in due course, 458, 471.

Indorser liability prerequisite, 415–416.

Notice,
Drawer liability prerequisite, 411–413.

Indorser liability prerequisite, 415–416, 419.

Time and Manner, 419.

Wrongful, 566–574.
Actual damages, extent, 573–574.

Defined, 567–568.

Mistake/willful, 569–572.

Post-dated checks, 561.

Trader rule, 568, 569–573.

**DIVERSION**
See Carrier; Stoppage in Transit.

**DOCUMENTS OF TITLE**
See also Bill of Lading; Warehouse Receipts.

Generally, 601–603.

Defined, 668, 711.

Documentary draft, 610.

Goods, tender of delivery, 93–94.

Goods held by bailee, risk of loss, 144.

Holder of negotiable warehouse receipt, 681.

Non-negotiable,
Defined, 695.

Notice to bailee, 697.

Title to goods, 695–697.

Person entitled under document, 681.

**DRAFTING**
See also Contract Formation.

Disclaimer of warranty, 358–359.

Form books under UCC, 19.

Limitation of remedy, 383.

Merger clause, 356.

Risk of loss agreement, 135.

Sale of goods forms, 31–32.

UCC, "Introduction", 1–5.

**DRAFTS**
See also Checks.

Introduction, 398.

**DRAWER**
Accommodation party, 425–443.

"Collection guaranteed", 428.

Contractual liability, 411–413.

Duty to examine and report, 539–540.

Forged signature, 499, 519–529.

Introduction, 398.

Negligent,
Contribute to forgery or alteration, 520, 537–540.

Estopped, 519, 537, 539.

**DRAWER**—Cont'd

Negligent—Cont'd
Fictitious payees, 541–550.
Impostors, 541–550.
Non-sufficient funds check, 529, 530.
"Payment guaranteed", 428.
Stolen and lost instruments,
Conversion suit, 500–501.
Introduction, 492–495.
Liability, 496–498.
Rights against drawee, 498–499.
Warranty plaintiff, 513–514.

**ELECTION OF REMEDIES**

Buyer's damages formula, 190–191.
Creditor's alternatives upon default, 961–965.
Judicial sale, 965.
Seller's damages for breach, 222–225.

**ENTRUSTING**

See also Warehouseman.

**EQUIPMENT**

See also Classification of Property.
Equipment trust, 774.

**ESTOPPEL**

Drawer negligent, 519, 537, 539.
Equitable, statute of frauds exception, 48–49, 59–60.
Inconsistent warranties, 373.
Negotiable instruments, agent's signature, 402.
Payor bank negligent, 537.
Promissory estoppel, contract formation, 33–34.

**EVIDENCE**

See also Parol Evidence Rule.
Accommodation status, proof of, 429–432.
Admissibility,
Course of dealing, 73–75, 86–87.
Course of performance, 73–75, 86–87.
Oral agreement, 60–61.
Trade usage, 73–75, 86–87.
Basis of bargain, 279.
Burden of going forward, defense to warranty, 326–327.
Close-connectedness, 480–483.
Commercially unreasonable completion, 241.
Credibility of oral evidence, 63–65, 65–67.
Damages, proof of market price, 190.
Implied warranty of merchantability, 292, 295–296.
Lost profit damages, 237–238.
Negotiable instruments, agent signature, 407–408.
Oral,
Admissibility, with merger clause, 76–81.
Evidence of contract terms, 65–68.
Proof of,
Suretyship, 429–432.
Trade usage, course of performance, 87.

**EVIDENCE**—Cont'd

Proof of—Cont'd
Unconscionable price, 123–124.
"Representative capacity", 407–408.
Value,
Contract price, 309.
Cost of repair, 308.
Price quotations, 309.
Written terms preferred, 65–68.

**EXCUSE**

Notice of dishonor, 419–423.

**EXPRESS WARRANTY**

See also Implied Warranty of Merchantability.
Generally, 273–286.
Advertisements, 279–280, 281–282.
Basic case, 273–274.
Basis of bargain, 273, 276, 277–282, 283, 284.
Breach, 112–113.
Conditions, 273–274.
Creation, by disclaimer examination, 368–369.
Defense,
Assumption of risk, 272, 335–337, 338–339.
Contributory negligence, 272, 335–337, 338–339.
Failure to give notice, 272, 343–348.
Lack of privity, 272, 335.
Statute of limitations, 272, 286, 339–343.
Description cases, 273–274, 276–277.
Disclaimer, 351–356.
Fraud, distinguished, 272.
Implied warranty,
Contradicting, 72.
Inconsistent, 372–375.
Inconsistent, 372–375.
Misrepresentation, distinguished, 272.
Models, 282–286.
Opinion not guarantee, 274–275.
Post-agreement statements, 280–282.
Proof, burden of, 278–279, 282.
Puffing, 273, 274–275, 282.
Reliance, 275–276, 277–282.
Samples, 282–286.

**EXTENSION BY ANALOGY**

Implied warranty of merchantability, 286–289.
Resale of goods, notice, 97, 220.
Statute of frauds, 45–46.
Unconscionability in bank-customer relationship, 556.

**FACTORS**

"Factor's lien", 755–756.

**FARM PRODUCTS**

See also Classification of Property.
Where to file, 821.

**FEDERAL COMMERCIAL LAW**

Article seven, UCC, 670–671.
Article nine, UCC, 782–783.

**FEDERAL COMMERCIAL LAW**—C't'd
Bankruptcy, 864–898.
Bill of lading, 710–713, 714–716, 724–726, 729, 731–737, 739, 750, 753.
Bulk sales, 643, 656, 659–660, 662, 664–665.
Consumer Credit Protection Act, 996.
Federal Aviation Act, 948.
Rights of shipper against carrier, 714–716, 724–726, 729, 731–739, 741.
Ship Mortgage Act, 782–783.
Supercedes UCC, 6.

**FICTITIOUS PAYEE**
See Impostor.
Banker's provision, 549–550.
Indorsement effective, 541–542, 543.
Padded payroll, 542, 543–547, 549.
Scope, 543–547.

**FIELD WAREHOUSE**
See Warehouse receipts; Warehouse-man.

**FILING**
Classifying the collateral, 823–825.
First to file rule, 828.
Fixtures owned by tenant, 933–934.
In wrong place, 829–833.
Kinds of collateral, 820.
Not required for true leases, 759.
Notoriety test, 826–827.
Place of business, 825–829.
Places to file, 818–820.
Pure race statute, 906–907.
What to file, 833–846.

**FINANCE CHARGES**
See Retail Installment Sales.

**FINANCING STATEMENT**
See also Filing.
As a security agreement, 790–791.
Description of collateral, 787–788, 843–846.
Formal requisites, 833–846.
Installment sales, leases, 759–760.
Minor errors, 834–835.
Name requirements, 837–841.
Signature requirements, 835–837.
Where to file, 820–823.

**FIXTURES**
Construction mortgagee, 934–935, 936–938.
Definition of, 771–772, 924–926.
Landlord's liens, 934–935.
Meaning of term, "subsequent", 932–933.
Owned by tenant, 933–935.
Purchase money security interests, 927–931, 934, 936–938.
Repossession by secured creditor, 930–931.
Where to file, 821.

**FLOATING LIEN**
Attachment of security interest, 793–794.
Bankrupt debtor, 876–883.
Definition of, 877.
Entity theory, 879.
Pre-code problems, 756.
Priority upon buyer's insolvency, 245.
Substitution theory, 879–880.

**F.O.B. CONTRACT**
Defined, 88, 140–141.
Risk of loss, 140–144.
Seller's damages, 222.

**FORECLOSURE**
See Default; Repossession; Secured Party's Remedies.

**FORGERY**
Drawer negligent, 402, 520, 537–540.
Drawer's signature, 499, 519–529.
Negligent drawer estopped, 519, 537, 539.
Notice of defenses, 475.
Statute of frauds, 63–64.
Stolen and lost instruments, 492–518.

**FORMS**
Containing conflicting contract terms, "Battle of the Forms", 23–33, 35–36.
Drafting aids, 19.
Sale of goods, drafting strategy, 31–32.

**FRAUD**
See also Statute of Frauds.
Bulk sales, 641–642.
Defense, holder in due course, 487–488.
Discharge negotiable instruments, 448.
Merger clause limitation, 78–79.
Misrepresentation, 113.
Parol evidence rule, exception, 75.
Proof, 113.
Registration motor vehicle title, 859–862.
Rescission, cause of, 248–249.
Warranty, distinguished from misrepresentation, 272.

**FRAUDULENT CONVEYANCES**
See also Bankruptcy; Bulk Sales.
Uniform Fraudulent Conveyance Act, 893–897.

**FREEDOM OF CONTRACT**
See also Unconscionability.
Article seven, UCC, 669–670.
Express agreement, 82–83.
Limitations, 109–111.
Damage agreements, 110–111.
Good faith requirement, 109, 111.
Notice of contract breach, 110.
Remedies, 376.
Third party rights, 110, 111.
Unconscionability, 109.
Notice requirements, 345–346.
Preserved, 6–7.
Reasonable standards of performance, 111.
Sale of goods, 23–33.
Warranty avoidance, 349.

**FUTURE ADVANCES**
Priority conflicts, 907–909, 913.

**GARNISHMENT**
Account priority conflicts, 589–590, 591–592.

**GENERAL INTANGIBLES**
See also Classification of Property.
Application of article nine, 775–776.

**GOOD FAITH**
Acceleration clauses, 959–961.
Bank may not disclaim, 555.
Buyer in ordinary course, 940–942.
Close-connectedness, 480.
Contract modification, 41–42.
Cover, 177–178.
Disclaimer of warranty policing, 390–391.
Estoppel exception, statute of frauds, 60.
Filing in wrong place, 829–830.
Final payment, 522, 523, 524–525.
Holder in due course, 458, 471–477.
Merger clause, limitation, 79–80.
Misdelivery by warehouseman, 680.
Not disclaimable, 109, 111.
Reasonable price set by party, 101.
Requirements contracts, 105, 106–107, 108–109.
Resale of repossessed collateral, 1003.
Seller's resale damages, 225.
Stale checks, 563–564.
Unconscionability prohibited, 113.

**GOOD FAITH PURCHASER**
Bulk sales, 642, 661–662.
Fungible, 702–703.
Negotiable bills of lading, 742–749.
Seller "subject to" under 2–702, p. 243.

**GOODS**
See also Carrier.
Accepted, action for the price, 208–213.
Conforming,
  Revocation of acceptance, 212–213.
  Risk of loss, 148.
Cover, reasonable substitutes, 178–180.
Damaged or lost, action for the price, 213.
Defective, acceptance, 250, 251–253.
Defined, 45.
Identified,
  Completing manufacture, 215–216.
  Specific performance, 195–196.
In warehouseman's hands, 671–682.
Misdelivery by warehouseman, 679–682.
Misdescription of, warehouse receipts, 691–692.
Nonconforming,
  Risk of loss, 146–150.
  Tender of delivery, 96.
Not reasonably resalable, action for the price, 213–216.
Sale of, Article two, Chapter one.
Unique,
  Action for the price, 213–216.
  Specific performance, 192–194.
Vis-a-vis fixtures, 771, 924–926.

**HISTORICAL DEVELOPMENT**
Drafting the UCC, 1–5.
Prior drafts of UCC, 9–10.
Statute of frauds, 43–44.

**HOLDER IN DUE COURSE**
Generally, Chapter fourteen.
Accommodation party,
  Defenses, 441–443.
  Oral proof prevented, 430.
Bona fide purchaser, 456.
Close-connectedness, 479–484.
  Circumstances, 481–483.
  Theories, 480.
Conditions, 458.
Defense, stop-order payment, 580–588.
Definition, 458.
Final payment, 522, 526–527.
Good faith, 471–477.
Holder, 458–459.
  Legal consequences, 490–491.
Indorsement required, 414–415, 459, 496–497.
Instrument, 459–465.
  Defined, 459–460.
  Negotiable, 952–953.
  "Payable to order or to bearer", 464–465.
  "Unconditional promise", etc., 460–463.
Introduction, 456–457.
Legal consequences, 486–489.
Legislative limitations on doctrine, 484–486.
Letters of credit, 632.
Negotiability, 460–465.
Payee, 478–479, 523–524.
Personal defenses, 487, 489.
Policy, 457.
Real defenses, 487–489.
Retail installment contract attached, 463.
Stolen and lost instruments, 497, 506, 509.
Uniform Consumer Credit Code, 484–486.
Value, 465–471.
  Antecedent debt, 465, 466.
  Defined, 465.
  Depository banks, 467–471.
  Irrevocable commitment, 465, 466.
  Partial interest, 465, 466.
  Policy, 465–466.
"Without notice", 471–477.
  Classification of knowable facts, 471, 474–477.
  "Notice of a fact", 472–473.
  Notice to purchaser, 473.

**IDENTIFICATION**
Goods,
  Risk of loss, 149.
  Specific performance, 195–196.
Uncompleted, right to identify upon buyer's breach, 238–239.

## IMPLIED WARRANTY OF FITNESS

Generally, 296–299.
Conditions, 297.
Disclaimer, 356–375.
Express warranty inconsistent, 374–375.
Implied warranty of merchantability distinguished, 296–297.
Knowledge requirement, 297, 298–299.
Reliance requirement, 297, 298–299.
Typical case, 297–298.

## IMPLIED WARRANTY OF MERCHANTABILITY

Generally, 286–296.
Basic case, 286, 292, 295–296.
Causation, 295–296.
Defective goods, 290, 291–292.
Defense,
    Assumption of risk, 272, 335–337, 338–339.
    Contributory negligence, 272, 335–337, 338–339.
    Failure to give notice, 272, 343–348.
    Lack of privity, 272, 327–335.
    Statute of limitations, 272, 286, 339–343.
Definition, merchantability, 289–295.
Disclaimer, 356–375.
Express warranty inconsistent, 372–374.
Fit for ordinary purpose, 290–292, 293, 294.
Implied warranty of fitness distinguished, 296–297.
Merchant requirement, 286, 289.
Nonsale transactions, analogy, 286–289.
No-worse-than-anybody-else ethic, 290–292, 293.
Price, index of obligation, 294.
Proof, burden of, 286, 290, 292, 295–296.
Services, sale of, 287–289.
Standard, 290–295.
Strict tort liability,
    Compared, 328–329.
    Distinguished, 271, 286, 295.
Trade usage, 294.

## IMPOSSIBILITY OF PERFORMANCE

Repudiation, 171, 173–174.

## IMPOSTOR

See also Fictitious Payee.
Banker's provision, 549–550.
Indorsement effective, 541–542.
Scope, 543, 547–548, 549.

## INDEFINITE QUANTITY CONTRACTS

Generally, 103–109.

## INDORSEMENT AND INDORSERS

Accommodation party, generally, 425–443.
Blank, definition, 413.
"Collection guaranteed", 428, 430.
Contractual liability, generally, 413–425.
Conversion suits, 503.
Definition, 413.
Effective, 543.

## INDORSEMENT AND INDORSERS—Cont'd

Fictitious payee, 541–550.
Forged,
    Liability generally, 492–518.
    Warehouse receipts, 686–687.
Holder requirement, 416–417, 459, 496–497.
Impostor, 541–550.
Notice of dishonor,
    Excused, 419–423.
    Reasonable diligence, 423.
    Required for liability, 415–416, 419.
"Payment guaranteed", 428, 430.
Presentment,
    Excused, 419–423.
    Reasonable diligence, 423.
    Required for liability, 416–419.
"Properly payable", 559.
Qualified, 423–425.
Restrictive, 423–425.
    Conversion, 507–508.
Special,
    Definition, 413, 415.
    Effect, 415.
Stolen instrument suit, 454–455.
Surety, generally, 425–443.
"Without recourse", 423.

## INSOLVENCY

Bulk sales, 641.
Buyer's, seller's damages, 241–245.
Misrepresentation of solvency, 241, 242–243.
Notice of dishonor not excused, 422–423.
Presentment not excused, 422–423.

## INSPECTION

Consequential damages, foreseeability test, 315–318.
Contents of financing statement, 829–833.
Cure, 267, 268–269.
Customer death or incompetence, 565.
Disclaimer of warranty, examination, 368.
Goods,
    Acceptance, 250–251.
    Buyer's right of, 92–94.
    Withholding payment until, 96.
Implied warranty of fitness, 297, 298–299.
Merchant, definition, 289.
Notice, holder in due course, 471, 472–473, 474–477.
Of breach, 183.
    Damages, 197–202.
Priority conflicts, 902.
Warranty of title, extent of claim, 301–302.

## INSTALLMENT CONTRACTS

Definition, 258.
"Impairs value of whole", 258–259.
Installment sale as security interest, 759–765.

## INSTALLMENT CONTRACTS—Cont'd

Rejection, 256, 257–259.
  Single installment, 258.
Repudiation, 173.

## INSURANCE

  See also Contribution; Subrogation.
Sale of goods,
  Contribution, 161–166.
  "Other clauses", 163–166.
  Subrogation, 150–158.
    Collateral rights, 152, 154–158.
Shipper's insurance, 727–729.
Warranty, distinguished, 272.

## INTANGIBLES

See Classification of Property.

## INTERNATIONAL COMMERCIAL TRANSACTIONS

Letters of credit, 601–607, 614–615.

## INTERPRETATION OF CONTRACTS

Express warranty, sample or model, 285.
Indefinite quantity term, 103–109.
Merger clauses, limitation by construction, 81.
Open price term, 98–103.
Terms, 84–88.

## INVENTORY

  See also Bulk Sales; Floating Lien.
Definition of, 917–918.
Proceeds thereof, 910–911.
Purchase money security interest, 916–918.

## JUDGMENT AND EXECUTION

Secured creditor, 962–964.

## JUDGMENT LIEN

Bankruptcy, 889–892.
Non-applicability of Article nine, 757–758.

## KNOWLEDGE

  See also Notice.
Acceptance, defective goods, 251–253.
Account priority conflicts, 591.
Bulk sales, 649.
Buyer in ordinary course, 940.
Chattel paper, 949–950.
Consequential damages, foreseeability test, 315–318.
Contents of financing statement, 829–833.
Cure, 267, 268–269.
Customer death or incompetence, 565.
Disclaimer of warranty, examination, 368.
Implied warranty of fitness, 297, 298.
Merchant, definition, 289.
Notice, holder in due course, 471, 472–473, 474–477.
Of breach, 183.
  Damages, 197–202.
Priority conflicts, 901–902.
Warranty of title, extent of claim, 301–302.

## LEASES

As security agreement, 789–790.
As security interests, 759–765.
Economic realities test, 763–764.
Reservation of title, 760–762.
True leases, 760–762.

## LETTERS OF CREDIT

Basic variations, 605–606.
Beneficiary nonperformance, 630–632.
Clean bill of lading, 621.
Conflicts of laws problems, 612–614.
Conformity to underlying contract, 616.
Documentary draft defined, 610.
"Established", meaning of, 617–618.
Financing function, 605, 633–639.
Formal requirements, 615–616.
Holder in due course, 632.
Introduction, 601–607.
Invalid terms, 616–617.
Legal nature of, 607–608.
Parties, 604.
Payment function, 601–605, 618.
Payment procedure, 604–607, 618–620.
Relevant law,
  Domestic transactions, 609–614.
  International transactions, 614–615.
Transfer and assignment,
  Generally, 633–634.
  Issuance of second letter, 638–639.
  Proceeds as security, 636–638.
  Supplier *qua* beneficiary, 634–636.
Uniform customs and practice (UCP), 611–614.
Warranty of presentment, 632–633.
Wrongful dishonor,
  As affecting customer, 628–630, 631–632.
  As affecting issuer, 632–633.
  Compliance with terms, 620–623.
  Forged documents, 624–625.
  Fraud in transaction, 624, 625–626.
  General principle, 620.
  Non-performance of underlying obligation, 626.
  Recognized exceptions, 624–626.
  Remedies, 627–628.

## LIEN CREDITOR

Bankruptcy, 889–892.
Conflicts with secured creditor, 901–902.
Priority over consignor, 768.
Seller "subject to" under, 2–702, pp. 243–245.
Trustee in bankruptcy, 867–871.

## LIMITATION OF ACTION

  See also Statute of Limitations.
Remedies, 375–396.

## LIQUIDATED DAMAGES

  Generally, 375–396.
Penalty, 125.
Seller's lost profits, 233.
Unconscionable, 125.

## LLEWELLYN, KARL N.

Chief reporter UCC project, 3.

**LLEWELLYN, KARL N.**—Cont'd
Draft of Article nine, 754–756.
Principal draftsman articles one and two, 3.

**MERCHANT**
Definition, 289.
"Firm offer" rule, 33.
Good faith, cover, 177–178.
Implied warranty of merchantability requirement, 286, 289.
Offer and acceptance, conflicting contract terms, 23–33.
Risk of loss, goods received, 145–146.
Statute of frauds exception, 46–48.
Warranty against infringement requirement, 302.

**MERCHANTABILITY**
See Implied Warranty of Merchantability.

**MERGER CLAUSE**
See also Parol Evidence Rule.
Generally, 76–81.
Disclaimer of oral warranties, 354–356.
Final written expression of agreement, 76–78.
Parol evidence, admissibility, 69–71.
Limitations,
Bad faith, 79–80.
Fraud, 78–79.
Judicial construction, 81.
Mistake, 80–81.
Subsequent contract modification, 81.
Unconscionability, 80.
Sample, 76, 77.

**MISTAKE**
Merger clause limitation, 80–81.
Parol Evidence Rule, exception, 76.
Remedy for overreaching, 113.
Rescission, cause of, 248–249.
Wrongful dishonor, 566, 569–570.

**MODIFICATION OF CONTRACT**
Acceptance of defective goods, 252–253.
Accommodation party, effect on status, 432–437.
Express warranty, 280–282.

**MONEY**
Cash sale presumed for goods, 41.

**MOTOR VEHICLES**
See also Registration of Motor Vehicle Title.
Perfection in multiple state transactions, 855–862.
Resale of repossessed collateral, 982–983, 984.
Secured creditor versus purchaser, 946–948.

**NEGLIGENCE**
Contributory defense,
Strict tort liability, 335–337.
Warranty actions, 335–337, 338–339.
Depositary bank, fictitious payee, 548–549.

**NEGLIGENCE**—Cont'd
Fictitious payees, 541–550.
Final payment, 524–525.
Forged or altered instruments, 537–540.
Impostors, 541–550.
Of shipper, rights of shipper against carrier, 718–720.
Risk of loss, 149–150.
Warehouseman's liability, 672–676.
Warranty, similarity of proof, 272, 286.

**NEGOTIABILITY**
Bill of lading, 713, 741–742.
Chattel paper, 952.
Letters of credit, 608.
"Payable to order or to bearer", 464–465.
Requirements, 398–399, 460–465.
"Unconditional promise", etc., 460–463.
Warehouse receipts,
Generally, 682–694.
Indorsement, 686–687.
Legal significance, 684–697.
Thief, 687.

**NEW VALUE**
Antecedent debt, 874.
Buyer in ordinary course, 940.
Chattel paper, 949–950.
Voidable preference, 878, 881.

**NOTICE**
See also Knowledge.
Acceptance, nonconforming goods, 343–348.
Account priority conflicts, 591, 593.
Address requirements in financing statement, 842–843.
Breach of contract, 110, 183–184.
Breach of warranty, damages requirement, 306.
Bulk sales law, 643–644, 651–653.
Burden of proof, defense to warranty, 327.
Consignments, 765–769.
Cure, seasonable, 266.
Defense, warranty stolen and altered instruments, 515, 517.
Deficiency judgment, 1002–1003, 1004.
Failure to give,
Defense, 343–348.
Resale, 224.
Filing, 907.
Financing statement, 833–846.
Holder in due course, defenses, 458, 471–477.
Implied warranty of merchantability, 286.
Letters of credit, assignment of proceeds, 636–637.
Meaning of "send", 985.
Negotiable warehouse receipts, 684.
Notice race statute, 831.
Of a fact, 472–473.
Of dishonor,
Drawer liability a prerequisite, 411–413.

**NOTICE**—Cont'd

Of dishonor—Cont'd

Excused, 419–423.

Indorser liability prerequisite, 415–416, 419.

Reasonable diligence, 423.

Time and manner, 419.

Purchase money security in inventory, 917–918, 919–920.

Purchasers of instruments and documents, 952–953.

Reasonable time, 343–345.

Rejection, 264, 265.

Resale of repossessed collateral, 982–983, 983–987.

Revocation of acceptance, 265.

Security agreement, 788, 789.

Seller's resale, 217.

Strict foreclosure, 979–980.

Sufficiency, 347–348.

Third party suits, 346–347.

To bailee, non-negotiable documents, 697.

"To purchaser", 473.

To third party creditors, 824–825.

**OFFER AND ACCEPTANCE**

See also Contract Formation.

"Battle of the Forms", 23–33, 35–36.

"Counteroffer" becomes acceptance, 24.

Contract formation, 22.

"Firm offer" by merchant, 33–34.

Methods of acceptance, 34–36.

Nonconforming goods, 35.

Performance, 35.

Reasonable medium when not specified, 34–35.

Shipment of conforming goods, 35.

"Unilateral Contract Trick" curtailed, 35.

Nonaccepting answers, 32.

Oral agreements, 30–31.

Unaccepted offer lapsed, 35.

Unilateral contracts, performance as acceptance, 35.

**OPEN PRICE TERM**

Supplied by code, 98–103.

**OUTPUT CONTRACTS**

See also Requirements Contracts.

Specific performance, 193–194.

**PAROL EVIDENCE RULE**

See also Merger Clause.

Generally, Chapter two.

Accommodation party, 430–432.

Agreement, final written expression, 66, 68–69.

Article two version, 66.

Burden of proof, completeness of agreement, 60, 69.

Contradictory terms, admissibility of extrinsic evidence, 69–73.

Creation of a security interest, 759.

Defenses to warranty actions, 326.

Disclaimer of oral warranties, 354–355.

**PAROL EVIDENCE RULE**—Cont'd

Explaining or supplementing evidence, 72–75.

Fraud exception, 75.

Merger clause,

Generally, 76–81.

Admissibility of oral evidence, 69–71.

Mistake, 76.

Negotiable instruments, agent signature, 404, 406–408.

"Representative capacity", 404, 406–408.

Security agreement, 788.

Suretyship, 430–432.

Writing, "Complete and exclusive" expression, 69–70.

Written terms preferred? 65–68.

**PASSAGE OF TITLE**

Risk of loss, Uniform Sales Act, 135–136.

**PAYEE**

Fictitious, 541–550.

Holder in due course, 478–479, 523–524.

Impostor, 541–550.

Introduction, 398.

Stolen and lost instruments, 494, 496–498, 503.

Stolen instrument, 454–455.

**PAYMENT**

Cash sale presumed for goods, 95.

Check, conditional tender, 97–98.

Discharge of instrument, 444–446, 450–451.

Final,

"Accountable for", 525–529.

Cash over counter, 531–532.

Clearing house rule, 533–534.

Completed process of posting, 531, 534–536.

Defense to restitution action, 523–524.

Midnight deadline, 531, 533–534.

Negligence of holder, 524–525.

Not bar recovery on stop order, 586.

Reliance, 523, 524, 526–527.

Settled without reservation, 531, 532–533.

Nonconforming goods tendered, 96.

Opportunity to inspect goods, 92–94.

Payor bank, condition to restitution, 523.

Sale of goods,

Place, 95–97.

Time, 95–97.

Terms supplied by code, 95–103.

**PAYOR BANK**

See also Banks.

Acceptance, 410–411, 520.

"Accountable for", 525–529.

Bank check, 578–580.

Cashier check, 578–580.

Certification, 411.

Certified checks, 564, 578–580.

Contractual liability as acceptor, 410–411.

Contractual liability before acceptance, 410.

**PAYOR BANK**—Cont'd
Deposit contract, 552–558.
Estoppel, negligence, 537.
Final payment, 522, 523–525, 529, 530–537.
Forged drawer signature, 519–529.
  Discovery before final payment, 520.
  Final payment prerequisite to liability, 522–523.
  Legal consequences of payment, 520.
  Liable to drawer, 520.
  Restitution action, 521–529.
Non-sufficient funds check, 529, 530.
Priority conflicts, 588–600.
  Cash payment, 594.
  Certification, 594.
  Completed posting process, 597–600.
  Death or incompetency, 564–566, 589.
  Decision to pay, 597–600.
  Legal process, 589–592.
  Settlement, 594–597.
  Stop-order, 574–588, 589.
  Timing of the "Legals", 591–594.
Properly payable, 498–499, 520, 558–566.
  Altered check, 559.
  Customer adjudicated incompetent, 564–566.
  Customer dead, 564–566.
  Drawer signature incorrect, 559.
  Overdrafts, 562.
  Post-dated checks, 560–562.
  Stale checks, 562–564.
Restrictive indorsements, 424–425.
Stolen and lost instruments,
  Conversion defendant, 501–502.
  Introduction, 492–495.
  Liability to drawer, 498–499.
  Warranty suits, 509–517.
Stop-order, 574–588.
  After customer dead, 566.
  Burden on customer, 582–583.
  Certified checks, 564, 578–580.
  Disclaimableness, 554, 555, 556–557.
  Form, 576–578.
  Liability, 580–588.
  Re-credit obligation, 582–588.
  Subrogation, 580–588.
  Theory, 575.
  Who may issue, 575–576.
  Wrongful dishonor liability, 566–574.

**PERFECTION, AUTOMATIC**
Assignment of accounts and contract rights, 805–809.
Bankrupt debtor, 868–869.
Consumer goods, 797–805.
"Day loans" to stock brokers, 809–810.
Farm equipment, 797–805.
Negotiable instruments and documents, 701, 810–813.
Warehouse receipts, 812–813.

**PERFECTION BY FILING**
See also Filing.
Classifying the collateral, 820, 823–825.
Field warehousing, 708–709.

**PERFECTION BY FILING**—Cont'd
Financing statement, nature of, 796–797.
First to file rule, 828.
Fixtures, 927–931.
In wrong place, 829–833.
Motor vehicle registration, 946–948.
Multiple state transactions, 846–862.
Negotiable documents, 698–699, 702.
Notice race statute, 831.
Peskind's law, 863.
Place of business, 825–829.
Places to file, 818–820.
Priorities, 903–923.
Pure race statute, 905–907.
What to file, 833–846.
When to file, 820–823.

**PERFECTION BY POSSESSION**
Generally, 814–818.
Need for, 814–815.
Negotiable documents, 698–699, 702.
Priority conflicts, 817.

**PLEADING**
Buyer's insolvency, 241.
Signatures, instruments, 491.
Statute of frauds, 60.
Stop-order disobeyed, 584.

**PLEDGE**
Generally, 814–818.
Bill of lading, 750–753.
Definition of, 754–755.
Warehouse receipts,
  Field warehousing, 704–709.
  Fungible goods, 702–703.
  Negotiable, 699–703.
  Non-negotiable, 703–704, 707–709.

**POSSESSION**
See also Perfection by Possession; Pledge.
Article Two, security interest, 781.
Collateral, 786–787.
Definition, 816–817.
Perfection by, 698–699, 702, 814–818.
Risk of loss,
  Goods held by bailee, 144–145.
  Goods received, 145–146.
Seller's right to retain goods, 96.

**PREFERENCES**
See Bankruptcy.

**PRESENTMENT**
Dishonor prerequisite, 416–417.
Excused, 419–423.
Indorser liability requirement, 416–419.
Methods, 418–419.
Reasonable diligence, 423.
Warranties, 509–517.

**PRICE**
See also Damages; Remedies.
Action for the, 208–216.
Cure, method of, 259, 268, 269.
Fair market price, 100–103.

**PRICE**—Cont'd

Implied warranty of merchantability, index of obligation, 294.

Methods of fixing, 98–103.

Reasonable, 99, 100–102.

Resale of repossessed collateral, 987–991.

Resale reasonable, 213–215.

Term supplied by code, for goods, 98–103.

Unconscionable remedy, 131–133.

Unconscionably excessive, 120–124.

**PRIORITIES**

Accounts, 921.

Article two security interests, 781.

Attachment, 911.

Basic priorities among secured creditors, 903–913.

Bulk sales, 661–662.

Conflicts between purchasers and secured creditors, 944–946.

Crops, 903, 922–924.

Fixtures, 924, 927–938.

Perfection in multiple state transactions, 848–852.

Purchase money security interest, 903–904, 910, 913–922.

Purchasers of goods, 938–948.

Pure race statute, 905–907.

Rule of Moore v. Bay, 890–891, 895.

Secured creditor vis-a-vis unsecured creditor, 901–902.

Security interests in personal property, 899–953.

Shelter principle, 900–901.

Trustee in bankruptcy, 864–898.

**PRIVATE SALE**

Notice requirement, 983–987.

Seller's remedy, 216–218.

Solicitation of bidders, 993–994.

**PRIVITY OF CONTRACT**

Defense, warranty actions, 327–335.
  Economic loss, 332, 333–335.
  Express, 280, 335.
  Personal injury, 329, 330–332.
  Property damage, 332–333.

Definition, 327–328.

Economic loss cases, 332, 333–335.

Express warranty, 280, 335.

Personal injury cases, 329, 330–331.

Property damage cases, 332–333.

Strict tort liability, non-privity plaintiffs, 328–331, 333.

Warranty versus tort, 328–329.

**PROCEEDS**

Accounts, 921.

Bank accounts, 885–886.

Chattel paper, 949–952.

Floating liens and bankruptcy, 877–880.

Identifiable, definition of, 884–885.

Letters of credit, transfer and assignment, 636–638.

**PROCEEDS**—Cont'd

Non-identifiable, 886–888.

Priority conflicts, 908–913.

Security interest in, 883–888.

Voidable preference, 887.

**PRODUCTS LIABILITY**

See also Strict Tort Liability.

Warranty actions, 328–335.

**PROMISSORY NOTE**

Altered, warranty, 514.

Contractual liability of maker, 408–410.

Discharge, generally, 443–454.

Final payment, 522, 523–525, 529, 530–537.

Introduction, 397–398.

Maker's liability, 408–410.

Stolen and lost, negotiable, 492–518.
  Conversion, 509–517.
  Introduction, 492–495.
  Maker's liability, 496–498.
  Uniform Consumer Credit Code, 484–
  Warranty liability, 509–517.
    486.

**PROSPECTIVE INABILITY TO PERFORM**

See Impossibility of Performance.

**PUBLIC SALE**

Notice requirement, 983–987.

Seller's remedy, 216–218.

Vis-a-vis private sale, 992–993.

**PURCHASE MONEY SECURITY INTEREST**

Auomatic perfection, 797–805.

Cross-collateral provisions, 914.

Definition of, 914–915.

"Enabling" requirement, 915–916.

Fixtures, 927–931, 934, 936–938.

Identification of, 799–800.

Inventory, 916–918.

Non-inventory collateral, 918–922.

Notice, 917–918, 919–920.

Priorities, 903–904, 910, 913–922.

Proration of purchase price, 800–802.

**PURCHASERS**

See also Bill of Lading.

Buyer in ordinary course, 940–943.

Chattel paper and non-negotiable instruments, 949–952.

Conflicts with secured creditors, 944–946.

Consumer goods, 943–944.

Holder in due course, close-connectedness, 479–484.

Motor vehicles, 946–948.

Security interests, 940–953.

Warehouse receipts,
  Negotiable, 682–694.
  Non-negotiable, 694–697.

**QUANTITY**

See Indefinite Quantity Contracts; Requirements Contracts.

**REAL ESTATE INTERESTS**
Application of Article Nine, 771–773.
Fixtures, 924–938.
Landlord's lien, 773, 934–935.
Not covered by UCC, 5.
Oil, gas, timber, minerals, 772–773.
Security interests in crops, 722.

**REASONABLE TIME**
Acceptance, time to inspect, 250.
Account priority conflicts, 593–594.
Action for price, risk of loss passed, 213.
Cover, 178.
Cure, 266.
Delivery, 89.
Notice, after acceptance, 343–345.
Presentment, 417–418.
Rejection, 260–264.
Revocation of acceptance, 260–264.
Risk of loss,
    After repudiation or buyer's breach, 149.
    Presenting document of title to bailee, 144.
Specific performance, anticipatory repudiation, 198–199.
Waiting for repudiator's performance, 202–206.
Warranty, stolen and altered instruments, 515–517.

**RECEIPT OF GOODS**
See Revocation of Acceptance.

**RECEIVABLES FINANCING**
See Accounts.

**RECORDING**
See Financing Statement; Notice; Security Interest.

**REGISTRATION OF MOTOR VEHICLE TITLE**
Conflicts between purchasers and secured creditors, 946–948.
Fraud, 859–862.
In lieu of filing, 820.
Perfection in multiple state transactions, 855–862.

**REJECTION OF GOODS**
See also Revocation of Acceptance.
Generally, 253–266.
Action for the price, 210–213.
Commercial units, 265.
Conditions, 254.
Damages after acceptance mutually exclusive, 306.
Definition, 247.
Duty afterwards, 265.
Effective, 210–212.
Ineffective, 251, 264–265.
Installment contract, 256, 257–259.
Material breach, analogy, 257–258.
Nonconforming goods, 92.
Nonconformity, substantiality of, 256–258.
Notice, seasonable, 265.

**REJECTION OF GOODS—Cont'd**
Perfect tender rule, 256–257.
Procedure, 264–266.
Rescission, distinguished, 246, 248–249.
Risk of loss, right of rejection, 146–149.
Self-help remedy, 246–247.
Substituted method, of tender, 95.
Time, reasonable, 260–264.
Writing, advisability of, 265.
Wrongful, 264–265.

**REMEDIES**
See also Breach of Contract; Buyer's Remedies; Creditor's Rights; Damages; Debtor's Remedies; Secured Party's Remedies; Seller's Remedies.
Action for the price, 208–216.
Basic principles, 178.
Bulk sales law, 653–666.
Buyer insolvent, 241–245.
Buyer's, Chapter six.
    Limitation of, 376–386, 392–396.
Contract, market differential, 180–191.
Cover, damage formula, 175–180.
Incidental damages, 312–314.
Letters of credit, 619, 627–628, 631–632.
Matching performance, 178.
Minimum adequate requirement, 379–382.
Mitigating damages, 205–206.
Modification, generally, 375–396.
Oral agreement, unenforceable, 61–63.
Person entitled under negotiable document, 681.
Policing seller's choice, 224–225.
Reasonable time, waiting for performance, 202–206.
Relationship between seller's remedies, 222–225.
Seller's,
    Action for lost profits, 225–238.
    Lost profits formula, 234–238.
Specific performance, 192–196.
Suspending performance, 205.
Unconscionability, 130–133.
Warranty of title, breach, 302.

**REPLEVIN**
Outlawed, 974.
Repossession by judicial action, 975–977.

**REPOSSESSION**
Breach of peace, 964, 966–975.
Creditor misbehavior, 995–1007.
Debtor's consent, 969–970.
Due process, 974–975.
Fixtures, 930–931.
Judicial action, 975–977.
Resale,
    In general, 981–983.
    "Commercially reasonable," 982–983, 987–995.
    Notice requirement, 983–987.
Self-help, 966–975.
Third party consent, 970–971.
Unconscionable creditor conduct, 125.

**REPUDIATION**
See also Anticipatory Repudiation.
Damages, seller's right, 220–225.
Defined, 170–174.
Impossibility of performance, 171.
Intent, 171.
Reasonable time waiting for performance, 202–206.
Retraction, 174–175.
Risk of loss, 149.

**REQUIREMENTS CONTRACTS**
Generally, 103–109.
Good faith, 105, 106–107, 108–109.

**RESCISSION**
Grounds for,
Fraud, 75, 248–249.
Mistake, 248–249.
Rejection distinguished, 246, 248–249.
Revocation distinguished, 246, 248–249.

**RESTITUTION**
Letters of credit, 632–633.
Oral agreement, enforcing, 61–63.
Payor bank, faked drawer signature, 521–529.

**RETAIL INSTALLMENT SALES**
Non-negotiable, 399, 463.
Notice of defenses, 475–476.
Purchase money security interests, 800–802.
Unconscionability, 801–802.

**REVOCATION OF ACCEPTANCE**
See also Rejection of Goods.
Generally, 253–266.
Action for the price, 210–213.
Assurances, 264.
Commercial units, 265.
Conditions, 254–255.
Cover, 175.
Damages after acceptance mutually exclusive, 306.
Duty afterwards, 266.
Effective, 210–212.
Material breach analogy, 259–260.
Nonconformity, substantiality of, 259–260.
Notice, seasonable, 265.
Policy, 253–254.
Procedure, 264–266.
Rescission, distinguished, 246, 248–249.
Risk of loss, 149.
Self-help remedy, 247.
Standards, 260.
Time, reasonable, 260–264.
Writing, advisability of, 265.
Wrongful, 211–213.

**RISK OF LOSS**
Generally, Chapter five.
Allocation to insurable party, 138.
Breach of contract consequences, 146–150.
Buyer repudiates, 149.
Contribution, 161–166.

**RISK OF LOSS**—Cont'd
Damage formula, time and place of tender, 185–187.
Defective goods, 147–149.
Defined, 134.
Destination contract, 140–143.
Fault, 149–150.
F.O.B. contracts, 140–143.
Goods held by bailee, 144–145.
Negligence, 149–150.
Revocation of acceptance, 149.
Shipment contract, 140–143.
Subrogation, 150–158.
Terms supplied by code, 91–92.
Theory, 134–140.

**SALE OF GOODS**
Defined, scope of Article Two, 21–23.
Negotiable instruments, underlying obligation, 398, 400.

**SALE ON APPROVAL**
See also Consignment.
As security interest, 766–768.

**SALE OR RETURN**
See also Consignment.
As security interest, 766–768.

**SCOPE OF ARTICLES**
Generally, 754, 756, 757.
Article Two,
Sale of goods, 21–23.
Security interests, 780–781.
Article Five, 609–615, 620, 626.
Article Six, 644–649, 656.
Article Seven, 668–671, 711–713, 715, 748–749, 753.
Article Nine,
Assignment of accounts and contract rights, 806–807.
Chattel paper, 775–778.
Conflict of laws problems, 778–780.
Conflicts between purchasers and secured creditors, 944–946.
Conflicts with state law, 783–784.
Consignments, 765–769.
Contract rights, 775–778.
Crops, 772.
Exclusions, 773–774.
Federal commercial law, 782–783, 864–898.
Fixtures, 771–772, 773, 927–938.
General intangible, 775–776.
Landlord's liens and fixtures, 773, 934–935.
Patents, copyrights, 775–776.
Proposed changes, fixtures, 931–932, 935–938.
Purchasers of instruments and documents, 952–953.
Real estate interests, 771–773, 922–924, 927.
Right of set-off, 774.
Sales of accounts, 775–778.
Bill of lading, 711–713, 748–749, 753.
Bulk sales, 656.

**SCOPE OF ARTICLES**—Cont'd

Comments, unofficial but illuminating, 11–13.
Conflicts between purchasers and secured creditors, 944–946.
Constitutional law, 974–975.
Documents of title, security interests, 698–699.
Field warehousing, 708–709.
Freedom of contract, 669–670.
Letters of credit, 609, 611–612, 636–638.
Negotiable documents, 952–953.
Purchaser of a security, 952–953.
Security interest in bills of lading, 752–753.
Security interests in aircraft, 948.
Statute of frauds, 44–46.
Transactions not covered, 5–6.
Warehouse receipts, 671.

**SECURED CREDITOR**

See also Creditor's Rights; Secured Party's Remedies; Security Interest.
Bulk sales law, 656.
Conflicts with purchasers, 944–946.
Creditor misbehavior, 995–1007.
Denial of deficiency, 1000–1007.
Fixtures, 927–938.
Priorities among, 903–922.
Rights in default, 954–956, 958–995.
Strict foreclosure, 977–980.
Subordinate to purchasers of goods, 938–948.
Versus trustee in bankruptcy, 864–898.
Vis-a-vis unsecured creditor, 901–902.

**SECURED PARTY'S REMEDIES**

See also Creditor's Rights; Default; Repossession.
Against a purchaser of the collateral, 976–977.
Denial of deficiency, 1000–1007.
Election of remedies, 964–965.
Priority upon buyer's insolvency, 243–244, 245.
Replevin, 974–977.
Resale of repossessed collateral, 981–983.
Rights in default, 954–956, 958–995.
Strict foreclosure, 977–981.

**SECURITY AGREEMENT**

As a financing statement, 834.
As collateral, chattel paper, 949.
Default clauses, 956–961.
Description of the collateral, 787–789.
Disclaimer of warranty, 362.
Signature requirement, 787.
Unconscionable, cross-collateral clause, 117–118.

**SECURITY INTEREST**

See also Financing Statement; Pledge; Priorities; Repossession.
Actual fraud, 895.

**SECURITY INTEREST**—Cont'd

Aircraft, 946, 948.
Attachment, 791–795.
Automatic perfection, 797–813.
Bank accounts, 885–886.
Bankruptcy, fraudulent conveyance, 892–897.
Buyer in ordinary course, 940–943.
Chattel paper, 949–952.
Conflict of laws problems, 778–780.
Consignments, 765–769.
Consumer goods, 797–805, 943–944.
Creation and perfection, 785–863.
Crops, 772, 903, 922–924.
Debtor's rights in collateral, 791–796.
Default and its consequences, 954–1007.
Definition of, 757.
Enforceability, 795–796.
"Factor's lien", 755–796.
Farm equipment, 798–805.
Federal commercial law, 782–783.
Financing statement, contents of, 833–845.
Fixtures, 771–773, 924–938.
Good faith purchaser, bills of lading, 748–749.
Landlord's lien, 773.
Leases, 759–765.
Letters of credit, assignment of proceeds, 636–638.
Mortgages, 773.
Motor vehicles, 946–948.
Multiple state transactions, 846–862.
"Negative pledge", 758.
Negotiable documents and instruments, 687, 809–813.
Oil, gas, timber, minerals, 772–773.
Perfection by filing, 818–863.
Perfection by possession, 814–818.
Pre-code devices, 754–756.
Priority conflicts, 899–953.
Proceeds, 883–888.
Purchasers of goods, 938–948.
Realty, 771–773.
Rejected goods, 266.
Revoked goods, 266.
Security agreement, 876.
Sham debts, 897–898.
Shelter principle, 900–901.
Temporary perfection in documents, 701, 752–753, 809–813.
"Trust receipt", 755.
Types of collateral, 756.
Under article two, 780–781.
Uniform Fraudulent Conveyance Act, 893–897.
Value, 791–796.
Warehouse receipts, 697–699, 812–813.
Warranty of title breach, 299–300.

**SELLER OF GOODS**

As bailee of goods sold, 144–145.
Buyer in ordinary course, 940–941.
Delivery terms option, 88–95.
Retaining control of shipped goods, 93, 96–97.

**SELLER'S REMEDIES**
See also Buyer's Remedies; Damages; Remedies.
Generally, chapter 7.
Action for the price, 208–216.
  Accepted goods, 210–213.
  Damaged or lost goods, 213.
  Goods not reasonably resalable, 213–216.
Allowance for overhead, 235–236.
Alternative responses to repudiation, 207.
"As good a position as performance", 229–233.
Buyer's insolvency, 241–245.
  Bank as claimant, 243.
  Misrepresentation of solvency, 241, 242–243.
  "Subject to", 243–245.
  Ten day demand, 241, 242.
Components and jobber sellers, 227–229, 236–237.
Contract-market differential, 220–225.
Damage formula under 2–708(2), pp. 234–238.
"Due allowance for costs reasonably incurred," 236.
"Due credit", 230–231, 234–236.
Inadequate under 2–708(1), pp. 229–232.
Jobbers and components sellers, 227–229, 236–237.
Lost profits, 225–238.
  Components and jobber sellers, 227–229, 236–237.
  Damage formula, 234–238.
  Inadequate under 2–708(1), pp. 229–232.
  Jobbers and components sellers, 227–229, 236–237.
  Lost volume seller, 226–227, 234–236.
  Overcompensation under 2–708(1), pp. 232–233.
  Overhead, 235–236.
Lost volume seller, 226–227, 234–236.
Mitigating damages, 215–216.
Overcompensation under 2–708(1), pp. 232–233.
Policing seller's choice, 224–225.
Private sale, 216–218.
Public sale, 216–218.
Relationship between, 222–225.
Resale, good faith requirement, 225.
Resale rights, 216–220.
  Commercially reasonable, 217, 218.
Standard priced goods, 226–227.
Unidentified and incomplete goods,
  Generally, 238–241.
  Commercially reasonable completion, 218–241.

**SET-OFF**
Account priority conflicts, 589.
Deficiency judgment, 1004–1006.

**SHIPMENT**
Rights of shipper against carrier, see Carrier.

**SHIPMENT CONTRACT**
Breach of tender requirement, 91.
Defined, 88, 90.
Distinguished from destination contract, 90, 140–141.
Presumed unless otherwise agreed, 141.
Risk of loss, 140–141.
Tender of documents, 93–94.

**SIGHT DRAFT**
See also Checks.
Bill of lading, 742, 752.
"Documentary sales", 93–94.
Meaning and use of, 601–603.

**SIGNATURES**
See also Financing Statement; Security Agreement.
Accommodation party, 429–430.
Definition, 400.
Drawer, forged, 499, 519–529.
Effective, impostor, 541–542.
Financing statement, 835–837.
Instruments,
  Burden of proof, 491.
  Pleadings, 491.
Negotiable instruments,
  Personal liability of agent, 403–406.
  Principal's liability for agent, 400–406.
  "Representative capacity", 403–405, 408.
  Required, 399–400.
  Unauthorized, 400–403.
Properly payable, 559.
Security agreement, 787.
Statute of frauds, 46–47, 51.
Surety, 429–430.
Unauthorized, drawer negligence, 402, 520, 537–540.

**SPECIFIC PERFORMANCE**
Anticipatory repudiation, 197.
Buyer's remedy, 192–196.
Goods "identified" to contract, 195.
Insolvent seller, 195.
Output contract, 193, 194.
Unavailable, unconscionability, 130.

**STATUTE OF FRAUDS**
Generally, Chapter two.
Burden of proof, 60.
Confirming oral agreement, 30–31, 51–52.
Consequences, 49–50.
Contract modification, 46.
Evaluation, 63–65.
Evidence, oral agreements, 60–61.
Exceptions, 47–49, 54–60.
  Admission of party exception, 48, 57–58.
  Equitable estoppel, common law, 48–49, 59–60.
  Merchant after reasonable conformation, 47–48, 54–55.
  Performance accepted exception, 48, 58.
  Specially manufactured goods, 48.
Extension by analogy, 45–46.

References are to Pages

**STATUTE OF FRAUDS**—Cont'd
Oral agreement,
  Confirming memo, 47–48.
  Enforcing restitution, 61–63.
Pleading, 60.
Quantity term limitation, 54.
Sale of personal property, 46.
Scope, 44–46.
Security agreement, 787–788.
Signature requirement, 46–47, 51.
Terms of agreement, 51–54.
Writing requirement, 46–47, 51–54.

**STATUTE OF LIMITATIONS**
Generally, 339–343.
Bulk sales, 656–657.
Defense to warranty suit, 272, 286, 339–343.
Prospective warranties, 341–342.
Trustee in bankruptcy versus secured creditor, 898.
Warranty versus tort, 339–340, 341.

**STATUTORY LIENS**
Non-applicability of Article Nine, 758.
Pledgee of negotiable receipts, 702.

**STOPPAGE IN TRANSIT**
Rights of shipper against carrier, 734.

**STRICT FORECLOSURE**
Notice requirements, 978, 979–980.
Use and advantages of, 977–981.

**STRICT TORT LIABILITY**
See also Products Liability.
Disclaimer, 350–351.
Implied warranty of merchantability, distinguished, 271, 286, 295.
Non-privity plaintiffs, 328–335.
Notice not required, 345.
Personal injury, 329–330, 331.
Plaintiff's contributory behavior, defense, 335–337.
Rights of shipper against carrier, 714–716, 724, 728, 729–730, 731–732, 737, 748.
Statute of limitations, UCC does not apply, 339–340, 341.
Warehouseman's liability, 674, 708.

**SUBORDINATION**
See also Priorities.
Not creating a security interest, 758.

**SUBROGATION**
Accommodation party, 438–440.
Banks, post-dated checks, 561–562.
Collateral rights, 152, 154–156, 157–158.
Payor bank, stop-order paid, 580–588.
Rights of surety, 769–771.
Risk of loss, 150–161.
  Limitations, 67–68.
Trustee as subrogee of creditors, 893.

**SUBSTANTIAL PERFORMANCE**
See Rejection of Goods; Revocation of Acceptance.

**SURETY BONDS**
See Suretyship.

**SURETYSHIP**
See also Accommodation Parties.
Generally, 425–443.
Defenses, 432–435, 440–443.
Description of basic obligation, 425–429.
Establishing status, 429–432.
Letters of credit, 608.
Not security interest, 769–770.
Signature and symbols, 429–430.
Subrogation rights, 769–771.

**TEMPORARY PERFECTION**
See also Perfection, Automatic.
Negotiable instruments and documents, 701, 752–753, 809–813.

**TENDER OF DELIVERY**
"Documentary sales", 93–94.
Documents covering goods, 93–94.
Excused, 95.
Measure of damages, 220–222.
Nonconforming goods, 96.
Place and time, damages formula, 184–188.
Statute of limitations, 341.
Terms supplied by code, 88–95.

**THIEF**
Contract modification, extortion trick, 40–41.
Conversion, bearer instruments, 506–507, 509.
Discharge of stolen instrument, 444–445.
General liability, stolen and lost instruments, 492–495.
Warehouse receipts, 687.

**THIRD PARTY BENEFICIARY**
Letters of credit, 607.

**TITLE TO GOODS**
See also Documents of Title; Passage of Title.
Acceptance, 249.
Common law supplements UCC, 6.
Negotiable bill of lading, 742.
Negotiable warehouse receipts, 684–688.
Non-negotiable documents, 695–697.
Risk of loss, Uniform Sales Act, 135–137.
Straight bill of lading, 749.
Warranty of, 299–305.

**TORT LAW**
See also Strict Tort Liability.
Creditor misbehavior, repossession, 996–997.
Repossession, 966–974.
Wrongfully inducing another to contract, 113.

**TRADE USAGE**
Admissibility, 73–75, 86–87.
Contract terms supplied by, 84–88.
Cure, 267–268, 269.
Defined, 84, 369.

**TRADE USAGE**—Cont'd
Disclaimer,
"As is" clauses, 365.
Implied warranty, 365, 369–372.
Express warranty, sample or model, 285.
Implied warranty of merchantability, 294.
Letters of credit, 609, 612–613.
Rejection, restriction, 256.

**TRANSACTION PLANNING**
Contract modification, 41–42.
Desired contract terms, 32–33.
Last resort martini, 32–33.
Open price term, 98–99.
Requirements contracts, 103–109.
Sale of goods,
Contract terms, 23–33.
Risk of loss insurance policy, 159.
Seller retaining control of shipped goods, 93, 96–97.
Statute of frauds requirements, 51–54.

**TRUTH-IN-LENDING**
See Uniform Consumer Credit Code.

**UNCONSCIONABILITY**
Generally, Chapter four.
Bank-customer relationship, 555, 556.
Bargaining power, 119, 125.
Burden of proof, excessive price, 123–124.
Commercially reasonable test, 116.
Consumers,
Non-English speaking, 118, 126–127.
Poor or ignorant, 118–119.
Contract modification, extorted, 40.
Defense, holder in due course, 487, 489.
Definitional attempt, 116–117.
Disclaimer of warranty, 125–127, 350, 356, 358, 383–384, 386–396.
Evidence of excessive price, 123–124.
Examples,
Choice of jurisdiction, 125, 127.
Contract rights and remedies, 125–128.
Cross-collateral clause, 117–118.
Disclaimer of warranty, 125–127.
Excessive price, 120–124.
Liquidated damages, 125.
Repossession conduct, 125, 127.
Waiver of warranties, 118, 125–127.
Freedom of contract limitation, 109–110.
Good faith requirement, 113.
Injunctive relief, 130–131.
Limitation,
Buyer's remedies, 377, 379, 383–386, 392–396.
Merger clause, 80.
"Meaningful choice", 118.
Price excessive, 120–124.
Procedural, 118–119.
Defined, 116–117.
Procedure for raising, 115–116.
Proration of purchase price, 801–802.
Punitive damages, 132–133.
Purchase money security interests, 801–802.

**UNCONSCIONABILITY**—Cont'd
Relationship of procedural and substantive, 128–130.
Relief, 115, 130–133.
Resale of repossessed collateral, 991–992.
Substantive, 119–128.
Defined, 116–117.
Unenforceable, 130–131.
Use by trustee in bankruptcy, 866–867.
Victims, 114–115.
Waiver of defense clause, 125, 127.

**UNIFORM CONSUMER CREDIT CODE**
Consumer credit lease defined, 485–486.
Consumer credit sale defined, 485–486.
Excessive price test, 123.
Holder in due course limitations, 484–486.
Proration of purchase price, 801–802.
Purchase money security interest, 801–802.
Remedy for overreaching, 113.

**UNIFORM MOTOR VEHICLE CERTIFICATE OF TITLE ACT**
See Registration of Motor Vehicle Title.

**UNPERFECTED SECURITY INTEREST**
See also Consignment; Leases.
Bankrupt debtor, 868–871.
Leases, installment sales, 759–760.

**UNSECURED CREDITOR**
See also Secured Creditor.
Bankruptcy, 867–868.
Vis-a-vis secured creditor, 901–902.

**USURY LAWS**
Trustee in bankruptcy versus secured creditor, 898.

**VALUE**
Attachment of security interest, 791–796.
Bailed goods, 677–678.
Banks, holder in due course, 467–471.
Breach of warranty, subjective-objective test, 310–311.
Evidence,
Contract price, 309.
Cost of repair, 308.
Price quotations, 309.
Goods, rights of shipper against carrier, 718–719, 721–723.
Holder in due course, 458, 465–471.
Measure of, breach of warranty, 308–311.
Purchase money security interest, 914–915.

**VOIDABLE PREFERENCE**
See also Antecedent Debt; Bankruptcy.
Proceeds, 887.

**WAIVER**
Contract modification operating as, 39.
Dishonor, 420.

**WAIVER**—Cont'd
Notice of dishonor, 420.
Presentment, 420.
Unconscionable,
  Of defense clause, 125, 127.
  Of warranties, 118, 125–127.

**WAREHOUSE RECEIPTS**
Absence of due negotiation, 693–697.
Altered or unauthorized, 689–690.
Bailee's liability for lost or injured
  goods, 672–679.
Defined, 668–669.
Field warehousing, 704–709.
Forged indorsement, 686–687.
Introduction, 667–668.
Lost or stolen, 689.
Misdescription of goods, 691–692.
Negotiability, 683–694.
Negotiable, rights of transferee, 702–703.
Non-negotiable,
  Rights of transferee, 703–704, 707–709.
  Title to goods, 695–697.
Non-receipt of goods by bailee, 690–691.
Perfected security interest in goods, 688.
Purchasers,
  Negotiable receipts, 682–694.
  Non-negotiable receipts, 694–697.
Rights of pledgee,
  Fungible goods, 702–703.
  Negotiable receipts, 699–703.
  Non-negotiable receipts, 703–704, 707–
  709.
Secured creditor versus transferee, 952–
  953.
Uniform Warehouse Receipts Act, 671,
  672.

**WAREHOUSEMAN**
Apparent authority to sell or store, 688.
Damages, 676–679.
Field warehousing, 704–709.
Goods held by, risk of loss, 144–145.
Liability for goods, "lawful excuse",
  680–682.
Liability to purchasers,
  Disclaimers, 691–692.
  Inspection of goods, 692–693.
Misdelivery of goods, 679–682.
Rights of storer against, 671–682.
Standard of care, 672–674.

**WARRANTY OF QUALITY**
  See also Express Warranty; Implied
    Warranty of Merchantability.
Breach, nonconforming goods tendered,
  96.
Defenses, generally, Chapter eleven.
Disclaimer, 349–375, 386–396.
Express, 273–286.
  Contradictory implied, 71–72.

**WARRANTY OF QUALITY**—Cont'd
Implied, 286–296.
  Contradicting express warranty, 72.
Oral representations, parol evidence
  rule, 71–72.
Resale of repossessed collateral, 992.

**WARRANTY OF TITLE**
  Generally, 299–305.
Auctioneers, 303–304.
Basic case, 299.
Breach, consequences, 302.
Cause of action, 299–303.
Claim of title requirement, 303–305.
Disclaimer, 303–305.
Drawer signature forged, 519, 520–521.
Insurance companies, 303.
Knowledge, possible limit on liability,
  301–302.
Quiet possession, disturbance of, 300–
  302, 303.
Security interest, breach, 299–300.
Stolen instruments, 495, 503, 504–505,
  509–517.
  Depository bank, 495, 503, 509–517.
  "Good title", 509–510.
  Potential plaintiffs, 513–514.
  Reasonable time, 515–517.
  Transferee-payor distinguished, 511–
  512.
Warranty against infringement, 302.

**WARRANTY UPON TRANSFER**
  See also Warranty of Title.
Stolen checks and notes, 509–517.

**WRITING**
  See also "Battle of the Forms"; Mer-
    ger Clause; Parol Evidence Rule.
Acceptance, means of, 250.
"Complete and exclusive expression" of
  contract, 69–70.
Confirming oral agreement, 30–31.
Defined, Parol Evidence Rule, 68–69.
Disclaimer of oral warranties, complete-
  ness, 354–355.
Embodies complete agreement, burden of
  proof, 67–68.
Evidence of contract terms, 65–68.
Express warranty, 274, 279.
Final written expression of agreement,
  76–78.
Notice, sufficiency, 347–348.
Rejection, 265.
Representative capacity, 403–406.
Revocation of acceptance, 265.
Security interest,
  Generally, 786–791.
  Chattel paper, 949.
  Fixtures, 929–930.
Sufficiency, for statute of frauds, 46–47,
  51–54.